A SOCIAL HISTORY OF THE WELSH LANGUAGE

CYFRES HANES CYMDEITHASOL YR IAITH GYMRAEG

GENERAL EDITOR / GOLYGYDD CYFFREDINOL: Geraint H. Jenkins

Statistical Evidence relating to the Welsh Language 1801–1911

Tystiolaeth Ystadegol yn ymwneud â'r Iaith Gymraeg 1801–1911

DOT JONES

UNIVERSITY OF WALES PRESS, CARDIFF
GWASG PRIFYSGOL CYMRU, CAERDYDD
1998

British Library Cataloguing in Publication Data

A catalogue record for this book is available from the British Library.

Manylion Catalogio Cyhoeddi'r Llyfrgell Brydeinig

Y mae cofnod catalogio'r llyfr hwn ar gael gan y Llyfrgell Brydeinig.

ISBN 0–7083–1460–0

The financial assistance of the University of Wales Board of Celtic Studies towards the publication of this book is gratefully acknowledged.
Diolchir i Fwrdd Gwybodau Celtaidd Prifysgol Cymru am gymorth ariannol tuag at gostau cynhyrchu'r gyfrol hon.

Cover designed by Elgan Davies, Welsh Books Council.
Dyluniwyd y clawr gan Elgan Davies, Cyngor Llyfrau Cymru.
Typeset in Llanilar by Andrew Hawke.
Cysodwyd yn Llanilar gan Andrew Hawke.
Printed in Wales by Dinefwr Press, Llandybïe.
Argraffwyd yng Nghymru gan Wasg Dinefwr, Llandybïe.

Bare statistics by themselves are poor food, but when studied in the light of other facts they gradually become appetizing, and can furnish the text for many a sermon.

J. E. Southall

Cynnwys / *Contents*

Rhagair

Mewn ysgrif bryfoclyd braidd dan y teitl 'Figures in Welsh History', a gyhoeddwyd ym 1995, galwodd John Williams haneswyr Cymru i gyfrif am naill ai osgoi data meintiol yn gyfan gwbl neu am fodloni ar ffigurau crynion neu ddyfaliadau deallus. Anodd gwadu'r ffaith fod llawer o haneswyr cymdeithasol ar gael o hyd y byddai'n well ganddynt swpera gyda'r Diafol nag ymroi i chwarae â ffigurau neu gyfaddef eu bod yn ddibynnol ar ystadegau. Fodd bynnag, y mae'r ffaith fod pecynnau cyfrifiadurol ystadegol grymus ar gael yn rhwydd wedi ei gwneud yn haws nag erioed o'r blaen i'r hanesydd mwyaf cyndyn gyfoethogi ei ddealltwriaeth hanesyddol trwy ddefnyddio deunydd meintiol. Ar gychwyn prosiect ymchwil y Ganolfan hon ar hanes cymdeithasol yr iaith Gymraeg, sylweddolwyd y byddai angen cyfrol sylweddol ar ddeunydd ystadegol yn ymwneud â'r iaith Gymraeg yn y bedwaredd ganrif ar bymtheg yn sail i gyfrolau diweddarach ar natur ieithyddol gyfnewidiol Cymru yn y cyfnod modern. Yr oedd y gwaith o ddethol, crynhoi, trefnu a dehongli'r wybodaeth amrywiol a chymhleth hon yn gryn dasg a haedda Mrs Dot Jones y clod mwyaf am gynhyrchu cyfrol sy'n torri tir newydd yn hanes demograffig ac ieithyddol Cymru. Bydd yr holl ddeunydd ystadegol a gyflwynir ynddi yn galluogi'r sawl sy'n astudio hanes Cymru yn y cyfnod modern i werthfawrogi yn llawnach nag erioed o'r blaen y symudiadau yn nosbarthiad y cyfrannau a siaradai Gymraeg a'r canlyniadau o ran patrymau cymdeithasol-ddiwylliannol o fewn Cymru.

Y mae'r holl waith ymchwil hanesyddol a llenyddol yr ymgymerir ag ef yn y Ganolfan Uwchefrydiau Cymreig a Cheltaidd yn ffrwyth cydweithrediad, ac y mae'r awdur wedi derbyn pob cefnogaeth gan y tîm o gymrodyr ymchwil ifainc sy'n rhan o'r prosiect. Y mae aelodau'r Pwyllgor Ymgynghorol, yn enwedig yr Athro Emeritws Ieuan Gwynedd Jones, wedi rhoi yn hael o'u hamser a'u harbenigedd yn ystod y cyfnod o baratoi'r gyfrol hon, ac y mae hefyd yn bleser diolch i'r Athro Emeritws John Williams, y bodiwyd ei gyfrol feistrolgar *Digest of Welsh Historical Statistics* yn helaeth gan bawb sy'n ymwneud â'r prosiect, am ei gyngor a'i anogaeth. Ymgymerwyd â'r rhan fwyaf o'r gwaith ymchwil yn Llyfrgell Genedlaethol Cymru a mawr yw ein dyled i staff y sefydliad hwnnw am eu cymorth cwrtais a diflino. Bu Mr Robert Davies, Mr Glyn

Foreword

In a gently provocative essay entitled 'Figures in Welsh History', published in 1995, John Williams took Welsh historians to task for either avoiding quantitative data altogether or plumping for round figures or relying on informed guesswork. It is hard to deny the fact that there are still many social historians who would rather sup with the Devil than indulge in number-crunching exercises or style themselves cliometricians. Nevertheless, the widespread availability of powerful computerized statistical packages has made it easier than ever before for even the most reluctant historian to enhance his historical understanding by using quantitative material. At the inception of this Centre's research project on the social history of the Welsh language, it was recognized that a substantial volume on statistical material relating to the Welsh language in the nineteenth century would be required to underpin subsequent volumes on the changing linguistic character of Wales in modern times. The task of extracting, assembling, tabulating and interpreting this diverse and complex material has been exceptionally difficult and Mrs Dot Jones deserves the highest praise for producing a volume which breaks new ground in the demographic and linguistic history of Wales. The copious statistical material presented here will enable all students of modern Welsh history to appreciate more fully than ever before the distributional shifts in the proportions who spoke Welsh and the consequences for socio-cultural patterns within Wales.

All historical and literary research conducted at the Centre for Advanced Welsh and Celtic Studies is collaborative in nature, and the author has received every support from the community of young research fellows involved in this project. Members of the Advisory Panel, notably Professor Emeritus Ieuan Gwynedd Jones, have generously given of their time and expertise during the preparation of this volume, and it is also a pleasure to thank Professor Emeritus John Williams, whose magisterial *Digest of Welsh Historical Statistics* has been heavily thumbed by everyone associated with the project, for his advice and encouragement. The bulk of the research was undertaken in the National Library of Wales and a special debt of gratitude is owed to its staff for their unfailingly courteous assistance. In particular Mr Robert Davies, Mr

Parry, Dr Michael J. Pearson a Dr Huw Walters yn hynod barod eu cymwynas wrth ateb ymholiadau a darparu deunydd. Yr ydym yn dra dyledus hefyd i aelodau o staff Prifysgol Cymru, Aberystwyth, ac yn enwedig i Dr Philip Henry Jones o'r Adran Astudiaethau Gwybodaeth a Llyfrgellyddiaeth am rannu o'i wybodaeth eang ar gyhoeddi yn yr iaith Gymraeg yn oes Victoria, i staff y Gwasanaeth Paratoi Data, yn enwedig Ms Christine Hughes, am fwydo setiau sylweddol o ddata ar daenlenni Excel dros gyfnod hir, ac i Mr Antony Smith, Cartograffydd yn y Sefydliad Astudiaethau Daear, am lunio amryw o'r mapiau. Yn ogystal, cafwyd cymorth amhrisiadwy yn y gwaith o baratoi'r mapiau gan Mr John R. Hunt, Swyddog Prosiect (Cartograffeg), Cyfadran y Gwyddorau Cymdeithasol, Y Brifysgol Agored, a luniodd fapiau iaith a ddiwygiwyd yn arbennig ar gyfer y gyfrol hon gan Dr W. T. R. Pryce, Y Brifysgol Agored yng Nghymru, a chan Dr Roger Griffiths, a luniodd y gyfres o fapiau'r siroedd yn yr adran ar Boblogaeth.

Cydnabyddir yn ddiolchgar gymorth gweinyddol Mrs Aeres Bowen Davies a Ms Siân Evans yn y Ganolfan, ac y mae diwyg y copi terfynol ar ei ennill yn ddirfawr oherwydd sgiliau manwl Mr Andrew Hawke a Mrs Glenys Howells. Yn olaf, cydnabyddir yn ddiolchgar arweiniad Mrs Susan Jenkins, Gwasg Prifysgol Cymru.

Hydref 1997 — *Geraint H. Jenkins*

Glyn Parry, Dr Michael J. Pearson and Dr Huw Walters were immensely helpful in answering queries and supplying material. Debts are owed, too, to members of staff of the University of Wales, Aberystwyth, notably to Dr Philip Henry Jones of the Department of Information and Library Studies, who shared his extensive knowledge of Welsh language publishing in Victorian times, to the staff of the Data Preparation Service, especially Ms Christine Hughes, who entered substantial datasets into Excel spreadsheet form over an extensive period of time, and to Mr Antony Smith, Cartographer in the Institute of Geography and Earth Sciences, who drew several of the maps. Invaluable help in the preparation of maps was also given by Mr John R. Hunt, Project Officer (Cartography), Faculty of Social Sciences, The Open University, who produced language maps specially revised for this volume by Dr W. T. R. Pryce, The Open University of Wales, and by Dr Roger Griffiths, who traced the series of county maps in the section on Population.

The administrative assistance of Mrs Aeres Bowen Davies and Ms Siân Evans at the Centre is gratefully acknowledged and the presentation of the final copy has benefited immeasurably from the meticulous skills of Mr Andrew Hawke and Mrs Glenys Howells. Finally, the guidance of Mrs Susan Jenkins of the University of Wales Press is gratefully acknowledged.

October 1997 — *Geraint H. Jenkins*

Rhagymadrodd Cyffredinol

Y mae'r gyfrol hon yn dwyn ynghyd amrywiaeth cyfoethog o ddeunydd ystadegol yn ymwneud â'r defnydd o'r iaith Gymraeg yn ystod cyfnod o gryn newid economaidd a chymdeithasol. Ar ddechrau'r bedwaredd ganrif ar bymtheg Cymraeg oedd iaith y mwyafrif helaeth o bobl Cymru. Tystiai teithwyr o Loegr – â gwahanol raddau o syndod, difyrrwch neu ddiddordeb – pa mor anodd oedd cyfathrebu â'r trigolion lleol. Serch hynny, erbyn 1911, ar drothwy'r Rhyfel Byd Cyntaf, deg y cant yn unig o'r boblogaeth a'u disgrifiai eu hunain yn siaradwyr 'Cymraeg yn unig' ac yr oedd clychau braw ynghylch goroesiad yr iaith yn seinio ers sawl cenhedlaeth. Y mae'r dystiolaeth ystadegol a ddangosir yma nid yn unig yn mesur y patrwm symudol o ddefnydd o'r Gymraeg/Saesneg, ond hefyd y grymoedd hynny a oedd yn effeithio ar y newid iaith hwn, ac yr effeithid arnynt ganddo, sef demograffeg, economi, addysg, crefydd a diwylliant. Y mae'r nod yn ddeublyg, sef darparu corff o ddeunydd cyfeirio, ynghyd â gosod sylfaen ar gyfer cyfrolau diweddarach yn y gyfres a fydd yn ymwneud â defnydd o'r Gymraeg yn y cyfnod diweddar.

Y mae, yn sicr, helaethrwydd o ddeunydd i'w hidlo a'i grynhoi. Yn ystod y bedwaredd ganrif ar bymtheg y cydnabuwyd bod cynnal arolwg cymdeithasol a chasglu ystadegau yn gam cyntaf angenrheidiol mewn unrhyw ymateb i broblem gymdeithasol dybiedig.[1] Ymhlith y cymhellion a oedd wrth wraidd cynnal y cyfrifiad poblogaeth cyntaf ym 1801, er enghraifft, oedd yr angen i wybod maint y galw am rawn ar adeg o ryfel, yn ogystal ag i ddarparu tystiolaeth ar gyfer y ddadl ynghylch twf mewn poblogaeth. Yn yr oes wyddonol newydd llifai ffrwd o gyfrifiadau a gwaith dosbarthu cymdeithasol o du unigolion selog, cymdeithasau ystadegol, asiantaethau lleol a chenedlaethol a'r llywodraeth. Daeth plant, merched, dynion, genedigaethau, marwolaethau, priodasau, oedran, galwedigaethau, salwch, ysgolion, tai, addoldai, a hyd yn oed iaith, yn achlysurol, oll yn destunau arolygon a dadansoddiad.

Ffrwydrodd y mudiad ystadegol ym Mhrydain yn y 1830au pan sefydlwyd Cymdeithasau Ystadegol yn y dinasoedd mawr a'r trefi yn sgil y problemau cymdeithasol a ddaethai i'w rhan o ganlyniad i dwf diwydiannol cyflym ar ddechrau'r bedwaredd ganrif ar bymtheg.[2] Yng Nghymru anfonwyd cynrychiolwyr gan Gymdeithas Athronyddol a Llenyddol Abertawe (y

General Introduction

This volume brings together a rich variety of statistical material relating to the use of the Welsh language during a period of considerable economic and social change. At the beginning of the nineteenth century the people of Wales were overwhelmingly Welsh-speaking. Travellers from England noted with varying degrees of astonishment, amusement or fascination the difficulty of communicating with local inhabitants. However, by 1911, on the eve of the First World War, only ten per cent of the population described themselves as speaking 'Welsh only' and alarm bells had been sounding regarding the survival of the language for several generations. The statistical evidence displayed here not only quantifies the changing pattern of Welsh/English use, but also those forces which both affected and were affected by this language shift, namely demography, economy, education, religion, and culture. The aim is twofold: to provide a body of reference material and also to lay the foundations for subsequent volumes in the series devoted to Welsh language use in the modern period.

There is certainly an abundance of material to sift and assemble. It was during the nineteenth century that conducting a social survey and gathering statistics was first recognized as a necessary initial step in any response to a perceived social problem.[1] The motives behind conducting the first population census in 1801, for example, included the need to ascertain the level of demand for grain at a time of war and to provide evidence for the debate concerning population growth. In the new scientific age a stream of social countings and classifications poured forth from zealous individuals, statistical societies, local, national and government agencies. Children, women, men, births, deaths, marriages, ages, occupations, sickness, schools, houses, places of religious worship, even occasionally language, all became subjects of survey and scrutiny.

The statistical movement in Britain exploded in the 1830s with the establishment of Statistical Societies in major cities and towns whose first concerns were the social problems associated with rapid urban industrial growth in the early nineteenth century.[2] In Wales the Philosophical and Literary Society of Swansea, founded 'to promote the cultivation and advancement of the several branches of Natural Science, the elucidation of the History and Antiquities of Wales, the

'Philosophical and Literary Society') – a sefydlwyd i hyrwyddo a meithrin y Gwyddorau Naturiol, i egluro Hanes a Hynafiaethau Cymru, i hybu Llenyddiaeth a'r Celfyddydau Cain, ac i ledaenu Gwybodaeth yn gyffredinol – i'r British Association a oedd yn cwrdd ym Mryste ym Mai 1836.[3] Wedi iddynt ddychwelyd, newidiwyd enw'r Gymdeithas yn Royal Institution of South Wales, a phenodwyd is-bwyllgor ystadegol. O safbwynt yr hanesydd iaith cymdeithasol, siomedig oedd canlyniadau ymdrechion yr is-bwyllgor. Un yn unig o'r ddau arolwg cymdeithasol cyfyngedig yr ymgymerwyd â hwy sy'n cynnwys manylion am y defnydd o'r Gymraeg/Saesneg.[4] Cyhoeddwyd arolygon cymdeithasol eraill yn y *Journal of the Statistical Society of London* (a alwyd yn ddiweddarach yn *Journal of the Royal Statistical Society*) – sef arolygon G. S. Kenrick o Bont-y-pŵl a Blaenafon, ac o Ferthyr Tudful, yn y 1840au, a'r arolwg hynod uchelgeisiol o'r ieithoedd Celtaidd a wnaethpwyd gan E. G. Ravenstein yng nghanol y 1870au.[5]

Fodd bynnag, cyhoeddiadau swyddogol, rhai'r llywodraeth a rhai eraill, yw'r ffynonellau pwysicaf ar gyfer ystadegau cymdeithasol y bedwaredd ganrif ar bymtheg. Y mae'r rhain yn cynnwys y cyfrifiadau poblogaeth a wneid bob deng mlynedd, ystadegau rheolaidd adrannau'r llywodraeth, ac ymchwiliadau achlysurol megis Comisiynau Brenhinol neu Ymholiadau Adrannol. Hon yn wir oedd oes y 'gwella trwy rifau'.[6] Gallai ymchwilwyr swyddogol foddi mewn môr o ffigurau; er enghraifft, yr oedd Adroddiad y Comisiynwyr yn Ymchwilio i Gyflwr Addysg yng Nghymru ym 1847 yn cynnwys dros bum can tudalen o dystiolaeth ystadegol. Gallent hefyd fod mor unllygeidiog o ganlyniad i'w rhagdybiaethau fel eu bod yn mynnu anwybyddu'r dystiolaeth ystadegol a gyflwynid. Ni chafodd peth o'r dystiolaeth a gasglwyd â mawr ofal ei ddosbarthu na'i gyhoeddi o gwbl. Y mae cyfoeth o ddeunydd ystadegol ar gyfer y bedwaredd ganrif ar bymtheg naill ai wedi mynd ar ddifancoll neu wedi ei anwybyddu.

O safbwynt yr ymchwilydd sy'n ymddiddori mewn deunydd Cymreig, y mae ystadegau Prydeinig swyddogol y bedwaredd ganrif ar bymtheg yn gyforiog o anawsterau. Yr enghraifft enwocaf yw'r cofnod 'WALES, see ENGLAND' yn y nawfed argraffiad o'r *Encyclopaedia Britannica* (1888). Nid yw'r ffaith mai dim ond 'England' a geir yn nheitl rhyw ymholiad llywodraethol neu'i gilydd yn golygu o anghenraid na fu'r ymchwilwyr yn ymweld â Chymru. Er enghraifft, yr oedd Comisiwn Newcastle, a adroddodd ym 1861 ar gyflwr addysg boblogaidd yn Lloegr, yn cynnwys adroddiad gwerthfawr gan y Comisiynydd Cynorthwyol, John Jenkins, ar 'The Mining Districts of Neath and Merthyr ... and the Agricultural District in the County of Merioneth'. Nid oedd yr esgeuluso ar Gymru wedi ei gyfyngu i weinyddiaeth ganolog. Yn Eisteddfod Genedlaethol Aberhonddu ym 1889

encouragement of Literature and the Fine Arts, and the general diffusion of Knowledge', sent representatives to the British Association meeting in Bristol in May 1836.[3] On their return the Society's name was changed to the Royal Institution of South Wales, and a statistical sub-committee was appointed. From the perspective of the social historian of language, the results of the sub-committee's efforts are disappointing. Only one of the two limited social surveys undertaken by the sub-committee includes details about Welsh/English language use.[4] Other social surveys, of Pontypool and Blaenafon, and of Merthyr Tydfil, undertaken by G. S. Kenrick in the 1840s, and the highly ambitious survey of the Celtic languages by E. G. Ravenstein in the mid-1870s, were published in the *Journal of the Statistical Society of London* (later the *Journal of the Royal Statistical Society*).[5]

The most important sources of social statistics for the nineteenth century, however, are official governmental and non-governmental publications. These include decennial censuses of population, regular returns from government departments, and occasional investigations such as Royal Commissions or Departmental Inquiries. This was truly the age of 'improvement by numbers'.[6] Official enquirers could be swamped by figures; for instance, the Report of the Commissioners of Inquiry into the State of Education in Wales in 1847 contained over five hundred pages of statistical evidence. They could also be so blinded by their preconceptions that they chose to ignore the statistical evidence presented. Some evidence, painstakingly collected, was never collated or published. A wealth of statistical material for the nineteenth century has either been lost or overlooked.

Official British statistics for the nineteenth century are fraught with difficulties for the searcher of Welsh material. The most infamous example is the 'WALES, See ENGLAND' entry in the 1888 (9th) edition of the *Encyclopaedia Britannica*. A government inquiry with only 'England' as part of its official title does not necessarily preclude the possibility that the investigators also visited Wales. For example, the Newcastle Commission, which reported in 1861 on the state of popular education in England, contained a valuable report by Assistant Commissioner John Jenkins on 'The Mining Districts of Neath and Merthyr ... and the Agricultural District in the County of Merioneth'. The neglect of Wales was not confined to central administration. An essay entered by 'Giraldus' in the National Eisteddfod held at Brecon in 1889 was severely criticized by the adjudicators for stating that 'The principality of Wales ... occupies a considerable area of the West of England'.[7] More discouraging is the fact that Ireland and Scotland are treated separately in official British statistics, but the figures for Wales are often included with those for England and are therefore impossible to disaggregate.[8]

beirniadwyd 'Giraldus' yn llym am ddatgan yn ei draethawd: 'The principality of Wales ... occupies a considerable area of the West of England'.[7] Mwy digalon fyth yw'r ffaith fod Iwerddon a'r Alban yn cael eu trin ar wahân mewn ystadegau Prydeinig swyddogol, ond bod y ffigurau ar gyfer Cymru yn aml yn cael eu cynnwys gyda rhai Lloegr ac felly yn amhosibl i'w gwahanu.[8]

Yr oedd tuedd hefyd i drin gogledd a de Cymru, a hyd yn oed Gymru gyfan weithiau, fel un o siroedd Lloegr, gan bylu'r gwahaniaethau rhwng siroedd Cymru trwy eu cyfuno. Yn ogystal, yr oedd awdurdodau'r cyfrifiad – am ran helaeth o'r bedwaredd ganrif ar bymtheg – yn cynnwys sir Fynwy fel sir o fewn Lloegr yn hytrach na Chymru. Ar wahân i broblemau diffinio a statws, ychydig o ddiddordeb a oedd gan y llywodraeth ganolog yng nghyflwr cymdeithasol Cymru yn ystod yn bedwaredd ganrif ar bymtheg, ac eithrio'r adegau hynny pan gâi swyddogion eu sbarduno i weithredu gan fygythiad terfysg.

Y tu allan i'r llywodraeth, cynhyrchodd awdurdodau canolog nifer o sefydliadau adroddiadau blynyddol neu lawlyfrau a oedd hefyd yn cynnwys gwybodaeth ystadegol. Yn ystod ail hanner y bedwaredd ganrif ar bymtheg – a chyn hynny yn achos y Methodistiaid Calfinaidd a'r Wesleaid – cyhoeddodd y rhan fwyaf o'r enwadau crefyddol ffigurau ar gyfer eglwysi, capeli, aelodau a disgyblion ysgol Sul. Ond ni fu pob sefydliad, gwaetha'r modd, mor garedig wrth haneswyr y dyfodol. Hyd yma, ni ddaethpwyd o hyd i ffigurau swyddogol am nifer y bobl a fynychai eisteddfodau, na ffigurau cylchrediad papurau newydd, na manylion am aelodaeth cymdeithasau a sefydlwyd i hyrwyddo'r Gymraeg yn y bedwaredd ganrif ar bymtheg. Diffyg tystiolaeth ystadegol, felly, sy'n gyfrifol am y ffaith nad yw'r adran ar Ddiwylliant yn adlewyrchu gwir bwysigrwydd bywyd diwylliannol Cymru o safbwynt cynnal yr iaith yn ystod y cyfnod hwn.

Newidiwyd y bwriad gwreiddiol o seilio'r gyfrol hon ar ffynonellau cyhoeddedig yn unig yn sgil darganfod dau arolwg amhrisiadwy mewn llawysgrif yn Llyfrgell Genedlaethol Cymru. Y mae'r cyntaf, sef arolwg a wnaed o bob tŷ yn nhri o blwyfi sir Drefaldwyn yn Rhagfyr 1846, yn cofnodi medr ieithyddol Cymraeg/ Saesneg yr holl breswylwyr. Trefnwyd yr arolwg gan y Parchedig Robert David Thomas, gweinidog eglwys Annibynnol Penarth, Llanfair Caereinion, a'i gyflwyno i'r Comisiwn Brenhinol ar Gyflwr Addysg yng Nghymru.[9] Er bod bras ganlyniadau'r arolwg yn ymddangos mewn atodiad i Adroddiad y Comisiwn, y mae'r ffynhonnell lawysgrif wedi ein galluogi i gyflwyno set arall o dablau yn seiliedig ar fedr ieithyddol.[10] Casgliad o atebion gan glerigwyr o fewn esgobaeth Tyddewi i holiadur printiedig ar wasanaethau Sul dwyieithog, a anfonwyd allan gan Gomisiynwyr yr Eglwys ym 1908, yw'r ail arolwg.[11] Hyd y gwyddys, ni chyhoeddwyd dim o'r wybodaeth

There was also a tendency to treat north and south Wales, and even sometimes the whole of Wales, on the same terms as an English county, thereby blurring Welsh county differences by aggregation. For much of the nineteenth century, too, census authorities included Monmouthshire as a county within England rather than within Wales. Apart from problems of definition and status, central government was little interested in the social condition of Wales during the nineteenth century, except on those occasions when the threat of civil unrest prodded officials into action.

Outside government, the central authorities of various organizations also produced annual reports or handbooks containing statistical information. In particular, most of the religious denominations published figures for churches, chapels, members, and Sunday school scholars during the second half of the nineteenth century, although Calvinistic Methodists and Wesleyan Methodists published relatively full figures from an earlier period. Unfortunately, not every organization was so obliging to future historians. Official figures for attendance at eisteddfodau, the circulation of newspapers, and the membership of societies established to promote the Welsh language in the nineteenth century, have so far eluded us. The slimness of the section on Culture is therefore a reflection of the lack of statistical evidence rather than of the importance of Welsh cultural life to language maintenance during this period.

The original intention of this volume was to confine the contents to published sources. However, two invaluable manuscript surveys held in the National Library of Wales were discovered and it was felt that their exclusion could not be justified. The first, a survey of every household in three Montgomeryshire parishes undertaken in December 1846, lists the Welsh/English language ability of each household member. The survey was organized by the Reverend Robert David Thomas, minister of Penarth Congregational chapel, Llanfair Caereinion, and was presented to the Royal Commission on the State of Education in Wales.[9] Although the broad results of the survey appear as an appendix to the Report of the Commission, by obtaining the manuscript source we have been able to present an alternative set of tabulations based on language ability.[10] The second survey is the collection of answers from clergymen within the diocese of St David's to a printed questionnaire on bilingual Sunday services sent out by the Church Commissioners in 1908.[11] As far as is known, none of the information contained in this questionnaire has been published previously.

Most of the material presented here has been compiled from original sources. The treasure trove known as the *Digest of Welsh Historical Statistics*, compiled by John Williams, however, has also been plundered, particularly for the section on Population.[12] His

a gynhwysir yn yr holiadur hwn o'r blaen.

Y mae'r rhan fwyaf o'r deunydd a gyflwynir yma wedi ei gywain o ffynonellau gwreiddiol. Manteisiwyd hefyd ar y *Digest of Welsh Historical Statistics*, y drysorfa o wybodaeth a gasglwyd ynghyd gan John Williams, yn enwedig ar gyfer yr adran ar Boblogaeth.[12] Y mae ei ddwy gyfrol werthfawr ef o ystadegau yn llenwi llawer o'r bylchau yn y deunydd cymdeithasol ac economaidd sy'n ymddangos yma. Yr ydym yn ddyledus hefyd i Dr W. T. Rees Pryce, y gosododd ei waith arloesol ar newid ieithyddol yng Nghymru sylfaen gadarn ar gyfer pob astudiaeth a'i dilynodd. Ailargreffir ei fapiau clasurol o barthau ieithyddol ym 1750 a 1900 yn y gyfrol hon, yn ogystal â nifer o dablau yn yr adran ar Iaith.[13]

Y maen prawf sylfaenol wrth benderfynu pa ffynonellau i'w defnyddio oedd perthnasedd i hanes cymdeithasol y Gymraeg. Felly, ceir yn y tablau naill ai fesur o ddefnydd o'r Gymraeg neu'r graddau y mae pwnc arbennig wedi dylanwadu ar y defnydd o iaith mewn cyfnod o newid yn ei hanes. Rhannwyd rhifau cyfansymiol yn elfennau mor lleol ag yr oedd ffynhonnell a gofod yn caniatáu. Trwy gydol y bedwaredd ganrif ar bymtheg, datblygodd Cymru fwyfwy yn wlad o wrthgyferbyniadau; os oedd rhannau o Gymru ar flaen y gad o ran newid a datblygiad diwydiannol, yr oedd eraill fel petaent heb eu cyffwrdd. Gwnaed pob ymdrech i gynnwys y dystiolaeth ystadegol sy'n amlygu'r patrwm symudol hwn. Er mwyn gallu cymharu'n well, ychwanegwyd cyfrifiadau canran at lawer o'r tablau. Ychwanegwyd mapiau at yr adrannau ar boblogaeth ac iaith. Yn anochel, bu'n rhaid hepgor llawer, a chywasgwyd mwy weithiau ar y deunydd a ddetholwyd nag y byddem wedi ei ddymuno. Gobeithio bod cynnwys manylion llawn am y ffynonellau yn gwneud peth iawn am y diffygion hyn. Y mae'r rhagarweiniad i bob adran yn cynnwys esboniad ar y ffynonellau gwreiddiol a gwerthfawrogiad beirniadol o'u dibynadwyedd. Er na cheisiwyd eu dadansoddi'n fanwl, rhoddir awgrym hefyd o'r prif nodweddion a ddatgelir ganddynt. Gall ystadegau weithiau ymddangos yn oer ac amhersonol, ond cyfeiriant at bobl o gig a gwaed, dynion, merched a phlant yr oedd rhai ohonynt, ond nid pawb, yn siarad Cymraeg fel eu dewis iaith.

1 Yn ôl G. S. Kenrick: 'A knowledge of the physical condition, the habits and attainments of a people, are necessary for the purpose of framing any sound plan for improving their condition by benevolent institutions, or restraining their excesses by penal enactments', 'Statistics of the Population in the Parish of Trevethin (Pontypool) and at the Neighbouring Works of Blaenavon in Monmouthshire, chiefly employed in the Iron Trade, and inhabiting part of the District recently disturbed', *Journal of the Statistical Society of London*, III (1840–1), 366.

2 Am hanes cynnar y Cymdeithasau Ystadegol, gw. Michael J. Cullen, *The Statistical Movement in Early Victorian Britain: The Foundations of Empirical Social Research* (Hassocks, 1975).

3 Gw. W. A. Beanland, *The History of the Royal Institution of*

valuable two-volume collection of statistics fills many of the gaps in the social and economic material that appear here. Another debt is owed to Dr W. T. Rees Pryce, whose pioneering work on language change in Wales has provided a firm foundation for all subsequent studies. His classic maps of language zones in 1750 and 1900 are reprinted here, as well as several tables in the Language section.[13]

In determining which sources would be used, the basic criteria was relevance to the social history of the Welsh language. Therefore, either a measure of Welsh language use is included in a table, or the subject of the table represents an important factor in language use in a situation of potential or actual language change. Aggregates have been broken down to as local a level as source and space permit. Throughout the nineteenth century, Wales increasingly became a land of contrasts; if parts of Wales were at the forefront of industrial change and progress, others seemingly remained untouched. Every effort has been made to include the statistical evidence which illustrates this changing pattern. To aid comparison, percentage calculations have been appended to many tables. Maps have been inserted in the sections on population and language. Inevitably, much has been left out, and even the material selected has sometimes been condensed more than one might have wished. It is hoped that these shortcomings have been at least partly mitigated by the inclusion of full details of the source material for further reference. Introductions to each section include an explanation of the original sources and a critical appraisal of their reliability. Although no detailed analysis is attempted, some indication of the main features which they reveal is also given. Statistics may sometimes appear cold and detached, but they refer to living people of their time; men, women and children, some of whom, but not all, spoke Welsh as their language of preference.

1 According to G. S. Kenrick, 'A knowledge of the physical condition, the habits and attainments of a people, are necessary for the purpose of framing any sound plan for improving their condition by benevolent institutions, or restraining their excesses by penal enactments', 'Statistics of the Population in the Parish of Trevethin (Pontypool) and at the Neighbouring Works of Blaenavon in Monmouthshire, chiefly employed in the Iron Trade, and inhabiting part of the District recently disturbed', *Journal of the Statistical Society of London*, III (1840–1), 366.

2 For the early history of Statistical Societies, see Michael J. Cullen, *The Statistical Movement in Early Victorian Britain: The Foundations of Empirical Social Research* (Hassocks, 1975).

3 See W. A. Beanland, *The History of the Royal Institution of South Wales, Swansea* (Swansea, 1935).

4 'Description and Amount of Religious Accommodation and Instruction in the Town of Swansea, May A.D. 1839', in the appendix to the *Annual Report of the Royal Institution of South Wales, 1838–39*, p. 90.

5 Kenrick, 'Statistics of the Population in the Parish of Trevethin'; idem, 'Statistics of Merthyr Tydvil', *Journal of the Statistical Society of London*, IX (1846), 14–21. E. G. Ravenstein, 'On

South Wales, Swansea (Swansea, 1935).

4 'Description and Amount of Religious Accommodation and Instruction in the Town of Swansea, May A.D. 1839', yn yr atodiad i adroddiad blynyddol y Royal Institution of South Wales, 1838–9, t. 90.

5 Kenrick, 'Statistics of the Population in the Parish of Trevethin'; idem, 'Statistics of Merthyr Tydvil', *Journal of the Statistical Society of London*, IX (1846), 14–21. E. G. Ravenstein, 'On the Celtic Languages in the British Isles, a Statistical Survey', *Journal of the Royal Statistical Society*, XLII (1879), 579–636. Gw. Iaith, Tabl 4.1 a Thablau 2.1–2.3.

6 Cullen, *The Statistical Movement*, t. 149.

7 *Cofnodion a Chyfansoddiadau Buddugol Eisteddfod Aberhonddu, 1889* (Cardiff, 1890), t. 227.

8 E.e., 'Emigration and immigration in the year 1882', *Journal of the Royal Statistical Society*, XLVI (1883), 380–7 (un o gyfres).

9 LlGC Llsgr. 23220E, Arolwg o gyflwr addysg ym mhlwyfi Castell Caereinion, Llanfair Caereinion a Manafon yn sir Drefaldwyn, a gyflawnwyd ym mis Rhagfyr 1846 gan gynrychiolwyr yr enwadau ymneilltuol lleol dan gyfarwyddyd y Parchedig Robert David Thomas ('Iorthryn Gwynedd', 1817–88), gweinidog eglwys Annibynnol Penarth, Llanfair Caereinion. Gw. Iaith, Tablau 4.2–4.5.

10 Gw. *Reports of the Commissioners of Inquiry into the State of Education in Wales. Part III, North Wales* (London, 1847), Atodiad H, 'Memorials from the Dissenters of Llanfair Caereinion, Castle Caereinion and Manavon, in the County of Montgomery, respecting the want of Education in those Parishes', tt. 337–58. PP 1847 (872) XXVII rhan II.

11 LlGC, Comisiwn yr Eglwys yng Nghymru, Holiadur ynglŷn â gwasanaethau dwyieithog ar y Sul, 1908. Gw. Crefydd, Tabl 2.8.

12 John Williams, *Digest of Welsh Historical Statistics* (2 gyf., Cardiff, 1985). Gw. Poblogaeth, Tablau 1.4 a 5.1.

13 Gw. yn arbennig, W. T. R. Pryce, 'Welsh and English in Wales, 1750–1971: A Spatial Analysis Based on the Linguistic Affiliation of Parochial Communities', *Bulletin of the Board of Celtic Studies*, XXVIII, rhan 1 (1978), 1–36; 'Yr Iaith Gymraeg 1750–1961', adran 3.1 yn H. Carter (gol.), *Atlas Cenedlaethol Cymru* (Caerdydd, 1981–9). Gw. Iaith, Tablau 1.1 ac 1.2, a Mapiau A a B.

the Celtic Languages in the British Isles, a Statistical Survey', *Journal of the Royal Statistical Society*, XLII (1879), 579–636. See Language, Table 4.1 and Tables 2.1–2.3.

6 Cullen, *The Statistical Movement*, p. 149.

7 *Transactions of the National Eisteddfod of Wales Brecknock, 1889* (Cardiff, 1890), p. 227.

8 For example, 'Emigration and immigration in the year 1882', *Journal of the Royal Statistical Society*, XLVI (1883), 380–7 (one of a series).

9 NLW MS 23220E, A survey of the state of education in and around the parishes of Castle Caereinion, Llanfair Caereinion and Manafon, county Montgomery, carried out, December 1846, by representatives of local nonconformist denominations under the supervision of the Reverend Robert David Thomas ('Iorthryn Gwynedd', 1817–88), minister of Penarth Congregational chapel, Llanfair Caereinion. See Language, Tables 4.2–4.5.

10 See *Reports of the Commissioners of Inquiry into the State of Education in Wales. Part III, North Wales* (London, 1847), Appendix H, 'Memorials from the Dissenters of Llanfair Caereinion, Castle Caereinion and Manavon, in the County of Montgomery, respecting the want of Education in those Parishes', pp. 337–58. PP 1847 (872) XXVII pt. II.

11 NLW, Welsh Church Commission, Questionnaire on Bilingual Sunday Services, 1908. See Religion, Table 2.8.

12 John Williams, *Digest of Welsh Historical Statistics* (2 vols., Cardiff, 1985). See Population, Tables 1.4 and 5.1.

13 See in particular, W. T. R. Pryce, 'Welsh and English in Wales, 1750–1971: A Spatial Analysis Based on the Linguistic Affiliation of Parochial Communities', *Bulletin of the Board of Celtic Studies*, XXVIII, pt. 1 (1978), 1–36; 'The Welsh language 1750–1961', section 3.1 in H. Carter (ed.), *National Atlas of Wales* (Cardiff, 1981–9). See Language, Tables 1.1 and 1.2, and Maps A and B.

I

Population

Poblogaeth

Rhagymadrodd

Yn unrhyw astudiaeth o'r dystiolaeth ystadegol sy'n ymwneud â newid ieithyddol, y mae deunydd demograffig o'r pwysigrwydd mwyaf. Patrwm symudol dosbarthiad, twf a symudiad poblogaeth, ffrwythlondeb, a strwythur y tylwyth yw'r deunydd sylfaenol y mae pob grym cymdeithasol ac economaidd arall yn gweithredu arno. Yng Nghymru'r bedwaredd ganrif ar bymtheg, lle'r oedd dwy iaith yn cystadlu â'i gilydd, cyfrannodd tueddiadau demograffig at y cymysgedd o ffactorau a benderfynai pa iaith a siaredid â phwy, ac ym mha amgylchiadau.

Prif ffynhonnell y tablau yn yr adran hon yw adroddiadau a chrynodebau'r cyfrifiad poblogaeth a gynhelid bob deng mlynedd. Yn achos y cyfrifiad cyntaf, a gynhaliwyd ym 1801, dibynnid ar swyddogion plwyf lleol i ddarparu gwybodaeth gyfyngedig am y nifer o dai, teuluoedd a phersonau (yn ddynion a merched) yn eu plwyf, treflan neu le, a'r nifer o bobl a gyflogid mewn tri dosbarth yn unig, sef amaethyddiaeth, masnach neu gynhyrchu neu grefft llaw, a galwedigaethau eraill. Gofynnwyd i glerigwyr roi gwybodaeth am nifer y bedyddiadau, claddedigaethau a phriodasau. Credir i'r cyfrifwyr cynnar dangyfrif cyfanswm y boblogaeth o gymaint â 5 y cant ym 1801 ac o 3 y cant ym 1811. Wedi hynny daeth gwell dibynadwyedd yn sgil dulliau amgenach o gasglu data.[1]

Er y gellir tybio bod cyfrifiadau diweddarach, at ei gilydd, yn ddibynadwy, cyfyd problem bosibl o ran cofnodi tueddiadau dros gyfnod yn sgil newidiadau yn yr unedau cyfansymiol. Yn ogystal â gwneud cofrestru sifil ar enedigaethau, priodasau a marwolaethau yn orfodol, daeth Deddf Cofrestru Genedigaethau, Marwolaethau a Phriodasau 1836 â chyfundrefn newydd i fodolaeth, a osodwyd dan gyfrifoldeb cofrestrydd goruchwyliol, ac a oedd yn seiliedig ar ddosbarthau cofrestru yr oedd eu ffiniau fel rheol yn cydredeg ag Undebau Deddf y Tlodion. Câi dosbarthau cofrestru eu rhannu yn is-ddosbarthau, pob un â'i gofrestrydd sefydlog, a chaent eu casglu ynghyd i ffurfio siroedd cofrestru. O 1851 ymlaen y sir gofrestru oedd y brif uned gyfansymiol yn y tablau cyfrifiad a gyhoeddid. Anaml y byddai'r sir gofrestru yn cyfateb i ffiniau'r sir hynafol, ddaearyddol neu 'gywir'. Mewn rhai achosion, megis siroedd Môn a'r Fflint, er enghraifft, yr oedd y gwahaniaeth yn sylweddol. Yr oedd creadigaeth arall, y sir seneddol, yn seiliedig ar y

Introduction

In any study of the statistical evidence relating to language change, demographic material is of principal importance. The changing patterns of population distribution, growth and movement, fertility, and household structure, form the basic material upon which all other social and economic forces operate. In nineteenth-century Wales, where two languages were in competition, demographic trends contributed to the mix of factors which determined which language was spoken to whom, and in what circumstances.

The main source of the tables in this section are the decennial population census reports and abstracts. The first census, conducted in 1801, relied on local parish officials to supply limited information on the number of houses, families and persons (male and female) in their parish, township or place, and the number of persons employed in just three classes – agriculture, trade or manufactures or handicraft, and other occupations. Clergymen were asked to supply information on the number of baptisms, burials and marriages. Early census-takers are believed to have undercounted the total population by as much as 5 per cent in 1801 and by 3 per cent in 1811. Thereafter improved methods of data collection led to increased reliability.[1]

Although the reliability of later census-taking can be generally assumed, a potential problem in charting trends over time arises with changes in the units of aggregation. Besides making the civil registration of births, marriages and deaths compulsory, the 1836 Act for the Registering of Births, Deaths and Marriages introduced a new system of local administration based on registration districts, placed under the responsibility of a superintendent registrar, whose boundaries were usually coterminous with the Poor Law Unions. Registration districts were divided into subdistricts, each with a resident registrar, and were collected together to form registration counties. From 1851 the registration county became the main unit of aggregation in the published census tables. The registration county rarely coincided with the boundaries of the ancient, geographical, or 'proper' county. In some cases, for example Anglesey and Flint, it was significantly different. Another creation, the parliamentary county, was based on the ancient county but, for the purposes of parliamentary seats, it included the detached areas of other counties located within its

sir hynafol ond, at ddibenion seddau seneddol, cynhwysai rannau ar wahân o siroedd eraill a leolid o fewn ei ffiniau. Daeth Deddf Llywodraeth Leol 1888 â rhaniadau eraill: Siroedd Gweinyddol, yn cynnwys Bwrdeistrefi, Dosbarthau Iechydol Trefol a Gwledig, a Dosbarthau Gwledig. Newidiodd Deddf Llywodraeth Leol 1894 enwau'r Dosbarthau Iechydol yn Ddosbarthau Trefol neu Wledig. Yr oedd y siroedd gweinyddol yn nes o ran arwynebedd i'r siroedd hynafol nag i'r sir gofrestru.

Newidiwyd ffiniau hefyd, a hynny mewn ymateb i ddosbarthiad newydd y boblogaeth, ac o ganlyniad i dacluso cyffredinol ar rannau o blwyfi rhanedig. Mewn materion yn ymwneud ag iaith, efallai nad oedd y newidiadau hyn yn arwyddocaol ar gyfer Cymru gyfan, ond yn lleol, gallent fod yn bwysig. Er enghraifft, collodd dosbarthau cofrestru Caerdydd a Merthyr Tudful boblogaethau o 16,000 yn y naill achos a 14,000 yn y llall yn sgil creu dosbarth Pontypridd ym 1863. Y mae'r mapiau, y rhestri a'r tablau yn yr atodiadau yn ein galluogi i gymharu'r gwahanol ardaloedd gweinyddol ac yn ei gwneud yn haws i olrhain newidiadau mewn ffiniau.[2]

Y mae'n amlwg fod twf a dosbarthiad poblogaeth yn ffactorau pwysig a ddylanwadai ar newid iaith. Dengys y tablau yng ngrŵp 1 raddfa a lleoliad newidiadau poblogaeth sylfaenol. Dengys Tablau 1.1 i 1.3 gyfansymiau poblogaeth ar gyfer Cymru, y siroedd, y dosbarthau cofrestru a'r is-ddosbarthau ym mhob cyfrifiad o 1801 hyd 1911. Dyblodd poblogaeth Cymru o 600,000 i 1,200,000 yn hanner cyntaf y bedwaredd ganrif ar bymtheg, a dyblu eto i dros ddwy filiwn ym 1911. O ganlyniad, er i'r ganran o siaradwyr Cymraeg ostwng, yr oedd cynnydd yn nifer y rhai a rifwyd, gan gyrraedd mwyafswm o 977,366 ym 1911 (gw. Iaith, Tabl 3.1). Serch hynny, y mae cyfansymiau cyfansawdd yn celu sefyllfaoedd gwrthgyferbyniol o fewn Cymru. Y mae'r gwahaniaethau lleol sylweddol a ddatgelir gan y ffigurau ar gyfer is-ddosbarthau (Tabl 1.3) yn gyfiawnhad dros eu cynnwys. Yn is-ddosbarth Ystradyfodwg (y Rhondda) rhwng 1861 a 1881, er enghraifft, bu cynnydd rhyfeddol i bymtheg gwaith y boblogaeth, tra arhosodd nifer trigolion is-ddosbarth Llansadwrn yn sir Gaerfyrddin fwy neu lai yn ei unfan rhwng 1801 a 1901. Yn ogystal â llanw a thrai cynnydd naturiol a phatrymau mudo cyson, gwelir effaith chwim a byrhoedlog safleoedd adeiladu mawr yn y cyfansymiau hyn hefyd, er mai cipluniau bob deng mlynedd a geir. Er enghraifft, rhwng 1881 a 1891, sef cyfnod adeiladu Dociau'r Barri a'r rheilffyrdd, treblodd poblogaeth wrywaidd is-ddosbarth Sain Nicolas yng Nghaerdydd. Ar lefel plwyf, yr oedd yr effaith hyd yn oed yn fwy trawiadol, gyda phoblogaeth plwyf Tregatwg ger Y Barri yn cynyddu o 303 ym 1881 i 8,228 ym 1891.

Wrth i boblogaeth Cymru gynyddu, yn enwedig o'r 1840au ymlaen, daeth hefyd yn fwyfwy trefol. Yn

boundaries. The Local Government Act of 1888 introduced further divisions: Administrative Counties, containing Municipal Boroughs, Urban and Rural Sanitary Districts, and Rural Districts. The subsequent Local Government Act of 1894 changed the name of Sanitary Districts to Urban or Rural Districts. Administrative counties were closer in area to the ancient counties than to the registration county.

Boundaries were also changed, both in response to changing population distribution, and as a result of a general tidying-up of detached parts of divided parishes. For matters relating to language, these changes might not have been significant for Wales as a whole, but at the local level, they could be important. For example, the registration districts of Cardiff and Merthyr Tydfil lost populations of 16,000 and 14,000 respectively following the formation of the district of Pontypridd in 1863. The maps, listings and tables in the appendices enable comparison of the different administrative areas and facilitate the tracing of boundary changes.[2]

Population growth and distribution were clearly important factors in determining language shift. The tables in group 1 indicate the scale and location of basic population changes. Tables 1.1 to 1.3 show population totals, for Wales, for counties, and for registration districts and subdistricts in each census from 1801 to 1911. The population of Wales doubled in the first half of the nineteenth century, from 600,000 to 1,200,000, and then doubled again to over two million in 1911. One linguistic consequence was that although the proportion of Welsh speakers decreased, the total number of Welsh speakers enumerated actually increased, and reached a maximum of 977,366 in 1911 (see Language, Table 3.1). However, overall totals conceal contrasting experiences within Wales. The figures for subdistricts, in Table 1.3, reveal appreciable local differences which justify their inclusion. For example, the subdistrict of Ystradyfodwg (Rhondda) experienced an astonishing fifteen-fold increase in population between 1861 and 1881, whereas the subdistrict of Llansadwrn in Carmarthenshire contained more or less the same number of inhabitants in 1901 as was the case in 1801, with little variation in the intervening years. Apart from the ebb and flow of natural increase and sustained migration patterns, the swift and fleeting impact of large construction sites is also revealed in these totals, albeit as decennial snapshots only. For instance, the male population in the St Nicholas subdistrict of Cardiff trebled between 1881 and 1891, a period which saw the construction of Barry Docks and railways. At parish level the impact was even more dramatic. The total population of the parish of Cadoxton near Barry increased from a mere 303 in 1881 to 8,228 in 1891.

As the population of Wales increased, particularly from the 1840s onwards, it also became increasingly

Nhabl 1.4 olrheinir datblygiad Cymru drefol rhwng 1801 – pan nad oedd gan ond un dref, sef Abertawe, boblogaeth o dros 10,000 – a 1911, pan oedd Caerdydd yn ganolfan fasnachol ryngwladol a chanddi boblogaeth o 180,000, a phan oedd poblogaeth tri ar ddeg ar hugain o ddosbarthau trefol a bwrdeistrefol Cymru dros 10,000. Dengys ffigur 1.1 ddau o brif nodweddion twf a dosbarthiad poblogaeth yng Nghymru yn y bedwaredd ganrif ar bymtheg, sef, yn gyntaf, y graddau y bu modd i siroedd gwledig dderbyn cynnydd sylweddol yn eu poblogaeth yn hanner cyntaf y ganrif, ac yn ail, y symud trawiadol diweddarach yng 'nghanolbwynt disgyrchiant' y boblogaeth i dde Cymru. Ym 1911 yr oedd bron deuparth poblogaeth Cymru wedi ei wasgu i ddwy sir, sef Morgannwg a Mynwy.

Yn achos y rhan fwyaf o'r tablau sy'n weddill, bu'n rhaid dewis rhwng atgynhyrchu'r holl ffigurau degmlwyddol ar draul eu rhannu yn elfennau, neu hepgor rhai blynyddoedd cyfrifiad. Gan ei bod yn haws dangos yr amrywiaeth o fewn Cymru trwy gyfrwng ffigurau gwahanedig, dewiswyd yr ail ddull. Rhydd tablau yng ngrwpiau 2–4, sy'n ymwneud ag oedran, statws priodasol, a man geni, ffigurau am flynyddoedd 1851, 1881 a 1911 ar gyfer Cymru, ei siroedd, a'i dosbarthau cofrestru. Y mae'r rhain yn ddigon i ddangos y prif dueddiadau demograffig. Ceir yr wybodaeth gyfatebol am y blynyddoedd eraill yn y tablau cyfrifiad cyhoeddedig neu yn y *Digest of Welsh Historical Statistics*.

Yn Nhablau 2.1 i 2.4, a ddengys y niferoedd a'r cyfraneddau mewn rhai grwpiau oedran, tynnir sylw at oedran cymharol ifanc y boblogaeth yng Nghymru oes Victoria, pryd yr oedd traean y boblogaeth dan bymtheg oed a llai nag un mewn pump o bobl dros bump a deugain. Unwaith eto y mae'n werth nodi amrywiadau lleol mewn proffiliau oedran a rhyw. Er enghraifft, y mae'r ffigurau ar gyfer is-ddosbarthau Tredegar ym 1851 ac Ystradyfodwg (y Rhondda) ym 1881 yn tystio i'r nifer anghymesur o ddynion ifainc rhwng 15 a 30 oed yn y canolfannau diwydiannol a oedd yn ehangu. Rhydd y pyramidiau poblogaeth diagramatig yn ffigur 2.1 ddarlun gweledol cliriach o fframwaith demograffig dwy ardal wrthgyferbyniol o fewn Cymru – Tregaron yn sir Aberteifi, a'r Rhondda – ynghyd â'r darlun cyffredinol ar gyfer Cymru gyfan er cymharu. O safbwynt y proses o drosglwyddo iaith, yr oedd y prinder cymharol yn nifer y bobl ifainc yn un o gadarnleoedd yr iaith yn sir Aberteifi yn arwyddocaol, ynghyd â'r diffyg cymharol yn nifer y bobl hŷn yn y cymunedau trefol diwydiannol a oedd ar gynnydd yn y de.

Y mae Tablau 3.1 a 3.2, ar statws priodasol, hefyd yn datgelu amrywiadau diddorol o fewn Cymru a hynny dros gyfnod sydd, mewn rhai ardaloedd, yn bwysig o safbwynt ystyriaethau iaith. Er gwaethaf y clodfori ar y wraig a'r 'gymhares' yn oes Victoria, y gwir oedd fod hanner y merched o oedran planta yng Nghymru yn

urbanized. Table 1.4 traces the development of urban Wales, from small beginnings in 1801, when only the town of Swansea could boast a population of over 10,000, to 1911 when Cardiff, with a population of 180,000, had become a world trading centre, and when thirty-three urban districts and municipal boroughs contained over 10,000 inhabitants. The diagrammatic representation of population growth and distribution, in figure 1.1, shows at a glance two of the major characteristics of population growth and distribution in Wales in the nineteenth century: first, the extent to which rural counties were able to absorb an appreciable population increase in the first half of the century, and second, the later dramatic shift of the population 'centre of gravity' to south Wales. In 1911 almost two-thirds of the population of Wales was concentrated in the two counties of Glamorgan and Monmouth.

For most of the remaining tables a choice had to be made between reproducing all decennial figures at the expense of disaggregation or omitting some census years. As the variation within Wales is better illustrated by disaggregated figures, the latter course of action has been pursued. Tables in groups 2–4, concerning age, marital status, and birthplace, give figures for the years 1851, 1881 and 1911 for Wales, counties, and registration districts. These adequately indicate the main demographic trends. For the intervening years, the equivalent information can be found in the published census tables or in the *Digest of Welsh Historical Statistics*.

Tables 2.1 to 2.4 show the number and proportions in certain age groups. They highlight the relative youthfulness of the population in Victorian Wales. Children under the age of fifteen comprised a third of the total population; fewer than one in five of the population were over the age of forty-five. Again, local variations in age and sex profiles are worth noting. For example, figures for the subdistricts of Tredegar in 1851 and Ystradyfodwg (Rhondda) in 1881 quantify the imbalance of young men in the age group 15–30 years in expanding industrial centres. The diagrammatic population pyramids shown in figure 2.1 give a more immediate visual representation of the demographic structure of two contrasting areas within Wales – Tregaron, in Cardiganshire, and the Rhondda – together with the overall picture for Wales for comparative purposes. Significant in the process of language transmission was, for example, the relative lack of young people in the Welsh-speaking stronghold of rural Cardiganshire, and the relative lack of older people in the growing industrial urban communities of the south.

Tables 3.1 and 3.2, on marital status, also reveal interesting variations within Wales and over time which, in some areas, have a bearing on language concerns. Despite the glorification of the role of the

ddibriod. Yn sir Aberteifi, golygai'r ffaith fod mwy o ddynion nag o ferched yn mudo o ardaloedd gwledig, ynghyd â'r arfer o ohirio priodi, mai traean yn unig o'r merched rhwng 15 a 45 oed a oedd yn briod. Mewn gwrthgyferbyniad, yr oedd dros 60 y cant o'r grŵp cyfatebol o ferched ym Medwellte a Phontypridd yn briod. Ysgrifennwyd llawer am y cyfraddau ffrwythlonder uchel yn y cymunedau glofaol, a chryfhawyd treftadaeth ddiwylliannol Gymreig cymunedau'r maes glo gan deuluoedd mawrion y don gyntaf o Gymry Cymraeg a fudodd i weithfeydd haearn a glo de Cymru.[3]

Ond efallai mai'r ffactor demograffig mwyaf grymus o safbwynt newid iaith yng Nghymru'r bedwaredd ganrif ar bymtheg oedd mudo – ymfudiad pobloedd o'r man lle y cawsant eu geni a'u magu. Cyfyd nifer o gwestiynau pwysig: i ble yr âi'r ymfudwyr a phaham? A oedd mwy nag un cam i'w mudo? A ddychwelent i fan eu geni? A briodent cyn neu ar ôl symud, a gynhalient eu cysylltiadau teuluol neu eu torri, ac a fyddent yn annog eraill i ymuno â hwy ai peidio? Y mae'r rhain yn gwestiynau hanfodol yn y cyd-destun ieithyddol Cymraeg/Saesneg. Gwaetha'r modd, tri yn unig o'r cwestiynau mwyaf sylfaenol a atebir gan ffigurau cyhoeddedig y cyfrifiad, sef: beth oedd y gwir nifer a ymfudodd rhwng cyfrifiadau ym mhob dosbarth (h.y. y newid yng nghyfanswm y boblogaeth nad yw'n ganlyniad i fwy o enedigaethau na marwolaethau), mannau geni trigolion siroedd Cymru, a mannau geni Cymry a rifwyd yn Lloegr. Y mae'r atebion i'r cwestiynau hyn, fel y'u darperir gan y cyfansymiau yn Nhablau 4.1 i 4.4, naill ai'n hepgor neu'n methu adnabod grwpiau pwysig o fudwyr dros-dro neu dymhorol, megis gweithwyr adeiladu neu weithwyr cynhaeaf neu'r rheini a chanddynt alwedigaethau teithiol. Nid yw'r gwir ffigurau ymfudo, sef y gwahaniaeth rhwng ymfudo i mewn ac allan, yn rhoi syniad o gwbl o wir raddfa'r symud. Yng nghanol mis Ebrill, fel rheol, y cynhelid y cyfrifiad ac, o ganlyniad, ni châi'r niferoedd cynyddol o ymwelwyr a lifai o Loegr i drefi gwyliau Cymru ym misoedd yr haf yn niwedd y bedwaredd ganrif ar bymtheg eu rhifo. Nid oes modd gwybod ychwaith faint o'r bobl a aned yn lleol a oedd yn ddychweledigion.

Ac eto, pa mor amherffaith bynnag yw'r data, gellir cywain llawer o wybodaeth ddefnyddiol o ddeunydd cyfrifiadau. Dengys Tablau 4.1 a 4.2 faint o'r cynnydd mewn poblogaeth yn ail hanner y bedwaredd ganrif ar bymtheg oedd yn ganlyniad cynnydd naturiol yn hytrach na mewnfudo. Yn llawer o'r dosbarthau cofrestru yr oedd y ffaith fod mwy o enedigaethau nag o farwolaethau yn egluro cynnydd o ddeg i ugain y cant mewn cyfnod rhwng dau gyfrifiad. Mewn geiriau eraill, yr oedd yn bosibl i newid bychan yng nghyfanswm y boblogaeth, neu hyd yn oed ddim newid o gwbl, awgrymu allfudo sylweddol. Yn Nosbarth Merthyr Tudful, er enghraifft, lleihad bychan (–2.7 y

Victorian wife and 'helpmeet', half the women of childbearing age in Wales remained unmarried. In Cardiganshire, the excess of male over female migration from rural areas, coupled with the custom of delayed marriage, meant that only a third of women aged 15–45 years were married. In contrast, over 60 per cent of the corresponding group of women were married in Bedwellte and Pontypridd. The high fertility rates in mining communities have been well documented, and the large families of the first wave of Welsh-speaking migrants to the ironworks and collieries of south Wales strengthened the Welsh cultural heritage of the coalfield communities.[3]

Perhaps the most powerful demographic factor affecting language change in nineteenth-century Wales, however, was migration – the movement of peoples beyond their place of birth or upbringing. Certain important questions arise: where did the migrants go and why? Did their migration involve more than one stage? Did they return to their place of origin? Did they marry before or after moving, maintain or sever their family ties, encourage or discourage others from joining them? These are vital questions in the English/Welsh language context. Unfortunately, the published census figures answer only three of the most basic questions, namely, what was the net intercensal migration figure for each district (i.e. change in total population not accounted for by an excess of births over deaths), what were the places of birth of inhabitants of counties of Wales, and what were the places of birth of Welsh people enumerated in England? The answers to these questions, as provided by the totals given in Tables 4.1 to 4.4, either omit or fail to identify important groups of temporary or seasonal migrants such as construction or harvest workers and those with travelling occupations. Net migration figures, the difference between inward and outward migration, give no indication of the actual scale of movement. Census day was usually in early April, thereby leaving uncounted the increasing numbers of English tourists flocking to the Welsh resorts in the summer months of the late nineteenth century. There is also no way of knowing how many of the local born were returnees.

Yet, however imperfect the data, much useful information can be gleaned from census material. Tables 4.1 and 4.2 reveal how much of the increase in population in the second half of the nineteenth century was the result of natural increase rather than in-migration. In many registration districts an increase of 10–20 per cent during an intercensal period could be supported by the surplus of births over deaths. In other words, a small total population change, or even no change at all, might actually indicate a substantial out-migration. The district of Merthyr Tydfil, for example, experienced a modest decrease in population (–2.7%) between 1871 and 1881, but the net outward

cant) a gafwyd yn y boblogaeth rhwng 1871 a 1881, er bod y gwir nifer a allfudodd yn y cyfnod hwnnw – llawer ohonynt i'r cymoedd glo ager cyfagos – bron yn 20,000.

Yn Nhablau 4.3 i 4.5 canolbwyntir ar fan geni trigolion. Gan fod y ffigurau hyn yn seiliedig ar dri diffiniad gwahanol o 'sir', dylid darllen y tablau yn ochelgar a'u hystyried yn fynegbyst i lwybrau ymfudo yn hytrach nag yn setiau o ffigurau i'w cymharu. Y mae cyfiawnhad dros y geiriau hyn o rybudd. Y mae gwahanol ddeongliadau o dystiolaeth cyfrifiadau a thystiolaeth arall o fewnfudo wedi cyfrannu at ddadl boeth ynglŷn ag ymfudo ac iaith ym Maes Glo De Cymru, a ysgogwyd gan Brinley Thomas mewn erthygl ar gysylltiadau economaidd rhwng Cymru ac America.[4] Er i ddilysrwydd y dystiolaeth ystadegol a'r dull dadansoddi a ddefnyddiwyd gan Thomas gael eu herio, y mae cyfiawnhad o hyd dros hanfod ei ddadl, sef bod y Cymry Cymraeg a ymfudodd o'r Gymru wledig i aneddiadau gweithfeydd haearn a glo de Cymru yn y bedwaredd ganrif ar bymtheg, yn hytrach nag i gyrchfannau yn Lloegr neu dramor, wedi creu crynoadau newydd o siaradwyr Cymraeg trefol a roddodd fywyd newydd i ddiwylliant Cymraeg a oedd fwyfwy dan fygythiad. Mewn gwrthgyferbyniad, denodd yr ehangu diweddarach ymfudwyr o'r tu allan i Gymru, gan atgyfnerthu pwysau cyferbyniol er Seisnigo. Y mae'r ffigurau yn Nhabl 4.3a ar gyfer Morgannwg yn sicr yn ategu'r farn hon.

Dengys Tabl 4.3b ddosbarthiad yr ymfudwyr o Gymru a rifwyd yn Lloegr, gan amlygu'n glir gyfeiriad y llwybrau mudo a ddilynai'r llinellau cyfathrebu naturiol tua'r dwyrain. Symudodd brodorion o ogledd Cymru i Lerpwl[5] ac i drefi eraill yn swydd Gaerhirfryn; symudodd brodorion o dde a chanolbarth Cymru i ganolbarth Lloegr neu Lundain. Ym 1851 cafodd un o bob deg person a aned yng Nghymru ei rifo yn Lloegr. Erbyn 1881 a 1911, yr oedd y gyfran hon wedi codi i un o bob wyth. Byddai bron pob cartref yng Nghymru mewn cysylltiad ag aelodau o'r teulu a oedd wedi ymgartrefu yn Lloegr – ewythrod, modrybedd, cefndryd, neu frodyr neu chwiorydd – ac ni allai eu llythyrau a'u hymweliadau gartref lai na chyfleu amgylchedd anghymreig.

Yr oedd llawer o ymfudwyr o Gymru yn fwy anturus na'r rhai a groesodd Glawdd Offa yn unig. Y mae Tabl 4.5 yn ein hatgoffa am y rhai hynny a fentrodd ar y daith fwy ansicr dros Fôr Iwerydd. O'u cymharu â phobloedd eraill Ewrop, amharod, at ei gilydd, fu'r Cymry i fentro oddi cartref[6] ac efallai nad yw'r nifer yn ymddangos yn fawr o'i gymharu â niferoedd y Gwyddelod a'r Albanwyr. Serch hynny, y mae dosbarthiad a dwysedd y Cymry yn ffactorau arwyddocaol o safbwynt cadw iaith. Mewn rhai aneddiadau, yn enwedig ym maes glo carreg Pennsylvania, cadwodd y Cymry eu traddodiadau mor daer, os nad yn fwy taer, na'r cymunedau a adawsent yng Nghymru.

migration figure for that period was almost 20,000, many of whom moved the short distance to the neighbouring and rapidly filling steam coal valleys.

Tables 4.3 to 4.5 focus on the birthplace of inhabitants. As the figures in these tables are based on three different definitions of 'county', these tables should be read with caution and regarded as separate indicators of migration paths rather than as sets of comparable figures. These words of caution are justified. Differing interpretations of census and other migration evidence have contributed to a vigorous debate about migration and language in the South Wales Coalfield initiated by Brinley Thomas in an article on Welsh economic links with America.[4] Although the validity of statistical evidence and method of analysis used by Thomas has been challenged, the essence of his argument remains justified – that the migration of Welsh speakers from rural Wales to the ironworks and colliery settlements of south Wales in the nineteenth century, in preference to destinations in England or abroad, established new concentrations of urban Welsh speakers who gave fresh vitality to an increasingly threatened Welsh culture. By contrast, later expansion drew in migrants from outside Wales, thereby reinforcing contrary pressures of Anglicization. Figures in Table 4.3a for Glamorgan certainly support this view.

Table 4.3b shows the distribution of Welsh migrants enumerated in England. The figures clearly indicate the direction of migration paths following natural lines of communication eastward. Natives of north Wales moved to the growing city of Liverpool[5] and to other towns in Lancashire; natives of south and mid-Wales moved to the Midlands or London. In 1851, one of every ten persons born in Wales was enumerated in England. By 1881 and 1911, this proportion had risen to one in eight. Almost every household would have had links with family members settled in England – uncles, aunts, cousins, or siblings – whose visits and letters home could only represent a non-Welsh environment.

Many Welsh migrants were more adventurous than those who simply crossed Offa's Dyke. Table 4.5 is a reminder of those who undertook the more uncertain voyage across the Atlantic. The Welsh, compared with other European peoples, could be still be labelled 'stay-at-homes'[6] and the total figures may not seem large in comparison with the Irish or the Scots. However, the distribution and concentration of Welsh people are significant factors for language maintenance. Welsh immigrants in certain settlements, particularly the anthracite coalfield of Pennsylvania, sustained Welsh cultural traditions as fervently, if not more so, than the communities they had left in Wales. Although there is no doubt that most migrants were motivated by a complex mixture of economic, social and psychological factors, settlements such as Chubut in Patagonia were founded specifically for cultural reasons, to renew

Diau fod cyfuniad cymhleth o ffactorau economaidd, cymdeithasol a seicolegol yn gyrru'r rhan fwyaf o ymfudwyr, ond rhesymau diwylliannol a oedd yn bennaf wrth wraidd trefedigaethau megis Chubut ym Mhatagonia, sef adnewyddu a chynnal y ffordd Gymreig o fyw mewn tiroedd cymharol wag a diogel rhag y bygythiadau cynyddol a wynebai'r Gymraeg a'i diwylliant yng Nghymru yn ail hanner y bedwaredd ganrif ar bymtheg.

Y mae'r tabl sy'n weddill yn yr adran ar Boblogaeth, sef 5.1, yn dosbarthu niferoedd y gwrywod a'r benywod yn ôl galwedigaeth, ar gyfer Cymru a'i siroedd o 1851 hyd 1911. Unwaith eto rhaid datgan rhybudd: cipluniau yw'r rhain a dynnwyd ym mis Ebrill bob deng mlynedd ac nid ydynt felly yn cynnwys galwedigaethau tymhorol fel gwaith cynhaeaf a diwydiannau gwasanaeth yn gysylltiedig â thwristiaeth. Y mae'r anghysondeb a'r dryswch o ran dosbarthu gwaith fferm a gwasanaeth i fenywod yn un o lawer agwedd anfoddhaol ar dablau cyfrifiad fel tystiolaeth o waith gan ferched. Ac eto, serch yr amherffeithrwydd, y mae'r ffigurau yn y tablau hyn yn ddefnyddiol o safbwynt dangos tueddiadau pwysig sy'n berthnasol i ddefnydd o iaith. Yr oedd rhai galwedigaethau o anghenraid yn dadwreiddio pobl; yr oedd rhai yn golygu defnyddio naill ai'r Gymraeg neu'r Saesneg yn gyfrwng cyfathrebu. Y mae'r ffigurau'n cadarnhau'n glir y newidiadau ategol yng nghryfderau'r sectorau amaethyddiaeth a mwyngloddio yn economi Cymru yn ail hanner y bedwaredd ganrif ar bymtheg. Y mae dechreuadau grwpiau galwedigaethol newydd yn ystod y cyfnod hwn, yn enwedig yng ngwasanaeth y llywodraeth, mân-werthu a masnach, cludiant a chyfathrebu, hefyd yn arwyddocaol o ran dylanwad ar iaith a newid ieithyddol.

1 Gw. Michael Drake, 'The census, 1801–1891' a Peter M. Tillott, 'Sources of inaccuracy in the 1851 and 1861 censuses' yn E. A. Wrigley (gol.), *Nineteenth-century society: Essays in the use of quantitative methods for the study of social data* (Cambridge, 1972), tt. 7–46, 82–133.

2 Am eglurhad defnyddiol ar weinyddu cyfrifiad a data cyfrifiad, gw. Edward Higgs, *Making Sense of the Census: The Manuscript Returns for England and Wales, 1801–1901* (London, 1989).

3 E.e., Dov Friedlander, 'Demographic patterns and socio-economic characteristics of the coal mining population of England and Wales in the nineteenth century', *Economic Development and Cultural Change*, 22 (1973), 39–51; Michael R. Haines, 'Fertility, nuptiality, and occupation: a study of coal-mining populations and regions in England and Wales in the mid-nineteenth century', *The Journal of Interdisciplinary History*, VIII, no. 2 (1977), 245–80.

4 Brinley Thomas, 'Wales and the Atlantic Economy', *Scottish Journal of Political Economy*, VI (1959), 169–72; ailadroddir ei ddadl yn 'The Industrial Revolution and the Welsh Language' yn Colin Baber ac L. J. Williams (goln.), *Modern South Wales: Essays in Economic History* (Cardiff, 1986), tt. 6–21. Am drafodaeth, gw. Dudley Baines, *Migration in a Mature Economy. Emigration and Internal Migration in England and Wales, 1861–1900* (Cambridge, 1985) ac ateb Brinley Thomas yn 'A Cauldron of Rebirth: Population and the Welsh Language in

and maintain the Welsh way of life in relatively empty lands safe from the growing threats to the Welsh language and culture in Wales in the second half of the nineteenth century.

The remaining Table 5.1 in the Population section classifies the numbers of males and females by occupation, for Wales and each county, 1851–1911. Once again a cautionary note must be sounded: these are snapshot figures taken in April in each decennial year and therefore do not reflect seasonal occupations like harvest work and service industries associated with tourism. The inconsistency and confusion in classifying female farm and service labour is one of the many unsatisfactory aspects of census tables as evidence of work by women. Yet, despite the many imperfections, the figures in these tables usefully identify important trends of relevance to language use. Some occupations necessarily uprooted people; some necessarily involved the use of English or Welsh as the language of communication. The complementary changes in strengths in the agriculture and the mining sectors which occurred in the Welsh economy in the second half of the nineteenth century are clearly quantified. The introduction of new occupational groups during this period, notably in government service, retailing and commerce, transport and communications, are also significant in terms of language influence and change.

1 See Michael Drake, 'The census, 1801–1891' and Peter M. Tillott, 'Sources of inaccuracy in the 1851 and 1861 censuses' in E. A. Wrigley (ed.), *Nineteenth-century society: Essays in the use of quantitative methods for the study of social data* (Cambridge, 1972), pp. 7–46, 82–133.

2 For a useful explanation of census-taking and census data, see Edward Higgs, *Making Sense of the Census: The Manuscript Returns for England and Wales, 1801–1901* (London, 1989).

3 For example, Dov Friedlander, 'Demographic patterns and socio-economic characteristics of the coal mining population of England and Wales in the nineteenth century', *Economic Development and Cultural Change*, 22 (1973), 39–51; Michael R. Haines, 'Fertility, nuptiality, and occupation: a study of coal-mining populations and regions in England and Wales in the mid-nineteenth century', *The Journal of Interdisciplinary History*, VIII, no. 2 (1977), 245–80.

4 Brinley Thomas, 'Wales and the Atlantic Economy', *Scottish Journal of Political Economy*, VI (1959), 169–72; his argument is restated in 'The Industrial Revolution and the Welsh Language' in Colin Baber and L. J. Williams (eds.), *Modern South Wales: Essays in Economic History* (Cardiff, 1986), pp. 6–21. For a critique, see Dudley Baines, *Migration in a Mature Economy. Emigration and Internal Migration in England and Wales, 1861–1900* (Cambridge, 1985) and a riposte by Brinley Thomas in 'A Cauldron of Rebirth: Population and the Welsh Language in the Nineteenth Century', *Welsh History Review*, 13, no. 4 (1987), 418–37. The matter is clearly resolved in Philip N. Jones, 'Population Migration into Glamorgan 1861–1911: a Reassessment' in Prys Morgan (ed.), *Glamorgan County History, Vol. VI, Glamorgan Society 1780–1980* (Cardiff, 1988), pp. 173–202.

5 In *The Welsh Builder on Merseyside* (Liverpool, 1946), J. R. Jones describes how Welsh-speaking young men from north Wales were able to find work in a Welsh-speaking environment in the building trade in Liverpool.

the Nineteenth Century', *Cylchgrawn Hanes Cymru*, 13, rhifyn 4 (1987), 418–37. Torrir y ddadl yn Philip N. Jones, 'Population Migration into Glamorgan 1861–1911: a Reassessment' yn Prys Morgan (gol.), *Glamorgan County History, Vol. VI, Glamorgan Society 1780–1980* (Cardiff, 1988), tt. 173–202.

[5] Yn *The Welsh Builder on Merseyside* (Liverpool, 1946), y mae J. R. Jones yn disgrifio sut y llwyddai Cymry Cymraeg ifainc o ogledd Cymru i gael gwaith mewn amgylchedd Cymraeg yn y diwydiant adeiladu yn Lerpwl.

[6] Anne Kelly Knowles, 'The Making of Ethnic Capitalists: Welsh Iron-Makers in Southern Ohio' (traethawd PhD anghyhoeddedig Prifysgol Wisconsin, 1993), t. 19.

[6] Anne Kelly Knowles, 'The Making of Ethnic Capitalists: Welsh Iron-Makers in Southern Ohio' (unpublished University of Wisconsin PhD thesis, 1993), p. 19.

Population 1.1 Total population. Persons, males, females. Number and percentage change. Number of females per 1000 males. Wales and Registration Counties. Census years 1801–1911

	Year	Number Persons	Males	Females	Females/ 1000 males	Intercensal period	*Percentage change* Persons	*Males*	*Females*
WALES	1801	**601767**	286667	315100	1099				
	1811	**688774**	330085	358689	1087	1801–11	***14.5***	*15.1*	*13.8*
	1821	**811381**	399596	411785	1031	1811–21	***17.8***	*21.1*	*14.8*
	1831	**924329**	455736	468593	1028	1821–31	***13.9***	*14.0*	*13.8*
	1841	**1068547**	529616	538931	1018	1831–41	***15.6***	*16.2*	*15.0*
	1851	**1188914**	594793	594121	999	1841–51	***11.3***	*12.3*	*10.2*
		(1186697)	(593690)	(593007)					
	1861	**1312834**	655145	657689	1004	1851–61	***10.6***	*10.4*	*10.9*
		(1296001)	(646560)	(649441)					
	1871	**1421670**	710601	711069	1001	1861–71	***9.7***	*9.9*	*9.5*
		(1420408)	(709938)	(710470)					
	1881	**1577559**	789074	788485	999	1871–81	***11.1***	*11.1*	*11.0*
		(1577533)	(789062)	(788471)					
	1891	**1776405**	894509	881896	986	1881–91	***12.6***	*13.4*	*11.8*
		(1774810)	(893759)	(881051)					
	1901	**2015012**	1012187	1002825	991	1891–1901	***13.5***	*13.3*	*13.8*
		(2033287)	(1021737)	(1011550)					
	1911	**2442041**	1242387	1199654	966	1901–11	***20.1***	*21.6*	*18.6*

Boundary changes: 1851–61 loss of 2217 from Denbighshire to Shropshire (pop. 1851)
1861–71 loss of 11930 from Radnorshire to Herefordshire, loss of 4903 from Denbighshire to Cheshire (pop. 1861)
1871–81 loss of 1262 from Radnorshire to Herefordshire (pop. 1871)
1881–91 gain of 27 from Gloucestershire to Monmouthshire, gain of 42 from Cheshire to Denbighshire, loss of 55 from Monmouthshire to Herefordshire, loss of 40 from Montgomeryshire to Shropshire (pop. 1881)
1891–1901 loss of 316 from Denbighshire to Cheshire, loss of 979 from Denbighshire to Shropshire (pop. 1891)
1901–11 gain of 18275 from Cheshire to Flintshire (pop. 1901)

Registration Counties

	Year	Persons	Males	Females	Females/ 1000 males	Intercensal period	Persons	Males	Females
MONMOUTH	1801	**54750**	26903	27847	1035				
	1811	**72927**	36518	36409	997	1801–11	***33.2***	*35.7*	*30.7*
	1821	**88639**	45848	42791	933	1811–21	***21.5***	*25.5*	*17.5*
	1831	**112686**	58437	54249	928	1821–31	***27.1***	*27.5*	*26.8*
	1841	**151021**	79034	71987	911	1831–41	***34.0***	*35.2*	*32.7*
	1851	**177130**	92301	84829	919	1841–51	***17.3***	*16.8*	*17.8*
	1861	**196977**	101010	95967	950	1851–61	***11.2***	*9.4*	*13.1*
	1871	**219708**	113862	105846	930	1861–71	***11.5***	*12.7*	*10.3*
	1881	**234332**	119965	114367	953	1871–81	***6.7***	*5.4*	*8.1*
		(234304)	(119949)	(114355)					
	1891	**275242**	142332	132910	934	1881–91	***17.5***	*18.7*	*16.2*
		(275612)	(142511)	(133101)					
	1901	**316864**	162737	154127	947	1891–1901	***15.0***	*14.2*	*15.8*
	1911	**414666**	216906	197760	912	1901–11	***30.9***	*33.3*	*28.3*

Boundary changes: 1881–91 loss of 93 to Herefordshire, gain of 38 from Herefordshire, gain of 27 from Gloucestershire (pop. 1871)
1891–1901 loss of 550 to Glamorgan, loss of 270 to Breconshire, gain of 1190 from Glamorgan (pop. 1881)

	Year	Persons	Males	Females	Females/ 1000 males	Intercensal period	Persons	Males	Females
GLAMORGAN	1801	**74189**	35572	38617	1086				
	1811	**89099**	43440	45659	1051	1801–11	***20.1***	*22.1*	*18.2*
	1821	**107263**	53482	53781	1006	1811–21	***20.4***	*23.1*	*17.8*
	1831	**132161**	66137	66024	998	1821–31	***23.2***	*23.7*	*22.8*
	1841	**178050**	91430	86620	947	1831–41	***34.7***	*38.2*	*31.2*
	1851	**240095**	125087	115008	919	1841–51	***34.8***	*36.8*	*32.8*
	1861	**326254**	167835	158419	944	1851–61	***35.9***	*34.2*	*37.7*
	1871	**405798**	209616	196182	936	1861–71	***24.4***	*24.9*	*23.8*
	1881	**518383**	266128	252255	948	1871–81	***27.7***	*27.0*	*28.6*
	1891	**693072**	363252	329820	908	1881–91	***33.7***	*36.5*	*30.7*
		(692432)	(362930)	(329502)					
	1901	**866250**	447103	419147	937	1891–1901	***25.1***	*23.2*	*27.2*
	1911	**1130668**	587666	543002	924	1901–11	***30.5***	*31.4*	*29.5*

Boundary changes: 1891–1901 loss of 1190 to Monmouthshire, gain of 550 from Monmouthshire (pop. 1891)

	Year	Number Persons	Males	Females	Females/ 1000 males	Intercensal period	*Percentage change* Persons	*Males*	*Females*
CARMARTHEN	1801	**55571**	25861	29710	1149				
	1811	**64642**	30187	34455	1141	1801–11	***16.3***	*16.7*	*16.0*
	1821	**75363**	36264	39099	1078	1811–21	***16.6***	*20.1*	*13.5*
	1831	**84339**	40711	43628	1072	1821–31	***11.9***	*12.3*	*11.6*
	1841	**89559**	42694	46865	1098	1831–41	***6.2***	*4.9*	*7.4*
	1851	**94672**	45519	49153	1080	1841–51	***5.7***	*6.6*	*4.9*
	1861	**96651**	46149	50502	1094	1851–61	***2.1***	*1.4*	*2.7*
	1871	**101381**	48350	53031	1097	1861–71	***4.9***	*4.8*	*5.0*
	1881	**111255**	53489	57766	1080	1871–81	***9.7***	*10.6*	*8.9*
	1891	**118624**	56922	61702	1084	1881–91	***6.6***	*6.4*	*6.8*
		(117721)	(56504)	(61217)					
	1901	**123570**	59339	64231	1082	1891–1901	***5.0***	*5.0*	*4.9*
	1911	**151050**	76017	75033	987	1901–11	***22.2***	*28.1*	*16.8*

Boundary changes: 1891–1901 loss of 903 to Breconshire (pop. 1891)

	Year	Number Persons	Males	Females	Females/ 1000 males	Intercensal period	Persons	Males	Females
PEMBROKE	1801	**50270**	22712	27558	1213				
	1811	**54213**	24684	29529	1196	1801–11	***7.8***	*8.7*	*7.2*
	1821	**65442**	30727	34715	1130	1811–21	***20.7***	*24.5*	*17.6*
	1831	**72946**	34203	38743	1133	1821–31	***11.5***	*11.3*	*11.6*
	1841	**78557**	36401	42156	1158	1831–41	***7.7***	*6.4*	*8.8*
	1851	**84472**	39620	44852	1132	1841–51	***7.5***	*8.8*	*6.4*
	1861	**87690**	42388	45302	1069	1851–61	***3.8***	*7.0*	*1.0*
	1871	**83873**	39474	44399	1125	1861–71	***–4.4***	*–6.9*	*–2.0*
	1881	**83679**	40085	43594	1088	1871–81	***–0.2***	*1.5*	*–1.8*
	1891	**82003**	38771	43232	1115	1881–91	***–2.0***	*–3.3*	*–0.8*
	1901	**82424**	39356	43068	1094	1891–1901	***0.5***	*1.5*	*–0.4*
	1911	**84874**	41219	43655	1059	1901–11	***3.0***	*4.7*	*1.4*

No boundary changes

	Year	Number Persons	Males	Females	Females/ 1000 males	Intercensal period	Persons	Males	Females
CARDIGAN	**1801**	**61290**	**28921**	**32369**	**1119**				
	1811	**70067**	32830	37237	1134	1801–11	***14.3***	*13.5*	*15.0*
	1821	**81765**	39318	42447	1080	1811–21	***16.7***	*19.8*	*14.0*
	1831	**90690**	43118	47572	1103	1821–31	***10.9***	*9.7*	*12.1*
	1841	**96002**	44492	51510	1158	1831–41	***5.9***	*3.2*	*8.3*
	1851	**97614**	45155	52459	1162	1841–51	***1.7***	*1.5*	*1.8*
	1861	**97401**	44446	52955	1191	1851–61	***–0.2***	*–1.6*	*0.9*
	1871	**97869**	44247	53622	1212	1861–71	***0.5***	*–0.4*	*1.3*
	1881	**95137**	42717	52420	1227	1871–81	***–2.8***	*–3.5*	*–2.2*
	1891	**86383**	37992	48391	1274	1881–91	***–9.2***	*–11.1*	*–7.7*
	1901	**82707**	36603	46104	1260	1891–1901	***–4.3***	*–3.7*	*–4.7*
	1911	**80769**	36526	44243	1211	1901–11	***–2.3***	*–0.2*	*–4.0*

No boundary changes

	Year	Number Persons	Males	Females	Females/ 1000 males	Intercensal period	Persons	Males	Females
BRECON	1801	**34791**	16848	17943	1065				
	1811	**39495**	19251	20244	1052	1801–11	***13.5***	*14.3*	*12.8*
	1821	**44853**	22507	22346	993	1811–21	***13.6***	*16.9*	*10.4*
	1831	**48799**	24401	24398	1000	1821–31	***8.8***	*8.4*	*9.2*
	1841	**55420**	27858	27562	989	1831–41	***13.6***	*14.2*	*13.0*
	1851	**59178**	29993	29185	973	1841–51	***6.8***	*7.7*	*5.9*
	1861	**58860**	29640	29220	986	1851–61	***–0.5***	*–1.2*	*0.1*
	1871	**56932**	28494	28438	998	1861–71	***–3.3***	*–3.9*	*–2.7*
	1881	**54140**	26991	27149	1006	1871–81	***–4.9***	*–5.3*	*–4.5*
	1891	**52872**	26333	26539	1008	1881–91	***–2.3***	*–2.4*	*–2.2*
		(54045)	(26894)	(27151)					
	1901	**53951**	26970	26981	1000	1891–1901	***–0.2***	*0.3*	*–0.6*
	1911	**56370**	28308	28062	991	1901–11	***4.5***	*5.0*	*4.0*

Boundary changes: 1891–1901 gain of 270 from Monmouthshire, gain of 903 from Carmarthenshire (pop. 1891)

	Year	Number Persons	Males	Females	Females/ 1000 males	Intercensal period	*Percentage change* Persons	*Males*	*Females*
RADNOR	1801	**23533**	11587	11946	1031				
	1811	**25108**	12230	12878	1053	1801–11	***6.7***	*5.5*	*7.8*
	1821	**28065**	14069	13996	995	1811–21	***11.8***	*15.0*	*8.7*
	1831	**30640**	15421	15219	987	1821–31	***9.2***	*9.6*	*8.7*
	1841	**31776**	16116	15660	972	1831–41	***3.7***	*4.5*	*2.9*
	1851	**31425**	16118	15307	950	1841–51	***–1.1***	*0.0*	*–2.3*
	1861	**32866**	17056	15810	927	1851–61	***4.6***	*5.8*	*3.3*
		(20936)	(10965)	(9971)					
	1871	**21016**	10811	10205	944	1861–71	***0.4***	*–1.4*	*2.3*
		(19754)	(10148)	(9606)					
	1881	**18523**	9404	9119	970	1871–81	***–6.2***	*–7.3*	*–5.1*
	1891	**17119**	8486	8633	1017	1881–91	***–7.6***	*–9.8*	*–5.3*
	1901	**20241**	10711	9530	890	1891–1901	***18.2***	*26.2*	*10.4*
	1911	**17505**	8796	8709	990	1901–11	***–13.5***	*–17.9*	*–8.6*

Boundary changes: 1861–71 loss of 11930 to Herefordshire (pop. 1861)
1871–81 loss of 1262 to Herefordshire (pop. 1871)

	Year	Number Persons	Males	Females	Females/ 1000 males	Intercensal period	*Persons*	*Males*	*Females*
MONTGOMERY	1801	**56041**	26885	29156	1084				
	1811	**60331**	29452	30879	1048	1801–11	***7.7***	*9.5*	*5.9*
	1821	**69349**	34440	34909	1014	1811–21	***14.9***	*16.9*	*13.1*
	1831	**77121**	38412	38709	1008	1821–31	***11.2***	*11.5*	*10.9*
	1841	**79756**	39488	40268	1020	1831–41	***3.4***	*2.8*	*4.0*
	1851	**77142**	38541	38601	1002	1841–51	***–3.3***	*–2.4*	*–4.1*
	1861	**76923**	38887	38036	978	1851–61	***–0.3***	*0.9*	*–1.5*
	1871	**78400**	39507	38893	984	1861–71	***1.9***	*1.6*	*2.3*
	1881	**76196**	38295	37901	990	1871–81	***–2.8***	*–3.1*	*–2.6*
		(76197)	(38295)	(37902)	990				
	1891	**67297**	32721	34576	1057	1881–91	***–11.7***	*–14.6*	*–8.8*
		(67418)	(32777)	(34641)					
	1901	**63994**	31195	32799	1051	1891–1901	***–5.1***	*–4.8*	*–5.3*
	1911	**62201**	30536	31665	1037	1901–11	***–2.8***	*–2.1*	*–3.5*

Boundary changes: 1881–91 loss of 40 to Shropshire, gain of 41 from Merioneth (pop. 1881)
1891–1901 gain of 121 from Merioneth (pop. 1891)

	Year	Number Persons	Males	Females	Females/ 1000 males	Intercensal period	*Persons*	*Males*	*Females*
FLINT	1801	**22163**	10781	11382	1056				
	1811	**26632**	13013	13619	1047	1801–11	***20.2***	*20.7*	*19.7*
	1821	**31178**	15479	15699	1014	1811–21	***17.1***	*19.0*	*15.3*
	1831	**35307**	17627	17680	1003	1821–31	***13.2***	*13.9*	*12.6*
	1841	**40798**	20673	20125	973	1831–41	***15.6***	*17.3*	*13.8*
	1851	**41047**	20787	20260	975	1841–51	***0.6***	*0.6*	*0.7*
	1861	**39941**	19997	19944	997	1851–61	***–2.7***	*–3.8*	*–1.6*
	1871	**43517**	22119	21398	967	1861–71	***9.0***	*10.6*	*7.3*
	1881	**45774**	23217	22557	972	1871–81	***5.2***	*5.0*	*5.4*
	1891	**42565**	21373	21192	992	1881–91	***–7.0***	*–7.9*	*–6.1*
	1901	**42261**	21129	21132	1000	1891–1901	***–0.7***	*–1.1*	*–0.3*
		(60536)	(30679)	(29857)					
	1911	**69722**	35440	34282	967	1901–11	***15.2***	*15.5*	*14.8*

Boundary changes: 1901–11 loss of 3326 to Cheshire, gain of 21601 from Cheshire (pop. 1901)

	Year	Number Persons	Males	Females	Females/ 1000 males	Intercensal period	*Percentage change* Persons	*Males*	*Females*
DENBIGH	1801	**61624**	29876	31748	1063				
	1811	**66059**	31765	34294	1080	1801–11	***7.2***	*6.3*	*8.0*
	1821	**78626**	38933	39693	1020	1811–21	***19.0***	*22.6*	*15.7*
	1831	**84650**	41806	42844	1025	1821–31	***7.7***	*7.4*	*7.9*
	1841	**92036**	45826	46210	1008	1831–41	***8.7***	*9.6*	*7.9*
	1851	**96915**	48639	48276	993	1841–51	***5.3***	*6.1*	*4.5*
		(94698)	(47536)	(47162)					
	1861	**104346**	52508	51838	987	1851–61	***10.2***	*10.5*	*9.9*
		(99443)	(50014)	(49429)					
	1871	**105164**	52389	52775	1007	1861–71	***5.8***	*4.7*	*6.8*
	1881	**112940**	56501	56439	999	1871–81	***7.4***	*7.8*	*6.9*
		(112982)	(56527)	(56455)					
	1891	**116698**	58433	58265	997	1881–91	***3.3***	*3.4*	*3.2*
		(115103)	(57683)	(57420)					
	1901	**126458**	63351	63107	996	1891–1901	***9.9***	*9.8*	*9.9*
	1911	**136810**	68298	68512	1003	1901–11	***8.2***	*7.8*	*8.6*

Boundary changes: 1851–61 loss of 2217 to Shropshire (pop. 1851)
1861–71 loss of 4903 to Cheshire (pop. 1861)
1881–91 gain of 42 from Cheshire (pop. 1881)
1891–1901 loss of 316 to Cheshire, loss of 979 to Shropshire (pop. 1891)

	Year	Number Persons	Males	Females	Females/ 1000 males	Intercensal period	*Percentage change* Persons	*Males*	*Females*
MERIONETH	1801	**35847**	16991	18856	1110				
	1811	**38644**	18167	20477	1127	1801–11	***7.8***	*6.9*	*8.6*
	1821	**42721**	20657	22064	1068	1811–21	***10.6***	*13.7*	*7.8*
	1831	**45217**	22120	23097	1044	1821–31	***5.8***	*7.1*	*4.7*
	1841	**50713**	25061	25652	1024	1831–41	***12.2***	*13.3*	*11.1*
	1851	**51307**	25389	25918	1021	1841–51	***1.2***	*1.3*	*1.0*
	1861	**53230**	26308	26922	1023	1851–61	***3.7***	*3.6*	*3.9*
	1871	**61507**	30765	30742	999	1861–71	***15.5***	*16.9*	*14.2*
	1881	**68278**	34350	33928	988	1871–81	***11.0***	*11.7*	*10.4*
		(68237)	(34328)	(33909)					
	1891	**64726**	31841	32885	1033	1881–91	***–5.1***	*–7.2*	*–3.0*
		(64605)	(31785)	(32820)					
	1901	**64248**	31504	32744	1039	1891–1901	***–0.6***	*–0.9*	*–0.2*
	1911	**60280**	29076	31204	1073	1901–11	***–6.2***	*–7.7*	*–4.7*

Boundary changes: 1881–91 loss of 41 to Montgomeryshire (pop. 1881)
1891–1901 loss of 121 to Montgomeryshire (pop. 1891)

	Year	Number Persons	Males	Females	Females/ 1000 males	Intercensal period	*Percentage change* Persons	*Males*	*Females*
CAERNARFON	1801	**46006**	21733	24273	1117				
	1811	**53447**	25294	28153	1113	1801–11	***16.2***	*16.4*	*16.0*
	1821	**63669**	31202	32467	1041	1811–21	***19.1***	*23.4*	*15.3*
	1831	**72475**	35160	37315	1061	1821–31	***13.8***	*12.7*	*14.9*
	1841	**86753**	42272	44481	1052	1831–41	***19.7***	*20.2*	*19.2*
	1851	**94674**	46472	48202	1037	1841–51	***9.1***	*9.9*	*8.4*
		(98185)	(48137)	(50048)					
	1861	**103538**	50420	53118	1054	1851–61	***5.5***	*4.7*	*6.1*
	1871	**111378**	54077	57301	1060	1861–71	***7.6***	*7.3*	*7.9*
	1881	**123781**	60742	63039	1038	1871–81	***11.1***	*12.3*	*10.0*
		(123800)	(60752)	(63048)					
	1891	**125585**	59731	65854	1103	1881–91	***1.4***	*–1.7*	*4.5*
	1901	**137236**	65368	71868	1099	1891–1901	***9.3***	*9.4*	*9.1*
	1911	**141767**	66619	75148	1128	1901–11	***3.3***	*1.9*	*4.6*

Boundary changes: 1851–61 gain of 3511 from Anglesey (pop. 1851)
1881–91 gain of 19 from Anglesey (pop. 1881)

	Year	Number Persons	Males	Females	Females/ 1000 males	Intercensal period	Percentage change Persons	Males	Females
ANGLESEY	1801	**25692**	11997	13695	1142				
	1811	**28110**	13254	14856	1121	1801–11	***9.4***	*10.5*	*8.5*
	1821	**34448**	16670	17778	1066	1811–21	***22.5***	*25.8*	*19.7*
	1831	**37298**	18183	19115	1051	1821–31	***8.3***	*9.1*	*7.5*
	1841	**38106**	18271	19835	1086	1831–41	***2.2***	*0.5*	*3.8*
	1851	**43243**	21172	22071	1042	1841–51	***13.5***	*15.9*	*11.3*
		(39732)	(19507)	(20225)					
	1861	**38157**	18501	19656	1062	1851–61	***–4.0***	*–5.2*	*–2.8*
	1871	**35127**	16890	18237	1080	1861–71	***–7.9***	*–8.7*	*–7.2*
	1881	**35141**	17190	17951	1044	1871–81	***0.0***	*1.8*	*–1.6*
		(35122)	(17180	17942)					
	1891	**34219**	16322	17897	1096	1881–91	***–2.6***	*–5.0*	*–0.3*
	1901	**34808**	16821	17987	1069	1891–1901	***1.7***	*3.1*	*0.5*
	1911	**35359**	16980	18379	1082	1901–11	***1.6***	*0.9*	*2.2*

Boundary changes: 1851–61 loss of 3511 to Caernarfonshire (pop. 1851)
1881–91 loss of 19 to Caernarfonshire (pop. 1881)

Sources: *Census of Population for England and Wales*: 1851, *Population Tables, Vol. I, XI Welsh Division* (HMSO, 1852) (for figures 1801–51); 1861, *Population Tables, Vol. I, part II, Division XI Monmouthshire and Wales* (HMSO, 1862); 1871, *Population Tables, Vol. II, Division XI Monmouthshire and Wales* (HMSO, 1872); 1881, *Vol. II, Division XI Monmouthshire and Wales* (HMSO, 1883); 1891, *Area, Housing and Population, Vol. II, Division XI Monmouthshire and Wales* (HMSO, 1893); 1901, County Volumes, *Anglesey-Radnor* (HMSO, 1902, 1903); 1911, County Volumes: *Anglesey, Carnarvon, Denbigh and Flint; Cardigan, Merioneth and Montgomery; Glamorgan; Brecknock, Carmarthen, Pembroke and Radnor; Monmouth* (HMSO, 1914) include tables taken from *Vol. II, Area, Families or Separate Occupiers and Population (Registration Areas)*, (HMSO, 1912).

These figures are for the Registration Division of Wales and Monmouthshire, and the constituent Registration Counties. In some cases the boundaries of registration counties differ considerably from the Ancient, Geographical, or 'Proper' county. See the County Maps in Appendix II (pp. 174–99) for details of the differences. Figures given in brackets represent the population of a changed area at the previous census. They are used to calculate the percentages shown in the last three columns. Details of boundary changes are given after the figures for each area.

Population 1.2 Total population. Persons, males, females. Number and percentage change. Number of females per 1000 males. Registration Districts. Census years 1801–1911

	Year	Number Persons	Males	Females	Females/ 1000 males	Intercensal period	*Percentage change* *Persons*	*Males*	*Females*
MONMOUTHSHIRE									
Chepstow	1801	**10604**	5355	5249	980				
	1811	**12296**	6089	6207	1019	1801–11	***16.0***	*13.7*	*18.3*
	1821	**14172**	7123	7049	990	1811–21	***15.3***	*17.0*	*13.6*
	1831	**15740**	7960	7780	977	1821–31	***11.1***	*11.8*	*10.4*
	1841	**16776**	8388	8388	1000	1831–41	***6.6***	*5.4*	*7.8*
	1851	**19057**	9696	9361	965	1841–51	***13.6***	*15.6*	*11.6*
	1861	**17941**	8961	8980	1002	1851–61	***–5.9***	*–7.6*	*–4.1*
	1871	**18341**	9262	9079	980	1861–71	***2.2***	*3.4*	*1.1*
	1881	**18701**	9461	9240	977	1871–81	***2.0***	*2.1*	*1.8*
	1891	**19464**	9642	9822	1019	1881–91	***4.1***	*1.9*	*6.3*
	1901	**19246**	9505	9741	1025	1891–1901	***–1.1***	*–1.4*	*–0.8*
	1911	**19929**	9866	10063	1020	1901–11	***3.5***	*3.8*	*3.3*

No boundary changes

	Year	Number Persons	Males	Females	Females/ 1000 males	Intercensal period	*Persons*	*Males*	*Females*
Monmouth	1801	**16391**	8041	8350	1038				
	1811	**17968**	8876	9092	1024	1801–11	***9.6***	*10.4*	*8.9*
	1821	**20725**	10520	10205	970	1811–21	***15.3***	*18.5*	*12.2*
	1831	**23310**	11676	11634	996	1821–31	***12.5***	*11.0*	*14.0*
	1841	**25305**	12771	12534	981	1831–41	***8.6***	*9.4*	*7.7*
	1851	**27379**	13705	13674	998	1841–51	***8.2***	*7.3*	*9.1*
	1861	**30244**	15283	14961	979	1851–61	***10.5***	*11.5*	*9.4*
	1871	**31598**	15955	15643	980	1861–71	***4.5***	*4.4*	*4.6*
	1881	**30340**	15377	14963	973	1871–81	***–4.0***	*–3.6*	*–4.3*
		(30312)	(15361)	(14951)					
	1891	**28281**	14200	14081	992	1881–91	***–6.7***	*–7.6*	*–5.8*
	1901	**28240**	14023	14217	1014	1891–1901	***–0.1***	*–1.2*	*1.0*
	1911	**29374**	14896	14478	972	1901–11	***4.0***	*6.2*	*1.8*

Boundary changes: 1881–91 loss of 93 to Ross (Her), gain of 27 from Westbury (Gloucs), gain of 32 from Ross (Her), gain of 6 from Hereford (Her) – overall loss of 28 (pop. 1881)

	Year	Number Persons	Males	Females	Females/ 1000 males	Intercensal period	*Persons*	*Males*	*Females*
Abergavenny[1]	1801	**8274**	3975	4299	1082				
	1811	**10599**	5189	5410	1043	1801–11	***28.1***	*30.5*	*25.8*
	1821	**12869**	6620	6249	944	1811–21	***21.4***	*27.6*	*15.5*
	1831	**14246**	7284	6962	956	1821–31	***10.7***	*10.0*	*11.4*
	1841	**17160**	8835	8325	942	1831–41	***20.5***	*21.3*	*19.6*
	1851	**17663**	8924	8739	979	1841–51	***2.9***	*1.0*	*5.0*
	1861	**19527**	9918	9609	969	1851–61	***10.6***	*11.1*	*10.0*
	1871	**22862**	11774	11088	942	1861–71	***17.1***	*18.7*	*15.4*
	1881	**23571**	11879	11692	984	1871–81	***3.1***	*0.9*	*5.4*
	1891	**26064**	13210	12854	973	1881–91	***10.6***	*11.2*	*9.9*
		(27654)	(14117)	(13537)					
	1901	**26729**	13291	13438	1011	1891–1901	***–3.3***	*–5.9*	*–0.7*
	1911	**28678**	14719	13959	948	1901–11	***7.3***	*10.7*	*3.9*

Boundary changes: 1851–61 loss of 41566 to new district of Bedwellte (pop. 1851). See note 1.
1891–1901 gain of 75 from Bedwellte, gain of 1515 from Pontypool – overall gain of 1590 (pop. 1891)

	Year	Number Persons	Males	Females	Females/ 1000 males	Intercensal period	*Persons*	*Males*	*Females*
Bedwellte[1]	1801	**2239**	1209	1030	852				
	1811	**6216**	3041	3175	1044	1801–11	***177.6***	*151.5*	*208.3*
	1821	**10441**	5947	4494	756	1811–21	***68.0***	*95.6*	*41.5*
	1831	**16629**	9192	7437	809	1821–31	***59.3***	*54.6*	*65.5*
	1841	**33685**	18834	14851	789	1831–41	***102.6***	*104.9*	*99.7*
	1851	**41566**	22819	18747	822	1841–51	***23.4***	*21.2*	*26.2*
	1861	**47565**	25511	22054	864	1851–61	***14.4***	*11.8*	*17.6*
	1871	**51763**	28081	23682	843	1861–71	***8.8***	*10.1*	*7.4*
	1881	**55840**	29793	26047	874	1871–81	***7.9***	*6.1*	*10.0*
	1891	**64866**	35091	29775	849	1881–91	***16.2***	*17.8*	*14.3*
		(64521)	(34902)	(29619)					
	1901	**81820**	43822	37998	867	1891–1901	***26.8***	*25.6*	*28.3*
	1911	**122288**	66225	56063	847	1901–11	***49.5***	*51.1*	*47.5*

Boundary changes: 1851–61 creation of new district from part of Abergavenny. See note 1.
1891–1901 loss of 75 to Abergavenny (pop. 1891)

	Year	Number Persons	Males	Females	Females/ 1000 males	Intercensal period	*Percentage change* *Persons*	*Males*	*Females*
Pontypool	1801	**6346**	3067	3279	1069				
	1811	**8749**	4392	4357	992	1801–11	***37.9***	*43.2*	*32.9*
	1821	**11437**	5918	5519	933	1811–21	***30.7***	*34.7*	*26.7*
	1831	**18549**	9950	8599	864	1821–31	***62.2***	*68.1*	*55.8*
	1841	**25038**	13189	11849	898	1831–41	***35.0***	*32.6*	*37.8*
	1851	**27993**	14563	13430	922	1841–51	***11.8***	*10.4*	*13.3*
	1861	**30288**	15484	14804	956	1851–61	***8.2***	*6.3*	*10.2*
	1871	**33892**	17686	16206	916	1861–71	***11.9***	*14.2*	*9.5*
	1881	**35338**	18258	17080	935	1871–81	***4.3***	*3.2*	*5.4*
	1891	**39771**	20555	19216	935	1881–91	***12.5***	*12.6*	*12.5*
		(38256)	19694	18562					
	1901	**45379**	23651	21728	919	1891–1901	***18.6***	*20.1*	*17.1*
	1911	**61868**	32566	29302	900	1901–11	***36.3***	*37.7*	*34.9*

Boundary changes: 1891–1901 loss of 1515 to Abergavenny (pop. 1891)

	Year	Number Persons	Males	Females	Females/ 1000 males	Intercensal period	*Persons*	*Males*	*Females*
Newport	1801	**10896**	5256	5640	1073				
	1811	**16180**	8012	8168	1019	1801–11	***48.5***	*52.4*	*44.8*
	1821	**18995**	9720	9275	954	1811–21	***17.4***	*21.3*	*13.6*
	1831	**24212**	12375	11837	957	1821–31	***27.5***	*27.3*	*27.6*
	1841	**33057**	17017	16040	943	1831–41	***36.5***	*37.5*	*35.5*
	1851	**43472**	22594	20878	924	1841–51	***31.5***	*32.8*	*30.2*
	1861	**51412**	25853	25559	989	1851–61	***18.3***	*14.4*	*22.4*
	1871	**61252**	31104	30148	969	1861–71	***19.1***	*20.3*	*18.0*
	1881	**70542**	35197	35345	1004	1871–81	***15.2***	*13.2*	*17.2*
	1891	**96796**	49634	47162	950	1881–91	***37.2***	*41.0*	*33.4*
		(97436)	(49956)	(47480)					
	1901	**115450**	58445	57005	975	1891–1901	***18.5***	*17.0*	*20.1*
	1911	**152529**	78634	73895	940	1901–11	***32.1***	*34.5*	*29.6*

Boundary changes: 1891–1901 gain of 1190 from Cardiff, loss of 550 to Cardiff – overall gain of 640 (pop. 1891)

	Year	Number Persons	Males	Females	Females/ 1000 males	Intercensal period	*Persons*	*Males*	*Females*
GLAMORGAN									
Cardiff	1801	**12054**	5763	6291	1092				
	1811	**13588**	6444	7144	1109	1801–11	***12.7***	*11.8*	*13.6*
	1821	**16099**	7916	8183	1034	1811–21	***18.5***	*22.8*	*14.5*
	1831	**19646**	9646	10000	1037	1821–31	***22.0***	*21.9*	*22.2*
	1841	**25006**	12666	12340	974	1831–41	***27.3***	*31.3*	*23.4*
	1851	**35778**	19228	16550	861	1841–51	***43.1***	*51.8*	*34.1*
	1861	**61671**	31922	29749	932	1851–61	***72.4***	*66.0*	*79.8*
		(58285)	(30174)	(28111)					
	1871	**76701**	39962	36739	919	1861–71	***31.6***	*32.4*	*30.7*
	1881	**106164**	54128	52036	961	1871–81	***38.4***	*35.4*	*41.6*
	1891	**173796**	89342	84454	945	1881–91	***63.7***	*65.1*	*62.3*
		(173156)	(89020)	(84136)					
	1901	**228638**	114027	114611	1005	1891–1901	***32.0***	*28.1*	*36.2*
	1911	**264710**	130502	134208	1028	1901–11	***15.8***	*14.4*	*17.1*

Boundary changes: 1861–71 loss of 16290 to Pontypridd (pop. 1861)
1891–1901 loss of 1190 to Newport, gain of 550 from Newport – overall gain of 640 (pop. 1891)

	Year	Number Persons	Males	Females	Females/ 1000 males	Intercensal period	*Persons*	*Males*	*Females*
Pontypridd[2]	1801	**3271**	1507	1764	1171				
	1811	**3840**	1959	1881	960	1801–11	***17.4***	*30.0*	*6.6*
	1821	**4785**	2452	2333	951	1811–21	***24.6***	*25.2*	*24.0*
	1831	**5346**	2753	2593	942	1821–31	***11.7***	*12.3*	*11.1*
	1841	**7551**	3946	3605	914	1831–41	***41.2***	*43.3*	*39.0*
	1851	**10713**	5674	5039	888	1841–51	***41.9***	*43.8*	*39.8*
	1861	**12904**	6843	6061	886	1851–61	***20.5***	*20.6*	*20.3*
		(30387)	(16267)	(14120)					
	1871	**51921**	27905	24016	861	1861–71	***70.9***	*71.5*	*70.1*
	1881	**93493**	50675	42818	845	1871–81	***80.1***	*81.6*	*78.3*
	1891	**146812**	82128	64684	788	1881–91	***57.0***	*62.1*	*51.1*
		(148374)	(82936)	(65438)					
	1901	**204824**	111264	93560	841	1891–1901	***38.0***	*34.2*	*43.0*
	1911	**288564**	155972	132592	850	1901–11	***40.9***	*40.2*	*41.7*

Boundary changes: 1861–71 creation of new district: 16290 from Cardiff, 14097 from Merthyr Tydfil (pop. 1861). See note 2.

	Year	Number Persons	Males	Females	Females/ 1000 males	Intercensal period	*Percentage change* *Persons*	*Males*	*Females*
Merthyr Tydfil	1801	**13655**	7398	6257	846				
	1811	**19861**	10438	9423	903	1801–11	***45.4***	*41.1*	*50.6*
	1821	**26738**	14341	12397	864	1811–21	***34.6***	*37.4*	*31.6*
	1831	**34181**	18114	16067	887	1821–31	***27.8***	*26.3*	*29.6*
	1841	**52863**	28629	24234	846	1831–41	***54.7***	*58.0*	*50.8*
	1851	**76804**	41425	35379	854	1841–51	***45.3***	*44.7*	*46.0*
	1861	**107105**	56362	50743	900	1851–61	***39.5***	*36.1*	*43.4*
		(93008)	(48686)	(44322)					
	1871	**104239**	55001	49238	895	1861–71	***12.1***	*13.0*	*11.1*
	1881	**101441**	52430	49011	935	1871–81	***–2.7***	*–4.7*	*–0.5*
	1891	**117205**	62315	54890	881	1881–91	***15.5***	*18.9*	*12.0*
		(115643)	(61507)	(54136)					
	1901	**135540**	71761	63779	889	1891–1901	***17.2***	*16.7*	*17.8*
	1911	**174147**	92477	81670	883	1901–11	***28.5***	*28.9*	*28.1*

Boundary changes: 1861–71 loss of 14097 to new district of Pontypridd (pop. 1861)
1891–1901 loss of 2486 to Pontypridd, gain of 924 from Pontypridd – overall loss of 1562 (pop. 1891)

	Year	Number Persons	Males	Females	Females/ 1000 males	Intercensal period	*Persons*	*Males*	*Females*
Bridgend	1801	**12352**	5708	6644	1164				
	1811	**13837**	6561	7276	1109	1801–11	***12.0***	*14.9*	*9.5*
	1821	**15920**	7748	8172	1055	1811–21	***15.1***	*18.1*	*12.3*
	1831	**17237**	8678	8559	986	1821–31	***8.3***	*12.0*	*4.7*
	1841	**21355**	10750	10605	987	1831–41	***23.9***	*23.9*	*23.9*
	1851	**23422**	11789	11633	987	1841–51	***9.7***	*9.7*	*9.7*
	1861	**26465**	13316	13149	987	1851–61	***13.0***	*13.0*	*13.0*
	1871	**31671**	16181	15490	957	1861–71	***19.7***	*21.5*	*17.8*
	1881	**38920**	20054	18866	941	1871–81	***22.9***	*23.9*	*21.8*
		(41004)	(21128)	(19876)					
	1891	**51453**	27288	24165	886	1881–91	***25.5***	*29.2*	*21.6*
	1901	**67453**	35912	31541	878	1891–1901	***31.1***	*31.6*	*30.5*
	1911	**94609**	49920	44689	895	1901–11	***40.3***	*39.0*	*41.7*

Boundary changes: 1881–91 gain of 2084 from Neath (pop. 1881)

	Year	Number Persons	Males	Females	Females/ 1000 males	Intercensal period	*Persons*	*Males*	*Females*
Neath	1801	**14478**	7320	7158	978				
	1811	**15359**	7804	7555	968	1801–11	***6.1***	*6.6*	*5.5*
	1821	**17428**	9048	8380	926	1811–21	***13.5***	*15.9*	*10.9*
	1831	**22939**	11950	10989	920	1821–31	***31.6***	*32.1*	*31.1*
	1841	**31304**	16920	14384	850	1831–41	***36.5***	*41.6*	*30.9*
	1851	**46471**	24208	22263	920	1841–51	***48.5***	*43.1*	*54.8*
	1861	**58533**	29984	28549	952	1851–61	***26.0***	*23.9*	*28.2*
	1871	**64619**	32505	32114	988	1861–71	***10.4***	*8.4*	*12.5*
		(44063)	(22130)	(21933)					
	1881	**52077**	26219	25858	986	1871–81	***18.2***	*18.5*	*17.9*
		(49993)	(25145)	(24848)					
	1891	**56673**	28855	27818	964	1881–91	***13.4***	*14.8*	*12.0*
	1901	**71604**	36551	35053	959	1891–1901	***26.3***	*26.7*	*26.0*
	1911	**100924**	52748	48176	913	1901–11	***40.9***	*44.3*	*37.4*

Boundary changes: 1871–81 loss of 14428 to new district of Pontardawe, loss of 6128 to Swansea – overall loss of 20556 (pop. 1871)
1881–91 loss of 2084 to Bridgend (pop. 1881)

	Year	Number Persons	Males	Females	Females/ 1000 males	Intercensal period	*Persons*	*Males*	*Females*
Pontardawe	1871	(17488)	(8742)	(8746)					
	1881	**20185**	10116	10069	995	1871–81	***15.4***	*15.7*	*15.1*
	1891	**21700**	10939	10761	984	1881–91	***7.5***	*8.1*	*6.9*
	1901	**26718**	13438	13280	988	1891–1901	***23.1***	*22.8*	*23.4*
	1911	**41969**	22252	19717	886	1901–11	***57.1***	*65.6*	*48.5*

Boundary changes: 1871–81 district created from part of Swansea (3060 pop. 1871) and part of Neath (14428 pop. 1871)

	Year	Number Persons	Males	Females	Females/ 1000 males	Intercensal period	*Percentage change* *Persons*	*Males*	*Females*
Swansea	1801	**17510**	7876	9634	1223				
	1811	**20810**	9431	11379	1207	1801–11	***18.8***	*19.7*	*18.1*
	1821	**24931**	11564	13367	1156	1811–21	***19.8***	*22.6*	*17.5*
	1831	**31211**	14567	16644	1143	1821–31	***25.2***	*26.0*	*24.5*
	1841	**38649**	18519	20130	1087	1831–41	***23.8***	*27.1*	*20.9*
	1851	**46907**	22763	24144	1061	1841–51	***21.4***	*22.9*	*19.9*
		(38420)	(18616)	(19804)					
	1861	**51260**	25372	25888	1020	1851–61	***33.4***	*36.3*	*30.7*
	1871	**67357**	33568	33789	1007	1861–71	***31.4***	*32.3*	*30.5*
		(70425)	(35201)	(35224)					
	1881	**95001**	47207	47794	1012	1871–81	***34.9***	*34.1*	*35.7*
	1891	**114326**	57047	57279	1004	1881–91	***20.3***	*20.8*	*19.8*
	1901	**119746**	58743	61003	1038	1891–1901	***4.7***	*3.0*	*6.5*
	1911	**151025**	76771	74254	967	1901–11	***26.1***	*30.7*	*21.7*

Boundary changes: 1851–61 loss of 8487 to new district of Gower (pop. 1851)
1871–81 loss of 3060 to Pontardawe, gain of 6128 from Neath – overall gain of 3068 (pop. 1871)

	Year	Number Persons	Males	Females	Females/ 1000 males	Intercensal period	*Persons*	*Males*	*Females*
Gower	1851	(8487)	(4147)	(4340)					
	1861	**8316**	4036	4280	1060	1851–61	***–2.0***	*–2.7*	*–1.4*
	1871	**9290**	4494	4796	1067	1861–71	***11.7***	*11.3*	*12.1*
	1881	**11102**	5299	5803	1095	1871–81	***19.5***	*17.9*	*21.0*
	1891	**11107**	5338	5769	1081	1881–91	***0.0***	*0.7*	*–0.6*
	1901	**11727**	5407	6320	1169	1891–1901	***5.6***	*1.3*	*9.6*
	1911	**14720**	7024	7696	1096	1901–11	***25.5***	*29.9*	*21.8*

Boundary changes: 1851–61 district created 1861 from part of Swansea (8487 pop. 1851)

CARMARTHENSHIRE

	Year	Number Persons	Males	Females	Females/ 1000 males	Intercensal period	*Persons*	*Males*	*Females*
Llanelli	1801	**8640**	3984	4656	1169				
	1811	**9953**	4543	5410	1191	1801–11	***15.2***	*14.0*	*16.2*
	1821	**12570**	6078	6492	1068	1811–21	***26.3***	*33.8*	*20.0*
	1831	**16170**	7979	8191	1027	1821–31	***28.6***	*31.3*	*26.2*
	1841	**20182**	9909	10273	1037	1831–41	***24.8***	*24.2*	*25.4*
	1851	**23507**	11618	11889	1023	1841–51	***16.5***	*17.2*	*15.7*
	1861	**27979**	13819	14160	1025	1851–61	***19.0***	*18.9*	*19.1*
	1871	**34732**	17102	17630	1031	1861–71	***24.1***	*23.8*	*24.5*
	1881	**44616**	22034	22582	1025	1871–81	***28.5***	*28.8*	*28.1*
	1891	**52382**	25912	26470	1022	1881–91	***17.4***	*17.6*	*17.2*
		(52225)	(25836)	(26389)					
	1901	**56897**	27762	29135	1049	1891–1901	***8.9***	*7.5*	*10.4*
	1911	**73999**	37893	36106	953	1901–11	***30.1***	*36.5*	*23.9*

Boundary changes: 1891–1901 loss of 157 to Carmarthen (pop. 1891)

	Year	Number Persons	Males	Females	Females/ 1000 males	Intercensal period	*Persons*	*Males*	*Females*
Llandovery	1801	**10902**	5125	5777	1127				
	1811	**12216**	5786	6430	1111	1801–11	***12.1***	*12.9*	*11.3*
	1821	**13713**	6744	6969	1033	1811–21	***12.3***	*16.6*	*8.4*
	1831	**14799**	7260	7539	1038	1821–31	***7.9***	*7.7*	*8.2*
	1841	**14726**	7105	7621	1073	1831–41	***–0.5***	*–2.1*	*1.1*
	1851	**15055**	7268	7787	1071	1841–51	***2.2***	*2.3*	*2.2*
	1861	**14775**	7133	7642	1071	1851–61	***–1.9***	*–1.9*	*–1.9*
	1871	**14046**	6734	7312	1086	1861–71	***–4.9***	*–5.6*	*–4.3*
		(12518)	(5945)	(6573)					
	1881	**12765**	6106	6659	1091	1871–81	***2.0***	*2.7*	*1.3*
	1891	**11622**	5460	6162	1129	1881–91	***–9.0***	*–10.6*	*–7.5*
		(10719)	(5042)	(5677)					
	1901	**9587**	4587	5000	1090	1891–1901	***–10.6***	*–9.0*	*–11.9*
	1911	**9353**	4657	4696	1008	1901–11	***–2.4***	*1.5*	*–6.1*

Boundary changes: 1871–81 loss of 1528 to Llandeilo Fawr (pop. 1871)
1891–1901 loss of 903 to Builth (pop. 1891)

	Year	Number Persons	Males	Females	Females/ 1000 males	Intercensal period	*Percentage change* Persons	Males	Females
Llandeilo Fawr	1801	**11940**	5693	6247	1097				
	1811	**13287**	6254	7033	1125	1801–11	***11.3***	*9.9*	*12.6*
	1821	**15695**	7549	8146	1079	1811–21	***18.1***	*20.7*	*15.8*
	1831	**16444**	7901	8543	1081	1821–31	***4.8***	*4.7*	*4.9*
	1841	**17128**	8186	8942	1092	1831–41	***4.2***	*3.6*	*4.7*
	1851	**17968**	8651	9317	1077	1841–51	***4.9***	*5.7*	*4.2*
	1861	**17222**	8202	9020	1100	1851–61	***–4.2***	*–5.2*	*–3.2*
	1871	**16976**	8063	8913	1105	1861–71	***–1.4***	*–1.7*	*–1.2*
		(18504)	(8852)	(9652)					
	1881	**18799**	9032	9767	1081	1871–81	***1.6***	*2.0*	*1.2*
	1891	**20483**	9892	10591	1071	1881–91	***9.0***	*9.5*	*8.4*
	1901	**23693**	11607	12086	1041	1891–1901	***15.7***	*17.3*	*14.1*
	1911	**33271**	17208	16063	933	1901–11	***40.4***	*48.3*	*32.9*

Boundary changes: 1871–81 gain of 1528 from Llandovery (pop. 1871)

	Year	Number Persons	Males	Females	Females/ 1000 males	Intercensal period	Persons	Males	Females
Carmarthen	1801	**24089**	11059	13030	1178				
	1811	**28283**	12701	15582	1227	1801–11	***17.4***	*14.8*	*19.6*
	1821	**33385**	15893	17492	1101	1811–21	***18.0***	*25.1*	*12.3*
	1831	**36926**	17571	19355	1102	1821–31	***10.6***	*10.6*	*10.7*
	1841	**37523**	17494	20029	1145	1831–41	***1.6***	*–0.4*	*3.5*
	1851	**38142**	17982	20160	1121	1841–51	***1.6***	*2.8*	*0.7*
	1861	**36675**	16995	19680	1158	1851–61	***–3.8***	*–5.5*	*–2.4*
	1871	**35627**	16451	19176	1166	1861–71	***–2.9***	*–3.2*	*–2.6*
	1881	**35075**	16317	18758	1150	1871–81	***–1.5***	*–0.8*	*–2.2*
	1891	**34137**	15658	18479	1180	1881–91	***–2.7***	*–4.0*	*–1.5*
		(34294)	(15734)	(18560)					
	1901	**33393**	15383	18010	1171	1891–1901	***–2.6***	*–2.2*	*–3.0*
	1911	**34427**	16259	18168	1117	1901–11	***3.1***	*5.7*	*0.9*

Boundary changes: 1891–1901 gain of 157 from Llanelli (pop. 1891)

	Year	Number Persons	Males	Females	Females/ 1000 males	Intercensal period	Persons	Males	Females
PEMBROKESHIRE									
Narberth	1801	**15809**	7303	8506	1165				
	1811	**16613**	7563	9050	1197	1801–11	***5.1***	*3.6*	*6.4*
	1821	**19606**	9355	10251	1096	1811–21	***18.0***	*23.7*	*13.3*
	1831	**20939**	10052	10887	1083	1821–31	***6.8***	*7.5*	*6.2*
	1841	**21748**	10263	11485	1119	1831–41	***3.9***	*2.1*	*5.5*
	1851	**22130**	10459	11671	1116	1841–51	***1.8***	*1.9*	*1.6*
	1861	**21344**	10036	11308	1127	1851–61	***–3.6***	*–4.0*	*–3.1*
	1871	**20332**	9471	10861	1147	1861–71	***–4.7***	*–5.6*	*–4.0*
	1881	**19541**	9149	10392	1136	1871–81	***–3.9***	*–3.4*	*–4.3*
	1891	**18190**	8402	9788	1165	1881–91	***–6.9***	*–8.2*	*–5.8*
	1901	**17362**	8071	9291	1151	1891–1901	***–4.6***	*–3.9*	*–5.1*
	1911	**17322**	8146	9176	1126	1901–11	***–0.2***	*0.9*	*–1.2*

No boundary changes

	Year	Number Persons	Males	Females	Females/ 1000 males	Intercensal period	Persons	Males	Females
Pembroke	1801	**10011**	4433	5578	1258				
	1811	**10061**	4450	5611	1261	1801–11	***0.5***	*0.4*	*0.6*
	1821	**14447**	6856	7591	1107	1811–21	***43.6***	*54.1*	*35.3*
	1831	**17231**	8042	9189	1143	1821–31	***19.3***	*17.3*	*21.1*
	1841	**19670**	9129	10541	1155	1831–41	***14.2***	*13.5*	*14.7*
	1851	**22960**	10778	12182	1130	1841–51	***16.7***	*18.1*	*15.6*
	1861	**29003**	14856	14147	952	1851–61	***26.3***	*37.8*	*16.1*
	1871	**29061**	14012	15049	1074	1861–71	***0.2***	*–5.7*	*6.4*
	1881	**30347**	14780	15567	1053	1871–81	***4.4***	*5.5*	*3.4*
	1891	**31283**	15136	16147	1067	1881–91	***3.1***	*2.4*	*3.7*
	1901	**31939**	15449	16490	1067	1891–1901	***2.1***	*2.1*	*2.1*
	1911	**30982**	15251	15731	1031	1901–11	***–3.0***	*–1.3*	*–4.6*

No boundary changes

	Year	Number Persons	Males	Females	Females/ 1000 males	Intercensal period	*Percentage change* Persons	Males	Females
Haverfordwest	1801	**24450**	10976	13474	1228				
	1811	**26848**	11980	14868	1241	1801–11	***9.8***	*9.1*	*10.3*
	1821	**31389**	14516	16873	1162	1811–21	***16.9***	*21.2*	*13.5*
	1831	**34776**	16109	18667	1159	1821–31	***10.8***	*11.0*	*10.6*
	1841	**37139**	17009	20130	1183	1831–41	***6.8***	*5.6*	*7.8*
	1851	**39382**	18383	20999	1142	1841–51	***6.0***	*8.1*	*4.3*
	1861	**37343**	17496	19847	1134	1851–61	***–5.2***	*–4.8*	*–5.5*
	1871	**34480**	15991	18489	1156	1861–71	***–7.7***	*–8.6*	*–6.8*
	1881	**33791**	16156	17635	1092	1871–81	***–2.0***	*1.0*	*–4.6*
	1891	**32530**	15233	17297	1135	1881–91	***–3.7***	*–5.7*	*–1.9*
	1901	**33123**	15836	17287	1092	1891–1901	***1.8***	*4.0*	*–0.1*
	1911	**36570**	17822	18748	1052	1901–11	***10.4***	*12.5*	*8.5*

No boundary changes

CARDIGANSHIRE

	Year	Number Persons	Males	Females	Females/ 1000 males	Intercensal period	Persons	Males	Females
Cardigan	1801	**14539**	6603	7936	1202				
	1811	**15313**	6796	8517	1253	1801–11	***5.3***	*2.9*	*7.3*
	1821	**17952**	8220	9732	1184	1811–21	***17.2***	*21.0*	*14.3*
	1831	**18786**	8564	10222	1194	1821–31	***4.6***	*4.2*	*5.0*
	1841	**19903**	8593	11310	1316	1831–41	***5.9***	*0.3*	*10.6*
	1851	**20186**	8812	11374	1291	1841–51	***1.4***	*2.5*	*0.6*
	1861	**18585**	7938	10647	1341	1851–61	***–7.9***	*–9.9*	*–6.4*
	1871	**17585**	7480	10105	1351	1861–71	***–5.4***	*–5.8*	*–5.1*
	1881	**17615**	7583	10032	1323	1871–81	***0.2***	*1.4*	*–0.7*
	1891	**16281**	6936	9345	1347	1881–91	***–7.6***	*–8.5*	*–6.8*
	1901	**15162**	6567	8595	1309	1891–1901	***–6.9***	*–5.3*	*–8.0*
	1911	**14732**	6548	8184	1250	1901–11	***–2.8***	*–0.3*	*–4.8*

No boundary changes

	Year	Number Persons	Males	Females	Females/ 1000 males	Intercensal period	Persons	Males	Females
Newcastle Emlyn	1801	**13585**	6558	7027	1072				
	1811	**15474**	7124	8350	1172	1801–11	***13.9***	*8.6*	*18.8*
	1821	**18598**	8891	9707	1092	1811–21	***20.2***	*24.8*	*16.3*
	1831	**20575**	9870	10705	1085	1821–31	***10.6***	*11.0*	*10.3*
	1841	**20863**	9694	11169	1152	1831–41	***1.4***	*–1.8*	*4.3*
	1851	**20173**	9385	10788	1149	1841–51	***–3.3***	*–3.2*	*–3.4*
	1861	**19081**	8727	10354	1186	1851–61	***–5.4***	*–7.0*	*–4.0*
	1871	**18818**	8494	10324	1215	1861–71	***–1.4***	*–2.7*	*–0.3*
	1881	**19014**	8643	10371	1200	1871–81	***1.0***	*1.8*	*0.5*
	1891	**19108**	8641	10467	1211	1881–91	***0.5***	*0.0*	*0.9*
	1901	**18135**	8173	9962	1219	1891–1901	***–5.1***	*–5.4*	*–4.8*
	1911	**17805**	8223	9582	1165	1901–11	***–1.8***	*0.6*	*–3.8*

No boundary changes

	Year	Number Persons	Males	Females	Females/ 1000 males	Intercensal period	Persons	Males	Females
Lampeter	1801	**6274**	3059	3215	1051				
	1811	**7009**	3365	3644	1083	1801–11	***11.7***	*10.0*	*13.3*
	1821	**8142**	4006	4136	1032	1811–21	***16.2***	*19.0*	*13.5*
	1831	**9437**	4579	4858	1061	1821–31	***15.9***	*14.3*	*17.5*
	1841	**9865**	4790	5075	1059	1831–41	***4.5***	*4.6*	*4.5*
	1851	**9874**	4705	5169	1099	1841–51	***0.1***	*–1.8*	*1.9*
	1861	**9994**	4759	5235	1100	1851–61	***1.2***	*1.1*	*1.3*
	1871	**9973**	4654	5319	1143	1861–71	***–0.2***	*–2.2*	*1.6*
	1881	**10087**	4671	5416	1159	1871–81	***1.1***	*0.4*	*1.8*
	1891	**9684**	4392	5292	1205	1881–91	***–4.0***	*–6.0*	*–2.3*
	1901	**9257**	4211	5046	1198	1891–1901	***–4.4***	*–4.1*	*–4.6*
	1911	**8967**	4175	4792	1148	1901–11	***–3.1***	*–0.9*	*–5.0*

No boundary changes

	Year	Number Persons	Males	Females	Females/ 1000 males	Intercensal period	*Percentage change* Persons	Males	Females
Aberaeron	1801	**7960**	3707	4253	1147				
	1811	**9420**	4362	5058	1160	1801–11	***18.3***	*17.7*	*18.9*
	1821	**10960**	5216	5744	1101	1811–21	***16.3***	*19.6*	*13.6*
	1831	**12308**	5883	6425	1092	1821–31	***12.3***	*12.8*	*11.9*
	1841	**12875**	6017	6858	1140	1831–41	***4.6***	*2.3*	*6.7*
	1851	**13224**	5991	7233	1207	1841–51	***2.7***	*–0.4*	*5.5*
	1861	**13540**	6046	7494	1239	1851–61	***2.4***	*0.9*	*3.6*
	1871	**13377**	5750	7627	1326	1861–71	***–1.2***	*–4.9*	*1.8*
	1881	**12543**	5278	7265	1376	1871–81	***–6.2***	*–8.2*	*–4.7*
	1891	**11595**	4873	6722	1379	1881–91	***–7.6***	*–7.7*	*–7.5*
	1901	**10735**	4497	6238	1387	1891–1901	***–7.4***	*–7.7*	*–7.2*
	1911	**10262**	4507	5755	1277	1901–11	***–4.4***	*0.2*	*–7.7*

No boundary changes

	Year	Number Persons	Males	Females	Females/ 1000 males	Intercensal period	Persons	Males	Females
Aberystwyth	1801	**12858**	6073	6785	1117				
	1811	**14914**	6878	8036	1168	1801–11	***16.0***	*13.3*	*18.4*
	1821	**17573**	8780	8793	1001	1811–21	***17.8***	*27.7*	*9.4*
	1831	**20026**	9584	10442	1090	1821–31	***14.0***	*9.2*	*18.8*
	1841	**22242**	10582	11660	1102	1831–41	***11.1***	*10.4*	*11.7*
	1851	**23753**	11359	12394	1091	1841–51	***6.8***	*7.3*	*6.3*
	1861	**25464**	11946	13518	1132	1851–61	***7.2***	*5.2*	*9.1*
	1871	**27439**	12840	14599	1137	1861–71	***7.8***	*7.5*	*8.0*
	1881	**25606**	11852	13754	1160	1871–81	***–6.7***	*–7.7*	*–5.8*
	1891	**21102**	9293	11809	1271	1881–91	***–17.6***	*–21.6*	*–14.1*
	1901	**21471**	9539	11932	1251	1891–1901	***1.7***	*2.6*	*1.0*
	1911	**21482**	9535	11947	1253	1901–11	***0.1***	*0.0*	*0.1*

No boundary changes

	Year	Number Persons	Males	Females	Females/ 1000 males	Intercensal period	Persons	Males	Females
Tregaron	1801	**6074**	2921	3153	1079				
	1811	**7057**	3425	3632	1060	1801–11	***16.2***	*17.3*	*15.2*
	1821	**8539**	4204	4335	1031	1811–21	***21.0***	*22.7*	*19.4*
	1831	**9558**	4638	4920	1061	1821–31	***11.9***	*10.3*	*13.5*
	1841	**10254**	4816	5438	1129	1831–41	***7.3***	*3.8*	*10.5*
	1851	**10404**	4903	5501	1122	1841–51	***1.5***	*1.8*	*1.2*
	1861	**10737**	5030	5707	1135	1851–61	***3.2***	*2.6*	*3.7*
	1871	**10677**	5029	5648	1123	1861–71	***–0.6***	*0.0*	*–1.0*
	1881	**10272**	4690	5582	1190	1871–81	***–3.8***	*–6.7*	*–1.2*
	1891	**8613**	3857	4756	1233	1881–91	***–16.2***	*–17.8*	*–14.8*
	1901	**7947**	3616	4331	1198	1891–1901	***–7.7***	*–6.2*	*–8.9*
	1911	**7521**	3538	3983	1126	1901–11	***–5.4***	*–2.2*	*–8.0*

No boundary changes

BRECONSHIRE

	Year	Number Persons	Males	Females	Females/ 1000 males	Intercensal period	Persons	Males	Females
Builth	1801	**7272**	3527	3745	1062				
	1811	**7606**	3586	4020	1121	1801–11	***4.6***	*1.7*	*7.3*
	1821	**8096**	4059	4037	995	1811–21	***6.4***	*13.2*	*0.4*
	1831	**8512**	4214	4298	1020	1821–31	***5.1***	*3.8*	*6.5*
	1841	**8714**	4261	4453	1045	1831–41	***2.4***	*1.1*	*3.6*
	1851	**8345**	4152	4193	1010	1841–51	***–4.2***	*–2.6*	*–5.8*
	1861	**8305**	4161	4144	996	1851–61	***–0.5***	*0.2*	*–1.2*
	1871	**8264**	4115	4149	1008	1861–71	***–0.5***	*–1.1*	*0.1*
	1881	**8182**	4015	4167	1038	1871–81	***–1.0***	*–2.4*	*0.4*
	1891	**7834**	3878	3956	1020	1881–91	***–4.3***	*–3.4*	*–5.1*
		(8737)	(4296)	(4441)					
	1901	**8976**	4448	4528	1018	1891–1901	***2.7***	*3.5*	*2.0*
	1911	**9482**	4630	4852	1048	1901–11	***5.6***	*4.1*	*7.2*

Boundary changes: 1891–1901 gain of 903 from Llandovery (pop. 1891)

	Year	Number Persons	Males	Females	Females/ 1000 males	Intercensal period	Percentage change *Persons*	*Males*	*Females*
Brecon	1801	**13642**	6559	7083	1080				
	1811	**14974**	7039	7935	1127	1801–11	***9.8***	*7.3*	*12.0*
	1821	**16722**	8096	8626	1065	1811–21	***11.7***	*15.0*	*8.7*
	1831	**17579**	8536	9043	1059	1821–31	***5.1***	*5.4*	*4.8*
	1841	**17701**	8657	9044	1045	1831–41	***0.7***	*1.4*	*0.0*
	1851	**18174**	8984	9190	1023	1841–51	***2.7***	*3.8*	*1.6*
	1861	**17279**	8555	8724	1020	1851–61	***–4.9***	*–4.8*	*–5.1*
	1871	**17724**	8836	8888	1006	1861–71	***2.6***	*3.3*	*1.9*
	1881	**17178**	8578	8600	1003	1871–81	***–3.1***	*–2.9*	*–3.2*
	1891	**15924**	7880	8044	1021	1881–91	***–7.3***	*–8.1*	*–6.5*
	1901	**15633**	7752	7881	1017	1891–1901	***–1.8***	*–1.6*	*–2.0*
	1911	**15063**	7525	7538	1002	1901–11	***–3.6***	*–2.9*	*–4.4*

No boundary changes

	Year	Number Persons	Males	Females	Females/ 1000 males	Intercensal period	*Persons*	*Males*	*Females*
Crickhowell	1801	**5201**	2606	2595	996				
	1811	**6632**	3307	3325	1005	1801–11	***27.5***	*26.9*	*28.1*
	1821	**9223**	4932	4291	870	1811–21	***39.1***	*49.1*	*29.1*
	1831	**11305**	5991	5314	887	1821–31	***22.6***	*21.5*	*23.8*
	1841	**17676**	9352	8324	890	1831–41	***56.4***	*56.1*	*56.6*
	1851	**21697**	11410	10287	902	1841–51	***22.7***	*22.0*	*23.6*
	1861	**22457**	11585	10872	938	1851–61	***3.5***	*1.5*	*5.7*
	1871	**20147**	10203	9944	975	1861–71	***–10.3***	*–11.9*	*–8.5*
	1881	**18558**	9370	9188	981	1871–81	***–7.9***	*–8.2*	*–7.6*
	1891	**19515**	9920	9595	967	1881–91	***5.2***	*5.9*	*4.4*
		(19785)	(10063)	(9722)					
	1901	**19941**	10144	9797	966	1891–1901	***0.8***	*0.8*	*0.8*
	1911	**22309**	11475	10834	944	1901–11	***11.9***	*13.1*	*10.6*

Boundary changes: 1891–1901 gain of 270 from Bedwellte (Mon) (pop. 1891)

	Year	Number Persons	Males	Females	Females/ 1000 males	Intercensal period	*Persons*	*Males*	*Females*
Hay	1801	**8676**	4156	4520	1088				
	1811	**9572**	4608	4964	1077	1801–11	***10.3***	*10.9*	*9.8*
	1821	**10599**	5207	5392	1036	1811–21	***10.7***	*13.0*	*8.6*
	1831	**11403**	5660	5743	1015	1821–31	***7.6***	*8.7*	*6.5*
	1841	**11329**	5588	5741	1027	1831–41	***–0.6***	*–1.3*	*0.0*
	1851	**10962**	5447	5515	1012	1841–51	***–3.2***	*–2.5*	*–3.9*
	1861	**10819**	5339	5480	1026	1851–61	***–1.3***	*–2.0*	*–0.6*
	1871	**10797**	5340	5457	1022	1861–71	***–0.2***	*0.0*	*–0.4*
	1881	**10222**	5028	5194	1033	1871–81	***–5.3***	*–5.8*	*–4.8*
	1891	**9599**	4655	4944	1062	1881–91	***–6.1***	*–7.4*	*–4.8*
	1901	**9401**	4626	4775	1032	1891–1901	***–2.1***	*–0.6*	*–3.4*
	1911	**9516**	4678	4838	1034	1901–11	***1.2***	*1.1*	*1.3*

No boundary changes

RADNORSHIRE

	Year	Number Persons	Males	Females	Females/ 1000 males	Intercensal period	*Persons*	*Males*	*Females*
Presteigne[3]	1801	**12107**	5920	6187	1045				
	1811	**12731**	6227	6504	1044	1801–11	***5.2***	*5.2*	*5.1*
	1821	**14370**	7207	7163	994	1811–21	***12.9***	*15.7*	*10.1*
	1831	**15584**	7776	7808	1004	1821–31	***8.4***	*7.9*	*9.0*
	1841	**15739**	7920	7819	987	1831–41	***1.0***	*1.9*	*0.1*
	1851	**15149**	7691	7458	970	1841–51	***–3.7***	*–2.9*	*–4.6*
	1861	**15671**	8006	7665	957	1851–61	***3.4***	*4.1*	*2.8*
		(3741)	(1915)	(1826)					
	1871	**3869**	1941	1928	993	1861–71	***3.4***	*1.4*	*5.6*
		(2607)	(1278)	(1329)					
	1881	**2336**	1142	1194	1046	1871–81	***–10.4***	*–10.6*	*–10.2*
	1891	**2042**	981	1061	1082	1881–91	***–12.6***	*–14.1*	*–11.1*
	1901	**1950**	964	986	1023	1891–1901	***–4.5***	*–1.7*	*–7.1*
	1911	**1809**	887	922	1039	1901–11	***–7.2***	*–8.0*	*–6.5*

Boundary changes: 1861–71 loss of 11930 to Kington (Her) (pop. 1861)
1871–81 district abolished; loss of 2607 to Knighton, 1262 to Kington (Her) (pop. 1871). See note 3.

	Year	Number Persons	Males	Females	Females/ 1000 males	Intercensal period	*Percentage change* Persons	Males	Females
Knighton[3]	1801	**6669**	3313	3356	1013				
	1811	**7251**	3551	3700	1042	1801–11	***8.7***	*7.2*	*10.3*
	1821	**7967**	4040	3927	972	1811–21	***9.9***	*13.8*	*6.1*
	1831	**8719**	4461	4258	954	1821–31	***9.4***	*10.4*	*8.4*
	1841	**9315**	4833	4482	927	1831–41	***6.8***	*8.3*	*5.3*
	1851	**9480**	4947	4533	916	1841–51	***1.8***	*2.4*	*1.1*
	1861	**10379**	5543	4836	872	1851–61	***9.5***	*12.0*	*6.7*
	1871	**10323**	5382	4941	918	1861–71	***–0.5***	*–2.9*	*2.2*
	1881	**9446**	4915	4531	922	1871–81	***–8.5***	*–8.7*	*–8.3*
		(9368)	(4878)	(4490)					
	1891	**8656**	4393	4263	970	1881–91	***–7.6***	*–9.9*	*–5.1*
	1901	**8945**	4631	4314	932	1891–1901	***3.3***	*5.4*	*1.2*
	1911	**8038**	4105	3933	958	1901–11	***–10.1***	*–11.4*	*–8.8*

Boundary changes: 1871–81 See note 3.
1881–91 loss of 78 to Rhayader (pop. 1881)

	Year	Number Persons	Males	Females	Females/ 1000 males	Intercensal period	Persons	Males	Females
Rhayader	1801	**4757**	2354	2403	1021				
	1811	**5126**	2452	2674	1091	1801–11	***7.8***	*4.2*	*11.3*
	1821	**5728**	2822	2906	1030	1811–21	***11.7***	*15.1*	*8.7*
	1831	**6337**	3184	3153	990	1821–31	***10.6***	*12.8*	*8.5*
	1841	**6722**	3363	3359	999	1831–41	***6.1***	*5.6*	*6.5*
	1851	**6796**	3480	3316	953	1841–51	***1.1***	*3.5*	*–1.3*
	1861	**6816**	3507	3309	944	1851–61	***0.3***	*0.8*	*–0.2*
	1871	**6824**	3488	3336	956	1861–71	***0.1***	*–0.5*	*0.8*
	1881	**6741**	3347	3394	1014	1871–81	***–1.2***	*–4.0*	*1.7*
		(6819)	(3384)	(3435)					
	1891	**6421**	3112	3309	1063	1881–91	***–5.8***	*–8.0*	*–3.7*
	1901	**9346**	5116	4230	827	1891–1901	***45.6***	*64.4*	*27.8*
	1911	**7658**	3804	3854	1013	1901–11	***–18.1***	*–25.6*	*–8.9*

Boundary changes: 1881–91 gain of 78 from Knighton (pop. 1891)

MONTGOMERYSHIRE

	Year	Number Persons	Males	Females	Females/ 1000 males	Intercensal period	Persons	Males	Females
Machynlleth	1801	**9888**	4661	5227	1121				
	1811	**9720**	4440	5280	1189	1801–11	***–1.7***	*–4.7*	*1.0*
	1821	**11382**	5574	5808	1042	1811–21	***17.1***	*25.5*	*10.0*
	1831	**12098**	5912	6186	1046	1821–31	***6.3***	*6.1*	*6.5*
	1841	**12307**	5946	6361	1070	1831–41	***1.7***	*0.6*	*2.8*
	1851	**12116**	5929	6187	1044	1841–51	***–1.6***	*–0.3*	*–2.7*
	1861	**12395**	6178	6217	1006	1851–61	***2.3***	*4.2*	*0.5*
	1871	**13317**	6569	6748	1027	1861–71	***7.4***	*6.3*	*8.5*
	1881	**12517**	6080	6437	1059	1871–81	***–6.0***	*–7.4*	*–4.6*
		(12558)	(6102)	(6456)					
	1891	**10826**	5110	5716	1119	1881–91	***–13.8***	*–16.3*	*–11.5*
		(10947)	(5166)	(5781)					
	1901	**11041**	5218	5823	1116	1891–1901	***0.9***	*1.0*	*0.7*
	1911	**10853**	5030	5823	1158	1901–11	***–1.7***	*–3.6*	*0.0*

Boundary changes: 1881–91 gain of 41 from Dolgellau (pop. 1881)
1891–1901 gain of 121 from Dolgellau (pop. 1891)

	Year	Number Persons	Males	Females	Females/ 1000 males	Intercensal period	Persons	Males	Females
Newtown	1801	**15616**	7341	8275	1127				
	1811	**17854**	8467	9387	1109	1801–11	***14.3***	*15.3*	*13.4*
	1821	**21493**	10612	10881	1025	1811–21	***20.4***	*25.3*	*15.9*
	1831	**25288**	12519	12769	1020	1821–31	***17.7***	*18.0*	*17.4*
	1841	**26016**	12863	13153	1023	1831–41	***2.9***	*2.7*	*3.0*
	1851	**25107**	12486	12621	1011	1841–51	***–3.5***	*–2.9*	*–4.0*
	1861	**23732**	11941	11791	987	1851–61	***–5.5***	*–4.4*	*–6.6*
	1871	**24554**	12464	12090	970	1861–71	***3.5***	*4.4*	*2.5*
	1881	**25439**	12732	12707	998	1871–81	***3.6***	*2.2*	*5.1*
	1891	**21722**	10409	11313	1087	1881–91	***–14.6***	*–18.2*	*–11.0*
	1901	**21118**	10233	10885	1064	1891–1901	***–2.8***	*–1.7*	*–3.8*
	1911	**20294**	9976	10318	1034	1901–11	***–3.9***	*–2.5*	*–5.2*

No boundary changes

	Year	Number Persons	Males	Females	Females/ 1000 males	Intercensal period	*Percentage change* Persons	*Males*	*Females*
Montgomery/ Forden	1801	**15392**	7472	7920	1060				
	1811	**15957**	7912	8045	1017	1801–11	***3.7***	*5.9*	*1.6*
	1821	**18280**	9215	9065	984	1811–21	***14.6***	*16.5*	*12.7*
	1831	**20197**	10145	10052	991	1821–31	***10.5***	*10.1*	*10.9*
	1841	**20983**	10520	10463	995	1831–41	***3.9***	*3.7*	*4.1*
	1851	**20381**	10302	10079	978	1841–51	***–2.9***	*–2.1*	*–3.7*
		(17984)	(9115)	(8869)					
	1861	**19097**	9864	9233	936	1851–61	***6.2***	*8.2*	*4.1*
	1871	**18858**	9573	9285	970	1861–71	***–1.3***	*–3.0*	*0.6*
	1881	**18281**	9445	8836	936	1871–81	***–3.1***	*–1.3*	*–4.8*
		(18276)	(9443)	(8833)					
	1891	**16313**	8142	8171	1004	1881–91	***–10.7***	*–13.8*	*–7.5*
	1901	**14844**	7354	7490	1018	1891–1901	***–9.0***	*–9.7*	*–8.3*
	1911	**14371**	7124	7247	1017	1901–11	***–3.2***	*–3.1*	*–3.2*

The name of this district was changed to Forden in 1871
Boundary changes: 1851–61 loss of 2397 to Llanfyllin (pop. 1851)
1881–91 loss of 5 to Atcham (Salop) (pop. 1881)

	Year	Number Persons	Males	Females	Females/ 1000 males	Intercensal period	Persons	Males	Females
Llanfyllin	1801	**15145**	7411	7734	1044				
	1811	**15834**	7667	8167	1065	1801–11	***4.5***	*3.5*	*5.6*
	1821	**18194**	9039	9155	1013	1811–21	***14.9***	*17.9*	*12.1*
	1831	**19538**	9836	9702	986	1821–31	***7.4***	*8.8*	*6.0*
	1841	**20450**	10159	10291	1013	1831–41	***4.7***	*3.3*	*6.1*
	1851	**19538**	9824	9714	989	1841–51	***–4.5***	*–3.3*	*–5.6*
		(21935)	(11011)	(10924)					
	1861	**21699**	10904	10795	990	1851–61	***–1.1***	*–1.0*	*–1.2*
	1871	**21671**	10901	10770	988	1861–71	***–0.1***	*0.0*	*–0.2*
	1881	**19959**	10038	9921	988	1871–81	***–7.9***	*–7.9*	*–7.9*
		(19924)	(10018)	(9906)					
	1891	**18436**	9060	9376	1035	1881–91	***–7.5***	*–9.6*	*–5.4*
	1901	**16991**	8390	8601	1025	1891–1901	***–7.8***	*–7.4*	*–8.3*
	1911	**16683**	8406	8277	985	1901–11	***–1.8***	*0.2*	*–3.8*

Boundary changes: 1851–61 gain of 2397 from Montgomery (pop. 1851)
1881–91 loss of 35 to Oswestry (Salop) (pop. 1881)

	Year	Number Persons	Males	Females	Females/ 1000 males	Intercensal period	Persons	Males	Females
FLINTSHIRE Holywell	1801	**22163**	10781	11382	1056				
	1811	**26157**	12538	13619	1086	1801–11	***18.0***	*16.3*	*19.7*
	1821	**31178**	15479	15699	1014	1811–21	***19.2***	*23.5*	*15.3*
	1831	**35307**	17627	17680	1003	1821–31	***13.2***	*13.9*	*12.6*
	1841	**40798**	20673	20125	973	1831–41	***15.6***	*17.3*	*13.8*
	1851	**41047**	20787	20260	975	1841–51	***0.6***	*0.6*	*0.7*
	1861	**39941**	19997	19944	997	1851–61	***–2.7***	*–3.8*	*–1.6*
	1871	**43517**	22119	21398	967	1861–71	***9.0***	*10.6*	*7.3*
	1881	**45774**	23217	22557	972	1871–81	***5.2***	*5.0*	*5.4*
	1891	**42565**	21373	21192	992	1881–91	***–7.0***	*–7.9*	*–6.1*
	1901	**42261**	21129	21132	1000	1891–1901	***–0.7***	*–1.1*	*–0.3*
		(38935)	(19412)	(19523)					
	1911	**42818**	21332	21486	1007	1901–11	***10.0***	*9.9*	*10.1*

Boundary changes: 1901–11 loss of 3326 to new district of Hawarden (previously transferred to Chester District, July 1901)

	Year	Number Persons	Males	Females	Females/ 1000 males	Intercensal period	Persons	Males	Females
Hawarden	1901	(21601)	(11267)	(10334)					
	1911	**26904**	14108	12796	907	1901–11	***24.5***	*25.2*	*23.8*

Boundary changes: 1901–11 creation of new district; gain of 21601 from Chester (Ches) (3326 of which had been transferred from Holywell in July 1901)

	Year	Number Persons	Males	Females	Females/ 1000 males	Intercensal period	*Percentage change* Persons	Males	Females
DENBIGHSHIRE									
Wrexham	1801	**24329**	11761	12568	1069				
	1811	**26192**	12674	13518	1067	1801–11	***7.7***	*7.8*	*7.6*
	1821	**32062**	15980	16082	1006	1811–21	***22.4***	*26.1*	*19.0*
	1831	**34839**	17303	17536	1013	1821–31	***8.7***	*8.3*	*9.0*
	1841	**39558**	19791	19767	999	1831–41	***13.5***	*14.4*	*12.7*
	1851	**42295**	21415	20880	975	1841–51	***6.9***	*8.2*	*5.6*
		(40078)	(20312)	(19766)					
	1861	**47975**	24551	23424	954	1851–61	***19.7***	*20.9*	*18.5*
		(43072)	(22057)	(21015)					
	1871	**48837**	24708	24129	977	1861–71	***13.4***	*12.0*	*14.8*
	1881	**55158**	28325	26833	947	1871–81	***12.9***	*14.6*	*11.2*
		(55200)	(28351)	(26849)					
	1891	**61795**	32101	29694	925	1881–91	***11.9***	*13.2*	*10.6*
		(60200)	(31351)	(28849)					
	1901	**70154**	36268	33886	934	1891–1901	***16.5***	*15.7*	*17.5*
	1911	**79054**	40903	38151	933	1901–11	***12.7***	*12.8*	*12.6*

Boundary changes: 1851–61 loss of 2217 to Whitchurch (Salop) (pop 1851)
1861–71 loss of 4903 to Chester (Ches) (pop. 1861)
1881–91 gain of 42 from Chester (Ches) (pop. 1881)
1891–1901 loss of 316 to Chester (Ches), loss of 306 to Whitchurch (Salop), loss of 973 to Ellesmere (Salop) – overall loss of 1595 (pop. 1891)

	Year	Number Persons	Males	Females	Females/ 1000 males	Intercensal period	Persons	Males	Females
Ruthin	1801	**13094**	6418	6676	1040				
	1811	**13417**	6553	6864	1047	1801–11	***2.5***	*2.1*	*2.8*
	1821	**15473**	7601	7872	1036	1811–21	***15.3***	*16.0*	*14.7*
	1831	**16113**	7947	8166	1028	1821–31	***4.1***	*4.6*	*3.7*
	1841	**16609**	8298	8311	1002	1831–41	***3.1***	*4.4*	*1.8*
	1851	**16853**	8394	8459	1008	1841–51	***1.5***	*1.2*	*1.8*
	1861	**16083**	8146	7937	974	1851–61	***–4.6***	*–3.0*	*–6.2*
	1871	**15399**	7814	7585	971	1861–71	***–4.3***	*–4.1*	*–4.4*
	1881	**14215**	7160	7055	985	1871–81	***–7.7***	*–8.4*	*–7.0*
	1891	**12938**	6462	6476	1002	1881–91	***–9.0***	*–9.7*	*–8.2*
	1901	**12088**	6069	6019	992	1891–1901	***–6.6***	*–6.1*	*–7.1*
	1911	**12204**	6049	6155	1018	1901–11	***1.0***	*–0.3*	*2.3*

No boundary changes

	Year	Number Persons	Males	Females	Females/ 1000 males	Intercensal period	Persons	Males	Females
St Asaph	1801	**15556**	7563	7993	1057				
	1811	**16710**	7944	8766	1103	1801–11	***7.4***	*5.0*	*9.7*
	1821	**19795**	9668	10127	1047	1811–21	***18.5***	*21.7*	*15.5*
	1831	**22017**	10674	11343	1063	1821–31	***11.2***	*10.4*	*12.0*
	1841	**23547**	11693	11854	1014	1831–41	***6.9***	*9.5*	*4.5*
	1851	**25288**	12613	12675	1005	1841–51	***7.4***	*7.9*	*6.9*
	1861	**27518**	13460	14058	1044	1851–61	***8.8***	*6.7*	*10.9*
	1871	**27878**	13356	14522	1087	1861–71	***1.3***	*–0.8*	*3.3*
	1881	**29458**	13935	15523	1114	1871–81	***5.7***	*4.3*	*6.9*
	1891	**28954**	13538	15416	1139	1881–91	***–1.7***	*–2.8*	*–0.7*
	1901	**31046**	14565	16481	1132	1891–1901	***7.2***	*7.6*	*6.9*
	1911	**33226**	15315	17911	1170	1901–11	***7.0***	*5.1*	*8.7*

No boundary changes

	Year	Number Persons	Males	Females	Females/ 1000 males	Intercensal period	Persons	Males	Females
Llanrwst	1801	**8645**	4134	4511	1091				
	1811	**9740**	4594	5146	1120	1801–11	***12.7***	*11.1*	*14.1*
	1821	**10924**	5312	5612	1056	1811–21	***12.2***	*15.6*	*9.1*
	1831	**11294**	5495	5799	1055	1821–31	***3.4***	*3.4*	*3.3*
	1841	**12322**	6044	6278	1039	1831–41	***9.1***	*10.0*	*8.3*
	1851	**12479**	6217	6262	1007	1841–51	***1.3***	*2.9*	*–0.3*
	1861	**12770**	6351	6419	1011	1851–61	***2.3***	*2.2*	*2.5*
	1871	**13050**	6511	6539	1004	1861–71	***2.2***	*2.5*	*1.9*
	1881	**14109**	7081	7028	993	1871–81	***8.1***	*8.8*	*7.5*
	1891	**13011**	6332	6679	1055	1881–91	***–7.8***	*–10.6*	*–5.0*
	1901	**13170**	6449	6721	1042	1891–1901	***1.2***	*1.8*	*0.6*
	1911	**12326**	6031	6295	1044	1901–11	***–6.4***	*–6.5*	*–6.3*

No boundary changes

	Year	Number Persons	Males	Females	Females/ 1000 males	Intercensal period	Percentage change Persons	Males	Females
MERIONETH									
Corwen	1801	**10331**	5025	5306	1056				
	1811	**10818**	5251	5567	1060	1801–11	***4.7***	*4.5*	*4.9*
	1821	**12408**	6176	6232	1009	1811–21	***14.7***	*17.6*	*11.9*
	1831	**14014**	7030	6984	993	1821–31	***12.9***	*13.8*	*12.1*
	1841	**15089**	7605	7484	984	1831–41	***7.7***	*8.2*	*7.2*
	1851	**15418**	7830	7588	969	1841–51	***2.2***	*3.0*	*1.4*
	1861	**16107**	8145	7962	978	1851–61	***4.5***	*4.0*	*4.9*
	1871	**16451**	8331	8120	975	1861–71	***2.1***	*2.3*	*2.0*
	1881	**16833**	8438	8395	995	1871–81	***2.3***	*1.3*	*3.4*
	1891	**16258**	8161	8097	992	1881–91	***–3.4***	*–3.3*	*–3.5*
	1901	**16313**	8145	8168	1003	1891–1901	***0.3***	*–0.2*	*0.9*
	1911	**16428**	8167	8261	1012	1901–11	***0.7***	*0.3*	*1.1*

No boundary changes

	Year	Number Persons	Males	Females	Females/ 1000 males	Intercensal period	Persons	Males	Females
Bala	1801	**6586**	3257	3329	1022				
	1811	**6903**	3218	3685	1145	1801–11	***4.8***	*–1.2*	*10.7*
	1821	**7113**	3440	3673	1068	1811–21	***3.0***	*6.9*	*–0.3*
	1831	**6654**	3200	3454	1079	1821–31	***–6.5***	*–7.0*	*–6.0*
	1841	**6953**	3372	3581	1062	1831–41	***4.5***	*5.4*	*3.7*
	1851	**6736**	3353	3383	1009	1841–51	***–3.1***	*–0.6*	*–5.5*
	1861	**6352**	3229	3123	967	1851–61	***–5.7***	*–3.7*	*–7.7*
	1871	**6604**	3345	3259	974	1861–71	***4.0***	*3.6*	*4.4*
	1881	**6740**	3498	3242	927	1871–81	***2.1***	*4.6*	*–0.5*
	1891	**6115**	3046	3069	1008	1881–91	***–9.3***	*–12.9*	*–5.3*
	1901	**5732**	2801	2931	1046	1891–1901	***–6.3***	*–8.0*	*–4.5*
	1911	**5609**	2781	2828	1017	1901–11	***–2.1***	*–0.7*	*–3.5*

No boundary changes

	Year	Number Persons	Males	Females	Females/ 1000 males	Intercensal period	Persons	Males	Females
Dolgellau	1801	**10792**	4937	5855	1186				
	1811	**11235**	5074	6161	1214	1801–11	***4.1***	*2.8*	*5.2*
	1821	**12566**	5971	6595	1105	1811–21	***11.8***	*17.7*	*7.0*
	1831	**12912**	6213	6699	1078	1821–31	***2.8***	*4.1*	*1.6*
	1841	**13211**	6286	6925	1102	1831–41	***2.3***	*1.2*	*3.4*
	1851	**12971**	6230	6741	1082	1841–51	***–1.8***	*–0.9*	*–2.7*
	1861	**12482**	5914	6568	1111	1851–61	***–3.8***	*–5.1*	*–2.6*
	1871	**14311**	6932	7379	1064	1861–71	***14.7***	*17.2*	*12.3*
	1881	**15180**	7273	7907	1087	1871–81	***6.1***	*4.9*	*7.2*
		(15139)	(7251)	(7888)					
	1891	**14492**	6822	7670	1124	1881–91	***–4.3***	*–5.9*	*–2.8*
		(14371)	(6766)	(7605)					
	1901	**14248**	6747	7501	1112	1891–1901	***–0.9***	*–0.3*	*–1.4*
	1911	**12998**	5920	7078	1196	1901–11	***–8.8***	*–12.3*	*–5.6*

Boundary changes: 1881–91 loss of 41 to Machynlleth (pop. 1881)
1891–1901 loss of 121 to Machynlleth (pop. 1891)

	Year	Number Persons	Males	Females	Females/ 1000 males	Intercensal period	Persons	Males	Females
Ffestiniog	1801	**8138**	3772	4366	1157				
	1811	**9688**	4624	5064	1095	1801–11	***19.0***	*22.6*	*16.0*
	1821	**10634**	5070	5564	1097	1811–21	***9.8***	*9.6*	*9.9*
	1831	**11558**	5598	5960	1065	1821–31	***8.7***	*10.4*	*7.1*
	1841	**15460**	7798	7662	983	1831–41	***33.8***	*39.3*	*28.6*
	1851	**16182**	7976	8206	1029	1841–51	***4.7***	*2.3*	*7.1*
	1861	**18289**	9020	9269	1028	1851–61	***13.0***	*13.1*	*13.0*
	1871	**24141**	12157	11984	986	1861–71	***32.0***	*34.8*	*29.3*
	1881	**29525**	15141	14384	950	1871–81	***22.3***	*24.5*	*20.0*
	1891	**27861**	13812	14049	1017	1881–91	***–5.6***	*–8.8*	*–2.3*
	1901	**27955**	13811	14144	1024	1891–1901	***0.3***	*0.0*	*0.7*
	1911	**25245**	12208	13037	1068	1901–11	***–9.7***	*–11.6*	*–7.8*

No boundary changes

	Year	Number Persons	Males	Females	Females/ 1000 males	Intercensal period	*Percentage change* *Persons*	*Males*	*Females*
CAERNARFONSHIRE									
Pwllheli	1801	**15820**	7436	8384	1127				
	1811	**17812**	8429	9383	1113	1801–11	***12.6***	*13.4*	*11.9*
	1821	**20159**	9778	10381	1062	1811–21	***13.2***	*16.0*	*10.6*
	1831	**20781**	10068	10713	1064	1821–31	***3.1***	*3.0*	*3.2*
	1841	**21637**	10298	11339	1101	1831–41	***4.1***	*2.3*	*5.8*
	1851	**21788**	10214	11574	1133	1841–51	***0.7***	*–0.8*	*2.1*
	1861	**20908**	9729	11179	1149	1851–61	***–4.0***	*–4.7*	*–3.4*
	1871	**20974**	10022	10952	1093	1861–71	***0.3***	*3.0*	*–2.0*
	1881	**22911**	11161	11750	1053	1871–81	***9.2***	*11.4*	*7.3*
	1891	**22273**	10481	11792	1125	1881–91	***–2.8***	*–6.1*	*0.4*
	1901	**21897**	10548	11349	1076	1891–1901	***–1.7***	*0.6*	*–3.8*
	1911	**22006**	10458	11548	1104	1901–11	***0.5***	*–0.9*	*1.8*

No boundary changes

	Year	Number Persons	Males	Females	Females/ 1000 males	Intercensal period	*Persons*	*Males*	*Females*
Caernarfon	1801	**12290**	5718	6572	1149				
	1811	**15307**	7119	8188	1150	1801–11	***24.5***	*24.5*	*24.6*
	1821	**17896**	8618	9278	1077	1811–21	***16.9***	*21.1*	*13.3*
	1831	**22019**	10685	11334	1061	1821–31	***23.0***	*24.0*	*22.2*
	1841	**28509**	13861	14648	1057	1831–41	***29.5***	*29.7*	*29.2*
	1851	**30446**	14912	15534	1042	1841–51	***6.8***	*7.6*	*6.0*
	1861	**32425**	15900	16525	1039	1851–61	***6.5***	*6.6*	*6.4*
	1871	**39137**	19360	19777	1022	1861–71	***20.7***	*21.8*	*19.7*
	1881	**43997**	22058	21939	995	1871–81	***12.4***	*13.9*	*10.9*
	1891	**40712**	19836	20876	1052	1881–91	***–7.5***	*–10.1*	*–4.8*
	1901	**42653**	21106	21547	1021	1891–1901	***4.8***	*6.4*	*3.2*
	1911	**40342**	19665	20677	1051	1901–11	***–5.4***	*–6.8*	*–4.0*

No boundary changes

	Year	Number Persons	Males	Females	Females/ 1000 males	Intercensal period	*Persons*	*Males*	*Females*
Bangor	1801	**11310**	5416	5894	1088				
	1811	**13061**	6264	6797	1085	1801–11	***15.5***	*15.7*	*15.3*
	1821	**16909**	8466	8443	997	1811–21	***29.5***	*35.2*	*24.2*
	1831	**19972**	9589	10383	1083	1821–31	***18.1***	*13.3*	*23.0*
	1841	**25901**	12796	13105	1024	1831–41	***29.7***	*33.4*	*26.2*
	1851	**30810**	15499	15311	988	1841–51	***19.0***	*21.1*	*16.8*
		(34321)	(17164)	(17157)					
	1861	**36309**	17980	18329	1019	1851–61	***5.8***	*4.8*	*6.8*
	1871	**36567**	17807	18760	1054	1861–71	***0.7***	*–1.0*	*2.4*
	1881	**38512**	18792	19720	1049	1871–81	***5.3***	*5.5*	*5.1*
		(38531)	(18802)	(19729)					
	1891	**38032**	18262	19770	1083	1881–91	***–1.3***	*–2.9*	*0.2*
	1901	**38655**	18350	20305	1107	1891–1901	***1.6***	*0.5*	*2.7*
	1911	**38165**	18375	19790	1077	1901–11	***–1.3***	*0.1*	*–2.5*

Boundary changes: 1851–61 gain of 3511 from Anglesey incl. Holyhead (pop. 1851)
1881–91 gain of 19 from Anglesey (pop. 1881)

	Year	Number Persons	Males	Females	Females/ 1000 males	Intercensal period	*Persons*	*Males*	*Females*
Conwy	1801	**6586**	3163	3423	1082				
	1811	**7267**	3482	3785	1087	1801–11	***10.3***	*10.1*	*10.6*
	1821	**8564**	4199	4365	1040	1811–21	***17.8***	*20.6*	*15.3*
	1831	**9703**	4818	4885	1014	1821–31	***13.3***	*14.7*	*11.9*
	1841	**10706**	5317	5389	1014	1831–41	***10.3***	*10.4*	*10.3*
	1851	**11630**	5847	5783	989	1841–51	***8.6***	*10.0*	*7.3*
	1861	**13896**	6811	7085	1040	1851–61	***19.5***	*16.5*	*22.5*
	1871	**14700**	6888	7812	1134	1861–71	***5.8***	*1.1*	*10.3*
	1881	**18361**	8731	9630	1103	1871–81	***24.9***	*26.8*	*23.3*
	1891	**24568**	11152	13416	1203	1881–91	***33.8***	*27.7*	*39.3*
	1901	**34031**	15364	18667	1215	1891–1901	***38.5***	*37.8*	*39.1*
	1911	**41254**	18121	23133	1277	1901–11	***21.2***	*17.9*	*23.9*

No boundary changes

	Year	Number Persons	Males	Females	Females/ 1000 males	Intercensal period	*Percentage change* Persons		
							Persons	*Males*	*Females*
ANGLESEY									
Anglesey[4]	1801	**21858**	10355	11503	1111				
	1811	**23084**	10934	12150	1111	1801–11	***5.6***	*5.6*	*5.6*
	1821	**27869**	13651	14218	1042	1811–21	***20.7***	*24.8*	*17.0*
	1831	**30552**	15020	15532	1034	1821–31	***9.6***	*10.0*	*9.2*
	1841	**31652**	15216	16436	1080	1831–41	***3.6***	*1.3*	*5.8*
	1851	**31709**	15254	16455	1079	1841–51	***0.2***	*0.2*	*0.1*
		(30381)	(14670)	(15711)					
	1861	**28922**	13924	14998	1077	1851–61	***–4.8***	*–5.1*	*–4.5*
	1871	**26532**	12741	13791	1082	1861–71	***–8.3***	*–8.5*	*–8.0*
	1881	**25010**	12006	13004	1083	1871–81	***–5.7***	*–5.8*	*–5.7*
		(24991)	(11996)	(12995)					
	1891	**24209**	11496	12713	1106	1881–91	***–3.1***	*–4.2*	*–2.2*
	1901	**23387**	11193	12194	1089	1891–1901	***–3.4***	*–2.6*	*–4.1*
	1911	**23272**	11056	12216	1105	1901–11	***–0.5***	*–1.2*	*0.2*

Boundary changes: 1851–61 loss of 1328 to Bangor
1881–91 loss of 19 to Bangor

	Year	Number Persons	Males	Females	Females/ 1000 males	Intercensal period	*Persons*	*Males*	*Females*
Holyhead[4]	1801	**3834**	1642	2192	1335				
	1811	**5026**	2320	2706	1166	1801–11	***31.1***	*41.3*	*23.4*
	1821	**6579**	3019	3560	1179	1811–21	***30.9***	*30.1*	*31.6*
	1831	**6746**	3163	3583	1133	1821–31	***2.5***	*4.8*	*0.6*
	1841	**6454**	3055	3399	1113	1831–41	***–4.3***	*–3.4*	*–5.1*
	1851	**11534**	5918	5616	949	1841–51	***78.7***	*93.7*	*65.2*
		(9351)	(4837)	(4514)					
	1861	**9235**	4577	4658	1018	1851–61	***–1.2***	*–5.4*	*3.2*
	1871	**8595**	4149	4446	1072	1861–71	***–6.9***	*–9.4*	*–4.6*
	1881	**10131**	5184	4947	954	1871–81	***17.9***	*24.9*	*11.3*
	1891	**10010**	4826	5184	1074	1881–91	***–1.2***	*–6.9*	*4.8*
	1901	**11421**	5628	5793	1029	1891–1901	***14.1***	*16.6*	*11.7*
	1911	**12087**	5924	6163	1040	1901–11	***5.8***	*5.3*	*6.4*

Boundary changes: 1851–61 loss of 2183 to Bangor

Sources: As for Table 1.1.

Figures given in brackets represent the population of a changed area at the previous census. They are used to calculate the percentages shown in the last three columns. Details of boundary changes are given after the figures for each registration district.

1. Until 1861 Bedwellte was part of Abergavenny District. Separate figures for the years 1801–51 are given here to provide a continuous series.
2. The district of Pontypridd was created in 1871 from part of Cardiff and Merthyr Tydfil districts. Figures given here for 1801–61 provide a continuous series.
3. The district of Presteigne was abolished in 1881 with the transfer of 1262 (pop. 1871) to Kington (Her). The remainder (2607) formed an additional subdistrict of Presteigne in the Knighton District. The later figures for this new subdistrict continue to be shown separately in this table (i.e. figures for Knighton in the table do not include Presteigne).
4. Until 1881 Holyhead was part of Anglesey District. Separate figures for the years 1801–71 are given here to provide a continuous series.

Population 1.3 Total population. Persons, males, females. Number and percentage change. Number of females per 1000 males. Registration Subdistricts. Census years 1801–1911

Subdistrict	Year	Number Persons	Males	Females	Females/ 1000 males	Intercensal period	*Percentage change* Persons	Males	Females
MONMOUTHSHIRE									
Chepstow District									
Shirenewton	1801	**3496**	1774	1722	971				
	1811	**3938**	1990	1948	979	1801–11	***12.6***	*12.2*	*13.1*
	1821	**4252**	2139	2113	988	1811–21	***8.0***	*7.5*	*8.5*
	1831	**4691**	2424	2267	935	1821–31	***10.3***	*13.3*	*7.3*
	1841	**4849**	2581	2268	879	1831–41	***3.4***	*6.5*	*0.0*
	1851	**5112**	2683	2429	905	1841–51	***5.4***	*4.0*	*7.1*
	1861	**4893**	2529	2364	935	1851–61	***–4.3***	*–5.7*	*–2.7*
	1871	**5096**	2656	2440	919	1861–71	***4.1***	*5.0*	*3.2*
	1881	**5541**	2906	2635	907	1871–81	***8.7***	*9.4*	*8.0*

Boundary changes: 1881–91 subdistrict abolished, loss of 5541 to Chepstow (pop. 1881)

Subdistrict	Year	Number Persons	Males	Females	Females/ 1000 males	Intercensal period	*Percentage change* Persons	Males	Females
Chepstow	1801	**4284**	2108	2176	1032				
	1811	**5123**	2441	2682	1099	1801–11	***19.6***	*15.8*	*23.3*
	1821	**5825**	2853	2972	1042	1811–21	***13.7***	*16.9*	*10.8*
	1831	**6695**	3367	3328	988	1821–31	***14.9***	*18.0*	*12.0*
	1841	**6862**	3252	3610	1110	1831–41	***2.5***	*–3.4*	*8.5*
	1851	**8197**	4041	4156	1028	1841–51	***19.5***	*24.3*	*15.1*
	1861	**7141**	3418	3723	1089	1851–61	***–12.9***	*–15.4*	*–10.4*
	1871	**6776**	3305	3471	1050	1861–71	***–5.1***	*–3.3*	*–6.8*
	1881	**7168**	3517	3651	1038	1871–81	***5.8***	*6.4*	*5.2*
		(11194)	(5708)	(5486)					
	1891	**11311**	5580	5731	1027	1881–91	***1.0***	*–2.2*	*4.5*
	1901	**10597**	5214	5383	1032	1891–1901	***–6.3***	*–6.6*	*–6.1*
	1911	**10924**	5427	5497	1013	1901–11	***3.1***	*4.1*	*2.1*

Boundary changes: 1881–91 loss of 1515 to Lydney, gain of 5541 from Shirenewton (pop. 1881)

Subdistrict	Year	Number Persons	Males	Females	Females/ 1000 males	Intercensal period	*Percentage change* Persons	Males	Females
Lydney	1801	**2824**	1473	1351	917				
	1811	**3235**	1658	1577	951	1801–11	***14.6***	*12.6*	*16.7*
	1821	**4095**	2131	1964	922	1811–21	***26.6***	*28.5*	*24.5*
	1831	**4354**	2169	2185	1007	1821–31	***6.3***	*1.8*	*11.3*
	1841	**5065**	2555	2510	982	1831–41	***16.3***	*17.8*	*14.9*
	1851	**5748**	2972	2776	934	1841–51	***13.5***	*16.3*	*10.6*
	1861	**5907**	3014	2893	960	1851–61	***2.8***	*1.4*	*4.2*
	1871	**6469**	3301	3168	960	1861–71	***9.5***	*9.5*	*9.5*
	1881	**5992**	3038	2954	972	1871–81	***–7.4***	*–8.0*	*–6.8*
		(7507)	(3753)	(3754)					
	1891	**8153**	4062	4091	1007	1881–91	***8.6***	*8.2*	*9.0*
	1901	**8649**	4291	4358	1016	1891–1901	***6.1***	*5.6*	*6.5*
	1911	**9005**	4439	4566	1029	1901–11	***4.1***	*3.4*	*4.8*

Boundary changes: 1881–91 gain of 1515 from Chepstow (pop. 1881)

Subdistrict	Year	Number Persons	Males	Females	Females/ 1000 males	Intercensal period	*Percentage change* Persons	Males	Females
Monmouth District									
Coleford	1801	**4830**	2498	2332	934				
	1811	**5780**	2968	2812	947	1801–11	***19.7***	*18.8*	*20.6*
	1821	**6826**	3494	3332	954	1811–21	***18.1***	*17.7*	*18.5*
	1831	**8027**	4062	3965	976	1821–31	***17.6***	*16.3*	*19.0*
	1841	**9163**	4658	4505	967	1831–41	***14.2***	*14.7*	*13.6*
	1851	**11296**	5688	5608	986	1841–51	***23.3***	*22.1*	*24.5*
	1861	**13964**	7150	6814	953	1851–61	***23.6***	*25.7*	*21.5*
	1871	**15376**	7923	7453	941	1861–71	***10.1***	*10.8*	*9.4*
	1881	**14887**	7652	7235	946	1871–81	***–3.2***	*–3.4*	*–2.9*
		(14821)	(7619)	(7202)					
	1891	**14147**	7287	6860	941	1881–91	***–4.5***	*–4.4*	*–4.7*
		(14282)	(7351)	(6931)					
	1901	**15256**	7804	7452	955	1891–1901	***6.8***	*6.2*	*7.5*
		(9204)							
	1911	**9365**	4774	4591	962	1901–11	***1.7***	–	–

Boundary changes: 1881–91 loss of 93 to Ross (Her), gain of 27 from Westbury (Gloucs) (pop. 1881)
1891 –1901 gain of 135 from Dingestow (pop. 1891)
1901–11 loss of 6052 to the new subdistrict of West Dean (all in Gloucs) (pop. 1901)

Subdistrict	Year	Number Persons	Males	Females	Females/ 1000 males	Intercensal period	Percentage change Persons	Males	Females
Dingestow	1801	**4355**	2147	2208	1028				
	1811	**4550**	2202	2348	1066	1801–11	***4.5***	*2.6*	*6.3*
	1821	**5036**	2610	2426	930	1811–21	***10.7***	*18.5*	*3.3*
	1831	**5172**	2645	2527	955	1821–31	***2.7***	*1.3*	*4.2*
	1841	**5298**	2788	2510	900	1831–41	***2.4***	*5.4*	*–0.7*
	1851	**5456**	2849	2607	915	1841–51	***3.0***	*2.2*	*3.9*
	1861	**5459**	2885	2574	892	1851–61	***0.1***	*1.3*	*–1.3*
	1871	**5465**	2836	2629	927	1861–71	***0.1***	*–1.7*	*2.1*
	1881	**4920**	2500	2420	968	1871–81	***–10.0***	*–11.8*	*–7.9*
		(5053)	(2562)	(2491)					
	1891	**4634**	2339	2295	981	1881–91	***–8.3***	*–8.7*	*–7.9*

Boundary changes: 1881–91 gain of 95 from Monmouth, gain of 32 from Ross (Her), gain of 6 from Hereford (Her) (pop. 1881)
1891–1901 subdistrict abolished; loss of 135 to Coleford, loss of 2482 to Monmouth, loss of 2017 to Trelleck (1891)

Subdistrict	Year	Number Persons	Males	Females	Females/ 1000 males	Intercensal period	Percentage change Persons	Males	Females
West Dean	1901	(6052)							
	1911	**6795**	3602	3193	886	1901–11	***12.3***	–	–

Boundary changes: 1901–11 subdistrict created from part of Coleford (all in Gloucs)

Subdistrict	Year	Number Persons	Males	Females	Females/ 1000 males	Intercensal period	Percentage change Persons	Males	Females
Monmouth	1801	**3898**	1755	2143	1221				
	1811	**3927**	1835	2092	1140	1801–11	***0.7***	*4.6*	*–2.4*
	1821	**4729**	2249	2480	1103	1811–21	***20.4***	*22.6*	*18.5*
	1831	**5588**	2668	2920	1094	1821–31	***18.2***	*18.6*	*17.7*
	1841	**6197**	2954	3243	1098	1831–41	***10.9***	*10.7*	*11.1*
	1851	**5967**	2797	3170	1133	1841–51	***–3.7***	*–5.3*	*–2.3*
	1861	**6024**	2849	3175	1114	1851–61	***1.0***	*1.9*	*0.2*
	1871	**6061**	2859	3202	1120	1861–71	***0.6***	*0.4*	*0.9*
	1881	**6358**	3126	3232	1034	1871–81	***4.9***	*9.3*	*0.9*
		(6263)	(3081)	(3182)					
	1891	**5611**	2639	2972	1126	1881–91	***–10.4***	*–14.3*	*–6.6*
		(8093)	(3888)	(4205)					
	1901	**7495**	3507	3988	1137	1891–1901	***–7.4***	*–9.8*	*–5.2*
	1911	**7708**	3786	3922	1036	1901–11	***2.8***	*8.0*	*–1.7*

Boundary changes: 1881–91 loss of 95 to Dingestow (pop. 1881)
1891–1901 gain of 2482 from Dingestow (pop. 1891)

Subdistrict	Year	Number Persons	Males	Females	Females/ 1000 males	Intercensal period	Percentage change Persons	Males	Females
Trelleck	1801	**3308**	1641	1667	1016				
	1811	**3711**	1871	1840	983	1801–11	***12.2***	*14.0*	*10.4*
	1821	**4134**	2167	1967	908	1811–21	***11.4***	*15.8*	*6.9*
	1831	**4523**	2301	2222	966	1821–31	***9.4***	*6.2*	*13.0*
	1841	**4647**	2371	2276	960	1831–41	***2.7***	*3.0*	*2.4*
	1851	**4660**	2371	2289	965	1841–51	***0.3***	*0.0*	*0.6*
	1861	**4797**	2399	2398	1000	1851–61	***2.9***	*1.2*	*4.8*
	1871	**4696**	2337	2359	1009	1861–71	***–2.1***	*–2.6*	*–1.6*
	1881	**4175**	2099	2076	989	1871–81	***–11.1***	*–10.2*	*–12.0*
	1891	**3889**	1935	1954	1010	1881–91	***–6.9***	*–7.8*	*–5.9*
		(5906)	(2961)	(2945)					
	1901	**5489**	2712	2777	1024	1891–1901	***–7.1***	*–8.4*	*–5.7*
	1911	**5506**	2734	2772	1014	1901–11	***0.3***	*0.8*	*–0.2*

Boundary changes: 1891–1901 gain of 2017 from Dingestow (1891)

Abergavenny District

Subdistrict	Year	Number Persons	Males	Females	Females/ 1000 males	Intercensal period	Percentage change Persons	Males	Females
Llan-arth	1801	**1443**	683	760	1113				
	1811	**1647**	797	850	1066	1801–11	***14.1***	*16.7*	*11.8*
	1821	**1705**	880	825	938	1811–21	***3.5***	*10.4*	*–2.9*
	1831	**1824**	957	867	906	1821–31	***7.0***	*8.8*	*5.1*
	1841	**1861**	915	946	1034	1831–41	***2.0***	*–4.4*	*9.1*
	1851	**1909**	963	946	982	1841–51	***2.6***	*5.2*	*0.0*
	1861	**1884**	961	923	960	1851–61	***–1.3***	*–0.2*	*–2.4*
	1871	**1891**	947	944	997	1861–71	***0.4***	*–1.5*	*2.3*
	1881	**1717**	843	874	1037	1871–81	***–9.2***	*–11.0*	*–7.4*
	1891	**1639**	785	854	1088	1881–91	***–4.5***	*–6.9*	*–2.3*
	1901	**1422**	664	758	1142	1891–1901	***–13.2***	*–15.4*	*–11.2*
	1911	**1393**	661	732	1107	1901–11	***–2.0***	*–0.5*	*–3.4*

No boundary changes

Subdistrict	Year	Number Persons	Males	Females	Females/ 1000 males	Intercensal period	*Percentage change* Persons	Males	Females
Llanfihangel	1801	**1616**	787	829	1053				
	1811	**1715**	870	845	971	1801–11	***6.1***	*10.5*	*1.9*
	1821	**1712**	881	831	943	1811–21	***–0.2***	*1.3*	*–1.7*
	1831	**1689**	870	819	941	1821–31	***–1.3***	*–1.2*	*–1.4*
	1841	**1820**	931	889	955	1831–41	***7.8***	*7.0*	*8.5*
	1851	**1957**	997	960	963	1841–51	***7.5***	*7.1*	*8.0*
	1861	**1860**	981	879	896	1851–61	***–5.0***	*–1.6*	*–8.4*
	1871	**1847**	952	895	940	1861–71	***–0.7***	*–3.0*	*1.8*
	1881	**1675**	874	801	916	1871–81	***–9.3***	*–8.2*	*–10.5*
	1891	**1698**	866	832	961	1881–91	***1.4***	*–0.9*	*3.9*
	1901	**1539**	792	747	943	1891–1901	***–9.4***	*–8.5*	*–10.2*
	1911	**1500**	779	721	926	1901–11	***–2.5***	*–1.6*	*–3.5*

No boundary changes

Subdistrict	Year	Number Persons	Males	Females	Females/ 1000 males	Intercensal period	*Percentage change* Persons	Males	Females
Abergavenny	1801	**3746**	1709	2037	1192				
	1811	**4618**	2159	2459	1139	1801–11	***23.3***	*26.3*	*20.7*
	1821	**5386**	2571	2815	1095	1811–21	***16.6***	*19.1*	*14.5*
	1831	**6351**	3074	3277	1066	1821–31	***17.9***	*19.6*	*16.4*
	1841	**7256**	3598	3658	1017	1831–41	***14.2***	*17.0*	*11.6*
	1851	**7942**	3885	4057	1044	1841–51	***9.5***	*8.0*	*10.9*
	1861	**8669**	4229	4440	1050	1851–61	***9.2***	*8.9*	*9.4*
	1871	**9131**	4462	4669	1046	1861–71	***5.3***	*5.5*	*5.2*
	1881	**10730**	5217	5513	1057	1871–81	***17.5***	*16.9*	*18.1*
	1891	**11686**	5630	6056	1076	1881–91	***8.9***	*7.9*	*9.8*
		(11807)	(5696)	(6111)					
	1901	**12014**	5705	6309	1106	1891–1901	***1.8***	*0.2*	*3.2*
	1911	**12812**	6351	6461	1017	1901–11	***6.6***	*11.3*	*2.4*

Boundary changes: 1891–1901 gain of 46 from Pontypool, gain of 75 from Aberystruth

Subdistrict	Year	Number Persons	Males	Females	Females/ 1000 males	Intercensal period	*Percentage change* Persons	Males	Females
Blaenafon	1801	**1469**	796	673	845				
	1811	**2619**	1363	1256	921	1801–11	***78.3***	*71.2*	*86.6*
	1821	**4066**	2288	1778	777	1811–21	***55.3***	*67.9*	*41.6*
	1831	**4382**	2383	1999	839	1821–31	***7.8***	*4.2*	*12.4*
	1841	**6223**	3391	2832	835	1831–41	***42.0***	*42.3*	*41.7*
	1851	**5855**	3079	2776	902	1841–51	***–5.9***	*–9.2*	*–2.0*
	1861	**7114**	3747	3367	899	1851–61	***21.5***	*21.7*	*21.3*
	1871	**9993**	5413	4580	846	1861–71	***40.5***	*44.5*	*36.0*
	1881	**9449**	4945	4504	911	1871–81	***–5.4***	*–8.6*	*–1.7*
	1891	**11041**	5929	5112	862	1881–91	***16.8***	*19.9*	*13.5*
		(12510)	(6770)	(5740)					
	1901	**11754**	6130	5624	917	1891–1901	***–6.0***	*–9.5*	*–2.0*
	1911	**12973**	6928	6045	873	1901–11	***10.4***	*13.0*	*7.5*

Boundary changes: 1891–1901 gain of 1469 from Pontypool

Subdistrict	Year	Number Persons	Males	Females	Females/ 1000 males	Intercensal period	*Percentage change* Persons	Males	Females
Abergavenny/Bedwellte District									
Aberystruth	1801	**805**	460	345	750				
	1811	**1626**	900	726	807	1801–11	***102.0***	*95.7*	*110.4*
	1821	**4059**	2394	1665	695	1811–21	***149.6***	*166.0*	*129.3*
	1831	**5992**	3334	2658	797	1821–31	***47.6***	*39.3*	*59.6*
	1841	**11272**	6365	4907	771	1831–41	***88.1***	*90.9*	*84.6*
	1851	**14383**	7994	6389	799	1841–51	***27.6***	*25.6*	*30.2*
	1861	**16055**	8742	7313	837	1851–61	***11.6***	*9.4*	*14.5*
	1871	**15468**	8532	6936	813	1861–71	***–3.7***	*–2.4*	*–5.2*
	1881	**18672**	9950	8722	877	1871–81	***20.7***	*16.6*	*25.7*
	1891	**25913**	14394	11519	800	1881–91	***38.8***	*44.7*	*32.1*
		(25568)	(14205)	(11363)					
	1901	**36806**	20009	16797	839	1891–1901	***44.0***	*40.9*	*47.8*
	1911	**51656**	27990	23666	846	1901–11	***40.3***	*39.9*	*40.9*

Boundary changes: 1861–71 whole subdistrict transferred from Abergavenny District to the new district of Bedwellte
1891–1901 loss of 75 to Abergavenny, loss of 270 to Llanelli

Subdistrict	Year	Number Persons	Males	Females	Females/ 1000 males	Intercensal period	*Percentage change* Persons	Males	Females
Tredegar	1801	**1132**	632	500	791				
	1811	**3958**	1829	2129	1164	1801–11	***249.6***	*189.4*	*325.8*
	1821	**5404**	3066	2338	763	1811–21	***36.5***	*67.6*	*9.8*
	1831	**8567**	4771	3796	796	1821–31	***58.5***	*55.6*	*62.4*
	1841	**19929**	11135	8794	790	1831–41	***132.6***	*133.4*	*131.7*
	1851	**24544**	13434	11110	827	1841–51	***23.2***	*20.6*	*26.3*
	1861	**28548**	15196	13352	879	1851–61	***16.3***	*13.1*	*20.2*
	1871	**33697**	18222	15475	849	1861–71	***18.0***	*19.9*	*15.9*
	1881	**34685**	18597	16088	865	1871–81	***2.9***	*2.1*	*4.0*
	1891	**35628**	18924	16704	883	1881–91	***2.7***	*1.8*	*3.8*
	1901	**40831**	21629	19202	888	1891–1901	***14.6***	*14.3*	*15.0*
	1911	**57008**	30784	26224	852	1901–11	***39.6***	*42.3*	*36.6*

Boundary changes: 1861–71 whole subdistrict transferred from Abergavenny District to the new district of Bedwellte

Subdistrict	Year	Number Persons	Males	Females	Females/ 1000 males	Intercensal period	Persons	Males	Females
Rock	1801	**302**	117	185	1581				
Bedwellte	1811	**632**	312	320	1026	1801–11	***109.3***	*166.7*	*73.0*
	1821	**978**	487	491	1008	1811–21	***54.7***	*56.1*	*53.4*
	1831	**2070**	1087	983	904	1821–31	***111.7***	*123.2*	*100.2*
	1841	**2484**	1334	1150	862	1831–41	***20.0***	*22.7*	*17.0*
	1851	**2639**	1391	1248	897	1841–51	***6.2***	*4.3*	*8.5*
	1861	**2962**	1573	1389	883	1851–61	***12.2***	*13.1*	*11.3*
	1871	**2598**	1327	1271	958	1861–71	***–12.3***	*–15.6*	*–8.5*
	1881	**2483**	1246	1237	993	1871–81	***–4.4***	*–6.1*	*–2.7*
	1891	**3325**	1773	1552	875	1881–91	***33.9***	*42.3*	*25.5*
	1901	**4183**	2184	1999	915	1891–1901	***25.8***	*23.2*	*28.8*
	1911	**13624**	7451	6173	828	1901–11	***225.7***	*241.2*	*208.8*

Boundary changes: 1861–71 whole subdistrict transferred from Abergavenny District to the new district of Bedwellte

Pontypool District

Subdistrict	Year	Number Persons	Males	Females	Females/ 1000 males	Intercensal period	Persons	Males	Females
Llanhilleth	1901	(5015)	(2832)	(2183)					
	1911	**9652**	5267	4385	833	1901–11	***92.5***	*86.1*	*100.9*

Boundary changes: 1901–11 subdistrict created from part of Pontypool

Subdistrict	Year	Number Persons	Males	Females	Females/ 1000 males	Intercensal period	Persons	Males	Females
Pontypool	1801	**2570**	1186	1384	1167				
	1811	**4252**	2202	2050	931	1801–11	***65.4***	*85.7*	*48.1*
	1821	**6242**	3351	2891	863	1811–21	***46.8***	*52.2*	*41.0*
	1831	**12835**	7014	5821	830	1821–31	***105.6***	*109.3*	*101.3*
	1841	**18280**	9647	8633	895	1831–41	***42.4***	*37.5*	*48.3*
	1851	**20614**	10690	9924	928	1841–51	***12.8***	*10.8*	*15.0*
	1861	**22633**	11547	11086	960	1851–61	***9.8***	*8.0*	*11.7*
	1871	**25287**	13195	12092	916	1861–71	***11.7***	*14.3*	*9.1*
	1881	**25297**	13048	12249	939	1871–81	***0.0***	*–1.1*	*1.3*
	1891	**29228**	15144	14084	930	1881–91	***15.5***	*16.1*	*15.0*
		(23967)	(12343)	(11624)					
	1901	**29798**	15624	14174	907	1891–1901	***24.3***	*26.6*	*21.9*
		(24783)	(12792)	(11991)					
	1911	**32594**	17146	15448	901	1901–11	***31.5***	*34.0*	*28.8*

Boundary changes: 1891–1901 loss of 46 to Abergavenny, loss of 1469 to Blaenafon, loss of 3746 to Llangybi (pop. 1891)
1901–11 loss of 5015 to new subdistrict of Llanhilleth (pop. 1901)

Subdistrict	Year	Number Persons	Males	Females	Females/ 1000 males	Intercensal period	Persons	Males	Females
Llangybi	1801	**1248**	605	643	1063				
	1811	**1648**	825	823	998	1801–11	***32.1***	*36.4*	*28.0*
	1821	**1966**	994	972	978	1811–21	***19.3***	*20.5*	*18.1*
	1831	**2147**	1088	1059	973	1821–31	***9.2***	*9.5*	*9.0*
	1841	**2632**	1385	1247	900	1831–41	***22.6***	*27.3*	*17.8*
	1851	**3599**	1934	1665	861	1841–51	***36.7***	*39.6*	*33.5*
	1861	**3620**	1908	1712	897	1851–61	***0.6***	*–1.3*	*2.8*
	1871	**4683**	2483	2200	886	1861–71	***29.4***	*30.1*	*28.5*
	1881	**6310**	3322	2988	899	1871–81	***34.7***	*33.8*	*35.8*
	1891	**7024**	3656	3368	921	1881–91	***11.3***	*10.1*	*12.7*
		(10770)	(5596)	(5174)					
	1901	**12015**	6255	5760	921	1891–1901	***11.6***	*11.8*	*11.3*
	1911	**15866**	8262	7604	920	1901–11	***32.1***	*32.1*	*32.0*

Boundary changes: 1891–1901 gain of 3746 from Pontypool (pop. 1891)

Subdistrict	Year	Number Persons	Males	Females	Females/ 1000 males	Intercensal period	*Percentage change* Persons	Males	Females
Usk	1801	**2528**	1276	1252	981				
	1811	**2849**	1365	1484	1087	1801–11	***12.7***	*7.0*	*18.5*
	1821	**3229**	1573	1656	1053	1811–21	***13.3***	*15.2*	*11.6*
	1831	**3567**	1848	1719	930	1821–31	***10.5***	*17.5*	*3.8*
	1841	**4126**	2157	1969	913	1831–41	***15.7***	*16.7*	*14.5*
	1851	**3780**	1939	1841	949	1841–51	***–8.4***	*–10.1*	*–6.5*
	1861	**4035**	2029	2006	989	1851–61	***6.7***	*4.6*	*9.0*
	1871	**3922**	2008	1914	953	1861–71	***–2.8***	*–1.0*	*–4.6*
	1881	**3731**	1888	1843	976	1871–81	***–4.9***	*–6.0*	*–3.7*
	1891	**3519**	1755	1764	1005	1881–91	***–5.7***	*–7.0*	*–4.3*
	1901	**3566**	1772	1794	1012	1891–1901	***1.3***	*1.0*	*1.7*
	1911	**3756**	1891	1865	986	1901–11	***5.3***	*6.7*	*4.0*
	No boundary changes								
Newport District									
Caerleon	1801	**3382**	1608	1774	1103				
	1811	**4307**	2118	2189	1034	1801–11	***27.4***	*31.7*	*23.4*
	1821	**4939**	2495	2444	980	1811–21	***14.7***	*17.8*	*11.6*
	1831	**5098**	2593	2505	966	1821–31	***3.2***	*3.9*	*2.5*
	1841	**5822**	3010	2812	934	1831–41	***14.2***	*16.1*	*12.3*
	1851	**6368**	3212	3156	983	1841–51	***9.4***	*6.7*	*12.2*
	1861	**7615**	3810	3805	999	1851–61	***19.6***	*18.6*	*20.6*
	1871	**8630**	4224	4406	1043	1861–71	***13.3***	*10.9*	*15.8*
	1881	**10709**	5157	5552	1077	1871–81	***24.1***	*22.1*	*26.0*
	1891	**18486**	9028	9458	1048	1881–91	***72.6***	*75.1*	*70.4*
		(5441)	(2653)	(2788)					
	1901	**5796**	2901	2895	998	1891–1901	***6.5***	*9.3*	*3.8*
	1911	**6895**	3366	3529	1048	1901–11	***19.0***	*16.0*	*21.9*
	Boundary changes: 1891–1901 loss of 13045 to Newport (pop. 1891)								
Newport	1801	**1423**	697	726	1042				
	1811	**3025**	1483	1542	1040	1801–11	***112.6***	*112.8*	*112.4*
	1821	**4951**	2431	2520	1037	1811–21	***63.7***	*63.9*	*63.4*
	1831	**7062**	3500	3562	1018	1821–31	***42.6***	*44.0*	*41.3*
	1841	**13766**	7037	6729	956	1831–41	***94.9***	*101.1*	*88.9*
	1851	**20279**	10536	9743	925	1841–51	***47.3***	*49.7*	*44.8*
	1861	**24756**	12216	12540	1027	1851–61	***22.1***	*15.9*	*28.7*
	1871	**29877**	15068	14809	983	1861–71	***20.7***	*23.3*	*18.1*
	1881	**33932**	16848	17084	1014	1871–81	***13.6***	*11.8*	*15.4*
	1891	**41903**	21350	20553	963	1881–91	***23.5***	*26.7*	*20.3*
		(54948)	(27725)	(27223)					
	1901	**67545**	33536	34009	1014	1891–1901	***22.9***	*21.0*	*24.9*
	1911	**83972**	42304	41668	985	1901–11	***24.3***	*26.1*	*22.5*
	Boundary changes: 1891–1901 gain of 13045 from Caerleon (pop. 1891)								
St Woollos	1801	**3309**	1614	1695	1050				
	1811	**4046**	1995	2051	1028	1801–11	***22.3***	*23.6*	*21.0*
	1821	**4144**	2113	2031	961	1811–21	***2.4***	*5.9*	*–1.0*
	1831	**4963**	2553	2410	944	1821–31	***19.8***	*20.8*	*18.7*
	1841	**5765**	2917	2848	976	1831–41	***16.2***	*14.3*	*18.2*
	1851	**7759**	4069	3690	907	1841–51	***34.6***	*39.5*	*29.6*
	1861	**8445**	4288	4157	969	1851–61	***8.8***	*5.4*	*12.7*
	1871	**11254**	5799	5455	941	1861–71	***33.3***	*35.2*	*31.2*
	1881	**12811**	6475	6336	979	1871–81	***13.8***	*11.7*	*16.2*
	1891	**16880**	8795	8085	919	1881–91	***31.8***	*35.8*	*27.6*
	Boundary changes: 1891–1901 subdistrict abolished; loss of 10771 to new subdistrict of Rogerstone, loss of 5834 to new subdistrict of Llantarnam, loss of 275 to Llandaff (pop. 1891)								
Rogerstone	1891	(15777)	(8302)	(7475)					
	1901	**17905**	9298	8607	926	1891–1901	***13.5***	*12.0*	*15.1*
	1911	**23824**	12504	11320	905	1901–11	***33.1***	*34.5*	*31.5*
	Boundary changes: 1891–1901 subdistrict created; gain of 10771 from St Woollos, gain of 3816 from Mynyddislwyn, gain of 1190 from Whitchurch (pop. 1891)								

Subdistrict	Year	Number Persons	Males	Females	Females/ 1000 males	Intercensal period	*Percentage change* *Persons*	*Males*	*Females*
Llantarnam	1891	(5834)	(3014)	(2820)					
	1901	**6180**	3206	2974	928	1891–1901	***5.9***	*6.4*	*5.5*
	1911	**8182**	4279	3903	912	1901–11	***32.4***	*33.5*	*31.2*

Boundary changes: 1891–1901 subdistrict created; gain of 5834 from St Woollos (pop. 1991)

Subdistrict	Year	Number Persons	Males	Females	Females/ 1000 males	Intercensal period	*Persons*	*Males*	*Females*
Mynyddislwyn	1801	**2782**	1337	1445	1081				
	1811	**4802**	2416	2386	988	1801–11	***72.6***	*80.7*	*65.1*
	1821	**4961**	2681	2280	850	1811–21	***3.3***	*11.0*	*–4.4*
	1831	**7089**	3729	3360	901	1821–31	***42.9***	*39.1*	*47.4*
	1841	**7704**	4053	3651	901	1831–41	***8.7***	*8.7*	*8.7*
	1851	**9066**	4777	4289	898	1841–51	***17.7***	*17.9*	*17.5*
	1861	**10596**	5539	5057	913	1851–61	***16.9***	*16.0*	*17.9*
	1871	**11491**	6013	5478	911	1861–71	***8.4***	*8.6*	*8.3*
	1881	**13090**	6717	6373	949	1871–81	***13.9***	*11.7*	*16.3*
	1891	**19527**	10461	9066	867	1881–91	***49.2***	*55.7*	*42.3*
		(15436)	(8262)	(7174)					
	1901	**18024**	9504	8520	896	1891–1901	***16.8***	*15.0*	*18.8*
	1911	**29656**	16181	13475	833	1901–11	***64.5***	*70.3*	*58.2*

Boundary changes: 1891–1901 loss of 3816 to Rogerstone, loss of 275 to Llandaff (pop. 1891)

GLAMORGAN
Cardiff District

Subdistrict	Year	Number Persons	Males	Females	Females/ 1000 males	Intercensal period	*Persons*	*Males*	*Females*
Caerphilly	1801	**3744**	1803	1941	1077				
	1811	**4456**	2207	2249	1019	1801–11	***19.0***	*22.4*	*15.9*
	1821	**4788**	2405	2383	991	1811–21	***7.5***	*9.0*	*6.0*
	1831	**5300**	2673	2627	983	1821–31	***10.7***	*11.1*	*10.2*
	1841	**6554**	3335	3219	965	1831–41	***23.7***	*24.8*	*22.5*
	1851	**8121**	4217	3904	926	1841–51	***23.9***	*26.4*	*21.3*
	1861	**10012**	5174	4838	935	1851–61	***23.3***	*22.7*	*23.9*

Boundary changes: 1861–71 subdistrict abolished; loss of 6383 to new subdistrict of Pontypridd, loss of 3629 to new subdistrict of Whitchurch (pop. 1861)

Subdistrict	Year	Number Persons	Males	Females	Females/ 1000 males	Intercensal period	*Persons*	*Males*	*Females*
Whitchurch	1861	(5739)	(2974)	(2765)					
	1871	**6432**	3293	3139	953	1861–71	***12.1***	*10.7*	*13.5*
	1881	**6474**	3311	3163	955	1871–81	***0.7***	*0.5*	*0.8*
		(6592)	(3374)	(3218)					
	1891	**6997**	3503	3494	997	1881–91	***6.1***	*3.8*	*8.6*

Boundary changes: 1861–71 subdistrict created; gain of 3629 from Caerphilly, gain of 2110 from Llantrisant (pop. 1861)
1881–91 gain of 118 from St Nicholas (pop. 1881)
1891–1901 subdistrict abolished; loss of 1190 to new subdistrict of Rogerstone, loss of 5807 to new subdistrict of Llandaff (pop. 1891)

Subdistrict	Year	Number Persons	Males	Females	Females/ 1000 males	Intercensal period	*Persons*	*Males*	*Females*
Cardiff	1801	**4672**	2173	2499	1150				
	1811	**5343**	2449	2894	1182	1801–11	***14.4***	*12.7*	*15.8*
	1821	**6892**	3300	3592	1088	1811–21	***29.0***	*34.7*	*24.1*
	1831	**9839**	4735	5104	1078	1821–31	***42.8***	*43.5*	*42.1*
	1841	**13922**	7083	6839	966	1831–41	***41.5***	*49.6*	*34.0*
	1851	**23085**	12696	10389	818	1841–51	***65.8***	*79.2*	*51.9*
	1861	**46954**	24390	22564	925	1851–61	***103.4***	*92.1*	*117.2*
	1871	**64972**	34004	30968	911	1861–71	***38.4***	*39.4*	*37.2*
	1881	**94666**	48299	46367	960	1871–81	***45.7***	*42.0*	*49.7*
		(94657)	(48294)	(46363)					
	1891	**148497**	75450	73047	968	1881–91	***56.9***	*56.2*	*57.6*

Boundary changes: 1881–91 loss of 9 to St Nicholas (pop. 1881)
1891–1901 subdistrict abolished with creation of new subdistricts – loss of 6856 to Llandaff, loss of 35294 to East Cardiff, loss of 53842 to Central Cardiff, loss of 39797 to West Cardiff, loss of 12726 to Penarth (pop. 1891)

Subdistrict	Year	Number Persons	Males	Females	Females/ 1000 males	Intercensal period	*Persons*	*Males*	*Females*
Llandaff	1891	(13213)	(6586)	(6627)					
	1901	**17333**	8417	8916	1059	1891–1901	***31.2***	*27.8*	*34.5*
	1911	**26599**	12836	13763	1072	1901–11	***53.5***	*52.5*	*54.4*

Boundary changes: 1891–1901 subdistrict created; gain of 275 from St Woollos, gain of 275 from Mynyddislwyn, gain of 5807 from Whitchurch, gain of 6856 from Cardiff (pop. 1891)

Subdistrict	Year	Number Persons	Males	Females	Females/ 1000 males	Intercensal period	*Percentage change* *Persons*	*Males*	*Females*
East Cardiff	1891	(35294)	(17180)	(18114)					
	1901	**52585**	25409	27176	1070	1891–1901	***49.0***	*47.9*	*50.0*
	1911	**59602**	28545	31057	1088	1901–11	***13.3***	*12.3*	*14.3*
	Boundary changes: 1891–1901	subdistrict created; gain of 35294 from Cardiff (pop. 1891)							
Central Cardiff	1891	(53824)	(28731)	(25093)					
	1901	**54316**	28240	26076	923	1891–1901	***0.9***	*–1.7*	*3.9*
	1911	**57506**	29577	27929	944	1901–11	***5.9***	*4.7*	*7.1*
	Boundary changes: 1891–1901	subdistrict created; gain of 53824 from Cardiff (pop. 1891)							
West Cardiff	1891	(39797)	(19834)	(19963)					
	1901	**57432**	27956	29476	1054	1891–1901	***44.3***	*40.9*	*47.7*
	1911	**65151**	31606	33545	1061	1901–11	***13.4***	*13.1*	*13.8*
	Boundary changes: 1891–1901	subdistrict created; gain of 39797 from Cardiff (pop. 1891)							
Penarth	1891	(12726)	(6300)	6426					
	1901	**14568**	6957	7611	1094	1891–1901	***14.5***	*10.4*	*18.4*
	1911	**15826**	7409	8417	1136	1901–11	***8.6***	*6.5*	*10.6*
	Boundary changes: 1891–1901	subdistrict created; gain of 12726 from Cardiff (pop. 1891)							
St Nicholas	1801	**3638**	1787	1851	1036				
	1811	**3789**	1788	2001	1119	1801–11	***4.2***	*0.1*	*8.1*
	1821	**4419**	2211	2208	999	1811–21	***16.6***	*23.7*	*10.3*
	1831	**4507**	2238	2269	1014	1821–31	***2.0***	*1.2*	*2.8*
	1841	**4530**	2248	2282	1015	1831–41	***0.5***	*0.4*	*0.6*
	1851	**4572**	2315	2257	975	1841–51	***0.9***	*3.0*	*–1.1*
	1861	**4705**	2358	2347	995	1851–61	***2.9***	*1.9*	*4.0*
		(5592)	(2810)	(2782)					
	1871	**5297**	2665	2632	988	1861–71	***–5.3***	*–5.2*	*–5.4*
	1881	**5024**	2518	2506	995	1871–81	***–5.2***	*–5.5*	*–4.8*
		(4915)	(2460)	(2455)					
	1891	**18302**	10389	7913	762	1881–91	***272.4***	*322.3*	*222.3*
	1901	**32404**	17048	15356	901	1891–1901	***77.1***	*64.1*	*94.1*
	1911	**40026**	20529	19497	950	1901–11	***23.5***	*20.4*	*27.0*
	Boundary changes: 1861–71	gain of 887 from Llantrisant							
	1881–91	loss of 118 to Whitchurch, gain of 9 from Cardiff							
Cardiff/Pontypridd District **Llantrisant**	1801	**3271**	1507	1764	1171				
	1811	**3840**	1959	1881	960	1801–11	***17.4***	*30.0*	*6.6*
	1821	**4785**	2452	2333	951	1811–21	***24.6***	*25.2*	*24.0*
	1831	**5346**	2753	2593	942	1821–31	***11.7***	*12.3*	*11.1*
	1841	**7551**	3946	3605	914	1831–41	***41.2***	*43.3*	*39.0*
	1851	**10713**	5674	5039	888	1841–51	***41.9***	*43.8*	*39.8*
	1861	**12904**	6843	6061	886	1851–61	***20.5***	*20.6*	*20.3*
		(9907)	(5252)	(4655)					
	1871	**13110**	6867	6243	909	1861–71	***32.3***	*30.8*	*34.1*
	1881	**19197**	10059	9138	908	1871–81	***46.4***	*46.5*	*46.4*
	1891	**28547**	15551	12996	836	1881–91	***48.7***	*54.6*	*42.2*
	1901	**34171**	18253	15918	872	1891–1901	***19.7***	*17.4*	*22.5*
	1911	**50929**	27061	23868	882	1901–11	***49.0***	*48.3*	*49.9*
	Boundary changes: 1861–71	subdistrict transferred from Cardiff District to the new district of Pontypridd; loss of 2110 to Whitchurch, loss of 887 to St Nicholas (pop. 1861)							
Pontypridd District **Pontypridd**	1861	(17445)	(9346)	(8099)					
	1871	**21897**	11479	10418	908	1861–71	***25.5***	*22.8*	*28.6*
	1881	**30250**	16146	14104	874	1871–81	***38.1***	*40.7*	*35.4*
	Boundary changes: 1861–71	subdistrict created; gain of 6383 from Caerphilly, gain of 11061 from Gelli-gaer (pop. 1861)							
	1881–91	subdistrict abolished; loss of 11598 to new subdistrict of Eglwysilan, loss of 18652 to new subdistrict of Llanwynno (pop. 1881)							

Subdistrict	Year	Number Persons	Males	Females	Females/ 1000 males	Intercensal period	*Percentage change* *Persons*	*Males*	*Females*
Eglwysilan	1881	(11598)	(5911)	(5687)					
	1891	**18832**	10202	8630	846	1881–91	***62.4***	*72.6*	*51.7*
		(17908)	(9695)	(8213)					
	1901	**30191**	16072	14119	878	1891–1901	***68.6***	*65.8*	*71.9*
	1911	**49765**	27064	22701	839	1901–11	***64.8***	*68.4*	*60.8*
	Boundary changes: 1881–91	subdistrict created; gain of 11598 from Pontypridd (pop. 1881)							
	1891–1901	loss of 924 to Lower Merthyr Tydfil (pop. 1891)							
Llanwynno	1881	(18652)	(10235)	(8417)					
	1891	**30712**	17203	13509	785	1881–91	***64.7***	*68.1*	*60.5*
		(33198)	(18518)	(14680)					
	1901	**51494**	28213	23281	825	1891–1901	***55.1***	*52.4*	*58.6*
	1911	**67094**	36012	31082	863	1901–11	***30.3***	*27.6*	*33.5*
	Boundary changes: 1881–91	subdistrict created: gain of 18652 from Pontypridd (pop. 1881)							
	1891–1901	gain of 2486 from Aberdare (pop. 1891)							
Ystradyfodwg (Rhondda)	1861	(3035)	(1669)	(1366)					
	1871	**16914**	9559	7355	769	1861–71	***457.3***	*472.7*	*438.4*
	1881	**44046**	24470	19576	800	1871–81	***160.4***	*156.0*	*166.2*
	1891	**68721**	39172	29549	754	1881–91	***56.0***	*60.1*	*50.9*
	1901	**88968**	48726	40242	826	1891–1901	***29.5***	*24.4*	*36.2*
	1911	**120776**	65835	54941	835	1901–11	***35.8***	*35.1*	*36.5*
	Boundary changes: 1861–71	subdistrict created; gain of 3035 from Aberdare (pop. 1861)							
	1901–1911	name changed to Rhondda							
Merthyr Tydfil District									
Gelli-gaer	1801	**1952**	1030	922	895				
	1811	**2391**	1232	1159	941	1801–11	***22.5***	*19.6*	*25.7*
	1821	**2972**	1480	1492	1008	1811–21	***24.3***	*20.1*	*28.7*
	1831	**3772**	1971	1801	914	1821–31	***26.9***	*33.2*	*20.7*
	1841	**6278**	3384	2894	855	1831–41	***66.4***	*71.7*	*60.7*
	1851	**8985**	4819	4166	864	1841–51	***43.1***	*42.4*	*44.0*
	1861	**16840**	9120	7720	846	1851–61	***87.4***	*89.3*	*85.3*
		(5778)	(3113)	(2665)					
	1871	**9193**	5016	4177	833	1861–71	***59.1***	*61.1*	*56.7*
	1881	**11592**	6201	5391	869	1871–81	***26.1***	*23.6*	*29.1*
	1891	**12754**	6831	5923	867	1881–91	***10.0***	*10.2*	*9.9*
	1901	**17242**	9175	8067	879	1891–1901	***35.2***	*34.3*	*36.2*
	1911	**35521**	19441	16080	827	1901–11	***106.0***	*111.9*	*99.3*
	Boundary changes: 1861–71	loss of 11061 to the new subdistrict of Pontypridd (pop. 1861)							
Merthyr Tydfil (Lower and Upper)[1]	1801	**8945**	4908	4037	823				
	1811	**12520**	6642	5878	885	1801–11	***40.0***	*35.3*	*45.6*
	1821	**19414**	10614	8800	829	1811–21	***55.1***	*59.8*	*49.7*
	1831	**24016**	12819	11197	873	1821–31	***23.7***	*20.8*	*27.2*
	1841	**37263**	20224	17039	842	1831–41	***55.1***	*57.8*	*52.2*
	No boundary changes								
Lower Merthyr Tydfil[1]	1841	**18289**	9696	8593	886				
	1851	**23147**	12170	10977	902	1841–51	***26.6***	*25.5*	*27.7*
	1861	**25300**	12875	12425	965	1851–61	***9.3***	*5.8*	*13.2*
	1871	**25777**	13128	12649	964	1861–71	***1.9***	*2.0*	*1.8*
	1881	**23904**	12033	11871	987	1871–81	***–7.3***	*–8.3*	*–6.2*
	1891	**31892**	16970	14922	879	1881–91	***33.4***	*41.0*	*25.7*
		(31489)	(16800)	(14689)					
	1901	**38579**	20722	17857	862	1891–1901	***22.5***	*23.3*	*21.6*
		(31307)							
	1911	**38646**	20849	17797	854	1901–11	***23.4***	–	–
	Boundary changes: 1891–1901	gain of 924 from Eglwysilan, loss of 1327 to Upper Merthyr Tydfil (pop. 1891)							

Subdistrict	Year	Number Persons	Males	Females	Females/ 1000 males	Intercensal period	*Percentage change* Persons	Males	Females
Upper Merthyr Tydfil[1]	1841	**18974**	10528	8446	802				
	1851	**25898**	13918	11980	861	1841–51	***36.5***	*32.2*	*41.8*
	1861	**27478**	14288	13190	923	1851–61	***6.1***	*2.7*	*10.1*
	1871	**28964**	15352	13612	887	1861–71	***5.4***	*7.4*	*3.2*
	1881	**27808**	14472	13336	922	1871–81	***–4.0***	*–5.7*	*–2.0*
	1891	**29245**	15470	13775	890	1881–91	***5.2***	*6.9*	*3.3*
		(30572)	(16147)	(14425)					
	1901	**34069**	18076	15993	885	1891–1901	***11.4***	*11.9*	*10.9*
		(41341)							
	1911	**46201**	24196	22005	909	1901–11	***11.7***	–	–

Boundary changes: 1891–1901 gain of 1327 from Lower Merthyr Tydfil (pop. 1891)
1901–11 gain of 7272 from Lower Merthyr Tydfil (pop. 1901)

Subdistrict	Year	Number Persons	Males	Females	Females/ 1000 males	Intercensal period	*Percentage change* Persons	Males	Females
Aberdare	1801	**2758**	1460	1298	889				
	1811	**4950**	2564	2386	931	1801–11	***79.5***	*75.6*	*83.8*
	1821	**4352**	2247	2105	937	1811–21	***–12.1***	*–12.4*	*–11.8*
	1831	**6393**	3324	3069	923	1821–31	***46.9***	*47.9*	*45.8*
	1841	**9322**	5021	4301	857	1831–41	***45.8***	*51.1*	*40.1*
	1851	**18774**	10518	8256	785	1841–51	***101.4***	*109.5*	*92.0*
	1861	**37487**	20079	17408	867	1851–61	***99.7***	*90.9*	*110.9*
		(34452)	(18410)	(16042)					
	1871	**40305**	21505	18800	874	1861–71	***17.0***	*16.8*	*17.2*
	1881	**38137**	19724	18413	934	1871–81	***–5.4***	*–8.3*	*–2.1*
	1891	**43314**	23044	20270	880	1881–91	***13.6***	*16.8*	*10.1*
		(40828)	(21729)	(19099)					
	1901	**45650**	23788	21862	919	1891–1901	***11.8***	*9.5*	*14.5*
	1911	**53779**	27991	25788	921	1901–11	***17.8***	*17.7*	*18.0*

Boundary changes: 1861–71 loss of 3035 to the new subdistrict of Ystradyfodwg (pop. 1861)
1891–1901 loss of 2486 to Llanwynno (pop. 1891)

Bridgend District

Subdistrict	Year	Number Persons	Males	Females	Females/ 1000 males	Intercensal period	*Percentage change* Persons	Males	Females
Maesteg	1801	**2855**	1364	1491	1093				
	1811	**3262**	1561	1701	1090	1801–11	***14.3***	*14.4*	*14.1*
	1821	**3839**	1897	1942	1024	1811–21	***17.7***	*21.5*	*14.2*
	1831	**4337**	2208	2129	964	1821–31	***13.0***	*16.4*	*9.6*
	1841	**6994**	3684	3310	898	1831–41	***61.3***	*66.8*	*55.5*
	1851	**7488**	3863	3625	938	1841–51	***7.1***	*4.9*	*9.5*
	1861	**8562**	4352	4210	967	1851–61	***14.3***	*12.7*	*16.1*
	1871	**12236**	6448	5788	898	1861–71	***42.9***	*48.2*	*37.5*
	1881	**18215**	9762	8453	866	1871–81	***48.9***	*51.4*	*46.0*
		(9422)	(4827)	(4595)					
	1891	**10560**	5654	4906	868	1881–91	***12.1***	*17.1*	*6.8*
	1901	**16341**	9032	7309	809	1891–1901	***54.7***	*59.7*	*49.0*
	1911	**27075**	14452	12623	873	1901–11	***65.7***	*60.0*	*72.7*

Boundary changes: 1881–91 loss of 880 to Cowbridge, loss of 1365 to Bridgend, loss of 8632 to new subdistrict of Ogmore, gain of 2084 from Margam (pop. 1881)

Subdistrict	Year	Number Persons	Males	Females	Females/ 1000 males	Intercensal period	*Percentage change* Persons	Males	Females
Ogmore	1881	(8632)	(4855)	(3777)					
	1891	**15920**	9074	6846	754	1881–91	***84.4***	*86.9*	*81.3*
	1901	**22250**	12384	9866	797	1891–1901	***39.8***	*36.5*	*44.1*
	1911	**29731**	16162	13569	840	1901–11	***33.6***	*30.5*	*37.5*

Boundary changes: 1881–91 subdistrict created; gain of 8632 from Maesteg (pop. 1881)

Subdistrict	Year	Number Persons	Males	Females	Females/ 1000 males	Intercensal period	*Percentage change* Persons	Males	Females
Cowbridge	1801	**4969**	2304	2665	1157				
	1811	**5379**	2534	2845	1123	1801–11	***8.3***	*10.0*	*6.8*
	1821	**6384**	3079	3305	1073	1811–21	***18.7***	*21.5*	*16.2*
	1831	**6563**	3362	3201	952	1821–31	***2.8***	*9.2*	*–3.1*
	1841	**6449**	3135	3314	1057	1831–41	***–1.7***	*–6.8*	*3.5*
	1851	**6516**	3205	3311	1033	1841–51	***1.0***	*2.2*	*–0.1*
	1861	**6486**	3154	3332	1056	1851–61	***–0.5***	*–1.6*	*0.6*
	1871	**6450**	3113	3337	1072	1861–71	***–0.6***	*–1.3*	*0.2*
	1881	**6165**	2946	3219	1093	1871–81	***–4.4***	*–5.4*	*–3.5*
		(7045)	(3401)	(3644)					
	1891	**7456**	3705	3751	1012	1881–91	***5.8***	*8.9*	*2.9*
	1901	**8014**	4037	3977	985	1891–1901	***7.5***	*9.0*	*6.0*
	1911	**9080**	4613	4467	968	1901–11	***13.3***	*14.3*	*12.3*

Boundary changes: 1881–91 gain of 880 from Maesteg (pop. 1881)

Subdistrict	Year	Number Persons	Males	Females	Females/ 1000 males	Intercensal period	*Percentage change Persons*	*Males*	*Females*
Bridgend	1801	**4528**	2040	2488	1220				
	1811	**5196**	2466	2730	1107	1801–11	***14.8***	*20.9*	*9.7*
	1821	**5697**	2772	2925	1055	1811–21	***9.6***	*12.4*	*7.1*
	1831	**6337**	3108	3229	1039	1821–31	***11.2***	*12.1*	*10.4*
	1841	**7912**	3931	3981	1013	1831–41	***24.9***	*26.5*	*23.3*
	1851	**9418**	4721	4697	995	1841–51	***19.0***	*20.1*	*18.0*
	1861	**11417**	5810	5607	965	1851–61	***21.2***	*23.1*	*19.4*
	1871	**12985**	6620	6365	961	1861–71	***13.7***	*13.9*	*13.5*
	1881	**14540**	7346	7194	979	1871–81	***12.0***	*11.0*	*13.0*
		(15905)	(8045)	(7860)					
	1891	**17517**	8855	8662	978	1881–91	***10.1***	*10.1*	*10.2*
	1901	**20848**	10459	10389	993	1891–1901	***19.0***	*18.1*	*19.9*
	1911	**28723**	14693	14030	955	1901–11	***37.8***	*40.5*	*35.0*

Boundary changes: 1881–91 gain of 1365 from Maesteg (pop. 1881)

Neath District

Subdistrict	Year	Number Persons	Males	Females	Females/ 1000 males	Intercensal period	*Percentage change Persons*	*Males*	*Females*
Margam	1801	**2476**	1158	1318	1138				
	1811	**2529**	1216	1313	1080	1801–11	***2.1***	*5.0*	*–0.4*
	1821	**2991**	1460	1531	1049	1811–21	***18.3***	*20.1*	*16.6*
	1831	**4785**	2502	2283	912	1821–31	***60.0***	*71.4*	*49.1*
	1841	**7944**	4263	3681	863	1831–41	***66.0***	*70.4*	*61.2*
	1851	**14697**	7962	6735	846	1841–51	***85.0***	*86.8*	*83.0*
	1861	**16815**	8749	8066	922	1851–61	***14.4***	*9.9*	*19.8*
	1871	**16675**	8378	8297	990	1861–71	***–0.8***	*–4.2*	*2.9*
	1881	**18326**	9272	9054	976	1871–81	***9.9***	*10.7*	*9.1*
		(15882)	(7976)	(7906)					
	1891	**18469**	9346	9123	976	1881–91	***16.3***	*17.2*	*15.4*
		(18326)	(9265)	(9061)					
	1901	**22421**	11298	11123	985	1891–1901	***22.3***	*21.9*	*22.8*
	1911	**32053**	16713	15340	918	1901–11	***43.0***	*47.9*	*37.9*

Boundary changes: 1881–91 loss of 2084 to Maesteg, loss of 360 to Ystradfellte (pop. 1881)
1891–1901 loss of 161 to Ystradfellte, gain of 18 from Neath (pop. 1891)

Subdistrict	Year	Number Persons	Males	Females	Females/ 1000 males	Intercensal period	*Percentage change Persons*	*Males*	*Females*
Neath	1801	**3816**	1685	2131	1265				
	1811	**4328**	1960	2368	1208	1801–11	***13.4***	*16.3*	*11.1*
	1821	**4520**	2188	2332	1066	1811–21	***4.4***	*11.6*	*–1.5*
	1831	**5986**	2804	3182	1135	1821–31	***32.4***	*28.2*	*36.4*
	1841	**7768**	3929	3839	977	1831–41	***29.8***	*40.1*	*20.6*
	1851	**10065**	5000	5065	1013	1841–51	***29.6***	*27.3*	*31.9*
	1861	**13462**	6740	6722	997	1851–61	***33.8***	*34.8*	*32.7*
	1871	**17236**	8638	8598	995	1861–71	***28.0***	*28.2*	*27.9*
	1881	**21548**	10768	10780	1001	1871–81	***25.0***	*24.7*	*25.4*
	1891	**22706**	11421	11285	988	1881–91	***5.4***	*6.1*	*4.7*
		(22741)	(11430)	(11311)					
	1901	**28015**	14146	13869	980	1891–1901	***23.2***	*23.8*	*22.6*
		(30417)	(15384)	(15033)					
	1911	**40856**	21149	19707	932	1901–11	***34.3***	*37.5*	*31.1*

Boundary changes: 1891–1901 loss of 18 to Margam, gain of 53 from Ystradfellte (pop. 1891)
1901–11 gain of 2402 from Ystradfellte (pop. 1901)

Subdistrict	Year	Number Persons	Males	Females	Females/ 1000 males	Intercensal period	*Percentage change Persons*	*Males*	*Females*
Ystradfellte	1801	**1740**	871	869	998				
	1811	**1949**	948	1001	1056	1801–11	***12.0***	*8.8*	*15.2*
	1821	**1956**	1007	949	942	1811–21	***0.4***	*6.2*	*–5.2*
	1831	**2367**	1195	1172	981	1821–31	***21.0***	*18.7*	*23.5*
	1841	**2738**	1416	1322	934	1831–41	***15.7***	*18.5*	*12.8*
	1851	**2865**	1482	1383	933	1841–51	***4.6***	*4.7*	*4.6*
	1861	**3303**	1730	1573	909	1851–61	***15.3***	*16.7*	*13.7*
	1871	**3598**	1843	1755	952	1861–71	***8.9***	*6.5*	*11.6*
	1881	**3916**	1996	1920	962	1871–81	***8.8***	*8.3*	*9.4*
		(4276)	(2218)	(2058)					
	1891	**6187**	3370	2817	836	1881–91	***44.7***	*51.9*	*36.9*
		(6348)	(3461)	(2887)					
	1901	**9353**	5013	4340	866	1891–1901	***47.3***	*44.8*	*50.3*

Boundary changes: 1881–91 gain of 360 from Margam (pop. 1881)
1891–1901 gain of 161 from Margam (pop. 1891)
1901–11 subdistrict abolished; loss of 2402 to Neath, loss of 499 to Cadoxton, loss of 6452 to the new subdistrict of Glyncorrwg (pop. 1901)

Subdistrict	Year	Number Persons	Males	Females	Females/ 1000 males	Intercensal period	*Percentage change* *Persons*	*Males*	*Females*
Glyncorrwg	1901	(6452)	(3518)	(2934)					
	1911	**8688**	4663	4025	863	1901–11	***34.7***	*32.5*	*37.2*

Boundary changes: 1901–11 subdistrict created from part of Ystradfellte, gain of 6452 (pop. 1901)

Subdistrict	Year	Number Persons	Males	Females	Females/ 1000 males	Intercensal period	*Percentage change* *Persons*	*Males*	*Females*
Ystradgynlais	1801	**1822**	869	953	1097				
	1811	**2241**	1078	1163	1079	1801–11	***23.0***	*24.1*	*22.0*
	1821	**2910**	1457	1453	997	1811–21	***29.9***	*35.2*	*24.9*
	1831	**3925**	1945	1980	1018	1821–31	***34.9***	*33.5*	*36.3*
	1841	**5698**	2967	2731	920	1831–41	***45.2***	*52.5*	*37.9*
	1851	**7987**	4183	3804	909	1841–51	***40.2***	*41.0*	*39.3*
	1861	**12328**	6332	5996	947	1851–61	***54.4***	*51.4*	*57.6*
	1871	**12433**	6210	6223	1002	1861–71	***0.9***	*–1.9*	*3.8*

Boundary changes: 1871–81 subdistrict abolished; loss of 12433 to the new subdistrict of Pontardawe (pop. 1871)

Subdistrict	Year	Number Persons	Males	Females	Females/ 1000 males	Intercensal period	*Percentage change* *Persons*	*Males*	*Females*
Cadoxton	1801	**2926**	1455	1471	1011				
	1811	**3006**	1466	1540	1050	1801–11	***2.7***	*0.8*	*4.7*
	1821	**3361**	1645	1716	1043	1811–21	***11.8***	*12.2*	*11.4*
	1831	**3861**	1933	1928	997	1821–31	***14.9***	*17.5*	*12.4*
	1841	**5103**	2629	2474	941	1831–41	***32.2***	*36.0*	*28.3*
	1851	**6581**	3392	3189	940	1841–51	***29.0***	*29.0*	*28.9*
	1861	**7522**	3836	3686	961	1851–61	***14.3***	*13.1*	*15.6*
	1871	**8549**	4284	4265	996	1861–71	***13.7***	*11.7*	*15.7*
		(6554)	(3271)	(3283)					
	1881	**8287**	4183	4104	981	1871–81	***26.4***	*27.9*	*25.0*
	1891	**9311**	4718	4593	974	1881–91	***12.4***	*12.8*	*11.9*
		(9258)	(4699)	(4559)					
	1901	**11815**	6094	5721	939	1891–1901	***27.6***	*29.7*	*25.5*
		(12314)	(6351)	(5963)					
	1911	**19327**	10223	9104	891	1901–11	***57.0***	*61.0*	*52.7*

Boundary changes: 1871–81 loss of 1995 to the new subdistrict of Pontardawe (pop. 1871)
1891–1901 loss of 53 to Neath (pop. 1891)
1901–11 gain of 499 from Ystradfellte (pop. 1901)

Neath/Swansea District

Subdistrict	Year	Number Persons	Males	Females	Females/ 1000 males	Intercensal period	*Percentage change* *Persons*	*Males*	*Females*
Llansamlet	1801	**2567**	1282	1285	1002				
	1811	**2307**	1136	1171	1031	1801–11	***–10.1***	*–11.4*	*–8.9*
	1821	**2639**	1291	1348	1044	1811–21	***14.4***	*13.6*	*15.1*
	1831	**3187**	1571	1616	1029	1821–31	***20.8***	*21.7*	*19.9*
	1841	**3375**	1716	1659	967	1831–41	***5.9***	*9.2*	*2.7*
	1851	**4276**	2189	2087	953	1841–51	***26.7***	*27.6*	*25.8*
	1861	**5103**	2597	2506	965	1851–61	***19.3***	*18.6*	*20.1*
	1871	**6128**	3152	2976	944	1861–71	***20.1***	*21.4*	*18.8*
	1881	**8392**	4324	4068	941	1871–81	***36.9***	*37.2*	*36.7*
	1891	**9721**	5049	4672	925	1881–91	***15.8***	*16.8*	*14.8*
		(6100)	(3183)	(2917)					
	1901	**6142**	3143	2999	954	1891–1901	***0.7***	*–1.3*	*2.8*
	1911	**7411**	3801	3610	950	1901–11	***20.7***	*20.9*	*20.4*

Boundary changes: 1871–81 subdistrict transferred from Neath District to Swansea District
1891–1901 loss of 342 to Llangyfelach, loss of 3279 to Swansea (pop. 1891)

Pontardawe District

Subdistrict	Year	Number Persons	Males	Females	Females/ 1000 males	Intercensal period	*Percentage change* *Persons*	*Males*	*Females*
Pontardawe	1871	(17488)	(8742)	(8746)					
	1881	**20185**	10116	10069	995	1871–81	***15.4***	*15.7*	*15.1*
	1891	**21700**	10939	10761	984	1881–91	***7.5***	*8.1*	*6.9*
	1901	**26718**	13438	13280	988	1891–1901	***23.1***	*22.8*	*23.4*
		(20933)	(10450)	(10483)					
	1911	**31498**	16461	15037	913	1901–11	***50.5***	*57.5*	*43.4*

Boundary changes: 1871–81 new district created containing one subdistrict; gain of 12433 from Ystradgynlais, gain of 1995 from Cadoxton, gain of 3060 from Llandeilo Tal-y-bont
1901–11 loss of 5785 to the new subdistrict of Ystradgynlais (pop. 1901)

Subdistrict	Year	Number Persons	Males	Females	Females/ 1000 males	Intercensal period	*Percentage change* *Persons*	*Males*	*Females*
Ystradgynlais	1901	(5785)	(2988)	(2797)					
	1911	**10471**	5791	4680	808	1901–11	***81.0***	*93.8*	*67.3*

Boundary changes: 1901–11 subdistrict created; gain of 5785 from Pontardawe (pop. 1901)

Subdistrict	Year	Number Persons	Males	Females	Females/ 1000 males	Intercensal period	*Percentage change* Persons	Males	Females
Swansea District									
Llandeilo Tal-y-bont	1801	**2655**	1245	1410	1133				
	1811	**3273**	1522	1751	1150	1801–11	***23.3***	*22.2*	*24.2*
	1821	**3422**	1713	1709	998	1811–21	***4.6***	*12.5*	*–2.4*
	1831	**4224**	2077	2147	1034	1821–31	***23.4***	*21.2*	*25.6*
	1841	**4880**	2394	2486	1038	1831–41	***15.5***	*15.3*	*15.8*
	1851	**5001**	2503	2498	998	1841–51	***2.5***	*4.6*	*0.5*
	1861	**5114**	2525	2589	1025	1851–61	***2.3***	*0.9*	*3.6*
	1871	**6587**	3269	3318	1015	1861–71	***28.8***	*29.5*	*28.2*
		(7211)	(3614)	(3597)					
	1881	**11336**	5778	5558	962	1871–81	***57.2***	*59.9*	*54.5*
	1891	**15452**	7796	7656	982	1881–91	***36.3***	*34.9*	*37.7*
	1901	**16890**	8383	8507	1015	1891–1901	***9.3***	*7.5*	*11.1*
		(15001)	(7375)	(7626)					
	1911	**23303**	12095	11208	927	1901–11	***55.3***	*64.0*	*47.0*

Boundary changes: 1871–81 loss of 3060 to new subdistrict of Pontardawe, gain of 3684 from Llangyfelach (pop. 1871)
1901–1911 loss of 1889 to Llangyfelach (pop. 1901)

Subdistrict	Year	Number Persons	Males	Females	Females/ 1000 males	Intercensal period	Persons	Males	Females
Llangyfelach	1801	**4122**	1964	2158	1099				
	1811	**4408**	2054	2354	1146	1801–11	***6.9***	*4.6*	*9.1*
	1821	**5468**	2599	2869	1104	1811–21	***24.0***	*26.5*	*21.9*
	1831	**7183**	3547	3636	1025	1821–31	***31.4***	*36.5*	*26.7*
	1841	**9001**	4430	4571	1032	1831–41	***25.3***	*24.9*	*25.7*
	1851	**11255**	5551	5704	1028	1841–51	***25.0***	*25.3*	*24.8*
		(9812)	(4869)	(4943)					
	1861	**14553**	7350	7203	980	1851–61	***48.3***	*51.0*	*45.7*
	1871	**21284**	10796	10488	971	1861–71	***46.3***	*46.9*	*45.6*
		(17600)	(8932)	(8668)					
	1881	**25153**	12820	12333	962	1871–81	***42.9***	*43.5*	*42.3*
	1891	**32266**	16360	15906	972	1881–91	***28.3***	*27.6*	*29.0*
		(32608)	(16538)	(16070)					
	1901	**32009**	15897	16112	1014	1891–1901	***–1.8***	*–3.9*	*0.3*
		(35921)	(17825)	(18096)					
	1911	**39739**	20414	19325	947	1901–11	***10.6***	*14.5*	*6.8*

Boundary changes: 1851–61 loss of 1443 to Gower Eastern (pop. 1851)
1871–81 loss of 3684 to Llandeilo Tal-y-bont (pop. 1871)
1891–1901 gain of 342 from Llansamlet (pop. 1891)
1901–1911 gain of 1889 from Llandeilo Tal-y-bont, gain of 2023 from Swansea (pop. 1901)

Subdistrict	Year	Number Persons	Males	Females	Females/ 1000 males	Intercensal period	Persons	Males	Females
Swansea	1801	**6420**	2683	3737	1393				
	1811	**8515**	3827	4688	1225	1801–11	***32.6***	*42.6*	*25.4*
	1821	**10669**	4728	5941	1257	1811–21	***25.3***	*23.5*	*26.7*
	1831	**14253**	6340	7913	1248	1821–31	***33.6***	*34.1*	*33.2*
	1841	**18278**	8606	9672	1124	1831–41	***28.2***	*35.7*	*22.2*
	1851	**23607**	11244	12363	1100	1841–51	***29.2***	*30.7*	*27.8*
	1861	**31593**	15497	16096	1039	1851–61	***33.8***	*37.8*	*30.2*
	1871	**39486**	19503	19983	1025	1861–71	***25.0***	*25.9*	*24.1*
	1881	**50120**	24285	25835	1064	1871–81	***26.9***	*24.5*	*29.3*
	1891	**56887**	27842	29045	1043	1881–91	***13.5***	*14.6*	*12.4*
		(60166)	(29530)	(30636)					
	1901	**64705**	31320	33385	1066	1891–1901	***7.5***	*6.1*	*9.0*
		(62682)	(30400)	(32282)					
	1911	**80572**	40461	40111	991	1901–11	***28.5***	*33.1*	*24.3*

Boundary changes: 1891–1901 gain of 3279 from Llansamlet (pop. 1891)
1901–1911 loss of 2023 to Llangyfelach (pop. 1901)

Subdistrict	Year	Number Persons	Males	Females	Females/ 1000 males	Intercensal period	Persons	Males	Females
Gower	1801	**4313**	1984	2329	1174				
	1811	**4614**	2028	2586	1275	1801–11	***7.0***	*2.2*	*11.0*
	1821	**5372**	2524	2848	1128	1811–21	***16.4***	*24.5*	*10.1*
	1831	**5551**	2603	2948	1133	1821–31	***3.3***	*3.1*	*3.5*
	1841	**6490**	3089	3401	1101	1831–41	***16.9***	*18.7*	*15.4*
	1851	**7044**	3465	3579	1033	1841–51	***8.5***	*12.2*	*5.2*

Boundary changes: 1851–61 subdistrict abolished; loss of 3155 to new subdistrict of Gower Eastern, loss of 3889 to new subdistrict of Gower Western, in the new district of Gower (pop. 1851)

Subdistrict	Year	Number Persons	Males	Females	Females/ 1000 males	Intercensal period	*Percentage change* Persons	*Percentage change* Males	*Percentage change* Females
Gower District									
Gower Eastern	1851	(4598)	(2245)	(2353)					
	1861	**4962**	2397	2565	1070	1851–61	***7.9***	*6.8*	*9.0*
	1871	**6277**	3026	3251	1074	1861–71	***26.5***	*26.2*	*26.7*
		(6307)	(3041)	(3266)					
	1881	**8248**	3890	4358	1120	1871–81	***30.8***	*27.9*	*33.4*
	1891	**8386**	4037	4349	1077	1881–91	***1.7***	*3.8*	*–0.2*
	1901	**9174**	4169	5005	1201	1891–1901	***9.4***	*3.3*	*15.1*
	1911	**12153**	5784	6369	1101	1901–11	***32.5***	*38.7*	*27.3*

Boundary changes: 1851–61 subdistrict created in the new district of Gower; gain of 3155 from Gower, gain of 1443 from Llangyfelach (pop. 1851)
1871–81 gain of 30 from Gower Western (pop. 1871)

Subdistrict	Year	Number Persons	Males	Females	Females/ 1000 males	Intercensal period	*Percentage change* Persons	*Percentage change* Males	*Percentage change* Females
Gower Western	1851	(3889)	(1902)	(1987)					
	1861	**3354**	1639	1715	1046	1851–61	***–13.8***	*–13.8*	*–13.7*
	1871	**3013**	1468	1545	1052	1861–71	***–10.2***	*–10.4*	*–9.9*
		(2983)	(1453)	(1530)					
	1881	**2854**	1409	1445	1026	1871–81	***–4.3***	*–3.0*	*–5.6*
	1891	**2721**	1301	1420	1091	1881–91	***–4.7***	*–7.7*	*–1.7*
	1901	**2553**	1238	1315	1062	1891–1901	***–6.2***	*–4.8*	*–7.4*
	1911	**2567**	1240	1327	1070	1901–11	***0.5***	*0.2*	*0.9*

Boundary changes: 1851–61 subdistrict created in the new district of Gower; gain of 3889 from Gower (pop. 1851)
1871–81 loss of 30 to Gower Eastern (pop. 1871)

Subdistrict	Year	Number Persons	Males	Females	Females/ 1000 males	Intercensal period	*Percentage change* Persons	*Percentage change* Males	*Percentage change* Females
CARMARTHENSHIRE									
Llanelli District									
Loughor	1801	**1171**	537	634	1181				
	1811	**1521**	705	816	1157	1801–11	***29.9***	*31.3*	*28.7*
	1821	**1681**	811	870	1073	1811–21	***10.5***	*15.0*	*6.6*
	1831	**2417**	1212	1205	994	1821–31	***43.8***	*49.4*	*38.5*
	1841	**2728**	1346	1382	1027	1831–41	***12.9***	*11.1*	*14.7*
	1851	**3582**	1799	1783	991	1841–51	***31.3***	*33.7*	*29.0*
	1861	**3970**	1966	2004	1019	1851–61	***10.8***	*9.3*	*12.4*
	1871	**5328**	2639	2689	1019	1861–71	***34.2***	*34.2*	*34.2*
	1881	**7541**	3765	3776	1003	1871–81	***41.5***	*42.7*	*40.4*
	1891	**9184**	4567	4617	1011	1881–91	***21.8***	*21.3*	*22.3*
	1901	**10049**	4979	5070	1018	1891–1901	***9.4***	*9.0*	*9.8*
		(4781)	(2365)	(2416)					
	1911	**6866**	3533	3333	943	1901–11	***43.6***	*49.4*	*38.0*

Boundary changes: 1901–11 loss of 2224 to Llan-non, loss of 3044 to new subdistrict of Llanelli Rural (pop. 1901)

Subdistrict	Year	Number Persons	Males	Females	Females/ 1000 males	Intercensal period	*Percentage change* Persons	*Percentage change* Males	*Percentage change* Females
Llanelli	1801	**2072**	958	1114	1163				
	1811	**2791**	1316	1475	1121	1801–11	***34.7***	*37.4*	*32.4*
	1821	**4300**	2142	2158	1007	1811–21	***54.1***	*62.8*	*46.3*
	1831	**6079**	3055	3024	990	1821–31	***41.4***	*42.6*	*40.1*
	1841	**9266**	4628	4638	1002	1831–41	***52.4***	*51.5*	*53.4*
	1851	**11285**	5633	5652	1003	1841–51	***21.8***	*21.7*	*21.9*
	1861	**14619**	7279	7340	1008	1851–61	***29.5***	*29.2*	*29.9*
	1871	**18519**	9166	9353	1020	1861–71	***26.7***	*25.9*	*27.4*
	1881	**23933**	11847	12086	1020	1871–81	***29.2***	*29.2*	*29.2*
	1891	**28169**	13926	14243	1023	1881–91	***17.7***	*17.5*	*17.8*
	1901	**30216**	14735	15481	1051	1891–1901	***7.3***	*5.8*	*8.7*

Boundary changes: 1901–11 subdistrict abolished; loss of 4599 and 25617 to the new subdistricts of Llanelli Rural and Llanelli Urban respectively (pop. 1901)

Subdistrict	Year	Number Persons	Males	Females	Females/ 1000 males	Intercensal period	*Percentage change* Persons	*Percentage change* Males	*Percentage change* Females
Llanelli Rural	1901[2]	(8954)							
	1911	**11681**	5878	5803	987	1901–11[2]	***30.5***	–	–

Boundary changes: 1901–11 subdistrict created; gain of 4599 from Llanelli, gain of 3044 from Loughor (pop. 1901)

Subdistrict	Year	Number Persons	Males	Females	Females/ 1000 males	Intercensal period	*Percentage change* Persons	*Percentage change* Males	*Percentage change* Females
Llanelli Urban	1901[2]	(25617)							
	1911	**32071**	16441	15630	951	1901–11[2]	***25.2***	–	–

Boundary changes: 1901–11 subdistrict created; gain of 25617 from Llanelli (pop. 1901)

Subdistrict	Year	Number Persons	Males	Females	Females/ 1000 males	Intercensal period	*Percentage change* Persons	Males	Females
Pembrey	1801	**2843**	1273	1570	1233				
	1811	**2969**	1276	1693	1327	1801–11	***4.4***	*0.2*	*7.8*
	1821	**3500**	1629	1871	1149	1811–21	***17.9***	*27.7*	*10.5*
	1831	**4326**	2086	2240	1074	1821–31	***23.6***	*28.1*	*19.7*
	1841	**4413**	2062	2351	1140	1831–41	***2.0***	*–1.2*	*5.0*
	1851	**4958**	2394	2564	1071	1841–51	***12.3***	*16.1*	*9.1*
	1861	**5797**	2829	2968	1049	1851–61	***16.9***	*18.2*	*15.8*
	1871	**6845**	3308	3537	1069	1861–71	***18.1***	*16.9*	*19.2*
	1881	**8173**	3958	4215	1065	1871–81	***19.4***	*19.6*	*19.2*
	1891	**9337**	4562	4775	1047	1881–91	***14.2***	*15.3*	*13.3*
		(9180)	(4486)	(4694)					
	1901	**9798**	4696	5102	1086	1891–1901	***6.7***	*4.7*	*8.7*
	1911	**12181**	6130	6051	987	1901–11	***24.3***	*30.5*	*18.6*

Boundary changes: 1891–1901 loss of 157 to Llangyndeyrn (pop. 1891)

Subdistrict	Year	Number Persons	Males	Females	Females/ 1000 males	Intercensal period	Persons	Males	Females
Llan-non	1801	**2554**	1216	1338	1100				
	1811	**2672**	1246	1426	1144	1801–11	***4.6***	*2.5*	*6.6*
	1821	**3089**	1496	1593	1065	1811–21	***15.6***	*20.1*	*11.7*
	1831	**3348**	1626	1722	1059	1821–31	***8.4***	*8.7*	*8.1*
	1841	**3775**	1873	1902	1015	1831–41	***12.8***	*15.2*	*10.5*
	1851	**3682**	1792	1890	1055	1841–51	***–2.5***	*–4.3*	*–0.6*
	1861	**3593**	1745	1848	1059	1851–61	***–2.4***	*–2.6*	*–2.2*
	1871	**4040**	1989	2051	1031	1861–71	***12.4***	*14.0*	*11.0*
	1881	**4969**	2464	2505	1017	1871–81	***23.0***	*23.9*	*22.1*
	1891	**5692**	2857	2835	992	1881–91	***14.6***	*15.9*	*13.2*
	1901	**6834**	3352	3482	1039	1891–1901	***20.1***	*17.3*	*22.8*
		(7747)	(3839)	(3908)					
	1911	**11200**	5911	5289	895	1901–11	***44.6***	*54.0*	*35.3*

Boundary changes: 1901–11 loss of 1311 to Llanelli Rural, gain of 2224 from Loughor (pop. 1901)

Subdistrict	Year	Number Persons	Males	Females	Females/ 1000 males	Intercensal period	Persons	Males	Females
Llandovery District									
Llanddeusant	1801	**682**	314	368	1172				
	1811	**807**	376	431	1146	1801–11	***18.3***	*19.7*	*17.1*
	1821	**854**	427	427	1000	1811–21	***5.8***	*13.6*	*–0.9*
	1831	**1006**	500	506	1012	1821–31	***17.8***	*17.1*	*18.5*
	1841	**942**	452	490	1084	1831–41	***–6.4***	*–9.6*	*–3.2*
	1851	**851**	416	435	1046	1841–51	***–9.7***	*–8.0*	*–11.2*
	1861	**848**	413	435	1053	1851–61	***–0.4***	*–0.7*	*0.0*
	1871	**703**	352	351	997	1861–71	***–17.1***	*–14.8*	*–19.3*
	1881	**647**	325	322	991	1871–81	***–8.0***	*–7.7*	*–8.3*
	1891	**561**	278	283	1018	1881–91	***–13.3***	*–14.5*	*–12.1*
	1901	**490**	242	248	1025	1891–1901	***–12.7***	*–12.9*	*–12.4*
	1911	**485**	251	234	932	1901–11	***–1.0***	*3.7*	*–5.6*

No boundary changes

Subdistrict	Year	Number Persons	Males	Females	Females/ 1000 males	Intercensal period	Persons	Males	Females
Llangadog	1801	**1821**	846	975	1152				
	1811	**1964**	935	1029	1101	1801–11	***7.9***	*10.5*	*5.5*
	1821	**2484**	1221	1263	1034	1811–21	***26.5***	*30.6*	*22.7*
	1831	**2476**	1206	1270	1053	1821–31	***–0.3***	*–1.2*	*0.6*
	1841	**2604**	1271	1333	1049	1831–41	***5.2***	*5.4*	*5.0*
	1851	**2820**	1365	1455	1066	1841–51	***8.3***	*7.4*	*9.2*
	1861	**2789**	1367	1422	1040	1851–61	***–1.1***	*0.1*	*–2.3*
	1871	**2830**	1384	1446	1045	1861–71	***1.5***	*1.2*	*1.7*
		(1302)	(595)	(707)					
	1881	**1911**	909	1002	1102	1871–81	***46.8***	*52.8*	*41.7*
	1891	**1730**	825	905	1097	1881–91	***–9.5***	*–9.2*	*–9.7*
	1901	**1578**	756	822	1087	1891–1901	***–8.8***	*–8.4*	*–9.2*
	1911	**1589**	810	779	962	1901–11	***0.7***	*7.1*	*–5.2*

Boundary changes: 1871–81 loss of 1528 to Llandybïe (pop. 1871)

Subdistrict	Year	Number Persons	Males	Females	Females/ 1000 males	Intercensal period	*Percentage change* Persons	Males	Females
Llansadwrn	1801	**1302**	626	676	1080				
	1811	**1449**	695	754	1085	1801–11	***11.3***	*11.0*	*11.5*
	1821	**1774**	920	854	928	1811–21	***22.4***	*32.4*	*13.3*
	1831	**1781**	857	924	1078	1821–31	***0.4***	*–6.8*	*8.2*
	1841	**1745**	862	883	1024	1831–41	***–2.0***	*0.6*	*–4.4*
	1851	**1699**	822	877	1067	1841–51	***–2.6***	*–4.6*	*–0.7*
	1861	**1710**	819	891	1088	1851–61	***0.6***	*–0.4*	*1.6*
	1871	**1674**	783	891	1138	1861–71	***–2.1***	*–4.4*	*0.0*
	1881	**1502**	707	795	1124	1871–81	***–10.3***	*–9.7*	*–10.8*
	1891	**1447**	695	752	1082	1881–91	***–3.7***	*–1.7*	*–5.4*
	1901	**1234**	569	665	1169	1891–1901	***–14.7***	*–18.1*	*–11.6*
	1911	**1190**	568	622	1095	1901–11	***–3.6***	*–0.2*	*–6.5*

No boundary changes

Subdistrict	Year	Number Persons	Males	Females	Females/ 1000 males	Intercensal period	*Percentage change* Persons	Males	Females
Myddfai	1801	**934**	451	483	1071				
	1811	**1085**	548	537	980	1801–11	***16.2***	*21.5*	*11.2*
	1821	**1110**	537	573	1067	1811–21	***2.3***	*–2.0*	*6.7*
	1831	**1192**	594	598	1007	1821–31	***7.4***	*10.6*	*4.4*
	1841	**1073**	533	540	1013	1831–41	***–10.0***	*–10.3*	*–9.7*
	1851	**1069**	520	549	1056	1841–51	***–0.4***	*–2.4*	*1.7*
	1861	**1118**	553	565	1022	1851–61	***4.6***	*6.3*	*2.9*
	1871	**964**	461	503	1091	1861–71	***–13.8***	*–16.6*	*–11.0*

Boundary changes: 1871–81 subdistrict abolished; loss of 964 to Llandingad (pop. 1871)

Subdistrict	Year	Number Persons	Males	Females	Females/ 1000 males	Intercensal period	*Percentage change* Persons	Males	Females
Llandingad	1801	**1395**	615	780	1268				
	1811	**1618**	775	843	1088	1801–11	***16.0***	*26.0*	*8.1*
	1821	**1917**	884	1033	1169	1811–21	***18.5***	*14.1*	*22.5*
	1831	**2465**	1159	1306	1127	1821–31	***28.6***	*31.1*	*26.4*
	1841	**2345**	1097	1248	1138	1831–41	***–4.9***	*–5.3*	*–4.4*
	1851	**2542**	1178	1364	1158	1841–51	***8.4***	*7.4*	*9.3*
	1861	**2389**	1090	1299	1192	1851–61	***–6.0***	*–7.5*	*–4.8*
	1871	**2379**	1115	1264	1134	1861–71	***–0.4***	*2.3*	*–2.7*
		(3343)	(1576)	(1767)					
	1881	**3416**	1635	1781	1089	1871–81	***2.2***	*3.7*	*0.8*
	1891	**3002**	1359	1643	1209	1881–91	***–12.1***	*–16.9*	*–7.7*
	1901	**2834**	1389	1445	1040	1891–1901	***–5.6***	*2.2*	*–12.1*
	1911	**3069**	1539	1530	994	1901–11	***8.3***	*10.8*	*5.9*

Boundary changes: 1871–81 gain of 964 from Myddfai (pop. 1871)

Subdistrict	Year	Number Persons	Males	Females	Females/ 1000 males	Intercensal period	*Percentage change* Persons	Males	Females
Llanfair-ar-y-bryn	1801	**1062**	546	516	945				
	1811	**1483**	660	823	1247	1801–11	***39.6***	*20.9*	*59.5*
	1821	**1426**	705	721	1023	1811–21	***–3.8***	*6.8*	*–12.4*
	1831	**1485**	742	743	1001	1821–31	***4.1***	*5.2*	*3.1*
	1841	**1649**	790	859	1087	1831–41	***11.0***	*6.5*	*15.6*
	1851	**1705**	834	871	1044	1841–51	***3.4***	*5.6*	*1.4*
	1861	**1559**	787	772	981	1851–61	***–8.6***	*–5.6*	*–11.4*
	1871	**1421**	678	743	1096	1861–71	***–8.9***	*–13.9*	*–3.8*
	1881	**1281**	615	666	1083	1871–81	***–9.9***	*–9.3*	*–10.4*
	1891	**1157**	555	602	1085	1881–91	***–9.7***	*–9.8*	*–9.6*
	1901	**997**	476	521	1095	1891–1901	***–13.8***	*–14.2*	*–13.5*
	1911	**871**	446	425	953	1901–11	***–12.6***	*–6.3*	*–18.4*

Subdistrict	Year	Number Persons	Males	Females	Females/ 1000 males	Intercensal period	*Percentage change* Persons	Males	Females
Llanwrtyd	1801	**553**	255	298	1169				
	1811	**680**	326	354	1086	1801–11	***23.0***	*27.8*	*18.8*
	1821	**809**	405	404	998	1811–21	***19.0***	*24.2*	*14.1*
	1831	**786**	377	409	1085	1821–31	***–2.8***	*–6.9*	*1.2*
	1841	**779**	361	418	1158	1831–41	***–0.9***	*–4.2*	*2.2*
	1851	**684**	317	367	1158	1841–51	***–12.2***	*–12.2*	*–12.2*
	1861	**731**	348	383	1101	1851–61	***6.9***	*9.8*	*4.4*
	1871	**844**	411	433	1054	1861–71	***15.5***	*18.1*	*13.1*
	1881	**942**	455	487	1070	1871–81	***11.6***	*10.7*	*12.5*
	1891	**903**	418	485	1160	1881–91	***–4.1***	*–8.1*	*–0.4*

Boundary changes: 1891–1901 whole subdistrict transferred to the district of Builth (Brec)

Subdistrict	Year	Number Persons	Males	Females	Females/ 1000 males	Intercensal period	*Percentage change* Persons	Males	Females
Cil-y-cwm	1801	**1485**	686	799	1165				
	1811	**1434**	678	756	1115	1801–11	***–3.4***	*–1.2*	*–5.4*
	1821	**1459**	714	745	1043	1811–21	***1.7***	*5.3*	*–1.5*
	1831	**1637**	849	788	928	1821–31	***12.2***	*18.9*	*5.8*
	1841	**1481**	712	769	1080	1831–41	***–9.5***	*–16.1*	*–2.4*
	1851	**1487**	721	766	1062	1841–51	***0.4***	*1.3*	*–0.4*
	1861	**1380**	670	710	1060	1851–61	***–7.2***	*–7.1*	*–7.3*
	1871	**1229**	585	644	1101	1861–71	***–10.9***	*–12.7*	*–9.3*
	1881	**1087**	512	575	1123	1871–81	***–11.6***	*–12.5*	*–10.7*
	1891	**1019**	483	536	1110	1881–91	***–6.3***	*–5.7*	*–6.8*
	1901	**860**	409	451	1103	1891–1901	***–15.6***	*–15.3*	*–15.9*
	1911	**715**	344	371	1078	1901–11	***–16.9***	*–15.9*	*–17.7*

No boundary changes

Subdistrict	Year	Number Persons	Males	Females	Females/ 1000 males	Intercensal period	Persons	Males	Females
Cynwyl Gaeo	1801	**1668**	786	882	1122				
	1811	**1696**	793	903	1139	1801–11	***1.7***	*0.9*	*2.4*
	1821	**1880**	931	949	1019	1811–21	***10.8***	*17.4*	*5.1*
	1831	**1971**	976	995	1019	1821–31	***4.8***	*4.8*	*4.8*
	1841	**2108**	1027	1081	1053	1831–41	***7.0***	*5.2*	*8.6*
	1851	**2198**	1095	1103	1007	1841–51	***4.3***	*6.6*	*2.0*
	1861	**2251**	1086	1165	1073	1851–61	***2.4***	*–0.8*	*5.6*
	1871	**2002**	965	1037	1075	1861–71	***–11.1***	*–11.1*	*–11.0*
	1881	**1979**	948	1031	1088	1871–81	***–1.1***	*–1.8*	*–0.6*
	1891	**1803**	847	956	1129	1881–91	***–8.9***	*–10.7*	*–7.3*
	1901	**1594**	746	848	1137	1891–1901	***–11.6***	*–11.9*	*–11.3*
	1911	**1434**	699	735	1052	1901–11	***–10.0***	*–6.3*	*–13.3*

No boundary changes

Llandeilo Fawr District

Subdistrict	Year	Number Persons	Males	Females	Females/ 1000 males	Intercensal period	Persons	Males	Females
Talley	1801	**1595**	756	839	1110				
	1811	**1729**	834	895	1073	1801–11	***8.4***	*10.3*	*6.7*
	1821	**2003**	969	1034	1067	1811–21	***15.8***	*16.2*	*15.5*
	1831	**2082**	991	1091	1101	1821–31	***3.9***	*2.3*	*5.5*
	1841	**2050**	991	1059	1069	1831–41	***–1.5***	*0.0*	*–2.9*
	1851	**2056**	1019	1037	1018	1841–51	***0.3***	*2.8*	*–2.1*
	1861	**2025**	972	1053	1083	1851–61	***–1.5***	*–4.6*	*1.5*
	1871	**1818**	883	935	1059	1861–71	***–10.2***	*–9.2*	*–11.2*
	1881	**1783**	856	927	1083	1871–81	***–1.9***	*–3.1*	*–0.9*
	1891	**1652**	782	870	1113	1881–91	***–7.3***	*–8.6*	*–6.1*
	1901	**1324**	628	696	1108	1891–1901	***–19.9***	*–19.7*	*–20.0*
	1911	**1145**	555	590	1063	1901–11	***–13.5***	*–11.6*	*–15.2*

No boundary changes

Subdistrict	Year	Number Persons	Males	Females	Females/ 1000 males	Intercensal period	Persons	Males	Females
Llanfynydd	1801	**1282**	628	654	1041				
	1811	**1327**	612	715	1168	1801–11	***3.5***	*–2.5*	*9.3*
	1821	**1587**	778	809	1040	1811–21	***19.6***	*27.1*	*13.1*
	1831	**1598**	804	794	988	1821–31	***0.7***	*3.3*	*–1.9*
	1841	**1528**	751	777	1035	1831–41	***–4.4***	*–6.6*	*–2.1*
	1851	**1540**	742	798	1075	1841–51	***0.8***	*–1.2*	*2.7*
	1861	**1410**	678	732	1080	1851–61	***–8.4***	*–8.6*	*–8.3*
	1871	**1289**	610	679	1113	1861–71	***–8.6***	*–10.0*	*–7.2*
	1881	**1169**	559	610	1091	1871–81	***–9.3***	*–8.4*	*–10.2*
	1891	**1075**	505	570	1129	1881–91	***–8.0***	*–9.7*	*–6.6*
		(990)	(471)	(519)					
	1901	**859**	415	444	1070	1891–1901	***–13.2***	*–11.9*	*–14.5*
	1911	**802**	400	402	1005	1901–11	***–6.6***	*–3.6*	*–9.5*

Boundary changes: 1891–1901 loss of 85 to Llangathen (pop. 1891)

Subdistrict	Year	Number Persons	Males	Females	Females/ 1000 males	Intercensal period	*Percentage change* Persons	Males	Females
Llangathen	1801	**2465**	1222	1243	1017				
	1811	**2820**	1343	1477	1100	1801–11	***14.4***	*9.9*	*18.8*
	1821	**3241**	1583	1658	1047	1811–21	***14.9***	*17.9*	*12.3*
	1831	**3396**	1665	1731	1040	1821–31	***4.8***	*5.2*	*4.4*
	1841	**3221**	1527	1694	1109	1831–41	***–5.2***	*–8.3*	*–2.1*
	1851	**3043**	1434	1609	1122	1841–51	***–5.5***	*–6.1*	*–5.0*
	1861	**2897**	1351	1546	1144	1851–61	***–4.8***	*–5.8*	*–3.9*
	1871	**2638**	1214	1424	1173	1861–71	***–8.9***	*–10.1*	*–7.9*
	1881	**2506**	1137	1369	1204	1871–81	***–5.0***	*–6.3*	*–3.9*
	1891	**2258**	1041	1217	1169	1881–91	***–9.9***	*–8.4*	*–11.1*
		(2343)	(1075)	(1268)					
	1901	**2163**	1014	1149	1133	1891–1901	***–7.7***	*–5.7*	*–9.4*
	1911	**2016**	964	1052	1091	1901–11	***–6.8***	*–4.9*	*–8.4*

Boundary changes: 1891–1901 gain of 85 from Llanfynydd (pop. 1891)

Subdistrict	Year	Number Persons	Males	Females	Females/ 1000 males	Intercensal period	*Percentage change* Persons	Males	Females
Llandeilo	1801	**3214**	1491	1723	1156				
	1811	**3597**	1693	1904	1125	1801–11	***11.9***	*13.5*	*10.5*
	1821	**4114**	1954	2160	1105	1811–21	***14.4***	*15.4*	*13.4*
	1831	**4528**	2107	2421	1149	1821–31	***10.1***	*7.8*	*12.1*
	1841	**4793**	2227	2566	1152	1831–41	***5.9***	*5.7*	*6.0*
	1851	**4812**	2215	2597	1172	1841–51	***0.4***	*–0.5*	*1.2*
	1861	**4546**	2094	2452	1171	1851–61	***–5.5***	*–5.5*	*–5.6*
	1871	**4619**	2133	2486	1165	1861–71	***1.6***	*1.9*	*1.4*
	1881	**4511**	2084	2427	1165	1871–81	***–2.3***	*–2.3*	*–2.4*
	1891	**4735**	2179	2556	1173	1881–91	***5.0***	*4.6*	*5.3*
	1901	**4930**	2240	2690	1201	1891–1901	***4.1***	*2.8*	*5.2*
		(5074)							
	1911	**5053**	2382	2671	1121	1901–11	***–0.4***	–	–

Boundary changes: 1901–11 gain of 144 from Llandybïe (pop. 1901)

Subdistrict	Year	Number Persons	Males	Females	Females/ 1000 males	Intercensal period	*Percentage change* Persons	Males	Females
Cwarter Bach	1901	(3515)							
	1911	**5212**	2709	2503	924	1901–11	***48.3***	–	–

Boundary changes: 1901–11 subdistrict created; gain of 3515 from Llandybïe (pop. 1901)

Subdistrict	Year	Number Persons	Males	Females	Females/ 1000 males	Intercensal period	*Percentage change* Persons	Males	Females
Llandybïe	1801	**3384**	1596	1788	1120				
	1811	**3814**	1772	2042	1152	1801–11	***12.7***	*11.0*	*14.2*
	1821	**4750**	2265	2485	1097	1811–21	***24.5***	*27.8*	*21.7*
	1831	**4840**	2334	2506	1074	1821–31	***1.9***	*3.0*	*0.8*
	1841	**5536**	2690	2846	1058	1831–41	***14.4***	*15.3*	*13.6*
	1851	**6517**	3241	3276	1011	1841–51	***17.7***	*20.5*	*15.1*
	1861	**6344**	3107	3237	1042	1851–61	***–2.7***	*–4.1*	*–1.2*
	1871	**6612**	3223	3389	1052	1861–71	***4.2***	*3.7*	*4.7*
		(8140)	(4012)	(4128)					
	1881	**8830**	4396	4434	1009	1871–81	***8.5***	*9.6*	*7.4*
	1891	**10763**	5385	5378	999	1881–91	***21.9***	*22.5*	*21.3*
	1901	**14417**	7310	7107	972	1891–1901	***33.9***	*35.7*	*32.1*
		(10758)							
	1911	**19043**	10198	8845	867	1901–11	***77.0***	–	–

Boundary changes: 1871–81 gain of 1528 from Llangadog (pop. 1871)
1901–11 loss of 144 to Llandeilo, loss of 3515 to the new subdistrict of Cwarter Bach (pop. 1901)

Carmarthen District

Subdistrict	Year	Number Persons	Males	Females	Females/ 1000 males	Intercensal period	*Percentage change* Persons	Males	Females
Llangyndeyrn	1801	**6205**	2945	3260	1107				
	1811	**7132**	3182	3950	1241	1801–11	***14.9***	*8.0*	*21.2*
	1821	**7834**	3850	3984	1035	1811–21	***9.8***	*21.0*	*0.9*
	1831	**8551**	4169	4382	1051	1821–31	***9.2***	*8.3*	*10.0*
	1841	**9269**	4436	4833	1089	1831–41	***8.4***	*6.4*	*10.3*
	1851	**8981**	4288	4693	1094	1841–51	***–3.1***	*–3.3*	*–2.9*
	1861	**9034**	4249	4785	1126	1851–61	***0.6***	*–0.9*	*2.0*
	1871	**8642**	4011	4631	1155	1861–71	***–4.3***	*–5.6*	*–3.2*
	1881	**8549**	3989	4560	1143	1871–81	***–1.1***	*–0.5*	*–1.5*
	1891	**8625**	4113	4512	1097	1881–91	***0.9***	*3.1*	*–1.1*
		(8782)	(4189)	(4593)					
	1901	**9142**	4369	4773	1092	1891–1901	***4.1***	*4.3*	*3.9*
	1911	**10774**	5315	5459	1027	1901–11	***17.9***	*21.7*	*14.4*

Boundary changes: 1891–1901 gain of 157 from Pembrey (pop. 1891)

Subdistrict	Year	Number Persons	Males	Females	Females/ 1000 males	Intercensal period	*Percentage change* Persons	Males	Females
St Clears	1801	**5085**	2358	2727	1156				
	1811	**5486**	2453	3033	1236	1801–11	***7.9***	*4.0*	*11.2*
	1821	**6618**	3131	3487	1114	1811–21	***20.6***	*27.6*	*15.0*
	1831	**7297**	3486	3811	1093	1821–31	***10.3***	*11.3*	*9.3*
	1841	**7187**	3332	3855	1157	1831–41	***–1.5***	*–4.4*	*1.2*
	1851	**7313**	3447	3866	1122	1841–51	***1.8***	*3.5*	*0.3*
	1861	**6862**	3161	3701	1171	1851–61	***–6.2***	*–8.3*	*–4.3*
	1871	**6352**	2890	3462	1198	1861–71	***–7.4***	*–8.6*	*–6.5*
	1881	**6181**	2840	3341	1176	1871–81	***–2.7***	*–1.7*	*–3.5*
		(6192)	(2847)	(3345)					
	1891	**5790**	2533	3257	1286	1881–91	***–6.5***	*–11.0*	*–2.6*
	1901	**5568**	2442	3126	1280	1891–1901	***–3.8***	*–3.6*	*–4.0*
	1911	**5422**	2429	2993	1232	1901–11	***–2.6***	*–0.5*	*–4.3*

Boundary changes: 1881–91 gain of 11 from Cynwyl (pop. 1881)

Subdistrict	Year	Number Persons	Males	Females	Females/ 1000 males	Intercensal period	Persons	Males	Females
Carmarthen	1801	**7486**	3243	4243	1308				
	1811	**9365**	4076	5289	1298	1801–11	***25.1***	*25.7*	*24.7*
	1821	**11508**	5278	6230	1180	1811–21	***22.9***	*29.5*	*17.8*
	1831	**13053**	6047	7006	1159	1821–31	***13.4***	*14.6*	*12.5*
	1841	**12295**	5574	6721	1206	1831–41	***–5.8***	*–7.8*	*–4.1*
	1851	**13294**	6162	7132	1157	1841–51	***8.1***	*10.5*	*6.1*
	1861	**12583**	5714	6869	1202	1851–61	***–5.3***	*–7.3*	*–3.7*
	1871	**12915**	5931	6984	1178	1861–71	***2.6***	*3.8*	*1.7*
	1881	**12872**	5950	6922	1163	1871–81	***–0.3***	*0.3*	*–0.9*
		(12621)	5823	6798					
	1891	**12272**	5624	6648	1182	1881–91	***–2.8***	*–3.4*	*–2.2*
	1901	**11921**	5442	6479	1191	1891–1901	***–2.9***	*–3.2*	*–2.5*
	1911	**11944**	5513	6431	1167	1901–11	***0.2***	*1.3*	*–0.7*

Boundary changes: 1881–91 loss of 251 to Cynwyl (pop. 1881)

Subdistrict	Year	Number Persons	Males	Females	Females/ 1000 males	Intercensal period	Persons	Males	Females
Cynwyl Elfed	1801	**5313**	2513	2800	1114				
	1811	**6300**	2990	3310	1107	1801–11	***18.6***	*19.0*	*18.2*
	1821	**7425**	3634	3791	1043	1811–21	***17.9***	*21.5*	*14.5*
	1831	**8025**	3869	4156	1074	1821–31	***8.1***	*6.5*	*9.6*
	1841	**8772**	4152	4620	1113	1831–41	***9.3***	*7.3*	*11.2*
	1851	**8554**	4085	4469	1094	1841–51	***–2.5***	*–1.6*	*–3.3*
	1861	**8196**	3871	4325	1117	1851–61	***–4.2***	*–5.2*	*–3.2*
	1871	**7718**	3619	4099	1133	1861–71	***–5.8***	*–6.5*	*–5.2*
	1881	**7473**	3538	3935	1112	1871–81	***–3.2***	*–2.2*	*–4.0*
		(7713)	(3658)	(4055)					
	1891	**7450**	3388	4062	1199	1881–91	***–3.4***	*–7.4*	*0.2*
	1901	**6762**	3130	3632	1160	1891–1901	***–9.2***	*–7.6*	*–10.6*
	1911	**6287**	3002	3285	1094	1901–11	***–7.0***	*–4.1*	*–9.6*

Boundary changes: 1881–91 gain of 251 from Carmarthen, loss of 11 to St Clears (pop. 1881)

PEMBROKESHIRE
Narberth District

Subdistrict	Year	Number Persons	Males	Females	Females/ 1000 males	Intercensal period	Persons	Males	Females
Llanboidy	1801	**2830**	1360	1470	1081				
	1811	**3125**	1407	1718	1221	1801–11	***10.4***	*3.5*	*16.9*
	1821	**3434**	1682	1752	1042	1811–21	***9.9***	*19.5*	*2.0*
	1831	**3708**	1785	1923	1077	1821–31	***8.0***	*6.1*	*9.8*
	1841	**3801**	1790	2011	1123	1831–41	***2.5***	*0.3*	*4.6*
	1851	**3715**	1734	1981	1142	1841–51	***–2.3***	*–3.1*	*–1.5*
	1861	**3635**	1714	1921	1121	1851–61	***–2.2***	*–1.2*	*–3.0*
	1871	**3455**	1608	1847	1149	1861–71	***–5.0***	*–6.2*	*–3.9*
	1881	**3447**	1609	1838	1142	1871–81	***–0.2***	*0.1*	*–0.5*
		(6391)	(2992)	(3399)					
	1891	**6070**	2835	3235	1141	1881–91	***–5.0***	*–5.2*	*–4.8*
	1901	**5630**	2631	2999	1140	1891–1901	***–7.2***	*–7.2*	*–7.3*
	1911	**5498**	2621	2877	1098	1901–11	***–2.3***	*–0.4*	*–4.1*

Boundary changes: 1881–91 gain of 2944 from Llandysilio (pop. 1881)

Subdistrict	Year	Number Persons	Males	Females	Females/ 1000 males	Intercensal period	*Percentage change* *Persons*	*Males*	*Females*
Llandysilio	1801	**2607**	1224	1383	1130				
	1811	**2715**	1231	1484	1206	1801–11	***4.1***	*0.6*	*7.3*
	1821	**3267**	1557	1710	1098	1811–21	***20.3***	*26.5*	*15.2*
	1831	**3565**	1693	1872	1106	1821–31	***9.1***	*8.7*	*9.5*
	1841	**3618**	1708	1910	1118	1831–41	***1.5***	*0.9*	*2.0*
	1851	**3491**	1634	1857	1136	1841–51	***–3.5***	*–4.3*	*–2.8*
	1861	**3340**	1522	1818	1194	1851–61	***–4.3***	*–6.9*	*–2.1*
	1871	**3312**	1541	1771	1149	1861–71	***–0.8***	*1.2*	*–2.6*
	1881	**3334**	1550	1784	1151	1871–81	***0.7***	*0.6*	*0.7*
Boundary changes:	1881–91	subdistrict abolished; loss of 2944 to Llanboidy, loss of 390 to Narberth (pop. 1881)							
Amroth	1801	**2872**	1349	1523	1129				
	1811	**2820**	1330	1490	1120	1801–11	***–1.8***	*–1.4*	*–2.2*
	1821	**3233**	1610	1623	1008	1811–21	***14.6***	*21.1*	*8.9*
	1831	**3327**	1679	1648	982	1821–31	***2.9***	*4.3*	*1.5*
	1841	**3290**	1591	1699	1068	1831–41	***–1.1***	*–5.2*	*3.1*
	1851	**3363**	1645	1718	1044	1841–51	***2.2***	*3.4*	*1.1*
	1861	**3265**	1556	1709	1098	1851–61	***–2.9***	*–5.4*	*–0.5*
	1871	**3102**	1462	1640	1122	1861–71	***–5.0***	*–6.0*	*–4.0*
	1881	**3084**	1454	1630	1121	1871–81	***–0.6***	*–0.5*	*–0.6*
	1891	**2968**	1368	1600	1170	1881–91	***–3.8***	*–5.9*	*–1.8*
Boundary changes:	1891–1901	subdistrict abolished; loss of 2968 to Narberth (pop. 1891)							
Narberth	1801	**2247**	1029	1218	1184				
	1811	**2487**	1063	1424	1340	1801–11	***10.7***	*3.3*	*16.9*
	1821	**3297**	1482	1815	1225	1811–21	***32.6***	*39.4*	*27.5*
	1831	**3717**	1725	1992	1155	1821–31	***12.7***	*16.4*	*9.8*
	1841	**3752**	1702	2050	1204	1831–41	***0.9***	*–1.3*	*2.9*
	1851	**3859**	1788	2071	1158	1841–51	***2.9***	*5.1*	*1.0*
	1861	**3620**	1650	1970	1194	1851–61	***–6.2***	*–7.7*	*–4.9*
	1871	**3646**	1660	1986	1196	1861–71	***0.7***	*0.6*	*0.8*
	1881	**3383**	1565	1818	1162	1871–81	***–7.2***	*–5.7*	*–8.5*
		(3773)	(1732)	(2041)					
	1891	**3542**	1597	1945	1218	1881–91	***–6.1***	*–7.8*	*–4.7*
		(6510)	(2965)	(3545)					
	1901	**6385**	2948	3437	1166	1891–1901	***–1.9***	*–0.6*	*–3.0*
	1911	**6381**	2963	3418	1154	1901–11	***–0.1***	*0.5*	*–0.6*
Boundary changes:	1881–91	gain of 390 from Llandysilio (pop. 1881)							
	1891–1901	gain of 2968 from Amroth (pop. 1881)							
Slebech	1801	**2464**	1071	1393	1301				
	1811	**2682**	1251	1431	1144	1801–11	***8.8***	*16.8*	*2.7*
	1821	**3227**	1541	1686	1094	1811–21	***20.3***	*23.2*	*17.8*
	1831	**3306**	1599	1707	1068	1821–31	***2.4***	*3.8*	*1.2*
	1841	**3511**	1653	1858	1124	1831–41	***6.2***	*3.4*	*8.8*
	1851	**3497**	1634	1863	1140	1841–51	***–0.4***	*–1.1*	*0.3*
	1861	**3171**	1506	1665	1106	1851–61	***–9.3***	*–7.8*	*–10.6*
	1871	**2809**	1286	1523	1184	1861–71	***–11.4***	*–14.6*	*–8.5*
	1881	**2483**	1145	1338	1169	1871–81	***–11.6***	*–11.0*	*–12.1*
	1891	**2289**	1049	1240	1182	1881–91	***–7.8***	*–8.4*	*–7.3*
Boundary changes:	1891–1901	subdistrict abolished; loss of 2289 to Begeli (pop. 1891)							
Begeli	1801	**2789**	1270	1519	1196				
	1811	**2784**	1281	1503	1173	1801–11	***–0.2***	*0.9*	*–1.1*
	1821	**3148**	1483	1665	1123	1811–21	***13.1***	*15.8*	*10.8*
	1831	**3316**	1571	1745	1111	1821–31	***5.3***	*5.9*	*4.8*
	1841	**3776**	1819	1957	1076	1831–41	***13.9***	*15.8*	*12.1*
	1851	**4205**	2024	2181	1078	1841–51	***11.4***	*11.3*	*11.4*
	1861	**4313**	2088	2225	1066	1851–61	***2.6***	*3.2*	*2.0*
	1871	**4008**	1914	2094	1094	1861–71	***–7.1***	*–8.3*	*–5.9*
	1881	**3810**	1826	1984	1087	1871–81	***–4.9***	*–4.6*	*–5.3*
	1891	**3321**	1553	1768	1138	1881–91	***–12.8***	*–15.0*	*–10.9*
		(5610)	(2602)	(3008)					
	1901	**5347**	2492	2855	1146	1891–1901	***–4.7***	*–4.2*	*–5.1*
	1911	**5443**	2562	2881	1125	1901–11	***1.8***	*2.8*	*0.9*
Boundary changes:	1891–1901	gain of 2289 from Slebech (pop. 1891)							

Subdistrict	Year	Number Persons	Males	Females	Females/ 1000 males	Intercensal period	Percentage change Persons	Males	Females
Pembroke District									
Tenby	1801	**5080**	2288	2792	1220				
	1811	**5256**	2338	2918	1248	1801–11	***3.5***	*2.2*	*4.5*
	1821	**6497**	2995	3502	1169	1811–21	***23.6***	*28.1*	*20.0*
	1831	**7552**	3480	4072	1170	1821–31	***16.2***	*16.2*	*16.3*
	1841	**8436**	3786	4650	1228	1831–41	***11.7***	*8.8*	*14.2*
	1851	**8949**	3983	4966	1247	1841–51	***6.1***	*5.2*	*6.8*
	1861	**9219**	4224	4995	1183	1851–61	***3.0***	*6.1*	*0.6*
	1871	**9667**	4298	5369	1249	1861–71	***4.9***	*1.8*	*7.5*
	1881	**10341**	4586	5755	1255	1871–81	***7.0***	*6.7*	*7.2*
	1891	**9740**	4332	5408	1248	1881–91	***–5.8***	*–5.5*	*–6.0*
	1901	**9560**	4233	5327	1258	1891–1901	***–1.8***	*–2.3*	*–1.5*
	1911	**9559**	4391	5168	1177	1901–11	***0.0***	*3.7*	*–3.0*

No boundary changes

Subdistrict	Year	Number Persons	Males	Females	Females/ 1000 males	Intercensal period	Percentage change Persons	Males	Females
Pembroke	1801	**3771**	1649	2122	1287				
	1811	**3790**	1696	2094	1235	1801–11	***0.5***	*2.9*	*–1.3*
	1821	**6173**	3012	3161	1049	1811–21	***62.9***	*77.6*	*51.0*
	1831	**7796**	3692	4104	1112	1821–31	***26.3***	*22.6*	*29.8*
	1841	**9082**	4319	4763	1103	1831–41	***16.5***	*17.0*	*16.1*
	1851	**11662**	5658	6004	1061	1841–51	***28.4***	*31.0*	*26.1*
	1861	**16559**	8962	7597	848	1851–61	***42.0***	*58.4*	*26.5*
	1871	**15525**	7794	7731	992	1861–71	***–6.2***	*–13.0*	*1.8*
	1881	**15689**	7989	7700	964	1871–81	***1.1***	*2.5*	*–0.4*
	1891	**16493**	8333	8160	979	1881–91	***5.1***	*4.3*	*6.0*
	1901	**16988**	8521	8467	994	1891–1901	***3.0***	*2.3*	*3.8*
	1911	**16568**	8493	8075	951	1901–11	***–2.5***	*–0.3*	*–4.6*

No boundary changes

Subdistrict	Year	Number Persons	Males	Females	Females/ 1000 males	Intercensal period	Percentage change Persons	Males	Females
Roose	1801	**1160**	496	664	1339				
	1811	**1015**	416	599	1440	1801–11	***–12.5***	*–16.1*	*–9.8*
	1821	**1777**	849	928	1093	1811–21	***75.1***	*104.1*	*54.9*
	1831	**1883**	870	1013	1164	1821–31	***6.0***	*2.5*	*9.2*
	1841	**2152**	1024	1128	1102	1831–41	***14.3***	*17.7*	*11.4*
	1851	**2349**	1137	1212	1066	1841–51	***9.2***	*11.0*	*7.4*
	1861	**3225**	1670	1555	931	1851–61	***37.3***	*46.9*	*28.3*
	1871	**3869**	1920	1949	1015	1861–71	***20.0***	*15.0*	*25.3*
	1881	**4317**	2205	2112	958	1871–81	***11.6***	*14.8*	*8.4*
	1891	**5050**	2471	2579	1044	1881–91	***17.0***	*12.1*	*22.1*
	1901	**5391**	2695	2696	1000	1891–1901	***6.8***	*9.1*	*4.5*
	1911	**4855**	2367	2488	1051	1901–11	***–9.9***	*–12.2*	*–7.7*

No boundary changes

Subdistrict	Year	Number Persons	Males	Females	Females/ 1000 males	Intercensal period	Percentage change Persons	Males	Females
Haverfordwest District									
Milford	1801	**5367**	2393	2974	1243				
	1811	**6450**	2956	3494	1182	1801–11	***20.2***	*23.5*	*17.5*
	1821	**7443**	3499	3944	1127	1811–21	***15.4***	*18.4*	*12.9*
	1831	**8348**	3891	4457	1145	1821–31	***12.2***	*11.2*	*13.0*
	1841	**8998**	4167	4831	1159	1831–41	***7.8***	*7.1*	*8.4*
	1851	**9815**	4858	4957	1020	1841–51	***9.1***	*16.6*	*2.6*
	1861	**9771**	4954	4817	972	1851–61	***–0.4***	*2.0*	*–2.8*
	1871	**8951**	4396	4555	1036	1861–71	***–8.4***	*–11.3*	*–5.4*
	1881	**9507**	5066	4441	877	1871–81	***6.2***	*15.2*	*–2.5*
	1891	**9711**	4917	4794	975	1881–91	***2.1***	*–2.9*	*7.9*
	1901	**10922**	5542	5380	971	1891–1901	***12.5***	*12.7*	*12.2*
	1911	**12038**	5988	6050	1010	1901–11	***10.2***	*8.0*	*12.5*

No boundary changes

Subdistrict	Year	Number Persons	Males	Females	Females/ 1000 males	Intercensal period	*Percentage change* *Persons*	*Males*	*Females*
Haverfordwest	1801	**7672**	3305	4367	1321				
	1811	**8480**	3739	4741	1268	1801–11	***10.5***	*13.1*	*8.6*
	1821	**9862**	4562	5300	1162	1811–21	***16.3***	*22.0*	*11.8*
	1831	**11042**	5140	5902	1148	1821–31	***12.0***	*12.7*	*11.4*
	1841	**12129**	5543	6586	1188	1831–41	***9.8***	*7.8*	*11.6*
	1851	**12376**	5603	6773	1209	1841–51	***2.0***	*1.1*	*2.8*
	1861	**12330**	5689	6641	1167	1851–61	***–0.4***	*1.5*	*–1.9*
	1871	**11408**	5281	6127	1160	1861–71	***–7.5***	*–7.2*	*–7.7*
	1881	**10755**	5008	5747	1148	1871–81	***–5.7***	*–5.2*	*–6.2*
	1891	**10261**	4696	5565	1185	1881–91	***–4.6***	*–6.2*	*–3.2*
	1901	**9946**	4621	5325	1152	1891–1901	***–3.1***	*–1.6*	*–4.3*
	1911	**9647**	4561	5086	1115	1901–11	***–3.0***	*–1.3*	*–4.5*

No boundary changes

Subdistrict	Year	Number Persons	Males	Females	Females/ 1000 males	Intercensal period	*Persons*	*Males*	*Females*
St David's	1801	**5387**	2536	2851	1124				
	1811	**5722**	2563	3159	1233	1801–11	***6.2***	*1.1*	*10.8*
	1821	**6755**	3118	3637	1166	1811–21	***18.1***	*21.7*	*15.1*
	1831	**7231**	3354	3877	1156	1821–31	***7.0***	*7.6*	*6.6*
	1841	**7732**	3534	4198	1188	1831–41	***6.9***	*5.4*	*8.3*
	1851	**8297**	3846	4451	1157	1841–51	***7.3***	*8.8*	*6.0*
	1861	**7347**	3323	4024	1211	1851–61	***–11.4***	*–13.6*	*–9.6*
	1871	**6684**	3007	3677	1223	1861–71	***–9.0***	*–9.5*	*–8.6*
	1881	**6282**	2868	3414	1190	1871–81	***–6.0***	*–4.6*	*–7.2*
	1891	**5803**	2634	3169	1203	1881–91	***–7.6***	*–8.2*	*–7.2*
	1901	**5405**	2493	2912	1168	1891–1901	***–6.9***	*–5.4*	*–8.1*
	1911	**5406**	2595	2811	1083	1901–11	***0.0***	*4.1*	*–3.5*

No boundary changes

Subdistrict	Year	Number Persons	Males	Females	Females/ 1000 males	Intercensal period	*Persons*	*Males*	*Females*
Fishguard	1801	**6024**	2742	3282	1197				
	1811	**6196**	2722	3474	1276	1801–11	***2.9***	*–0.7*	*5.9*
	1821	**7329**	3337	3992	1196	1811–21	***18.3***	*22.6*	*14.9*
	1831	**8155**	3724	4431	1190	1821–31	***11.3***	*11.6*	*11.0*
	1841	**8280**	3765	4515	1199	1831–41	***1.5***	*1.1*	*1.9*
	1851	**8894**	4076	4818	1182	1841–51	***7.4***	*8.3*	*6.7*
	1861	**7895**	3530	4365	1237	1851–61	***–11.2***	*–13.4*	*–9.4*
	1871	**7437**	3307	4130	1249	1861–71	***–5.8***	*–6.3*	*–5.4*
	1881	**7247**	3214	4033	1255	1871–81	***–2.6***	*–2.8*	*–2.3*
	1891	**6755**	2986	3769	1262	1881–91	***–6.8***	*–7.1*	*–6.5*
	1901	**6850**	3180	3670	1154	1891–1901	***1.4***	*6.5*	*–2.6*
	1911	**9479**	4678	4801	1026	1901–11	***38.4***	*47.1*	*30.8*

No boundary changes

CARDIGANSHIRE
Cardigan District

Subdistrict	Year	Number Persons	Males	Females	Females/ 1000 males	Intercensal period	*Persons*	*Males*	*Females*
Newport	1801	**4842**	2173	2669	1228				
	1811	**5094**	2095	2999	1432	1801–11	***5.2***	*–3.6*	*12.4*
	1821	**6073**	2742	3331	1215	1811–21	***19.2***	*30.9*	*11.1*
	1831	**6075**	2660	3415	1284	1821–31	***0.0***	*–3.0*	*2.5*
	1841	**6227**	2587	3640	1407	1831–41	***2.5***	*–2.7*	*6.6*
	1851	**6130**	2589	3541	1368	1841–51	***–1.6***	*0.1*	*–2.7*
	1861	**5566**	2314	3252	1405	1851–61	***–9.2***	*–10.6*	*–8.2*
	1871	**5432**	2293	3139	1369	1861–71	***–2.4***	*–0.9*	*–3.5*
	1881	**5219**	2170	3049	1405	1871–81	***–3.9***	*–5.4*	*–2.9*
	1891	**4684**	1968	2716	1380	1881–91	***–10.3***	*–9.3*	*–10.9*
	1901	**4189**	1789	2400	1342	1891–1901	***–10.6***	*–9.1*	*–11.6*
	1911	**4062**	1808	2254	1247	1901–11	***–3.0***	*1.1*	*–6.1*

No boundary changes

Subdistrict	Year	Number Persons	Males	Females	Females/ 1000 males	Intercensal period	Percentage change *Persons*	*Males*	*Females*
Cardigan	1801	**6376**	2889	3487	1207				
	1811	**6869**	3225	3644	1130	1801–11	***7.7***	*11.6*	*4.5*
	1821	**7947**	3622	4325	1194	1811–21	***15.7***	*12.3*	*18.7*
	1831	**8564**	3921	4643	1184	1821–31	***7.8***	*8.3*	*7.4*
	1841	**9417**	4072	5345	1313	1831–41	***10.0***	*3.9*	*15.1*
	1851	**9723**	4258	5465	1283	1841–51	***3.2***	*4.6*	*2.2*
	1861	**8886**	3816	5070	1329	1851–61	***–8.6***	*–10.4*	*–7.2*
	1871	**8323**	3529	4794	1358	1861–71	***–6.3***	*–7.5*	*–5.4*
	1881	**8705**	3828	4877	1274	1871–81	***4.6***	*8.5*	*1.7*
	1891	**8085**	3431	4654	1356	1881–91	***–7.1***	*–10.4*	*–4.6*
		(7890)	(3373)	(4517)					
	1901	**7573**	3279	4294	1310	1891–1901	***–4.0***	*–2.8*	*–4.9*
		(10973)	(4778)	(6195)					
	1911	**10670**	4740	5930	1251	1901–11	***–2.8***	*–0.8*	*–4.3*

Boundary changes: 1891–1901 loss of 1206 to Llandygwydd, gain of 1011 from Llandygwydd (pop. 1891)
1901–11 gain of 3400 from Llandygwydd (pop. 1901)

Subdistrict	Year	Number Persons	Males	Females	Females/ 1000 males	Intercensal period	*Persons*	*Males*	*Females*
Llandygwydd	1801	**3321**	1541	1780	1155				
	1811	**3350**	1476	1874	1270	1801–11	***0.9***	*–4.2*	*5.3*
	1821	**3932**	1856	2076	1119	1811–21	***17.4***	*25.7*	*10.8*
	1831	**4147**	1983	2164	1091	1821–31	***5.5***	*6.8*	*4.2*
	1841	**4259**	1934	2325	1202	1831–41	***2.7***	*–2.5*	*7.4*
	1851	**4333**	1965	2368	1205	1841–51	***1.7***	*1.6*	*1.8*
	1861	**4133**	1808	2325	1286	1851–61	***–4.6***	*–8.0*	*–1.8*
	1871	**3830**	1658	2172	1310	1861–71	***–7.3***	*–8.3*	*–6.6*
	1881	**3691**	1585	2106	1329	1871–81	***–3.6***	*–4.4*	*–3.0*
	1891	**3512**	1537	1975	1285	1881–91	***–4.8***	*–3.0*	*–6.2*
		(3707)	(1595)	(2112)					
	1901	**3400**	1499	1901	1268	1891–1901	***–8.3***	*–6.0*	*–10.0*

Boundary changes: 1891–1901 loss of 1011 to Cardigan, gain of 1206 from Cardigan (pop. 1891)
1901–11 subdistrict abolished; loss of 3400 to Cardigan (pop. 1901)

Newcastle Emlyn District

Subdistrict	Year	Number Persons	Males	Females	Females/ 1000 males	Intercensal period	*Persons*	*Males*	*Females*
Cenarth	1801	**5822**	2673	3149	1178				
	1811	**6211**	2806	3405	1213	1801–11	***6.7***	*5.0*	*8.1*
	1821	**7839**	3712	4127	1112	1811–21	***26.2***	*32.3*	*21.2*
	1831	**8980**	4326	4654	1076	1821–31	***14.6***	*16.5*	*12.8*
	1841	**9125**	4265	4860	1140	1831–41	***1.6***	*–1.4*	*4.4*
	1851	**8686**	4088	4598	1125	1841–51	***–4.8***	*–4.2*	*–5.4*
	1861	**8072**	3772	4300	1140	1851–61	***–7.1***	*–7.7*	*–6.5*
	1871	**7964**	3662	4302	1175	1861–71	***–1.3***	*–2.9*	*0.0*
	1881	**8233**	3800	4433	1167	1871–81	***3.4***	*3.8*	*3.0*
	1891	**8202**	3772	4430	1174	1881–91	***–0.4***	*–0.7*	*–0.1*
	1901	**7918**	3614	4304	1191	1891–1901	***–3.5***	*–4.2*	*–2.8*
		(5445)	(2488)	(2957)					
	1911	**5440**	2494	2946	1181	1901–11	***–0.1***	*0.2*	*–0.4*

Boundary changes: 1901–11 loss of 2473 to the new subdistrict of Clydau (pop. 1901)

Subdistrict	Year	Number Persons	Males	Females	Females/ 1000 males	Intercensal period	*Persons*	*Males*	*Females*
Clydau	1901	(2473)	(1126)	(1347)					
	1911	**2422**	1155	1267	1097	1901–11	***–2.1***	*2.6*	*–5.9*

Boundary changes: 1901–11 subdistrict created; gain of 2473 from Cenarth (pop. 1901)

Subdistrict	Year	Number Persons	Males	Females	Females/ 1000 males	Intercensal period	*Persons*	*Males*	*Females*
Penbryn	1801	**3446**	1835	1611	878				
	1811	**4193**	1924	2269	1179	1801–11	***21.7***	*4.9*	*40.8*
	1821	**4990**	2362	2628	1113	1811–21	***19.0***	*22.8*	*15.8*
	1831	**5478**	2624	2854	1088	1821–31	***9.8***	*11.1*	*8.6*
	1841	**5413**	2478	2935	1184	1831–41	***–1.2***	*–5.6*	*2.8*
	1851	**5360**	2418	2942	1217	1841–51	***–1.0***	*–2.4*	*0.2*
	1861	**5075**	2208	2867	1298	1851–61	***–5.3***	*–8.7*	*–2.5*
	1871	**4733**	2070	2663	1286	1861–71	***–6.7***	*–6.3*	*–7.1*
	1881	**4547**	2030	2517	1240	1871–81	***–3.9***	*–1.9*	*–5.5*
	1891	**4427**	1932	2495	1291	1881–91	***–2.6***	*–4.8*	*–0.9*
	1901	**4071**	1772	2299	1297	1891–1901	***–8.0***	*–8.3*	*–7.9*
	1911	**3957**	1769	2188	1237	1901–11	***–2.8***	*–0.2*	*–4.8*

No boundary changes

Subdistrict	Year	Number Persons	Males	Females	Females/ 1000 males	Intercensal period	*Percentage change* Persons	Males	Females
Llandysul	1801	**4317**	2050	2267	1106				
	1811	**5070**	2394	2676	1118	1801–11	***17.4***	*16.8*	*18.0*
	1821	**5769**	2817	2952	1048	1811–21	***13.8***	*17.7*	*10.3*
	1831	**6117**	2920	3197	1095	1821–31	***6.0***	*3.7*	*8.3*
	1841	**6325**	2951	3374	1143	1831–41	***3.4***	*1.1*	*5.5*
	1851	**6127**	2879	3248	1128	1841–51	***–3.1***	*–2.4*	*–3.7*
	1861	**5934**	2747	3187	1160	1851–61	***–3.1***	*–4.6*	*–1.9*
	1871	**6121**	2762	3359	1216	1861–71	***3.2***	*0.5*	*5.4*
	1881	**6234**	2813	3421	1216	1871–81	***1.8***	*1.8*	*1.8*
	1891	**6479**	2937	3542	1206	1881–91	***3.9***	*4.4*	*3.5*
	1901	**6146**	2787	3359	1205	1891–1901	***–5.1***	*–5.1*	*–5.2*
	1911	**5986**	2805	3181	1134	1901–11	***–2.6***	*0.6*	*–5.3*

No boundary changes

Subdistrict	Year	Number Persons	Males	Females	Females/ 1000 males	Intercensal period	*Percentage change* Persons	Males	Females
Lampeter District									
Llanybydder	1801	**1752**	830	922	1111				
	1811	**1989**	946	1043	1103	1801–11	***13.5***	*14.0*	*13.1*
	1821	**2275**	1111	1164	1048	1811–21	***14.4***	*17.4*	*11.6*
	1831	**2593**	1243	1350	1086	1821–31	***14.0***	*11.9*	*16.0*
	1841	**2737**	1308	1429	1093	1831–41	***5.6***	*5.2*	*5.9*
	1851	**2630**	1234	1396	1131	1841–51	***–3.9***	*–5.7*	*–2.3*
	1861	**2541**	1195	1346	1126	1851–61	***–3.4***	*–3.2*	*–3.6*
	1871	**2580**	1191	1389	1166	1861–71	***1.5***	*–0.3*	*3.2*
	1881	**2690**	1244	1446	1162	1871–81	***4.3***	*4.5*	*4.1*
	1891	**2489**	1150	1339	1164	1881–91	***–7.5***	*–7.6*	*–7.4*
	1901	**2358**	1099	1259	1146	1891–1901	***–5.3***	*–4.4*	*–6.0*
	1911	**2264**	1066	1198	1124	1901–11	***–4.0***	*–3.0*	*–4.8*

No boundary changes

Subdistrict	Year	Number Persons	Males	Females	Females/ 1000 males	Intercensal period	*Percentage change* Persons	Males	Females
Pencarreg	1801	**1798**	865	933	1079				
	1811	**1927**	928	999	1077	1801–11	***7.2***	*7.3*	*7.1*
	1821	**2228**	1130	1098	972	1811–21	***15.6***	*21.8*	*9.9*
	1831	**2402**	1182	1220	1032	1821–31	***7.8***	*4.6*	*11.1*
	1841	**2534**	1229	1305	1062	1831–41	***5.5***	*4.0*	*7.0*
	1851	**2706**	1304	1402	1075	1841–51	***6.8***	*6.1*	*7.4*
	1861	**2878**	1382	1496	1082	1851–61	***6.4***	*6.0*	*6.7*
	1871	**2790**	1286	1504	1170	1861–71	***–3.1***	*–6.9*	*0.5*
	1881	**2600**	1188	1412	1189	1871–81	***–6.8***	*–7.6*	*–6.1*
	1891	**2429**	1099	1330	1210	1881–91	***–6.6***	*–7.5*	*–5.8*
	1901	**2281**	1034	1247	1206	1891–1901	***–6.1***	*–5.9*	*–6.2*
	1911	**2086**	963	1123	1166	1901–11	***–8.5***	*–6.9*	*–9.9*

No boundary changes

Subdistrict	Year	Number Persons	Males	Females	Females/ 1000 males	Intercensal period	*Percentage change* Persons	Males	Females
Lampeter	1801	**1432**	706	726	1028				
	1811	**1641**	783	858	1096	1801–11	***14.6***	*10.9*	*18.2*
	1821	**1926**	932	994	1067	1811–21	***17.4***	*19.0*	*15.9*
	1831	**2467**	1222	1245	1019	1821–31	***28.1***	*31.1*	*25.3*
	1841	**2691**	1347	1344	998	1831–41	***9.1***	*10.2*	*8.0*
	1851	**2634**	1264	1370	1084	1841–51	***–2.1***	*–6.2*	*1.9*
	1861	**2710**	1321	1389	1051	1851–61	***2.9***	*4.5*	*1.4*
	1871	**2813**	1340	1473	1099	1861–71	***3.8***	*1.4*	*6.0*
	1881	**2938**	1392	1546	1111	1871–81	***4.4***	*3.9*	*5.0*
	1891	**3030**	1361	1669	1226	1881–91	***3.1***	*–2.2*	*8.0*
	1901	**3024**	1366	1658	1214	1891–1901	***–0.2***	*0.4*	*–0.7*
	1911	**3006**	1373	1633	1189	1901–11	***–0.6***	*0.5*	*–1.5*

No boundary changes

Subdistrict	Year	Number Persons	Males	Females	Females/ 1000 males	Intercensal period	*Percentage change* *Persons*	*Males*	*Females*
Llanwenog	1801	**1292**	658	634	964				
	1811	**1452**	708	744	1051	1801–11	***12.4***	*7.6*	*17.4*
	1821	**1713**	833	880	1056	1811–21	***18.0***	*17.7*	*18.3*
	1831	**1975**	932	1043	1119	1821–31	***15.3***	*11.9*	*18.5*
	1841	**1903**	906	997	1100	1831–41	***–3.6***	*–2.8*	*–4.4*
	1851	**1904**	903	1001	1109	1841–51	***0.1***	*–0.3*	*0.4*
	1861	**1865**	861	1004	1166	1851–61	***–2.0***	*–4.7*	*0.3*
	1871	**1790**	837	953	1139	1861–71	***–4.0***	*–2.8*	*–5.1*
	1881	**1859**	847	1012	1195	1871–81	***3.9***	*1.2*	*6.2*
	1891	**1736**	782	954	1220	1881–91	***–6.6***	*–7.7*	*–5.7*
	1901	**1594**	712	882	1239	1891–1901	***–8.2***	*–9.0*	*–7.5*
	1911	**1611**	773	838	1084	1901–11	***1.1***	*8.6*	*–5.0*

No boundary changes

Subdistrict	Year	Number Persons	Males	Females	Females/ 1000 males	Intercensal period	*Persons*	*Males*	*Females*
Aberaeron District									
Llandysilio	1801	**3618**	1674	1944	1161				
	1811	**4477**	2059	2418	1174	1801–11	***23.7***	*23.0*	*24.4*
	1821	**5304**	2491	2813	1129	1811–21	***18.5***	*21.0*	*16.3*
	1831	**6064**	2907	3157	1086	1821–31	***14.3***	*16.7*	*12.2*
	1841	**6268**	2929	3339	1140	1831–41	***3.4***	*0.8*	*5.8*
	1851	**6415**	2903	3512	1210	1841–51	***2.3***	*–0.9*	*5.2*
	1861	**6459**	2868	3591	1252	1851–61	***0.7***	*–1.2*	*2.2*
	1871	**6269**	2681	3588	1338	1861–71	***–2.9***	*–6.5*	*–0.1*
	1881	**5934**	2477	3457	1396	1871–81	***–5.3***	*–7.6*	*–3.7*
		(5963)	(2489)	(3474)					
	1891	**5592**	2376	3216	1354	1881–91	***–6.2***	*–4.5*	*–7.4*
	1901	**5117**	2138	2979	1393	1891–1901	***–8.5***	*–10.0*	*–7.4*
	1911	**4853**	2158	2695	1249	1901–11	***–5.2***	*0.9*	*–9.5*

Boundary changes: 1881–91 gain of 29 from Llansanffraid (pop. 1881)

Subdistrict	Year	Number Persons	Males	Females	Females/ 1000 males	Intercensal period	*Persons*	*Males*	*Females*
Llansanffraid	1801	**4342**	2033	2309	1136				
	1811	**4943**	2303	2640	1146	1801–11	***13.8***	*13.3*	*14.3*
	1821	**5656**	2725	2931	1076	1811–21	***14.4***	*18.3*	*11.0*
	1831	**6244**	2976	3268	1098	1821–31	***10.4***	*9.2*	*11.5*
	1841	**6607**	3088	3519	1140	1831–41	***5.8***	*3.8*	*7.7*
	1851	**6809**	3088	3721	1205	1841–51	***3.1***	*0.0*	*5.7*
	1861	**7081**	3178	3903	1228	1851–61	***4.0***	*2.9*	*4.9*
	1871	**7108**	3069	4039	1316	1861–71	***0.4***	*–3.4*	*3.5*
	1881	**6609**	2801	3808	1360	1871–81	***–7.0***	*–8.7*	*–5.7*
		(6580)	(2789)	(3791)					
	1891	**6003**	2497	3506	1404	1881–91	***–8.8***	*–10.5*	*–7.5*
	1901	**5618**	2359	3259	1382	1891–1901	***–6.4***	*–5.5*	*–7.0*
	1911	**5409**	2349	3060	1303	1901–11	***–3.7***	*–0.4*	*–6.1*

Boundary changes: 1881–91 loss of 29 to Llandysilio (pop. 1881)

Subdistrict	Year	Number Persons	Males	Females	Females/ 1000 males	Intercensal period	*Persons*	*Males*	*Females*
Aberystwyth District									
Llanrhystud	1801	**2714**	1297	1417	1093				
	1811	**2996**	1406	1590	1131	1801–11	***10.4***	*8.4*	*12.2*
	1821	**3240**	1556	1684	1082	1811–21	***8.1***	*10.7*	*5.9*
	1831	**3458**	1721	1737	1009	1821–31	***6.7***	*10.6*	*3.1*
	1841	**3653**	1770	1883	1064	1831–41	***5.6***	*2.8*	*8.4*
	1851	**3409**	1615	1794	1111	1841–51	***–6.7***	*–8.8*	*–4.7*
	1861	**3419**	1594	1825	1145	1851–61	***0.3***	*–1.3*	*1.7*
	1871	**3470**	1615	1855	1149	1861–71	***1.5***	*1.3*	*1.6*
	1881	**3128**	1419	1709	1204	1871–81	***–9.9***	*–12.1*	*–7.9*
	1891	**2686**	1255	1431	1140	1881–91	***–14.1***	*–11.6*	*–16.3*
	1901	**2525**	1207	1318	1092	1891–1901	***–6.0***	*–3.8*	*–7.9*
	1911	**2422**	1212	1210	998	1901–11	***–4.1***	*0.4*	*–8.2*

No boundary changes

Subdistrict	Year	Number Persons	Males	Females	Females/ 1000 males	Intercensal period	*Percentage change* Persons	Males	Females
Aberystwyth	1801	**4036**	1811	2225	1229				
	1811	**4848**	2181	2667	1223	1801–11	***20.1***	*20.4*	*19.9*
	1821	**6482**	3477	3005	864	1811–21	***33.7***	*59.4*	*12.7*
	1831	**7393**	3399	3994	1175	1821–31	***14.1***	*–2.2*	*32.9*
	1841	**8211**	3709	4502	1214	1831–41	***11.1***	*9.1*	*12.7*
	1851	**8442**	3862	4580	1186	1841–51	***2.8***	*4.1*	*1.7*
	1861	**8772**	3936	4836	1229	1851–61	***3.9***	*1.9*	*5.6*
	1871	**10086**	4552	5534	1216	1861–71	***15.0***	*15.7*	*14.4*
	1881	**10271**	4603	5668	1231	1871–81	***1.8***	*1.1*	*2.4*
	1891	**9453**	3999	5454	1364	1881–91	***–8.0***	*–13.1*	*–3.8*
	1901	**10899**	4713	6186	1313	1891–1901	***15.3***	*17.9*	*13.4*
	1911	**11509**	4889	6620	1354	1901–11	***5.6***	*3.7*	*7.0*

No boundary changes

Subdistrict	Year	Number Persons	Males	Females	Females/ 1000 males	Intercensal period	*Percentage change* Persons	Males	Females
Genau'r-glyn	1801	**2477**	1218	1259	1034				
	1811	**2799**	1311	1488	1135	1801–11	***13.0***	*7.6*	*18.2*
	1821	**3287**	1560	1727	1107	1811–21	***17.4***	*19.0*	*16.1*
	1831	**3880**	1876	2004	1068	1821–31	***18.0***	*20.3*	*16.0*
	1841	**4358**	2131	2227	1045	1831–41	***12.3***	*13.6*	*11.1*
	1851	**4502**	2182	2320	1063	1841–51	***3.3***	*2.4*	*4.2*
	1861	**4638**	2197	2441	1111	1851–61	***3.0***	*0.7*	*5.2*
	1871	**5023**	2399	2624	1094	1861–71	***8.3***	*9.2*	*7.5*
	1881	**4527**	2132	2395	1123	1871–81	***–9.9***	*–11.1*	*–8.7*
	1891	**3621**	1613	2008	1245	1881–91	***–20.0***	*–24.3*	*–16.2*
	1901	**3387**	1513	1874	1239	1891–1901	***–6.5***	*–6.2*	*–6.7*
	1911	**3445**	1592	1853	1164	1901–11	***1.7***	*5.2*	*–1.1*

No boundary changes

Subdistrict	Year	Number Persons	Males	Females	Females/ 1000 males	Intercensal period	*Percentage change* Persons	Males	Females
Rheidol	1801	**3631**	1747	1884	1078				
	1811	**4271**	1980	2291	1157	1801–11	***17.6***	*13.3*	*21.6*
	1821	**4564**	2187	2377	1087	1811–21	***6.9***	*10.5*	*3.8*
	1831	**5295**	2588	2707	1046	1821–31	***16.0***	*18.3*	*13.9*
	1841	**6020**	2972	3048	1026	1831–41	***13.7***	*14.8*	*12.6*
	1851	**7400**	3700	3700	1000	1841–51	***22.9***	*24.5*	*21.4*
	1861	**8635**	4219	4416	1047	1851–61	***16.7***	*14.0*	*19.4*
	1871	**8860**	4274	4586	1073	1861–71	***2.6***	*1.3*	*3.8*
	1881	**7680**	3698	3982	1077	1871–81	***–13.3***	*–13.5*	*–13.2*
	1891	**5342**	2426	2916	1202	1881–91	***–30.4***	*–34.4*	*–26.8*
	1901	**4660**	2106	2554	1213	1891–1901	***–12.8***	*–13.2*	*–12.4*
	1911	**4106**	1842	2264	1229	1901–11	***–11.9***	*–12.5*	*–11.4*

No boundary changes

Subdistrict	Year	Number Persons	Males	Females	Females/ 1000 males	Intercensal period	*Percentage change* Persons	Males	Females
Tregaron District									
Gwnnws	1801	**1660**	805	855	1062				
	1811	**1763**	836	927	1109	1801–11	***6.2***	*3.9*	*8.4*
	1821	**2370**	1182	1188	1005	1811–21	***34.4***	*41.4*	*28.2*
	1831	**2713**	1326	1387	1046	1821–31	***14.5***	*12.2*	*16.8*
	1841	**3018**	1443	1575	1091	1831–41	***11.2***	*8.8*	*13.6*
	1851	**3147**	1524	1623	1065	1841–51	***4.3***	*5.6*	*3.0*
	1861	**3423**	1604	1819	1134	1851–61	***8.8***	*5.2*	*12.1*
	1871	**3597**	1749	1848	1057	1861–71	***5.1***	*9.0*	*1.6*
	1881	**3314**	1556	1758	1130	1871–81	***–7.9***	*–11.0*	*–4.9*
	1891	**2475**	1120	1355	1210	1881–91	***–25.3***	*–28.0*	*–22.9*
	1901	**2264**	1048	1216	1160	1891–1901	***–8.5***	*–6.4*	*–10.3*
	1911	**2172**	1054	1118	1061	1901–11	***–4.1***	*0.6*	*–8.1*

No boundary changes

Subdistrict	Year	Number Persons	Males	Females	Females/ 1000 males	Intercensal period	*Percentage change* *Persons*	*Males*	*Females*
Llangeitho	1801	**2094**	996	1098	1102				
	1811	**2442**	1190	1252	1052	1801–11	***16.6***	*19.5*	*14.0*
	1821	**2817**	1366	1451	1062	1811–21	***15.4***	*14.8*	*15.9*
	1831	**3176**	1537	1639	1066	1821–31	***12.7***	*12.5*	*13.0*
	1841	**3257**	1549	1708	1103	1831–41	***2.6***	*0.8*	*4.2*
	1851	**3293**	1555	1738	1118	1841–51	***1.1***	*0.4*	*1.8*
	1861	**3336**	1570	1766	1125	1851–61	***1.3***	*1.0*	*1.6*
	1871	**3189**	1462	1727	1181	1861–71	***–4.4***	*–6.9*	*–2.2*
	1881	**3187**	1433	1754	1224	1871–81	***–0.1***	*–2.0*	*1.6*
	1891	**2792**	1265	1527	1207	1881–91	***–12.4***	*–11.7*	*–12.9*
	1901	**2603**	1192	1411	1184	1891–1901	***–6.8***	*–5.8*	*–7.6*
	1911	**2413**	1149	1264	1100	1901–11	***–7.3***	*–3.6*	*–10.4*

No boundary changes

Subdistrict	Year	Number Persons	Males	Females	Females/ 1000 males	Intercensal period	*Persons*	*Males*	*Females*
Tregaron	1801	**2320**	1120	1200	1071				
	1811	**2852**	1399	1453	1039	1801–11	***22.9***	*24.9*	*21.1*
	1821	**3352**	1656	1696	1024	1811–21	***17.5***	*18.4*	*16.7*
	1831	**3669**	1775	1894	1067	1821–31	***9.5***	*7.2*	*11.7*
	1841	**3979**	1824	2155	1181	1831–41	***8.4***	*2.8*	*13.8*
	1851	**3964**	1824	2140	1173	1841–51	***–0.4***	*0.0*	*–0.7*
	1861	**3978**	1856	2122	1143	1851–61	***0.4***	*1.8*	*–0.8*
	1871	**3891**	1818	2073	1140	1861–71	***–2.2***	*–2.0*	*–2.3*
	1881	**3771**	1701	2070	1217	1871–81	***–3.1***	*–6.4*	*–0.1*
	1891	**3346**	1472	1874	1273	1881–91	***–11.3***	*–13.5*	*–9.5*
	1901	**3080**	1376	1704	1238	1891–1901	***–7.9***	*–6.5*	*–9.1*
	1911	**2936**	1335	1601	1199	1901–11	***–4.7***	*–3.0*	*–6.0*

No boundary changes

BRECONSHIRE
Builth District

Subdistrict	Year	Number Persons	Males	Females	Females/ 1000 males	Intercensal period	*Persons*	*Males*	*Females*
Llanwrtyd	1891	(903)	(418)	(485)					
	1901	**942**	442	500	1131	1891–1901	***4.3***	*5.7*	*3.1*
		(1258)	(608)	(650)					
	1911	**1339**	654	685	1047	1901–11	***6.4***	*7.6*	*5.4*

Boundary changes: 1891–1901 whole subdistrict transferred from Llandovery District (Carm), 903 (pop. 1891)
1901–11 gain of 316 from Treflys (pop. 1901)

Subdistrict	Year	Number Persons	Males	Females	Females/ 1000 males	Intercensal period	*Persons*	*Males*	*Females*
Abergwesyn/ Treflys	1801	**2478**	1207	1271	1053				
	1811	**2570**	1166	1404	1204	1801–11	***3.7***	*–3.4*	*10.5*
	1821	**2823**	1410	1413	1002	1811–21	***9.8***	*20.9*	*0.6*
	1831	**3007**	1472	1535	1043	1821–31	***6.5***	*4.4*	*8.6*
	1841	**2955**	1432	1523	1064	1831–41	***–1.7***	*–2.7*	*–0.8*
	1851	**2890**	1419	1471	1037	1841–51	***–2.2***	*–0.9*	*–3.4*
	1861	**2897**	1430	1467	1026	1851–61	***0.2***	*0.8*	*–0.3*
	1871	**2851**	1387	1464	1056	1861–71	***–1.6***	*–3.0*	*–0.2*
	1881	**2679**	1294	1385	1070	1871–81	***–6.0***	*–6.7*	*–5.4*
	1891	**2351**	1163	1188	1021	1881–91	***–12.2***	*–10.1*	*–14.2*
	1901	**2130**	1090	1040	954	1891–1901	***–9.4***	*–6.3*	*–12.5*
		(1814)	(924)	(890)					
	1911	**1813**	924	889	962	1901–11	***–0.1***	*0.0*	*–0.1*

Boundary changes: 1901–11 change of name to Treflys, loss of 316 to Llanwrtyd (pop. 1901)

Subdistrict	Year	Number Persons	Males	Females	Females/ 1000 males	Intercensal period	*Persons*	*Males*	*Females*
Colwyn	1801	**1962**	959	1003	1046				
	1811	**1922**	929	993	1069	1801–11	***–2.0***	*–3.1*	*–1.0*
	1821	**1940**	1028	912	887	1811–21	***0.9***	*10.7*	*–8.2*
	1831	**2118**	1070	1048	979	1821–31	***9.2***	*4.1*	*14.9*
	1841	**2172**	1082	1090	1007	1831–41	***2.5***	*1.1*	*4.0*
	1851	**1995**	1017	978	962	1841–51	***–8.1***	*–6.0*	*–10.3*
	1861	**1964**	1024	940	918	1851–61	***–1.6***	*0.7*	*–3.9*
	1871	**2077**	1081	996	921	1861–71	***5.8***	*5.6*	*6.0*
	1881	**1847**	959	888	926	1871–81	***–11.1***	*–11.3*	*–10.8*
	1891	**1714**	871	843	968	1881–91	***–7.2***	*–9.2*	*–5.1*
	1901	**1765**	856	909	1062	1891–1901	***3.0***	*–1.7*	*7.8*
	1911	**2323**	1115	1208	1083	1901–11	***31.6***	*30.3*	*32.9*

No boundary changes

Subdistrict	Year	Number Persons	Males	Females	Females/ 1000 males	Intercensal period	*Percentage change* Persons	Males	Females
Builth	1801	**2832**	1361	1471	1081				
	1811	**3114**	1491	1623	1089	1801–11	***10.0***	*9.6*	*10.3*
	1821	**3333**	1621	1712	1056	1811–21	***7.0***	*8.7*	*5.5*
	1831	**3387**	1672	1715	1026	1821–31	***1.6***	*3.1*	*0.2*
	1841	**3587**	1747	1840	1053	1831–41	***5.9***	*4.5*	*7.3*
	1851	**3460**	1716	1744	1016	1841–51	***–3.5***	*–1.8*	*–5.2*
	1861	**3444**	1707	1737	1018	1851–61	***–0.5***	*–0.5*	*–0.4*
	1871	**3336**	1647	1689	1026	1861–71	***–3.1***	*–3.5*	*–2.8*
	1881	**3656**	1762	1894	1075	1871–81	***9.6***	*7.0*	*12.1*
	1891	**3769**	1844	1925	1044	1881–91	***3.1***	*4.7*	*1.6*
	1901	**4139**	2060	2079	1009	1891–1901	***9.8***	*11.7*	*8.0*
	1911	**4007**	1937	2070	1069	1901–11	***–3.2***	*–6.0*	*–0.4*

No boundary changes

Brecon District

Subdistrict	Year	Number Persons	Males	Females	Females/ 1000 males	Intercensal period	*Percentage change* Persons	Males	Females
Merthyr Cynog	1801	**1669**	830	839	1011				
	1811	**1667**	810	857	1058	1801–11	***–0.1***	*–2.4*	*2.1*
	1821	**1813**	901	912	1012	1811–21	***8.8***	*11.2*	*6.4*
	1831	**1712**	871	841	966	1821–31	***–5.6***	*–3.3*	*–7.8*
	1841	**1672**	837	835	998	1831–41	***–2.3***	*–3.9*	*–0.7*
	1851	**1653**	858	795	927	1841–51	***–1.1***	*2.5*	*–4.8*
	1861	**1593**	822	771	938	1851–61	***–3.6***	*–4.2*	*–3.0*
	1871	**1591**	794	797	1004	1861–71	***–0.1***	*–3.4*	*3.4*
	1881	**1371**	685	686	1001	1871–81	***–13.8***	*–13.7*	*–13.9*

Boundary changes: 1881–91 subdistrict abolished; loss of 386 to Defynnog, loss of 985 to Brecon (pop. 1881)

Subdistrict	Year	Number Persons	Males	Females	Females/ 1000 males	Intercensal period	*Percentage change* Persons	Males	Females
Defynnog	1801	**3956**	1904	2052	1078				
	1811	**4244**	1992	2252	1131	1801–11	***7.3***	*4.6*	*9.7*
	1821	**4477**	2156	2321	1077	1811–21	***5.5***	*8.2*	*3.1*
	1831	**4629**	2266	2363	1043	1821–31	***3.4***	*5.1*	*1.8*
	1841	**4420**	2098	2322	1107	1831–41	***–4.5***	*–7.4*	*–1.7*
	1851	**4440**	2147	2293	1068	1841–51	***0.5***	*2.3*	*–1.2*
	1861	**4075**	1974	2101	1064	1851–61	***–8.2***	*–8.1*	*–8.4*
	1871	**3974**	1953	2021	1035	1861–71	***–2.5***	*–1.1*	*–3.8*
	1881	**3727**	1805	1922	1065	1871–81	***–6.2***	*–7.6*	*–4.9*
		(4113)	(2003)	(2110)					
	1891	**3786**	1869	1917	1026	1881–91	***–8.0***	*–6.7*	*–9.1*
	1901	**3876**	1950	1926	988	1891–1901	***2.4***	*4.3*	*0.5*
	1911	**3467**	1745	1722	987	1901–11	***–10.6***	*–10.5*	*–10.6*

Boundary changes: 1881–91 gain of 386 from Merthyr Cynog (pop. 1881)

Subdistrict	Year	Number Persons	Males	Females	Females/ 1000 males	Intercensal period	*Percentage change* Persons	Males	Females
Brecon	1801	**4343**	1976	2367	1198				
	1811	**4945**	2246	2699	1202	1801–11	***13.9***	*13.7*	*14.0*
	1821	**6110**	2886	3224	1117	1811–21	***23.6***	*28.5*	*19.5*
	1831	**6821**	3222	3599	1117	1821–31	***11.6***	*11.6*	*11.6*
	1841	**7243**	3569	3674	1029	1831–41	***6.2***	*10.8*	*2.1*
	1851	**7515**	3704	3811	1029	1841–51	***3.8***	*3.8*	*3.7*
	1861	**7054**	3376	3678	1089	1851–61	***–6.1***	*–8.9*	*–3.5*
	1871	**7715**	3868	3847	995	1861–71	***9.4***	*14.6*	*4.6*
	1881	**7987**	4024	3963	985	1871–81	***3.5***	*4.0*	*3.0*
		(8972)	(4511)	(4461)					
	1891	**8512**	4211	4301	1021	1881–91	***–5.1***	*–6.7*	*–3.6*
	1901	**8113**	3946	4167	1056	1891–1901	***–4.7***	*–6.3*	*–3.1*
	1911	**8009**	3991	4018	1007	1901–11	***–1.3***	*1.1*	*–3.6*

Boundary changes: 1881–91 gain of 985 from Merthyr Cynog (pop. 1881)

Subdistrict	Year	Number Persons	Males	Females	Females/ 1000 males	Intercensal period	*Percentage change* Persons	Males	Females
Pencelli	1801	**1000**	509	491	965				
	1811	**1236**	590	646	1095	1801–11	***23.6***	*15.9*	*31.6*
	1821	**1487**	737	750	1018	1811–21	***20.3***	*24.9*	*16.1*
	1831	**1520**	755	765	1013	1821–31	***2.2***	*2.4*	*2.0*
	1841	**1532**	772	760	984	1831–41	***0.8***	*2.3*	*–0.7*
	1851	**1541**	754	787	1044	1841–51	***0.6***	*–2.3*	*3.6*
	1861	**1657**	891	766	860	1851–61	***7.5***	*18.2*	*–2.7*
	1871	**1574**	761	813	1068	1861–71	***–5.0***	*–14.6*	*6.1*
	1881	**1456**	747	709	949	1871–81	***–7.5***	*–1.8*	*–12.8*
	1891	**1223**	600	623	1038	1881–91	***–16.0***	*–19.7*	*–12.1*
	1901	**1356**	692	664	960	1891–1901	***10.9***	*15.3*	*6.6*
	1911	**1264**	615	649	1055	1901–11	***–6.8***	*–11.1*	*–2.3*

No boundary changes

Subdistrict	Year	Number Persons	Males	Females	Females/ 1000 males	Intercensal period	*Percentage change* *Persons*	*Males*	*Females*
Llan-gors	1801	**2674**	1340	1334	996				
	1811	**2882**	1401	1481	1057	1801–11	***7.8***	*4.6*	*11.0*
	1821	**2835**	1416	1419	1002	1811–21	***–1.6***	*1.1*	*–4.2*
	1831	**2897**	1422	1475	1037	1821–31	***2.2***	*0.4*	*3.9*
	1841	**2834**	1381	1453	1052	1831–41	***–2.2***	*–2.9*	*–1.5*
	1851	**3025**	1521	1504	989	1841–51	***6.7***	*10.1*	*3.5*
	1861	**2900**	1492	1408	944	1851–61	***–4.1***	*–1.9*	*–6.4*
	1871	**2870**	1460	1410	966	1861–71	***–1.0***	*–2.1*	*0.1*
	1881	**2637**	1317	1320	1002	1871–81	***–8.1***	*–9.8*	*–6.4*
	1891	**2403**	1200	1203	1003	1881–91	***–8.9***	*–8.9*	*–8.9*
	1901	**2288**	1164	1124	966	1891–1901	***–4.8***	*–3.0*	*–6.6*
	1911	**2323**	1174	1149	979	1901–11	***1.5***	*0.9*	*2.2*

No boundary changes

Crickhowell District

Subdistrict	Year	Number Persons	Males	Females	Females/ 1000 males	Intercensal period	*Persons*	*Males*	*Females*
Cwm-du	1801	**969**	462	507	1097				
	1811	**928**	423	505	1194	1801–11	***–4.2***	*–8.4*	*–0.4*
	1821	**1010**	502	508	1012	1811–21	***8.8***	*18.7*	*0.6*
	1831	**1103**	570	533	935	1821–31	***9.2***	*13.5*	*4.9*
	1841	**1039**	522	517	990	1831–41	***–5.8***	*–8.4*	*–3.0*
	1851	**1066**	560	506	904	1841–51	***2.6***	*7.3*	*–2.1*
	1861	**1056**	535	521	974	1851–61	***–0.9***	*–4.5*	*3.0*
	1871	**975**	495	480	970	1861–71	***–7.7***	*–7.5*	*–7.9*
	1881	**957**	465	492	1058	1871–81	***–1.8***	*–6.1*	*2.5*
	1891	**850**	412	438	1063	1881–91	***–11.2***	*–11.4*	*–11.0*
	1901	**826**	409	417	1020	1891–1901	***–2.8***	*–0.7*	*–4.8*
	1911	**840**	427	413	967	1901–11	***1.7***	*4.4*	*–1.0*

No boundary changes

Subdistrict	Year	Number Persons	Males	Females	Females/ 1000 males	Intercensal period	*Persons*	*Males*	*Females*
Llangynidr	1801	**775**	416	359	863				
	1811	**1126**	574	552	962	1801–11	***45.3***	*38.0*	*53.8*
	1821	**1345**	705	640	908	1811–21	***19.4***	*22.8*	*15.9*
	1831	**1440**	758	682	900	1821–31	***7.1***	*7.5*	*6.6*
	1841	**2775**	1468	1307	890	1831–41	***92.7***	*93.7*	*91.6*
	1851	**3246**	1756	1490	849	1841–51	***17.0***	*19.6*	*14.0*
	1861	**3594**	1849	1745	944	1851–61	***10.7***	*5.3*	*17.1*
	1871	**3928**	2004	1924	960	1861–71	***9.3***	*8.4*	*10.3*
	1881	**3625**	1810	1815	1003	1871–81	***–7.7***	*–9.7*	*–5.7*
	1891	**3642**	1849	1793	970	1881–91	***0.5***	*2.2*	*–1.2*

Boundary changes: 1891–1901 subdistrict abolished; loss of 488 to Crickhowell, loss of 3154 to new subdistrict of Beaufort (pop. 1891)

Subdistrict	Year	Number Persons	Males	Females	Females/ 1000 males	Intercensal period	*Persons*	*Males*	*Females*
Llangatwg	1801	**1046**	502	544	1084				
	1811	**1263**	621	642	1034	1801–11	***20.7***	*23.7*	*18.0*
	1821	**1947**	1139	808	709	1811–21	***54.2***	*83.4*	*25.9*
	1831	**2690**	1467	1223	834	1821–31	***38.2***	*28.8*	*51.4*
	1841	**4334**	2390	1944	813	1831–41	***61.1***	*62.9*	*59.0*
	1851	**5415**	2907	2508	863	1841–51	***24.9***	*21.6*	*29.0*
	1861	**5759**	2962	2797	944	1851–61	***6.4***	*1.9*	*11.5*
	1871	**5303**	2709	2594	958	1861–71	***–7.9***	*–8.5*	*–7.3*
	1881	**4731**	2411	2320	962	1871–81	***–10.8***	*–11.0*	*–10.6*

Boundary changes: 1881–91 subdistrict abolished; loss of 3661 to Llanelli, loss of 1070 to Crickhowell (pop. 1881)

Subdistrict	Year	Number Persons	Males	Females	Females/ 1000 males	Intercensal period	*Persons*	*Males*	*Females*
Beaufort	1891	(5908)	(3019)	(2889)					
	1901	**5993**	3138	2855	910	1891–1901	***1.4***	*3.9*	*–1.2*
	1911	**7008**	3690	3318	899	1901–11	***16.9***	*17.6*	*16.2*

Boundary changes: 1891–1901 subdistrict created; gain of 3154 from Llangynidr, gain of 2754 from Llanelli (pop. 1891)

Subdistrict	Year	Number Persons	Males	Females	Females/ 1000 males	Intercensal period	*Percentage change* *Persons*	*Males*	*Females*
Llanelli	1801	**937**	517	420	812				
	1811	**1821**	988	833	843	1801–11	***94.3***	*91.1*	*98.3*
	1821	**2962**	1653	1309	792	1811–21	***62.7***	*67.3*	*57.1*
	1831	**4041**	2181	1860	853	1821–31	***36.4***	*31.9*	*42.1*
	1841	**7366**	3912	3454	883	1831–41	***82.3***	*79.4*	*85.7*
	1851	**9644**	5064	4580	904	1841–51	***30.9***	*29.4*	*32.6*
	1861	**9603**	5063	4540	897	1851–61	***–0.4***	*0.0*	*–0.9*
	1871	**7541**	3889	3652	939	1861–71	***–21.5***	*–23.2*	*–19.6*
	1881	**6979**	3605	3374	936	1871–81	***–7.5***	*–7.3*	*–7.6*
		(10640)	(5476)	(5164)					
	1891	**11976**	6209	5767	929	1881–91	***12.6***	*13.4*	*11.7*
		(9492)	(4948)	(4544)					
	1901	**9909**	5110	4799	939	1891–1901	***4.4***	*3.3*	*5.6*
	1911	**11040**	5708	5332	934	1901–11	***11.4***	*11.7*	*11.1*

Boundary changes: 1881–91 gain of 3661 from Llangatwg (pop. 1881)
1891–1901 loss of 2754 to new subdistrict of Beaufort, gain of 270 from Aberystruth (Mon) (pop. 1891)

Subdistrict	Year	Number Persons	Males	Females	Females/ 1000 males	Intercensal period	*Percentage change* *Persons*	*Males*	*Females*
Crickhowell	1801	**1474**	709	765	1079				
	1811	**1494**	701	793	1131	1801–11	***1.4***	*–1.1*	*3.7*
	1821	**1959**	933	1026	1100	1811–21	***31.1***	*33.1*	*29.4*
	1831	**2031**	1015	1016	1001	1821–31	***3.7***	*8.8*	*–1.0*
	1841	**2162**	1060	1102	1040	1831–41	***6.5***	*4.4*	*8.5*
	1851	**2326**	1123	1203	1071	1841–51	***7.6***	*5.9*	*9.2*
	1861	**2445**	1176	1269	1079	1851–61	***5.1***	*4.7*	*5.5*
	1871	**2400**	1106	1294	1170	1861–71	***–1.8***	*–6.0*	*2.0*
	1881	**2266**	1079	1187	1100	1871–81	***–5.6***	*–2.4*	*–8.3*
		(3336)	(1619)	(1717)					
	1891	**3047**	1450	1597	1101	1881–91	***–8.7***	*–10.4*	*–7.0*
		(3535)	(1684)	(1851)					
	1901	**3213**	1487	1726	1161	1891–1901	***–9.1***	*–11.7*	*–6.8*
	1911	**3421**	1650	1771	1073	1901–11	***6.5***	*11.0*	*2.6*

Boundary changes: 1881–91 gain of 1070 from Llangatwg (pop. 1881)
1891–1901 gain of 488 from Llangynidr (pop. 1891)

Subdistrict	Year	Number Persons	Males	Females	Females/ 1000 males	Intercensal period	*Percentage change* *Persons*	*Males*	*Females*
Hay District									
Talgarth	1801	**2114**	997	1117	1120				
	1811	**2315**	1120	1195	1067	1801–11	***9.5***	*12.3*	*7.0*
	1821	**2560**	1247	1313	1053	1811–21	***10.6***	*11.3*	*9.9*
	1831	**2676**	1323	1353	1023	1821–31	***4.5***	*6.1*	*3.0*
	1841	**2539**	1269	1270	1001	1831–41	***–5.1***	*–4.1*	*–6.1*
	1851	**2549**	1280	1269	991	1841–51	***0.4***	*0.9*	*–0.1*
	1861	**2476**	1236	1240	1003	1851–61	***–2.9***	*–3.4*	*–2.3*
	1871	**2635**	1305	1330	1019	1861–71	***6.4***	*5.6*	*7.3*
	1881	**2513**	1256	1257	1001	1871–81	***–4.6***	*–3.8*	*–5.5*
		(2735)	(1353)	(1382)					
	1891	**2639**	1285	1354	1054	1881–91	***–3.5***	*–5.0*	*–2.0*
		(3708)	(1810)	(1898)					
	1901	**3769**	1857	1912	1030	1891–1901	***1.6***	*2.6*	*0.7*
	1911	**4117**	2009	2108	1049	1901–11	***9.2***	*8.2*	*10.3*

Boundary changes: 1881–91 gain of 222 from Clyro (pop. 1881)
1891–1901 gain of 1069 from Clyro (pop. 1891)

Subdistrict	Year	Number Persons	Males	Females	Females/ 1000 males	Intercensal period	*Percentage change* *Persons*	*Males*	*Females*
Clyro	1801	**3023**	1469	1554	1058				
	1811	**3304**	1589	1715	1079	1801–11	***9.3***	*8.2*	*10.4*
	1821	**3474**	1749	1725	986	1811–21	***5.1***	*10.1*	*0.6*
	1831	**3903**	1977	1926	974	1821–31	***12.3***	*13.0*	*11.7*
	1841	**3837**	1912	1925	1007	1831–41	***–1.7***	*–3.3*	*–0.1*
	1851	**3628**	1850	1778	961	1841–51	***–5.4***	*–3.2*	*–7.6*
	1861	**3521**	1761	1760	999	1851–61	***–2.9***	*–4.8*	*–1.0*
	1871	**3407**	1691	1716	1015	1861–71	***–3.2***	*–4.0*	*–2.5*
	1881	**3113**	1571	1542	982	1871–81	***–8.6***	*–7.1*	*–10.1*
		(2891)	(1474)	(1417)					
	1891	**2529**	1270	1259	991	1881–91	***–12.5***	*–13.8*	*–11.2*

Boundary changes: 1881–91 loss of 222 to Talgarth (pop. 1881)
1891–1901 subdistrict abolished; loss of 1069 to Talgarth, loss of 1460 to Hay (pop. 1891)

Subdistrict	Year	Number Persons	Males	Females	Females/ 1000 males	Intercensal period	*Percentage change* Persons	Males	Females
Hay	1801	3539	1690	1849	1094				
	1811	3953	1899	2054	1082	1801–11	11.7	12.4	11.1
	1821	4565	2211	2354	1065	1811–21	15.5	16.4	14.6
	1831	4824	2360	2464	1044	1821–31	5.7	6.7	4.7
	1841	4953	2407	2546	1058	1831–41	2.7	2.0	3.3
	1851	4785	2317	2468	1065	1841–51	–3.4	–3.7	–3.1
	1861	4822	2342	2480	1059	1851–61	0.8	1.1	0.5
	1871	4755	2344	2411	1029	1861–71	–1.4	0.1	–2.8
	1881	4596	2201	2395	1088	1871–81	–3.3	–6.1	–0.7
	1891	4431	2100	2331	1110	1881–91	–3.6	–4.6	–2.7
		(5891)	(2845)	(3046)					
	1901	5632	2769	2863	1034	1891–1901	–4.4	–2.7	–6.0
	1911	5399	2669	2730	1023	1901–11	–4.1	–3.6	–4.6

Boundary changes: 1891–1901 gain of 1460 from Clyro (pop. 1891)

RADNORSHIRE

Presteigne District

Subdistrict	Year	Number Persons	Males	Females	Females/ 1000 males	Intercensal period	*Percentage change* Persons	Males	Females
Brilley	1801	1717	857	860	1004				
	1811	1750	875	875	1000	1801–11	1.9	2.1	1.7
	1821	1908	998	910	912	1811–21	9.0	14.1	4.0
	1831	2122	1052	1070	1017	1821–31	11.2	5.4	17.6
	1841	2117	1094	1023	935	1831–41	–0.2	4.0	–4.4
	1851	2095	1065	1030	967	1841–51	–1.0	–2.7	0.7
	1861	2067	1083	984	909	1851–61	–1.3	1.7	–4.5

Boundary changes: 1861–71 whole subdistrict transferred to the new district of Kington (Her)

Subdistrict	Year	Number Persons	Males	Females	Females/ 1000 males	Intercensal period	*Percentage change* Persons	Males	Females
Radnor	1801	3116	1546	1570	1016				
	1811	3286	1636	1650	1009	1801–11	5.5	5.8	5.1
	1821	3657	1850	1807	977	1811–21	11.3	13.1	9.5
	1831	3895	2017	1878	931	1821–31	6.5	9.0	3.9
	1841	3972	2069	1903	920	1831–41	2.0	2.6	1.3
	1851	3714	1947	1767	908	1841–51	–6.5	–5.9	–7.1
	1861	3567	1855	1712	923	1851–61	–4.0	–4.7	–3.1

Boundary changes: 1861–71 whole subdistrict transferred to the new district of Kington (Her)

Subdistrict	Year	Number Persons	Males	Females	Females/ 1000 males	Intercensal period	*Percentage change* Persons	Males	Females
Kington	1801	4510	2185	2325	1064				
	1811	4867	2364	2503	1059	1801–11	7.9	8.2	7.7
	1821	5601	2753	2848	1035	1811–21	15.1	16.5	13.8
	1831	6005	2948	3057	1037	1821–31	7.2	7.1	7.3
	1841	6128	3007	3121	1038	1831–41	2.0	2.0	2.1
	1851	5847	2916	2931	1005	1841–51	–4.6	–3.0	–6.1
	1861	6296	3153	3143	997	1851–61	7.7	8.1	7.2

Boundary changes: 1861–71 whole subdistrict transferred to the new district of Kington (Her)

Presteigne/Knighton District

Subdistrict	Year	Number Persons	Males	Females	Females/ 1000 males	Intercensal period	*Percentage change* Persons	Males	Females
Presteigne	1801	2764	1332	1432	1075				
	1811	2828	1352	1476	1092	1801–11	2.3	1.5	3.1
	1821	3204	1606	1598	995	1811–21	13.3	18.8	8.3
	1831	3562	1759	1803	1025	1821–31	11.2	9.5	12.8
	1841	3522	1750	1772	1013	1831–41	–1.1	–0.5	–1.7
	1851	3493	1763	1730	981	1841–51	–0.8	0.7	–2.4
	1861	3741	1915	1826	954	1851–61	7.1	8.6	5.5
	1871	3869	1941	1928	993	1861–71	3.4	1.4	5.6
		(2607)	(1278)	(1329)					
	1881	2336	1142	1194	1046	1871–81	–10.4	–10.6	–10.2
	1891	2042	981	1061	1082	1881–91	–12.6	–14.1	–11.1
	1901	1950	964	986	1023	1891–1901	–4.5	–1.7	–7.1
	1911	1809	887	922	1039	1901–11	–7.2	–8.0	–6.5

Boundary changes: 1871–81 loss of 1262 to Kington District (Her), remainder (2607) transferred to Knighton District with the abolition of Presteigne District (pop. 1871)

Subdistrict	Year	Number Persons	Males	Females	Females/ 1000 males	Intercensal period	*Percentage change* Persons	Males	Females
Knighton District									
Knighton	1801	**3691**	1811	1880	1038				
	1811	**3975**	1960	2015	1028	1801–11	***7.7***	*8.2*	*7.2*
	1821	**4277**	2194	2083	949	1811–21	***7.6***	*11.9*	*3.4*
	1831	**4645**	2394	2251	940	1821–31	***8.6***	*9.1*	*8.1*
	1841	**5038**	2614	2424	927	1831–41	***8.5***	*9.2*	*7.7*
	1851	**5316**	2748	2568	934	1841–51	***5.5***	*5.1*	*5.9*
	1861	**6009**	3190	2819	884	1851–61	***13.0***	*16.1*	*9.8*
	1871	**5966**	3053	2913	954	1861–71	***–0.7***	*–4.3*	*3.3*
	1881	**5724**	2940	2784	947	1871–81	***–4.1***	*–3.7*	*–4.4*
		(6115)	(3141)	(2974)					
	1891	**5768**	2883	2885	1001	1881–91	***–5.7***	*–8.2*	*–3.0*
	1901	**5927**	3006	2921	972	1891–1901	***2.8***	*4.3*	*1.2*
	1911	**5369**	2683	2686	1001	1901–11	***–9.4***	*–10.7*	*–8.0*

Boundary changes: 1881–91 gain of 391 from Llanbister (pop. 1881)

Subdistrict	Year	Number Persons	Males	Females	Females/ 1000 males	Intercensal period	Persons	Males	Females
Llanbister	1801	**2978**	1502	1476	983				
	1811	**3276**	1591	1685	1059	1801–11	***10.0***	*5.9*	*14.2*
	1821	**3690**	1846	1844	999	1811–21	***12.6***	*16.0*	*9.4*
	1831	**4074**	2067	2007	971	1821–31	***10.4***	*12.0*	*8.8*
	1841	**4277**	2219	2058	927	1831–41	***5.0***	*7.4*	*2.5*
	1851	**4164**	2199	1965	894	1841–51	***–2.6***	*–0.9*	*–4.5*
	1861	**4370**	2353	2017	857	1851–61	***4.9***	*7.0*	*2.6*
	1871	**4357**	2329	2028	871	1861–71	***–0.3***	*–1.0*	*0.5*
	1881	**3722**	1975	1747	885	1871–81	***–14.6***	*–15.2*	*–13.9*
		(3253)	(1737)	(1516)					
	1891	**2888**	1510	1378	913	1881–91	***–11.2***	*–13.1*	*–9.1*
	1901	**3018**	1625	1393	857	1891–1901	***4.5***	*7.6*	*1.1*
	1911	**2669**	1422	1247	877	1901–11	***–11.6***	*–12.5*	*–10.5*

Boundary changes: 1881–91 loss of 391 to Knighton, loss of 78 to Nantmel (pop. 1881)

Subdistrict	Year	Number Persons	Males	Females	Females/ 1000 males	Intercensal period	Persons	Males	Females
Rhayader District									
Rhayader	1801	**2282**	1067	1215	1139				
	1811	**2708**	1294	1414	1093	1801–11	***18.7***	*21.3*	*16.4*
	1821	**3094**	1533	1561	1018	1811–21	***14.3***	*18.5*	*10.4*
	1831	**3409**	1723	1686	979	1821–31	***10.2***	*12.4*	*8.0*
	1841	**3702**	1830	1872	1023	1831–41	***8.6***	*6.2*	*11.0*
	1851	**3689**	1862	1827	981	1841–51	***–0.4***	*1.7*	*–2.4*
	1861	**3639**	1829	1810	990	1851–61	***–1.4***	*–1.8*	*–0.9*
	1871	**3626**	1832	1794	979	1861–71	***–0.4***	*0.2*	*–0.9*
	1881	**3439**	1696	1743	1028	1871–81	***–5.2***	*–7.4*	*–2.8*
	1891	**3089**	1497	1592	1063	1881–91	***–10.2***	*–11.7*	*–8.7*
	1901[3]	**5328**	3178	2150	677	1891–1901	***72.5***	*112.3*	*35.1*
	1911	**2979**	1505	1474	979	1901–11	***–44.1***	*–52.6*	*–31.4*

No boundary changes

Subdistrict	Year	Number Persons	Males	Females	Females/ 1000 males	Intercensal period	Persons	Males	Females
Nantmel	1801	**2475**	1287	1188	923				
	1811	**2418**	1158	1260	1088	1801–11	***–2.3***	*–10.0*	*6.1*
	1821	**2634**	1289	1345	1043	1811–21	***8.9***	*11.3*	*6.7*
	1831	**2928**	1461	1467	1004	1821–31	***11.2***	*13.3*	*9.1*
	1841	**3020**	1533	1487	970	1831–41	***3.1***	*4.9*	*1.4*
	1851	**3107**	1618	1489	920	1841–51	***2.9***	*5.5*	*0.1*
	1861	**3177**	1678	1499	893	1851–61	***2.3***	*3.7*	*0.7*
	1871	**3198**	1656	1542	931	1861–71	***0.7***	*–1.3*	*2.9*
	1881	**3302**	1651	1651	1000	1871–81	***3.3***	*–0.3*	*7.1*
		(3380)	(1688)	(1692)					
	1891	**3332**	1615	1717	1063	1881–91	***–1.4***	*–4.3*	*1.5*
	1901	**4018**	1938	2080	1073	1891–1901	***20.6***	*20.0*	*21.1*
	1911	**4679**	2299	2380	1035	1901–11	***16.5***	*18.6*	*14.4*

Boundary changes: 1881–91 gain of 78 from Llanbister (pop. 1881)

Subdistrict	Year	Number Persons	Males	Females	Females/ 1000 males	Intercensal period	Percentage change *Persons*	*Males*	*Females*
MONTGOMERYSHIRE									
Machynlleth District									
Machynlleth	1801	**3077**	1394	1683	1207				
	1811	**3247**	1488	1759	1182	1801–11	***5.5***	*6.7*	*4.5*
	1821	**3851**	1857	1994	1074	1811–21	***18.6***	*24.8*	*13.4*
	1831	**3908**	1844	2064	1119	1821–31	***1.5***	*–0.7*	*3.5*
	1841	**3905**	1867	2038	1092	1831–41	***–0.1***	*1.2*	*–1.3*
	1851	**3981**	1939	2042	1053	1841–51	***1.9***	*3.9*	*0.2*
	1861	**4068**	2012	2056	1022	1851–61	***2.2***	*3.8*	*0.7*
	1871	**4624**	2291	2333	1018	1861–71	***13.7***	*13.9*	*13.5*
	1881	**4307**	2076	2231	1075	1871–81	***–6.9***	*–9.4*	*–4.4*
		(4335)	(2089)	(2246)					
	1891	**3599**	1695	1904	1123	1881–91	***–17.0***	*–18.9*	*–15.2*
	1901	**3525**	1680	1845	1098	1891–1901	***–2.1***	*–0.9*	*–3.1*
		(2564)	(1207)	(1357)					
	1911	**2411**	1120	1291	1153	1901–11	***–6.0***	*–7.2*	*–4.9*

Boundary changes: 1881–91 gain of 28 from Darowen (pop. 1881)
1901–11 loss of 581 to Darowen, loss of 380 to Tywyn (pop. 1901)

Subdistrict	Year	Number Persons	Males	Females	Females/ 1000 males	Intercensal period	Percentage change *Persons*	*Males*	*Females*
Pennal/Tywyn	1801	**3390**	1609	1781	1107				
	1811	**3232**	1491	1741	1168	1801–11	***–4.7***	*–7.3*	*–2.2*
	1821	**3858**	1913	1945	1017	1811–21	***19.4***	*28.3*	*11.7*
	1831	**4272**	2135	2137	1001	1821–31	***10.7***	*11.6*	*9.9*
	1841	**4407**	2144	2263	1056	1831–41	***3.2***	*0.4*	*5.9*
	1851	**4143**	2017	2126	1054	1841–51	***–6.0***	*–5.9*	*–6.1*
	1861	**4167**	2023	2144	1060	1851–61	***0.6***	*0.3*	*0.8*
	1871	**4730**	2258	2472	1095	1861–71	***13.5***	*11.6*	*15.3*
	1881	**4713**	2289	2424	1059	1871–81	***–0.4***	*1.4*	*–1.9*
		(4754)	(2311)	(2443)					
	1891	**4508**	2095	2413	1152	1881–91	***–5.2***	*–9.3*	*–1.2*
	1901	**4825**	2223	2602	1170	1891–1901	***7.0***	*6.1*	*7.8*
		(4646)	(2137)	(2509)					
	1911	**4777**	2127	2650	1246	1901–11	***2.8***	*–0.5*	*5.6*

Boundary changes: 1881–91 subdistrict renamed Tywyn; gain of 41 from Tal-y-llyn (Mer) (pop. 1881)
1901–11 gain of 380 from Machynlleth, loss of 559 to Darowen (pop. 1901)

Subdistrict	Year	Number Persons	Males	Females	Females/ 1000 males	Intercensal period	Percentage change *Persons*	*Males*	*Females*
Darowen	1801	**3421**	1658	1763	1063				
	1811	**3241**	1461	1780	1218	1801–11	***–5.3***	*–11.9*	*1.0*
	1821	**3673**	1804	1869	1036	1811–21	***13.3***	*23.5*	*5.0*
	1831	**3918**	1933	1985	1027	1821–31	***6.7***	*7.2*	*6.2*
	1841	**3995**	1935	2060	1065	1831–41	***2.0***	*0.1*	*3.8*
	1851	**3992**	1973	2019	1023	1841–51	***–0.1***	*2.0*	*–2.0*
	1861	**4160**	2143	2017	941	1851–61	***4.2***	*8.6*	*–0.1*
	1871	**3963**	2020	1943	962	1861–71	***–4.7***	*–5.7*	*–3.7*
	1881	**3497**	1715	1782	1039	1871–81	***–11.8***	*–15.1*	*–8.3*
		(3469)	(1702)	(1767)					
	1891	**2719**	1320	1399	1060	1881–91	***–21.6***	*–22.4*	*–20.8*
		(2840)	(1376)	(1464)					
	1901	**2691**	1315	1376	1046	1891–1901	***–5.2***	*–4.4*	*–6.0*
		(3831)	(1874)	(1957					
	1911	**3665**	1783	1882	1056	1901–11	***–4.3***	*–4.9*	*–3.8*

Boundary changes: 1881–91 loss of 28 to Machynlleth (pop. 1881)
1891–1901 gain of 121 from Tal-y-llyn (Mer) (pop. 1891)
1901–11 gain of 581 from Machynlleth, gain of 559 from Tywyn (pop. 1901)

Subdistrict	Year	Number Persons	Males	Females	Females/ 1000 males	Intercensal period	Percentage change *Persons*	*Males*	*Females*
Newtown District									
Upper and Lower Llanidloes[4]	1801	**5210**	2400	2810	1171				
	1811	**5599**	2665	2934	1101	1801–11	***7.5***	*11.0*	*4.4*
	1821	**6733**	3235	3498	1081	1811–21	***20.3***	*21.4*	*19.2*
	1831	**7856**	3788	4068	1074	1821–31	***16.7***	*17.1*	*16.3*
	1841	**8065**	3920	4145	1057	1831–41	***2.7***	*3.5*	*1.9*

Subdistrict	Year	Number Persons	Males	Females	Females/ 1000 males	Intercensal period	*Percentage change* *Persons*	*Males*	*Females*
Upper Llanidloes	1841	**4234**	2044	2190	1071	1831–41			
	1851	**4236**	2072	2164	1044	1841–51	***0.0***	*1.4*	*–1.2*
	1861	**3663**	1831	1832	1001	1851–61	***–13.5***	*–11.6*	*–15.3*
	1871	**4184**	2128	2056	966	1861–71	***14.2***	*16.2*	*12.2*
	1881	**3896**	1913	1983	1037	1871–81	***–6.9***	*–10.1*	*–3.6*
	1891	**3042**	1435	1607	1120	1881–91	***–21.9***	*–25.0*	*–19.0*

Boundary changes: 1891–1901 subdistrict joined with Lower Llanidloes to create the new subdistrict of Llanidloes

Subdistrict	Year	Number Persons	Males	Females	Females/ 1000 males	Intercensal period	*Persons*	*Males*	*Females*
Lower Llanidloes	1841	**3831**	1876	1955	1042	1831–41			
	1851	**3963**	2008	1955	974	1841–51	***3.4***	*7.0*	*0.0*
	1861	**3666**	1837	1829	996	1851–61	***–7.5***	*–8.5*	*–6.4*
	1871	**4207**	2154	2053	953	1861–71	***14.8***	*17.3*	*12.2*
	1881	**4471**	2236	2235	1000	1871–81	***6.3***	*3.8*	*8.9*
	1891	**3412**	1599	1813	1134	1881–91	***–23.7***	*–28.5*	*–18.9*

Boundary changes: 1891–1901 subdistrict joined with Upper Llanidloes to create the new subdistrict of Llanidloes

Subdistrict	Year	Number Persons	Males	Females	Females/ 1000 males	Intercensal period	*Persons*	*Males*	*Females*
Llanidloes	1891	(6454)	(3034)	(3420)					
	1901	**6313**	3039	3274	1077	1891–1901	***–2.2***	*0.2*	*–4.3*
	1911	**5881**	2843	3038	1069	1901–11	***–6.8***	*–6.4*	*–7.2*

Boundary changes: 1891–1901 subdistrict created from the joining subdistricts of Lower Llanidloes and Upper Llanidloes

Subdistrict	Year	Number Persons	Males	Females	Females/ 1000 males	Intercensal period	*Persons*	*Males*	*Females*
Llanwnnog	1801	**4109**	1951	2158	1106				
	1811	**4335**	2078	2257	1086	1801–11	***5.5***	*6.5*	*4.6*
	1821	**4582**	2250	2332	1036	1811–21	***5.7***	*8.3*	*3.3*
	1831	**4838**	2411	2427	1007	1821–31	***5.6***	*7.2*	*4.1*
	1841	**5111**	2552	2559	1003	1831–41	***5.6***	*5.8*	*5.4*
	1851	**4807**	2399	2408	1004	1841–51	***–5.9***	*–6.0*	*–5.9*
	1861	**4802**	2451	2351	959	1851–61	***–0.1***	*2.2*	*–2.4*
	1871	**4894**	2534	2360	931	1861–71	***1.9***	*3.4*	*0.4*
	1881	**4720**	2392	2328	973	1871–81	***–3.6***	*–5.6*	*–1.4*
	1891	**3971**	1987	1984	998	1881–91	***–15.9***	*–16.9*	*–14.8*
	1901	**3864**	1934	1930	998	1891–1901	***–2.7***	*–2.7*	*–2.7*
	1911	**4058**	2089	1969	943	1901–11	***5.0***	*8.0*	*2.0*

No boundary changes

Subdistrict	Year	Number Persons	Males	Females	Females/ 1000 males	Intercensal period	*Persons*	*Males*	*Females*
Kerry	1801	**2240**	1090	1150	1055				
	1811	**2331**	1099	1232	1121	1801–11	***4.1***	*0.8*	*7.1*
	1821	**2552**	1317	1235	938	1811–21	***9.5***	*19.8*	*0.2*
	1831	**2743**	1455	1288	885	1821–31	***7.5***	*10.5*	*4.3*
	1841	**2743**	1427	1316	922	1831–41	***0.0***	*–1.9*	*2.2*
	1851	**2449**	1265	1184	936	1841–51	***–10.7***	*–11.4*	*–10.0*
	1861	**2601**	1371	1230	897	1851–61	***6.2***	*8.4*	*3.9*
	1871	**2619**	1384	1235	892	1861–71	***0.7***	*0.9*	*0.4*
	1881	**2601**	1339	1262	942	1871–81	***–0.7***	*–3.3*	*2.2*
	1891	**2324**	1177	1147	975	1881–91	***–10.6***	*–12.1*	*–9.1*
	1901	**2128**	1067	1061	994	1891–1901	***–8.4***	*–9.3*	*–7.5*
	1911	**2086**	1072	1014	946	1901–11	***–2.0***	*0.5*	*–4.4*

No boundary changes

Subdistrict	Year	Number Persons	Males	Females	Females/ 1000 males	Intercensal period	*Persons*	*Males*	*Females*
Newtown	1801	**1665**	783	882	1126				
	1811	**2724**	1240	1484	1197	1801–11	***63.6***	*58.4*	*68.3*
	1821	**4493**	2232	2261	1013	1811–21	***64.9***	*80.0*	*52.4*
	1831	**6555**	3199	3356	1049	1821–31	***45.9***	*43.3*	*48.4*
	1841	**6842**	3309	3533	1068	1831–41	***4.4***	*3.4*	*5.3*
	1851	**6559**	3151	3408	1082	1841–51	***–4.1***	*–4.8*	*–3.5*
	1861	**6086**	2963	3123	1054	1851–61	***–7.2***	*–6.0*	*–8.4*
	1871	**5886**	2844	3042	1070	1861–71	***–3.3***	*–4.0*	*–2.6*
	1881	**7170**	3495	3675	1052	1871–81	***21.8***	*22.9*	*20.8*
	1891	**6610**	3051	3559	1167	1881–91	***–7.8***	*–12.7*	*–3.2*
	1901	**6500**	3011	3489	1159	1891–1901	***–1.7***	*–1.3*	*–2.0*
	1911	**6068**	2842	3226	1135	1901–11	***–6.6***	*–5.6*	*–7.5*

No boundary changes

Subdistrict	Year	Number Persons	Males	Females	Females/ 1000 males	Intercensal period	*Percentage change Persons*	*Males*	*Females*
Tregynon	1801	**2392**	1117	1275	1141				
	1811	**2865**	1385	1480	1069	1801–11	***19.8***	*24.0*	*16.1*
	1821	**3133**	1578	1555	985	1811–21	***9.4***	*13.9*	*5.1*
	1831	**3296**	1666	1630	978	1821–31	***5.2***	*5.6*	*4.8*
	1841	**3255**	1655	1600	967	1831–41	***–1.2***	*–0.7*	*–1.8*
	1851	**3093**	1591	1502	944	1841–51	***–5.0***	*–3.9*	*–6.1*
	1861	**2914**	1488	1426	958	1851–61	***–5.8***	*–6.5*	*–5.1*
	1871	**2764**	1420	1344	946	1861–71	***–5.1***	*–4.6*	*–5.8*
	1881	**2581**	1357	1224	902	1871–81	***–6.6***	*–4.4*	*–8.9*
	1891	**2363**	1160	1203	1037	1881–91	***–8.4***	*–14.5*	*–1.7*
	1901	**2313**	1182	1131	957	1891–1901	***–2.1***	*1.9*	*–6.0*
	1911	**2201**	1130	1071	948	1901–11	***–4.8***	*–4.4*	*–5.3*

No boundary changes

Subdistrict	Year	Number Persons	Males	Females	Females/ 1000 males	Intercensal period	*Persons*	*Males*	*Females*
Montgomery District									
Montgomery	1801	**4997**	2348	2649	1128				
	1811	**5456**	2692	2764	1027	1801–11	***9.2***	*14.7*	*4.3*
	1821	**6066**	3054	3012	986	1811–21	***11.2***	*13.4*	*9.0*
	1831	**6451**	3274	3177	970	1821–31	***6.3***	*7.2*	*5.5*
	1841	**6280**	3164	3116	985	1831–41	***–2.7***	*–3.4*	*–1.9*
	1851	**6109**	3096	3013	973	1841–51	***–2.7***	*–2.1*	*–3.3*
	1861	**6121**	3178	2943	926	1851–61	***0.2***	*2.6*	*–2.3*
	1871	**5914**	2982	2932	983	1861–71	***–3.4***	*–6.2*	*–0.4*
	1881	**5721**	2932	2789	951	1871–81	***–3.3***	*–1.7*	*–4.9*
	1891	**5144**	2589	2555	987	1881–91	***–10.1***	*–11.7*	*–8.4*
	1901	**4717**	2327	2390	1027	1891–1901	***–8.3***	*–10.1*	*–6.5*
		(4631)	(2279)	(2352)					
	1911	**4515**	2248	2267	1008	1901–11	***–2.5***	*–1.4*	*–3.6*

Boundary changes: 1901–11 loss of 86 to Welshpool (pop. 1901)

Subdistrict	Year	Number Persons	Males	Females	Females/ 1000 males	Intercensal period	*Persons*	*Males*	*Females*
Chirbury	1801	**4242**	2185	2057	941				
	1811	**3934**	2022	1912	946	1801–11	***–7.3***	*–7.5*	*–7.0*
	1821	**4159**	2151	2008	934	1811–21	***5.7***	*6.4*	*5.0*
	1831	**4887**	2556	2331	912	1821–31	***17.5***	*18.8*	*16.1*
	1841	**5395**	2786	2609	936	1831–41	***10.4***	*9.0*	*11.9*
	1851	**5441**	2834	2607	920	1841–51	***0.9***	*1.7*	*–0.1*
	1861	**5756**	3019	2737	907	1851–61	***5.8***	*6.5*	*5.0*
	1871	**5921**	3127	2794	894	1861–71	***2.9***	*3.6*	*2.1*
	1881	**5712**	3042	2670	878	1871–81	***–3.5***	*–2.7*	*–4.4*
		(5707)	(3040)	(2667)					
	1891	**4863**	2473	2390	966	1881–91	***–14.8***	*–18.7*	*–10.4*
	1901	**4188**	2146	2042	952	1891–1901	***–13.9***	*–13.2*	*–14.6*
	1911	**3997**	2021	1976	978	1901–11	***–4.6***	*–5.8*	*–3.2*

Boundary changes: 1881–91 loss of 5 to Atcham District (Salop) (pop. 1881)

Subdistrict	Year	Number Persons	Males	Females	Females/ 1000 males	Intercensal period	*Persons*	*Males*	*Females*
Welshpool	1801	**6153**	2939	3214	1094				
	1811	**6567**	3198	3369	1053	1801–11	***6.7***	*8.8*	*4.8*
	1821	**8055**	4010	4045	1009	1811–21	***22.7***	*25.4*	*20.1*
	1831	**8859**	4315	4544	1053	1821–31	***10.0***	*7.6*	*12.3*
	1841	**9308**	4570	4738	1037	1831–41	***5.1***	*5.9*	*4.3*
	1851	**8831**	4372	4459	1020	1841–51	***–5.1***	*–4.3*	*–5.9*
		(6434)	(3185)	(3249)					
	1861	**7220**	3667	3553	969	1851–61	***12.2***	*15.1*	*9.4*
	1871	**7023**	3464	3559	1027	1861–71	***–2.7***	*–5.5*	*0.2*
	1881	**6848**	3471	3377	973	1871–81	***–2.5***	*0.2*	*–5.1*
	1891	**6306**	3080	3226	1047	1881–91	***–7.9***	*–11.3*	*–4.5*
	1901	**5939**	2881	3058	1061	1891–1901	***–5.8***	*–6.5*	*–5.2*
		(6025)	(2929)	(3096)					
	1911	**5859**	2855	3004	1052	1901–11	***–2.8***	*–2.5*	*–3.0*

Boundary changes: 1851–61 loss of 2397 to Llansanffraid (pop. 1851)
1901–11 gain of 86 from Montgomery (pop. 1901)

Subdistrict	Year	Number Persons	Males	Females	Females/ 1000 males	Intercensal period	*Percentage change* Persons	Males	Females
Llanfyllin District									
Llanfair	1801	**5600**	2739	2861	1045				
	1811	**5349**	2577	2772	1076	1801–11	***–4.5***	*–5.9*	*–3.1*
	1821	**6395**	3153	3242	1028	1811–21	***19.6***	*22.4*	*17.0*
	1831	**6666**	3348	3318	991	1821–31	***4.2***	*6.2*	*2.3*
	1841	**6888**	3427	3461	1010	1831–41	***3.3***	*2.4*	*4.3*
	1851	**6697**	3385	3312	978	1841–51	***–2.8***	*–1.2*	*–4.3*
	1861	**6375**	3197	3178	994	1851–61	***–4.8***	*–5.6*	*–4.0*
	1871	**6100**	3118	2982	956	1861–71	***–4.3***	*–2.5*	*–6.2*
	1881	**5587**	2808	2779	990	1871–81	***–8.4***	*–9.9*	*–6.8*
	1891	**5033**	2507	2526	1008	1881–91	***–9.9***	*–10.7*	*–9.1*
	1901	**4496**	2244	2252	1004	1891–1901	***–10.7***	*–10.5*	*–10.8*
	1911	**4391**	2236	2155	964	1901–11	***–2.3***	*–0.4*	*–4.3*

No boundary changes

Subdistrict	Year	Number Persons	Males	Females	Females/ 1000 males	Intercensal period	Persons	Males	Females
Llansanffraid	1801	**5791**	2861	2930	1024				
	1811	**6182**	2980	3202	1074	1801–11	***6.8***	*4.2*	*9.3*
	1821	**6947**	3485	3462	993	1811–21	***12.4***	*16.9*	*8.1*
	1831	**7590**	3778	3812	1009	1821–31	***9.3***	*8.4*	*10.1*
	1841	**7989**	3935	4054	1030	1831–41	***5.3***	*4.2*	*6.3*
	1851	**7466**	3711	3755	1012	1841–51	***–6.5***	*–5.7*	*–7.4*
		(9863)	(4898)	(4965)					
	1861	**10223**	5115	5108	999	1851–61	***3.7***	*4.4*	*2.9*
	1871	**10447**	5186	5261	1014	1861–71	***2.2***	*1.4*	*3.0*
	1881	**9583**	4786	4797	1002	1871–81	***–8.3***	*–7.7*	*–8.8*
	1891	**9098**	4398	4700	1069	1881–91	***–5.1***	*–8.1*	*–2.0*
	1901	**8616**	4158	4458	1072	1891–1901	***–5.3***	*–5.5*	*–5.1*
	1911	**8405**	4154	4251	1023	1901–11	***–2.4***	*–0.1*	*–4.6*

Boundary changes: 1851–61 gain of 2397 from Welshpool (pop. 1851)

Subdistrict	Year	Number Persons	Males	Females	Females/ 1000 males	Intercensal period	Persons	Males	Females
Llanrhaeadr	1801	**3754**	1811	1943	1073				
	1811	**4303**	2110	2193	1039	1801–11	***14.6***	*16.5*	*12.9*
	1821	**4852**	2401	2451	1021	1811–21	***12.8***	*13.8*	*11.8*
	1831	**5282**	2710	2572	949	1821–31	***8.9***	*12.9*	*4.9*
	1841	**5573**	2797	2776	992	1831–41	***5.5***	*3.2*	*7.9*
	1851	**5375**	2728	2647	970	1841–51	***–3.6***	*–2.5*	*–4.6*
	1861	**5101**	2592	2509	968	1851–61	***–5.1***	*–5.0*	*–5.2*
	1871	**5124**	2597	2527	973	1861–71	***0.5***	*0.2*	*0.7*
	1881	**4789**	2444	2345	959	1871–81	***–6.5***	*–5.9*	*–7.2*
		(4754)	(2424)	(2330)					
	1891	**4305**	2155	2150	998	1881–91	***–9.4***	*–11.1*	*–7.7*
	1901	**3879**	1988	1891	951	1891–1901	***–9.9***	*–7.7*	*–12.0*
	1911	**3887**	2016	1871	928	1901–11	***0.2***	*1.4*	*–1.1*

Boundary changes: 1881–91 loss of 35 to Oswestry District (Salop) (pop. 1881)

Subdistrict	Year	Number Persons	Males	Females	Females/ 1000 males	Intercensal period	Persons	Males	Females
FLINTSHIRE									
Holywell District									
Whitford	1801	**5322**	2650	2672	1008				
	1811	**5479**	2688	2791	1038	1801–11	***3.0***	*1.4*	*4.5*
	1821	**6430**	3217	3213	999	1811–21	***17.4***	*19.7*	*15.1*
	1831	**7569**	3840	3729	971	1821–31	***17.7***	*19.4*	*16.1*
	1841	**8758**	4497	4261	948	1831–41	***15.7***	*17.1*	*14.3*
	1851	**8583**	4364	4219	967	1841–51	***–2.0***	*–3.0*	*–1.0*
	1861	**8043**	4031	4012	995	1851–61	***–6.3***	*–7.6*	*–4.9*
	1871	**8623**	4339	4284	987	1861–71	***7.2***	*7.6*	*6.8*
	1881	**8437**	4212	4225	1003	1871–81	***–2.2***	*–2.9*	*–1.4*
	1891	**7113**	3457	3656	1058	1881–91	***–15.7***	*–17.9*	*–13.5*
	1901	**7544**	3683	3861	1048	1891–1901	***6.1***	*6.5*	*5.6*
	1911	**7728**	3752	3976	1060	1901–11	***2.4***	*1.9*	*3.0*

No boundary changes

Subdistrict	Year	Number Persons	Males	Females	Females/ 1000 males	Intercensal period	*Percentage change* *Persons*	*Males*	*Females*
Holywell	1801	**6616**	3085	3531	1145				
	1811	**8387**	3899	4488	1151	1801–11	***26.8***	*26.4*	*27.1*
	1821	**10574**	5142	5432	1056	1811–21	***26.1***	*31.9*	*21.0*
	1831	**11213**	5486	5727	1044	1821–31	***6.0***	*6.7*	*5.4*
	1841	**12950**	6595	6355	964	1831–41	***15.5***	*20.2*	*11.0*
	1851	**13342**	6733	6609	982	1841–51	***3.0***	*2.1*	*4.0*
	1861	**12100**	6113	5987	979	1851–61	***–9.3***	*–9.2*	*–9.4*
	1871	**11680**	5920	5760	973	1861–71	***–3.5***	*–3.2*	*–3.8*
	1881	**11566**	5778	5788	1002	1871–81	***–1.0***	*–2.4*	*0.5*
	1891	**10929**	5400	5529	1024	1881–91	***–5.5***	*–6.5*	*–4.5*
		(10607)	(5233)	(5374)					
	1901	**9311**	4565	4746	1040	1891–1901	***–12.2***	*–12.8*	*–11.7*
	1911	**9809**	4877	4932	1011	1901–11	***5.3***	*6.8*	*3.9*

Boundary changes: 1891–1901 loss of 322 to Flint (pop. 1891)

Subdistrict	Year	Number Persons	Males	Females	Females/ 1000 males	Intercensal period	*Persons*	*Males*	*Females*
Flint	1801	**4537**	2298	2239	974				
	1811	**5483**	2753	2730	992	1801–11	***20.9***	*19.8*	*21.9*
	1821	**6348**	3237	3111	961	1811–21	***15.8***	*17.6*	*14.0*
	1831	**6780**	3449	3331	966	1821–31	***6.8***	*6.5*	*7.1*
	1841	**8239**	4151	4088	985	1831–41	***21.5***	*20.4*	*22.7*
	1851	**8189**	4188	4001	955	1841–51	***–0.6***	*0.9*	*–2.1*
	1861	**8079**	4015	4064	1012	1851–61	***–1.3***	*–4.1*	*1.6*
	1871	**9380**	4794	4586	957	1861–71	***16.1***	*19.4*	*12.8*
	1881	**11162**	5743	5419	944	1871–81	***19.0***	*19.8*	*18.2*
	1891	**11386**	5813	5573	959	1881–91	***2.0***	*1.2*	*2.8*
		(11708)	(5980)	(5728)					
	1901	**12071**	6083	5988	984	1891–1901	***3.1***	*1.7*	*4.5*
	1911	**14216**	7204	7012	973	1901–11	***17.8***	*18.4*	*17.1*

Boundary changes: 1891–1901 gain of 322 from Holywell (pop. 1891)

Subdistrict	Year	Number Persons	Males	Females	Females/ 1000 males	Intercensal period	*Persons*	*Males*	*Females*
Mold	1801	**5688**	2748	2940	1070				
	1811	**6808**	3198	3610	1129	1801–11	***19.7***	*16.4*	*22.8*
	1821	**7826**	3883	3943	1015	1811–21	***15.0***	*21.4*	*9.2*
	1831	**9745**	4852	4893	1008	1821–31	***24.5***	*25.0*	*24.1*
	1841	**10851**	5430	5421	998	1831–41	***11.3***	*11.9*	*10.8*
	1851	**10933**	5502	5431	987	1841–51	***0.8***	*1.3*	*0.2*
	1861	**11719**	5838	5881	1007	1851–61	***7.2***	*6.1*	*8.3*
	1871	**13834**	7066	6768	958	1861–71	***18.0***	*21.0*	*15.1*
	1881	**14609**	7484	7125	952	1871–81	***5.6***	*5.9*	*5.3*
	1891	**13137**	6703	6434	960	1881–91	***–10.1***	*–10.4*	*–9.7*
	1901	**13335**	6798	6537	962	1891–1901	***1.5***	*1.4*	*1.6*
		(10009)	(5081)	(4928)					
	1911	**11065**	5499	5566	1012	1901–11	***10.6***	*8.2*	*12.9*

Boundary changes: 1901–11 loss of 3326 to the new subdistrict of Hawarden (previously transferred to Chester District, July 1901)

Subdistrict	Year	Number Persons	Males	Females	Females/ 1000 males	Intercensal period	*Persons*	*Males*	*Females*
Hawarden District									
Hawarden	1901	(21601)	(11267)	(10334)					
	1911	**26904**	14108	12796	907	1901–11	***24.5***	*25.2*	*23.8*

Boundary changes: 1901–11 new district with one subdistrict created, from Chester District (Ches) (3326 of which had been transferred from Mold in July 1901)

Subdistrict	Year	Number Persons	Males	Females	Females/ 1000 males	Intercensal period	*Persons*	*Males*	*Females*
DENBIGHSHIRE									
Wrexham District									
Hope	1801	**5932**	2963	2969	1002				
	1811	**6638**	3263	3375	1034	1801–11	***11.9***	*10.1*	*13.7*
	1821	**7324**	3703	3621	978	1811–21	***10.3***	*13.5*	*7.3*
	1831	**8290**	4170	4120	988	1821–31	***13.2***	*12.6*	*13.8*
	1841	**8874**	4588	4286	934	1831–41	***7.0***	*10.0*	*4.0*
	1851	**9566**	4904	4662	951	1841–51	***7.8***	*6.9*	*8.8*
	1861	**11297**	5747	5550	966	1851–61	***18.1***	*17.2*	*19.0*

Boundary changes: 1861–71 subdistrict abolished; loss of 2117 to Holt, loss of 4277 to Wrexham, loss of 4903 to Hawarden (Ches) (pop. 1861)

Subdistrict	Year	Number Persons	Males	Females	Females/ 1000 males	Intercensal period	*Percentage change* *Persons*	*Males*	*Females*
Malpas/Holt	1801	**5930**	2885	3045	1055				
	1811	**6136**	2955	3181	1076	1801–11	***3.5***	*2.4*	*4.5*
	1821	**6910**	3466	3444	994	1811–21	***12.6***	*17.3*	*8.3*
	1831	**7142**	3523	3619	1027	1821–31	***3.4***	*1.6*	*5.1*
	1841	**7009**	3465	3544	1023	1831–41	***–1.9***	*–1.6*	*–2.1*
	1851	**6824**	3417	3407	997	1841–51	***–2.6***	*–1.4*	*–3.9*
		(4607)	(2314)	(2293)					
	1861	**4452**	2200	2252	1024	1851–61	***–3.4***	*–4.9*	*–1.8*
		(6569)	(3216)	(3353)					
	1871	**6760**	3247	3513	1082	1861–71	***2.9***	*1.0*	*4.8*
	1881	**6616**	3211	3405	1060	1871–81	***–2.1***	*–1.1*	*–3.1*
		(6658)	(3237)	(3421)					
	1891	**6901**	3333	3568	1071	1881–91	***3.6***	*3.0*	*4.3*
		(5306)	(2583)	(2723)					
	1901	**5406**	2634	2772	1052	1891–1901	***1.9***	*2.0*	*1.8*
	1911	**5852**	2876	2976	1035	1901–11	***8.3***	*9.2*	*7.4*

Boundary changes: 1851–61 subdistrict renamed Holt; loss of 2217 to Whitchurch District (Salop) (pop. 1851)
1861–71 gain of 2117 from Hope (pop. 1861)
1881–91 gain of 42 from Chester District (Ches) (pop. 1881)
1891–1901 loss of 316 to Chester (Ches), loss of 973 to Ellesmere (Salop), loss of 306 to Whitchurch (Salop) (pop. 1891)

Subdistrict	Year	Number Persons	Males	Females	Females/ 1000 males	Intercensal period	*Persons*	*Males*	*Females*
Ruabon	1801	**4795**	2281	2514	1102				
	1811	**5146**	2552	2594	1016	1801–11	***7.3***	*11.9*	*3.2*
	1821	**7581**	3807	3774	991	1811–21	***47.3***	*49.2*	*45.5*
	1831	**8751**	4416	4335	982	1821–31	***15.4***	*16.0*	*14.9*
	1841	**11715**	5863	5852	998	1831–41	***33.9***	*32.8*	*35.0*
	1851	**11875**	6070	5805	956	1841–51	***1.4***	*3.5*	*–0.8*
	1861	**14680**	7601	7079	931	1851–61	***23.6***	*25.2*	*21.9*
	1871	**15494**	7976	7518	943	1861–71	***5.5***	*4.9*	*6.2*
	1881	**15485**	8046	7439	925	1871–81	***–0.1***	*0.9*	*–1.1*
	1891	**17609**	9199	8410	914	1881–91	***13.7***	*14.3*	*13.1*
	1901	**21721**	11443	10278	898	1891–1901	***23.4***	*24.4*	*22.2*
	1911	**23928**	12516	11412	912	1901–11	***10.2***	*9.4*	*11.0*

No boundary changes

Subdistrict	Year	Number Persons	Males	Females	Females/ 1000 males	Intercensal period	*Persons*	*Males*	*Females*
Wrexham	1801	**7672**	3632	4040	1112				
	1811	**8272**	3904	4368	1119	1801–11	***7.8***	*7.5*	*8.1*
	1821	**10247**	5004	5243	1048	1811–21	***23.9***	*28.2*	*20.0*
	1831	**10656**	5194	5462	1052	1821–31	***4.0***	*3.8*	*4.2*
	1841	**11960**	5875	6085	1036	1831–41	***12.2***	*13.1*	*11.4*
	1851	**14030**	7024	7006	997	1841–51	***17.3***	*19.6*	*15.1*
	1861	**17546**	9003	8543	949	1851–61	***25.1***	*28.2*	*21.9*
		(21823)	(11240)	(10583)					
	1871	**26583**	13485	13098	971	1861–71	***21.8***	*20.0*	*23.8*
	1881	**33057**	17068	15989	937	1871–81	***24.4***	*26.6*	*22.1*
	1891	**37285**	19569	17716	905	1881–91	***12.8***	*14.7*	*10.8*
	1901	**43027**	22191	20836	939	1891–1901	***15.4***	*13.4*	*17.6*
	1911	**49274**	25511	23763	931	1901–11	***14.5***	*15.0*	*14.0*

Boundary changes: 1861–71 gain of 4277 from Hope (pop. 1861)

Ruthin District

Subdistrict	Year	Number Persons	Males	Females	Females/ 1000 males	Intercensal period	*Persons*	*Males*	*Females*
Llanarmon	1801	**2022**	1012	1010	998				
	1811	**2216**	1096	1120	1022	1801–11	***9.6***	*8.3*	*10.9*
	1821	**2608**	1320	1288	976	1811–21	***17.7***	*20.4*	*15.0*
	1831	**2651**	1385	1266	914	1821–31	***1.6***	*4.9*	*–1.7*
	1841	**3018**	1580	1438	910	1831–41	***13.8***	*14.1*	*13.6*
	1851	**3360**	1731	1629	941	1841–51	***11.3***	*9.6*	*13.3*
	1861	**3198**	1648	1550	941	1851–61	***–4.8***	*–4.8*	*–4.8*
	1871	**3128**	1606	1522	948	1861–71	***–2.2***	*–2.5*	*–1.8*
	1881	**2714**	1404	1310	933	1871–81	***–13.2***	*–12.6*	*–13.9*
	1891	**2264**	1152	1112	965	1881–91	***–16.6***	*–17.9*	*–15.1*
	1901	**2010**	1020	990	971	1891–1901	***–11.2***	*–11.5*	*–11.0*
	1911	**1838**	925	913	987	1901–11	***–8.6***	*–9.3*	*–7.8*

No boundary changes

Subdistrict	Year	Number Persons	Males	Females	Females/ 1000 males	Intercensal period	*Percentage change Persons*	*Males*	*Females*
Ruthin	1801	**3477**	1618	1859	1149				
	1811	**3507**	1662	1845	1110	1801–11	***0.9***	*2.7*	*–0.8*
	1821	**4276**	2012	2264	1125	1811–21	***21.9***	*21.1*	*22.7*
	1831	**4676**	2206	2470	1120	1821–31	***9.4***	*9.6*	*9.1*
	1841	**4592**	2205	2387	1083	1831–41	***–1.8***	*0.0*	*–3.4*
	1851	**4666**	2222	2444	1100	1841–51	***1.6***	*0.8*	*2.4*
	1861	**4438**	2163	2275	1052	1851–61	***–4.9***	*–2.7*	*–6.9*
	1871	**4422**	2205	2217	1005	1861–71	***–0.4***	*1.9*	*–2.5*
	1881	**4038**	1946	2092	1075	1871–81	***–8.7***	*–11.7*	*–5.6*
	1891	**3716**	1781	1935	1086	1881–91	***–8.0***	*–8.5*	*–7.5*
	1901	**3474**	1670	1804	1080	1891–1901	***–6.5***	*–6.2*	*–6.8*
		(3935)	(1914)	(2021)					
	1911	**4257**	2050	2207	1077	1901–11	***8.2***	*7.1*	*9.2*

Boundary changes: 1901–11 gain of 12 from Llanelidan, gain of 438 from Gyffylliog, gain of 11 from Llanrhaeadr (pop. 1901)

Subdistrict	Year	Number Persons	Males	Females	Females/ 1000 males	Intercensal period	*Percentage change Persons*	*Males*	*Females*
Llanelidan	1801	**2189**	1072	1117	1042				
	1811	**2238**	1132	1106	977	1801–11	***2.2***	*5.6*	*–1.0*
	1821	**2672**	1303	1369	1051	1811–21	***19.4***	*15.1*	*23.8*
	1831	**2509**	1233	1276	1035	1821–31	***–6.1***	*–5.4*	*–6.8*
	1841	**2785**	1389	1396	1005	1831–41	***11.0***	*12.7*	*9.4*
	1851	**2818**	1423	1395	980	1841–51	***1.2***	*2.4*	*–0.1*
	1861	**2684**	1361	1323	972	1851–61	***–4.8***	*–4.4*	*–5.2*
	1871	**2598**	1344	1254	933	1861–71	***–3.2***	*–1.2*	*–5.2*
	1881	**2418**	1199	1219	1017	1871–81	***–6.9***	*–10.8*	*–2.8*
	1891	**2148**	1091	1057	969	1881–91	***–11.2***	*–9.0*	*–13.3*
	1901	**2054**	1018	1036	1018	1891–1901	***–4.4***	*–6.7*	*–2.0*
		(2415)	(1212)	(1203)					
	1911	**2372**	1181	1191	1008	1901–11	***–1.8***	*–2.6*	*–1.0*

Boundary changes: 1901–11 gain of 373 from Gyffylliog, loss of 12 to Ruthin (pop. 1901)

Subdistrict	Year	Number Persons	Males	Females	Females/ 1000 males	Intercensal period	*Percentage change Persons*	*Males*	*Females*
Gyffylliog	1801	**1239**	608	631	1038				
	1811	**1321**	663	658	992	1801–11	***6.6***	*9.0*	*4.3*
	1821	**1399**	727	672	924	1811–21	***5.9***	*9.7*	*2.1*
	1831	**1442**	720	722	1003	1821–31	***3.1***	*–1.0*	*7.4*
	1841	**1481**	752	729	969	1831–41	***2.7***	*4.4*	*1.0*
	1851	**1376**	687	689	1003	1841–51	***–7.1***	*–8.6*	*–5.5*
	1861	**1326**	674	652	967	1851–61	***–3.6***	*–1.9*	*–5.4*
	1871	**1294**	670	624	931	1861–71	***–2.4***	*–0.6*	*–4.3*
	1881	**1189**	621	568	915	1871–81	***–8.1***	*–7.3*	*–9.0*
	1891	**1038**	524	514	981	1881–91	***–12.7***	*–15.6*	*–9.5*
	1901	**1050**	565	485	858	1891–1901	***1.2***	*7.8*	*–5.6*

Boundary changes: 1901–11 subdistrict abolished; loss of 438 to Ruthin, loss of 373 to Llanelidan, loss of 239 to Llanrhaeadr (pop. 1901)

Subdistrict	Year	Number Persons	Males	Females	Females/ 1000 males	Intercensal period	*Percentage change Persons*	*Males*	*Females*
Llanrhaeadr	1801	**2476**	1226	1250	1020				
	1811	**2462**	1210	1252	1035	1801–11	***–0.6***	*–1.3*	*0.2*
	1821	**2704**	1312	1392	1061	1811–21	***9.8***	*8.4*	*11.2*
	1831	**2874**	1429	1445	1011	1821–31	***6.3***	*8.9*	*3.8*
	1841	**2788**	1412	1376	975	1831–41	***–3.0***	*–1.2*	*–4.8*
	1851	**2678**	1360	1318	969	1841–51	***–3.9***	*–3.7*	*–4.2*
	1861	**2611**	1382	1229	889	1851–61	***–2.5***	*1.6*	*–6.8*
	1871	**2371**	1197	1174	981	1861–71	***–9.2***	*–13.4*	*–4.5*
	1881	**2379**	1238	1141	922	1871–81	***0.3***	*3.4*	*–2.8*
	1891	**2294**	1169	1125	962	1881–91	***–3.6***	*–5.6*	*–1.4*
	1901	**2079**	1053	1026	974	1891–1901	***–9.4***	*–9.9*	*–8.8*
		(2307)	(1180)	(1127)					
	1911	**2411**	1236	1175	951	1901–11	***4.5***	*4.7*	*4.3*

Boundary changes: 1901–11 loss of 11 to Ruthin, gain of 239 from Gyffylliog (pop. 1901)

Subdistrict	Year	Number Persons	Males	Females	Females/ 1000 males	Intercensal period	*Percentage change Persons*	*Males*	*Females*
Llandyrnog	1801	**1691**	882	809	917				
	1811	**1673**	790	883	1118	1801–11	***–1.1***	*–10.4*	*9.1*
	1821	**1814**	927	887	957	1811–21	***8.4***	*17.3*	*0.5*
	1831	**1961**	974	987	1013	1821–31	***8.1***	*5.1*	*11.3*
	1841	**1945**	960	985	1026	1831–41	***–0.8***	*–1.4*	*–0.2*
	1851	**1955**	971	984	1013	1841–51	***0.5***	*1.1*	*–0.1*
	1861	**1826**	918	908	989	1851–61	***–6.6***	*–5.5*	*–7.7*
	1871	**1586**	792	794	1003	1861–71	***–13.1***	*–13.7*	*–12.6*
	1881	**1477**	752	725	964	1871–81	***–6.9***	*–5.1*	*–8.7*
	1891	**1478**	745	733	984	1881–91	***0.1***	*–0.9*	*1.1*
	1901	**1421**	743	678	913	1891–1901	***–3.9***	*–0.3*	*–7.5*
	1911	**1326**	657	669	1018	1901–11	***–6.7***	*–11.6*	*–1.3*

No boundary changes

St Asaph District

Subdistrict	Year	Number Persons	Males	Females	Females/ 1000 males	Intercensal period	*Percentage change Persons*	*Males*	*Females*
St Asaph	1801	**5068**	2543	2525	993				
	1811	**5390**	2592	2798	1079	1801–11	***6.4***	*1.9*	*10.8*
	1821	**6787**	3340	3447	1032	1811–21	***25.9***	*28.9*	*23.2*
	1831	**7559**	3749	3810	1016	1821–31	***11.4***	*12.2*	*10.5*
	1841	**9040**	4502	4538	1008	1831–41	***19.6***	*20.1*	*19.1*
	1851	**10518**	5210	5308	1019	1841–51	***16.3***	*15.7*	*17.0*
	1861	**11922**	5738	6184	1078	1851–61	***13.3***	*10.1*	*16.5*
	1871	**12722**	5928	6794	1146	1861–71	***6.7***	*3.3*	*9.9*
	1881	**14230**	6579	7651	1163	1871–81	***11.9***	*11.0*	*12.6*
	1891	**13993**	6335	7658	1209	1881–91	***–1.7***	*–3.7*	*0.1*
	1901	**16372**	7474	8898	1191	1891–1901	***17.0***	*18.0*	*16.2*
	1911	**18284**	8055	10229	1270	1901–11	***11.7***	*7.8*	*15.0*

No boundary changes

Subdistrict	Year	Number Persons	Males	Females	Females/ 1000 males	Intercensal period	*Percentage change Persons*	*Males*	*Females*
Abergele	1801	**4038**	1981	2057	1038				
	1811	**4263**	2053	2210	1076	1801–11	***5.6***	*3.6*	*7.4*
	1821	**4961**	2488	2473	994	1811–21	***16.4***	*21.2*	*11.9*
	1831	**5456**	2742	2714	990	1821–31	***10.0***	*10.2*	*9.7*
	1841	**5899**	3010	2889	960	1831–41	***8.1***	*9.8*	*6.4*
	1851	**6163**	3104	3059	986	1841–51	***4.5***	*3.1*	*5.9*
	1861	**6543**	3225	3318	1029	1851–61	***6.2***	*3.9*	*8.5*
	1871	**6083**	2973	3110	1046	1861–71	***–7.0***	*–7.8*	*–6.3*
	1881	**6004**	2897	3107	1072	1871–81	***–1.3***	*–2.6*	*–0.1*
	1891	**5938**	2883	3055	1060	1881–91	***–1.1***	*–0.5*	*–1.7*
	1901	**5740**	2786	2954	1060	1891–1901	***–3.3***	*–3.4*	*–3.3*
	1911	**5572**	2676	2896	1082	1901–11	***–2.9***	*–3.9*	*–2.0*

No boundary changes

Subdistrict	Year	Number Persons	Males	Females	Females/ 1000 males	Intercensal period	*Percentage change Persons*	*Males*	*Females*
Denbigh	1801	**6450**	3039	3411	1122				
	1811	**7057**	3299	3758	1139	1801–11	***9.4***	*8.6*	*10.2*
	1821	**8047**	3840	4207	1096	1811–21	***14.0***	*16.4*	*11.9*
	1831	**9002**	4183	4819	1152	1821–31	***11.9***	*8.9*	*14.5*
	1841	**8608**	4181	4427	1059	1831–41	***–4.4***	*0.0*	*–8.1*
	1851	**8607**	4299	4308	1002	1841–51	***0.0***	*2.8*	*–2.7*
	1861	**9053**	4497	4556	1013	1851–61	***5.2***	*4.6*	*5.8*
	1871	**9073**	4455	4618	1037	1861–71	***0.2***	*–0.9*	*1.4*
	1881	**9224**	4459	4765	1069	1871–81	***1.7***	*0.1*	*3.2*
	1891	**9023**	4320	4703	1089	1881–91	***–2.2***	*–3.1*	*–1.3*
	1901	**8934**	4305	4629	1075	1891–1901	***–1.0***	*–0.3*	*–1.6*
	1911	**9370**	4584	4786	1044	1901–11	***4.9***	*6.5*	*3.4*

No boundary changes

Subdistrict	Year	Number Persons	Males	Females	Females/ 1000 males	Intercensal period	*Percentage change Persons*	*Males*	*Females*
Llanrwst									
Llanrwst District	1801	**5151**	2500	2651	1060				
	1801	**5151**	2500	2651	1060				
	1811	**5448**	2575	2873	1116	1801–11	***5.8***	*3.0*	*8.4*
	1821	**6173**	3008	3165	1052	1811–21	***13.3***	*16.8*	*10.2*
	1831	**6477**	3200	3277	1024	1821–31	***4.9***	*6.4*	*3.5*
	1841	**6927**	3364	3563	1059	1831–41	***6.9***	*5.1*	*8.7*
	1851	**7083**	3538	3545	1002	1841–51	***2.3***	*5.2*	*–0.5*
	1861	**7100**	3500	3600	1029	1851–61	***0.2***	*–1.1*	*1.6*
	1871	**7001**	3441	3560	1035	1861–71	***–1.4***	*–1.7*	*–1.1*
	1881	**7367**	3665	3702	1010	1871–81	***5.2***	*6.5*	*4.0*
	1891	**6934**	3404	3530	1037	1881–91	***–5.9***	*–7.1*	*–4.6*
	1901	**6756**	3273	3483	1064	1891–1901	***–2.6***	*–3.8*	*–1.3*
	1911	**6486**	3158	3328	1054	1901–11	***–4.0***	*–3.5*	*–4.5*

No boundary changes

Subdistrict	Year	Number Persons	Males	Females	Females/ 1000 males	Intercensal period	*Percentage change Persons*	*Males*	*Females*
Betws-y-coed	1801	**1844**	893	951	1065				
	1811	**2123**	974	1149	1180	1801–11	***15.1***	*9.1*	*20.8*
	1821	**2269**	1078	1191	1105	1811–21	***6.9***	*10.7*	*3.7*
	1831	**2297**	1082	1215	1123	1821–31	***1.2***	*0.4*	*2.0*
	1841	**2563**	1261	1302	1033	1831–41	***11.6***	*16.5*	*7.2*
	1851	**2601**	1292	1309	1013	1841–51	***1.5***	*2.5*	*0.5*
	1861	**2735**	1385	1350	975	1851–61	***5.2***	*7.2*	*3.1*
	1871	**2923**	1489	1434	963	1861–71	***6.9***	*7.5*	*6.2*
	1881	**3649**	1828	1821	996	1871–81	***24.8***	*22.8*	*27.0*
	1891	**3299**	1539	1760	1144	1881–91	***–9.6***	*–15.8*	*–3.3*
	1901	**3624**	1759	1865	1060	1891–1901	***9.9***	*14.3*	*6.0*
	1911	**3220**	1529	1691	1106	1901–11	***–11.1***	*–13.1*	*–9.3*

No boundary changes

Subdistrict	Year	Number Persons	Males	Females	Females/ 1000 males	Intercensal period	*Percentage change Persons*	*Males*	*Females*
Ysbyty	1801	**1650**	741	909	1227				
	1811	**2169**	1045	1124	1076	1801–11	***31.5***	*41.0*	*23.7*
	1821	**2482**	1226	1256	1024	1811–21	***14.4***	*17.3*	*11.7*
	1831	**2520**	1213	1307	1077	1821–31	***1.5***	*–1.1*	*4.1*
	1841	**2832**	1419	1413	996	1831–41	***12.4***	*17.0*	*8.1*
	1851	**2795**	1387	1408	1015	1841–51	***–1.3***	*–2.3*	*–0.4*
	1861	**2935**	1466	1469	1002	1851–61	***5.0***	*5.7*	*4.3*
	1871	**3126**	1581	1545	977	1861–71	***6.5***	*7.8*	*5.2*
	1881	**3093**	1588	1505	948	1871–81	***–1.1***	*0.4*	*–2.6*
	1891	**2778**	1389	1389	1000	1881–91	***–10.2***	*–12.5*	*–7.7*
	1901	**2790**	1417	1373	969	1891–1901	***0.4***	*2.0*	*–1.2*
	1911	**2620**	1344	1276	949	1901–11	***–6.1***	*–5.2*	*–7.1*

No boundary changes

Subdistrict	Year	Number Persons	Males	Females	Females/ 1000 males	Intercensal period	*Percentage change Persons*	*Males*	*Females*
MERIONETH									
Corwen District									
Gwyddelwern	1801	**4469**	2106	2363	1122				
	1811	**4718**	2277	2441	1072	1801–11	***5.6***	*8.1*	*3.3*
	1821	**5102**	2493	2609	1047	1811–21	***8.1***	*9.5*	*6.9*
	1831	**5334**	2654	2680	1010	1821–31	***4.5***	*6.5*	*2.7*
	1841	**5575**	2794	2781	995	1831–41	***4.5***	*5.3*	*3.8*
	1851	**5526**	2787	2739	983	1841–51	***–0.9***	*–0.3*	*–1.5*
	1861	**5479**	2791	2688	963	1851–61	***–0.9***	*0.1*	*–1.9*
	1871	**5382**	2725	2657	975	1861–71	***–1.8***	*–2.4*	*–1.2*

Boundary changes: 1871–81 subdistrict abolished; all parts transferred to the new subdistrict of Llangollen (pop. 1871)

Subdistrict	Year	Number Persons	Males	Females	Females/ 1000 males	Intercensal period	*Percentage change* *Persons*	*Males*	*Females*
Corwen	1801	**5862**	2919	2943	1008				
	1811	**6100**	2974	3126	1051	1801–11	***4.1***	*1.9*	*6.2*
	1821	**7306**	3683	3623	984	1811–21	***19.8***	*23.8*	*15.9*
	1831	**8680**	4376	4304	984	1821–31	***18.8***	*18.8*	*18.8*
	1841	**9514**	4811	4703	978	1831–41	***9.6***	*9.9*	*9.3*
	1851	**9892**	5043	4849	962	1841–51	***4.0***	*4.8*	*3.1*
	1861	**10628**	5354	5274	985	1851–61	***7.4***	*6.2*	*8.8*
	1871	**11069**	5606	5463	974	1861–71	***4.1***	*4.7*	*3.6*
		(8048)	(4089)	(3959)					
	1881	**8068**	4037	4031	999	1871–81	***0.2***	*–1.3*	*1.8*
	1891	**7479**	3794	3685	971	1881–91	***–7.3***	*–6.0*	*–8.6*
	1901	**7364**	3757	3607	960	1891–1901	***–1.5***	*–1.0*	*–2.1*
	1911	**7375**	3751	3624	966	1901–11	***0.1***	*–0.2*	*0.5*

Boundary changes: 1871–81 loss of 3021 to the new subdistrict of Llangollen (pop. 1871)

Subdistrict	Year	Number Persons	Males	Females	Females/ 1000 males	Intercensal period	*Persons*	*Males*	*Females*
Llangollen	1871	(8403)	(4242)	(4161)					
	1881	**8765**	4401	4364	992	1871–81	***4.3***	*3.7*	*4.9*
	1891	**8779**	4367	4412	1010	1881–91	***0.2***	*–0.8*	*1.1*
	1901	**8949**	4388	4561	1039	1891–1901	***1.9***	*0.5*	*3.4*
	1911	**9053**	4416	4637	1050	1901–11	***1.2***	*0.6*	*1.7*

Boundary changes: 1871–81 subdistrict created; gain of 5382 from Gwyddelwern, gain of 3021 from Corwen (pop. 1871)

Bala District

Subdistrict	Year	Number Persons	Males	Females	Females/ 1000 males	Intercensal period	*Persons*	*Males*	*Females*
Bala	1801	**6586**	3257	3329	1022				
	1811	**6903**	3218	3685	1145	1801–11	***4.8***	*–1.2*	*10.7*
	1821	**7113**	3440	3673	1068	1811–21	***3.0***	*6.9*	*–0.3*
	1831	**6654**	3200	3454	1079	1821–31	***–6.5***	*–7.0*	*–6.0*
	1841	**6953**	3372	3581	1062	1831–41	***4.5***	*5.4*	*3.7*
	1851	**6736**	3353	3383	1009	1841–51	***–3.1***	*–0.6*	*–5.5*
	1861	**6352**	3229	3123	967	1851–61	***–5.7***	*–3.7*	*–7.7*
	1871	**6604**	3345	3259	974	1861–71	***4.0***	*3.6*	*4.4*
	1881	**6740**	3498	3242	927	1871–81	***2.1***	*4.6*	*–0.5*
	1891	**6115**	3046	3069	1008	1881–91	***–9.3***	*–12.9*	*–5.3*
	1901	**5732**	2801	2931	1046	1891–1901	***–6.3***	*–8.0*	*–4.5*
	1911	**5609**	2781	2828	1017	1901–11	***–2.1***	*–0.7*	*–3.5*

No boundary changes

Tal-y-llyn District

Subdistrict	Year	Number Persons	Males	Females	Females/ 1000 males	Intercensal period	*Persons*	*Males*	*Females*
Tal-y-llyn	1801	**4038**	1871	2167	1158				
	1811	**4297**	2023	2274	1124	1801–11	***6.4***	*8.1*	*4.9*
	1821	**5026**	2548	2478	973	1811–21	***17.0***	*26.0*	*9.0*
	1831	**4812**	2381	2431	1021	1821–31	***–4.3***	*–6.6*	*–1.9*
	1841	**5021**	2511	2510	1000	1831–41	***4.3***	*5.5*	*3.2*
	1851	**5053**	2605	2448	940	1841–51	***0.6***	*3.7*	*–2.5*
	1861	**4839**	2412	2427	1006	1851–61	***–4.2***	*–7.4*	*–0.9*
	1871	**5991**	3013	2978	988	1861–71	***23.8***	*24.9*	*22.7*
	1881	**6437**	3239	3198	987	1871–81	***7.4***	*7.5*	*7.4*
		(6396)	(3217)	(3179)					
	1891	**5467**	2675	2792	1044	1881–91	***–14.5***	*–16.8*	*–12.2*
		(5346)	(2619)	(2727)					
	1901	**5147**	2524	2623	1039	1891–1901	***–3.7***	*–3.6*	*–3.8*
	1911	**4306**	2014	2292	1138	1901–11	***–16.3***	*–20.2*	*–12.6*

Boundary changes: 1881–91 loss of 41 to Tywyn (Mer) (pop. 1881)
1891–1901 loss of 121 to Darowen (Mont) (pop. 1891)

Subdistrict	Year	Number Persons	Males	Females	Females/ 1000 males	Intercensal period	*Percentage change* *Persons*	*Males*	*Females*
Barmouth	1801	**6754**	3066	3688	1203				
	1811	**6938**	3051	3887	1274	1801–11	***2.7***	*–0.5*	*5.4*
	1821	**7540**	3423	4117	1203	1811–21	***8.7***	*12.2*	*5.9*
	1831	**8100**	3832	4268	1114	1821–31	***7.4***	*11.9*	*3.7*
	1841	**8190**	3775	4415	1170	1831–41	***1.1***	*–1.5*	*3.4*
	1851	**7918**	3625	4293	1184	1841–51	***–3.3***	*–4.0*	*–2.8*
	1861	**7643**	3502	4141	1182	1851–61	***–3.5***	*–3.4*	*–3.5*
	1871	**8320**	3919	4401	1123	1861–71	***8.9***	*11.9*	*6.3*
	1881	**8743**	4034	4709	1167	1871–81	***5.1***	*2.9*	*7.0*
	1891	**9025**	4147	4878	1176	1881–91	***3.2***	*2.8*	*3.6*
	1901	**9101**	4223	4878	1155	1891–1901	***0.8***	*1.8*	*0.0*
	1911	**8692**	3906	4786	1225	1901–11	***–4.5***	*–7.5*	*–1.9*

No boundary changes

Subdistrict	Year	Number Persons	Males	Females	Females/ 1000 males	Intercensal period	*Persons*	*Males*	*Females*
Ffestiniog District									
Llanfihangel-y-	1801	**2205**	1009	1196	1185				
traethau/	1811	**2446**	1142	1304	1142	1801–11	***10.9***	*13.2*	*9.0*
Deudraeth	1821	**2824**	1301	1523	1171	1811–21	***15.5***	*13.9*	*16.8*
	1831	**2934**	1372	1562	1138	1821–31	***3.9***	*5.5*	*2.6*
	1841	**3489**	1674	1815	1084	1831–41	***18.9***	*22.0*	*16.2*
	1851	**3669**	1745	1924	1103	1841–51	***5.2***	*4.2*	*6.0*
	1861	**3658**	1701	1957	1150	1851–61	***–0.3***	*–2.5*	*1.7*
	1871	**4500**	2196	2304	1049	1861–71	***23.0***	*29.1*	*17.7*
	1881	**5094**	2482	2612	1052	1871–81	***13.2***	*13.0*	*13.4*
	1891	**4892**	2341	2551	1090	1881–91	***–4.0***	*–5.7*	*–2.3*
		(5824)	(2805)	(3019)					
	1901	**5669**	2724	2945	1081	1891–1901	***–2.7***	*–2.9*	*–2.5*
	1911	**5433**	2558	2875	1124	1901–11	***–4.2***	*–6.1*	*–2.4*

Boundary changes: 1891–1901 subdistrict renamed Deudraeth; gain of 932 from Ffestiniog (pop. 1891)

Subdistrict	Year	Number Persons	Males	Females	Females/ 1000 males	Intercensal period	*Persons*	*Males*	*Females*
Ffestiniog	1801	**3203**	1471	1732	1177				
	1811	**3789**	1835	1954	1065	1801–11	***18.3***	*24.7*	*12.8*
	1821	**4056**	1937	2119	1094	1811–21	***7.0***	*5.6*	*8.4*
	1831	**4500**	2244	2256	1005	1821–31	***10.9***	*15.8*	*6.5*
	1841	**6419**	3417	3002	879	1831–41	***42.6***	*52.3*	*33.1*
	1851	**6654**	3455	3199	926	1841–51	***3.7***	*1.1*	*6.6*
	1861	**7783**	4036	3747	928	1851–61	***17.0***	*16.8*	*17.1*
	1871	**11484**	5985	5499	919	1861–71	***47.6***	*48.3*	*46.8*
	1881	**15115**	8132	6983	859	1871–81	***31.6***	*35.9*	*27.0*
	1891	**14389**	7315	7074	967	1881–91	***–4.8***	*–10.0*	*1.3*
		(13457)	(6851)	(6606)					
	1901	**13805**	6988	6817	976	1891–1901	***2.6***	*2.0*	*3.2*
	1911	**12034**	6047	5987	990	1901–11	***–12.8***	*–13.5*	*–12.2*

Boundary changes: 1891–1901 loss of 932 to Deudraeth (pop. 1891)

Subdistrict	Year	Number Persons	Males	Females	Females/ 1000 males	Intercensal period	*Persons*	*Males*	*Females*
Tremadoc	1801	**2730**	1292	1438	1113				
	1811	**3453**	1647	1806	1097	1801–11	***26.5***	*27.5*	*25.6*
	1821	**3754**	1832	1922	1049	1811–21	***8.7***	*11.2*	*6.4*
	1831	**4124**	1982	2142	1081	1821–31	***9.9***	*8.2*	*11.4*
	1841	**5552**	2707	2845	1051	1831–41	***34.6***	*36.6*	*32.8*
	1851	**5859**	2776	3083	1111	1841–51	***5.5***	*2.5*	*8.4*
	1861	**6848**	3283	3565	1086	1851–61	***16.9***	*18.3*	*15.6*
	1871	**8157**	3976	4181	1052	1861–71	***19.1***	*21.1*	*17.3*
	1881	**9316**	4527	4789	1058	1871–81	***14.2***	*13.9*	*14.5*
	1891	**8580**	4156	4424	1064	1881–91	***–7.9***	*–8.2*	*–7.6*
	1901	**8481**	4099	4382	1069	1891–1901	***–1.2***	*–1.4*	*–0.9*
	1911	**7778**	3603	4175	1159	1901–11	***–8.3***	*–12.1*	*–4.7*

No boundary changes

Subdistrict	Year	Number Persons	Males	Females	Females/ 1000 males	Intercensal period	*Percentage change* *Persons*	*Males*	*Females*
CAERNARFONSHIRE									
Pwllheli District									
Cricieth	1801	**4332**	2018	2314	1147				
	1811	**4467**	2197	2270	1033	1801–11	***3.1***	*8.9*	*–1.9*
	1821	**5230**	2519	2711	1076	1811–21	***17.1***	*14.7*	*19.4*
	1831	**5235**	2606	2629	1009	1821–31	***0.1***	*3.5*	*–3.0*
	1841	**5759**	2770	2989	1079	1831–41	***10.0***	*6.3*	*13.7*
	1851	**5789**	2752	3037	1104	1841–51	***0.5***	*–0.6*	*1.6*
	1861	**5591**	2649	2942	1111	1851–61	***–3.4***	*–3.7*	*–3.1*
	1871	**5904**	2871	3033	1056	1861–71	***5.6***	*8.4*	*3.1*
	1881	**6865**	3371	3494	1036	1871–81	***16.3***	*17.4*	*15.2*
	1891	**6964**	3295	3669	1114	1881–91	***1.4***	*–2.3*	*5.0*
	1901	**6769**	3299	3470	1052	1891–1901	***–2.8***	*0.1*	*–5.4*
	1911	**6807**	3228	3579	1109	1901–11	***0.6***	*–2.2*	*3.1*
	No boundary changes								
Pwllheli	1801	**4474**	2141	2333	1090				
	1811	**5450**	2564	2886	1126	1801–11	***21.8***	*19.8*	*23.7*
	1821	**6101**	2916	3185	1092	1811–21	***11.9***	*13.7*	*10.4*
	1831	**6506**	3082	3424	1111	1821–31	***6.6***	*5.7*	*7.5*
	1841	**6896**	3233	3663	1133	1831–41	***6.0***	*4.9*	*7.0*
	1851	**6837**	3173	3664	1155	1841–51	***–0.9***	*–1.9*	*0.0*
	1861	**6579**	3026	3553	1174	1851–61	***–3.8***	*–4.6*	*–3.0*
	1871	**6722**	3226	3496	1084	1861–71	***2.2***	*6.6*	*–1.6*
	1881	**7228**	3500	3728	1065	1871–81	***7.5***	*8.5*	*6.6*
	1891	**7009**	3309	3700	1118	1881–91	***–3.0***	*–5.5*	*–0.8*
		(6888)	(3249)	(3639)					
	1901	**6980**	3284	3696	1125	1891–1901	***1.3***	*1.1*	*1.6*
	1911	**7145**	3391	3754	1107	1901–11	***2.4***	*3.3*	*1.6*
	Boundary changes: 1891–1901 loss of 121 to Aberdaron (pop. 1891)								
Aberdaron	1801	**3413**	1617	1796	1111				
	1811	**3937**	1822	2115	1161	1801–11	***15.4***	*12.7*	*17.8*
	1821	**4045**	1983	2062	1040	1811–21	***2.7***	*8.8*	*–2.5*
	1831	**4063**	1947	2116	1087	1821–31	***0.4***	*–1.8*	*2.6*
	1841	**4075**	1944	2131	1096	1831–41	***0.3***	*–0.2*	*0.7*
	1851	**3967**	1905	2062	1082	1841–51	***–2.7***	*–2.0*	*–3.2*
	1861	**3800**	1822	1978	1086	1851–61	***–4.2***	*–4.4*	*–4.1*
	1871	**3651**	1781	1870	1050	1861–71	***–3.9***	*–2.3*	*–5.5*
	1881	**3618**	1813	1805	996	1871–81	***–0.9***	*1.8*	*–3.5*
	1891	**3532**	1708	1824	1068	1881–91	***–2.4***	*–5.8*	*1.1*
		(3653)	(1768)	(1885)					
	1901	**3551**	1767	1784	1010	1891–1901	***–2.8***	*–0.1*	*–5.4*
	1911	**3371**	1636	1735	1061	1901–11	***–5.1***	*–7.4*	*–2.7*
	Boundary changes: 1891–1901 gain of 121 from Pwllheli (pop. 1891)								
Nefyn	1801	**3601**	1660	1941	1169				
	1811	**3958**	1846	2112	1144	1801–11	***9.9***	*11.2*	*8.8*
	1821	**4783**	2360	2423	1027	1811–21	***20.8***	*27.8*	*14.7*
	1831	**4977**	2433	2544	1046	1821–31	***4.1***	*3.1*	*5.0*
	1841	**4907**	2351	2556	1087	1831–41	***–1.4***	*–3.4*	*0.5*
	1851	**5195**	2384	2811	1179	1841–51	***5.9***	*1.4*	*10.0*
	1861	**4938**	2232	2706	1212	1851–61	***–4.9***	*–6.4*	*–3.7*
	1871	**4697**	2144	2553	1191	1861–71	***–4.9***	*–3.9*	*–5.7*
	1881	**5200**	2477	2723	1099	1871–81	***10.7***	*15.5*	*6.7*
	1891	**4768**	2169	2599	1198	1881–91	***–8.3***	*–12.4*	*–4.6*
	1901	**4597**	2198	2399	1091	1891–1901	***–3.6***	*1.3*	*–7.7*
	1911	**4683**	2203	2480	1126	1901–11	***1.9***	*0.2*	*3.4*
	No boundary changes								

Subdistrict	Year	Number Persons	Males	Females	Females/ 1000 males	Intercensal period	Percentage change Persons	Males	Females
Caernarfon District									
Llandwrog	1801	**4122**	1969	2153	1093				
	1811	**5252**	2526	2726	1079	1801–11	***27.4***	*28.3*	*26.6*
	1821	**5767**	2884	2883	1000	1811–21	***9.8***	*14.2*	*5.8*
	1831	**6489**	3198	3291	1029	1821–31	***12.5***	*10.9*	*14.2*
	1841	**8080**	3998	4082	1021	1831–41	***24.5***	*25.0*	*24.0*
	1851	**8090**	4041	4049	1002	1841–51	***0.1***	*1.1*	*–0.8*
	1861	**8518**	4262	4256	999	1851–61	***5.3***	*5.5*	*5.1*
	1871	**10995**	5606	5389	961	1861–71	***29.1***	*31.5*	*26.6*
	1881	**13456**	6901	6555	950	1871–81	***22.4***	*23.1*	*21.6*
	1891	**12400**	6125	6275	1024	1881–91	***–7.8***	*–11.2*	*–4.3*
		(12192)	(6022)	(6170)					
	1901	**13612**	7010	6602	942	1891–1901	***11.6***	*16.4*	*7.0*
	1911	**12844**	6423	6421	1000	1901–11	***–5.6***	*–8.4*	*–2.7*
	Boundary changes: 1891–1901 loss of 208 to Caernarfon (pop. 1891)								
Llanrug	1801	**2203**	1072	1131	1055				
	1811	**2766**	1339	1427	1066	1801–11	***25.6***	*24.9*	*26.2*
	1821	**3431**	1714	1717	1002	1811–21	***24.0***	*28.0*	*20.3*
	1831	**5046**	2616	2430	929	1821–31	***47.1***	*52.6*	*41.5*
	1841	**7646**	3935	3711	943	1831–41	***51.5***	*50.4*	*52.7*
	1851	**8683**	4379	4304	983	1841–51	***13.6***	*11.3*	*16.0*
	1861	**10404**	5366	5038	939	1851–61	***19.8***	*22.5*	*17.1*
	1871	**13467**	6850	6617	966	1861–71	***29.4***	*27.7*	*31.3*
	1881	**14794**	7542	7252	962	1871–81	***9.9***	*10.1*	*9.6*
	1891	**13397**	6638	6759	1018	1881–91	***–9.4***	*–12.0*	*–6.8*
		(13273)	(6566)	(6707)					
	1901	**13844**	6933	6911	997	1891–1901	***4.3***	*5.6*	*3.0*
	1911	**13250**	6601	6649	1007	1901–11	***–4.3***	*–4.8*	*–3.8*
	Boundary changes: 1891–1901 loss of 124 to Caernarfon (pop. 1891)								
Caernarfon	1801	**3818**	1679	2139	1274				
	1811	**4786**	2061	2725	1322	1801–11	***25.4***	*22.8*	*27.4*
	1821	**5979**	2729	3250	1191	1811–21	***24.9***	*32.4*	*19.3*
	1831	**7798**	3565	4233	1187	1821–31	***30.4***	*30.6*	*30.2*
	1841	**9397**	4301	5096	1185	1831–41	***20.5***	*20.6*	*20.4*
	1851	**10137**	4760	5377	1130	1841–51	***7.9***	*10.7*	*5.5*
	1861	**10190**	4707	5483	1165	1851–61	***0.5***	*–1.1*	*2.0*
	1871	**11281**	5294	5987	1131	1861–71	***10.7***	*12.5*	*9.2*
	1881	**12253**	5929	6324	1067	1871–81	***8.6***	*12.0*	*5.6*
	1891	**11744**	5590	6154	1101	1881–91	***–4.2***	*–5.7*	*–2.7*
		(12076)	(5765)	(6311)					
	1901	**12142**	5725	6417	1121	1891–1901	***0.5***	*–0.7*	*1.7*
	1911	**11258**	5263	5995	1139	1901–11	***–7.3***	*–8.1*	*–6.6*
	Boundary changes: 1891–1901 gain of 208 from Llandwrog, gain of 124 from Llanrug (pop. 1891)								
Llanidan	1801	**2147**	998	1149	1151				
	1811	**2503**	1193	1310	1098	1801–11	***16.6***	*19.5*	*14.0*
	1821	**2719**	1291	1428	1106	1811–21	***8.6***	*8.2*	*9.0*
	1831	**2686**	1306	1380	1057	1821–31	***–1.2***	*1.2*	*–3.4*
	1841	**3386**	1627	1759	1081	1831–41	***26.1***	*24.6*	*27.5*
	1851	**3536**	1732	1804	1042	1841–51	***4.4***	*6.5*	*2.6*
	1861	**3313**	1565	1748	1117	1851–61	***–6.3***	*–9.6*	*–3.1*
	1871	**3394**	1610	1784	1108	1861–71	***2.4***	*2.9*	*2.1*
	1881	**3494**	1686	1808	1072	1871–81	***2.9***	*4.7*	*1.3*
	1891	**3171**	1483	1688	1138	1881–91	***–9.2***	*–12.0*	*–6.6*
	1901	**3055**	1438	1617	1124	1891–1901	***–3.7***	*–3.0*	*–4.2*
	1911	**2990**	1378	1612	1170	1901–11	***–2.1***	*–4.2*	*–0.3*
	No boundary changes								

Subdistrict	Year	Number Persons	Males	Females	Females/ 1000 males	Intercensal period	*Percentage change Persons*	*Males*	*Females*
Bangor District									
Beaumaris	1801	**5967**	2780	3187	1146				
	1811	**6432**	2997	3435	1146	1801–11	***7.8***	*7.8*	*7.8*
	1821	**7896**	3823	4073	1065	1811–21	***22.8***	*27.6*	*18.6*
	1831	**8341**	3986	4355	1093	1821–31	***5.6***	*4.3*	*6.9*
	1841	**9399**	4476	4923	1100	1831–41	***12.7***	*12.3*	*13.0*
	1851	**10548**	5197	5351	1030	1841–51	***12.2***	*16.1*	*8.7*
		(14059)	(6862)	(7197)					
	1861	**13139**	6228	6911	1110	1851–61	***–6.5***	*–9.2*	*–4.0*
	1871	**12519**	5900	6619	1122	1861–71	***–4.7***	*–5.3*	*–4.2*
	1881	**12781**	6227	6554	1053	1871–81	***2.1***	*5.5*	*–1.0*
		(12800)	(6237)	(6563)					
	1891	**12708**	6136	6572	1071	1881–91	***–0.7***	*–1.6*	*0.1*
	1901	**12743**	6228	6515	1046	1891–1901	***0.3***	*1.5*	*–0.9*
	1911	**12579**	6240	6339	1016	1901–11	***–1.3***	*0.2*	*–2.7*

Boundary changes: 1851–61 gain of 2548 from Llangefni (Angl), gain of 963 from Llandyfrydog (Angl) (pop. 1851)
1881–91 gain of 19 from Bryngwran (Angl) (pop. 1881)

Subdistrict	Year	Number Persons	Males	Females	Females/ 1000 males	Intercensal period	*Percentage change Persons*	*Males*	*Females*
Bangor	1801	**3050**	1501	1549	1032				
	1811	**4153**	2019	2134	1057	1801–11	***36.2***	*34.5*	*37.8*
	1821	**5920**	3007	2913	969	1811–21	***42.5***	*48.9*	*36.5*
	1831	**7351**	3298	4053	1229	1821–31	***24.2***	*9.7*	*39.1*
	1841	**10242**	5012	5230	1043	1831–41	***39.3***	*52.0*	*29.0*
	1851	**12962**	6505	6457	993	1841–51	***26.6***	*29.8*	*23.5*
	1861	**14043**	6945	7098	1022	1851–61	***8.3***	*6.8*	*9.9*
	1871	**14218**	6874	7344	1068	1861–71	***1.2***	*–1.0*	*3.5*
	1881	**14957**	7165	7792	1088	1871–81	***5.2***	*4.2*	*6.1*
		(13853)	(6587)	(7266)					
	1891	**15090**	7116	7974	1121	1881–91	***8.9***	*8.0*	*9.7*
		(12261)	(5790)	(6471)					
	1901	**13539**	6322	7217	1142	1891–1901	***10.4***	*9.2*	*11.5*
	1911	**13466**	6253	7213	1154	1901–11	***–0.5***	*–1.1*	*–0.1*

Boundary changes: 1881–91 gain of 2483 from Llanllechid, loss of 3587 to Llanllechid (pop. 1881)
1891–1901 loss of 2829 to new subdistrict of Llanfairfechan (pop. 1891)

Subdistrict	Year	Number Persons	Males	Females	Females/ 1000 males	Intercensal period	*Percentage change Persons*	*Males*	*Females*
Llanfairfechan	1891	(2829)	(1326)	(1503)					
	1901	**3151**	1507	1644	1091	1891–1901	***11.4***	*13.7*	*9.4*
	1911	**3373**	1598	1775	1111	1901–11	***7.0***	*6.0*	*8.0*

Boundary changes: 1891–1901 subdistrict created from part of Bangor

Subdistrict	Year	Number Persons	Males	Females	Females/ 1000 males	Intercensal period	*Percentage change Persons*	*Males*	*Females*
Llanllechid	1801	**2293**	1135	1158	1020				
	1811	**2476**	1248	1228	984	1801–11	***8.0***	*10.0*	*6.0*
	1821	**3093**	1636	1457	891	1811–21	***24.9***	*31.1*	*18.6*
	1831	**4280**	2305	1975	857	1821–31	***38.4***	*40.9*	*35.6*
	1841	**6260**	3308	2952	892	1831–41	***46.3***	*43.5*	*49.5*
	1851	**7300**	3797	3503	923	1841–51	***16.6***	*14.8*	*18.7*
	1861	**9127**	4807	4320	899	1851–61	***25.0***	*26.6*	*23.3*
	1871	**9830**	5033	4797	953	1861–71	***7.7***	*4.7*	*11.0*
	1881	**10774**	5400	5374	995	1871–81	***9.6***	*7.3*	*12.0*
		(11878)	(5978)	(5900)					
	1891	**10234**	5010	5224	1043	1881–91	***–13.8***	*–16.2*	*–11.5*
	1901	**9222**	4293	4929	1148	1891–1901	***–9.9***	*–14.3*	*–5.6*
	1911	**8747**	4284	4463	1042	1901–11	***–5.2***	*–0.2*	*–9.5*

Boundary changes: 1881–91 gain of 3587 from Bangor, loss of 2483 to Bangor (pop. 1881)

Subdistrict	Year	Number Persons	Males	Females	Females/ 1000 males	Intercensal period	*Percentage change* *Persons*	*Males*	*Females*
Conwy District									
Conwy	1801	**1642**	785	857	1092				
	1811	**1831**	843	988	1172	1801–11	***11.5***	*7.4*	*15.3*
	1821	**2094**	992	1102	1111	1811–21	***14.4***	*17.7*	*11.5*
	1831	**2330**	1099	1231	1120	1821–31	***11.3***	*10.8*	*11.7*
	1841	**2702**	1324	1378	1041	1831–41	***16.0***	*20.5*	*11.9*
	1851	**3127**	1544	1583	1025	1841–51	***15.7***	*16.6*	*14.9*
	1861	**3956**	1982	1974	996	1851–61	***26.5***	*28.4*	*24.7*
	1871	**4047**	1942	2105	1084	1861–71	***2.3***	*–2.0*	*6.6*
	1881	**5127**	2552	2575	1009	1871–81	***26.7***	*31.4*	*22.3*
		(6801)	(3384)	(3417)					
	1891	**7246**	3518	3728	1060	1881–91	***6.5***	*4.0*	*9.1*
	1901	**8496**	4154	4342	1045	1891–1901	***17.3***	*18.1*	*16.5*
		(10182)	(4921)	(5261)					
	1911	**11409**	5467	5942	1087	1901–11	***12.1***	*11.1*	*12.9*

Boundary changes: 1881–91 gain of 1674 from Llechwedd Isaf (pop. 1881)
1901–11 gain of 1686 from Creuddyn (pop. 1901)

Subdistrict	Year	Persons	Males	Females	Females/ 1000 males	Intercensal period	Persons	Males	Females
Creuddyn	1801	**3458**	1670	1788	1071				
	1811	**3767**	1839	1928	1048	1801–11	***8.9***	*10.1*	*7.8*
	1821	**4728**	2340	2388	1021	1811–21	***25.5***	*27.2*	*23.9*
	1831	**5501**	2797	2704	967	1821–31	***16.3***	*19.5*	*13.2*
	1841	**6021**	3045	2976	977	1831–41	***9.5***	*8.9*	*10.1*
	1851	**6565**	3322	3243	976	1841–51	***9.0***	*9.1*	*9.0*
	1861	**7903**	3799	4104	1080	1851–61	***20.4***	*14.4*	*26.5*
	1871	**8779**	4020	4759	1184	1861–71	***11.1***	*5.8*	*16.0*
	1881	**11560**	5347	6213	1162	1871–81	***31.7***	*33.0*	*30.6*
	1891	**17322**	7634	9688	1269	1881–91	***49.8***	*42.8*	*55.9*
	1901	**25535**	11210	14325	1278	1891–1901	***47.4***	*46.8*	*47.9*

Boundary changes: 1901–11 subdistrict abolished: loss of 1686 to Conwy, loss of 11477 to the new subdistrict of Llandudno, loss of 12372 to the new subdistrict of Colwyn Bay (pop. 1901)

Subdistrict	Year	Persons	Males	Females	Females/ 1000 males	Intercensal period	Persons	Males	Females
Llechwedd Isaf	1801	**1486**	708	778	1099				
	1811	**1669**	800	869	1086	1801–11	***12.3***	*13.0*	*11.7*
	1821	**1742**	867	875	1009	1811–21	***4.4***	*8.4*	*0.7*
	1831	**1872**	922	950	1030	1821–31	***7.5***	*6.3*	*8.6*
	1841	**1983**	948	1035	1092	1831–41	***5.9***	*2.8*	*8.9*
	1851	**1938**	981	957	976	1841–51	***–2.3***	*3.5*	*–7.5*
	1861	**2037**	1030	1007	978	1851–61	***5.1***	*5.0*	*5.2*
	1871	**1874**	926	948	1024	1861–71	***–8.0***	*–10.1*	*–5.9*
	1881	**1674**	832	842	1012	1871–81	***–10.7***	*–10.2*	*–11.2*

Boundary changes: 1881–91 subdistrict abolished, all parts transferred to Conwy (pop. 1881)

Subdistrict	Year	Persons	Males	Females	Females/ 1000 males	Intercensal period	Persons	Males	Females
Llandudno	1901	**(11477)**	(5005)	(6472)					
	1911	**13054**	5529	7525	1361	1901–11	**13.7**	10.5	16.3

Boundary changes: 1901–11 subdistrict created from part of Creuddyn

Subdistrict	Year	Persons	Males	Females	Females/ 1000 males	Intercensal period	Persons	Males	Females
Colwyn Bay	1901	**(12372)**	(5438)	(6934)					
	1911	**16791**	7125	9666	1357	1901–11	**35.7**	31.0	39.4

Boundary changes: 1901–11 subdistrict created from part of Creuddyn

Subdistrict	Year	Number Persons	Males	Females	Females/ 1000 males	Intercensal period	Percentage change Persons	Males	Females
ANGLESEY									
Anglesey District									
Llangefni	1801	**4067**	1807	2260	1251				
	1811	**4749**	2187	2562	1171	1801–11	***16.8***	*21.0*	*13.4*
	1821	**5997**	2945	3052	1036	1811–21	***26.3***	*34.7*	*19.1*
	1831	**6556**	3238	3318	1025	1821–31	***9.3***	*9.9*	*8.7*
	1841	**6996**	3384	3612	1067	1831–41	***6.7***	*4.5*	*8.9*
	1851	**7204**	3449	3755	1089	1841–51	***3.0***	*1.9*	*4.0*
		(5827)	(2799)	(3028)					
	1861	**5431**	2637	2794	1060	1851–61	***–6.8***	*–5.8*	*–7.7*
	1871	**4938**	2350	2588	1101	1861–71	***–9.1***	*–10.9*	*–7.4*
	1881	**4891**	2320	2571	1108	1871–81	***–1.0***	*–1.3*	*–0.7*
	1891	**5003**	2362	2641	1118	1881–91	***2.3***	*1.8*	*2.7*
	1901	**5034**	2399	2635	1098	1891–1901	***0.6***	*1.6*	*–0.2*
	1911	**5033**	2345	2688	1146	1901–11	***0.0***	*–2.3*	*2.0*

Boundary changes: 1851–61 loss of 2548 to Beaumaris (Caern), loss of 2422 to Bryngwran, gain of 3582 from Llandyfrydog (pop. 1851)

Subdistrict	Year	Number Persons	Males	Females	Females/ 1000 males	Intercensal period	Percentage change Persons	Males	Females
Anglesey/Holyhead District									
Bryngwran	1801	**3477**	1629	1848	1134				
	1811	**3949**	1894	2055	1085	1801–11	***13.6***	*16.3*	*11.2*
	1821	**4512**	2262	2250	995	1811–21	***14.3***	*19.4*	*9.5*
	1831	**4701**	2279	2422	1063	1821–31	***4.2***	*0.8*	*7.6*
	1841	**5106**	2502	2604	1041	1831–41	***8.6***	*9.8*	*7.5*
	1851	**5209**	2602	2607	1002	1841–51	***2.0***	*4.0*	*0.1*
		(6164)	(3029)	(3135)					
	1861	**5746**	2787	2959	1062	1851–61	***–6.8***	*–8.0*	*–5.6*
	1871	**5261**	2556	2705	1058	1861–71	***–8.4***	*–8.3*	*–8.6*
	1881	**5069**	2472	2597	1051	1871–81	***–3.6***	*–3.3*	*–4.0*
		(5050)	(2462)	(2588)					
	1891	**4933**	2377	2556	1075	1881–91	***–2.3***	*–3.5*	*–1.2*
	1901	**4858**	2349	2509	1068	1891–1901	***–1.5***	*–1.2*	*–1.8*
	1911	**5129**	2512	2617	1042	1901–11	***5.6***	*6.9*	*4.3*

Boundary changes: 1851–61 gain of 2411 from Llangefni, loss of 613 to Llanddeusant, loss of 843 to Llandyfrydog (pop. 1851)
1881–91 subdistrict transferred to the new district of Holyhead; loss of 19 to Beaumaris (Caern) (pop. 1881)

Subdistrict	Year	Number Persons	Males	Females	Females/ 1000 males	Intercensal period	Percentage change Persons	Males	Females
Anglesey District									
Llandyfrydog /	1801	**3697**	1796	1901	1058				
Llanfechell	1811	**4191**	2025	2166	1070	1801–11	***13.4***	*12.8*	*13.9*
	1821	**5290**	2623	2667	1017	1811–21	***26.2***	*29.5*	*23.1*
	1831	**5564**	2750	2814	1023	1821–31	***5.2***	*4.8*	*5.5*
	1841	**5459**	2646	2813	1063	1831–41	***–1.9***	*–3.8*	*0.0*
	1851	**5608**	2729	2879	1055	1841–51	***2.7***	*3.1*	*2.3*
		(5043)	(2448)	(2595)					
	1861	**4580**	2203	2377	1079	1851–61	***–9.2***	*–10.0*	*–8.4*
	1871	**4244**	2094	2150	1027	1861–71	***–7.3***	*–4.9*	*–9.5*
	1881	**4025**	1950	2075	1064	1871–81	***–5.2***	*–6.9*	*–3.5*
		(4115)	(1994)	(2121)					
	1891	**4111**	2014	2097	1041	1881–91	***–0.1***	*1.0*	*–1.1*
		(4284)	(2075)	(2209)					
	1901	**3917**	1885	2032	1078	1891–1901	***–8.6***	*–9.2*	*–8.0*
	1911	**3955**	1876	2079	1108	1901–11	***1.0***	*–0.5*	*2.3*

Boundary changes: 1851–61 gain of 843 from Bryngwran, gain of 3137 from Llanddeusant, loss of 963 to Beaumaris (Caern), loss of 3582 to Llangefni (pop. 1851)
1881–91 gain of 69 from Llanddeusant, gain of 22 from Amlwch (pop. 1881)
1891–1901 subdistrict renamed Llanfechell; gain of 685 from Amlwch, loss of 512 to Amlwch (pop. 1901)

Subdistrict	Year	Number Persons	Males	Females	Females/ 1000 males	Intercensal period	*Percentage change Persons*	*Males*	*Females*
Amlwch	1801	**6647**	3165	3482	1100				
	1811	**5563**	2591	2972	1147	1801–11	***–16.3***	*–18.1*	*–14.6*
	1821	**6970**	3426	3544	1034	1811–21	***25.3***	*32.2*	*19.2*
	1831	**8225**	4011	4214	1051	1821–31	***18.0***	*17.1*	*18.9*
	1841	**8218**	3841	4377	1140	1831–41	***–0.1***	*–4.2*	*3.9*
	1851	**7691**	3575	4116	1151	1841–51	***–6.4***	*–6.9*	*–6.0*
	1861	**7777**	3614	4163	1152	1851–61	***1.1***	*1.1*	*1.1*
	1871	**7082**	3266	3816	1168	1861–71	***–8.9***	*–9.6*	*–8.3*
	1881	**6198**	2825	3373	1194	1871–81	***–12.5***	*–13.5*	*–11.6*
		(6176)	(2813)	(3363)					
	1891	**5567**	2492	3075	1234	1881–91	***–9.9***	*–11.4*	*–8.6*
		(5394)	(2431)	(2963)					
	1901	**5306**	2450	2856	1166	1891–1901	***–1.6***	*0.8*	*–3.6*
	1911	**4837**	2174	2663	1225	1901–11	***–8.8***	*–11.3*	*–6.8*

Boundary changes: 1881–91 loss of 22 to Llandyfrydog (pop. 1881)
1891–1901 loss of 685 to Llanfechell, gain of 512 from Llanfechell (pop. 1891)

Subdistrict	Year	Number Persons	Males	Females	Females/ 1000 males	Intercensal period	*Percentage change Persons*	*Males*	*Females*
Anglesey/Holyhead District									
Llanddeusant	1801	**3970**	1958	2012	1028				
	1811	**4632**	2237	2395	1071	1801–11	***16.7***	*14.2*	*19.0*
	1821	**5100**	2395	2705	1129	1811–21	***10.1***	*7.1*	*12.9*
	1831	**5506**	2742	2764	1008	1821–31	***8.0***	*14.5*	*2.2*
	1841	**5873**	2843	3030	1066	1831–41	***6.7***	*3.7*	*9.6*
	1851	**5997**	2899	3098	1069	1841–51	***2.1***	*2.0*	*2.2*
		(5656)	(2819)	(2837)					
	1861	**5388**	2683	2705	1008	1851–61	***–4.7***	*–4.8*	*–4.7*
	1871	**5007**	2475	2532	1023	1861–71	***–7.1***	*–7.8*	*–6.4*
	1881	**4827**	2439	2388	979	1871–81	***–3.6***	*–1.5*	*–5.7*
		(4759)	(2407)	(2352)					
	1891	**4595**	2251	2344	1041	1881–91	***–3.4***	*–6.5*	*–0.3*
	1901	**4272**	2110	2162	1025	1891–1901	***–7.0***	*–6.3*	*–7.8*
	1911	**4318**	2149	2169	1009	1901–11	***1.1***	*1.8*	*0.3*

Boundary changes: 1851–61 gain of 2183 from Holyhead, gain of 613 from Bryngwran, loss of 3137 to Llandyfrydog (pop. 1851)
1881–91 subdistrict transferred to new district of Holyhead; loss of 68 to Llandyfrydog (pop. 1881)

Subdistrict	Year	Number Persons	Males	Females	Females/ 1000 males	Intercensal period	*Percentage change Persons*	*Males*	*Females*
Holyhead	1801	**3834**	1642	2192	1335				
	1811	**5026**	2320	2706	1166	1801–11	***31.1***	*41.3*	*23.4*
	1821	**6579**	3019	3560	1179	1811–21	***30.9***	*30.1*	*31.6*
	1831	**6746**	3163	3583	1133	1821–31	***2.5***	*4.8*	*0.6*
	1841	**6454**	3055	3399	1113	1831–41	***–4.3***	*–3.4*	*–5.1*
	1851	**11534**	5918	5616	949	1841–51	***78.7***	*93.7*	*65.2*
		(9351)	(4837)	(4514)					
	1861	**9235**	4577	4658	1018	1851–61	***–1.2***	*–5.4*	*3.2*
	1871	**8595**	4149	4446	1072	1861–71	***–6.9***	*–9.4*	*–4.6*
	1881	**10131**	5184	4947	954	1871–81	***17.9***	*24.9*	*11.3*
	1891	**10010**	4826	5184	1074	1881–91	***–1.2***	*–6.9*	*4.8*
	1901	**11421**	5628	5793	1029	1891–1901	***14.1***	*16.6*	*11.7*
	1911	**12087**	5924	6163	1040	1901–11	***5.8***	*5.3*	*6.4*

Boundary changes: 1851–61 loss of 2183 to Llanddeusant (pop. 1851)
1881–91 subdistrict transferred from Anglesey District to the new district of Holyhead

Sources: As for Table 1.1.

[1] Figures for Upper and Lower Merthyr Tydfil are not given separately before 1841.

[2] The 1911 census does not give separate figures for males and females for 1901 on the basis of boundaries in 1911. However, figures for Llanelli Rural and Llanelli Urban together can be calculated and are given as follows:

Subdistrict	Year	Number Males	Females	Females/ 1000 males	Intercensal period	*Percentage change Males*	*Females*
Llanelli Rural and Llanelli Urban	1901	16862	17709	1050			
	1911	22319	21433	960	1901–11	*32.4*	*21.0*

[3] The large increase and subsequent decrease in population, 1901–11, in this subdistrict was caused by the construction of a waterworks at the time of the 1901 census.

[4] Figures for Upper and Lower Llanidloes are not given separately before 1841.

Population 1.4 Urban population. Total population and percentage change. Towns. 1801–1911

Town		1801	1811	1821	1831	1841	1851	1861	1871	1881	1891	1901	1911
MONMOUTHSHIRE													
Abergavenny	P	1472	3036										
	P	–	2815	3388	3940	4689	5204						
	Town, ICD, USD, MB	–	–	–	–	–	4797	4621	4803	6941	7743	7795	8511
	% change		*106.3*	*20.4*	*16.3*	*19.0*	*11.0*	*–3.7*	*3.9*	*44.5*	*11.6*	*0.7*	*9.2*
Abersychan	LB, USD, UD	–	–	–	–	–	–	–	14569	13496	15296	17768	24656
	% change									*–7.4*	*13.3*	*16.2*	*38.8*
Abertillery	USD	–	–	–	–	–	–	–	5696	6003	9138		
	UD	–	–	–	–	–	–	–	–	–	10846	21945	35415
	% change									*5.4*	*52.2*	*102.3*	*61.4*
Bedwellte	USD	–	–	–	–	–	–	–	–	3622	6773		
	UD	–	–	–	–	–	–	–	–	–	6743	9988	22547
	% change										*87.0*	*48.1*	*125.7*
Blaenafon	LB, USD	–	–	–	–	–	–	–	9376	9451			
	USD (new boundaries), UD	–	–	–	–	–	–	–	–	9522	11452	10869	12010
	% change									*0.8*	*20.3*	*–5.1*	*10.5*
Chepstow	Town	–	–	–	–	–	4295	3364					
	LB, USD, UD	–	–	–	–	–	–	3455	3347	3591	3378	3067	2953
	% change							*–21.7*	*–3.1*	*7.3*	*–5.9*	*–9.2*	*–3.7*
Ebbw Vale	USD	–	–	–	–	–	–	–	14505[1]	14700	17034		
	UD	–	–	–	–	–	–	–	–	–	17312	20994	30541
	% change									*1.3*	*15.9*	*21.3*	*45.5*
Mynyddislwyn	UD (1903)	–	–	–	–	–	–	–	–	–	–	3337	9980
	% change												*199.1*
Nant-y-glo and	USD, UD	–	–	–	–	–	–	–	–	9267	12410	13489	15395
Blaenau	*% change*										*33.9*	*8.7*	*14.1*
Newport[2]	B, MB	1135	2346	4000	7062	10492	19323	23249	27069	35313			
	CB	–	–	–	–	–	–	–	–	–	38469	54707	67270	83691
	% change		*106.7*	*70.5*	*76.6*	*48.6*	*84.2*	*20.3*	*16.4*	*30.5*	*42.2*	*23.0*	*24.4*
Pant-teg	LB, UDS	–	–	–	–	–	–	–	2761	3321			
	USD (new boundaries), UD	–	–	–	–	–	–	–	–	5539	6479	7484	10098
	% change									*20.3*	*17.0*	*15.5*	*34.9*
Pontypool	Town, LB, USD, UD	–	–	–	–	–	3708	4661	4834	5244	5842	6126	6452
	% change							*25.7*	*3.7*	*8.5*	*11.4*	*4.9*	*5.3*
Rhymni	USD, UD	–	–	–	–	–	–	–	8138	8663	7733	7915	11449
	% change									*6.5*	*–10.7*	*2.4*	*44.6*
Risca	USD	–	–	–	–	–	–	–	5396[3]	5540			
	USD (new boundaries), UD	–	–	–	–	–	–	–	–	5556	7783	9661	14149
	% change									*2.7*	*40.1*	*24.1*	*46.5*
Tredegar	Town	–	–	–	–	–	8305	9383	12389				
	USD, UD	–	–	–	–	–	–	–	16989	18771	17341	18497	23601
	% change							*13.0*	*32.0*	*10.5*	*–7.6*	*6.7*	*27.6*

Town		1801	1811	1821	1831	1841	1851	1861	1871	1881	1891	1901	1911
GLAMORGAN													
Aberafan	P, B, MB	275	321	365	573	1290	2380	2916	3574	4859	6300	7553	10505
	% change		*16.7*	*13.7*	*57.0*	*125.1*	*84.5*	*22.5*	*22.6*	*36.0*	*29.7*	*19.9*	*39.1*
Aberdare	LB, USD, UD	–	–	–	–	–	–	–	36112	33804	38431	43365	50830
	% change									*–6.4*	*13.7*	*12.8*	*17.2*
Barry	USD, UD	–	–	–	–	–	–	–	–	494	13278	27030	33763
	% change										*2587.9*	*103.6*	*24.9*
Bridgend	LB, USD, UD	–	–	–	–	–	–	–	3539	4153	4676	6062	
	UD (new boundaries)	–	–	–	–	–	–	–	–	–	–	6299	8021
	% change									*17.3*	*12.6*	*29.6*	*27.3*
Briton Ferry	LB, USD, UD	–	–	–	–	–	–	–	4803	6061	5778	6973	8472
	% change									*26.2*	*–4.7*	*20.7*	*21.5*
Caerphilly	UD	–	–	–	–	–	–	–	–	–	8064	15835	32844
	% change											*96.4*	*107.4*
Cardiff	Town, B, MB	1870	2457	3521	6187	10077	18351	32954	39536				
	MB (new boundaries), UD	–	–	–	–	–	–	–	57363	82761	128915	164333	182259
	% change		*31.4*	*43.3*	*75.7*	*62.9*	*82.1*	*79.6*	*20.0*	*44.3*	*55.8*	*27.5*	*10.9*
Gelli-gaer	UD	–	–	–	–	–	–	–	–	–	–	17242	35521
	% change												*106*
Glyncorrwg	Hamlet, P	102	116	124	133	136	93	322	734	1288	2277[3]		
	UD	–	–	–	–	–	–	–	–	–	3683	6452	8688
	% change		*13.7*	*6.9*	*7.3*	*2.3*	*–31.6*	*246.2*	*128*	*75.5*	*76.8*	*75.2*	*34.7*
Maesteg	USD, UD	–	–	–	–	–	–	–	7667	8310	9417	15012	24977
	% change									*8.4*	*13.3*	*59.4*	*66.4*
Merthyr Tydfil	P, LB, USD	7705	11104	17404	22083	34977	46378	49794	51949	48861	58080		
	UD, CB	–	–	–	–	–	–	–	–	–	59004	69228	80990
	% change		*44.1*	*56.7*	*26.9*	*58.4*	*32.6*	*7.4*	*4.3*	*–5.9*	*18.9*	*17.3*	*17.0*
Mountain Ash	LB, USD	–	–	–	–	–	–	–	7457	10295	17590		
	UD	–	–	–	–	–	–	–	–	–	17826	31093	42246
	% change									*38.1*	*70.9*	*74.4*	*35.9*
Neath	P	2502	2740	2823	4043	4970							
	B, MB	–	–	–	–	4967	5841	6810	9319	10409	11113	13720	17586
	% change		*9.5*	*3.0*	*43.2*	*22.9*	*17.6*	*16.6*	*36.8*	*11.7*	*6.8*	*23.5*	*28.2*
Ogmore and Garw	USD, UD	–	–	–	–	–	–	–	–	6894	13800	19907	26741
	% change										*100.2*	*44.3*	*34.3*
Penarth	P	72	75	77	68	110	105	1406	2612				
	USD, UD	–	–	–	–	–	–	–	3104	6228	12424	14228	15488
	% change		*4.2*	*2.7*	*–11.7*	*61.8*	*–4.5*	*1239.0*	*85.8*	*100.6*	*99.5*	*14.5*	*8.9*
Pontypridd	USD	–	–	–	–	–	–	–	11000[1]	12317	19969		
	UD	–	–	–	–	–	–	–	–	–	24763	32316	43211
	% change									*12.0*	*62.1*	*30.5*	*33.7*
Porthcawl	UD	–	–	–	–	–	–	–	–	–	1758	1872	3444
	% change											*6.5*	*84*

Town		1801	1811	1821	1831	1841	1851	1861	1871	1881	1891	1901	1911
Rhondda[4]	P	542	973	985	1047	1363	1998	3857	17777				
	USD, UD	–	–	–	–	–	–	–	23950	55632	88351	113735	152781
	% change		*79.5*	*1.2*	*6.3*	*30.2*	*46.6*	*93.0*	*360.9*	*132.3*	*58.8*	*28.7*	*34.3*
Swansea	Town, B	6099	8196	10255	13694	16787							
	MB[5 6]	10117	11963	14896	19672	24604	31461	41606					
	MB[5]	–	–	–	–	–	–	40802	51702	65597			
	CB	–	–	–	–	–	–	–	–	76430	90349		
	CB (new boundaries)	–	–	–	–	–	–	–	–	–	91034	94537	114663
	% change		*18.2*	*24.5*	*32.1*	*25.1*	*27.9*	*32.2*	*26.7*	*26.9*	*18.2*	*3.8*	*21.3*
CARMARTHENSHIRE													
Carmarthen	Town, B, MB	5548	7275	8906	9955	9526	10524	9993	10488	10514	10300		
	MB (new boundaries)	–	–	–	–	–	–	–	–	–	10338	10025	10221
	% change		*31.1*	*22.4*	*11.8*	*–4.3*	*10.5*	*–5.0*	*5.0*	*0.2*	*–2.0*	*3.0*	*2.0*
Llanelli[7]	B	2072	2791	2621	4173	6846	8415	11084	13958				
	USD, UD	–	–	–	–	–	–	–	15021	19760	23937	25617	32071
	% change		*34.7*	*–6.1*	*59.2*	*64.1*	*22.9*	*31.7*	*25.9*	*31.5*	*21.1*	*7.0*	*25.2*
PEMBROKESHIRE													
Haverfordwest	Town, B, MB	2880	3093	2280	3915	5941	6580	7019	6622	6398	6179	6007	5919
	% change		*7.4*	*–26.3*	*71.7*	*51.7*	*10.8*	*6.7*	*–5.7*	*–3.4*	*–3.4*	*–2.8*	*–1.5*
Milford Haven	PB	–	–	–	–	2377	2837	3007	2836				
	USD, UD	–	–	–	–	–	–	–	3348	3812	4070	5102	6399
	% change						*19.4*	*6.0*	*–5.7*	*13.9*	*6.8*	*25.4*	*25.4*
Pembroke[8]	B, MB	1842	2415	2527	6511	7412	10107	15071	13704	14156	14978	15853	15673
	% change		*31.1*	*4.6*	*157.7*	*13.8*	*36.4*	*49.1*	*–9.1*	*3.3*	*5.8*	*5.8*	*–1.1*
CARDIGANSHIRE													
Aberystwyth	Chapelry	1758	2264	3556	4128	4916							
	B, MB	–	–	–	–	4975	5231	5641	6898	7088	6725	8014	8411
	% change		*28.8*	*57.1*	*16.1*	*19.1*	*5.1*	*7.8*	*22.3*	*2.8*	*–5.1*	*19.2*	*5.0*
BRECONSHIRE													
Brecon	Town, MB	2576	3196	4193	5026	5701	5673	5235	5845	6247	5646	5875	5908
	% change		*24.1*	*31.2*	*19.9*	*13.4*	*–0.5*	*–7.7*	*11.7*	*6.9*	*–9.6*	*4.1*	*0.6*
MONTGOMERYSHIRE													
Newtown[9]	P, USD, UD	1665	2724	3593	6555	6842	6559	6086	5886	7170	6610	6500	6068
	% change		*63.6*	*31.9*	*82.4*	*4.4*	*–4.1*	*–7.2*	*–3.3*	*21.8*	*–7.8*	*–1.7*	*–6.6*
Welshpool	Town, B, MB	2872	3440	4255	5255	6185	6564	7304	6983[10]	7107	6501	6121	5917
	% change		*19.8*	*23.7*	*23.5*	*17.7*	*6.1*	*11.3*	*–4.4*	*1.8*	*–8.5*	*–5.8*	*–3.3*
DENBIGHSHIRE													
Colwyn Bay	USD, UD	–	–	–	–	–	–	–	–	2418	4754	8689	12630
	% change										*96.6*	*82.8*	*45.4*
Wrexham	Township, PB, MB	2575[11]	4524[11]	4795	5484	5831	6714	7562	8576	10978	12552	14966	18377
	% change			*6.0*	*14.4*	*6.3*	*15.1*	*12.6*	*13.4*	*28*	*14.3*	*19.2*	*22.8*

Town		1801	1811	1821	1831	1841	1851	1861	1871	1881	1891	1901	1911
FLINTSHIRE													
Flint	B, MB	1961	1433	1612	2216	2860	3296	3428	4269	5096	5247	4625	5472
	% change		*−26.9*	*12.5*	*37.5*	*29.1*	*15.2*	*4.0*	*24.5*	*19.4*	*3.0*	*−11.9*	*18.3*
Mold	PB	–	–	–	–	3557	3432	3735	4534				
	LB, USD, UD	–	–	–	–	–	–	–	3978	4320	4457	4263	4873
	% change						*−3.5*	*8.8*	*21.4*	*8.6*	*3.2*	*−4.4*	*14.3*
Rhyl	USD, UD	–	–	–	–	–	–	–	4500	6029	6491	8473	9005
	% change									*34.0*	*7.7*	*30.5*	*6.3*
MERIONETH													
Ffestiniog	P, USD, UD	732	961	1168	1648	3138	3460	4553	8055	11274	11073	11435	9674
	% change		*31.3*	*21.5*	*41.1*	*90.4*	*10.3*	*31.6*	*76.9*	*40.0*	*−1.8*	*3.3*	*−15.4*
CAERNARFONSHIRE													
Bangor	City	1770	2383	3579	4751	7232							
	PB	–	–	–	–	5058	6338	6738	9856				
	USD	–	–	–	–	–	–	–	7939	8247			
	MB	–	–	–	–	–	–	–	–	9005	9892	11269	11236
	% change		*34.6*	*50.2*	*32.7*	*52.2*	*25.3*	*6.3*	*46.3*	*3.9*	*9.9*	*13.9*	*−0.3*
Caernarfon	[12] P, B	3626	4595	5788	7642	9192							
	B, MB	–	–	–	–	8001	8674	8512	9449	10258	9804	9760	9119
	% change		*26.7*	*26.0*	*32.0*	*20.3*	*8.4*	*−1.9*	*11.0*	*8.6*	*−4.4*	*−0.4*	*−6.6*
Conwy	PB	–	–	–	–	1828	2105	2523	2620				
	MB	–	–	–	–	–	–	–	2512	3254	3442	4681	5242
	% change						*15.2*	*19.9*	*3.8*	*29.5*	*5.8*	*36.0*	*12.0*
Llandudno	USD, UD	–	–	–	–	–	–	–	3695	4839[13]	7348	9279	10469
	% change									*31.0*	*51.8*	*26.3*	*12.8*
ANGLESEY													
Beaumaris	B, MB	–	–	–	2675	2701	2599	2558	2291	2239	2202	2326	2231
	% change					*1.1*	*−3.8*	*−1.6*	*−10.4*	*−2.3*	*−1.7*	*5.6*	*−4.1*
Holyhead	Town, B	2132	3005	4071	4282	3869							
	PB, USD, UD	–	–	–	–	2974	5622	6193	7191	8680	8745	1007	1063
	% change		*40.9*	*35.5*	*5.2*	*−9.6*	*89.0*	*10.2*	*16.1*	*20.7*	*0.7*	*−88.5*	*5.6*

Source: John Williams, *Digest of Welsh Historical Statistics* (2 vols., Cardiff, 1985), I, Population Table 12, pp. 62–7. The original sources for this table, from the Census Reports, are given as follows: 1801–31, Enumeration. County Tables; 1841, Enumeration and County Tables and Appendix I; 1851, Enumeration II, Welsh Division County Tables and pp. 84–9 for PBs and MBs; 1861, Volume I. Welsh Division. County Tables and p. xxi, Table IX; 1871, Area etc. Vol. I, Table VII, Vol. II, County Tables; 1881: Area etc. Vol. I, Table VI, Vol. II, Table II and County Tables; 1891 Area etc. Vol. I, Table VI, Vol. II, Table II ; 1901 Summary Tables, XI Wales and Monmouthshire, County Tables; 1911, Administrative Areas, Table 10.
The following notes are those attached to the *Digest* table for the relevant years.

No attempt has been made to calculate at each census date the population of the particular geographical area covered by any particular town at one given date. The figures given throughout relate solely to the administrative areas, and may thus not always reflect the true growth of an urban area.

As far as possible, however, figures have been taken in a consistent basis for each town. In some cases, this presents no problem – figures are available throughout for the same area even though there may be a change in the administrative unit. For example, an Urban Sanitary District may become an Urban District but still cover the same area. In other cases it has been impossible to obtain figures on a consistent basis. Such breaks in continuity are indicated by starting a new line. For the year of changeover two sets of figures have been given to facilitate comparison.

The administrative units to which the figures relate are indicated after the name of each town and in the line or lines below where there is a break in continuity. Where more than one type of unit is given on the same line, these units are consecutive, not

concurrent, but the actual area involved remains the same. The types of administrative units with the abbreviations used are as follows:

> Parish, Town, Borough, used 1801–41 and, in a few cases, 1851–71; 'Town' – used 1851–61 for Pontypool, Tredegar, Chepstow and Abergavenny. The limits were defined by the Superintendent Registrar of the Division; MB (Municipal Borough) used 1851–1911; CB (County Borough), used 1891–1911; LBd (Local Board District), used 1871 only; ICD (Improvement Commissioners District), used 1871 only; USD (Urban Sanitary District), used 1881–91; UD (Urban District), used 1901–11; PB (Parliamentary Borough), used 1841–71.

1801–41. For some towns figures are readily obtained for these years: they are described in the census as towns or boroughs and distinguished from the parishes. In a few other cases the boundaries of a town appear to be the same as the parish under which it appeared in the early censuses. In most cases, however, parish boundaries do not coincide with the boundaries of what later became towns. For this reason no figures are given for 1801–41 for many of the towns included in the table. And caution is needed in interpreting any figures which are given for 1801–41, partly because it is often impossible to tell if the figures disguise boundary changes but also, and more important, because the figures in the first three censuses underestimated the true size of the population. The county population figures were later revised but (with the exceptions of Merthyr Tydfil and Swansea) the figures for towns and parishes were not revised.

[1] These are only approximate figures, given in 1881.

[2] All figures for Newport 1801–51 are taken from the 1851 census, and may be for the area as constituted in 1851, since they differ considerably from the figures given in individual censuses. There was a boundary change at some time before 1851. The 1821 figure is an estimate made by Rickman in 1831.

[3] The figure 2277 is the population of the area in 1891, for the area as in 1881. It has been calculated from figures in the 1891 census.

[4] Called Ystradyfodwg until 1891.

[5] No boundary change between 1861 and 1871 is mentioned in the 1871 census, but the large difference in the figures given for 1861 in the 1861 and 1871 censuses would seem to indicate a change – unless there was an error or a revision in 1871.

[6] The figures for 1801–41 are taken from the 1851 census and relate as nearly as possible to the area as constituted in 1851.

[7] The Llanelli figures for 1801 and 1811 reflect later (1851) attempts to place population on the same boundary basis.

[8] The sum of the two parishes making up the borough of Pembroke.

[9] The present UD is Newtown and Llanllwchaearn. The USD covered the same area. The two parishes were added together to obtain the figures 1801–71; together they are the same area as the USD and UD.

[10] The 1881 census gives 7199 as population for 1871, but does not indicate any boundary change.

[11] The figures given for 1811–31 are the totals of the figures for Wrexham Regis and Wrexham Abbot for these years, since the population of these two parishes corresponded with that of Wrexham Parliamentary Borough in 1841. The percentage figure for 1801, however, is only that for Wrexham Regis, since Wrexham Abbot is not given in the census for this year; this accounts for the apparently large increase in population between 1801 and 1811.

[12] Parish of Llanbeblig, which includes the Borough of Caernarfon, and the townships of Bontnewydd and Treflan.

[13] The figure 4807 is given for 1881 in 1891; however, no boundary change is indicated. 4807 may be a revision or an error.

Population Figure a Population distribution. Wales and Registration Counties. 1801, 1851, 1911

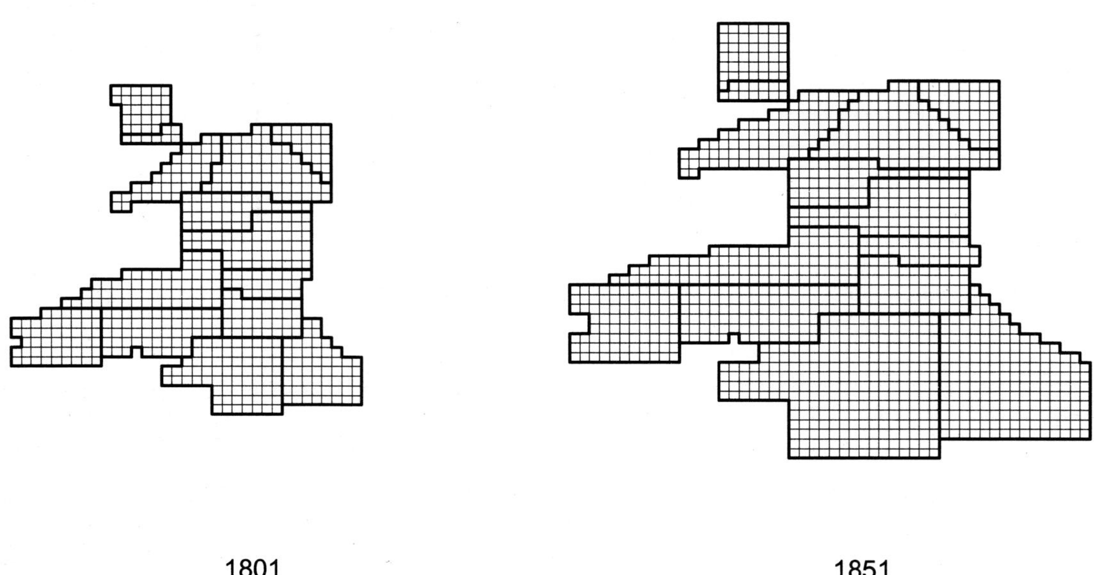

1801

1851

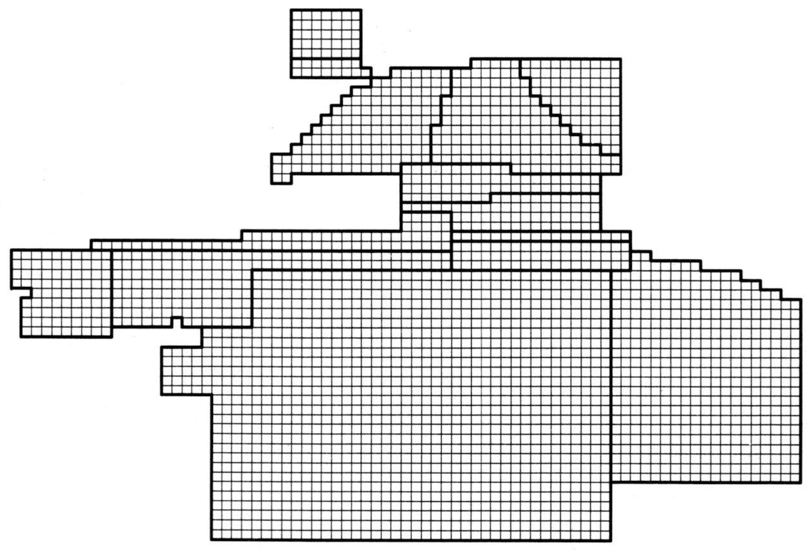

1911

1 square = 1,000 people

Population 2.1 Ages. Persons, males, females. Number and percentage. Wales and Registration Counties. 1851, 1881, 1911

			Number						Percentage				
		Year	All ages	under 15	15–	30–	45–	60–	< 15	15–	30–	45–	60–
WALES	Persons	1851	1188914	430467	315882	211027	132304	99234	*36.2*	*26.6*	*17.7*	*11.1*	*8.3*
		1881	1577559	586091	409965	271453	181748	128302	*37.2*	*26.0*	*17.2*	*11.5*	*8.1*
		1911	2442041	805100	653381	507292	300001	176267	*33.0*	*26.8*	*20.8*	*12.3*	*7.2*
	Males	1851	594793	217805	159061	107363	65868	44696	*36.6*	*26.7*	*18.1*	*11.1*	*7.5*
		1881	789074	294301	209802	135813	89275	59883	*37.3*	*26.6*	*17.2*	*11.3*	*7.6*
		1911	1242387	403177	338163	263659	154931	82457	*32.5*	*27.2*	*21.2*	*12.5*	*6.6*
	Females	1851	594121	212662	156821	103664	66436	54538	*35.8*	*26.4*	*17.4*	*11.2*	*9.2*
		1881	788485	291790	200163	135640	92473	68419	*37.0*	*25.4*	*17.2*	*11.7*	*8.7*
		1911	1199654	401923	315218	243633	145070	93810	*33.5*	*26.3*	*20.3*	*12.1*	*7.8*
Registration Counties													
MONMOUTH	Persons	1851	177130	63277	49655	33852	18564	11782	*35.7*	*28.0*	*19.1*	*10.5*	*6.7*
		1881	234332	89798	59808	40300	26713	17713	*38.3*	*25.5*	*17.2*	*11.4*	*7.6*
		1911	414666	145154	112479	84888	47024	25121	*35.0*	*27.1*	*20.5*	*11.3*	*6.1*
	Males	1851	92301	31759	26590	18325	9901	5726	*34.4*	*28.8*	*19.9*	*10.7*	*6.2*
		1881	119965	44962	31690	20893	13608	8812	*37.5*	*26.4*	*17.4*	*11.3*	*7.3*
		1911	216906	73018	60089	45896	25398	12505	*33.7*	*27.7*	*21.2*	*11.7*	*5.8*
	Females	1851	84829	31518	23065	15527	8663	6056	*37.2*	*27.2*	*18.3*	*10.2*	*7.1*
		1881	114367	44836	28118	19407	13105	8901	*39.2*	*24.6*	*17.0*	*11.5*	*7.8*
		1911	197760	72136	52390	38992	21626	12616	*36.5*	*26.5*	*19.7*	*10.9*	*6.4*
GLAMORGAN	Persons	1851	240095	86526	70113	45855	23761	13840	*36.0*	*29.2*	*19.1*	*9.9*	*5.8*
		1881	518383	199494	142890	92907	53907	29185	*38.5*	*27.6*	*17.9*	*10.4*	*5.6*
		1911	1130668	389015	313530	240566	127223	60334	*34.4*	*27.7*	*21.3*	*11.3*	*5.3*
	Males	1851	125087	43683	37676	24999	12451	6278	*34.9*	*30.1*	*20.0*	*10.0*	*5.0*
		1881	266128	99955	75639	49149	27518	13867	*37.6*	*28.4*	*18.5*	*10.3*	*5.2*
		1911	587666	194395	165276	130051	68859	29085	*33.1*	*28.1*	*22.1*	*11.7*	*4.9*
	Females	1851	115008	42843	32437	20856	11310	7562	*37.3*	*28.2*	*18.1*	*9.8*	*6.6*
		1881	252255	99539	67251	43758	26389	15318	*39.5*	*26.7*	*17.3*	*10.5*	*6.1*
		1911	543002	194620	148254	110515	58364	31249	*35.8*	*27.3*	*20.4*	*10.7*	*5.8*
CARMARTHEN	Persons	1851	94672	35653	24483	15423	10501	8612	*37.7*	*25.9*	*16.3*	*11.1*	*9.1*
		1881	111255	42286	28862	17989	12263	9855	*38.0*	*25.9*	*16.2*	*11.0*	*8.9*
		1911	151050	47876	42291	30565	18497	11821	*31.7*	*28.0*	*20.2*	*12.2*	*7.8*
	Males	1851	45519	18051	11432	7384	4980	3672	*39.7*	*25.1*	*16.2*	*10.9*	*8.1*
		1881	53489	21454	13625	8333	5741	4336	*40.1*	*25.5*	*15.6*	*10.7*	*8.1*
		1911	76017	23761	21980	15768	9285	5223	*31.3*	*28.9*	*20.7*	*12.2*	*6.9*
	Females	1851	49153	17602	13051	8039	5521	4940	*35.8*	*26.6*	*16.4*	*11.2*	*10.1*
		1881	57766	20832	15237	9656	6522	5519	*36.1*	*26.4*	*16.7*	*11.3*	*9.6*
		1911	75033	24115	20311	14797	9212	6598	*32.1*	*27.1*	*19.7*	*12.3*	*8.8*
PEMBROKE	Persons	1851	84472	31520	21172	14025	9703	8052	*37.3*	*25.1*	*16.6*	*11.5*	*9.5*
		1881	83679	29847	21695	13177	10216	8744	*35.7*	*25.9*	*15.7*	*12.2*	*10.4*
		1911	84874	25575	22799	16319	11763	8418	*30.1*	*26.9*	*19.2*	*13.9*	*9.9*
	Males	1851	39620	15937	9364	6498	4427	3394	*40.2*	*23.6*	*16.4*	*11.2*	*8.6*
		1881	40085	15052	10408	5987	4754	3884	*37.6*	*26.0*	*14.9*	*11.9*	*9.7*
		1911	41219	12841	11304	7742	5571	3761	*31.2*	*27.4*	*18.8*	*13.5*	*9.1*
	Females	1851	44852	15583	11808	7527	5276	4658	*34.7*	*26.3*	*16.8*	*11.8*	*10.4*
		1881	43594	14795	11287	7190	5462	4860	*33.9*	*25.9*	*16.5*	*12.5*	*11.1*
		1911	43655	12734	11495	8577	6192	4657	*29.2*	*26.3*	*19.6*	*14.2*	*10.7*

		Year	Number All ages	under 15	15–	30–	45–	60–	Percentage < 15	15–	30–	45–	60–
CARDIGAN	Persons	1851	97614	35720	24178	16319	11697	9700	*36.6*	*24.8*	*16.7*	*12.0*	*9.9*
		1881	95137	33405	23204	15242	12248	11038	*35.1*	*24.4*	*16.0*	*12.9*	*11.6*
		1911	80769	21541	19910	15460	12720	11138	*26.7*	*24.7*	*19.1*	*15.7*	*13.8*
	Males	1851	45155	18004	10667	7135	5261	4088	*39.9*	*23.6*	*15.8*	*11.7*	*9.1*
		1881	42717	16766	10168	6089	5126	4568	*39.2*	*23.8*	*14.3*	*12.0*	*10.7*
		1911	36526	10768	9069	6573	5544	4572	*29.5*	*24.8*	*18.0*	*15.2*	*12.5*
	Females	1851	52459	17716	13511	9184	6436	5612	*33.8*	*25.8*	*17.5*	*12.3*	*10.7*
		1881	52420	16639	13036	9153	7122	6470	*31.7*	*24.9*	*17.5*	*13.6*	*12.3*
		1911	44243	10773	10841	8887	7176	6566	*24.3*	*24.5*	*20.1*	*16.2*	*14.8*
BRECON	Persons	1851	49178	20295	16150	10566	6593	5574	*34.3*	*27.3*	*17.9*	*11.1*	*9.4*
		1881	54140	19521	13688	8877	6717	5337	*36.1*	*25.3*	*16.4*	*12.4*	*9.9*
		1911	56370	17609	14547	11236	7629	5349	*31.2*	*25.8*	*19.9*	*13.5*	*9.5*
	Males	1851	29993	10294	8191	5508	3402	2598	*34.3*	*27.3*	*18.4*	*11.3*	*8.7*
		1881	26991	9768	6842	4486	3323	2572	*36.2*	*25.3*	*16.6*	*12.3*	*9.5*
		1911	28308	8816	7226	5730	3912	2624	*31.1*	*25.5*	*20.2*	*13.8*	*9.3*
	Females	1851	29185	10001	7959	5058	3191	2976	*34.3*	*27.3*	*17.3*	*10.9*	*10.2*
		1881	27149	9753	6846	4391	3394	2765	*35.9*	*25.2*	*16.2*	*12.5*	*10.2*
		1911	28062	8793	7321	5506	3717	2725	*31.3*	*26.1*	*19.6*	*13.2*	*9.7*
RADNOR	Persons	1851	31425	11273	8227	5163	3655	3107	*35.9*	*26.2*	*16.4*	*11.6*	*9.9*
		1881	18523	6725	4724	2893	2258	1923	*36.3*	*25.5*	*15.6*	*12.2*	*10.4*
		1911	17505	5277	4359	3403	2445	2021	*30.1*	*24.9*	*19.4*	*14.0*	*11.5*
	Males	1851	16118	5814	4197	2701	1876	1530	*36.1*	*26.0*	*16.8*	*11.6*	*9.5*
		1881	9404	3386	2405	1488	1158	967	*36.0*	*25.6*	*15.8*	*12.3*	*10.3*
		1911	8796	2697	2083	1703	1245	1068	*30.7*	*23.7*	*19.4*	*14.2*	*12.1*
	Females	1851	15307	5459	4030	2462	1779	1577	*35.7*	*26.3*	*16.1*	*11.6*	*10.3*
		1881	9119	3339	2319	1405	1100	956	*36.6*	*25.4*	*15.4*	*12.1*	*10.5*
		1911	8709	2580	2276	1700	1200	953	*29.6*	*26.1*	*19.5*	*13.8*	*10.9*
MONTGOMERY	Persons	1851	77142	27353	19905	12529	9302	8053	*35.5*	*25.8*	*16.2*	*12.1*	*10.4*
		1881	76196	27764	18777	12088	9502	8065	*36.4*	*24.6*	*15.9*	*12.5*	*10.6*
		1911	62201	18733	15013	11975	9166	7314	*30.1*	*24.1*	*19.3*	*14.7*	*11.8*
	Males	1851	38541	13734	10066	6290	4688	3763	*35.6*	*26.1*	*16.3*	*12.2*	*9.8*
		1881	38295	13998	9653	5962	4789	3893	*36.6*	*25.2*	*15.6*	*12.5*	*10.2*
		1911	30536	9474	7303	5717	4527	3515	*31.0*	*23.9*	*18.7*	*14.8*	*11.5*
	Females	1851	38601	13619	9839	6239	4614	4290	*35.3*	*25.5*	*16.2*	*12.0*	*11.1*
		1881	37901	13766	9124	6126	4713	4172	*36.3*	*24.1*	*16.2*	*12.4*	*11.0*
		1911	31665	9259	7710	6258	4639	3799	*29.2*	*24.3*	*19.8*	*14.7*	*12.0*
FLINT	Persons	1851	41047	15768	9906	7096	4929	3348	*38.4*	*24.1*	*17.3*	*12.0*	*8.2*
		1881	45774	17346	10889	8160	5504	3875	*37.9*	*23.8*	*17.8*	*12.0*	*8.5*
		1911	69722	23314	17298	14136	8852	6122	*33.4*	*24.8*	*20.3*	*12.7*	*8.8*
	Males	1851	20787	8081	5255	3650	2458	1343	*38.9*	*25.3*	*17.6*	*11.8*	*6.5*
		1881	23217	8645	5983	4180	2689	1720	*37.2*	*25.8*	*18.0*	*11.6*	*7.4*
		1911	35440	11585	9332	7173	4481	2869	*32.7*	*26.3*	*20.2*	*12.6*	*8.1*
	Females	1851	20260	7687	4651	3446	2471	2005	*37.9*	*23.0*	*17.0*	*12.2*	*9.9*
		1881	22557	8701	4906	3980	2815	2155	*38.6*	*21.7*	*17.6*	*12.5*	*9.6*
		1911	34282	11729	7966	6963	4371	3253	*34.2*	*23.2*	*20.3*	*12.8*	*9.5*

		Year	Number All ages	under 15	15–	30–	45–	60–	Percentage < 15	15–	30–	45–	60–
DENBIGH	Persons	1851	96915	34782	24747	16928	11503	8955	*35.9*	*25.5*	*17.5*	*11.9*	*9.2*
		1881	112940	40973	28138	19624	14138	10067	*36.3*	*24.9*	*17.4*	*12.5*	*8.9*
		1911	136810	43417	34000	28696	18496	12201	*31.7*	*24.9*	*21.0*	*13.5*	*8.9*
	Males	1851	48639	17786	12503	8495	5734	4121	*36.6*	*25.7*	*17.5*	*11.8*	*8.5*
		1881	56501	20468	14555	9774	6962	4742	*36.2*	*25.8*	*17.3*	*12.3*	*8.4*
		1911	68298	21963	17495	14117	9148	5575	*32.2*	*25.6*	*20.7*	*13.4*	*8.2*
	Females	1851	48276	16996	12244	8433	5769	4834	*35.2*	*25.4*	*17.5*	*12.0*	*10.0*
		1881	56439	20505	13583	9850	7176	5325	*36.3*	*24.1*	*17.5*	*12.7*	*9.4*
		1911	68512	21454	16505	14579	9348	6626	*31.3*	*24.1*	*21.3*	*13.6*	*9.7*
MERIONETH	Persons	1851	51307	18528	12371	8829	6053	5526	*36.1*	*24.1*	*17.2*	*11.8*	*10.8*
		1881	68278	24654	16957	12373	7972	6322	*36.1*	*24.8*	*18.1*	*11.7*	*9.3*
		1911	60280	17523	14239	12408	9139	6971	*29.1*	*23.6*	*20.6*	*15.2*	*11.6*
	Males	1851	25389	9426	6128	4387	2940	2508	*37.1*	*24.1*	*17.3*	*11.6*	*9.9*
		1881	34350	12248	8869	6301	3981	2951	*35.7*	*25.8*	*18.3*	*11.6*	*8.6*
		1911	29076	8621	6994	5900	4422	3139	*29.6*	*24.1*	*20.3*	*15.2*	*10.8*
	Females	1851	25918	9102	6243	4442	3113	3018	*35.1*	*24.1*	*17.1*	*12.0*	*11.6*
		1881	33928	12406	8088	6072	3991	3371	*36.6*	*23.8*	*17.9*	*11.8*	*9.9*
		1911	31204	8902	7245	6508	4717	3832	*28.5*	*23.2*	*20.9*	*15.1*	*12.3*
CAERNARFON	Persons	1851	94674	34149	24109	16843	11058	8515	*36.1*	*25.5*	*17.8*	*11.7*	*9.0*
		1881	123781	42672	31783	21904	15537	11885	*34.5*	*25.7*	*17.7*	*12.6*	*9.6*
		1911	141767	39608	34440	30737	21655	15327	*27.9*	*24.3*	*21.7*	*15.3*	*10.8*
	Males	1851	46472	17372	11647	8331	5313	3809	*37.4*	*25.1*	*17.9*	*11.4*	*8.2*
		1881	60742	21741	15708	10385	7371	5537	*35.8*	*25.9*	*17.1*	*12.1*	*9.1*
		1911	66619	19883	16006	14069	9999	6662	*29.8*	*24.0*	*21.1*	*15.0*	*10.0*
	Females	1851	48202	16777	12462	8512	5745	4706	*34.8*	*25.9*	*17.7*	*11.9*	*9.8*
		1881	63039	20931	16075	11519	8166	6348	*33.2*	*25.5*	*18.3*	*13.0*	*10.1*
		1911	75148	19725	18434	16668	11656	8665	*26.2*	*24.5*	*22.2*	*15.5*	*11.5*
ANGLESEY	Persons	1851	43243	15623	10866	7599	4985	4170	*36.1*	*25.1*	*17.6*	*11.5*	*9.6*
		1881	35141	11606	8550	5919	4773	4293	*33.0*	*24.3*	*16.8*	*13.6*	*12.2*
		1911	35359	10458	8476	6903	5392	4130	*29.6*	*24.0*	*19.5*	*15.2*	*11.7*
	Males	1851	21172	7864	5345	3660	2437	1866	*37.1*	*25.2*	*17.3*	*11.5*	*8.8*
		1881	17190	5858	4257	2786	2255	2034	*34.1*	*24.8*	*16.2*	*13.1*	*11.8*
		1911	16980	5355	4006	3220	2540	1859	*31.5*	*23.6*	*19.0*	*15.0*	*10.9*
	Females	1851	22071	7759	5521	3939	2548	2304	*35.2*	*25.0*	*17.8*	*11.5*	*10.4*
		1881	17951	5748	4293	3133	2518	2259	*32.0*	*23.9*	*17.5*	*14.0*	*12.6*
		1911	18379	5103	4470	3683	2852	2271	*27.8*	*24.3*	*20.0*	*15.5*	*12.4*

Sources: *Census of Population for England and Wales*: 1851, *Population Tables II, Ages, Civil Condition, Occupations, and Birthplace of the People. Vol. II,* (HMSO, 1854), p. 813; 1881, *Vol. III, Ages, Condition as to Marriage, Occupations, and Birthplaces of the People* (HMSO, 1883), Division XI – Wales and Monmouthshire, Table 1; 1911, County Volumes: *Anglesey, Carnarvon, Denbigh and Flint; Cardigan, Merioneth and Montgomery; Glamorgan; Brecknock, Carmarthen, Pembroke and Radnor; Monmouth* (HMSO, 1914), Table 19.

These figures are for the Registration Division of Wales and Monmouthshire, and the constituent Registration Counties. In some cases the boundaries differ considerably from those of the Ancient, Geographical or 'Proper' county. (See the County Maps and Appendix II (pp. 174–99) for details of the differences.)

Population 2.2 Ages. Persons, males, females. Number and percentage. Registration Districts. 1851, 1881, 1911

Registration District[1]		Year	Number All ages	under 15	15–	30–	45–	60–	Percentage under 15	15–	30–	45–	60–
MONMOUTHSHIRE													
Chepstow	Persons	1851	19057	6702	4997	3507	2169	1682	*35.2*	*26.2*	*18.4*	*11.4*	*8.8*
		1881	18701	6853	4409	3137	2372	1930	*36.6*	*23.6*	*16.8*	*12.7*	*10.3*
		1911	19929	6490	4789	3863	2802	1985	*32.6*	*24.0*	*19.4*	*14.1*	*10.0*
	Males	1851	9696	3355	2578	1840	1111	812	*34.6*	*26.6*	*19.0*	*11.5*	*8.4*
		1881	9461	3459	2281	1549	1222	950	*36.6*	*24.1*	*16.4*	*12.9*	*10.0*
		1911	9866	3253	2376	1888	1386	963	*33.0*	*24.1*	*19.1*	*14.0*	*9.8*
	Females	1851	9361	3347	2419	1667	1058	870	*35.8*	*25.8*	*17.8*	*11.3*	*9.3*
		1881	9240	3394	2128	1588	1150	980	*36.7*	*23.0*	*17.2*	*12.4*	*10.6*
		1911	10063	3237	2413	1975	1416	1022	*32.2*	*24.0*	*19.6*	*14.1*	*10.2*
Monmouth	Persons	1851	27379	9857	6862	4885	3160	2615	*36.0*	*25.1*	*17.8*	*11.5*	*9.6*
		1881	30340	11694	6938	4827	3804	3077	*38.5*	*22.9*	*15.9*	*12.5*	*10.1*
		1911	29374	9681	7063	5600	3976	3054	*33.0*	*24.0*	*19.1*	*13.5*	*10.4*
	Males	1851	13705	4885	3432	2521	1609	1258	*35.6*	*25.0*	*18.4*	*11.7*	*9.2*
		1881	15377	5964	3637	2408	1866	1502	*38.8*	*23.7*	*15.7*	*12.1*	*9.8*
		1911	14896	4895	3800	2795	1991	1415	*32.9*	*25.5*	*18.8*	*13.4*	*9.5*
	Females	1851	13674	4972	3430	2364	1551	1357	*36.4*	*25.1*	*17.3*	*11.3*	*9.9*
		1881	14963	5730	3301	2419	1938	1575	*38.3*	*22.1*	*16.2*	*13.0*	*10.5*
		1911	14478	4786	3263	2805	1985	1639	*33.1*	*22.5*	*19.4*	*13.7*	*11.3*
Abergavenny	Persons	1851	59229	21095	17680	11400	5882	3172	*35.6*	*29.9*	*19.2*	*9.9*	*5.4*
		1881	23571	8474	5823	4286	2916	2072	*36.0*	*24.7*	*18.2*	*12.4*	*8.8*
		1911	28678	8872	7309	5846	4006	2645	*30.9*	*25.5*	*20.4*	*14.0*	*9.2*
	Males	1851	31743	10625	9985	6371	3233	1529	*33.5*	*31.5*	*20.1*	*10.2*	*4.8*
		1881	11879	4211	2962	2209	1444	1053	*35.4*	*24.9*	*18.6*	*12.2*	*8.9*
		1911	14719	4549	3742	2996	2108	1324	*30.9*	*25.4*	*20.4*	*14.3*	*9.0*
	Females	1851	27486	10470	7695	5029	2649	1643	*38.1*	*28.0*	*18.3*	*9.6*	*6.0*
		1881	11692	4263	2861	2077	1472	1019	*36.5*	*24.5*	*17.8*	*12.6*	*8.7*
		1911	13959	4323	3567	2850	1898	1321	*31.0*	*25.6*	*20.4*	*13.6*	*9.5*
Bedwellte	Persons	1881	55840	21950	14798	9734	6044	3314	*39.3*	*26.5*	*17.4*	*10.8*	*5.9*
		1911	122288	46103	33829	25329	11737	5290	*37.7*	*27.7*	*20.7*	*9.6*	*4.3*
	Males	1881	29793	11022	8465	5357	3225	1724	*37.0*	*28.4*	*18.0*	*10.8*	*5.8*
		1911	66225	23223	19077	14434	6720	2771	*35.1*	*28.8*	*21.8*	*10.1*	*4.2*
	Females	1881	26047	10928	6333	4377	2819	1590	*42.0*	*24.3*	*16.8*	*10.8*	*6.1*
		1911	56063	22880	14752	10895	5017	2519	*40.8*	*26.3*	*19.4*	*8.9*	*4.5*
Pontypool	Persons	1851	27993	10410	7548	5315	2983	1737	*37.2*	*27.0*	*19.0*	*10.7*	*6.2*
		1881	35338	13959	8996	5762	4009	2612	*39.5*	*25.5*	*16.3*	*11.3*	*7.4*
		1911	61868	22369	16925	12338	6791	3445	*36.2*	*27.4*	*19.9*	*11.0*	*5.6*
	Males	1851	14563	5262	3993	2857	1589	862	*36.1*	*27.4*	*19.6*	*10.9*	*5.9*
		1881	18258	7011	4901	2979	2042	1325	*38.4*	*26.8*	*16.3*	*11.2*	*7.3*
		1911	32566	11154	9181	6825	3667	1739	*34.3*	*28.2*	*21.0*	*11.3*	*5.3*
	Females	1851	13430	5148	3555	2458	1394	875	*38.3*	*26.5*	*18.3*	*10.4*	*6.5*
		1881	17080	6948	4095	2783	1967	1287	*40.7*	*24.0*	*16.3*	*11.5*	*7.5*
		1911	29302	11215	7744	5513	3124	1706	*38.3*	*26.4*	*18.8*	*10.7*	*5.8*

Registration District[1]		Year	Number All ages	under 15	15–	30–	45–	60–	*Percentage under 15*	*15–*	*30–*	*45–*	*60–*
Newport	Persons	1851	43472	15213	12568	8745	4370	2576	*35.0*	*28.9*	*20.1*	*10.1*	*5.9*
		1881	70542	26868	18844	12554	7568	4708	*38.1*	*26.7*	*17.8*	*10.7*	*6.7*
		1911	152529	51639	42564	31912	17712	8702	*33.9*	*27.9*	*20.9*	*11.6*	*5.7*
	Males	1851	22594	7632	6602	4736	2359	1265	*33.8*	*29.2*	*21.0*	*10.4*	*5.6*
		1881	35197	13295	9444	6391	3809	2258	*37.8*	*26.8*	*18.2*	*10.8*	*6.4*
		1911	78634	25944	21913	16958	9526	4293	*33.0*	*27.9*	*21.6*	*12.1*	*5.5*
	Females	1851	20878	7581	5966	4009	2011	1311	*36.3*	*28.6*	*19.2*	*9.6*	*6.3*
		1881	35345	13573	9400	6163	3759	2450	*38.4*	*26.6*	*17.4*	*10.6*	*6.9*
		1911	73895	25695	20651	14954	8186	4409	*34.8*	*27.9*	*20.2*	*11.1*	*6.0*
GLAMORGAN													
Cardiff	Persons	1851	46491	15160	14136	9451	4800	2944	*32.6*	*30.4*	*20.3*	*10.3*	*6.3*
		1881	106164	38538	30848	20198	11147	5433	*36.3*	*29.1*	*19.0*	*10.5*	*5.1*
		1911	264710	85182	73233	56487	33471	16337	*32.2*	*27.7*	*21.3*	*12.6*	*6.2*
	Males	1851	24902	7683	7777	5379	2638	1425	*30.9*	*31.2*	*21.6*	*10.6*	*5.7*
		1881	54128	19272	15706	10766	5758	2626	*35.6*	*29.0*	*19.9*	*10.6*	*4.9*
		1911	130502	42266	34993	28110	17278	7855	*32.4*	*26.8*	*21.5*	*13.2*	*6.0*
	Females	1851	21589	7477	6359	4072	2162	1519	*34.6*	*29.5*	*18.9*	*10.0*	*7.0*
		1881	52036	19266	15142	9432	5389	2807	*37.0*	*29.1*	*18.1*	*10.4*	*5.4*
		1911	134208	42916	38240	28377	16193	8482	*32.0*	*28.5*	*21.1*	*12.1*	*6.3*
Pontypridd	Persons	1881	93493	36797	26648	16982	8981	4085	*39.4*	*28.5*	*18.2*	*9.6*	*4.4*
		1911	288564	105670	80068	61712	29581	11533	*36.6*	*27.7*	*21.4*	*10.3*	*4.0*
	Males	1881	50675	18661	15537	9528	4845	2104	*36.8*	*30.7*	*18.8*	*9.6*	*4.2*
		1911	155972	52807	45006	35474	16954	5731	*33.9*	*28.9*	*22.7*	*10.9*	*3.7*
	Females	1881	42818	18136	11111	7454	4136	1981	*42.4*	*25.9*	*17.4*	*9.7*	*4.6*
		1911	132592	52863	35062	26238	12627	5802	*39.9*	*26.4*	*19.8*	*9.5*	*4.4*
Merthyr Tydfil	Persons	1851	76804	27119	23806	15559	6956	3364	*35.3*	*31.0*	*20.3*	*9.1*	*4.4*
		1881	101441	38993	27316	17801	11120	6211	*38.4*	*26.9*	*17.5*	*11.0*	*6.1*
		1911	174147	60997	47795	37402	18961	8992	*35.0*	*27.4*	*21.5*	*10.9*	*5.2*
	Males	1851	41425	13655	13551	8847	3792	1580	*33.0*	*32.7*	*21.4*	*9.2*	*3.8*
		1881	52430	19511	14846	9505	5640	2928	*37.2*	*28.3*	*18.1*	*10.8*	*5.6*
		1911	92477	30623	26111	20791	10545	4407	*33.1*	*28.2*	*22.5*	*11.4*	*4.8*
	Females	1851	35379	13464	10255	6712	3164	1784	*38.1*	*29.0*	*19.0*	*8.9*	*5.0*
		1881	49011	19482	12470	8296	5480	3283	*39.8*	*25.4*	*16.9*	*11.2*	*6.7*
		1911	81670	30374	21684	16611	8416	4585	*37.2*	*26.6*	*20.3*	*10.3*	*5.6*
Bridgend	Persons	1851	23422	8502	6198	4008	2726	1988	*36.3*	*26.5*	*17.1*	*11.6*	*8.5*
		1881	38920	14609	10117	6813	4390	2991	*37.5*	*26.0*	*17.5*	*11.3*	*7.7*
		1911	94609	33497	25373	20073	10492	5174	*35.4*	*26.8*	*21.2*	*11.1*	*5.5*
	Males	1851	11789	4293	3121	2066	1394	915	*36.4*	*26.5*	*17.5*	*11.8*	*7.8*
		1881	20054	7310	5389	3619	2243	1493	*36.5*	*26.9*	*18.0*	*11.2*	*7.4*
		1911	49920	16790	13619	11148	5748	2615	*33.6*	*27.3*	*22.3*	*11.5*	*5.2*
	Females	1851	11633	4209	3077	1942	1332	1073	*36.2*	*26.5*	*16.7*	*11.5*	*9.2*
		1881	18866	7299	4728	3194	2147	1498	*38.7*	*25.1*	*16.9*	*11.4*	*7.9*
		1911	44689	16707	11754	8925	4744	2559	*37.4*	*26.3*	*20.0*	*10.6*	*5.7*

Registration District[1]		Year	Number All ages	under 15	15–	30–	45–	60–	*Percentage* *under 15*	*15–*	*30–*	*45–*	*60–*
Neath	Persons	1851	46471	18266	13229	8401	4290	2285	*39.3*	*28.5*	*18.1*	*9.2*	*4.9*
		1881	52077	20650	13840	8984	5442	3161	*39.7*	*26.6*	*17.3*	*10.4*	*6.1*
		1911	100924	35747	28241	20757	10845	5334	*35.4*	*28.0*	*20.6*	*10.7*	*5.3*
	Males	1851	24208	9212	7178	4565	2246	1007	*38.1*	*29.7*	*18.9*	*9.3*	*4.2*
		1881	26219	10317	7132	4581	2740	1449	*39.3*	*27.2*	*17.5*	*10.5*	*5.5*
		1911	52748	17935	15148	11293	5829	2543	*34.0*	*28.7*	*21.4*	*11.1*	*4.8*
	Females	1851	22263	9054	6051	3836	2044	1278	*40.7*	*27.2*	*17.2*	*9.2*	*5.7*
		1881	25858	10333	6708	4403	2702	1712	*40.0*	*25.9*	*17.0*	*10.4*	*6.6*
		1911	48176	17812	13093	9464	5016	2791	*37.0*	*27.2*	*19.6*	*10.4*	*5.8*
Pontardawe	Persons	1881	20185	8456	5217	3165	2025	1322	*41.9*	*25.8*	*15.7*	*10.0*	*6.5*
		1911	41969	14863	12023	8885	4135	2063	*35.4*	*28.6*	*21.2*	*9.9*	*4.9*
	Males	1881	10116	4252	2663	1556	1026	619	*42.0*	*26.3*	*15.4*	*10.1*	*6.1*
		1911	22252	7398	6614	4978	2282	980	*33.2*	*29.7*	*22.4*	*10.3*	*4.4*
	Females	1881	10069	4204	2554	1609	999	703	*41.8*	*25.4*	*16.0*	*9.9*	*7.0*
		1911	19717	7465	5409	3907	1853	1083	*37.9*	*27.4*	*19.8*	*9.4*	*5.5*
Swansea	Persons	1851	46907	17479	12744	8436	4989	3259	*37.3*	*27.2*	*18.0*	*10.6*	*6.9*
		1881	95001	37222	26227	17126	9496	4930	*39.2*	*27.6*	*18.0*	*10.0*	*5.2*
		1911	151025	48427	43049	32122	17963	9464	*32.1*	*28.5*	*21.3*	*11.9*	*6.3*
	Males	1851	22763	8840	6049	4142	2381	1351	*38.8*	*26.6*	*18.2*	*10.5*	*5.9*
		1881	47207	18534	13122	8743	4656	2152	*39.3*	*27.8*	*18.5*	*9.9*	*4.6*
		1911	76771	24239	22045	16811	9377	4299	*31.6*	*28.7*	*21.9*	*12.2*	*5.6*
	Females	1851	24144	8639	6695	4294	2608	1908	*35.8*	*27.7*	*17.8*	*10.8*	*7.9*
		1881	47794	18688	13105	8383	4840	2778	*39.1*	*27.4*	*17.5*	*10.1*	*5.8*
		1911	74254	24188	21004	15311	8586	5165	*32.6*	*28.3*	*20.6*	*11.6*	*7.0*
Gower	Persons	1881	11102	4229	2677	1838	1306	1052	*38.1*	*24.1*	*16.6*	*11.8*	*9.5*
		1911	14720	4632	3748	3128	1775	1437	*31.5*	*25.5*	*21.3*	*12.1*	*9.8*
	Males	1881	5299	2098	1244	851	610	496	*39.6*	*23.5*	*16.1*	*11.5*	*9.4*
		1911	7024	2337	1740	1446	846	655	*33.3*	*24.8*	*20.6*	*12.0*	*9.3*
	Females	1881	5803	2131	1433	987	696	556	*36.7*	*24.7*	*17.0*	*12.0*	*9.6*
		1911	7696	2295	2008	1682	929	782	*29.8*	*26.1*	*21.9*	*12.1*	*10.2*
CARMARTHENSHIRE													
Llanelli	Persons	1851	23507	9515	5949	3951	2454	1638	*40.5*	*25.3*	*16.8*	*10.4*	*7.0*
		1881	44616	18340	11705	7483	4375	2713	*41.1*	*26.2*	*16.8*	*9.8*	*6.1*
		1911	73999	24620	20857	15227	8542	4753	*33.3*	*28.2*	*20.6*	*11.5*	*6.4*
	Males	1851	11618	4856	2877	1981	1168	736	*41.8*	*24.8*	*17.1*	*10.1*	*6.3*
		1881	22034	9161	5897	3665	2095	1216	*41.6*	*26.8*	*16.6*	*9.5*	*5.5*
		1911	37893	12298	11031	7994	4401	2169	*32.5*	*29.1*	*21.1*	*11.6*	*5.7*
	Females	1851	11889	4659	3072	1970	1286	902	*39.2*	*25.8*	*16.6*	*10.8*	*7.6*
		1881	22582	9179	5808	3818	2280	1497	*40.6*	*25.7*	*16.9*	*10.1*	*6.6*
		1911	36106	12322	9826	7233	4141	2584	*34.1*	*27.2*	*20.0*	*11.5*	*7.2*

Registration District[1]		Year	Number All ages	under 15	15–	30–	45–	60–	Percentage under 15	15–	30–	45–	60–
Llandovery	Persons	1851	15055	5472	4025	2438	1664	1456	*36.3*	*26.7*	*16.2*	*11.1*	*9.7*
		1881	12765	4475	3317	2014	1515	1444	*35.1*	*26.0*	*15.8*	*11.9*	*11.3*
		1911	9353	2516	2550	1810	1330	1147	*26.9*	*27.3*	*19.4*	*14.2*	*12.3*
	Males	1851	7268	2742	1890	1198	803	635	*37.7*	*26.0*	*16.5*	*11.0*	*8.7*
		1881	6106	2303	1494	899	756	654	*37.7*	*24.5*	*14.7*	*12.4*	*10.7*
		1911	4657	1276	1335	894	639	513	*27.4*	*28.7*	*19.2*	*13.7*	*11.0*
	Females	1851	7787	2730	2135	1240	861	821	*35.1*	*27.4*	*15.9*	*11.1*	*10.5*
		1881	6659	2172	1823	1115	759	790	*32.6*	*27.4*	*16.7*	*11.4*	*11.9*
		1911	4696	1240	1215	916	691	634	*26.4*	*25.9*	*19.5*	*14.7*	*13.5*
Llandeilo Fawr	Persons	1851	17968	6622	4613	2893	2059	1781	*36.9*	*25.7*	*16.1*	*11.5*	*9.9*
		1881	18799	7169	4639	2989	2127	1875	*38.1*	*24.7*	*15.9*	*11.3*	*10.0*
		1911	33271	11025	9446	6807	3705	2288	*33.1*	*28.4*	*20.5*	*11.1*	*6.9*
	Males	1851	8651	3380	2153	1386	1001	731	*39.1*	*24.9*	*16.0*	*11.6*	*8.4*
		1881	9032	3672	2167	1373	970	850	*40.7*	*24.0*	*15.2*	*10.7*	*9.4*
		1911	17208	5548	5070	3617	1938	1035	*32.2*	*29.5*	*21.0*	*11.3*	*6.0*
	Females	1851	9317	3242	2460	1507	1058	1050	*34.8*	*26.4*	*16.2*	*11.4*	*11.3*
		1881	9767	3497	2472	1616	1157	1025	*35.8*	*25.3*	*16.5*	*11.8*	*10.5*
		1911	16063	5477	4376	3190	1767	1253	*34.1*	*27.2*	*19.9*	*11.0*	*7.8*
Carmarthen	Persons	1851	38142	14044	9896	6141	4324	3737	*36.8*	*25.9*	*16.1*	*11.3*	*9.8*
		1881	35075	12302	9201	5503	4246	3823	*35.1*	*26.2*	*15.7*	*12.1*	*10.9*
		1911	34427	9715	9438	6721	4920	3633	*28.2*	*27.4*	*19.5*	*14.3*	*10.6*
	Males	1851	17982	7073	4512	2819	2008	1570	*39.3*	*25.1*	*15.7*	*11.2*	*8.7*
		1881	16317	6318	4067	2396	1920	1616	*38.7*	*24.9*	*14.7*	*11.8*	*9.9*
		1911	16259	4639	4544	3263	2307	1506	*28.5*	*27.9*	*20.1*	*14.2*	*9.3*
	Females	1851	20160	6971	5384	3322	2316	2167	*34.6*	*26.7*	*16.5*	*11.5*	*10.7*
		1881	18758	5984	5134	3107	2326	2207	*31.9*	*27.4*	*16.6*	*12.4*	*11.8*
		1911	18168	5076	4894	3458	2613	2127	*27.9*	*26.9*	*19.0*	*14.4*	*11.7*
PEMBROKESHIRE													
Narberth	Persons	1851	22130	8575	5262	3569	2523	2201	*38.7*	*23.8*	*16.1*	*11.4*	*9.9*
		1881	19541	7198	4771	2937	2341	2294	*36.8*	*24.4*	*15.0*	*12.0*	*11.7*
		1911	17322	4987	4450	3254	2592	2039	*28.8*	*25.7*	*18.8*	*15.0*	*11.8*
	Males	1851	10459	4371	2415	1607	1162	904	*41.8*	*23.1*	*15.4*	*11.1*	*8.6*
		1881	9149	3655	2163	1318	1033	980	*39.9*	*23.6*	*14.4*	*11.3*	*10.7*
		1911	8146	2484	2121	1483	1167	891	*30.5*	*26.0*	*18.2*	*14.3*	*10.9*
	Females	1851	11671	4204	2847	1962	1361	1297	*36.0*	*24.4*	*16.8*	*11.7*	*11.1*
		1881	10392	3543	2608	1619	1308	1314	*34.1*	*25.1*	*15.6*	*12.6*	*12.6*
		1911	9176	2503	2329	1771	1425	1148	*27.3*	*25.4*	*19.3*	*15.5*	*12.5*
Pembroke	Persons	1851	22960	8464	5895	4111	2473	2017	*36.9*	*25.7*	*17.9*	*10.8*	*8.8*
		1881	30347	10869	8180	4991	3653	2654	*35.8*	*27.0*	*16.4*	*12.0*	*8.7*
		1911	30982	8977	8632	5907	4420	3046	*29.0*	*27.9*	*19.1*	*14.3*	*9.8*
	Males	1851	10778	4274	2530	1966	1142	866	*39.7*	*23.5*	*18.2*	*10.6*	*8.0*
		1881	14780	5532	3981	2331	1741	1195	*37.4*	*26.9*	*15.8*	*11.8*	*8.1*
		1911	15251	4540	4398	2825	2102	1386	*29.8*	*28.8*	*18.5*	*13.8*	*9.1*
	Females	1851	12182	4190	3365	2145	1331	1151	*34.4*	*27.6*	*17.6*	*10.9*	*9.4*
		1881	15567	5337	4199	2660	1912	1459	*34.3*	*27.0*	*17.1*	*12.3*	*9.4*
		1911	15731	4437	4234	3082	2318	1660	*28.2*	*26.9*	*19.6*	*14.7*	*10.6*

Registration District[1]		Year	Number All ages	under 15	15–	30–	45–	60–	*Percentage* *under 15*	*15–*	*30–*	*45–*	*60–*
Haverfordwest	Persons	1851	39382	14481	10015	6345	4707	3834	*36.8*	*25.4*	*16.1*	*12.0*	*9.7*
		1881	33791	11780	8744	5249	4222	3796	*34.9*	*25.9*	*15.5*	*12.5*	*11.2*
		1911	36570	11611	9717	7158	4751	3333	*31.8*	*26.6*	*19.6*	*13.0*	*9.1*
	Males	1851	18383	7292	4419	2925	2123	1624	*39.7*	*24.0*	*15.9*	*11.5*	*8.8*
		1881	16156	5865	4264	2338	1980	1709	*36.3*	*26.4*	*14.5*	*12.3*	*10.6*
		1911	17822	5817	4785	3434	2302	1484	*32.6*	*26.8*	*19.3*	*12.9*	*8.3*
	Females	1851	20999	7189	5596	3420	2584	2210	*34.2*	*26.6*	*16.3*	*12.3*	*10.5*
		1881	17635	5915	4480	2911	2242	2087	*33.5*	*25.4*	*16.5*	*12.7*	*11.8*
		1911	18748	5794	4932	3724	2449	1849	*30.9*	*26.3*	*19.9*	*13.1*	*9.9*
CARDIGANSHIRE													
Cardigan	Persons	1851	20186	7351	4705	3376	2545	2209	*36.4*	*23.3*	*16.7*	*12.6*	*10.9*
		1881	17615	5956	4047	2979	2307	2326	*33.8*	*23.0*	*16.9*	*13.1*	*13.2*
		1911	14732	3935	3513	2888	2279	2117	*26.7*	*23.8*	*19.6*	*15.5*	*14.4*
	Males	1851	8812	3725	1842	1293	1076	876	*42.3*	*20.9*	*14.7*	*12.2*	*9.9*
		1881	7583	2999	1658	1116	922	888	*39.5*	*21.9*	*14.7*	*12.2*	*11.7*
		1911	6548	1981	1562	1204	926	875	*30.3*	*23.9*	*18.4*	*14.1*	*13.4*
	Females	1851	11374	3626	2863	2083	1469	1333	*31.9*	*25.2*	*18.3*	*12.9*	*11.7*
		1881	10032	2957	2389	1863	1385	1438	*29.5*	*23.8*	*18.6*	*13.8*	*14.3*
		1911	8184	1954	1951	1684	1353	1242	*23.9*	*23.8*	*20.6*	*16.5*	*15.2*
Newcastle Emlyn	Persons	1851	20173	7334	4895	3275	2529	2140	*36.4*	*24.3*	*16.2*	*12.5*	*10.6*
		1881	19014	6636	4691	2880	2408	2399	*34.9*	*24.7*	*15.1*	*12.7*	*12.6*
		1911	17805	4895	4531	3390	2751	2238	*27.5*	*25.4*	*19.0*	*15.5*	*12.6*
	Males	1851	9385	3785	2140	1441	1113	906	*40.3*	*22.8*	*15.4*	*11.9*	*9.7*
		1881	8643	3381	2083	1168	1004	1007	*39.1*	*24.1*	*13.5*	*11.6*	*11.7*
		1911	8223	2505	2086	1505	1209	918	*30.5*	*25.4*	*18.3*	*14.7*	*11.2*
	Females	1851	10788	3549	2755	1834	1416	1234	*32.9*	*25.5*	*17.0*	*13.1*	*11.4*
		1881	10371	3255	2608	1712	1404	1392	*31.4*	*25.1*	*16.5*	*13.5*	*13.4*
		1911	9582	2390	2445	1885	1542	1320	*24.9*	*25.5*	*19.7*	*16.1*	*13.8*
Lampeter	Persons	1851	9874	3642	2457	1613	1183	979	*36.9*	*24.9*	*16.3*	*12.0*	*9.9*
		1881	10087	3553	2524	1635	1274	1101	*35.2*	*25.0*	*16.2*	*12.6*	*10.9*
		1911	8967	2357	2208	1750	1381	1271	*26.3*	*24.6*	*19.5*	*15.4*	*14.2*
	Males	1851	4705	1825	1138	758	546	438	*38.8*	*24.2*	*16.1*	*11.6*	*9.3*
		1881	4671	1730	1178	694	569	500	*37.0*	*25.2*	*14.9*	*12.2*	*10.7*
		1911	4175	1206	1076	752	606	535	*28.9*	*25.8*	*18.0*	*14.5*	*12.8*
	Females	1851	5169	1817	1319	855	637	541	*35.2*	*25.5*	*16.5*	*12.3*	*10.5*
		1881	5416	1823	1346	941	705	601	*33.7*	*24.9*	*17.4*	*13.0*	*11.1*
		1911	4792	1151	1132	998	775	736	*24.0*	*23.6*	*20.8*	*16.2*	*15.4*
Aberaeron	Persons	1851	13224	4940	3119	2234	1564	1367	*37.4*	*23.6*	*16.9*	*11.8*	*10.3*
		1881	12543	4451	2780	1964	1715	1633	*35.5*	*22.2*	*15.7*	*13.7*	*13.0*
		1911	10262	2727	2303	1859	1726	1647	*26.6*	*22.4*	*18.1*	*16.8*	*16.0*
	Males	1851	5991	2497	1299	927	693	575	*41.7*	*21.7*	*15.5*	*11.6*	*9.6*
		1881	5278	2206	1102	664	648	658	*41.8*	*20.9*	*12.6*	*12.3*	*12.5*
		1911	4507	1367	1040	688	748	664	*30.3*	*23.1*	*15.3*	*16.6*	*14.7*
	Females	1851	7233	2443	1820	1307	871	792	*33.8*	*25.2*	*18.1*	*12.0*	*10.9*
		1881	7265	2245	1678	1300	1067	975	*30.9*	*23.1*	*17.9*	*14.7*	*13.4*
		1911	5755	1360	1263	1171	978	983	*23.6*	*21.9*	*20.3*	*17.0*	*17.1*

Registration District[1]		Year	Number All ages	under 15	15–	30–	45–	60–	Percentage under 15	15–	30–	45–	60–
Aberystwyth	Persons	1851	23753	8551	6317	4089	2752	2044	*36.0*	*26.6*	*17.2*	*11.6*	*8.6*
		1881	25606	9112	6677	4144	3253	2420	*35.6*	*26.1*	*16.2*	*12.7*	*9.5*
		1911	21482	5619	5494	4280	3396	2693	*26.2*	*25.6*	*19.9*	*15.8*	*12.5*
	Males	1851	11359	4249	3011	1911	1287	901	*37.4*	*26.5*	*16.8*	*11.3*	*7.9*
		1881	11852	4590	3049	1757	1447	1009	*38.7*	*25.7*	*14.8*	*12.2*	*8.5*
		1911	9535	2726	2370	1844	1521	1074	*28.6*	*24.9*	*19.3*	*16.0*	*11.3*
	Females	1851	12394	4302	3306	2178	1465	1143	*34.7*	*26.7*	*17.6*	*11.8*	*9.2*
		1881	13754	4522	3628	2387	1806	1411	*32.9*	*26.4*	*17.4*	*13.1*	*10.3*
		1911	11947	2893	3124	2436	1875	1619	*24.2*	*26.1*	*20.4*	*15.7*	*13.6*
Tregaron	Persons	1851	10404	3902	2685	1732	1124	961	*37.5*	*25.8*	*16.6*	*10.8*	*9.2*
		1881	10272	3697	2485	1640	1291	1159	*36.0*	*24.2*	*16.0*	*12.6*	*11.3*
		1911	7521	2008	1861	1293	1187	1172	*26.7*	*24.7*	*17.2*	*15.8*	*15.6*
	Males	1851	4903	1923	1237	805	546	392	*39.2*	*25.2*	*16.4*	*11.1*	*8.0*
		1881	4690	1860	1098	690	536	506	*39.7*	*23.4*	*14.7*	*11.4*	*10.8*
		1911	3538	983	935	580	534	506	*27.8*	*26.4*	*16.4*	*15.1*	*14.3*
	Females	1851	5501	1979	1448	927	578	569	*36.0*	*26.3*	*16.9*	*10.5*	*10.3*
		1881	5582	1837	1387	950	755	653	*32.9*	*24.8*	*17.0*	*13.5*	*11.7*
		1911	3983	1025	926	713	653	666	*25.7*	*23.2*	*17.9*	*16.4*	*16.7*
BRECONSHIRE													
Builth	Persons	1851	8345	2970	2256	1299	923	897	*35.6*	*27.0*	*15.6*	*11.1*	*10.7*
		1881	8182	3009	2063	1304	1012	794	*36.8*	*25.2*	*15.9*	*12.4*	*9.7*
		1911	9482	2633	2515	1915	1428	991	*27.8*	*26.5*	*20.2*	*15.1*	*10.5*
	Males	1851	4152	1540	1064	667	451	430	*37.1*	*25.6*	*16.1*	*10.9*	*10.4*
		1881	4015	1491	947	660	501	416	*37.1*	*23.6*	*16.4*	*12.5*	*10.4*
		1911	4630	1323	1187	933	697	490	*28.6*	*25.6*	*20.2*	*15.1*	*10.6*
	Females	1851	4193	1430	1192	632	472	467	*34.1*	*28.4*	*15.1*	*11.3*	*11.1*
		1881	4167	1518	1116	644	511	378	*36.4*	*26.8*	*15.5*	*12.3*	*9.1*
		1911	4852	1310	1328	982	731	501	*27.0*	*27.4*	*20.2*	*15.1*	*10.3*
Brecon	Persons	1851	18174	5847	5088	3107	2125	2007	*32.2*	*28.0*	*17.1*	*11.7*	*11.0*
		1881	17178	5885	4673	2802	2148	1670	*34.3*	*27.2*	*16.3*	*12.5*	*9.7*
		1911	15063	4414	3949	3051	2015	1634	*29.3*	*26.2*	*20.3*	*13.4*	*10.8*
	Males	1851	8984	2946	2504	1546	1069	919	*32.8*	*27.9*	*17.2*	*11.9*	*10.2*
		1881	8578	2996	2362	1403	1025	792	*34.9*	*27.5*	*16.4*	*11.9*	*9.2*
		1911	7525	2225	1968	1522	1006	804	*29.6*	*26.2*	*20.2*	*13.4*	*10.7*
	Females	1851	9190	2901	2584	1561	1056	1088	*31.6*	*28.1*	*17.0*	*11.5*	*11.8*
		1881	8600	2889	2311	1399	1123	878	*33.6*	*26.9*	*16.3*	*13.1*	*10.2*
		1911	7538	2189	1981	1529	1009	830	*29.0*	*26.3*	*20.3*	*13.4*	*11.0*
Crickhowell	Persons	1851	21697	7751	6099	4224	2242	1381	*35.7*	*28.1*	*19.5*	*10.3*	*6.4*
		1881	18558	7034	4489	3107	2256	1672	*37.9*	*24.2*	*16.7*	*12.2*	*9.0*
		1911	22309	7887	5774	4413	2719	1516	*35.4*	*25.9*	*19.8*	*12.2*	*6.8*
	Males	1851	11410	3924	3297	2343	1212	634	*34.4*	*28.9*	*20.5*	*10.6*	*5.6*
		1881	9370	3495	2343	1590	1139	803	*37.3*	*25.0*	*17.0*	*12.2*	*8.6*
		1911	11475	3939	2973	2355	1469	739	*34.3*	*25.9*	*20.5*	*12.8*	*6.4*
	Females	1851	10287	3827	2802	1881	1030	747	*37.2*	*27.2*	*18.3*	*10.0*	*7.3*
		1881	9188	3539	2146	1517	1117	869	*38.5*	*23.4*	*16.5*	*12.2*	*9.5*
		1911	10834	3948	2801	2058	1250	777	*36.4*	*25.9*	*19.0*	*11.5*	*7.2*

Registration District[1]		Year	Number All ages	under 15	15–	30–	45–	60–	*Percentage* *under 15*	*15–*	*30–*	*45–*	*60–*
Hay	Persons	1851	10962	3727	2707	1936	1303	1289	*34.0*	*24.7*	*17.7*	*11.9*	*11.8*
		1881	10222	3593	2463	1664	1301	1201	*35.1*	*24.1*	*16.3*	*12.7*	*11.7*
		1911	9516	2675	2309	1857	1467	1208	*28.1*	*24.3*	*19.5*	*15.4*	*12.7*
	Males	1851	5447	1884	1326	952	670	615	*34.6*	*24.3*	*17.5*	*12.3*	*11.3*
		1881	5028	1786	1190	833	658	561	*35.5*	*23.7*	*16.6*	*13.1*	*11.2*
		1911	4678	1329	1098	920	740	591	*28.4*	*23.5*	*19.7*	*15.8*	*12.6*
	Females	1851	5515	1843	1381	984	633	674	*33.4*	*25.0*	*17.8*	*11.5*	*12.2*
		1881	5194	1807	1273	831	643	640	*34.8*	*24.5*	*16.0*	*12.4*	*12.3*
		1911	4838	1346	1211	937	727	617	*27.8*	*25.0*	*19.4*	*15.0*	*12.8*
RADNORSHIRE													
Presteigne	Persons	1851	15149	5089	4048	2606	1838	1568	*33.6*	*26.7*	*17.2*	*12.1*	*10.4*
	Males	1851	7691	2593	2040	1362	927	769	*33.7*	*26.5*	*17.7*	*12.1*	*10.0*
	Females	1851	7458	2496	2008	1244	911	799	*33.5*	*26.9*	*16.7*	*12.2*	*10.7*
Knighton	Persons	1851	9480	3507	2553	1486	1085	849	*37.0*	*26.9*	*15.7*	*11.4*	*9.0*
		1881	11782	4246	3043	1803	1495	1195	*36.0*	*25.8*	*15.3*	*12.7*	*10.1*
		1911	9847	3078	2361	1795	1446	1167	*31.3*	*24.0*	*18.2*	*14.7*	*11.9*
	Males	1851	4947	1824	1330	794	569	430	*36.9*	*26.9*	*16.1*	*11.5*	*8.7*
		1881	6057	2142	1595	935	774	611	*35.4*	*26.3*	*15.4*	*12.8*	*10.1*
		1911	4992	1564	1144	907	747	630	*31.3*	*22.9*	*18.2*	*15.0*	*12.6*
	Females	1851	4533	1683	1223	692	516	419	*37.1*	*27.0*	*15.3*	*11.4*	*9.2*
		1881	5725	2104	1448	868	721	584	*36.8*	*25.3*	*15.2*	*12.6*	*10.2*
		1911	4855	1514	1217	888	699	537	*31.2*	*25.1*	*18.3*	*14.4*	*11.1*
Rhayader	Persons	1851	6796	2677	1626	1071	732	690	*39.4*	*23.9*	*15.8*	*10.8*	*10.2*
		1881	6741	2479	1681	1090	763	728	*36.8*	*24.9*	*16.2*	*11.3*	*10.8*
		1911	7658	2199	1998	1608	999	854	*28.7*	*26.1*	*21.0*	*13.0*	*11.2*
	Males	1851	3480	1397	827	545	380	331	*40.1*	*23.8*	*15.7*	*10.9*	*9.5*
		1881	3347	1244	810	553	384	356	*37.2*	*24.2*	*16.5*	*11.5*	*10.6*
		1911	3804	1133	939	796	498	438	*29.8*	*24.7*	*20.9*	*13.1*	*11.5*
	Females	1851	3316	1280	799	526	352	359	*38.6*	*24.1*	*15.9*	*10.6*	*10.8*
		1881	3394	1235	871	537	379	372	*36.4*	*25.7*	*15.8*	*11.2*	*11.0*
		1911	3854	1066	1059	812	501	416	*27.7*	*27.5*	*21.1*	*13.0*	*10.8*
MONTGOMERYSHIRE													
Machynlleth	Persons	1851	12116	4121	3029	2061	1459	1446	*34.0*	*25.0*	*17.0*	*12.0*	*11.9*
		1881	12517	4423	3159	1973	1626	1336	*35.3*	*25.2*	*15.8*	*13.0*	*10.7*
		1911	10853	2990	2590	2276	1681	1316	*27.5*	*23.9*	*21.0*	*15.5*	*12.1*
	Males	1851	5929	2129	1442	1012	698	648	*35.9*	*24.3*	*17.1*	*11.8*	*10.9*
		1881	6080	2207	1547	932	782	612	*36.3*	*25.4*	*15.3*	*12.9*	*10.1*
		1911	5030	1493	1182	997	786	572	*29.7*	*23.5*	*19.8*	*15.6*	*11.4*
	Females	1851	6187	1992	1587	1049	761	798	*32.2*	*25.7*	*17.0*	*12.3*	*12.9*
		1881	6437	2216	1612	1041	844	724	*34.4*	*25.0*	*16.2*	*13.1*	*11.2*
		1911	5823	1497	1408	1279	895	744	*25.7*	*24.2*	*22.0*	*15.4*	*12.8*

Registration District[1]		Year	Number All ages	under 15	15–	30–	45–	60–	*Percentage under 15*	*15–*	*30–*	*45–*	*60–*
Newtown	Persons	1851	25107	9150	6674	3942	2891	2450	*36.4*	*26.6*	*15.7*	*11.5*	*9.8*
		1881	25439	9671	6387	3988	2933	2460	*38.0*	*25.1*	*15.7*	*11.5*	*9.7*
		1911	20294	6265	5169	3831	2796	2233	*30.9*	*25.5*	*18.9*	*13.8*	*11.0*
	Males	1851	12486	4583	3407	1951	1444	1101	*36.7*	*27.3*	*15.6*	*11.6*	*8.8*
		1881	12732	4896	3229	1970	1466	1171	*38.5*	*25.4*	*15.5*	*11.5*	*9.2*
		1911	9976	3229	2477	1797	1371	1102	*32.4*	*24.8*	*18.0*	*13.7*	*11.0*
	Females	1851	12621	4567	3267	1991	1447	1349	*36.2*	*25.9*	*15.8*	*11.5*	*10.7*
		1881	12707	4775	3158	2018	1467	1289	*37.6*	*24.9*	*15.9*	*11.5*	*10.1*
		1911	10318	3036	2692	2034	1425	1131	*29.4*	*26.1*	*19.7*	*13.8*	*11.0*
Montgomery/ Forden	Persons	1851	20381	7083	5237	3480	2488	2093	*34.8*	*25.7*	*17.1*	*12.2*	*10.3*
		1881	18281	6527	4481	2972	2328	1973	*35.7*	*24.5*	*16.3*	*12.7*	*10.8*
		1911	14371	4277	3383	2739	2199	1773	*29.8*	*23.5*	*19.1*	*15.3*	*12.3*
	Males	1851	10302	3533	2690	1800	1283	996	*34.3*	*26.1*	*17.5*	*12.5*	*9.7*
		1881	9445	3333	2428	1487	1210	987	*35.3*	*25.7*	*15.7*	*12.8*	*10.4*
		1911	7124	2141	1676	1344	1106	857	*30.1*	*23.5*	*18.9*	*15.5*	*12.0*
	Females	1851	10079	3550	2547	1680	1205	1097	*35.2*	*25.3*	*16.7*	*12.0*	*10.9*
		1881	8836	3194	2053	1485	1118	986	*36.1*	*23.2*	*16.8*	*12.7*	*11.2*
		1911	7247	2136	1707	1395	1093	916	*29.5*	*23.6*	*19.2*	*15.1*	*12.6*
Llanfyllin	Persons	1851	19538	6999	4965	3046	2464	2064	*35.8*	*25.4*	*15.6*	*12.6*	*10.6*
		1881	19959	7143	4750	3155	2615	2296	*35.8*	*23.8*	*15.8*	*13.1*	*11.5*
		1911	16683	5201	3871	3129	2490	1992	*31.2*	*23.2*	*18.8*	*14.9*	*11.9*
	Males	1851	9824	3489	2527	1527	1263	1018	*35.5*	*25.7*	*15.5*	*12.9*	*10.4*
		1881	10038	3562	2449	1573	1331	1123	*35.5*	*24.4*	*15.7*	*13.3*	*11.2*
		1911	8406	2611	1968	1579	1264	984	*31.1*	*23.4*	*18.8*	*15.0*	*11.7*
	Females	1851	9714	3510	2438	1519	1201	1046	*36.1*	*25.1*	*15.6*	*12.4*	*10.8*
		1881	9921	3581	2301	1582	1284	1173	*36.1*	*23.2*	*15.9*	*12.9*	*11.8*
		1911	8277	2590	1903	1550	1226	1008	*31.3*	*23.0*	*18.7*	*14.8*	*12.2*
FLINTSHIRE													
Holywell	Persons	1851	41047	15768	9906	7096	4929	3348	*38.4*	*24.1*	*17.3*	*12.0*	*8.2*
		1881	45774	17346	10889	8160	5504	3875	*37.9*	*23.8*	*17.8*	*12.0*	*8.5*
		1911	42818	14061	10506	8512	5613	4126	*32.8*	*24.5*	*19.9*	*13.1*	*9.6*
	Males	1851	20787	8081	5255	3650	2458	1343	*38.9*	*25.3*	*17.6*	*11.8*	*6.5*
		1881	23217	8645	5983	4180	2689	1720	*37.2*	*25.8*	*18.0*	*11.6*	*7.4*
		1911	21332	6904	5473	4254	2801	1900	*32.4*	*25.7*	*19.9*	*13.1*	*8.9*
	Females	1851	20260	7687	4651	3446	2471	2005	*37.9*	*23.0*	*17.0*	*12.2*	*9.9*
		1881	22557	8701	4906	3980	2815	2155	*38.6*	*21.7*	*17.6*	*12.5*	*9.6*
		1911	21486	7157	5033	4258	2812	2226	*33.3*	*23.4*	*19.8*	*13.1*	*10.4*
Hawarden	Persons	1911	26904	9253	6792	5624	3239	1996	*34.4*	*25.2*	*20.9*	*12.0*	*7.4*
	Males	1911	14108	4681	3859	2919	1680	969	*33.2*	*27.4*	*20.7*	*11.9*	*6.9*
	Females	1911	12796	4572	2933	2705	1559	1027	*35.7*	*22.9*	*21.1*	*12.2*	*8.0*

Registration District[1]		Year	Number All ages	under 15	15–	30–	45–	60–	*Percentage under 15*	*15–*	*30–*	*45–*	*60–*
DENBIGHSHIRE													
Wrexham	Persons	1851	42295	15496	10997	7442	4914	3446	*36.6*	*26.0*	*17.6*	*11.6*	*8.1*
		1881	55158	21546	13546	9706	6516	3844	*39.1*	*24.6*	*17.6*	*11.8*	*7.0*
		1911	79054	27706	19793	16356	9671	5528	*35.0*	*25.0*	*20.7*	*12.2*	*7.0*
	Males	1851	21415	7956	5678	3772	2463	1546	*37.2*	*26.5*	*17.6*	*11.5*	*7.2*
		1881	28325	10745	7519	4958	3298	1805	*37.9*	*26.5*	*17.5*	*11.6*	*6.4*
		1911	40903	14044	10902	8351	5002	2604	*34.3*	*26.7*	*20.4*	*12.2*	*6.4*
	Females	1851	20880	7540	5319	3670	2451	1900	*36.1*	*25.5*	*17.6*	*11.7*	*9.1*
		1881	26833	10801	6027	4748	3218	2039	*40.3*	*22.5*	*17.7*	*12.0*	*7.6*
		1911	38151	13662	8891	8005	4669	2924	*35.8*	*23.3*	*21.0*	*12.2*	*7.7*
Ruthin	Persons	1851	16853	5923	4231	2789	2090	1820	*35.1*	*25.1*	*16.5*	*12.4*	*10.8*
		1881	14215	4832	3563	2239	1983	1598	*34.0*	*25.1*	*15.8*	*14.0*	*11.2*
		1911	12204	3265	3112	2493	1884	1450	*26.8*	*25.5*	*20.4*	*15.4*	*11.9*
	Males	1851	8394	2959	2156	1398	1031	850	*35.3*	*25.7*	*16.7*	*12.3*	*10.1*
		1881	7160	2424	1870	1105	979	782	*33.9*	*26.1*	*15.4*	*13.7*	*10.9*
		1911	6049	1612	1607	1202	942	686	*26.6*	*26.6*	*19.9*	*15.6*	*11.3*
	Females	1851	8459	2964	2075	1391	1059	970	*35.0*	*24.5*	*16.4*	*12.5*	*11.5*
		1881	7055	2408	1693	1134	1004	816	*34.1*	*24.0*	*16.1*	*14.2*	*11.6*
		1911	6155	1653	1505	1291	942	764	*26.9*	*24.5*	*21.0*	*15.3*	*12.4*
St Asaph	Persons	1851	25288	8847	6496	4483	3067	2395	*35.0*	*25.7*	*17.7*	*12.1*	*9.5*
		1881	29458	9781	7366	5199	3977	3135	*33.2*	*25.0*	*17.6*	*13.5*	*10.6*
		1911	33226	8916	8162	7223	5104	3821	*26.8*	*24.6*	*21.7*	*15.4*	*11.5*
	Males	1851	12613	4580	3183	2226	1513	1111	*36.3*	*25.2*	*17.6*	*12.0*	*8.8*
		1881	13935	4869	3325	2455	1860	1426	*34.9*	*23.9*	*17.6*	*13.3*	*10.2*
		1911	15315	4558	3581	3252	2284	1640	*29.8*	*23.4*	*21.2*	*14.9*	*10.7*
	Females	1851	12675	4267	3313	2257	1554	1284	*33.7*	*26.1*	*17.8*	*12.3*	*10.1*
		1881	15523	4912	4041	2744	2117	1709	*31.6*	*26.0*	*17.7*	*13.6*	*11.0*
		1911	17911	4358	4581	3971	2820	2181	*24.3*	*25.6*	*22.2*	*15.7*	*12.2*
Llanrwst	Persons	1851	12479	4516	3023	2214	1432	1294	*36.2*	*24.2*	*17.7*	*11.5*	*10.4*
		1881	14109	4814	3663	2480	1662	1490	*34.1*	*26.0*	*17.6*	*11.8*	*10.6*
		1911	12326	3530	2933	2624	1837	1402	*28.6*	*23.8*	*21.3*	*14.9*	*11.4*
	Males	1851	6217	2291	1486	1099	727	614	*36.9*	*23.9*	*17.7*	*11.7*	*9.9*
		1881	7081	2430	1841	1256	825	729	*34.3*	*26.0*	*17.7*	*11.7*	*10.3*
		1911	6031	1749	1405	1312	920	645	*29.0*	*23.3*	*21.8*	*15.3*	*10.7*
	Females	1851	6262	2225	1537	1115	705	680	*35.5*	*24.5*	*17.8*	*11.3*	*10.9*
		1881	7028	2384	1822	1224	837	761	*33.9*	*25.9*	*17.4*	*11.9*	*10.8*
		1911	6295	1781	1528	1312	917	757	*28.3*	*24.3*	*20.8*	*14.6*	*12.0*
MERIONETH													
Corwen	Persons	1851	15418	5594	3803	2653	1836	1532	*36.3*	*24.7*	*17.2*	*11.9*	*9.9*
		1881	16833	6091	4030	2783	2162	1767	*36.2*	*23.9*	*16.5*	*12.8*	*10.5*
		1911	16428	4783	3988	3361	2467	1829	*29.1*	*24.3*	*20.5*	*15.0*	*11.1*
	Males	1851	7830	2850	1948	1349	926	757	*36.4*	*24.9*	*17.2*	*11.8*	*9.7*
		1881	8438	2987	2119	1391	1083	858	*35.4*	*25.1*	*16.5*	*12.8*	*10.2*
		1911	8167	2378	2010	1635	1262	882	*29.1*	*24.6*	*20.0*	*15.5*	*10.8*
	Females	1851	7588	2744	1855	1304	910	775	*36.2*	*24.4*	*17.2*	*12.0*	*10.2*
		1881	8395	3104	1911	1392	1079	909	*37.0*	*22.8*	*16.6*	*12.9*	*10.8*
		1911	8261	2405	1978	1726	1205	947	*29.1*	*23.9*	*20.9*	*14.6*	*11.5*

Registration District[1]		Year	Number All ages	under 15	15–	30–	45–	60–	Percentage under 15	15–	30–	45–	60–
Bala	Persons	1851	6736	2301	1686	1094	857	798	*34.2*	*25.0*	*16.2*	*12.7*	*11.8*
		1881	6740	2137	1756	1201	859	787	*31.7*	*26.1*	*17.8*	*12.7*	*11.7*
		1911	5609	1436	1481	1110	827	755	*25.6*	*26.4*	*19.8*	*14.7*	*13.5*
	Males	1851	3353	1165	857	531	423	377	*34.7*	*25.6*	*15.8*	*12.6*	*11.2*
		1881	3498	1036	985	638	452	387	*29.6*	*28.2*	*18.2*	*12.9*	*11.1*
		1911	2781	693	748	547	415	378	*24.9*	*26.9*	*19.7*	*14.9*	*13.6*
	Females	1851	3383	1136	829	563	434	421	*33.6*	*24.5*	*16.6*	*12.8*	*12.4*
		1881	3242	1101	771	563	407	400	*34.0*	*23.8*	*17.4*	*12.6*	*12.3*
		1911	2828	743	733	563	412	377	*26.3*	*25.9*	*19.9*	*14.6*	*13.3*
Dolgellau	Persons	1851	12971	4502	2970	2195	1597	1707	*34.7*	*22.9*	*16.9*	*12.3*	*13.2*
		1881	15180	5438	3594	2763	1810	1575	*35.8*	*23.7*	*18.2*	*11.9*	*10.4*
		1911	12998	3475	3040	2679	2118	1686	*26.7*	*23.4*	*20.6*	*16.3*	*13.0*
	Males	1851	6230	2292	1408	1046	751	733	*36.8*	*22.6*	*16.8*	*12.1*	*11.8*
		1881	7273	2663	1703	1353	847	707	*36.6*	*23.4*	*18.6*	*11.6*	*9.7*
		1911	5920	1693	1377	1165	958	727	*28.6*	*23.3*	*19.7*	*16.2*	*12.3*
	Females	1851	6741	2210	1562	1149	846	974	*32.8*	*23.2*	*17.0*	*12.6*	*14.4*
		1881	7907	2775	1891	1410	963	868	*35.1*	*23.9*	*17.8*	*12.2*	*11.0*
		1911	7078	1782	1663	1514	1160	959	*25.2*	*23.5*	*21.4*	*16.4*	*13.5*
Ffestiniog	Persons	1851	16182	6131	3912	2887	1763	1489	*37.9*	*24.2*	*17.8*	*10.9*	*9.2*
		1881	29525	10988	7577	5626	3141	2193	*37.2*	*25.7*	*19.1*	*10.6*	*7.4*
		1911	25245	7829	5730	5258	3727	2701	*31.0*	*22.7*	*20.8*	*14.8*	*10.7*
	Males	1851	7976	3119	1915	1461	840	641	*39.1*	*24.0*	*18.3*	*10.5*	*8.0*
		1881	15141	5562	4062	2919	1599	999	*36.7*	*26.8*	*19.3*	*10.6*	*6.6*
		1911	12208	3857	2859	2553	1787	1152	*31.6*	*23.4*	*20.9*	*14.6*	*9.4*
	Females	1851	8206	3012	1997	1426	923	848	*36.7*	*24.3*	*17.4*	*11.2*	*10.3*
		1881	14384	5426	3515	2707	1542	1194	*37.7*	*24.4*	*18.8*	*10.7*	*8.3*
		1911	13037	3972	2871	2705	1940	1549	*30.5*	*22.0*	*20.7*	*14.9*	*11.9*
CAERNARFONSHIRE													
Pwllheli	Persons	1851	21788	7673	5142	3831	2680	2462	*35.2*	*23.6*	*17.6*	*12.3*	*11.3*
		1881	22911	7728	5570	3928	2960	2725	*33.7*	*24.3*	*17.1*	*12.9*	*11.9*
		1911	22006	5926	5284	4473	3492	2831	*26.9*	*24.0*	*20.3*	*15.9*	*12.9*
	Males	1851	10214	3877	2298	1732	1205	1102	*38.0*	*22.5*	*17.0*	*11.8*	*10.8*
		1881	11161	3974	2739	1806	1364	1278	*35.6*	*24.5*	*16.2*	*12.2*	*11.5*
		1911	10458	3018	2496	2045	1629	1270	*28.9*	*23.9*	*19.6*	*15.6*	*12.1*
	Females	1851	11574	3796	2844	2099	1475	1360	*32.8*	*24.6*	*18.1*	*12.7*	*11.8*
		1881	11750	3754	2831	2122	1596	1447	*31.9*	*24.1*	*18.1*	*13.6*	*12.3*
		1911	11548	2908	2788	2428	1863	1561	*25.2*	*24.1*	*21.0*	*16.1*	*13.5*
Caernarfon	Persons	1851	30446	11329	7666	5419	3519	2513	*37.2*	*25.2*	*17.8*	*11.6*	*8.3*
		1881	43997	15838	11430	8105	4970	3654	*36.0*	*26.0*	*18.4*	*11.3*	*8.3*
		1911	40342	11858	9036	8639	6262	4547	*29.4*	*22.4*	*21.4*	*15.5*	*11.3*
	Males	1851	14912	5702	3748	2677	1716	1069	*38.2*	*25.1*	*18.0*	*11.5*	*7.2*
		1881	22058	8108	5875	3962	2419	1694	*36.8*	*26.6*	*18.0*	*11.0*	*7.7*
		1911	19665	5963	4478	4161	3033	2030	*30.3*	*22.8*	*21.2*	*15.4*	*10.3*
	Females	1851	15534	5627	3918	2742	1803	1444	*36.2*	*25.2*	*17.7*	*11.6*	*9.3*
		1881	21939	7730	5555	4143	2551	1960	*35.2*	*25.3*	*18.9*	*11.6*	*8.9*
		1911	20677	5895	4558	4478	3229	2517	*28.5*	*22.0*	*21.7*	*15.6*	*12.2*

Registration District[1]		Year	Number All ages	under 15	15–	30–	45–	60–	*Percentage under 15*	*15–*	*30–*	*45–*	*60–*
Bangor	Persons	1851	30810	10962	8332	5644	3474	2398	*35.6*	*27.0*	*18.3*	*11.3*	*7.8*
		1881	38512	12948	9820	6703	5167	3874	*33.6*	*25.5*	*17.4*	*13.4*	*10.1*
		1911	38165	10966	9165	8044	5791	4199	*28.7*	*24.0*	*21.1*	*15.2*	*11.0*
	Males	1851	15499	5627	4134	2932	1718	1088	*36.3*	*26.7*	*18.9*	*11.1*	*7.0*
		1881	18792	6548	4810	3172	2456	1806	*34.8*	*25.6*	*16.9*	*13.1*	*9.6*
		1911	18375	5559	4447	3770	2761	1838	*30.3*	*24.2*	*20.5*	*15.0*	*10.0*
	Females	1851	15311	5335	4198	2712	1756	1310	*34.8*	*27.4*	*17.7*	*11.5*	*8.6*
		1881	19720	6400	5010	3531	2711	2068	*32.5*	*25.4*	*17.9*	*13.7*	*10.5*
		1911	19790	5407	4718	4274	3030	2361	*27.3*	*23.8*	*21.6*	*15.3*	*11.9*
Conwy	Persons	1851	11630	4185	2969	1949	1385	1142	*36.0*	*25.5*	*16.8*	*11.9*	*9.8*
		1881	18361	6158	4963	3168	2440	1632	*33.5*	*27.0*	*17.3*	*13.3*	*8.9*
		1911	41254	10858	10955	9581	6110	3750	*26.3*	*26.6*	*23.2*	*14.8*	*9.1*
	Males	1851	5847	2166	1467	990	674	550	*37.0*	*25.1*	*16.9*	*11.5*	*9.4*
		1881	8731	3111	2284	1445	1132	759	*35.6*	*26.2*	*16.6*	*13.0*	*8.7*
		1911	18121	5343	4585	4093	2576	1524	*29.5*	*25.3*	*22.6*	*14.2*	*8.4*
	Females	1851	5783	2019	1502	959	711	592	*34.9*	*26.0*	*16.6*	*12.3*	*10.2*
		1881	9630	3047	2679	1723	1308	873	*31.6*	*27.8*	*17.9*	*13.6*	*9.1*
		1911	23133	5515	6370	5488	3534	2226	*23.8*	*27.5*	*23.7*	*15.3*	*9.6*
ANGLESEY													
Anglesey	Persons	1851	43243	15623	10866	7599	4985	4170	*36.1*	*25.1*	*17.6*	*11.5*	*9.6*
		1881	35141	11606	8550	5919	4773	4293	*33.0*	*24.3*	*16.8*	*13.6*	*12.2*
		1911	13825	3950	3231	2556	2211	1877	*28.6*	*23.4*	*18.5*	*16.0*	*13.6*
	Males	1851	21172	7864	5345	3660	2437	1866	*37.1*	*25.2*	*17.3*	*11.5*	*8.8*
		1881	17190	5858	4257	2786	2255	2034	*34.1*	*24.8*	*16.2*	*13.1*	*11.8*
		1911	6395	1986	1434	1145	1002	828	*31.1*	*22.4*	*17.9*	*15.7*	*12.9*
	Females	1851	22071	7759	5521	3939	2548	2304	*35.2*	*25.0*	*17.8*	*11.5*	*10.4*
		1881	17951	5748	4293	3133	2518	2259	*32.0*	*23.9*	*17.5*	*14.0*	*12.6*
		1911	7430	1964	1797	1411	1209	1049	*26.4*	*24.2*	*19.0*	*16.3*	*14.1*
Holyhead	Persons	1911	21534	6508	5245	4347	3181	2253	*30.2*	*24.4*	*20.2*	*14.8*	*10.5*
	Males	1911	10585	3369	2572	2075	1538	1031	*31.8*	*24.3*	*19.6*	*14.5*	*9.7*
	Females	1911	10949	3139	2673	2272	1643	1222	*28.7*	*24.4*	*20.8*	*15.0*	*11.2*

Sources: *Census of Population for England and Wales*: 1851, *Population Tables II, Ages, Civil Condition, Occupations, and Birth-place of the People. Vol. II* (HMSO, 1854) pp. 813–14; 1881, *Vol. III, Ages, Condition as to Marriage, Occupations, and Birthplaces of the People* (HMSO, 1883) Division XI – Wales and Monmouthshire, Table 2; 1911, County Volumes: *Anglesey, Carnarvon, Denbigh and Flint; Cardigan, Merioneth and Montgomery; Glamorgan; Brecknock, Carmarthen, Pembroke and Radnor; Monmouth* (HMSO, 1914) Table 19.

[1] See Table 1.2 for details of boundary changes.

Population 2.3 Ages. Persons, males, females. Number and percentage. Registration Subdistricts. 1851, 1881

Registration Subdistrict[1]		Year	Number All ages	under 15	15–	30–	45–	60–	*Percentage under 15*	*15–*	*30–*	*45–*	*60–*
MONMOUTHSHIRE													
Chepstow													
Shirenewton	Persons	1851	5112	1804	1238	896	661	513	*35.3*	*24.2*	*17.5*	*12.9*	*10.0*
		1881	5541	2075	1276	913	727	550	*37.4*	*23.0*	*16.5*	*13.1*	*9.9*
	Males	1851	2683	907	685	479	334	278	*33.8*	*25.5*	*17.9*	*12.4*	*10.4*
		1881	2906	1042	697	479	390	298	*35.9*	*24.0*	*16.5*	*13.4*	*10.3*
	Females	1851	2429	897	553	417	327	235	*36.9*	*22.8*	*17.2*	*13.5*	*9.7*
		1881	2635	1033	579	434	337	252	*39.2*	*22.0*	*16.5*	*12.8*	*9.6*
Chepstow	Persons	1851	8197	2798	2288	1553	876	682	*34.1*	*27.9*	*18.9*	*10.7*	*8.3*
		1881	7168	2532	1766	1228	870	772	*35.3*	*24.6*	*17.1*	*12.1*	*10.8*
	Males	1851	4041	1386	1117	794	433	311	*34.3*	*27.6*	*19.6*	*10.7*	*7.7*
		1881	3517	1287	868	572	426	364	*36.6*	*24.7*	*16.3*	*12.1*	*10.3*
	Females	1851	4156	1412	1171	759	443	371	*34.0*	*28.2*	*18.3*	*10.7*	*8.9*
		1881	3651	1245	898	656	444	408	*34.1*	*24.6*	*18.0*	*12.2*	*11.2*
Lydney	Persons	1851	5748	2100	1471	1058	632	487	*36.5*	*25.6*	*18.4*	*11.0*	*8.5*
		1881	5992	2246	1367	996	775	608	*37.5*	*22.8*	*16.6*	*12.9*	*10.1*
	Males	1851	2972	1062	776	567	344	223	*35.7*	*26.1*	*19.1*	*11.6*	*7.5*
		1881	3038	1130	716	498	406	288	*37.2*	*23.6*	*16.4*	*13.4*	*9.5*
	Females	1851	2776	1038	695	491	288	264	*37.4*	*25.0*	*17.7*	*10.4*	*9.5*
		1881	2954	1116	651	498	369	320	*37.8*	*22.0*	*16.9*	*12.5*	*10.8*
Monmouth													
Coleford	Persons	1851	11296	4405	2844	1972	1195	880	*39.0*	*25.2*	*17.5*	*10.6*	*7.8*
		1881	14887	6185	3277	2328	1764	1333	*41.5*	*22.0*	*15.6*	*11.8*	*9.0*
	Males	1851	5688	2188	1471	1027	590	412	*38.5*	*25.9*	*18.1*	*10.4*	*7.2*
		1881	7652	3142	1852	1170	869	619	*41.1*	*24.2*	*15.3*	*11.4*	*8.1*
	Females	1851	5608	2217	1373	945	605	468	*39.5*	*24.5*	*16.9*	*10.8*	*8.3*
		1881	7235	3043	1425	1158	895	714	*42.1*	*19.7*	*16.0*	*12.4*	*9.9*
Dingestow	Persons	1851	5456	1870	1299	1036	687	564	*34.3*	*23.8*	*19.0*	*12.6*	*10.3*
		1881	4920	1786	1085	811	639	599	*36.3*	*22.1*	*16.5*	*13.0*	*12.2*
	Males	1851	2849	949	719	545	368	268	*33.3*	*25.2*	*19.1*	*12.9*	*9.4*
		1881	2500	889	573	405	326	307	*35.6*	*22.9*	*16.2*	*13.0*	*12.3*
	Females	1851	2607	921	580	491	319	296	*35.3*	*22.2*	*18.8*	*12.2*	*11.4*
		1881	2420	897	512	406	313	292	*37.1*	*21.2*	*16.8*	*12.9*	*12.1*
Monmouth	Persons	1851	5967	1979	1609	1097	715	567	*33.2*	*27.0*	*18.4*	*12.0*	*9.5*
		1881	6358	2218	1660	1019	833	628	*34.9*	*26.1*	*16.0*	*13.1*	*9.9*
	Males	1851	2797	955	675	534	369	264	*34.1*	*24.1*	*19.1*	*13.2*	*9.4*
		1881	3126	1159	762	492	400	313	*37.1*	*24.4*	*15.7*	*12.8*	*10.0*
	Females	1851	3170	1024	934	563	346	303	*32.3*	*29.5*	*17.8*	*10.9*	*9.6*
		1881	3232	1059	898	527	433	315	*32.8*	*27.8*	*16.3*	*13.4*	*9.7*
Trelleck	Persons	1851	4660	1603	1110	780	563	604	*34.4*	*23.8*	*16.7*	*12.1*	*13.0*
		1881	4175	1505	916	669	568	517	*36.0*	*21.9*	*16.0*	*13.6*	*12.4*
	Males	1851	2371	793	567	415	282	314	*33.4*	*23.9*	*17.5*	*11.9*	*13.2*
		1881	2099	774	450	341	271	263	*36.9*	*21.4*	*16.2*	*12.9*	*12.5*
	Females	1851	2289	810	543	365	281	290	*35.4*	*23.7*	*15.9*	*12.3*	*12.7*
		1881	2076	731	466	328	297	254	*35.2*	*22.4*	*15.8*	*14.3*	*12.2*
Abergavenny													
Llan-arth	Persons	1851	1909	602	518	322	249	218	*31.5*	*27.1*	*16.9*	*13.0*	*11.4*
		1881	1717	552	427	292	233	213	*32.1*	*24.9*	*17.0*	*13.6*	*12.4*
	Males	1851	963	306	257	169	132	99	*31.8*	*26.7*	*17.5*	*13.7*	*10.3*
		1881	843	292	185	144	110	112	*34.6*	*21.9*	*17.1*	*13.0*	*13.3*
	Females	1851	946	296	261	153	117	119	*31.3*	*27.6*	*16.2*	*12.4*	*12.6*
		1881	874	260	242	148	123	101	*29.7*	*27.7*	*16.9*	*14.1*	*11.6*
Llanfihangel	Persons	1851	1957	645	518	337	246	211	*33.0*	*26.5*	*17.2*	*12.6*	*10.8*
		1881	1675	579	414	284	217	181	*34.6*	*24.7*	*17.0*	*13.0*	*10.8*
	Males	1851	997	318	257	188	140	94	*31.9*	*25.8*	*18.9*	*14.0*	*9.4*
		1881	874	285	217	151	117	104	*32.6*	*24.8*	*17.3*	*13.4*	*11.9*
	Females	1851	960	327	261	149	106	117	*34.1*	*27.2*	*15.5*	*11.0*	*12.2*
		1881	801	294	197	133	100	77	*36.7*	*24.6*	*16.6*	*12.5*	*9.6*

Registration Subdistrict[1]		Year	Number All ages	under 15	15–	30–	45–	60–	Percentage under 15	15–	30–	45–	60–
Abergavenny	Persons	1851	7942	2550	2191	1492	1042	667	*32.1*	*27.6*	*18.8*	*13.1*	*8.4*
		1881	10730	3588	2685	2061	1379	1017	*33.4*	*25.0*	*19.2*	*12.9*	*9.5*
	Males	1851	3885	1249	1024	761	550	301	*32.1*	*26.4*	*19.6*	*14.2*	*7.7*
		1881	5217	1792	1252	1032	651	490	*34.3*	*24.0*	*19.8*	*12.5*	*9.4*
	Females	1851	4057	1301	1167	731	492	366	*32.1*	*28.8*	*18.0*	*12.1*	*9.0*
		1881	5513	1796	1433	1029	728	527	*32.6*	*26.0*	*18.7*	*13.2*	*9.6*
Blaenafon	Persons	1851	5855	2236	1591	1104	576	348	*38.2*	*27.2*	*18.9*	*9.8*	*5.9*
		1881	9449	3755	2297	1649	1087	661	*39.7*	*24.3*	*17.5*	*11.5*	*7.0*
	Males	1851	3079	1134	872	600	305	168	*36.8*	*28.3*	*19.5*	*9.9*	*5.5*
		1881	4945	1842	1308	882	566	347	*37.2*	*26.5*	*17.8*	*11.4*	*7.0*
	Females	1851	2776	1102	719	504	271	180	*39.7*	*25.9*	*18.2*	*9.8*	*6.5*
		1881	4504	1913	989	767	521	314	*42.5*	*22.0*	*17.0*	*11.6*	*7.0*
Aberystruth	Persons	1851	14383	5134	4654	2724	1275	596	*35.7*	*32.4*	*18.9*	*8.9*	*4.1*
		1881	18672	7667	4940	3185	1945	935	*41.1*	*26.5*	*17.1*	*10.4*	*5.0*
	Males	1851	7994	2593	2786	1610	712	293	*32.4*	*34.9*	*20.1*	*8.9*	*3.7*
		1881	9950	3814	2906	1723	1036	471	*38.3*	*29.2*	*17.3*	*10.4*	*4.7*
	Females	1851	6389	2541	1868	1114	563	303	*39.8*	*29.2*	*17.4*	*8.8*	*4.7*
		1881	8722	3853	2034	1462	909	464	*44.2*	*23.3*	*16.8*	*10.4*	*5.3*
Tredegar	Persons	1851	24544	8939	7505	4904	2241	955	*36.4*	*30.6*	*20.0*	*9.1*	*3.9*
		1881	34685	13297	9270	6118	3827	2173	*38.3*	*26.7*	*17.6*	*11.0*	*6.3*
	Males	1851	13434	4533	4407	2769	1243	482	*33.7*	*32.8*	*20.6*	*9.3*	*3.6*
		1881	18597	6713	5271	3410	2052	1151	*36.1*	*28.3*	*18.3*	*11.0*	*6.2*
	Females	1851	11110	4406	3098	2135	998	473	*39.7*	*27.9*	*19.2*	*9.0*	*4.3*
		1881	16088	6584	3999	2708	1775	1022	*40.9*	*24.9*	*16.8*	*11.0*	*6.4*
Rock Bedwellte	Persons	1851	2639	989	703	517	253	177	*37.5*	*26.6*	*19.6*	*9.6*	*6.7*
	Males	1851	1391	492	382	274	151	92	*35.4*	*27.5*	*19.7*	*10.9*	*6.6*
	Females	1851	1248	497	321	243	102	85	*39.8*	*25.7*	*19.5*	*8.2*	*6.8*
Bedwellte	Persons	1881	2483	986	588	431	272	206	*39.7*	*23.7*	*17.4*	*11.0*	*8.3*
	Males	1881	1246	495	288	224	137	102	*39.7*	*23.1*	*18.0*	*11.0*	*8.2*
	Females	1881	1237	491	300	207	135	104	*39.7*	*24.3*	*16.7*	*10.9*	*8.4*
Pontypool													
Pontypool	Persons	1851	20614	7923	5524	3930	2147	1090	*38.4*	*26.8*	*19.1*	*10.4*	*5.3*
		1881	25297	10264	6390	4118	2804	1721	*40.6*	*25.3*	*16.3*	*11.1*	*6.8*
	Males	1851	10690	3987	2904	2114	1153	532	*37.3*	*27.2*	*19.8*	*10.8*	*5.0*
		1881	13048	5126	3519	2128	1435	840	*39.3*	*27.0*	*16.3*	*11.0*	*6.4*
	Females	1851	9924	3936	2620	1816	994	558	*39.7*	*26.4*	*18.3*	*10.0*	*5.6*
		1881	12249	5138	2871	1990	1369	881	*41.9*	*23.4*	*16.2*	*11.2*	*7.2*
Llangybi	Persons	1851	3599	1259	1056	672	352	260	*35.0*	*29.3*	*18.7*	*9.8*	*7.2*
		1881	6310	2430	1683	1052	696	449	*38.5*	*26.7*	*16.7*	*11.0*	*7.1*
	Males	1851	1934	644	586	370	193	141	*33.3*	*30.3*	*19.1*	*10.0*	*7.3*
		1881	3322	1246	924	551	351	250	*37.5*	*27.8*	*16.6*	*10.6*	*7.5*
	Females	1851	1665	615	470	302	159	119	*36.9*	*28.2*	*18.1*	*9.5*	*7.1*
		1881	2988	1184	759	501	345	199	*39.6*	*25.4*	*16.8*	*11.5*	*6.7*
Usk	Persons	1851	3780	1228	968	713	484	387	*32.5*	*25.6*	*18.9*	*12.8*	*10.2*
		1881	3731	1265	923	592	509	442	*33.9*	*24.7*	*15.9*	*13.6*	*11.8*
	Males	1851	1939	631	503	373	243	189	*32.5*	*25.9*	*19.2*	*12.5*	*9.7*
		1881	1888	639	458	300	256	235	*33.8*	*24.3*	*15.9*	*13.6*	*12.4*
	Females	1851	1841	597	465	340	241	198	*32.4*	*25.3*	*18.5*	*13.1*	*10.8*
		1881	1843	626	465	292	253	207	*34.0*	*25.2*	*15.8*	*13.7*	*11.2*
Newport													
Caerleon	Persons	1851	6368	2191	1635	1228	708	606	*34.4*	*25.7*	*19.3*	*11.1*	*9.5*
		1881	10709	4176	2538	1897	1191	907	*39.0*	*23.7*	*17.7*	*11.1*	*8.5*
	Males	1851	3212	1054	828	629	387	314	*32.8*	*25.8*	*19.6*	*12.0*	*9.8*
		1881	5157	2043	1160	899	611	444	*39.6*	*22.5*	*17.4*	*11.8*	*8.6*
	Females	1851	3156	1137	807	599	321	292	*36.0*	*25.6*	*19.0*	*10.2*	*9.3*
		1881	5552	2133	1378	998	580	463	*38.4*	*24.8*	*18.0*	*10.4*	*8.3*

Registration Subdistrict[1]		Year	Number All ages	under 15	15–	30–	45–	60–	Percentage under 15	15–	30–	45–	60–
Newport	Persons	1851	20279	6842	6200	4463	1929	845	*33.7*	*30.6*	*22.0*	*9.5*	*4.2*
		1881	33932	12263	9789	6313	3575	1992	*36.1*	*28.8*	*18.6*	*10.5*	*5.9*
	Males	1851	10536	3452	3187	2468	1033	396	*32.8*	*30.2*	*23.4*	*9.8*	*3.8*
		1881	16848	6026	4867	3274	1766	915	*35.8*	*28.9*	*19.4*	*10.5*	*5.4*
	Females	1851	9743	3390	3013	1995	896	449	*34.8*	*30.9*	*20.5*	*9.2*	*4.6*
		1881	17084	6237	4922	3039	1809	1077	*36.5*	*28.8*	*17.8*	*10.6*	*6.3*
St Woollos	Persons	1851	7759	2799	2162	1444	828	526	*36.1*	*27.9*	*18.6*	*10.7*	*6.8*
		1881	12811	5144	3196	2098	1436	937	*40.2*	*24.9*	*16.4*	*11.2*	*7.3*
	Males	1851	4069	1424	1159	773	446	267	*35.0*	*28.5*	*19.0*	*11.0*	*6.6*
		1881	6475	2563	1646	1063	749	454	*39.6*	*25.4*	*16.4*	*11.6*	*7.0*
	Females	1851	3690	1375	1003	671	382	259	*37.3*	*27.2*	*18.2*	*10.4*	*7.0*
		1881	6336	2581	1550	1035	687	483	*40.7*	*24.5*	*16.3*	*10.8*	*7.6*
Mynyddislwyn	Persons	1851	9066	3381	2571	1610	905	599	*37.3*	*28.4*	*17.8*	*10.0*	*6.6*
		1881	13090	5285	3321	2246	1366	872	*40.4*	*25.4*	*17.2*	*10.4*	*6.7*
	Males	1851	4777	1702	1428	866	493	288	*35.6*	*29.9*	*18.1*	*10.3*	*6.0*
		1881	6717	2663	1771	1155	683	445	*39.6*	*26.4*	*17.2*	*10.2*	*6.6*
	Females	1851	4289	1679	1143	744	412	311	*39.1*	*26.6*	*17.3*	*9.6*	*7.3*
		1881	6373	2622	1550	1091	683	427	*41.1*	*24.3*	*17.1*	*10.7*	*6.7*
GLAMORGAN													
Cardiff													
Caerphilly	Persons	1851	8121	2811	2349	1497	850	614	*34.6*	*28.9*	*18.4*	*10.5*	*7.6*
	Males	1851	4217	1416	1232	817	451	301	*33.6*	*29.2*	*19.4*	*10.7*	*7.1*
	Females	1851	3904	1395	1117	680	399	313	*35.7*	*28.6*	*17.4*	*10.2*	*8.0*
Cardiff	Persons	1851	23085	6841	7511	5188	2337	1208	*29.6*	*32.5*	*22.5*	*10.1*	*5.2*
		1881	94666	34381	27902	18378	9681	4324	*36.3*	*29.5*	*19.4*	*10.2*	*4.6*
	Males	1851	12696	3478	4210	3068	1349	591	*27.4*	*33.2*	*24.2*	*10.6*	*4.7*
		1881	48299	17202	14194	9818	5028	2057	*35.6*	*29.4*	*20.3*	*10.4*	*4.3*
	Females	1851	10389	3363	3301	2120	988	617	*32.4*	*31.8*	*20.4*	*9.5*	*5.9*
		1881	46367	17179	13708	8560	4653	2267	*37.1*	*29.6*	*18.5*	*10.0*	*4.9*
St Nicholas	Persons	1851	4572	1563	1259	733	557	460	*34.2*	*27.5*	*16.0*	*12.2*	*10.1*
		1881	5024	1693	1354	760	660	557	*33.7*	*27.0*	*15.1*	*13.1*	*11.1*
	Males	1851	2315	789	643	375	291	217	*34.1*	*27.8*	*16.2*	*12.6*	*9.4*
		1881	2518	853	657	383	334	291	*33.9*	*26.1*	*15.2*	*13.3*	*11.6*
	Females	1851	2257	774	616	358	266	243	*34.3*	*27.3*	*15.9*	*11.8*	*10.8*
		1881	2506	840	697	377	326	266	*33.5*	*27.8*	*15.0*	*13.0*	*10.6*
Llantrisant	Persons	1851	10713	3945	3017	2033	1056	662	*36.8*	*28.2*	*19.0*	*9.9*	*6.2*
		1881	19197	7690	4968	3435	1998	1106	*40.1*	*25.9*	*17.9*	*10.4*	*5.8*
	Males	1851	5674	2000	1692	1119	547	316	*35.2*	*29.8*	*19.7*	*9.6*	*5.6*
		1881	10059	3867	2729	1848	1053	562	*38.4*	*27.1*	*18.4*	*10.5*	*5.6*
	Females	1851	5039	1945	1325	914	509	346	*38.6*	*26.3*	*18.1*	*10.1*	*6.9*
		1881	9138	3823	2239	1587	945	544	*41.8*	*24.5*	*17.4*	*10.3*	*6.0*
Whitchurch	Persons	1881	6474	2464	1592	1060	806	552	*38.1*	*24.6*	*16.4*	*12.4*	*8.5*
	Males	1881	3311	1217	855	565	396	278	*36.8*	*25.8*	*17.1*	*12.0*	*8.4*
	Females	1881	3163	1247	737	495	410	274	*39.4*	*23.3*	*15.6*	*13.0*	*8.7*
Pontypridd	Persons	1881	30250	11730	8399	5480	3052	1589	*38.8*	*27.8*	*18.1*	*10.1*	*5.3*
	Males	1881	16146	5886	4831	3017	1606	806	*36.5*	*29.9*	*18.7*	*9.9*	*5.0*
	Females	1881	14104	5844	3568	2463	1446	783	*41.4*	*25.3*	*17.5*	*10.3*	*5.6*
Ystradyfodwg	Persons	1881	44046	17377	13281	8067	3931	1390	*39.5*	*30.2*	*18.3*	*8.9*	*3.2*
	Males	1881	24470	8908	7977	4663	2186	736	*36.4*	*32.6*	*19.1*	*8.9*	*3.0*
	Females	1881	19576	8469	5304	3404	1745	654	*43.3*	*27.1*	*17.4*	*8.9*	*3.3*
Merthyr Tydfil													
Gelli-gaer	Persons	1851	8985	3271	2567	1779	903	465	*36.4*	*28.6*	*19.8*	*10.1*	*5.2*
		1881	11592	4569	3190	2003	1217	613	*39.4*	*27.5*	*17.3*	*10.5*	*5.3*
	Males	1851	4819	1666	1383	1018	515	237	*34.6*	*28.7*	*21.1*	*10.7*	*4.9*
		1881	6201	2292	1809	1114	664	322	*37.0*	*29.2*	*18.0*	*10.7*	*5.2*
	Females	1851	4166	1605	1184	761	388	228	*38.5*	*28.4*	*18.3*	*9.3*	*5.5*
		1881	5391	2277	1381	889	553	291	*42.2*	*25.6*	*16.5*	*10.3*	*5.4*

Registration Subdistrict[1]		Year	Number All ages	under 15	15–	30–	45–	60–	*Percentage under 15*	*15–*	*30–*	*45–*	*60–*
Lower Merthyr Tydfil	Persons	1851	23147	8352	6870	4551	2278	1096	*36.1*	*29.7*	*19.7*	*9.8*	*4.7*
		1881	23904	9123	6262	4226	2569	1724	*38.2*	*26.2*	*17.7*	*10.7*	*7.2*
	Males	1851	12170	4175	3746	2518	1225	506	*34.3*	*30.8*	*20.7*	*10.1*	*4.2*
		1881	12033	4530	3243	2205	1271	784	*37.6*	*27.0*	*18.3*	*10.6*	*6.5*
	Females	1851	10977	4177	3124	2033	1053	590	*38.1*	*28.5*	*18.5*	*9.6*	*5.4*
		1881	11871	4593	3019	2021	1298	940	*38.7*	*25.4*	*17.0*	*10.9*	*7.9*
Upper Merthyr Tydfil	Persons	1851	25898	9197	7931	5446	2266	1058	*35.5*	*30.6*	*21.0*	*8.7*	*4.1*
		1881	27808	10248	7680	4907	3147	1826	*36.9*	*27.6*	*17.6*	*11.3*	*6.6*
	Males	1851	13918	4634	4531	3043	1232	478	*33.3*	*32.6*	*21.9*	*8.9*	*3.4*
		1881	14472	5126	4249	2640	1583	874	*35.4*	*29.4*	*18.2*	*10.9*	*6.0*
	Females	1851	11980	4563	3400	2403	1034	580	*38.1*	*28.4*	*20.1*	*8.6*	*4.8*
		1881	13336	5122	3431	2267	1564	952	*38.4*	*25.7*	*17.0*	*11.7*	*7.1*
Aberdare	Persons	1851	18774	6299	6438	3783	1509	745	*33.6*	*34.3*	*20.2*	*8.0*	*4.0*
		1881	38137	15053	10184	6665	4187	2048	*39.5*	*26.7*	*17.5*	*11.0*	*5.4*
	Males	1851	10518	3180	3891	2268	820	359	*30.2*	*37.0*	*21.6*	*7.8*	*3.4*
		1881	19724	7563	5545	3546	2122	948	*38.3*	*28.1*	*18.0*	*10.8*	*4.8*
	Females	1851	8256	3119	2547	1515	689	386	*37.8*	*30.9*	*18.4*	*8.3*	*4.7*
		1881	18413	7490	4639	3119	2065	1100	*40.7*	*25.2*	*16.9*	*11.2*	*6.0*
Bridgend													
Maesteg	Persons	1851	7488	2862	2053	1270	795	508	*38.2*	*27.4*	*17.0*	*10.6*	*6.8*
		1881	18215	7305	4893	3182	1816	1019	*40.1*	*26.9*	*17.5*	*10.0*	*5.6*
	Males	1851	3863	1443	1107	669	417	227	*37.4*	*28.7*	*17.3*	*10.8*	*5.9*
		1881	9762	3703	2823	1750	976	510	*37.9*	*28.9*	*17.9*	*10.0*	*5.2*
	Females	1851	3625	1419	946	601	378	281	*39.1*	*26.1*	*16.6*	*10.4*	*7.8*
		1881	8453	3602	2070	1432	840	509	*42.6*	*24.5*	*16.9*	*9.9*	*6.0*
Cowbridge	Persons	1851	6516	2139	1784	1041	869	683	*32.8*	*27.4*	*16.0*	*13.3*	*10.5*
		1881	6165	2063	1589	975	825	713	*33.5*	*25.8*	*15.8*	*13.4*	*11.6*
	Males	1851	3205	1071	876	521	416	321	*33.4*	*27.3*	*16.3*	*13.0*	*10.0*
		1881	2946	989	721	489	408	339	*33.6*	*24.5*	*16.6*	*13.8*	*11.5*
	Females	1851	3311	1068	908	520	453	362	*32.3*	*27.4*	*15.7*	*13.7*	*10.9*
		1881	3219	1074	868	486	417	374	*33.4*	*27.0*	*15.1*	*13.0*	*11.6*
Bridgend	Persons	1851	9418	3501	2361	1697	1062	797	*37.2*	*25.1*	*18.0*	*11.3*	*8.5*
		1881	14540	5241	3635	2656	1749	1259	*36.0*	*25.0*	*18.3*	*12.0*	*8.7*
	Males	1851	4721	1779	1138	876	561	367	*37.7*	*24.1*	*18.6*	*11.9*	*7.8*
		1881	7346	2618	1845	1380	859	644	*35.6*	*25.1*	*18.8*	*11.7*	*8.8*
	Females	1851	4697	1722	1223	821	501	430	*36.7*	*26.0*	*17.5*	*10.7*	*9.2*
		1881	7194	2623	1790	1276	890	615	*36.5*	*24.9*	*17.7*	*12.4*	*8.5*
Neath													
Margam	Persons	1851	14697	5704	4497	2643	1319	534	*38.8*	*30.6*	*18.0*	*9.0*	*3.6*
		1881	18326	7282	4925	2985	1984	1150	*39.7*	*26.9*	*16.3*	*10.8*	*6.3*
	Males	1851	7962	2913	2588	1475	730	256	*36.6*	*32.5*	*18.5*	*9.2*	*3.2*
		1881	9272	3706	2526	1533	982	525	*40.0*	*27.2*	*16.5*	*10.6*	*5.7*
	Females	1851	6735	2791	1909	1168	589	278	*41.4*	*28.3*	*17.3*	*8.7*	*4.1*
		1881	9054	3576	2399	1452	1002	625	*39.5*	*26.5*	*16.0*	*11.1*	*6.9*
Neath	Persons	1851	10065	3741	2847	1943	967	567	*37.2*	*28.3*	*19.3*	*9.6*	*5.6*
		1881	21548	8334	5807	3954	2200	1253	*38.7*	*26.9*	*18.3*	*10.2*	*5.8*
	Males	1851	5000	1822	1413	1046	482	237	*36.4*	*28.3*	*20.9*	*9.6*	*4.7*
		1881	10768	4105	2990	2006	1104	563	*38.1*	*27.8*	*18.6*	*10.3*	*5.2*
	Females	1851	5065	1919	1434	897	485	330	*37.9*	*28.3*	*17.7*	*9.6*	*6.5*
		1881	10780	4229	2817	1948	1096	690	*39.2*	*26.1*	*18.1*	*10.2*	*6.4*
Ystradfellte	Persons	1851	2865	1023	816	560	275	191	*35.7*	*28.5*	*19.5*	*9.6*	*6.7*
		1881	3916	1528	1072	622	429	265	*39.0*	*27.4*	*15.9*	*11.0*	*6.8*
	Males	1851	1482	494	432	320	151	85	*33.3*	*29.1*	*21.6*	*10.2*	*5.7*
		1881	1996	746	577	308	235	130	*37.4*	*28.9*	*15.4*	*11.8*	*6.5*
	Females	1851	1383	529	384	240	124	106	*38.3*	*27.8*	*17.4*	*9.0*	*7.7*
		1881	1920	782	495	314	194	135	*40.7*	*25.8*	*16.4*	*10.1*	*7.0*
Ystradgynlais	Persons	1851	7987	3338	2134	1419	719	377	*41.8*	*26.7*	*17.8*	*9.0*	*4.7*
	Males	1851	4183	1722	1173	757	371	160	*41.2*	*28.0*	*18.1*	*8.9*	*3.8*
	Females	1851	3804	1616	961	662	348	217	*42.5*	*25.3*	*17.4*	*9.1*	*5.7*

Registration Subdistrict[1]		Year	Number All ages	under 15	15–	30–	45–	60–	Percentage under 15	15–	30–	45–	60–
Cadoxton	Persons	1851	6581	2740	1753	1141	591	356	*41.6*	*26.6*	*17.3*	*9.0*	*5.4*
		1881	8287	3506	2036	1423	829	493	*42.3*	*24.6*	*17.2*	*10.0*	*5.9*
	Males	1851	3392	1408	922	609	297	156	*41.5*	*27.2*	*18.0*	*8.8*	*4.6*
		1881	4183	1760	1039	734	419	231	*42.1*	*24.8*	*17.5*	*10.0*	*5.5*
	Females	1851	3189	1332	831	532	294	200	*41.8*	*26.1*	*16.7*	*9.2*	*6.3*
		1881	4104	1746	997	689	410	262	*42.5*	*24.3*	*16.8*	*10.0*	*6.4*
Pontardawe	Persons	1881	20185	8456	5217	3165	2025	1322	*41.9*	*25.8*	*15.7*	*10.0*	*6.5*
	Males	1881	10116	4252	2663	1556	1026	619	*42.0*	*26.3*	*15.4*	*10.1*	*6.1*
	Females	1881	10069	4204	2554	1609	999	703	*41.8*	*25.4*	*16.0*	*9.9*	*7.0*
Llansamlet	Persons	1851	4276	1720	1182	695	419	260	*40.2*	*27.6*	*16.3*	*9.8*	*6.1*
		1881	8392	3550	2179	1420	817	426	*42.3*	*26.0*	*16.9*	*9.7*	*5.1*
	Males	1851	2189	853	650	358	215	113	*39.0*	*29.7*	*16.4*	*9.8*	*5.2*
		1881	4324	1774	1209	755	407	179	*41.0*	*28.0*	*17.5*	*9.4*	*4.1*
	Females	1851	2087	867	532	337	204	147	*41.5*	*25.5*	*16.1*	*9.8*	*7.0*
		1881	4068	1776	970	665	410	247	*43.7*	*23.8*	*16.3*	*10.1*	*6.1*
Swansea													
Llandeilo Tal-y-bont	Persons	1851	5001	1986	1292	764	546	413	*39.7*	*25.8*	*15.3*	*10.9*	*8.3*
		1881	11336	4954	2874	1872	1059	577	*43.7*	*25.4*	*16.5*	*9.3*	*5.1*
	Males	1851	2503	1043	626	385	274	175	*41.7*	*25.0*	*15.4*	*10.9*	*7.0*
		1881	5778	2502	1541	952	526	257	*43.3*	*26.7*	*16.5*	*9.1*	*4.4*
	Females	1851	2498	943	666	379	272	238	*37.8*	*26.7*	*15.2*	*10.9*	*9.5*
		1881	5558	2452	1333	920	533	320	*44.1*	*24.0*	*16.6*	*9.6*	*5.8*
Llangyfelach	Persons	1851	11255	4754	2887	1895	1058	661	*42.2*	*25.7*	*16.8*	*9.4*	*5.9*
		1881	25153	10497	6838	4351	2363	1104	*41.7*	*27.2*	*17.3*	*9.4*	*4.4*
	Males	1851	5551	2365	1473	937	510	266	*42.6*	*26.5*	*16.9*	*9.2*	*4.8*
		1881	12820	5324	3617	2247	1179	453	*41.5*	*28.2*	*17.5*	*9.2*	*3.5*
	Females	1851	5704	2389	1414	958	548	395	*41.9*	*24.8*	*16.8*	*9.6*	*6.9*
		1881	12333	5173	3221	2104	1184	651	*41.9*	*26.1*	*17.1*	*9.6*	*5.3*
Swansea	Persons	1851	23607	8122	6845	4666	2503	1471	*34.4*	*29.0*	*19.8*	*10.6*	*6.2*
		1881	50120	18221	14336	9483	5257	2823	*36.4*	*28.6*	*18.9*	*10.5*	*5.6*
	Males	1851	11244	4085	3130	2291	1158	580	*36.3*	*27.8*	*20.4*	*10.3*	*5.2*
		1881	24285	8934	6755	4789	2544	1263	*36.8*	*27.8*	*19.7*	*10.5*	*5.2*
	Females	1851	12363	4037	3715	2375	1345	891	*32.7*	*30.0*	*19.2*	*10.9*	*7.2*
		1881	25835	9287	7581	4694	2713	1560	*35.9*	*29.3*	*18.2*	*10.5*	*6.0*
Gower	Persons	1851	7044	2617	1720	1111	882	714	*37.2*	*24.4*	*15.8*	*12.5*	*10.1*
	Males	1851	3465	1347	820	529	439	330	*38.9*	*23.7*	*15.3*	*12.7*	*9.5*
	Females	1851	3579	1270	900	582	443	384	*35.5*	*25.1*	*16.3*	*12.4*	*10.7*
Gower Eastern	Persons	1881	8248	3321	2033	1381	893	620	*40.3*	*24.6*	*16.7*	*10.8*	*7.5*
	Males	1881	3890	1643	926	634	409	278	*42.2*	*23.8*	*16.3*	*10.5*	*7.1*
	Females	1881	4358	1678	1107	747	484	342	*38.5*	*25.4*	*17.1*	*11.1*	*7.8*
Gower Western	Persons	1881	2854	908	644	457	413	432	*31.8*	*22.6*	*16.0*	*14.5*	*15.1*
	Males	1881	1409	455	318	217	201	218	*32.3*	*22.6*	*15.4*	*14.3*	*15.5*
	Females	1881	1445	453	326	240	212	214	*31.3*	*22.6*	*16.6*	*14.7*	*14.8*
CARMARTHENSHIRE													
Llanelli													
Loughor	Persons	1851	3582	1487	925	560	374	236	*41.5*	*25.8*	*15.6*	*10.4*	*6.6*
		1881	7541	3197	1992	1293	646	413	*42.4*	*26.4*	*17.1*	*8.6*	*5.5*
	Males	1851	1799	774	451	289	172	113	*43.0*	*25.1*	*16.1*	*9.6*	*6.3*
		1881	3765	1588	1012	646	324	195	*42.2*	*26.9*	*17.2*	*8.6*	*5.2*
	Females	1851	1783	713	474	271	202	123	*40.0*	*26.6*	*15.2*	*11.3*	*6.9*
		1881	3776	1609	980	647	322	218	*42.6*	*26.0*	*17.1*	*8.5*	*5.8*
Llanelli	Persons	1851	11285	4624	2896	1999	1085	681	*41.0*	*25.7*	*17.7*	*9.6*	*6.0*
		1881	23933	9663	6520	4090	2351	1309	*40.4*	*27.2*	*17.1*	*9.8*	*5.5*
	Males	1851	5633	2366	1419	1021	517	310	*42.0*	*25.2*	*18.1*	*9.2*	*5.5*
		1881	11847	4763	3369	1999	1126	590	*40.2*	*28.4*	*16.9*	*9.5*	*5.0*
	Females	1851	5652	2258	1477	978	568	371	*40.0*	*26.1*	*17.3*	*10.0*	*6.6*
		1881	12086	4900	3151	2091	1225	719	*40.5*	*26.1*	*17.3*	*10.1*	*5.9*

Registration Subdistrict[1]		Year	Number All ages	under 15	15–	30–	45–	60–	*Percentage under 15*	*15–*	*30–*	*45–*	*60–*
Pembrey	Persons	1851	4958	1879	1228	827	592	432	*37.9*	*24.8*	*16.7*	*11.9*	*8.7*
		1881	8173	3418	1908	1352	887	608	*41.8*	*23.3*	*16.5*	*10.9*	*7.4*
	Males	1851	2394	942	571	402	291	188	*39.3*	*23.9*	*16.8*	*12.2*	*7.9*
		1881	3958	1764	881	650	400	263	*44.6*	*22.3*	*16.4*	*10.1*	*6.6*
	Females	1851	2564	937	657	425	301	244	*36.5*	*25.6*	*16.6*	*11.7*	*9.5*
		1881	4215	1654	1027	702	487	345	*39.2*	*24.4*	*16.7*	*11.6*	*8.2*
Llan-non	Persons	1851	3682	1525	900	565	403	289	*41.4*	*24.4*	*15.3*	*10.9*	*7.8*
		1881	4969	2062	1285	748	491	383	*41.5*	*25.9*	*15.1*	*9.9*	*7.7*
	Males	1851	1792	774	436	269	188	125	*43.2*	*24.3*	*15.0*	*10.5*	*7.0*
		1881	2464	1046	635	370	245	168	*42.5*	*25.8*	*15.0*	*9.9*	*6.8*
	Females	1851	1890	751	464	296	215	164	*39.7*	*24.6*	*15.7*	*11.4*	*8.7*
		1881	2505	1016	650	378	246	215	*40.6*	*25.9*	*15.1*	*9.8*	*8.6*
Llandovery													
Llanddeusant	Persons	1851	851	267	257	126	96	105	*31.4*	*30.2*	*14.8*	*11.3*	*12.3*
		1881	647	184	190	87	93	93	*28.4*	*29.4*	*13.4*	*14.4*	*14.4*
	Males	1851	416	131	116	67	44	58	*31.5*	*27.9*	*16.1*	*10.6*	*13.9*
		1881	325	105	87	35	51	47	*32.3*	*26.8*	*10.8*	*15.7*	*14.5*
	Females	1851	435	136	141	59	52	47	*31.3*	*32.4*	*13.6*	*12.0*	*10.8*
		1881	322	79	103	52	42	46	*24.5*	*32.0*	*16.1*	*13.0*	*14.3*
Llangadog	Persons	1851	2820	1056	715	487	297	265	*37.4*	*25.4*	*17.3*	*10.5*	*9.4*
		1881	1911	676	482	298	231	224	*35.4*	*25.2*	*15.6*	*12.1*	*11.7*
	Males	1851	1365	518	339	247	158	103	*37.9*	*24.8*	*18.1*	*11.6*	*7.5*
		1881	909	339	217	139	114	100	*37.3*	*23.9*	*15.3*	*12.5*	*11.0*
	Females	1851	1455	538	376	240	139	162	*37.0*	*25.8*	*16.5*	*9.6*	*11.1*
		1881	1002	337	265	159	117	124	*33.6*	*26.4*	*15.9*	*11.7*	*12.4*
Llansadwrn	Persons	1851	1699	609	461	270	189	170	*35.8*	*27.1*	*15.9*	*11.1*	*10.0*
		1881	1502	518	405	207	186	186	*34.5*	*27.0*	*13.8*	*12.4*	*12.4*
	Males	1851	822	322	217	126	83	74	*39.2*	*26.4*	*15.3*	*10.1*	*9.0*
		1881	707	271	175	88	92	81	*38.3*	*24.8*	*12.4*	*13.0*	*11.5*
	Females	1851	877	287	244	144	106	96	*32.7*	*27.8*	*16.4*	*12.1*	*10.9*
		1881	795	247	230	119	94	105	*31.1*	*28.9*	*15.0*	*11.8*	*13.2*
Myddfai	Persons	1851	1069	375	276	172	116	130	*35.1*	*25.8*	*16.1*	*10.9*	*12.2*
	Males	1851	520	193	118	80	65	64	*37.1*	*22.7*	*15.4*	*12.5*	*12.3*
	Females	1851	549	182	158	92	51	66	*33.2*	*28.8*	*16.8*	*9.3*	*12.0*
Llandingad	Persons	1851	2542	865	708	449	281	239	*34.0*	*27.9*	*17.7*	*11.1*	*9.4*
		1881	3416	1202	915	533	393	373	*35.2*	*26.8*	*15.6*	*11.5*	*10.9*
	Males	1851	1178	421	319	213	124	101	*35.7*	*27.1*	*18.1*	*10.5*	*8.6*
		1881	1635	615	442	233	188	157	*37.6*	*27.0*	*14.3*	*11.5*	*9.6*
	Females	1851	1364	444	389	236	157	138	*32.6*	*28.5*	*17.3*	*11.5*	*10.1*
		1881	1781	587	473	300	205	216	*33.0*	*26.6*	*16.8*	*11.5*	*12.1*
Llanfair-ar-y-bryn	Persons	1851	1705	660	467	254	184	140	*38.7*	*27.4*	*14.9*	*10.8*	*8.2*
		1881	1281	447	358	193	152	131	*34.9*	*27.9*	*15.1*	*11.9*	*10.2*
	Males	1851	834	338	223	128	83	62	*40.5*	*26.7*	*15.3*	*10.0*	*7.4*
		1881	615	227	159	87	80	62	*36.9*	*25.9*	*14.1*	*13.0*	*10.1*
	Females	1851	871	322	244	126	101	78	*37.0*	*28.0*	*14.5*	*11.6*	*9.0*
		1881	666	220	199	106	72	69	*33.0*	*29.9*	*15.9*	*10.8*	*10.4*
Llanwrtyd	Persons	1851	684	262	175	101	82	64	*38.3*	*25.6*	*14.8*	*12.0*	*9.4*
		1881	942	340	234	177	107	84	*36.1*	*24.8*	*18.8*	*11.4*	*8.9*
	Males	1851	317	119	81	48	41	28	*37.5*	*25.6*	*15.1*	*12.9*	*8.8*
		1881	455	175	100	84	53	43	*38.5*	*22.0*	*18.5*	*11.6*	*9.5*
	Females	1851	367	143	94	53	41	36	*39.0*	*25.6*	*14.4*	*11.2*	*9.8*
		1881	487	165	134	93	54	41	*33.9*	*27.5*	*19.1*	*11.1*	*8.4*
Cil-y-cwm	Persons	1851	1487	571	387	215	165	149	*38.4*	*26.0*	*14.5*	*11.1*	*10.0*
		1881	1087	384	268	194	123	118	*35.3*	*24.7*	*17.8*	*11.3*	*10.9*
	Males	1851	721	291	186	107	81	56	*40.4*	*25.8*	*14.8*	*11.2*	*7.8*
		1881	512	197	116	91	59	49	*38.5*	*22.7*	*17.8*	*11.5*	*9.6*
	Females	1851	766	280	201	108	84	93	*36.6*	*26.2*	*14.1*	*11.0*	*12.1*
		1881	575	187	152	103	64	69	*32.5*	*26.4*	*17.9*	*11.1*	*12.0*

Registration Subdistrict[1]		Year	Number All ages	under 15	15–	30–	45–	60–	*Percentage under 15*	*15–*	*30–*	*45–*	*60–*
Cynwyl Gaeo	Persons	1851	2198	807	579	364	254	194	*36.7*	*26.3*	*16.6*	*11.6*	*8.8*
		1881	1979	724	465	325	230	235	*36.6*	*23.5*	*16.4*	*11.6*	*11.9*
	Males	1851	1095	409	291	182	124	89	*37.4*	*26.6*	*16.6*	*11.3*	*8.1*
		1881	948	374	198	142	119	115	*39.5*	*20.9*	*15.0*	*12.6*	*12.1*
	Females	1851	1103	398	288	182	130	105	*36.1*	*26.1*	*16.5*	*11.8*	*9.5*
		1881	1031	350	267	183	111	120	*33.9*	*25.9*	*17.7*	*10.8*	*11.6*
Llandeilo Fawr													
Talley	Persons	1851	2056	766	546	324	238	182	*37.3*	*26.6*	*15.8*	*11.6*	*8.9*
		1881	1783	688	449	283	185	178	*38.6*	*25.2*	*15.9*	*10.4*	*10.0*
	Males	1851	1019	405	256	161	118	79	*39.7*	*25.1*	*15.8*	*11.6*	*7.8*
		1881	856	348	216	129	80	83	*40.7*	*25.2*	*15.1*	*9.3*	*9.7*
	Females	1851	1037	361	290	163	120	103	*34.8*	*28.0*	*15.7*	*11.6*	*9.9*
		1881	927	340	233	154	105	95	*36.7*	*25.1*	*16.6*	*11.3*	*10.2*
Llanfynydd	Persons	1851	1540	544	452	238	172	134	*35.3*	*29.4*	*15.5*	*11.2*	*8.7*
		1881	1169	381	289	182	168	149	*32.6*	*24.7*	*15.6*	*14.4*	*12.7*
	Males	1851	742	266	217	123	84	52	*35.8*	*29.2*	*16.6*	*11.3*	*7.0*
		1881	559	199	125	81	77	77	*35.6*	*22.4*	*14.5*	*13.8*	*13.8*
	Females	1851	798	278	235	115	88	82	*34.8*	*29.4*	*14.4*	*11.0*	*10.3*
		1881	610	182	164	101	91	72	*29.8*	*26.9*	*16.6*	*14.9*	*11.8*
Llangathen	Persons	1851	3043	1064	805	468	341	365	*35.0*	*26.5*	*15.4*	*11.2*	*12.0*
		1881	2506	883	613	391	324	295	*35.2*	*24.5*	*15.6*	*12.9*	*11.8*
	Males	1851	1434	531	373	206	167	157	*37.0*	*26.0*	*14.4*	*11.6*	*10.9*
		1881	1137	432	273	168	139	125	*38.0*	*24.0*	*14.8*	*12.2*	*11.0*
	Females	1851	1609	533	432	262	174	208	*33.1*	*26.8*	*16.3*	*10.8*	*12.9*
		1881	1369	451	340	223	185	170	*32.9*	*24.8*	*16.3*	*13.5*	*12.4*
Llandeilo	Persons	1851	4812	1623	1260	772	633	524	*33.7*	*26.2*	*16.0*	*13.2*	*10.9*
		1881	4511	1535	1168	715	558	535	*34.0*	*25.9*	*15.9*	*12.4*	*11.9*
	Males	1851	2215	813	537	360	304	201	*36.7*	*24.2*	*16.3*	*13.7*	*9.1*
		1881	2084	785	486	320	255	238	*37.7*	*23.3*	*15.4*	*12.2*	*11.4*
	Females	1851	2597	810	723	412	329	323	*31.2*	*27.8*	*15.9*	*12.7*	*12.4*
		1881	2427	750	682	395	303	297	*30.9*	*28.1*	*16.3*	*12.5*	*12.2*
Llandybïe	Persons	1851	6517	2625	1550	1091	675	576	*40.3*	*23.8*	*16.7*	*10.4*	*8.8*
		1881	8830	3682	2120	1418	892	718	*41.7*	*24.0*	*16.1*	*10.1*	*8.1*
	Males	1851	3241	1365	770	536	328	242	*42.1*	*23.8*	*16.5*	*10.1*	*7.5*
		1881	4396	1908	1067	675	419	327	*43.4*	*24.3*	*15.4*	*9.5*	*7.4*
	Females	1851	3276	1260	780	555	347	334	*38.5*	*23.8*	*16.9*	*10.6*	*10.2*
		1881	4434	1774	1053	743	473	391	*40.0*	*23.7*	*16.8*	*10.7*	*8.8*
Carmarthen													
Llangyndeyrn	Persons	1851	8981	3274	2347	1383	1048	929	*36.5*	*26.1*	*15.4*	*11.7*	*10.3*
		1881	8549	3200	2204	1278	967	900	*37.4*	*25.8*	*14.9*	*11.3*	*10.5*
	Males	1851	4288	1669	1094	645	484	396	*38.9*	*25.5*	*15.0*	*11.3*	*9.2*
		1881	3989	1629	976	540	467	377	*40.8*	*24.5*	*13.5*	*11.7*	*9.5*
	Females	1851	4693	1605	1253	738	564	533	*34.2*	*26.7*	*15.7*	*12.0*	*11.4*
		1881	4560	1571	1228	738	500	523	*34.5*	*26.9*	*16.2*	*11.0*	*11.5*
St Clears	Persons	1851	7313	2812	1700	1173	865	763	*38.5*	*23.2*	*16.0*	*11.8*	*10.4*
		1881	6181	2145	1520	962	772	782	*34.7*	*24.6*	*15.6*	*12.5*	*12.7*
	Males	1851	3447	1413	778	527	405	324	*41.0*	*22.6*	*15.3*	*11.7*	*9.4*
		1881	2840	1113	638	413	347	329	*39.2*	*22.5*	*14.5*	*12.2*	*11.6*
	Females	1851	3866	1399	922	646	460	439	*36.2*	*23.8*	*16.7*	*11.9*	*11.4*
		1881	3341	1032	882	549	425	453	*30.9*	*26.4*	*16.4*	*12.7*	*13.6*
Carmarthen	Persons	1851	13294	4670	3578	2278	1468	1300	*35.1*	*26.9*	*17.1*	*11.0*	*9.8*
		1881	12872	4155	3556	2149	1677	1335	*32.3*	*27.6*	*16.7*	*13.0*	*10.4*
	Males	1851	6162	2347	1577	1037	687	514	*38.1*	*25.6*	*16.8*	*11.1*	*8.3*
		1881	5950	2127	1603	953	730	537	*35.7*	*26.9*	*16.0*	*12.3*	*9.0*
	Females	1851	7132	2323	2001	1241	781	786	*32.6*	*28.1*	*17.4*	*11.0*	*11.0*
		1881	6922	2028	1953	1196	947	798	*29.3*	*28.2*	*17.3*	*13.7*	*11.5*

Registration Subdistrict[1]		Year	Number All ages	under 15	15–	30–	45–	60–	Percentage under 15	15–	30–	45–	60–
Cynwyl	Persons	1851	8554	3288	2271	1307	943	745	*38.4*	*26.5*	*15.3*	*11.0*	*8.7*
		1881	7473	2802	1921	1114	830	806	*37.5*	*25.7*	*14.9*	*11.1*	*10.8*
	Males	1851	4085	1644	1063	610	432	336	*40.2*	*26.0*	*14.9*	*10.6*	*8.2*
		1881	3538	1449	850	490	376	373	*41.0*	*24.0*	*13.8*	*10.6*	*10.5*
	Females	1851	4469	1644	1208	697	511	409	*36.8*	*27.0*	*15.6*	*11.4*	*9.2*
		1881	3935	1353	1071	624	454	433	*34.4*	*27.2*	*15.9*	*11.5*	*11.0*
PEMBROKESHIRE													
Narberth													
Llanboidy	Persons	1851	3715	1436	883	614	426	356	*38.7*	*23.8*	*16.5*	*11.5*	*9.6*
		1881	3447	1225	872	534	456	360	*35.5*	*25.3*	*15.5*	*13.2*	*10.4*
	Males	1851	1734	732	393	270	188	151	*42.2*	*22.7*	*15.6*	*10.8*	*8.7*
		1881	1609	617	393	244	207	148	*38.3*	*24.4*	*15.2*	*12.9*	*9.2*
	Females	1851	1981	704	490	344	238	205	*35.5*	*24.7*	*17.4*	*12.0*	*10.3*
		1881	1838	608	479	290	249	212	*33.1*	*26.1*	*15.8*	*13.5*	*11.5*
Llandysilio	Persons	1851	3491	1408	803	568	380	332	*40.3*	*23.0*	*16.3*	*10.9*	*9.5*
		1881	3334	1306	792	509	402	325	*39.2*	*23.8*	*15.3*	*12.1*	*9.7*
	Males	1851	1634	707	354	261	169	143	*43.3*	*21.7*	*16.0*	*10.3*	*8.8*
		1881	1550	675	336	224	188	127	*43.5*	*21.7*	*14.5*	*12.1*	*8.2*
	Females	1851	1857	701	449	307	211	189	*37.7*	*24.2*	*16.5*	*11.4*	*10.2*
		1881	1784	631	456	285	214	198	*35.4*	*25.6*	*16.0*	*12.0*	*11.1*
Amroth	Persons	1851	3363	1255	813	548	421	326	*37.3*	*24.2*	*16.3*	*12.5*	*9.7*
		1881	3084	1157	736	477	334	380	*37.5*	*23.9*	*15.5*	*10.8*	*12.3*
	Males	1851	1645	641	406	255	206	137	*39.0*	*24.7*	*15.5*	*12.5*	*8.3*
		1881	1454	576	350	205	153	170	*39.6*	*24.1*	*14.1*	*10.5*	*11.7*
	Females	1851	1718	614	407	293	215	189	*35.7*	*23.7*	*17.1*	*12.5*	*11.0*
		1881	1630	581	386	272	181	210	*35.6*	*23.7*	*16.7*	*11.1*	*12.9*
Narberth	Persons	1851	3859	1407	965	626	458	403	*36.5*	*25.0*	*16.2*	*11.9*	*10.4*
		1881	3383	1169	855	496	426	437	*34.6*	*25.3*	*14.7*	*12.6*	*12.9*
	Males	1851	1788	722	397	280	212	177	*40.4*	*22.2*	*15.7*	*11.9*	*9.9*
		1881	1565	606	361	233	173	192	*38.7*	*23.1*	*14.9*	*11.1*	*12.3*
	Females	1851	2071	685	568	346	246	226	*33.1*	*27.4*	*16.7*	*11.9*	*10.9*
		1881	1818	563	494	263	253	245	*31.0*	*27.2*	*14.5*	*13.9*	*13.5*
Slebech	Persons	1851	3497	1360	800	548	385	404	*38.9*	*22.9*	*15.7*	*11.0*	*11.6*
		1881	2483	844	616	387	285	351	*34.0*	*24.8*	*15.6*	*11.5*	*14.1*
	Males	1851	1634	684	363	246	181	160	*41.9*	*22.2*	*15.1*	*11.1*	*9.8*
		1881	1145	423	274	171	121	156	*36.9*	*23.9*	*14.9*	*10.6*	*13.6*
	Females	1851	1863	676	437	302	204	244	*36.3*	*23.5*	*16.2*	*11.0*	*13.1*
		1881	1338	421	342	216	164	195	*31.5*	*25.6*	*16.1*	*12.3*	*14.6*
Begeli	Persons	1851	4205	1709	998	665	453	380	*40.6*	*23.7*	*15.8*	*10.8*	*9.0*
		1881	3810	1497	900	534	438	441	*39.3*	*23.6*	*14.0*	*11.5*	*11.6*
	Males	1851	2024	885	502	295	206	136	*43.7*	*24.8*	*14.6*	*10.2*	*6.7*
		1881	1826	758	449	241	191	187	*41.5*	*24.6*	*13.2*	*10.5*	*10.2*
	Females	1851	2181	824	496	370	247	244	*37.8*	*22.7*	*17.0*	*11.3*	*11.2*
		1881	1984	739	451	293	247	254	*37.2*	*22.7*	*14.8*	*12.4*	*12.8*
Pembroke													
Tenby	Persons	1851	8949	3139	2291	1553	1082	884	*35.1*	*25.6*	*17.4*	*12.1*	*9.9*
		1881	10341	3554	2769	1771	1199	1048	*34.4*	*26.8*	*17.1*	*11.6*	*10.1*
	Males	1851	3983	1551	887	710	480	355	*38.9*	*22.3*	*17.8*	*12.1*	*8.9*
		1881	4586	1750	1111	762	522	441	*38.2*	*24.2*	*16.6*	*11.4*	*9.6*
	Females	1851	4966	1588	1404	843	602	529	*32.0*	*28.3*	*17.0*	*12.1*	*10.7*
		1881	5755	1804	1658	1009	677	607	*31.3*	*28.8*	*17.5*	*11.8*	*10.5*
Pembroke	Persons	1851	11662	4340	3099	2172	1142	909	*37.2*	*26.6*	*18.6*	*9.8*	*7.8*
		1881	15689	5556	4370	2533	1943	1287	*35.4*	*27.9*	*16.1*	*12.4*	*8.2*
	Males	1851	5658	2201	1428	1075	545	409	*38.9*	*25.2*	*19.0*	*9.6*	*7.2*
		1881	7989	2843	2333	1245	963	605	*35.6*	*29.2*	*15.6*	*12.1*	*7.6*
	Females	1851	6004	2139	1671	1097	597	500	*35.6*	*27.8*	*18.3*	*9.9*	*8.3*
		1881	7700	2713	2037	1288	980	682	*35.2*	*26.5*	*16.7*	*12.7*	*8.9*

Registration Subdistrict[1]		Year	Number All ages	under 15	15–	30–	45–	60–	*Percentage under 15*	*15–*	*30–*	*45–*	*60–*
Roose	Persons	1851	2349	985	505	386	249	224	*41.9*	*21.5*	*16.4*	*10.6*	*9.5*
		1881	4317	1759	1041	687	511	319	*40.7*	*24.1*	*15.9*	*11.8*	*7.4*
	Males	1851	1137	522	215	181	117	102	*45.9*	*18.9*	*15.9*	*10.3*	*9.0*
		1881	2205	939	537	324	256	149	*42.6*	*24.4*	*14.7*	*11.6*	*6.8*
	Females	1851	1212	463	290	205	132	122	*38.2*	*23.9*	*16.9*	*10.9*	*10.1*
		1881	2112	820	504	363	255	170	*38.8*	*23.9*	*17.2*	*12.1*	*8.0*
Haverfordwest													
Milford	Persons	1851	9815	3509	2693	1600	1146	867	*35.8*	*27.4*	*16.3*	*11.7*	*8.8*
		1881	9507	3356	2623	1574	1101	853	*35.3*	*27.6*	*16.6*	*11.6*	*9.0*
	Males	1851	4858	1783	1344	794	539	398	*36.7*	*27.7*	*16.3*	*11.1*	*8.2*
		1881	5066	1718	1522	844	585	397	*33.9*	*30.0*	*16.7*	*11.5*	*7.8*
	Females	1851	4957	1726	1349	806	607	469	*34.8*	*27.2*	*16.3*	*12.2*	*9.5*
		1881	4441	1638	1101	730	516	456	*36.9*	*24.8*	*16.4*	*11.6*	*10.3*
Haverfordwest	Persons	1851	12376	4403	3223	1967	1542	1241	*35.6*	*26.0*	*15.9*	*12.5*	*10.0*
	Males	1851	5603	2162	1351	897	671	522	*38.6*	*24.1*	*16.0*	*12.0*	*9.3*
	Females	1851	6773	2241	1872	1070	871	719	*33.1*	*27.6*	*15.8*	*12.9*	*10.6*
St David's	Persons	1851	8297	3061	2045	1399	966	826	*36.9*	*24.6*	*16.9*	*11.6*	*10.0*
		1881	6282	2210	1500	958	823	791	*35.2*	*23.9*	*15.2*	*13.1*	*12.6*
	Males	1851	3846	1546	881	640	434	345	*40.2*	*22.9*	*16.6*	*11.3*	*9.0*
		1881	2868	1096	663	366	379	364	*38.2*	*23.1*	*12.8*	*13.2*	*12.7*
	Females	1851	4451	1515	1164	759	532	481	*34.0*	*26.2*	*17.1*	*12.0*	*10.8*
		1881	3414	1114	837	592	444	427	*32.6*	*24.5*	*17.3*	*13.0*	*12.5*
Fishguard	Persons	1851	8894	3508	2054	1379	1053	900	*39.4*	*23.1*	*15.5*	*11.8*	*10.1*
		1881	7247	2614	1684	1125	896	928	*36.1*	*23.2*	*15.5*	*12.4*	*12.8*
	Males	1851	4076	1801	843	594	479	359	*44.2*	*20.7*	*14.6*	*11.8*	*8.8*
		1881	3214	1263	710	455	396	390	*39.3*	*22.1*	*14.2*	*12.3*	*12.1*
	Females	1851	4818	1707	1211	785	574	541	*35.4*	*25.1*	*16.3*	*11.9*	*11.2*
		1881	4033	1351	974	670	500	538	*33.5*	*24.2*	*16.6*	*12.4*	*13.3*
CARDIGANSHIRE													
Cardigan													
Newport	Persons	1851	6130	2245	1389	1002	800	694	*36.6*	*22.7*	*16.3*	*13.1*	*11.3*
		1881	5219	1801	1131	860	743	684	*34.5*	*21.7*	*16.5*	*14.2*	*13.1*
	Males	1851	2589	1142	501	344	338	264	*44.1*	*19.4*	*13.3*	*13.1*	*10.2*
		1881	2170	890	412	325	290	253	*41.0*	*19.0*	*15.0*	*13.4*	*11.7*
	Females	1851	3541	1103	888	658	462	430	*31.1*	*25.1*	*18.6*	*13.0*	*12.1*
		1881	3049	911	719	535	453	431	*29.9*	*23.6*	*17.5*	*14.9*	*14.1*
Cardigan	Persons	1851	9723	3425	2375	1634	1240	1049	*35.2*	*24.4*	*16.8*	*12.8*	*10.8*
		1881	8705	2923	2075	1490	1090	1127	*33.6*	*23.8*	*17.1*	*12.5*	*12.9*
	Males	1851	4258	1743	937	650	523	405	*40.9*	*22.0*	*15.3*	*12.3*	*9.5*
		1881	3828	1500	903	558	434	433	*39.2*	*23.6*	*14.6*	*11.3*	*11.3*
	Females	1851	5465	1682	1438	984	717	644	*30.8*	*26.3*	*18.0*	*13.1*	*11.8*
		1881	4877	1423	1172	932	656	694	*29.2*	*24.0*	*19.1*	*13.5*	*14.2*
Llandygwydd	Persons	1851	4333	1681	941	740	505	466	*38.8*	*21.7*	*17.1*	*11.7*	*10.8*
		1881	3691	1232	841	629	474	515	*33.4*	*22.8*	*17.0*	*12.8*	*14.0*
	Males	1851	1965	840	404	299	215	207	*42.7*	*20.6*	*15.2*	*10.9*	*10.5*
		1881	1585	609	343	233	198	202	*38.4*	*21.6*	*14.7*	*12.5*	*12.7*
	Females	1851	2368	841	537	441	290	259	*35.5*	*22.7*	*18.6*	*12.2*	*10.9*
		1881	2106	623	498	396	276	313	*29.6*	*23.6*	*18.8*	*13.1*	*14.9*
Newcastle Emlyn													
Cenarth	Persons	1851	8686	3230	2123	1345	1093	895	*37.2*	*24.4*	*15.5*	*12.6*	*10.3*
		1881	8233	3038	2039	1206	988	962	*36.9*	*24.8*	*14.6*	*12.0*	*11.7*
	Males	1851	4088	1672	949	605	492	370	*40.9*	*23.2*	*14.8*	*12.0*	*9.1*
		1881	3800	1532	900	516	427	425	*40.3*	*23.7*	*13.6*	*11.2*	*11.2*
	Females	1851	4598	1558	1174	740	601	525	*33.9*	*25.5*	*16.1*	*13.1*	*11.4*
		1881	4433	1506	1139	690	561	537	*34.0*	*25.7*	*15.6*	*12.7*	*12.1*

Registration Subdistrict[1]		Year	Number All ages	under 15	15–	30–	45–	60–	*Percentage under 15*	*15–*	*30–*	*45–*	*60–*
Penbryn	Persons	1851	5360	1958	1225	877	666	634	*36.5*	*22.9*	*16.4*	*12.4*	*11.8*
		1881	4547	1517	1078	691	617	644	*33.4*	*23.7*	*15.2*	*13.6*	*14.2*
	Males	1851	2418	998	512	365	272	271	*41.3*	*21.2*	*15.1*	*11.2*	*11.2*
		1881	2030	793	469	261	244	263	*39.1*	*23.1*	*12.9*	*12.0*	*13.0*
	Females	1851	2942	960	713	512	394	363	*32.6*	*24.2*	*17.4*	*13.4*	*12.3*
		1881	2517	724	609	430	373	381	*28.8*	*24.2*	*17.1*	*14.8*	*15.1*
Llandysul	Persons	1851	6127	2146	1547	1053	770	611	*35.0*	*25.2*	*17.2*	*12.6*	*10.0*
		1881	6234	2081	1574	983	803	793	*33.4*	*25.2*	*15.8*	*12.9*	*12.7*
	Males	1851	2879	1115	679	471	349	265	*38.7*	*23.6*	*16.4*	*12.1*	*9.2*
		1881	2813	1056	714	391	333	319	*37.5*	*25.4*	*13.9*	*11.8*	*11.3*
	Females	1851	3248	1031	868	582	421	346	*31.7*	*26.7*	*17.9*	*13.0*	*10.7*
		1881	3421	1025	860	592	470	474	*30.0*	*25.1*	*17.3*	*13.7*	*13.9*
Lampeter													
Llanybydder	Persons	1851	2630	989	645	377	332	287	*37.6*	*24.5*	*14.3*	*12.6*	*10.9*
		1881	2690	1008	644	426	334	278	*37.5*	*23.9*	*15.8*	*12.4*	*10.3*
	Males	1851	1234	500	293	168	151	122	*40.5*	*23.7*	*13.6*	*12.2*	*9.9*
		1881	1244	500	287	179	158	120	*40.2*	*23.1*	*14.4*	*12.7*	*9.6*
	Females	1851	1396	489	352	209	181	165	*35.0*	*25.2*	*15.0*	*13.0*	*11.8*
		1881	1446	508	357	247	176	158	*35.1*	*24.7*	*17.1*	*12.2*	*10.9*
Pencarreg	Persons	1851	2706	998	644	457	323	284	*36.9*	*23.8*	*16.9*	*11.9*	*10.5*
		1881	2600	925	589	395	377	314	*35.6*	*22.7*	*15.2*	*14.5*	*12.1*
	Males	1851	1304	503	292	223	143	143	*38.6*	*22.4*	*17.1*	*11.0*	*11.0*
		1881	1188	445	258	166	163	156	*37.5*	*21.7*	*14.0*	*13.7*	*13.1*
	Females	1851	1402	495	352	234	180	141	*35.3*	*25.1*	*16.7*	*12.8*	*10.1*
		1881	1412	480	331	229	214	158	*34.0*	*23.4*	*16.2*	*15.2*	*11.2*
Lampeter	Persons	1851	2634	912	699	463	313	247	*34.6*	*26.5*	*17.6*	*11.9*	*9.4*
		1881	2938	954	850	503	327	304	*32.5*	*28.9*	*17.1*	*11.1*	*10.3*
	Males	1851	1264	465	332	216	154	97	*36.8*	*26.3*	*17.1*	*12.2*	*7.7*
		1881	1392	449	425	232	149	137	*32.3*	*30.5*	*16.7*	*10.7*	*9.8*
	Females	1851	1370	447	367	247	159	150	*32.6*	*26.8*	*18.0*	*11.6*	*10.9*
		1881	1546	505	425	271	178	167	*32.7*	*27.5*	*17.5*	*11.5*	*10.8*
Llanwenog	Persons	1851	1904	743	469	316	215	161	*39.0*	*24.6*	*16.6*	*11.3*	*8.5*
		1881	1859	666	441	311	236	205	*35.8*	*23.7*	*16.7*	*12.7*	*11.0*
	Males	1851	903	357	221	151	98	76	*39.5*	*24.5*	*16.7*	*10.9*	*8.4*
		1881	847	336	208	117	99	87	*39.7*	*24.6*	*13.8*	*11.7*	*10.3*
	Females	1851	1001	386	248	165	117	85	*38.6*	*24.8*	*16.5*	*11.7*	*8.5*
		1881	1012	330	233	194	137	118	*32.6*	*23.0*	*19.2*	*13.5*	*11.7*
Aberaeron													
Llandysilio	Persons	1851	6415	2409	1543	1079	736	648	*37.6*	*24.1*	*16.8*	*11.5*	*10.1*
		1881	5934	2105	1321	915	814	779	*35.5*	*22.3*	*15.4*	*13.7*	*13.1*
	Males	1851	2903	1247	620	449	320	267	*43.0*	*21.4*	*15.5*	*11.0*	*9.2*
		1881	2477	1044	519	298	300	316	*42.1*	*21.0*	*12.0*	*12.1*	*12.8*
	Females	1851	3512	1162	923	630	416	381	*33.1*	*26.3*	*17.9*	*11.8*	*10.8*
		1881	3457	1061	802	617	514	463	*30.7*	*23.2*	*17.8*	*14.9*	*13.4*
Llansanffraid	Persons	1851	6809	2531	1576	1155	828	719	*37.2*	*23.1*	*17.0*	*12.2*	*10.6*
		1881	6609	2346	1459	1049	901	854	*35.5*	*22.1*	*15.9*	*13.6*	*12.9*
	Males	1851	3088	1250	679	478	373	308	*40.5*	*22.0*	*15.5*	*12.1*	*10.0*
		1881	2801	1162	583	366	348	342	*41.5*	*20.8*	*13.1*	*12.4*	*12.2*
	Females	1851	3721	1281	897	677	455	411	*34.4*	*24.1*	*18.2*	*12.2*	*11.0*
		1881	3808	1184	876	683	553	512	*31.1*	*23.0*	*17.9*	*14.5*	*13.4*
Aberystwyth													
Llanrhystud	Persons	1851	3409	1221	906	528	436	318	*35.8*	*26.6*	*15.5*	*12.8*	*9.3*
		1881	3128	1092	787	489	411	349	*34.9*	*25.2*	*15.6*	*13.1*	*11.2*
	Males	1851	1615	606	420	245	204	140	*37.5*	*26.0*	*15.2*	*12.6*	*8.7*
		1881	1419	529	338	218	174	160	*37.3*	*23.8*	*15.4*	*12.3*	*11.3*
	Females	1851	1794	615	486	283	232	178	*34.3*	*27.1*	*15.8*	*12.9*	*9.9*
		1881	1709	563	449	271	237	189	*32.9*	*26.3*	*15.9*	*13.9*	*11.1*

Registration Subdistrict[1]		Year	Number All ages	under 15	15–	30–	45–	60–	*Percentage under 15*	*15–*	*30–*	*45–*	*60–*
Aberystwyth	Persons	1851	8442	2830	2219	1512	1045	836	*33.5*	*26.3*	*17.9*	*12.4*	*9.9*
		1881	10271	3403	2846	1749	1332	941	*33.1*	*27.7*	*17.0*	*13.0*	*9.2*
	Males	1851	3862	1392	980	651	475	364	*36.0*	*25.4*	*16.9*	*12.3*	*9.4*
		1881	4603	1684	1231	698	582	408	*36.6*	*26.7*	*15.2*	*12.6*	*8.9*
	Females	1851	4580	1438	1239	861	570	472	*31.4*	*27.1*	*18.8*	*12.4*	*10.3*
		1881	5668	1719	1615	1051	750	533	*30.3*	*28.5*	*18.5*	*13.2*	*9.4*
Genau'r-glyn	Persons	1851	4502	1667	1142	730	534	429	*37.0*	*25.4*	*16.2*	*11.9*	*9.5*
		1881	4527	1683	1070	717	604	453	*37.2*	*23.6*	*15.8*	*13.3*	*10.0*
	Males	1851	2182	843	544	358	237	200	*38.6*	*24.9*	*16.4*	*10.9*	*9.2*
		1881	2132	872	499	295	273	193	*40.9*	*23.4*	*13.8*	*12.8*	*9.1*
	Females	1851	2320	824	598	372	297	229	*35.5*	*25.8*	*16.0*	*12.8*	*9.9*
		1881	2395	811	571	422	331	260	*33.9*	*23.8*	*17.6*	*13.8*	*10.9*
Rheidol	Persons	1851	7400	2833	2050	1319	737	461	*38.3*	*27.7*	*17.8*	*10.0*	*6.2*
		1881	7680	2934	1974	1189	906	677	*38.2*	*25.7*	*15.5*	*11.8*	*8.8*
	Males	1851	3700	1408	1067	657	371	197	*38.1*	*28.8*	*17.8*	*10.0*	*5.3*
		1881	3698	1505	981	546	418	248	*40.7*	*26.5*	*14.8*	*11.3*	*6.7*
	Females	1851	3700	1425	983	662	366	264	*38.5*	*26.6*	*17.9*	*9.9*	*7.1*
		1881	3982	1429	993	643	488	429	*35.9*	*24.9*	*16.1*	*12.3*	*10.8*
Tregaron													
Gwnnws	Persons	1851	3147	1136	906	504	335	266	*36.1*	*28.8*	*16.0*	*10.6*	*8.5*
		1881	3314	1238	866	493	419	298	*37.4*	*26.1*	*14.9*	*12.6*	*9.0*
	Males	1851	1524	566	455	236	161	106	*37.1*	*29.9*	*15.5*	*10.6*	*7.0*
		1881	1556	610	434	208	185	119	*39.2*	*27.9*	*13.4*	*11.9*	*7.6*
	Females	1851	1623	570	451	268	174	160	*35.1*	*27.8*	*16.5*	*10.7*	*9.9*
		1881	1758	628	432	285	234	179	*35.7*	*24.6*	*16.2*	*13.3*	*10.2*
Llangeitho	Persons	1851	3293	1246	788	559	396	304	*37.8*	*23.9*	*17.0*	*12.0*	*9.2*
		1881	3187	1110	720	539	409	409	*34.8*	*22.6*	*16.9*	*12.8*	*12.8*
	Males	1851	1555	618	349	269	199	120	*39.7*	*22.4*	*17.3*	*12.8*	*7.7*
		1881	1433	554	298	225	163	193	*38.7*	*20.8*	*15.7*	*11.4*	*13.5*
	Females	1851	1738	628	439	290	197	184	*36.1*	*25.3*	*16.7*	*11.3*	*10.6*
		1881	1754	556	422	314	246	216	*31.7*	*24.1*	*17.9*	*14.0*	*12.3*
Tregaron	Persons	1851	3964	1520	991	669	393	391	*38.3*	*25.0*	*16.9*	*9.9*	*9.9*
		1881	3771	1349	899	608	463	452	*35.8*	*23.8*	*16.1*	*12.3*	*12.0*
	Males	1851	1824	739	433	300	186	166	*40.5*	*23.7*	*16.4*	*10.2*	*9.1*
		1881	1701	696	366	257	188	194	*40.9*	*21.5*	*15.1*	*11.1*	*11.4*
	Females	1851	2140	781	558	369	207	225	*36.5*	*26.1*	*17.2*	*9.7*	*10.5*
		1881	2070	653	533	351	275	258	*31.5*	*25.7*	*17.0*	*13.3*	*12.5*
BRECONSHIRE													
Builth													
Abergwesyn	Persons	1851	2890	1024	801	450	308	307	*35.4*	*27.7*	*15.6*	*10.7*	*10.6*
		1881	2679	963	686	424	339	267	*35.9*	*25.6*	*15.8*	*12.7*	*10.0*
	Males	1851	1419	539	365	227	148	140	*38.0*	*25.7*	*16.0*	*10.4*	*9.9*
		1881	1294	462	331	204	169	128	*35.7*	*25.6*	*15.8*	*13.1*	*9.9*
	Females	1851	1471	485	436	223	160	167	*33.0*	*29.6*	*15.2*	*10.9*	*11.4*
		1881	1385	501	355	220	170	139	*36.2*	*25.6*	*15.9*	*12.3*	*10.0*
Colwyn	Persons	1851	1995	723	524	331	227	190	*36.2*	*26.3*	*16.6*	*11.4*	*9.5*
		1881	1847	720	446	273	236	172	*39.0*	*24.1*	*14.8*	*12.8*	*9.3*
	Males	1851	1017	369	262	174	114	98	*36.3*	*25.8*	*17.1*	*11.2*	*9.6*
		1881	959	369	228	138	124	100	*38.5*	*23.8*	*14.4*	*12.9*	*10.4*
	Females	1851	978	354	262	157	113	92	*36.2*	*26.8*	*16.1*	*11.6*	*9.4*
		1881	888	351	218	135	112	72	*39.5*	*24.5*	*15.2*	*12.6*	*8.1*
Builth	Persons	1851	3460	1223	931	518	388	400	*35.3*	*26.9*	*15.0*	*11.2*	*11.6*
		1881	3656	1326	931	607	437	355	*36.3*	*25.5*	*16.6*	*12.0*	*9.7*
	Males	1851	1716	632	437	266	189	192	*36.8*	*25.5*	*15.5*	*11.0*	*11.2*
		1881	1762	660	388	318	208	188	*37.5*	*22.0*	*18.0*	*11.8*	*10.7*
	Females	1851	1744	591	494	252	199	208	*33.9*	*28.3*	*14.4*	*11.4*	*11.9*
		1881	1894	666	543	289	229	167	*35.2*	*28.7*	*15.3*	*12.1*	*8.8*

Registration Subdistrict[1]		Year	Number All ages	under 15	15–	30–	45–	60–	*Percentage under 15*	*15–*	*30–*	*45–*	*60–*
Brecon													
Merthyr Cynog	Persons	1851	1653	544	478	270	176	185	*32.9*	*28.9*	*16.3*	*10.6*	*11.2*
		1881	1371	499	372	219	147	134	*36.4*	*27.1*	*16.0*	*10.7*	*9.8*
	Males	1851	858	281	244	145	91	97	*32.8*	*28.4*	*16.9*	*10.6*	*11.3*
		1881	685	243	188	108	75	71	*35.5*	*27.4*	*15.8*	*10.9*	*10.4*
	Females	1851	795	263	234	125	85	88	*33.1*	*29.4*	*15.7*	*10.7*	*11.1*
		1881	686	256	184	111	72	63	*37.3*	*26.8*	*16.2*	*10.5*	*9.2*
Defynnog	Persons	1851	4440	1545	1155	672	547	521	*34.8*	*26.0*	*15.1*	*12.3*	*11.7*
		1881	3727	1309	964	605	477	372	*35.1*	*25.9*	*16.2*	*12.8*	*10.0*
	Males	1851	2147	765	550	321	277	234	*35.6*	*25.6*	*15.0*	*12.9*	*10.9*
		1881	1805	645	475	294	221	170	*35.7*	*26.3*	*16.3*	*12.2*	*9.4*
	Females	1851	2293	780	605	351	270	287	*34.0*	*26.4*	*15.3*	*11.8*	*12.5*
		1881	1922	664	489	311	256	202	*34.5*	*25.4*	*16.2*	*13.3*	*10.5*
Brecon	Persons	1851	7515	2223	2242	1375	862	813	*29.6*	*29.8*	*18.3*	*11.5*	*10.8*
		1881	7987	2659	2314	1331	964	719	*33.3*	*29.0*	*16.7*	*12.1*	*9.0*
	Males	1851	3704	1136	1103	679	430	356	*30.7*	*29.8*	*18.3*	*11.6*	*9.6*
		1881	4024	1408	1183	670	445	318	*35.0*	*29.4*	*16.7*	*11.1*	*7.9*
	Females	1851	3811	1087	1139	696	432	457	*28.5*	*29.9*	*18.3*	*11.3*	*12.0*
		1881	3963	1251	1131	661	519	401	*31.6*	*28.5*	*16.7*	*13.1*	*10.1*
Pencelli	Persons	1851	1541	534	393	276	179	159	*34.7*	*25.5*	*17.9*	*11.6*	*10.3*
		1881	1456	495	344	225	218	174	*34.0*	*23.6*	*15.5*	*15.0*	*12.0*
	Males	1851	754	251	198	138	93	74	*33.3*	*26.3*	*18.3*	*12.3*	*9.8*
		1881	747	244	175	119	121	88	*32.7*	*23.4*	*15.9*	*16.2*	*11.8*
	Females	1851	787	283	195	138	86	85	*36.0*	*24.8*	*17.5*	*10.9*	*10.8*
		1881	709	251	169	106	97	86	*35.4*	*23.8*	*15.0*	*13.7*	*12.1*
Llan-gors	Persons	1851	3025	1001	820	514	361	329	*33.1*	*27.1*	*17.0*	*11.9*	*10.9*
		1881	2637	923	679	422	342	271	*35.0*	*25.7*	*16.0*	*13.0*	*10.3*
	Males	1851	1521	513	409	263	178	158	*33.7*	*26.9*	*17.3*	*11.7*	*10.4*
		1881	1317	456	341	212	163	145	*34.6*	*25.9*	*16.1*	*12.4*	*11.0*
	Females	1851	1504	488	411	251	183	171	*32.4*	*27.3*	*16.7*	*12.2*	*11.4*
		1881	1320	467	338	210	179	126	*35.4*	*25.6*	*15.9*	*13.6*	*9.5*
Crickhowell													
Cwm-du	Persons	1851	1066	368	272	184	126	116	*34.5*	*25.5*	*17.3*	*11.8*	*10.9*
		1881	957	353	206	153	112	133	*36.9*	*21.5*	*16.0*	*11.7*	*13.9*
	Males	1851	560	197	144	95	70	54	*35.2*	*25.7*	*17.0*	*12.5*	*9.6*
		1881	465	173	91	78	55	68	*37.2*	*19.6*	*16.8*	*11.8*	*14.6*
	Females	1851	506	171	128	89	56	62	*33.8*	*25.3*	*17.6*	*11.1*	*12.3*
		1881	492	180	115	75	57	65	*36.6*	*23.4*	*15.2*	*11.6*	*13.2*
Llangynidr	Persons	1851	3246	1200	882	648	312	204	*37.0*	*27.2*	*20.0*	*9.6*	*6.3*
		1881	3625	1467	864	628	387	279	*40.5*	*23.8*	*17.3*	*10.7*	*7.7*
	Males	1851	1756	638	494	367	165	92	*36.3*	*28.1*	*20.9*	*9.4*	*5.2*
		1881	1810	713	446	324	202	125	*39.4*	*24.6*	*17.9*	*11.2*	*6.9*
	Females	1851	1490	562	388	281	147	112	*37.7*	*26.0*	*18.9*	*9.9*	*7.5*
		1881	1815	754	418	304	185	154	*41.5*	*23.0*	*16.7*	*10.2*	*8.5*
Llangatwg	Persons	1851	5415	1903	1543	1110	560	299	*35.1*	*28.5*	*20.5*	*10.3*	*5.5*
		1881	4731	1816	1169	772	538	436	*38.4*	*24.7*	*16.3*	*11.4*	*9.2*
	Males	1851	2907	937	871	651	319	129	*32.2*	*30.0*	*22.4*	*11.0*	*4.4*
		1881	2411	902	623	402	268	216	*37.4*	*25.8*	*16.7*	*11.1*	*9.0*
	Females	1851	2508	966	672	459	241	170	*38.5*	*26.8*	*18.3*	*9.6*	*6.8*
		1881	2320	914	546	370	270	220	*39.4*	*23.5*	*15.9*	*11.6*	*9.5*
Llanelli	Persons	1851	9644	3535	2752	1871	954	532	*36.7*	*28.5*	*19.4*	*9.9*	*5.5*
		1881	6979	2636	1696	1190	898	559	*37.8*	*24.3*	*17.1*	*12.9*	*8.0*
	Males	1851	5064	1782	1491	1023	512	256	*35.2*	*29.4*	*20.2*	*10.1*	*5.1*
		1881	3605	1327	944	609	458	267	*36.8*	*26.2*	*16.9*	*12.7*	*7.4*
	Females	1851	4580	1753	1261	848	442	276	*38.3*	*27.5*	*18.5*	*9.7*	*6.0*
		1881	3374	1309	752	581	440	292	*38.8*	*22.3*	*17.2*	*13.0*	*8.7*

Registration Subdistrict[1]		Year	Number All ages	under 15	15–	30–	45–	60–	Percentage under 15	15–	30–	45–	60–
Crickhowell	Persons	1851	2326	745	650	411	290	230	*32.0*	*27.9*	*17.7*	*12.5*	*9.9*
		1881	2266	762	554	364	321	265	*33.6*	*24.4*	*16.1*	*14.2*	*11.7*
	Males	1851	1123	370	297	207	146	103	*32.9*	*26.4*	*18.4*	*13.0*	*9.2*
		1881	1079	380	239	177	156	127	*35.2*	*22.2*	*16.4*	*14.5*	*11.8*
	Females	1851	1203	375	353	204	144	127	*31.2*	*29.3*	*17.0*	*12.0*	*10.6*
		1881	1187	382	315	187	165	138	*32.2*	*26.5*	*15.8*	*13.9*	*11.6*
Hay													
Talgarth	Persons	1851	2549	842	644	438	324	301	*33.0*	*25.3*	*17.2*	*12.7*	*11.8*
		1881	2513	868	607	417	311	310	*34.5*	*24.2*	*16.6*	*12.4*	*12.3*
	Males	1851	1280	434	311	213	174	148	*33.9*	*24.3*	*16.6*	*13.6*	*11.6*
		1881	1256	433	303	214	156	150	*34.5*	*24.1*	*17.0*	*12.4*	*11.9*
	Females	1851	1269	408	333	225	150	153	*32.2*	*26.2*	*17.7*	*11.8*	*12.1*
		1881	1257	435	304	203	155	160	*34.6*	*24.2*	*16.1*	*12.3*	*12.7*
Clyro	Persons	1851	3628	1285	921	630	400	392	*35.4*	*25.4*	*17.4*	*11.0*	*10.8*
		1881	3113	1104	789	465	421	334	*35.5*	*25.3*	*14.9*	*13.5*	*10.7*
	Males	1851	1850	655	488	308	199	200	*35.4*	*26.4*	*16.6*	*10.8*	*10.8*
		1881	1571	553	406	240	211	161	*35.2*	*25.8*	*15.3*	*13.4*	*10.2*
	Females	1851	1778	630	433	322	201	192	*35.4*	*24.4*	*18.1*	*11.3*	*10.8*
		1881	1542	551	383	225	210	173	*35.7*	*24.8*	*14.6*	*13.6*	*11.2*
Hay	Persons	1851	4785	1600	1142	868	579	596	*33.4*	*23.9*	*18.1*	*12.1*	*12.5*
		1881	4596	1621	1067	782	569	557	*35.3*	*23.2*	*17.0*	*12.4*	*12.1*
	Males	1851	2317	795	527	431	297	267	*34.3*	*22.7*	*18.6*	*12.8*	*11.5*
		1881	2201	800	481	379	291	250	*36.3*	*21.9*	*17.2*	*13.2*	*11.4*
	Females	1851	2468	805	615	437	282	329	*32.6*	*24.9*	*17.7*	*11.4*	*13.3*
		1881	2395	821	586	403	278	307	*34.3*	*24.5*	*16.8*	*11.6*	*12.8*
RADNORSHIRE													
Presteigne													
Brilley	Persons	1851	2095	730	567	314	254	230	*34.8*	*27.1*	*15.0*	*12.1*	*11.0*
	Males	1851	1065	375	284	167	125	114	*35.2*	*26.7*	*15.7*	*11.7*	*10.7*
	Females	1851	1030	355	283	147	129	116	*34.5*	*27.5*	*14.3*	*12.5*	*11.3*
Radnor	Persons	1851	3714	1268	1050	590	443	363	*34.1*	*28.3*	*15.9*	*11.9*	*9.8*
	Males	1851	1947	655	552	323	221	196	*33.6*	*28.4*	*16.6*	*11.4*	*10.1*
	Females	1851	1767	613	498	267	222	167	*34.7*	*28.2*	*15.1*	*12.6*	*9.5*
Kington	Persons	1851	5847	1903	1526	1067	727	624	*32.5*	*26.1*	*18.2*	*12.4*	*10.7*
	Males	1851	2916	960	757	535	365	299	*32.9*	*26.0*	*18.3*	*12.5*	*10.3*
	Females	1851	2931	943	769	532	362	325	*32.2*	*26.2*	*18.2*	*12.4*	*11.1*
Presteigne	Persons	1851	3493	1188	905	635	414	351	*34.0*	*25.9*	*18.2*	*11.9*	*10.0*
		1881	2336	839	538	384	296	279	*35.9*	*23.0*	*16.4*	*12.7*	*11.9*
	Males	1851	1763	603	447	337	216	160	*34.2*	*25.4*	*19.1*	*12.3*	*9.1*
		1881	1142	400	251	192	156	143	*35.0*	*22.0*	*16.8*	*13.7*	*12.5*
	Females	1851	1730	585	458	298	198	191	*33.8*	*26.5*	*17.2*	*11.4*	*11.0*
		1881	1194	439	287	192	140	136	*36.8*	*24.0*	*16.1*	*11.7*	*11.4*
Knighton													
Knighton	Persons	1851	5316	1833	1441	897	631	514	*34.5*	*27.1*	*16.9*	*11.9*	*9.7*
		1881	5724	2004	1522	886	735	577	*35.0*	*26.6*	*15.5*	*12.8*	*10.1*
	Males	1851	2748	936	754	476	322	260	*34.1*	*27.4*	*17.3*	*11.7*	*9.5*
		1881	2940	1014	814	446	377	289	*34.5*	*27.7*	*15.2*	*12.8*	*9.8*
	Females	1851	2568	897	687	421	309	254	*34.9*	*26.8*	*16.4*	*12.0*	*9.9*
		1881	2784	990	708	440	358	288	*35.6*	*25.4*	*15.8*	*12.9*	*10.3*
Llanbister	Persons	1851	4164	1674	1112	589	454	335	*40.2*	*26.7*	*14.1*	*10.9*	*8.0*
		1881	3722	1403	983	533	464	339	*37.7*	*26.4*	*14.3*	*12.5*	*9.1*
	Males	1851	2199	888	576	318	247	170	*40.4*	*26.2*	*14.5*	*11.2*	*7.7*
		1881	1975	728	530	297	241	179	*36.9*	*26.8*	*15.0*	*12.2*	*9.1*
	Females	1851	1965	786	536	271	207	165	*40.0*	*27.3*	*13.8*	*10.5*	*8.4*
		1881	1747	675	453	236	223	160	*38.6*	*25.9*	*13.5*	*12.8*	*9.2*

Registration Subdistrict[1]		Year	Number All ages	under 15	15–	30–	45–	60–	*Percentage under 15*	*15–*	*30–*	*45–*	*60–*
Rhayader													
Rhayader	Persons	1851	3689	1434	870	589	410	386	*38.9*	*23.6*	*16.0*	*11.1*	*10.5*
		1881	3439	1230	886	528	399	396	*35.8*	*25.8*	*15.4*	*11.6*	*11.5*
	Males	1851	1862	738	434	300	215	175	*39.6*	*23.3*	*16.1*	*11.5*	*9.4*
		1881	1696	605	441	264	202	184	*35.7*	*26.0*	*15.6*	*11.9*	*10.8*
	Females	1851	1827	696	436	289	195	211	*38.1*	*23.9*	*15.8*	*10.7*	*11.5*
		1881	1743	625	445	264	197	212	*35.9*	*25.5*	*15.1*	*11.3*	*12.2*
Nantmel	Persons	1851	3107	1243	756	482	322	304	*40.0*	*24.3*	*15.5*	*10.4*	*9.8*
		1881	3302	1249	795	562	364	332	*37.8*	*24.1*	*17.0*	*11.0*	*10.1*
	Males	1851	1618	659	393	245	165	156	*40.7*	*24.3*	*15.1*	*10.2*	*9.6*
		1881	1651	639	369	289	182	172	*38.7*	*22.4*	*17.5*	*11.0*	*10.4*
	Females	1851	1489	584	363	237	157	148	*39.2*	*24.4*	*15.9*	*10.5*	*9.9*
		1881	1651	610	426	273	182	160	*36.9*	*25.8*	*16.5*	*11.0*	*9.7*
MONTGOMERYSHIRE													
Machynlleth													
Machynlleth	Persons	1851	3981	1376	985	684	480	456	*34.6*	*24.7*	*17.2*	*12.1*	*11.5*
		1881	4307	1634	989	711	528	445	*37.9*	*23.0*	*16.5*	*12.3*	*10.3*
	Males	1851	1939	709	462	336	224	208	*36.6*	*23.8*	*17.3*	*11.6*	*10.7*
		1881	2076	813	481	328	258	196	*39.2*	*23.2*	*15.8*	*12.4*	*9.4*
	Females	1851	2042	667	523	348	256	248	*32.7*	*25.6*	*17.0*	*12.5*	*12.1*
		1881	2231	821	508	383	270	249	*36.8*	*22.8*	*17.2*	*12.1*	*11.2*
Pennal	Persons	1851	4143	1384	970	718	529	542	*33.4*	*23.4*	*17.3*	*12.8*	*13.1*
		1881	4713	1546	1308	720	630	509	*32.8*	*27.8*	*15.3*	*13.4*	*10.8*
	Males	1851	2017	722	451	359	247	238	*35.8*	*22.4*	*17.8*	*12.2*	*11.8*
		1881	2289	778	644	340	295	232	*34.0*	*28.1*	*14.9*	*12.9*	*10.1*
	Females	1851	2126	662	519	359	282	304	*31.1*	*24.4*	*16.9*	*13.3*	*14.3*
		1881	2424	768	664	380	335	277	*31.7*	*27.4*	*15.7*	*13.8*	*11.4*
Darowen	Persons	1851	3992	1361	1074	659	450	448	*34.1*	*26.9*	*16.5*	*11.3*	*11.2*
		1881	3497	1243	862	542	468	382	*35.5*	*24.6*	*15.5*	*13.4*	*10.9*
	Males	1851	1973	698	529	317	227	202	*35.4*	*26.8*	*16.1*	*11.5*	*10.2*
		1881	1715	616	422	264	229	184	*35.9*	*24.6*	*15.4*	*13.4*	*10.7*
	Females	1851	2019	663	545	342	223	246	*32.8*	*27.0*	*16.9*	*11.0*	*12.2*
		1881	1782	627	440	278	239	198	*35.2*	*24.7*	*15.6*	*13.4*	*11.1*
Newtown													
Upper Llanidloes	Persons	1851	4236	1612	1108	670	466	380	*38.1*	*26.2*	*15.8*	*11.0*	*9.0*
		1881	3896	1509	934	631	463	359	*38.7*	*24.0*	*16.2*	*11.9*	*9.2*
	Males	1851	2072	814	531	341	234	152	*39.3*	*25.6*	*16.5*	*11.3*	*7.3*
		1881	1913	766	448	300	235	164	*40.0*	*23.4*	*15.7*	*12.3*	*8.6*
	Females	1851	2164	798	577	329	232	228	*36.9*	*26.7*	*15.2*	*10.7*	*10.5*
		1881	1983	743	486	331	228	195	*37.5*	*24.5*	*16.7*	*11.5*	*9.8*
Lower Llanidloes	Persons	1851	3963	1506	1061	608	422	366	*38.0*	*26.8*	*15.3*	*10.6*	*9.2*
		1881	4471	1866	989	759	453	404	*41.7*	*22.1*	*17.0*	*10.1*	*9.0*
	Males	1851	2008	773	554	302	214	165	*38.5*	*27.6*	*15.0*	*10.7*	*8.2*
		1881	2236	932	514	377	234	179	*41.7*	*23.0*	*16.9*	*10.5*	*8.0*
	Females	1851	1955	733	507	306	208	201	*37.5*	*25.9*	*15.7*	*10.6*	*10.3*
		1881	2235	934	475	382	219	225	*41.8*	*21.3*	*17.1*	*9.8*	*10.1*
Llanwnnog	Persons	1851	4807	1898	1194	735	469	511	*39.5*	*24.8*	*15.3*	*9.8*	*10.6*
		1881	4720	1874	1118	689	535	504	*39.7*	*23.7*	*14.6*	*11.3*	*10.7*
	Males	1851	2399	954	608	350	233	254	*39.8*	*25.3*	*14.6*	*9.7*	*10.6*
		1881	2392	961	561	344	268	258	*40.2*	*23.5*	*14.4*	*11.2*	*10.8*
	Females	1851	2408	944	586	385	236	257	*39.2*	*24.3*	*16.0*	*9.8*	*10.7*
		1881	2328	913	557	345	267	246	*39.2*	*23.9*	*14.8*	*11.5*	*10.6*
Kerry	Persons	1851	2449	886	677	370	290	226	*36.2*	*27.6*	*15.1*	*11.8*	*9.2*
		1881	2601	1037	612	391	310	251	*39.9*	*23.5*	*15.0*	*11.9*	*9.7*
	Males	1851	1265	433	376	192	153	111	*34.2*	*29.7*	*15.2*	*12.1*	*8.8*
		1881	1339	506	342	196	165	130	*37.8*	*25.5*	*14.6*	*12.3*	*9.7*
	Females	1851	1184	453	301	178	137	115	*38.3*	*25.4*	*15.0*	*11.6*	*9.7*
		1881	1262	531	270	195	145	121	*42.1*	*21.4*	*15.5*	*11.5*	*9.6*

Registration Subdistrict[1]		Year	Number All ages	under 15	15–	30–	45–	60–	Percentage under 15	15–	30–	45–	60–
Newtown	Persons	1851	6559	2130	1791	1143	867	628	*32.5*	*27.3*	*17.4*	*13.2*	*9.6*
		1881	7170	2426	2049	1124	865	706	*33.8*	*28.6*	*15.7*	*12.1*	*9.8*
	Males	1851	3151	1033	879	557	422	260	*32.8*	*27.9*	*17.7*	*13.4*	*8.3*
		1881	3495	1238	981	548	402	326	*35.4*	*28.1*	*15.7*	*11.5*	*9.3*
	Females	1851	3408	1097	912	586	445	368	*32.2*	*26.8*	*17.2*	*13.1*	*10.8*
		1881	3675	1188	1068	576	463	380	*32.3*	*29.1*	*15.7*	*12.6*	*10.3*
Tregynon	Persons	1851	3093	1118	843	416	377	339	*36.1*	*27.3*	*13.4*	*12.2*	*11.0*
		1881	2581	959	685	394	307	236	*37.2*	*26.5*	*15.3*	*11.9*	*9.1*
	Males	1851	1591	576	459	209	188	159	*36.2*	*28.8*	*13.1*	*11.8*	*10.0*
		1881	1357	493	383	205	162	114	*36.3*	*28.2*	*15.1*	*11.9*	*8.4*
	Females	1851	1502	542	384	207	189	180	*36.1*	*25.6*	*13.8*	*12.6*	*12.0*
		1881	1224	466	302	189	145	122	*38.1*	*24.7*	*15.4*	*11.8*	*10.0*
Montgomery													
Montgomery	Persons	1851	6109	2140	1591	1038	702	638	*35.0*	*26.0*	*17.0*	*11.5*	*10.4*
		1881	5721	2051	1390	902	738	640	*35.9*	*24.3*	*15.8*	*12.9*	*11.2*
	Males	1851	3096	1083	821	526	354	312	*35.0*	*26.5*	*17.0*	*11.4*	*10.1*
		1881	2932	1049	737	427	394	325	*35.8*	*25.1*	*14.6*	*13.4*	*11.1*
	Females	1851	3013	1057	770	512	348	326	*35.1*	*25.6*	*17.0*	*11.5*	*10.8*
		1881	2789	1002	653	475	344	315	*35.9*	*23.4*	*17.0*	*12.3*	*11.3*
Chirbury	Persons	1851	5441	2028	1337	919	646	511	*37.3*	*24.6*	*16.9*	*11.9*	*9.4*
		1881	5712	2149	1335	930	693	605	*37.6*	*23.4*	*16.3*	*12.1*	*10.6*
	Males	1851	2834	1011	738	508	332	245	*35.7*	*26.0*	*17.9*	*11.7*	*8.6*
		1881	3042	1116	754	505	347	320	*36.7*	*24.8*	*16.6*	*11.4*	*10.5*
	Females	1851	2607	1017	599	411	314	266	*39.0*	*23.0*	*15.8*	*12.0*	*10.2*
		1881	2670	1033	581	425	346	285	*38.7*	*21.8*	*15.9*	*13.0*	*10.7*
Welshpool	Persons	1851	8831	2915	2309	1523	1140	944	*33.0*	*26.1*	*17.2*	*12.9*	*10.7*
		1881	6848	2327	1756	1140	897	728	*34.0*	*25.6*	*16.6*	*13.1*	*10.6*
	Males	1851	4372	1439	1131	766	597	439	*32.9*	*25.9*	*17.5*	*13.7*	*10.0*
		1881	3471	1168	937	555	469	342	*33.7*	*27.0*	*16.0*	*13.5*	*9.9*
	Females	1851	4459	1476	1178	757	543	505	*33.1*	*26.4*	*17.0*	*12.2*	*11.3*
		1881	3377	1159	819	585	428	386	*34.3*	*24.3*	*17.3*	*12.7*	*11.4*
Llanfyllin													
Llanfair	Persons	1851	6697	2467	1627	1044	830	729	*36.8*	*24.3*	*15.6*	*12.4*	*10.9*
		1881	5587	2047	1333	861	711	635	*36.6*	*23.9*	*15.4*	*12.7*	*11.4*
	Males	1851	3385	1234	822	531	423	375	*36.5*	*24.3*	*15.7*	*12.5*	*11.1*
		1881	2808	1019	687	434	353	315	*36.3*	*24.5*	*15.5*	*12.6*	*11.2*
	Females	1851	3312	1233	805	513	407	354	*37.2*	*24.3*	*15.5*	*12.3*	*10.7*
		1881	2779	1028	646	427	358	320	*37.0*	*23.2*	*15.4*	*12.9*	*11.5*
Llansanffraid	Persons	1851	7466	2552	2011	1119	963	821	*34.2*	*26.9*	*15.0*	*12.9*	*11.0*
		1881	9583	3412	2259	1507	1274	1131	*35.6*	*23.6*	*15.7*	*13.3*	*11.8*
	Males	1851	3711	1269	1002	558	481	401	*34.2*	*27.0*	*15.0*	*13.0*	*10.8*
		1881	4786	1719	1129	733	649	556	*35.9*	*23.6*	*15.3*	*13.6*	*11.6*
	Females	1851	3755	1283	1009	561	482	420	*34.2*	*26.9*	*14.9*	*12.8*	*11.2*
		1881	4797	1693	1130	774	625	575	*35.3*	*23.6*	*16.1*	*13.0*	*12.0*
Llanrhaeadr	Persons	1851	5375	1980	1327	883	671	514	*36.8*	*24.7*	*16.4*	*12.5*	*9.6*
		1881	4789	1684	1158	787	630	530	*35.2*	*24.2*	*16.4*	*13.2*	*11.1*
	Males	1851	2728	986	703	438	359	242	*36.1*	*25.8*	*16.1*	*13.2*	*8.9*
		1881	2444	824	633	406	329	252	*33.7*	*25.9*	*16.6*	*13.5*	*10.3*
	Females	1851	2647	994	624	445	312	272	*37.6*	*23.6*	*16.8*	*11.8*	*10.3*
		1881	2345	860	525	381	301	278	*36.7*	*22.4*	*16.2*	*12.8*	*11.9*
FLINTSHIRE													
Holywell													
Whitford	Persons	1851	8583	3275	2058	1463	1028	759	*38.2*	*24.0*	*17.0*	*12.0*	*8.8*
		1881	8437	3151	1951	1427	1094	814	*37.3*	*23.1*	*16.9*	*13.0*	*9.6*
	Males	1851	4364	1643	1120	753	536	312	*37.6*	*25.7*	*17.3*	*12.3*	*7.1*
		1881	4212	1498	1106	727	524	357	*35.6*	*26.3*	*17.3*	*12.4*	*8.5*
	Females	1851	4219	1632	938	710	492	447	*38.7*	*22.2*	*16.8*	*11.7*	*10.6*
		1881	4225	1653	845	700	570	457	*39.1*	*20.0*	*16.6*	*13.5*	*10.8*

Registration Subdistrict[1]		Year	Number All ages	under 15	15–	30–	45–	60–	*Percentage under 15*	*15–*	*30–*	*45–*	*60–*
Holywell	Persons	1851	13342	5093	3297	2353	1539	1060	*38.2*	*24.7*	*17.6*	*11.5*	*7.9*
		1881	11566	4188	2835	1993	1433	1117	*36.2*	*24.5*	*17.2*	*12.4*	*9.7*
	Males	1851	6733	2664	1716	1202	753	398	*39.6*	*25.5*	*17.9*	*11.2*	*5.9*
		1881	5778	2059	1500	1025	694	500	*35.6*	*26.0*	*17.7*	*12.0*	*8.7*
	Females	1851	6609	2429	1581	1151	786	662	*36.8*	*23.9*	*17.4*	*11.9*	*10.0*
		1881	5788	2129	1335	968	739	617	*36.8*	*23.1*	*16.7*	*12.8*	*10.7*
Flint	Persons	1851	8189	3223	1920	1454	1001	591	*39.4*	*23.4*	*17.8*	*12.2*	*7.2*
		1881	11162	4311	2642	2061	1306	842	*38.6*	*23.7*	*18.5*	*11.7*	*7.5*
	Males	1851	4188	1627	1044	777	500	240	*38.8*	*24.9*	*18.6*	*11.9*	*5.7*
		1881	5743	2203	1465	1057	639	379	*38.4*	*25.5*	*18.4*	*11.1*	*6.6*
	Females	1851	4001	1596	876	677	501	351	*39.9*	*21.9*	*16.9*	*12.5*	*8.8*
		1881	5419	2108	1177	1004	667	463	*38.9*	*21.7*	*18.5*	*12.3*	*8.5*
Mold	Persons	1851	10933	4177	2631	1826	1361	938	*38.2*	*24.1*	*16.7*	*12.4*	*8.6*
		1881	14609	5696	3461	2679	1671	1102	*39.0*	*23.7*	*18.3*	*11.4*	*7.5*
	Males	1851	5502	2147	1375	918	669	393	*39.0*	*25.0*	*16.7*	*12.2*	*7.1*
		1881	7484	2885	1912	1371	832	484	*38.5*	*25.5*	*18.3*	*11.1*	*6.5*
	Females	1851	5431	2030	1256	908	692	545	*37.4*	*23.1*	*16.7*	*12.7*	*10.0*
		1881	7125	2811	1549	1308	839	618	*39.5*	*21.7*	*18.4*	*11.8*	*8.7*
DENBIGHSHIRE													
Wrexham													
Hope	Persons	1851	9566	3625	2374	1630	1092	845	*37.9*	*24.8*	*17.0*	*11.4*	*8.8*
	Males	1851	4904	1860	1275	827	550	392	*37.9*	*26.0*	*16.9*	*11.2*	*8.0*
	Females	1851	4662	1765	1099	803	542	453	*37.9*	*23.6*	*17.2*	*11.6*	*9.7*
Malpas	Persons	1851	6824	2434	1728	1117	861	684	*35.7*	*25.3*	*16.4*	*12.6*	*10.0*
	Males	1851	3417	1259	838	561	440	319	*36.8*	*24.5*	*16.4*	*12.9*	*9.3*
	Females	1851	3407	1175	890	556	421	365	*34.5*	*26.1*	*16.3*	*12.4*	*10.7*
Ruabon	Persons	1851	11875	4494	3013	2164	1370	834	*37.8*	*25.4*	*18.2*	*11.5*	*7.0*
		1881	15485	6197	3581	2651	1919	1137	*40.0*	*23.1*	*17.1*	*12.4*	*7.3*
	Males	1851	6070	2317	1602	1104	688	359	*38.2*	*26.4*	*18.2*	*11.3*	*5.9*
		1881	8046	3160	2096	1359	934	497	*39.3*	*26.1*	*16.9*	*11.6*	*6.2*
	Females	1851	5805	2177	1411	1060	682	475	*37.5*	*24.3*	*18.3*	*11.7*	*8.2*
		1881	7439	3037	1485	1292	985	640	*40.8*	*20.0*	*17.4*	*13.2*	*8.6*
Wrexham	Persons	1851	14030	4943	3882	2531	1591	1083	*35.2*	*27.7*	*18.0*	*11.3*	*7.7*
		1881	33057	12932	8394	5969	3741	2021	*39.1*	*25.4*	*18.1*	*11.3*	*6.1*
	Males	1851	7024	2520	1963	1280	785	476	*35.9*	*27.9*	*18.2*	*11.2*	*6.8*
		1881	17068	6371	4703	3085	1938	971	*37.3*	*27.6*	*18.1*	*11.4*	*5.7*
	Females	1851	7006	2423	1919	1251	806	607	*34.6*	*27.4*	*17.9*	*11.5*	*8.7*
		1881	15989	6561	3691	2884	1803	1050	*41.0*	*23.1*	*18.0*	*11.3*	*6.6*
Holt	Persons	1881	6616	2417	1571	1086	856	686	*36.5*	*23.7*	*16.4*	*12.9*	*10.4*
	Males	1881	3211	1214	720	514	426	337	*37.8*	*22.4*	*16.0*	*13.3*	*10.5*
	Females	1881	3405	1203	851	572	430	349	*35.3*	*25.0*	*16.8*	*12.6*	*10.2*
Ruthin													
Llanarmon	Persons	1851	3360	1304	828	572	376	280	*38.8*	*24.6*	*17.0*	*11.2*	*8.3*
		1881	2714	1018	662	426	357	251	*37.5*	*24.4*	*15.7*	*13.2*	*9.2*
	Males	1851	1731	643	449	304	194	141	*37.1*	*25.9*	*17.6*	*11.2*	*8.1*
		1881	1404	533	353	223	175	120	*38.0*	*25.1*	*15.9*	*12.5*	*8.5*
	Females	1851	1629	661	379	268	182	139	*40.6*	*23.3*	*16.5*	*11.2*	*8.5*
		1881	1310	485	309	203	182	131	*37.0*	*23.6*	*15.5*	*13.9*	*10.0*
Ruthin	Persons	1851	4666	1475	1249	750	610	582	*31.6*	*26.8*	*16.1*	*13.1*	*12.5*
		1881	4038	1350	1001	660	582	445	*33.4*	*24.8*	*16.3*	*14.4*	*11.0*
	Males	1851	2222	754	575	360	288	245	*33.9*	*25.9*	*16.2*	*13.0*	*11.0*
		1881	1946	657	491	319	273	206	*33.8*	*25.2*	*16.4*	*14.0*	*10.6*
	Females	1851	2444	721	674	390	322	337	*29.5*	*27.6*	*16.0*	*13.2*	*13.8*
		1881	2092	693	510	341	309	239	*33.1*	*24.4*	*16.3*	*14.8*	*11.4*

Registration Subdistrict[1]		Year	Number All ages	under 15	15–	30–	45–	60–	*Percentage under 15*	*15–*	*30–*	*45–*	*60–*
Llanelidan	Persons	1851	2818	1050	635	453	385	295	*37.3*	*22.5*	*16.1*	*13.7*	*10.5*
		1881	2418	811	611	369	336	291	*33.5*	*25.3*	*15.3*	*13.9*	*12.0*
	Males	1851	1423	534	344	212	195	138	*37.5*	*24.2*	*14.9*	*13.7*	*9.7*
		1881	1199	383	318	191	163	144	*31.9*	*26.5*	*15.9*	*13.6*	*12.0*
	Females	1851	1395	516	291	241	190	157	*37.0*	*20.9*	*17.3*	*13.6*	*11.3*
		1881	1219	428	293	178	173	147	*35.1*	*24.0*	*14.6*	*14.2*	*12.1*
Gyffylliog	Persons	1851	1376	509	319	239	166	143	*37.0*	*23.2*	*17.4*	*12.1*	*10.4*
		1881	1189	407	303	195	138	146	*34.2*	*25.5*	*16.4*	*11.6*	*12.3*
	Males	1851	687	233	177	122	80	75	*33.9*	*25.8*	*17.8*	*11.6*	*10.9*
		1881	621	209	174	97	74	67	*33.7*	*28.0*	*15.6*	*11.9*	*10.8*
	Females	1851	689	276	142	117	86	68	*40.1*	*20.6*	*17.0*	*12.5*	*9.9*
		1881	568	198	129	98	64	79	*34.9*	*22.7*	*17.3*	*11.3*	*13.9*
Llanrhaeadr	Persons	1851	2678	937	691	435	324	291	*35.0*	*25.8*	*16.2*	*12.1*	*10.9*
		1881	2379	798	618	371	328	264	*33.5*	*26.0*	*15.6*	*13.8*	*11.1*
	Males	1851	1360	479	352	224	163	142	*35.2*	*25.9*	*16.5*	*12.0*	*10.4*
		1881	1238	409	350	175	165	139	*33.0*	*28.3*	*14.1*	*13.3*	*11.2*
	Females	1851	1318	458	339	211	161	149	*34.7*	*25.7*	*16.0*	*12.2*	*11.3*
		1881	1141	389	268	196	163	125	*34.1*	*23.5*	*17.2*	*14.3*	*11.0*
Llandyrnog	Persons	1851	1955	648	509	340	229	229	*33.1*	*26.0*	*17.4*	*11.7*	*11.7*
		1881	1477	448	368	218	242	201	*30.3*	*24.9*	*14.8*	*16.4*	*13.6*
	Males	1851	971	316	259	176	111	109	*32.5*	*26.7*	*18.1*	*11.4*	*11.2*
		1881	752	233	184	100	129	106	*31.0*	*24.5*	*13.3*	*17.2*	*14.1*
	Females	1851	984	332	250	164	118	120	*33.7*	*25.4*	*16.7*	*12.0*	*12.2*
		1881	725	215	184	118	113	95	*29.7*	*25.4*	*16.3*	*15.6*	*13.1*
St Asaph													
St Asaph	Persons	1851	10518	3780	2775	1872	1248	843	*35.9*	*26.4*	*17.8*	*11.9*	*8.0*
		1881	14230	4759	3656	2432	1922	1461	*33.4*	*25.7*	*17.1*	*13.5*	*10.3*
	Males	1851	5210	1902	1365	940	604	399	*36.5*	*26.2*	*18.0*	*11.6*	*7.7*
		1881	6579	2406	1556	1121	859	637	*36.6*	*23.7*	*17.0*	*13.1*	*9.7*
	Females	1851	5308	1878	1410	932	644	444	*35.4*	*26.6*	*17.6*	*12.1*	*8.4*
		1881	7651	2353	2100	1311	1063	824	*30.8*	*27.4*	*17.1*	*13.9*	*10.8*
Abergele	Persons	1851	6163	2146	1600	1052	750	615	*34.8*	*26.0*	*17.1*	*12.2*	*10.0*
		1881	6004	2006	1395	1055	827	721	*33.4*	*23.2*	*17.6*	*13.8*	*12.0*
	Males	1851	3104	1132	783	524	389	276	*36.5*	*25.2*	*16.9*	*12.5*	*8.9*
		1881	2897	975	685	499	396	342	*33.7*	*23.6*	*17.2*	*13.7*	*11.8*
	Females	1851	3059	1014	817	528	361	339	*33.1*	*26.7*	*17.3*	*11.8*	*11.1*
		1881	3107	1031	710	556	431	379	*33.2*	*22.9*	*17.9*	*13.9*	*12.2*
Denbigh	Persons	1851	8607	2921	2121	1559	1069	937	*33.9*	*24.6*	*18.1*	*12.4*	*10.9*
		1881	9224	3016	2315	1712	1228	953	*32.7*	*25.1*	*18.6*	*13.3*	*10.3*
	Males	1851	4299	1546	1035	762	520	436	*36.0*	*24.1*	*17.7*	*12.1*	*10.1*
		1881	4459	1488	1084	835	605	447	*33.4*	*24.3*	*18.7*	*13.6*	*10.0*
	Females	1851	4308	1375	1086	797	549	501	*31.9*	*25.2*	*18.5*	*12.7*	*11.6*
		1881	4765	1528	1231	877	623	506	*32.1*	*25.8*	*18.4*	*13.1*	*10.6*
Llanrwst													
Llanrwst	Persons	1851	7083	2475	1723	1251	883	751	*34.9*	*24.3*	*17.7*	*12.5*	*10.6*
		1881	7367	2525	1869	1225	914	834	*34.3*	*25.4*	*16.6*	*12.4*	*11.3*
	Males	1851	3538	1270	835	624	436	373	*35.9*	*23.6*	*17.6*	*12.3*	*10.5*
		1881	3665	1285	916	608	447	409	*35.1*	*25.0*	*16.6*	*12.2*	*11.2*
	Females	1851	3545	1205	888	627	447	378	*34.0*	*25.0*	*17.7*	*12.6*	*10.7*
		1881	3702	1240	953	617	467	425	*33.5*	*25.7*	*16.7*	*12.6*	*11.5*
Betws-y-coed	Persons	1851	2601	974	612	494	257	264	*37.4*	*23.5*	*19.0*	*9.9*	*10.1*
		1881	3649	1212	989	688	403	357	*33.2*	*27.1*	*18.9*	*11.0*	*9.8*
	Males	1851	1292	483	307	248	139	115	*37.4*	*23.8*	*19.2*	*10.8*	*8.9*
		1881	1828	585	516	353	203	171	*32.0*	*28.2*	*19.3*	*11.1*	*9.4*
	Females	1851	1309	491	305	246	118	149	*37.5*	*23.3*	*18.8*	*9.0*	*11.4*
		1881	1821	627	473	335	200	186	*34.4*	*26.0*	*18.4*	*11.0*	*10.2*

Registration Subdistrict[1]		Year	Number All ages	under 15	15–	30–	45–	60–	*Percentage under 15*	*15–*	*30–*	*45–*	*60–*
Ysbyty	Persons	1851	2795	1067	688	469	292	279	*38.2*	*24.6*	*16.8*	*10.4*	*10.0*
		1881	3093	1077	796	576	345	299	*34.8*	*25.7*	*18.6*	*11.2*	*9.7*
	Males	1851	1387	538	344	227	152	126	*38.8*	*24.8*	*16.4*	*11.0*	*9.1*
		1881	1588	560	409	295	175	149	*35.3*	*25.8*	*18.6*	*11.0*	*9.4*
	Females	1851	1408	529	344	242	140	153	*37.6*	*24.4*	*17.2*	*9.9*	*10.9*
		1881	1505	517	387	281	170	150	*34.4*	*25.7*	*18.7*	*11.3*	*10.0*
MERIONETH													
Corwen													
Gwyddelwern	Persons	1851	5526	2064	1340	897	631	594	*37.4*	*24.2*	*16.2*	*11.4*	*10.7*
	Males	1851	2787	1039	689	449	312	298	*37.3*	*24.7*	*16.1*	*11.2*	*10.7*
	Females	1851	2739	1025	651	448	319	296	*37.4*	*23.8*	*16.4*	*11.6*	*10.8*
Corwen	Persons	1851	9892	3530	2463	1756	1205	938	*35.7*	*24.9*	*17.8*	*12.2*	*9.5*
		1881	8068	2924	1950	1327	995	872	*36.2*	*24.2*	*16.4*	*12.3*	*10.8*
	Males	1851	5043	1811	1259	900	614	459	*35.9*	*25.0*	*17.8*	*12.2*	*9.1*
		1881	4037	1401	1041	660	512	423	*34.7*	*25.8*	*16.3*	*12.7*	*10.5*
	Females	1851	4849	1719	1204	856	591	479	*35.5*	*24.8*	*17.7*	*12.2*	*9.9*
		1881	4031	1523	909	667	483	449	*37.8*	*22.6*	*16.5*	*12.0*	*11.1*
Llangollen	Persons	1881	8765	3167	2080	1456	1167	895	*36.1*	*23.7*	*16.6*	*13.3*	*10.2*
	Males	1881	4401	1586	1078	731	571	435	*36.0*	*24.5*	*16.6*	*13.0*	*9.9*
	Females	1881	4364	1581	1002	725	596	460	*36.2*	*23.0*	*16.6*	*13.7*	*10.5*
Bala													
Bala	Persons	1851	6736	2301	1686	1094	857	798	*34.2*	*25.0*	*16.2*	*12.7*	*11.8*
		1881	6740	2137	1756	1201	859	787	*31.7*	*26.1*	*17.8*	*12.7*	*11.7*
	Males	1851	3353	1165	857	531	423	377	*34.7*	*25.6*	*15.8*	*12.6*	*11.2*
		1881	3498	1036	985	638	452	387	*29.6*	*28.2*	*18.2*	*12.9*	*11.1*
	Females	1851	3383	1136	829	563	434	421	*33.6*	*24.5*	*16.6*	*12.8*	*12.4*
		1881	3242	1101	771	563	407	400	*34.0*	*23.8*	*17.4*	*12.6*	*12.3*
Dolgellau													
Tal-y-llyn	Persons	1851	5053	1818	1156	848	624	607	*36.0*	*22.9*	*16.8*	*12.3*	*12.0*
		1881	6437	2512	1474	1176	713	562	*39.0*	*22.9*	*18.3*	*11.1*	*8.7*
	Males	1851	2605	964	599	438	314	290	*37.0*	*23.0*	*16.8*	*12.1*	*11.1*
		1881	3239	1252	757	612	354	264	*38.7*	*23.4*	*18.9*	*10.9*	*8.2*
	Females	1851	2448	854	557	410	310	317	*34.9*	*22.8*	*16.7*	*12.7*	*12.9*
		1881	3198	1260	717	564	359	298	*39.4*	*22.4*	*17.6*	*11.2*	*9.3*
Barmouth	Persons	1851	7918	2684	1814	1347	973	1100	*33.9*	*22.9*	*17.0*	*12.3*	*13.9*
		1881	8743	2926	2120	1587	1097	1013	*33.5*	*24.2*	*18.2*	*12.5*	*11.6*
	Males	1851	3625	1328	809	608	437	443	*36.6*	*22.3*	*16.8*	*12.1*	*12.2*
		1881	4034	1411	946	741	493	443	*35.0*	*23.5*	*18.4*	*12.2*	*11.0*
	Females	1851	4293	1356	1005	739	536	657	*31.6*	*23.4*	*17.2*	*12.5*	*15.3*
		1881	4709	1515	1174	846	604	570	*32.2*	*24.9*	*18.0*	*12.8*	*12.1*
Ffestiniog													
Llanfihangel-y-traethau	Persons	1851	3669	1354	872	600	468	375	*36.9*	*23.8*	*16.4*	*12.8*	*10.2*
		1881	5094	1972	1189	913	567	453	*38.7*	*23.3*	*17.9*	*11.1*	*8.9*
	Males	1851	1745	679	403	288	213	162	*38.9*	*23.1*	*16.5*	*12.2*	*9.3*
		1881	2482	957	620	429	278	198	*38.6*	*25.0*	*17.3*	*11.2*	*8.0*
	Females	1851	1924	675	469	312	255	213	*35.1*	*24.4*	*16.2*	*13.3*	*11.1*
		1881	2612	1015	569	484	289	255	*38.9*	*21.8*	*18.5*	*11.1*	*9.8*
Ffestiniog	Persons	1851	6654	2512	1628	1246	678	590	*37.8*	*24.5*	*18.7*	*10.2*	*8.9*
		1881	15115	5548	4132	3034	1481	920	*36.7*	*27.3*	*20.1*	*9.8*	*6.1*
	Males	1851	3455	1340	851	662	348	254	*38.8*	*24.6*	*19.2*	*10.1*	*7.4*
		1881	8132	2830	2372	1716	772	442	*34.8*	*29.2*	*21.1*	*9.5*	*5.4*
	Females	1851	3199	1172	777	584	330	336	*36.6*	*24.3*	*18.3*	*10.3*	*10.5*
		1881	6983	2718	1760	1318	709	478	*38.9*	*25.2*	*18.9*	*10.2*	*6.8*

Registration Subdistrict[1]		Year	Number All ages	under 15	15–	30–	45–	60–	Percentage under 15	15–	30–	45–	60–
Tremadoc	Persons	1851	5859	2265	1412	1041	617	524	*38.7*	*24.1*	*17.8*	*10.5*	*8.9*
		1881	9316	3468	2256	1679	1093	820	*37.2*	*24.2*	*18.0*	*11.7*	*8.8*
	Males	1851	2776	1100	661	511	279	225	*39.6*	*23.8*	*18.4*	*10.1*	*8.1*
		1881	4527	1775	1070	774	549	359	*39.2*	*23.6*	*17.1*	*12.1*	*7.9*
	Females	1851	3083	1165	751	530	338	299	*37.8*	*24.4*	*17.2*	*11.0*	*9.7*
		1881	4789	1693	1186	905	544	461	*35.4*	*24.8*	*18.9*	*11.4*	*9.6*
CAERNARFONSHIRE													
Pwllheli													
Cricieth	Persons	1851	5789	1996	1408	1014	701	670	*34.5*	*24.3*	*17.5*	*12.1*	*11.6*
		1881	6865	2366	1713	1223	809	754	*34.5*	*25.0*	*17.8*	*11.8*	*11.0*
	Males	1851	2752	979	660	474	335	304	*35.6*	*24.0*	*17.2*	*12.2*	*11.0*
		1881	3371	1199	869	576	363	364	*35.6*	*25.8*	*17.1*	*10.8*	*10.8*
	Females	1851	3037	1017	748	540	366	366	*33.5*	*24.6*	*17.8*	*12.1*	*12.1*
		1881	3494	1167	844	647	446	390	*33.4*	*24.2*	*18.5*	*12.8*	*11.2*
Pwllheli	Persons	1851	6837	2473	1600	1217	799	748	*36.2*	*23.4*	*17.8*	*11.7*	*10.9*
		1881	7228	2486	1734	1242	931	835	*34.4*	*24.0*	*17.2*	*12.9*	*11.6*
	Males	1851	3173	1258	696	535	348	336	*39.6*	*21.9*	*16.9*	*11.0*	*10.6*
		1881	3500	1285	836	560	451	368	*36.7*	*23.9*	*16.0*	*12.9*	*10.5*
	Females	1851	3664	1215	904	682	451	412	*33.2*	*24.7*	*18.6*	*12.3*	*11.2*
		1881	3728	1201	898	682	480	467	*32.2*	*24.1*	*18.3*	*12.9*	*12.5*
Aberdaron	Persons	1851	3967	1365	967	682	506	447	*34.4*	*24.4*	*17.2*	*12.8*	*11.3*
		1881	3618	1145	812	627	536	498	*31.6*	*22.4*	*17.3*	*14.8*	*13.8*
	Males	1851	1905	713	444	310	228	210	*37.4*	*23.3*	*16.3*	*12.0*	*11.0*
		1881	1813	617	401	303	247	245	*34.0*	*22.1*	*16.7*	*13.6*	*13.5*
	Females	1851	2062	652	523	372	278	237	*31.6*	*25.4*	*18.0*	*13.5*	*11.5*
		1881	1805	528	411	324	289	253	*29.3*	*22.8*	*18.0*	*16.0*	*14.0*
Nefyn	Persons	1851	5195	1839	1167	918	674	597	*35.4*	*22.5*	*17.7*	*13.0*	*11.5*
		1881	5200	1731	1311	836	684	638	*33.3*	*25.2*	*16.1*	*13.2*	*12.3*
	Males	1851	2384	927	498	413	294	252	*38.9*	*20.9*	*17.3*	*12.3*	*10.6*
		1881	2477	873	633	367	303	301	*35.2*	*25.6*	*14.8*	*12.2*	*12.2*
	Females	1851	2811	912	669	505	380	345	*32.4*	*23.8*	*18.0*	*13.5*	*12.3*
		1881	2723	858	678	469	381	337	*31.5*	*24.9*	*17.2*	*14.0*	*12.4*
Caernarfon													
Llandwrog	Persons	1851	8090	3095	1859	1445	924	767	*38.3*	*23.0*	*17.9*	*11.4*	*9.5*
		1881	13456	5126	3377	2570	1353	1030	*38.1*	*25.1*	*19.1*	*10.1*	*7.7*
	Males	1851	4041	1570	940	731	460	340	*38.9*	*23.3*	*18.1*	*11.4*	*8.4*
		1881	6901	2616	1811	1321	654	499	*37.9*	*26.2*	*19.1*	*9.5*	*7.2*
	Females	1851	4049	1525	919	714	464	427	*37.7*	*22.7*	*17.6*	*11.5*	*10.5*
		1881	6555	2510	1566	1249	699	531	*38.3*	*23.9*	*19.1*	*10.7*	*8.1*
Llanrug	Persons	1851	8683	3447	2231	1527	937	541	*39.7*	*25.7*	*17.6*	*10.8*	*6.2*
		1881	14794	5512	3695	2645	1723	1219	*37.3*	*25.0*	*17.9*	*11.6*	*8.2*
	Males	1851	4379	1729	1166	764	476	244	*39.5*	*26.6*	*17.4*	*10.9*	*5.6*
		1881	7542	2856	1967	1296	855	568	*37.9*	*26.1*	*17.2*	*11.3*	*7.5*
	Females	1851	4304	1718	1065	763	461	297	*39.9*	*24.7*	*17.7*	*10.7*	*6.9*
		1881	7252	2656	1728	1349	868	651	*36.6*	*23.8*	*18.6*	*12.0*	*9.0*
Caernarfon	Persons	1851	10137	3540	2714	1830	1222	831	*34.9*	*26.8*	*18.1*	*12.1*	*8.2*
		1881	12253	3942	3598	2279	1445	989	*32.2*	*29.4*	*18.6*	*11.8*	*8.1*
	Males	1851	4760	1757	1228	882	573	320	*36.9*	*25.8*	*18.5*	*12.0*	*6.7*
		1881	5929	1986	1750	1073	695	425	*33.5*	*29.5*	*18.1*	*11.7*	*7.2*
	Females	1851	5377	1783	1486	948	649	511	*33.2*	*27.6*	*17.6*	*12.1*	*9.5*
		1881	6324	1956	1848	1206	750	564	*30.9*	*29.2*	*19.1*	*11.9*	*8.9*
Llanidan	Persons	1851	3536	1247	862	617	436	374	*35.3*	*24.4*	*17.4*	*12.3*	*10.6*
		1881	3494	1258	760	611	449	416	*36.0*	*21.8*	*17.5*	*12.9*	*11.9*
	Males	1851	1732	646	414	300	207	165	*37.3*	*23.9*	*17.3*	*12.0*	*9.5*
		1881	1686	650	347	272	215	202	*38.6*	*20.6*	*16.1*	*12.8*	*12.0*
	Females	1851	1804	601	448	317	229	209	*33.3*	*24.8*	*17.6*	*12.7*	*11.6*
		1881	1808	608	413	339	234	214	*33.6*	*22.8*	*18.8*	*12.9*	*11.8*

Registration Subdistrict[1]		Year	Number All ages	under 15	15–	30–	45–	60–	Percentage under 15	15–	30–	45–	60–
Bangor													
Beaumaris	Persons	1851	10548	3656	2712	1901	1249	1030	*34.7*	*25.7*	*18.0*	*11.8*	*9.8*
		1881	12781	4250	3125	2048	1716	1642	*33.3*	*24.5*	*16.0*	*13.4*	*12.8*
	Males	1851	5197	1873	1301	966	598	459	*36.0*	*25.0*	*18.6*	*11.5*	*8.8*
		1881	6227	2222	1523	932	783	767	*35.7*	*24.5*	*15.0*	*12.6*	*12.3*
	Females	1851	5351	1783	1411	935	651	571	*33.3*	*26.4*	*17.5*	*12.2*	*10.7*
		1881	6554	2028	1602	1116	933	875	*30.9*	*24.4*	*17.0*	*14.2*	*13.4*
Bangor	Persons	1851	12962	4490	3679	2440	1425	928	*34.6*	*28.4*	*18.8*	*11.0*	*7.2*
		1881	14957	4910	4023	2695	2001	1328	*32.8*	*26.9*	*18.0*	*13.4*	*8.9*
	Males	1851	6505	2300	1808	1275	704	418	*35.4*	*27.8*	*19.6*	*10.8*	*6.4*
		1881	7165	2412	1926	1290	937	600	*33.7*	*26.9*	*18.0*	*13.1*	*8.4*
	Females	1851	6457	2190	1871	1165	721	510	*33.9*	*29.0*	*18.0*	*11.2*	*7.9*
		1881	7792	2498	2097	1405	1064	728	*32.1*	*26.9*	*18.0*	*13.7*	*9.3*
Llanllechid	Persons	1851	7300	2816	1941	1303	800	440	*38.6*	*26.6*	*17.8*	*11.0*	*6.0*
		1881	10774	3788	2672	1960	1450	904	*35.2*	*24.8*	*18.2*	*13.5*	*8.4*
	Males	1851	3797	1454	1025	691	416	211	*38.3*	*27.0*	*18.2*	*11.0*	*5.6*
		1881	5400	1914	1361	950	736	439	*35.4*	*25.2*	*17.6*	*13.6*	*8.1*
	Females	1851	3503	1362	916	612	384	229	*38.9*	*26.1*	*17.5*	*11.0*	*6.5*
		1881	5374	1874	1311	1010	714	465	*34.9*	*24.4*	*18.8*	*13.3*	*8.7*
Conwy													
Conwy	Persons	1851	3127	1144	814	565	350	254	*36.6*	*26.0*	*18.1*	*11.2*	*8.1*
		1881	5127	1687	1405	909	678	448	*32.9*	*27.4*	*17.7*	*13.2*	*8.7*
	Males	1851	1544	582	381	288	173	120	*37.7*	*24.7*	*18.7*	*11.2*	*7.8*
		1881	2552	886	695	443	314	214	*34.7*	*27.2*	*17.4*	*12.3*	*8.4*
	Females	1851	1583	562	433	277	177	134	*35.5*	*27.4*	*17.5*	*11.2*	*8.5*
		1881	2575	801	710	466	364	234	*31.1*	*27.6*	*18.1*	*14.1*	*9.1*
Creuddyn	Persons	1851	6565	2394	1648	1082	786	655	*36.5*	*25.1*	*16.5*	*12.0*	*10.0*
		1881	11560	3927	3143	1999	1521	970	*34.0*	*27.2*	*17.3*	*13.2*	*8.4*
	Males	1851	3322	1232	841	544	384	321	*37.1*	*25.3*	*16.4*	*11.6*	*9.7*
		1881	5347	1954	1374	880	699	440	*36.5*	*25.7*	*16.5*	*13.1*	*8.2*
	Females	1851	3243	1162	807	538	402	334	*35.8*	*24.9*	*16.6*	*12.4*	*10.3*
		1881	6213	1973	1769	1119	822	530	*31.8*	*28.5*	*18.0*	*13.2*	*8.5*
Llechwedd Isaf	Persons	1851	1938	647	507	302	249	233	*33.4*	*26.2*	*15.6*	*12.8*	*12.0*
		1881	1674	544	415	260	241	214	*32.5*	*24.8*	*15.5*	*14.4*	*12.8*
	Males	1851	981	352	245	158	117	109	*35.9*	*25.0*	*16.1*	*11.9*	*11.1*
		1881	832	271	215	122	119	105	*32.6*	*25.8*	*14.7*	*14.3*	*12.6*
	Females	1851	957	295	262	144	132	124	*30.8*	*27.4*	*15.0*	*13.8*	*13.0*
		1881	842	273	200	138	122	109	*32.4*	*23.8*	*16.4*	*14.5*	*12.9*
ANGLESEY													
Anglesey													
Llangefni	Persons	1851	7204	2652	1658	1267	856	771	*36.8*	*23.0*	*17.6*	*11.9*	*10.7*
		1881	4891	1574	1120	850	638	709	*32.2*	*22.9*	*17.4*	*13.0*	*14.5*
	Males	1851	3449	1310	785	589	397	368	*38.0*	*22.8*	*17.1*	*11.5*	*10.7*
		1881	2320	780	518	389	289	344	*33.6*	*22.3*	*16.8*	*12.5*	*14.8*
	Females	1851	3755	1342	873	678	459	403	*35.7*	*23.2*	*18.1*	*12.2*	*10.7*
		1881	2571	794	602	461	349	365	*30.9*	*23.4*	*17.9*	*13.6*	*14.2*
Bryngwran	Persons	1851	5209	1912	1344	853	591	509	*36.7*	*25.8*	*16.4*	*11.3*	*9.8*
		1881	5069	1686	1235	784	687	677	*33.3*	*24.4*	*15.5*	*13.6*	*13.4*
	Males	1851	2602	1011	666	407	295	223	*38.9*	*25.6*	*15.6*	*11.3*	*8.6*
		1881	2472	853	604	367	315	333	*34.5*	*24.4*	*14.8*	*12.7*	*13.5*
	Females	1851	2607	901	678	446	296	286	*34.6*	*26.0*	*17.1*	*11.4*	*11.0*
		1881	2597	833	631	417	372	344	*32.1*	*24.3*	*16.1*	*14.3*	*13.2*
Llandyfrydog	Persons	1851	5608	2102	1235	962	678	631	*37.5*	*22.0*	*17.2*	*12.1*	*11.3*
		1881	4025	1255	970	662	559	579	*31.2*	*24.1*	*16.4*	*13.9*	*14.4*
	Males	1851	2729	1060	588	466	326	289	*38.8*	*21.5*	*17.1*	*11.9*	*10.6*
		1881	1950	639	479	287	273	272	*32.8*	*24.6*	*14.7*	*14.0*	*13.9*
	Females	1851	2879	1042	647	496	352	342	*36.2*	*22.5*	*17.2*	*12.2*	*11.9*
		1881	2075	616	491	375	286	307	*29.7*	*23.7*	*18.1*	*13.8*	*14.8*

Registration Subdistrict[1]		Year	Number All ages	under 15	15–	30–	45–	60–	*Percentage under 15*	*15–*	*30–*	*45–*	*60–*
Amlwch	Persons	1851	7691	2844	1867	1222	966	792	*37.0*	*24.3*	*15.9*	*12.6*	*10.3*
		1881	6198	2078	1425	963	955	777	*33.5*	*23.0*	*15.5*	*15.4*	*12.5*
	Males	1851	3575	1432	832	528	472	311	*40.1*	*23.3*	*14.8*	*13.2*	*8.7*
		1881	2825	1025	647	406	413	334	*36.3*	*22.9*	*14.4*	*14.6*	*11.8*
	Females	1851	4116	1412	1035	694	494	481	*34.3*	*25.1*	*16.9*	*12.0*	*11.7*
		1881	3373	1053	778	557	542	443	*31.2*	*23.1*	*16.5*	*16.1*	*13.1*
Llanddeusant	Persons	1851	5997	2120	1478	1047	714	638	*35.4*	*24.6*	*17.5*	*11.9*	*10.6*
		1881	4827	1569	1208	750	644	656	*32.5*	*25.0*	*15.5*	*13.3*	*13.6*
	Males	1851	2899	1046	724	484	351	294	*36.1*	*25.0*	*16.7*	*12.1*	*10.1*
		1881	2439	824	612	349	316	338	*33.8*	*25.1*	*14.3*	*13.0*	*13.9*
	Females	1851	3098	1074	754	563	363	344	*34.7*	*24.3*	*18.2*	*11.7*	*11.1*
		1881	2388	745	596	401	328	318	*31.2*	*25.0*	*16.8*	*13.7*	*13.3*
Holyhead	Persons	1851	11534	3993	3284	2248	1180	829	*34.6*	*28.5*	*19.5*	*10.2*	*7.2*
		1881	10131	3444	2592	1910	1290	895	*34.0*	*25.6*	*18.9*	*12.7*	*8.8*
	Males	1851	5918	2005	1750	1186	596	381	*33.9*	*29.6*	*20.0*	*10.1*	*6.4*
		1881	5184	1737	1397	988	649	413	*33.5*	*26.9*	*19.1*	*12.5*	*8.0*
	Females	1851	5616	1988	1534	1062	584	448	*35.4*	*27.3*	*18.9*	*10.4*	*8.0*
		1881	4947	1707	1195	922	641	482	*34.5*	*24.2*	*18.6*	*13.0*	*9.7*

Sources: *Census of Population for England and Wales*: 1851, *Population Tables II, Ages, Civil Condition, Occupations, and Birthplace of the People. Vol. II* (HMSO, 1854) pp. 815–19; 1881, *Vol. III, Ages, Condition as to Marriage, Occupations, and Birthplaces of the People* (HMSO, 1883) Division XI – Wales and Monmouthshire, Table 3.

[1] See Table 1.3 for details of boundary changes.

Population 2.4 Ages. Persons, males, females. Number and percentage. Major Urban Areas. 1851, 1881, 1911

Urban areas		Year	Number All ages	under 15	15–	30–	45–	60–	*Percentage under 15*	*15–*	*30–*	*45–*	*60–*
Newport	Persons	1851	19323	6584	5839	4224	1863	813	*34.1*	*30.2*	*21.9*	*9.6*	*4.2*
		1881	35313	12868	10088	6598	3691	2068	*36.4*	*28.6*	*18.7*	*10.5*	*5.9*
		1911	83691	27425	23750	17666	10010	4840	*32.8*	*28.4*	*21.1*	*12.0*	*5.8*
	Males	1851	9879	3308	2901	2294	996	380	*33.5*	*29.4*	*23.2*	*10.1*	*3.8*
		1881	17503	6320	4999	3409	1819	956	*36.1*	*28.6*	*19.5*	*10.4*	*5.5*
		1911	42174	13586	11806	9133	5258	2391	*32.2*	*28.0*	*21.7*	*12.5*	*5.7*
	Females	1851	9444	3276	2938	1930	867	433	*34.7*	*31.1*	*20.4*	*9.2*	*4.6*
		1881	17810	6548	5089	3189	1872	1112	*36.8*	*28.6*	*17.9*	*10.5*	*6.2*
		1911	41517	13839	11944	8533	4752	2449	*33.3*	*28.8*	*20.6*	*11.4*	*5.9*
Cardiff	Persons	1851	18351	5298	6135	4342	1806	770	*28.9*	*33.4*	*23.7*	*9.8*	*4.2*
		1881	82761	29820	24583	16148	8492	3718	*36.0*	*29.7*	*19.5*	*10.3*	*4.5*
		1911	182259	58309	51030	38493	23266	11161	*32.0*	*28.0*	*21.1*	*12.8*	*6.1*
	Males	1851	10286	2712	3510	2611	1065	388	*26.4*	*34.1*	*25.4*	*10.4*	*3.8*
		1881	42316	14941	12543	8658	4408	1766	*35.3*	*29.6*	*20.5*	*10.4*	*4.2*
		1911	89728	28806	24540	19197	11916	5269	*32.1*	*27.3*	*21.4*	*13.3*	*5.9*
	Females	1851	8065	2586	2625	1731	741	382	*32.1*	*32.5*	*21.5*	*9.2*	*4.7*
		1881	40445	14879	12040	7490	4084	1952	*36.8*	*29.8*	*18.5*	*10.1*	*4.8*
		1911	92531	29503	26490	19296	11350	5892	*31.9*	*28.6*	*20.9*	*12.3*	*6.4*
Merthyr Tydfil	Persons	1851	63080	22278	19716	12842	5631	2613	*35.3*	*31.3*	*20.4*	*8.9*	*4.1*
		1881	48861	18269	13266	8656	5400	3270	*37.4*	*27.2*	*17.7*	*11.1*	*6.7*
		1911	80990	28162	22061	17367	8911	4489	*34.8*	*27.2*	*21.4*	*11.0*	*5.5*
	Males	1851	34009	11196	11287	7274	3051	1201	*32.9*	*33.2*	*21.4*	*9.0*	*3.5*
		1881	25056	9077	7152	4606	2702	1519	*36.2*	*28.5*	*18.4*	*10.8*	*6.1*
		1911	43026	14162	11968	9653	4958	2285	*32.9*	*27.8*	*22.4*	*11.5*	*5.3*
	Females	1851	29071	11082	8429	5568	2580	1412	*38.1*	*29.0*	*19.2*	*8.9*	*4.9*
		1881	23805	9192	6114	4050	2698	1751	*38.6*	*25.7*	*17.0*	*11.3*	*7.4*
		1911	37964	14000	10093	7714	3953	2204	*36.9*	*26.6*	*20.3*	*10.4*	*5.8*
Swansea	Persons	1851	31461	11389	8915	5976	3250	1931	*36.2*	*28.3*	*19.0*	*10.3*	*6.1*
		1881	65597	24696	18531	12102	6769	3499	*37.6*	*28.2*	*18.4*	*10.3*	*5.3*
		1911	114663	36016	32915	24533	13954	7245	*31.4*	*28.7*	*21.4*	*12.2*	*6.3*
	Males	1851	15212	5717	4252	2964	1522	757	*37.6*	*28.0*	*19.5*	*10.0*	*5.0*
		1881	32222	12215	9037	6164	3284	1522	*37.9*	*28.0*	*19.1*	*10.2*	*4.7*
		1911	57853	18035	16655	12686	7268	3209	*31.2*	*28.8*	*21.9*	*12.6*	*5.5*
	Females	1851	16249	5672	4663	3012	1728	1174	*34.9*	*28.7*	*18.5*	*10.6*	*7.2*
		1881	33375	12481	9494	5938	3485	1977	*37.4*	*28.4*	*17.8*	*10.4*	*5.9*
		1911	56810	17981	16260	11847	6686	4036	*31.7*	*28.6*	*20.9*	*11.8*	*7.1*
Aberdare	Persons	1881	33804	13418	9051	5854	3687	1794	*39.7*	*26.8*	*17.3*	*10.9*	*5.3*
		1911	50830	17366	13745	11101	5876	2742	*34.2*	*27.0*	*21.8*	*11.6*	*5.4*
	Males	1881	17446	6717	4898	3123	1871	837	*38.5*	*28.1*	*17.9*	*10.7*	*4.8*
		1911	26418	8669	7283	6013	3193	1260	*32.8*	*27.6*	*22.8*	*12.1*	*4.8*
	Females	1881	16358	6701	4153	2731	1816	957	*41.0*	*25.4*	*16.7*	*11.1*	*5.9*
		1911	24412	8697	6462	5088	2683	1482	*35.6*	*26.5*	*20.8*	*11.0*	*6.1*

Urban areas		Year	Number All ages	under 15	15–	30–	45–	60–	Percentage under 15	15–	30–	45–	60–
Ystradyfodwg (Rhondda)	Persons	1881	55632	22048	16548	10300	4937	1799	*39.6*	*29.7*	*18.5*	*8.9*	*3.2*
		1911	152781	55725	42747	32638	15655	6016	*36.5*	*28.0*	*21.4*	*10.2*	*3.9*
	Males	1881	30877	11294	9967	5937	2743	936	*36.6*	*32.3*	*19.2*	*8.9*	*3.0*
		1881	24755	10754	6581	4363	2194	863	*43.4*	*26.6*	*17.6*	*8.9*	*3.5*
	Females	1911	83209	27863	24313	18969	9061	3003	*33.5*	*29.2*	*22.8*	*10.9*	*3.6*
		1911	69572	27862	18434	13669	6594	3013	*40.0*	*26.5*	*19.6*	*9.5*	*4.3*

Sources: *Census of Population for England and Wales*: 1851, *Population Tables II, Ages, Civil Condition, Occupations, and Birthplace of the People. Vol. II* (HMSO, 1854), p. 820; 1881, *Vol. III, Ages, Condition as to Marriage, Occupations, and Birthplaces of the People* (HMSO, 1883), Division XI – Wales and Monmouthshire, Table 6; 1911, County Volumes: *Anglesey, Carnarvon, Denbigh and Flint; Cardigan, Merioneth and Montgomery; Glamorgan; Brecknock, Carmarthen, Pembroke and Radnor; Monmouth* (HMSO, 1914), Table 16.

The boundaries are as follows: 1851, Municipal Borough – Newport, Cardiff, Swansea; Parliamentary – Merthyr Tydfil; 1881, Urban Sanitary District, 1911, County Borough – Newport, Cardiff, Merthyr Tydfil, Swansea; Urban District – Mountain Ash, Aberdare, Rhondda. The table excludes the 'Principal Towns' of Pembroke and Caernarfon, for which ages are given in the 1851 census. It includes Urban (Sanitary) Districts with a total population of over 30,000 in 1881, and over 40,000 in 1911.

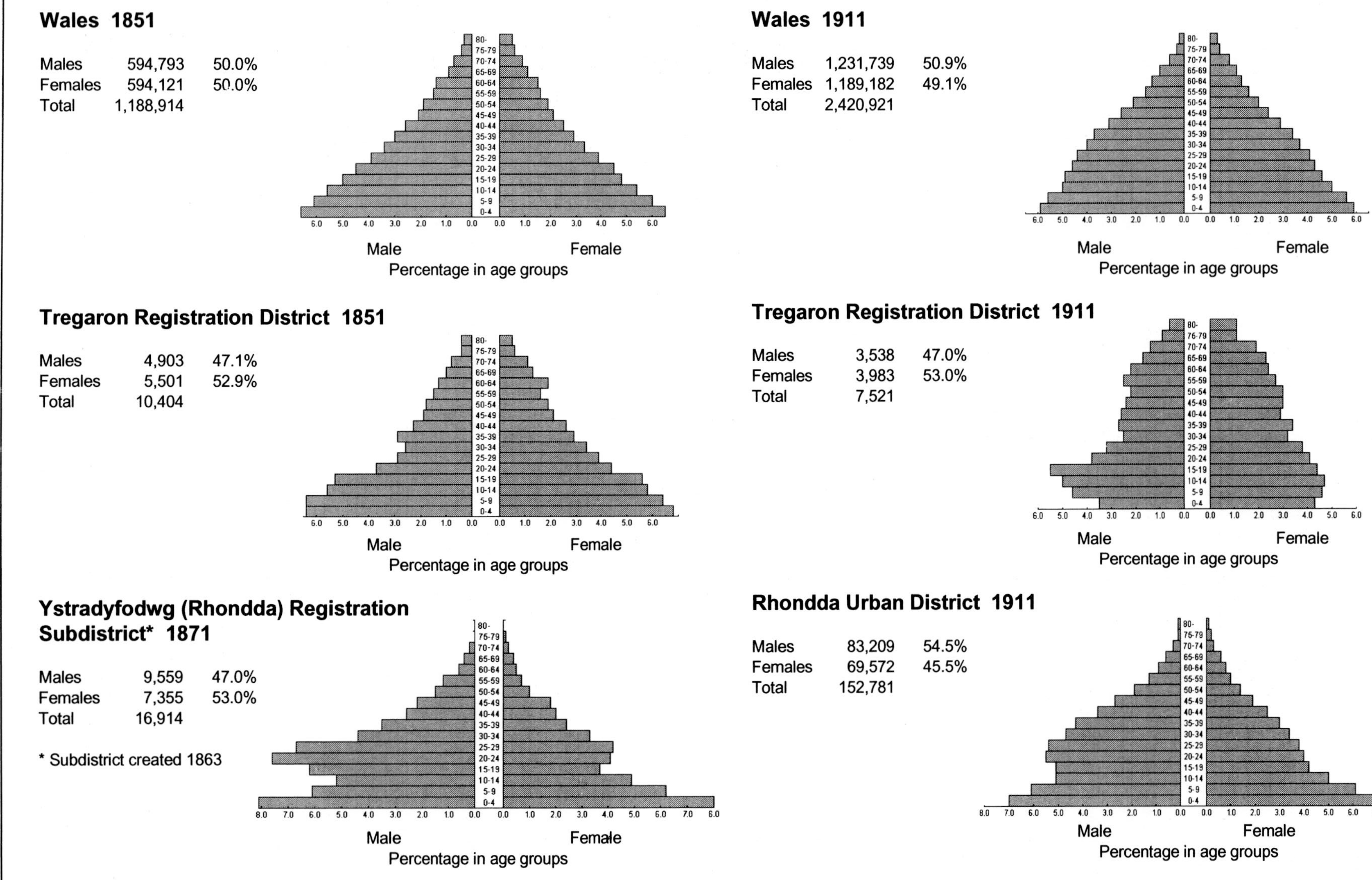

Population Figure b Distribution by age and sex. Percentages. Wales and selected areas. 1851, 1911

Wales 1851

Males	594,793	50.0%
Females	594,121	50.0%
Total	1,188,914	

Wales 1911

Males	1,231,739	50.9%
Females	1,189,182	49.1%
Total	2,420,921	

Tregaron Registration District 1851

Males	4,903	47.1%
Females	5,501	52.9%
Total	10,404	

Tregaron Registration District 1911

Males	3,538	47.0%
Females	3,983	53.0%
Total	7,521	

Ystradyfodwg (Rhondda) Registration Subdistrict* 1871

Males	9,559	47.0%
Females	7,355	53.0%
Total	16,914	

* Subdistrict created 1863

Rhondda Urban District 1911

Males	83,209	54.5%
Females	69,572	45.5%
Total	152,781	

Population 3.1 Marital status. Males and females. Wales and Registration Counties. 1851, 1881, 1911

	Year	Number[1] Unmarried Males	Females	Married Males	Females	Widowed Males	Females	*Percentage married*[2] *Males*	*Females age 15–45*
WALES	1851	164763	145702	189580	192256	22645	43501	*50.3*	*46.1*
	1881	206711	175364	258345	260792	29717	60539	*52.2*	*49.3*
	1911	368668	290183	425431	427832	45111	79716	*50.7*	*51.1*
Registration Counties									
MONMOUTH	1851	26975	17693	30160	30138	3407	5480	*49.8*	*53.9*
	1881	31164	21747	39422	39483	4417	8301	*52.6*	*54.2*
	1911	62982	41562	73769	73036	7137	11026	*51.3*	*55.8*
GLAMORGAN	1851	37229	25278	39774	39319	4401	7568	*48.9*	*52.3*
	1881	69073	48567	88429	87295	8671	16854	*53.2*	*55.1*
	1911	171929	116085	202168	201275	19174	31022	*51.4*	*55.6*
CARMARTHEN	1851	11280	12877	14536	14870	1652	3804	*52.9*	*41.6*
	1881	12857	14663	17275	17738	1903	4533	*53.9*	*43.7*
	1911	23695	20286	25718	25484	2843	5148	*49.2*	*46.5*
PEMBROKE	1851	9566	12513	12750	13341	1367	3415	*53.8*	*39.5*
	1881	10112	11853	13254	13396	1667	3550	*52.9*	*40.6*
	1911	12353	12917	14272	14714	1753	3290	*50.3*	*42.8*
CARDIGAN	1851	11411	15337	13969	15160	1771	4246	*51.4*	*37.0*
	1881	11130	15889	12956	14731	1865	5161	*49.9*	*35.7*
	1911	11940	15912	11882	13152	1936	4406	*46.1*	*33.6*
BRECON	1851	8864	7382	9543	9595	1292	2207	*48.4*	*45.7*
	1881	7424	6422	8629	8727	1170	2247	*50.1*	*45.9*
	1911	8876	7709	9446	9513	1170	2047	*48.5*	*45.4*
RADNOR	1851	4955	4107	4696	4689	653	1052	*45.6*	*41.7*
	1881	2870	2319	2755	2777	393	684	*45.8*	*42.1*
	1911	2836	2655	2880	2896	383	578	*47.2*	*41.1*
MONTGOMERY	1851	11275	10061	11869	11927	1663	2994	*47.8*	*40.9*
	1881	10738	8973	11868	12031	1693	3131	*48.8*	*44.4*
	1911	9636	9399	9929	10253	1497	2754	*47.1*	*40.0*
FLINT	1851	5543	4239	6470	6543	693	1791	*50.9*	*49.6*
	1881	6204	4263	7579	7625	789	1968	*52.0*	*53.1*
	1911	10507	7926	11971	12106	1377	2521	*50.2*	*50.7*
DENBIGH	1851	13080	11878	15666	15687	2107	3715	*50.8*	*45.1*
	1881	15088	12712	18598	18673	2347	4549	*51.6*	*48.2*
	1911	20270	17954	23329	23730	2736	5374	*50.3*	*47.4*
MERIONETH	1851	6807	6522	8076	8267	1080	2027	*50.6*	*43.2*
	1881	9568	7570	11154	11296	1380	2656	*50.5*	*49.1*
	1911	9083	8960	9972	10323	1400	3019	*48.8*	*41.5*
CAERNARFON	1851	12214	12284	15126	15551	1760	3590	*52.0*	*43.9*
	1881	15972	15910	20406	20940	2623	5258	*52.3*	*45.6*
	1911	19635	23462	24202	25131	2899	6830	*51.8*	*41.2*
ANGLESEY	1851	5564	5531	6945	7169	799	1612	*52.2*	*45.0*
	1881	4513	4476	6020	6080	799	1647	*53.1*	*44.6*
	1911	4926	5356	5893	6219	806	1701	*50.7*	*42.6*

Sources: *Census of Population for England and Wales*: 1851, *Population Tables II, Ages, Civil Condition, Occupations, and Birthplace of the People. Vol. II* (HMSO, 1854), pp. 821–2; 1881, *Vol. III, Ages, Condition as to Marriage, Occupations, and Birthplaces of the People* (HMSO, 1883), Division XI – Wales and Monmouthshire, Table 7; 1911, County Volumes: *Anglesey, Carnarvon, Denbigh and Flint; Cardigan, Merioneth and Montgomery; Glamorgan; Brecknock, Carmarthen, Pembroke and Radnor; Monmouth* (HMSO, 1914), Table 20.

These figures are for the Registration Division of Wales and Monmouthshire, and the constituent Registration Counties. In some cases the boundaries differ considerably from those of the Ancient, Geographical or 'Proper' county. (See the County Maps in Appendix II (pp. 174–99). Details of boundary changes affecting registration counties are given in Table 1.1.

[1] For 1851, those aged 20 years and over; for 1881 and 1911, those aged 15 years and over.

[2] For males, this is the number married as a percentage of the total number of males in the age group (i.e. 20 years and over in 1851, 15 years and over in 1881 and 1911). For females, as a measure of married women of childbearing age, this is the number married as a percentage of the total in the age group 15–45 years.

Population 3.2 Marital status. Males and females. Registration Districts. 1851, 1881, 1911

Registration District	Year	Number[1] Unmarried Males	Females	Married Males	Females	Widowed Males	Females	*Percentage married[2] Males*	*Females age 15–45*
MONMOUTHSHIRE									
Chepstow	1851	1818	1284	3218	3200	368	664	*59.5*	–
	1881	2410	1980	3211	3166	381	700	*53.5*	*49.6*
	1911	2703	2589	3535	3541	375	696	*53.5*	*47.0*
Monmouth	1851	2359	1864	4604	4634	548	965	*61.3*	–
	1881	3806	2930	5953	5053	554	1150	*57.7*	*51.6*
	1911	4286	3338	5164	5202	551	1152	*51.6*	*49.7*
Abergavenny	1851	6690	3104	10110	9902	1140	1728	*56.4*	–
	1881	3222	2500	3947	4036	499	893	*51.5*	*51.4*
	1911	4533	3586	5024	5040	613	1010	*49.4*	*48.9*
Bedwellte	1881	8188	4076	9429	9293	1154	1750	*50.2*	*60.2*
	1911	19139	9315	21777	21310	2086	2558	*50.6*	*67.1*
Pontypool	1851	2490	1379	4847	4805	541	816	*61.5*	–
	1881	4756	2985	5860	5946	631	1201	*52.1*	*55.7*
	1911	9472	5750	10927	10819	1013	1518	*51.0*	*57.4*
Newport	1851	4654	2598	7348	7331	809	1303	*57.4*	–
	1881	8782	7276	11922	11889	1198	2607	*54.4*	*52.3*
	1911	22849	16984	27342	27124	2499	4092	*51.9*	*53.3*
GLAMORGAN									
Cardiff	1851	6166	3068	7680	7521	867	1369	*52.2*	–
	1881	14396	11236	18874	18247	1586	3287	*54.1*	*53.3*
	1911	37087	34484	46901	48261	4248	8547	*53.2*	*49.1*
Pontypridd	1881	14026	6572	16360	15801	1628	2309	*51.1*	*62.2*
	1911	46083	22582	52315	51073	4767	6074	*50.7*	*62.5*
Merthyr Tydfil	1851	9100	3743	13367	12729	1472	2251	*55.8*	–
	1881	13821	8761	17137	16979	1961	3789	*52.1*	*55.6*
	1911	27381	15696	31094	30848	3379	4752	*50.3*	*58.8*
Bridgend	1851	2124	1783	3785	3782	458	767	*59.4*	–
	1881	5523	3883	6454	6404	767	1280	*50.6*	*51.7*
	1911	14729	9115	16743	16586	1658	2281	*50.5*	*57.3*
Neath	1851	4139	2349	7574	7368	779	1331	*60.6*	–
	1881	6379	5071	8632	8666	891	1788	*54.3*	*53.3*
	1911	15180	9908	17969	17756	1664	2700	*51.6*	*56.7*
Pontardawe	1881	2265	1849	3267	3306	332	710	*55.7*	*53.8*
	1911	586	3934	7569	7318	699	1000	*51.0*	*57.9*
Swansea	1851	3526	3647	7313	7608	823	1849	*62.7*	–
	1881	1497	9798	15887	16032	1289	3276	*55.4*	*53.5*
	1911	3002	18112	27039	26841	2491	5113	*51.5*	*51.0*
Gower	1881	1166	1397	1818	1860	217	415	*56.8*	*45.6*
	1911	1881	2254	2538	2592	268	555	*54.1*	*44.4*
CARMARTHENSHIRE									
Llanelli	1851	1507	1481	3726	3783	339	763	*66.9*	–
	1881	5064	4613	7158	7325	651	1465	*55.6*	*52.1*
	1911	1301	8753	13029	12835	1265	2196	*50.9*	*50.2*
Llandovery	1851	1187	1366	2288	2303	282	591	*60.9*	–
	1881	1611	1949	1933	1971	259	567	*50.8*	*36.4*
	1911	1739	1600	1423	1413	219	443	*42.1*	*33.7*

Registration District	Year	Number[1] Unmarried Males	Females	Married Males	Females	Widowed Males	Females	*Percentage married[2] Males*	*Females age 15–45*
Llandeilo Fawr	1851	1230	1510	2816	2832	311	742	*64.6*	–
	1881	2087	2483	2945	3009	328	778	*54.9*	*43.1*
	1911	5269	3968	5753	5621	638	997	*49.3*	*50.9*
Carmarthen	1851	2617	3538	5693	5909	720	1708	*63.0*	–
	1881	4095	5618	5239	5433	665	1723	*52.4*	*36.9*
	1911	5386	5965	5513	5615	721	1512	*47.4*	*38.3*
PEMBROKESHIRE									
Narberth	1851	1257	1948	3343	3469	372	968	*67.2*	–
	1881	2157	2880	2956	3080	381	889	*53.8*	*38.8*
	1911	2465	3038	2819	2891	378	744	*49.8*	*37.5*
Pembroke	1851	1559	2232	3630	3748	367	843	*65.3*	–
	1881	3726	4059	4947	5015	575	1156	*53.5*	*43.6*
	1911	4762	4646	5300	5435	649	1213	*49.5*	*42.0*
Haverfordwest	1851	2791	3953	5772	6094	628	1604	*62.8*	–
	1881	4229	4914	5351	5301	711	1505	*52.0*	*39.0*
	1911	5126	5233	6153	6388	726	1333	*51.3*	*45.9*
CARDIGANSHIRE									
Cardigan	1851	1212	2409	2678	3241	385	1013	*62.6*	–
	1881	1839	3080	2386	2905	359	1090	*52.1*	*36.4*
	1911	1996	2827	2227	2583	344	820	*48.8*	*35.2*
Newcastle Emlyn	1851	1294	2207	2950	3107	384	869	*63.7*	–
	1881	2232	3293	2653	2835	377	988	*50.4*	*33.7*
	1911	2593	3482	2681	2872	445	838	*46.9*	*34.4*
Lampeter	1851	775	912	1467	1515	165	411	*60.9*	–
	1881	1309	1601	1438	1516	194	476	*48.9*	*36.2*
	1911	1366	1696	1386	1462	216	483	*46.7*	*35.0*
Aberaeron	1851	854	1385	1857	2080	233	620	*63.1*	–
	1881	1248	2198	1579	2051	245	771	*51.4*	*35.3*
	1911	1439	2080	1414	1680	287	635	*45.0*	*32.1*
Aberystwyth	1851	1932	2302	3549	3635	429	915	*60.1*	–
	1881	3239	4001	3544	3905	479	1326	*48.8*	*37.2*
	1911	3199	4396	3153	3434	457	1224	*46.3*	*32.9*
Tregaron	1851	792	974	1460	1547	175	418	*60.2*	–
	1881	1263	1716	1356	1519	211	510	*47.9*	*34.7*
	1911	1347	1431	1021	1121	187	406	*40.0*	*31.2*
BRECONSHIRE									
Builth	1851	806	752	1219	1227	158	311	*55.8*	–
	1881	1129	1128	1226	1232	169	289	*48.6*	*40.6*
	1911	1571	1594	1539	1573	197	375	*46.5*	*38.6*
Brecon	1851	1888	1749	2804	2839	400	743	*55.1*	–
	1881	2616	2344	2633	2655	333	712	*47.2*	*41.0*
	1911	2537	2317	2446	2450	317	582	*46.2*	*40.9*
Crickhowell	1851	2232	1066	3783	3730	443	697	*58.6*	–
	1881	2337	1679	3108	3170	430	800	*52.9*	*54.2*
	1911	3213	2296	3899	3889	424	701	*51.7*	*54.1*
Hay	1851	1027	951	1732	1746	291	456	*56.8*	–
	1881	1342	1271	1662	1670	238	446	*51.3*	*44.3*
	1911	1555	1502	1562	1601	232	389	*46.6*	*40.1*

Registration District	Year	Number[1] Unmarried Males	Females	Married Males	Females	Widowed Males	Females	*Percentage married*[2] *Males*	*Females age 15–45*
RADNORSHIRE									
Presteigne	1851	1584	1290	2381	2361	346	563	*55.2*	–
Knighton	1851	1110	764	1322	1343	184	275	*50.5*	–
	1881	1883	1407	1782	1775	250	439	*45.5*	*43.1*
	1911	1559	1365	1648	1664	221	312	*48.1*	*42.3*
Rhayader	1851	635	555	990	968	123	214	*56.6*	–
	1881	987	912	973	1002	143	245	*46.3*	*40.3*
	1911	1277	1290	1232	1232	162	266	*46.1*	*39.8*
MONTGOMERYSHIRE									
Machynlleth	1851	1030	1127	1918	1932	251	537	*60.0*	–
	1881	1699	1623	1883	1980	291	618	*48.6*	*42.1*
	1911	1608	1943	1707	1824	222	559	*48.3*	*37.0*
Newtown	1851	2310	2000	3705	3733	522	992	*56.7*	–
	1881	3472	3006	3850	3923	514	1003	*49.1*	*44.7*
	1911	3118	3151	3175	3294	454	837	*47.1*	*39.0*
Montgomery/ Forden	1851	2084	1625	3197	3181	451	761	*55.8*	–
	1881	2715	2024	2985	2943	412	675	*48.8*	*46.5*
	1911	2214	1993	2431	2462	338	656	*48.8*	*42.9*
Llanfyllin	1851	1731	1439	3047	3056	439	704	*58.4*	–
	1881	2850	2320	3150	3185	476	835	*48.6*	*43.6*
	1911	2696	2312	2616	2673	483	702	*45.1*	*41.0*
FLINTSHIRE									
Holywell	1851	3430	2500	6465	6521	693	1791	*61.1*	–
	1881	6204	4263	7579	7625	789	1968	*52.0*	*53.1*
	1911	6372	5253	7176	7306	880	1770	*49.7*	*47.9*
Hawarden	1911	4135	2673	4795	4800	497	751	*50.9*	*55.4*
DENBIGHSHIRE									
Wrexham	1851	3451	2903	7033	6986	831	1530	*62.2*	–
	1881	7230	4795	9342	9316	1008	1921	*53.1*	*55.9*
	1911	1541	7984	13834	13977	1484	2528	*51.5*	*54.5*
Ruthin	1851	1467	1372	2677	2656	387	680	*59.1*	–
	1881	2029	1696	2352	2328	355	623	*49.7*	*43.5*
	1911	2059	1853	2077	2093	301	556	*46.8*	*41.0*
St Asaph	1851	2125	2107	4029	4053	594	1028	*59.7*	–
	1881	3802	4425	4623	4745	641	1441	*51.0*	*39.5*
	1911	4766	6307	5327	5553	664	1693	*49.5*	*36.8*
Llanrwst	1851	1095	1009	1916	1940	295	476	*58.0*	–
	1881	2027	1796	2281	2284	343	564	*49.0*	*44.7*
	1911	1904	1810	2091	2107	287	597	*48.8*	*43.2*
MERIONETH									
Corwen	1851	1391	1066	2446	2455	380	564	*58.0*	–
	1881	2321	1835	2753	2797	377	659	*50.5*	*47.4*
	1911	2594	2333	2809	2840	386	683	*48.5*	*42.5*
Bala	1851	630	614	1025	1052	160	255	*56.5*	–
	1881	1297	859	1009	1006	156	276	*41.0*	*41.5*
	1911	1039	937	902	899	147	249	*43.2*	*37.5*
Dolgellau	1851	1011	1198	2053	2133	268	594	*61.6*	–
	1881	1811	1929	2503	2564	296	639	*54.3*	*46.7*
	1911	1844	2347	2073	2204	310	745	*49.0*	*36.4*

Registration District	Year	Number[1] Unmarried Males	Females	Married Males	Females	Widowed Males	Females	*Percentage married*[2] *Males*	*Females age 15–45*
Ffestiniog	1851	1300	1245	2548	2610	272	613	*61.8*	–
	1881	4139	2947	4889	4929	551	1082	*51.0*	*52.8*
	1911	3606	3343	4188	4380	557	1342	*50.1*	*44.7*
CAERNARFONSHIRE									
Pwllheli	1851	1651	2193	3307	3550	430	937	*61.4*	–
	1881	3060	3232	3585	3770	542	994	*49.9*	*42.9*
	1911	3463	3784	3484	3752	493	1104	*46.8*	*38.0*
Caernarfon	1851	2251	2198	4935	5056	509	1201	*64.1*	–
	1881	5756	4916	7291	7518	903	1775	*52.3*	*50.2*
	1911	5612	5273	7187	7488	903	2021	*52.5*	*47.0*
Bangor	1851	2712	2299	5071	5072	560	1034	*60.8*	–
	1881	4865	4932	6573	6698	806	1690	*53.7*	*45.2*
	1911	5417	5767	6578	6767	821	1849	*51.3*	*42.7*
Conwy	1851	1048	941	1807	1825	261	417	*58.0*	–
	1881	2291	2830	2957	2954	372	799	*52.6*	*39.4*
	1911	5143	8638	6953	7124	682	1856	*54.4*	*36.9*
ANGLESEY									
Anglesey	1851	3497	3536	6940	7149	799	1611	*61.8*	–
	1881	4513	4476	6020	6080	799	1647	*53.1*	*44.6*
	1911	1869	2293	2207	2415	333	758	*50.1*	*38.5*
Holyhead	1911	3057	3063	2686	3804	473	943	*43.2*	*45.3*

Sources: *Census of Population for England and Wales*: 1851, *Population Tables II, Ages, Civil Condition, Occupations, and Birthplace of the People. Vol. II* (HMSO, 1854), p. 825; 1881, *Vol. III, Ages, Condition as to Marriage, Occupations, and Birthplaces of the People* (HMSO, 1883), Division XI – Wales and Monmouthshire, Table 8; 1911, County Volumes: *Anglesey, Carnarvon, Denbigh and Flint; Cardigan, Merioneth and Montgomery; Glamorgan; Brecknock, Carmarthen, Pembroke and Radnor; Monmouth* (HMSO, 1914), Table 21.

Details of boundary changes affecting Registration Districts are given in Table 1.2.

1 For 1851, those aged 20 years and over; for 1881 and 1911, those aged 15 years and over.

2 For males, this is the number married as a percentage of the total number of males in the age group (i.e. 20 years and over in 1851, 15 years and over in 1881 and 1911). For females, as a measure of married women of childbearing age, this is the number married as a percentage of the total in the age group 15–45 years.

Population 4.1 Population change. Natural increase and net migration. Wales and Registration Counties. 1841–1911

	Intercensal period	Total population change Number	*Percentage*	Natural increase (births – deaths) Number	*Percentage*	Net migration (change – natural increase) Number	*Percentage*
WALES	1841–51	120367	*11.26*	111312	*10.42*	9055	*0.85*
	1851–61	126137	*10.63*	145951	*12.30*	–19814	*–1.67*
	1861–71	125669	*9.70*	175204	*13.52*	–49535	*–3.82*
	1871–81	157151	*11.06*	209284	*14.73*	–52133	*–3.67*
	1881–91	198872	*12.61*	216666	*13.73*	–17794	*–1.13*
	1891–1901	240202	*13.53*	249552	*14.06*	–9350	*–0.53*
	1901–1911	408754	*20.10*	310262	*15.26*	98492	*4.84*

Boundary changes: 1851–61 loss of 2217 from Denbighshire to Shropshire (pop. 1851)
1861–71 loss of 11930 from Radnorshire to Herefordshire, loss of 4903 from Denbighshire to Cheshire (pop 1861)
1871–81 loss of 1262 from Radnorshire to Herefordshire (pop. 1871)
1881–91 gain of 27 from Gloucestershire to Monmouthshire, gain of 42 from Cheshire to Denbighshire, loss of 55 from Monmouthshire to Herefordshire, loss of 40 from Montgomeryshire to Shropshire (pop. 1881)
1891–1901 loss of 316 from Denbighshire to Cheshire, loss of 1279 from Denbighshire to Shropshire (pop. 1891)
1901–11 gain of 18275 from Cheshire to Flintshire (pop. 1901)

Registration Counties

	Intercensal period	Total population change Number	*Percentage*	Natural increase (births – deaths) Number	*Percentage*	Net migration (change – natural increase) Number	*Percentage*
MONMOUTH	1841–51	26109	*17.29*	16509	*10.93*	9600	*6.36*
	1851–61	19847	*11.20*	25956	*14.65*	–6109	*–3.45*
	1861–71	22731	*11.54*	29919	*15.19*	–7188	*–3.65*
	1871–81	14624	*6.66*	36349	*16.54*	–21725	*–9.89*
	1881–91	40938	*17.47*	37237	*15.89*	3701	*1.58*
	1891–1901	41252	*14.97*	46387	*16.83*	–5135	*–1.86*
	1901–1911	97802	*30.87*	63394	*20.01*	34408	*10.86*

Boundary changes: 1881–91 overall loss of 28 to Herefordshire and Gloucestershire (pop. 1881)
1891–1901 overall gain of 370 from Glamorgan and Breconshire (pop. 1891)

	Intercensal period	Total population change Number	*Percentage*	Natural increase (births – deaths) Number	*Percentage*	Net migration (change – natural increase) Number	*Percentage*
GLAMORGAN	1841–51	62045	*34.85*	20170	*11.33*	41875	*23.52*
	1851–61	86159	*35.89*	41924	*17.46*	44235	*18.42*
	1861–71	79544	*24.38*	60563	*18.56*	18981	*5.82*
	1871–81	112585	*27.74*	82276	*20.28*	30309	*7.47*
	1881–91	174689	*33.70*	97222	*18.75*	77467	*14.94*
	1891–1901	173718	*25.09*	132748	*19.17*	40970	*5.92*
	1901–1911	264418	*30.52*	172297	*19.89*	92121	*10.63*

Boundary changes: 1891–1901 overall loss of 640 to Monmouthshire (pop. 1891)

	Intercensal period	Total population change Number	*Percentage*	Natural increase (births – deaths) Number	*Percentage*	Net migration (change – natural increase) Number	*Percentage*
CARMARTHEN	1841–51	5113	*5.71*	11588	*12.94*	–6475	*–7.23*
	1851–61	1979	*2.09*	15,803	*16.69*	–13824	*–14.60*
	1861–71	4730	*4.89*	12961	*13.41*	–8231	*–8.52*
	1871–81	9874	*9.74*	15326	*15.12*	–5452	*–5.38*
	1881–91	7369	*6.62*	15239	*13.70*	–7870	*–7.07*
	1891–1901	5794	*4.92*	14382	*12.22*	–8588	*–7.30*
	1901–1911	27480	*22.24*	16816	*13.61*	10664	*8.63*

Boundary changes: 1891–1901 loss of 903 to Breconshire (pop. 1891)

	Intercensal period	Total population change Number	*Percentage*	Natural increase (births – deaths) Number	*Percentage*	Net migration (change – natural increase) Number	*Percentage*
PEMBROKE	1841–51	5915	*7.53*	10622	*13.52*	–4707	*–5.99*
	1851–61	3218	*3.81*	8965	*10.61*	–5747	*–6.80*
	1861–71	–3817	*–4.35*	10009	*11.41*	–13826	*–15.77*
	1871–81	–194	*–0.23*	9198	*10.97*	–9392	*–11.20*
	1881–91	–1676	*–2.00*	9914	*11.85*	–11590	*–13.85*
	1891–1901	421	*0.51*	7629	*9.30*	–7208	*–8.79*
	1901–1911	2450	*2.97*	7922	*9.61*	–5472	*–6.64*

No boundary changes

	Intercensal period	Total population change Number	Percentage	Natural increase (births – deaths) Number	Percentage	Net migration (change – natural increase) Number	Percentage
CARDIGAN	1841–51	1612	*1.68*	11040	*11.50*	–9428	*–9.82*
	1851–61	–213	*–.022*	9100	*9.32*	–9313	*–9.54*
	1861–71	468	*0.48*	10628	*10.91*	–10160	*–10.43*
	1871–81	–2732	*–2.79*	8582	*8.77*	–11314	*–11.56*
	1881–91	–8754	*–9.20*	6968	*7.32*	–15722	*–16.53*
	1891–1901	–3676	*–4.26*	6968	*7.32*	–15722	*–16.53*
	1901–1911	–1938	*–2.34*	1809	*2.19*	–3747	*–4.53*

No boundary changes

	Intercensal period	Total population change Number	Percentage	Natural increase (births – deaths) Number	Percentage	Net migration (change – natural increase) Number	Percentage
BRECON	1841–51	3758	*6.78*	6124	*11.05*	–2366	*–4.27*
	1851–61	–318	*–0.54*	6300	*10.65*	–6618	*–11.18*
	1861–71	–1928	*–3.28*	7057	*11.99*	–8985	*–15.27*
	1871–81	–2792	*–4.90*	6683	*11.74*	–9475	*–16.64*
	1881–91	–1268	*–2.34*	5691	*10.51*	–6959	*–12.85*
	1891–1901	–94	*–0.17*	5485	*10.15*	–5579	*–10.32*
	1901–1911	2419	*4.48*	5944	*11.02*	–3525	*–6.53*

Boundary changes: 1891–1901 gain of 1173 from Carmarthenshire and Monmouthshire (pop. 1891)

	Intercensal period	Total population change Number	Percentage	Natural increase (births – deaths) Number	Percentage	Net migration (change – natural increase) Number	Percentage
RADNOR	1841–51	–351	*–1.10*	3403	*10.71*	–3754	*–11.81*
	1851–61	1441	*4.59*	4330	*13.78*	–2889	*–9.19*
	1861–71	80	*0.38*	3236	*15.46*	–3156	*–15.07*
	1871–81	–1231	*–6.23*	2479	*12.55*	–3710	*–18.78*
	1881–91	–1404	*–7.58*	2019	*10.90*	–3423	*–18.48*
	1891–1901[1]	3122	*18.24*	2085	*12.18*	1037	*6.06*
	1901–1911	–2736	*–13.52*	1951	*9.64*	–4687	*–23.16*

Boundary changes: 1861–71 loss of 11930 to Herefordshire (pop. 1861)
1871–81 loss of 1262 to Herefordshire (pop. 1871)

[1] The 1901 census notes that the abnormal increase in population for that year was caused by a large number of men (accompanied by their families) temporarily engaged in waterworks construction.

	Intercensal period	Total population change Number	Percentage	Natural increase (births – deaths) Number	Percentage	Net migration (change – natural increase) Number	Percentage
MONTGOMERY	1841–51	–2614	*–3.28*	5009	*6.28*	–7623	*–9.56*
	1851–61	–219	*–0.28*	7116	*9.22*	–7335	*–9.51*
	1861–71	1477	*1.92*	8117	*10.55*	–6640	*–8.63*
	1871–81	–2204	*–2.81*	8961	*11.43*	–11165	*–14.24*
	1881–91	–8900	*–11.68*	6886	*9.04*	–15786	*–20.72*
	1891–1901	–3424	*–5.08*	5263	*7.81*	–8687	*–12.89*
	1901–1911	–1793	*–2.80*	4808	*7.51*	–6601	*–10.32*

Boundary changes: 1891–1901 gain of 121 from Merioneth (pop. 1891)

	Intercensal period	Total population change Number	Percentage	Natural increase (births – deaths) Number	Percentage	Net migration (change – natural increase) Number	Percentage
FLINT	1841–51	249	*0.61*	4650	*11.40*	–4401	*–10.79*
	1851–61	–1106	*–2.69*	3275	*7.98*	–4381	*–10.67*
	1861–71	3576	*8.95*	4555	*11.40*	–979	*–2.45*
	1871–81	2257	*5.19*	5466	*12.56*	–3209	*–7.37*
	1881–91	–3209	*–7.01*	4592	*10.03*	–7801	*–17.04*
	1891–1901	–304	*–0.71*	4064	*9.55*	–4368	*–10.26*
	1901–1911	9186	*15.17*	7613	*12.58*	1573	*2.60*

Boundary changes: 1901–11 overall gain of 18,275 from Cheshire

	Intercensal period	Total population change Number	Percentage	Natural increase (births – deaths) Number	Percentage	Net migration (change – natural increase) Number	Percentage
DENBIGH	1841–51	4879	*5.30*	3327	*3.61*	1552	*1.69*
	1851–61	9648	*10.19*	9286	*9.81*	362	*0.38*
	1861–71	5721	*5.75*	11845	*11.91*	–6124	*–6.16*
	1871–81	7776	*7.39*	11893	*11.31*	–4117	*–3.91*
	1881–91	3716	*3.29*	11172	*9.89*	–7456	*–6.60*
	1891–1901	11355	*9.87*	12582	*10.93*	–1227	*–1.07*
	1901–1911	10352	*8.19*	13706	*10.84*	–3354	*–2.65*

Boundary changes: 1851–61 loss of 2217 to Shropshire (pop. 1851)
1861–71 loss of 4903 to Cheshire (pop. 1861)
1881–91 gain of 42 from Merioneth (pop. 1881)
1891–1901 loss of 1595 to Cheshire and Shropshire (pop. 1891)

	Intercensal period	Total population change Number	Percentage	Natural increase (births – deaths) Number	Percentage	Net migration (change – natural increase) Number	Percentage
MERIONETH	1841–51	594	*1.17*	4781	*9.43*	–4187	*–8.26*
	1851–61	1923	*3.75*	4703	*9.17*	–2780	*–5.42*
	1861–71	8277	*5.55*	6534	*12.28*	1743	*3.27*
	1871–81	6771	*11.01*	8319	*13.53*	–1548	*–2.52*
	1881–91	–3511	*–5.15*	7202	*10.55*	–10713	*–15.70*
	1891–1901	–357	*–0.55*	4871	*7.54*	–5228	*–8.09*
	1901–1911	–3968	*–6.18*	4397	*6.84*	–8365	*–13.02*

Boundary changes: 1881–91 loss of 41 to Denbighshire (pop. 1881)
1891–1901 loss of 121 to Montgomeryshire (pop. 1891)

	Intercensal period	Total population change Number	Percentage	Natural increase (births – deaths) Number	Percentage	Net migration (change – natural increase) Number	Percentage
CAERNARFON	1841–51	7921	*9.13*	10453	*12.05*	–2532	*–2.92*
	1851–61	5353	*5.45*	9820	*10.00*	–4467	*–4.55*
	1861–71	7840	*7.57*	10462	*10.10*	–2622	*–2.53*
	1871–81	12403	*11.14*	11188	*10.05*	1215	*1.09*
	1881–91	1785	*1.44*	10244	*8.27*	–8459	*–6.83*
	1891–1901	11651	*9.28*	8839	*7.04*	2812	*2.24*
	1901–1911	4531	*3.30*	9424	*6.87*	–4893	*–3.57*

Boundary changes: 1851–61 gain of 3511 from Anglesey (pop. 1851)
1881–91 gain of 19 from Anglesey (pop. 1881)

	Intercensal period	Total population change Number	Percentage	Natural increase (births – deaths) Number	Percentage	Net migration (change – natural increase) Number	Percentage
ANGLESEY	1841–51	5137	*13.48*	3935	*10.33*	1202	*3.15*
	1851–61	–1575	*–3.96*	3384	*8.52*	–4959	*–12.48*
	1861–71	–3030	*–7.94*	1963	*5.14*	–4993	*–13.09*
	1871–81	14	*0.04*	2432	*6.92*	–2418	*–6.88*
	1881–91	–903	*–2.57*	2320	*6.61*	–3223	*–9.18*
	1891–1901	589	*1.72*	2127	*6.22*	–1538	*–4.49*
	1901–1911	551	*1.58*	2439	*7.01*	–1888	*–5.42*

Boundary changes: 1851–61 loss of 3511 to Caernarfonshire (pop. 1851)
1881–91 loss of 19 to Caernarfonshire (pop. 1881)

Sources: *Census Reports* 1851–1911, Registrar General, *Annual Reports,* 1841–1911, as tabulated in John Williams, *Digest of Welsh Historical Statistics* (2 vols., Cardiff, 1985), I, Population Table 14, pp. 68–75.

The figures relate to the Registration Division of Wales and the constituent Registration Counties. (See County Maps in Appendix II (pp. 999–999) for the difference between Registration and Ancient or Geographical county boundaries.)

Where there has been a boundary change between censuses, the population increase or decrease has been calculated from the figures relating to the population of the county as constituted at the later date. However, the Registrar-General's annual figures of births and deaths (from which the figures for natural increase have been calculated) relate to the original area until the actual date of any boundary change. In a few cases this could be a significant source of error. All boundary changes have been noted.

No allowance has been made for the under-registration of births.

The figures for net migration are simply the total intercensal change in population minus the natural increase.

The percentages are of the relevant total population at the beginning of each ten-year period.

Population 4.2 Population change. Natural increase and net migration. Registration Districts. 1851–1911

Registration District	Intercensal period	Total population change Number	*Percentage*	Natural increase (births – deaths) Number	*Percentage*	Net migration (change – natural increase) Number	*Percentage*
MONMOUTHSHIRE							
Chepstow	1851–61	–1116	*–5.9*	2204	*11.6*	–3320	*–17.4*
	1861–71	400	*2.2*	2291	*12.8*	–1891	*–10.5*
	1871–81	360	*2.0*	2315	*12.6*	–1955	*–10.7*
	1881–91	763	*4.1*	2638	*14.1*	–1875	*–10.0*
	1891–1901	–218	*–1.1*	2529	*13.0*	–2747	*–14.1*
	1901–1911	683	*3.5*	2318	*12.0*	–1635	*–8.5*
Monmouth	1851–61	2865	*10.5*	3503	*12.8*	–638	*–2.3*
	1861–71	1354	*4.5*	3908	*12.9*	–2554	*–8.4*
	1871–81	–1258	*–4.0*	4913	*15.5*	–6171	*–19.5*
	1881–91	–2031	*–6.7*	3509	*11.6*	–5540	*–18.3*
	1891–1901	–41	*–0.1*	3488	*12.3*	–3529	*–12.5*
	1901–1911	1134	*4.0*	3336	*11.8*	–2202	*–7.8*

Boundary changes: 1881–91 loss of 93 to Ross (Her), gain of 27 from Westbury (Gloucs), gain of 32 from Ross (Her), gain of 6 from Hereford (Her) – overall loss of 28 (pop. 1881)

Registration District	Intercensal period	Total population change Number	*Percentage*	Natural increase (births – deaths) Number	*Percentage*	Net migration (change – natural increase) Number	*Percentage*
Abergavenny	1851–61	7863	*13.3*	8860	*15.0*	–997	*–1.7*
	1861–71	3335	*17.1*	2558	*13.1*	777	*4.0*
	1871–81	709	*3.1*	2789	*12.2*	–2080	*–9.1*
	1881–91	2493	*10.6*	2268	*9.6*	225	*1.0*
	1891–1901	–896	*–3.2*	1906	*6.9*	–2802	*–10.1*
	1901–1911	1949	*7.3*	2255	*8.4*	–306	*–1.1*

Boundary changes: 1851–61 loss of 41566 to new district of Bedwellte (pop. 1851)
1891–1901 gain of 75 from Bedwellte, gain of 1515 from Pontypool – overall gain of 1590 (pop. 1891)

Registration District	Intercensal period	Total population change Number	*Percentage*	Natural increase (births – deaths) Number	*Percentage*	Net migration (change – natural increase) Number	*Percentage*
Bedwellte	1861–71	4198	*8.8*	8170	*17.2*	–3972	*–8.4*
	1871–81	4077	*7.9*	9128	*17.6*	–5051	*–9.8*
	1881–91	9026	*16.2*	7779	*13.9*	1247	*2.2*
	1891–1901	17317	*26.8*	13089	*20.3*	4228	*6.6*
	1901–1911	40468	*49.5*	22309	*27.3*	18159	*22.2*

Boundary changes: 1851–61 creation of new district from part of Abergavenny
1891–1901 loss of 75 to Abergavenny (pop. 1891)

Registration District	Intercensal period	Total population change Number	*Percentage*	Natural increase (births – deaths) Number	*Percentage*	Net migration (change – natural increase) Number	*Percentage*
Pontypool	1851–61	2295	*8.2*	4769	*17.0*	–2474	*–8.8*
	1861–71	3604	*11.9*	5034	*16.6*	–1430	*–4.7*
	1871–81	1446	*4.3*	6372	*18.8*	–4926	*–14.5*
	1881–91	4433	*12.5*	5915	*16.7*	–1482	*–4.2*
	1891–1901	7103	*18.6*	7629	*19.9*	–526	*–1.4*
	1901–1911	16489	*36.3*	10430	*23.0*	6059	*13.4*

Boundary changes: 1891–1901 loss of 1515 to Abergavenny (pop. 1891)

Registration District	Intercensal period	Total population change Number	*Percentage*	Natural increase (births – deaths) Number	*Percentage*	Net migration (change – natural increase) Number	*Percentage*
Newport	1851–61	7940	*18.3*	6560	*15.1*	1380	*3.2*
	1861–71	9840	*19.1*	7958	*15.5*	1882	*3.7*
	1871–81	9290	*15.2*	10832	*17.7*	–1542	*–2.5*
	1881–91	26254	*37.2*	15128	*21.4*	11126	*15.8*
	1891–1901	17991	*18.5*	17746	*18.2*	245	*0.3*
	1901–1911	37079	*32.1*	22746	*19.7*	14333	*12.4*

Boundary changes: 1891–1901 gain of 1190 from Cardiff, loss of 550 to Cardiff – overall gain of 640 (pop. 1891)

Registration District	Intercensal period	Total population change Number	*Percentage*	Natural increase (births – deaths) Number	*Percentage*	Net migration (change – natural increase) Number	*Percentage*
GLAMORGAN							
Cardiff	1851–61	28084	*60.4*	8540	*18.4*	19544	*42.0*
	1861–71	18416	*31.6*	10392	*17.8*	8024	*13.8*
	1871–81	29463	*38.4*	14739	*19.2*	14724	*19.2*
	1881–91	67632	*63.7*	24618	*23.2*	43014	*40.5*
	1891–1901	55505	*32.1*	36321	*21.0*	19184	*11.1*
	1901–1911	36072	*15.8*	36258	*15.9*	–186	*–0.1*

Boundary changes: 1861–71 loss of 16290 to Pontypridd (pop. 1861)
1891–1901 loss of 1190 to Newport, gain of 550 from Newport – overall gain of 640 (pop. 1891)

Registration District	Intercensal period	Total population change Number	Percentage	Natural increase (births – deaths) Number	Percentage	Net migration (change – natural increase) Number	Percentage
Pontypridd	1861–71	21534	*70.9*	7640	*25.1*	13894	*45.7*
	1871–81	41572	*80.1*	15050	*29.0*	26522	*51.1*
	1881–91	53319	*57.0*	21901	*23.4*	31418	*33.6*
	1891–1901	55835	*37.6*	35008	*23.6*	20827	*14.0*
	1901–1911	83740	*40.9*	52365	*25.6*	31375	*15.3*

Boundary changes: 1871 creation of new district: 16290 from Cardiff, 14097 from Merthyr Tydfil (pop. 1861)
1891–1901 loss of 924 to Merthyr Tydfil, gain of 2486 from Merthyr Tydfil – overall gain of 1562 (pop. 1891)

Registration District	Intercensal period	Total population change Number	Percentage	Natural increase (births – deaths) Number	Percentage	Net migration (change – natural increase) Number	Percentage
Merthyr Tydfil	1851–61	30301	*39.5*	13644	*17.8*	16657	*21.7*
	1861–71	11231	*12.1*	16228	*17.4*	–4997	*–5.4*
	1871–81	–2798	*–2.7*	16082	*15.4*	–18880	*–18.1*
	1881–91	15764	*15.5*	12924	*12.7*	2840	*2.8*
	1891–1901	20512	*17.7*	18465	*16.0*	2047	*1.8*
	1901–1911	38607	*28.5*	26590	*19.6*	12017	*8.9*

Boundary changes: 1861–71 loss of 14097 to new district of Pontypridd (pop. 1861)
1891–1901 loss of 2486 to Pontypridd, gain of 924 from Pontypridd – overall loss of 1562 (pop. 1891)

Registration District	Intercensal period	Total population change Number	Percentage	Natural increase (births – deaths) Number	Percentage	Net migration (change – natural increase) Number	Percentage
Bridgend	1851–61	3043	*13.0*	3095	*13.2*	–52	*–0.2*
	1861–71	5206	*19.7*	3936	*14.9*	1270	*4.8*
	1871–81	7249	*22.9*	5452	*17.2*	1797	*5.7*
	1881–91	10449	*25.5*	5549	*13.5*	4900	*12.0*
	1891–1901	16000	*31.1*	8639	*16.8*	7361	*14.3*
	1901–1911	27156	*40.3*	13816	*20.5*	13340	*19.8*

Boundary changes: 1881–91 gain of 2084 from Neath (pop. 1881)

Registration District	Intercensal period	Total population change Number	Percentage	Natural increase (births – deaths) Number	Percentage	Net migration (change – natural increase) Number	Percentage
Neath	1851–61	12062	*26.0*	9510	*20.5*	2552	*5.5*
	1861–71	6086	*10.4*	11622	*19.9*	–5536	*–9.5*
	1871–81	8014	*18.2*	–	–	–	–
	1881–91	6680	*13.4*	9109	*18.2*	–2429	*–4.9*
	1891–1901	14931	*26.3*	11515	*20.3*	3416	*6.0*
	1901–1911	29320	*40.9*	16396	*22.9*	12924	*18.0*

Boundary changes: 1871–81 loss of 14428 to new district of Pontardawe, loss of 6128 to Swansea – overall loss of 20556 (pop. 1871)
1881–91 loss of 2084 to Bridgend (pop. 1881)

Registration District	Intercensal period	Total population change Number	Percentage	Natural increase (births – deaths) Number	Percentage	Net migration (change – natural increase) Number	Percentage
Pontardawe	1871–81	2697	*15.4*	29252	*167.3*	6035	*34.5*
	1881–91	1515	*7.5*	3509	*17.4*	–1994	*–9.9*
	1891–1901	5018	*23.1*	4343	*20.0*	675	*3.1*
	1901–1911	15251	*57.1*	6612	*24.7*	8639	*32.3*

Boundary changes: 1881 district created from part of Swansea (3060 pop. 1871) and part of Neath (14428 pop. 1871)

Registration District	Intercensal period	Total population change Number	Percentage	Natural increase (births – deaths) Number	Percentage	Net migration (change – natural increase) Number	Percentage
Swansea	1851–61	12840	*33.4*	7135	*18.6*	5705	*14.8*
	1861–71	16097	*31.4*	9813	*19.1*	6284	*12.3*
	1871–81	24576	*34.9*	–	–	–	–
	1881–91	19325	*20.3*	18252	*19.2*	1073	*1.1*
	1891–1901	5420	*4.7*	17081	*14.9*	–11661	*–10.2*
	1901–1911	31279	*26.1*	18661	*15.6*	12618	*10.5*

Boundary changes: 1851–61 loss of 8487 to new district of Gower (pop. 1851)
1871–81 loss of 3060 to Pontardawe, gain of 6128 from Neath – overall gain of 3068 (pop. 1871)

Registration District	Intercensal period	Total population change Number	Percentage	Natural increase (births – deaths) Number	Percentage	Net migration (change – natural increase) Number	Percentage
Gower	1861–71	974	*11.7*	932	*11.2*	42	*0.5*
	1871–81	1812	*19.5*	1701	*18.3*	111	*1.2*
	1881–91	5	*0.0*	1360	*12.3*	–1355	*–12.2*
	1891–1901	620	*5.6*	1376	*12.4*	–756	*–6.8*
	1901–1911	2993	*25.5*	1599	*13.6*	1394	*11.9*

Boundary changes: district created 1861 from part of Swansea (8487 pop. 1851)

Registration District	Intercensal period	Total population change Number	*Percentage*	Natural increase (births – deaths) Number	*Percentage*	Net migration (change – natural increase) Number	*Percentage*
CARMARTHENSHIRE							
Llanelli	1851–61	4472	*19.0*	4207	*17.9*	265	*1.1*
	1861–71	6753	*24.1*	5862	*21.0*	891	*3.2*
	1871–81	9884	*28.5*	7926	*22.8*	1958	*5.6*
	1881–91	7766	*17.4*	8748	*19.6*	–982	*–2.2*
	1891–1901	4675	*9.0*	8994	*17.2*	–4322	*–8.3*
	1901–1911	17102	*30.1*	10338	*18.2*	6764	*11.9*
	Boundary changes: 1891–1901 loss of 157 to Carmarthen (pop. 1891)						
Llandovery	1851–61	–280	*–1.9*	1781	*11.8*	–2061	*–13.7*
	1861–71	–729	*–4.9*	1733	*11.7*	–2462	*–16.7*
	1871–81	–1281	*–9.1*	1761	*12.5*	–3042	*–21.7*
	1881–91	–1143	*–9.0*	1109	*8.7*	–2252	*–17.6*
	1891–1901	–1109	*–10.3*	505	*4.7*	–1614	*–15.1*
	1901–1911	–234	*–2.4*	481	*5.0*	–715	*–7.5*
	Boundary changes: 1871–81 loss of 1528 to Llandeilo Fawr (pop. 1871) 1891–1901 loss of 903 to Builth (pop. 1891)						
Llandeilo Fawr	1851–61	–746	*–4.2*	1955	*10.9*	–2701	*–15.0*
	1861–71	–246	*–1.4*	1977	*11.5*	–2223	*–12.9*
	1871–81	1823	*10.7*	2370	*14.0*	–547	*–3.2*
	1881–91	1684	*9.0*	2399	*12.8*	–715	*–3.8*
	1891–1901	3210	*15.7*	2859	*14.0*	351	*1.7*
	1901–1911	9578	*40.4*	4249	*17.9*	5329	*22.5*
	Boundary changes: 1871–81 gain of 1528 from Llandovery (pop. 1871)						
Carmarthen	1851–61	–1467	*–3.8*	3860	*10.1*	–5327	*–14.0*
	1861–71	–1048	*–2.9*	3389	*9.2*	–4437	*–12.1*
	1871–81	–552	*–1.5*	3269	*9.2*	–3821	*–10.7*
	1881–91	–938	*–2.7*	2978	*8.5*	–3916	*–11.2*
	1891–1901	–904	*–2.6*	2021	*5.9*	–2925	*–8.5*
	1901–1911	1034	*3.1*	1748	*5.2*	–714	*–2.1*
	Boundary changes: 1891–1901 gain of 157 from Llanelli (pop. 1891)						
PEMBROKESHIRE							
Narberth	1851–61	–786	*–3.6*	2554	*11.5*	–3340	*–15.1*
	1861–71	–1012	*–4.7*	2375	*11.1*	–3387	*–15.9*
	1871–81	–791	*–3.9*	2299	*11.3*	–3090	*–15.2*
	1881–91	–1351	*–6.9*	1931	*9.9*	–3282	*–16.8*
	1891–1901	–828	*–4.6*	1155	*6.3*	–1983	*–10.9*
	1901–1911	–40	*–0.2*	1207	*7.0*	–1247	*–7.2*
Pembroke	1851–61	6043	*26.3*	3207	*14.0*	2836	*12.4*
	1861–71	58	*0.2*	4269	*14.7*	–4211	*–14.5*
	1871–81	1286	*4.4*	3804	*13.1*	–2518	*–8.7*
	1881–91	936	*3.1*	4360	*14.4*	–3424	*–11.3*
	1891–1901	656	*2.1*	3274	*10.5*	–2618	*–8.4*
	1901–1911	–957	*–3.0*	2895	*9.1*	–3852	*–12.1*
Haverfordwest	1851–61	–2039	*–5.2*	3204	*8.1*	–5243	*–13.3*
	1861–71	–2863	*–7.7*	3365	*9.0*	–6228	*–16.7*
	1871–81	–689	*–2.0*	3095	*9.0*	–3784	*–11.0*
	1881–91	–1261	*–3.7*	3623	*10.7*	–4884	*–14.5*
	1891–1901	593	*1.8*	3200	*9.8*	–2607	*–8.0*
	1901–1911	3447	*10.4*	3820	*11.5*	–373	*–1.1*
CARDIGANSHIRE							
Cardigan	1851–61	–1601	*–7.9*	1075	*5.3*	–2676	*–13.3*
	1861–71	–1000	*–5.4*	1022	*5.5*	–2022	*–10.9*
	1871–81	30	*0.2*	1221	*6.9*	–1191	*–6.8*
	1881–91	–1334	*–7.6*	1074	*6.1*	–2408	*–13.7*
	1891–1901	–1119	*–6.9*	473	*2.9*	–1592	*–9.8*
	1901–1911	–430	*–2.8*	208	*1.4*	–638	*–4.2*

Registration District	Intercensal period	Total population change Number	Percentage	Natural increase (births – deaths) Number	Percentage	Net migration (change – natural increase) Number	Percentage
Newcastle Emlyn	1851–61	–1092	*–5.4*	1801	*8.9*	–2893	*–14.3*
	1861–71	–263	*–1.4*	1879	*9.8*	–2142	*–11.2*
	1871–81	196	*1.0*	1811	*9.6*	–1615	*–8.6*
	1881–91	94	*0.5*	1777	*9.3*	–1683	*–8.9*
	1891–1901	–973	*–5.1*	1142	*6.0*	–2115	*–11.1*
	1901–1911	–330	*–1.8*	617	*3.4*	–947	*–5.2*
Lampeter	1851–61	120	*1.2*	839	*8.5*	–719	*–7.3*
	1861–71	–21	*–0.2*	1075	*10.8*	–1096	*–11.0*
	1871–81	114	*1.1*	1022	*10.2*	–908	*–9.1*
	1881–91	–403	*–4.0*	1090	*10.8*	–1493	*–14.8*
	1891–1901	–427	*–4.4*	440	*4.5*	–867	*–9.0*
	1901–1911	–290	*–3.1*	259	*2.8*	–549	*–5.9*
Aberaeron	1851–61	316	*2.4*	1310	*9.9*	–994	*–7.5*
	1861–71	–163	*–1.2*	1505	*11.1*	–1668	*–12.3*
	1871–81	–834	*–6.2*	1144	*8.6*	–1978	*–14.8*
	1881–91	–948	*–7.6*	989	*7.9*	–1937	*–15.4*
	1891–1901	–860	*–7.4*	492	*4.2*	–1352	*–11.7*
	1901–1911	–473	*–4.4*	1	*0.0*	–474	*–4.4*
Aberystwyth	1851–61	1711	*7.2*	2761	*11.6*	–1050	*–4.4*
	1861–71	1975	*7.8*	3763	*14.8*	–1788	*–7.0*
	1871–81	–1833	*–6.7*	2244	*8.2*	–4077	*–14.9*
	1881–91	–4504	*–17.6*	1231	*4.8*	–5735	*–22.4*
	1891–1901	369	*1.7*	643	*3.0*	–274	*–1.3*
	1901–1911	11	*0.1*	566	*2.6*	–555	*–2.6*
Tregaron	1851–61	333	*3.2*	1314	*12.6*	–981	*–9.4*
	1861–71	–60	*–0.6*	1384	*12.9*	–1444	*–13.4*
	1871–81	–405	*–3.8*	1140	*10.7*	–1545	*–14.5*
	1881–91	–1659	*–16.2*	810	*7.9*	–2469	*–24.0*
	1891–1901	–666	*–7.7*	402	*4.7*	–1068	*–12.4*
	1901–1911	–426	*–5.4*	158	*2.0*	–584	*–7.3*
BRECONSHIRE							
Builth	1851–61	–40	*–0.5*	1006	*12.1*	–1046	*–12.5*
	1861–71	–41	*–0.5*	1122	*13.5*	–1163	*–14.0*
	1871–81	–82	*–1.0*	1038	*12.6*	–1120	*–13.6*
	1881–91	–348	*–4.3*	961	*11.7*	–1309	*–16.0*
	1891–1901	216	*2.5*	797	*9.1*	–581	*–6.6*
	1901–1911	506	*5.6*	814	*9.1*	–308	*–3.4*
	Boundary changes: 1891–1901 gain of 903 from Llandovery (pop. 1891)						
Brecon	1851–61	–895	*–4.9*	1413	*7.8*	–2308	*–12.7*
	1861–71	445	*2.6*	1899	*11.0*	–1454	*–8.4*
	1871–81	–546	*–3.1*	1752	*9.9*	–2298	*–13.0*
	1881–91	–1254	*–7.3*	1417	*8.2*	–2671	*–15.5*
	1891–1901	–291	*–1.8*	1268	*8.0*	–1559	*–9.8*
	1901–1911	–570	*–3.6*	1301	*8.3*	–1871	*–12.0*
Crickhowell	1851–61	760	*3.5*	3277	*15.1*	–2517	*–11.6*
	1861–71	–2310	*–10.3*	2895	*12.9*	–5205	*–23.2*
	1871–81	–1589	*–7.9*	2908	*14.4*	–4497	*–22.3*
	1881–91	957	*5.2*	2315	*12.5*	–1358	*–7.3*
	1891–1901	130	*0.7*	2658	*13.4*	–2528	*–12.8*
	1901–1911	2368	*11.9*	3439	*17.2*	–1071	*–5.4*
	Boundary changes: 1891–1901 gain of 270 from Bedwellte (Mon) (pop. 1891)						
Hay	1851–61	–143	*–1.3*	604	*5.5*	–747	*–6.8*
	1861–71	–22	*–0.2*	1141	*10.5*	–1163	*–10.7*
	1871–81	–575	*–5.3*	985	*9.1*	–1560	*–14.4*
	1881–91	–623	*–6.1*	998	*9.8*	–1621	*–15.9*
	1891–1901	–198	*–2.1*	762	*7.9*	–960	*–10.0*
	1901–1911	115	*1.2*	390	*4.1*	–275	*–2.9*

Registration District	Intercensal period	Total population change Number	Percentage	Natural increase (births – deaths) Number	Percentage	Net migration (change – natural increase) Number	Percentage
Presteigne	1851–61	522	*3.4*	1659	*11.0*	–1137	*–7.5*
	1861–71	128	*3.4*	552	*14.8*	–424	*–11.3*

Boundary changes: 1861–71 loss of 11930 to Kington (Her) (pop. 1861)
1871–81 district abolished; loss of 2607 to Knighton, 1262 to Kington (Her) (pop. 1871)

Registration District	Intercensal period	Total population change Number	Percentage	Natural increase (births – deaths) Number	Percentage	Net migration (change – natural increase) Number	Percentage
Knighton	1851–61	899	*9.5*	1605	*16.9*	–706	*–7.4*
	1861–71	–56	*–0.5*	1623	*15.6*	–1679	*–16.2*
	1871–81	–1148	*–8.9*	1591	*12.3*	–2739	*–21.2*
	1881–91	–1006	*–8.6*	1399	*12.0*	–2405	*–20.5*
	1891–1901	197	*1.8*	1277	*11.9*	–1080	*–10.1*
	1901–1911	–1048	*–9.6*	1035	*9.5*	–2083	*–19.1*

Boundary changes: 1871–81 gain of 2607 from Presteigne (pop. 1871); 1881–91 loss of 78 to Rhayader (pop. 1881)

Registration District	Intercensal period	Total population change Number	Percentage	Natural increase (births – deaths) Number	Percentage	Net migration (change – natural increase) Number	Percentage
Rhayader	1851–61	20	*0.3*	1066	*15.7*	–1046	*–15.4*
	1861–71	8	*0.1*	1061	*15.6*	–1053	*–15.4*
	1871–81	–83	*–1.2*	888	*13.0*	–971	*–14.2*
	1881–91	–398	*–5.8*	620	*9.1*	–1018	*–14.9*
	1891–1901	2925	*45.6*	808	*12.6*	2117	*33.0*
	1901–1911	–1688	*–18.1*	916	*9.8*	–2604	*–27.9*

Boundary changes: 1881–91 gain of 78 from Knighton (pop. 1891)

MONTGOMERYSHIRE

Registration District	Intercensal period	Total population change Number	Percentage	Natural increase (births – deaths) Number	Percentage	Net migration (change – natural increase) Number	Percentage
Machynlleth	1851–61	279	*2.3*	999	*8.2*	–720	*–5.9*
	1861–71	922	*7.4*	1360	*11.0*	–438	*–3.5*
	1871–81	–800	*–6.0*	1364	*10.2*	–2164	*–16.2*
	1881–91	–1732	*–13.8*	670	*5.3*	–2402	*–19.1*
	1891–1901	93	*0.8*	564	*5.2*	–471	*–4.3*
	1901–1911	–188	*–1.7*	407	*3.7*	–595	*–5.4*

Boundary changes: 1881–91 gain of 41 from Dolgellau (pop. 1881); 1891–1901 gain of 121 from Dolgellau (pop. 1891)

Registration District	Intercensal period	Total population change Number	Percentage	Natural increase (births – deaths) Number	Percentage	Net migration (change – natural increase) Number	Percentage
Newtown	1851–61	–1375	*–5.5*	2408	*9.6*	–3783	*–15.1*
	1861–71	822	*3.5*	2868	*12.1*	–2046	*–8.6*
	1871–81	885	*3.6*	3555	*14.5*	–2670	*–10.9*
	1881–91	–3717	*–14.6*	2490	*9.8*	–6207	*–24.4*
	1891–1901	–604	*–2.8*	2068	*9.5*	–2672	*–12.3*
	1901–1911	–824	*–3.9*	1904	*9.0*	–2728	*–12.9*
Montgomery/ Forden	1851–61	1113	*6.2*	2091	*11.6*	–978	*–5.4*
	1861–71	–239	*–1.3*	1990	*10.4*	–2229	*–11.7*
	1871–81	–577	*–3.1*	2156	*11.4*	–2733	*–14.5*
	1881–91	–1963	*–10.7*	1801	*9.9*	–3764	*–20.6*
	1891–1901	–1469	*–9.0*	1244	*7.6*	–2713	*–16.6*
	1901–1911	–473	*–3.2*	1147	*7.7*	–1620	*–10.9*

The name of this district was changed to Forden in 1871
Boundary changes: 1851–61 loss of 2397 to Llanfyllin (pop. 1851); 1881–91 loss of 5 to Atcham (Salop) (pop. 1881)

Registration District	Intercensal period	Total population change Number	Percentage	Natural increase (births – deaths) Number	Percentage	Net migration (change – natural increase) Number	Percentage
Llanfyllin	1851–61	–236	*–1.1*	1618	*7.4*	–1854	*–8.5*
	1861–71	–28	*–0.1*	1899	*8.8*	–1927	*–8.9*
	1871–81	–1712	*–7.9*	1886	*8.7*	–3598	*–16.6*
	1881–91	–1488	*–7.5*	1925	*9.7*	–3413	*–17.1*
	1891–1901	–1445	*–7.8*	1387	*7.5*	–2832	*–15.4*
	1901–1911	–308	*–1.8*	1350	*7.9*	–1658	*–9.8*

Boundary changes: 1851–61 gain of 2397 from Montgomery (pop. 1851); 1881–91 loss of 35 to Oswestry (Salop) (pop. 1881)

FLINTSHIRE

Registration District	Intercensal period	Total population change Number	Percentage	Natural increase (births – deaths) Number	Percentage	Net migration (change – natural increase) Number	Percentage
Holywell	1851–61	–1106	*–2.7*	3275	*8.0*	–4381	*–10.7*
	1861–71	3576	*9.0*	4555	*11.4*	–979	*–2.5*
	1871–81	2257	*5.2*	5466	*12.6*	–3209	*–7.4*
	1881–91	–3209	*–7.0*	4592	*10.0*	–7801	*–17.0*
	1891–1901	–304	*–0.7*	4064	*9.5*	–4368	*–10.3*
	1901–1911	3892	*10.0*	4308	*11.1*	–416	*–1.1*

Boundary changes: 1901–11 loss of 3326 to new district of Hawarden (previously transferred to Chester District, July 1901)

Registration District	Intercensal period	Total population change Number	Percentage	Natural increase (births – deaths) Number	Percentage	Net migration (change – natural increase) Number	Percentage
Hawarden	1901–1911	4375	*20.3*	3305	*15.3*	1070	*5.0*

Boundary changes: 1901–11 creation of new district; gain of 21601 from Chester (Ches) (3326 of which had been transferred from Holywell in July 1901)

Registration District	Intercensal period	Total population change Number	Percentage	Natural increase (births – deaths) Number	Percentage	Net migration (change – natural increase) Number	Percentage
DENBIGHSHIRE							
Wrexham	1851–61	7897	*19.7*	5236	*13.1*	2661	*6.6*
	1861–71	5765	*13.4*	7749	*18.0*	–1984	*–4.6*
	1871–81	6321	*12.9*	8228	*16.8*	–1907	*–3.9*
	1881–91	6595	*11.9*	7717	*14.0*	–1122	*–2.0*
	1891–1901	9937	*16.5*	10397	*17.3*	–460	*–0.8*
	1901–1911	8900	*12.7*	11775	*16.8*	–2875	*–4.1*

Boundary changes: 1851–61 loss of 2217 to Whitchurch (Salop) (pop. 1851)
1861–71 loss of 4903 to Chester (Ches) (pop. 1861)
1881–91 gain of 42 from Chester (Ches) (pop. 1881)
1891–1901 loss of 316 to Chester (Ches), loss of 306 to Whitchurch (Salop), loss of 973 to Ellesmere (Salop) – overall loss of 1595 (pop. 1891)

Registration District	Intercensal period	Total population change Number	Percentage	Natural increase (births – deaths) Number	Percentage	Net migration (change – natural increase) Number	Percentage
Ruthin	1851–61	–770	*–4.6*	1069	*6.3*	–1839	*–10.9*
	1861–71	–684	*–4.3*	1253	*7.8*	–1937	*–12.0*
	1871–81	–1184	*–7.7*	1050	*6.8*	–2234	*–14.5*
	1881–91	–1277	*–9.0*	999	*7.0*	–2276	*–16.0*
	1891–1901	–850	*–6.6*	613	*4.7*	–1463	*–11.3*
	1901–1911	116	*1.0*	455	*3.8*	–339	*–2.8*
St Asaph	1851–61	2230	*8.8*	1820	*7.2*	410	*1.6*
	1861–71	360	*1.3*	1640	*6.0*	–1280	*–4.7*
	1871–81	1580	*5.7*	1436	*5.2*	144	*0.5*
	1881–91	–504	*–1.7*	1336	*4.5*	–1840	*–6.2*
	1891–1901	2092	*7.2*	821	*2.8*	1271	*4.4*
	1901–1911	2180	*7.0*	820	*2.6*	1360	*4.4*
Llanrwst	1851–61	291	*2.3*	1171	*9.4*	–880	*–7.1*
	1861–71	280	*2.2*	1203	*9.4*	–923	*–7.2*
	1871–81	1059	*8.1*	1179	*9.0*	–120	*–0.9*
	1881–91	–1098	*–7.8*	1120	*7.9*	–2218	*–15.7*
	1891–1901	159	*1.2*	751	*5.8*	–592	*–4.5*
	1901–1911	–844	*–6.4*	656	*5.0*	–1500	*–11.4*
Corwen	1851–61	689	*4.5*	1135	*7.4*	–446	*–2.9*
	1861–71	344	*2.1*	1707	*10.6*	–1363	*–8.5*
	1871–81	382	*2.3*	2062	*12.5*	–1680	*–10.2*
	1881–91	–575	*–3.4*	1563	*9.3*	–2138	*–12.7*
	1891–1901	55	*0.3*	1223	*7.5*	–1168	*–7.2*
	1901–1911	115	*0.7*	1355	*8.3*	–1240	*–7.6*
Bala	1851–61	–384	*–5.7*	526	*7.8*	–910	*–13.5*
	1861–71	252	*4.0*	589	*9.3*	–337	*–5.3*
	1871–81	136	*2.1*	554	*8.4*	–418	*–6.3*
	1881–91	–625	*–9.3*	497	*7.4*	–1122	*–16.6*
	1891–1901	–383	*–6.3*	315	*5.2*	–698	*–11.4*
	1901–1911	–123	*–2.1*	174	*3.0*	–297	*–5.2*
Dolgellau	1851–61	–489	*–3.8*	763	*5.9*	–1252	*–9.7*
	1861–71	1829	*14.7*	1166	*9.3*	663	*5.3*
	1871–81	869	*6.1*	1653	*11.6*	–784	*–5.5*
	1881–91	–647	*–4.3*	1213	*8.0*	–1860	*–12.3*
	1891–1901	–122	*–0.8*	726	*5.1*	–848	*–5.9*
	1901–1911	–1250	*–8.8*	557	*3.9*	–1807	*–12.7*

Boundary changes: 1881–91 loss of 41 to Machynlleth (pop. 1881)
1891–1901 loss of 121 to Machynlleth (pop. 1891)

Registration District	Intercensal period	Total population change Number	Percentage	Natural increase (births – deaths) Number	Percentage	Net migration (change – natural increase) Number	Percentage
Ffestiniog	1851–61	2107	*13.0*	2279	*14.1*	–172	*–1.1*
	1861–71	5852	*32.0*	3072	*16.8*	2780	*15.2*
	1871–81	5384	*22.3*	4050	*16.8*	1334	*5.5*
	1881–91	–1664	*–5.6*	3819	*12.9*	–5483	*–18.6*
	1891–1901	94	*0.3*	2607	*9.4*	–2513	*–9.0*
	1901–1911	–2710	*–9.7*	2311	*8.3*	–5021	*–18.0*

Registration District	Intercensal period	Total population change Number	Percentage	Natural increase (births – deaths) Number	Percentage	Net migration (change – natural increase) Number	Percentage
CAERNARFONSHIRE							
Pwllheli	1851–61	–880	*–4.0*	1759	*8.1*	–2639	*–12.1*
	1861–71	66	*0.3*	1768	*8.5*	–1702	*–8.1*
	1871–81	1937	*9.2*	2017	*9.6*	–80	*–0.4*
	1881–91	–638	*–2.8*	1870	*8.2*	–2508	*–10.9*
	1891–1901	–376	*–1.7*	934	*4.2*	–1310	*–5.9*
	1901–1911	109	*0.5*	1030	*4.7*	–921	*–4.2*
Caernarfon	1851–61	1979	*6.5*	2968	*9.7*	–989	*–3.2*
	1861–71	6712	*20.7*	3856	*11.9*	2856	*8.8*
	1871–81	4860	*12.4*	4756	*12.2*	104	*0.3*
	1881–91	–3285	*–7.5*	3609	*8.2*	–6894	*–15.7*
	1891–1901	1941	*4.8*	3062	*7.5*	–1121	*–2.8*
	1901–1911	–2311	*–5.4*	3061	*7.2*	–5372	*–12.6*
Bangor	1851–61	1988	*5.8*	3676	*10.7*	–1688	*–4.9*
	1861–71	258	*0.7*	3052	*8.4*	–2794	*–7.7*
	1871–81	1945	*5.3*	2949	*8.1*	–1004	*–2.7*
	1881–91	–499	*–1.3*	2588	*6.7*	–3087	*–8.0*
	1891–1901	623	*1.6*	2387	*6.3*	–1764	*–4.6*
	1901–1911	–490	*–1.3*	2484	*6.4*	–2974	*–7.7*
	Boundary changes: 1851–61	gain of 3511 from Anglesey (pop. 1851)					
	1881–91	gain of 19 from Anglesey (pop. 1881)					
Conwy	1851–61	2266	*19.5*	1417	*12.2*	849	*7.3*
	1861–71	804	*5.8*	1792	*12.9*	–988	*–7.1*
	1871–81	3661	*24.9*	1466	*10.0*	2195	*14.9*
	1881–91	6207	*33.8*	2177	*11.9*	4030	*21.9*
	1891–1901	9463	*38.5*	2456	*10.0*	7007	*28.5*
	1901–1911	7223	*21.2*	2849	*8.4*	4374	*12.9*
ANGLESEY							
Anglesey	1851–61	–1575	*–4.0*	3384	*8.5*	–4959	*–12.5*
	1861–71	–3030	*–7.9*	1963	*5.1*	–4993	*–13.1*
	1871–81	14	*0.0*	2432	*6.9*	–2418	*–6.9*
	1881–91	–501	*–3.3*	801	*5.3*	–1302	*–8.6*
	1891–1901	–424	*–2.9*	602	*4.1*	–1026	*–7.0*
	1901–1911	–432	*–3.0*	727	*5.1*	–1159	*–8.1*
	Boundary changes: 1851–61	loss of 3511 to Bangor (pop. 1851)					
	1871–81	loss of 8595 to Holyhead (pop. 1871)					
	1881–91	loss of 19 to Bangor (pop. 1881)					
Holyhead	1881–91	–402	*–2.0*	1591	*8.0*	–1993	*–10.0*
	1891–1901	1013	*5.2*	1525	*7.8*	–512	*–2.6*
	1901–1911	983	*4.8*	1712	*8.3*	–729	*–3.5*
	Boundary changes:	district created 1881 from part of Anglesey					

Sources: *Census of Population for England and Wales*: 1851–61, *Population Tables, Vol. I part II, Division XI Monmouthshire and Wales* (HMSO, 1862), table E; 1871, *Population Tables, Vol. II, Division XI Monmouthshire and Wales* (HMSO, 1872), table 9; 1881, *Vol. II, Division XI Monmouthshire and Wales* (HMSO, 1883), table 10; 1891, *Area, Housing and Population, Vol. II, Division XI Monmouthshire and Wales* (HMSO, 1893), Table 12; 1901, County Volumes, *Anglesey-Radnor* (HMSO, 1902, 1903), Table 22; 1911, County Volumes: *Anglesey, Carnarvon, Denbigh and Flint; Cardigan, Merioneth and Montgomery; Glamorgan; Brecknock, Carmarthen, Pembroke and Radnor; Monmouth* (HMSO, 1914), Table 15.

Where there has been a boundary change between censuses, the population increase or decrease has been calculated from the figures relating to the population of the county as constituted at the later date. However, the Registrar-General's annual figures of births and deaths (from which the figures for natural increase have been calculated) relate to the original area until the actual date of any boundary change. In a few cases this could be a significant source of error. All boundary changes have been noted.

The figures for net migration are simply the total intercensal change in population minus the natural increase.

The percentages are of the relevant total population at the beginning of each ten-year period.

Population 4.3 Population change. Migration. Wales and Counties. 1851, 1881, 1911; a) Birthplace of those enumerated in Wales b) Place of enumeration in England and Wales of those born in Wales

a) Birthplace of those enumerated in **Wales**

Birthplace	**1851** under 20 yrs	20 yrs and over	All ages Number	*as % total enumerated*
Wales[1]	**501037**	**545236**	**1046273**	***88.0***
Monmouthshire	61679	46732	108411	*9.1*
Glamorgan	90059	78609	168668	*14.2*
Carmarthenshire	56514	73271	129785	*10.9*
Pembrokeshire	45117	54056	99173	*8.3*
Cardiganshire	33766	43380	77146	*6.5*
Breconshire	25300	29876	55176	*4.6*
Radnorshire	12170	15296	27466	*2.3*
Montgomeryshire	29830	34846	64676	*5.4*
Flintshire	25486	25103	50589	*4.3*
Denbighshire	38552	45288	83840	*7.1*
Merioneth	17701	23281	40982	*3.4*
Caernarfonshire	39813	43651	83464	*7.0*
Anglesey	25050	31847	56897	*4.8*
England[1]	**39326**	**77553**	**116879**	***9.8***
London	1501	3433	4934	*0.4*
South East	818	2626	3444	*0.3*
South Midland	374	1408	1782	*0.1*
East	205	1153	1358	*0.1*
South West	6521	19279	25800	*2.2*
West Midland	24321	40668	64989	*5.5*
North Midland	236	939	1175	*0.1*
North West	4663	5950	10613	*0.9*
Yorkshire	276	917	1193	*0.1*
North	314	1014	1328	*0.1*
Ireland	**5540**	**15198**	**20738**	***1.7***
Scotland	**449**	**1759**	**2208**	***0.2***
Other	**882**	**1934**	**2816**	***0.3***
Total	**547234**	**641680**	**1188914**	***100.0***

Birthplace	**1881** Males	Females	Total	*as % total enumerated*	**1911** Males	Females	Total	*as % total enumerated*
Wales	**671425**	**690288**	**1361713**	***86.6***	**971621**	**982087**	**1953708**	***80.7***
Monmouthshire	81825	82361	164186	*10.4*	149625	149146	298771	*12.3*
Glamorgan	172720	177937	350657	*22.3*	385574	391785	777359	*32.1*
Carmarthenshire	69512	74199	143711	*9.1*	79483	83248	162731	*6.7*
Pembrokeshire	47736	52894	100630	*6.4*	49191	51298	100489	*4.2*
Cardiganshire	38070	43396	81466	*5.2*	34670	38383	73053	*3.0*
Breconshire	30204	29952	60156	*3.8*	31093	30317	61410	*2.5*
Radnorshire	12705	11766	24471	*1.6*	12176	11125	23301	*1.0*
Montgomeryshire	32452	31145	63597	*4.0*	29245	27680	56925	*2.4*
Flintshire	33814	32018	65832	*4.2*	35963	34184	70147	*2.9*
Denbighshire	49810	48154	97964	*6.2*	59932	56933	116865	*4.8*
Merioneth	23510	23664	47174	*3.0*	23382	24012	47394	*2.0*
Caernarfonshire	50668	53407	104075	*6.6*	55082	56978	112060	*4.6*
Anglesey	26321	27482	53803	*3.4*	25204	26077	51281	*2.1*
England[1]	**92253**	**79852**	**172105**	***10.9***	**213855**	**174383**	**388238**	***16.0***
London	4656	4727	9383	*0.6*	15584	11834	27418	*1.1*
South East	3927	3598	7525	*0.5*	10908	8725	19633	*0.8*
South Midland	2380	1965	4345	*0.3*	7022	5469	12491	*0.5*
East	1576	1271	2847	*0.2*	4376	3414	7790	*0.3*
South West	32844	25358	58202	*3.7*	57099	41814	98913	*4.1*
West Midland	29854	27141	56995	*3.6*	78724	64510	143234	*5.9*
North Midland	1807	1537	3344	*0.2*	4479	4086	8565	*0.4*
North West	10541	10527	21068	*1.3*	23280	23825	47105	*1.9*
Yorkshire	1972	1685	3657	*0.2*	6848	5926	12774	*0.5*
North	2031	1639	3670	*0.2*	5001	4436	9437	*0.4*
Ireland	**13095**	**9777**	**22872**	***1.5***	**13338**	**7526**	**20864**	***0.9***
Scotland	**3278**	**2162**	**5440**	***0.3***	**5678**	**3904**	**9582**	***0.4***
Other	**6271**	**3379**	**9650**	***0.6***	**27247**	**21282**	**48529**	***2.0***
Total	**786322**	**785458**	**1571780**	***100.0***	**1231739**	**1189182**	**2420921**	***100.0***

b) Place of enumeration of those born in **Wales**

Place of enumeration	1851 Total	1881 Males	1881 Females	1881 Total	1911 Males	1911 Females	1911 Total
Wales	**1046273**[2]	**671425**	**690288**	**1361713**	**971621**	**982087**	**1953708**
% in Wales	*89.7*	*88.0*	*85.8*	*86.8*	*88.9*	*86.4*	*87.6*
Monmouthshire	122666	82454	82325	164779	148779	145598	294377
Glamorgan	208525	211429	211269	422698	443687	438159	881846
Carmarthenshire	91459	57318	63211	120529	71559	75535	147094
Pembrokeshire	80104	38835	45085	83920	36755	41336	78091
Cardiganshire	95724	30523	37581	68104	24290	30650	54940
Breconshire	50951	25295	25964	51259	24972	24724	49696
Radnorshire	19788	10214	9835	20049	8796	8786	17582
Montgomeryshire	68686	29652	29331	58983	22747	23173	45920
Flintshire	38197	33748	33118	66866	35224	34445	69669
Denbighshire	86814	49218	47913	97131	59547	57279	116826
Merioneth	50112	24920	24542	49462	20101	21613	41714
Caernarfonshire	91341	54797	56364	111161	53000	57019	110019
Anglesey	41596	23022	24750	47772	22164	23770	45934
England	**120202**	**91861**	**114640**	**206501**	**121150**	**154439**	**275589**
% in England	*10.3*	*12.0*	*14.2*	*13.2*	*11.1*	*13.6*	*12.4*
London	17575	11829	16216	28045	13393	18262	31655
South East	3771	4835	5696	10531	9980	12433	22413
South Midland	1651	2059	2782	4841	6149	8261	14410
East	772	1219	1303	2522	3330	3791	7121
South West	5303	6151	6823	12974	9027	11144	20171
West Midland	38505	24194	28935	53129	27573	33826	61399
North Midland	1011	1729	1948	3677	3719	3952	7671
North West	48454	29991	41777	71768	36093	51084	87177
Yorkshire	1381	4821	5123	9944	7079	7485	14564
North	1779	5033	4037	9070	4807	4201	9008
Total	**1166475**	**763286**	**804928**	**1568214**	**1092771**	**1136526**	**2229297**

MONMOUTHSHIRE

a) Birthplace of those enumerated in **Monmouthshire**

Birthplace	1851[3] Total	%	1881 Males	Females	Total	%	1911 Males	Females	Total	%
Wales[1]	**122666**	*69.3*	**82454**	**82325**	**164779**	*78.0*	**148779**	**145598**	**294377**	*74.4*
Monmouthshire	**96800**	*54.6*	**69327**	**69976**	**139303**	*65.9*	**126794**	**125175**	**251969**	*63.7*
Glamorgan	8212		4772	4810	9582		12096	12068	24164	
Carmarthenshire	3419		1127	1003	2130		1170	954	2124	
Pembrokeshire	2041		895	569	1464		1078	895	1973	
Cardiganshire	2494		979	702	1681		823	634	1457	
Breconshire	6844		3800	3774	7574		4123	4047	8170	
Radnorshire	1212		784	565	1349		930	673	1603	
Montgomeryshire	890		282	238	520		448	277	725	
Flintshire	156		86	50	136		339	232	571	
Denbighshire	236		66	52	118		155	113	268	
Merioneth	215		43	28	71		267	180	447	
Caernarfonshire	86		80	57	137		354	217	571	
Anglesey	61		31	25	56		107	59	166	
England[1]	**47609**	*26.9*	**21444**	**17681**	**39125**	*18.5*	**51083**	**37522**	**88605**	*22.4*
London	1157		711	728	1439		2637	1947	4584	
South East	800		675	621	1296		2211	1636	3847	
South Midland	398		418	365	783		1471	1035	2506	
East	338		223	203	426		832	628	1460	
South West	11116		8087	5981	14068		12764	8766	21530	
West Midland	32599		9597	8480	18077		26127	19596	45723	
North Midland	292		283	251	534		808	655	1463	
North West	389		507	435	942		1862	1378	3240	
Yorkshire	224		315	233	548		1275	1039	2314	
North	296		373	242	615		955	766	1721	
Ireland	5868		2930	2288	5218		1962	1070	3032	
Scotland	318		431	246	677		946	596	1542	
Other	649		1003	465	1468		4659	3504	8163	
Total	**177130**	*100.0*	**108262**	**103005**	**211267**	*100.0*	**207429**	**188290**	**395719**	*100.0*

b) Place of enumeration of those born in **Monmouthshire**

Birthplace	1851 Total	%	1881 Males	Females	Total	%	1911 Males	Females	Total	%
Wales	**108411**	*91.1*	**81825**	**82361**	**164186**	*84.4*	**149625**	**149146**	**298771**	*88.4*
Monmouthshire	**96800**	*81.3*	**69327**	**69976**	**139303**	*71.6*	**126794**	**125175**	**251969**	*74.6*
Glamorgan	7696		10323	10137	20460		19967	21002	40969	
Carmarthenshire	180		335	325	660		615	506	1121	
Pembrokeshire	92		119	138	257		214	205	419	
Cardiganshire	113		61	73	134		92	112	204	
Breconshire	3283		1365	1442	2807		1462	1612	3074	
Radnorshire	60		47	65	112		84	108	192	
Montgomeryshire	41		28	35	63		31	36	67	
Flintshire	21		58	53	111		100	93	193	
Denbighshire	64		56	37	93		94	93	187	
Merioneth	11		40	26	66		32	37	69	
Caernarfonshire	33		47	43	90		75	66	141	
Anglesey	7		19	11	30		65	101	166	
England	**10606**	*8.9*	13434	16825	**30259**	*15.6*	16871	22234	**39105**	*11.6*
London	1964		1736	2762	4498		1750	2812	4562	
South East	477		853	990	1843		1697	2192	3889	
South Midland	207		354	535	889		988	1458	2446	
East	88		216	230	446		508	658	1166	
South West	1459		1685	2067	3752		1852	2617	4469	
West Midland	5514		5206	6750	11956		5678	7688	13366	
North Midland	98		325	317	642		589	580	1169	
North West	454		1241	1533	2774		1656	2150	3806	
Yorkshire	160		983	913	1896		1386	1332	2718	
North	185		835	728	1563		767	747	1514	
Total	**119017**	*100.0*	**95259**	**99186**	**194445**	*100.0*	**166496**	**171380**	**337876**	*100.0*

GLAMORGAN

a) Birthplace of those enumerated in **Glamorgan**

Birthplace	1851[3] Total	%	1881 Males	1881 Females	1881 Total	%	1911 Males	1911 Females	1911 Total	%
Wales[1]	**208726**	*86.9*	**211429**	**210269**	**421698**	*82.5*	**443687**	**438159**	**881846**	*78.7*
Monmouthshire	7696		10323	10137	20460		19967	21002	40969	
Glamorgan	**155507**	*64.8*	**162900**	**167739**	**330639**	*64.6*	**362196**	**367773**	**729969**	*65.1*
Carmarthenshire	21151		14304	13297	27601		15300	14452	29752	
Pembrokeshire	7297		8275	7023	15298		11349	9502	20851	
Cardiganshire	3610		5124	3642	8766		8997	7111	16108	
Breconshire	10278		5804	5235	11039		7600	6879	14479	
Radnorshire	701		973	643	1616		2177	1569	3746	
Montgomeryshire	1022		18522	986	19508		4840	3072	7912	
Flintshire	265		232	155	387		1509	886	2395	
Denbighshire	210		265	166	431		613	390	1003	
Merioneth	232		293	161	454		3027	1912	4939	
Caernarfonshire	215		293	198	491		4203	2371	6574	
Anglesey	341		203	130	333		1247	632	1879	
England[1]	**19777**	*8.3*	39354	31357	**70711**	*13.8*	110392	83649	**194041**	*17.3*
London	1168		1819	1775	3594		8368	6301	14669	
South East	974		1627	1346	2973		5907	4617	10524	
South Midland	512		884	673	1557		3689	2692	6381	
East	341		581	451	1032		2067	1586	3653	
South West	10482		21384	16519	37903		40479	29832	70311	
West Midland	4812		9237	7644	16881		35610	27304	62914	
North Midland	225		505	412	917		2022	1647	3669	
North West	529		1351	1043	2394		5825	4476	10301	
Yorkshire	256		719	539	1258		3247	2543	5790	
North	478		949	772	1721		2889	2455	5344	
Ireland	9737		6832	5126	11958		8596	4279	12875	
Scotland	785		1309	710	2019		3064	1834	4898	
Other	1170		3655	1392	5047		16441	10809	27250	
Total	**240095**	*100.0*	**262579**	**248854**	**511433**	*100.0*	**582180**	**538730**	**1120910**	*100.0*

b) Place of enumeration of those born in **Glamorgan**

Birthplace	1851 Total	%	1881 Males	1881 Females	1881 Total	%	1911 Males	1911 Females	1911 Total	%
Wales	**168668**	*96.3*	**172720**	**177937**	**350657**	*93.5*	**385574**	**391785**	**777359**	*93.2*
Monmouthshire	8212		4772	4810	9582		12096	12068	24164	
Glamorgan	**155507**	*88.8*	**162900**	**167739**	**330639**	*88.1*	**362196**	**367773**	**729969**	*87.5*
Carmarthenshire	3129		2366	2486	4852		5551	5624	11175	
Pembrokeshire	254		597	662	1259		1248	1470	2718	
Cardiganshire	205		205	227	432		615	835	1450	
Breconshire	1073		1335	1510	2845		2578	2523	5101	
Radnorshire	37		52	56	108		176	252	428	
Montgomeryshire	89		80	94	174		193	231	424	
Flintshire	24		96	112	208		274	256	530	
Denbighshire	60		81	67	148		224	213	437	
Merioneth	26		85	64	149		138	163	301	
Caernarfonshire	28		118	88	206		216	308	524	
Anglesey	24		33	22	55		69	69	138	
England	**6452**	*3.7*	11349	13147	24496	*6.5*	26176	30920	57096	*6.8*
London	1578		1869	2427	4296		3565	4599	8164	
South East	457		933	969	1902		3095	3591	6686	
South Midland	188		367	439	806		1833	2245	4078	
East	97		275	267	542		1001	1134	2135	
South West	1174		1910	2099	4009		4040	4853	8893	
West Midland	2017		2472	3286	5758		5695	7080	12775	
North Midland	97		349	349	698		931	968	1899	
North West	544		1299	1640	2939		2916	3378	6294	
Yorkshire	113		856	805	1661		1844	1877	3721	
North	187		1019	866	1885		1256	1195	2451	
Total	**175120**	*100.0*	**184069**	**191084**	**375153**	*100.0*	**411750**	**422705**	**834455**	*100.0*

CARMARTHENSHIRE

a) Birthplace of those enumerated in **Carmarthenshire**

Birthplace	1851[3] Total	%	1881 Males	Females	Total	%	1911 Males	Females	Total	%
Wales[1]	**91462**	*96.6*	**57318**	**63211**	**120529**	*96.5*	**71559**	**75535**	**147094**	*91.7*
Monmouthshire	180		335	325	660		615	506	1121	
Glamorgan	3129		2366	2486	4852		5551	5624	11175	
Carmarthenshire	**83506**	*88.2*	**50651**	**55887**	**106538**	*85.3*	**59808**	**64329**	**124137**	*77.4*
Pembrokeshire	1974		1828	2041	3869		2360	2133	4493	
Cardiganshire	1337		1517	1871	3388		1878	1992	3870	
Breconshire	1127		334	363	697		481	433	914	
Radnorshire	36		29	42	71		90	65	155	
Montgomeryshire	51		52	31	83		155	93	248	
Flintshire	18		24	14	38		160	79	239	
Denbighshire	29		42	30	72		80	56	136	
Merioneth	24		24	16	40		101	67	168	
Caernarfonshire	32		33	30	63		217	121	338	
Anglesey	16		16	12	28		40	27	67	
England[1]	**2159**	*2.3*	**1939**	**1556**	**3495**	*2.8*	**6803**	**3618**	**10421**	*6.5*
London	299		193	195	388		1255	469	1724	
South East	184		162	155	317		525	311	836	
South Midland	113		106	80	186		319	159	478	
East	113		67	43	110		195	115	310	
South West	588		563	419	982		969	583	1552	
West Midland	549		495	424	919		2031	1199	3230	
North Midland	52		62	50	112		222	128	350	
North West	106		161	106	267		793	402	1195	
Yorkshire	78		61	41	102		317	147	464	
North	77		62	37	99		161	99	260	
Ireland	514		196	166	362		507	128	635	
Scotland	97		148	91	239		212	125	337	
Other	48		108	131	239		964	955	1919	
Total	**94672**	*100.0*	**59709**	**65155**	**124864**	*100.0*	**80045**	**80361**	**160406**	*100.0*

b) Place of enumeration of those born in **Carmarthenshire**

Birthplace	1851 Total	%	1881 Males	Females	Total	%	1911 Males	Females	Total	%
Wales	**129785**	*97.8*	**69512**	**74199**	**143711**	*96.3*	**79483**	**83248**	**162731**	*94.6*
Monmouthshire	3419		1127	1003	2130		1170	954	2124	
Glamorgan	21151		14304	13297	27601		15300	14452	29752	
Carmarthenshire	**83506**	*62.9*	**50651**	**55887**	**106538**	*71.4*	**59808**	**64329**	**124137**	*72.2*
Pembrokeshire	6856		1303	1597	2900		1077	1343	2420	
Cardiganshire	12296		761	893	1654		821	930	1751	
Breconshire	1979		1049	1255	2304		858	842	1700	
Radnorshire	52		50	48	98		64	64	128	
Montgomeryshire	62		35	41	76		52	40	92	
Flintshire	19		46	31	77		105	65	170	
Denbighshire	35		58	52	110		87	85	172	
Merioneth	54		61	41	102		48	57	105	
Caernarfonshire	35		46	39	85		67	68	135	
Anglesey	21		21	15	36		26	19	45	
England	**2897**	*2.2*	**2759**	**2765**	**5524**	*3.7*	**4534**	**4761**	**9295**	*5.4*
London	959		818	784	1602		1057	1064	2121	
South East	190		243	253	496		539	623	1162	
South Midland	96		133	131	264		490	547	1037	
East	45		59	59	118		205	203	408	
South West	281		268	253	521		383	461	844	
West Midland	833		549	673	1222		867	930	1797	
North Midland	50		71	78	149		178	148	326	
North West	334		358	329	687		460	494	954	
Yorkshire	29		135	106	241		224	202	426	
North	80		125	99	224		131	89	220	
Total	**132682**	*100.0*	**72271**	**76964**	**149235**	*100.0*	**84017**	**88009**	**172026**	*100.0*

PEMBROKESHIRE

a) Birthplace of those enumerated in **Pembrokeshire**

Birthplace	1851[3] Total	%	1881 Males	Females	Total	%	1911 Males	Females	Total	%
Wales[1]	**80130**	*94.8*	**38835**	**45085**	**83920**	*91.4*	**36755**	**41336**	**78091**	*86.8*
Monmouthshire	92		119	138	257		214	205	419	
Glamorgan	254		597	662	1259		1248	1470	2718	
Carmarthenshire	6856		1303	1597	2900		1077	1343	2420	
Pembrokeshire	**72304**	*85.6*	**35833**	**41841**	**77674**	*84.6*	**33436**	**37520**	**70956**	*78.9*
Cardiganshire	362		590	596	1186		451	488	939	
Breconshire	41		55	53	108		64	96	160	
Radnorshire	17		14	15	29		36	30	66	
Montgomeryshire	29		37	26	63		43	34	77	
Flintshire	15		35	14	49		29	30	59	
Denbighshire	11		25	14	39		17	24	41	
Merioneth	18		24	6	30		24	18	42	
Caernarfonshire	83		83	22	105		59	26	85	
Anglesey	22		49	13	62		36	30	66	
England[1]	**3240**	*3.9*	**3463**	**2606**	**6069**	*6.6*	**5212**	**3798**	**9010**	*10.0*
London	436		568	443	1011		897	538	1435	
South East	514		604	457	1061		714	559	1273	
South Midland	136		191	123	314		245	189	434	
East	144		200	137	337		534	283	817	
South West	1110		868	697	1565		1080	848	1928	
West Midland	516		451	407	858		820	631	1451	
North Midland	79		137	57	194		171	119	290	
North West	141		236	173	409		362	242	604	
Yorkshire	61		82	61	143		245	263	508	
North	103		111	46	157		142	120	262	
Ireland	703		669	322	991		542	380	922	
Scotland	201		200	105	305		216	168	384	
Other	185		282	257	539		737	816	1553	
Total	**84472**	*100.0*	**43449**	**48375**	**91824**	*100.0*	**43462**	**46498**	**89960**	*100.0*

b) Place of enumeration of those born in **Pembrokeshire**

Birthplace	1851 Total	%	1881 Males	Females	Total	%	1911 Males	Females	Total	%
Wales	**99173**	*94.5*	**47736**	**52894**	**100630**	*89.7*	**49191**	**51298**	**100489**	*86.5*
Monmouthshire	2041		895	869	1764		1078	895	1973	
Glamorgan	7297		8275	7023	15298		11349	9502	20851	
Carmarthenshire	1974		1828	2041	3869		2360	2133	4493	
Pembrokeshire	**72304**	*68.9*	**35833**	**41841**	**77674**	*69.2*	**33436**	**37520**	**70956**	*61.1*
Cardiganshire	14866		513	678	1191		585	821	1406	
Breconshire	472		169	200	369		176	159	335	
Radnorshire	17		9	27	36		30	54	84	
Montgomeryshire	27		30	21	51		20	21	41	
Flintshire	6		28	39	67		24	26	50	
Denbighshire	17		26	27	53		39	50	89	
Merioneth	34		18	28	46		11	22	33	
Caernarfonshire	57		79	61	140		56	61	117	
Anglesey	61		33	39	72		27	34	61	
England	**5799**	*5.5*	**5273**	**6335**	**11608**	*10.3*	**7108**	**8562**	**15670**	*13.5*
London	1521		1246	1586	2832		1234	1671	2905	
South East	712		930	1019	1949		1668	1890	3558	
South Midland	158		186	286	472		538	697	1235	
East	100		169	180	349		386	432	818	
South West	878		632	773	1405		1058	1119	2177	
West Midland	1347		701	1025	1726		860	1136	1996	
North Midland	65		100	134	234		145	200	345	
North West	849		881	947	1828		786	906	1692	
Yorkshire	69		235	247	482		240	315	555	
North	100		193	138	331		193	196	389	
Total	**104972**	*100.0*	**53009**	**59229**	**112238**	*100.0*	**56299**	**59860**	**116159**	*100.0*

CARDIGANSHIRE

a) Birthplace of those enumerated in **Cardiganshire**

Birthplace	1851[3] Total	%	1881 Males	Females	Total	%	1911 Males	Females	Total	%
Wales[1]	**95725**	*98.1*	**30523**	**37581**	**68104**	*96.9*	**24290**	**30650**	**54940**	*91.8*
Monmouthshire	113		61	73	134		92	112	204	
Glamorgan	205		205	227	432		615	835	1450	
Carmarthenshire	12296		761	893	1654		821	930	1751	
Pembrokeshire	14866		513	678	1191		585	821	1406	
Cardiganshire	**66727**	*68.4*	**28151**	**34962**	**63113**	*89.8*	**21341**	**26955**	**48296**	*80.7*
Breconshire	148		78	64	142		73	111	184	
Radnorshire	64		38	45	83		28	41	69	
Montgomeryshire	704		317	288	605		275	354	629	
Flintshire	57		40	31	71		79	78	157	
Denbighshire	80		52	33	85		47	32	79	
Merioneth	307		139	135	274		176	216	392	
Caernarfonshire	96		69	57	126		111	106	217	
Anglesey	61		33	25	58		34	44	78	
England[1]	**1464**	*1.5*	**868**	**946**	**1814**	*2.6*	**2131**	**1868**	**3999**	*6.7*
London	316		159	187	346		555	417	972	
South East	107		61	70	131		165	124	289	
South Midland	51		54	38	92		104	79	183	
East	62		36	27	63		89	52	141	
South West	436		139	148	287		156	143	299	
West Midland	283		225	311	536		565	631	1196	
North Midland	41		24	20	44		65	70	135	
North West	108		119	107	226		307	252	559	
Yorkshire	28		27	24	51		88	66	154	
North	32		20	10	30		32	34	66	
Ireland	279		65	38	103		114	59	173	
Scotland	74		55	54	109		71	49	120	
Other	72		64	76	140		312	335	647	
Total	**97614**	*100.0*	**31575**	**38695**	**70270**	*100.0*	**26918**	**32961**	**59879**	*100.0*

b) Place of enumeration of those born in **Cardiganshire**

Birthplace	1851 Total	%	1881 Males	Females	Total	%	1911 Males	Females	Total	%
Wales	**77146**	*96.3*	**38070**	**43396**	**81466**	*93.6*	**34670**	**38383**	**73053**	*89.0*
Monmouthshire	2494		979	702	1681		823	634	1457	
Glamorgan	3610		5124	3642	8766		8997	7111	16108	
Carmarthenshire	1337		1517	1871	3388		1878	1992	3870	
Pembrokeshire	362		590	596	1186		451	488	939	
Cardiganshire	**66727**	*83.3*	**28151**	**34962**	**63113**	*72.5*	**21341**	**26955**	**48296**	*58.8*
Breconshire	800		385	368	753		284	268	552	
Radnorshire	185		35	61	96		43	49	92	
Montgomeryshire	1190		341	438	779		180	226	406	
Flintshire	59		93	41	134		80	65	145	
Denbighshire	60		124	84	208		163	123	286	
Merioneth	147		439	464	903		224	294	518	
Caernarfonshire	140		225	144	369		170	143	313	
Anglesey	35		67	23	90		36	35	71	
England	**2935**	*3.7*	**2937**	**2660**	**5597**	*6.4*	**4304**	**4765**	**9069**	*11.0*
London	1488		1176	1176	2352		1852	2076	3928	
South East	117		165	137	302		293	339	632	
South Midland	59		98	95	193		337	402	739	
East	15		59	29	88		206	207	413	
South West	154		210	96	306		156	168	324	
West Midland	447		364	341	705		503	539	1042	
North Midland	25		30	40	70		79	76	155	
North West	522		638	643	1281		679	794	1473	
Yorkshire	47		104	73	177		131	119	250	
North	61		93	30	123		68	45	113	
Total	**80081**	*100.0*	**41007**	**46056**	**87063**	*100.0*	**38974**	**43148**	**82122**	*100.0*

BRECONSHIRE

a) Birthplace of those enumerated in **Breconshire**

Birthplace	1851[3] Total	%	1881 Males	Females	Total	%	1911 Males	Females	Total	%
Wales[1]	**50954**	*86.1*	**25295**	**25964**	**51259**	*88.8*	**24972**	**24724**	**49696**	*83.8*
Monmouthshire	3283		1365	1442	2807		1462	1612	3074	
Glamorgan	1073		1335	1510	2845		2578	2523	5101	
Carmarthenshire	1979		1049	1255	2304		858	842	1700	
Pembrokeshire	472		169	200	369		176	159	335	
Cardiganshire	800		385	368	753		284	268	552	
Breconshire	**35783**	*60.5*	**19525**	**19801**	**39326**	*68.1*	**18178**	**18049**	**36227**	*61.1*
Radnorshire	6980		1141	115	1256		941	978	1919	
Montgomeryshire	297		160	134	294		214	141	355	
Flintshire	43		28	13	41		61	31	92	
Denbighshire	90		26	15	41		30	21	51	
Merioneth	54		29	20	49		68	33	101	
Caernarfonshire	30		36	12	48		81	48	129	
Anglesey	67		11	10	21		26	12	38	
England[1]	**7330**	*12.4*	**3085**	**2552**	**5637**	*9.8*	**4430**	**3480**	**7910**	*13.3*
London	307		180	171	351		342	283	625	
South East	197		138	153	291		265	231	496	
South Midland	122		119	107	226		223	149	372	
East	92		70	52	122		129	96	225	
South West	1226		621	471	1092		634	427	1061	
West Midland	5101		1675	1385	3060		2195	1830	4025	
North Midland	85		62	53	115		136	109	245	
North West	82		115	77	192		274	178	452	
Yorkshire	63		52	38	90		155	102	257	
North	55		39	38	77		74	73	147	
Ireland	674		263	181	444		200	85	285	
Scotland	110		116	87	203		192	109	301	
Other	110		102	101	203		572	523	1095	
Total	**59178**	*100.0*	**28861**	**28885**	**57746**	*100.0*	**30366**	**28921**	**59287**	*100.0*

b) Place of enumeration of those born in **Breconshire**

Birthplace	1851 Total	%	1881 Males	Females	Total	%	1911 Males	Females	Total	%
Wales	**55176**	*95.5*	**30204**	**29952**	**60156**	*90.9*	**31093**	**30317**	**61410**	*89.3*
Monmouthshire	6844		3800	3774	7574		4123	4047	8170	
Glamorgan	10278		5804	5235	11039		7600	6879	14479	
Carmarthenshire	1127		334	363	697		481	433	914	
Pembrokeshire	41		55	53	108		64	96	160	
Cardiganshire	148		78	64	142		73	111	184	
Breconshire	**35783**	*61.9*	**19525**	**19801**	**39326**	*59.4*	**18178**	**18049**	**36227**	*52.7*
Radnorshire	846		463	520	983		428	519	947	
Montgomeryshire	49		39	55	94		49	64	113	
Flintshire	13		10	14	24		21	25	46	
Denbighshire	20		36	30	66		30	32	62	
Merioneth	9		25	18	43		10	21	31	
Caernarfonshire	12		30	19	49		30	35	65	
Anglesey	6		5	6	11		6	6	12	
England	**2594**	*4.5*	2642	3399	6041	*9.1*	3137	4199	7336	*10.7*
London	759		487	713	1200		450	679	1129	
South East	188		201	259	460		328	499	827	
South Midland	90		108	158	266		229	321	550	
East	22		55	49	104		99	130	229	
South West	194		169	200	369		220	311	531	
West Midland	1137		981	1340	2321		1091	1407	2498	
North Midland	33		70	82	152		166	180	346	
North West	96		238	304	542		319	411	730	
Yorkshire	39		185	166	351		162	195	357	
North	36		148	128	276		73	66	139	
Total	**57770**	*100.0*	**32846**	**33351**	**66197**	*100.0*	**34230**	**34516**	**68746**	*100.0*

RADNORSHIRE

a) Birthplace of those enumerated in **Radnorshire**

	1851[3]		1881				1911			
Birthplace	Total	%	Males	Females	Total	%	Males	Females	Total	%
Wales[1]	**19788**	*63.1*	**10214**	**9835**	**20049**	*85.2*	**88796**	**8786**	**17582**	*77.8*
Monmouthshire	60		47	65	112		84	108	192	
Glamorgan	37		52	56	108		176	252	428	
Carmarthenshire	52		50	48	98		64	64	128	
Pembrokeshire	17		9	27	36		30	54	84	
Cardiganshire	185		35	61	96		43	49	92	
Breconshire	846		463	520	983		428	519	947	
Radnorshire	**17739**	*56.5*	**9259**	**8793**	**18052**	*76.7*	**7568**	**76318**	**14886**	*65.9*
Montgomeryshire	796		248	222	470		303	321	624	
Flintshire	13		4	3	7		30	35	65	
Denbighshire	14		16	11	27		14	13	27	
Merioneth	11		3	7	10		9	16	25	
Caernarfonshire	12		3	3	6		32	19	51	
Anglesey	6		2	0	2		13	17	30	
England[1]	**11425**	*36.4*	**1660**	**1747**	**3407**	*14.5*	**2339**	**2257**	**4596**	*20.3*
London	195		60	162	222		88	125	213	
South East	86		42	48	90		83	69	152	
South Midland	49		42	37	79		79	63	142	
East	18		15	25	40		33	36	69	
South West	78		66	65	131		77	91	168	
West Midland	10889		1348	1319	2667		1714	1613	3327	
North Midland	36		22	21	43		51	50	101	
North West	52		45	49	94		135	147	282	
Yorkshire	13		9	12	21		54	38	92	
North	9		7	6	13		23	25	48	
Ireland	90		28	19	47		32	31	63	
Scotland	45		22	21	43		32	31	63	
Other	27		15	27	42		141	145	286	
Total	**31375***	*100.0*	**11939**	**11589**	**23528**	*100.0*	**11340**	**11250**	**22590**	*100.0*

b) Place of enumeration of those born in **Radnorshire**

	1851		1881				1911			
Birthplace	Total	%	Males	Females	Total	%	Males	Females	Total	%
Wales	**27466**	*85.8*	**12705**	**11766**	**24471**	*72.4*	**12176**	**11125**	**23301**	*70.9*
Monmouthshire	1212		784	565	1349		930	673	1603	
Glamorgan	701		973	643	1616		2177	1569	3746	
Carmarthenshire	36		29	42	71		90	65	155	
Pembrokeshire	17		14	15	29		36	30	66	
Cardiganshire	64		38	45	83		28	41	69	
Breconshire	6980		1141	1157	2298		941	978	1919	
Radnorshire	**17739**	*55.4*	**9259**	**8793**	**18052**	*53.4*	**7568**	**7318**	**14886**	*45.3*
Montgomeryshire	672		407	438	845		308	349	657	
Flintshire	8		15	14	29		29	25	54	
Denbighshire	19		26	34	60		45	47	92	
Merioneth	13		8	5	13		6	13	19	
Caernarfonshire	5		8	13	21		16	13	29	
Anglesey	0		3	2	5		2	4	6	
England	**4546**	*14.2*	**4173**	**5150**	**9323**	*27.6*	**4133**	**5435**	**9568**	*29.1*
London	743		270	388	658		192	376	568	
South East	107		77	130	207		179	308	487	
South Midland	83		67	87	154		115	211	326	
East	35		13	33	46		90	67	157	
South West	60		67	84	151		84	146	230	
West Midland	3327		3325	3868	7193		2809	3409	6218	
North Midland	34		41	55	96		149	145	294	
North West	124		220	384	604		366	562	928	
Yorkshire	21		63	93	156		108	164	272	
North	12		30	28	58		41	47	88	
Total	**32012**	*100.0*	**16878**	**16916**	**33794**	*100.0*	**16309**	**16560**	**32869**	*100.0*

MONTGOMERYSHIRE

a) Birthplace of those enumerated in **Montgomeryshire**

Birthplace	1851[3] Total	%	1881 Males	Females	Total	%	1911 Males	Females	Total	%
Wales[1]	**68691**	*89.0*	**29652**	**29331**	**58983**	*89.8*	**22747**	**23173**	**45920**	*86.4*
Monmouthshire	41		28	35	63		31	36	67	
Glamorgan	89		80	94	174		193	231	424	
Carmarthenshire	62		35	41	76		52	40	92	
Pembrokeshire	27		30	21	51		20	21	41	
Cardiganshire	1190		341	438	779		180	226	406	
Breconshire	49		39	55	94		49	64	113	
Radnorshire	672		407	438	845		308	349	657	
Montgomeryshire	**59134**	*76.7*	**27415**	**26896**	**54311**	*82.6*	**20911**	**21049**	**41960**	*79.0*
Flintshire	192		99	74	173		389	400	789	
Denbighshire	2695		462	472	934		73	82	155	
Merioneth	4339		537	625	1162		405	509	914	
Caernarfonshire	131		83	72	155		100	133	233	
Anglesey	65		36	21	57		32	28	60	
England[1]	**8082**	*10.5*	**3070**	**3155**	**6225**	*9.5*	**3063**	**3280**	**6343**	*11.9*
London	212		122	162	284		144	175	319	
South East	87		77	94	171		95	93	188	
South Midland	53		68	60	128		80	88	168	
East	53		35	32	67		56	59	115	
South West	196		145	144	289		62	86	148	
West Midland	6998		2050	2107	4157		1880	2033	3913	
North Midland	43		73	55	128		55	66	121	
North West	363		346	376	722		549	543	1092	
Yorkshire	51		101	89	190		100	81	181	
North	26		48	33	81		37	49	86	
Ireland	205		117	82	199		66	48	114	
Scotland	84		113	77	190		84	74	158	
Other	70		52	69	121		272	339	611	
Total	**77142**	*100.0*	**33004**	**32714**	**65718**	*100.0*	**26232**	**26914**	**53146**	*100.0*

b) Place of enumeration of those born in **Montgomeryshire**

Birthplace	1851 Total	%	1881 Males	Females	Total	%	1911 Males	Females	Total	%
Wales	**64676**	*83.9*	**32452**	**31145**	**63597**	*77.7*	**29245**	**27680**	**56925**	*73.7*
Monmouthshire	890		282	238	520		448	277	725	
Glamorgan	1022		1522	986	2508		4840	3072	7912	
Carmarthenshire	51		52	31	83		155	93	248	
Pembrokeshire	29		37	26	63		43	34	77	
Cardiganshire	704		317	288	605		275	354	629	
Breconshire	297		160	134	294		214	141	355	
Radnorshire	796		248	222	470		303	321	624	
Montgomeryshire	**59134**	*76.7*	**27415**	**26896**	**54311**	*66.4*	**20911**	**21049**	**41960**	*54.3*
Flintshire	100		168	225	393		216	250	466	
Denbighshire	459		881	855	1736		908	891	1799	
Merioneth	1040		1101	979	2080		693	849	1542	
Caernarfonshire	126		244	223	467		197	291	488	
Anglesey	28		25	42	67		42	58	100	
England	**12372**	*16.1*	**7897**	**10334**	**18231**	*22.3*	**8570**	**11756**	**20326**	*26.3*
London	1593		629	1022	1651		517	898	1415	
South East	257		194	306	500		360	548	908	
South Midland	156		110	210	320		264	456	720	
East	64		43	51	94		132	145	277	
South West	104		86	91	177		145	152	297	
West Midland	7790		4599	5167	9766		4033	4822	8855	
North Midland	80		125	171	296		241	276	517	
North West	2180		1865	2943	4808		2435	3883	6318	
Yorkshire	117		186	319	505		361	483	844	
North	31		60	54	114		82	93	175	
Total	**77048**	*100.0*	**40349**	**41479**	**81828**	*100.0*	**37815**	**39436**	**77251**	*100.0*

FLINTSHIRE

a) Birthplace of those enumerated in **Flintshire**

Birthplace	1851[3] Total	%	1881 Males	Females	Total	%	1911 Males	Females	Total	%
Wales[1]	**38208**	*93.1*	**33748**	**33118**	**66866**	*83.0*	**35224**	**34445**	**69669**	*75.2*
Monmouthshire	21		58	53	111		100	93	193	
Glamorgan	24		96	112	208		274	256	530	
Carmarthenshire	19		46	31	77		105	65	170	
Pembrokeshire	6		28	39	67		24	26	50	
Cardiganshire	59		93	41	134		80	65	145	
Breconshire	13		10	14	24		21	25	46	
Radnorshire	8		15	14	29		29	25	54	
Montgomeryshire	100		168	225	393		216	250	466	
Flintshire	**33772**	*82.3*	**29507**	**28116**	**57623**	*71.5*	**30664**	**29084**	**59748**	*64.4*
Denbighshire	3281		2961	3497	6458		2757	3360	6117	
Merioneth	260		156	225	381		210	286	496	
Caernarfonshire	389		356	437	793		453	558	1011	
Anglesey	245		180	2385	2565		212	268	480	
England[1]	**2102**	*5.1*	**5429**	**6054**	**11483**	*14.2*	**9215**	**10851**	**20066**	*21.6*
London	120		171	242	413		291	364	655	
South East	76		123	143	266		213	266	479	
South Midland	57		123	132	255		232	258	490	
East	21		51	68	119		103	117	220	
South West	123		227	232	459		211	259	470	
West Midland	329		1414	1597	3011		2591	3035	5626	
North Midland	25		153	177	330		248	313	561	
North West	1233		2828	3068	5896		4723	5510	10233	
Yorkshire	75		173	210	383		366	450	816	
North	43		151	169	320		217	263	480	
Ireland	612		786	608	1394		392	400	792	
Scotland	72		191	208	399		206	263	469	
Other	53		255	190	445		743	966	1709	
Total	**41047**	*100.0*	**40409**	**40178**	**80587**	*100.0*	**45780**	**46925**	**92705**	*100.0*

b) Place of enumeration of those born in **Flintshire**

Birthplace	1851 Total	%	1881 Males	Females	Total	%	1911 Males	Females	Total	%
Wales	**50589**	*68.4*	**33814**	**32018**	**65832**	*74.4*	**35963**	**34184**	**70147**	*69.3*
Monmouthshire	156		86	50	136		155	113	268	
Glamorgan	265		232	155	387		613	390	1003	
Carmarthenshire	18		24	14	38		80	56	136	
Pembrokeshire	15		35	14	49		17	24	41	
Cardiganshire	57		40	31	71		47	32	79	
Breconshire	43		28	13	41		30	21	51	
Radnorshire	13		4	3	7		14	13	27	
Montgomeryshire	192		99	74	173		73	82	155	
Flintshire	**33772**	*45.6*	**29507**	**28116**	**57623**	*65.1*	**30664**	**29084**	**59748**	*59.1*
Denbighshire	14949		2845	2793	5638		3330	3367	6697	
Merioneth	208		197	122	319		130	143	273	
Caernarfonshire	678		578	524	1102		680	730	1410	
Anglesey	223		139	109	248		130	129	259	
England	**23396**	*31.6*	**10079**	**12584**	**22663**	*25.6*	**13963**	**17054**	**31017**	*30.7*
London	514		373	373	746		386	434	820	
South East	117		185	179	364		332	394	726	
South Midland	101		87	114	201		263	334	597	
East	36		43	41	84		139	128	267	
South West	75		107	85	192		175	190	365	
West Midland	5570		1611	1549	3160		1674	1782	3456	
North Midland	121		138	157	295		369	379	748	
North West	16242		6628	9247	15875		8976	11979	20955	
Yorkshire	145		314	397	711		794	837	1631	
North	475		593	442	1035		855	597	1452	
Total	**73985**	*100.0*	**43893**	**44602**	**88495**	*100.0*	**49926**	**51238**	**101164**	*100.0*

DENBIGHSHIRE

a) Birthplace of those enumerated in **Denbighshire**

Birthplace	1851[3] Total	%	1881 Males	Females	Total	%	1911 Males	Females	Total	%
Wales[1]	**86815**	*89.6*	**49218**	**47913**	**97131**	*86.9*	**59547**	**57279**	**116826**	*80.7*
Monmouthshire	64		56	37	93		94	93	187	
Glamorgan	60		81	67	148		224	213	437	
Carmarthenshire	35		58	52	110		87	85	172	
Pembrokeshire	17		26	27	53		39	50	89	
Cardiganshire	60		124	84	208		163	123	286	
Breconshire	20		36	30	66		30	32	62	
Radnorshire	19		26	34	60		45	47	92	
Montgomeryshire	459		881	855	1736		908	891	1799	
Flintshire	14949		8545	2793	11338		3330	3367	6697	
Denbighshire	**62999**	*65.0*	**42151**	**40489**	**82640**	*74.0*	**51119**	**48195**	**99314**	*68.6*
Merioneth	2087		1371	1664	3035		1567	1744	3311	
Caernarfonshire	5701		1134	1313	2447		1571	1968	3539	
Anglesey	344		266	305	571		316	421	737	
England[1]	**8674**	*9.0*	**6257**	**6465**	**12722**	*11.4*	**10858**	**13138**	**23996**	*16.6*
London	326		229	270	499		390	481	871	
South East	176		183	219	402		296	334	630	
South Midland	123		158	150	308		266	340	606	
East	81		102	104	206		131	215	346	
South West	153		251	238	489		274	342	616	
West Midland	1982		2416	2336	4752		3477	4022	7499	
North Midland	141		166	178	344		368	482	850	
North West	5413		2445	2592	5037		4815	6001	10816	
Yorkshire	170		182	198	380		542	626	1168	
North	107		112	167	279		255	269	524	
Ireland	1036		528	445	973		425	384	809	
Scotland	229		266	284	550		297	332	629	
Other	161		159	205	364		1081	1442	2523	
Total	**96915**	*100.0*	**56428**	**55312**	**111740**	*100.0*	**72208**	**72575**	**144783**	*100*

b) Place of enumeration of those born in **Denbighshire**

Birthplace	1851 Total	%	1881 Males	Females	Total	%	1911 Males	Females	Total	%
Wales	**83840**	*81.6*	**49810**	**48154**	**97964**	*81.0*	**59932**	**56933**	**116865**	*77.5*
Monmouthshire	236		66	52	118		339	232	571	
Glamorgan	210		265	166	431		1509	886	2395	
Carmarthenshire	29		42	30	72		160	79	239	
Pembrokeshire	11		25	14	39		29	30	59	
Cardiganshire	80		52	33	85		79	78	157	
Breconshire	90		26	15	41		61	31	92	
Radnorshire	14		16	11	27		30	35	65	
Montgomeryshire	2695		462	472	934		389	400	789	
Flintshire	3281		2961	3497	6458		2757	3360	6117	
Denbighshire	**62999**	*61.3*	**42151**	**40489**	**82640**	*68.3*	**51119**	**48195**	**99314**	*65.9*
Merioneth	9479		1549	1289	2838		1172	1094	2266	
Caernarfonshire	4379		2039	1913	3952		2066	2283	4349	
Anglesey	337		156	173	329		222	230	452	
England	**18882**	*18.4*	**10133**	**12889**	**23022**	*19.0*	**14447**	**19463**	**33910**	*22.5*
London	833		508	604	1112		603	757	1360	
South East	194		190	225	415		494	588	1082	
South Midland	135		123	142	265		388	455	843	
East	59		45	49	94		131	194	325	
South West	89		110	106	216		213	245	458	
West Midland	7100		2130	2325	4455		2469	2841	5310	
North Midland	88		113	135	248		441	419	860	
North West	10078		6171	8623	14794		8194	12626	20820	
Yorkshire	182		403	415	818		934	871	1805	
North	124		340	265	605		580	467	1047	
Total	**102722**	*100.0*	**59943**	**61043**	**120986**	*100.0*	**74379**	**76396**	**150775**	*100.0*

MERIONETH

a) Birthplace of those enumerated in **Merioneth**

Birthplace	1851[3] Total	%	1881 Males	Females	Total	%	1911 Males	Females	Total	%
Wales[1]	**50114**	*97.7*	**24920**	**24542**	**49462**	*95.0*	**20101**	**21613**	**41714**	*91.5*
Monmouthshire	11		40	26	66		32	37	69	
Glamorgan	26		85	64	149		138	163	301	
Carmarthenshire	54		61	41	102		48	57	105	
Pembrokeshire	34		18	28	46		11	22	33	
Cardiganshire	147		439	464	903		224	294	518	
Breconshire	9		25	18	43		10	21	31	
Radnorshire	13		8	5	13		6	13	19	
Montgomeryshire	1040		1101	979	2080		693	849	1542	
Flintshire	208		197	155	352		130	143	273	
Denbighshire	9479		1549	1289	2838		1172	1094	2266	
Merioneth	**32156**	*62.7*	**19659**	**19406**	**39065**	*75.1*	**16199**	**17338**	**33537**	*73.6*
Caernarfonshire	6647		1332	1806	3138		1265	1399	2664	
Anglesey	288		362	243	605		170	176	346	
England[1]	**1036**	*2.0*	**1046**	**1040**	**2086**	*4.0*	**1414**	**1786**	**3200**	*7.0*
London	103		66	117	183		181	178	359	
South East	40		41	45	86		85	81	166	
South Midland	33		60	34	94		63	74	137	
East	21		30	33	63		38	37	75	
South West	41		97	91	188		62	85	147	
West Midland	428		317	301	618		426	606	1032	
North Midland	32		64	39	103		58	58	116	
North West	315		287	307	594		407	560	967	
Yorkshire	14		50	45	95		63	76	139	
North	9		26	25	51		29	29	58	
Ireland	77		95	41	136		39	45	84	
Scotland	41		64	48	112		40	49	89	
Other	39		144	98	242		208	270	478	
Total	**51307**	*100.0*	**26269**	**25769**	**52038**	*100.0*	**21802**	**23763**	**45565**	*100.0*

b) Place of enumeration of those born in **Merioneth**

Birthplace	1851 Total	%	1881 Males	Females	Total	%	1911 Males	Females	Total	%
Wales	**40982**	*94.2*	**23510**	**23664**	**47174**	*92.3*	**23382**	**24012**	**47394**	*85.8*
Monmouthshire	215		43	28	71		267	180	447	
Glamorgan	232		293	161	454		3027	1912	4939	
Carmarthenshire	24		24	16	40		101	67	168	
Pembrokeshire	18		24	6	30		24	18	42	
Cardiganshire	307		139	135	274		176	216	392	
Breconshire	54		29	20	49		68	33	101	
Radnorshire	11		3	7	10		9	16	25	
Montgomeryshire	4339		537	625	1162		405	509	914	
Flintshire	260		156	225	381		210	286	496	
Denbighshire	2087		1371	1664	3035		1567	1744	3311	
Merioneth	**32156**	*73.9*	**19659**	**19406**	**39065**	*76.4*	**16199**	**17338**	**33537**	*60.7*
Caernarfonshire	1124		1148	1266	2414		1207	1559	2766	
Anglesey	155		84	105	189		122	134	256	
England	**2532**	*5.8*	**1717**	**2234**	**3951**	*7.7*	**3250**	**4625**	**7875**	*14.2*
London	384		221	337	558		407	629	1036	
South East	70		74	76	150		189	271	460	
South Midland	33		38	51	89		163	277	440	
East	10		20	16	36		78	69	147	
South West	24		59	29	88		75	91	166	
West Midland	592		277	293	570		478	507	985	
North Midland	16		28	28	56		62	84	146	
North West	1347		926	1324	2250		1540	2443	3983	
Yorkshire	35		41	55	96		109	151	260	
North	21		33	25	58		149	103	252	
Total	**43514**	*100.0*	**25227**	**25898**	**51125**	*100.0*	**26632**	**28637**	**55269**	*100.0*

CAERNARFONSHIRE

a) Birthplace of those enumerated in **Caernarfonshire**

Birthplace	1851[3] Total	%	1881 Males	Females	Total	%	1911 Males	Females	Total	%
Wales[1]	**91342**	*96.5*	**54797**	**56364**	**111161**	*93.1*	**53000**	**57019**	**110019**	*88.0*
Monmouthshire	33		47	43	90		75	66	141	
Glamorgan	28		118	88	206		216	308	524	
Carmarthenshire	35		46	39	85		67	68	135	
Pembrokeshire	57		79	61	140		56	61	117	
Cardiganshire	140		225	144	369		170	143	313	
Breconshire	12		30	19	49		30	35	65	
Radnorshire	5		8	13	21		16	13	29	
Montgomeryshire	126		244	223	467		197	291	488	
Flintshire	678		578	524	1102		680	730	1410	
Denbighshire	4379		2039	1913	3952		2066	2283	4349	
Merioneth	1124		1148	1266	2414		1207	1559	2766	
Caernarfonshire	**68522**	*72.4*	**46173**	**48145**	**94318**	*79.0*	**45588**	**48568**	**94156**	*75.3*
Anglesey	16202		3741	3564	7305		2620	2877	5497	
England[1]	**2481**	*2.6*	**3077**	**3502**	**6579**	*5.5*	**5103**	**7237**	**12340**	*9.9*
London	199		215	232	447		309	448	757	
South East	135		116	163	279		243	276	519	
South Midland	104		99	130	229		191	284	475	
East	45		99	61	160		130	152	282	
South West	115		266	262	528		188	241	429	
West Midland	344		493	701	1194		1052	1777	2829	
North Midland	87		215	197	412		208	339	547	
North West	1271		1314	1508	2822		2327	3084	5411	
Yorkshire	115		161	157	318		306	418	724	
North	66		79	76	155		145	212	357	
Ireland	583		313	308	621		256	370	626	
Scotland	170		261	182	443		250	232	482	
Other	98		287	258	545		770	806	1576	
Total	**94674**	*100.0*	**58735**	**60614**	**119349**	*100.0*	**59379**	**65664**	**125043**	*100.0*

b) Place of enumeration of those born in **Caernarfonshire**

Birthplace	1851 Total	%	1881 Males	Females	Total	%	1911 Males	Females	Total	%
Wales	**83464**	*94.7*	**50668**	**53407**	**104075**		**55082**	**56978**	**112060**	
Monmouthshire	86		80	57	137		354	217	571	
Glamorgan	215		293	198	491		4203	2371	6574	
Carmarthenshire	32		33	30	63		217	121	338	
Pembrokeshire	83		83	22	105		59	26	85	
Cardiganshire	96		69	57	126		111	106	217	
Breconshire	30		36	12	48		81	48	129	
Radnorshire	12		3	3	6		32	19	51	
Montgomeryshire	131		83	72	155		100	133	233	
Flintshire	389		356	437	793		453	558	1011	
Denbighshire	5701		1134	1313	2447		1571	1968	3539	
Merioneth	6647		1332	1806	3138		1265	1399	2664	
Caernarfonshire	**68522**	*77.8*	**46173**	**48145**	**94318**	*83.3*	**45588**	**48568**	**94156**	*73.0*
Anglesey	1520		993	1255	2248		1048	1444	2492	
England	**4661**	*5.3*	**3960**	**5206**	**9166**	*8.1*	**7014**	**9980**	**16994**	*13.2*
London	451		354	430	784		591	851	1442	
South East	159		154	192	346		382	492	874	
South Midland	44		75	100	175		284	454	738	
East	31		59	46	105		162	172	334	
South West	112		177	67	244		180	194	374	
West Midland	242		301	351	652		630	701	1331	
North Midland	57		65	60	125		165	237	402	
North West	3436		2530	3697	6227		4129	6363	10492	
Yorkshire	80		121	187	308		280	361	641	
North	49		124	76	200		211	155	366	
Total	**88125**	*100.0*	**54628**	**58613**	**113241**	*100.0*	**62096**	**66958**	**129054**	*100.0*

ANGLESEY

a) Birthplace of those enumerated in **Anglesey**

Birthplace	1851[3] Total	%	1881 Males	Females	Total	%	1911 Males	Females	Total	%
Wales[1]	**41603**	*96.2*	**23022**	**24750**	**47772**	*92.9*	**22164**	**23770**	**45934**	*90.2*
Monmouthshire	7		19	11	30		65	101	166	
Glamorgan	24		33	22	55		69	69	138	
Carmarthenshire	21		21	15	36		26	19	45	
Pembrokeshire	61		33	39	72		27	34	61	
Cardiganshire	35		67	23	90		36	35	71	
Breconshire	6		5	6	11		6	6	12	
Radnorshire	0		3	2	5		2	4	6	
Montgomeryshire	28		25	42	67		42	58	100	
Flintshire	223		139	109	248		130	129	259	
Denbighshire	337		156	173	329		222	230	452	
Merioneth	155		84	105	189		122	134	256	
Caernarfonshire	1520		993	1255	2248		1048	1444	2492	
Anglesey	**39179**	*90.6*	**21391**	**22899**	**44290**	*86.1*	**20351**	**21486**	**41837**	*82.1*
England[1]	**1189**	*2.8*	**1561**	**1251**	**2812**	*5.5*	**1812**	**1899**	**3711**	*7.3*
London	96		163	103	266		127	108	235	
South East	68		78	84	162		106	128	234	
South Midland	31		58	36	94		60	59	119	
East	29		67	35	102		39	38	77	
South West	136		130	91	221		143	111	254	
West Midland	109		136	129	265		236	233	469	
North Midland	37		41	27	68		67	50	117	
North West	611		787	686	1473		901	1052	1953	
Yorkshire	45		40	38	78		90	77	167	
North	27		54	18	72		42	42	84	
Ireland	340		273	153	426		207	247	454	
Scotland	82		102	49	151		68	42	110	
Other	29		145	110	255		347	372	719	
Total	**43243**	*100.0*	**25103**	**26313**	**51416**	*100.0*	**24598**	**26330**	**50928**	*100.0*

b) Place of enumeration of those born in **Anglesey**

Birthplace	1851 Total	%	1881 Males	Females	Total	%	1911 Males	Females	Total	%
Wales	**56897**	*92.6*	**26321**	**27482**	**53803**	*87.2*	**25204**	**26077**	**51281**	*84.6*
Monmouthshire	61		31	25	56		107	59	166	
Glamorgan	341		203	130	333		1247	632	1879	
Carmarthenshire	16		16	12	28		40	27	67	
Pembrokeshire	22		49	13	62		36	30	66	
Cardiganshire	61		33	25	58		34	44	78	
Breconshire	67		11	10	21		26	12	38	
Radnorshire	6		2	0	2		13	17	30	
Montgomeryshire	65		36	21	57		32	28	60	
Flintshire	245		180	235	415		212	268	480	
Denbighshire	344		266	305	571		316	421	737	
Merioneth	288		362	243	605		170	176	346	
Caernarfonshire	16202		3741	3564	7305		2620	2877	5497	
Anglesey	**39179**	*63.8*	**21391**	**22899**	**44290**	*71.8*	**20351**	**21486**	**41837**	*69.0*
England	**4556**	*7.4*	**3521**	**4398**	**7919**	*12.8*	**4098**	**5256**	**9354**	*15.4*
London	264		188	250	438		250	295	545	
South East	147		81	99	180		186	241	427	
South Midland	40		39	39	78		119	184	303	
East	32		31	30	61		79	103	182	
South West	57		118	49	167		177	164	341	
West Midland	141		131	135	266		221	221	442	
North Midland	28		40	41	81		44	72	116	
North West	3777		2714	3578	6292		2844	3753	6597	
Yorkshire	47		60	94	154		105	146	251	
North	23		119	83	202		73	77	150	
Total	**61453**	*100.0*	**29842**	**31880**	**61722**	*100.0*	**29302**	**31333**	**60635**	*100.0*

Sources: *Census of Population*: *1851, Population Tables II, Ages, Civil Condition, Occupation, and Birth-place of the People: Vol. I, Summary Tables,* Table xxxix*; Vol. II, Division XI,* Birthplaces of the inhabitants of Districts, pp. 886–91. 1881, *Vol. II, Ages, Condition as to Marriage, Occupations, and Birthplaces of the People* (HMSO 1883), Division XI – Wales and Monmouthshire, Table 11 and Table 12. 1911, *Vol. IX, Birthplaces of Persons Enumerated in Administrative Counties, County Boroughs, etc.*, Table 2.

There are various pitfalls for the unwary in the interpretation of these figures. One is the different areas to which the county figures refer. The 1851 figures refer to Registration Districts as headings for those enumerated. In the absence of Welsh county totals in the 1851 census, the totals for Registration Counties have been calculated simply as the sum of the relevant Registration Districts. Yet footnotes imply that the birthplace has been classified according to Ancient County (see note 1). The 1881 figures refer to the Ancient or 'Proper' counties. The 1911 figures refer to Administration Counties and associated County Boroughs, set up by the 1888 Local Government Board Act, which more closely follow the boundaries of Ancient Counties than Registration Counties. Where there is a significant difference between Registration County and the Ancient County boundaries it could be misleading to compare the 1851 figures with later ones which are calculated on a different basis.

English counties are grouped according to the census as follows: South East – Surrey (excl. London), Kent (excl. London), Sussex, Hampshire, Berkshire; South Midland – Middlesex (excl. London), Hertford, Buckingham, Oxford, Northampton, Huntingdon, Bedford, Cambridge; East – Essex, Suffolk, Norfolk; South West – Wiltshire, Dorset, Devon, Cornwall, Somerset; West Midland – Gloucester, Hereford, Shropshire, Stafford, Worcester, Warwick; North Midland – Leicester, Rutland, Lincoln, Nottingham, Derby; North West – Cheshire, Lancashire; Yorkshire; North – Durham, Northumberland, Cumberland, Westmoreland.

[1] The 1851 census figures include Wales with England for the small number of those entered as born 'county not stated'. Here the totals have been included in the total for Wales. For 1881 and 1911 these numbers are given separately and therefore can be included in the relevant totals.

[2] The figures for each county of Wales and the remainder of this table are compiled from different census sources. There is a discrepancy of 310 between this total figure for Wales, calculated from the census Summary Table xxxix, and the sum of Welsh natives enumerated in Wales calculated from the sum of separate Registration Districts (1045963). The summary table does not provide separate figures for Welsh counties.

[3] The 1851 census table, 'Birth-places of the Inhabitants of Districts', gives information on the number of inhabitants of other counties contained in Registration Counties as follows:

Registration County of Monmouth:	Gloucestershire 18797, Herefordshire 2149, Glamorgan 513.
Registration County of Glamorgan:	Monmouthshire 945, Breconshire 8913.
Registration County of Carmarthen:	Glamorgan 1099, Breconshire 684.
Registration County of Pembroke:	Carmarthenshire 5871.
Registration County of Cardigan:	Pembrokeshire 15539, Carmarthenshire 11872.
Registration County of Brecon:	Radnorshire 5585, Herefordshire 2315.
Registration County of Radnor:	Breconshire 599, Herefordshire 873, Shropshire 1891.
Registration County of Montgomery:	Cardiganshire 593, Merioneth 3375, Denbighshire 2241, Shropshire 4595
Registration County of Flint:	Denbighshire 49.
Registration County of Denbigh:	Flintshire 15627, Caernarfonshire 4717, Cheshire 2816.
Registration County of Merioneth:	Montgomeryshire 116, Denbighshire 10170, Caernarfonshire 5553.
Registration County of Caernarfon:	Denbighshire 2990, Anglesey 17074.
Registration County of Anglesey:	wholly within Anglesey Ancient County.

Population 4.4 Population change. Migration. Birthplace of those enumerated in the major urban areas. Available years 1851, 1881, 1911

Newport[3]

Birthplace	1851 Total	%	1911 Males	Females	Total	%
Wales[1]	**10974**	***56.8***	**27086**	**29444**	**56530**	***67.5***
Monmouthshire	9144	*47.3*	24188	26192	50380	*60.2*
Glamorgan	734	*3.8*	1929	2281	4210	*5.0*
Carmarthenshire	173	*0.9*	192	184	376	*0.4*
Pembrokeshire	437	*2.3*	240	230	470	*0.6*
Cardiganshire	210	*1.1*	119	109	228	*0.3*
Breconshire	193	*1.0*	178	252	430	*0.5*
Radnorshire	21	*0.1*	50	58	108	*0.1*
Montgomeryshire	21	*0.1*	43	35	78	*0.1*
Flintshire	4	*0.0*	32	21	53	*0.1*
Denbighshire	7	*0.0*	34	30	64	*0.1*
Merioneth	20	*0.1*	22	14	36	*0.0*
Caernarfonshire	5	*0.0*	28	24	52	*0.1*
Anglesey	5	*0.0*	26	6	32	*0.0*
England[2]	**5915**	***30.6***	**12263**	**10725**	**22988**	***27.5***
London	296	*1.5*	781	585	1366	*1.6*
South East	199	*1.0*	678	520	1198	*1.4*
South Midland	91	*0.5*	379	317	696	*0.8*
East	60	*0.3*	261	199	460	*0.5*
South West	2949	*15.3*	3025	2669	5694	*6.8*
West Midland	1996	*10.3*	5491	5049	10540	*12.6*
North Midland	51	*0.3*	228	214	442	*0.5*
North West	110	*0.6*	996	853	1849	*2.2*
Yorkshire	63	*0.3*	409	357	766	*0.9*
North	100	*0.5*	409	303	712	*0.9*
Ireland	2069	*10.7*	683	461	1144	*1.4*
Scotland	136	*0.7*	426	241	667	*0.8*
Other	229	*1.2*	1716	646	2362	*2.8*
Total	**19323**	***100.0***	**42174**	**41517**	**83691**	***100.0***

Merthyr Tydfil[4]

Birthplace	1851	%	1911 Males	Females	Total	%
Wales[1]	**56421**	***89.4***	**34862**	**33190**	**68052**	***84.0***
Monmouthshire	2242	*3.6*	1378	1386	2764	*3.4*
Glamorgan	33679	*53.4*	27557	27495	55052	*68.0*
Carmarthenshire	9103	*14.4*	810	677	1487	*1.8*
Pembrokeshire	3069	*4.9*	546	425	971	*1.2*
Cardiganshire	2292	*3.6*	695	518	1213	*1.5*
Breconshire	4147	*6.6*	1278	1186	2464	*3.0*
Radnorshire	495	*0.8*	419	315	734	*0.9*
Montgomeryshire	799	*1.3*	816	493	1309	*1.6*
Flintshire	89	*0.1*	39	23	62	*0.1*
Denbighshire	102	*0.2*	167	77	244	*0.3*
Merioneth	146	*0.2*	348	178	526	*0.6*
Caernarfonshire	112	*0.2*	632	339	971	*1.2*
Anglesey	146	*0.2*	140	53	193	*0.2*
England[2]	**3251**	***5.2***	**5566**	**3477**	**9043**	***11.2***
London	148	*0.2*	447	283	730	*0.9*
South East	120	*0.2*	247	153	400	*0.5*
South Midland	69	*0.1*	179	91	270	*0.3*
East	35	*0.0*	92	56	148	*0.2*
South West	1499	*2.4*	1384	855	2239	*2.8*
West Midland	1108	*1.8*	2504	1600	4104	*5.1*
North Midland	40	*0.1*	88	52	140	*0.2*
North West	98	*0.2*	514	298	812	*1.0*
Yorkshire	48	*0.1*	190	106	296	*0.4*
North	86	*0.1*	97	85	182	*0.2*
Ireland	3051	*4.8*	1674	633	2307	*2.8*
Scotland	143	*0.2*	153	66	219	*0.3*
Other	224	*0.4*	771	598	1369	*1.7*
Total	**63080**	***100.0***	**43026**	**37964**	**80990**	***100.0***

Swansea[5]

Birthplace	1851 Total	%	1881 Males	Females	Total	%	1911 Males	Females	Total	%
Wales[1]	**25446**	***80.9***	**24020**	**26713**	**50733**	***77.3***	**44515**	**47140**	**91655**	***79.9***
Monmouthshire	242	*0.8*	458	506	964	*1.5*	718	812	1530	*1.3*
Glamorgan	21098	*67.1*	19899	22191	42090	*64.2*	39613	41863	81476	*71.1*
Carmarthenshire	2581	*8.2*	1594	1958	3552	*5.4*	1776	2113	3889	*3.4*
Pembrokeshire	937	*3.0*	1222	1294	2516	*3.8*	1226	1250	2476	*2.2*
Cardiganshire	193	*0.6*	355	309	664	*1.0*	375	367	742	*0.6*
Breconshire	130	*0.4*	201	235	436	*0.7*	309	382	691	*0.6*
Radnorshire	20	*0.1*	44	27	71	*0.1*	110	77	187	*0.2*
Montgomeryshire	25	*0.1*	42	22	64	*0.1*	49	48	97	*0.1*
Flintshire	124	*0.4*	60	45	105	*0.2*	52	28	80	*0.1*
Denbighshire	40	*0.1*	26	26	52	*0.1*	81	50	131	*0.1*
Merioneth	6	*0.0*	13	6	19	*0.0*	32	33	65	*0.1*
Caernarfonshire	12	*0.0*	24	22	46	*0.1*	73	41	114	*0.1*
Anglesey	383	*0.1*	18	23	41	*0.1*	37	17	54	*0.0*
England[2]	**4375**	***13.9***	**6241**	**5498**	**11739**	***17.9***	**9434**	**7491**	**16925**	***14.8***
London	341	*1.1*	397	390	787	*1.2*	958	732	1690	*1.5*
South East	276	*0.9*	277	254	531	*0.8*	622	497	1119	*1.0*
South Midland	90	*0.3*	179	142	321	*0.5*	361	296	657	*0.6*
East	85	*0.3*	131	79	210	*0.3*	278	186	464	*0.4*
South West	2341	*7.4*	3346	2908	6254	*9.5*	3064	2519	5583	*4.9*
West Midland	887	*2.8*	1220	1172	2392	*3.6*	2291	1947	4238	*3.7*
North Midland	46	*0.1*	118	100	218	*0.3*	292	192	484	*0.4*
North West	140	*0.4*	313	225	538	*0.8*	1268	864	2132	*1.9*
Yorkshire	56	*0.2*	96	100	196	*0.3*	393	308	701	*0.6*
North	113	*0.4*	137	111	248	*0.4*	275	238	513	*0.4*
Ireland	1333	*4.2*	1084	740	1824	*2.8*	947	517	1464	*1.3*
Scotland	129	*0.4*	258	138	396	*0.6*	395	198	593	*0.5*
Other	178	*0.6*	619	286	905	*1.4*	2562	1464	4026	*3.5*
Total	**43243**	***100.0***	**32222**	**33375**	**65597**	***100.0***	**57853**	**56810**	**114663**	***100.0***

Cardiff[6]

Birthplace	1881 Males	Females	Total	%	1911 Males	Females	Total	%
Wales[1]	**24084**	**26026**	**50110**	***60.5***	**59194**	**64930**	**124124**	***68.1***
Monmouthshire	1919	2368	4287	*5.2*	3163	4381	7544	*4.1*
Glamorgan	19910	21334	41244	*49.8*	52478	56601	109079	*59.8*
Carmarthenshire	440	443	883	*1.1*	759	850	1609	*0.9*
Pembrokeshire	870	961	1831	*2.2*	1164	1404	2568	*1.4*
Cardiganshire	422	320	742	*0.9*	550	521	1071	*0.6*
Breconshire	206	288	494	*0.6*	396	552	948	*0.5*
Radnorshire	46	59	105	*0.1*	101	114	215	*0.1*
Montgomeryshire	45	39	84	*0.1*	126	132	258	*0.1*
Flintshire	21	15	36	*0.0*	42	37	79	*0.0*
Denbighshire	31	23	54	*0.1*	94	75	169	*0.1*
Merioneth	15	7	22	*0.0*	75	62	137	*0.1*
Caernarfonshire	48	34	82	*0.1*	143	92	235	*0.1*
Anglesey	22	23	45	*0.1*	42	41	83	*0.0*
England[2]	**13255**	**11637**	**24892**	***30.1***	**23133**	**22833**	**45966**	***25.2***
London	766	702	1468	*1.8*	1824	1754	3578	*2.0*
South East	681	546	1227	*1.5*	1367	1288	2655	*1.5*
South Midland	263	223	486	*0.6*	703	653	1356	*0.7*
East	211	162	373	*0.5*	418	407	825	*0.5*
South West	6728	5951	12679	*15.3*	9033	8757	17790	*9.8*
West Midland	3124	2924	6048	*7.3*	6144	6514	12658	*6.9*
North Midland	151	125	276	*0.3*	477	439	916	*0.5*
North West	484	403	887	*1.1*	2135	1998	4133	*2.3*
Yorkshire	303	197	500	*0.6*	796	718	1514	*0.8*
North	431	312	743	*0.9*	983	986	1969	*1.1*
Ireland	2211	2048	4259	*5.1*	1657	1467	3124	*1.7*
Scotland	538	248	786	*0.9*	996	686	1682	*0.9*
Other	2228	486	2714	*3.3*	4748	2615	7363	*4.0*
Total	**42316**	**40445**	**82761**	***100.0***	**89728**	**92531**	**182259**	***100.0***

Rhondda[7]

Birthplace	1881 Males	Females	Total	%	1911 Males	Females	Total	%
Wales[1]	**27306**	**22730**	**50036**	***89.9***	**66010**	**59780**	**125790**	***82.3***
Monmouthshire	2234	1818	4052	*7.3*	2637	2438	5075	*3.3*
Glamorgan	17194	15973	33167	*59.6*	48822	47427	96249	*63.0*
Carmarthenshire	2468	1582	4050	*7.3*	2622	1979	4601	*3.0*
Pembrokeshire	1229	819	2048	*3.7*	2185	1471	3656	*2.4*
Cardiganshire	1712	972	2684	*4.8*	3210	2395	5605	*3.7*
Breconshire	1215	873	2088	*3.8*	1122	899	2021	*1.3*
Radnorshire	200	112	312	*0.6*	332	234	566	*0.4*
Montgomeryshire	687	401	1088	*2.0*	1789	1041	2830	*1.9*
Flintshire	30	13	43	*0.1*	106	71	177	*0.1*
Denbighshire	47	17	64	*0.1*	323	158	481	*0.3*
Merioneth	90	41	131	*0.2*	1096	676	1772	*1.2*
Caernarfonshire	56	30	86	*0.2*	1241	696	1937	*1.3*
Anglesey	41	16	57	*0.1*	439	239	678	*0.4*
England[2]	**3249**	**1853**	**5102**	***9.2***	**15212**	**8689**	**23901**	***15.6***
London	70	48	118	*0.2*	1105	576	1681	*1.1*
South East	70	47	117	*0.2*	541	347	888	*0.6*
South Midland	56	18	74	*0.1*	369	202	571	*0.4*
East	15	12	27	*0.0*	219	136	355	*0.2*
South West	1961	1074	3035	*5.5*	6414	3472	9886	*6.5*
West Midland	865	530	1395	*2.5*	5472	3196	8668	*5.7*
North Midland	25	15	40	*0.1*	153	100	253	*0.2*
North West	73	35	108	*0.2*	772	530	1302	*0.9*
Yorkshire	45	19	64	*0.1*	229	168	397	*0.3*
North	30	34	64	*0.1*	152	119	271	*0.2*
Ireland	182	80	262	*0.5*	721	208	929	*0.6*
Scotland	37	17	54	*0.1*	177	86	263	*0.2*
Other	103	75	178	*0.3*	1089	809	1898	*1.2*
Total	**30877**	**24755**	**55632**	***100.0***	**83209**	**69572**	**152781**	***100.0***

Source: *Census of Population*: *1851, Population Tables II, Ages, Civil Condition, Occupation, and Birth-place of the People: Vol. II, Division XI*, Birthplaces of the inhabitants of principal towns, p. 892. 1881, *Vol. II, Ages, Condition as to Marriage, Occupations, and Birthplaces of the People* (HMSO 1883), Division XI – Wales and Monmouthshire, Table 11. 1911, *Vol. IX, Birthplaces of Persons Enumerated in Administrative Counties, County Boroughs, etc.*, Table 2.

English counties are grouped according to the Divisions I–X given in the census as follows: South East – Surrey (excl. London), Kent (excl. London), Sussex, Hampshire, Berkshire; South Midland – Middlesex (excl. London), Hertford, Buckingham, Oxford, Northampton, Huntingdon, Bedford, Cambridge; East – Essex, Suffolk, Norfolk; South West – Wiltshire, Dorset, Devon, Cornwall, Somerset; West Midland – Gloucester, Hereford, Shropshire, Stafford, Worcester, Warwick; North Midland – Leicester, Rutland, Lincoln, Nottingham, Derby; North West – Cheshire, Lancashire; Yorkshire; North – Durham, Northumberland, Cumberland, Westmoreland.

1 Includes Wales, county not stated.
2 Includes England, county not stated.
3 Newport: 1851, Borough; 1911, County Borough. Minor boundary change. No figures given in 1881.
4 Merthyr Tydfil: 1851, 'Town' (Parliamentary limits); 1911, County Borough. Boundary change. No figures given in 1881.
5 Swansea: 1851, Borough; 1881, Municipal Borough; 1911, County Borough. Boundary changes.
6 Cardiff: 1881, Urban Sanitary District; 1911, County Borough. No boundary change. No figures given in 1851.
7 Rhondda: 1881 (Ystradyfodwg), Urban Sanitary District; 1911, Urban District. No boundary change. No figures given in 1851.

Population 4.5 Population change. Migration. Inhabitants of the USA born in Wales. 1850–1910

State	Inhabitants of the USA born in Wales 1850	1860	1870[1]	1880[1]	1890	1900	1910
Total USA	**29868**	**45763**	**74533**	**83302**	**100079**	**93586**	**82479**
Alabama	67	11	39	69	398	306	230
Arizona	–	–	3	57	85	136	210
Arkansas	11	10	24	99	130	113	148
California	182	1262	1517	1920	1860	1949	2415
Colorado		38	165	1212	2082	1955	1989
Connecticut	111	176	288	407	629	650	616
Delaware	17	30	43	51	63	43	34
District of Columbia	20	28	29	56	71	82	86
Florida	11	6	6	23	56	169	63
Georgia	13	56	61	52	108	65	89
Idaho	–	–	335	641	770	732	722
Illinois	572	1528	3146	3694	4138	4364	4091
Indiana	169	226	556	927	888	2083	1498
Iowa	352	913	1967	3031	3601	3091	2434
Kansas	–	163	1021	2088	2488	2005	1615
Kentucky	171	420	347	394	380	337	222
Louisiana	48	97	114	71	99	126	82
Maine	60	88	279	283	215	199	204
Maryland	260	701	994	924	761	674	583
Massachusetts	214	320	576	873	1527	1680	1513
Michigan	127	348	558	830	769	838	786
Minnesota	2	422	944	1103	1470	1288	1023
Mississippi	10	21	25	12	21	30	25
Missouri	176	305	1524	1766	1862	1613	1219
Montana	–	–	197	246	719	935	884
Nebraska	–	128	220	624	1182	922	824
Nevada	–	21	301	315	212	128	168
New Hampshire	11	14	27	21	79	68	58
New Jersey	166	371	804	863	1069	1195	1201
New Mexico	1	2	9	28	122	105	93
New York	7582	7998	7857	7223	8108	7304	7462
North Carolina	7	20	10	12	23	20	35
North Dakota	–	–	–	–	108	147	222
Ohio	5849	8365	12939	13763	12905	11481	9376
Oklahoma	–	–	–	–	19	269	365
Oregon	9	32	63	165	374	401	585
Pennsylvania	8920	13101	27633	29447	38301	35453	29253
Rhode Island	12	19	56	167	194	256	268
South Carolina	10	11	15	10	7	8	11
South Dakota	–	–	–	–	695	549	503
Tennessee	17	86	314	302	620	300	252
Texas	17	48	55	221	321	313	301
Utah	125	945	1783	2390	2387	2141	1672
Vermont	57	384	565	514	959	1056	1043
Virginia	173	584	148	135	300	267	225
Washington	–	11	44	193	1676	1509	1975
West Virginia	–	–	321	369	398	482	880
Wisconsin	4319	6454	6550	5352	4297	3356	2507
Wyoming			58	154	533	393	419

Source: *Sixteenth Census of the USA, 1940, Population Vol. II, Characteristics of the Population*, Reports by States, Parts 1–7, Table 15 (except District of Colombia, Table 10).

[1] There is a discrepancy at source in the figures for these years. The USA total is given as 74533 for 1870 and 83302 for 1880, whereas the sum of the states is 74530 and 83097 respectively.

Population 5.1 Occupations. Males and Females. Wales and Counties. 1851, 1881, 1911

WALES

Class	Number 1851	1881	1911	*Percentage* 1851	1881	1911
Males						
Agriculture, fishing	136212	100918	97248	*35.3*	*20.6*	*12.0*
Mines, Quarries	65398	101675	256250	*16.9*	*20.8*	*31.7*
Metals, Machines, Implements	35659	55503	90845	*9.2*	*11.3*	*11.2*
Textile fabrics, Dress	29748	23079	24499	*7.7*	*4.7*	*3.0*
Building, Construction	26102	39871	59958	*6.8*	*8.1*	*7.4*
Conveyance of men, goods, etc.	16144	36644	85481	*4.2*	*7.5*	*10.6*
Food, Drink, Tobacco, Lodging	14710	21016	44422	*3.8*	*4.3*	*5.5*
Wood, Brick, Chemicals, Skins, Paper	11963	15055	25295	*3.1*	*3.1*	*3.1*
Professional Occupations	6820	12413	22367	*1.8*	*2.5*	*2.8*
Government, Defence, Public Utilities	5492	8075	17976	*1.4*	*1.6*	*2.2*
Domestic Offices or Services	5259	10240	14792	*1.4*	*2.1*	*1.8*
Commercial Occupations	1921	9673	27057	*0.5*	*2.0*	*3.3*
Other, General and Undefined Workers	30530	55477	42404	*7.9*	*11.3*	*5.2*
TOTAL OCCUPIED	385958	489639	808594	*100.0*	*100.0*	*100.0*
Unoccupied	208835	299435	114895			
Females						
Agriculture, fishing	33748	10817	20249	*26.8*	*7.0*	*9.4*
Mines, Quarries	1816	1320	268	*1.4*	*0.9*	*0.1*
Metals, Machines, Implements	2127	3710	3525	*1.7*	*2.4*	*1.6*
Textile fabrics, Dress	30733	29139	40865	*24.4*	*18.8*	*18.9*
Building, Construction	645	58	27	*0.5*	*0.0*	*0.0*
Conveyance of men, goods, etc.	496	416	683	*0.4*	*0.3*	*0.3*
Food, Drink, Tobacco, Lodging	8707	9561	28287	*6.9*	*6.2*	*13.1*
Wood, Brick, Chemicals, Skins, Paper	701	1695	3689	*0.6*	*1.1*	*1.7*
Professional Occupations	1870	6512	18453	*1.5*	*4.2*	*8.6*
Government, Defence, Public Utilities	152	389	2744	*0.1*	*0.3*	*1.3*
Domestic Offices or Services	41948	88221	90496	*33.3*	*57.0*	*42.0*
Commercial Occupations	138	148	2269	*0.1*	*0.1*	*1.1*
Other, General and Undefined Workers	2781	2771	4126	*2.2*	*1.8*	*1.9*
TOTAL OCCUPIED	125862	154757	215681	*100.0*	*100.0*	*100.0*
Unoccupied	468259	633702	696687			

MONMOUTHSHIRE

Class	Number 1851	1881	1911	*Percentage* 1851	1881	1911
Males						
Agriculture, fishing	13396	9576	7842	*21.2*	*12.8*	*5.8*
Mines, Quarries	15771	16208	53504	*25.0*	*21.6*	*39.4*
Metals, Machines, Implements	10038	13089	18147	*15.9*	*17.5*	*13.4*
Textile fabrics, Dress	3508	2422	2824	*5.6*	*3.2*	*2.1*
Building, Construction	4187	5694	9956	*6.6*	*7.6*	*7.3*
Conveyance of men, goods, etc.	2301	6663	14426	*3.6*	*8.9*	*10.6*
Food, Drink, Tobacco, Lodging	2502	3399	6870	*4.0*	*4.5*	*5.1*
Wood, Brick, Chemicals, Skins, Paper	2018	2063	3747	*3.2*	*2.8*	*2.8*
Professional Occupations	974	1579	3023	*1.5*	*2.1*	*2.2*
Government, Defence, Public Utilities	855	980	2390	*1.4*	*1.3*	*1.8*
Domestic Offices or Services	851	1383	2071	*1.3*	*1.8*	*1.5*
Commercial Occupations	393	1576	4087	*0.6*	*2.1*	*3.0*
Other, General and Undefined Workers	6370	10236	6928	*10.1*	*13.7*	*5.1*
TOTAL OCCUPIED	63164	74868	135815	*100.0*	*100.0*	*100.0*
Unoccupied	29137	45097	22057			
Females						
Agriculture, fishing	2088	540	940	*12.9*	*2.8*	*3.5*
Mines, Quarries	525	346	86	*3.2*	*1.8*	*0.3*
Metals, Machines, Implements	653	732	294	*4.0*	*3.8*	*1.1*
Textile fabrics, Dress	4418	3584	5096	*27.3*	*18.4*	*18.8*
Building, Construction	156	15	4	*1.0*	*0.1*	*0.0*
Conveyance of men, goods, etc.	56	60	99	*0.3*	*0.3*	*0.4*
Food, Drink, Tobacco, Lodging	1142	1039	3484	*7.1*	*5.3*	*12.8*
Wood, Brick, Chemicals, Skins, Paper	123	317	612	*0.8*	*1.6*	*2.3*
Professional Occupations	427	1204	2951	*2.6*	*6.2*	*10.9*
Government, Defence, Public Utilities	19	69	456	*0.1*	*0.4*	*1.7*
Domestic Offices or Services	6213	11130	12102	*38.4*	*57.1*	*44.6*
Commercial Occupations	13	27	361	*0.1*	*0.1*	*1.3*
Other, General and Undefined Workers	340	415	649	*2.1*	*2.1*	*2.4*
TOTAL OCCUPIED	16173	19478	27134	*100.0*	*100.0*	*100.0*
Unoccupied	68656	94889	112392			

GLAMORGAN

Class	Number 1851	1881	1911	Percentage 1851	1881	1911
Males						
Agriculture, fishing	13237	10186	9718	*15.6*	*6.1*	*2.5*
Mines, Quarries	22320	48380	150694	*26.3*	*28.9*	*39.3*
Metals, Machines, Implements	13670	26709	48461	*16.1*	*15.9*	*12.6*
Textile fabrics, Dress	5081	6088	9918	*6.0*	*3.6*	*2.6*
Building, Construction	6320	13195	26441	*7.5*	*7.9*	*6.9*
Conveyance of men, goods, etc.	5629	17663	48376	*6.6*	*10.5*	*12.6*
Food, Drink, Tobacco, Lodging	3291	7004	21156	*3.9*	*4.2*	*5.5*
Wood, Brick, Chemicals, Skins, Paper	2623	4740	10989	*3.1*	*2.8*	*2.9*
Professional Occupations	1275	3674	9622	*1.5*	*2.2*	*2.5*
Government, Defence, Public Utilities	734	2010	7680	*0.9*	*1.2*	*2.0*
Domestic Offices or Services	686	2140	4271	*0.8*	*1.3*	*1.1*
Commercial Occupations	608	4464	15886	*0.7*	*2.7*	*4.1*
Other, General and Undefined Workers	9313	21235	19970	*11.0*	*12.7*	*5.2*
TOTAL OCCUPIED	84787	167488	383182	*100.0*	*100.0*	*100.0*
Unoccupied	40300	98640	62575			
Females						
Agriculture, fishing	3030	964	1607	*13.2*	*2.2*	*2.0*
Mines, Quarries	678	558	92	*3.0*	*1.3*	*0.1*
Metals, Machines, Implements	888	2095	2157	*3.9*	*4.8*	*2.6*
Textile fabrics, Dress	6027	9122	18509	*26.3*	*20.9*	*22.7*
Building, Construction	186	12	11	*0.8*	*0.0*	*0.0*
Conveyance of men, goods, etc.	74	112	363	*0.3*	*0.3*	*0.4*
Food, Drink, Tobacco, Lodging	1941	2582	10906	*8.5*	*5.9*	*13.4*
Wood, Brick, Chemicals, Skins, Paper	166	695	1896	*0.7*	*1.6*	*2.3*
Professional Occupations	397	2437	8297	*1.7*	*5.6*	*10.2*
Government, Defence, Public Utilities	17	65	1066	*0.1*	*0.1*	*1.3*
Domestic Offices or Services	8834	23999	33079	*38.6*	*55.1*	*40.6*
Commercial Occupations	51	44	1404	*0.2*	*0.1*	*1.7*
Other, General and Undefined Workers	604	860	2022	*2.6*	*2.0*	*2.5*
TOTAL OCCUPIED	22893	43545	81409	*100.0*	*100.0*	*100.0*
Unoccupied	92115	208710	320998			

CARMARTHENSHIRE

Class	Number 1851	1881	1911	Percentage 1851	1881	1911
Males						
Agriculture, fishing	13060	9295	11372	*46.7*	*29.8*	*21.4*
Mines, Quarries	2793	3163	11340	*10.0*	*10.1*	*21.3*
Metals, Machines, Implements	1971	5476	9505	*7.1*	*17.6*	*17.9*
Textile fabrics, Dress	2439	2025	2287	*8.7*	*6.5*	*4.3*
Building, Construction	2162	2536	4272	*7.7*	*8.1*	*8.0*
Conveyance of men, goods, etc.	781	1388	3747	*2.8*	*4.5*	*7.1*
Food, Drink, Tobacco, Lodging	953	1199	2189	*3.4*	*3.8*	*4.1*
Wood, Brick, Chemicals, Skins, Paper	999	1052	1624	*3.6*	*3.4*	*3.1*
Professional Occupations	544	894	1389	*1.9*	*2.9*	*2.6*
Government, Defence, Public Utilities	512	381	885	*1.8*	*1.2*	*1.7*
Domestic Offices or Services	305	553	823	*1.1*	*1.8*	*1.5*
Commercial Occupations	118	559	1190	*0.4*	*1.8*	*2.2*
Other, General and Undefined Workers	1304	2663	2516	*4.7*	*8.5*	*4.7*
TOTAL OCCUPIED	27941	31184	53139	*100.0*	*100.0*	*100.0*
Unoccupied	17578	22305	9690			
Females						
Agriculture, fishing	4398	1636	4055	*38.1*	*13.0*	*21.6*
Mines, Quarries	24	29	13	*0.2*	*0.2*	*0.1*
Metals, Machines, Implements	67	766	893	*0.6*	*6.1*	*4.7*
Textile fabrics, Dress	2384	2198	4046	*20.6*	*17.4*	*21.5*
Building, Construction	29	2	4	*0.3*	*0.0*	*0.0*
Conveyance of men, goods, etc.	31	39	28	*0.3*	*0.3*	*0.1*
Food, Drink, Tobacco, Lodging	807	730	1930	*7.0*	*5.8*	*10.3*
Wood, Brick, Chemicals, Skins, Paper	84	145	178	*0.7*	*1.2*	*0.9*
Professional Occupations	135	364	996	*1.2*	*2.9*	*5.3*
Government, Defence, Public Utilities	11	27	177	*0.1*	*0,2*	*0.9*
Domestic Offices or Services	3322	6492	6189	*28.8*	*51.5*	*32.9*
Commercial Occupations	7	4	71	*0.1*	*0.0*	*0.4*
Other, General and Undefined Workers	255	176	231	*2.2*	*1.4*	*1.2*
TOTAL OCCUPIED	11554	12608	18811	*100.0*	*100.0*	*100.0*
Unoccupied	37599	45158	44174			

PEMBROKESHIRE

Class	Number 1851	1881	1911	Percentage 1851	1881	1911
Males						
Agriculture, fishing	9865	7820	8906	*41.7*	*32.4*	*31.7*
Mines, Quarries	1139	666	1017	*4.8*	*2.8*	*3.6*
Metals, Machines, Implements	1232	2337	2974	*5.2*	*9.7*	*10.6*
Textile fabrics, Dress	1935	1411	1120	*8.2*	*5.8*	*4.0*
Building, Construction	1873	2275	2493	*7.9*	*9.4*	*8.9*
Conveyance of men, goods, etc.	1306	1939	2851	*5.5*	*8.0*	*10.2*
Food, Drink, Tobacco, Lodging	878	1018	1646	*3.7*	*4.2*	*5.9*
Wood, Brick, Chemicals, Skins, Paper	742	727	726	*3.1*	*3.0*	*2.6*
Professional Occupations	544	694	885	*2.3*	*2.9*	*3.2*
Government, Defence, Public Utilities	1558	1621	2100	*6.6*	*6.7*	*7.5*
Domestic Offices or Services	437	630	710	*1.8*	*2.6*	*2.5*
Commercial Occupations	125	319	559	*0.5*	*1.3*	*2.0*
Other, General and Undefined Workers	2036	2671	2096	*8.6*	*11.1*	*7.5*
TOTAL OCCUPIED	23670	24128	28083	*100.0*	*100.0*	*100.0*
Unoccupied	15950	15957	6217			
Females						
Agriculture, fishing	3298	1256	2517	*31.9*	*12.3*	*21.9*
Mines, Quarries	273	35	8	*2.6*	*0.3*	*0.1*
Metals, Machines, Implements	6	7	15	*0.1*	*0.1*	*0.1*
Textile fabrics, Dress	2303	1826	2060	*22.2*	*17.8*	*18.0*
Building, Construction	33	5	1	*0.3*	*0.0*	*0.0*
Conveyance of men, goods, etc.	35	22	18	*0.3*	*0.2*	*0.2*
Food, Drink, Tobacco, Lodging	677	721	1262	*6.5*	*7.0*	*11.0*
Wood, Brick, Chemicals, Skins, Paper	42	46	77	*0.4*	*0.4*	*0.7*
Professional Occupations	171	322	678	*1.7*	*3.1*	*5.9*
Government, Defence, Public Utilities	14	25	162	*0.1*	*0.2*	*1.4*
Domestic Offices or Services	3321	5882	4519	*32.1*	*57.4*	*39.4*
Commercial Occupations	14	8	31	*0.1*	*0.1*	*0.3*
Other, General and Undefined Workers	165	97	127	*1.6*	*0.9*	*1.1*
TOTAL OCCUPIED	10352	10252	11475	*100.0*	*100.0*	*100.0*
Unoccupied	34500	33342	26001			

CARDIGANSHIRE

Class	Number 1851	1881	1911	Percentage 1851	1881	1911
Males						
Agriculture, fishing	13544	11744	7965	*49.7*	*47.3*	*45.7*
Mines, Quarries	1883	1972	788	*6.9*	*7.9*	*4.5*
Metals, Machines, Implements	850	835	640	*3.1*	*3.4*	*3.7*
Textile fabrics, Dress	2646	2099	1085	*9.7*	*8.5*	*6.2*
Building, Construction	1931	2164	1626	*7.1*	*8.7*	*9.3*
Conveyance of men, goods, etc.	1074	975	1014	*3.9*	*3.9*	*5.8*
Food, Drink, Tobacco, Lodging	722	910	966	*2.7*	*3.7*	*5.5*
Wood, Brick, Chemicals, Skins, Paper	644	658	469	*2.4*	*2.7*	*2.7*
Professional Occupations	535	813	792	*2.0*	*3.3*	*4.5*
Government, Defence, Public Utilities	330	348	397	*1.2*	*1.4*	*2.3*
Domestic Offices or Services	344	488	466	*1.3*	*2.0*	*2.7*
Commercial Occupations	102	247	364	*0.4*	*1.0*	*2.1*
Other, General and Undefined Workers	2635	1570	848	*9.7*	*6.3*	*4.9*
TOTAL OCCUPIED	27240	24823	17420	*100.0*	*100.0*	*100.0*
Unoccupied	17915	17894	4452			
Females						
Agriculture, fishing	4868	2351	2571	*42.4*	*17.2*	*25.9*
Mines, Quarries	9	151	3	*0.1*	*1.1*	*0.0*
Metals, Machines, Implements	258	8	19	*2.2*	*0.1*	*0.2*
Textile fabrics, Dress	2521	2884	1521	*22.0*	*21.1*	*15.3*
Building, Construction	19	4	1	*0.2*	*0.0*	*0.0*
Conveyance of men, goods, etc.	29	22	9	*0.3*	*0.2*	*0.1*
Food, Drink, Tobacco, Lodging	607	829	1304	*5.3*	*6.1*	*13.2*
Wood, Brick, Chemicals, Skins, Paper	28	35	56	*0.2*	*0.3*	*0.6*
Professional Occupations	67	205	459	*0.6*	*1.5*	*4.6*
Government, Defence, Public Utilities	15	43	148	*0.1*	*0.3*	*1.5*
Domestic Offices or Services	2601	6898	3680	*22.7*	*50.5*	*37.1*
Commercial Occupations	8	10	21	*0.1*	*0.1*	*0.2*
Other, General and Undefined Workers	445	216	121	*3.9*	*1.6*	*1.2*
TOTAL OCCUPIED	11475	13656	9913	*100.0*	*100.0*	*100.0*
Unoccupied	40984	38764	17929			

BRECONSHIRE

Class	Number 1851	1881	1911	*Percentage* 1851	1881	1911
Males						
Agriculture, fishing	8177	6002	4837	*40.6*	*35.6*	*24.1*
Mines, Quarries	3584	4212	5945	*17.8*	*25.0*	*29.6*
Metals, Machines, Implements	1523	910	896	*7.6*	*5.4*	*4.5*
Textile fabrics, Dress	1410	883	636	*7.0*	*5.2*	*3.2*
Building, Construction	1186	1467	1762	*5.9*	*8.7*	*8.8*
Conveyance of men, goods, etc.	235	695	1270	*1.2*	*4.1*	*6.3*
Food, Drink, Tobacco, Lodging	835	734	1061	*4.1*	*4.4*	*5.3*
Wood, Brick, Chemicals, Skins, Paper	614	466	489	*3.0*	*2.8*	*2.4*
Professional Occupations	404	497	565	*2.0*	*3.0*	*2.8*
Government, Defence, Public Utilities	427	498	585	*2.1*	*3.0*	*2.9*
Domestic Offices or Services	367	590	709	*1.8*	*3.5*	*3.5*
Commercial Occupations	58	212	429	*0.3*	*1.3*	*2.1*
Other, General and Undefined Workers	1342	1481	888	*6.7*	*8.8*	*4.4*
TOTAL OCCUPIED	20162	16847	20070	*100.0*	*100.0*	*100.0*
Unoccupied	9831	10144	3718			
Females						
Agriculture, fishing	1748	342	832	*26.9*	*6.1*	*13.4*
Mines, Quarries	101	56	9	*1.6*	*1.0*	*0.1*
Metals, Machines, Implements	152	12	34	*2.3*	*0.2*	*0.5*
Textile fabrics, Dress	1594	827	905	*24.5*	*14.8*	*14.6*
Building, Construction	37	1	1	*0.6*	*0.0*	*0.0*
Conveyance of men, goods, etc.	31	15	11	*0.5*	*0.3*	*0.2*
Food, Drink, Tobacco, Lodging	458	334	788	*7.0*	*6.0*	*12.7*
Wood, Brick, Chemicals, Skins, Paper	20	76	66	*0.3*	*1.4*	*1.1*
Professional Occupations	74	218	468	*1.1*	*3.9*	*7.5*
Government, Defence, Public Utilities	12	23	95	*0.2*	*0.4*	*1.5*
Domestic Offices or Services	2166	3582	2910	*33.3*	*64.2*	*46.8*
Commercial Occupations	1	2	27	*0.0*	*0.0*	*0.4*
Other, General and Undefined Workers	108	94	72	*1.7*	*1.7*	*1.2*
TOTAL OCCUPIED	6502	5582	6218	*100.0*	*100.0*	*100.0*
Unoccupied	22683	21547	16285			

RADNORSHIRE

Class	Number 1851	1881	1911	*Percentage* 1851	1881	1911
Males						
Agriculture, fishing	6472	3347	3951	*63.4*	*57.7*	*52.0*
Mines, Quarries	52	45	152	*0.5*	*0.8*	*2.0*
Metals, Machines, Implements	378	177	267	*3.7*	*3.1*	*3.5*
Textile fabrics, Dress	695	306	255	*6.8*	*5.3*	*3.4*
Building, Construction	672	545	704	*6.6*	*9.4*	*9.3*
Conveyance of men, goods, etc.	70	95	428	*0.7*	*1.6*	*5.6*
Food, Drink, Tobacco, Lodging	398	249	424	*3.9*	*4.3*	*5.6*
Wood, Brick, Chemicals, Skins, Paper	357	133	174	*3.5*	*2.3*	*2.3*
Professional Occupations	182	141	256	*1.8*	*2.4*	*3.4*
Government, Defence, Public Utilities	73	66	196	*0.7*	*1.1*	*2.6*
Domestic Offices or Services	237	225	377	*2.3*	*3.9*	*5.0*
Commercial Occupations	33	32	123	*0.3*	*0.6*	*1.6*
Other, General and Undefined Workers	585	441	295	*5.7*	*7.6*	*3.9*
TOTAL OCCUPIED	10204	5802	7602	*100.0*	*100.0*	*100.0*
Unoccupied	5914	3602	1478			
Females						
Agriculture, fishing	1273	142	503	*38.1*	*7.2*	*16.4*
Mines, Quarries	1	0	1	*0.0*	*0.0*	*0.0*
Metals, Machines, Implements	3	0	0	*0.1*	*0.0*	*0.0*
Textile fabrics, Dress	670	278	289	*20.0*	*14.1*	*9.4*
Building, Construction	9	0	1	*0.3*	*0.0*	*0.0*
Conveyance of men, goods, etc.	13	7	7	*0.4*	*0.4*	*0.2*
Food, Drink, Tobacco, Lodging	124	87	489	*3.7*	*4.4*	*15.9*
Wood, Brick, Chemicals, Skins, Paper	12	7	25	*0.4*	*0.4*	*0.8*
Professional Occupations	66	75	184	*2.0*	*3.8*	*6.0*
Government, Defence, Public Utilities	6	4	37	*0.2*	*0.2*	*1.2*
Domestic Offices or Services	1112	1354	1496	*33.3*	*68.7*	*48.7*
Commercial Occupations	2	2	12	*0.1*	*0.1*	*0.4*
Other, General and Undefined Workers	52	15	25	*1.6*	*0.8*	*0.8*
TOTAL OCCUPIED	3343	1971	3069	*100.0*	*100.0*	*100.0*
Unoccupied	11964	7148	6017			

MONTGOMERYSHIRE

Class	Number 1851	1881	1911	*Percentage* 1851	1881	1911
Males						
Agriculture, fishing	14293	10777	8503	*56.0*	*45.3*	*49.3*
Mines, Quarries	1250	1683	517	*4.9*	*7.1*	*3.0*
Metals, Machines, Implements	936	857	630	*3.7*	*3.6*	*3.7*
Textile fabrics, Dress	3889	1961	1034	*15.2*	*8.2*	*6.0*
Building, Construction	1230	1763	1306	*4.8*	*7.4*	*7.6*
Conveyance of men, goods, etc.	393	543	1013	*1.5*	*2.3*	*5.9*
Food, Drink, Tobacco, Lodging	1083	1088	948	*4.2*	*4.6*	*5.5*
Wood, Brick, Chemicals, Skins, Paper	754	643	471	*3.0*	*2.7*	*2.7*
Professional Occupations	430	682	554	*1.7*	*2.9*	*3.2*
Government, Defence, Public Utilities	203	392	399	*0.8*	*1.6*	*2.3*
Domestic Offices or Services	403	752	671	*1.6*	*3.2*	*3.9*
Commercial Occupations	63	281	348	*0.2*	*1.2*	*2.0*
Other, General and Undefined Workers	581	2363	861	*2.3*	*9.9*	*5.0*
TOTAL OCCUPIED	25508	23785	17255	*100.0*	*100.0*	*100.0*
Unoccupied	13033	14510	3520			
Females						
Agriculture, fishing	3031	769	1543	*30.7*	*9.1*	*21.6*
Mines, Quarries	9	16	9	*0.1*	*0.2*	*0.1*
Metals, Machines, Implements	63	8	13	*0.6*	*0.1*	*0.2*
Textile fabrics, Dress	3323	1767	1227	*33.7*	*21.0*	*17.1*
Building, Construction	30	4	0	*0.3*	*0.0*	*0.0*
Conveyance of men, goods, etc.	40	24	13	*0.4*	*0.3*	*0.2*
Food, Drink, Tobacco, Lodging	506	441	617	*5.1*	*5.2*	*8.6*
Wood, Brick, Chemicals, Skins, Paper	19	42	41	*0.2*	*0.5*	*0.6*
Professional Occupations	89	261	395	*0.9*	*3.1*	*5.5*
Government, Defence, Public Utilities	10	24	73	*0.1*	*0.3*	*1.0*
Domestic Offices or Services	2631	4950	3129	*26.7*	*58.8*	*43.7*
Commercial Occupations	0	7	24	*0.0*	*0.1*	*0.3*
Other, General and Undefined Workers	118	99	71	*1.2*	*1.2*	*1.0*
TOTAL OCCUPIED	9869	8412	7155	*100.0*	*100.0*	*100.0*
Unoccupied	28732	29489	14523			

FLINTSHIRE

Class	Number 1851	1881	1911	*Percentage* 1851	1881	1911
Males						
Agriculture, fishing	3225	2261	5213	*24.8*	*15.8*	*17.8*
Mines, Quarries	3541	3503	5057	*27.2*	*24.5*	*17.2*
Metals, Machines, Implements	1135	1132	4409	*8.7*	*7.9*	*15.0*
Textile fabrics, Dress	779	514	995	*6.0*	*3.6*	*3.4*
Building, Construction	710	946	2237	*5.5*	*6.6*	*7.6*
Conveyance of men, goods, etc.	520	662	2350	*4.0*	*4.6*	*8.0*
Food, Drink, Tobacco, Lodging	606	665	1911	*4.7*	*4.6*	*6.5*
Wood, Brick, Chemicals, Skins, Paper	609	1331	2060	*4.7*	*9.3*	*7.0*
Professional Occupations	195	353	975	*1.5*	*2.5*	*3.3*
Government, Defence, Public Utilities	97	171	545	*0.7*	*1.2*	*1.9*
Domestic Offices or Services	226	366	903	*1.7*	*2.6*	*3.1*
Commercial Occupations	81	249	918	*0.6*	*1.7*	*3.1*
Other, General and Undefined Workers	1285	2150	1786	*9.9*	*15.0*	*6.1*
TOTAL OCCUPIED	13009	14303	29359	*100.0*	*100.0*	*100.0*
Unoccupied	7778	8914	6440			
Females						
Agriculture, fishing	713	194	825	*19.7*	*5.0*	*8.9*
Mines, Quarries	8	16	5	*0.2*	*0.4*	*0.1*
Metals, Machines, Implements	14	45	32	*0.4*	*1.2*	*0.3*
Textile fabrics, Dress	786	722	1430	*21.7*	*18.8*	*15.5*
Building, Construction	24	5	1	*0.7*	*0.1*	*0.0*
Conveyance of men, goods, etc.	35	29	31	*1.0*	*0.8*	*0.3*
Food, Drink, Tobacco, Lodging	347	280	1317	*9.6*	*7.3*	*14.3*
Wood, Brick, Chemicals, Skins, Paper	67	107	218	*1.9*	*2.8*	*2.4*
Professional Occupations	67	183	912	*1.9*	*4.8*	*9.9*
Government, Defence, Public Utilities	7	17	111	*0.2*	*0.4*	*1.2*
Domestic Offices or Services	1455	2148	4109	*40.2*	*55.9*	*44.6*
Commercial Occupations	23	2	47	*0.6*	*0.1*	*0.5*
Other, General and Undefined Workers	74	95	185	*2.0*	*2.5*	*2.0*
TOTAL OCCUPIED	3620	3843	9223	*100.0*	*100.0*	*100.0*
Unoccupied	16640	18714	27671			

DENBIGHSHIRE

Class	Number 1851	1881	1911	Percentage 1851	1881	1911
Males						
Agriculture, fishing	14117	9475	10149	*44.9*	*26.6*	*21.7*
Mines, Quarries	4637	7719	11978	*14.7*	*21.7*	*25.6*
Metals, Machines, Implements	1750	1587	2350	*5.6*	*4.5*	*5.0*
Textile fabrics, Dress	2483	1637	1584	*7.9*	*4.6*	*3.4*
Building, Construction	1822	2823	3388	*5.8*	*7.9*	*7.2*
Conveyance of men, goods, etc.	573	1008	2899	*1.8*	*2.8*	*6.2*
Food, Drink, Tobacco, Lodging	1465	1947	3073	*4.7*	*5.5*	*6.6*
Wood, Brick, Chemicals, Skins, Paper	1130	1550	2802	*3.6*	*4.4*	*6.0*
Professional Occupations	699	1101	1598	*2.2*	*3.1*	*3.4*
Government, Defence, Public Utilities	272	766	1063	*0.9*	*2.2*	*2.3*
Domestic Offices or Services	688	1338	1714	*2.2*	*3.8*	*3.7*
Commercial Occupations	137	648	1451	*0.4*	*1.8*	*3.1*
Other, General and Undefined Workers	1669	4001	2696	*5.3*	*11.2*	*5.8*
TOTAL OCCUPIED	31442	35600	46745	*100.0*	*100.0*	*100.0*
Unoccupied	17197	20901	9940			
Females						
Agriculture, fishing	3015	684	1576	*28.0*	*6.1*	*10.8*
Mines, Quarries	115	57	5	*1.1*	*0.5*	*0.0*
Metals, Machines, Implements	6	9	16	*0.1*	*0.1*	*0.1*
Textile fabrics, Dress	2323	1645	1884	*21.6*	*14.7*	*12.9*
Building, Construction	55	1	0	*0.5*	*0.0*	*0.0*
Conveyance of men, goods, etc.	62	26	39	*0.6*	*0.2*	*0.3*
Food, Drink, Tobacco, Lodging	854	759	1983	*7.9*	*6.8*	*13.6*
Wood, Brick, Chemicals, Skins, Paper	76	120	253	*0.7*	*1.1*	*1.7*
Professional Occupations	187	504	1280	*1.7*	*4.5*	*8.8*
Government, Defence, Public Utilities	18	39	135	*0.2*	*0.3*	*0.9*
Domestic Offices or Services	3852	7178	7095	*35.8*	*64.3*	*48.6*
Commercial Occupations	3	10	128	*0.0*	*0.1*	*0.9*
Other, General and Undefined Workers	185	224	216	*1.7*	*2.0*	*1.5*
TOTAL OCCUPIED	10751	11156	14610	*100.0*	*100.0*	*100.0*
Unoccupied	37525	45283	42524			

MERIONETH

Class	Number 1851	1881	1911	Percentage 1851	1881	1911
Males						
Agriculture, fishing	8498	6784	4734	*53.0*	*31.2*	*32.5*
Mines, Quarries	1658	5072	3368	*10.3*	*23.4*	*23.1*
Metals, Machines, Implements	582	659	367	*3.6*	*3.0*	*2.5*
Textile fabrics, Dress	1549	1268	561	*9.7*	*5.8*	*3.9*
Building, Construction	772	2096	1228	*4.8*	*9.7*	*8.4*
Conveyance of men, goods, etc.	436	878	987	*2.7*	*4.0*	*6.8*
Food, Drink, Tobacco, Lodging	498	783	739	*3.1*	*3.6*	*5.1*
Wood, Brick, Chemicals, Skins, Paper	416	553	360	*2.6*	*2.5*	*2.5*
Professional Occupations	295	641	546	*1.8*	*3.0*	*3.7*
Government, Defence, Public Utilities	117	196	328	*0.7*	*0.9*	*2.3*
Domestic Offices or Services	237	555	506	*1.5*	*2.6*	*3.5*
Commercial Occupations	39	311	296	*0.2*	*1.4*	*2.0*
Other, General and Undefined Workers	936	1916	542	*5.8*	*8.8*	*3.7*
TOTAL OCCUPIED	16033	21712	14562	*100.0*	*100.0*	*100.0*
Unoccupied	9356	12638	3151			
Females						
Agriculture, fishing	2155	632	901	*38.9*	*9.4*	*15.7*
Mines, Quarries	6	9	4	*0.1*	*0.1*	*0.1*
Metals, Machines, Implements	7	5	9	*0.1*	*0.1*	*0.2*
Textile fabrics, Dress	1188	993	766	*21.4*	*14.7*	*13.4*
Building, Construction	14	0	0	*0.3*	*0.0*	*0.0*
Conveyance of men, goods, etc.	31	15	12	*0.6*	*0.2*	*0.2*
Food, Drink, Tobacco, Lodging	322	420	857	*5.8*	*6.2*	*15.0*
Wood, Brick, Chemicals, Skins, Paper	22	31	44	*0.4*	*0.5*	*0.8*
Professional Occupations	50	192	388	*0.9*	*2.8*	*6.8*
Government, Defence, Public Utilities	8	20	76	*0.1*	*0.3*	*1.3*
Domestic Offices or Services	1659	4314	2575	*29.9*	*64.0*	*45.0*
Commercial Occupations	0	6	15	*0.0*	*0.1*	*0.3*
Other, General and Undefined Workers	80	105	75	*1.4*	*1.6*	*1.3*
TOTAL OCCUPIED	5542	6742	5722	*100.0*	*100.0*	*100.0*
Unoccupied	20376	27180	13813			

CAERNARFONSHIRE

Class	Number 1851	1881	1911	*Percentage* 1851	1881	1911
Males						
Agriculture, fishing	11755	9155	7755	*39.8*	*24.0*	*19.6*
Mines, Quarries	5698	10463	11172	*19.3*	*27.5*	*28.2*
Metals, Machines, Implements	1136	1271	1535	*3.8*	*3.3*	*3.9*
Textile fabrics, Dress	2219	1887	1663	*7.5*	*5.0*	*4.2*
Building, Construction	2057	3500	3267	*7.0*	*9.2*	*8.2*
Conveyance of men, goods, etc.	1981	2474	3664	*6.7*	*6.5*	*9.2*
Food, Drink, Tobacco, Lodging	984	1604	2591	*3.3*	*4.2*	*6.5*
Wood, Brick, Chemicals, Skins, Paper	772	938	1116	*2.6*	*2.5*	*2.8*
Professional Occupations	524	1090	1621	*1.8*	*2.9*	*4.1*
Government, Defence, Public Utilities	196	501	991	*0.7*	*1.3*	*2.5*
Domestic Offices or Services	383	1075	1103	*1.3*	*2.8*	*2.8*
Commercial Occupations	109	668	1157	*0.4*	*1.8*	*2.9*
Other, General and Undefined Workers	1747	3454	1984	*5.9*	*9.1*	*5.0*
TOTAL OCCUPIED	29561	38080	39619	*100.0*	*100.0*	*100.0*
Unoccupied	16911	22662	7936			
Females						
Agriculture, fishing	2661	917	1310	*28.1*	*6.5*	*8.8*
Mines, Quarries	2	32	30	*0.0*	*0.2*	*0.2*
Metals, Machines, Implements	10	12	31	*0.1*	*0.1*	*0.2*
Textile fabrics, Dress	2174	2567	2243	*22.9*	*18.3*	*15.1*
Building, Construction	37	6	1	*0.4*	*0.0*	*0.0*
Conveyance of men, goods, etc.	47	24	37	*0.5*	*0.2*	*0.2*
Food, Drink, Tobacco, Lodging	614	1077	2647	*6.5*	*7.7*	*17.9*
Wood, Brick, Chemicals, Skins, Paper	31	59	184	*0.3*	*0.4*	*1.2*
Professional Occupations	101	447	1043	*1.1*	*3.2*	*7.0*
Government, Defence, Public Utilities	11	21	156	*0.1*	*0.1*	*1.1*
Domestic Offices or Services	3561	8581	6807	*37.5*	*61.2*	*45.9*
Commercial Occupations	15	24	117	*0.2*	*0.2*	*0.8*
Other, General and Undefined Workers	220	244	223	*2.3*	*1.7*	*1.5*
TOTAL OCCUPIED	9484	14011	14829	*100.0*	*100.0*	*100.0*
Unoccupied	38718	49028	38999			

ANGLESEY

Class	Number 1851	1881	1911	*Percentage* 1851	1881	1911
Males						
Agriculture, fishing	6573	4496	6303	*49.7*	*40.8*	*40.0*
Mines, Quarries	1072	389	718	*8.1*	*3.5*	*4.6*
Metals, Machines, Implements	458	464	664	*3.5*	*4.2*	*4.2*
Textile fabrics, Dress	1115	578	537	*8.4*	*5.2*	*3.4*
Building, Construction	1180	867	1278	*8.9*	*7.9*	*8.1*
Conveyance of men, goods, etc.	845	1661	2456	*6.4*	*15.1*	*15.6*
Food, Drink, Tobacco, Lodging	495	416	848	*3.7*	*3.8*	*5.4*
Wood, Brick, Chemicals, Skins, Paper	285	201	268	*2.2*	*1.8*	*1.7*
Professional Occupations	219	254	541	*1.7*	*2.3*	*3.4*
Government, Defence, Public Utilities	118	145	417	*0.9*	*1.3*	*2.6*
Domestic Offices or Services	95	145	468	*0.7*	*1.3*	*3.0*
Commercial Occupations	55	107	249	*0.4*	*1.0*	*1.6*
Other, General and Undefined Workers	727	1296	994	*5.5*	*11.8*	*6.3*
TOTAL OCCUPIED	13237	11019	15741	*100.0*	*100.0*	*100.0*
Unoccupied	7935	6171	3721			
Females						
Agriculture, fishing	1470	390	1069	*34.2*	*11.1*	*17.5*
Mines, Quarries	65	15	3	*1.5*	*0.4*	*0.0*
Metals, Machines, Implements	0	11	12	*0.0*	*0.3*	*0.2*
Textile fabrics, Dress	1022	726	889	*23.7*	*20.7*	*14.5*
Building, Construction	16	3	2	*0.4*	*0.1*	*0.0*
Conveyance of men, goods, etc.	12	21	16	*0.3*	*0.6*	*0.3*
Food, Drink, Tobacco, Lodging	308	262	703	*7.2*	*7.5*	*11.5*
Wood, Brick, Chemicals, Skins, Paper	11	15	39	*0.3*	*0.4*	*0.6*
Professional Occupations	39	100	402	*0.9*	*2.9*	*6.6*
Government, Defence, Public Utilities	4	12	52	*0.1*	*0.3*	*0.9*
Domestic Offices or Services	1221	1813	2806	*28.4*	*51.8*	*45.9*
Commercial Occupations	1	2	11	*0.0*	*0.1*	*0.2*
Other, General and Undefined Workers	135	131	109	*3.1*	*3.7*	*1.8*
TOTAL OCCUPIED	4304	3501	6113	*100.0*	*100.0*	*100.0*
Unoccupied	17767	14450	15361			

Source: Census figures, as presented in John Williams, *Digest of Welsh Historical Statistics* (2 vols., Cardiff, 1985), I, Tables: Labour 1B and Labour 2C, pp. 96–102, 106–18.

At source, the census occupation categories have been painstakingly reclassified for earlier censuses in order to provide a continuous series 1851–1911 on the basis of the census classification of 1911. Full details of the adjustments are given in Williams (1985), pp. 98–9. Here, in order to indicate the main structural changes in the economy of Wales, and the different experience of men and women in the work domain, classes have been amalgamated. The percentages are the class total as a percentage of the total number occupied.

The figures for 1851 and 1881 are on the basis of Registration Counties; those for 1911 are on the basis of Administrative Counties.

The classes are listed in order of importance for males in Wales in 1851. Instructions on the household schedule for entering details of occupation varied between censuses. Particular care should be taken in the interpretation of figures for women in agriculture and domestic occupations. There is evidence to suggest that living-in female farm servants were more likely to be classified as domestic servants in 1881, and there is inconsistency in the degree of inclusion of female members of the family helping on farms.

Appendix I Wales. Registration Districts. 1851

Source: 1851 Census.

Appendix II. Boundaries. Registration Counties, Ancient Counties, Registration Districts and Subdistricts, and Civil Parishes. 1851

MONMOUTHSHIRE

Monmouth Registration County Registration Districts and Subdistricts

576 Chepstow
1. *Shirenewton*
2. *Chepstow*
3. *Lydney*

577 Monmouth
1. *Coleford*
2. *Dingestow*
3. *Monmouth*
4. *Trelleck*

578 Abergavenny
1. *Llan-arth*
2. *Llanfihangel*
3. *Abergavenny*
4. *Blaenafon*
5. *Aberystruth*
6. *Tredegar*
7. *Rock Bedwellte*

579 Pontypool
1. *Pontypool*
2. *Llangybi*
3. *Usk*

580 Newport
1. *Caerleon*
2. *Newport*
3. *St Woollos*
4. *Mynyddislwyn*

NUMERICAL KEY TO PARISHES
(* indicates part of parish)

576 Chepstow

576.1 Shirenewton

1. Portskewett
2. Caldicot
3. Ifton
4. Roggiett
5. Llanvihangel near Roggiett
6. Undy

45. Llangattock Vibon Avel
46. Llanfihangel Ystum Llywern
47. Llantilio Crossenny
48. Pen-rhos
49. Tregara
50. Dingestow
51. Grace Dieu Park (ExP)
52. Rockfield

577.3 Monmouth

53. Dixton Newton
54. Monmouth

577.4 Trelleck

55. Wonastow
56. Mitchel Troy
57. Pen-allt
58. Llandogo
59. Trelleck* (excl. Trelleck Grange C)
60. Llanishen
61. Llangofen
62. Cwmcarfan
63. Pen-clawdd
64. Raglan
65. Llandenny

578 Abergavenny

578.1 Llan-arth

66. Betws Newydd
67. Bryngwyn
68. Llan-arth
69. Llanfair Cilgedin
70. Llanfihangel-nigh-Usk
71. Llansanffraid
72. Llanddewi Rhydderch

578.2 Llanfihangel

73. Llanvapley
74. Llanddewi Skyrryd
75. Llanvetherine
76. Llangattock Lingoed
77. Llanvihangel Crucorney
78. Cwm-iou* (U. Cwm-iou, L. Cwm-iou, Bwlch-tre-wyn H, Fwthog H (Her))
79. Oldcastle

578.5 Aberystruth

90. Aberystruth

578.6 Tredegar

91. Bedwellte* (Man-moel H, Uwchlaw'r-coed H)

578.7 Rock Bedwellte

92. Bedwellte* (Islaw'r-coed H)

579 Pontypool

579.1 Pontypool

93. Llanhilleth
94. Trevethin (with Pontypool)
95. Mamheilad
96. Llanfihangel Pont-y-moel
97. Pant-teg

579.2 Llangybi

98. Llanfrechfa
99. Llanddewi Fach
100. Llandegveth
101. Llangybi
102. Usk* (Glasgoed H)

579.3 Usk

103. Usk* (Usk, Gwehelog H)
104. Llanbadog Fawr
105. Monkswood
106. Goytre
107. Kemeys Commander
108. Trostre
109. Gwernesni
110. Llangeview
111. Llanhowel
112. Llantrisant

580 Newport

580.1 Caerleon

113. Llanvaches
114. Pen-how
115. Llanmartin with Llandevaud
116. Llan-wern
117. Bishton
118. Wilcrick
119. St Bride's Netherwent* (Llandevenny)
120. Magor
121. Whitson
122. Goldcliff
123. Nash
124. Christchurch
125. Langstone
126. Kemeys Inferior
127. Tredunnock
128. Llanhennock
129. Llangattock (incl. Caerleon T)

580.2 Newport

130. St Woollos (incl. Newport Bor.)
131. St Bride's Wentlloog
133. Marshfield
134. Coedcernyw
135. Basaleg
136. Michaelston-y-Vedw* (incl. Llanfedw (Glam))
137. Risca
138. Henllys
139. Betws
140. Malpas
141. Llanfihangel Llantarnam

580.4 Mynyddislwyn

142. Mynyddislwyn
143. Bedwas* (Lower Bedwas, Upper Bedwas)
144. Machen (incl. Rhyd-y-gwern (Glam))

Parts of Monmouthshire Ancient County in other Registration Counties

Glamorgan

581.2 Cardiff

145. St Mellons
146. Rumney

Herefordshire

348.6 Hereford

147. Grosmont
148. Llangua

7. St Bride's Netherwent* (excl. Llandevenny)
8. Caer-went
9. Llanvair Discoed
10. Shirenewton
11. Itton
12. Newchurch
13. Kilgwrrwg
14. Wolvesnewton
15. Llan-gwm
16. Llansoy
17. Llanvihangel Torymynydd

576.2 Chepstow

18. Trelleck* (Trelleck Grange C)
19. Little Tintern
20. Chapel Hill
21. Penteri
22. St Arvans
23. Chepstow
24. Mounton
25. Matharn and Runston
26. St Pierre
27. Tidenham (Gloucs)

576.3 Lydney

28. Woollaston (Gloucs)
29. Alvington (Gloucs)
30. Lydney (Gloucs)
31. Hewelsfield (Gloucs)
32. St Briavels (Gloucs)

577 Monmouth

577.1 Coleford

33. Newland* (Bream, Clearwell, Newland, Coleford) (Gloucs)
34. West Dean (Gloucs)
35. Staunton (Gloucs)
36. English Bicknor (Gloucs)

577.2 Dingestow

37. Welsh Bicknor (Her)
38. Whitchurch (Her)
39. Ganarew (Her)
40. Welsh Newton (Her)
41. Llanrothal (Her)
42. Garway (Her)
43. Skenfrith
44. St Maughan's

578.3 Abergavenny

80. Llantilio Pertholey
81. Abergavenny
82. Llangattock nigh Usk
83. Llanover* (Lower Division)
84. Llanelen
85. Llanwenarth* (Citra Division)
86. Llanfoist* (First Part)

578.4 Blaenafon

87. Llanfoist* (Second Part)
88. Llanwenarth* (Ultra Division)
89. Llanover* (Upper Division)

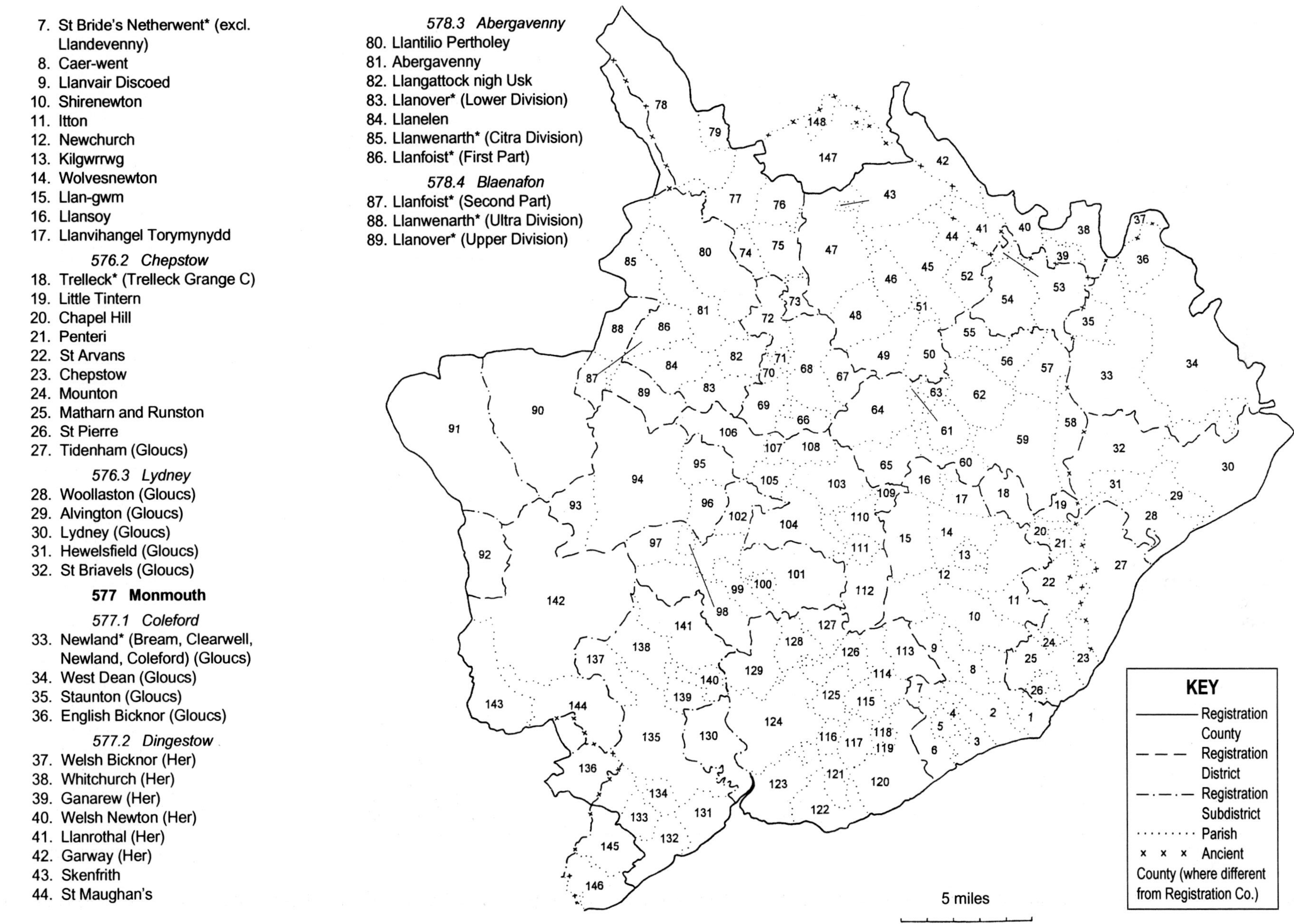

Glamorgan Registration County Registration Districts and Subdistricts

581 Cardiff

1. *Caerphilly*
2. *Cardiff*
3. *St Nicholas*
4. *Llantrisant*

582 Merthyr Tydfil

1. *Gelli-gaer*
2. *L Merthyr Tydfil*
3. *U Merthyr Tydfil*
4. *Aberdare*

583 Bridgend

1. *Maesteg*
2. *Cowbridge*
3. *Bridgend*

584 Neath

1. *Margam*
2. *Neath*
3. *Ystradfellte*
4. *Ystradgynlais*
5. *Cadoxton*
6. *Llansamlet*

585 Swansea

1. *Llandeilo Tal-y-bont*
2. *Llangyfelach*
3. *Swansea*
4. *Gower*

NUMERICAL KEY TO PARISHES
(* indicates part of parish)

581 Cardiff

581.1 Caerphilly

1. Eglwysilan
2. Rudry
3. Bedwas* (Van H)
4. Lisvane
5. Llanedern
6. Llanishen
7. Whitchurch

33. Llanvithyn ExP
34. St Nicholas
35. St Lythan's
36. Wenvoe
37. St Andrews Major
38. Michaelston-super-Ely
39. St George

581.4 Llantrisant

40. St Brides-super-Ely
41. Peterston-super-Ely
42. Pendoylan
43. Llanilltern
44. Pen-tyrch
45. Llantrisant
46. Llantwit Fardre

582 Merthyr Tydfil

582.1 Gelli-gaer

47. Llanwynno
48. Llanfabon
49. Gelli-gaer

582.2 L Merthyr Tydfil

50. Merthyr Tydfil* (Lower)

582.3 U Merthyr Tydfil

51. Merthyr Tydfil* (Upper)
52. Vaynor (Brec)

582.4 Aberdare

53. Penderyn (Brec)
54. Aberdare
55. Ystradyfodwg

583 Bridgend

583.1 Maesteg

56. Llangynwyd
57. Betws
58. Llangeinor
59. Llandyfodwg
60. Llanharan
61. Llanilid
62. Coychurch
63. St Brides Minor

583.2 Cowbridge

64. Llan-gan

85. Llanblethian
86. Llysworney
87. Nash ExP
88. Stembridge ExP
89. Colwinston

583.3 Bridgend

90. St Andrews Minor
91. Wick
92. St Brides Major
93. Ewenni
94. Coety
95. Newcastle
96. Laleston
97. Merthyr Mawr
98. Tythegston
99. Newton Nottage
100. Pyle and Kenfig

584 Neath

584.1 Margam

101. Margam
102. Llangynwyd* (Higher)
103. Aberafan
104. Michaelston-super-Avan

584.2 Neath

105. Baglan
106. Briton Ferry
107. Neath
108. Llantwit-juxta-Neath

584.3 Ystradfellte

109. Cadoxton* (Lower Neath H, Middle Neath H, Upper Neath H)
110. Glyncorrwg
111. Ystradfellte (Brec)

584.4 Ystradgynlais

112. Ystradgynlais (Brec)
113. Llanguicke

584.5 Cadoxton

114. Cadoxton*(Blaenhonddan H, Dyffryn Clydach H, Coed-ffranc H, Ynysymwn H, Upper Dulais H, Lower Dulais H)
115. Cilybebyll

584.6 Llansamlet

116. Llansamlet

585 Swansea

585.1 Llandeilo Tal-y-bont

117. Llangyfelach* (Rhyndwyglydach H, Mawr H, Penderi H)
118. Llandeilo Tal-y-bont

585.2 Llangyfelach

119. Llangyfelach* (Clas H)
120. Llanrhidian* (Llanrhidian Higher Div)
121. St John's near Swansea
122. Swansea* (Swansea Higher)

585.3 Swansea

123. Swansea* (Swansea Town and Franchise)

585.4 Gower

124. Oystermouth
125. Bishopston
126. Pennard
127. Ilston
128. Pen-maen
129. Nicholaston
130. Penrice
131. Oxwich
132. Port Einon
133. Knelston
134. Reynoldston
135. Llanddewi
136. Rhosili
137. Llangennith
138. Llanmadog
139. Cheriton
140. Llanrhidian* (Llanrhidian Lower)

Parts of Glamorgan Ancient County in other Registration Counties

Monmouthshire

580.3 St Woollos

141. Michaelston-y-Vedw* (incl. Llanfedw)

580.4 Mynyddislwyn

142. Machen (incl. Rhyd-y-gwern)

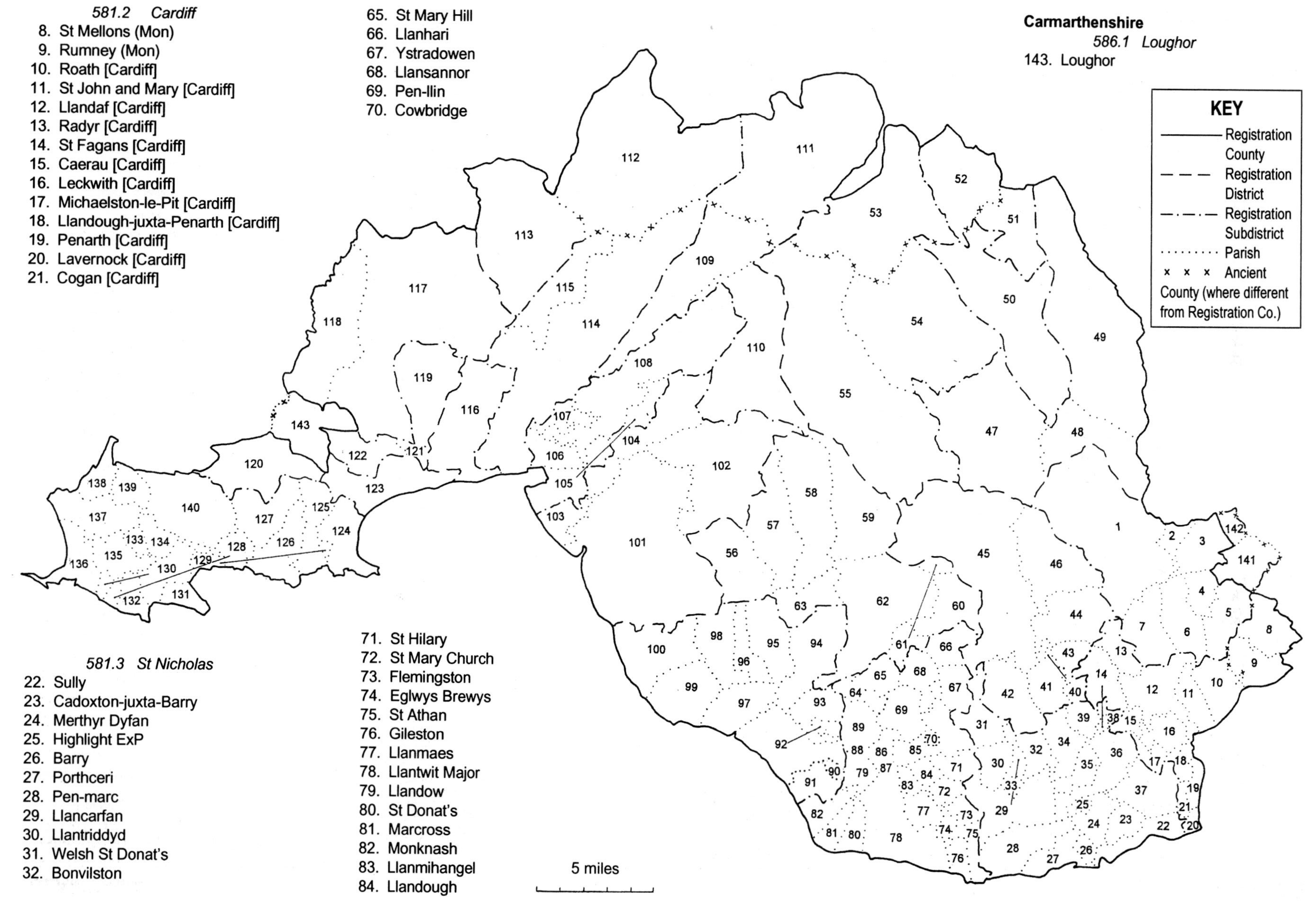
581.2 Cardiff
8. St Mellons (Mon)
9. Rumney (Mon)
10. Roath [Cardiff]
11. St John and Mary [Cardiff]
12. Llandaf [Cardiff]
13. Radyr [Cardiff]
14. St Fagans [Cardiff]
15. Caerau [Cardiff]
16. Leckwith [Cardiff]
17. Michaelston-le-Pit [Cardiff]
18. Llandough-juxta-Penarth [Cardiff]
19. Penarth [Cardiff]
20. Lavernock [Cardiff]
21. Cogan [Cardiff]
581.3 St Nicholas
22. Sully
23. Cadoxton-juxta-Barry
24. Merthyr Dyfan
25. Highlight ExP
26. Barry
27. Porthceri
28. Pen-marc
29. Llancarfan
30. Llantriddyd
31. Welsh St Donat's
32. Bonvilston
65. St Mary Hill
66. Llanhari
67. Ystradowen
68. Llansannor
69. Pen-llin
70. Cowbridge
71. St Hilary
72. St Mary Church
73. Flemingston
74. Eglwys Brewys
75. St Athan
76. Gileston
77. Llanmaes
78. Llantwit Major
79. Llandow
80. St Donat's
81. Marcross
82. Monknash
83. Llanmihangel
84. Llandough
Carmarthenshire
586.1 Loughor
143. Loughor
KEY
Registration County
Registration District
Registration Subdistrict
Parish
Ancient County (where different from Registration Co.)
5 miles

Carmarthen Registration County Registration Districts and Subdistricts

586 Llanelli
1. *Loughor*
2. *Llanelli*
3. *Pembrey*
4. *Llan-non*

587 Llandovery
1. *Llanddeusant*
2. *Llangadog*
3. *Llansadwrn*
4. *Myddfai*
5. *Llandingad*
6. *Llanfair-ar-y-bryn*
7. *Llanwrtyd*
8. *Cil-y-cwm*
9. *Cynwyl Gaeo*

588 Llandeilo Fawr
1. *Talley*
2. *Llanfynydd*
3. *Llangathen*
4. *Llandeilo*
5. *Llandybïe*

589 Carmarthen
1. *Llangyndeyrn*
2. *St Clears*
3. *Carmarthen*
4. *Cynwyl*

NUMERICAL KEY TO PARISHES
(* indicates part of parish)

586 Llanelli

586.1 Loughor
1. Loughor (Glam)
2. Llangennech
3. Llanelli* (Berwick H)

586.2 Llanelli
4. Llanelli* (Llanelli Bor, Hengoed H, Westfa H)

586.3 Pembrey
5. Pembrey
6. St Mary, Kidwelly

586.4 Llan-non
7. Llanelli* (Glyn H)
8. Llan-non
9. Llanedi

587 Llandovery

587.1 Llanddeusant
10. Llanddeusant

587.2 Llangadog
11. Llangadog

587.3 Llansadwrn
12. Llansadwrn
13. Llanwrda

587.4 Myddfai
14. Myddfai

587.5 Llandingad
15. Llandingad (incl. Llandovery Bor)

587.6 Llanfair-ar-y-bryn
16. Llanfair-ar-y-bryn

587.7 Llanwrtyd
17. Llanddulas (Brec)
18. Llanwrtyd (Brec)

587.8 Cil-y-cwm
19. Cil-y-cwm

587.9 Cynwyl Gaeo
20. Cynwyl Gaeo

588 Llandeilo Fawr

588.1 Talley
21. Llansawel
22. Talley

588.2 Llanfynydd
23. Brechfa
24. Llanfynydd
25. Llanfihangel Cilfargen

588.3 Llangathen
26. Llanegwad
27. Llangathen

588.4 Llandeilo
28. Llandyfeisant
29. Llandeilo Fawr* (incl. Llandeilo T)

588.5 Llandybïe
30. Llandeilo Fawr*
31. Llanfihangel Aberbythych
32. Llandybïe
33. Betws

589 Carmarthen

589.1 Llangyndeyrn
34. Llanddarog
35. Llanarthne
36. Llangynnwr
37. Llangyndeyrn
38. Llandyfaelog
39. St Ishmael

589.2 St Clears
40. Llansteffan
41. Laugharne P with Laugharne T
42. Llansadyrnin
43. Llan-dawg
44. Llanddowror
45. Llangynin
46. St Clears
47. Llanfihangel Abercywyn
48. Llandeilo Abercywyn
49. Llangynog

589.3 Carmarthen
50. Llan-gain
51. Carmarthen (St Peter's)
52. Abergwili

589.4 Cynwyl
53. Llanllawddog
54. Llanpumsaint
55. Newchurch
56. Merthyr
57. Aber-nant
58. Cynwyl Elfed PC
59. Tre-lech a'r Betws
60. Meidrim
61. Llanwinio

Parts of Carmarthenshire Ancient County in other Registration Counties

Pembrokeshire

590.1 Llanboidy
62. Llanboidy
63. Henllan Amgoed* (Eglwys Fair a Churig C)
64. Llanglydwen
65. Cilymaenllwyd*
66. Llanfallteg*

590.2 Llandysilio
67. Llandysilio*
68. Egremont

590.3 Amroth
69. Henllan Amgoed*
70. Llan-gan*
71. Cyffig
72. Eglwys Gymyn
73. Pendine
74. Marros

590.4 Narberth
75. Cilymaenllwyd* (Castelldwyran H)

Cardiganshire

594.1 Cenarth
76. Cilrhedyn*
77. Cenarth (incl. Newcastle T)
78. Pen-boyr
79. Llangeler

594.3 Llandysul
80. Llanfihangel-ar-arth

595.1 Llanybydder
81. Llanllwni
82. Llanfihangel Rhos-y-corn
83. Llanybydder

595.2 Pencarreg
84. Pencarreg
85. Llan-y-crwys

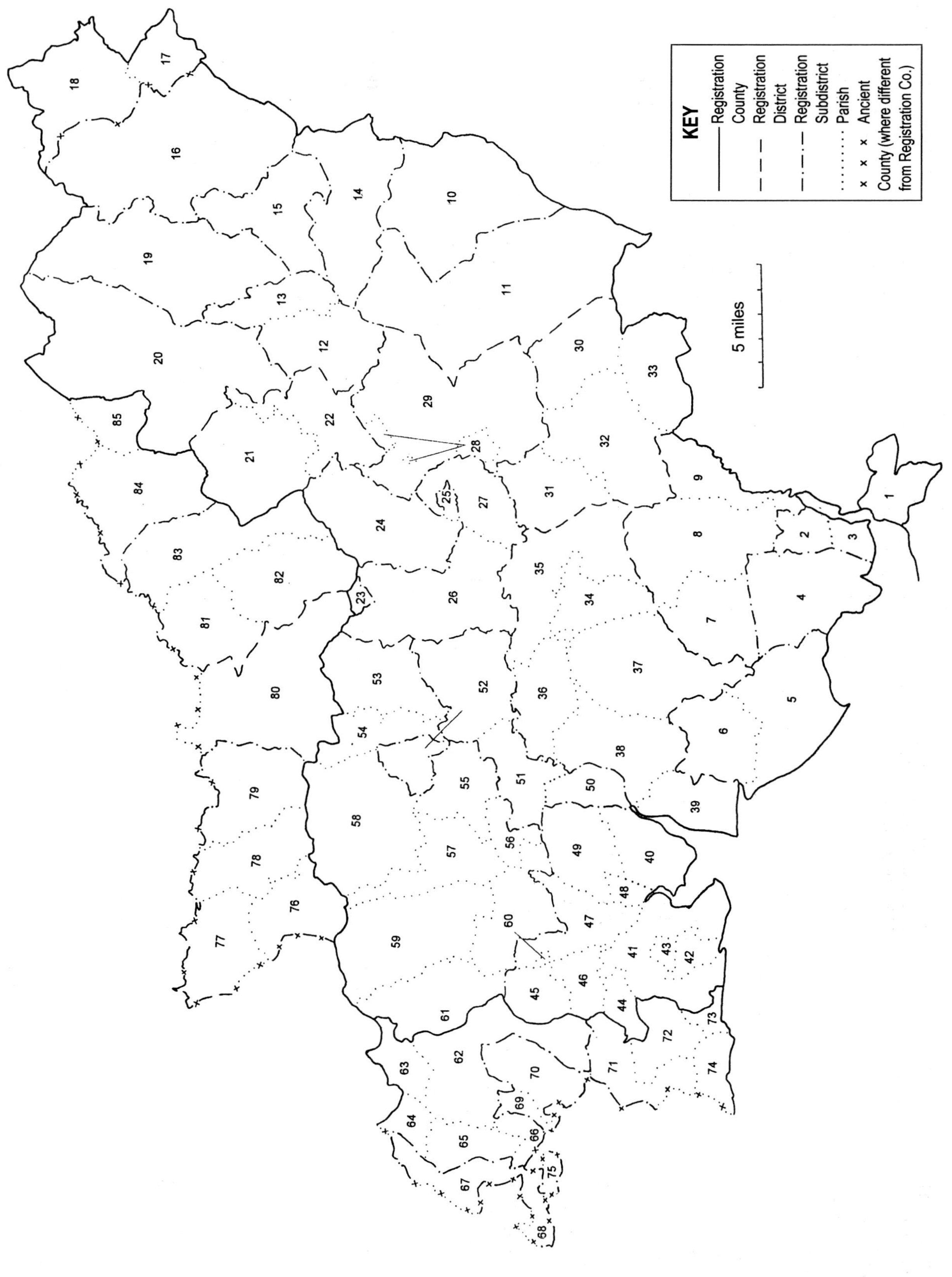
KEY
Registration County
Registration District
Registration Subdistrict
Parish
Ancient County (where different from Registration Co.)
5 miles

PEMBROKESHIRE

Pembroke Registration County Registration Districts and Subdistricts

590 Narberth
1. *Llanboidy*
2. *Llandysilio*
3. *Amroth*
4. *Narberth*
5. *Slebech*
6. *Begeli*

591 Pembroke
1. *Tenby*
2. *Pembroke*
3. *Roose*

592 Haverfordwest
1. *Milford*
2. *Haverfordwest*
3. *St David's*
4. *Fishguard*

NUMERICAL KEY TO PARISHES
(* indicates part of parish)

590 Narberth

590.1 Llanboidy

1. Llanboidy (Carm)
2. Henllan Amgoed* (Eglwys Fair a Churig C (Carm))
3. Llanglydwen (Carm)
4. Cilymaenllwyd* (Carm)
5. Llanfallteg (Carm and Pemb)
6. Mynachlog-ddu

590.2 Llandysilio

7. Llangolman
8. Llandeilo
9. Maenclochog with Forlan H
10. New Moat
11. Llys-y-frân
12. Clarbeston
13. Bletherston
14. Llan-y-cefn
15. Llandysilio (Carm and Pemb)
16. Egremont (Carm)
50. Caldy Island and St Margaret's Island (ExP)
51. Penally
52. Manorbier
53. Hodgeston
54. Lamphey
55. St Florence
56. Carew
57. Lawrenni
58. Nash (with Upton H)
59. Cosheston
60. St Michael, Pembroke

591.2 Pembroke

61. St Mary, Pembroke
62. Monkton
63. St Petrox
64. Stackpole Elidir
65. Bosheston
66. St Twinnels
67. Warren
68. Castlemartin
69. Angle
70. Rhoscrowther
71. Pwllcrochan

591.3 Roose

72. Burton
73. Rosemarket
74. Llanstadwel

592 Haverfordwest

592.1 Milford

75. Steynton (incl. Milford)
76. Hubberston
77. Herbrandston
78. St Ishmaels
79. Dale
80. Marloes
81. St Brides
82. Hasguard
83. Talbenny
84. West Walton
85. Walwyn's Castle
86. West Robeston
87. Johnston
88. Llangwm
89. Freystrop

592.2 Haverfordwest

90. St Issells, Haroldston
91. Haverfordwest (incl. St Thomas, St Mary, St Martin, Furzy Park and Portfield ExP)
92. Prendergast
93. Uzmaston
94. Boulston
95. Wiston
96. Rudbaxton
97. Camrose
98. Lambston
99. Haroldston West
100. Nolton
101. Roch
102. Trefgarn

592.3 St David's

103. St Lawrence
104. Hayscastle
105. St Edrens
106. Llanrheithan
107. Llandeloy
108. Brawdy
109. St Elvis
110. Whitchurch
111. St David's
112. Llanhowel
113. Llanrhian
114. Mathry
115. Granston

592.4 Fishguard

116. St Nicholas
117. Manorowen
118. Llanwnda
119. Fishguard
120. Llanllawer
121. Llanychâr
122. Llanstinan
123. Jordanston
124. Llanfair Nant-y-gof
125. Letterston
126. Little Newcastle
127. St Dogwells
128. Ambleston
129. Spital
130. East Walton
131. Henry's Moat
132. Castlebythe
133. Puncheston
134. Morfil
135. Pont-faen

Parts of Pembrokeshire Ancient County in other Registration Counties

Cardiganshire

593.1 Newport

136. Llanychlwydog
137. Dinas
138. Newport
139. Nevern
140. Bayvil
141. Meline
142. Eglwyswrw
143. Whitechurch
144. Llanfair Nant-gwyn

593.2 Cardigan

145. Llantood
146. Bridell
147. Cilgerran
148. Monington
149. Moylgrove
150. St Dogmaels

593.3 Llandygwydd

151. Maenordeifi
152. Llanfihangel Penbedw

594.1 Cenarth

153. Capel Colman
154. Penrhydd
155. Llanfyrnach
156. Cilrhedyn*
157. Clydau

17. Cilymaenllwyd* (Grondre H)

590.3 Amroth

18. Henllan Amgoed* (Carm)
19. Llan-gan (Carm and Pemb)
20. Cyffig (Carm)
21. Eglwys Gymyn (Carm)
22. Pendine (Carm)
23. Marros (Carm)
24. Amroth
25. Crunwear
26. Ludchurch

590.4 Narberth

27. Crinow
28. Lampeter Velfrey
29. Llanddewi Velfrey with Henllan H
30. Cilymaenllwyd* (Castelldwyran H (Carm))
31. Narberth* (Narberth North)

590.5 Slebech

32. Narberth* (Narberth South)
33. Robeston Wathen PC
34. Llawhaden
35. Newton North
36. Slebech
37. Mounton
38. Minwear
39. Martletwy
40. Coedcanlas

590.6 Begeli

41. Yerbeston
42. Loveston
43. Reynoldston
44. Jeffreston
45. Begeli (incl. Williamston C)
46. St Issells

591 Pembroke

591.1 Tenby

47. Redberth
48. Gumfreston
49. St Mary, Tenby

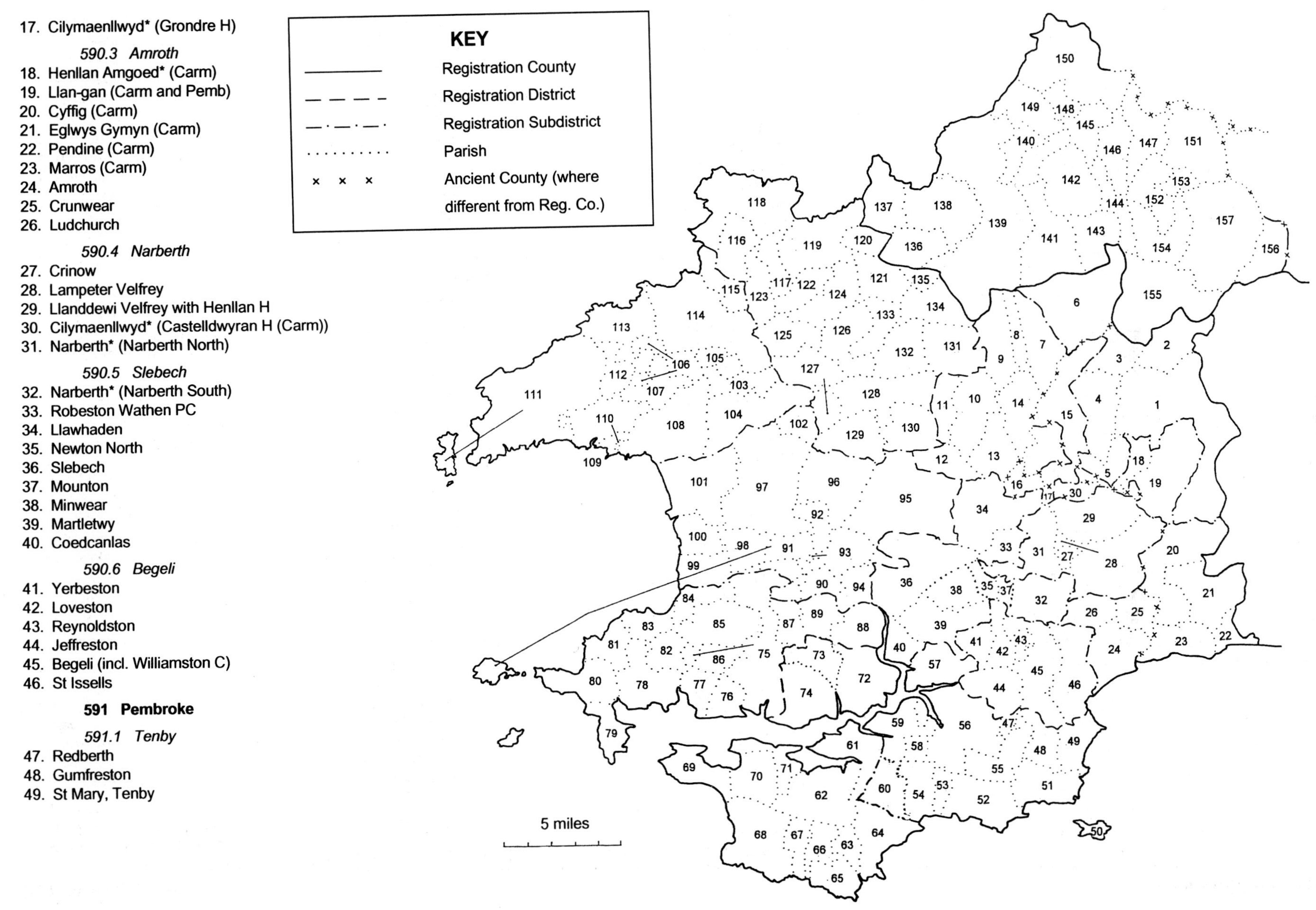

Cardigan Registration County Registration Districts and Subdistricts

593 Cardigan
1. Newport
2. Cardigan
3. Llandygwydd

594 Newcastle Emlyn
1. Cenarth
2. Penbryn
3. Llandysul

595 Lampeter
1. Llanybydder
2. Pencarreg
3. Lampeter
4. Llanwenog

596 Aberaeron
1. Llandysilio
2. Llansanffraid

597 Aberystwyth
1. Llanrhystud
2. Aberystwyth
3. Genau'r-glyn
4. Rheidol

598 Tregaron
1. Gwnnws
2. Llangeitho
3. Tregaron

NUMERICAL KEY TO PARISHES
(* indicates part of parish)

593 Cardigan

593.1 Newport

1. Llanychlwydog (Pemb)
2. Dinas (Pemb)
3. Newport (Pemb)
4. Nevern (Pemb)
5. Bayvil (Pemb)
6. Meline (Pemb)
7. Eglwyswrw (Pemb)

593.2 Cardigan

10. Llantood (Pemb)
11. Bridell (Pemb)
12. Cilgerran (Pemb)
13. Monington (Pemb)
14. Moylgrove (Pemb)
15. St Dogmaels (Pemb)
16. Cardigan (St Mary P, Cardigan Bor)
17. Llangoedmor
18. Verwick
19. Mount

593.3 Llandygwydd

20. Aber-porth
21. Blaen-porth
22. Tre-main
23. Llechryd PC
24. Llandygwydd
25. Maenordeifi (Pemb)
26. Llanfihangel Penbedw (Pemb)

594 Newcastle Emlyn

594.1 Cenarth

27. Capel Colman (Pemb)
28. Penrhydd (Pemb)
29. Llanfyrnach (Pemb)
30. Cilrhedyn (Pemb and Carm)
31. Clydau (Pemb)
32. Cenarth (incl. Newcastle T) (Carm)
33. Pen-boyr (Carm)
34. Llangeler (Carm)

594.2 Penbryn

35. Llanfair Trelygen
36. Llandyfrïog
37. Bron-gwyn
38. Troed-yr-aur
39. Betws Ifan
40. Penbryn
41. Llangrannog

594.3 Llandysul

42. Llangynllo
43. Henllan
44. Llanfairorllwyn
45. Bangor
46. Llandysul
47. Llanfihangel-ar-arth (Carm)

595 Lampeter

595.1 Llanybydder

48. Llanllwni (Carm)
49. Llanfihangel Rhos-y-corn (Carm)
50. Llanybydder (Carm)

595.2 Pencarreg

51. Pencarreg (Carm)
52. Llan-y-crwys (Carm)
53. Cellan
54. Llanfair Clydogau

595.3 Lampeter

55. Betws Bledrws
56. Llangybi
57. Trefilan
58. Silian
59. Lampeter

595.4 Llanwenog

60. Llanwenog
61. Llanwnnen

596 Aberaeron

596.1 Llandysilio

62. Dihewyd
63. Llannarth
64. Llandysiliogogo
65. Llanllwchaearn
66. Llanina

596.2 Llansanffraid

67. Llanfihangel Ystrad
68. Cilcennin
69. Ciliau Aeron
70. Llannerch Aeron
71. Henfynyw
72. Llanddewi Aber-arth
73. Llanbadarn Trefeglwys
74. Llansanffraid

597 Aberystwyth

597.1 Llanrhystud

75. Llanrhystud
76. Llanddeiniol
77. Llangwyryfon
78. Llanilar
79. Rhostïe

597.2 Aberystwyth

80. Llanychaearn
81. Llanbadarn Fawr* (Aberystwyth Ch and Bor, Isaf-yn-dre, Faenor, Broncastellan, Clarach, Lower Llanbadarn-y-Creuddyn)

597.3 Genau'r-glyn

82. Llanbadarn Fawr* (Elerch T)
83. Llanfihangel Genau'r-glyn* (Henllys, Ceulan a Maes-mawr, Cyfoethybrenin, Tirymynech)
84. Llangynfelyn

597.4 Rheidol

85. Llanbadarn Fawr* (Upper Llanbadarn-y-Creuddyn, Cwmrheidol, Melindwr, Parsel Canol, Trefeurig)
86. Llanafan
87. Llanfihangel-y-Creuddyn

598 Tregaron

598.1 Gwnnws

88. Llanfihangel Lledrod
89. Gwnnws
90. Ysbyty Ystwyth
91. Ysbyty Ystradmeurig PC

598.2 Llangeitho

92. Llanbadarn Odwyn
93. Llangeitho
94. Nancwnlle
95. Llanddewibrefi* (Gartheli C, Gwynfil T, Blaenpennal C) and Betws Leucu PC

598.3 Tregaron

96. Llanddewibrefi* (Llanio, Gogoean, Garth and Ystrad, Prysg and Carfan, Gorwydd, Doethïe C. and P.)
97. Caron-is-clawdd

Parts of Cardiganshire Ancient County in other Registration Counties

Montgomeryshire

98. Llanfihangel Genau'r-glyn* (Ysgubor-y-coed)

8. Whitechurch (Pemb)
9. Llanfair Nant-gwyn (Pemb)

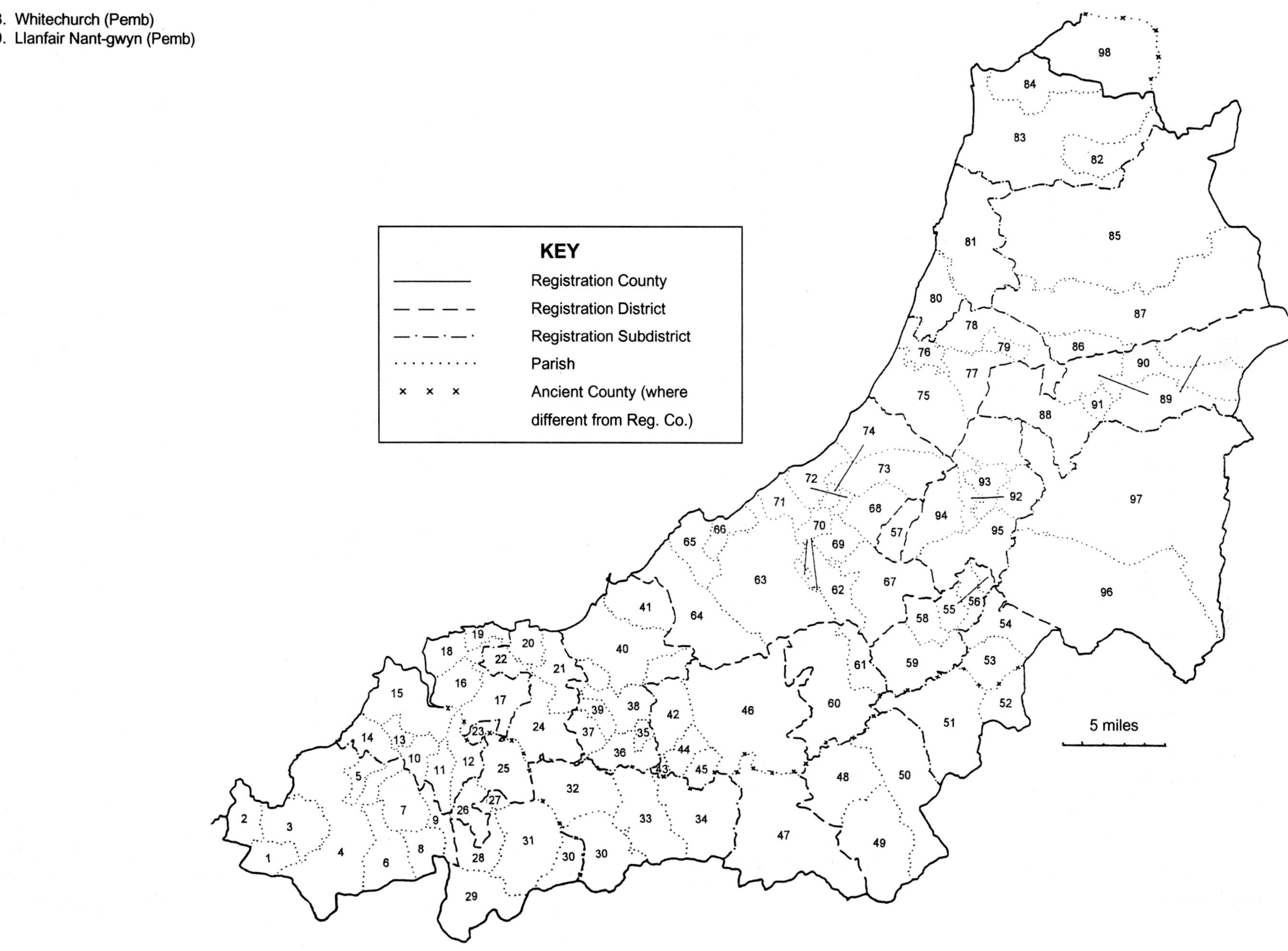

Brecon Registration County Registration Districts and Subdistricts

599 Builth
1. *Abergwesyn*
2. *Colwyn*
3. *Builth*

600 Brecon
1. *Merthyr Cynog*
2. *Defynnog*
3. *Brecon*
4. *Pencelli*
5. *Llan-gors*

601 Crickhowell
1. *Cwm-du*
2. *Llangynidr*
3. *Llangatwg*
4. *Llanelli*
5. *Crickhowell*

602 Hay
1. *Talgarth*
2. *Clyro*
3. *Hay*

NUMERICAL KEY TO PARISHES
(* indicates part of parish)

599 Builth

599.1 Abergwesyn
1. Llanddewi Abergwesyn
2. Llanfihangel Abergwesyn
3. Llangamarch
4. Llanlleonfel
5. Llanafan Fechan
6. Llanafan Fawr* (excl. Llysdinam)
7. Llanfihangel Brynpabuan* (Llanfihangel H)

599.2 Colwyn
8. Diserth (Rad)
9. Llandrindod (Rad)
10. Betws Diserth PC (Rad)
11. Llansanffraid-yn-Elfael (Rad)
12. Cregrina (Rad)
13. Rhulen PC (Rad)
14. Llanbadarn-y-garreg PC
15. Aberedw (Rad)
16. Llanfaredd

599.3 Builth
17. Llanelwedd (Rad)
18. Builth
19. Llanganten
20. Llanafan Fawr* (Llysdinam H)
21. Llanfihangel Brynpabuan* (Rhosferig H)
22. Llanynys
23. Maesmynys
24. Llanddewi'r-cwm
25. Allt-mawr
26. Llangynog
27. Gwenddwr* (excl. Trawsgoed)
28. Crucadarn

600 Brecon

600.1 Merthyr Cynog
29. Merthyr Cynog
30. Garthbrengi
31. Llandyfaelog Fach* (Llanfihangel Fechan C)
32. Llanfihangel Nant Brân

600.2 Defynnog
33. Llandeilo'r-fân
34. Llywel
35. Trallong
36. Defynnog

600.3 Brecon
37. Llansbyddyd
38. Aberysgir
39. Battle
40. Llandyfaelog Fach*
41. Llan-ddew
42. Brecon: St John the Evangelist, St Mary, St David
43. Brecon: Cantref

600.4 Pencelli
44. Llanfrynach
45. Llanfigan
46. Llanddeti

600.5 Llan-gors
47. Llansanffraid
48. Llanhamlach
49. Llan-y-wern
50. Talach-ddu
51. Gwenddwr* (Trawsgoed H)
52. Llanfellte
53. Llanfilo
54. Llanfihangel Tal-y-llyn
55. Llan-gors (incl. Llandyfaelog Tre'r-graig)
56. Llangasty Tal-y-llyn
57. Cathedin

601 Crickhowell

601.1 Cwm-du
58. Llanfihangel Cwm Du

601.2 Llangynidr
59. Llangynidr

601.3 Llangatwg
60. Llangatwg

601.4 Llanelli
61. Llanelli PC

601.5 Crickhowell
62. Crickhowell
63. Llangenni PC
64. Llanbedr
65. Partrishow PC
66. Talgarth* (Grwyne-fawr H, Grwynefechan H)

602 Hay

602.1 Talgarth
67. Talgarth* (Talgarth Bor H, Forest H, Pwll-y-wrach H, Trefeca H)
68. Llaneleu
69. Brwynllys
70. Llys-wen
71. Aberllynfi
72. Glasbury* (Tre-goed and Felindre H, Pipton H)

602.2 Clyro
73. Glasbury* (pt in Rad)
74. Boughrood (Rad)
75. Llansteffan (Rad)
76. Llandeilo Graban (Rad)
77. Llanbedr Painscastle (Rad)
78. Llanddewi Fach (Rad)
79. Bryn-gwyn (Rad)
80. Clyro (Rad)
81. Llowes (Rad)
82. Llanigon
83. Hay
84. Cusop (Her)
85. Dorstone (Her)
86. Bredwardine (Her)
87. Clifford (Her)
88. Whitney (Her)

Parts of Breconshire Ancient County in other Registration Counties

Glamorgan

582.3 U Merthyr Tydfil
89. Vaynor

582.4 Aberdare
90. Penderyn

584.3 Ystradfellte
91. Ystradfellte

584.4 Ystradgynlais
92. Ystradgynlais

Carmarthenshire

587.7 Llanwrtyd
93. Llandulas
94. Llanwrtyd

Radnorshire

605.1 Rhayader
95. Llanwrthwl

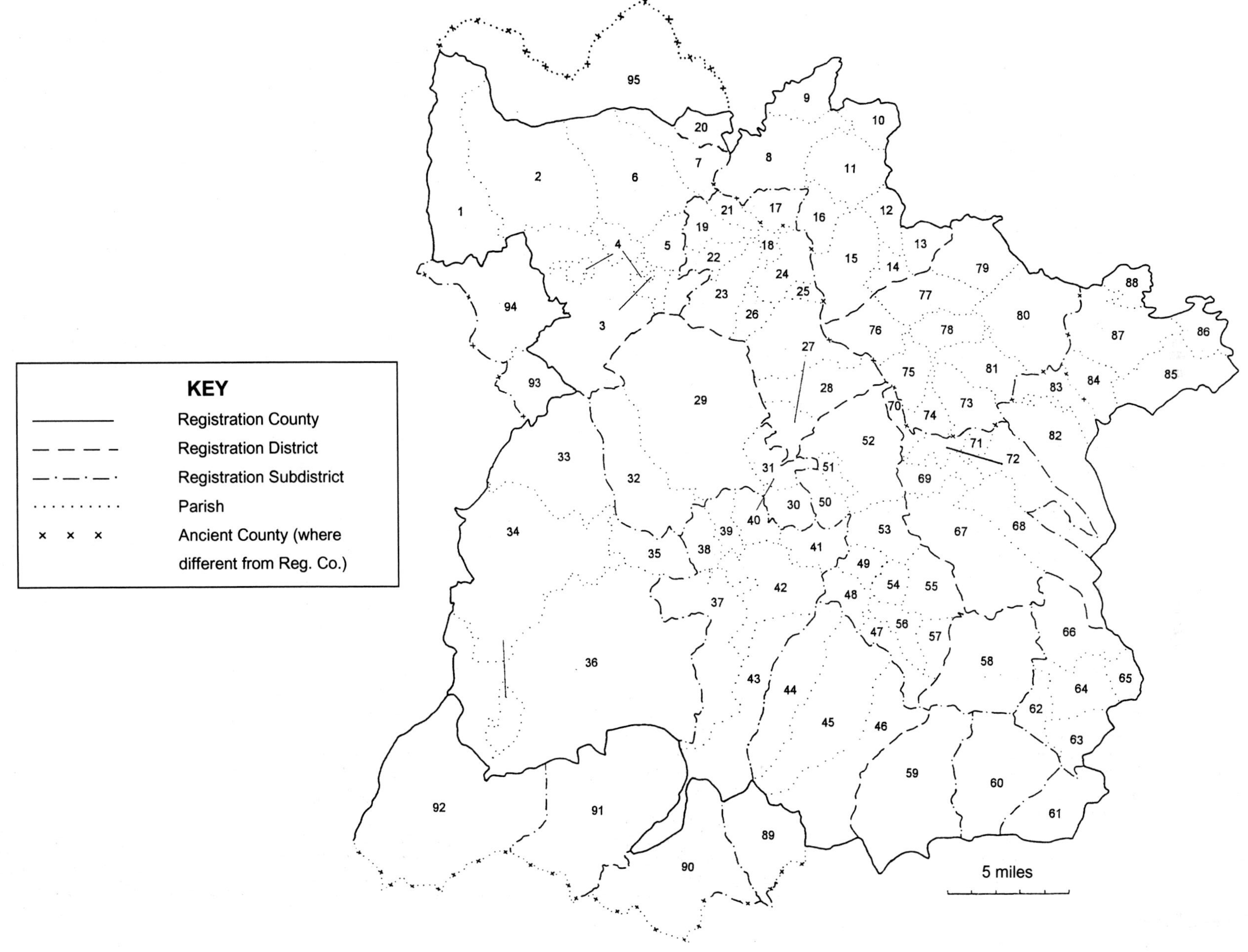
KEY
Registration County
Registration District
Registration Subdistrict
Parish
Ancient County (where different from Reg. Co.)
5 miles

RADNORSHIRE

Radnor Registration County Registration Districts and Subdistricts

603 Presteigne
1. Brilley
2. Radnor
3. Kington
4. Presteigne

604 Knighton
1. Knighton
2. Llanbister

605 Rhayader
1. Rhayader
2. Nantmel

NUMERICAL KEY TO PARISHES
(* indicates part of parish)

603 Presteigne

603.1 Brilley

1. Winforton (Her)
2. Willersley (Her)
3. Eardisley (Her)
4. Brilley (Her)
5. Huntington (Her)
6. Michaelchurch-on-Arrow
7. Newchurch

603.2 Radnor

8. Glasgwm
9. Colva PC
10. Gladestry
11. Llanfihangel Nant Melan
12. Llandegley
13. New Radnor
14. Old Radnor (incl. L. Harpton (Her))

603.3 Kington

15. Kington (Her)
16. Lyonshall (Her)
17. Pembridge (Her)
18. Stanton-upon-Arrow (Her)
19. Titley (Her)

603.4 Presteigne

20. Knill (Her)
21. Presteigne (Rad and Her)
22. Casgob
23. Pilleth
24. Whitton
25. Norton
26. Upper Kinsham (Her)
27. Byton (Her)
28. Lingeu (Her)

604 Knighton

604.1 Knighton

29. Brampton Bryan (Rad and Her)
30. Leintwardine (Her)
31. Bedstone (Salop)
32. Bucknell (Her and Salop)
33. Stowe (Salop)
34. Knighton
35. Llanfair Waterdine (Salop)
36. Betws-y-crwyn (Salop)
37. Llanfihangel-y-Bugeildy* (Lower)

604.2 Llanbister

38. Llanfihangel-y-Bugeildy* (Upper)
39. Llangynllo
40. Bleddfa
41. Llanfihangel Rhydieithon
42. Llanddewi Ystradenni
43. Llanbister
44. Llananno
45. Llanbadarn Fynydd

605 Rhayader

605.1 Rhayader

46. Abaty Cwm-hir
47. St Harmon
48. Rhayader
49. Cwmteuddwr
50. Llanwrthwl (Brec)

605.2 Nantmel

51. Nantmel
52. Llanfihangel Helygen
53. Llanyre
54. Cefn-llys
55. Llanbadarn Fawr

Parts of Radnorshire Ancient County in other Registration Counties

Breconshire

599.2 Colwyn

56. Diserth
57. Llandrindod
58. Betws Diserth PC
59. Llansanffraid-yn-Elfael
60. Cregrina
61. Rhulen PC
62. Llanbadarn-y-garreg PC
63. Aberedw
64. Llanfaredd PC

599.3 Builth

65. Llanelwedd

602.2 Clyro

66. Glasbury*
67. Boughrood
68. Llansteffan
69. Llandeilo Graban
70. Llanbedr Painscastle
71. Llanddewi Fach
72. Bryn-gwyn
73. Clyro
74. Llowes

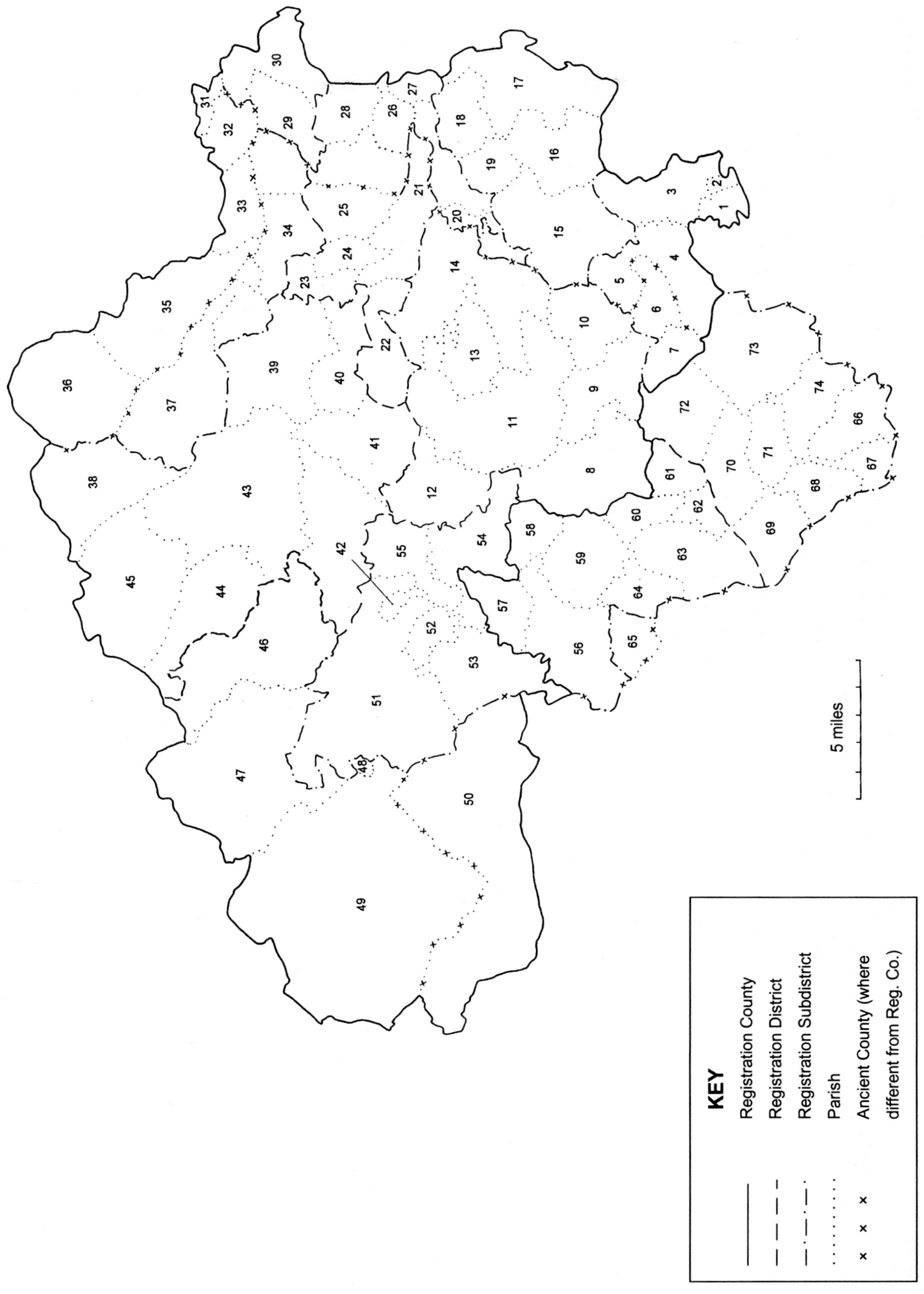
5 miles
KEY
Registration County
Registration District
Registration Subdistrict
Parish
Ancient County (where different from Reg. Co.)

MONTGOMERYSHIRE

Montgomery Registration County Registration Districts and Subdistricts

606 Machynlleth
1. Machynlleth
2. Pennal
3. Darowen

607 Newtown
1. Upper Llanidloes
2. Lower Llanidloes
3. Llanwnnog
4. Ceri
5. Newtown
6. Tregynon

608 Montgomery
1. Montgomery
2. Chirbury
3. Welshpool

609 Llanfyllin
1. Llanfair
2. Llansanffraid
3. Llanrhaeadr

NUMERICAL KEY TO PARISHES
(* indicates part of parish)

606 Machynlleth

606.1 Machynlleth

1. Llanfihangel Genau'r-glyn* (Ysgubor-y-coed)
2. Machynlleth
3. Penegoes

606.2 Pennal

4. Pennal (Mer)
5. Tywyn (Mer)
6. Llanwrin

606.3 Darowen

7. Cemais
8. Darowen
9. Llanbryn-mair

607 Newtown

607.1 Upper Llanidloes

10. Llangurig
11. Llanidloes* (Upper Div)

607.2 Lower Llanidloes

12. Llanidloes* (Lower Div)
13. Trefeglwys

607.3 Llanwnnog

14. Carno
15. Llanwnnog
16. Llandinam
17. Penstrowed
18. Aberhafesb

607.4 Ceri

19. Mochdre
20. Ceri

607.5 Newtown

21. Newtown
22. Llanllwchaearn

607.6 Tregynon

23. Betws
24. Tregynon
25. Llanwyddelan
26. Llanllugan
27. Manafon

608 Montgomery

608.1 Montgomery

28. Berriew
29. Montgomery (incl. Montgomery T)
30. Llandysul
31. Llanmerewig
32. Mainstone* (Castlewright T)
33. Lydham* (Aston T)
34. Churchstoke (Mont and Salop)

608.2 Chirbury

35. Chirbury (Salop)
36. Worthen* (Worthen (Salop), Rhos-goch T, Trelystan T)
37. Forden

608.3 Welshpool

38. Worthen* (Leighton T)
39. Buttington
40. Alberbury* (Middletown T, Uppington T)
41. Guilsfield
42. Welshpool (incl. Welshpool T)
43. Castle Caereinion

609 Llanfyllin

609.1 Llanfair

44. Llangyniew
45. Llanfair Caereinion
46. Llanerfyl
47. Llangadfan
48. Garthbeibio
49. Llanfihangel

609.2 Llansanffraid

50. Meifod
51. Llanfyllin
52. Llanfechain
53. Llansanffraid
54. Llandrinio
55. Llandysilio
56. Llanymynech* (Carreghofa T)

609.3 Llanrhaeadr

57. Llangedwyn (Denb)
58. Llangadwaladr (Denb)
59. Llanarmon Mynydd Mawr (Denb)
60. Llanrhaeadr-ym-Mochnant (Denb and Mont)
61. Hirnant
62. Llanwddyn
63. Pennant
64. Llangynog

Parts of Montgomeryshire Ancient County in other Registration Counties

Merioneth

617.1 Tal-y-llyn

65. Mallwyd*

Shropshire

353.2 Bishops Castle

66. Snead
67. Hyssington*

359.4 Alderbury

68. Alberbury* (Bausley T, Crugion T)

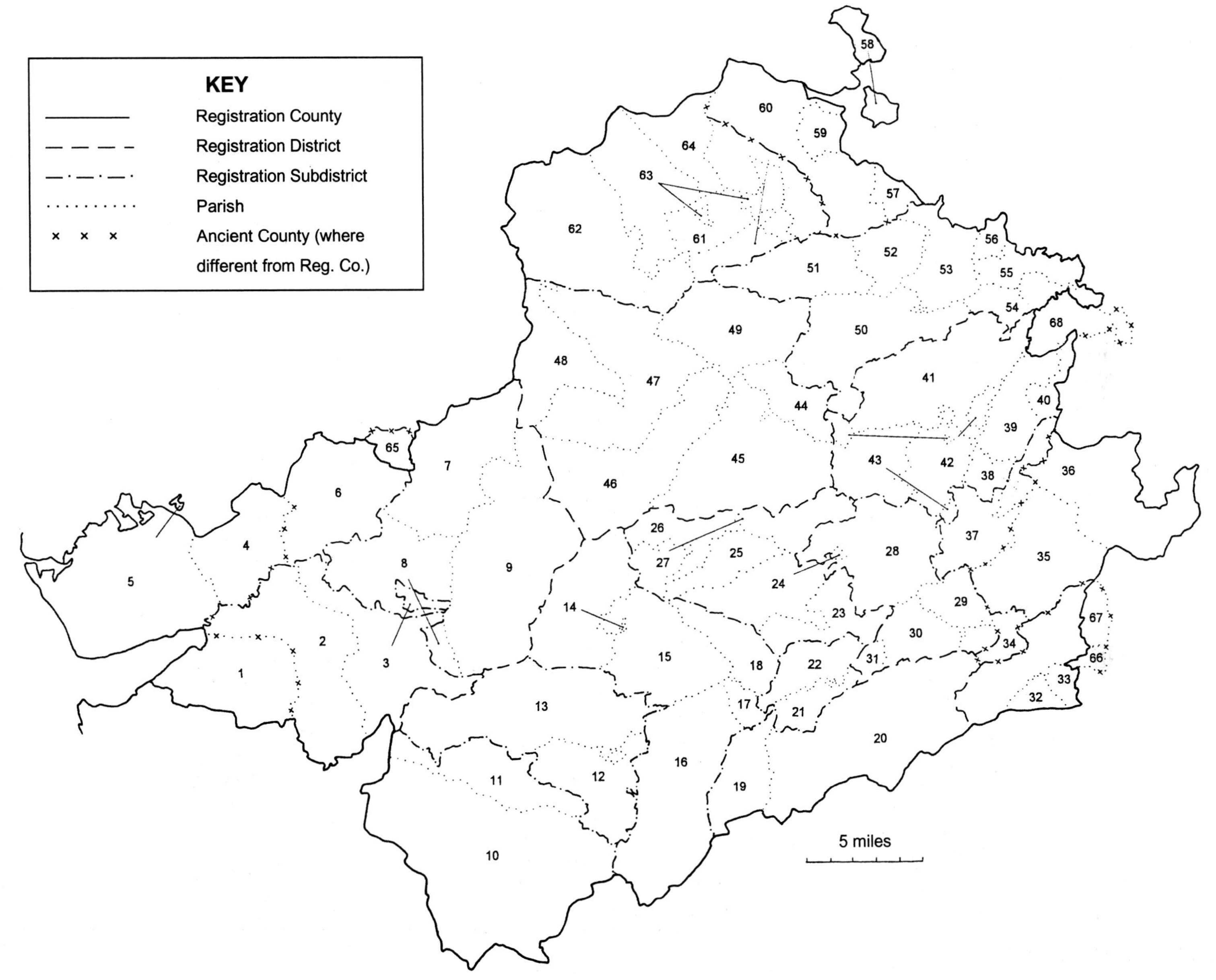
KEY
Registration County
Registration District
Registration Subdistrict
Parish
Ancient County (where different from Reg. Co.)
5 miles

FLINTSHIRE

Flint Registration County Registration Districts and Subdistricts

610 Holywell

1. *Whitford*
2. *Holywell*
3. *Flint*
4. *Mold*

NUMERICAL KEY TO PARISHES

(* indicates part of parish)

610 Holywell

610.1 Whitford

1. Gwaunysgor
2. Newmarket
3. Llanasa
4. Whitford
5. Caerwys

610.2 Holywell

6. Holywell
7. Ysgeifiog
8. Nannerch (Flint and Denb)

610.3 Flint

9. Halkyn
10. Flint PC
11. Northop

610.4 Mold

12. Cilcain
13. Mold* (excl. Treuddyn C)

Parts of Flintshire Ancient County located in other Registration Counties

Denbighshire

611.1 Hope

14. Mold* (Treuddyn C)
15. Hope (Flint)
16. Gresford* (Marford and Hosely)

611.2 Malpas

17. Bangor* (Bangor T)
18. Worthenbury

613.1 St Asaph

19. Bodfari* (Bodfari T)
20. Tremeirchion
21. Cwm
22. Diserth
23. Meliden
24. Rhuddlan
25. St Asaph* (excl. Meiriadog T, Wigfair T)

Shropshire

362.1 Overton

26. Overton
27. Ellesmere* (Penley C)

362.2 Hanmer

28. Malpas* (Is-coed C)
29. Hanmer

Cheshire

459.4 Hawarden

30. Hawarden
31. Doddleston* (Higher Kinnerton)

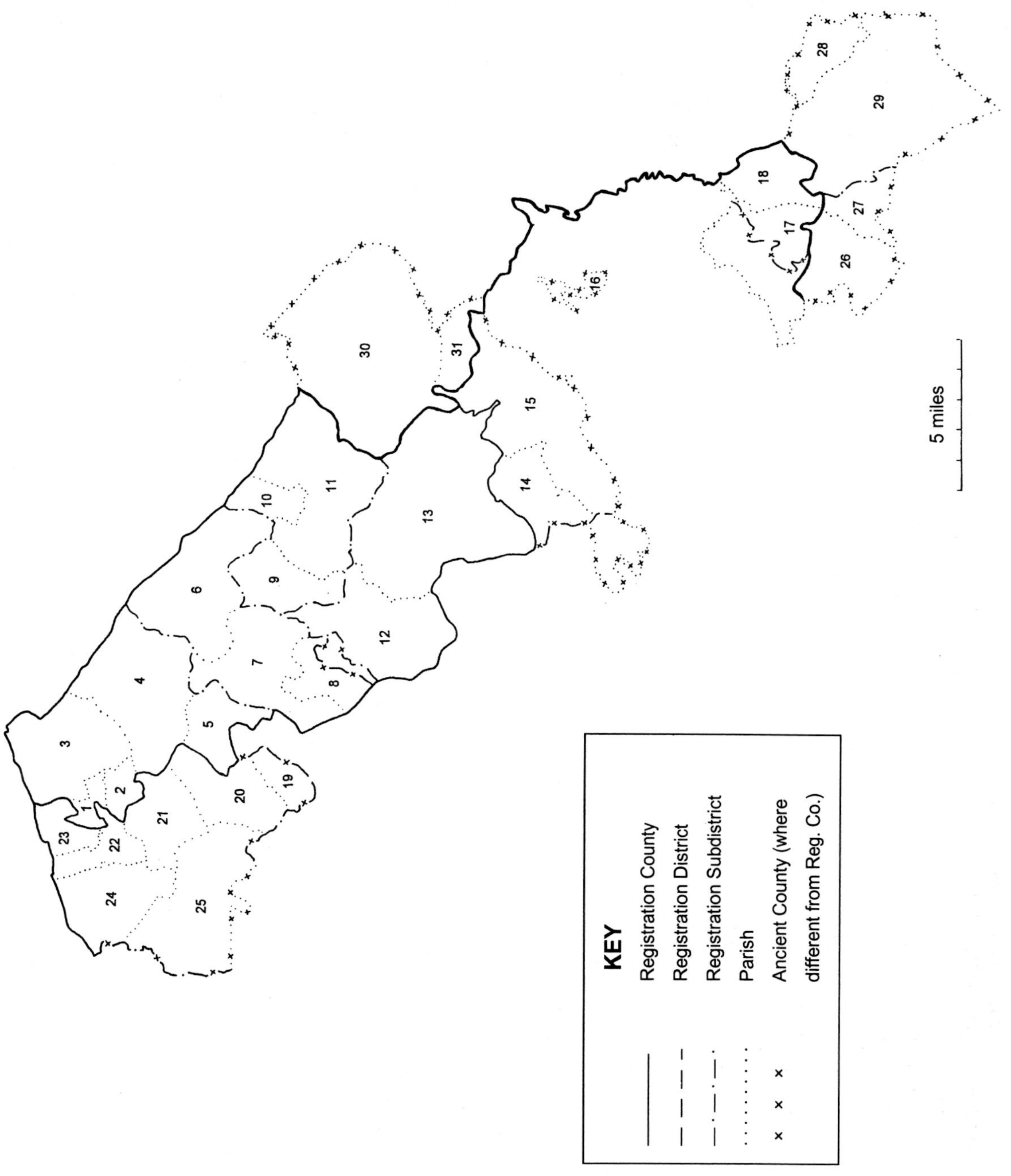

KEY
Registration County
Registration District
Registration Subdistrict
Parish
Ancient County (where different from Reg. Co.)
5 miles
1
2
3
4
5
6
7
8
9
10
11
12
13
14
15
16
17
18
19
20
21
22
23
24
25
26
27
28
29
30
31

DENBIGHSHIRE

Denbigh Registration County Registration Districts and Subdistricts

611 Wrexham
1. Hope
2. Malpas
3. Ruabon
4. Wrexham

612 Ruthin
1. Llanarmon
2. Ruthin
3. Llanelidan
4. Gyffylliog
5. Llanrhaeadr
6. Llandyrnog

613 St Asaph
1. St Asaph
2. Abergele
3. Denbigh

614 Llanrwst
1. Llanrwst
2. Betws-y-coed
3. Ysbyty

NUMERICAL KEY TO PARISHES
(* indicates part of parish)

611 Wrexham

611.1 Hope

1. Mold* (Treuddyn C (Flint))
2. Hope (Flint)
3. Gresford* (Marford and Hosely (Flint), Llai, Burton, Allington, Gresford, Gwersyllt)
4. Wrexham* (Brymbo T)

611.2 Malpas

5. Shocklach* (Ches)
6. Malpas* (Ches)
7. Worthenbury (Flint)
8. Threapwood ExP C (Ches and Flint)
9. Bangor (incl. Bangor T (Flint))
10. Holt
11. Marchwiail

611.3 Ruabon

12. Erbistock (Flint and Denb)
13. Ruabon

611.4 Wrexham

14. Gresford* (Erddig, Borras Riffri, Erlas)
15. Wrexham* (excl. Brymbo T, incl. Abenburyfechan T (Flint))

612 Ruthin

612.1 Llanarmon

16. Llandegla
17. Llanarmon
18. Llanferres

612.2 Ruthin

19. Llanbedr Dyffryn Clwyd
20. Llanhychan
21. Llanfwrog
22. Ruthin
23. Llan-rhudd
24. Efenechdyd

612.3 Llanelidan

25. Llanfair Dyffryn Clwyd
26. Llanelidan
27. Derwen

612.4 Gyffylliog

28. Clocaenog
29. Gyffylliog
30. Nantglyn

612.5 Llanrhaeadr

31. Llanrhaeadr-yng-Nghinmeirch
32. Llanynys

612.6 Llandyrnog

33. Llangynhafal
34. Llandyrnog
35. Llangwyfan
36. Bodfari* (Aberwheeler T)

613 St Asaph

613.1 St Asaph

37. Bodfari* (Flint)
38. Tremeirchion (Flint)
39. Cwm (Flint)
40. Diserth (Flint)
41. Meliden (Flint)
42. Rhuddlan (Flint)
43. St Asaph (Flint and Denb)

613.2 Abergele

44. St George
45. Abergele
46. Llanddulas
47. Betws-yn-Rhos
48. Llanfair Talhaearn

613.3 Denbigh

49. Llanefydd
50. Henllan
51. Denbigh
52. Llansannan

614 Llanrwst

614.1 Llanrwst

53. Gwytherin
54. Llangernyw
55. Eglwys-fach (Denb and Caern)
56. The Abbey ExP (Caern)
57. Llanddoged
58. Llanrwst* (excl. Gwydir T)

614.2 Betws-y-coed

59. Llanrwst* (Gwydir T) (Caern)
60. Trefriw and Llanrhychwyn (Caern)
61. Betws-y-coed (Caern)
62. Dolwyddelan (Caern)

614.3 Ysbyty

63. Penmachno (Caern)
64. Ysbyty (Caern and Denb)
65. Pentrefoelas
66. Gwernhywel ExP

Parts of Denbighshire Ancient County in other Registration Counties

Montgomeryshire

609.3 Llanrhaeadr

67. Llangedwyn
68. Llangadwaladr
69. Llanarmon Mynydd Mawr
70. Llanrhaeadr-ym-Mochnant*

Flintshire

610.2 Holywell

71. Nannerch* (Penbedw T)

Merioneth

615.1 Gwyddelwern

72. Cerrigydrudion
73. Llanfihangel Glyn Myfyr*
74. Llangwm

615.2 Corwen

75. Bryneglwys
76. Llandysilio
77. Llangollen
78. Llanarmon Dyffryn Ceiriog
79. Llansanffraid Glynceiriog

Caernarfonshire

622.2 Creuddyn

80. Llandrillo-yn-Rhos*
81. Llaneilian
82. Llansanffraid Glan Conwy

Shropshire

361.2 Llansilin

83. Llansilin*

361.4 St Martin

84. Chirk

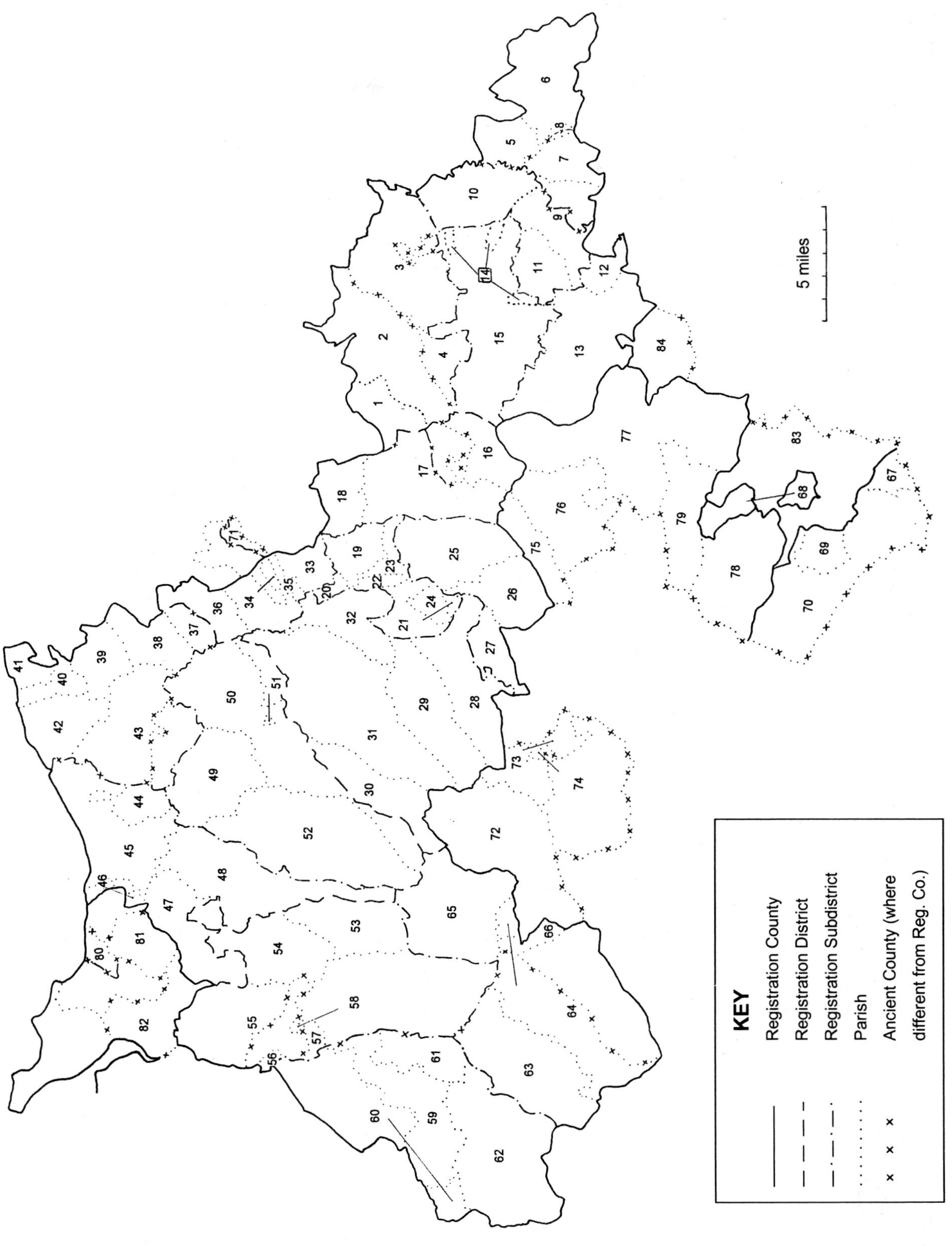
KEY
Registration County
Registration District
Registration Subdistrict
Parish
Ancient County (where different from Reg. Co.)
5 miles

MERIONETH

Merioneth Registration County Registration Districts and Subdistricts

615 Corwen
1. Gwyddelwern
2. Corwen

616 Bala
1. Bala

617 Dolgellau
1. Tal-y-llyn
2. Barmouth

618 Ffestiniog
1. Llanfihangel-y-traethau
2. Ffestiniog
3. Tremadoc

NUMERICAL KEY TO PARISHES
(* indicates part of parish)

615 Corwen

615.1 Gwyddelwern

1. Cerrigydrudion (Denb)
2. Llanfihangel Glyn Myfyr (Denb and Mer)
3. Llangwm (Denb)
4. Betws Gwerful Goch
5. Gwyddelwern
6. Llangar
7. Llandrillo

615.2 Corwen

8. Corwen
9. Llansanffraid Glyndyfrdwy
10. Bryneglwys (Denb)
11. Llandysilio (Denb)
12. Llangollen
13. Llansanffraid Glynceiriog (Denb)
14. Llanarmon Dyffryn Ceiriog

616 Bala

616.1 Bala

15. Llandderfel
16. Llanfor
17. Llanycil
18. Llanuwchllyn
19. Llangywer

617 Dolgellau

617.1 Tal-y-llyn

20. Llanymawddwy
21. Mallwyd (Mer and Mont)
22. Tal-y-llyn
23. Llanfihangel-y-Pennant
24. Llanegryn
25. Llangelynnin

617.2 Barmouth

26. Dolgellau
27. Llanfachreth
28. Llanelltud
29. Llanaber (incl. Barmouth T)
30. Llanddwywe
31. Llanenddwyn

618 Ffestiniog

618.1 Llanfihangel-y-traethau

32. Llanbedr
33. Llanfair
34. Llandanwg
35. Llanfihangel-y-traethau
36. Llandecwyn

618.2 Ffestiniog

37. Trawsfynydd
38. Ffestiniog
39. Maentwrog
40. Llanfrothen

618.3 Tremadoc

41. Beddgelert (Mer and Caern)
42. Llanfihangel-y-Pennant (Caern)
43. Dolbenmaen (Caern)
44. Penmorfa (Caern)
45. Ynyscynhaearn (Caern)
46. Treflys (Caern)

Parts of Merioneth Ancient County in other Registration Counties

Montgomeryshire

606.2 Pennal

47. Pennal (Mer)
48. Tywyn (Mer)

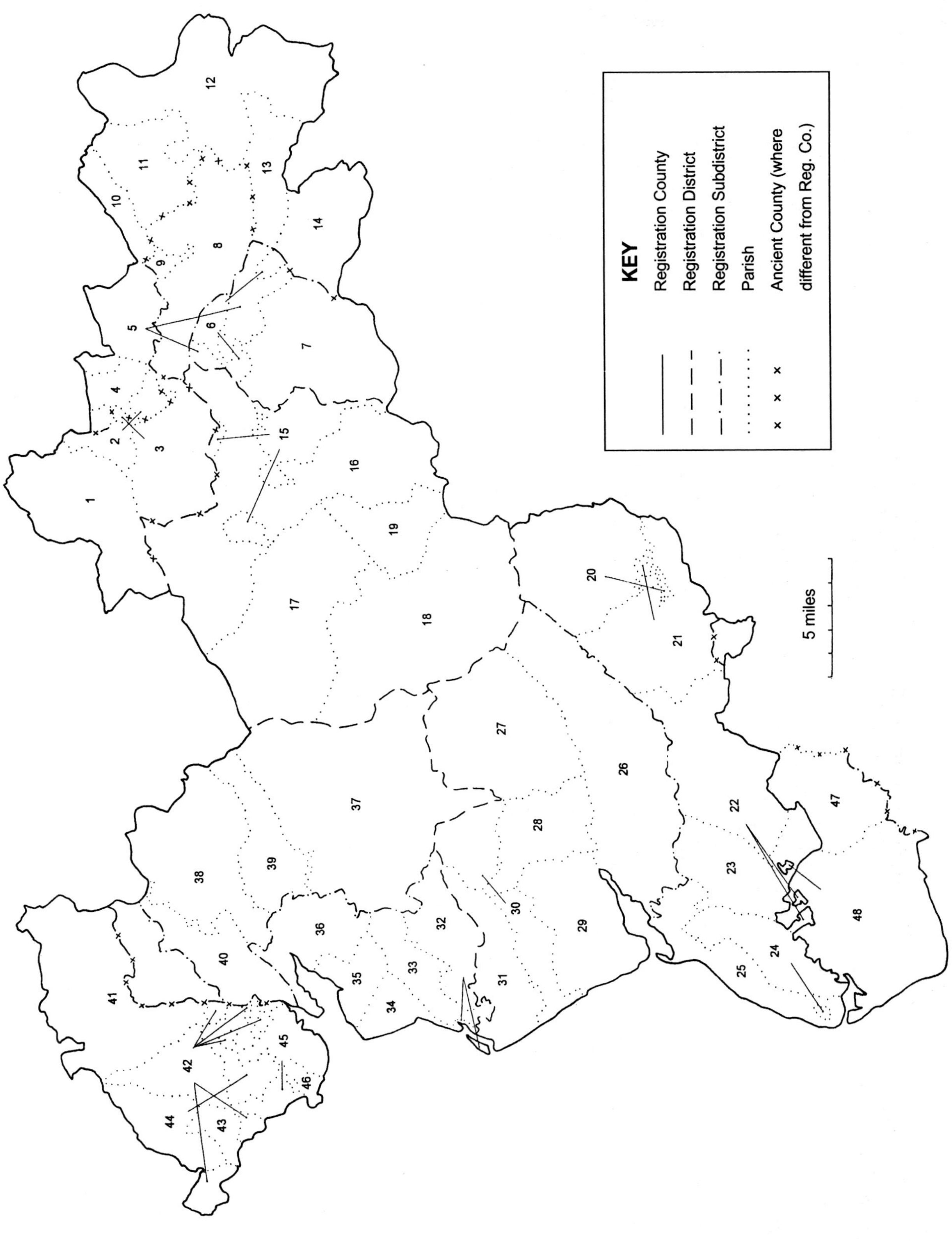

KEY
Registration County
Registration District
Registration Subdistrict
Parish
Ancient County (where different from Reg. Co.)
5 miles

Caernarfon Registration County Registration Districts and Subdistricts

619 Pwllheli
1. Cricieth
2. Pwllheli
3. Aberdaron
4. Nefyn

620 Caernarfon
1. Llandwrog
2. Llanrug
3. Caernarfon
4. Llanidan

621 Bangor
1. Beaumaris
2. Bangor
3. Llanllechid

622 Conwy
1. Conwy
2. Creuddyn
3. Llechwedd Isaf

NUMERICAL KEY TO PARISHES
(* indicates part of parish)

619 Pwllheli

619.1 Cricieth
1. Cricieth
2. Llanystumdwy
3. Aber-erch
4. Llanarmon
5. Llangybi
6. Llanaelhaearn
7. Carnguwch

619.2 Pwllheli
8. Llannor
9. Pwllheli Bor (in Deneio P)
10. Penrhos
11. Llanfihangel Bachellaeth
12. Llanbedrog
13. Llan-gain
14. Llanengan
15. Llandygwnning

619.3 Aberdaron
16. Rhiw
17. Llanfaelrhys
18. Aberdaron
19. Bardsey Island ExP
20. Bryncroes
21. Bodferin
22. Llangwnnadl
23. Penllech PC
24. Mellteyrn
25. Botwnnog

619.4 Nefyn
26. Llaniestyn
27. Tudweiliog
28. Edern
29. Llandudwen
30. Boduan
31. Ceidio
32. Nefyn
33. Pistyll PC

620 Caernarfon

620.1 Llandwrog
34. Clynnog
35. Llanllyfni
36. Llandwrog
37. Llanwnda

620.2 Llanrug
38. Betws Garmon
39. Llanberis
40. Llanrug
41. Llanddeiniolen
42. Llanfair-is-gaer

620.3 Caernarfon
43. Llanbeblig (incl. Caernarfon Bor)
44. Llanfaglan

620.4 Llanidan
45. Llangeinwen (Angl)
46. St Peter, Newborough (Angl)
47. Llangaffo (Angl)
48. Llanidan (Angl)
49. Llanfair-yn-y-cwmwd (Angl)

621 Bangor

621.1 Beaumaris
50. Llanedwen PC (Angl)
51. Llanddaniel-fab PC (Angl)
52. Llanfihangel Ysgeifiog (Angl)
53. Llanffinan PC (Angl)
54. Penmynydd (Angl)
55. Llansadwrn (Angl)
56. Llaniestyn (Angl)
57. Llanddona (Angl)
58. Llanfihangel Dinsylwy (Angl)
59. Penmon (Angl)
60. Llangoed PC (Angl)
61. Llan-faes (Angl)
62. Beaumaris (Angl)
63. Llandegfan (Angl)
64. Llandysilio (Angl)
65. Llanfair Pwllgwyngyll (Angl)

621.2 Bangor
66. Bangor
67. Llandygái

621.3 Llanllechid
68. Llanllechid
69. Aber
70. Llanfairfechan

622 Conwy

622.1 Conwy
71. Dwygyfylchi
72. Conwy
73. Gyffin

622.2 Creuddyn
74. Eglwys-rhos
75. Llandudno
76. Llandrillo-yn-Rhos (Denb and Caern)
77. Llangystennin
78. Llysfaen
79. Llaneilian (Denb)
80. Llansanffraid Glan Conwy (Denb)

622.3 Llechwedd Isaf
81. Llangelynnin
82. Caerhun
83. Llanbedrycennin

Parts of Caernarfonshire Ancient County in other Registration Counties

Denbighshire

614.1 Llanrwst
84. Eglwys-fach (Eglwys-fach T, Maenan T)
85. The Abbey ExP

614.2 Betws-y-coed
86. Llanrwst* (Gwydir T)
87. Trefriw and Llanrhychwyn
88. Betws-y-coed
89. Dolwyddelan

614.3 Ysbyty
90. Penmachno
91. Ysbyty*

Merioneth

618.3 Tremadoc
92. Beddgelert*
93. Llanfihangel-y-Pennant
94. Dolbenmaen
95. Penmorfa
96. Ynyscynhaearn
97. Treflys

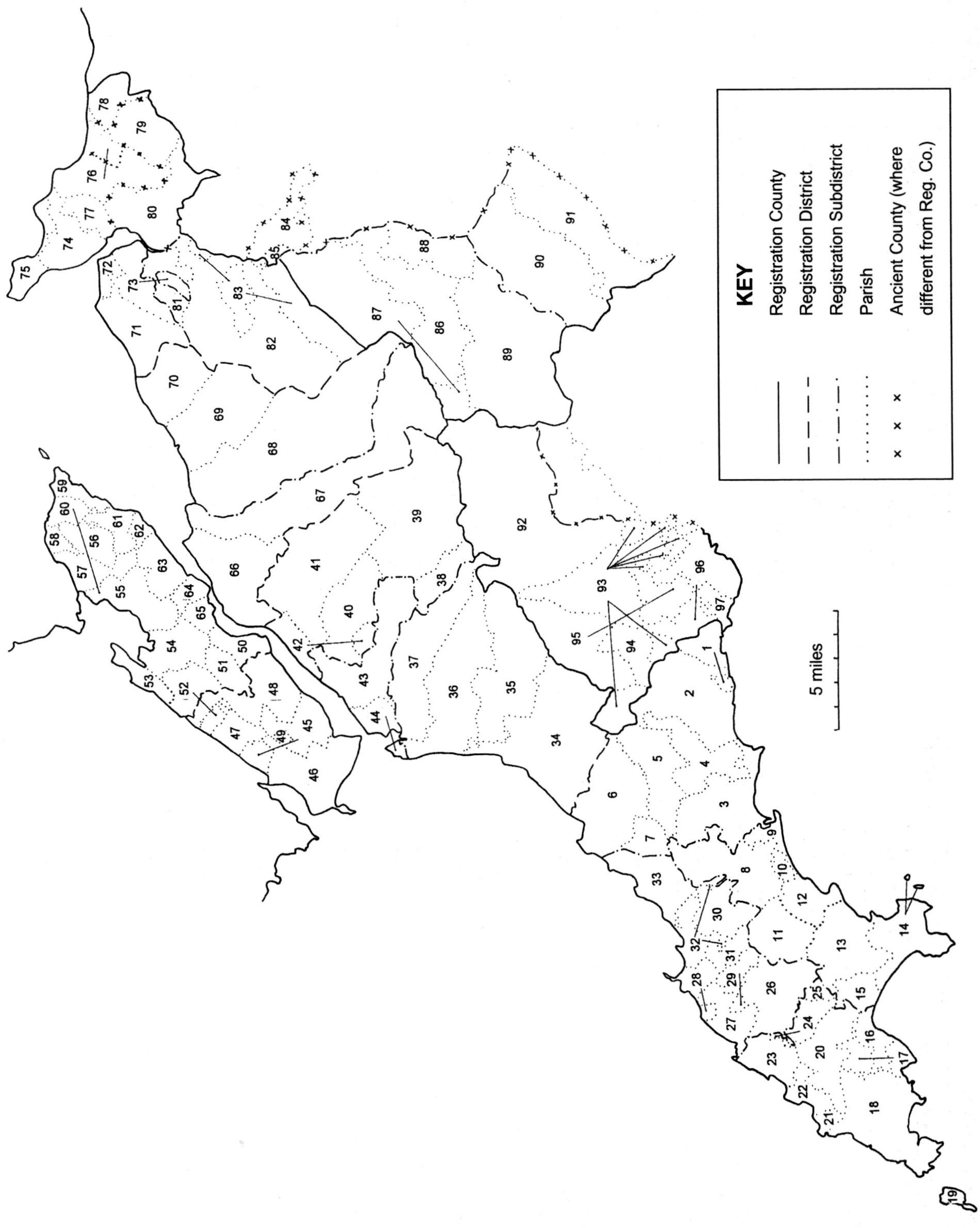
KEY
Registration County
Registration District
Registration Subdistrict
Parish
Ancient County (where different from Reg. Co.)
5 miles

Anglesey Registration County Registration Districts and Subdistricts

623 Anglesey

1. *Llangefni*
2. *Bryngwran*
3. *Llandyfrydog*
4. *Amlwch*
5. *Llanddeusant*
6. *Holyhead*

NUMERICAL KEY TO PARISHES

(* indicates part of parish)

623 Anglesey

623.1 Llangefni

1. Tregaean PC
2. Llangwyllog
3. Llangefni
4. Llangristiolus
5. Heneglwys
6. Cerrigceinwen
7. Trefdraeth
8. Llangadwaladr
9. Aberffraw

623.2 Bryngwran

10. Llangwyfan PC
11. Llanfaelog PC
12. Llechylched PC
13. Ceirchiog PC
14. Llanbeulan
15. Trewalchmai PC
16. Bodwrog PC
17. Llandrygarn
18. Llanllibio PC
19. Llantrisaint
20. Llechgynfarwy PC
21. Rhodogeidio PC
22. Llannerch-y-medd Village (ExP)
23. Gwredog ExP

623.3 Llandyfrydog

24. Llandyfrydog and Llanfihangel Tre'r-beirdd PC
25. Coedana PC
26. Llanfair Mathafarn Eithaf PC
27. Llanddyfnan
28. Pentraeth PC
29. Llanbedr-goch PC
30. Llaneugrad
31. Llanallgo PC
32. Penrhosllugwy

623.4 Amlwch

33. Llaneilian
34. Llanwenllwyfo PC
35. Rhosymynach District (undivided lands)
36. Amlwch

623.5 Llanddeusant

37. Rhosbeirio PC
38. Bodewryd PC
39. Llanbadrig
40. Llanfechell
41. Llanrhwydrys PC
42. Llanfair-yng-Nghornwy PC
43. Llanrhuddlad
44. Llanfflewin
45. Llanbabo
46. Llanddeusant
47. Llanfaethlu
48. Llanfwrog PC
49. Llanfachreth
50. Llanfigel PC

623.6 Holyhead

51. Bodedern
52. Llanynghenedl PC
53. Llanfair-yn-neubwll PC
54. Llanfihangel-yn-Nhywyn
55. Rhoscolyn
56. Holyhead

Parts of Anglesey Ancient County in other Registration Counties

Caernarfonshire

620.4 Llanidan

57. Llangeinwen
58. St Peter, Newborough
59. Llangaffo
60. Llanidan
61. Llanfair-yn-y-cwmwd

621.1 Beaumaris

62. Llanedwen PC
63. Llanddaniel-fab PC
64. Llanfihangel Ysgeifiog
65. Llanffinan PC
66. Penmynydd
67. Llansadwrn
68. Llaniestyn
69. Llanddona
70. Llanfihangel Dinsylwy
71. Penmon
72. Llangoed PC
73. Llan-faes
74. Beaumaris
75. Llandegfan
76. Llandysilio
77. Llanfair Pwllgwyngyll

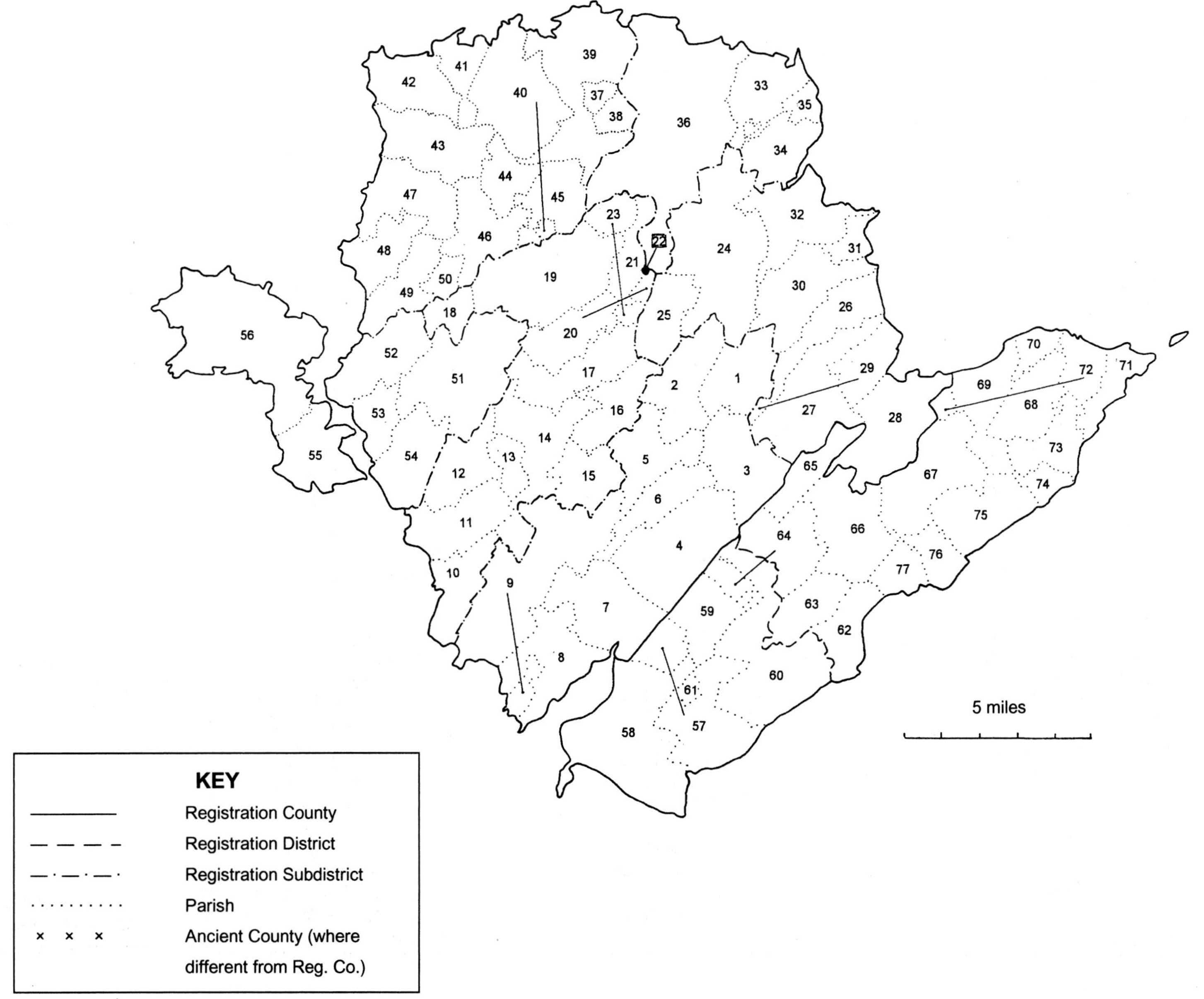
5 miles
KEY
Registration County
Registration District
Registration Subdistrict
Parish
Ancient County (where different from Reg. Co.)

Appendix III Boundary changes affecting Registration Areas, 1851–1911

A. Boundary changes between the Welsh and English Divisions

	Civil parishes affected	Registration Districts and Subdistricts affected From	To	Population
1851–61				
Denb → Salop	Part of Malpas (Ches)	WREXHAM: Malpas	WHITCHURCH: Malpas	2217 (1851)
1861–71				
Rad → Her	All parishes	PRESTEIGNE: Brilley	KINGTON: Brilley	2067 (1861)
	All parishes	PRESTEIGNE: Radnor	KINGTON: Radnor	3567 (1861)
	All parishes	PRESTEIGNE: Kington	KINGTON: Kington	6296 (1861)
Denb → Ches	Hope parish, townships: Treuddyn, Marford and Hosely	WREXHAM: Hope	CHESTER: Hawarden	4903 (1861)
1871–81				
Rad → Her	Parishes: Knill, Upper Kinsham, Byton and Lingen; townships: Combe, Lower Kinsham, Willey and Stapleton	PRESTEIGNE: Presteigne	KINGTON: Kinsham	1262 (1871)
1881–91				
Mon → Her	Newland (pt)	MONMOUTH: Coleford	ROSS: St Weonards	93 (1881)
Her → Mon	Whitchurch	ROSS: St Weonards	MONMOUTH: Dingestow	32 (1881)
Her → Mon	Llantilio Crossenny	HEREFORD: Kentchurch	MONMOUTH: Dingestow	6 (1881)
Gloucs → Mon	West Dean	WESTBURY: Newnham	MONMOUTH: Coleford	27 (1881)
	Overall loss from Monmouth 28 (1881)			
Mont→ Salop	Llangadwaladr → Llansilin	LLANFYLLIN: Llanrhaeadr	OSWESTRY: Llansilin	35 (1881)
	Worthen → Pontesbury	MONTGOMERY: Chirbury	ATCHAM: Pontesbury	5 (1881)
	Overall loss from Montgomery 40 (1881)			
Ches → Denb	Marford and Hosely → Allingham	CHESTER: Hawarden	WREXHAM: Holt	65 (1881)
Denb → Ches	Gresford → Marford and Hosely	WREXHAM: Holt	CHESTER: Hawarden	23 (1881)
	Overall gain to Denbigh 42 (1881)			
1891–1901				
Denb → Ches	Shocklach Church) Shocklach Oviatt)	WREXHAM: Holt	CHESTER: Tattenhall	316 (1891)
Denb → Salop	Threapwood	WREXHAM: Holt	WHITCHURCH: Malpas	306 (1891)
Denb → Salop	Bangor, Worthenbury	WREXHAM: Holt	ELLESMERE: Overton	973 (1891)
	Overall loss from Denbigh 1595 (1891)			
1901–11				
Flint → Ches	(1/7/01) Buckley Mold	HOLYWELL: Mold	CHESTER: Hawarden	3326 (1901)
Ches → Flint	(1/2/03) Whole subdistrict	CHESTER: Hawarden	HAWARDEN: Hawarden	21601 (1901)
	Overall gain to Flint 18275 (1901)			

B. Boundary Changes within the Welsh Division affecting Registration Districts and Subdistricts, 1861–1911

Area affected	From	To	Population
1851–61			
Monmouthshire			
A new District of BEDWELLTE *created with the transfer of* Aberystruth,Tredegar, *and* Rock Bedwellte *subdistricts from* ABERGAVENNY *District.*			
Glamorgan			
A new District of GOWER *created from the old subdistrict of* Gower *and a small part of the subdistrict of* Llangyfelach.			
Llanrhidian Higher (pt Llanrhidian P)	SWANSEA: Llangyfelach	GOWER: Gower Eastern	1443 (1851)
Oystermouth, Bishopston, Pennard, Ilston, Pen-maen	SWANSEA: Gower	GOWER: Gower Eastern	3155 (1851)

Area affected	From	To	Population
Glamorgan cont.			
Nicholaston, Penrice, Oxwich, Port Einon, Knelston, Reynoldston, Llanddewi, Rhosili, Llangennith, Llanmadog, Cheriton, Llanrhidian L (pt Llanrhidian P)	SWANSEA: Gower	GOWER: Gower Western	3889 (1851)
Montgomeryshire			
Guilsfield	MONTGOMERY: Pool	LLANFYLLIN: Llansanffraid	2397 (1851)
Denbighshire			
WREXHAM: Malpas *subdistrict renamed* Holt *with the transfer of part to* Shropshire. *See A.*			
Denbighshire → Shropshire See A			
Anglesey			
Anglesey *subdistricts completely reformed. Only* Amlwch *subdistrict remained unchanged.*			
Heneglwys, Cerrigceinwen, Aberffraw	ANGLESEY: Llangefni	ANGLESEY: Bryngwran	2411 (1851)
Llanllibio, Llantrisaint	ANGLESEY: Bryngwran	ANGLESEY: Llanddeusant	613 (1851)
Llechgynfarwy, Rhodogeidio, Llannerch-y-medd, Gwredog	ANGLESEY: Bryngwran	ANGLESEY: Llandyfrydog	843 (1851)
Llanfihangel Tre'r-beirdd, Llanfair Mathafarn Eithaf, Llanddyfnan, Llanbedr-goch, Llaneugrad, Llanallgo, Penrhosllugwy	ANGLESEY: Llandyfrydog	ANGLESEY: Llangefni	3582 (1851)
Llanbadrig, Llanfechell, Llanrhwydrys, Llanfair-yng-Nghornwy, Llanfflewin, Llanbabo	ANGLESEY: Llanddeusant	ANGLESEY: Llandyfrydog	3137 (1851)
Bodedern, Llanynghenedl, Llanfair-yn-neubwll, Llanfihangel-yn-Nhywyn	ANGLESEY: Holyhead	ANGLESEY: Llanddeusant	2183 (1851)
Anglesey → Caernarfonshire			
Llangristiolus, Trefdraeth, Llangadwaladr	ANGLESEY: Llangefni	BANGOR: Beaumaris	2548 (1851)
Pentraeth	ANGLESEY: Llandyfrydog	BANGOR: Beaumaris	963 (1851)

1861–71 Districts were renumbered for the 1871 census.

Montmouthshire

Subdistricts of Aberystruth, Tredegar, *and* Rock Bedwellte *transferred from* ABERGAVENNY *to the new* BEDWELLTE *District.*

Area affected	From	To	Population
Glamorgan			
New District of PONTYPRIDD *created from parts of* CARDIFF *and* MERTHYR TYDFIL, *with subdistricts* Pontypridd, Llantrisant, Ystradyfodwg.			
Eglwysilan	CARDIFF: Caerphilly	PONTYPRIDD: Pontypridd	6383 (1861)
Llanfabon, Llanwynno	MERTHYR TYDFIL: Gelli-gaer	PONTYPRIDD: Pontypridd	11062 (1861)
Llantrisant, Llantwit Fardre	CARDIFF: Llantrisant	PONTYPRIDD: Llantrisant	9907 (1861)
Ystradyfodwg (excl. Rhigos H)	MERTHYR TYDFIL: Aberdare	PONTYPRIDD: Ystradyfodwg	3035 (1861)
CARDIFF *District reorganized*: Caerphilly *subdistrict abolished and new subdistrict* Whitchurch *created.*			
Lisvane, Llanedern, Llanishen, Rudry, Van, Whitchurch	CARDIFF: Caerphilly	CARDIFF: Whitchurch	3629 (1861)
Pen-tyrch	CARDIFF: Llantrisant	CARDIFF: Whitchurch	2110 (1861)
Llanilltern, Pendoylan, Peterston-super-Ely, St Brides-super-Ely	CARDIFF: Llantrisant	CARDIFF: St Nicholas	887 (1861)
Montgomeryshire			
District of MONTGOMERY *renamed* FORDEN.			
Denbighshire (See also A above)			
Subdistrict of WREXHAM: Hope *abolished with parts transferred to the subdistricts of* Holt, Wrexham *and* Hawarden (Ches).			
Townships Burton, Allington, Gresford	WREXHAM: Hope	WREXHAM: Holt	2117 (1861)
Townships Llai, Gwersyllt, Brymbo	WREXHAM: Hope	WREXHAM: Wrexham	4277 (1861)

1871–81

Area affected	From	To	Population
Glamorgan			
New District of PONTARDAWE *formed with one subdistrict,* Pontardawe.			
All parishes	BRIDGEND: Ystradgynlais	PONTARDAWE: Pontardawe	12433 (1871)
Cilybebyll, Ynysymwn H	NEATH: Cadoxton	PONTARDAWE: Pontardawe	1995 (1871)
Rhyndwyglydach H, Mawr H	SWANSEA: Llandeilo Tal-y-bont	PONTARDAWE: Pontardawe	3060 (1871)
Swansea Higher	SWANSEA: Llangyfelach	SWANSEA: Llandeilo Tal-y-bont	3684 (1871)
All parishes	NEATH: Llansamlet	SWANSEA: Llansamlet	6128 (1871)
Nicholaston → Bishopston*	GOWER: Gower Western	GOWER: Gower Eastern	30 (1871)

Area affected	From	To	Population
Carmarthenshire			
Llangadog → Cwarter Bach*	LLANDOVERY: Llangadog	LLANDEILO FAWR: Llandybïe	1528 (1871)
Subdistricts of Myddfai *and* Llandingad *joined to comprise the new subdistrict of* Llandingad.			
All parishes	LLANDOVERY: Myddfai	}	964 (1871)
All parishes	LLANDOVERY: Llandingad	}LLANDOVERY: Llandingad	2379 (1871)
Radnorshire			
The District of PRESTEIGNE *(with one subdistrict,* Presteigne*) abolished, parts transferred to* KINGTON: Kinsham (Hereford – *See A) and the District of* KNIGHTON.			
Parishes: Casgob, Norton, Pilleth, Whitton; townships: Disgoed, Litton and Casgob, Presteigne	PRESTEIGNE: Presteigne	KNIGHTON: Presteigne	2607 (1871)
Merioneth			
A new subdistrict of Llangollen *created from part of* Corwen. *The subdistrict of* Gwyddelwern *abolished, all parts transferred to* Corwen *subdistrict.*			
Bryneglwys, Llandysilio, Glyntraean, Llangollen Traean, Llansanffraid Glynceiriog, Llanarmon Dyffryn Ceiriog	CORWEN: Corwen	CORWEN: Llangollen	8403 (1971)
1881–91			
Monmouthshire			
Subdistrict of Shirenewton *abolished.*			
All parishes	CHEPSTOW: Shirenewton	CHEPSTOW: Chepstow	5541 (1881)
Tiddenham (Gloucs), Lancant (Gloucs)	CHEPSTOW: Chepstow	CHEPSTOW: Lydney	1515 (1881)
Pt Dixton Newton	MONMOUTH: Monmouth	MONMOUTH: Dingestow	95 (1881)
Glamorgan			
Llanilltern	CARDIFF: St Nicholas	CARDIFF: Whitchurch	118 (1881)
pt St Fagans → Michaelston-super-Ely*	CARDIFF: Cardiff	CARDIFF: St Nicholas	9 (1881)
Pt Higher Llangynwyd → Glyncorrwg*	NEATH: Margam	NEATH: Ystradfellte	360 (1881)
Pontypridd subdistrict divided:			
Llanfabon, Eglwysilan	PONTYPRIDD: Pontypridd	PONTYPRIDD: Eglwysilan	11598 (1881)
Llanwynno	PONTYPRIDD: Pontypridd	PONTYPRIDD: Llanwynno	18652 (1881)
Llanharan, Llanilid, Peterston	BRIDGEND: Maesteg	BRIDGEND: Cowbridge	880 (1881)
Coychurch Higher, Coychurch Lower, Pen-coed	BRIDGEND: Maesteg	BRIDGEND: Bridgend	1365 (1881)
Higher Llangynwyd	NEATH: Margam	BRIDGEND: Maesteg	2084 (1881)
Betws, Llangeinor, Llandyfodwg, St Brides Minor, Ynysawdre	BRIDGEND: Maesteg	BRIDGEND: Ogmore (new)	8632 (1881)
Carmarthenshire			
pt Meidrim → Llanfihangel Abercywyn	CARMARTHEN: Cynwyl	CARMARTHEN: St Clears	11 (1881)
pt Abergwili → Llanpumsaint	CARMARTHEN: Carmarthen	CARMARTHEN: Cynwyl	251 (1881)
Pembrokeshire			
Subdistrict of Llandysilio *transferred to the subdistrict of* Llanboidy.			
All parishes	NARBERTH: Llandysilio	NARBERTH: Llanboidy	3334 (1881)
Llanfallteg (East and West)	NARBERTH: Llanboidy	NARBERTH: Narberth	390 (1881)
Cardiganshire			
Llannerch Aeron → Dihewyd	ABERAERON: Llansanffraid	ABERAERON: Llandysilio	29 (1881)
Breconshire			
Subdistrict of Merthyr Cynog *abolished with parts transferred to* Defynnog *and* Brecon *subdistricts.*			
Llanfihangel Nant Brân	BRECON: Merthyr Cynog	BRECON: Defynnog	386 (1881)
Merthyr Cynog, Garthbrengi, Llanfihangel Fechan	BRECON: Merthyr Cynog	BRECON: Brecon	985 (1881)
Subdistrict of Llangatwg *abolished with parts transferred to* Llanelli *and* Crickhowell *subdistricts.*			
Llangatwg (pt)	CRICKHOWELL: Llangatwg	CRICKHOWELL: Llanelli	3661 (1881)
Llangatwg (pt)	CRICKHOWELL: Llangatwg	CRICKHOWELL: Crickhowell	1070 (1881)
Glasbury → Tre-goed and Felindre*	HAY: Clyro	HAY: Talgarth	222 (1881)
Radnorshire			
Llanfihangel-y-Bugeildy (pt)	KNIGHTON: Llanbister	KNIGHTON: Knighton	391 (1881)
Llanddewi Ystradenni → Nantmel*	KNIGHTON: Llanbister	RHAYADER: Nantmel	78 (1881)
Montgomeryshire (see also A above)			
MACHYNLLETH: Pennal *subdistrict renamed* Tywyn.			
Penegoes → Darowen, Darowen→ Penegoes	MACHYNLLETH: Darowen	MACHYNLLETH: Machynlleth	28 (1881)
Denbighshire See A above			

Area affected	From	To	Population
Merioneth → Montgomeryshire			
Llannerchgoediog Isaf etc.	DOLGELLAU: Tal-y-llyn	MACHYNLLETH: Tywyn	44 (1881)
Caernarfonshire			
Llandygái	BANGOR: Bangor	BANGOR: Llanllechid	3587 (1881)
Aber, Llanfairfechan	BANGOR: Llanllechid	BANGOR: Bangor	2483 (1881)
CONWY: Conwy *and* CONWY: Llechwedd Isaf *subdistricts united under the name* Conwy.			
Anglesey → Caernarfonshire			
Aberffraw (pt) → Llangadwaladr	ANGLESEY: Bryngwran	BANGOR: Beaumaris	19 (1881)
Anglesey			
Bryngwran, Llanddeusant, *and* Holyhead *subdistricts transferred from* ANGLESEY *District to the new District of* HOLYHEAD.			
Bodewryd, Rhosbeirio	HOLYHEAD: Llanddeusant	ANGLESEY: Llandyfrydog	68 (1881)
Amlwch (pt) → Llanbadrig	ANGLESEY: Amlwch	ANGLESEY: Llandyfrydog	22 (1881)
1891–1901			
Monmouthshire → Glamorgan			
Rhyd-y-gwern (Glam)	NEWPORT: Mynyddislwyn	CARDIFF: Llandaff	275 (1891)
Llanfedw, Rhyd-y-gwern	NEWPORT: St Woollos	CARDIFF: Llandaff	275 (1891)
Monmouthshire → Breconshire			
Aberystruth Bryn-mawr Urban	BEDWELLTE: Aberystruth	CRICKHOWELL: Llanelli	270 (1891)
Monmouthshire			
Subdistrict of Dingestow *abolished and parts divided between subdistricts of* Coleford, Monmouth, *and* Trelleck.			
Welsh Bicknor	MONMOUTH: Dingestow	MONMOUTH: Coleford	135 (1891)
Ganarew, Garway, Llanrothal, Welsh Newton, Whitchurch, Rockfield, St Maughan's, Skenfrith	MONMOUTH: Dingestow	MONMOUTH: Monmouth	2482 (1891)
Dingestow, Llangattock Vibon Avel, Llantilio Crossenny, Llanfihangel Ystum Llywern, Grace Dieu Park, Pen-rhos, Tregara	MONMOUTH: Dingestow	MONMOUTH: Trelleck	2017 (1891)
Subdistrict of St Woollos *abolished and parts transferred to new subdistricts of* Rogerstone, Llantarnam, *and* Llandaff.			
Coedcernyw, Dyffryn, Graig, Marshfield, Michaelston-y-Vedw, Peterston, Risca, Rogerstone, St Bride's Wentlloog	NEWPORT: St Woollos	NEWPORT: Rogerstone	10771 (1891)
Betws, Henllys, Llanfihangel Llantarnam, Malpas	NEWPORT: St Woollos	NEWPORT: Llantarnam	5834 (1891)
Upper, Lower Machen	NEWPORT: Mynyddislwyn	NEWPORT: Rogerstone	1680 (1891)
	NEWPORT: Caerleon	NEWPORT: Newport	13045 (1891)
Aberystruth (pt)	BEDWELLTE: Aberystruth	ABERGAVENNY: Abergavenny	75 (1891)
Trevethin with Pontypool (pt)	PONTYPOOL: Pontypool	ABERGAVENNY: Abergavenny	46 (1891)
Trevethin with Pontypool (pt)	PONTYPOOL: Pontypool	ABERGAVENNY: Blaenafon	1469 (1891)
Pant-teg	PONTYPOOL: Pontypool	PONTYPOOL: Llangybi	3746 (1891)
Glamorgan			
Subdistricts of Whitchurch *and* Cardiff *abolished with the creation of new subdistricts of* Llandaff, East Cardiff, Central Cardiff, West Cardiff, *and* Penarth.			
All parishes	CARDIFF: Whitchurch	CARDIFF: Llandaff	6997 (1891)
Caerau, Llandaff, St Fagans, Radyr	CARDIFF: Cardiff	CARDIFF: Llandaff	5666 (1891)
Roath (pt), St John (pt)	CARDIFF: Cardiff	CARDIFF: East Cardiff	35294 (1891)
Roath (pt), St John (pt), St Mary (pt)	CARDIFF: Cardiff	CARDIFF: Central Cardiff	53824 (1891)
Canton, St John (pt), St Mary (pt)	CARDIFF: Cardiff	CARDIFF: West Cardiff	39797 (1891)
Cogan, Lavernock, Leckwith, Penarth, Michaelston-le-Pit, Llandough	CARDIFF: Cardiff	CARDIFF: Penarth	12726 (1891)
Llanfabon (pt)	PONTYPRIDD: Egwysilan	MERTHYR TYDFIL: Lower M.T.	924 (1891)
Merthyr Tydfil (pt)	MERTHYR TYDFIL: Lower M.T.	MERTHYR TYDFIL: Upper M.T.	1327 (1891)
Aberdare (pt)	MERTHYR TYDFIL: Aberdare	PONTYPRIDD: Llanwynno	2486 (1891)
pt Michaelston Upper → Glyncorrwg*	NEATH: Margam	NEATH: Ystradfellte	161 (1891)
pt Baglan Lower → Aberafan*	NEATH: Neath	NEATH: Margam	18 (1891)
pt Blaenrhondda → Neath*	NEATH: Cadoxton	NEATH: Neath	53 (1891)
pt Llansamlet Higher, pt Llansamlet Lower	SWANSEA: Llansamlet	SWANSEA: Llangyfelach	342 (1891)
pt Llansamlet Higher	SWANSEA: Llansamlet	SWANSEA: Swansea	3279 (1891)
Glamorgan → Monmouthshire			
St Mellons, Rumney	CARDIFF: Cardiff	NEWPORT: Rogerstone	1190 (1891)
Carmarthenshire			
Kidwelly St Mary (pt)	LLANELLI: Pembrey	CARMARTHEN: Llangyndeyrn	157 (1891)
Brechfa	LLANDEILO FAWR: Llanfynydd	LLANDEILO FAWR: Llangathen	85 (1891)

Area affected	From	To	Population
Carmarthenshire → Breconshire			
The whole subdistrict of Llanwrtyd *transferred to the District of* BUILTH.			
Llanddulas, Llanwrtyd	LLANDOVERY: Llanwrtyd	BUILTH: Llanwrtyd	903 (1891)
Pembrokeshire			
In the District of NARBERTH, *the subdistricts of* Amroth *and* Slebech *abolished, all parts transferred to* Narberth *and* Begeli *subdistricts respectively.*			
Cardiganshire			
Verwick, Llangoedmor, Mount	CARDIGAN: Cardigan	CARDIGAN: Llandygwydd	1206 (1891)
Maenordeifi, Llanfihangel Penbedw	CARDIGAN: Llandygwydd	CARDIGAN: Cardigan	1011 (1891)
Breconshire			
The subdistrict of Llangynidr *abolished, parts transferred to* Crickhowell *and the new subdistrict of* Beaufort.			
Llangynidr (the pt in Brec)	CRICKHOWELL: Llangynidr	CRICKHOWELL: Crickhowell	488 (1891)
Llangynidr (the pt in Mon)	CRICKHOWELL: Llangynidr	CRICKHOWELL: Beaufort	3154 (1891)
Llangatwg (the pt in Mon)	CRICKHOWELL: Llanelli	CRICKHOWELL: Beaufort	2754 (1891)
Subdistrict of Clyro *abolished, parts transferred to* Talgarth *and* Hay *subdistricts.*			
Boughrood, Glasbury, Llandeilo, Llansteffan	HAY: Clyro	HAY: Talgarth	1069 (1891)
Bryn-gwyn, Clyro, Llanbedr Painscastle Llanddewi Fach, Llowes	HAY: Clyro	HAY: Hay	1460 (1891)
Montgomeryshire			
Subdistricts of Upper Llanidloes *and* Lower Llanidloes *joined to form the subdistrict of* Llanidloes.			
Flintshire			
pt Holywell → Coleshill Fawr (new)	HOLYWELL: Holywell	HOLYWELL: Flint	322 (1891)
Denbighshire See A above.			
Merioneth → Montgomeryshire			
Caereinion Fechan (pt Mallwyd)	DOLGELLAU: Tal-y-llyn	MACHYNLLETH: Darowen	121 (1891)
Merioneth			
Subdistrict of Llanfihangel-y-traethau *renamed* Deudraeth.			
Llanfrothen	FFESTINIOG: Ffestiniog	FFESTINIOG: Deudraeth	932 (1891)
Caernarfonshire			
Llandygwnning	PWLLHELI: Pwllheli	PWLLHELI: Aberdaron	121 (1891)
pt Llanwnda → Betws Garmon	CAERNARFON: Llandwrog	CAERNARFON: Caernarfon	208 (1891)
Betws Garmon	CAERNARFON: Llanrug	CAERNARFON: Caernarfon	124 (1891)
Creation of a new subdistrict, Llanfairfechan, *from part of the subdistrict of* Bangor.			
Aber, Llanfairfechan	BANGOR: Bangor	BANGOR: Llanfairfechan	2829 (1891)
1901–11			
Monmouthshire			
New subdistrict of West Dean *created from part of* Coleford *subdistrict.*			
pt Newland (Gloucs), pt West Dean (Gloucs)	MONMOUTH: Coleford	MONMOUTH: West Dean	6052 (1901)
New subdistrict of Llanhilleth *created from part of* Pontypool *subdistrict.*			
Llanhilleth	PONTYPOOL: Pontypool	PONTYPOOL: Llanhilleth	5015 (1901)
Glamorgan			
Merthyr Tydfil (pt)	MERTHYR TYDFIL: Lower M.T.	MERTHYR TYDFIL: Upper M.T.	7272 (1901)
Subdistrict of Ystradfellte *abolished and parts transferred to* Neath, Cadoxton *and the new subdistrict of* Glyncorrwg.			
Blaengwrach, Neath Higher (pt), Ystradfellte (Brec)	NEATH: Ystradfellte	NEATH: Neath	2402 (1901)
Glyncorrwg	NEATH: Ystradfellte	NEATH: Glyncorrwg	6452 (1901)
Neath Higher (pt), Neath Lower	NEATH: Ystradfellte	NEATH: Cadoxton	499 (1901)
New subdistrict, Ystradgynlais, *formed from part of* Pontardawe *subdistrict.*			
Ystradgynlais Higher, Ystradgynlais Lower	PONTARDAWE: Pontardawe	PONTARDAWE: Ystradgynlais	5785 (1901)
Swansea (pt)	SWANSEA: Llandeilo Tal-y-bont	SWANSEA: Llangyfelach	1889 (1901)
Cockett (pt)	SWANSEA: Swansea	SWANSEA: Llangyfelach	2023 (1901)
Carmarthenshire			
Llangennech	LLANELLI: Loughor	LLANELLI: Llan-non	2224 (1901)
Subdistrict of Llanelli *divided into separate subdistricts* Llanelli Rural *and* Llanelli Urban.			
Llanelli Urban	LLANELLI: Llanelli	LLANELLI: Llanelli Urban	25617 (1901)
Llanelli Rural (pt)	LLANELLI: Llanelli	LLANELLI: Llanelli Rural	4599 (1901)
Llanelli Rural (pt)	LLANELLI: Loughor	LLANELLI: Llanelli Rural	3044 (1901)
Llanelli Rural (pt)	LLANELLI: Llan-non	LLANELLI: Llanelli Rural	1311 (1901)

Area affected	From	To	Population
New subdistrict of Cwarter Bach *created from part of* Llandybïe.			
Llandeilo Rural (pt), Cwarter Bach	LLANDEILO FAWR: Llandybïe	LLANDEILO FAWR: Cwarter Bach	3515 (1901)
Llandeilo Rural (pt)	LLANDEILO FAWR: Llandybïe	LLANDEILO FAWR: Llandeilo	144 (1901)
Cardiganshire			
Subdistrict of Llandygwydd *abolished, all parts transferred to* Cardigan.			
New subdistrict of Clydau *created from part of* Cenarth.			
Capel Colman, Castellan, Clydau, Llanfyrnach, Penrhydd, West Cilrhedyn (all Pemb)	NEWCASTLE EMLYN: Cenarth	NEWCASTLE EMLYN: Clydau	2473 (1901)
Breconshire			
Name of the subdistrict of Abergwesyn *changed to* Treflys *with part transferred to* Llanwrtyd.			
Llanddewi Abergwesyn, Llanfihangel Abergwesyn	BUILTH: Abergwesyn	BUILTH: Llanwrtyd	316 (1901)
Montgomeryshire			
Ysgubor-y-coed (Card)	MACHYNLLETH: Machynlleth	MACHYNLLETH: Tywyn	380 (1901)
Penegoes	MACHYNLLETH: Machynlleth	MACHYNLLETH: Darowen	581 (1901)
Llanwrin	MACHYNLLETH: Tywyn	MACHYNLLETH: Darowen	559 (1901)
Brithdir	FORDEN: Montgomery	FORDEN: Welshpool	86 (1901)
Flintshire			
Creation of new District of HAWARDEN *with one subdistrict named* Hawarden (see A above). *The following part had been transferred to* CHESTER *in July 1901*:			
Buckley Mold	HOLYWELL: Mold	HAWARDEN: Hawarden	3326 (1901)
Denbighshire			
Subdistrict of Gyffylliog *abolished with parts transferred to the subdistricts of* Ruthin, Llanelidan, *and* Llanrhaeadr.			
Gyffylliog	RUTHIN: Gyffylliog	RUTHIN: Ruthin	438 (1901)
Clocaenog	RUTHIN: Gyffylliog	RUTHIN: Llanelidan	373 (1901)
Nantglyn	RUTHIN: Gyffylliog	RUTHIN: Llanrhaeadr	239 (1901)
Llanfair Dyffryn Clwyd Urban	RUTHIN: Llanelidan	RUTHIN: Ruthin	12 (1901)
Llanynys Urban	RUTHIN: Llanrhaeadr	RUTHIN: Ruthin	11 (1901)
Caernarfonshire			
Subdistrict of Creuddyn *abolished with parts transferred to* Conwy *and new subdistricts of* Llandudno *and* Colwyn Bay.			
Llan-rhos	CONWY: Creuddyn	CONWY: Conwy	1686 (1901)
Llandudno, Llangystennin, Penrhyn	CONWY: Creuddyn	CONWY: Llandudno	11477 (1901)
Llandrillo (Denb), Llanelian (Denb) Llansanffraid (Denb), Llysfaen	CONWY: Creuddyn	CONWY: Colwyn Bay	12372 (1901)
Anglesey			
Subdistrict of Llandyfrydog *renamed* Llanfechell.			
Amlwch (pt)	ANGLESEY: Amlwch	ANGLESEY: Llanfechell	685 (1901)
Bodewryd, Llandyfrydog	ANGLESEY: Llandyfrydog	ANGLESEY: Amlwch	512 (1901)

Source: Census Reports, Registrar-General's Decennial Supplements

* Changes in parish boundaries affecting Registration areas. Details of other changes in parish boundaries may be found in the census.

Appendix IV Area and total population. Registration, Administrative and Parliamentary Counties. 1911

Counties	Area (acres) Registration	Administrative	Parliamentary	Total population Registration	Administrative	Parliamentary
Monmouthshire	395593	349552	341497	414666	395719	388944
Glamorgan	576540	518865	518872	1130668	1120910	1120910
Carmarthenshire	465226	588472	588472	151050	160406	160406
Pembrokeshire	357419	393003	395446	84874	89960	90797
Cardiganshire	595412	443189	440746	80769	59879	59042
Breconshire	473080	469281	475228	56370	59287	65999
Radnorshire	238663	301165	301165	17505	22590	22590
Montgomeryshire	591999	510110	510168	62201	53146	53146
Flintshire	106878	163025	164745	69722	92705	92889
Denbighshire	378309	426084	423498	136810	144783	142246
Merioneth	422372	524035	428106	60280	45565	45849
Caernarfonshire	322742	365986	361156	141767	125043	127212
Anglesey	120417	176630	176630	35359	50928	50928

Source: Census 1911. County Reports, Table 1.

Census material was aggregated in a variety of ways during the nineteenth century. Registration divisions formed the basis of most census tables from 1851 to 1901. The Administrative County was created by the Local Government Act of 1888 and was more closely aligned to the Ancient than the Registration County. The Ancient, Geographical, or 'Proper' county divisions formed the basis of the Parliamentary county. The comparison between the Ancient and Parliamentary County boundaries was so close that the 1911 census did not give separate figures for Ancient counties.

II

Language

Iaith

Rhagymadrodd

Ni fu arolwg swyddogol o'r iaith a siaredid gan unigolion yng Nghymru tan gyfrifiad poblogaeth 1891. Golyga hyn fod yn rhaid cywain tystiolaeth ystadegol ynglŷn â defnydd o iaith am y rhan helaethaf o'r bedwaredd ganrif ar bymtheg o amrywiaeth o ffynonellau. At hynny, nid yw'r dystiolaeth ystadegol sydd ar gael bob amser yn rhwydd ei dehongli. Boed yn hunanasesiad neu'n farn pobl eraill, y mae cwestiynau am fedr mewn iaith a defnydd o iaith mewn amgylchiadau lle y mae dwy iaith yn cydfodoli yn anos eu hateb yn fanwl-gywir na chwestiynau demograffig ynglŷn ag oedran neu fan geni. Yn wir, parodd yr holiaduron a baratowyd gan Alexander Ellis wrth iddo geisio pennu'r ffin rhwng ardaloedd Cymraeg a Saesneg eu hiaith ym 1879–80 ddryswch weithiau i'r bobl a'u derbyniodd. Atebodd y Parchedig John Griffith, rheithor Merthyr Tudful, fel hyn: '1. It is difficult to answer your questions, as they do not apply to a district like this. 2. ... You will find it very difficult to trace a boundary in towns. The English is peculiarly "Welsh-English", ... in fact English in a Welsh idiom.'[1] Dengys y dadlau yn sgil cyhoeddi canlyniadau'r cyfrifiad iaith cyntaf ym 1891 fod unigolyn yr un mor anodd ei asesu, o safbwynt ieithyddol, â lle. Serch hynny, y mae'r ystadegau a gyflwynir yn yr adran hon yn ceisio mesur, yn fras, y cynnydd yn niferoedd siaradwyr y Gymraeg yn erbyn y lleihad yn y gyfran o Gymry Cymraeg, yn ogystal â dangos cymhlethdodau'r proses o newid ieithyddol mewn termau gofodol a chymdeithasol.

Yn Nhabl 1.1 cyflwynir arolwg ystadegol o'r defnydd o'r Gymraeg yng Nghymru dros yr holl gyfnod. Cyfuna ddeunydd o dair ffynhonnell wahanol iawn: dosbarthiad ffigurau eglwysig am y cyfnod *c.*1800–1880, canlyniadau arolwg rhyfeddol a gynhaliwyd gan un ymchwilydd yn y 1870au, a chanlyniadau cyfrifiadau 1891–1911. Er gwaethaf y diffyg dilyniant anorfod yn Nhabl 1.1, dadlenna'r ffigurau'n glir yr eithafion rhwng y siroedd mwyaf Cymraeg a mwyaf Saesneg eu hiaith a dangosant raddfa'r newid iaith trwy gydol y bedwaredd ganrif ar bymtheg. Yng Nghymru gyfan, yr oedd tua 71.8 y cant o'r boblogaeth yn byw mewn ardaloedd 'Cymraeg a dwyieithog' ym 1801. Erbyn 1911, yn ôl canlyniadau'r cyfrifiadau, disgynasai'r gyfran o'r boblogaeth a 'fedrai'r Gymraeg' i 43.5 y cant. Er i'r Gymraeg barhau yn brif iaith ymhlith

Introduction

No official survey of the language spoken by individuals in Wales was undertaken until the 1891 population census. This means that statistical evidence of language use for the greater part of the nineteenth century has necessarily to be assembled from a variety of sources. Moreover, the statistical evidence which does exist is not always easy to interpret. Whether self-assessed or the opinion of others, questions of language ability and language use in circumstances where two languages coexist are more difficult to answer precisely than demographic questions of age or birthplace. Indeed, when Alexander Ellis attempted to determine the boundary between Welsh-speaking and English-speaking areas in 1879–80, the recipients of his questionnaires were sometimes puzzled. The Reverend John Griffith, rector of Merthyr Tydfil, replied: '1. It is difficult to answer your questions, as they do not apply to a district like this. 2. ... You will find it very difficult to trace a boundary in towns. The English is peculiarly "Welsh English", ... in fact English in a Welsh idiom.'[1] The debate which ensued when the results of the first language census in 1891 were made public illustrates that, in linguistic terms, individuals were as difficult to assess as were places. Nevertheless, the statistics presented in this section attempt both to measure the broad trend of increasing numbers of Welsh speakers against the decreasing proportion of Welsh speakers as well as to illustrate the complexities of the process of language change in spatial and social terms.

Table 1.1 presents a statistical overview of the use of the Welsh language in Wales over the whole period. It combines material from three very different sources: the classification of ecclesiastical returns for the period *c.*1800–1880, the results of a remarkable survey conducted by one investigator in the 1870s, and the census returns for 1891–1911. Despite the inevitable discontinuities in Table 1.1, the figures clearly reveal the extremes between the most Welsh and the most English counties and indicate the scale of language shift through the nineteenth century. In Wales as a whole, approximately 71.8 per cent of the population lived in 'Welsh and bilingual' areas in 1801. By 1911, according to census returns, the proportion of the population 'able to speak Welsh' had fallen to 43.5 per cent. Although the population of some counties, for

trigolion siroedd megis Aberteifi, Meirionnydd, a Môn, er enghraifft, daethai'r Saesneg bellach yn brif iaith trigolion siroedd eraill, megis Morgannwg a Brycheiniog yn enwedig.

Ar gyfer y rhan helaethaf o'r bedwaredd ganrif ar bymtheg, dibynnwn ar ddadansoddiad medrus W. T. Rees Pryce o ffigurau eglwysig, a gyhoeddwyd mewn cyfres o erthyglau arloesol.[2] Bob tro y byddai esgob yn ymweld â'i esgobaeth, gofynnid i'r offeiriaid lleol ddarparu ffigurau a gynhwysai fanylion am yr iaith a ddefnyddid yng ngwasanaethau'r eglwysi. Y mae adroddiadau gan ddeoniaid gwlad ar blwyfi o fewn eu hardaloedd yn ategu'r wybodaeth hon ac yn ffynhonnell werthfawr lle'r aeth ffigurau'r ymweliadau gofwy ar ddifancoll. Yn ogystal â'r ffaith fod gan yr Eglwys sefydledig gyfrifoldeb statudol i ddarparu gwasanaethau yn yr iaith a oedd yn briodol i'r plwyf, yr oedd cystadleuaeth o du'r Ymneilltuwyr yn cymell clerigwyr Anglicanaidd i gydymffurfio â dymuniadau eu cynulleidfaoedd. Wedi cymharu'n ofalus â ffynonellau eraill, daw Pryce i'r canlyniad fod lle cryf i gredu bod yr iaith neu'r ieithoedd a ddefnyddid yng ngwasanaethau'r eglwys yn adlewyrchu amgylchiadau plwyfi unigol yn y cyfnod hwnnw.[3] Y mae Tabl 1.2 yn dosbarthu ffigurau yn ôl siroedd am y blynyddoedd 1801, 1851 a 1881 yn fanylach na Thabl 1.1. O gymharu'r canrannau â chyfanswm y boblogaeth, gwelir cynnydd ym mhoblogaeth y plwyfi Cymraeg neu Gymraeg yn bennaf o 300,000 ym 1801 i oddeutu 500,000 ym 1851. Defnyddiwyd yr un ffynhonnell ar gyfer mapiau A a B i ddangos parthau ieithyddol yng nghanol y bedwaredd ganrif ar bymtheg a'r newidiadau a gafwyd mewn plwyfi unigol yn y cyfnod rhwng 1749 a *c.*1900.

Ym 1879 cyhoeddodd y daearyddwr Ernst Ravenstein ganlyniadau arolwg uchelgeisiol o'r ieithoedd Celtaidd a siaredid ym Mhrydain yn y *Journal of the Royal Statistical Society*.[4] Defnyddiodd Ravenstein ffigurau cyfrifiad swyddogol i edrych ar y defnydd o'r Wyddeleg yn Iwerddon ond, yn achos Cymru a'r Alban, anfonodd '1,200 circulars to registrars of births, clergymen, schoolmasters, and others, likely to be intimately acquainted with the linguistic condition of their neighbourhood, besides carrying on a voluminous correspondence with gentlemen whom, in the course of my inquiry, I found to take a special interest in the subject'. Atebwyd hanner ei holiaduron, a phan na chafwyd ateb holwyd y tafarnwr lleol am wybodaeth. Gwaetha'r modd, ni nododd Ravenstein union ddyddiad ei arolwg, ond y mae'n debygol mai yng nghanol y 1870au y'i cynhaliwyd. Er cadarnhau i raddau helaeth ei farn fod canlyniadau ei arolwg yn 'bur agos i'r gwirionedd', mynegir rhai amheuon yn y troednodiadau ar ei dablau. Yn Nhabl 2.2, y mae'r ffigurau ar gyfer Cymru gyfan, sy'n dangos bod canran y siaradwyr Saesneg yn uwch na chanran y siaradwyr Cymraeg, yn cadarnhau bod y cydbwysedd ieithyddol wedi dechrau pendilio oddi wrth y Gymraeg cyn y

example, Cardigan, Merioneth, and Anglesey remained predominantly Welsh-speaking, others, notably Glamorgan and Brecon, became predominantly English-speaking.

For the greater part of the nineteenth century, we rely on the skilful analysis of ecclesiastical returns by W. T. Rees Pryce, published in a series of pioneering articles.[2] In advance of the bishop's regular visits to his diocese, local clergy were required to provide returns which included details of the language used in church services. Reports by rural deans on parishes within their districts supplement this information and are a valuable source where visitation returns have failed to survive. Not only did the established Church have a statutory obligation to provide services in the language appropriate to the parish, but competition from Nonconformist alternatives motivated Anglican clergy to comply with the wishes of their congregations. Following careful comparison with other sources, Pryce concludes: 'there exist strong grounds for accepting that the language or languages as used in Anglican church services closely reflected contemporary circumstances in individual parishes'.[3] Table 1.2 classifies returns on a county basis for the years 1801, 1851 and 1881 in more detail than Table 1.1. Comparison of the percentages with the total population suggests an increase of population in Welsh or mainly Welsh parishes from 300,000 to approximately 500,000 between 1801 and 1851. Maps A and B use the same source to indicate language zones in the mid-nineteenth century and the changes which occurred in individual parishes during the period from 1749 to *c.*1900.

In 1879 the geographer Ernst Ravenstein published in the *Journal of the Royal Statistical Society* the results of an ambitious survey of the Celtic languages spoken in Britain.[4] Ravenstein was able to use official census returns to examine the use of Irish in Ireland but, for Wales and Scotland, he dispatched '1,200 circulars to registrars of births, clergymen, schoolmasters, and others, likely to be intimately acquainted with the linguistic condition of their neighbourhood, besides carrying on a voluminous correspondence with gentlemen whom, in the course of my inquiry, I found to take a special interest in the subject'. Half his circulars were answered and, where information was not forthcoming, the local innkeeper was solicited for information. Unfortunately, Ravenstein failed to state the precise date of his survey, but it was probably conducted in the mid-1870s. Although his view that the results of the survey were 'a close approximation to the truth' has been largely confirmed, some qualifying comments are included in the footnotes to his tables. In Table 2.2, the figures for Wales as a whole, which show a percentage of English speakers greater than the percentage of Welsh speakers, confirm that the linguistic balance had begun to swing away from Welsh

1870au. Dylid nodi hefyd y gwahaniaethau rhwng siroedd a thwf yr ardaloedd dwyieithog. Hyd yn oed yn y siroedd Cymreiciaf, megis Caernarfon a Môn, er enghraifft, lle y medrai dros 90 y cant siarad Cymraeg, yr oedd cyfran arwyddocaol (43.5 y cant yn y naill achos a 38 y cant yn y llall) yn medru siarad Saesneg.

Er bod awdurdodau'r cyfrifiad wedi bod yn awyddus er 1801 i gyfrif y boblogaeth yn ôl mesurau demograffig ac economaidd, nid oedd ganddynt unrhyw ddiddordeb mewn dosbarthu poblogaeth Cymru yn ôl medr mewn iaith. Pan osodwyd y dasg ger eu bron ym 1891, prin oedd eu brwdfrydedd o hyd. Ychydig o arweiniad a roddasant i rifwyr lleol, a diwerth oedd y canlyniadau yn eu golwg. Mewn gwirionedd, penderfyniad munud olaf oedd ychwanegu cwestiwn ar yr 'iaith a siaredir' yn ffurflenni cyfrifiad Cymru ar gyfer 1891. Yr oedd cwestiwn ar iaith wedi ei gynnwys ar gyfer Iwerddon er 1851 ac ar gyfer yr Alban er 1881, ond ni chafodd hyn ei ystyried hyd yn oed gan y pwyllgor seneddol ar y cyfrifiad a adroddodd ym 1890. Codwyd y mater wrth fynd heibio yn ystod yr ail ddarlleniad ar Fesur y Cyfrifiad (Cymru a Lloegr) yn Nhŷ'r Cyffredin yng Ngorffennaf 1890 gan yr AS Gwyddelig dros Queen's County, W. A. MacDonald, na allai weld paham y cydnabyddid heniaith yr Alban heb roi sylw o gwbl i heniaith Cymru, er nad oedd am wasgu os oedd gan Aelodau Cymru wrthwynebiad. Siaradodd dau o'r aelodau Cymreig hynny, Samuel T. Evans a D. A. Thomas, o blaid ac ychwanegwyd yr unig newidiad at y Trydydd Darlleniad, sef y ddarpariaeth 'that a Return shall be made in Wales of the persons who can speak Welsh and English or English only', a hynny heb drafodaeth bellach. Bu newid bychan arall yn Nhŷ'r Arglwyddi a'i gwnaeth yn gwbl glir mai yn y ffurflenni ar gyfer cartrefi yng Nghymru yn unig y cynhwysid y cwestiwn.[5] Maes o law, ymddangosodd ffurflenni ar gyfer Cymru ac arnynt golofn dan y pennawd 'Iaith a siaredir', ynghyd â'r cyfarwyddiadau, 'Os Saesneg yn unig, ysgrifennwch "Saesneg", os Cymraeg yn unig, ysgrifennwch "Cymraeg", os Saesneg a Chymraeg, ysgrifennwch "Y Ddwy".'

Nid oedd y senedd wedi rhag-weld nac ymbaratoi ar gyfer y rhyferthwy o gŵynion a chyhuddiadau a ddaeth o Gymru y mis Ebrill canlynol yn sgil ychwanegu'r cwestiwn iaith annisgwyl at Gyfrifiad 1891. Parodd pryderon ynglŷn â diffyg ffurflenni Cymraeg a'r cwestiwn iaith ferw gwyllt wrth i ddiwrnod y cyfrifiad agosáu. Bu crïwr tref Machynlleth yn tramwyo'r strydoedd y diwrnod cyn dydd y cyfrifiad yn annog y trigolion i gofio eu gwlad, eu hiaith a'u cenedl. O ganlyniad, defnyddiodd rhifwyr Machynlleth eu hawl i newid 57 o gofrestrau ac arnynt enwau 284 o bobl y gwyddent eu bod yn medru siarad Saesneg yn ogystal â Chymraeg o 'Cymraeg yn unig' i 'Y Ddwy'.[6] Er y cafwyd gwahaniaeth barn yn ddiweddarach ynglŷn â'r rhugldér gofynnol, honnai'r *South Wales Daily News* mai'r maen prawf sylfaenol i'r

before the 1870s. Other points to note are the differences between counties and the growth of bilingual areas. Even in the most Welsh counties, for example Caernarfon and Anglesey, where over 90 per cent could speak Welsh, a significant proportion (43.5 per cent and 38 per cent respectively) were able to speak English.

Although census authorities had been eager since 1801 to count the population by demographic and economic measures, they showed no interest in classifying the population of Wales by language ability. When presented with the task in 1891, they remained unenthusiastic, gave little guidance to local enumerators, and were dismissive of the results. In fact, the addition of a question on 'language spoken' in the Welsh census schedules for 1891 was very much a last-minute decision. A language question had been included for Ireland since 1851 and for Scotland since 1881, but it was not even considered by the parliamentary committee on the census which reported in 1890. The issue was simply raised casually during the second reading of the Census (England and Wales) Bill in the House of Commons in July 1890 by the Irish MP for Queen's County, W. A. MacDonald, who could not see 'why you should recognise the ancient language of Scotland and take no account of the ancient language of Wales', though he 'would not press it if the Welsh Members object to it'. Two Welsh members, Samuel T. Evans and D. A. Thomas, then spoke in support and, without further discussion, the provision 'that a Return shall be made in Wales of the persons who can speak Welsh and English or English only' became the only amendment to the Third Reading. A further minor amendment in the House of Lords made it absolutely clear that the question was to be included only in household schedules for Wales.[5] In due course, household schedules for Wales appeared with a final column headed 'Language spoken', with instructions, 'If only English, write "English"; if only Welsh, write "Welsh"; if English and Welsh, write "Both".'

The unheralded introduction of the language question to the 1891 census gave parliament no preparation for the barrage of complaints and accusations which emanated from Wales around census day in April the following year. Concern over the lack of Welsh schedules and the language return reached panic proportions as census day loomed. The town crier at Machynlleth, Montgomeryshire, paraded the streets the day before census day urging citizens: 'Remember our country, our language, our nation.' As a consequence, Machynlleth enumerators used their powers to change 57 schedules, containing the entries of 284 persons whom they knew were able to speak English as well as Welsh from 'Welsh only' to 'Both'.[6] Although conflicting views later emerged regarding the proficiency required, the *South Wales Daily News*

awdurdodau ar y pryd oedd y gallu i roi tystiolaeth mewn llys barn.[7]

Y gŵyn fwyaf cyffredin, fodd bynnag, oedd prinder ffurflenni Cymraeg, a oedd wedi eu cynhyrchu ar gyfer pob cyfrifiad er 1851.[8] Mewn ymateb i feirniadaeth yn Nhŷ'r Cyffredin honnodd swyddogion Bwrdd y Llywodraeth fod pob cofrestrydd yng Nghymru yn gyfrifol am amcangyfrif y nifer o ffurflenni Cymraeg angenrheidiol a bod 'an extraordinary desire' wedi arwain at brinder. Trwy amryfusedd yr oedd siroedd Caernarfon a'r Fflint wedi derbyn ffurflenni Saesneg a fwriadwyd ar gyfer Lloegr, ac nad oeddynt, o'r herwydd, yn cynnwys y cwestiwn iaith. Sicrhawyd y Senedd y cymerid camau i gasglu'r wybodaeth angenrheidiol.[9]

Digon rhwydd oedd egluro camgymeriadau gweinyddol. Materion anos a mwy tringar oedd sut y cawsai atebion i'r cwestiwn 'iaith a siaredir' eu dewis, gan eu bod yn cyffwrdd â materion megis balchder cenedlaethol, y gallu i wneud hunanasesiad dibynadwy, ac amharodrwydd swyddogion cyfrifiad o Saeson i dderbyn bod y defnydd o'r iaith Gymraeg mor eang ag y dangosai'r ffigurau. Parodd cyhoeddi'r Adroddiad Cyffredinol ym 1894, a neilltuodd ddau dudalen yn unig ar gyfer 'Languages in Wales and Monmouthshire', fwy fyth o ddadlau. Honnodd y Cofrestrydd Cyffredinol, Brydges Henniker, fod y ffigurau yn annibynadwy, gan ddadlau bod y cwestiwn iaith, mewn rhai achosion, wedi ei ateb ar ran babanod a bod llawer wedi ateb 'Cymraeg yn unig', gan mai'r Gymraeg oedd eu hiaith arferol neu eu dewis iaith, pan fyddai 'Y Ddwy' wedi bod yn gywirach. Er iddo fethu taflu goleuni ar y safonau angenrheidiol na dyfynnu tystiolaeth, credai Henniker fod nifer y Cymry uniaith yn sylweddol is nag a ddangosai'r canlyniadau, ac mai'r unig ffordd ddibynadwy o'u defnyddio oedd cyfuno'r nifer a atebodd 'Cymraeg yn unig' ac 'Y Ddwy' er mwyn cael cyfanswm y siaradwyr Cymraeg, boed y rheini'n siarad Saesneg hefyd ai peidio.[10] Parodd yr ensyniad yn yr Adroddiad fod y Cymry yn fwriadol wedi rhoi atebion ffug ferw gwyllt. Unwaith eto, gofynnwyd cwestiynau yn y Senedd, a bu'n rhaid i'r Cofrestrydd Cyffredinol gyhoeddi llythyr o ymddiheuriad ac eglurhad.[11] Yr oedd sylwedyddion eraill a chanddynt ddiddordeb uniongyrchol yn ffigurau'r cyfrifiad ac a oedd yn gyfarwydd â materion Cymreig yn fwy tueddol i dderbyn y canlyniadau. Ystyriai Thomas Darlington, a ysgrifennai yn *Wales*, fod y ffigurau mor agos i'r gwir ag y gellid disgwyl i ffigurau ar fater fel iaith fod.[12] Er bod J. E. Southall, awdur *Wales and her Language*, yn fwy amheus, yr oedd, serch hynny, yn 'dueddol' o dderbyn cywirdeb y canlyniadau.[13] Yr oedd aelodau'r Comisiwn Brenhinol ar Dir yng Nghymru a Mynwy, a adroddodd ym 1896, ychydig yn fwy cadarnhaol. Datganodd yr adroddiad yn hyderus fod y canlyniadau at ei gilydd yn gywir, gan nodi y byddai'r rhai hynny a oedd â chrap ar y Gymraeg ynghyd â'r sawl a oedd â chrap ar y Saesneg

claimed that the authorities at the time considered the ability to give evidence in a court of law as the basic criterion.[7]

However, there is no doubt that the most widespread complaint was the lack of Welsh household schedules, which had been produced for each census since 1851.[8] Local Government Board officials rebutted criticism in the House of Commons by replying that each Registrar in Wales was responsible for estimating the number of Welsh forms required and that 'an extraordinary desire' had resulted in supply falling short of demand. In Caernarfonshire and Flintshire, errors in packing had led to the receipt of English forms intended for England, which did not contain the final column including the language question. Parliament was assured that steps would be taken to collect the necessary information.[9]

Administrative errors could be straightforwardly explained. How answers to the 'language spoken' question were chosen, and how to interpret the choices made were more difficult and delicate issues to discuss, since they involved matters such as Welsh national pride, the ability to make a reliable self-assessment, and the reluctance of English census officials to believe that the use of the Welsh language was as widespread as the returns indicated. The publication of the General Report in 1894, which devoted two pages only for 'Languages in Wales and Monmouthshire', caused yet more controversy. The Registrar General, Brydges Henniker, claimed that the returns were 'untrustworthy' on the grounds that the language question had, in some cases, been filled in for infants and many had entered 'Welsh only' because they spoke Welsh habitually or preferably when the more correct entry would have been 'Both'. Although he failed both to clarify standards required or to cite evidence, Henniker believed the number of monoglot Welsh people had been considerably overstated and that the figures could only be reliably used by combining the number of 'Welsh only' and 'Both' together in order to arrive at the number of people able to speak Welsh, with or without English.[10] The implication in the Report that Welsh people had deliberately falsified the returns caused uproar. Once again questions were asked in Parliament, and the Registrar General was obliged to publish a letter of apology and explanation.[11] Other commentators with a direct interest in the census figures and familiar with Welsh affairs were more disposed to endorse the results. Thomas Darlington, writing in *Wales*, considered the returns 'quite as near the truth as returns on such a matter as language can ever be expected to be'.[12] Although J. E. Southall, the author of *Wales and her Language,* was more sceptical, he was nevertheless 'inclined' to accept the correctness of the returns.[13] Members of the Royal Commission on Land in Wales and Monmouthshire, reporting in 1896, were rather more positive. Their

yn cael eu hepgor pe defnyddid y gallu i roi tystiolaeth mewn llys barn fel y maen prawf sylfaenol.[14] Y mae astudiaeth o lyfrau rhifwyr y cyfrifiad, sydd bellach ar gael ar gyfer 1891, yn cadarnhau'r farn honno. Y mae'r gofal a gymerwyd dros lenwi ffurflenni'r cartrefi yn amlwg. Yn achos iaith, nodwyd yn aml wahaniaethau mewn medr ieithyddol rhwng preswylwyr y tŷ, a'r cofnod arferol wrth nodi gallu ieithyddol babanod (un o'r pwyntiau a ddefnyddiwyd gan y Cofrestrydd i fwrw amheuaeth ar y ffigurau) oedd 'Cymraeg yn unig' neu 'Saesneg yn unig', atebion a ddatgelai iaith y cartref. Gellid dadlau hefyd y gallai'r prinder ffurflenni Cymraeg fod wedi annog pobl i roi 'Y Ddwy' yn hytrach na 'Cymraeg yn unig', gyda'r canlyniad fod nifer y siaradwyr Cymraeg uniaith mewn gwirionedd yn uwch na'r hyn a amcangyfrifwyd, yn hytrach nag fel arall.[15]

I'r hanesydd cymdeithasol, efallai'r mai'r siom fwyaf o safbwynt cyfrifiad 1891 yw nid yn gymaint y cwestiwn ynglŷn â chywirdeb ond yn hytrach y diffyg gwahanu ar ffigurau yn y tabl un-tudalen a gyhoeddwyd. Cyhoeddir ffigurau ar gyfer cyfanswm y boblogaeth a oedd yn ddwy oed a throsodd, a hynny yn ôl siroedd cofrestru a 52 o ddosbarthau cofrestru, heb ddadansoddiad pellach yn ôl oedran, rhyw, nac ardal. Y mae hyn yn creu anawsterau wrth geisio cymharu ffigurau 1891 â chanlyniadau cyfrifiadau diweddarach, a gyhoeddwyd yn ôl siroedd gweinyddol ac nad oeddynt yn cynnwys plant dwy oed. Serch hynny, y mae Tablau 3.1 a 3.2 yn dangos yn eglur barhad cryfder y Gymraeg yn y gogledd a'r gorllewin, a hefyd y twf absoliwt (yn hytrach na chanran y twf) yn niferoedd y siaradwyr Cymraeg yn llawer o ardaloedd diwydiannol y de. Dyma'r ardal a alwodd Brinley Thomas yn 'bair y dadeni', h.y. ailgartrefu siaradwyr Cymraeg a allai, heb y cyfleoedd economaidd a gynigiai Maes Glo De Cymru, fod wedi ymfudo o Gymru.[16] Er bod Caerdydd yn datblygu yn ganolfan fasnach a busnes ryngwladol ac yn sgil hynny yn ddinas a oedd bron yn gwbl Saesneg ei hiaith, yr oedd mwy o siaradwyr Cymraeg (86,994) yn byw o fewn ffiniau Dosbarth Cofrestru cyfagos Pontypridd, a oedd yn cynnwys y Rhondda, nag yn Sir Gofrestru Aberteifi, lle'r oedd 95 y cant o'r boblogaeth yn siarad Cymraeg.

Achoswyd llai o gythrwfl gan gyfrifiadau diweddarach 1901 a 1911. Yn ei Adroddiad Cyffredinol ar gyfrifiad 1901, daliai'r Cofrestrydd Cyffredinol, William Dunbar, i gael anhawster i dderbyn dilysrwydd y ffigurau ynglŷn â siaradwyr Cymraeg uniaith, er y sylweddolai fod y ffaith fod cymaint o Gymraeg yn cael ei siarad ymhlith y trigolion, yn eu cartrefi ac mewn mannau eraill, yn enwedig yn y rhannau mwyaf anghysbell o Gymru, yn siŵr o wneud argraff ar unrhyw un a ymwelai â'r wlad.[17] Yr oedd adroddiad llawnach 1911, a gyhoeddwyd yn gyfrol ar wahân, yn cyfaddef na sefydlwyd unrhyw feini prawf pendant i fesur rhuglder ieithyddol ac nad oedd yn amlwg o'r

report confidently declared that 'the Returns are substantially correct', and pointed out that if the basic criterion was the ability to give evidence in a court of law then it would omit both those who had a smattering of Welsh as well as those who had a smattering of English.[14] Examination of the census enumerators' books, now available for 1891, corroborates this view. The care with which the household schedules were generally completed is apparent. Regarding language, distinctions in language ability between household members were often entered and, where the language ability of infants was entered (one of the points used by the Registrar to discredit the returns), the entry was usually 'Welsh only' or 'English only', thereby indicating the language of the home. It could also be argued that the scarcity of Welsh census forms may have discouraged the entry of 'Welsh only' in favour of 'Both' and therefore resulted in the underestimation rather than the overestimation of the number of monoglot Welsh speakers.[15]

For the social historian, perhaps the biggest disappointment of the 1891 census is less the question of accuracy than the lack of disaggregation in the one-page published table. The returns are published only for the total population aged two years and over on the basis of registration counties and 52 registration districts, without further breakdown by age, sex, or area. This creates difficulties when attempting to compare the 1891 figures with later census returns, which were published on the basis of administrative counties and excluded children aged two. Nevertheless, Tables 3.1 and 3.2 clearly reveal the continuing strength of the Welsh language in the north and the west, and also the absolute growth (rather than percentage growth) in the numbers of Welsh speakers in many of the industrial areas of the south. The latter was the principal location of what Brinley Thomas called the 'cauldron of rebirth', i.e. the resettlement of Welsh-speaking people who, without the economic opportunities afforded by the South Wales Coalfield, might otherwise have emigrated.[16] Although the development of Cardiff as an international trading and business centre was creating an almost entirely English-speaking city, the adjacent Registration District of Pontypridd, which included the Rhondda, contained more Welsh speakers (86,994) than the entire Registration County of Cardiganshire, where 95 per cent of the population were able to speak Welsh.

Subsequent censuses, in 1901 and 1911, aroused less controversy. In his General Report on the 1901 census, the Registrar General, William Dunbar, still found it difficult to accept the authenticity of the returns relating to monoglot Welsh speakers, but his scepticism was tempered by the recognition that 'anyone travelling in Wales, especially the remoter districts, cannot but be impressed by the frequency with which he hears the native language spoken by the

canlyniadau a oedd unrhyw orliwio a fu ar nifer siaradwyr uniaith yn fwy ymhlith y personau a gofnodwyd fel siaradwyr 'Saesneg yn unig' neu ymhlith y rhai a gofnodwyd fel siaradwyr 'Cymraeg yn unig'.[18]

Ym 1901 – am y tro cyntaf – yr oedd y tablau cyfrifiad a gyhoeddwyd ar yr iaith a siaredid yng Nghymru yn gwahaniaethu rhwng dynion a merched ac yn rhoi manylion am wahanol grwpiau oedran mewn Dosbarthau Trefol a Gwledig. Ym 1911, hefyd, gan fod yr ardal gyfansymiol sylfaenol yr un fath, yr oedd modd gwneud cymariaethau uniongyrchol yn hyderus am y tro cyntaf rhwng dechrau a diwedd cyfnod o ddeng mlynedd ar lefel leol. Rhydd Tabl 3.3 ffigurau cymaradwy cyffredinol ar gyfer Cymru, y siroedd gweinyddol, a'r dosbarthau lleol ar gyfer 1901 a 1911. Y mae Tabl 3.4 yn aildrefnu'r ffigurau canrannol a roddwyd yn Nhabl 3.3 i ddadlennu tabl cynghrair o ddosbarthau lleol a restrir yn ôl gallu'r trigolion i siarad Cymraeg ym 1911. Dengys Tabl 3.5 ffigurau cymaradwy ar gyfer personau, dynion a merched, yn ôl grŵp oedran, ar gyfer Cymru a'r siroedd gweinyddol, ym 1901 a 1911. Yn Nhablau 3.6 a 3.7 cyflwynir dadansoddiad llawn o'r ffigurau, yn ôl rhyw a grŵp oedran, ar gyfer Dosbarthau Trefol a Gwledig am 1901 a 1911. Dengys mapiau D ac E y nifer o bobl a fedrai'r Gymraeg ym 1901 a 1911, mewn canrannau mewn ardaloedd dosbarth lleol.

Nid oedd y darlun cyffredinol rhwng 1901 a 1911 yn argoeli'n dda i ddyfodol y Gymraeg. Er bod y nifer absoliwt a siaradai'r iaith wedi cynyddu fymryn o 929,824 i 976,966, yr oedd canran y siaradwyr Cymraeg wedi disgyn o 49.9 y cant i 44.6 y cant. At hynny, yr oedd y gronfa o siaradwyr uniaith Gymraeg, a oedd wedi disgyn i 8.7 y cant, bron yn sych erbyn 1911. Yn ddaearyddol, yr oedd cylchfa'r iaith Gymraeg yn crebachu a darnio.

Ar y lefel leol, y mae Tablau 3.3 i 3.7 yn cynnwys llawer o wybodaeth fanwl ar gyfer 1901 a 1911, ac ychydig nodweddion yn unig a ellir eu pwysleisio yma. Y mae'r dadansoddiad yn ôl oedran a lleoliad yn ddiddorol ac yn darparu gwybodaeth bwysig ynglŷn â'r prosesau newid iaith sylfaenol mewn ardaloedd arbennig. Er enghraifft, dengys Tabl 3.4 mai Dosbarth Trefol Bethesda oedd y dosbarth mwyaf Cymraeg yng Nghymru ym 1911. Ar yr olwg gyntaf, ymddengys fod y Gymraeg mor ddiogel ym Methesda ym 1911 ag yr oedd ym 1901, gyda 99 y cant o'r boblogaeth a oedd yn dair oed a throsodd yn medru'r iaith. Ond o edrych yn fanylach, amlyga'r ffigurau sefyllfa ieithyddol ansefydlog, gan fod nifer y siaradwyr Cymraeg uniaith wedi disgyn o 64.4 y cant i 56.1 y cant yn ystod y degawd. Dengys cymhariaeth rhwng ffigurau medrieithyddol y gwahanol grwpiau oedran yn Nosbarth Trefol Bethesda ym 1911 (Tabl 3.7) sut yr oedd y Saesneg yn treiddio i'r ardaloedd Cymreiciaf yn ystod y cyfnod hwn. Y mae'r ffaith mai un plentyn rhwng tair a phedair oed yn unig a gofnodwyd yn Saesneg ei

people when conversing amongst themselves in their homes or elsewhere'.[17] The fuller 1911 language report, published as a separate volume, admitted that no definite criteria had been established for language proficiency and that it was not obvious from the returns whether any exaggeration of the monoglot population was greater among persons returned as able to speak 'English only' or among those returned as able to speak 'Welsh only'.[18]

In 1901 – for the first time – the published census tables on language spoken in Wales distinguished males from females and gave details for different age groups in Urban and Rural Districts. In 1911, too, continuity in the basic area of aggregation meant that, for the first time, direct comparisons could confidently be made between the beginning and the end of a decennial period at a local level. Table 3.3 gives comparable overall figures for Wales, administrative counties, and local districts for 1901 and 1911. Table 3.4 reorders the percentage figures given in Table 3.3 to present a league table of local districts listed according to ability to speak Welsh in 1911. Table 3.5 shows comparable figures for persons, males, and females, by age group, for Wales and administrative counties, in 1901 and 1911. Tables 3.6 and 3.7 present the full breakdown of the returns, by sex and age group, for Urban and Rural Districts for 1901 and 1911 respectively. Maps D and E display the number of people able to speak Welsh, in 1901 and 1911, in percentage terms in local district areas.

The overall picture between 1901 and 1911 did not promise well for the future of the Welsh language. Although the absolute number of those able to speak Welsh had increased slightly from 929,824 to 976,966, the percentage of those able to speak Welsh had decreased from 49.9 per cent to 44.6 per cent. Moreover, the reservoir of monoglot Welsh speakers, which had fallen to 8.7 per cent, had almost dried up by 1911. Geographically, the Welsh language zone was shrinking and fragmenting.

At the local level, Tables 3.3 to 3.7 contain much valuable detailed information for 1901 and 1911, and only a few significant features can be stressed here. The breakdown by age and locality is interesting and provides important information regarding the underlying processes of language change in particular areas. For example, Bethesda Urban District heads the list in Table 3.4 as the most Welsh district in Wales in 1911. At first glance the position of the Welsh language in Bethesda seems to have been as unassailable in 1911 as it was in 1901, with 99 per cent of the population aged three and above able to speak Welsh. However, on closer inspection, the figures reveal an unstable linguistic situation, for the number of monoglot Welsh speakers had fallen from 64.4 per cent to 56.1 per cent during the decade. A comparison of language-ability figures between different age groups in Bethesda

iaith (ac un ar ddeg yn ddwyieithog) yn awgrymu mai Cymraeg oedd iaith y cartref i bob pwrpas o hyd. Mewn grwpiau oedran hŷn, fodd bynnag, y mae'r gyfran a fedrai'r Saesneg yn codi'n sydyn, o 20.2 y cant o'r plant rhwng pump a naw oed, i 56.8 y cant o'r plant rhwng deg a phedair ar ddeg, ac i fwyafswm o 62.7 y cant ymhlith pobl ifainc rhwng pymtheg a phedair ar hugain oed. Mewn ardal yr oedd ei phoblogaeth wedi disgyn ddeg y cant ac nad oedd nemor ddim mewnfudwyr wedi ymgartrefu ynddi yn ystod y deng mlynedd hyd at 1911, ymddengys y byddai'n rhesymol casglu bod y modd y dysgid Saesneg mewn ysgolion wedi bod yn ddigon llwyddiannus i 'Y Ddwy' gael ei gofnodi ar ffurflen y cyfrifiad yn hytrach na 'Cymraeg yn unig'. Er y byddai bron pawb ym Methesda wedi teimlo'n fwy cysurus o lawer yn siarad Cymraeg, yr oedd gan fwyafrif y bobl ifainc grap o leiaf ar y Saesneg. Cyfyd cymhariaeth o'r ffigurau ar gyfer dynion a merched gwestiynau diddorol hefyd. Paham, er enghraifft, yr oedd merched ifainc rhwng pymtheg a phedair ar hugain oed yn fwy tebygol o gael eu cofnodi yn ddwyieithog (68.8 y cant) na dynion ifainc yn yr un grŵp oedran (54.8 y cant)? Un rheswm posibl, yn achos dynion ifainc, oedd Cymreictod y gweithle; rheswm arall oedd y gallai merched ifainc ei hystyried hi'n ddymunol i feistroli'r Saesneg er mwyn codi yn y byd.[19] Y mae'r ffigurau yn y tablau hyn yn codi rhagor o gwestiynau nag y gallant eu hateb, ond y mae cyfiawnhad dros eu cynnwys gan eu bod yn datgelu cymhlethdod y proses o newid ieithyddol ar lefel leol mewn ffyrdd a gelir gan y cyfansymiau.

Y mae'r tablau olaf yn yr adran hon yn cynnwys gwybodaeth yn ymwneud ag iaith a gasglwyd mewn arolygon cymdeithasol yn y 1840au. Cyhoeddodd G. S. Kenrick, rheolwr Gweithfeydd Haearn y Farteg, ei arolygon o weithwyr haearn Pont-y-pŵl, Blaenafon a Merthyr Tudful yn y *Journal of the Statistical Society of London* ym 1841 a 1846.[20] Ei nod oedd: 'to display to the wealthy classes of society the real condition of the mass of their labouring and necessitous neighbours, and to produce a feeling of commiseration in the one, and of thankfulness and good-will in the other'.[21] Cynhwysir canlyniadau'r arolwg yn llawn yn Nhabl 4.1. Yng nghyd-destun iaith, un o'r nodweddion mwyaf trawiadol yw Cymreictod trigolion Merthyr Tudful o'i gymharu â Seisnigrwydd trigolion Pont-y-pŵl a Blaenafon.

Gwnaethpwyd arolwg manylach ym 1846 dan gyfarwyddyd y Parchedig Robert David Thomas ('Iorthryn Gwynedd'), gweinidog gyda'r Annibynwyr, mewn ymateb i gylchlythyrau a ddosbarthwyd gan y Comisiynwyr a benodwyd yn yr un flwyddyn i ymchwilio i gyflwr addysg yng Nghymru. Ymwelwyd â phob cartref ym mhlwyfi Llanfair Caereinion, Castell Caereinion, a Manafon yn sir Drefaldwyn, a rhestrwyd gwybodaeth am bob person dan y penawdau canlynol:

Urban District in 1911 (Table 3.7) indicates ways in which English was infiltrating even the most Welsh districts during this period. The fact that, among children aged three and four, only one child was entered as monoglot English (and eleven as bilingual) suggests that the language of the home remained overwhelmingly Welsh. In subsequent age groups, however, the proportion of those able to speak English rises sharply, from 20.2 per cent of those aged between five and nine, to 56.8 per cent of those aged between ten and fourteen, and to a maximum of 62.7 per cent among those aged between fifteen and twenty-four. In an area which had experienced a ten per cent decrease in population and which saw few settling incomers in the decennial period up to 1911, it seems reasonable to conclude that the teaching of English within schools had been sufficiently successful for 'Both' to be entered in the census schedule rather than 'Welsh only'. Although nearly everyone living in Bethesda would have been much more comfortable speaking Welsh, the majority of young people could, at the very least, 'get by' in English. A comparison of figures for males and females also begs interesting questions. Why, for example, should young women aged between fifteen and twenty-four be more likely to be entered as bilingual (68.8 per cent) than young men in the same age group (54.8 per cent)? One reason might be the Welshness of the workplace for young men; another that the acquisition of English might have been considered desirable by women who sought to improve their status.[19] The figures in these tables raise more questions than they are able to answer, but their inclusion is justified because they reveal at local level the complexity of the process of language change in ways that are obscured by the aggregated totals.

The final tables in this section contain information relating to language assembled in social surveys conducted in the 1840s. G. S. Kenrick, manager of the Varteg Ironworks, conducted surveys amongst the iron workers of Pontypool, Blaenafon, and Merthyr Tydfil, which he published in the *Journal of the Statistical Society of London* in 1841 and 1846.[20] His aim was 'to display to the wealthy classes of society the real condition of the mass of their labouring and necessitous neighbours, and to produce a feeling of commiseration in the one, and of thankfulness and good-will in the other'.[21] The complete survey results are included in Table 4.1. In the context of language, one of the most striking features is the Welshness of the inhabitants in Merthyr Tydfil as opposed to the Englishness of the inhabitants of Pontypool and Blaenafon.

A more detailed survey was carried out in 1846 under the direction of the Reverend Robert David Thomas ('Iorthryn Gwynedd'), a Congregational minister, in response to circulars which were distributed by the Commissioners appointed in the same year to investigate the state of education in Wales. Every

enw, oedran, galwedigaeth, cenedl, iaith, yr wyddor, sillafu, darllen, ysgrifennu, rhifyddeg, gramadeg, daearyddiaeth, canu, addysg ysgol Sul, llyfrau, mynychu ysgol ddyddiol ac ysgol Sul, man addoliad, a cholofn olaf ar gyfer sylwadau. Rhoddwyd y cyfarwyddiadau canlynol i'r 'arolygwyr' a bennwyd i gasglu'r wybodaeth: 'Mark w for Welsh; and e for English. Make any remarks you think proper. Write plainly with good ink. Do it faithfully and accurately.'[22] Y mae canlyniadau eu hymdrechion gofalus a thrylwyr i restru gwybodaeth am ryw 4,216 o drigolion y tri phlwyf yn rhoi cyfle unigryw i archwilio patrwm cymdeithasol cymuned wledig gymysg ei hiaith, mewn cyfnod cyn dyfodiad y rheilffyrdd, a lle'r oedd y llwybrau cyfathrebu naturiol yn rhedeg tua'r dwyrain i Loegr. Yr oedd i bob un o'r plwyfi batrwm tebyg o aneddiadau o fân ffermydd gwasgaredig a gynhaliai liaws o grefftwyr gwlad. Yr oedd plwyf Llanfair Caereinion, fodd bynnag, hefyd yn cynnwys pentref mawr Llanfair Caereinion, 'tref embryonig' yng nghanol y bedwaredd ganrif ar bymtheg, a oedd yn ganolfan farchnad ar gyfer cynnyrch fferm a nwyddau gwlân, ac yn darparu cyfleusterau gwasanaeth a mân-werthu i'r gymuned ehangach.[23] Casglwyd yr wybodaeth yn yr arolwg er mwyn cyflwyno tystiolaeth ar gyflwr addysg yn yr amryfal dreflannau, ac fe'i cyhoeddwyd gan y Comisiynwyr fel rhan o atodiad o lythyrau a deisebau.[24] Yn Nhablau 4.2 i 4.5 aildrefnwyd yr wybodaeth o'r ffurflenni llawysgrif er mwyn cyflwyno iaith fel y prif fater, mewn perthynas â nifer o newidynnau cymdeithasol ac economaidd yn achos pob un o'r tri phlwyf. Rhoddir gwybodaeth am iaith yn ôl oedran, pennaeth cartref, cenedl, a galwedigaeth, gan wahaniaethu rhwng dynion a merched, ym mhob plwyf. At ei gilydd, ymddengys fod yr ardal yn ddwyieithog, ond awgryma dadansoddiad manylach o Dabl 4.2, sy'n rhannu'r ffigurau yn ôl oedran, mai'r Gymraeg a ddefnyddid helaethaf yn y cartref. Awgryma gweddill y tablau gysylltiadau diddorol rhwng iaith a chenedl, galwedigaeth a statws cymdeithasol.

[1] Alexander J. Ellis, 'On the Delimitation of the English and Welsh Languages', *Y Cymmrodor*, V (1882), 173–208. Dyma'r cwestiynau a holwyd yn ne Cymru: 1. Yn gyffredinol, ai Cymraeg neu Saesneg a siaredir gan y werin? 2. Os Cymraeg yw'r iaith, ble yw'r man agosaf lle y siaredir Saesneg, i'r dwyrain neu'r gorllewin? 3. Os Saesneg yw'r iaith, ble yw'r man agosaf lle y siaredir y Gymraeg, ac ai Saesneg llyfr ydyw, neu iaith debyg i'r un a siaredir yn Henffordd neu Gaerloyw? 4. Os ceir cymysgedd o'r ddwy iaith, pa mor aml y ceir gwasanaethau neu bregethau Cymraeg? (Yn yr erthygl eglura Ellis mai Saesneg 'llyfr' yw'r Saesneg a ddysgwyd yn yr ysgol yn hytrach na thrwy gyfathrebu.)

[2] Gw. W. T. R. Pryce, 'Approaches to the Linguistic Geography of Northeast Wales, 1750–1846', *Cylchgrawn Llyfrgell Genedlaethol Cymru*, XVII (1971–2), 343–63; idem, 'Welsh and English in Wales, 1750–1971: A Spatial Analysis Based on the Linguistic Affiliation of Parochial Communities', *Bulletin of the Board of Celtic Studies*, XXVIII, rhan 1 (1978), 1–36; idem, 'Wales as a Culture Region: Patterns of Change 1750–

household in the Montgomeryshire parishes of Llanfair Caereinion, Castle Caereinion, and Manafon was visited, and information for each household member was listed under the following headings: name, age, occupation, nation, language, alphabet, spelling, reading, writing, arithmetic, grammar, geography, singing, Sunday school teaching, books, attendance at day school and Sunday school, place of worship, and a final column for remarks. The 'inspectors' who were detailed to collect the information were instructed to 'Mark w for Welsh; and e for English. Make any remarks you think proper. Write plainly with good ink. Do it faithfully and accurately.'[22] The results of their diligent and careful efforts in listing information about some 4,216 inhabitants of the three parishes offers a unique opportunity to examine the social structure of a mixed language, pre-railway, rural community where the natural lines of communication ran eastwards to England. Each of the parishes displays a similar settlement pattern of small scattered farms supporting a range of rural craftsmen. The parish of Llanfair Caereinion, however, also contained the large village of Llanfair Caereinion, an 'embryonic town' in the mid-nineteenth century, which acted as a marketing centre for farm produce and woollen manufactures, and provided service and retail facilities for the wider community.[23] Information collected in the survey was compiled in order to present evidence of the state of education in the various townships, and it was published by the Commissioners as part of an appendix of letters and memorials.[24] In Tables 4.2 to 4.5 the information from the manuscript returns has been reassembled to present language as the main concern, in relation to a number of social and economic variables for each of the three parishes. Information is given on language according to age, head of household, nationality, and occupation, distinguishing males from females, within each parish. Overall the district appears to have been bilingual, but a closer analysis of Table 4.2, which breaks down the overall figures by age, suggests that Welsh was more widely used in the home. The remainder of the tables indicate interesting relationships between language and nationality, occupation and social status.

[1] Alexander J. Ellis, 'On the Delimitation of the English and Welsh Languages', *Y Cymmrodor,* V (1882), 173–208. Questions asked in south Wales were as follows: 1. Is Welsh or English generally spoken by the peasantry of ... to one another? 2. If Welsh, where is the nearest English speaking place, East or West? 3. If English, where is the nearest Welsh speaking place? and is it book English, or like Hereford and Gloucester? 4. If mixed, how often have you Welsh Services or Sermons? (In the article Ellis explained that 'book' English had been learnt at school and not by communication.)

[2] See W. T. R. Pryce, 'Approaches to the Linguistic Geography of Northeast Wales, 1750–1846', *National Library of Wales Journal*, XVII (1971–2), 343–63; idem, 'Welsh and English in Wales, 1750–1971: A Spatial Analysis Based on the Linguistic Affiliation of Parochial Communities', *Bulletin of the*

1971', *Transactions of the Honourable Society of Cymmrodorion* (1978), 229–61.

[3] Pryce, 'Welsh and English in Wales, 1750–1971', 3.

[4] E. G. Ravenstein, 'On the Celtic Languages in the British Isles, a Statistical Survey', *Journal of the Royal Statistical Society*, XLII (1879), 579–636.

[5] *Parliamentary Debates* (Hansard), 3edd gyfres, cyf. 347, 399–421 (21 Gorffennaf 1890); ibid., 534–5 (22 Gorffennaf 1890); ibid., 743 (24 Gorffennaf 1890); ibid., 1722 (4 Awst 1890).

[6] *Parliamentary Debates* (Hansard), 3edd gyfres, cyf. 352, 1743–4 (30 Ebrill 1891).

[7] *South Wales Daily News*, 2 Ebrill 1891.

[8] Honnid mai 14,000 yn unig o ffurflenni cyfrifiad a argraffwyd yn Gymraeg. *South Wales Daily News*, 4 Ebrill 1891.

[9] *Parliamentary Debates* (Hansard), 3edd gyfres, cyf. 352, 132–3 (9 Ebrill 1891); ibid., 908–9 (20 Ebrill 1891); ibid., 1743–6 (30 Ebrill 1891). Ceir tystiolaeth bellach fod ffurflenni Saesneg a'r golofn olaf wedi ei hepgor wedi cael eu hanfon i rannau o siroedd Mynwy a Phenfro.

[10] Census of England and Wales, 1891, *Vol. IV. General Report, with Summary Tables and Appendices* (HMSO, 1893), 'Languages in Wales and Monmouthshire', tt. 81–3. Ceir y canlyniadau yn Nhabl 24 (ar ôl tablau ar boblogaeth tlotai a charchardai), Census of England and Wales, 1891, *Vol. III, Ages, Condition as to Marriage, Occupations, Birth-places, and Infirmities* (HMSO, 1893), tt. 561–2.

[11] *Parliamentary Debates* (Hansard), 4edd gyfres, cyf. 29, 31–8 (20 Awst 1891); ibid., 319–24 (22 Awst 1891). *Copy 'of Explanatory letter of the Registrar General of England and Wales relative to the Census of 1891'*, PP 1894 (331) LXIX, t. 1.

[12] Thomas Darlington, 'The English-speaking Population of Wales', *Wales*, I (1894), 16.

[13] J. E. Southall, *The Welsh Language Census of 1891* (Newport, 1895), t. 4.

[14] Royal Commission on Land in Wales and Monmouthshire, *Report*, PP 1896 (c8221) XXXIV, tt. 94–7. Atgynhyrchwyd canlyniadau llawn y cyfrifiad mewn perthynas â'r iaith Gymraeg yn Atodiad E, *Report*, PP 1896 (c8242) XXXII, t. 293.

[15] Y mae llyfrau rhifwyr cyfrifiad 1891 yng Nghymru yn cael eu dadansoddi'n fanwl mewn project dan nawdd y Cyngor Ymchwil Economaidd a Chymdeithasol yng Nghanolfan Uwchefrydiau Cymreig a Cheltaidd Prifysgol Cymru. Cyhoeddir y canlyniadau mewn cyfrolau eraill yn y gyfres hon.

[16] Brinley Thomas, 'A Cauldron of Rebirth: Population and the Welsh Language in the Nineteenth Century', *Cylchgrawn Hanes Cymru*, 13, rhifyn 4 (1987), 418–37.

[17] Census of England and Wales, 1901, *General Report* (HMSO, 1904), 'Languages in Wales and Monmouthshire', tt. 165–70.

[18] Census of England and Wales, 1911, *Vol. XII, Language Spoken in Wales and Monmouthshire* (HMSO, 1913), Adroddiad i–xi; Tablau 1–51. Atgynhyrchwyd y tablau yng nghyfrolau'r siroedd, Tablau 33 a 34.

[19] Y mae digon o dystiolaeth i gadarnhau'r posibilrwydd hwn. E.e. adroddodd y Pwyllgor Adrannol a benodwyd ym Mawrth 1925 i wneud ymholiadau ynglŷn â sefyllfa'r iaith Gymraeg ac i roi cyngor ynglŷn â hybu'r iaith o fewn y gyfundrefn addysg yng Nghymru: 'A phan fo'r Gymraeg yn bwnc dibwys a dirmygedig yn yr ysgol, naturiol i'r merched ym mlodau eu hieuenctid ac yn nyddiau caru dybied eu bod yn arddangos mwy o ledneisrwydd wrth siarad Saesneg.' Pwyllgor Adrannol ar y Gymraeg yng Nghyfundrefn Addysg Cymru, *Y Gymraeg mewn Addysg a Bywyd* (Llundain, 1927), t. 176.

[20] G. S. Kenrick, 'Statistics of the Population in the Parish of Trevethin (Pontypool) and at the Neighbouring Works of Blaenavon in Monmouthshire, chiefly employed in the Iron Trade, and inhabiting part of the District recently disturbed', *Journal of the Statistical Society of London*, III (1840–1), 366–75; idem, 'Statistics of Merthyr Tydvil', *Journal of the Statistical Board of Celtic Studies*, XXVIII, pt. 1 (1978), 1–36; idem, 'Wales as a Culture Region: Patterns of Change 1750–1971', *Transactions of the Honourable Society of Cymmrodorion* (1978), 229–61.

[3] Pryce, 'Welsh and English in Wales, 1750–1971', 3.

[4] E. G. Ravenstein, 'On the Celtic Languages in the British Isles, a Statistical Survey', *Journal of the Royal Statistical Society*, XLII (1879), 579–636.

[5] *Parliamentary Debates* (Hansard), 3rd series, vol. 347, 399–421 (21 July 1890); ibid., 534–5 (22 July 1890); ibid., 743 (24 July 1890); ibid., 1722 (4 August 1890).

[6] *Parliamentary Debates* (Hansard), 3rd series, vol. 352, 1743–4 (30 April 1891).

[7] *South Wales Daily News*, 2 April 1891.

[8] It was claimed that only 14,000 Welsh census schedules were printed. *South Wales Daily News*, 4 April 1891.

[9] *Parliamentary Debates* (Hansard), 3rd series, vol. 352, 132–3 (9 April 1891); ibid., 908–9 (20 April 1891); ibid., 1743–6 (30 April 1891). There is further evidence of English forms bereft of the last column being sent to parts of Monmouthshire and Pembrokeshire.

[10] Census of England and Wales, 1891, *Vol. IV. General Report, with Summary Tables and Appendices* (HMSO, 1893), 'Languages in Wales and Monmouthshire', pp. 81–3. The results are tabulated in Table 24 (following tables on the population in workhouses and prisons), in Census of England and Wales, 1891, *Vol. III, Ages, Condition as to Marriage, Occupations, Birth-places, and Infirmities* (HMSO, 1893), pp. 561–2.

[11] *Parliamentary Debates* (Hansard), 4th series, vol. 29, 31–8 (20 August 1891); ibid., 319–24 (22 August 1891). *Copy 'of Explanatory letter of the Registrar General of England and Wales relative to the Census of 1891'*, PP 1894 (331) LXIX, p. 1.

[12] Thomas Darlington, 'The English-speaking Population of Wales', *Wales*, I (1894), 16.

[13] J. E. Southall, *The Welsh Language Census of 1891* (Newport, 1895), p.4.

[14] Royal Commission on Land in Wales and Monmouthshire, *Report*, PP 1896 (c8221) XXXIV, pp. 94–7. The full results of the census regarding the Welsh language were reproduced in the *Report*, Appendix E, PP 1896 (c8242) XXXII, p. 293.

[15] Enumerators' books from the 1891 census in Wales are being examined in detail in an ESRC project at the Centre for Advanced Welsh and Celtic Studies of the University of Wales. The results will be published in separate volumes in this series.

[16] Brinley Thomas, 'A Cauldron of Rebirth: Population and the Welsh Language in the Nineteenth Century', *Welsh History Review*, 13, no. 4 (1987), 418–37.

[17] Census of England and Wales, 1901, *General Report* (HMSO, 1904), 'Languages in Wales and Monmouthshire', pp. 165–70.

[18] Census of England and Wales, 1911, *Vol. XII, Language Spoken in Wales and Monmouthshire* (HMSO, 1913), Report i–xi; Tables 1–51. Tables are reprinted in the County Volumes as Tables 33 and 34.

[19] There is plenty of evidence to support such a possibility. For example, the Departmental Committee appointed in March 1925 to inquire into the position of the Welsh language and to advise as to its promotion in the educational system of Wales, reported that 'the Welsh girl, in whose education Welsh has played but a small and despised part, naturally, in the years of adolescence, and during the time of courtship, thinks that she shows a greater delicacy in speaking English'. Departmental Committee on Welsh in the Educational System of Wales, *Welsh in Education and Life* (London, 1927), p. 188.

[20] G. S. Kenrick, 'Statistics of the Population in the Parish of Trevethin (Pontypool) and at the Neighbouring Works of Blaenavon in Monmouthshire, chiefly employed in the Iron

Society of London, IX (1846), 14–21.

[21] Kenrick, 'Statistics of the Population in the Parish of Trevethin', 367.

[22] LlGC Llsgr. 23220E, Arolwg o gyflwr addysg ym mhlwyfi Castell Caereinion, Llanfair Caereinion a Manafon yn sir Drefaldwyn, a gyflawnwyd ym mis Rhagfyr 1846 gan gynrychiolwyr yr enwadau Ymneilltuol lleol dan gyfarwyddyd y Parchedig Robert David Thomas ('Iorthryn Gwynedd', 1817–88), gweinidog eglwys Annibynnol Penarth, Llanfair Caereinion.

[23] W. T. R. Pryce a John Arwel Edwards, 'The Social Structure of the Embryonic Town in Rural Wales: Llanfair Caereinion in the mid-nineteenth century', *Montgomeryshire Collections*, 67 (1979), 45–90; idem, 'Familiar and Household Structures in the Embryonic Town: Llanfair Caereinion in the mid-nineteenth century', ibid., 68 (1980), 39–65.

[24] *Reports of the Commissioners of Inquiry into the State of Education in Wales. Part III. North Wales* (London, 1847), Atodiad H, 'Memorials from the Dissenters of Llanfair Caereinion, Castle Caereinion and Manavon, in the County of Montgomery, respecting the want of Education in those Parishes', tt. 337–58.

Trade, and inhabiting part of the District recently disturbed', *Journal of the Statistical Society of London*, III (1840–1), 366–75; idem, 'Statistics of Merthyr Tydvil', *Journal of the Statistical Society of London*, IX (1846), 14–21.

[21] Kenrick, 'Statistics of the Population in the Parish of Trevethin', 367.

[22] NLW MS 23220E, A survey of the state of education in and around the parishes of Castle Caereinion, Llanfair Caereinion and Manafon, county Montgomery, carried out, December 1846, by representatives of local Nonconformist denominations under the supervision of the Reverend Robert David Thomas ('Iorthryn Gwynedd', 1817–88), minister of Penarth Congregational chapel, Llanfair Caereinion.

[23] W. T. R. Pryce and John Arwel Edwards, 'The Social Structure of the Embryonic Town in Rural Wales: Llanfair Caereinion in the mid-nineteenth century', *Montgomery Collections*, 67 (1979), 45–90; idem, 'Familiar and Household Structures in the Embryonic Town: Llanfair Caereinion in the mid-nineteenth century', ibid., 68 (1980), 39–65.

[24] *Reports of the Commissioners of Inquiry into the State of Education in Wales. Part III. North Wales* (London, 1847), Appendix H, 'Memorials from the Dissenters of Llanfair Caereinion, Castle Caereinion and Manavon, in the County of Montgomery, respecting the want of Education in those Parishes', pp. 337–58.

Language 1.1 Visitation Returns. The Welsh-speaking population. Wales and Counties. 1801–1911

	Living in Welsh and bilingual[1] areas				*Population able to speak Welsh*	
	Percentage				*Percentage*	
	1801	*1851*	*1871*	*1881*	*1901*	*1911*
Wales	*71.8*	*69.0*	***71.2***	*36.8*	*49.9*	*43.5*
Counties						
Monmouth	*35.8*	*34.5*	***28.9***	–	*13.0*	*9.6*
Glamorgan	*79.4*	*66.7*	***68.2***	*18.1*	*43.5*	*38.1*
Carmarthen	*88.7*	*97.5*	***94.0***	*83.3*	*90.4*	*84.9*
Pembroke	*39.7*	*36.4*	***35.6***	*24.7*	*34.4*	*32.4*
Cardigan	*100.0*	*100.0*	***95.5***	*100.0*	*93.0*	*89.6*
Brecon	*76.7*	*78.6*	***66.6***	*25.1*	*45.9*	*41.5*
Radnor	*11.0*	*6.9*	***4.0***	–	*6.2*	*5.4*
Montgomery	*58.0*	*46.7*	***43.9***	*27.9*	*47.5*	*44.8*
Flint	*77.0*	*82.1*	***69.9***	*33.7*	*49.1*	*42.2*
Denbigh	*67.6*	*73.9*	***77.1***	*40.8*	*61.9*	*56.7*
Merioneth	*100.0*	*100.0*	***94.4***	*95.8*	*93.7*	*90.3*
Caernarfon	*100.0*	*88.8*	***92.9***	*80.1*	*89.6*	*85.6*
Anglesey	*95.4*	*100.0*	***93.1***	*74.2*	*91.7*	*88.7*

Source: W. T. R. Pryce, 'Welsh and English in Wales, 1750–1971: A Spatial Analysis Based on the Linguistic Affiliation of Parochial Communities', *Bulletin of the Board of Celtic Studies,* XXVIII, pt. 1 (1978), Table 4, 27. Figures for 1801, 1851, 1881 are estimates based on parochial returns (see introduction and below); 1871 are (corrected) from E. G. Ravenstein (see notes to Tables 2.1–2.3); 1901, 1911 are from census Summary Tables.

The figures for 1801, 1851, 1881 are based on the classification of returns as follows:

Welsh	All services in Welsh; Welsh but not more than one English service in three months; Welsh but some English in summer months for visitors
Mainly Welsh	Welsh but one English service each month; Welsh always in the evenings but morning services alternately Welsh or bilingual; Welsh always in the evenings but two morning services, one in Welsh and one in English; bilingual services but more Welsh than English
Bilingual[1]	Two services every Sunday, one in each language; alternating Welsh/English services
Mainly English	English always in the evenings but morning services alternately English/Welsh; bilingual services but more English than Welsh; main services in English but afternoon services alternately English/Welsh; English but one or two services in Welsh each month
English	English with the rare use of Welsh (at most four times a year)

[1] The definition of 'bilingual' in this context indicates the presence of two languages in a locality rather than individuals able to speak two languages.

Detailed discussion of the classification appears in W. T. R. Pryce, 'Approaches to the Linguistic Geography of Northeast Wales, 1750–1846', *National Library of Wales Journal*, XVII (1971–2), 343–63.

Language 1.2 Visitation Returns. Linguistic classification of ecclesiastical parishes. Wales and Counties. 1801, 1851, 1881

	Census	Enumerated Population	*Percentage living in language areas* Welsh	*Mainly Welsh*	*Bilingual*	*Mainly English*	*English*
Wales	1801	587245	*44.2*	*10.4*	*17.2*	*4.4*	*23.8*
	1851	1163139	*27.5*	*14.2*	*27.3*	*3.2*	*27.8*
	1881	1571780	*7.3*	*14.5*	*15.0*	*28.7*	*34.5*
Counties							
Monmouth	1801	45568	*13.2*	*5.6*	*17.0*	*8.5*	*55.7*
	1851	157418	*0.1*	*3.8*	*30.6*	*13.2*	*52.3*
	1881	211267	–	–	–	–	*100.0*
Glamorgan	1801	70879	*33.2*	*8.2*	*29.9*	*5.0*	*23.7*
	1851	231849	*11.1*	*25.3*	*30.3*	*0.5*	*32.8*
	1881	511433	*2.1*	*7.0*	*9.0*	*52.6*	*29.3*
Carmarthen	1801	67317	*51.8*	*14.3*	*22.6*	*0.4*	*10.9*
	1851	110632	*47.3*	*16.2*	*34.0*	–	*2.5*
	1881	124864	*14.7*	*11.3*	*57.4*	*13.1*	*3.5*
Pembroke	1801	56280	*22.0*	*7.3*	*10.4*	*0.9*	*59.4*
	1851	94140	*19.2*	*5.0*	*12.2*	*0.6*	*63.0*
	1881	91824	*6.8*	*8.7*	*9.2*	*5.7*	*69.6*
Cardigan	1801	42956	*73.7*	*17.8*	*8.5*	–	–
	1851	70796	*63.8*	*9.9*	*26.3*	–	–
	1881	70270	*25.0*	*45.8*	*29.2*	–	–
Brecon	1801	32325	*48.5*	*10.0*	*18.2*	–	*23.3*
	1851	61474	*15.3*	*12.8*	*50.4*	–	*21.5*
	1881	57746	–	*2.2*	*23.0*	*33.5*	*41.3*
Radnor	1801	19135	*4.5*	*3.5*	*3.0*	–	*89.0*
	1851	24716	–	–	*6.9*	–	*93.1*
	1881	23528	–	–	–	*3.3*	*96.7*
Montgomery	1801	48184	*27.5*	*6.1*	*24.4*	*6.8*	*35.2*
	1851	67335	*19.2*	*4.8*	*22.7*	*7.0*	*46.3*
	1881	65718	*6.7*	*15.5*	*5.7*	*20.3*	*51.8*
Flint	1801	39469	*14.4*	*11.7*	*50.9*	–	*23.0*
	1851	68156	*23.1*	*5.5*	*53.5*	–	*17.9*
	1881	80587	*0.3*	*8.8*	*24.5*	*40.5*	*25.9*
Denbigh	1801	60299	*41.9*	*21.9*	*3.8*	*20.5*	*11.9*
	1851	92583	*39.4*	*12.6*	*21.9*	–	*26.1*
	1881	111740	*3.5*	*13.4*	*23.9*	*48.2*	*11.1*
Merioneth	1801	29506	*100.0*	–	–	–	–
	1851	38843	*60.1*	*27.6*	*12.3*	–	–
	1881	52038	*12.4*	*51.6*	*31.8*	*4.2*	–
Caernarfon	1801	41521	*84.1*	*9.6*	*6.3*	–	–
	1851	87870	*52.0*	*28.9*	*7.9*	*11.0*	*0.2*
	1881	119349	*22.7*	*52.4*	*5.0*	*19.8*	*0.1*
Anglesey	1801	33806	*74.1*	*6.4*	*14.9*	*4.6*	–
	1851	57327	*60.6*	*13.6*	*25.8*	–	–
	1881	51416	*39.6*	*31.5*	*3.1*	*25.8*	–

Source: W. T. R. Pryce, 'Welsh and English in Wales, 1750–1971: A Spatial Analysis Based on the Linguistic Affiliation of Parochial Communities', *Bulletin of the Board of Celtic Studies,* XXVIII, pt. 1 (1978), 34–5 (Appendix A).

See notes to Table 1.1.

Language 2.1 Ravenstein's Language Survey. The Welsh-speaking population. Language districts. Wales. 1871

District in which	Area sq mls	%	Population 1871 Total	%	Persons speaking Welsh Total	%
Welsh spoken by a majority	6050	*76.5*	1025573	*78.1*	887870	*94.9*
Welsh spoken by 25–50%	357	*4.5*	113030	*8.7*	38046	*4.1*
Welsh spoken by less than 25%	1501	*19.0*	174080	*13.2*	8614	*1.0*
Total Wales	**7908**	***100.0***	**1312583**	***100.0***	**934530**	***100.0***

Language 2.2 Ravenstein's Language Survey. The Welsh-speaking population. Wales and Counties. 1871

	Area sq mls	%	Population 1871	Persons speaking Welsh only	Persons speaking Welsh and English	*Percentage speaking Welsh Welsh only*	*Percentage speaking Welsh Welsh and English*	*Percentage speaking Welsh English only*
Wales	7908	*100.0*	1412583	294110	640420	*22.4*	*48.8*	*28.8*
Counties								
Monmouth	576	*7.3*	195448	1500	55000	*0.8*	*28.1*	*71.1*
Glamorgan	810	*10.2*	397859	48350	223110	*12.2*	*56.1*	*31.8*
Carmarthen	947	*12.0*	115710	37800	70920	*32.7*	*61.3*	*6.0*
Pembroke	615	*7.8*	91998	5430	27320	*5.9*	*29.7*	*64.4*
Cardigan	693	*8.8*	73441	34500	35600	*47.0*	*48.5*	*4.5*
Brecon	719	*9.1*	59901	6340	33530	*10.6*	*56.0*	*33.4*
Radnor	432	*5.5*	25430	20	1000	*0.1*	*3.9*	*96.0*
Montgomery	758	*9.6*	67623	6600	23100	*9.8*	*34.2*	*56.1*
Flint	264	*3.3*	76312	5420	47890	*7.1*	*62.8*	*30.1*
Denbigh	612	*7.7*	105102	39500	41500	*37.6*	*39.5*	*22.9*
Merioneth	602	*7.6*	46598	17000	27000	*36.5*	*57.9*	*5.6*
Caernarfon	578	*7.3*	106121	60000	38600	*56.5*	*36.4*	*7.1*
Anglesey	302	*3.8*	51040	31650	15850	*62.0*	*31.1*	*6.9*

Language 2.3 Ravenstein's Language Survey. The Welsh-speaking population. Language districts. Wales and Counties. 1871

	Language district[1]	Area sq mls	Population 1871	Persons speaking Welsh only	Persons speaking Welsh and English	*Percentage speaking Welsh Welsh only*	*Percentage speaking Welsh Welsh and English*	*Percentage speaking Welsh English only*
Wales	Welsh	6050	1025573	887870		*86.6*		*13.4*
	Mixed	357	113030	38040		*33.7*		*66.3*
	English	1501	174080	8620		*5.0*		*95.0*
Counties								
Monmouth	Welsh	83	61525	1500	44850	*2.4*	*72.9*	*24.7*
	Mixed	32	17713	–	6380	–	*36.0*	*64.0*
	English	461	116210	–	3770	–	*3.2*	*96.8*
Glamorgan	Welsh	581	323617	44950	204640	*13.9*	*63.2*	*22.9*
	Mixed	147	63731	3400	18010	*5.3*	*28.3*	*66.4*
	English	82	10511	–	460	–	*4.4*	*95.6*
Carmarthen	Welsh	915	113484	108150		*95.3*		*4.7*
	English	32	2226	570		*25.6*		*74.4*
Pembroke	Welsh	337	32935	5430	25620	*16.5*	*77.8*	*5.7*
	English	278	59063	–	1700	–	*2.9*	*97.1*
Cardigan	Welsh	693	73441	34500	35600	*47.0*	*48.5*	*4.5*

	Language district[1]	Area sq mls	Population 1871	Persons speaking Welsh only	Persons speaking Welsh and English	*Percentage speaking Welsh: Welsh only*	*Welsh and English*	*English only*
Brecon	Welsh	650	45194	36290		*80.3*		*19.7*
	Mixed	18	9149	3230		*35.3*		*64.7*
	English	41	5558	350		*6.3*		*93.7*
Radnor	Welsh	54	713	470		*65.9*		*34.1*
	Mixed	20	2000	520		*26.0*		*74.0*
	English	358	22717	30		*0.1*		*99.9*
Montgomery	Welsh[2]	461	27917	6270	16740	*22.5*	*60.0*	*17.5*
	Mixed	137	18536	280	5470	*1.5*	*29.5*	*68.0*
	English	160	21170	50	890	*0.2*	*4.2*	*95.6*
Flint	Welsh	211	58201	52560		*90.3*		*9.7*
	Mixed	3	1901	750		*39.5*		*60.5*
	English	50	16210	–		–		*100.0*
Denbigh	Welsh	583	84787	80200		*94.6*		*5.4*
	English	39	20315	800		*3.9*		*96.1*
Merioneth	Welsh	602	46598	17000	27000	*36.5*	*57.9*	*5.6*
Caernarfon	Welsh	578	106121	60000	38600	*56.5*	*36.4*	*7.1*
Anglesey	Welsh	302	51040	31650	15850	*62.0*	*31.1*	*6.9*
Shropshire	Mixed[3]	19	2469	900		*36.5*		*63.5*

Source: E. G. Ravenstein, 'On the Celtic Languages in the British Isles, a Statistical Survey', *Journal of the Royal Statistical Society*, XLII (1879), 579–636. Table 2.1, Ravenstein, Table 1, 620. Tables 2.2, 2.3 have been compiled from Ravenstein, Table 2, Table 3, and appendix Table IV, together with figures incorporated in the text. Following the example of W. T. R. Pryce (1978), arithmetical corrections, mostly minor, have been made. The last columns of both tables, the percentage of the population able to speak only English, do not appear at source. They have been calculated by subtraction, as an aid to further analysis.

W. T. R. Pryce (1978), gives a thorough comparison of Ravenstein's figures with his own work on visitation returns and later census figures. He suggests that Ravenstein underestimated the population living in the Welsh and Mixed areas of Radnorshire, and possibly overestimated the equivalent population in Monmouthshire.

Ravenstein also considered the Welsh-speaking population in England. He estimated that 62,000 (37%) of the 166,717 natives of Wales residing in England in 1871 'had some knowledge of Welsh when they came to England', and suggested that the total of 'Welsh speaking Welsh' was no fewer than 996,530 within the limits of England and Wales (Ravenstein, 1879, 621).

1 District criteria: 'Welsh', in which Welsh is spoken by a majority; 'Mixed', in which Welsh is spoken by more than 25% and by less than 50%; 'English', in which Welsh is spoken by no more than 25%.

2 This district is subdivided as follows:

	sq mls	population	Speaking: Welsh only	Welsh and English
Cyfeiliog	115	8,794	4,000	4,000
Eastern slope	346	19,123	1,570	12,740

3 Includes the western parishes of Selatyn and Llanyblodwel, and the township of Sychdyn.

Language 3.1 Census Returns. Ability to speak Welsh and English. Number and percentage. Wales and Counties. 1891, 1901, 1911

	Year	Number: Population over 2 yrs[1]	Welsh only	Both	English only	*Percentage: Welsh only*	*Both*	*English only*	*Able to speak Welsh*
Wales	1891[1]	1685614	508036	402253	759416	*30.4*	*24.0*	*45.4*	*54.5*
	1901	1864696	280905	648919	928222	*15.1*	*34.9*	*49.9*	*49.9*
	1911	2247927	190292	787074	1208282	*8.7*	*35.9*	*55.2*	*44.6*
Counties									
Monmouth	1891[1]	260033	9816	29743	217664	*3.8*	*11.5*	*84.5*	*15.4*
	1901	274415	2013	33677	238131	*0.7*	*12.3*	*86.8*	*13.0*
	1911	364590	1496	33751	314530	*0.4*	*9.6*	*89.8*	*10.1*
Glamorgan	1891[1]	653889	142346	177726	326481	*21.9*	*27.4*	*50.3*	*49.5*
	1901	791847	52493	292399	442107	*6.6*	*37.0*	*56.0*	*43.7*
	1911	1033717	31719	361973	608919	*3.2*	*36.0*	*60.6*	*39.2*
Carmarthen	1891[1]	112685	63345	36937	11751	*56.5*	*32.9*	*10.5*	*89.5*
	1901	126166	44901	69046	12018	*35.6*	*54.8*	*9.5*	*90.4*
	1911	149691	30705	96531	19991	*20.8*	*65.5*	*13.6*	*86.4*
Pembroke	1891[1]	78163	13673	10804	51959	*17.9*	*14.1*	*67.9*	*32.0*
	1901	82223	9797	18536	53796	*11.9*	*22.6*	*65.5*	*34.5*
	1911	84463	6511	20879	55124	*7.9*	*25.3*	*66.8*	*33.2*
Cardigan	1891[1]	82979	61624	17111	3979	*74.5*	*20.7*	*4.8*	*95.2*
	1901	57664	29081	24557	3880	*50.5*	*42.7*	*6.7*	*93.2*
	1911	57039	19497	31580	4966	*34.8*	*56.3*	*8.9*	*91.1*
Brecon	1891[1]	50335	5228	13699	31086	*10.5*	*27.4*	*62.1*	*37.8*
	1901	50409	4674	18445	27245	*9.3*	*36.6*	*54.1*	*45.9*
	1911	55315	3015	19881	31583	*5.5*	*36.4*	*57.9*	*42.0*
Radnor	1891[1]	16326	75	924	15270	*0.5*	*5.7*	*93.8*	*6.1*
	1901	21754	51	1309	20370	*0.2*	*6.0*	*93.7*	*6.3*
	1911	21279	11	1128	19884	*0.1*	*5.4*	*94.6*	*5.4*
Montgomery	1891[1]	64359	16414	15846	31770	*25.6*	*24.7*	*49.6*	*50.4*
	1901	51310	7980	16361	26913	*15.6*	*31.9*	*52.5*	*47.5*
	1911	50008	5367	17039	27003	*10.9*	*34.5*	*54.6*	*45.3*
Flint	1891[1]	40601	10484	16879	12862	*26.0*	*41.9*	*31.9*	*68.0*
	1901	75931	5722	31568	38544	*7.5*	*41.6*	*50.8*	*49.2*
	1911	86570	2946	33587	47886	*3.5*	*39.8*	*56.7*	*43.3*
Denbigh	1891[1]	111191	37195	35030	38310	*33.6*	*31.7*	*34.6*	*65.3*
	1901	122195	22366	53238	46435	*18.3*	*43.6*	*38.0*	*61.9*
	1911	135607	13637	63224	56499	*10.2*	*47.4*	*42.3*	*57.6*
Merioneth	1891[1]	61903	45856	12023	3621	*74.5*	*19.5*	*5.9*	*94.1*
	1901	45631	23081	19674	2825	*50.6*	*43.2*	*6.2*	*93.8*
	1911	43209	15857	23119	3340	*37.5*	*54.6*	*7.9*	*92.1*
Caernarfon	1891[1]	120314	78780	28330	12604	*65.8*	*23.7*	*10.5*	*89.5*
	1901	117647	55955	49346	12165	*47.6*	*42.0*	*10.4*	*89.6*
	1911	118344	42097	59150	14464	*36.4*	*51.1*	*12.5*	*87.5*
Anglesey	1891[1]	32836	23200	7201	2059	*71.4*	*22.2*	*6.3*	*93.7*
	1901	47504	22791	20763	3793	*48.0*	*43.8*	*8.0*	*91.8*
	1911	48095	17434	25232	4093	*37.3*	*54.0*	*8.8*	*91.2*

Source: *Census of Population for England and Wales*: 1891, *Vol. III, Ages, condition as to marriage, occupations, birth-places and infirmities* (HMSO, 1893),Table 24, pp. 561–2; 1901, *County Reports* (HMSO, 1902/3), Table 40; 1911, *Vol. XII, Language Spoken in Wales and Monmouthshire* (HMSO, 1913), Table 1.

[1] The figures for 1891 are not strictly comparable with those for subsequent years. They are based on registration counties and include children aged two years. Figures for 1901 and 1911 are for administrative counties and exclude children aged two years.

Language 3.2 Census Returns. Ability to speak Welsh and English. Number and percentage. Registration Districts. 1891

Registration District	Number Population aged 2 years and over	Welsh only	Both	English only	*Percentage* *Welsh only*	*Both*	*English only*	*Able to speak Welsh*
MONMOUTHSHIRE								
Chepstow	18477	30	249	18042	*0.2*	*1.4*	*98.5*	*1.5*
Monmouth	26903	29	306	26098	*0.1*	*1.2*	*98.7*	*1.3*
Abergavenny	24883	361	2420	21985	*1.5*	*9.8*	*88.7*	*11.2*
Bedwellte	61078	6805	15105	38833	*11.2*	*24.8*	*63.9*	*36.1*
Pontypool	37470	351	3499	33426	*0.9*	*9.4*	*89.7*	*10.3*
Newport	91222	2240	8164	79280	*2.5*	*9.1*	*88.2*	*11.6*
GLAMORGAN								
Cardiff	164134	3120	19395	138276	*1.9*	*11.9*	*85.1*	*14.0*
Pontypridd	137814	40507	46487	50005	*29.6*	*33.9*	*36.5*	*63.5*
Merthyr Tydfil	110569	35244	39812	34651	*32.1*	*36.3*	*31.6*	*68.4*
Bridgend	48776	11806	17329	19243	*24.4*	*35.8*	*39.8*	*60.2*
Neath	53574	14740	20493	17793	*27.7*	*38.5*	*33.5*	*66.4*
Pontardawe	20479	13655	5132	1590	*67.0*	*25.2*	*7.8*	*92.2*
Swansea	107963	22417	27229	57099	*20.9*	*25.4*	*53.2*	*46.5*
Gower	10580	857	1849	7824	*8.1*	*17.6*	*74.3*	*25.7*
CARMARTHENSHIRE								
Llanelli	49415	25366	17630	6161	*51.5*	*35.8*	*12.5*	*87.5*
Llandovery	11127	6804	3570	688	*61.5*	*32.3*	*6.2*	*93.8*
Llandeilo Fawr	19497	13327	5151	926	*68.7*	*26.5*	*4.8*	*95.2*
Carmarthen	32646	17848	10586	3976	*55.1*	*32.7*	*12.3*	*87.7*
PEMBROKESHIRE								
Narberth	17410	6520	3392	7445	*37.6*	*19.5*	*42.9*	*57.1*
Pembroke	29797	67	1430	26871	*0.2*	*5.0*	*94.6*	*5.3*
Haverfordwest	30956	7086	5982	17643	*23.1*	*19.5*	*57.4*	*42.6*
CARDIGANSHIRE								
Cardigan	15617	10285	4575	679	*66.2*	*29.4*	*4.4*	*95.6*
Newcastle Emlyn	18302	15501	2231	549	*84.8*	*12.2*	*3.0*	*97.0*
Lampeter	9304	7230	1713	328	*78.0*	*18.5*	*3.5*	*96.5*
Aberaeron	11107	9369	1549	148	*84.7*	*14.0*	*1.3*	*98.7*
Aberystwyth	20357	11971	6136	2169	*59.0*	*30.3*	*10.7*	*89.3*
Tregaron	8292	7268	907	106	*87.8*	*11.0*	*1.3*	*98.7*
BRECONSHIRE								
Builth	7472	858	1828	4745	*11.5*	*24.6*	*63.8*	*36.1*
Brecon	15273	2767	5347	7095	*18.2*	*35.2*	*46.6*	*53.3*
Crickhowell	18438	1585	5781	10921	*8.7*	*31.6*	*59.7*	*40.3*
Hay	9152	18	743	8325	*0.2*	*8.2*	*91.6*	*8.4*
RADNORSHIRE								
Knighton	10171	1	102	10048	*0.0*	*1.0*	*99.0*	*1.0*
Rhayader	6155	74	822	5222	*1.2*	*13.4*	*85.3*	*14.6*
MONTGOMERYSHIRE								
Machynlleth	10380	6548	3144	645	*63.3*	*30.4*	*6.2*	*93.8*
Newtown	20768	2784	5870	12000	*13.5*	*28.4*	*58.1*	*41.9*
Forden	15572	91	1254	14172	*0.6*	*8.1*	*91.3*	*8.7*
Llanfyllin	17639	6991	5578	4953	*39.9*	*31.8*	*28.3*	*71.7*
FLINTSHIRE								
Holywell	40601	10484	16879	12862	*26.0*	*41.9*	*31.9*	*68.0*
DENBIGHSHIRE								
Wrexham	58444	10604	16641	30810	*18.3*	*28.6*	*53.0*	*46.9*
Ruthin	12436	7283	4037	1053	*58.8*	*32.6*	*8.5*	*91.5*
St Asaph	27840	10410	11452	5820	*37.6*	*41.4*	*21.0*	*79.0*
Llanrwst	12471	8898	2900	627	*71.6*	*23.3*	*5.0*	*95.0*

Registration District	Number Population aged 2 years and over	Welsh only	Both	English only	*Percentage* *Welsh only*	*Both*	*English only*	*Able to speak Welsh*
MERIONETH								
Corwen	15576	9642	4179	1645	*62.3*	*27.0*	*10.6*	*89.4*
Bala	5881	4762	818	275	*81.3*	*14.0*	*4.7*	*95.3*
Dolgellau	13902	9995	2810	1016	*72.3*	*20.3*	*7.3*	*92.6*
Ffestiniog	26544	21457	4216	685	*81.3*	*16.0*	*2.6*	*97.4*
CAERNARFONSHIRE								
Pwllheli	21333	17568	2783	860	*82.8*	*13.1*	*4.1*	*95.9*
Caernarfon	38974	30767	6633	1500	*79.1*	*17.1*	*3.9*	*96.1*
Bangor	36476	22137	10640	3504	*61.0*	*29.3*	*9.7*	*90.3*
Conwy	23531	8308	8274	6740	*35.6*	*35.4*	*28.9*	*71.1*
ANGLESEY								
Anglesey	14130	11589	2077	327	*82.8*	*14.8*	*2.3*	*97.7*
Holyhead	18706	11611	5124	1732	*62.8*	*27.7*	*9.4*	*90.6*

Source: *Census of Population for England and Wales*: 1891, *Vol. III, Ages, condition as to marriage, occupations, birth-places and infirmities* (HMSO, 1893),Table 24, pp. 561–2.

Language 3.3 Census Returns. Ability to speak Welsh and English. Number and percentage. Wales and Administrative Counties, Urban and Rural Districts. 1901, 1911

District[1]	Year	Number[2] Population 3 years and over	Welsh only	Both	English only	*Percentage[3]* *Welsh only*	*Both*	*English only*	*Able to speak Welsh[4]*
WALES									
Urban Districts[5]	1901	1186656	75467	390211	715505	*6.4*	*32.9*	*60.4*	*39.3*
	1911	1483588	47385	449259	941250	*3.3*	*31.2*	*65.3*	*34.5*
Rural Districts	1901	685040	205438	258708	212717	*30.0*	*37.8*	*31.1*	*67.9*
	1911	764339	142907	337815	267032	*19.1*	*45.2*	*35.7*	*64.3*
MONMOUTHSHIRE									
Urban Districts									
Total	1901	234161	1902	30027	201669	*0.8*	*12.8*	*86.2*	*13.6*
	1911	320071	1443	30650	274740	*0.5*	*10.0*	*89.4*	*10.4*
Aber-carn UD	1901	11516	158	2197	9159	*1.4*	*19.1*	*79.5*	*20.5*
	1911	15072	47	2026	12648	*0.3*	*13.8*	*85.9*	*14.1*
Abergavenny MB	1901	7307	2	348	6946	*0.0*	*4.8*	*95.1*	*4.8*
	1911	8029	11	361	7415	*0.1*	*4.6*	*95.1*	*4.8*
Abersychan UD	1901	16210	36	1056	15111	*0.2*	*6.5*	*93.2*	*6.7*
	1911	22540	8	905	21370	*0.0*	*4.1*	*95.9*	*4.1*
Abertillery UD	1901	19820	117	2157	17537	*0.6*	*10.9*	*88.5*	*11.5*
	1911	32078	79	2164	28284	*0.3*	*7.1*	*92.6*	*7.3*
Bedwellte UD[3]	1901	9069	177	2980	5911	*2.0*	*32.9*	*65.2*	*34.8*
	1911	20506	229	4141	14939	*1.2*	*21.4*	*77.3*	*22.6*
Blaenafon UD	1901	10012	9	857	9137	*0.1*	*8.6*	*91.3*	*8.6*
	1911	11087	11	616	10080	*0.1*	*5.7*	*94.1*	*5.9*
Caerleon UD	1901	1270	0	44	1226	*0.0*	*3.5*	*96.5*	*3.5*
	1911	1935	2	73	1828	*0.1*	*3.8*	*95.9*	*3.9*
Chepstow UD	1901	2896	0	40	2849	*0.0*	*1.4*	*98.5*	*1.4*
	1911	2809	1	41	2660	*0.0*	*1.5*	*98.4*	*1.6*
Ebbw Vale UD	1901	19261	146	4108	14973	*0.8*	*21.4*	*77.8*	*22.1*
	1911	27857	113	3435	23035	*0.4*	*12.9*	*86.5*	*13.3*
Llanfrechfa Upper UD	1901	2699	7	132	2560	*0.3*	*4.9*	*94.8*	*5.2*
	1911	4093	8	203	3774	*0.2*	*5.1*	*94.7*	*5.3*
Llantarnam UD	1901	4868	15	237	4604	*0.3*	*4.9*	*94.8*	*5.2*
	1911	6475	10	250	5962	*0.2*	*4.0*	*95.7*	*4.2*
Monmouth MB[3]	1901	4794	0	42	4716	*0.0*	*0.9*	*99.1*	*0.9*
	1911	4985	6	54	3124	*0.2*	*1.7*	*97.5*	*1.9*
Mynyddislwyn UD	1901	3072	92	1179	1801	*3.0*	*38.4*	*58.6*	*41.4*
	1911	9014	60	2061	6766	*0.7*	*23.2*	*76.1*	*23.9*
Nant-y-glo and	1901	12255	98	2370	9740	*0.8*	*19.4*	*79.5*	*20.2*
Blaenau UD	1911	14055	79	1544	11796	*0.6*	*11.5*	*87.8*	*12.1*
Newport CB	1901	62181	55	2215	59576	*0.1*	*3.6*	*95.8*	*3.7*
	1911	77686	26	2032	72891	*0.0*	*2.7*	*96.6*	*2.7*
Pant-teg UD	1901	6938	1	366	6565	*0.0*	*5.3*	*94.7*	*5.3*
	1911	9364	8	374	8833	*0.1*	*4.1*	*95.8*	*4.1*
Pontypool UD	1901	5658	10	256	5383	*0.2*	*4.5*	*95.2*	*4.7*
	1911	6021	4	246	5716	*0.1*	*4.1*	*95.8*	*4.2*
Rhymni UD[3]	1901	7246	713	4283	2245	*9.8*	*59.1*	*31.0*	*69.0*
	1911	10489	526	5340	4049	*5.3*	*53.8*	*40.8*	*59.1*
Risca UD	1901	8820	19	630	8167	*0.2*	*7.1*	*92.6*	*7.4*
	1911	12981	17	678	11848	*0.1*	*5.4*	*94.4*	*5.5*
Tredegar UD	1901	16889	246	4494	12120	*1.5*	*26.6*	*71.8*	*28.1*
	1911	21572	198	4063	16363	*1.0*	*19.7*	*79.3*	*20.7*
Usk UD	1901	1380	1	36	1343	*0.1*	*2.6*	*97.3*	*2.7*
	1911	1423	0	43	1359	*0.0*	*3.1*	*96.9*	*3.1*

District[1]	Year	Number[2] Population 3 years and over	Welsh only	Both	English only	*Percentage[3]* *Welsh only*	*Both*	*English only*	*Able to speak Welsh[4]*
Rural Districts									
Total	1901	40254	111	3650	36462	*0.3*	*9.1*	*90.6*	*9.3*
	1911	44519	53	3101	39790	*0.1*	*7.2*	*92.6*	*7.3*
Abergavenny RD	1901	8167	19	827	7317	*0.2*	*10.1*	*89.6*	*10.4*
	1911	8283	14	607	7363	*0.2*	*7.6*	*92.2*	*7.8*
Chepstow RD[3]	1901	6958	4	132	6820	*0.1*	*1.9*	*98.0*	*2.0*
	1911	7432	2	131	6884	*0.0*	*1.9*	*98.1*	*1.9*
Magor RD	1901	4157	4	119	4027	*0.1*	*2.9*	*97.0*	*3.0*
	1911	4551	3	100	4240	*0.1*	*2.3*	*97.6*	*2.4*
Monmouth RD	1901	6035	1	167	5864	*0.0*	*2.8*	*97.2*	*2.8*
	1911	6146	2	142	5716	*0.0*	*2.4*	*97.5*	*2.5*
Pontypool RD	1901	4224	8	295	3914	*0.2*	*7.0*	*92.7*	*7.2*
	1911	4754	3	224	4495	*0.1*	*4.7*	*95.2*	*4.8*
St Mellons RD	1901	10713	75	2110	8520	*0.7*	*19.7*	*79.5*	*20.4*
	1911	13353	29	1897	11092	*0.2*	*14.6*	*85.2*	*14.8*
GLAMORGAN									
Urban Districts									
Total	1901	658329	35069	225021	393832	*5.3*	*34.3*	*59.9*	*39.6*
	1911	843674	20766	268838	528069	*2.5*	*32.8*	*64.4*	*35.3*
Aberafan MB	1901	6952	70	2717	4152	*1.0*	*39.1*	*59.7*	*40.1*
	1911	9688	68	2992	6407	*0.7*	*31.5*	*67.5*	*32.2*
Aberdare UD	1901	39932	5382	23067	11307	*13.5*	*58.0*	*28.4*	*71.5*
	1911	46844	3068	26894	15988	*6.7*	*58.5*	*34.8*	*65.2*
Barry UD	1901	24671	152	3247	20502	*0.6*	*13.2*	*83.5*	*13.8*
	1911	31411	101	3537	26014	*0.3*	*11.8*	*86.8*	*12.1*
Bridgend UD	1901	5869	54	1656	4139	*0.9*	*28.3*	*70.7*	*29.2*
	1911	7453	43	1694	5602	*0.6*	*23.1*	*76.3*	*23.7*
Briton Ferry UD	1901	6402	178	2965	3241	*2.8*	*46.4*	*50.7*	*49.2*
	1911	7885	118	2969	4561	*1.5*	*38.7*	*59.5*	*40.3*
Caerphilly UD	1901	14493	599	5876	7944	*4.2*	*40.7*	*55.1*	*44.9*
	1911	29893	742	9281	18867	*2.6*	*32.1*	*65.3*	*34.7*
Cardiff CB	1901	151925	329	11966	138003	*0.2*	*7.9*	*91.0*	*8.1*
	1911	170016	262	11053	150547	*0.2*	*6.8*	*92.5*	*6.9*
Cowbridge MB	1901	1137	5	256	876	*0.4*	*22.5*	*77.0*	*23.0*
	1911	1113	6	215	891	*0.5*	*19.3*	*80.1*	*19.9*
Gelli-gaer UD	1901	15741	1357	7440	6916	*8.6*	*47.3*	*44.0*	*56.0*
	1911	32288	866	12391	18654	*2.7*	*38.8*	*58.4*	*41.5*
Glyncorrwg UD	1901	5851	741	3171	1890	*12.8*	*54.7*	*32.6*	*67.4*
	1911	7868	308	4170	3297	*4.0*	*53.6*	*42.4*	*57.6*
Maesteg UD	1901	13701	1506	8353	3830	*11.0*	*61.0*	*28.0*	*72.0*
	1911	22687	1196	12537	8411	*5.4*	*56.6*	*38.0*	*62.0*
Margam UD	1901	8295	400	4681	3164	*4.8*	*56.5*	*38.2*	*61.3*
	1911	13593	224	6252	6649	*1.7*	*47.0*	*50.0*	*48.7*
Merthyr Tydfil CB	1901	63681	4630	31763	27039	*7.3*	*49.9*	*42.5*	*57.2*
	1911	74597	2643	34826	35882	*3.6*	*47.3*	*48.7*	*50.9*
Mountain Ash UD	1901	28321	1937	11606	14726	*6.9*	*41.1*	*52.1*	*47.9*
	1911	38475	1161	14130	21997	*3.1*	*37.9*	*58.9*	*41.0*
Neath MB	1901	12740	279	4780	7647	*2.2*	*37.6*	*60.2*	*39.8*
	1911	16345	191	4742	11016	*1.2*	*29.7*	*69.0*	*30.9*
Ogmore and Garw UD	1901	18134	1731	8763	7620	*9.6*	*48.4*	*42.1*	*57.9*
	1911	24350	1016	10252	12346	*4.3*	*43.4*	*52.3*	*47.7*
Oystermouth UD	1901	4175	4	343	3823	*0.1*	*8.2*	*91.6*	*8.3*
	1911	5739	2	405	5248	*0.0*	*7.2*	*92.7*	*7.2*
Penarth UD	1901	13287	3	948	12141	*0.0*	*7.1*	*91.4*	*7.2*
	1911	14597	8	808	13130	*0.1*	*5.7*	*93.1*	*5.8*

District[1]	Year	Number[2] Population 3 years and over	Welsh only	Both	English only	*Percentage[3]* *Welsh only*	*Both*	*English only*	*Able to speak Welsh[4]*
Pontypridd UD	1901	29627	1003	10283	18248	*3.4*	*34.8*	*61.7*	*38.2*
	1911	39542	589	11265	26597	*1.5*	*29.3*	*69.1*	*30.8*
Porthcawl UD	1901	1770	7	667	1093	*0.4*	*37.7*	*61.9*	*38.1*
	1911	3279	41	869	2281	*1.3*	*27.2*	*71.4*	*28.5*
Rhondda UD	1901	103740	11841	54906	36754	*11.4*	*53.0*	*35.5*	*64.4*
	1911	139235	6100	70696	60056	*4.5*	*51.6*	*43.9*	*56.1*
Swansea CB	1901	87885	2861	25567	58777	*3.3*	*29.2*	*67.1*	*32.4*
	1911	106776	2013	26860	73628	*2.0*	*26.1*	*71.5*	*28.0*
Rural Districts **Total**	1901	143518	17424	67378	48275	*12.2*	*47.1*	*33.7*	*59.2*
	1911	190043	10953	93135	80850	*5.9*	*50.3*	*43.7*	*56.3*
Cowbridge RD	1901	6384	98	2595	3655	*1.5*	*40.7*	*57.4*	*42.3*
	1911	7396	41	2419	4799	*0.6*	*33.3*	*66.1*	*33.9*
Gower RD	1901	6729	349	2020	4341	*5.0*	*30.3*	*64.7*	*35.3*
	1911	8030	137	2873	4862	*1.7*	*36.5*	*61.8*	*38.2*
Llandaff and Dinas	1901	21385	176	4909	16268	*0.8*	*23.0*	*76.2*	*23.8*
Powys RD	1911	30974	134	5086	24824	*0.4*	*16.9*	*82.6*	*17.4*
Llantrisant and	1901	10879	579	5418	4864	*5.3*	*49.9*	*44.8*	*55.2*
Llantwit Fardre RD	1911	15984	273	6285	9058	*1.7*	*40.2*	*58.0*	*42.0*
Neath RD	1901	26040	3490	16105	6400	*13.4*	*62.0*	*24.6*	*75.4*
	1911	38176	1614	23784	12136	*4.3*	*63.4*	*32.3*	*67.7*
Pen-y-bont RD[3]	1901	15228	616	7847	6686	*4.1*	*51.7*	*44.1*	*55.8*
	1911	20649	393	9320	9738	*2.0*	*47.9*	*50.0*	*49.9*
Pontardawe RD	1901	19206	7192	10602	1344	*37.6*	*55.4*	*7.0*	*93.0*
	1911	28861	4835	18350	4742	*17.3*	*65.7*	*17.0*	*83.0*
Swansea RD	1901	27667	4924	17882	4717	*17.9*	*65.0*	*17.1*	*82.9*
	1911	39973	3526	25018	10691	*9.0*	*63.7*	*27.2*	*72.7*
CARMARTHENSHIRE									
Urban Districts **Total**	1901	46245	6155	32433	7600	*13.3*	*70.2*	*16.4*	*83.5*
	1911	56932	3890	40395	11755	*6.9*	*72.0*	*21.0*	*79.0*
Ammanford UD	1901	2827	626	1964	237	*22.1*	*69.5*	*8.4*	*91.6*
	1911	5574	498	3902	1091	*9.1*	*71.1*	*19.9*	*80.1*
Burry Port UD	1901	3611	599	2422	590	*16.6*	*67.1*	*16.3*	*83.7*
	1911	4258	410	3030	745	*9.8*	*72.4*	*17.8*	*82.2*
Carmarthen MB	1901	9523	1000	6661	1851	*10.5*	*70.0*	*19.4*	*80.5*
	1911	9731	686	6858	2118	*7.1*	*71.0*	*21.9*	*78.1*
Kidwelly MB	1901	2103	621	1331	148	*29.6*	*63.4*	*7.0*	*93.0*
	1911	2813	325	2095	320	*11.9*	*76.5*	*11.7*	*88.3*
Llandeilo UD	1901	1851	189	1432	229	*10.2*	*77.4*	*12.4*	*87.6*
	1911	1837	73	1446	287	*4.0*	*80.1*	*15.9*	*84.1*
Llandovery MB	1901	1699	102	1323	271	*6.0*	*78.0*	*16.0*	*84.0*
	1911	1870	102	1295	457	*5.5*	*69.8*	*24.6*	*75.4*
Llanelli UD	1901	23811	2829	16707	4237	*11.9*	*70.2*	*17.8*	*82.1*
	1911	29970	1653	21105	6667	*5.6*	*71.7*	*22.6*	*77.3*
Newcastle Emlyn UD	1901	820	189	593	37	*23.1*	*72.4*	*4.5*	*95.5*
	1911	879	143	664	70	*16.3*	*75.6*	*8.0*	*91.9*
Rural Districts **Total**	1901	79921	38746	36613	4418	*48.6*	*45.9*	*5.5*	*94.4*
	1911	92759	26815	56136	8236	*29.4*	*61.5*	*9.0*	*90.9*
Carmarthen RD	1901	21871	10325	9618	1892	*47.3*	*44.0*	*8.7*	*91.3*
	1911	22670	6773	13449	2200	*30.2*	*60.0*	*9.8*	*90.2*
Llandeilo Fawr RD	1901	17278	8190	8345	714	*47.5*	*48.4*	*4.1*	*95.8*
	1911	23373	6164	14468	2293	*26.9*	*63.1*	*10.0*	*90.0*

District[1]	Year	Number[2] Population 3 years and over	Welsh only	Both	English only	*Percentage[3]* *Welsh only*	*Both*	*English only*	*Able to speak Welsh[4]*
Llandovery RD	1901	7339	3130	3921	263	*42.8*	*53.6*	*3.6*	*96.4*
	1911	7013	1715	4505	710	*24.7*	*65.0*	*10.2*	*89.8*
Llanelli RD	1901	18715	8109	9768	817	*43.4*	*52.2*	*4.4*	*95.6*
	1911	25218	5836	16682	2080	*23.7*	*67.7*	*8.4*	*91.4*
Llanybydder RD	1901	3574	2419	1095	59	*67.7*	*30.6*	*1.7*	*98.3*
	1911	3421	1632	1624	119	*48.4*	*48.1*	*3.5*	*96.5*
Newcastle Emlyn RD	1901	6182	4531	1580	50	*73.5*	*25.6*	*0.8*	*99.2*
	1911	6134	3307	2655	116	*54.4*	*43.7*	*1.9*	*98.1*
Whitland RD	1901	4962	2042	2286	623	*41.2*	*46.2*	*12.6*	*87.4*
	1911	4930	1388	2753	718	*28.6*	*56.7*	*14.8*	*85.2*
PEMBROKESHIRE									
Urban Districts									
Total	1901	34528	278	3286	30935	*0.8*	*9.5*	*89.6*	*10.3*
	1911	36397	163	3759	31517	*0.5*	*10.6*	*88.8*	*11.1*
Fishguard UD	1901	1602	209	1238	155	*13.0*	*77.3*	*9.7*	*90.3*
	1911	2656	131	1819	661	*5.0*	*69.6*	*25.3*	*74.7*
Haverfordwest MB	1901	5616	9	590	5012	*0.2*	*10.5*	*89.3*	*10.7*
	1911	5613	9	559	4934	*0.2*	*10.2*	*89.7*	*10.3*
Milford Haven UD	1901	4711	6	259	4435	*0.1*	*5.5*	*94.2*	*5.6*
	1911	5877	3	218	5405	*0.1*	*3.9*	*95.6*	*3.9*
Narberth UD	1901	993	2	318	673	*0.2*	*32.0*	*67.8*	*32.2*
	1911	1052	4	320	718	*0.4*	*30.7*	*68.9*	*31.1*
Neyland UD	1901	2622	21	134	2467	*0.8*	*5.1*	*94.1*	*5.9*
	1911	2288	5	133	2100	*0.2*	*5.9*	*93.8*	*6.2*
Pembroke MB	1901	14783	25	538	14209	*0.2*	*3.6*	*96.1*	*3.8*
	1911	14755	9	515	13887	*0.1*	*3.6*	*96.3*	*3.6*
Tenby MB	1901	4201	6	209	3984	*0.1*	*5.0*	*94.8*	*5.1*
	1911	4156	2	195	3812	*0.0*	*4.9*	*94.8*	*4.9*
Rural Districts									
Total	1901	47695	9519	15250	22861	*20.0*	*32.0*	*48.0*	*52.0*
	1911	48066	6348	17120	23607	*13.5*	*36.4*	*50.1*	*49.8*
Haverfordwest RD	1901	18951	2856	7019	9057	*15.1*	*37.1*	*47.8*	*52.2*
	1911	19929	1682	7885	9881	*8.6*	*40.5*	*50.8*	*49.2*
Llanfyrnach RD	1901	2312	1771	508	30	*76.7*	*22.0*	*1.3*	*98.7*
	1911	2281	1254	979	41	*55.1*	*43.1*	*1.8*	*98.2*
Narberth RD	1901	10385	1271	3393	5708	*12.3*	*32.7*	*55.0*	*45.0*
	1911	10387	869	3373	5964	*8.5*	*33.0*	*58.4*	*41.6*
Pembroke RD	1901	8248	16	474	7747	*0.2*	*5.8*	*94.0*	*5.9*
	1911	7977	16	403	7375	*0.2*	*5.2*	*94.6*	*5.4*
St Dogmaels RD	1901	7799	3605	3856	319	*46.3*	*49.6*	*4.1*	*95.9*
	1911	7492	2527	4480	346	*34.4*	*60.9*	*4.7*	*95.3*
CARDIGANSHIRE									
Urban Districts									
Total	1901	15011	2287	10178	2511	*15.3*	*67.9*	*16.8*	*83.2*
	1911	15566	1401	10962	2922	*9.2*	*71.7*	*19.1*	*80.9*
Aberaeron UD	1901	1250	327	857	59	*26.3*	*68.9*	*4.7*	*95.3*
	1911	1289	225	964	87	*17.6*	*75.5*	*6.8*	*93.2*
Aberystwyth MB	1901	7649	587	5046	2005	*7.7*	*66.0*	*26.2*	*73.7*
	1911	8042	370	5192	2285	*4.7*	*66.1*	*29.1*	*70.8*
Cardigan MB	1901	3310	679	2355	267	*20.6*	*71.3*	*8.1*	*91.9*
	1911	3391	410	2642	297	*12.2*	*78.9*	*8.9*	*91.1*
New Quay UD	1901	1164	363	759	39	*31.3*	*65.4*	*3.4*	*96.6*
	1911	1132	184	864	64	*16.5*	*77.7*	*5.8*	*94.2*
Lampeter MB	1901	1638	331	1161	141	*20.3*	*71.1*	*8.6*	*91.3*
	1911	1712	212	1300	189	*12.5*	*76.4*	*11.1*	*88.9*

District[1]	Year	Number[2] Population 3 years and over	Welsh only	Both	English only	Percentage[3] Welsh only	Both	English only	Able to speak Welsh[4]
Rural Districts									
Total	1901	42653	26794	14379	1369	*62.9*	*33.8*	*3.2*	*96.7*
	1911	41473	18096	20618	2044	*44.4*	*50.6*	*5.0*	*95.0*
Aberaeron RD	1901	7722	5394	2199	109	*70.0*	*28.5*	*1.4*	*98.6*
	1911	7338	3821	3221	185	*52.9*	*44.6*	*2.6*	*97.4*
Aberystwyth RD	1901	12617	6703	5163	694	*53.2*	*40.9*	*5.5*	*94.1*
	1911	12429	4232	7043	924	*34.7*	*57.7*	*7.6*	*92.4*
Cardigan RD	1901	3222	1535	1513	161	*47.8*	*47.1*	*5.0*	*95.0*
	1911	3117	892	1876	274	*29.2*	*61.4*	*9.0*	*90.6*
Lampeter RD	1901	3518	2262	1172	82	*64.3*	*33.3*	*2.3*	*97.7*
	1911	3398	1527	1692	109	*45.9*	*50.8*	*3.3*	*96.7*
Llandysul RD	1901	7720	5201	2333	177	*67.4*	*30.3*	*2.3*	*97.7*
	1911	7617	3701	3515	278	*49.4*	*46.9*	*3.7*	*96.3*
Tregaron RD	1901	7494	5537	1824	123	*74.0*	*24.4*	*1.6*	*98.4*
	1911	7180	3772	3075	229	*53.3*	*43.5*	*3.2*	*96.8*
Ysgubor-y-coed CP (admin. by Machyn-lleth (Mont) RD)	1901	360	162	175	23	*45.0*	*48.6*	*6.4*	*93.6*
	1911	394	151	196	45	*38.5*	*50.0*	*11.5*	*88.5*
BRECONSHIRE									
Urban Districts									
Total	1901	15628	166	3344	12103	*1.1*	*21.4*	*77.5*	*22.5*
	1911	16481	155	2797	13282	*1.0*	*17.2*	*81.8*	*18.2*
Brecon UD	1901	5467	12	1180	4273	*0.2*	*21.6*	*78.2*	*21.8*
	1911	5587	18	954	4507	*0.3*	*17.4*	*82.2*	*17.7*
Bryn-mawr UD	1901	6265	54	1441	4758	*0.9*	*23.0*	*76.0*	*23.9*
	1911	6996	15	1129	5744	*0.2*	*16.4*	*83.3*	*16.6*
Builth Wells UD	1901	1714	6	259	1448	*0.4*	*15.1*	*84.5*	*15.5*
	1911	1635	3	228	1393	*0.2*	*14.0*	*85.8*	*14.2*
Hay UD	1901	1596	0	61	1535	*0.0*	*3.8*	*96.2*	*3.8*
	1911	1541	0	44	1488	*0.0*	*2.9*	*97.1*	*2.9*
Llanwrtyd UD	1901	586	94	403	89	*16.0*	*68.8*	*15.2*	*84.8*
	1911	722	119	442	150	*16.7*	*62.2*	*21.1*	*78.9*
Rural Districts									
Total	1901	34781	4508	15101	15142	*13.0*	*43.5*	*43.6*	*56.4*
	1911	38834	2860	17084	18301	*7.5*	*44.6*	*47.7*	*52.0*
Brecon RD	1901	9168	1032	4656	3471	*11.3*	*50.8*	*37.9*	*62.1*
	1911	8613	505	4242	3789	*5.9*	*49.7*	*44.4*	*55.6*
Builth Wells RD	1901	4048	404	1801	1842	*10.0*	*44.5*	*45.5*	*54.5*
	1911	3984	280	1647	2008	*7.1*	*41.9*	*51.0*	*49.0*
Crickhowell RD	1901	6602	78	1790	4729	*1.2*	*27.1*	*71.7*	*28.3*
	1911	7217	24	1299	5818	*0.3*	*18.2*	*81.5*	*18.5*
Hay RD	1901	3089	5	541	2540	*0.2*	*17.5*	*82.3*	*17.7*
	1911	3381	12	505	2808	*0.4*	*15.2*	*84.5*	*15.5*
Faenor and Penderyn RD	1901	4402	643	2888	865	*14.6*	*65.7*	*19.7*	*80.3*
	1911	5124	281	3179	1585	*5.6*	*63.0*	*31.4*	*68.6*
Ystradgynlais RD	1901	5285	2136	2736	409	*40.4*	*51.8*	*7.7*	*92.3*
	1911	9541	1701	5790	1814	*18.1*	*61.7*	*19.3*	*79.8*
Llanwrthwl CP (admin. by Rhayader (Rad) RD)	1901	1667	57	401	1208	*3.4*	*24.1*	*72.5*	*27.5*
	1911	387	5	80	301	*1.3*	*20.7*	*78.0*	*22.0*
Ystradfellte CP (admin. by Neath (Glam) RD)	1901	520	153	288	78	*29.5*	*55.5*	*15.0*	*85.0*
	1911	587	52	342	178	*9.1*	*59.7*	*31.1*	*68.8*

District[1]	Year	Number[2] Population 3 years and over	Welsh only	Both	English only	*Percentage[3]* *Welsh only*	*Both*	*English only*	*Able to speak Welsh[4]*
RADNORSHIRE									
Urban Districts									
Total	1901	4868	3	213	4648	*0.1*	*4.4*	*95.5*	*4.4*
	1911	5500	3	267	5168	*0.1*	*4.9*	*95.0*	*5.0*
Knighton UD	1901	1972	2	54	1914	*0.1*	*2.7*	*97.1*	*2.8*
	1911	1774	0	43	1681	*0.0*	*2.5*	*97.5*	*2.5*
Llandrindod Wells UD	1901	1732	1	152	1578	*0.1*	*8.8*	*91.1*	*8.8*
	1911	2644	3	210	2423	*0.1*	*8.0*	*91.9*	*8.1*
Presteigne UD	1901	1164	0	7	1156	*0.0*	*0.6*	*99.4*	*0.6*
	1911	1082	0	14	1064	*0.0*	*1.3*	*98.7*	*1.3*
Rural Districts									
Total	1901	16886	48	1096	15722	*0.3*	*6.5*	*93.2*	*6.8*
	1911	15779	8	861	14716	*0.1*	*5.5*	*94.4*	*5.6*
Colwyn RD	1901	1761	1	97	1661	*0.1*	*5.5*	*94.4*	*5.6*
	1911	1935	0	146	1742	*0.0*	*7.7*	*92.3*	*7.7*
Knighton RD	1901	4537	0	66	4469	*0.0*	*1.5*	*98.5*	*1.5*
	1911	4155	1	91	4034	*0.0*	*2.2*	*97.8*	*2.2*
New Radnor RD	1901	2760	0	42	2713	*0.0*	*1.5*	*98.5*	*1.5*
	1911	2604	0	36	2538	*0.0*	*1.4*	*98.6*	*1.4*
Painscastle RD	1901	2207	0	78	2127	*0.0*	*3.5*	*96.5*	*3.5*
	1911	2193	0	73	2090	*0.0*	*3.4*	*96.6*	*3.4*
Rhayader RD	1901	5621	47	813	4752	*0.8*	*14.5*	*84.7*	*15.3*
	1911	4892	7	515	4312	*0.1*	*10.6*	*89.1*	*10.8*
MONTGOMERYSHIRE									
Urban Districts									
Total	1901	18806	657	5062	13066	*3.5*	*26.9*	*69.6*	*30.4*
	1911	18089	387	4587	12824	*2.2*	*25.7*	*72.0*	*27.9*
Llanfyllin MB	1901	1526	275	920	329	*18.0*	*60.4*	*21.6*	*78.4*
	1911	1548	166	973	404	*10.8*	*63.1*	*26.2*	*73.8*
Llanidloes MB	1901	2578	57	1271	1243	*2.2*	*49.4*	*48.3*	*51.7*
	1911	2437	28	1018	1347	*1.2*	*42.5*	*56.3*	*43.7*
Machynlleth UD	1901	1907	302	1388	209	*15.9*	*73.1*	*11.0*	*89.0*
	1911	1859	168	1423	255	*9.1*	*77.1*	*13.8*	*86.2*
Montgomery MB	1901	977	1	61	913	*0.1*	*6.3*	*93.6*	*6.4*
	1911	942	9	48	873	*1.0*	*5.2*	*93.9*	*6.1*
Newtown and Llanllwchaearn UD	1901	6091	11	779	5299	*0.2*	*12.8*	*87.0*	*13.0*
	1911	5722	6	592	4984	*0.1*	*10.6*	*89.1*	*10.7*
Welshpool MB	1901	5727	11	643	5073	*0.2*	*11.2*	*88.6*	*11.4*
	1911	5581	10	533	4961	*0.2*	*9.7*	*90.0*	*9.9*
Rural Districts									
Total	1901	32504	7323	11299	13847	*22.6*	*34.8*	*42.6*	*57.3*
	1911	31919	4980	12452	14179	*15.8*	*39.4*	*44.9*	*55.1*
Forden RD	1901	5411	18	524	4862	*0.3*	*9.7*	*90.0*	*10.0*
	1911	5364	21	488	4800	*0.4*	*9.2*	*90.4*	*9.6*
Llanfyllin RD	1901	11971	3326	5103	3529	*27.8*	*42.7*	*29.5*	*70.5*
	1911	11773	2173	5775	3715	*18.6*	*49.5*	*31.9*	*68.1*
Machynlleth RD	1901	4095	2497	1483	112	*61.0*	*36.2*	*2.7*	*97.3*
	1911	3897	1917	1844	109	*49.5*	*47.6*	*2.8*	*97.2*
Newtown and Llanidloes RD	1901	11027	1482	4189	5344	*13.5*	*38.0*	*48.5*	*51.5*
	1911	10885	869	4345	5555	*8.1*	*40.3*	*51.6*	*48.4*
FLINTSHIRE									
Urban Districts									
Total	1901	28336	709	11086	16507	*2.5*	*39.2*	*58.3*	*41.7*
	1911	32525	443	10542	20651	*1.4*	*33.3*	*65.2*	*34.7*

District[1]	Year	Number[2] Population 3 years and over	Welsh only	Both	English only	*Percentage[3] Welsh only*	*Both*	*English only*	*Able to speak Welsh[4]*
Buckley UD	1901	5307	9	553	4743	*0.2*	*10.4*	*89.4*	*10.6*
	1911	5825	24	496	5162	*0.4*	*8.7*	*90.8*	*9.2*
Connah's Quay UD	1901	3095	16	385	2690	*0.5*	*12.5*	*87.0*	*13.0*
	1911	4216	29	478	3532	*0.7*	*11.8*	*87.4*	*12.5*
Flint MB	1901	4273	160	1891	2211	*3.8*	*44.3*	*51.9*	*48.1*
	1911	5062	77	1705	3152	*1.6*	*34.5*	*63.8*	*36.1*
Holywell UD	1901	2505	105	1643	755	*4.2*	*65.6*	*30.2*	*69.8*
	1911	2413	53	1387	920	*2.2*	*58.7*	*39.0*	*61.0*
Mold UD	1901	3960	121	2225	1613	*3.1*	*56.2*	*40.7*	*59.3*
	1911	4495	83	2267	2020	*1.9*	*51.9*	*46.2*	*53.8*
Prestatyn UD	1901	1187	74	662	449	*6.2*	*55.9*	*37.9*	*62.1*
	1911	1955	39	878	1003	*2.0*	*45.7*	*52.2*	*47.8*
Rhyl UD	1901	8009	224	3727	4046	*2.8*	*46.6*	*50.6*	*49.4*
	1911	8559	138	3331	4862	*1.7*	*40.0*	*58.3*	*41.6*
Rural Districts									
Total	1901	44595	5013	20482	22037	*11.3*	*46.0*	*49.5*	*57.2*
	1911	54045	2503	23045	27235	*4.7*	*43.6*	*51.6*	*48.4*
Hawarden RD	1901	11648	619	2700	11318	*5.3*	*23.2*	*97.2*	*28.5*
	1911	19064	301	3403	14827	*1.6*	*18.3*	*79.9*	*20.0*
Holywell RD	1901	22373	3560	13920	4858	*15.9*	*62.3*	*21.7*	*78.2*
	1911	23682	1711	15530	5912	*7.4*	*67.1*	*25.5*	*74.5*
Overton RD	1901	4752	0	135	4605	*0.0*	*2.8*	*97.2*	*2.8*
	1911	4878	4	127	4620	*0.1*	*2.7*	*97.2*	*2.8*
St Asaph (Flint) RD	1901	5822	834	3727	1256	*14.3*	*64.1*	*21.6*	*78.4*
	1911	6421	487	3985	1876	*7.7*	*62.8*	*29.5*	*70.4*
DENBIGHSHIRE									
Urban Districts									
Total	1901	38253	2862	16919	18408	*7.5*	*44.3*	*48.2*	*51.8*
	1911	45958	2169	18865	24087	*4.8*	*41.8*	*53.4*	*46.6*
Abergele and	1901	1958	170	1425	356	*8.7*	*72.8*	*18.2*	*81.5*
Pen-sarn UD	1911	2011	81	1474	418	*4.1*	*74.7*	*21.2*	*78.8*
Colwyn Bay and	1901	8265	567	3435	4244	*6.9*	*41.6*	*51.4*	*48.5*
Colwyn UD	1911	12108	419	4508	6849	*3.6*	*38.2*	*58.1*	*41.8*
Denbigh MB	1901	6064	988	4227	838	*16.3*	*69.8*	*13.8*	*86.1*
	1911	6564	900	4566	994	*13.9*	*70.7*	*15.4*	*84.6*
Llangollen UD	1901	3117	251	1954	911	*8.1*	*62.7*	*29.2*	*70.8*
	1911	3081	164	1939	919	*5.4*	*64.2*	*30.4*	*69.6*
Llanrwst UD	1901	2473	527	1754	188	*21.3*	*71.0*	*7.6*	*92.4*
	1911	2364	352	1751	208	*15.2*	*75.8*	*9.0*	*91.0*
Ruthin MB	1901	2486	294	1806	381	*11.9*	*72.8*	*15.4*	*84.6*
	1911	2678	181	1939	513	*6.9*	*73.6*	*19.5*	*80.4*
Wrexham MB	1901	13890	65	2318	11490	*0.5*	*16.7*	*82.7*	*17.2*
	1911	17152	72	2688	14186	*0.4*	*15.9*	*83.7*	*16.3*
Rural Districts									
Total	1901	83942	19504	36319	28027	*23.3*	*43.3*	*33.4*	*66.6*
	1911	89649	11468	44359	32412	*13.0*	*50.3*	*36.7*	*63.2*
Chirk RD	1901	4153	668	1333	2148	*16.1*	*32.1*	*51.8*	*48.2*
	1911	4271	495	1420	2274	*11.8*	*33.9*	*54.3*	*45.7*
Llangollen RD	1901	3285	773	1881	617	*23.6*	*57.5*	*18.9*	*81.1*
	1911	3389	499	2084	703	*15.2*	*63.4*	*21.4*	*78.6*
Llanrwst RD	1901	4302	2489	1587	221	*57.9*	*36.9*	*5.1*	*94.9*
	1911	4132	1950	1888	227	*48.0*	*46.4*	*5.6*	*94.4*
Llansilin RD	1901	3002	976	1802	223	*32.5*	*60.0*	*7.4*	*92.6*
	1911	3006	563	2159	262	*18.9*	*72.4*	*8.8*	*91.2*

District[1]	Year	Number[2] Population 3 years and over	Welsh only	Both	English only	Percentage[3] Welsh only	Both	English only	Able to speak Welsh[4]
Ruthin RD	1901	8652	3321	4004	715	*45.4*	*46.3*	*8.3*	*91.7*
	1911	8608	2212	5348	943	*26.0*	*62.9*	*11.1*	*88.9*
St Asaph (Denb) RD	1901	6481	3059	2737	671	*47.3*	*42.3*	*10.4*	*89.6*
	1911	6325	2095	3445	675	*33.7*	*55.4*	*10.9*	*89.1*
Uwchaled RD	1901	2091	1640	407	43	*78.5*	*19.5*	*2.1*	*97.9*
	1911	2115	1134	837	121	*54.2*	*40.0*	*5.8*	*94.2*
Wrexham RD	1901	50565	5358	21883	23288	*10.6*	*43.3*	*46.1*	*53.9*
	1911	56210	2196	26192	27004	*4.0*	*47.3*	*48.7*	*51.2*
Llaneilian CP and Llansanffraid CP (admin. by Conwy (Caern) RD)	1901	1411	620	685	101	*44.1*	*48.7*	*7.2*	*92.8*
	1911	1593	324	986	203	*21.4*	*65.2*	*13.4*	*86.6*
MERIONETH									
Urban Districts									
Total	1901	20766	8499	10730	1510	*41.0*	*51.7*	*7.3*	*92.7*
	1911	19113	5680	11407	1615	*30.4*	*61.0*	*8.6*	*91.3*
Bala UD	1901	1455	407	941	105	*28.0*	*64.8*	*7.2*	*92.8*
	1911	1462	256	1047	150	*17.6*	*72.0*	*10.3*	*89.6*
Barmouth UD	1901	2123	273	1371	478	*12.9*	*64.6*	*22.5*	*77.5*
	1911	2023	196	1299	450	*10.1*	*66.8*	*23.1*	*76.9*
Dolgellau UD	1901	2273	586	1469	212	*25.8*	*64.7*	*9.3*	*90.4*
	1911	2060	425	1418	165	*21.2*	*70.6*	*8.2*	*91.8*
Ffestiniog UD	1901	10556	5993	4368	186	*56.8*	*41.4*	*1.8*	*98.2*
	1911	9087	3995	4688	178	*45.1*	*52.9*	*2.0*	*98.0*
Mallwyd UD	1901	837	452	326	59	*54.0*	*38.9*	*7.0*	*93.0*
	1911	726	294	364	63	*40.8*	*50.5*	*8.7*	*91.3*
Tywyn UD	1901	3522	788	2255	470	*22.4*	*64.1*	*13.4*	*86.5*
	1911	3755	514	2591	609	*13.8*	*69.7*	*16.4*	*83.5*
Rural Districts									
Total	1901	24865	14582	8944	1315	*58.7*	*36.0*	*5.3*	*94.7*
	1911	24096	10177	11712	1725	*43.1*	*49.6*	*7.3*	*92.6*
Deudraeth RD	1901	7478	4964	2306	197	*66.5*	*30.9*	*2.6*	*97.3*
	1911	7361	3480	3222	405	*48.9*	*45.3*	*5.7*	*94.2*
Dolgellau RD	1901	8152	4582	2981	584	*56.2*	*36.6*	*7.2*	*92.8*
	1911	7595	3001	3757	671	*40.4*	*50.6*	*9.0*	*91.0*
Edeirnion RD	1901	4794	2187	2261	345	*45.6*	*47.2*	*7.2*	*92.8*
	1911	4860	1508	2878	436	*31.3*	*59.7*	*9.0*	*91.0*
Penllyn RD	1901	3947	2646	1151	143	*67.2*	*29.2*	*3.6*	*96.4*
	1911	3868	2074	1594	176	*53.9*	*41.5*	*4.6*	*95.4*
Pennal CP (admin. by Machynlleth (Mont) RD)	1901	494	203	245	46	*41.1*	*49.6*	*9.3*	*90.7*
	1911	412	114	261	37	*27.7*	*63.3*	*9.0*	*91.0*
CAERNARFONSHIRE									
Urban Districts									
Total	1901	54064	12735	31161	10058	*23.6*	*57.7*	*18.6*	*81.3*
	1911	55347	8281	34153	11837	*15.3*	*62.9*	*21.8*	*78.2*
Bangor City MB	1901	10565	1104	7329	2112	*10.5*	*69.4*	*20.0*	*79.9*
	1911	10658	597	7672	2238	*5.7*	*73.0*	*21.3*	*78.7*
Bethesda UD	1901	4903	3152	1705	38	*64.4*	*34.8*	*0.8*	*99.2*
	1911	4455	2467	1887	43	*56.1*	*42.9*	*1.0*	*99.0*
Betws-y-coed UD[3]	1901	1012	266	597	148	*26.3*	*59.1*	*14.6*	*85.4*
	1911	886	123	606	111	*14.6*	*72.1*	*13.2*	*86.8*
Caernarfon MB	1901	9175	2275	5911	973	*24.8*	*64.5*	*10.6*	*89.3*
	1911	8647	1469	6285	840	*17.1*	*73.1*	*9.8*	*90.2*
Conwy MB	1901	4367	707	2796	859	*16.2*	*64.1*	*19.7*	*80.3*
	1911	4962	229	3185	1452	*4.7*	*65.5*	*29.8*	*70.2*

District[1]	Year	Number[2] Population 3 years and over	Welsh only	Both	English only	*Percentage[3]* *Welsh only*	*Both*	*English only*	*Able to speak Welsh[4]*
Cricieth UD	1901	1345	357	878	107	*26.6*	*65.4*	*8.0*	*92.0*
	1911	1333	243	968	107	*18.4*	*73.4*	*8.1*	*91.9*
Llandudno UD	1901	8766	331	4031	4379	*3.8*	*46.0*	*50.0*	*49.8*
	1911	10008	129	4243	5410	*1.3*	*43.3*	*55.3*	*44.7*
Llanfairfechan UD	1901	2587	850	1388	342	*32.9*	*53.8*	*13.3*	*86.7*
	1911	2792	547	1712	454	*20.2*	*63.1*	*16.7*	*83.3*
Penmaen-mawr UD	1901	3278	838	1852	583	*25.6*	*56.5*	*17.8*	*82.1*
	1911	3826	482	2491	726	*13.0*	*67.3*	*19.6*	*80.3*
Pwllheli UD	1901	3475	1256	1968	248	*36.2*	*56.7*	*7.1*	*92.9*
	1911	3587	897	2332	255	*25.7*	*66.9*	*7.3*	*92.7*
Ynyscynhaearn UD	1901	4591	1599	2706	269	*34.9*	*59.0*	*5.9*	*93.9*
	1911	4193	1098	2772	201	*27.0*	*68.1*	*4.9*	*95.0*
Rural Districts									
Total	1901	63583	43220	18185	2107	*68.0*	*28.6*	*3.3*	*96.7*
	1911	62997	33816	24997	2627	*55.0*	*40.7*	*4.3*	*95.7*
Conwy RD	1901	5841	2036	3084	712	*34.9*	*52.9*	*12.2*	*87.8*
	1911	6698	1197	4141	1185	*18.3*	*63.5*	*18.2*	*81.8*
Geirionydd RD[3]	1901	4531	2620	1717	192	*57.8*	*37.9*	*4.2*	*95.8*
	1911	4251	2023	1712	230	*51.0*	*43.2*	*5.8*	*94.2*
Glaslyn RD	1901	3348	2496	752	94	*74.7*	*22.5*	*2.8*	*97.2*
	1911	3131	1950	1005	94	*63.9*	*33.0*	*3.1*	*96.9*
Gwyrfai RD	1901	27771	20423	6870	446	*73.6*	*24.8*	*1.6*	*98.4*
	1911	26661	16092	9576	418	*61.7*	*36.7*	*1.6*	*98.4*
Llŷn RD	1901	15891	12290	3272	313	*77.4*	*20.6*	*2.0*	*98.0*
	1911	15947	10138	5111	353	*65.0*	*32.8*	*2.3*	*97.7*
Ogwen RD	1901	6201	3355	2490	350	*54.1*	*40.2*	*5.6*	*94.3*
	1911	6309	2416	3452	347	*38.9*	*55.5*	*5.6*	*94.4*
ANGLESEY									
Urban Districts									
Total	1901	17661	4145	10751	2658	*23.5*	*61.0*	*15.1*	*84.5*
	1911	17935	2604	12037	2783	*14.9*	*69.0*	*16.0*	*84.0*
Amlwch UD	1901	2815	1401	1278	134	*49.8*	*45.4*	*4.8*	*95.2*
	1911	2570	884	1557	77	*35.1*	*61.8*	*3.1*	*96.9*
Beaumaris MB	1901	2210	205	1383	614	*9.3*	*62.8*	*27.9*	*72.1*
	1911	2131	101	1261	742	*4.8*	*59.9*	*35.2*	*64.7*
Holyhead UD	1901	9364	1455	6145	1675	*15.5*	*65.7*	*17.9*	*81.2*
	1911	10019	876	7078	1709	*9.1*	*73.2*	*17.7*	*82.3*
Llangefni UD	1901	1658	770	830	56	*46.5*	*50.1*	*3.4*	*96.6*
	1911	1658	572	990	67	*35.1*	*60.7*	*4.1*	*95.8*
Menai Bridge UD	1901	1614	314	1115	179	*19.5*	*69.3*	*11.1*	*88.8*
	1911	1557	171	1151	188	*11.3*	*76.2*	*12.5*	*87.5*
Rural Districts									
Total	1901	29843	18646	10012	1135	*62.6*	*33.6*	*3.8*	*96.1*
	1911	30160	14830	13195	1310	*50.6*	*45.0*	*4.5*	*95.5*
Aethwy RD	1901	8185	4279	3237	662	*52.3*	*39.6*	*8.1*	*91.9*
	1911	8212	3241	4017	693	*40.8*	*50.5*	*8.7*	*91.3*
Dwyran RD	1901	2870	2037	796	34	*71.0*	*27.8*	*1.2*	*98.8*
	1911	2819	1687	1026	37	*61.3*	*37.3*	*1.3*	*98.7*
Twrcelyn RD	1901	8973	6018	2736	189	*67.2*	*30.5*	*2.1*	*97.7*
	1911	8813	4618	3778	177	*53.9*	*44.1*	*2.1*	*97.9*
Valley RD	1901	9815	6312	3243	250	*64.4*	*33.1*	*2.5*	*97.5*
	1911	10316	5284	4374	403	*52.5*	*43.5*	*4.0*	*96.0*

Source: *Census of Population for England and Wales*: 1911, *Vol. XII, Language Spoken in Wales and Monmouthshire* (HMSO, 1913) Table 2; reprinted in *County Reports*, Table 34.

Administrative Counties and their constituent Urban and Rural Districts are not strictly comparable with the divisions of Registration Counties and Registration Districts given in Table 3.2. The figures for 1901 given here are on the basis of 1911 boundaries.

[1] Abbreviations as follows: UD Urban District; MB Municipal Borough; CB County Borough; RD Rural District.

[2] The total for population aged 3 years and over includes mostly small numbers of those who either gave no statement as to language spoken or who entered other languages. The totals for Wales are as follows: no language statement: 1901, 2,757; 1911, 58,517; other languages: 1901, 3,893; 1911, 3,762.

[3] The denominator excludes those who gave no language statement but includes those who entered other languages. In general the percentage giving no language statement was less than 3 per cent. In the following districts, however, in 1911 the percentage was greater than 5 per cent: Bedwellte UD (1,188, 5.8%), Monmouth MB (1,781, 35.7%), Rhymni (569, 5.4%), Chepstow RD (414, 5.6%), Pen-y-bont RD (1,185, 5.7%), Betws-y-coed UD (465, 5.2%), Geirionydd RD (285, 6.7%).

[4] Those entered as able to speak 'Welsh only' and 'Both'.

[5] Includes County Boroughs and Municipal Boroughs.

Language 3.4 Census Returns. Ability to speak Welsh. 1901, 1911. Local government districts listed in order of ability to speak Welsh in 1911

	Local government district	County	1911 Population 3 years and over Number	1911 Language spoken Welsh only %	1911 Language spoken Both %	1911 Language spoken English only %	1911 Able to speak Welsh %	1901 Population 3 years and over Number	1901 Language spoken Welsh only %	1901 Language spoken Both %	1901 Language spoken English only %	1901 Able to speak Welsh %
1	Bethesda UD	Caern	4455	*56.1*	*42.9*	*1.0*	*99.0*	4903	*64.4*	*34.8*	*0.8*	*99.2*
2	Dwyran RD	Angl	2819	*61.3*	*37.3*	*1.3*	*98.7*	2870	*71.0*	*27.8*	*1.2*	*98.8*
3	Gwyrfai RD	Caern	26661	*61.7*	*36.7*	*1.6*	*98.4*	27771	*73.6*	*24.8*	*1.6*	*98.4*
4	Llanfyrnach RD	Pemb	2281	*55.1*	*43.1*	*1.8*	*98.2*	2312	*76.7*	*22.0*	*1.3*	*98.7*
5	Newcastle Emlyn RD	Carm	6134	*54.4*	*43.7*	*1.9*	*98.1*	6182	*73.5*	*25.6*	*0.8*	*99.2*
6	Ffestiniog UD	Mer	9087	*45.1*	*52.9*	*2.0*	*98.0*	10556	*56.8*	*41.4*	*1.8*	*98.2*
7	Twrcelyn RD	Angl	8813	*53.9*	*44.1*	*2.1*	*97.9*	8973	*67.2*	*30.5*	*2.1*	*97.7*
8	Llŷn RD	Caern	15947	*65.0*	*32.8*	*2.3*	*97.7*	15891	*77.4*	*20.6*	*2.0*	*98.0*
9	Aberaeron RD	Card	7338	*52.9*	*44.6*	*2.6*	*97.4*	7722	*70.0*	*28.5*	*1.4*	*98.6*
10	Machynlleth RD	Mont	3897	*49.5*	*47.6*	*2.8*	*97.2*	4095	*61.0*	*36.2*	*2.7*	*97.3*
11	Glaslyn RD	Caern	3131	*63.9*	*33.0*	*3.1*	*96.9*	3348	*74.7*	*22.5*	*2.8*	*97.2*
12	Amlwch UD	Angl	2570	*35.1*	*61.8*	*3.1*	*96.9*	2815	*49.8*	*45.4*	*4.8*	*95.2*
13	Tregaron RD	Card	7180	*53.3*	*43.5*	*3.2*	*96.8*	7494	*74.0*	*24.4*	*1.6*	*98.4*
14	Lampeter RD	Card	3398	*45.9*	*50.8*	*3.3*	*96.7*	3518	*64.3*	*33.3*	*2.3*	*97.7*
15	Llanybydder RD	Carm	3421	*48.4*	*48.1*	*3.5*	*96.5*	3574	*67.7*	*30.6*	*1.7*	*98.3*
16	Llandysul RD	Card	7617	*49.4*	*46.9*	*3.7*	*96.3*	7720	*67.4*	*30.3*	*2.3*	*97.7*
17	Valley RD	Angl	10316	*52.5*	*43.5*	*4.0*	*96.0*	9815	*64.4*	*33.1*	*2.5*	*97.5*
18	Llangefni UD	Angl	1658	*35.1*	*60.7*	*4.1*	*95.8*	1658	*46.5*	*50.1*	*3.4*	*96.6*
19	Penllyn RD	Mer	3868	*53.9*	*41.5*	*4.6*	*95.4*	3947	*67.2*	*29.2*	*3.6*	*96.4*
20	St Dogmaels RD	Pemb	7492	*34.4*	*60.9*	*4.7*	*95.3*	7799	*46.3*	*49.6*	*4.1*	*95.9*
21	Ynyscynhaearn UD	Caern	4193	*27.0*	*68.1*	*4.9*	*95.0*	4591	*34.9*	*59.0*	*5.9*	*93.9*
22	Llanrwst RD	Denb	4132	*48.0*	*46.4*	*5.6*	*94.4*	4302	*57.9*	*36.9*	*5.1*	*94.9*
23	Ogwen RD	Caern	6309	*38.9*	*55.5*	*5.6*	*94.4*	6201	*54.1*	*40.2*	*5.6*	*94.3*
24	New Quay UD	Card	1132	*16.5*	*77.7*	*5.8*	*94.2*	1164	*31.3*	*65.4*	*3.4*	*96.6*
25	Uwchaled RD	Denb	2115	*54.2*	*40.0*	*5.8*	*94.2*	2091	*78.5*	*19.5*	*2.1*	*97.9*
26	Deudraeth RD	Mer	7361	*48.9*	*45.3*	*5.7*	*94.2*	7478	*66.5*	*30.9*	*2.6*	*97.3*
27	Geirionydd RD	Caern	4251	*51.0*	*43.2*	*5.8*	*94.2*	4531	*57.8*	*37.9*	*4.2*	*95.8*
28	Aberaeron UD	Card	1289	*17.6*	*75.5*	*6.8*	*93.2*	1250	*26.3*	*68.9*	*4.7*	*95.3*
29	Pwllheli UD	Caern	3587	*25.7*	*66.9*	*7.3*	*92.7*	3475	*36.2*	*56.7*	*7.1*	*92.9*
30	Aberystwyth RD	Card	12429	*34.7*	*57.7*	*7.6*	*92.4*	12617	*53.2*	*40.9*	*5.5*	*94.1*
31	Newcastle Emlyn UD	Carm	879	*16.3*	*75.6*	*8.0*	*91.9*	820	*23.1*	*72.4*	*4.5*	*95.5*
32	Cricieth UD	Caern	1333	*18.4*	*73.4*	*8.1*	*91.9*	1345	*26.6*	*65.4*	*8.0*	*92.0*
33	Dolgellau UD	Mer	2060	*21.2*	*70.6*	*8.2*	*91.8*	2273	*25.8*	*64.7*	*9.3*	*90.4*
34	Llanelli RD	Carm	25218	*23.7*	*67.7*	*8.4*	*91.4*	18715	*43.4*	*52.2*	*4.4*	*95.6*
35	Mallwyd UD	Mer	726	*40.8*	*50.5*	*8.7*	*91.3*	837	*54.0*	*38.9*	*7.0*	*93.0*
36	Aethwy RD	Angl	8212	*40.8*	*50.5*	*8.7*	*91.3*	8185	*52.3*	*39.6*	*8.1*	*91.9*
37	Llansilin RD	Denb	3006	*18.9*	*72.4*	*8.8*	*91.2*	3002	*32.5*	*60.0*	*7.4*	*92.6*
38	Cardigan MB	Card	3391	*12.2*	*78.9*	*8.9*	*91.1*	3310	*20.6*	*71.3*	*8.1*	*91.9*
39	Llanrwst UD	Denb	2364	*15.2*	*75.8*	*9.0*	*91.0*	2473	*21.3*	*71.0*	*7.6*	*92.4*
40	Dolgellau RD	Mer	7595	*40.4*	*50.6*	*9.0*	*91.0*	8152	*56.2*	*36.6*	*7.2*	*92.8*
41	Edeirnion RD	Mer	4860	*31.3*	*59.7*	*9.0*	*91.0*	4794	*45.6*	*47.2*	*7.2*	*92.8*
42	Pennal CP[1]	Mer	412	*27.7*	*63.3*	*9.0*	*91.0*	494	*41.1*	*49.6*	*9.3*	*90.7*
43	Cardigan RD	Card	3117	*29.2*	*61.4*	*9.0*	*90.6*	3222	*47.8*	*47.1*	*5.0*	*95.0*
44	Carmarthen RD	Carm	22670	*30.2*	*60.0*	*9.8*	*90.2*	21871	*47.3*	*44.0*	*8.7*	*91.3*
45	Caernarfon MB	Caern	8647	*17.1*	*73.1*	*9.8*	*90.2*	9175	*24.8*	*64.5*	*10.6*	*89.3*
46	Llandeilo Fawr RD	Carm	23373	*26.9*	*63.1*	*10.0*	*90.0*	17278	*47.5*	*48.4*	*4.1*	*95.8*
47	Llandovery RD	Carm	7013	*24.7*	*65.0*	*10.2*	*89.8*	7339	*42.8*	*53.6*	*3.6*	*96.4*
48	Bala UD	Mer	1462	*17.6*	*72.0*	*10.3*	*89.6*	1455	*28.0*	*64.8*	*7.2*	*92.8*
49	St Asaph (Denb) RD	Denb	6325	*33.7*	*55.4*	*10.9*	*89.1*	6481	*47.3*	*42.3*	*10.4*	*89.6*
50	Lampeter MB	Card	1712	*12.5*	*76.4*	*11.1*	*88.9*	1638	*20.3*	*71.1*	*8.6*	*91.3*
51	Ruthin RD	Denb	8608	*26.0*	*62.9*	*11.1*	*88.9*	8652	*45.4*	*46.3*	*8.3*	*91.7*
52	Ysgubor-y-coed CP[2]	Card	394	*38.5*	*50.0*	*11.5*	*88.5*	360	*45.0*	*48.6*	*6.4*	*93.6*
53	Kidwelly MB	Carm	2813	*11.9*	*76.5*	*11.7*	*88.3*	2103	*29.6*	*63.4*	*7.0*	*93.0*
54	Menai Bridge UD	Angl	1557	*11.3*	*76.2*	*12.5*	*87.5*	1614	*19.5*	*69.3*	*11.1*	*88.8*
55	Betws-y-coed UD	Caern	886	*14.6*	*72.1*	*13.2*	*86.8*	1012	*26.3*	*59.1*	*14.6*	*85.4*
56	Llaneilian CP and Llansanffraid CP[3]	Denb	1593	*21.4*	*65.2*	*13.4*	*86.6*	1411	*44.1*	*48.7*	*7.2*	*92.8*
57	Machynlleth UD	Mont	1859	*9.1*	*77.1*	*13.8*	*86.2*	1907	*15.9*	*73.1*	*11.0*	*89.0*
58	Whitland RD	Carm	4930	*28.6*	*56.7*	*14.8*	*85.2*	4962	*41.2*	*46.2*	*12.6*	*87.4*
59	Denbigh MB	Denb	6564	*13.9*	*70.7*	*15.4*	*84.6*	6064	*16.3*	*69.8*	*13.8*	*86.1*
60	Llandeilo UD	Carm	1837	*4.0*	*80.1*	*15.9*	*84.1*	1851	*10.2*	*77.4*	*12.4*	*87.6*

	Local government district	County	1911 Population 3 years and over Number	1911 Language spoken Welsh only %	1911 Language spoken Both %	1911 Language spoken English only %	1911 Able to speak Welsh %	1901 Population 3 years and over Number	1901 Language spoken Welsh only %	1901 Language spoken Both %	1901 Language spoken English only %	1901 Able to speak Welsh %
61	Tywyn UD	Mer	3755	*13.8*	*69.7*	*16.4*	*83.5*	3522	*22.4*	*64.1*	*13.4*	*86.5*
62	Llanfairfechan UD	Caern	2792	*20.2*	*63.1*	*16.7*	*83.3*	2587	*32.9*	*53.8*	*13.3*	*86.7*
63	Pontardawe RD	Glam	28861	*17.3*	*65.7*	*17.0*	*83.0*	19206	*37.6*	*55.4*	*7.0*	*93.0*
64	Holyhead UD	Angl	10019	*9.1*	*73.2*	*17.7*	*82.3*	9364	*15.5*	*65.7*	*17.9*	*81.2*
65	Burry Port UD	Carm	4258	*9.8*	*72.4*	*17.8*	*82.2*	3611	*16.6*	*67.1*	*16.3*	*83.7*
66	Conwy RD	Caern	6698	*18.3*	*63.5*	*18.2*	*81.8*	5841	*34.9*	*52.9*	*12.2*	*87.8*
67	Ruthin MB	Denb	2678	*6.9*	*73.6*	*19.5*	*80.4*	2486	*11.9*	*72.8*	*15.4*	*84.6*
68	Penmaen-mawr UD	Caern	3826	*13.0*	*67.3*	*19.6*	*80.3*	3278	*25.6*	*56.5*	*17.8*	*82.1*
69	Ammanford UD	Carm	5574	*9.1*	*71.1*	*19.9*	*80.1*	2827	*22.1*	*69.5*	*8.4*	*91.6*
70	Ystradgynlais RD	Brec	9541	*18.1*	*61.7*	*19.3*	*79.8*	5285	*40.4*	*51.8*	*7.7*	*92.3*
71	Llanwrtyd UD	Brec	722	*16.7*	*62.2*	*21.1*	*78.9*	586	*16.0*	*68.8*	*15.2*	*84.8*
72	Abergele and Pen-sarn UD	Denb	2011	*4.1*	*74.7*	*21.2*	*78.8*	1958	*8.7*	*72.8*	*18.2*	*81.5*
73	Bangor City MB	Caern	10658	*5.7*	*73.0*	*21.3*	*78.7*	10565	*10.5*	*69.4*	*20.0*	*79.9*
74	Llangollen RD	Denb	3389	*15.2*	*63.4*	*21.4*	*78.6*	3285	*23.6*	*57.5*	*18.9*	*81.1*
75	Carmarthen MB	Carm	9731	*7.1*	*71.0*	*21.9*	*78.1*	9523	*10.5*	*70.0*	*19.4*	*80.5*
76	Llanelli UD	Carm	29970	*5.6*	*71.7*	*22.6*	*77.3*	23811	*11.9*	*70.2*	*17.8*	*82.1*
77	Barmouth UD	Mer	2023	*10.1*	*66.8*	*23.1*	*76.9*	2123	*12.9*	*64.6*	*22.5*	*77.5*
78	Llandovery MB	Carm	1870	*5.5*	*69.8*	*24.6*	*75.4*	1699	*6.0*	*78.0*	*16.0*	*84.0*
79	Fishguard UD	Pemb	2656	*5.0*	*69.6*	*25.3*	*74.7*	1602	*13.0*	*77.3*	*9.7*	*90.3*
80	Holywell RD	Flint	23682	*7.4*	*67.1*	*25.5*	*74.5*	22373	*15.9*	*62.3*	*21.7*	*78.2*
81	Llanfyllin MB	Mont	1548	*10.8*	*63.1*	*26.2*	*73.8*	1526	*18.0*	*60.4*	*21.6*	*78.4*
82	Aberystwyth MB	Card	8042	*4.7*	*66.1*	*29.1*	*70.8*	7649	*7.7*	*66.0*	*26.2*	*73.7*
83	St Asaph (Flint) RD	Flint	6421	*7.7*	*62.8*	*29.5*	*70.4*	5822	*14.3*	*64.1*	*21.6*	*78.4*
84	Conwy MB	Caern	4962	*4.7*	*65.5*	*29.8*	*70.2*	4367	*16.2*	*64.1*	*19.7*	*80.3*
85	Llangollen UD	Denb	3081	*5.4*	*64.2*	*30.4*	*69.6*	3117	*8.1*	*62.7*	*29.2*	*70.8*
86	Ystradfellte CP[4]	Brec	587	*9.1*	*59.7*	*31.1*	*68.8*	520	*29.5*	*55.5*	*15.0*	*85.0*
87	Faenor and Penderyn RD	Brec	5124	*5.6*	*63.0*	*31.4*	*68.6*	4402	*14.6*	*65.7*	*19.7*	*80.3*
88	Llanfyllin RD	Mont	11773	*18.6*	*49.5*	*31.9*	*68.1*	11971	*27.8*	*42.7*	*29.5*	*70.5*
89	Neath RD	Glam	38176	*4.3*	*63.4*	*32.3*	*67.7*	26040	*13.4*	*62.0*	*24.6*	*75.4*
90	Aberdare UD	Glam	46844	*6.7*	*58.5*	*34.8*	*65.2*	39932	*13.5*	*58.0*	*28.4*	*71.5*
91	Beaumaris MB	Angl	2131	*4.8*	*59.9*	*35.2*	*64.7*	2210	*9.3*	*62.8*	*27.9*	*72.1*
92	Maesteg UD	Glam	22687	*5.4*	*56.6*	*38.0*	*62.0*	13701	*11.0*	*61.0*	*28.0*	*72.0*
93	Holywell UD	Flint	2413	*2.2*	*58.7*	*39.0*	*61.0*	2505	*4.2*	*65.6*	*30.2*	*69.8*
94	Rhymni UD	Mon	10489	*5.3*	*53.8*	*40.8*	*59.1*	7246	*9.8*	*59.1*	*31.0*	*69.0*
95	Glyncorrwg UD	Glam	7868	*4.0*	*53.6*	*42.4*	*57.6*	5851	*12.8*	*54.7*	*32.6*	*67.4*
96	Rhondda UD	Glam	139235	*4.5*	*51.6*	*43.9*	*56.1*	103740	*11.4*	*53.0*	*35.5*	*64.4*
97	Brecon RD	Brec	8613	*5.9*	*49.7*	*44.4*	*55.6*	9168	*11.3*	*50.8*	*37.9*	*62.1*
98	Mold UD	Flint	4495	*1.9*	*51.9*	*46.2*	*53.8*	3960	*3.1*	*56.2*	*40.7*	*59.3*
99	Wrexham RD	Denb	56210	*4.0*	*47.3*	*48.7*	*51.2*	50565	*10.6*	*43.3*	*46.1*	*53.9*
100	Merthyr Tydfil CB	Glam	74597	*3.6*	*47.3*	*48.7*	*50.9*	63681	*7.3*	*49.9*	*42.5*	*57.2*
101	Pen-y-bont RD	Glam	20649	*2.0*	*47.9*	*50.0*	*49.9*	15228	*4.1*	*51.7*	*44.1*	*55.8*
102	Haverfordwest RD	Pemb	19929	*8.6*	*40.5*	*50.8*	*49.2*	18951	*15.1*	*37.1*	*47.8*	*52.2*
103	Builth RD	Brec	3984	*7.1*	*41.9*	*51.0*	*49.0*	4048	*10.0*	*44.5*	*45.5*	*54.5*
104	Margam UD	Glam	13593	*1.7*	*47.0*	*50.0*	*48.7*	8295	*4.8*	*56.5*	*38.2*	*61.3*
105	Newtown and Llanidloes RD	Mont	10885	*8.1*	*40.3*	*51.6*	*48.4*	11027	*13.5*	*38.0*	*48.5*	*51.5*
106	Prestatyn UD	Flint	1955	*2.0*	*45.7*	*52.2*	*47.8*	1187	*6.2*	*55.9*	*37.9*	*62.1*
107	Ogmore and Garw UD	Glam	24350	*4.3*	*43.4*	*52.3*	*47.7*	18134	*9.6*	*48.4*	*42.1*	*57.9*
108	Chirk RD	Denb	4271	*11.8*	*33.9*	*54.3*	*45.7*	4153	*16.1*	*32.1*	*51.8*	*48.2*
109	Llandudno UD	Caern	10008	*1.3*	*43.3*	*55.3*	*44.7*	8766	*3.8*	*46.0*	*50.0*	*49.8*
110	Llanidloes MB	Mont	2437	*1.2*	*42.5*	*56.3*	*43.7*	2578	*2.2*	*49.4*	*48.3*	*51.7*
111	Llantrisant and Llantwit Fardre RD	Glam	15984	*1.7*	*40.2*	*58.0*	*42.0*	10879	*5.3*	*49.9*	*44.8*	*55.2*
112	Colwyn Bay and Colwyn UD	Denb	12108	*3.6*	*38.2*	*58.1*	*41.8*	8265	*6.9*	*41.6*	*51.4*	*48.5*
113	Narberth RD	Pemb	10387	*8.5*	*33.0*	*58.4*	*41.6*	10385	*12.3*	*32.7*	*55.0*	*45.0*
114	Rhyl UD	Flint	8559	*1.7*	*40.0*	*58.3*	*41.6*	8009	*2.8*	*46.6*	*50.6*	*49.4*
115	Gelli-gaer UD	Glam	32288	*2.7*	*38.8*	*58.4*	*41.5*	15741	*8.6*	*47.3*	*44.0*	*56.0*
116	Mountain Ash UD	Glam	38475	*3.1*	*37.9*	*58.9*	*41.0*	28321	*6.9*	*41.1*	*52.1*	*47.9*
117	Briton Ferry UD	Glam	7885	*1.5*	*38.7*	*59.5*	*40.3*	6402	*2.8*	*46.4*	*50.7*	*49.2*
118	Gower RD	Glam	8030	*1.7*	*36.5*	*61.8*	*38.2*	6729	*5.2*	*30.0*	*64.5*	*35.3*
119	Flint MB	Flint	5062	*1.6*	*34.5*	*63.8*	*36.1*	4273	*3.8*	*44.3*	*51.9*	*48.1*

	Local government district	County	Population 3 years and over Number (1911)	Language spoken: Welsh only % (1911)	Language spoken: Both % (1911)	Language spoken: English only % (1911)	Able to speak Welsh % (1911)	Population 3 years and over Number (1901)	Language spoken: Welsh only % (1901)	Language spoken: Both % (1901)	Language spoken: English only % (1901)	Able to speak Welsh % (1901)
120	Caerphilly UD	Glam	29893	*2.6*	*32.1*	*65.3*	*34.7*	14493	*4.2*	*40.7*	*55.1*	*44.9*
121	Cowbridge RD	Glam	7396	*0.6*	*33.3*	*66.1*	*33.9*	6384	*1.5*	*40.7*	*57.4*	*42.3*
122	Aberafan MB	Glam	9688	*0.7*	*31.5*	*67.5*	*32.2*	6952	*1.0*	*39.1*	*59.7*	*40.1*
123	Narberth UD	Pemb	1052	*0.4*	*30.7*	*68.9*	*31.1*	993	*0.2*	*32.0*	*67.8*	*32.2*
124	Neath MB	Glam	16345	*1.2*	*29.7*	*69.0*	*30.9*	12740	*2.2*	*37.6*	*60.2*	*39.8*
125	Pontypridd UD	Glam	39542	*1.5*	*29.3*	*69.1*	*30.8*	29627	*3.4*	*34.8*	*61.7*	*38.2*
126	Porthcawl UD	Glam	3279	*1.3*	*27.2*	*71.4*	*28.5*	1770	*0.4*	*37.7*	*61.9*	*38.1*
127	Swansea CB	Glam	106776	*2.0*	*26.1*	*71.5*	*28.0*	87885	*3.3*	*29.2*	*67.1*	*32.4*
128	Mynyddislwyn UD	Mon	9014	*0.7*	*23.2*	*76.1*	*23.9*	3072	*3.0*	*38.4*	*58.6*	*41.4*
129	Bridgend UD	Glam	7453	*0.6*	*23.1*	*76.3*	*23.7*	5869	*0.9*	*28.3*	*70.7*	*29.2*
130	Bedwellte UD	Mon	20506	*1.2*	*21.4*	*77.3*	*22.6*	9069	*2.0*	*32.9*	*65.2*	*34.8*
131	Llanwrthwl CP[5]	Brec	387	*1.3*	*20.7*	*78.0*	*22.0*	1677	*3.4*	*24.1*	*72.5*	*27.5*
132	Tredegar UD	Mon	21572	*1.0*	*19.7*	*79.3*	*20.7*	16889	*1.5*	*26.6*	*71.8*	*28.1*
133	Hawarden RD	Flint	19064	*1.6*	*18.3*	*79.9*	*20.0*	11648	*5.3*	*23.2*	*97.2*	*28.5*
134	Cowbridge MB	Glam	1113	*0.5*	*19.3*	*80.1*	*19.9*	1137	*0.4*	*22.5*	*77.0*	*23.0*
135	Crickhowell RD	Brec	7217	*0.3*	*18.2*	*81.5*	*18.5*	6602	*1.2*	*27.1*	*71.7*	*28.3*
136	Brecon UD	Brec	5587	*0.3*	*17.4*	*82.2*	*17.7*	5467	*0.2*	*21.6*	*78.2*	*21.8*
137	Llandaff and Dinas Powys RD	Glam	30974	*0.4*	*16.9*	*82.6*	*17.4*	21385	*0.8*	*23.0*	*76.2*	*23.8*
138	Bryn-mawr UD	Brec	6996	*0.2*	*16.4*	*83.3*	*16.6*	6265	*0.9*	*23.0*	*76.0*	*23.9*
139	Wrexham MB	Denb	17152	*0.4*	*15.9*	*83.7*	*16.3*	13890	*0.5*	*16.7*	*82.7*	*17.2*
140	Hay RD	Brec	3381	*0.4*	*15.2*	*84.5*	*15.5*	3089	*0.2*	*17.5*	*82.3*	*17.7*
141	St Mellons RD	Mon	13353	*0.2*	*14.6*	*85.2*	*14.8*	10713	*0.7*	*19.7*	*79.5*	*20.4*
142	Builth UD	Brec	1635	*0.2*	*14.0*	*85.8*	*14.2*	1714	*0.4*	*15.1*	*84.5*	*15.5*
143	Aber-carn UD	Mon	15072	*0.3*	*13.8*	*85.9*	*14.1*	11516	*1.4*	*19.1*	*79.5*	*20.5*
144	Ebbw Vale UD	Mon	27857	*0.4*	*12.9*	*86.5*	*13.3*	19261	*0.8*	*21.4*	*77.8*	*22.1*
145	Connah's Quay UD	Flint	4216	*0.7*	*11.8*	*87.4*	*12.5*	3095	*0.5*	*12.5*	*87.0*	*13.0*
146	Nant-y-glo and Blaenau UD	Mon	14055	*0.6*	*11.5*	*87.8*	*12.1*	12255	*0.8*	*19.4*	*79.5*	*20.2*
147	Barry UD	Glam	31411	*0.3*	*11.8*	*86.8*	*12.1*	24671	*0.6*	*13.2*	*83.5*	*13.8*
148	Rhayader RD	Rad	4892	*0.1*	*10.6*	*89.1*	*10.8*	5621	*0.8*	*14.5*	*84.7*	*15.3*
149	Newtown and Llanidloes UD	Mont	5722	*0.1*	*10.6*	*89.1*	*10.7*	6091	*0.2*	*12.8*	*87.0*	*13.0*
150	Haverfordwest MB	Pemb	5613	*0.2*	*10.2*	*89.7*	*10.3*	5616	*0.2*	*10.5*	*89.3*	*10.7*
151	Welshpool MB	Mont	5581	*0.2*	*9.7*	*90.0*	*9.9*	5727	*0.2*	*11.2*	*88.6*	*11.4*
152	Forden RD	Mont	5364	*0.4*	*9.2*	*90.4*	*9.6*	5411	*0.3*	*9.7*	*90.0*	*10.0*
153	Buckley UD	Flint	5825	*0.4*	*8.7*	*90.8*	*9.2*	5307	*0.2*	*10.4*	*89.4*	*10.6*
154	Llandrindod Wells UD	Rad	2644	*0.1*	*8.0*	*91.9*	*8.1*	1732	*0.1*	*8.8*	*91.1*	*8.8*
155	Abergavenny RD	Mon	8283	*0.2*	*7.6*	*92.2*	*7.8*	8167	*0.2*	*10.1*	*89.6*	*10.4*
156	Colwyn RD	Rad	1935	*0.0*	*7.7*	*92.3*	*7.7*	1761	*0.1*	*5.5*	*94.4*	*5.6*
157	Abertillery UD	Mon	32078	*0.3*	*7.1*	*92.6*	*7.3*	19820	*0.6*	*10.9*	*88.5*	*11.5*
158	Oystermouth UD	Glam	5739	*0.0*	*7.2*	*92.7*	*7.2*	4175	*0.1*	*8.2*	*91.6*	*8.3*
159	Cardiff City CB	Glam	170016	*0.2*	*6.8*	*92.5*	*6.9*	151925	*0.2*	*7.9*	*91.0*	*8.1*
160	Neyland UD	Pemb	2288	*0.2*	*5.9*	*93.8*	*6.2*	2622	*0.8*	*5.1*	*94.1*	*5.9*
161	Montgomery MB	Mont	942	*1.0*	*5.2*	*93.9*	*6.1*	977	*0.1*	*6.3*	*93.6*	*6.4*
162	Blaenafon UD	Mon	11087	*0.1*	*5.7*	*94.1*	*5.9*	10012	*0.1*	*8.6*	*91.3*	*8.6*
163	Penarth UD	Glam	14597	*0.1*	*5.7*	*93.1*	*5.8*	13287	*0.0*	*7.1*	*91.4*	*7.2*
164	Risca UD	Mon	12981	*0.1*	*5.4*	*94.4*	*5.5*	8820	*0.2*	*7.1*	*92.6*	*7.4*
165	Pembroke RD	Pemb	7977	*0.2*	*5.2*	*94.6*	*5.4*	8248	*0.2*	*5.8*	*94.0*	*5.9*
166	Upper Llanfrechfa UD	Mon	4093	*0.2*	*5.1*	*94.7*	*5.3*	2699	*0.3*	*4.9*	*94.8*	*5.2*
167	Tenby MB	Pemb	4156	*0.0*	*4.9*	*94.8*	*4.9*	4201	*0.1*	*5.0*	*94.8*	*5.1*
168	Abergavenny MB	Mon	8029	*0.1*	*4.6*	*95.1*	*4.8*	7307	*0.0*	*4.8*	*95.1*	*4.8*
169	Pontypool RD	Mon	4754	*0.1*	*4.7*	*95.2*	*4.8*	4224	*0.2*	*7.0*	*92.7*	*7.2*
170	Llantarnam UD	Mon	6475	*0.2*	*4.0*	*95.7*	*4.2*	4868	*0.3*	*4.9*	*94.8*	*5.2*
171	Pontypool UD	Mon	6021	*0.1*	*4.1*	*95.8*	*4.2*	5658	*0.2*	*4.5*	*95.2*	*4.7*
172	Abersychan UD	Mon	22540	*0.0*	*4.1*	*95.9*	*4.1*	16210	*0.2*	*6.5*	*93.2*	*6.7*
176	Pant-teg UD	Mon	9364	*0.1*	*4.1*	*95.8*	*4.1*	6938	*0.0*	*5.3*	*94.7*	*5.3*
177	Caerleon UD	Mon	1935	*0.1*	*3.8*	*95.9*	*3.9*	1270	*0.0*	*3.5*	*96.5*	*3.5*
178	Milford Haven UD	Pemb	5877	*0.1*	*3.9*	*95.6*	*3.9*	4711	*0.1*	*5.5*	*94.2*	*5.6*
179	Pembroke MB	Pemb	14755	*0.1*	*3.6*	*96.3*	*3.6*	14783	*0.2*	*3.6*	*96.1*	*3.8*
180	Painscastle RD	Rad	2193	*0.0*	*3.4*	*96.6*	*3.4*	2207	*0.0*	*3.5*	*96.5*	*3.5*
181	Usk UD	Mon	1423	*0.0*	*3.1*	*96.9*	*3.1*	1380	*0.1*	*2.6*	*97.3*	*2.7*

	Local government district	County	1911 Population 3 years and over Number	1911 Language spoken Welsh only %	1911 Language spoken Both %	1911 Language spoken English only %	1911 Able to speak Welsh %	1901 Population 3 years and over Number	1901 Language spoken Welsh only %	1901 Language spoken Both %	1901 Language spoken English only %	1901 Able to speak Welsh %
182	Hay UD	Brec	1541	*0.0*	*2.9*	*97.1*	*2.9*	1596	*0.0*	*3.8*	*96.2*	*3.8*
183	Overton RD	Flint	4878	*0.1*	*2.7*	*97.2*	*2.8*	4752	*0.0*	*2.8*	*97.2*	*2.8*
184	Newport CB	Mon	77686	*0.0*	*2.7*	*96.6*	*2.7*	62181	*0.1*	*3.6*	*95.8*	*3.7*
185	Monmouth RD	Mon	6146	*0.0*	*2.4*	*97.5*	*2.5*	6035	*0.0*	*2.8*	*97.2*	*2.8*
186	Knighton UD	Rad	1774	*0.0*	*2.5*	*97.5*	*2.5*	1972	*0.1*	*2.7*	*97.1*	*2.8*
187	Magor RD	Mon	4551	*0.1*	*2.3*	*97.6*	*2.4*	4157	*0.1*	*2.9*	*97.0*	*3.0*
188	Knighton RD	Rad	4155	*0.0*	*2.2*	*97.8*	*2.2*	4537	*0.0*	*1.5*	*98.5*	*1.5*
189	Monmouth MB	Mon	4985	*0.2*	*1.7*	*97.5*	*1.9*	4794	*0.0*	*0.9*	*99.1*	*0.9*
190	Chepstow RD	Mon	7432	*0.0*	*1.9*	*98.1*	*1.9*	6958	*0.1*	*1.9*	*98.0*	*2.0*
191	Chepstow UD	Mon	2809	*0.0*	*1.5*	*98.4*	*1.6*	2896	*0.0*	*1.4*	*98.5*	*1.4*
192	New Radnor RD	Rad	2604	*0.0*	*1.4*	*98.6*	*1.4*	2760	*0.0*	*1.5*	*98.5*	*1.5*
193	Presteigne UD	Rad	1082	*0.0*	*1.3*	*98.7*	*1.3*	1164	*0.0*	*0.6*	*99.4*	*0.6*

Source: As Table 3.3. Figures for this table have been taken from Table 3.3 and reordered according to ability to speak Welsh in 1911.

Abbreviations as follows: UD Urban District; MB Municipal Borough; CB County Borough; RD Rural District; CP Civil Parish.

[1] Area administered by Machynlleth (Mont) Rural District Council.
[2] Area administered by Machynlleth (Mont) Rural District Council.
[3] Area administered by Conwy (Caern) Rural District Council.
[4] Area administered by Neath (Glam) Rural District Council.
[5] Area administered by Rhayader (Rad) Rural District Council.

Language 3.5 Census Returns. Ability to speak Welsh and English. Persons, males and females, by age. Numbers and percentage. Wales and Administrative Counties. 1901, 1911

		Age last birthday	1901 Number[1] Total in age group	Welsh only	Welsh and English	English only	*Percentage[2] Welsh only*	*Able to speak Welsh*	1911 Number[1] Total in age group	Welsh only	Welsh and English	English only	*Percentage[2] Welsh only*	*Able to speak Welsh*
WALES														
	Persons	All 3+	1864696	280905	648919	928222	*15.1*	*49.9*	2247927	190292	786674	1208282	*8.7*	*44.6*
		3–4							112434	14594	19596	66343	*14.5*	*34.0*
		5–9							269636	26267	71285	159129	*10.2*	*38.0*
		10–14							242394	14609	81126	138180	*6.2*	*40.9*
		3–14	536259	84917	145977	303956	*15.9*	*43.2*	624464	55470	172007	363652	*9.4*	*38.5*
		15–24	385211	40228	144204	198983	*10.5*	*47.9*	443684	20506	159784	253128	*4.7*	*41.5*
		25–44	559745	70540	214045	272591	*12.6*	*50.9*	708404	44005	267664	384085	*6.3*	*44.7*
		45–64	290939	57858	112551	119803	*19.9*	*58.6*	358582	45063	144627	163837	*12.7*	*53.6*
		65–	92542	27362	32142	32889	*29.6*	*64.4*	112793	25248	42592	43580	*22.6*	*60.8*
	Males	All 3+	937236	137333	324539	470342	*14.7*	*49.4*	1144694	92737	395457	624466	*8.3*	*43.8*
		3–4							56044	7371	9597	33129	*14.7*	*33.9*
		5–9							135161	13500	35159	79986	*10.5*	*37.8*
		10–14							121123	7717	39631	69261	*6.6*	*40.6*
		3–14	268258	43554	72370	151576	*16.3*	*43.3*	312328	28588	84387	182376	*9.7*	*38.2*
		15–24	195792	21604	71492	101203	*11.0*	*47.6*	229050	11212	80059	131903	*5.0*	*40.7*
		25–44	286218	34669	108985	140404	*12.1*	*50.3*	368220	21797	137170	203008	*6.0*	*43.7*
		45–64	145407	26636	56515	61721	*18.3*	*57.2*	184261	21213	74022	86627	*11.6*	*52.3*
		65–	41561	10870	15177	15438	*26.2*	*62.7*	50835	9927	19819	20552	*19.7*	*59.1*
	Females	All 3+	927460	143572	324380	457880	*15.5*	*50.5*	1103233	97555	391217	583816	*9.1*	*45.5*
		3–4							56390	7223	9999	33214	*14.3*	*34.1*
		5–9							134475	12767	36126	79143	*10.0*	*38.2*
		10–14							121271	6892	41495	68919	*5.9*	*41.2*
		3–14	268001	41363	73607	152380	*15.5*	*43.0*	312136	26882	87620	181276	*9.1*	*38.7*
		15–24	189419	18624	72712	97780	*9.8*	*48.3*	214634	9294	79725	121225	*4.4*	*42.3*
		25–44	273527	35871	105060	132187	*13.1*	*51.6*	340184	22208	130494	181077	*6.6*	*45.7*
		45–64	145532	31222	56036	58082	*21.5*	*60.0*	174321	23850	70605	77210	*13.9*	*55.0*
		65–	50981	16492	16965	17451	*32.4*	*65.7*	61958	15321	22773	23028	*25.0*	*62.3*
MONMOUTHSHIRE														
	Persons	All 3+	274415	2013	33677	238131	*0.7*	*13.0*	364590	1496	33801	314530	*0.4*	*10.1*
		3–4							20245	53	610	17466	*0.3*	*3.7*
		5–9							46947	100	1837	41943	*0.2*	*4.4*
		10–14							40436	84	1909	36316	*0.2*	*5.2*
		3–14	83183	392	4464	78258	*0.5*	*5.8*	107628	237	4356	95725	*0.2*	*4.6*
		15–24	57106	275	5314	51355	*0.5*	*9.8*	73778	195	4528	66280	*0.3*	*6.6*
		25–44	82563	576	12076	69675	*0.7*	*15.3*	115682	464	12355	99744	*0.4*	*11.4*
		45–64	39987	493	8973	30432	*1.2*	*23.7*	53039	390	9360	42082	*0.8*	*18.8*
		65–	11576	277	2850	8411	*2.4*	*27.1*	14463	210	3202	10699	*1.5*	*24.2*
	Males	All 3+	141484	1037	17429	122551	*0.7*	*13.1*	191605	782	17832	165590	*0.4*	*10.1*
		3–4							10191	32	282	8830	*0.3*	*3.4*
		5–9							23542	41	884	21032	*0.2*	*4.2*
		10–14							20240	44	935	18188	*0.2*	*5.1*
		3–14	41555	181	2218	39120	*0.4*	*5.8*	53973	117	2101	48050	*0.2*	*4.4*
		15–24	29741	170	2737	26698	*0.6*	*9.8*	39073	106	2346	35077	*0.3*	*6.5*
		25–44	43759	329	6510	36714	*0.8*	*15.6*	62821	267	6826	54310	*0.4*	*11.5*
		45–64	20894	247	4611	15972	*1.2*	*23.3*	28729	208	5072	22858	*0.7*	*18.7*
		65–	5535	110	1353	4047	*2.0*	*26.5*	7009	84	1487	5295	*1.2*	*22.8*
	Females	All 3+	132931	976	16248	115580	*0.7*	*13.0*	172985	714	15969	148940	*0.4*	*10.1*
		3–4							10054	21	328	8636	*0.2*	*3.9*
		5–9							23405	59	953	20911	*0.3*	*4.6*
		10–14							20196	40	974	18128	*0.2*	*5.3*
		3–14	41628	211	2246	39138	*0.5*	*5.9*	53655	120	2255	47675	*0.2*	*4.7*
		15–24	27365	105	2577	24657	*0.4*	*9.8*	34705	89	2182	31203	*0.3*	*6.8*
		25–44	38804	247	5566	32961	*0.6*	*15.0*	52861	197	5529	45434	*0.4*	*11.2*
		45–64	19093	246	4362	14460	*1.3*	*24.2*	24310	182	4288	19224	*0.8*	*18.8*
		65–	6041	167	1497	4364	*2.8*	*27.6*	7454	126	1715	5404	*1.7*	*5.4*

Administrative County	Age last birthday	1901 Number[1] Total in age group	1901 Welsh only	1901 Welsh and English	1901 English only	1901 Percentage[2] *Welsh only*	1901 Percentage[2] *Able to speak Welsh*	1911 Number[1] Total in age group	1911 Welsh only	1911 Welsh and English	1911 English only	1911 Percentage[2] *Welsh only*	1911 Percentage[2] *Able to speak Welsh*
GLAMORGAN													
Persons	All 3+	791847	52493	292399	442107	*6.6*	*43.7*	1033717	31719	361973	608919	*3.2*	*39.2*
	3–4							55141	2560	11554	35195	*5.2*	*28.6*
	5–9							130412	3470	37098	83624	*2.8*	*32.6*
	10–14							112887	1989	36446	70634	*1.8*	*35.2*
	3–14	236126	14474	70443	150149	*6.2*	*36.1*	298440	8019	85098	189453	*2.8*	*32.9*
	15–24	169432	7546	64553	95998	*4.5*	*42.6*	210166	3687	71998	129073	*1.8*	*36.8*
	25–44	250250	15401	100388	132513	*6.2*	*46.3*	339149	8345	126798	197192	*2.5*	*40.5*
	45–64	109587	11163	46217	51751	*10.2*	*52.4*	149397	8029	62940	76001	*5.5*	*48.2*
	65–	26452	3909	10798	11696	*14.8*	*55.7*	36565	3639	15139	17200	*10.1*	*52.1*
Males	All 3+	409769	27416	151587	226940	*6.7*	*43.8*	538343	16199	187504	318379	*3.1*	*38.8*
	3–4							27411	1278	5667	17542	*5.2*	*28.3*
	5–9							65175	1763	18288	42020	*2.8*	*32.3*
	10–14							56225	994	17932	35389	*1.8*	*34.8*
	3–14	117748	7359	35041	74768	*6.3*	*36.2*	148811	4035	41887	94951	*2.9*	*32.6*
	15–24	88376	4463	33619	49141	*5.1*	*43.2*	109391	2061	36933	67168	*1.9*	*36.4*
	25–44	134292	8508	53945	70139	*6.3*	*46.6*	183085	4646	68228	106580	*2.6*	*40.4*
	45–64	57320	5541	23989	27417	*9.7*	*51.6*	80269	4074	33433	41540	*5.1*	*47.3*
	65–	12033	1545	4993	5475	*12.8*	*54.4*	16787	1383	7023	8140	*8.3*	*50.7*
Females	All 3+	382078	25077	140812	215167	*6.6*	*43.5*	495374	15520	174469	290540	*3.2*	*39.5*
	3–4							27730	1282	5887	17653	*5.2*	*28.9*
	5–9							65237	1707	18810	41604	*2.7*	*33.0*
	10–14							56662	995	18514	35245	*1.8*	*35.6*
	3–14	118378	7115	35402	75381	*6.0*	*36.1*	149629	3984	43211	94502	*2.8*	*33.3*
	15–24	81056	3083	30934	46857	*3.8*	*42.0*	100775	1626	35065	61905	*1.6*	*37.2*
	25–44	115958	6893	46443	62374	*6.0*	*46.1*	156064	3699	58570	90612	*2.4*	*40.7*
	45–64	52267	5622	22228	24334	*10.8*	*53.3*	69128	3955	29507	34461	*5.8*	*49.2*
	65–	14419	2364	5805	6221	*16.4*	*56.7*	19778	2256	8116	9060	*11.6*	*53.3*
CARMARTHENSHIRE													
Persons	All 3+	126166	44901	69046	12018	*35.6*	*90.4*	149691	30705	96531	19991	*20.8*	*86.4*
	3–4							7065	2839	2297	1099	*45.5*	*82.4*
	5–9							16812	4497	9603	2167	*27.6*	*86.7*
	10–14							15388	2262	11213	1727	*14.9*	*88.6*
	3–14	36253	14858	17505	3834	*41.0*	*89.4*	39265	9598	23113	4993	*25.5*	*86.8*
	15–24	26170	6542	17079	2507	*25.0*	*90.3*	31083	3320	22703	4774	*10.8*	*84.4*
	25–44	35326	10826	21133	3308	*30.7*	*90.6*	45849	6936	31667	6841	*15.2*	*84.8*
	45–64	20647	8459	10351	1811	*41.0*	*91.2*	24601	6976	14805	2649	*28.6*	*89.2*
	65–	7770	4216	2978	558	*54.4*	*92.8*	8893	3875	4243	734	*43.8*	*91.7*
Males	All 3+	60102	20409	33674	5907	*34.0*	*90.1*	74721	13882	48187	11328	*18.9*	*84.5*
	3–4							3523	1393	1158	525	*45.3*	*82.9*
	5–9							8369	2284	4757	1067	*28.2*	*86.8*
	10–14							7564	1174	5454	835	*15.7*	*88.8*
	3–14	18023	7476	8633	1886	*41.5*	*89.5*	19456	4851	11369	2427	*26.0*	*87.0*
	15–24	12469	3103	8100	1241	*24.9*	*89.9*	16089	1624	11255	3053	*10.2*	*80.7*
	25–44	16685	4739	10321	1590	*28.4*	*90.3*	23339	3116	15994	3988	*13.5*	*82.6*
	45–64	9564	3494	5128	926	*36.6*	*90.2*	12076	2925	7522	1529	*24.4*	*87.2*
	65–	3361	1597	1492	264	*47.6*	*92.1*	3761	1366	2047	331	*36.5*	*91.1*
Females	All 3+	66064	24492	35372	6111	*37.1*	*90.7*	74970	16823	48344	8663	*22.8*	*88.3*
	3–4							3542	1446	1139	574	*45.8*	*81.8*
	5–9							8443	2213	4846	1100	*27.1*	*86.5*
	10–14							7824	1088	5759	892	*14.1*	*88.5*
	3–14	18230	7382	8872	1948	*40.6*	*89.3*	19809	4747	11744	2566	*24.9*	*86.5*
	15–24	13701	3439	8979	1266	*25.1*	*90.7*	14994	1696	11448	1721	*11.4*	*88.4*
	25–44	18641	6087	10812	1718	*32.7*	*90.8*	22510	3820	15673	2853	*17.1*	*87.2*
	45–64	11083	4965	5223	885	*44.8*	*92.0*	12525	4051	7283	1120	*32.5*	*91.0*
	65–	4409	2619	1486	294	*59.5*	*93.3*	5132	2509	2196	403	*49.1*	*92.1*

Administrative County	Age last birthday	Number[1] Total in age group (1901)	Welsh only	Welsh and English	English only	Percentage[2] *Welsh only*	*Able to speak Welsh*	Number[1] Total in age group (1911)	Welsh only	Welsh and English	English only	Percentage[2] *Welsh only*	*Able to speak Welsh*
PEMBROKESHIRE													
Persons	All 3+	82223	9797	18536	53796	*11.9*	*34.5*	84463	6511	20879	55124	*7.9*	*33.2*
	3–4							3632	569	331	2378	*17.4*	*27.5*
	5–9							9055	937	1523	6225	*10.8*	*28.3*
	10–14							8790	449	2059	6014	*5.3*	*29.4*
	3–14	23212	3228	3680	16285	*13.9*	*29.8*	21477	1955	3913	14617	*9.5*	*28.6*
	15–24	16251	1248	3778	11204	*7.7*	*31.0*	16758	614	4123	11714	*3.7*	*28.7*
	25–44	22414	2084	5589	14710	*9.3*	*34.3*	24281	1311	6726	15830	*5.5*	*33.7*
	45–64	14305	1999	3835	8455	*14.0*	*40.8*	15512	1541	4324	9476	*10.0*	*38.2*
	65–	6041	1238	1654	3142	*20.5*	*47.9*	6435	1090	1793	3487	*17.1*	*45.3*
Males	All 3+	38778	4251	8370	26098	*11.0*	*32.6*	40694	2852	9735	27164	*7.2*	*31.6*
	3–4							1818	296	160	1204	*17.8*	*27.5*
	5–9							4576	505	733	3168	*11.5*	*28.1*
	10–14							4439	242	1059	3003	*5.6*	*30.2*
	3–14	11679	1731	1808	8131	*14.8*	*30.3*	10833	1043	1952	7375	*10.1*	*28.9*
	15–24	7680	547	1644	5474	*7.1*	*28.6*	8406	308	1919	5991	*3.7*	*27.0*
	25–44	10310	809	2412	7067	*7.9*	*31.3*	11452	537	3051	7661	*4.8*	*31.9*
	45–64	6508	741	1736	4022	*11.4*	*38.1*	7220	587	1985	4582	*8.2*	*36.0*
	65–	2601	423	770	1404	*16.3*	*45.9*	2783	377	828	1555	*13.7*	*43.6*
Females	All 3+	43445	5546	10166	27698	*12.8*	*36.2*	43769	3659	11144	27960	*8.6*	*34.6*
	3–4							1814	273	171	1174	*16.9*	*27.4*
	5–9							4479	432	790	3057	*10.1*	*28.6*
	10–14							4351	207	1000	3011	*4.9*	*28.6*
	3–14	11533	1497	1872	8154	*13.0*	*29.2*	10644	912	1961	7242	*9.0*	*28.4*
	15–24	8571	701	2134	5730	*8.2*	*33.1*	8352	306	2204	5723	*3.7*	*30.5*
	25–44	12104	1275	3177	7643	*10.5*	*36.8*	12829	774	3675	8169	*6.1*	*35.2*
	45–64	7797	1258	2099	4433	*16.1*	*43.1*	8292	954	2339	4894	*11.6*	*40.2*
	65–	3440	815	884	1738	*23.7*	*49.4*	3652	713	965	1932	*19.8*	*46.5*
CARDIGANSHIRE													
Persons	All 3+	57664	29081	24557	3880	*50.5*	*93.2*	57039	19497	31580	4966	*34.8*	*91.1*
	3–4							2008	1203	392	167	*68.3*	*90.5*
	5–9							5317	2605	2133	360	*51.1*	*92.9*
	10–14							5544	1504	3625	296	*27.7*	*94.5*
	3–14	14595	8610	5165	789	*59.1*	*94.6*	12869	5312	6150	823	*43.2*	*93.3*
	15–24	10986	3720	6213	1018	*33.9*	*90.5*	10698	1898	7378	1276	*18.0*	*87.9*
	25–44	15270	6407	7582	1233	*42.0*	*91.7*	15593	3737	10078	1645	*24.2*	*89.3*
	45–64	11467	6529	4244	669	*57.0*	*94.1*	11995	5059	5902	933	*42.5*	*92.1*
	65–	5346	3815	1353	171	*71.5*	*96.8*	5884	3491	2072	289	*59.6*	*95.0*
Males	All 3+	25147	12036	11257	1763	*47.9*	*92.8*	25537	8078	14508	2475	*32.2*	*90.1*
	3–4							1006	598	191	82	*68.7*	*90.6*
	5–9							2659	1354	1024	170	*53.1*	*93.3*
	10–14							2758	785	1775	136	*29.1*	*95.0*
	3–14	7293	4350	2559	372	*59.7*	*94.9*	6423	2737	2990	388	*44.7*	*93.6*
	15–24	4841	1684	2685	445	*34.8*	*90.4*	5017	899	3328	714	*18.2*	*85.5*
	25–44	6208	2384	3266	520	*38.5*	*91.2*	6518	1446	4287	743	*22.3*	*88.5*
	45–64	4742	2332	2048	352	*49.2*	*92.5*	5246	1887	2820	500	*36.2*	*90.3*
	65–	2063	1286	699	74	*62.5*	*96.4*	2333	1109	1083	130	*47.7*	*94.3*
Females	All 3+	32517	17045	13300	2117	*52.5*	*93.5*	31502	11419	17072	2491	*36.9*	*92.0*
	3–4							1002	605	201	85	*67.9*	*90.5*
	5–9							2658	1251	1109	190	*49.1*	*92.5*
	10–14							2786	719	1850	160	*26.3*	*94.1*
	3–14	7302	4260	2606	417	*58.5*	*94.3*	6446	2575	3160	435	*41.7*	*92.9*
	15–24	6145	2036	3528	573	*33.1*	*90.6*	5681	999	4050	562	*17.8*	*90.0*
	25–44	9062	4023	4316	713	*44.4*	*92.1*	9075	2291	5791	902	*25.5*	*89.9*
	45–64	6725	4197	2196	317	*62.5*	*95.3*	6749	3172	3082	433	*47.4*	*93.5*
	65–	3283	2529	654	97	*77.1*	*97.0*	3551	2382	989	159	*67.5*	*95.5*

Administrative County		Age last birthday	Number[1] Total in age group	Welsh only	Welsh and English	English only	Percentage[2] *Welsh only*	*Able to speak Welsh*	Number[1] Total in age group	Welsh only	Welsh and English	English only	Percentage[2] *Welsh only*	*Able to speak Welsh*
			1901						1911					
BRECONSHIRE														
	Persons	All 3+	50409	4674	18445	27245	*9.3*	*45.9*	55315	3015	19971	31583	*5.5*	*42.1*
		3–4							2636	288	447	1660	*12.0*	*30.6*
		5–9							6386	429	1650	4101	*6.9*	*33.6*
		10–14							5829	238	1795	3711	*4.1*	*35.4*
		3–14	13749	1406	3215	9109	*10.2*	*33.7*	14851	955	3892	9472	*6.7*	*33.8*
		15–24	10310	639	3539	6119	*6.2*	*40.6*	10703	302	3593	6779	*2.8*	*36.4*
		25–44	14701	1145	5945	7598	*7.8*	*48.2*	16942	688	6417	9720	*4.1*	*42.1*
		45–64	8387	936	4042	3409	*11.2*	*59.4*	9361	659	4360	4282	*7.1*	*53.9*
		65–	3262	548	1704	1010	*16.8*	*69.0*	3458	411	1709	1330	*11.9*	*61.4*
	Males	All 3+	25573	2292	9325	13930	*9.0*	*45.5*	28319	1476	10316	16225	*5.3*	*42.0*
		3–4							1277	149	201	832	*12.6*	*29.6*
		5–9							3252	225	849	2070	*7.1*	*34.1*
		10–14							2931	128	921	1843	*4.4*	*36.2*
		3–14	6830	739	1586	4496	*10.8*	*34.1*	7460	502	1971	4745	*6.9*	*34.2*
		15–24	5267	334	1774	3152	*6.3*	*40.1*	5461	156	1871	3469	*2.8*	*36.8*
		25–44	7598	577	3043	3970	*7.6*	*47.7*	8894	341	3382	5107	*3.9*	*42.0*
		45–64	4364	435	2093	1836	*10.0*	*57.9*	4905	337	2269	2271	*6.9*	*53.3*
		65–	1514	207	829	478	*13.7*	*68.4*	1599	140	823	633	*8.8*	*60.3*
	Females	All 3+	24836	2382	9120	13315	*9.6*	*46.3*	26996	1539	9655	15358	*5.8*	*42.1*
		3–4							1359	139	246	828	*11.4*	*31.7*
		5–9							3134	204	801	2031	*6.7*	*33.1*
		10–14							2898	110	874	1868	*3.9*	*34.5*
		3–14	6919	667	1629	4615	*9.7*	*33.2*	7391	453	1921	4727	*6.4*	*33.4*
		15–24	5043	305	1765	2967	*6.1*	*41.1*	5242	146	1722	3310	*2.8*	*36.0*
		25–44	7103	568	2902	3628	*8.0*	*48.9*	8048	347	3035	4613	*4.3*	*42.2*
		45–64	4023	501	1949	1573	*12.5*	*60.9*	4456	322	2091	2011	*7.3*	*54.5*
		65–	1748	341	875	532	*19.5*	*69.6*	1859	271	886	697	*14.6*	*62.4*
RADNORSHIRE														
	Persons	All 3+	21754	51	1309	20370	*0.2*	*6.3*	21279	11	1128	19884	*0.1*	*5.4*
		3–4							868	0	17	786	*0.0*	*2.1*
		5–9							2245	1	26	2158	*0.0*	*1.2*
		10–14							2198	0	41	2122	*0.0*	*1.9*
		3–14	5647	4	92	5544	*0.1*	*1.7*	5311	1	84	5066	*0.0*	*1.7*
		15–24	4406	12	171	4218	*0.3*	*4.2*	4045	1	144	3877	*0.0*	*3.6*
		25–44	6256	14	496	5738	*0.2*	*8.2*	6201	3	397	5765	*0.0*	*6.5*
		45–64	3836	16	354	3463	*0.4*	*9.7*	3998	1	310	3665	*0.0*	*7.8*
		65–	1609	5	196	1407	*0.3*	*12.5*	1724	5	193	1511	*0.3*	*11.6*
	Males	All 3+	11059	38	712	10292	*0.3*	*6.8*	10651	3	569	9953	*0.0*	*5.4*
		3–4							418	0	7	383	*0.0*	*1.8*
		5–9							1153	0	16	1111	*0.0*	*1.4*
		10–14							1125	0	18	1087	*0.0*	*1.6*
		3–14	2718	2	43	2670	*0.1*	*1.7*	2696	0	41	2581	*0.0*	*1.6*
		15–24	2211	10	99	2097	*0.5*	*4.9*	1964	0	68	1882	*0.0*	*3.5*
		25–44	3268	13	270	2979	*0.4*	*8.7*	3041	1	190	2833	*0.0*	*6.3*
		45–64	2035	12	204	1817	*0.6*	*10.6*	2051	0	164	1874	*0.0*	*8.0*
		65–	827	1	96	729	*0.1*	*11.7*	899	2	106	783	*0.2*	*12.1*
	Females	All 3+	10695	13	597	10078	*0.1*	*5.7*	10628	8	559	9931	*0.1*	*5.4*
		3–4							450	0	10	403	*0.0*	*2.4*
		5–9							1092	1	10	1047	*0.1*	*1.0*
		10–14							1073	0	23	1035	*0.0*	*2.2*
		3–14	2929	2	49	2874	*0.1*	*1.7*	2615	1	43	2485	*0.0*	*1.7*
		15–24	2195	2	72	2121	*0.1*	*3.4*	2081	1	76	1995	*0.0*	*3.7*
		25–44	2988	1	226	2759	*0.0*	*7.6*	3160	2	207	2932	*0.1*	*6.7*
		45–64	1801	4	150	1646	*0.2*	*8.6*	1947	1	146	1791	*0.1*	*7.6*
		65–	782	4	100	678	*0.5*	*13.3*	825	3	87	728	*0.4*	*11.0*

Administrative County		Age last birthday	Number[1] Total in age group	Welsh only	Welsh and English	English only	Percentage[2] *Welsh only*	*Able to speak Welsh*	Number[1] Total in age group	Welsh only	Welsh and English	English only	Percentage[2] *Welsh only*	*Able to speak Welsh*
			1901						1911					
MONTGOMERYSHIRE														
	Persons	All 3+	51310	7980	16361	26913	*15.6*	*47.5*	50008	5367	16499	27003	*11.0*	*44.7*
		3–4							2170	443	247	1329	*21.9*	*34.2*
		5–9							5385	815	1152	3276	*15.5*	*37.5*
		10–14							5436	443	1192	3192	*9.2*	*33.8*
		3–14	14155	2459	3102	8578	*17.4*	*39.3*	12991	1701	2591	7797	*14.1*	*35.5*
		15–24	9794	1146	3209	5423	*11.7*	*44.5*	9173	604	3170	5327	*6.6*	*41.4*
		25–44	13856	1793	5014	7037	*13.0*	*49.2*	13796	1131	5205	7373	*8.2*	*46.2*
		45–64	9198	1661	3400	4129	*18.1*	*55.1*	9670	1123	3878	4617	*11.7*	*52.0*
		65–	4307	921	1636	1746	*21.4*	*59.4*	4378	808	1655	1889	*18.6*	*56.6*
	Males	All 3+	24985	3977	7906	13070	*15.9*	*47.6*	24659	2730	7807	13280	*11.5*	*44.2*
		3–4							1141	238	149	669	*22.5*	*36.6*
		5–9							2743	450	565	1656	*16.8*	*38.0*
		10–14							2728	245	286	1617	*11.4*	*24.6*
		3–14	7050	1260	1502	4278	*17.9*	*39.2*	6612	933	1000	3942	*15.9*	*32.8*
		15–24	4681	618	1488	2566	*13.2*	*45.1*	4532	337	1553	2605	*7.5*	*42.0*
		25–44	6583	893	2363	3321	*13.6*	*49.5*	6605	576	2476	3520	*8.8*	*46.4*
		45–64	4567	798	1731	2034	*17.5*	*55.4*	4801	540	1954	2282	*11.3*	*52.2*
		65–	2104	408	822	871	*19.4*	*58.5*	2109	344	824	931	*16.4*	*55.6*
	Females	All 3+	26325	4003	8455	13843	*15.2*	*47.4*	25349	2637	8692	13723	*10.5*	*45.2*
		3–4							1029	205	98	660	*21.3*	*31.5*
		5–9							2642	365	587	1620	*14.2*	*37.0*
		10–14							2708	198	906	1575	*7.4*	*41.2*
		3–14	7105	1199	1600	4300	*16.9*	*39.4*	6379	768	1591	3855	*12.4*	*38.0*
		15–24	5113	528	1721	2857	*10.3*	*44.0*	4641	267	1617	2722	*5.8*	*40.9*
		25–44	7273	900	2651	3716	*12.4*	*48.9*	7191	555	2729	3853	*7.8*	*46.0*
		45–64	4631	863	1669	2095	*18.7*	*54.7*	4869	583	1924	2335	*12.0*	*51.8*
		65–	2203	513	814	875	*23.3*	*60.3*	2269	464	831	958	*20.6*	*57.5*
FLINTSHIRE														
	Persons	All 3+	75931	5722	31568	38544	*7.5*	*49.2*	86570	2946	33587	47886	*3.5*	*43.3*
		3–4							3959	313	790	2438	*8.8*	*31.1*
		5–9							9918	339	2905	6181	*3.6*	*34.4*
		10–14							9600	149	3211	5920	*1.6*	*36.2*
		3–14	21426	1690	6958	12758	*7.9*	*40.4*	23477	801	6906	14539	*3.6*	*34.6*
		15–24	14909	599	6435	7851	*4.0*	*47.2*	16042	254	6045	9458	*1.6*	*40.0*
		25–44	21318	1250	9588	10452	*5.9*	*50.9*	26100	581	10814	14331	*2.3*	*44.3*
		45–64	13412	1353	6389	5654	*10.1*	*57.8*	15122	702	7064	7155	*4.7*	*52.0*
		65–	4866	830	2198	1829	*17.1*	*62.3*	5829	608	2758	2403	*10.5*	*58.3*
	Males	All 3+	37549	3075	15542	18880	*8.2*	*49.6*	42682	1570	16794	23289	*3.8*	*44.1*
		3–4							1891	150	382	1148	*8.9*	*31.7*
		5–9							4992	175	1487	3076	*3.7*	*35.1*
		10–14							4855	84	1655	2966	*1.8*	*37.0*
		3–14	10776	888	3503	6370	*8.3*	*40.8*	11738	409	3524	7190	*3.7*	*35.4*
		15–24	7657	365	3269	4010	*4.8*	*47.5*	8279	152	3138	4842	*1.9*	*40.4*
		25–44	10439	707	4721	4998	*6.8*	*52.0*	12762	317	5448	6841	*2.5*	*45.7*
		45–64	6538	743	3109	2679	*11.4*	*59.0*	7351	394	3480	3387	*5.4*	*53.3*
		65–	2139	372	940	823	*17.4*	*61.5*	2552	298	1204	1029	*11.8*	*59.3*
	Females	All 3+	38382	2647	16026	19664	*6.9*	*48.7*	43888	1376	16793	24597	*3.2*	*42.5*
		3–4							2068	163	408	1290	*8.8*	*30.7*
		5–9							4926	164	1418	3105	*3.5*	*33.7*
		10–14							4745	65	1556	2954	*1.4*	*35.4*
		3–14	10650	802	3455	6388	*7.5*	*40.0*	11739	392	3382	7349	*3.5*	*33.9*
		15–24	7252	234	3166	3641	*3.2*	*46.9*	7763	102	2907	4616	*1.3*	*39.4*
		25–44	10879	543	4867	5454	*5.0*	*49.8*	13338	264	5366	7490	*2.0*	*42.9*
		45–64	6874	610	3280	2975	*8.9*	*56.6*	7771	308	3584	3768	*4.0*	*50.8*
		65–	2727	458	1258	1006	*16.8*	*63.0*	3277	310	1554	1374	*9.6*	*57.5*

Administrative County		Age last birthday	Number[1] Total in age group	Welsh only	Welsh and English	English only	Percentage[2] *Welsh only*	*Able to speak Welsh*	Number[1] Total in age group	Welsh only	Welsh and English	English only	Percentage[2] *Welsh only*	*Able to speak Welsh*
			1901						1911					
DENBIGHSHIRE														
	Persons	All 3+	122195	22366	53238	46435	*18.3*	*61.9*	135607	13637	63224	56499	*10.2*	*57.6*
		3–4							6256	1249	1456	2988	*21.9*	*47.5*
		5–9							15532	1956	5809	7230	*13.0*	*51.8*
		10–14							14746	924	7038	6497	*6.4*	*55.1*
		3–14	33981	7011	12473	14459	*20.7*	*57.4*	36534	4129	14303	16715	*11.7*	*52.4*
		15–24	24504	3031	11692	9745	*12.4*	*60.1*	24974	1421	12544	10733	*5.7*	*56.5*
		25–44	36096	5370	17149	13531	*14.9*	*62.4*	41841	2936	20856	17719	*7.1*	*57.3*
		45–64	20689	4616	9330	6713	*22.3*	*67.5*	23884	3221	11839	8628	*13.6*	*63.6*
		65–	6925	2338	2594	1987	*33.8*	*71.3*	8374	1930	3682	2704	*23.2*	*67.5*
	Males	All 3+	61281	11788	26827	22580	*19.3*	*63.1*	67674	7267	32023	27391	*10.9*	*58.9*
		3–4							3179	673	723	1504	*23.2*	*48.1*
		5–9							7810	1004	2860	3691	*13.3*	*51.1*
		10–14							7432	493	3534	3283	*6.7*	*55.1*
		3–14	17215	3638	6200	7358	*21.2*	*57.2*	18421	2170	7117	8478	*12.2*	*52.3*
		15–24	12710	1759	5990	4940	*13.9*	*61.0*	13117	832	6559	5573	*6.4*	*56.9*
		25–44	17988	2942	8789	6232	*16.4*	*65.3*	20568	1595	10627	8237	*7.8*	*59.7*
		45–64	10219	2389	4645	3168	*23.4*	*68.9*	11782	1741	6046	3938	*14.8*	*66.4*
		65–	3149	1060	1203	882	*33.7*	*71.9*	3786	929	1674	1165	*24.6*	*69.0*
	Females	All 3+	60914	10578	26411	23855	*17.4*	*60.8*	67933	6370	31201	29108	*9.5*	*56.3*
		3–4							3077	576	733	1484	*20.6*	*46.9*
		5–9							7722	952	2949	3539	*12.8*	*52.4*
		10–14							7314	431	3504	3214	*6.0*	*55.0*
		3–14	16766	3373	6273	7101	*20.1*	*57.6*	18113	1959	7186	8237	*11.3*	*52.6*
		15–24	11794	1272	5702	4805	*10.8*	*59.2*	11857	589	5985	5160	*5.0*	*56.0*
		25–44	18108	2428	8360	7299	*13.4*	*59.6*	21273	1341	10229	9482	*6.4*	*54.9*
		45–64	10470	2227	4685	3545	*21.3*	*66.1*	12102	1480	5793	4690	*12.4*	*60.8*
		65–	3776	1278	1391	1105	*33.8*	*70.7*	4588	1001	2008	1539	*22.0*	*66.1*
MERIONETH														
	Persons	All 3+	45631	23081	19674	2825	*50.6*	*93.8*	43209	15857	23119	3340	*37.5*	*92.1*
		3–4							1595	1064	229	104	*76.2*	*92.6*
		5–9							4366	2508	1388	250	*60.5*	*94.0*
		10–14							4569	1443	2791	210	*32.5*	*95.3*
		3–14	12142	7348	4181	602	*60.6*	*95.0*	10530	5015	4408	564	*50.2*	*94.4*
		15–24	8700	3141	5069	480	*36.1*	*94.5*	7460	1548	5202	589	*21.0*	*91.8*
		25–44	13035	5690	6301	1025	*43.7*	*92.1*	12713	3358	7963	1258	*26.7*	*90.0*
		45–64	8750	4892	3293	556	*56.0*	*93.6*	8833	3857	4205	703	*44.0*	*92.0*
		65–	3004	2010	830	162	*67.0*	*94.6*	3673	2079	1341	226	*57.0*	*93.8*
	Males	All 3+	22261	11630	9373	1232	*52.3*	*94.4*	20627	7905	10861	1461	*39.1*	*92.7*
		3–4							762	530	96	40	*79.6*	*94.0*
		5–9							2152	1245	675	115	*61.2*	*94.3*
		10–14							2252	771	1310	111	*35.2*	*94.9*
		3–14	6189	3796	2077	312	*61.4*	*95.0*	5166	2546	2081	266	*52.0*	*94.6*
		15–24	4334	1748	2384	196	*40.4*	*95.4*	3755	910	2518	273	*24.6*	*92.5*
		25–44	6209	2881	2898	419	*46.4*	*93.2*	5889	1683	3649	516	*28.8*	*91.1*
		45–64	4261	2406	1616	234	*56.5*	*94.5*	4229	1901	1993	313	*45.2*	*92.5*
		65–	1268	799	398	71	*63.0*	*94.4*	1588	865	620	93	*54.8*	*94.1*
	Females	All 3+	23370	11451	10301	1593	*49.0*	*93.2*	22582	7952	12258	1879	*36.0*	*91.4*
		3–4							833	534	133	64	*73.1*	*91.2*
		5–9							2214	1263	713	135	*59.8*	*93.6*
		10–14							2317	672	1481	99	*29.8*	*95.6*
		3–14	5953	3552	2104	290	*59.7*	*95.1*	5364	2469	2327	298	*48.5*	*94.1*
		15–24	4366	1393	2685	284	*31.9*	*93.5*	3705	638	2684	316	*17.5*	*91.1*
		25–44	6826	2809	3403	606	*41.2*	*91.1*	6824	1675	4314	742	*24.9*	*89.0*
		45–64	4489	2486	1677	322	*55.4*	*92.8*	4604	1956	2212	390	*42.9*	*91.4*
		65–	1736	1211	432	91	*69.8*	*94.8*	2085	1214	721	133	*58.7*	*93.6*

Administrative County		Age last birthday	1901 Number[1] Total in age group	Welsh only	Welsh and English	English only	Percentage[2] *Welsh only*	*Able to speak Welsh*	1911 Number[1] Total in age group	Welsh only	Welsh and English	English only	Percentage[2] *Welsh only*	*Able to speak Welsh*
CAERNARFONSHIRE														
	Persons	All 3+	117647	55955	49346	12165	*47.6*	*89.6*	118344	42097	59150	14464	*36.4*	*87.5*
		3–4							4839	2796	888	560	*65.9*	*86.8*
		5–9							12122	6007	4315	1217	*52.0*	*89.4*
		10–14							11873	3617	6855	1053	*31.4*	*90.9*
		3–14	29466	16418	10402	2598	*55.8*	*91.2*	28834	12420	12058	2830	*45.5*	*89.6*
		15–24	23683	8800	12458	2374	*37.2*	*89.9*	20434	4592	12972	2524	*22.8*	*87.4*
		25–44	35156	14561	16087	4455	*41.4*	*87.2*	36532	10550	20242	5291	*29.2*	*85.3*
		45–64	21801	11334	8309	2135	*52.0*	*90.2*	23544	9655	10737	2911	*41.4*	*87.5*
		65–	7541	4842	2090	603	*64.3*	*92.0*	9000	4880	3141	908	*54.6*	*89.8*
	Males	All 3+	56364	28089	23041	5130	*49.9*	*90.8*	56034	21291	27579	5913	*38.9*	*89.2*
		3–4							2397	1416	416	277	*67.1*	*86.8*
		5–9							6082	3092	2088	599	*53.5*	*89.6*
		10–14							5929	1952	3294	501	*34.0*	*91.3*
		3–14	14841	8435	5114	1269	*56.9*	*91.4*	14408	6460	5798	1377	*47.4*	*89.9*
		15–24	11481	4878	5660	911	*42.5*	*91.9*	9862	2679	6070	917	*27.7*	*90.4*
		25–44	16519	7289	7420	1775	*44.2*	*89.1*	16876	5351	9318	2034	*32.0*	*87.8*
		45–64	10256	5446	3867	931	*53.1*	*90.9*	11057	4744	5017	1209	*43.2*	*89.0*
		65–	3267	2041	980	244	*62.5*	*92.5*	3831	2057	1376	376	*54.0*	*90.1*
	Females	All 3+	61283	27866	26305	7035	*45.5*	*88.5*	62310	20806	31571	8551	*34.1*	*86.0*
		3–4							2442	1380	472	283	*64.6*	*86.7*
		5–9							6040	2915	2227	618	*50.6*	*89.3*
		10–14							5944	1665	3561	552	*28.8*	*90.4*
		3–14	14625	7983	5288	1329	*54.7*	*90.9*	14426	5960	6260	1453	*43.6*	*89.4*
		15–24	12202	3922	6798	1463	*32.2*	*88.0*	10572	1913	6902	1607	*18.4*	*84.6*
		25–44	18637	7272	8667	2680	*39.0*	*85.6*	19656	5199	10924	3257	*26.8*	*83.2*
		45–64	11545	5888	4442	1204	*51.0*	*89.5*	12487	4911	5720	1702	*39.8*	*86.2*
		65–	4274	2801	1110	359	*65.6*	*91.6*	5169	2823	1765	532	*55.1*	*89.6*
ANGLESEY														
	Persons	All 3+	47504	22791	20763	3793	*48.0*	*91.8*	48095	17434	25232	4093	*37.3*	*91.2*
		3–4							2020	1217	338	173	*70.4*	*90.0*
		5–9							5139	2603	1846	397	*53.7*	*91.8*
		10–14							5098	1507	2951	488	*30.5*	*90.1*
		3–14	12324	7019	4297	993	*57.0*	*91.9*	12257	5327	5135	1058	*46.2*	*90.8*
		15–24	8960	3529	4694	691	*39.4*	*91.9*	8370	2070	5384	724	*25.3*	*91.1*
		25–44	13504	5423	6697	1316	*40.2*	*89.9*	13725	3965	8146	1376	*29.4*	*89.8*
		45–64	8873	4407	3814	626	*49.8*	*92.8*	9626	3850	4903	735	*40.6*	*92.2*
		65–	3843	2413	1261	167	*62.8*	*95.7*	4117	2222	1664	200	*54.4*	*95.1*
	Males	All 3+	22884	11295	9496	1969	*49.4*	*91.0*	23148	8702	11742	2018	*38.7*	*91.0*
		3–4							1030	618	165	93	*70.5*	*89.4*
		5–9							2656	1362	933	211	*54.3*	*91.6*
		10–14							2645	805	1458	302	*31.4*	*88.2*
		3–14	6341	3699	2086	548	*58.4*	*91.3*	6331	2785	2556	606	*46.8*	*89.8*
		15–24	4344	1925	2043	332	*44.4*	*91.5*	4104	1148	2501	339	*28.7*	*91.4*
		25–44	6360	2598	3027	680	*40.9*	*88.6*	6370	1921	3694	638	*30.7*	*89.8*
		45–64	4139	2052	1738	333	*49.7*	*91.7*	4545	1875	2267	344	*41.8*	*92.3*
		65–	1700	1021	602	76	*60.1*	*95.5*	1798	973	724	91	*54.4*	*94.9*
	Females	All 3+	24620	11496	11267	1824	*46.7*	*92.6*	24947	8732	13490	2075	*35.9*	*91.5*
		3–4							990	599	173	80	*70.3*	*90.6*
		5–9							2483	1241	913	186	*53.0*	*92.1*
		10–14							2453	702	1493	186	*29.5*	*92.2*
		3–14	5983	3320	2211	445	*55.6*	*92.6*	5926	2542	2579	452	*45.6*	*91.9*
		15–24	4616	1604	2651	359	*34.8*	*92.2*	4266	922	2883	385	*22.0*	*90.8*
		25–44	7144	2825	3670	636	*39.6*	*91.0*	7355	2044	4452	738	*28.3*	*89.8*
		45–64	4734	2355	2076	293	*49.8*	*93.7*	5081	1975	2636	391	*39.5*	*92.2*
		65–	2143	1392	659	91	*65.0*	*95.8*	2319	1249	940	109	*54.4*	*95.3*

Source: 1901 Census, *County Reports*, Table 40. 1911 Census, *Vol. XII*, *Language Spoken in Wales and Monmouthshire* (HMSO, 1913), Table 1; reprinted in County Reports,Table 33.

[1] The total for population aged 3 years and over includes mostly small numbers of those who either gave no statement as to language spoken or who entered other languages. The totals for Wales are as follows: no language statement: 1901, 2,757; 1911, 58,517; other languages: 1901, 3,893; 1911, 3,762.

[2] The denominator excludes those who gave no language statement but includes those who entered other languages. In general the percentage giving no language statement was less than 3 per cent. In the following districts, however, in 1911 the percentage was greater than 5 per cent: Bedwellte UD (1,188, 5.8%), Monmouth MB (1,781, 35.7%), Rhymni (569, 5.4%), Chepstow RD (414, 5.6%), Pen-y-bont RD (1,185, 5.7%), Betws-y-coed UD (465, 5.2%), Geirionydd RD (285, 6.7%).

Language 3.6 Census Returns. Ability to speak Welsh and English. Persons, males and females, by age. Numbers and percentage. Urban and Rural Districts. 1901

District[1]	Age last birth-day	Persons: Number[2] Total in age group	Persons: Welsh only	Persons: Both	Persons: English only	Persons: Percentage[3] Welsh only	Persons: Percentage[3] Able to speak Welsh	Males: Number[2] Total in age group	Males: Welsh only	Males: Both	Males: English only	Males: Percentage[3] Welsh only	Males: Percentage[3] Able to speak Welsh	Females: Number[2] Total in age group	Females: Welsh only	Females: Both	Females: English only	Females: Percentage[3] Welsh only	Females: Percentage[3] Able to speak Welsh
MONMOUTHSHIRE																			
Aber-carn UD	All 3+	11516	158	2197	9159	*1.4*	*20.5*	6185	74	1172	4938	*1.2*	*20.1*	5331	84	1025	4221	*1.6*	*20.8*
	3–14	3791	32	295	3462	*0.8*	*8.6*	1940	11	147	1781	*0.6*	*8.1*	1851	21	148	1681	*1.1*	*9.1*
	15–24	2427	20	329	2078	*0.8*	*14.4*	1332	7	169	1156	*0.5*	*13.2*	1095	13	160	922	*1.2*	*15.8*
	25–44	3582	52	859	2671	*1.5*	*25.4*	2016	30	484	1502	*1.5*	*25.5*	1566	22	375	1169	*1.4*	*25.4*
	45–64	1411	28	572	811	*2.0*	*42.5*	761	15	304	442	*2.0*	*41.9*	650	13	268	369	*2.0*	*43.2*
	65–	305	26	142	137	*8.5*	*55.1*	136	11	68	57	*8.1*	*58.1*	169	15	74	80	*8.9*	*52.7*
Abergavenny MB	All 3+	7307	2	348	6946	*0.0*	*4.8*	3409	1	149	3251	*0.0*	*4.4*	3898	1	199	3695	*0.0*	*5.1*
	3–14	1901	0	17	1884	*0.0*	*0.9*	914	0	2	912	*0.0*	*0.2*	987	0	15	972	*0.0*	*1.5*
	15–24	1519	0	39	1480	*0.0*	*2.6*	645	0	13	632	*0.0*	*2.0*	874	0	26	848	*0.0*	*3.0*
	25–44	2101	1	138	1953	*0.0*	*6.6*	958	0	63	888	*0.0*	*6.6*	1143	1	75	1065	*0.1*	*6.6*
	45–64	1357	0	108	1247	*0.0*	*8.0*	686	0	54	631	*0.0*	*7.9*	671	0	54	616	*0.0*	*8.0*
	65–	429	1	46	382	*0.2*	*11.0*	206	1	17	188	*0.5*	*8.7*	223	0	29	194	*0.0*	*13.0*
Abersychan UD	All 3+	16210	36	1056	15111	*0.2*	*6.7*	8486	22	563	7896	*0.3*	*6.9*	7724	14	493	7215	*0.2*	*6.6*
	3–14	5540	4	110	5426	*0.1*	*2.1*	2792	3	50	2739	*0.1*	*1.9*	2748	1	60	2687	*0.0*	*2.2*
	15–24	3315	7	130	3176	*0.2*	*4.1*	1805	4	77	1722	*0.2*	*4.5*	1510	3	53	1454	*0.2*	*3.7*
	25–44	4622	12	309	4296	*0.3*	*6.9*	2470	8	161	2298	*0.3*	*6.8*	2152	4	148	1998	*0.2*	*7.1*
	45–64	2111	6	356	1749	*0.3*	*17.1*	1107	2	198	907	*0.2*	*18.1*	1004	4	158	842	*0.4*	*16.1*
	65–	622	7	151	464	*1.1*	*25.4*	312	5	77	230	*1.6*	*26.3*	310	2	74	234	*0.6*	*24.5*
Abertillery UD	All 3+	19820	117	2157	17537	*0.6*	*11.5*	11002	69	1210	9716	*0.6*	*11.6*	8818	48	947	7821	*0.5*	*11.3*
	3–14	6451	14	203	6233	*0.2*	*3.4*	3248	7	101	3139	*0.2*	*3.3*	3203	7	102	3094	*0.2*	*3.4*
	15–24	4357	22	374	3959	*0.5*	*9.1*	2525	12	218	2293	*0.5*	*9.1*	1832	10	156	1666	*0.5*	*9.1*
	25–44	6492	57	894	5535	*0.9*	*14.7*	3837	36	535	3262	*0.9*	*14.9*	2655	21	359	2273	*0.8*	*14.3*
	45–64	2158	22	559	1577	*1.0*	*26.9*	1220	13	303	904	*1.1*	*25.9*	938	9	256	673	*1.0*	*28.3*
	65–	362	2	127	233	*0.6*	*35.6*	172	1	53	118	*0.6*	*31.4*	190	1	74	115	*0.5*	*39.5*
Bedwellte UD	All 3+	9069	177	2980	5911	*2.0*	*34.8*	4866	101	1593	3171	*2.1*	*34.8*	4203	76	1387	2740	*1.8*	*34.8*
	3–14	2845	24	538	2283	*0.8*	*19.8*	1446	15	265	1166	*1.0*	*19.4*	1399	9	273	1117	*0.6*	*20.2*
	15–24	1917	24	571	1322	*1.3*	*31.0*	1037	18	300	719	*1.7*	*30.7*	880	6	271	603	*0.7*	*31.5*
	25–44	2877	56	1114	1707	*1.9*	*40.7*	1609	36	622	951	*2.2*	*40.9*	1268	20	492	756	*1.6*	*40.4*
	45–64	1170	47	639	483	*4.0*	*58.7*	649	24	348	276	*3.7*	*57.4*	521	23	291	207	*4.4*	*60.3*
	65–	260	26	118	116	*10.0*	*55.4*	125	8	58	59	*6.4*	*52.8*	135	18	60	57	*13.3*	*57.8*

Blaenafon UD	All 3+	10012	9	857	9137	*0.1*	*8.6*	5263	5	413	4841	*0.1*	*7.9*	4749	4	444	4296	*0.1*	*9.4*
	3–14	2937	0	26	2908	*0.0*	*0.9*	1516	0	9	1506	*0.0*	*0.6*	1421	0	17	1402	*0.0*	*1.2*
	15–24	2051	1	62	1987	*0.0*	*3.1*	1081	1	27	1052	*0.1*	*2.6*	970	0	35	935	*0.0*	*3.6*
	25–44	3005	3	243	2755	*0.1*	*8.2*	1614	1	118	1494	*0.1*	*7.4*	1391	2	125	1261	*0.1*	*9.1*
	45–64	1650	3	382	1265	*0.2*	*23.3*	880	2	186	692	*0.2*	*21.4*	770	1	196	573	*0.1*	*25.6*
	65–	369	2	144	222	*0.5*	*39.6*	172	1	73	97	*0.6*	*43.0*	197	1	71	125	*0.5*	*36.5*
Caerleon UD	All 3+	1270	0	44	1226	*0.0*	*3.5*	593	0	19	574	*0.0*	*3.2*	677	0	25	652	*0.0*	*3.7*
	3–14	424	0	0	424	*0.0*	*0.0*	214	0	0	214	*0.0*	*0.0*	210	0	0	210	*0.0*	*0.0*
	15–24	230	0	1	229	*0.0*	*0.4*	113	0	0	113	*0.0*	*0.0*	117	0	1	116	*0.0*	*0.9*
	25–44	315	0	13	302	*0.0*	*4.1*	132	0	4	128	*0.0*	*3.0*	183	0	9	174	*0.0*	*4.9*
	45–64	204	0	21	183	*0.0*	*10.3*	88	0	10	78	*0.0*	*11.4*	116	0	11	105	*0.0*	*9.5*
	65–	97	0	9	88	*0.0*	*9.3*	46	0	5	41	*0.0*	*10.9*	51	0	4	47	*0.0*	*7.8*
Chepstow UD	All 3+	2896	0	40	2849	*0.0*	*1.4*	1359	0	22	1332	*0.0*	*1.6*	1537	0	18	1517	*0.0*	*1.2*
	3–14	750	0	2	746	*0.0*	*0.3*	349	0	0	348	*0.0*	*0.0*	401	0	2	398	*0.0*	*0.5*
	15–24	570	0	7	559	*0.0*	*1.2*	258	0	4	251	*0.0*	*1.6*	312	0	3	308	*0.0*	*1.0*
	25–44	803	0	17	786	*0.0*	*2.1*	378	0	10	368	*0.0*	*2.6*	425	0	7	418	*0.0*	*1.6*
	45–64	537	0	11	526	*0.0*	*2.0*	255	0	7	248	*0.0*	*2.7*	282	0	4	278	*0.0*	*1.4*
	65–	236	0	3	232	*0.0*	*1.3*	119	0	1	117	*0.0*	*0.8*	117	0	2	115	*0.0*	*1.7*
Ebbw Vale UD	All 3+	19261	146	4108	14973	*0.8*	*22.1*	10437	76	2136	8202	*0.7*	*21.2*	8824	70	1972	6771	*0.8*	*23.2*
	3–14	5811	20	410	5371	*0.3*	*7.4*	2877	9	208	2654	*0.3*	*7.6*	2934	11	202	2717	*0.4*	*7.3*
	15–24	4138	24	579	3525	*0.6*	*14.6*	2360	16	296	2042	*0.7*	*13.2*	1778	8	283	1483	*0.5*	*16.4*
	25–44	5935	29	1570	4331	*0.5*	*27.0*	3393	22	835	2531	*0.6*	*25.3*	2542	7	735	1800	*0.3*	*29.2*
	45–64	2747	42	1254	1442	*1.5*	*47.3*	1515	20	662	827	*1.3*	*45.1*	1232	22	592	615	*1.8*	*49.9*
	65–	630	31	295	304	*4.9*	*51.7*	292	9	135	148	*3.1*	*49.3*	338	22	160	156	*6.5*	*53.8*
Llanfrechfa Upper UD	All 3+	2699	7	132	2560	*0.3*	*5.2*	1427	5	71	1351	*0.4*	*5.3*	1272	2	61	1209	*0.2*	*5.0*
	3–14	895	4	18	873	*0.4*	*2.5*	468	3	7	458	*0.6*	*2.1*	427	1	11	415	*0.2*	*2.8*
	15–24	551	1	13	537	*0.2*	*2.5*	295	1	9	285	*0.3*	*3.4*	256	0	4	252	*0.0*	*1.6*
	25–44	802	1	55	746	*0.1*	*7.0*	437	0	28	409	*0.0*	*6.4*	365	1	27	337	*0.3*	*7.7*
	45–64	359	1	34	324	*0.3*	*9.7*	188	1	21	166	*0.5*	*11.7*	171	0	13	158	*0.0*	*7.6*
	65–	92	0	12	80	*0.0*	*13.0*	39	0	6	33	*0.0*	*15.4*	53	0	6	47	*0.0*	*11.3*
Llantarnam UD	All 3+	4868	15	237	4604	*0.3*	*5.2*	2554	8	126	2413	*0.3*	*5.3*	2314	7	111	2191	*0.3*	*5.1*
	3–14	1565	4	20	1536	*0.3*	*1.5*	770	2	10	756	*0.3*	*1.6*	795	2	10	780	*0.3*	*1.5*
	15–24	1045	2	25	1018	*0.2*	*2.6*	595	2	16	577	*0.3*	*3.0*	450	0	9	441	*0.0*	*2.0*
	25–44	1353	6	79	1265	*0.4*	*6.3*	735	3	41	688	*0.4*	*6.0*	618	3	38	577	*0.5*	*6.6*
	45–64	736	2	80	650	*0.3*	*11.2*	373	1	45	325	*0.3*	*12.4*	363	1	35	325	*0.3*	*10.0*
	65–	169	1	33	135	*0.6*	*20.1*	81	0	14	67	*0.0*	*17.3*	88	1	19	68	*1.1*	*22.7*
Monmouth MB	All 3+	4794	0	42	4716	*0.0*	*0.9*	2179	0	23	2140	*0.0*	*1.1*	2615	0	19	2576	*0.0*	*0.7*
	3–14	1268	0	3	1259	*0.0*	*0.2*	647	0	0	644	*0.0*	*0.0*	621	0	3	615	*0.0*	*0.5*
	15–24	916	0	10	901	*0.0*	*1.1*	362	0	7	353	*0.0*	*1.9*	554	0	3	548	*0.0*	*0.5*
	25–44	1265	0	10	1252	*0.0*	*0.8*	537	0	7	530	*0.0*	*1.3*	728	0	3	722	*0.0*	*0.4*
	45–64	896	0	15	876	*0.0*	*1.7*	434	0	7	424	*0.0*	*1.6*	462	0	8	452	*0.0*	*1.7*
	65–	449	0	4	428	*0.0*	*0.9*	199	0	2	189	*0.0*	*1.0*	250	0	2	239	*0.0*	*0.8*

District[1]	Age last birth-day	Number[2] Total in age group	Welsh only	Both	English only	Percentage[3] Welsh only	Percentage[3] Able to speak Welsh	Number[2] Total in age group	Welsh only	Both	English only	Percentage[3] Welsh only	Percentage[3] Able to speak Welsh	Number[2] Total in age group	Welsh only	Both	English only	Percentage[3] Welsh only	Percentage[3] Able to speak Welsh
		Persons						Males						Females					
Nant-y-glo and Blaenau UD	All 3+	12255	98	2370	9740	*0.8*	*20.2*	6590	51	1240	5263	*0.8*	*19.6*	5665	47	1130	4477	*0.8*	*20.8*
	3–14	3945	18	238	3680	*0.5*	*6.5*	1956	10	113	1828	*0.5*	*6.3*	1989	8	125	1852	*0.4*	*6.7*
	15–24	2602	16	352	2221	*0.6*	*14.2*	1424	11	168	1235	*0.8*	*12.6*	1178	5	184	986	*0.4*	*16.1*
	25–44	3778	23	893	2845	*0.6*	*24.3*	2187	11	501	1660	*0.5*	*23.4*	1591	12	392	1185	*0.8*	*25.4*
	45–64	1594	24	716	848	*1.5*	*46.4*	871	10	376	480	*1.1*	*44.3*	723	14	340	368	*1.9*	*49.0*
	65–	336	17	171	146	*5.1*	*56.0*	152	9	82	60	*5.9*	*59.9*	184	8	89	86	*4.3*	*52.7*
Newport CB	All 3+	62181	55	2215	59576	*0.1*	*3.7*	30843	35	1129	29373	*0.1*	*3.8*	31338	20	1086	30203	*0.1*	*3.5*
	3–14	18313	2	193	18104	*0.0*	*1.1*	9031	1	90	8931	*0.0*	*1.0*	9282	1	103	9173	*0.0*	*1.1*
	15–24	13860	11	370	13368	*0.1*	*2.8*	6774	6	183	6482	*0.1*	*2.8*	7086	5	187	6886	*0.1*	*2.7*
	25–44	19382	25	889	18300	*0.1*	*4.7*	9731	15	485	9075	*0.2*	*5.1*	9651	10	404	9225	*0.1*	*4.3*
	45–64	8478	13	545	7883	*0.2*	*6.6*	4281	10	265	3973	*0.2*	*6.4*	4197	3	280	3910	*0.1*	*6.7*
	65–	2148	4	218	1921	*0.2*	*10.3*	1026	3	106	912	*0.3*	*10.6*	1122	1	112	1009	*0.1*	*10.1*
Pant-teg UD	All 3+	6938	1	366	6565	*0.0*	*5.3*	3581	0	184	3396	*0.0*	*5.1*	3357	1	182	3169	*0.0*	*5.5*
	3–14	2068	0	18	2045	*0.0*	*0.9*	998	0	7	990	*0.0*	*0.7*	1070	0	11	1055	*0.0*	*1.0*
	15–24	1506	0	51	1455	*0.0*	*3.4*	830	0	31	799	*0.0*	*3.7*	676	0	20	656	*0.0*	*3.0*
	25–44	2013	1	113	1899	*0.0*	*5.7*	1051	0	50	1001	*0.0*	*4.8*	962	1	63	898	*0.1*	*6.7*
	45–64	1050	0	128	921	*0.0*	*12.2*	550	0	69	481	*0.0*	*12.5*	500	0	59	440	*0.0*	*11.8*
	65–	301	0	56	245	*0.0*	*18.6*	152	0	27	125	*0.0*	*17.8*	149	0	29	120	*0.0*	*19.5*
Pontypool UD	All 3+	5658	10	256	5383	*0.2*	*4.7*	2862	6	143	2708	*0.2*	*5.2*	2796	4	113	2675	*0.1*	*4.2*
	3–14	1610	1	4	1604	*0.1*	*0.3*	786	1	2	783	*0.1*	*0.4*	824	0	2	821	*0.0*	*0.2*
	15–24	1314	2	27	1282	*0.2*	*2.2*	656	1	17	635	*0.2*	*2.7*	658	1	10	647	*0.2*	*1.7*
	25–44	1715	6	111	1596	*0.3*	*6.8*	895	4	61	830	*0.4*	*7.3*	820	2	50	766	*0.2*	*6.3*
	45–64	798	1	75	720	*0.1*	*9.5*	431	0	48	381	*0.0*	*11.1*	367	1	27	339	*0.3*	*7.6*
	65–	221	0	39	181	*0.0*	*17.7*	94	0	15	79	*0.0*	*16.0*	127	0	24	102	*0.0*	*19.0*
Rhymni UD	All 3+	7246	713	4283	2245	*9.8*	*69.0*	3780	343	2209	1225	*9.1*	*67.6*	3466	370	2074	1020	*10.7*	*70.6*
	3–14	2228	227	1139	861	*10.2*	*61.3*	1109	96	584	428	*8.7*	*61.4*	1119	131	555	433	*11.7*	*61.3*
	15–24	1488	82	908	496	*5.5*	*66.6*	833	54	476	302	*6.5*	*63.7*	655	28	432	194	*4.3*	*70.3*
	25–44	2213	185	1413	614	*8.4*	*72.2*	1194	97	746	351	*8.1*	*70.6*	1019	88	667	263	*8.6*	*74.2*
	45–64	1051	163	669	218	*15.5*	*79.2*	533	77	339	116	*14.5*	*78.2*	518	86	330	102	*16.6*	*80.3*
	65–	266	56	154	56	*21.1*	*78.9*	111	19	64	28	*17.1*	*74.8*	155	37	90	28	*23.9*	*81.9*
Risca UD	All 3+	8820	19	630	8167	*0.2*	*7.4*	4579	11	295	4271	*0.2*	*6.7*	4241	8	335	3896	*0.2*	*8.1*
	3–14	3159	3	33	3123	*0.1*	*1.1*	1591	1	10	1580	*0.1*	*0.7*	1568	2	23	1543	*0.1*	*1.6*
	15–24	1656	3	58	1595	*0.2*	*3.7*	899	2	25	872	*0.2*	*3.0*	757	1	33	723	*0.1*	*4.5*
	25–44	2640	4	225	2409	*0.2*	*8.7*	1393	3	106	1283	*0.2*	*7.8*	1247	1	119	1126	*0.1*	*9.6*
	45–64	1070	7	221	840	*0.7*	*21.3*	558	3	112	442	*0.5*	*20.6*	512	4	109	398	*0.8*	*22.1*
	65–	295	2	93	200	*0.7*	*32.2*	138	2	42	94	*1.4*	*31.9*	157	0	51	106	*0.0*	*32.5*

Tredegar UD	All 3+	16889	246	4494	12120	*1.5*	*28.1*	8926	135	2322	6450	*1.5*	*27.6*	7963	111	2172	5670	*1.4*	*28.7*
	3–14	5135	19	640	4473	*0.4*	*12.8*	2591	12	327	2251	*0.5*	*13.1*	2544	7	313	2222	*0.3*	*12.6*
	15–24	3495	34	753	2703	*1.0*	*22.6*	1862	21	385	1454	*1.1*	*21.8*	1633	13	368	1249	*0.8*	*23.4*
	25–44	4972	72	1538	3358	*1.4*	*32.4*	2724	48	832	1840	*1.8*	*32.4*	2248	24	706	1518	*1.1*	*32.5*
	45–64	2569	77	1204	1280	*3.0*	*49.9*	1383	40	595	743	*2.9*	*45.9*	1186	37	609	537	*3.1*	*54.6*
	65–	718	44	359	306	*6.1*	*56.2*	366	14	183	162	*3.8*	*53.8*	352	30	176	144	*8.5*	*58.7*
Usk UD	All 3+	1380	1	36	1343	*0.1*	*2.7*	690	0	14	676	*0.0*	*2.0*	690	1	22	667	*0.1*	*3.3*
	3–14	355	0	4	351	*0.0*	*1.1*	185	0	3	182	*0.0*	*1.6*	170	0	1	169	*0.0*	*0.6*
	15–24	262	0	2	260	*0.0*	*0.8*	130	0	1	129	*0.0*	*0.8*	132	0	1	131	*0.0*	*0.8*
	25–44	436	1	17	418	*0.2*	*4.1*	227	0	7	220	*0.0*	*3.1*	209	1	10	198	*0.5*	*5.3*
	45–64	218	0	9	209	*0.0*	*4.1*	103	0	1	102	*0.0*	*1.0*	115	0	8	107	*0.0*	*7.0*
	65–	109	0	4	105	*0.0*	*3.7*	45	0	2	43	*0.0*	*4.4*	64	0	2	62	*0.0*	*3.1*
Abergavenny RD	All 3+	8167	19	827	7317	*0.2*	*10.4*	3984	12	366	3603	*0.3*	*9.5*	4183	7	461	3714	*0.2*	*11.2*
	3–14	1925	5	68	1852	*0.3*	*3.8*	955	4	34	917	*0.4*	*4.0*	970	1	34	935	*0.1*	*3.6*
	15–24	1414	2	74	1338	*0.1*	*5.4*	659	2	35	622	*0.3*	*5.6*	755	0	39	716	*0.0*	*5.2*
	25–44	2359	3	255	2099	*0.1*	*10.9*	1167	1	104	1060	*0.1*	*9.0*	1192	2	151	1039	*0.2*	*12.8*
	45–64	1742	4	259	1477	*0.2*	*15.1*	868	3	119	745	*0.3*	*14.1*	874	1	140	732	*0.1*	*16.1*
	65–	727	5	171	551	*0.7*	*24.2*	335	2	74	259	*0.6*	*22.7*	392	3	97	292	*0.8*	*25.5*
Chepstow RD	All 3+	6958	4	132	6820	*0.1*	*2.0*	3487	0	64	3421	*0.0*	*1.8*	3471	4	68	3399	*0.1*	*2.1*
	3–14	2228	0	14	2214	*0.0*	*0.6*	1107	0	9	1098	*0.0*	*0.8*	1121	0	5	1116	*0.0*	*0.4*
	15–24	1164	1	14	1149	*0.1*	*1.3*	596	0	6	590	*0.0*	*1.0*	568	1	8	559	*0.2*	*1.6*
	25–44	1863	2	54	1806	*0.1*	*3.0*	924	0	26	897	*0.0*	*2.8*	939	2	28	909	*0.2*	*3.2*
	45–64	1202	1	42	1159	*0.1*	*3.6*	598	0	22	576	*0.0*	*3.7*	604	1	20	583	*0.2*	*3.5*
	65–	501	0	8	492	*0.0*	*1.6*	262	0	1	260	*0.0*	*0.4*	239	0	7	232	*0.0*	*2.9*
Magor RD	All 3+	4157	4	119	4027	*0.1*	*3.0*	2139	2	62	2072	*0.1*	*3.0*	2018	2	57	1955	*0.1*	*2.9*
	3–14	1105	0	6	1095	*0.0*	*0.5*	528	0	4	522	*0.0*	*0.8*	577	0	2	573	*0.0*	*0.3*
	15–24	808	1	7	798	*0.1*	*1.0*	383	0	2	380	*0.0*	*0.5*	425	1	5	418	*0.2*	*1.4*
	25–44	1162	2	48	1112	*0.2*	*4.3*	627	1	32	594	*0.2*	*5.3*	535	1	16	518	*0.2*	*3.2*
	45–64	799	1	32	765	*0.1*	*4.1*	446	1	9	436	*0.2*	*2.2*	353	0	23	329	*0.0*	*6.5*
	65–	283	0	26	257	*0.0*	*9.2*	155	0	15	140	*0.0*	*9.7*	128	0	11	117	*0.0*	*8.6*
Monmouth RD	All 3+	6035	1	167	5864	*0.0*	*2.8*	3001	0	89	2911	*0.0*	*3.0*	3034	1	78	2953	*0.0*	*2.6*
	3–14	1626	0	19	1607	*0.0*	*1.2*	822	0	12	810	*0.0*	*1.5*	804	0	7	797	*0.0*	*0.9*
	15–24	1057	0	25	1032	*0.0*	*2.4*	523	0	11	512	*0.0*	*2.1*	534	0	14	520	*0.0*	*2.6*
	25–44	1600	0	52	1548	*0.0*	*3.3*	777	0	27	750	*0.0*	*3.5*	823	0	25	798	*0.0*	*3.0*
	45–64	1191	0	45	1144	*0.0*	*3.8*	607	0	25	582	*0.0*	*4.1*	584	0	20	562	*0.0*	*3.4*
	65–	561	1	26	533	*0.2*	*4.8*	272	0	14	257	*0.0*	*5.2*	289	1	12	276	*0.3*	*4.5*
Pontypool RD	All 3+	4224	8	295	3914	*0.2*	*7.2*	2128	4	145	1975	*0.2*	*7.0*	2096	4	150	1939	*0.2*	*7.3*
	3–14	1121	1	31	1087	*0.1*	*2.9*	556	1	17	537	*0.2*	*3.2*	565	0	14	550	*0.0*	*2.5*
	15–24	776	2	38	735	*0.3*	*5.2*	392	1	17	374	*0.3*	*4.6*	384	1	21	361	*0.3*	*5.7*
	25–44	1213	2	72	1137	*0.2*	*6.1*	601	1	30	568	*0.2*	*5.2*	612	1	42	569	*0.2*	*7.0*
	45–64	752	3	90	657	*0.4*	*12.4*	397	1	42	353	*0.3*	*10.8*	355	2	48	304	*0.6*	*14.1*
	65–	362	0	64	298	*0.0*	*17.7*	182	0	39	143	*0.0*	*21.4*	180	0	25	155	*0.0*	*13.9*

District[1]	Age last birth-day	Number[2] Total in age group	Welsh only	Both	English only	Percentage[3] Welsh only	Able to speak Welsh	Number[2] Total in age group	Welsh only	Both	English only	Percentage[3] Welsh only	Able to speak Welsh	Number[2] Total in age group	Welsh only	Both	English only	Percentage[3] Welsh only	Able to speak Welsh
		Persons						Males						Females					
St Mellons RD	All 3+	13785	167	3289	10321	*1.2*	*25.1*	7134	77	1670	5382	*1.1*	*24.5*	6651	90	1619	4939	*1.4*	*25.7*
	3–14	4187	14	415	3757	*0.3*	*10.2*	2159	5	207	1946	*0.2*	*9.8*	2028	9	208	1811	*0.4*	*10.7*
	15–24	2668	20	495	2152	*0.7*	*19.3*	1372	11	244	1117	*0.8*	*18.6*	1296	9	251	1035	*0.7*	*20.1*
	25–44	4065	33	1095	2935	*0.8*	*27.7*	2145	12	595	1536	*0.6*	*28.3*	1920	21	500	1399	*1.1*	*27.1*
	45–64	2137	48	907	1178	*2.2*	*44.7*	1112	24	444	642	*2.2*	*42.1*	1025	24	463	536	*2.3*	*47.5*
	65–	728	52	377	299	*7.1*	*58.9*	346	25	180	141	*7.2*	*59.2*	382	27	197	158	*7.1*	*58.6*
GLAMORGAN																			
Aberafan MB	All 3+	6952	70	2717	4152	*1.0*	*40.1*	3502	30	1331	2131	*0.9*	*38.9*	3450	40	1386	2021	*1.2*	*41.3*
	3–14	2314	6	570	1736	*0.3*	*24.9*	1140	0	278	861	*0.0*	*24.4*	1174	6	292	875	*0.5*	*25.4*
	15–24	1411	10	566	829	*0.7*	*40.8*	714	4	282	422	*0.6*	*40.1*	697	6	284	407	*0.9*	*41.6*
	25–44	2040	21	928	1086	*1.0*	*46.5*	1057	12	454	588	*1.1*	*44.1*	983	9	474	498	*0.9*	*49.1*
	45–64	952	22	521	409	*2.3*	*57.0*	487	9	257	221	*1.8*	*54.6*	465	13	264	188	*2.8*	*59.6*
	65–	235	11	132	92	*4.7*	*60.9*	104	5	60	39	*4.8*	*62.5*	131	6	72	53	*4.6*	*59.5*
Aberdare UD	All 3+	39932	5382	23067	11307	*13.5*	*71.5*	20937	2743	12102	5988	*13.2*	*71.2*	18995	2639	10965	5319	*13.9*	*71.9*
	3–14	11453	1445	5966	3949	*12.7*	*65.2*	5635	721	2961	1896	*12.9*	*66.0*	5818	724	3005	2053	*12.5*	*64.5*
	15–24	8562	726	5378	2427	*8.5*	*71.5*	4633	423	2848	1343	*9.2*	*70.8*	3929	303	2530	1084	*7.7*	*72.3*
	25–44	12950	1610	8011	3302	*12.5*	*74.4*	7154	881	4387	1872	*12.3*	*73.8*	5796	729	3624	1430	*12.6*	*75.3*
	45–64	5570	1172	3057	1322	*21.1*	*76.2*	2913	567	1600	734	*19.5*	*74.7*	2657	605	1457	588	*22.8*	*77.8*
	65–	1397	429	655	307	*30.8*	*77.9*	602	151	306	143	*25.2*	*76.2*	795	278	349	164	*35.1*	*79.3*
Barry UD	All 3+	24671	152	3247	20502	*0.6*	*13.8*	13131	91	1641	10683	*0.7*	*13.2*	11540	61	1606	9819	*0.5*	*14.5*
	3–14	7918	18	509	7322	*0.2*	*6.7*	3913	8	249	3614	*0.2*	*6.6*	4005	10	260	3708	*0.3*	*6.8*
	15–24	4640	26	551	3824	*0.6*	*12.5*	2484	19	273	1959	*0.8*	*11.8*	2156	7	278	1865	*0.3*	*13.2*
	25–44	8740	54	1450	6841	*0.6*	*17.3*	4848	35	734	3700	*0.7*	*15.9*	3892	19	716	3141	*0.5*	*18.9*
	45–64	2896	40	613	2177	*1.4*	*22.6*	1665	24	329	1251	*1.4*	*21.2*	1231	16	284	926	*1.3*	*24.4*
	65–	477	14	124	338	*2.9*	*28.9*	221	5	56	159	*2.3*	*27.6*	256	9	68	179	*3.5*	*30.1*
Bridgend UD	All 3+	5649	54	1600	3975	*1.0*	*29.3*	2790	30	761	1987	*1.1*	*28.4*	2859	24	839	1988	*0.8*	*30.2*
	3–14	1526	6	187	1330	*0.4*	*12.7*	739	4	83	649	*0.5*	*11.8*	787	2	104	681	*0.3*	*13.5*
	15–24	1197	6	261	930	*0.5*	*22.3*	539	3	94	442	*0.6*	*18.0*	658	3	167	488	*0.5*	*25.8*
	25–44	1811	21	607	1169	*1.2*	*34.8*	919	13	301	597	*1.4*	*34.4*	892	8	306	572	*0.9*	*35.3*
	45–64	824	16	378	428	*1.9*	*47.9*	444	9	201	233	*2.0*	*47.3*	380	7	177	195	*1.8*	*48.5*
	65–	291	5	167	118	*1.7*	*59.3*	149	1	82	66	*0.7*	*55.7*	142	4	85	52	*2.8*	*63.1*
Briton Ferry UD	All 3+	6402	178	2965	3241	*2.8*	*49.2*	3233	79	1478	1662	*2.4*	*48.2*	3169	99	1487	1579	*3.1*	*50.1*
	3–14	1977	45	550	1377	*2.3*	*30.2*	1001	22	284	691	*2.2*	*30.7*	976	23	266	686	*2.4*	*29.6*
	15–24	1426	22	619	778	*1.5*	*45.0*	717	8	317	386	*1.1*	*45.4*	709	14	302	392	*2.0*	*44.6*
	25–44	1839	44	1044	746	*2.4*	*59.2*	940	19	519	399	*2.0*	*57.3*	899	25	525	347	*2.8*	*61.2*
	45–64	955	49	624	281	*5.1*	*70.5*	475	22	298	154	*4.6*	*67.4*	480	27	326	127	*5.6*	*73.5*
	65–	205	18	128	59	*8.8*	*71.2*	100	8	60	32	*8.0*	*68.0*	105	10	68	27	*9.5*	*74.3*

Caerphilly UD	All 3+	14493	599	5876	7944	*4.2*	*44.9*	7726	335	3079	4265	*4.4*	*44.4*	6767	264	2797	3679	*3.9*	*45.4*
	3–14	4391	129	1243	2977	*3.0*	*31.5*	2191	72	628	1465	*3.3*	*32.3*	2200	57	615	1512	*2.6*	*30.8*
	15–24	3030	77	1184	1759	*2.5*	*41.8*	1641	41	607	986	*2.5*	*39.7*	1389	36	577	773	*2.6*	*44.2*
	25–44	4707	197	2170	2320	*4.2*	*50.5*	2631	114	1192	1311	*4.4*	*49.8*	2076	83	978	1009	*4.0*	*51.3*
	45–64	1911	145	1007	758	*7.6*	*60.3*	1045	81	522	442	*7.8*	*57.7*	866	64	485	316	*7.4*	*63.5*
	65–	454	51	272	130	*11.3*	*71.3*	218	27	130	61	*12.4*	*72.0*	236	24	142	69	*10.2*	*70.6*
Cardiff CB	All 3+	151925	329	11966	138003	*0.2*	*8.1*	75496	172	5697	68207	*0.2*	*7.8*	76429	157	6269	69796	*0.2*	*8.4*
	3–14	44248	52	1255	42796	*0.1*	*3.0*	22055	25	594	21355	*0.1*	*2.8*	22193	27	661	21441	*0.1*	*3.1*
	15–24	32489	57	2051	29849	*0.2*	*6.5*	15489	33	939	14038	*0.2*	*6.3*	17000	24	1112	15811	*0.1*	*6.7*
	25–44	49382	110	4865	43654	*0.2*	*10.1*	25048	68	2390	21893	*0.3*	*9.8*	24334	42	2475	21761	*0.2*	*10.4*
	45–64	20957	75	2910	17790	*0.4*	*14.3*	10731	31	1397	9148	*0.3*	*13.3*	10226	44	1513	8642	*0.4*	*15.2*
	65–	4849	35	885	3914	*0.7*	*19.0*	2173	15	377	1773	*0.7*	*18.0*	2676	20	508	2141	*0.7*	*19.8*
Cowbridge MB	All 3+	1137	5	256	876	*0.4*	*23.0*	546	4	103	439	*0.7*	*19.6*	591	1	153	437	*0.2*	*26.1*
	3–14	309	0	9	300	*0.0*	*2.9*	154	0	3	151	*0.0*	*1.9*	155	0	6	149	*0.0*	*3.9*
	15–24	245	0	40	205	*0.0*	*16.3*	118	0	11	107	*0.0*	*9.3*	127	0	29	98	*0.0*	*22.8*
	25–44	318	0	83	235	*0.0*	*26.1*	143	0	32	111	*0.0*	*22.4*	175	0	51	124	*0.0*	*29.1*
	45–64	190	3	78	109	*1.6*	*42.6*	95	3	41	51	*3.2*	*46.3*	95	0	37	58	*0.0*	*38.9*
	65–	75	2	46	27	*2.7*	*64.0*	36	1	16	19	*2.8*	*47.2*	39	1	30	8	*2.6*	*79.5*
Glyncorrwg UD	All 3+	5851	741	3171	1890	*12.8*	*67.4*	3203	411	1712	1054	*12.9*	*66.8*	2648	330	1459	836	*12.6*	*68.2*
	3–14	1971	218	1010	715	*11.2*	*63.2*	954	111	487	344	*11.8*	*63.5*	1017	107	523	371	*10.7*	*62.9*
	15–24	1315	129	742	438	*9.9*	*66.5*	778	82	431	262	*10.6*	*66.2*	537	47	311	176	*8.8*	*67.0*
	25–44	1761	223	1011	514	*12.8*	*70.6*	1021	127	574	310	*12.6*	*69.3*	740	96	437	204	*13.0*	*72.3*
	45–64	678	132	353	192	*19.5*	*71.6*	383	73	192	117	*19.1*	*69.4*	295	59	161	75	*20.0*	*74.6*
	65–	126	39	55	31	*31.2*	*75.2*	67	18	28	21	*26.9*	*68.7*	59	21	27	10	*36.2*	*82.8*
Maesteg UD	All 3+	13701	1506	8353	3830	*11.0*	*72.0*	7665	847	4624	2187	*11.1*	*71.4*	6036	659	3729	1643	*10.9*	*72.8*
	3–14	4138	441	2313	1380	*10.7*	*66.6*	2109	221	1172	715	*10.5*	*66.1*	2029	220	1141	665	*10.9*	*67.2*
	15–24	3009	242	1965	798	*8.1*	*73.4*	1776	164	1119	490	*9.2*	*72.4*	1233	78	846	308	*6.3*	*75.0*
	25–44	4383	446	2779	1154	*10.2*	*73.6*	2566	277	1603	683	*10.8*	*73.4*	1817	169	1176	471	*9.3*	*74.1*
	45–64	1784	270	1116	398	*15.1*	*77.7*	1032	141	642	249	*13.7*	*75.9*	752	129	474	149	*17.2*	*80.2*
	65–	387	107	180	100	*27.6*	*74.2*	182	44	88	50	*24.2*	*72.5*	205	63	92	50	*30.7*	*75.6*
Margam UD	All 3+	8295	400	4681	3164	*4.8*	*61.3*	4234	210	2380	1596	*5.0*	*61.2*	4061	190	2301	1568	*4.7*	*61.4*
	3–14	2498	101	1210	1182	*4.0*	*52.5*	1227	56	604	564	*4.6*	*53.8*	1271	45	606	618	*3.5*	*51.3*
	15–24	1717	30	994	678	*1.7*	*59.6*	906	18	523	350	*2.0*	*59.7*	811	12	471	328	*1.5*	*59.6*
	25–44	2561	88	1521	929	*3.4*	*62.8*	1353	50	792	488	*3.7*	*62.2*	1208	38	729	441	*3.1*	*63.5*
	45–64	1196	113	776	300	*9.4*	*74.3*	618	55	394	162	*8.9*	*72.7*	578	58	382	138	*10.0*	*76.1*
	65–	323	68	180	75	*21.1*	*76.8*	130	31	67	32	*23.8*	*75.4*	193	37	113	43	*19.2*	*77.7*
Merthyr Tydfil UD	All 3+	63681	4630	31763	27039	*7.3*	*57.2*	34291	2468	16535	15134	*7.2*	*55.5*	29390	2162	15228	11905	*7.4*	*59.2*
	3–14	18386	1085	7762	9472	*5.9*	*48.2*	9252	554	3847	4822	*6.0*	*47.6*	9134	531	3915	4650	*5.8*	*48.8*
	15–24	13854	668	7133	6001	*4.8*	*56.3*	7729	419	3776	3501	*5.4*	*54.3*	6125	249	3357	2500	*4.1*	*58.9*
	25–44	20225	1334	10786	7988	*6.6*	*60.0*	11379	777	5785	4733	*6.8*	*57.8*	8846	557	5001	3255	*6.3*	*62.9*
	45–64	9142	1133	5046	2951	*12.4*	*67.6*	4954	561	2640	1746	*11.3*	*64.7*	4188	572	2406	1205	*13.7*	*71.2*
	65–	2074	410	1036	627	*19.8*	*69.8*	977	157	487	332	*16.1*	*66.0*	1097	253	549	295	*23.1*	*73.1*

District[1]	Age last birth-day	Number[2] Total in age group	Welsh only	Both	English only	Percentage[3] Welsh only	Able to speak Welsh	Number[2] Total in age group	Welsh only	Both	English only	Percentage[3] Welsh only	Able to speak Welsh	Number[2] Total in age group	Welsh only	Both	English only	Percentage[3] Welsh only	Able to speak Welsh
		Persons						Males						Females					
Mountain Ash UD	All 3+	28321	1937	11606	14726	*6.9*	*47.9*	15719	1090	6355	8245	*6.9*	*47.4*	12602	847	5251	6481	*6.7*	*48.5*
	3–14	8831	386	2791	5628	*4.4*	*36.1*	4440	197	1371	2860	*4.4*	*35.4*	4391	189	1420	2768	*4.3*	*36.8*
	15–24	6000	267	2516	3209	*4.5*	*46.4*	3553	187	1408	1953	*5.3*	*45.0*	2447	80	1108	1256	*3.3*	*48.6*
	25–44	9616	731	4388	4483	*7.6*	*53.3*	5659	436	2536	2678	*7.7*	*52.6*	3957	295	1852	1805	*7.5*	*54.3*
	45–64	3293	450	1674	1165	*13.7*	*64.6*	1818	234	934	647	*12.9*	*64.4*	1475	216	740	518	*14.7*	*64.9*
	65–	581	103	237	241	*17.7*	*58.5*	249	36	106	107	*14.5*	*57.0*	332	67	131	134	*20.2*	*59.6*
Neath MB	All 3+	12740	279	4780	7647	*2.2*	*39.8*	6280	115	2317	3822	*1.8*	*38.9*	6460	164	2463	3825	*2.5*	*40.7*
	3–14	3775	72	780	2913	*1.9*	*22.6*	1884	35	377	1466	*1.9*	*21.9*	1891	37	403	1447	*2.0*	*23.3*
	15–24	2728	33	911	1777	*1.2*	*34.7*	1293	11	439	837	*0.9*	*35.0*	1435	22	472	940	*1.5*	*34.4*
	25–44	3821	78	1765	1969	*2.0*	*48.3*	1912	36	859	1009	*1.9*	*47.0*	1909	42	906	960	*2.2*	*49.7*
	45–64	1864	66	1036	755	*3.6*	*59.3*	939	25	507	401	*2.7*	*57.0*	925	41	529	354	*4.4*	*61.7*
	65–	552	30	288	233	*5.4*	*57.7*	252	8	135	109	*3.2*	*56.7*	300	22	153	124	*7.4*	*58.5*
Ogmore and Garw UD	All 3+	18134	1731	8763	7620	*9.6*	*57.9*	10290	979	4905	4395	*9.5*	*57.2*	7844	752	3858	3225	*9.6*	*58.8*
	3–14	5531	377	2338	2809	*6.8*	*49.1*	2754	177	1160	1414	*6.4*	*48.6*	2777	200	1178	1395	*7.2*	*49.7*
	15–24	4066	289	1998	1775	*7.1*	*56.3*	2489	187	1149	1151	*7.5*	*53.7*	1577	102	849	624	*6.5*	*60.4*
	25–44	5961	628	3084	2240	*10.5*	*62.3*	3588	387	1823	1372	*10.8*	*61.7*	2373	241	1261	868	*10.2*	*63.3*
	45–64	2205	348	1176	681	*15.8*	*69.1*	1270	189	687	394	*14.9*	*69.0*	935	159	489	287	*17.0*	*69.3*
	65–	371	89	167	115	*24.0*	*69.0*	189	39	86	64	*20.6*	*66.1*	182	50	81	51	*27.5*	*72.0*
Oystermouth UD	All 3+	4175	4	343	3823	*0.1*	*8.3*	1782	1	94	1684	*0.1*	*5.3*	2393	3	249	2139	*0.1*	*10.5*
	3–14	1064	0	30	1034	*0.0*	*2.8*	505	0	6	499	*0.0*	*1.2*	559	0	24	535	*0.0*	*4.3*
	15–24	852	0	54	795	*0.0*	*6.3*	300	0	6	293	*0.0*	*2.0*	552	0	48	502	*0.0*	*8.7*
	25–44	1224	4	138	1080	*0.3*	*11.6*	524	1	39	482	*0.2*	*7.6*	700	3	99	598	*0.4*	*14.6*
	45–64	761	0	101	660	*0.0*	*13.3*	330	0	35	295	*0.0*	*10.6*	431	0	66	365	*0.0*	*15.3*
	65–	274	0	20	254	*0.0*	*7.3*	123	0	8	115	*0.0*	*6.5*	151	0	12	139	*0.0*	*7.9*
Penarth UD	All 3+	13287	3	948	12141	*0.0*	*7.2*	6311	0	392	5734	*0.0*	*6.2*	6976	3	556	6407	*0.0*	*8.0*
	3–14	3747	0	70	3673	*0.0*	*1.9*	1854	0	25	1825	*0.0*	*1.3*	1893	0	45	1848	*0.0*	*2.4*
	15–24	2967	0	179	2719	*0.0*	*6.0*	1295	0	57	1170	*0.0*	*4.4*	1672	0	122	1549	*0.0*	*7.3*
	25–44	4269	2	387	3778	*0.0*	*9.1*	2015	0	159	1761	*0.0*	*7.9*	2254	2	228	2017	*0.1*	*10.2*
	45–64	1878	0	234	1625	*0.0*	*12.5*	954	0	114	822	*0.0*	*11.9*	924	0	120	803	*0.0*	*13.0*
	65–	426	1	78	346	*0.2*	*18.6*	193	0	37	156	*0.0*	*19.2*	233	1	41	190	*0.4*	*18.1*
Pontypridd UD	All 3+	29627	1003	10283	18248	*3.4*	*38.2*	15853	583	5384	9831	*3.7*	*37.7*	13774	420	4899	8417	*3.1*	*38.7*
	3–14	9209	182	2136	6855	*2.0*	*25.3*	4595	97	1056	3423	*2.1*	*25.2*	4614	85	1080	3432	*1.8*	*25.3*
	15–24	6284	155	2010	4105	*2.5*	*34.5*	3451	95	1045	2301	*2.8*	*33.1*	2833	60	965	1804	*2.1*	*36.2*
	25–44	9567	346	3901	5287	*3.6*	*44.5*	5362	218	2120	3006	*4.1*	*43.7*	4205	128	1781	2281	*3.1*	*45.5*
	45–64	3710	227	1806	1668	*6.1*	*54.9*	2021	128	963	923	*6.4*	*54.1*	1689	99	843	745	*5.9*	*55.8*
	65–	857	93	430	333	*10.9*	*61.1*	424	45	200	178	*10.6*	*57.9*	433	48	230	155	*11.1*	*64.2*

Porthcawl UD	All 3+	1770	7	667	1093	*0.4*	*38.1*	780	5	285	489	*0.6*	*37.2*	990	2	382	604	*0.2*	*38.9*
	3–14	447	0	62	384	*0.0*	*13.9*	217	0	19	198	*0.0*	*8.8*	230	0	43	186	*0.0*	*18.8*
	15–24	365	0	103	261	*0.0*	*28.3*	154	0	42	112	*0.0*	*27.3*	211	0	61	149	*0.0*	*29.0*
	25–44	473	0	197	275	*0.0*	*41.7*	198	0	92	105	*0.0*	*46.7*	275	0	105	170	*0.0*	*38.2*
	45–64	335	1	215	119	*0.3*	*64.5*	144	0	95	49	*0.0*	*66.0*	191	1	120	70	*0.5*	*63.4*
	65–	150	6	90	54	*4.0*	*64.0*	67	5	37	25	*7.5*	*62.7*	83	1	53	29	*1.2*	*65.1*
Rhondda UD	All 3+	103740	11841	54906	36754	*11.4*	*64.4*	57292	6458	30117	20562	*11.3*	*64.0*	46448	5383	24789	16192	*11.6*	*65.1*
	3–14	31622	2921	15019	13581	*9.3*	*56.9*	15774	1486	7507	6727	*9.5*	*57.2*	15848	1435	7512	6854	*9.1*	*56.6*
	15–24	23049	1731	13067	8194	*7.5*	*64.3*	13381	1113	7267	4960	*8.3*	*62.7*	9668	618	5800	3234	*6.4*	*66.5*
	25–44	33966	3874	18989	11038	*11.4*	*67.4*	19948	2223	11045	6632	*11.2*	*66.6*	14018	1651	7944	4406	*11.8*	*68.5*
	45–64	12807	2643	6811	3337	*20.7*	*73.9*	7094	1374	3790	1918	*19.4*	*72.9*	5713	1269	3021	1419	*22.2*	*75.1*
	65–	2296	672	1020	604	*29.3*	*73.7*	1095	262	508	325	*23.9*	*70.3*	1201	410	512	279	*34.1*	*76.8*
Swansea CB	All 3+	87885	2861	25567	58777	*3.3*	*32.4*	42792	1334	12073	28860	*3.1*	*31.4*	45093	1527	13494	29917	*3.4*	*33.4*
	3–14	25136	805	5144	19033	*3.2*	*23.8*	12477	413	2484	9501	*3.3*	*23.3*	12659	392	2660	9532	*3.1*	*24.2*
	15–24	19277	372	5552	13143	*1.9*	*30.8*	9076	189	2518	6194	*2.1*	*29.9*	10201	183	3034	6949	*1.8*	*31.6*
	25–44	26567	746	8610	16974	*2.8*	*35.3*	13202	343	4172	8478	*2.6*	*34.3*	13365	403	4438	8496	*3.0*	*36.3*
	45–64	13469	673	4935	7787	*5.0*	*41.7*	6615	291	2360	3903	*4.4*	*40.2*	6854	382	2575	3884	*5.6*	*43.2*
	65–	3436	265	1326	1840	*7.7*	*46.3*	1422	98	539	784	*6.9*	*44.8*	2014	167	787	1056	*8.3*	*47.4*
Cowbridge RD	All 3+	6384	98	2595	3655	*1.5*	*42.3*	3229	49	1292	1860	*1.5*	*41.6*	3155	49	1303	1795	*1.6*	*43.0*
	3–14	1781	14	402	1354	*0.8*	*23.5*	865	7	203	651	*0.8*	*24.4*	916	7	199	703	*0.8*	*22.7*
	15–24	1295	13	429	844	*1.0*	*34.1*	638	11	191	427	*1.7*	*31.7*	657	2	238	417	*0.3*	*36.5*
	25–44	1861	23	837	988	*1.2*	*46.2*	974	13	422	527	*1.3*	*44.7*	887	10	415	461	*1.1*	*48.0*
	45–64	1033	20	638	372	*1.9*	*63.7*	546	9	328	206	*1.6*	*61.7*	487	11	310	166	*2.3*	*65.9*
	65–	414	28	289	97	*6.8*	*76.6*	206	9	148	49	*4.4*	*76.2*	208	19	141	48	*9.1*	*76.9*
Gelli-gaer and Rhigos RD	All 3+	16621	1652	7884	7057	*10.0*	*57.4*	8918	861	4198	3839	*9.7*	*56.8*	7703	791	3686	3218	*10.3*	*58.2*
	3–14	5323	461	1985	2864	*8.7*	*46.1*	2717	237	1011	1459	*8.8*	*46.1*	2606	224	974	1405	*8.6*	*46.0*
	15–24	3480	249	1748	1479	*7.2*	*57.4*	1909	139	917	849	*7.3*	*55.4*	1571	110	831	630	*7.0*	*59.9*
	25–44	5043	447	2677	1910	*8.9*	*62.0*	2819	249	1480	1085	*8.8*	*61.4*	2224	198	1197	825	*8.9*	*62.8*
	45–64	2265	360	1215	689	*15.9*	*69.6*	1234	185	658	391	*15.0*	*68.3*	1031	175	557	298	*17.0*	*71.1*
	65–	510	135	259	115	*26.5*	*77.4*	239	51	132	55	*21.4*	*76.9*	271	84	127	60	*31.0*	*77.9*
Gower RD	All 3+	6729	349	2020	4341	*5.2*	*35.3*	3237	161	977	2087	*5.0*	*35.3*	3492	188	1043	2254	*5.4*	*35.3*
	3–14	1962	157	550	1243	*8.1*	*36.3*	985	78	265	633	*8.0*	*35.1*	977	79	285	610	*8.1*	*37.4*
	15–24	1317	53	448	816	*4.0*	*38.0*	632	20	230	382	*3.2*	*39.6*	685	33	218	434	*4.8*	*36.6*
	25–44	1771	73	588	1106	*4.1*	*37.4*	818	36	267	514	*4.4*	*37.1*	953	37	321	592	*3.9*	*37.7*
	45–64	1206	52	334	818	*4.3*	*32.0*	575	25	165	383	*4.4*	*33.1*	631	27	169	435	*4.3*	*31.1*
	65–	473	14	100	358	*3.0*	*24.2*	227	2	50	175	*0.9*	*22.9*	246	12	50	183	*4.9*	*25.3*
Llandaff and Dinas Powys RD	All 3+	21385	176	4909	16268	*0.8*	*23.8*	10427	98	2431	7882	*0.9*	*24.3*	10958	78	2478	8386	*0.7*	*23.4*
	3–14	6357	20	699	5618	*0.3*	*11.3*	3153	11	372	2758	*0.4*	*12.2*	3204	9	327	2860	*0.3*	*10.5*
	15–24	4287	19	783	3481	*0.4*	*18.7*	1978	15	349	1612	*0.8*	*18.4*	2309	4	434	1869	*0.2*	*19.0*
	25–44	6534	43	1700	4787	*0.7*	*26.7*	3198	25	847	2325	*0.8*	*27.3*	3336	18	853	2462	*0.5*	*26.1*
	45–64	3108	41	1179	1887	*1.3*	*39.3*	1580	22	598	960	*1.4*	*39.2*	1528	19	581	927	*1.2*	*39.3*
	65–	1099	53	548	495	*4.8*	*54.8*	518	25	265	227	*4.8*	*56.1*	581	28	283	268	*4.8*	*53.7*

District[1]	Age last birth-day	Persons: Number[2] Total in age group	Welsh only	Both	English only	Percentage[3] Welsh only	Able to speak Welsh	Males: Number[2] Total in age group	Welsh only	Both	English only	Percentage[3] Welsh only	Able to speak Welsh	Females: Number[2] Total in age group	Welsh only	Both	English only	Percentage[3] Welsh only	Able to speak Welsh
Llangyfelach RD	All 3+	27667	4924	17882	4717	*17.9*	*82.9*	13799	2438	9000	2291	*17.8*	*83.3*	13868	2486	8882	2426	*18.0*	*82.4*
	3–14	8985	1655	5412	1803	*18.7*	*79.7*	4495	821	2751	865	*18.5*	*80.5*	4490	834	2661	938	*18.8*	*78.8*
	15–24	5741	636	4232	864	*11.1*	*84.9*	2896	356	2113	422	*12.3*	*85.4*	2845	280	2119	442	*9.9*	*84.4*
	25–44	7789	1245	5329	1204	*16.0*	*84.5*	3881	595	2695	586	*15.4*	*84.9*	3908	650	2634	618	*16.7*	*84.2*
	45–64	4116	1035	2400	676	*25.2*	*83.6*	2040	504	1195	339	*24.7*	*83.4*	2076	531	1205	337	*25.6*	*83.7*
	65–	1036	353	509	170	*34.2*	*83.5*	487	162	246	79	*33.3*	*83.8*	549	191	263	91	*35.0*	*83.3*
Llantrisant and Llantwit Fardre RD	All 3+	10879	579	5418	4864	*5.3*	*55.2*	5715	303	2821	2581	*5.3*	*54.7*	5164	276	2597	2283	*5.4*	*55.7*
	3–14	3387	120	1335	1924	*3.6*	*43.0*	1686	61	681	939	*3.6*	*44.1*	1701	59	654	985	*3.5*	*42.0*
	15–24	2231	82	1119	1028	*3.7*	*53.9*	1223	47	586	589	*3.8*	*51.8*	1008	35	533	439	*3.5*	*56.4*
	25–44	3284	160	1866	1252	*4.9*	*61.8*	1817	97	1006	711	*5.3*	*60.8*	1467	63	860	541	*4.3*	*63.0*
	45–64	1523	141	863	517	*9.3*	*66.0*	778	67	433	277	*8.6*	*64.4*	745	74	430	240	*9.9*	*67.7*
	65–	454	76	235	143	*16.7*	*68.5*	211	31	115	65	*14.7*	*69.2*	243	45	120	78	*18.5*	*67.9*
Neath RD	All 3+	25160	3195	15661	6259	*12.7*	*75.1*	12990	1644	8156	3167	*12.7*	*75.6*	12170	1551	7505	3092	*12.8*	*74.5*
	3–14	7849	1020	4444	2364	*13.0*	*69.8*	3997	552	2245	1188	*13.9*	*70.2*	3852	468	2199	1176	*12.2*	*69.4*
	15–24	5349	444	3600	1295	*8.3*	*75.7*	2851	253	1917	678	*8.9*	*76.2*	2498	191	1683	617	*7.7*	*75.2*
	25–44	7435	854	4888	1685	*11.5*	*77.3*	3895	459	2592	839	*11.8*	*78.4*	3540	395	2296	846	*11.2*	*76.1*
	45–64	3540	614	2187	735	*17.4*	*79.2*	1818	289	1150	377	*15.9*	*79.2*	1722	325	1037	358	*18.9*	*79.2*
	65–	987	263	542	180	*26.7*	*81.6*	429	91	252	85	*21.2*	*80.0*	558	172	290	95	*30.9*	*82.9*
Pen-y-bont RD	All 3+	15448	616	7903	6850	*4.0*	*55.3*	7986	324	4023	3578	*4.1*	*54.7*	7462	292	3880	3272	*3.9*	*56.0*
	3–14	4030	177	1699	2126	*4.4*	*46.9*	2050	98	874	1061	*4.8*	*47.8*	1980	79	825	1065	*4.0*	*45.9*
	15–24	2967	74	1484	1402	*2.5*	*52.6*	1564	42	759	756	*2.7*	*51.4*	1403	32	725	646	*2.3*	*54.0*
	25–44	4858	140	2598	2089	*2.9*	*56.5*	2592	83	1375	1107	*3.2*	*56.5*	2266	57	1223	982	*2.5*	*56.5*
	45–64	2749	128	1640	971	*4.7*	*64.4*	1384	65	791	520	*4.7*	*61.9*	1365	63	849	451	*4.6*	*66.9*
	65–	844	97	482	262	*11.5*	*68.6*	396	36	224	134	*9.1*	*65.7*	448	61	258	128	*13.6*	*71.2*
Pontardawe RD	All 3+	19206	7192	10602	1344	*37.6*	*93.0*	9615	3553	5324	700	*37.1*	*92.7*	9591	3639	5278	644	*38.1*	*93.3*
	3–14	5961	2561	2963	407	*43.2*	*93.1*	2930	1295	1444	174	*44.5*	*94.0*	3031	1266	1519	233	*41.9*	*92.3*
	15–24	4282	1136	2836	295	*26.6*	*93.1*	2169	584	1406	169	*27.0*	*92.2*	2113	552	1430	126	*26.2*	*94.0*
	25–44	5494	1859	3191	430	*33.9*	*92.2*	2831	934	1653	237	*33.1*	*91.6*	2663	925	1538	193	*34.8*	*92.7*
	45–64	2670	1194	1294	174	*44.9*	*93.5*	1338	558	673	104	*41.8*	*92.2*	1332	636	621	70	*47.9*	*94.7*
	65–	799	442	318	38	*55.4*	*95.2*	347	182	148	16	*52.6*	*95.4*	452	260	170	22	*57.5*	*95.1*
CARMARTHENSHIRE																			
Carmarthen MB	All 3+	9523	1000	6661	1851	*10.5*	*80.5*	4352	403	3050	891	*9.3*	*79.4*	5171	597	3611	960	*11.6*	*81.4*
	3–14	2243	233	1458	552	*10.4*	*75.4*	1084	114	700	270	*10.5*	*75.1*	1159	119	758	282	*10.3*	*75.7*
	15–24	1978	116	1516	343	*5.9*	*82.5*	921	44	714	160	*4.8*	*82.4*	1057	72	802	183	*6.8*	*82.7*
	25–44	2862	244	2080	533	*8.5*	*81.3*	1290	97	942	248	*7.5*	*80.7*	1572	147	1138	285	*9.4*	*81.8*
	45–64	1772	262	1175	333	*14.8*	*81.1*	788	94	522	170	*11.9*	*78.2*	984	168	653	163	*17.1*	*83.4*
	65–	668	145	432	90	*21.7*	*86.5*	269	54	172	43	*20.1*	*84.0*	399	91	260	47	*22.9*	*88.2*

Kidwelly MB	All 3+	2103	621	1331	148	*29.6*	*93.0*	961	283	615	61	*29.5*	*93.6*	1142	338	716	87	*29.6*	*92.4*
	3–14	700	240	423	34	*34.4*	*95.1*	349	116	216	15	*33.4*	*95.7*	351	124	207	19	*35.4*	*94.6*
	15–24	366	72	265	29	*19.7*	*92.1*	149	32	108	9	*21.5*	*94.0*	217	40	157	20	*18.4*	*90.8*
	25–44	556	150	363	43	*27.0*	*92.3*	252	74	160	18	*29.4*	*92.9*	304	76	203	25	*25.0*	*91.8*
	45–64	348	112	204	32	*32.2*	*90.8*	158	47	97	14	*29.7*	*91.1*	190	65	107	18	*34.2*	*90.5*
	65–	133	47	76	10	*35.3*	*92.5*	53	14	34	5	*26.4*	*90.6*	80	33	42	5	*41.3*	*93.8*
Llandeilo UD	All 3+	1851	189	1432	229	*10.2*	*87.6*	801	82	616	102	*10.3*	*87.3*	1050	107	816	127	*10.2*	*87.9*
	3–14	416	40	311	65	*9.6*	*84.4*	205	22	156	27	*10.7*	*86.8*	211	18	155	38	*8.5*	*82.0*
	15–24	490	36	407	47	*7.3*	*90.4*	183	14	149	20	*7.7*	*89.1*	307	22	258	27	*7.2*	*91.2*
	25–44	496	38	387	71	*7.7*	*85.7*	218	15	167	36	*6.9*	*83.5*	278	23	220	35	*8.3*	*87.4*
	45–64	330	41	251	38	*12.4*	*88.5*	145	19	109	17	*13.1*	*88.3*	185	22	142	21	*11.9*	*88.6*
	65–	119	34	76	8	*28.8*	*93.2*	50	12	35	2	*24.5*	*95.9*	69	22	41	6	*31.9*	*91.3*
Llandovery MB	All 3+	1699	102	1323	271	*6.0*	*84.0*	840	33	629	176	*3.9*	*79.0*	859	69	694	95	*8.0*	*88.9*
	3–14	411	10	312	86	*2.5*	*78.9*	242	4	182	54	*1.7*	*77.5*	169	6	130	32	*3.6*	*81.0*
	15–24	389	5	305	79	*1.3*	*79.7*	210	1	145	64	*0.5*	*69.5*	179	4	160	15	*2.2*	*91.6*
	25–44	457	21	369	67	*4.6*	*85.3*	207	7	161	39	*3.4*	*81.2*	250	14	208	28	*5.6*	*88.8*
	45–64	302	29	244	29	*9.6*	*90.4*	123	9	98	16	*7.3*	*87.0*	179	20	146	13	*11.2*	*92.7*
	65–	140	37	93	10	*26.4*	*92.9*	58	12	43	3	*20.7*	*94.8*	82	25	50	7	*30.5*	*91.5*
Llanelli UD	All 3+	23811	2829	16707	4237	*11.9*	*82.1*	11579	1347	8125	2079	*11.6*	*81.8*	12232	1482	8582	2158	*12.1*	*82.3*
	3–14	7078	883	4623	1571	*12.5*	*77.8*	3557	454	2317	785	*12.8*	*77.9*	3521	429	2306	786	*12.2*	*77.7*
	15–24	5054	338	3905	795	*6.7*	*84.0*	2403	179	1864	349	*7.4*	*85.0*	2651	159	2041	446	*6.0*	*83.1*
	25–44	7163	737	5275	1138	*10.3*	*84.0*	3462	342	2552	559	*9.9*	*83.6*	3701	395	2723	579	*10.7*	*84.3*
	45–64	3520	599	2361	553	*17.0*	*84.2*	1701	271	1127	297	*16.0*	*82.3*	1819	328	1234	256	*18.0*	*85.9*
	65–	996	272	543	180	*27.3*	*81.9*	456	101	265	89	*22.2*	*80.4*	540	171	278	91	*31.7*	*83.1*
Newcastle Emlyn UD	All 3+	820	189	593	37	*23.1*	*95.5*	375	79	273	22	*21.1*	*94.1*	445	110	320	15	*24.7*	*96.6*
	3–14	194	53	130	10	*27.5*	*94.8*	92	35	51	5	*38.5*	*94.5*	102	18	79	5	*17.6*	*95.1*
	15–24	161	25	129	7	*15.5*	*95.7*	69	8	58	3	*11.6*	*95.7*	92	17	71	4	*18.5*	*95.7*
	25–44	238	38	184	16	*16.0*	*93.3*	110	11	89	10	*10.0*	*90.9*	128	27	95	6	*21.1*	*95.3*
	45–64	167	52	111	4	*31.1*	*97.6*	78	16	58	4	*20.5*	*94.9*	89	36	53	0	*40.4*	*100.0*
	65–	60	21	39	0	*35.0*	*100.0*	26	9	17	0	*34.6*	*100.0*	34	12	22	0	*35.3*	*100.0*
Carmarthen RD	All 3+	21871	10325	9618	1892	*47.3*	*91.3*	10059	4542	4706	794	*45.2*	*92.0*	11812	5783	4912	1098	*49.0*	*90.7*
	3–14	6167	3300	2276	584	*53.6*	*90.5*	3032	1654	1121	254	*54.6*	*91.6*	3135	1646	1155	330	*52.6*	*89.5*
	15–24	4478	1628	2412	430	*36.4*	*90.3*	2013	714	1111	185	*35.5*	*90.8*	2465	914	1301	245	*37.1*	*90.0*
	25–44	5758	2416	2866	464	*42.0*	*91.8*	2596	992	1409	187	*38.3*	*92.6*	3162	1424	1457	277	*45.1*	*91.2*
	45–64	3838	2006	1537	290	*52.3*	*92.4*	1712	803	798	110	*46.9*	*93.6*	2126	1203	739	180	*56.7*	*91.5*
	65–	1630	975	527	124	*60.0*	*92.4*	706	379	267	58	*53.8*	*91.8*	924	596	260	66	*64.6*	*92.8*
Llandeilo Fawr RD	All 3+	20105	8816	10309	951	*43.9*	*95.3*	9929	4224	5181	510	*42.6*	*94.8*	10176	4592	5128	441	*45.2*	*95.7*
	3–14	5967	3098	2621	237	*52.0*	*96.0*	2975	1571	1289	111	*52.9*	*96.3*	2992	1527	1332	126	*51.2*	*95.8*
	15–24	4185	1258	2684	239	*30.1*	*94.3*	2157	681	1317	156	*31.6*	*92.8*	2028	577	1367	83	*28.5*	*95.9*
	25–44	5639	2112	3221	300	*37.5*	*94.6*	2797	984	1656	155	*35.2*	*94.4*	2842	1128	1565	145	*39.7*	*94.9*
	45–64	3158	1609	1405	142	*51.0*	*95.5*	1511	717	718	74	*47.5*	*95.1*	1647	892	687	68	*54.2*	*95.9*
	65–	1156	739	378	33	*64.3*	*97.1*	489	271	201	14	*55.8*	*97.1*	667	468	177	19	*70.5*	*97.1*

District[1]	Age last birth-day	Persons: Number[2] Total in age group	Welsh only	Both	English only	Percentage[3] Welsh only	Able to speak Welsh	Males: Number[2] Total in age group	Welsh only	Both	English only	Percentage[3] Welsh only	Able to speak Welsh	Females: Number[2] Total in age group	Welsh only	Both	English only	Percentage[3] Welsh only	Able to speak Welsh
Llandovery RD	All 3+	7339	3130	3921	263	*42.8*	*96.4*	3472	1397	1912	151	*40.4*	*95.6*	3867	1733	2009	112	*45.0*	*97.1*
	3–14	1933	981	897	45	*51.0*	*97.7*	965	483	454	23	*50.3*	*97.6*	968	498	443	22	*51.7*	*97.7*
	15–24	1525	405	1037	78	*26.6*	*94.9*	723	204	463	54	*28.3*	*92.5*	802	201	574	24	*25.2*	*97.0*
	25–44	1882	647	1158	73	*34.5*	*96.1*	870	282	555	31	*32.5*	*96.4*	1012	365	603	42	*36.1*	*95.8*
	45–64	1389	685	641	58	*49.5*	*95.8*	635	267	328	37	*42.2*	*94.1*	754	418	313	21	*55.6*	*97.2*
	65–	610	412	188	9	*67.7*	*98.5*	279	161	112	6	*57.7*	*97.8*	331	251	76	3	*76.1*	*99.1*
Llanelli RD	All 3+	22326	8708	12190	1407	*39.0*	*93.7*	10965	4126	6093	732	*37.7*	*93.3*	11361	4582	6097	675	*40.4*	*94.1*
	3–14	7071	3130	3467	471	*44.3*	*93.3*	3465	1556	1665	242	*44.9*	*93.0*	3606	1574	1802	229	*43.7*	*93.6*
	15–24	4598	1272	3058	265	*27.7*	*94.2*	2302	656	1514	131	*28.5*	*94.3*	2296	616	1544	134	*26.9*	*94.2*
	25–44	6375	2309	3658	395	*36.3*	*93.7*	3192	1099	1880	203	*34.5*	*93.5*	3183	1210	1778	192	*38.1*	*94.0*
	45–64	3272	1439	1609	222	*44.0*	*93.2*	1579	614	831	133	*38.9*	*91.5*	1693	825	778	89	*48.8*	*94.7*
	65–	1010	558	398	54	*55.2*	*94.7*	427	201	203	23	*47.1*	*94.6*	583	357	195	31	*61.2*	*94.7*
Llanybydder RD	All 3+	3574	2419	1095	59	*67.7*	*98.3*	1652	1050	561	40	*63.6*	*97.6*	1922	1369	534	19	*71.2*	*99.0*
	3–14	979	751	218	10	*76.7*	*99.0*	486	380	100	6	*78.2*	*98.8*	493	371	118	4	*75.3*	*99.2*
	15–24	641	306	317	18	*47.7*	*97.2*	313	127	170	16	*40.6*	*94.9*	328	179	147	2	*54.6*	*99.4*
	25–44	948	567	366	15	*59.8*	*98.4*	399	217	171	11	*54.4*	*97.2*	549	350	195	4	*63.8*	*99.3*
	45–64	644	470	159	15	*73.0*	*97.7*	290	191	93	6	*65.9*	*97.9*	354	279	66	9	*78.8*	*97.5*
	65–	362	325	35	1	*90.0*	*99.7*	164	135	27	1	*82.8*	*99.4*	198	190	8	0	*96.0*	*100.0*
Newcastle Emlyn RD	All 3+	6182	4531	1580	50	*73.5*	*99.2*	2828	1961	828	35	*69.4*	*98.8*	3354	2570	752	15	*77.0*	*99.6*
	3–14	1788	1492	283	5	*83.8*	*99.7*	916	759	151	5	*83.0*	*99.5*	872	733	132	0	*84.7*	*100.0*
	15–24	1254	753	483	16	*60.1*	*98.7*	542	291	238	12	*53.8*	*97.8*	712	462	245	4	*65.0*	*99.4*
	25–44	1640	1096	523	16	*67.0*	*99.0*	731	450	272	8	*61.6*	*98.9*	909	646	251	8	*71.4*	*99.1*
	45–64	1035	785	236	11	*76.1*	*98.9*	449	307	133	8	*68.5*	*98.2*	586	478	103	3	*81.8*	*99.5*
	65–	465	405	55	2	*87.7*	*99.6*	190	154	34	2	*81.1*	*98.9*	275	251	21	0	*92.3*	*100.0*
Whitland RD	All 3+	4962	2042	2286	623	*41.2*	*87.4*	2289	882	1085	314	*38.7*	*86.2*	2673	1160	1201	309	*43.4*	*88.4*
	3–14	1306	647	486	164	*49.9*	*87.4*	655	328	231	89	*50.6*	*86.3*	651	319	255	75	*49.2*	*88.4*
	15–24	1051	328	561	161	*31.2*	*84.7*	484	152	249	82	*31.5*	*83.0*	567	176	312	79	*31.0*	*86.1*
	25–44	1312	451	683	177	*34.4*	*86.5*	561	169	307	85	*30.1*	*84.8*	751	282	376	92	*37.6*	*87.7*
	45–64	872	370	418	84	*42.4*	*90.4*	395	139	216	40	*35.2*	*89.9*	477	231	202	44	*48.4*	*90.8*
	65–	421	246	138	37	*58.4*	*91.2*	194	94	82	18	*48.5*	*90.7*	227	152	56	19	*67.0*	*91 6*
PEMBROKESHIRE																			
Haverfordwest MB	All 3+	5616	9	590	5012	*0.2*	*10.7*	2535	1	250	2281	*0.0*	*9.9*	3081	8	340	2731	*0.3*	*11.3*
	3–14	1567	0	51	1515	*0.0*	*3.3*	798	0	28	770	*0.0*	*3.5*	769	0	23	745	*0.0*	*3.0*
	15–24	1050	1	106	943	*0.1*	*10.2*	448	0	52	396	*0.0*	*11.6*	602	1	54	547	*0.2*	*9.1*
	25–44	1591	2	218	1369	*0.1*	*13.8*	674	0	84	589	*0.0*	*12.5*	917	2	134	780	*0.2*	*14.8*
	45–64	971	5	139	826	*0.5*	*14.8*	422	1	55	365	*0.2*	*13.3*	549	4	84	461	*0.7*	*16.0*
	65–	437	1	76	359	*0.2*	*17.6*	193	0	31	161	*0.0*	*16.1*	244	1	45	198	*0.4*	*18.9*

Milford Haven UD	All 3+	4711	6	259	4435	0.1	5.6	2514	5	129	2369	0.2	5.3	2197	1	130	2066	0.0	6.0
	3–14	1269	0	16	1253	0.0	1.3	599	0	6	593	0.0	1.0	670	0	10	660	0.0	1.5
	15–24	1136	1	53	1079	0.1	4.8	652	1	28	620	0.2	4.4	484	0	25	459	0.0	5.2
	25–44	1516	5	114	1390	0.3	7.9	869	4	59	799	0.5	7.3	647	1	55	591	0.2	8.7
	45–64	607	0	48	558	0.0	7.9	314	0	25	288	0.0	8.0	293	0	23	270	0.0	7.8
	65–	183	0	28	155	0.0	15.3	80	0	11	69	0.0	13.8	103	0	17	86	0.0	16.5
Neyland UD	All 3+	2622	21	134	2467	0.8	5.9	1316	21	65	1230	1.6	6.5	1306	0	69	1237	0.0	5.3
	3–14	802	0	13	789	0.0	1.6	403	0	7	396	0.0	1.7	399	0	6	393	0.0	1.5
	15–24	563	1	18	544	0.2	3.4	289	1	10	278	0.3	3.8	274	0	8	266	0.0	2.9
	25–44	720	17	48	655	2.4	9.0	359	17	26	316	4.7	12.0	361	0	22	339	0.0	6.1
	45–64	432	3	43	386	0.7	10.6	211	3	17	191	1.4	9.5	221	0	26	195	0.0	11.8
	65–	105	0	12	93	0.0	11.4	54	0	5	49	0.0	9.3	51	0	7	44	0.0	13.7
Pembroke MB	All 3+	14783	25	538	14209	0.2	3.8	7404	9	267	7118	0.1	3.7	7379	16	271	7091	0.2	3.9
	3–14	4208	9	43	4156	0.2	1.2	2072	5	13	2054	0.2	0.9	2136	4	30	2102	0.2	1.6
	15–24	3064	8	73	2979	0.3	2.6	1575	2	34	1535	0.1	2.3	1489	6	39	1444	0.4	3.0
	25–44	4233	6	212	4011	0.1	5.2	2185	2	120	2059	0.1	5.6	2048	4	92	1952	0.2	4.7
	45–64	2430	2	167	2259	0.1	7.0	1188	0	83	1104	0.0	7.0	1242	2	84	1155	0.2	6.9
	65–	848	0	43	804	0.0	5.1	384	0	17	366	0.0	4.4	464	0	26	438	0.0	5.6
Tenby MB	All 3+	4201	6	209	3984	0.1	5.1	1711	1	89	1619	0.1	5.3	2490	5	120	2365	0.2	5.0
	3–14	997	0	2	995	0.0	0.2	524	0	1	523	0.0	0.2	473	0	1	472	0.0	0.2
	15–24	901	1	40	858	0.1	4.6	321	0	13	306	0.0	4.0	580	1	27	552	0.2	4.8
	25–44	1216	4	82	1130	0.3	7.1	430	1	35	394	0.2	8.4	786	3	47	736	0.4	6.4
	45–64	786	1	59	726	0.1	7.6	334	0	26	308	0.0	7.8	452	1	33	418	0.2	7.5
	65–	301	0	26	275	0.0	8.6	102	0	14	88	0.0	13.7	199	0	12	187	0.0	6.0
Haverfordwest RD	All 3+	20553	3065	8257	9212	14.9	55.1	9701	1382	3732	4579	14.3	52.8	10852	1683	4525	4633	15.5	57.3
	3–14	6052	1139	1828	3079	18.8	49.1	3050	622	908	1518	20.4	50.2	3002	517	920	1561	17.2	47.9
	15–24	3959	369	1748	1837	9.3	53.5	1845	174	744	925	9.4	49.8	2114	195	1004	912	9.2	56.8
	25–44	5382	583	2336	2457	10.8	54.3	2460	228	1003	1226	9.3	50.1	2922	355	1333	1231	12.2	57.8
	45–64	3511	586	1610	1314	16.7	62.6	1612	222	723	666	13.8	58.7	1899	364	887	648	19.2	65.9
	65–	1649	388	735	525	23.5	68.1	734	136	354	244	18.5	66.8	915	252	381	281	27.6	69.3
Llanfyrnach RD	All 3+	2312	1771	508	30	76.7	98.7	1032	758	259	15	73.4	98.5	1280	1013	249	15	79.3	98.8
	3–14	664	567	91	4	85.6	99.4	338	290	46	2	85.8	99.4	326	277	45	2	85.5	99.4
	15–24	399	257	131	11	64.4	97.2	169	102	60	7	60.4	95.9	230	155	71	4	67.4	98.3
	25–44	622	437	175	9	70.4	98.6	264	168	91	5	63.6	98.1	358	269	84	4	75.4	98.9
	45–64	423	330	88	5	78.0	98.8	178	127	50	1	71.3	99.4	245	203	38	4	82.9	98.4
	65–	204	180	23	1	88.2	99.5	83	71	12	0	85.5	100.0	121	109	11	1	90.1	99.2
Narberth RD	All 3+	11378	1273	3711	6381	11.2	43.9	5285	561	1731	2987	10.6	43.4	6093	712	1980	3394	11.7	44.2
	3–14	3143	436	715	1991	13.9	36.6	1619	242	367	1010	14.9	37.6	1524	194	348	981	12.7	35.6
	15–24	2161	175	708	1276	8.1	40.9	1018	73	344	599	7.2	41.0	1143	102	364	677	8.9	40.8
	25–44	3002	252	1097	1650	8.4	45.0	1304	92	477	734	7.1	43.7	1698	160	620	916	9.4	46.0
	45–64	2172	256	846	1064	11.8	50.9	983	100	396	484	10.2	50.6	1189	156	450	580	13.2	51.1
	65–	900	154	345	400	17.1	55.5	361	54	147	160	15.0	55.7	539	100	198	240	18.6	55.4

District[1]	Age last birth-day	Number[2] Total in age group	Welsh only	Both	English only	Percentage[3] Welsh only	Able to speak Welsh	Number[2] Total in age group	Welsh only	Both	English only	Percentage[3] Welsh only	Able to speak Welsh	Number[2] Total in age group	Welsh only	Both	English only	Percentage[3] Welsh only	Able to speak Welsh
		Persons						Males						Females					
Pembroke RD	All 3+	8248	16	474	7747	*0.2*	*5.9*	3950	12	182	3747	*0.3*	*4.9*	4298	4	292	4000	*0.1*	*6.9*
	3–14	2460	0	41	2416	*0.0*	*1.7*	1240	0	20	1217	*0.0*	*1.6*	1220	0	21	1199	*0.0*	*1.7*
	15–24	1677	4	55	1617	*0.2*	*3.5*	799	4	22	772	*0.5*	*3.3*	878	0	33	845	*0.0*	*3.8*
	25–44	2109	7	167	1931	*0.3*	*8.3*	968	5	62	898	*0.5*	*6.9*	1141	2	105	1033	*0.2*	*9.4*
	45–64	1402	3	129	1268	*0.2*	*9.4*	647	2	48	596	*0.3*	*7.7*	755	1	81	672	*0.1*	*10.9*
	65–	600	2	82	515	*0.3*	*14.0*	296	1	30	264	*0.3*	*10.5*	304	1	52	251	*0.3*	*17.4*
St Dogmaels RD	All 3+	7799	3605	3856	319	*46.3*	*95.9*	3330	1501	1666	153	*45.2*	*95.4*	4469	2104	2190	166	*47.2*	*96.3*
	3–14	2050	1077	880	87	*52.7*	*95.7*	1036	572	412	48	*55.4*	*95.3*	1014	505	468	39	*49.9*	*96.1*
	15–24	1341	431	846	60	*32.2*	*95.5*	564	190	337	36	*33.7*	*93.6*	777	241	509	24	*31.1*	*96.9*
	25–44	2023	771	1140	108	*38.2*	*94.6*	797	292	455	47	*36.8*	*94.1*	1226	479	685	61	*39.1*	*94.9*
	45–64	1571	813	706	49	*51.8*	*96.9*	619	286	313	19	*46.3*	*96.9*	952	527	393	30	*55.5*	*96.8*
	65–	814	513	284	15	*63.2*	*98.2*	314	161	149	3	*51.4*	*99.0*	500	352	135	12	*70.5*	*97.6*
CARDIGANSHIRE																			
Aberaeron UD	All 3+	1250	327	857	59	*26.3*	*95.3*	461	113	313	33	*24.6*	*92.8*	789	214	544	26	*27.3*	*96.7*
	3–14	315	91	212	8	*29.3*	*97.4*	149	40	105	3	*27.0*	*98.0*	166	51	107	5	*31.3*	*96.9*
	15–24	202	29	161	11	*14.4*	*94.5*	68	15	47	6	*22.1*	*91.2*	134	14	114	5	*10.5*	*96.2*
	25–44	344	63	254	27	*18.3*	*92.2*	110	24	71	15	*21.8*	*86.4*	234	39	183	12	*16.7*	*94.9*
	45–64	248	79	160	8	*32.0*	*96.8*	87	20	62	5	*23.0*	*94.3*	161	59	98	3	*36.9*	*98.1*
	65–	141	65	70	5	*46.4*	*96.4*	47	14	28	4	*30.4*	*91.3*	94	51	42	1	*54.3*	*98.9*
Aberystwyth MB	All 3+	7649	587	5046	2005	*7.7*	*73.7*	3258	237	2205	809	*7.3*	*75.0*	4391	350	2841	1196	*8.0*	*72.7*
	3–14	1482	134	952	393	*9.1*	*73.4*	712	70	454	188	*9.8*	*73.6*	770	64	498	205	*8.3*	*73.3*
	15–24	2037	62	1349	622	*3.0*	*69.3*	843	31	581	227	*3.7*	*72.7*	1194	31	768	395	*2.6*	*66.9*
	25–44	2450	149	1685	613	*6.1*	*74.9*	1035	69	733	231	*6.7*	*77.6*	1415	80	952	382	*5.7*	*72.9*
	45–64	1255	133	813	309	*10.6*	*75.4*	520	39	337	144	*7.5*	*72.3*	735	94	476	165	*12.8*	*77.6*
	65–	425	109	247	68	*25.7*	*84.0*	148	28	100	19	*19.0*	*87.1*	277	81	147	49	*29.2*	*82.3*
Cardigan MB	All 3+	3310	679	2355	267	*20.6*	*91.9*	1388	249	1023	113	*18.0*	*91.8*	1922	430	1332	154	*22.4*	*92.0*
	3–14	894	176	632	81	*19.8*	*90.9*	429	86	306	35	*20.1*	*91.8*	465	90	326	46	*19.5*	*90.0*
	15–24	603	70	509	24	*11.6*	*96.0*	253	28	215	10	*11.1*	*96.0*	350	42	294	14	*12.0*	*96.0*
	25–44	863	141	636	83	*16.4*	*90.3*	343	53	256	34	*15.5*	*90.1*	520	88	380	49	*17.0*	*90.5*
	45–64	670	181	431	57	*27.1*	*91.5*	250	49	175	25	*19.7*	*90.0*	420	132	256	32	*31.4*	*92.4*
	65–	280	111	147	22	*39.6*	*92.1*	113	33	71	9	*29.2*	*92.0*	167	78	76	13	*46.7*	*92.2*
Lampeter MB	All 3+	1638	331	1161	141	*20.3*	*91.3*	731	125	533	71	*17.1*	*90.3*	907	206	628	70	*22.8*	*92.2*
	3–14	385	83	267	31	*21.8*	*91.9*	193	43	138	10	*22.5*	*94.8*	192	40	129	21	*21.1*	*88.9*
	15–24	348	29	289	29	*8.3*	*91.4*	159	8	132	19	*5.0*	*88.1*	189	21	157	10	*11.1*	*94.2*
	25–44	478	63	356	59	*13.2*	*87.7*	187	15	145	27	*8.0*	*85.6*	291	48	211	32	*16.5*	*89.0*
	45–64	312	103	191	18	*33.0*	*94.2*	139	40	86	13	*28.8*	*90.6*	173	63	105	5	*36.4*	*97.1*
	65–	115	53	58	4	*46.1*	*96.5*	53	19	32	2	*35.8*	*96.2*	62	34	26	2	*54.8*	*96.8*

New Quay UD	All 3+	1164	363	759	39	*31.3*	*96.6*	424	113	289	19	*26.8*	*95.5*	740	250	470	20	*33.8*	*97.3*
	3–14	331	121	201	7	*36.8*	*97.9*	170	68	97	3	*40.5*	*98.2*	161	53	104	4	*32.9*	*97.5*
	15–24	168	16	141	10	*9.6*	*94.0*	43	1	37	4	*2.4*	*90.5*	125	15	104	6	*12.0*	*95.2*
	25–44	269	55	205	9	*20.4*	*96.7*	71	8	59	4	*11.3*	*94.4*	198	47	146	5	*23.7*	*97.5*
	45–64	261	89	164	8	*34.1*	*96.9*	94	15	74	5	*16.0*	*94.7*	167	74	90	3	*44.3*	*98.2*
	65–	135	82	48	5	*60.7*	*96.3*	46	21	22	3	*45.7*	*93.5*	89	61	26	2	*68.5*	*97.8*
Aberaeron RD	All 3+	7722	5394	2199	109	*70.0*	*98.6*	3314	2197	1051	60	*66.4*	*98.2*	4408	3197	1148	49	*72.7*	*98.9*
	3–14	2109	1647	441	18	*78.2*	*99.1*	1055	836	212	7	*79.2*	*99.3*	1054	811	229	11	*77.2*	*99.0*
	15–24	1305	647	630	26	*49.6*	*97.9*	573	289	267	17	*50.4*	*97.0*	732	358	363	9	*49.0*	*98.6*
	25–44	1850	1149	660	36	*62.3*	*98.0*	722	395	302	22	*54.9*	*96.9*	1128	754	358	14	*67.0*	*98.8*
	45–64	1612	1233	345	26	*76.9*	*98.4*	635	422	197	14	*66.7*	*97.8*	977	811	148	12	*83.5*	*98.8*
	65–	846	718	123	3	*85.1*	*99.6*	329	255	73	0	*77.7*	*100.0*	517	463	50	3	*89.7*	*99.4*
Aberystwyth RD	All 3+	12617	6703	5163	694	*53.2*	*94.1*	5701	2894	2421	337	*50.8*	*93.3*	6916	3809	2742	357	*55.1*	*94.8*
	3–14	3242	2046	1064	131	*63.1*	*96.0*	1617	1016	535	66	*62.8*	*95.9*	1625	1030	529	65	*63.4*	*96.0*
	15–24	2283	896	1221	145	*39.3*	*92.8*	1076	446	555	57	*41.5*	*93.1*	1207	450	666	88	*37.3*	*92.5*
	25–44	3318	1408	1647	236	*42.5*	*92.1*	1432	569	730	108	*39.8*	*90.8*	1886	839	917	128	*44.5*	*93.2*
	45–64	2581	1516	922	137	*58.8*	*94.5*	1122	590	449	78	*52.6*	*92.7*	1459	926	473	59	*63.5*	*96.0*
	65–	1193	837	309	45	*70.3*	*96.2*	454	273	152	28	*60.3*	*93.8*	739	564	157	17	*76.4*	*97.7*
Cardigan RD	All 3+	3222	1535	1513	161	*47.8*	*95.0*	1400	609	713	73	*43.7*	*94.8*	1822	926	800	88	*51.0*	*95.1*
	3–14	808	477	292	35	*59.3*	*95.6*	430	241	170	17	*56.3*	*96.0*	378	236	122	18	*62.8*	*95.2*
	15–24	622	185	387	48	*29.8*	*92.3*	267	80	159	27	*30.1*	*89.8*	355	105	228	21	*29.7*	*94.1*
	25–44	863	371	443	45	*43.2*	*94.8*	340	136	187	15	*40.2*	*95.6*	523	235	256	30	*45.1*	*94.2*
	45–64	646	322	295	27	*50.0*	*95.8*	256	99	144	13	*38.7*	*94.9*	390	223	151	14	*57.5*	*96.4*
	65–	283	180	96	6	*63.8*	*97.9*	107	53	53	1	*49.5*	*99.1*	176	127	43	5	*72.6*	*97.1*
Lampeter RD	All 3+	3518	2262	1172	82	*64.3*	*97.7*	1552	903	602	47	*58.2*	*97.0*	1966	1359	570	35	*69.2*	*98.2*
	3–14	884	638	227	17	*72.3*	*98.1*	433	313	112	8	*72.3*	*98.2*	451	325	115	9	*72.4*	*98.0*
	15–24	658	306	333	19	*46.5*	*97.1*	290	117	158	15	*40.3*	*94.8*	368	189	175	4	*51.4*	*98.9*
	25–44	887	498	364	25	*56.1*	*97.2*	385	188	185	12	*48.8*	*96.9*	502	310	179	13	*61.8*	*97.4*
	45–64	740	523	196	21	*70.7*	*97.2*	302	178	112	12	*58.9*	*96.0*	438	345	84	9	*78.8*	*97.9*
	65–	349	297	52	0	*85.1*	*100.0*	142	107	35	0	*75.4*	*100.0*	207	190	17	0	*91.8*	*100.0*
Llandysul RD	All 3+	7720	5201	2333	177	*67.4*	*97.7*	3355	2136	1109	105	*63.8*	*96.9*	4365	3065	1224	72	*70.3*	*98.3*
	3–14	1990	1466	478	45	*73.7*	*97.7*	1004	752	226	25	*75.0*	*97.5*	986	714	252	20	*72.4*	*98.0*
	15–24	1346	709	596	40	*52.7*	*97.0*	608	314	263	30	*51.7*	*95.1*	738	395	333	10	*53.5*	*98.6*
	25–44	2096	1271	762	61	*60.7*	*97.1*	836	461	346	27	*55.3*	*96.8*	1260	810	416	34	*64.3*	*97.3*
	45–64	1508	1089	391	23	*72.5*	*98.5*	612	386	206	19	*63.2*	*96.9*	896	703	185	4	*78.8*	*99.6*
	65–	780	666	106	8	*85.4*	*99.0*	295	223	68	4	*75.6*	*98.6*	485	443	38	4	*91.3*	*99.2*
Tregaron RD	All 3+	7494	5537	1824	123	*74.0*	*98.4*	3382	2382	907	84	*70.6*	*97.5*	4112	3155	917	39	*76.7*	*99.1*
	3–14	2064	1671	374	17	*81.0*	*99.2*	1050	855	187	6	*81.6*	*99.4*	1014	816	187	11	*80.5*	*98.9*
	15–24	1350	759	547	42	*56.3*	*96.9*	626	347	245	32	*55.6*	*94.9*	724	412	302	10	*56.9*	*98.6*
	25–44	1760	1203	523	30	*68.5*	*98.3*	710	450	234	22	*63.7*	*96.9*	1050	753	289	8	*71.7*	*99.2*
	45–64	1555	1228	294	31	*79.1*	*98.0*	685	481	182	21	*70.3*	*96.9*	870	747	112	10	*86.0*	*98.8*
	65–	765	676	86	3	*88.4*	*99.6*	311	249	59	3	*80.1*	*99.0*	454	427	27	0	*94.1*	*100.0*

District[1]	Age last birth-day	Number[2] Total in age group	Welsh only	Both	English only	Percentage[3] Welsh only	Percentage[3] Able to speak Welsh	Number[2] Total in age group	Welsh only	Both	English only	Percentage[3] Welsh only	Percentage[3] Able to speak Welsh	Number[2] Total in age group	Welsh only	Both	English only	Percentage[3] Welsh only	Percentage[3] Able to speak Welsh
		Persons						Males						Females					
Ysgubor-y-coed CP (admin. by Machynlleth (Mont) RD)	All 3+	360	162	175	23	*45.0*	*93.6*	181	78	91	12	*43.1*	*93.4*	179	84	84	11	*46.9*	*93.9*
	3–14	91	60	25	6	*65.9*	*93.4*	51	30	17	4	*58.8*	*92.2*	40	30	8	2	*75.0*	*95.0*
	15–24	64	12	50	2	*18.8*	*96.9*	35	8	26	1	*22.9*	*97.1*	29	4	24	1	*13.8*	*96.6*
	25–44	92	36	47	9	*39.1*	*90.2*	37	16	18	3	*43.2*	*91.9*	55	20	29	6	*36.4*	*89.1*
	45–64	79	33	42	4	*41.8*	*94.9*	40	13	24	3	*32.5*	*92.5*	39	20	18	1	*51.3*	*97.4*
	65–	34	21	11	2	*61.8*	*94.1*	18	11	6	1	*61.1*	*94.4*	16	10	5	1	*62.5*	*93.8*
BRECONSHIRE																			
Brecon UD	All 3+	5467	12	1180	4273	*0.2*	*21.8*	2614	3	513	2096	*0.1*	*19.8*	2853	9	667	2177	*0.3*	*23.7*
	3–14	1393	0	65	1326	*0.0*	*4.7*	690	0	36	652	*0.0*	*5.2*	703	0	29	674	*0.0*	*4.1*
	15–24	1251	1	172	1078	*0.1*	*13.8*	621	0	67	554	*0.0*	*10.8*	630	1	105	524	*0.2*	*16.8*
	25–44	1525	2	362	1161	*0.1*	*23.9*	711	1	164	546	*0.1*	*23.2*	814	1	198	615	*0.1*	*24.4*
	45–64	912	1	362	549	*0.1*	*39.8*	441	0	165	276	*0.0*	*37.4*	471	1	197	273	*0.2*	*42.0*
	65–	386	8	219	159	*2.1*	*58.8*	151	2	81	68	*1.3*	*55.0*	235	6	138	91	*2.6*	*61.3*
Bryn-mawr UD	All 3+	6265	54	1441	4758	*0.9*	*23.9*	3262	27	752	2472	*0.8*	*23.9*	3003	27	689	2286	*0.9*	*23.9*
	3–14	1869	15	126	1725	*0.8*	*7.6*	913	10	60	841	*1.1*	*7.7*	956	5	66	884	*0.5*	*7.4*
	15–24	1332	2	202	1125	*0.2*	*15.3*	690	1	103	583	*0.1*	*15.1*	642	1	99	542	*0.2*	*15.6*
	25–44	1953	14	576	1357	*0.7*	*30.2*	1085	9	322	748	*0.8*	*30.5*	868	5	254	609	*0.6*	*29.8*
	45–64	896	15	420	461	*1.7*	*48.5*	471	6	214	251	*1.3*	*46.7*	425	9	206	210	*2.1*	*50.6*
	65–	215	8	117	90	*3.7*	*58.1*	103	1	53	49	*1.0*	*52.4*	112	7	64	41	*6.3*	*63.4*
Builth Wells UD	All 3+	1714	6	259	1448	*0.4*	*15.5*	815	3	138	673	*0.4*	*17.3*	899	3	121	775	*0.3*	*13.8*
	3–14	382	0	14	367	*0.0*	*3.7*	193	0	8	184	*0.0*	*4.2*	189	0	6	183	*0.0*	*3.2*
	15–24	382	2	39	341	*0.5*	*10.7*	168	0	23	145	*0.0*	*13.7*	214	2	16	196	*0.9*	*8.4*
	25–44	533	1	99	433	*0.2*	*18.8*	257	1	55	201	*0.4*	*21.8*	276	0	44	232	*0.0*	*15.9*
	45–64	304	3	74	227	*1.0*	*25.3*	145	2	35	108	*1.4*	*25.5*	159	1	39	119	*0.6*	*25.2*
	65–	113	0	33	80	*0.0*	*29.2*	52	0	17	35	*0.0*	*32.7*	61	0	16	45	*0.0*	*26.2*
Hay UD	All 3+	1596	0	61	1535	*0.0*	*3.8*	744	0	38	706	*0.0*	*5.1*	852	0	23	829	*0.0*	*2.7*
	3–14	454	0	11	443	*0.0*	*2.4*	223	0	7	216	*0.0*	*3.1*	231	0	4	227	*0.0*	*1.7*
	15–24	277	0	5	272	*0.0*	*1.8*	113	0	5	108	*0.0*	*4.4*	164	0	0	164	*0.0*	*0.0*
	25–44	439	0	21	418	*0.0*	*4.8*	211	0	11	200	*0.0*	*5.2*	228	0	10	218	*0.0*	*4.4*
	45–64	295	0	15	280	*0.0*	*5.1*	142	0	10	132	*0.0*	*7.0*	153	0	5	148	*0.0*	*3.3*
	65–	131	0	9	122	*0.0*	*6.9*	55	0	5	50	*0.0*	*9.1*	76	0	4	72	*0.0*	*5.3*
Brecon RD	All 3+	9168	1032	4656	3471	*11.3*	*62.1*	4664	479	2312	1869	*10.3*	*59.9*	4504	553	2344	1602	*12.3*	*64.4*
	3–14	2272	246	773	1247	*10.9*	*45.0*	1160	124	399	635	*10.7*	*45.2*	1112	122	374	612	*11.0*	*44.8*
	15–24	1894	130	923	838	*6.9*	*55.7*	943	61	427	453	*6.5*	*51.9*	951	69	496	385	*7.3*	*59.5*
	25–44	2598	244	1448	906	*9.4*	*65.1*	1323	115	714	494	*8.7*	*62.7*	1275	129	734	412	*10.1*	*67.7*
	45–64	1661	228	1055	378	*13.7*	*77.2*	873	103	540	230	*11.8*	*73.7*	788	125	515	148	*15.9*	*81.2*
	65–	743	184	457	102	*24.8*	*86.3*	365	76	232	57	*20.8*	*84.4*	378	108	225	45	*28.6*	*88.1*

Builth RD	All 3+	4634	498	2204	1931	10.7	58.3	2344	238	1090	1015	10.2	56.7	2290	260	1114	916	11.4	60.0
	3–14	1262	126	419	717	10.0	43.2	652	75	196	381	11.5	41.6	610	51	223	336	8.4	44.9
	15–24	918	44	413	461	4.8	49.8	474	20	200	254	4.2	46.4	444	24	213	207	5.4	53.4
	25–44	1248	99	673	475	7.9	61.9	591	49	309	232	8.3	60.7	657	50	364	243	7.6	63.0
	45–64	832	143	477	212	17.2	74.5	433	57	266	110	13.2	74.6	399	86	211	102	21.6	74.4
	65–	374	86	222	66	23.0	82.4	194	37	119	38	19.1	80.4	180	49	103	28	27.2	84.4
Crickhowell RD	All 3+	6602	78	1790	4729	1.2	28.3	3196	42	887	2265	1.3	29.1	3406	36	903	2464	1.1	27.6
	3–14	1883	14	131	1736	0.7	7.7	909	8	65	835	0.9	8.0	974	6	66	901	0.6	7.4
	15–24	1190	7	211	971	0.6	18.3	551	6	96	449	1.1	18.5	639	1	115	522	0.2	18.2
	25–44	1863	15	548	1298	0.8	30.2	906	6	268	631	0.7	30.3	957	9	280	667	0.9	30.2
	45–64	1137	20	576	541	1.8	52.4	576	12	292	272	2.1	52.8	561	8	284	269	1.4	52.0
	65–	529	22	324	183	4.2	65.4	254	10	166	78	3.9	69.3	275	12	158	105	4.4	61.8
Hay RD	All 3+	3089	5	541	2540	0.2	17.7	1538	2	260	1276	0.1	17.0	1551	3	281	1264	0.2	18.3
	3–14	874	1	43	828	0.1	5.0	425	0	17	408	0.0	4.0	449	1	26	420	0.2	6.0
	15–24	554	1	75	477	0.2	13.7	266	1	38	227	0.4	14.7	288	0	37	250	0.0	12.9
	25–44	856	2	150	704	0.2	17.8	442	0	76	366	0.0	17.2	414	2	74	338	0.5	18.4
	45–64	580	1	181	398	0.2	31.4	296	1	84	211	0.3	28.7	284	0	97	187	0.0	34.2
	65–	225	0	92	133	0.0	40.9	109	0	45	64	0.0	41.3	116	0	47	69	0.0	40.5
Faenor and Penderyn RD	All 3+	4402	643	2888	865	14.6	80.3	2223	314	1459	448	14.1	79.8	2179	329	1429	417	15.1	80.8
	3–14	1211	153	782	275	12.6	77.2	605	85	391	128	14.0	78.7	606	68	391	147	11.2	75.7
	15–24	916	87	654	172	9.5	81.2	493	52	342	98	10.6	80.1	423	35	312	74	8.3	82.4
	25–44	1340	154	897	287	11.5	78.6	683	74	455	154	10.8	77.5	657	80	442	133	12.2	79.7
	45–64	712	162	446	104	22.8	85.4	364	76	230	58	20.9	84.1	348	86	216	46	24.7	86.8
	65–	223	87	109	27	39.0	87.9	78	27	41	10	34.6	87.2	145	60	68	17	41.4	88.3
Ystradgynlais RD	All 3+	5285	2136	2736	409	40.4	92.3	2725	1055	1439	230	38.7	91.6	2560	1081	1297	179	42.3	93.0
	3–14	1690	803	770	117	47.5	93.1	835	414	369	52	49.6	93.8	855	389	401	65	45.5	92.4
	15–24	1090	325	664	99	29.9	90.9	584	162	355	66	27.8	88.7	506	163	309	33	32.3	93.5
	25–44	1583	553	898	130	35.0	91.8	854	284	493	77	33.3	91.0	729	269	405	53	37.0	92.7
	45–64	682	319	314	49	46.8	92.8	348	147	173	28	42.2	92.0	334	172	141	21	51.5	93.7
	65–	240	136	90	14	56.7	94.2	104	48	49	7	46.2	93.3	136	88	41	7	64.7	94.9
Llanwrthwl CP (admin. by Rhayader (Rad) RD)	All 3+	1667	57	401	1208	3.4	27.5	1183	54	291	837	4.6	29.2	484	3	110	371	0.6	23.3
	3–14	332	1	22	308	0.3	6.9	165	1	7	156	0.6	4.9	167	0	15	152	0.0	9.0
	15–24	397	16	107	274	4.0	31.0	314	16	90	208	5.1	33.8	83	0	17	66	0.0	20.5
	25–44	589	22	166	401	3.7	31.9	443	21	118	304	4.7	31.4	146	1	48	97	0.7	33.6
	45–64	295	17	84	194	5.8	34.2	228	16	62	150	7.0	34.2	67	1	22	44	1.5	34.3
	65–	54	1	22	31	1.9	42.6	33	0	14	19	0.0	42.4	21	1	8	12	4.8	42.9
Ystradfellte CP (admin. by Neath (Glam) RD)	All 3+	520	153	288	78	29.5	85.0	265	75	146	43	28.4	83.7	255	78	142	35	30.6	86.3
	3–14	127	47	59	20	37.3	84.1	60	22	31	6	37.3	89.8	67	25	28	14	37.3	79.1
	15–24	109	24	74	11	22.0	89.9	50	15	28	7	30.0	86.0	59	9	46	4	15.3	93.2
	25–44	174	39	107	28	22.4	83.9	92	17	58	17	18.5	81.5	82	22	49	11	26.8	86.6
	45–64	81	27	38	16	33.3	80.2	47	15	22	10	31.9	78.7	34	12	16	6	35.3	82.4
	65–	29	16	10	3	55.2	89.7	16	6	7	3	37.5	81.3	13	10	3	0	76.9	100.0

District[1]	Age last birth-day	Number[2] Total in age group	Welsh only	Both	English only	Percentage[3] Welsh only	Able to speak Welsh	Number[2] Total in age group	Welsh only	Both	English only	Percentage[3] Welsh only	Able to speak Welsh	Number[2] Total in age group	Welsh only	Both	English only	Percentage[3] Welsh only	Able to speak Welsh
		Persons						Males						Females					
RADNORSHIRE																			
Knighton UD	All 3+	1972	2	54	1914	*0.1*	*2.8*	940	1	30	907	*0.1*	*3.3*	1032	1	24	1007	*0.1*	*2.4*
	3–14	512	0	2	510	*0.0*	*0.4*	236	0	0	236	*0.0*	*0.0*	276	0	2	274	*0.0*	*0.7*
	15–24	431	1	18	410	*0.2*	*4.4*	196	1	13	180	*0.5*	*7.1*	235	0	5	230	*0.0*	*2.1*
	25–44	549	0	20	529	*0.0*	*3.6*	267	0	9	258	*0.0*	*3.4*	282	0	11	271	*0.0*	*3.9*
	45–64	312	1	9	302	*0.3*	*3.2*	160	0	4	156	*0.0*	*2.5*	152	1	5	146	*0.7*	*3.9*
	65–	168	0	5	163	*0.0*	*3.0*	81	0	4	77	*0.0*	*4.9*	87	0	1	86	*0.0*	*1.1*
Llandrindod Wells UD	All 3+	1732	1	152	1578	*0.1*	*8.8*	764	1	61	701	*0.1*	*8.1*	968	0	91	877	*0.0*	*9.4*
	3–14	344	0	10	334	*0.0*	*2.9*	156	0	5	151	*0.0*	*3.2*	188	0	5	183	*0.0*	*2.7*
	15–24	465	0	35	429	*0.0*	*7.5*	194	0	16	177	*0.0*	*8.2*	271	0	19	252	*0.0*	*7.0*
	25–44	597	0	68	529	*0.0*	*11.4*	265	0	26	239	*0.0*	*9.8*	332	0	42	290	*0.0*	*12.7*
	45–64	264	1	32	231	*0.4*	*12.5*	116	1	11	104	*0.9*	*10.3*	148	0	21	127	*0.0*	*14.2*
	65–	62	0	7	55	*0.0*	*11.3*	33	0	3	30	*0.0*	*9.1*	29	0	4	25	*0.0*	*13.8*
Presteigne UD	All 3+	1164	0	7	1156	*0.0*	*0.6*	556	0	2	554	*0.0*	*0.4*	608	0	5	602	*0.0*	*0.8*
	3–14	293	0	0	293	*0.0*	*0.0*	151	0	0	151	*0.0*	*0.0*	142	0	0	142	*0.0*	*0.0*
	15–24	205	0	1	204	*0.0*	*0.5*	93	0	0	93	*0.0*	*0.0*	112	0	1	111	*0.0*	*0.9*
	25–44	319	0	2	317	*0.0*	*0.6*	146	0	0	146	*0.0*	*0.0*	173	0	2	171	*0.0*	*1.2*
	45–64	243	0	4	238	*0.0*	*1.7*	117	0	2	115	*0.0*	*1.7*	126	0	2	123	*0.0*	*1.6*
	65–	104	0	0	104	*0.0*	*0.0*	49	0	0	49	*0.0*	*0.0*	55	0	0	55	*0.0*	*0.0*
Colwyn RD	All 3+	1761	1	97	1661	*0.1*	*5.6*	884	1	48	834	*0.1*	*5.5*	877	0	49	827	*0.0*	*5.6*
	3–14	506	0	10	494	*0.0*	*2.0*	237	0	5	231	*0.0*	*2.1*	269	0	5	263	*0.0*	*1.9*
	15–24	354	0	14	340	*0.0*	*4.0*	181	0	8	173	*0.0*	*4.4*	173	0	6	167	*0.0*	*3.5*
	25–44	499	1	38	460	*0.2*	*7.8*	263	1	20	242	*0.4*	*8.0*	236	0	18	218	*0.0*	*7.6*
	45–64	279	0	23	256	*0.0*	*8.2*	137	0	11	126	*0.0*	*8.0*	142	0	12	130	*0.0*	*8.5*
	65–	123	0	12	111	*0.0*	*9.8*	66	0	4	62	*0.0*	*6.1*	57	0	8	49	*0.0*	*14.0*
Knighton RD	All 3+	4537	0	66	4469	*0.0*	*1.5*	2402	0	42	2358	*0.0*	*1.8*	2135	0	24	2111	*0.0*	*1.1*
	3–14	1298	0	1	1297	*0.0*	*0.1*	603	0	0	603	*0.0*	*0.0*	695	0	1	694	*0.0*	*0.1*
	15–24	931	0	4	927	*0.0*	*0.4*	521	0	3	518	*0.0*	*0.6*	410	0	1	409	*0.0*	*0.2*
	25–44	1230	0	33	1196	*0.0*	*2.7*	677	0	20	656	*0.0*	*3.0*	553	0	13	540	*0.0*	*2.4*
	45–64	741	0	24	717	*0.0*	*3.2*	415	0	19	396	*0.0*	*4.6*	326	0	5	321	*0.0*	*1.5*
	65–	337	0	4	332	*0.0*	*1.2*	186	0	0	185	*0.0*	*0.0*	151	0	4	147	*0.0*	*2.6*
New Radnor RD	All 3+	2760	0	42	2713	*0.0*	*1.5*	1415	0	26	1385	*0.0*	*1.8*	1345	0	16	1328	*0.0*	*1.2*
	3–14	765	0	1	763	*0.0*	*0.1*	395	0	0	394	*0.0*	*0.0*	370	0	1	369	*0.0*	*0.3*
	15–24	537	0	4	532	*0.0*	*0.7*	272	0	2	269	*0.0*	*0.7*	265	0	2	263	*0.0*	*0.8*
	25–44	720	0	19	698	*0.0*	*2.6*	371	0	13	356	*0.0*	*3.5*	349	0	6	342	*0.0*	*1.7*
	45–64	529	0	15	514	*0.0*	*2.8*	271	0	9	262	*0.0*	*3.3*	258	0	6	252	*0.0*	*2.3*
	65–	209	0	3	206	*0.0*	*1.4*	106	0	2	104	*0.0*	*1.9*	103	0	1	102	*0.0*	*1.0*

Painscastle RD	All 3+	2207	0	78	2127	0.0	3.5	1118	0	34	1084	0.0	3.0	1089	0	44	1043	0.0	4.0
	3–14	573	0	5	567	0.0	0.9	282	0	2	280	0.0	0.7	291	0	3	287	0.0	1.0
	15–24	404	0	7	397	0.0	1.7	198	0	2	196	0.0	1.0	206	0	5	201	0.0	2.4
	25–44	627	0	35	591	0.0	5.6	316	0	12	304	0.0	3.8	311	0	23	287	0.0	7.4
	45–64	413	0	21	392	0.0	5.1	219	0	11	208	0.0	5.0	194	0	10	184	0.0	5.2
	65–	190	0	10	180	0.0	5.3	103	0	7	96	0.0	6.8	87	0	3	84	0.0	3.4
Rhayader RD	All 3+	5621	47	813	4752	0.8	15.3	2980	35	469	2469	1.2	16.9	2641	12	344	2283	0.5	13.5
	3–14	1356	4	63	1286	0.3	5.0	658	2	31	624	0.3	5.0	698	2	32	662	0.3	4.9
	15–24	1079	11	88	979	1.0	9.2	556	9	55	491	1.6	11.5	523	2	33	488	0.4	6.7
	25–44	1715	13	281	1418	0.8	17.2	963	12	170	778	1.2	18.9	752	1	111	640	0.1	14.9
	45–64	1055	14	226	813	1.3	22.8	600	11	137	450	1.8	24.7	455	3	89	363	0.7	20.2
	65–	416	5	155	256	1.2	38.5	203	1	76	126	0.5	37.9	213	4	79	130	1.9	39.0
MONTGOMERYSHIRE																			
Llanfyllin MB	All 3+	1526	275	920	329	18.0	78.4	728	137	442	149	18.8	79.5	798	138	478	180	17.3	77.4
	3–14	384	72	200	112	18.8	70.8	196	32	110	54	16.3	72.4	188	40	90	58	21.3	69.1
	15–24	296	33	204	59	11.1	80.1	137	20	89	28	14.6	79.6	159	13	115	31	8.2	80.5
	25–44	435	73	273	89	16.8	79.5	194	34	126	34	17.5	82.5	241	39	147	55	16.2	77.2
	45–64	281	61	166	52	21.9	81.4	128	29	74	25	22.7	80.5	153	32	92	27	21.2	82.1
	65–	130	36	77	17	27.7	86.9	73	22	43	8	30.1	89.0	57	14	34	9	24.6	84.2
Llanidloes MB	All 3+	2578	57	1271	1243	2.2	51.7	1168	13	572	581	1.1	50.2	1410	44	699	662	3.1	52.9
	3–14	677	7	153	515	1.0	23.7	355	2	82	271	0.6	23.7	322	5	71	244	1.6	23.8
	15–24	492	1	197	294	0.2	40.2	209	0	85	124	0.0	40.7	283	1	112	170	0.4	39.9
	25–44	744	15	429	296	2.0	60.0	316	4	189	121	1.3	61.5	428	11	240	175	2.6	58.9
	45–64	461	14	336	110	3.0	76.1	204	2	149	53	1.0	74.0	257	12	187	57	4.7	77.7
	65–	204	20	156	28	9.8	86.3	84	5	67	12	6.0	85.7	120	15	89	16	12.5	86.7
Machynlleth UD	All 3+	1907	302	1388	209	15.9	89.0	878	121	647	105	13.9	88.0	1029	181	741	104	17.6	89.9
	3–14	465	84	340	39	18.1	91.6	221	44	160	15	20.1	93.2	244	40	180	24	16.4	90.2
	15–24	373	27	307	36	7.3	90.3	172	12	142	17	7.0	90.1	201	15	165	19	7.5	90.5
	25–44	608	66	458	84	10.9	86.2	274	24	211	39	8.8	85.8	334	42	247	45	12.6	86.5
	45–64	321	64	216	39	20.1	87.8	152	22	102	27	14.6	82.1	169	42	114	12	25.0	92.9
	65–	140	61	67	11	43.9	92.1	59	19	32	7	32.8	87.9	81	42	35	4	51.9	95.1
Montgomery MB	All 3+	977	1	61	913	0.1	6.4	461	0	27	432	0.0	5.9	516	1	34	481	0.2	6.8
	3–14	275	0	7	266	0.0	2.6	134	0	2	130	0.0	1.5	141	0	5	136	0.0	3.5
	15–24	185	0	7	178	0.0	3.8	81	0	4	77	0.0	4.9	104	0	3	101	0.0	2.9
	25–44	251	0	27	224	0.0	10.8	123	0	12	111	0.0	9.8	128	0	15	113	0.0	11.7
	45–64	147	1	11	135	0.7	8.2	68	0	6	62	0.0	8.8	79	1	5	73	1.3	7.6
	65–	119	0	9	110	0.0	7.6	55	0	3	52	0.0	5.5	64	0	6	58	0.0	9.4
Newtown and Llanllwchaearn UD	All 3+	6091	11	779	5299	0.2	13.0	2815	1	332	2482	0.0	11.8	3276	10	447	2817	0.3	14.0
	3–14	1687	3	87	1597	0.2	5.3	867	1	43	823	0.1	5.1	820	2	44	774	0.2	5.6
	15–24	1291	2	136	1152	0.2	10.7	560	0	55	505	0.0	9.8	731	2	81	647	0.3	11.4
	25–44	1762	3	253	1505	0.2	14.5	769	0	96	673	0.0	12.5	993	3	157	832	0.3	16.1
	45–64	939	2	188	749	0.2	20.2	437	0	89	348	0.0	20.4	502	2	99	401	0.4	20.1
	65–	412	1	115	296	0.2	28.2	182	0	49	133	0.0	26.9	230	1	66	163	0.4	29.1

District[1]	Age last birth-day	Persons: Number[2] Total in age group	Persons: Welsh only	Persons: Both	Persons: English only	Persons: Percentage[3] *Welsh only*	Persons: Percentage[3] *Able to speak Welsh*	Males: Number[2] Total in age group	Males: Welsh only	Males: Both	Males: English only	Males: Percentage[3] *Welsh only*	Males: Percentage[3] *Able to speak Welsh*	Females: Number[2] Total in age group	Females: Welsh only	Females: Both	Females: English only	Females: Percentage[3] *Welsh only*	Females: Percentage[3] *Able to speak Welsh*
Welshpool MB	All 3+	5727	11	643	5073	*0.2*	*11.4*	2759	4	320	2435	*0.1*	*11.7*	2968	7	323	2638	*0.2*	*11.1*
	3–14	1527	0	44	1483	*0.0*	*2.9*	759	0	23	736	*0.0*	*3.0*	768	0	21	747	*0.0*	*2.7*
	15–24	1118	2	97	1019	*0.2*	*8.9*	531	1	57	473	*0.2*	*10.9*	587	1	40	546	*0.2*	*7.0*
	25–44	1625	4	205	1416	*0.2*	*12.9*	786	3	107	676	*0.4*	*14.0*	839	1	98	740	*0.1*	*11.8*
	45–64	993	4	169	820	*0.4*	*17.4*	471	0	77	394	*0.0*	*16.3*	522	4	92	426	*0.8*	*18.4*
	65–	464	1	128	335	*0.2*	*27.8*	212	0	56	156	*0.0*	*26.4*	252	1	72	179	*0.4*	*29.0*
Forden RD	All 3+	5411	18	524	4862	*0.3*	*10.0*	2716	9	252	2449	*0.3*	*9.6*	2695	9	272	2413	*0.3*	*10.4*
	3–14	1488	2	64	1421	*0.1*	*4.4*	738	1	31	705	*0.1*	*4.3*	750	1	33	716	*0.1*	*4.5*
	15–24	929	3	61	862	*0.3*	*6.9*	472	1	22	447	*0.2*	*4.9*	457	2	39	415	*0.4*	*9.0*
	25–44	1420	2	163	1253	*0.1*	*11.6*	696	1	84	609	*0.1*	*12.2*	724	1	79	644	*0.1*	*11.0*
	45–64	1064	8	158	897	*0.8*	*15.6*	541	4	76	460	*0.7*	*14.8*	523	4	82	437	*0.8*	*16.4*
	65–	510	3	78	429	*0.6*	*15.9*	269	2	39	228	*0.7*	*15.2*	241	1	39	201	*0.4*	*16.6*
Llanfyllin RD	All 3+	11971	3326	5103	3529	*27.8*	*70.5*	5932	1737	2512	1677	*29.3*	*71.7*	6039	1589	2591	1852	*26.3*	*69.3*
	3–14	3395	1076	1053	1260	*31.7*	*62.8*	1670	565	499	603	*33.9*	*63.8*	1725	511	554	657	*29.7*	*61.8*
	15–24	2137	485	982	666	*22.7*	*68.7*	1045	268	456	319	*25.7*	*69.4*	1092	217	526	347	*19.9*	*68.1*
	25–44	3075	718	1515	840	*23.4*	*72.7*	1494	377	732	384	*25.3*	*74.3*	1581	341	783	456	*21.6*	*71.1*
	45–64	2286	680	1052	554	*29.7*	*75.8*	1182	352	559	271	*29.8*	*77.1*	1104	328	493	283	*29.7*	*74.4*
	65–	1078	367	501	209	*34.1*	*80.6*	541	175	266	100	*32.3*	*81.5*	537	192	235	109	*35.8*	*79.7*
Machynlleth RD	All 3+	4095	2497	1483	112	*61.0*	*97.3*	2006	1237	714	52	*61.8*	*97.4*	2089	1260	769	60	*60.3*	*97.1*
	3–14	1039	729	282	27	*70.2*	*97.4*	534	371	150	12	*69.6*	*97.7*	505	358	132	15	*70.9*	*97.0*
	15–24	732	368	343	21	*50.3*	*97.1*	362	207	142	13	*57.2*	*96.4*	370	161	201	8	*43.5*	*97.8*
	25–44	1155	600	519	36	*51.9*	*96.9*	549	295	241	13	*53.7*	*97.6*	606	305	278	23	*50.3*	*96.2*
	45–64	786	524	238	24	*66.7*	*96.9*	387	250	126	11	*64.6*	*97.2*	399	274	112	13	*68.7*	*96.7*
	65–	383	276	101	4	*72.4*	*99.0*	174	114	55	3	*66.3*	*98.3*	209	162	46	1	*77.5*	*99.5*
Newtown and Llanidloes RD	All 3+	11027	1482	4189	5344	*13.5*	*51.5*	5522	718	2088	2708	*13.0*	*50.9*	5505	764	2101	2636	*13.9*	*52.1*
	3–14	3218	486	872	1858	*15.1*	*42.2*	1576	244	402	929	*15.5*	*41.0*	1642	242	470	929	*14.7*	*43.4*
	15–24	2241	225	875	1136	*10.1*	*49.2*	1112	109	436	563	*9.8*	*49.2*	1129	116	439	573	*10.3*	*49.2*
	25–44	2781	312	1172	1294	*11.2*	*53.4*	1382	155	565	661	*11.2*	*52.1*	1399	157	607	633	*11.2*	*54.7*
	45–64	1920	303	866	749	*15.8*	*60.9*	997	139	473	383	*14.0*	*61.5*	923	164	393	366	*17.8*	*60.3*
	65–	867	156	404	307	*18.0*	*64.6*	455	71	212	172	*15.6*	*62.2*	412	85	192	135	*20.6*	*67.2*
FLINTSHIRE																			
Buckley UD	All 3+	5307	9	553	4743	*0.2*	*10.6*	2780	4	272	2504	*0.1*	*9.9*	2527	5	281	2239	*0.2*	*11.3*
	3–14	1691	0	71	1620	*0.0*	*4.2*	887	0	33	854	*0.0*	*3.7*	804	0	38	766	*0.0*	*4.7*
	15–24	996	0	66	930	*0.0*	*6.6*	592	0	35	557	*0.0*	*5.9*	404	0	31	373	*0.0*	*7.7*
	25–44	1447	1	187	1257	*0.1*	*13.0*	742	0	89	653	*0.0*	*12.0*	705	1	98	604	*0.1*	*14.1*
	45–64	908	3	172	733	*0.3*	*19.3*	458	1	89	368	*0.2*	*19.7*	450	2	83	365	*0.4*	*18.9*
	65–	265	5	57	203	*1.9*	*23.4*	101	3	26	72	*3.0*	*28.7*	164	2	31	131	*1.2*	*20.1*

Connah's Quay UD	All 3+	3095	16	385	2690	0.5	13.0	1537	10	202	1322	0.7	13.8	1558	6	183	1368	0.4	12.1
	3–14	989	1	55	933	0.1	5.7	470	0	22	448	0.0	4.7	519	1	33	485	0.2	6.6
	15–24	609	3	58	546	0.5	10.0	328	2	36	288	0.6	11.7	281	1	22	258	0.4	8.2
	25–44	926	4	132	788	0.4	14.7	464	3	68	392	0.6	15.3	462	1	64	396	0.2	14.1
	45–64	449	3	112	334	0.7	25.6	216	3	62	151	1.4	30.1	233	0	50	183	0.0	21.5
	65–	122	5	28	89	4.1	27.0	59	2	14	43	3.4	27.1	63	3	14	46	4.8	27.0
Flint MB	All 3+	4273	160	1891	2211	3.8	48.1	2162	79	957	1120	3.7	48.0	2111	81	934	1091	3.8	48.2
	3–14	1291	45	332	911	3.5	29.3	657	21	182	451	3.2	31.0	634	24	150	460	3.8	27.4
	15–24	823	17	327	475	2.1	42.0	454	9	182	260	2.0	42.3	369	8	145	215	2.2	41.6
	25–44	1141	31	604	505	2.7	55.7	574	15	311	248	2.6	56.8	567	16	293	257	2.8	54.6
	45–64	781	39	478	261	5.0	66.4	385	20	233	132	5.2	65.7	396	19	245	129	4.8	67.0
	65–	237	28	150	59	11.8	75.1	92	14	49	29	15.2	68.5	145	14	101	30	9.7	79.3
Holywell UD	All 3+	2505	105	1643	755	4.2	69.8	1143	53	786	304	4.6	73.4	1362	52	857	451	3.8	66.8
	3–14	640	26	362	251	4.1	60.7	318	14	183	121	4.4	61.9	322	12	179	130	3.7	59.5
	15–24	541	12	377	151	2.2	72.0	241	7	180	54	2.9	77.6	300	5	197	97	1.7	67.6
	25–44	656	19	437	200	2.9	69.5	291	9	205	77	3.1	73.5	365	10	232	123	2.7	66.3
	45–64	510	32	359	119	6.3	76.7	226	17	168	41	7.5	81.9	284	15	191	78	5.3	72.5
	65–	158	16	108	34	10.1	78.5	67	6	50	11	9.0	83.6	91	10	58	23	11.0	74.7
Mold UD	All 3+	3960	121	2225	1613	3.1	59.3	1893	54	1087	751	2.9	60.3	2067	67	1138	862	3.2	58.3
	3–14	1138	26	446	665	2.3	41.5	587	16	233	337	2.7	42.5	551	10	213	328	1.8	40.5
	15–24	800	10	455	335	1.3	58.1	359	5	218	136	1.4	62.1	441	5	237	199	1.1	54.9
	25–44	1101	30	695	376	2.7	65.8	522	13	333	176	2.5	66.3	579	17	362	200	2.9	65.5
	45–64	685	29	459	197	4.2	71.2	324	10	230	84	3.1	74.1	361	19	229	113	5.3	68.7
	65–	236	26	170	40	11.0	83.1	101	10	73	18	9.9	82.2	135	16	97	22	11.9	83.7
Prestatyn UD	All 3+	1187	74	662	449	6.2	62.1	532	43	307	181	8.1	65.9	655	31	355	268	4.7	59.0
	3–14	253	17	129	105	6.8	58.2	137	10	62	64	7.4	52.9	116	7	67	41	6.1	64.3
	15–24	226	8	142	76	3.5	66.4	98	4	66	28	4.1	71.4	128	4	76	48	3.1	62.5
	25–44	417	20	241	156	4.8	62.6	178	13	116	49	7.3	72.5	239	7	125	107	2.9	55.2
	45–64	219	14	116	89	6.4	59.4	91	9	50	32	9.9	64.8	128	5	66	57	3.9	55.5
	65–	72	15	34	23	20.8	68.1	28	7	13	8	25.0	71.4	44	8	21	15	18.2	65.9
Rhyl UD	All 3+	8009	224	3727	4046	2.8	49.4	3462	116	1663	1679	3.4	51.4	4547	108	2064	2367	2.4	47.8
	3–14	1915	34	691	1187	1.8	37.9	935	14	341	578	1.5	38.0	980	20	350	609	2.0	37.8
	15–24	1820	29	919	870	1.6	52.1	757	18	410	329	2.4	56.5	1063	11	509	541	1.0	48.9
	25–44	2427	51	1170	1201	2.1	50.4	1028	26	525	476	2.5	53.6	1399	25	645	725	1.8	48.0
	45–64	1389	62	708	618	4.5	55.4	565	35	296	234	6.2	58.6	824	27	412	384	3.3	53.3
	65–	458	48	239	170	10.5	62.8	177	23	91	62	13.1	64.8	281	25	148	108	8.9	61.6
Hawarden RD	All 3+	14648	619	2700	11318	4.2	22.7	7628	323	1390	5908	4.2	22.5	7020	296	1310	5410	4.2	22.9
	3–14	4547	215	598	3734	4.7	17.9	2269	112	275	1882	4.9	17.1	2278	103	323	1852	4.5	18.7
	15–24	2822	81	488	2250	2.9	20.2	1585	48	269	1266	3.0	20.0	1237	33	219	984	2.7	20.4
	25–44	4166	139	854	3170	3.3	23.8	2161	74	441	1644	3.4	23.9	2005	65	413	1526	3.2	23.8
	45–64	2327	135	560	1629	5.8	29.9	1233	63	306	862	5.1	30.0	1094	72	254	767	6.6	29.8
	65–	786	49	200	535	6.3	31.8	380	26	99	254	6.9	33.0	406	23	101	281	5.7	30.6

District[1]	Age last birth-day	Persons: Number[2] Total in age group	Persons: Welsh only	Persons: Both	Persons: English only	Persons: Percentage[3] Welsh only	Persons: Percentage[3] Able to speak Welsh	Males: Number[2] Total in age group	Males: Welsh only	Males: Both	Males: English only	Males: Percentage[3] Welsh only	Males: Percentage[3] Able to speak Welsh	Females: Number[2] Total in age group	Females: Welsh only	Females: Both	Females: English only	Females: Percentage[3] Welsh only	Females: Percentage[3] Able to speak Welsh
Holywell RD	All 3+	22373	3560	13920	4858	*15.9*	*78.2*	11327	1960	7021	2325	*17.3*	*79.4*	11046	1600	6899	2533	*14.5*	*77.0*
	3–14	6207	1085	3403	1712	*17.5*	*72.4*	3121	570	1718	827	*18.3*	*73.5*	3086	515	1685	885	*16.7*	*71.3*
	15–24	4276	357	2804	1109	*8.4*	*74.0*	2297	225	1484	585	*9.8*	*74.4*	1979	132	1320	524	*6.7*	*73.4*
	25–44	6112	799	4162	1139	*13.1*	*81.3*	3103	470	2126	499	*15.2*	*83.9*	3009	329	2036	640	*10.9*	*78.6*
	45–64	4179	819	2667	686	*19.6*	*83.5*	2111	470	1324	314	*22.3*	*85.0*	2068	349	1343	372	*16.9*	*81.9*
	65–	1599	500	884	212	*31.3*	*86.7*	695	225	369	100	*32.4*	*85.6*	904	275	515	112	*30.5*	*87.6*
Overton RD	All 3+	4752	0	135	4605	*0.0*	*2.8*	2277	0	47	2223	*0.0*	*2.1*	2475	0	88	2382	*0.0*	*3.6*
	3–14	1275	0	8	1264	*0.0*	*0.6*	623	0	3	618	*0.0*	*0.5*	652	0	5	646	*0.0*	*0.8*
	15–24	947	0	24	919	*0.0*	*2.5*	437	0	9	425	*0.0*	*2.1*	510	0	15	494	*0.0*	*2.9*
	25–44	1352	0	62	1289	*0.0*	*4.6*	641	0	21	620	*0.0*	*3.3*	711	0	41	669	*0.0*	*5.8*
	45–64	786	0	29	755	*0.0*	*3.7*	381	0	12	367	*0.0*	*3.2*	405	0	17	388	*0.0*	*4.2*
	65–	392	0	12	378	*0.0*	*3.1*	195	0	2	193	*0.0*	*1.0*	197	0	10	185	*0.0*	*5.1*
St Asaph (Flint) RD	All 3+	5822	834	3727	1256	*14.3*	*78.4*	2808	433	1810	563	*15.4*	*79.9*	3014	401	1917	693	*13.3*	*77.0*
	3–14	1480	241	863	376	*16.3*	*74.6*	772	131	451	190	*17.0*	*75.4*	708	110	412	186	*15.5*	*73.7*
	15–24	1049	82	775	190	*7.8*	*81.9*	509	47	380	82	*9.2*	*83.9*	540	35	395	108	*6.5*	*79.9*
	25–44	1573	156	1044	371	*9.9*	*76.4*	735	84	486	164	*11.4*	*77.7*	838	72	558	207	*8.6*	*75.3*
	45–64	1179	217	729	233	*18.4*	*80.2*	548	115	339	94	*21.0*	*82.8*	631	102	390	139	*16.2*	*78.0*
	65–	541	138	316	86	*25.6*	*84.1*	244	56	154	33	*23.0*	*86.4*	297	82	162	53	*27.6*	*82.2*
DENBIGHSHIRE																			
Abergele and Pen-sarn UD	All 3+	1958	170	1425	356	*8.7*	*81.5*	882	84	648	147	*9.5*	*83.0*	1076	86	777	209	*8.0*	*80.2*
	3–14	540	48	398	91	*8.9*	*82.6*	280	30	196	53	*10.7*	*80.7*	260	18	202	38	*6.9*	*84.6*
	15–24	370	7	313	49	*1.9*	*86.5*	158	3	139	16	*1.9*	*89.9*	212	4	174	33	*1.9*	*84.0*
	25–44	523	33	358	132	*6.3*	*74.8*	218	17	156	45	*7.8*	*79.4*	305	16	202	87	*5.2*	*71.5*
	45–64	375	40	273	59	*10.7*	*83.5*	166	21	119	24	*12.7*	*84.3*	209	19	154	35	*9.1*	*82.8*
	65–	150	42	83	25	*28.0*	*83.3*	60	13	38	9	*21.7*	*85.0*	90	29	45	16	*32.2*	*82.2*
Colwyn Bay and Colwyn UD	All 3+	8265	567	3435	4244	*6.9*	*48.5*	3373	289	1548	1527	*8.6*	*54.5*	4892	278	1887	2717	*5.7*	*44.3*
	3–14	1790	170	767	849	*9.5*	*52.5*	890	74	380	434	*8.3*	*51.1*	900	96	387	415	*10.7*	*53.8*
	15–24	1933	74	916	938	*3.8*	*51.3*	737	45	379	311	*6.1*	*57.6*	1196	29	537	627	*2.4*	*47.4*
	25–44	2818	132	1171	1511	*4.7*	*46.3*	1077	72	533	470	*6.7*	*56.2*	1741	60	638	1041	*3.4*	*40.1*
	45–64	1307	130	463	709	*10.0*	*45.5*	503	73	200	228	*14.5*	*54.4*	804	57	263	481	*7.1*	*39.9*
	65–	417	61	118	237	*14.6*	*42.9*	166	25	56	84	*15.1*	*48.8*	251	36	62	153	*14.3*	*39.0*
Denbigh MB	All 3+	6064	988	4227	838	*16.3*	*86.1*	2828	522	2025	273	*18.5*	*90.3*	3236	466	2202	565	*14.4*	*82.5*
	3–14	1421	213	1004	203	*15.0*	*85.7*	678	121	487	70	*17.8*	*89.7*	743	92	517	133	*12.4*	*82.1*
	15–24	1149	88	908	149	*7.7*	*87.0*	557	45	468	41	*8.1*	*92.6*	592	43	440	108	*7.3*	*81.7*
	25–44	1782	224	1291	263	*12.6*	*85.2*	807	120	607	77	*14.9*	*90.3*	975	104	684	186	*10.7*	*80.9*
	45–64	1296	312	806	178	*24.1*	*86.3*	596	163	359	74	*27.3*	*87.6*	700	149	447	104	*21.3*	*85.1*
	65–	416	151	218	45	*36.5*	*89.1*	190	73	104	11	*38.8*	*94.1*	226	78	114	34	*34.5*	*85.0*

Llangollen UD	All 3+	3117	251	1954	911	*8.1*	*70.8*	1391	120	910	360	*8.6*	*74.1*	1726	131	1044	551	*7.6*	*68.1*
	3–14	693	64	398	230	*9.2*	*66.8*	343	34	193	115	*9.9*	*66.4*	350	30	205	115	*8.6*	*67.1*
	15–24	667	26	466	175	*3.9*	*73.8*	268	10	201	57	*3.7*	*78.7*	399	16	265	118	*4.0*	*70.4*
	25–44	944	54	623	267	*5.7*	*71.7*	427	30	296	101	*7.0*	*76.3*	517	24	327	166	*4.6*	*67.9*
	45–64	589	56	336	197	*9.5*	*66.6*	258	27	164	67	*10.5*	*74.0*	331	29	172	130	*8.8*	*60.7*
	65–	224	51	131	42	*22.8*	*81.3*	95	19	56	20	*20.0*	*78.9*	129	32	75	22	*24.8*	*82.9*
Llanrwst UD	All 3+	2473	527	1754	188	*21.3*	*92.4*	1146	242	823	79	*21.2*	*93.1*	1327	285	931	109	*21.5*	*91.8*
	3–14	599	173	381	44	*28.9*	*92.6*	297	89	187	21	*30.0*	*92.9*	302	84	194	23	*27.9*	*92.4*
	15–24	525	55	444	26	*10.5*	*95.0*	243	31	204	8	*12.8*	*96.7*	282	24	240	18	*8.5*	*93.6*
	25–44	727	91	567	66	*12.6*	*90.9*	338	47	261	28	*14.0*	*91.7*	389	44	306	38	*11.3*	*90.2*
	45–64	462	123	300	39	*26.6*	*91.6*	219	51	150	18	*23.3*	*91.8*	243	72	150	21	*29.6*	*91.4*
	65–	160	85	62	13	*53.1*	*91.9*	49	24	21	4	*49.0*	*91.8*	111	61	41	9	*55.0*	*91.9*
Ruthin MB	All 3+	2486	294	1806	381	*11.9*	*84.6*	1187	142	862	181	*12.0*	*84.7*	1299	152	944	200	*11.7*	*84.6*
	3–14	657	91	445	120	*13.9*	*81.7*	339	50	220	68	*14.8*	*79.9*	318	41	225	52	*12.9*	*83.6*
	15–24	468	23	392	53	*4.9*	*88.7*	227	11	186	30	*4.8*	*86.8*	241	12	206	23	*5.0*	*90.5*
	25–44	680	46	500	133	*6.8*	*80.4*	318	19	251	48	*6.0*	*84.9*	362	27	249	85	*7.5*	*76.5*
	45–64	460	70	330	57	*15.3*	*87.5*	208	31	149	27	*15.0*	*87.0*	252	39	181	30	*15.6*	*88.0*
	65–	221	64	139	18	*29.0*	*91.9*	95	31	56	8	*32.6*	*91.6*	126	33	83	10	*26.2*	*92.1*
Wrexham MB	All 3+	13890	65	2318	11490	*0.5*	*17.2*	6887	30	1093	5750	*0.4*	*16.3*	7003	35	1225	5740	*0.5*	*18.0*
	3–14	3699	15	319	3364	*0.4*	*9.0*	1869	5	156	1708	*0.3*	*8.6*	1830	10	163	1656	*0.5*	*9.5*
	15–24	3117	10	562	2539	*0.3*	*18.4*	1538	6	235	1292	*0.4*	*15.7*	1579	4	327	1247	*0.3*	*21.0*
	25–44	4400	16	838	3540	*0.4*	*19.4*	2158	6	407	1739	*0.3*	*19.1*	2242	10	431	1801	*0.4*	*19.7*
	45–64	2166	18	491	1654	*0.8*	*23.5*	1102	11	254	834	*1.0*	*24.0*	1064	7	237	820	*0.7*	*22.9*
	65–	508	6	108	393	*1.2*	*22.4*	220	2	41	177	*0.9*	*19.5*	288	4	67	216	*1.4*	*24.7*
Chirk RD	All 3+	4153	668	1333	2148	*16.1*	*48.2*	2183	355	677	1149	*16.3*	*47.3*	1970	313	656	999	*15.9*	*49.2*
	3–14	1281	237	300	743	*18.5*	*42.0*	634	111	145	378	*17.5*	*40.4*	647	126	155	365	*19.5*	*43.5*
	15–24	806	82	249	473	*10.2*	*41.2*	459	53	129	276	*11.6*	*39.7*	347	29	120	197	*8.4*	*43.1*
	25–44	1159	179	422	558	*15.4*	*51.9*	622	93	220	309	*15.0*	*50.3*	537	86	202	249	*16.0*	*53.6*
	45–64	697	113	283	300	*16.2*	*56.9*	372	67	144	160	*18.1*	*56.9*	325	46	139	140	*14.2*	*56.9*
	65–	210	57	79	74	*27.1*	*64.8*	96	31	39	26	*32.3*	*72.9*	114	26	40	48	*22.8*	*57.9*
Llangollen RD	All 3+	3285	773	1881	617	*23.6*	*81.1*	1704	428	977	290	*25.2*	*82.8*	1581	345	904	327	*21.9*	*79.2*
	3–14	949	219	524	202	*23.2*	*78.6*	491	127	265	97	*26.0*	*80.2*	458	92	259	105	*20.2*	*77.0*
	15–24	598	96	397	104	*16.1*	*82.6*	329	60	216	52	*18.3*	*84.1*	269	36	181	52	*13.4*	*80.7*
	25–44	963	188	581	188	*19.6*	*80.2*	491	104	301	82	*21.3*	*83.0*	472	84	280	106	*17.8*	*77.3*
	45–64	559	176	287	93	*31.7*	*83.3*	291	100	146	43	*34.6*	*85.1*	268	76	141	50	*28.5*	*81.3*
	65–	216	94	92	30	*43.5*	*86.1*	102	37	49	16	*36.3*	*84.3*	114	57	43	14	*50.0*	*87.7*
Llanrwst RD	All 3+	4302	2489	1587	221	*57.9*	*94.9*	2165	1312	763	89	*60.6*	*95.9*	2137	1177	824	132	*55.2*	*93.8*
	3–14	1098	710	337	51	*64.7*	*95.4*	545	354	165	26	*65.0*	*95.2*	553	356	172	25	*64.4*	*95.5*
	15–24	839	383	421	33	*45.8*	*96.1*	421	220	190	11	*52.3*	*97.4*	418	163	231	22	*39.2*	*94.7*
	25–44	1172	596	499	75	*50.9*	*93.6*	601	338	242	21	*56.2*	*96.5*	571	258	257	54	*45.3*	*90.5*
	45–64	842	530	264	47	*63.0*	*94.4*	420	269	128	22	*64.2*	*94.7*	422	261	136	25	*61.8*	*94.1*
	65–	351	270	66	15	*76.9*	*95.7*	178	131	38	9	*73.6*	*94.9*	173	139	28	6	*80.3*	*96.5*

District[1]	Age last birth-day	Persons: Number[2] Total in age group	Persons: Welsh only	Persons: Both	Persons: English only	Persons: Percentage[3] *Welsh only*	Persons: Percentage[3] *Able to speak Welsh*	Males: Number[2] Total in age group	Males: Welsh only	Males: Both	Males: English only	Males: Percentage[3] *Welsh only*	Males: Percentage[3] *Able to speak Welsh*	Females: Number[2] Total in age group	Females: Welsh only	Females: Both	Females: English only	Females: Percentage[3] *Welsh only*	Females: Percentage[3] *Able to speak Welsh*
Llansilin RD	All 3+	3002	976	1802	223	*32.5*	*92.6*	1556	551	908	96	*35.4*	*93.8*	1446	425	894	127	*29.4*	*91.2*
	3–14	834	314	431	89	*37.6*	*89.3*	432	186	201	45	*43.1*	*89.6*	402	128	230	44	*31.8*	*89.1*
	15–24	568	139	385	43	*24.5*	*92.4*	291	86	194	10	*29.7*	*96.6*	277	53	191	33	*19.1*	*88.1*
	25–44	813	225	538	50	*27.7*	*93.8*	419	120	280	19	*28.6*	*95.5*	394	105	258	31	*26.6*	*92.1*
	45–64	560	202	322	36	*36.1*	*93.6*	296	107	171	18	*36.1*	*93.9*	264	95	151	18	*36.0*	*93.2*
	65–	227	96	126	5	*42.3*	*97.8*	118	52	62	4	*44.1*	*96.6*	109	44	64	1	*40.4*	*99.1*
Ruthin RD	All 3+	8652	3921	4004	715	*45.4*	*91.7*	4412	2049	2061	294	*46.5*	*93.3*	4240	1872	1943	421	*44.2*	*90.0*
	3–14	2093	1187	773	130	*56.8*	*93.8*	1097	625	413	56	*57.1*	*94.9*	996	562	360	74	*56.4*	*92.6*
	15–24	1677	541	959	173	*32.3*	*89.7*	852	295	480	75	*34.7*	*91.2*	825	246	479	98	*29.9*	*88.1*
	25–44	2421	919	1274	227	*38.0*	*90.6*	1248	492	673	82	*39.5*	*93.4*	1173	427	601	145	*36.4*	*87.6*
	45–64	1672	813	718	137	*48.7*	*91.7*	832	421	354	55	*50.7*	*93.4*	840	392	364	82	*46.7*	*90.1*
	65–	789	461	280	48	*58.4*	*93.9*	383	216	141	26	*56.4*	*93.2*	406	245	139	22	*60.3*	*94.6*
St Asaph (Denb) RD	All 3+	6481	3059	2737	671	*47.3*	*89.6*	3275	1632	1330	309	*49.9*	*90.5*	3206	1427	1407	362	*44.6*	*88.6*
	3–14	1668	907	596	160	*54.5*	*90.4*	846	469	276	100	*55.5*	*88.2*	822	438	320	60	*53.5*	*92.7*
	15–24	1273	492	651	127	*38.7*	*89.9*	659	279	322	56	*42.4*	*91.3*	614	213	329	71	*34.7*	*88.4*
	25–44	1833	742	850	237	*40.5*	*87.0*	916	417	408	91	*45.5*	*90.1*	917	325	442	146	*35.6*	*83.9*
	45–64	1228	612	501	114	*49.9*	*90.7*	633	324	259	49	*51.3*	*92.2*	595	288	242	65	*48.4*	*89.1*
	65–	479	306	139	33	*63.9*	*92.9*	221	143	65	13	*64.7*	*94.1*	258	163	74	20	*63.2*	*91.9*
Uwchaled RD	All 3+	2091	1640	407	43	*78.5*	*97.9*	1073	855	199	18	*79.8*	*98.3*	1018	785	208	25	*77.1*	*97.5*
	3–14	571	476	88	7	*83.4*	*98.8*	298	245	46	7	*82.2*	*97.7*	273	231	42	0	*84.6*	*100.0*
	15–24	385	276	98	11	*71.7*	*97.1*	185	143	42	0	*77.3*	*100.0*	200	133	56	11	*66.5*	*94.5*
	25–44	578	431	131	16	*74.6*	*97.2*	293	229	59	5	*78.2*	*98.3*	285	202	72	11	*70.9*	*96.1*
	45–64	387	311	70	6	*80.4*	*98.4*	214	168	40	6	*78.5*	*97.2*	173	143	30	0	*82.7*	*100.0*
	65–	170	146	20	3	*86.4*	*98.2*	83	70	12	0	*85.4*	*100.0*	87	76	8	3	*87.4*	*96.6*
Wrexham RD	All 3+	50565	5358	21883	23288	*10.6*	*53.9*	26525	2864	11663	11979	*10.8*	*54.8*	24040	2494	10220	11309	*10.4*	*52.9*
	3–14	15727	1988	5580	8151	*12.6*	*48.1*	8005	1022	2807	4170	*12.8*	*47.9*	7722	966	2773	3981	*12.5*	*48.4*
	15–24	9834	665	4326	4836	*6.8*	*50.8*	5628	429	2494	2701	*7.6*	*52.0*	4206	236	1832	2135	*5.6*	*49.2*
	25–44	14891	1340	7300	6236	*9.0*	*58.1*	7865	760	3994	3104	*9.7*	*60.5*	7026	580	3306	3132	*8.3*	*55.4*
	45–64	7852	998	3777	3071	*12.7*	*60.9*	4000	502	1962	1534	*12.6*	*61.6*	3852	496	1815	1537	*12.9*	*60.1*
	65–	2261	367	900	994	*16.2*	*56.0*	1027	151	406	470	*14.7*	*54.2*	1234	216	494	524	*17.5*	*57.5*
Llaneilian CP and Llansanffraid CP (admin. by Conwy (Caern) RD)	All 3+	1411	620	685	101	*44.1*	*92.8*	694	313	340	39	*45.2*	*94.4*	717	307	345	62	*43.0*	*91.3*
	3–14	361	199	132	25	*55.9*	*93.0*	171	96	63	10	*56.8*	*94.1*	190	103	69	15	*55.1*	*92.0*
	15–24	295	74	205	16	*25.1*	*94.6*	158	43	111	4	*27.2*	*97.5*	137	31	94	12	*22.6*	*91.2*
	25–44	392	154	206	32	*39.3*	*91.8*	190	78	101	11	*41.1*	*94.2*	202	76	105	21	*37.6*	*89.6*
	45–64	237	112	109	16	*47.3*	*93.2*	109	54	46	9	*49.5*	*91.7*	128	58	63	7	*45.3*	*94.5*
	65–	126	81	33	12	*64.3*	*90.5*	66	42	19	5	*63.6*	*92.4*	60	39	14	7	*65.0*	*88.3*

MERIONETH

Bala UD	All 3+	1455	407	941	105	*28.0*	*92.8*	679	191	433	54	*28.2*	*92.0*	776	216	508	51	*27.9*	*93.4*
	3–14	334	114	196	24	*34.1*	*92.8*	175	66	95	14	*37.7*	*92.0*	159	48	101	10	*30.2*	*93.7*
	15–24	300	48	234	17	*16.1*	*94.3*	130	25	95	10	*19.2*	*92.3*	170	23	139	7	*13.6*	*95.9*
	25–44	420	78	311	31	*18.6*	*92.6*	203	38	150	15	*18.7*	*92.6*	217	40	161	16	*18.4*	*92.6*
	45–64	293	111	155	26	*38.0*	*91.1*	132	46	74	11	*35.1*	*91.6*	161	65	81	15	*40.4*	*90.7*
	65–	108	56	45	7	*51.9*	*93.5*	39	16	19	4	*41.0*	*89.7*	69	40	26	3	*58.0*	*95.7*
Barmouth UD	All 3+	2123	273	1371	478	*12.9*	*77.5*	909	134	591	184	*14.7*	*79.8*	1214	139	780	294	*11.5*	*75.8*
	3–14	443	99	267	77	*22.3*	*82.6*	220	57	117	46	*25.9*	*79.1*	223	42	150	31	*18.8*	*86.1*
	15–24	453	32	329	92	*7.1*	*79.7*	186	16	142	28	*8.6*	*84.9*	267	16	187	64	*6.0*	*76.0*
	25–44	642	37	420	185	*5.8*	*71.2*	254	14	173	67	*5.5*	*73.6*	388	23	247	118	*5.9*	*69.6*
	45–64	455	78	281	96	*17.1*	*78.9*	197	36	129	32	*18.3*	*83.8*	258	42	152	64	*16.3*	*75.2*
	65–	130	27	74	28	*20.9*	*78.3*	52	11	30	11	*21.2*	*78.8*	78	16	44	17	*20.8*	*77.9*
Dolgellau UD	All 3+	2273	586	1469	212	*25.8*	*90.4*	1037	266	678	90	*25.7*	*91.1*	1236	320	791	122	*25.9*	*89.9*
	3–14	548	195	298	54	*35.6*	*90.0*	284	100	160	24	*35.2*	*91.5*	264	95	138	30	*36.0*	*88.3*
	15–24	429	48	352	27	*11.2*	*93.5*	199	28	161	8	*14.1*	*95.5*	230	20	191	19	*8.7*	*91.7*
	25–44	654	121	453	78	*18.5*	*87.8*	276	47	195	33	*17.0*	*87.7*	378	74	258	45	*19.6*	*87.8*
	45–64	465	144	278	42	*31.0*	*90.8*	214	62	131	21	*29.0*	*90.2*	251	82	147	21	*32.7*	*91.2*
	65–	177	78	88	11	*44.1*	*93.8*	64	29	31	4	*45.3*	*93.8*	113	49	57	7	*43.4*	*93.8*
Ffestiniog UD	All 3+	10556	5993	4368	186	*56.8*	*98.2*	5350	3111	2139	94	*58.2*	*98.2*	5206	2882	2229	92	*55.4*	*98.2*
	3–14	3017	1931	1050	35	*64.0*	*98.8*	1493	976	500	17	*65.4*	*98.9*	1524	955	550	18	*62.7*	*98.8*
	15–24	2088	800	1255	32	*38.3*	*98.5*	1147	478	652	16	*41.7*	*98.6*	941	322	603	16	*34.2*	*98.3*
	25–44	3087	1616	1405	62	*52.4*	*98.0*	1558	862	665	28	*55.4*	*98.1*	1529	754	740	34	*49.3*	*97.8*
	45–64	1943	1320	572	48	*68.0*	*97.5*	984	673	279	30	*68.5*	*96.9*	959	647	293	18	*67.5*	*98.1*
	65–	421	326	86	9	*77.4*	*97.9*	168	122	43	3	*72.6*	*98.2*	253	204	43	6	*80.6*	*97.6*
Mallwyd UD	All 3+	837	452	326	59	*54.0*	*93.0*	406	208	159	39	*51.2*	*90.4*	431	244	167	20	*56.6*	*95.4*
	3–14	203	128	70	5	*63.1*	*97.5*	102	60	37	5	*58.8*	*95.1*	101	68	33	0	*67.3*	*100.0*
	15–24	121	41	69	11	*33.9*	*90.9*	63	27	29	7	*42.9*	*88.9*	58	14	40	4	*24.1*	*93.1*
	25–44	250	92	130	28	*36.8*	*88.8*	121	43	62	16	*35.5*	*86.8*	129	49	68	12	*38.0*	*90.7*
	45–64	192	134	45	13	*69.8*	*93.2*	92	58	24	10	*63.0*	*89.1*	100	76	21	3	*76.0*	*97.0*
	65–	71	57	12	2	*80.3*	*97.2*	28	20	7	1	*71.4*	*96.4*	43	37	5	1	*86.0*	*97.7*
Tywyn UD	All 3+	3522	788	2255	470	*22.4*	*86.5*	1606	397	1009	196	*24.8*	*87.7*	1916	391	1246	274	*20.4*	*85.6*
	3–14	891	258	524	107	*29.0*	*88.0*	442	144	245	53	*32.6*	*88.0*	449	114	279	54	*25.5*	*87.9*
	15–24	653	83	509	60	*12.7*	*90.8*	300	42	235	22	*14.0*	*92.6*	353	41	274	38	*11.6*	*89.2*
	25–44	1053	169	701	178	*16.1*	*82.8*	445	79	289	75	*17.8*	*82.7*	608	90	412	103	*14.9*	*82.8*
	45–64	656	163	406	86	*24.9*	*86.9*	305	87	187	30	*28.6*	*90.1*	351	76	219	56	*21.7*	*84.0*
	65–	269	115	115	39	*42.8*	*85.5*	114	45	53	16	*39.5*	*86.0*	155	70	62	23	*45.2*	*85.2*
Deudraeth RD	All 3+	7478	4964	2306	197	*66.5*	*97.3*	3659	2423	1130	100	*66.3*	*97.2*	3819	2541	1176	97	*66.6*	*97.5*
	3–14	2150	1642	453	51	*76.5*	*97.6*	1105	844	223	36	*76.5*	*96.7*	1045	798	230	15	*76.5*	*98.6*
	15–24	1399	719	641	39	*51.4*	*97.2*	678	370	288	20	*54.6*	*97.1*	721	349	353	19	*48.4*	*97.4*
	25–44	2106	1284	756	60	*61.1*	*97.1*	1034	627	380	23	*60.8*	*97.7*	1072	657	376	37	*61.4*	*96.5*
	45–64	1319	919	368	32	*69.7*	*97.6*	631	431	187	13	*68.3*	*97.9*	688	488	181	19	*70.9*	*97.2*
	65–	504	400	88	15	*79.5*	*97.0*	211	151	52	8	*71.6*	*96.2*	293	249	36	7	*85.3*	*97.6*

District[1]	Age last birth-day	Number[2] Total in age group	Welsh only	Both	English only	Percentage[3] Welsh only	Able to speak Welsh	Number[2] Total in age group	Welsh only	Both	English only	Percentage[3] Welsh only	Able to speak Welsh	Number[2] Total in age group	Welsh only	Both	English only	Percentage[3] Welsh only	Able to speak Welsh
		Persons						Males						Females					
Dolgellau RD	All 3+	8152	4582	2981	584	*56.2*	*92.8*	3993	2308	1454	228	*57.8*	*94.3*	4159	2274	1527	356	*54.7*	*91.4*
	3–14	2138	1454	552	132	*68.0*	*93.8*	1123	764	295	64	*68.0*	*94.3*	1015	690	257	68	*68.0*	*93.3*
	15–24	1503	630	764	106	*42.0*	*92.9*	759	354	359	44	*46.8*	*94.2*	744	276	405	62	*37.1*	*91.7*
	25–44	2301	1087	1002	210	*47.3*	*90.8*	1095	546	478	70	*49.9*	*93.6*	1206	541	524	140	*44.9*	*88.3*
	45–64	1634	999	522	113	*61.1*	*93.1*	769	479	249	41	*62.3*	*94.7*	865	520	273	72	*60.1*	*91.7*
	65–	576	412	141	23	*71.5*	*96.0*	247	165	73	9	*66.8*	*96.4*	329	247	68	14	*75.1*	*95.7*
Edeirnion RD	All 3+	4794	2187	2261	345	*45.6*	*92.8*	2431	1148	1119	164	*47.2*	*93.3*	2363	1039	1142	181	*44.0*	*92.3*
	3–14	1297	728	488	81	*56.1*	*93.8*	676	382	260	34	*56.5*	*95.0*	621	346	228	47	*55.7*	*92.4*
	15–24	901	297	544	59	*33.0*	*93.4*	470	178	260	32	*37.9*	*93.2*	431	119	284	27	*27.7*	*93.7*
	25–44	1329	507	693	129	*38.1*	*90.3*	631	261	309	61	*41.4*	*90.3*	698	246	384	68	*35.2*	*90.3*
	45–64	892	416	420	56	*46.6*	*93.7*	482	219	236	27	*45.4*	*94.4*	410	197	184	29	*48.0*	*92.9*
	65–	375	239	116	20	*63.7*	*94.7*	172	108	54	10	*62.8*	*94.2*	203	131	62	10	*64.5*	*95.1*
Penllyn RD	All 3+	3947	2646	1151	143	*67.2*	*96.4*	1961	1348	548	62	*68.8*	*96.8*	1986	1298	603	81	*65.5*	*95.9*
	3–14	1004	750	221	30	*74.9*	*97.0*	519	384	116	17	*74.3*	*96.7*	485	366	105	13	*75.6*	*97.3*
	15–24	754	418	311	24	*55.5*	*96.8*	352	217	130	5	*61.6*	*98.6*	402	201	181	19	*50.1*	*95.3*
	25–44	1064	649	366	49	*61.0*	*95.4*	531	338	172	21	*63.7*	*96.0*	533	311	194	28	*58.3*	*94.7*
	45–64	797	559	201	34	*70.4*	*95.7*	404	290	98	15	*72.0*	*96.3*	393	269	103	19	*68.8*	*95.1*
	65–	328	270	52	6	*82.3*	*98.2*	155	119	32	4	*76.8*	*97.4*	173	151	20	2	*87.3*	*98.8*
Pennal CP (admin. by Machynlleth (Mont) RD	All 3+	494	203	245	46	*41.1*	*90.7*	230	96	113	21	*41.7*	*90.9*	264	107	132	25	*40.5*	*90.5*
	3–14	117	49	62	6	*41.9*	*94.9*	50	19	29	2	*38.0*	*96.0*	67	30	33	4	*44.8*	*94.0*
	15–24	99	25	61	13	*25.3*	*86.9*	50	13	33	4	*26.0*	*92.0*	49	12	28	9	*24.5*	*81.6*
	25–44	129	50	64	15	*38.8*	*88.4*	61	26	25	10	*42.6*	*83.6*	68	24	39	5	*35.3*	*92.6*
	45–64	104	49	45	10	*47.1*	*90.4*	51	25	22	4	*49.0*	*92.2*	53	24	23	6	*45.3*	*88.7*
	65–	45	30	13	2	*66.7*	*95.6*	18	13	4	1	*72.2*	*94.4*	27	17	9	1	*63.0*	*96.3*
CAERNARFONSHIRE																			
Bangor City MB	All 3+	10565	1104	7329	2112	*10.5*	*79.9*	4849	512	3410	913	*10.6*	*81.0*	5716	592	3919	1199	*10.4*	*79.0*
	3–14	2653	364	1683	606	*13.7*	*77.2*	1339	189	845	305	*14.1*	*77.2*	1314	175	838	301	*13.3*	*77.1*
	15–24	2297	130	1748	413	*5.7*	*81.9*	995	58	793	139	*5.9*	*85.9*	1302	72	955	274	*5.5*	*78.9*
	25–44	3310	253	2329	717	*7.7*	*78.1*	1512	117	1082	306	*7.7*	*79.4*	1798	136	1247	411	*7.6*	*77.0*
	45–64	1722	222	1212	285	*12.9*	*83.4*	769	98	538	131	*12.8*	*82.8*	953	124	674	154	*13.0*	*83.8*
	65–	583	135	357	91	*23.2*	*84.4*	234	50	152	32	*21.4*	*86.3*	349	85	205	59	*24.4*	*83.1*
Bethesda UD	All 3+	4903	3152	1705	38	*64.4*	*99.2*	2201	1477	705	12	*67.3*	*99.5*	2702	1675	1000	26	*62.0*	*99.0*
	3–14	1369	964	399	4	*70.5*	*99.7*	675	488	184	2	*72.4*	*99.7*	694	476	215	2	*68.7*	*99.7*
	15–24	723	315	406	2	*43.6*	*99.7*	336	168	167	1	*50.0*	*99.7*	387	147	239	1	*38.0*	*99.7*
	25–44	1356	788	550	15	*58.2*	*98.9*	547	321	219	4	*59.0*	*99.3*	809	467	331	11	*57.7*	*98.6*
	45–64	1074	769	295	8	*71.7*	*99.3*	478	359	116	1	*75.4*	*99.8*	596	410	179	7	*68.8*	*98.8*
	65–	381	316	55	9	*83.2*	*97.6*	165	141	19	4	*86.0*	*97.6*	216	175	36	5	*81.0*	*97.7*

Betws-y-coed UD	All 3+	835	195	500	139	*23.4*	*83.3*	371	100	209	61	*27.0*	*83.5*	464	95	291	78	*20.5*	*83.2*
	3–14	163	53	89	20	*32.7*	*87.7*	71	26	36	8	*37.1*	*88.6*	92	27	53	12	*29.3*	*87.0*
	15–24	195	25	142	28	*12.8*	*85.6*	79	13	53	13	*16.5*	*83.5*	116	12	89	15	*10.3*	*87.1*
	25–44	263	56	152	55	*21.3*	*79.1*	122	31	67	24	*25.4*	*80.3*	141	25	85	31	*17.7*	*78.0*
	45–64	173	43	102	28	*24.9*	*83.8*	82	23	47	12	*28.0*	*85.4*	91	20	55	16	*22.0*	*82.4*
	65–	41	18	15	8	*43.9*	*80.5*	17	7	6	4	*41.2*	*76.5*	24	11	9	4	*45.8*	*83.3*
Caernarfon MB	All 3+	9175	2275	5911	973	*24.8*	*89.3*	4213	1031	2743	431	*24.5*	*89.7*	4962	1244	3168	542	*25.1*	*89.1*
	3–14	2211	783	1193	231	*35.5*	*89.5*	1068	390	585	92	*36.6*	*91.4*	1143	393	608	139	*34.5*	*87.8*
	15–24	1933	334	1434	159	*17.3*	*91.6*	851	145	628	74	*17.1*	*90.9*	1082	189	806	85	*17.5*	*92.1*
	25–44	2791	492	1943	352	*17.6*	*87.3*	1255	209	888	155	*16.7*	*87.5*	1536	283	1055	197	*18.4*	*87.2*
	45–64	1708	452	1086	168	*26.5*	*90.2*	809	204	528	77	*25.2*	*90.5*	899	248	558	91	*27.6*	*89.9*
	65–	532	214	255	63	*40.2*	*88.2*	230	83	114	33	*36.1*	*85.7*	302	131	141	30	*43.4*	*90.1*
Conwy MB	All 3+	4387	707	2796	879	*16.1*	*79.9*	2079	351	1240	484	*16.9*	*76.6*	2308	356	1556	395	*15.4*	*82.8*
	3–14	1115	254	702	158	*22.8*	*85.8*	559	136	319	103	*24.4*	*81.5*	556	118	383	55	*21.2*	*90.1*
	15–24	943	83	693	166	*8.8*	*82.3*	436	51	306	78	*11.7*	*81.9*	507	32	387	88	*6.3*	*82.6*
	25–44	1392	150	878	362	*10.8*	*73.9*	656	68	398	189	*10.4*	*71.0*	736	82	480	173	*11.1*	*76.4*
	45–64	706	130	410	165	*18.4*	*76.6*	331	64	171	95	*19.4*	*71.2*	375	66	239	70	*17.6*	*81.3*
	65–	231	90	113	28	*39.0*	*87.9*	97	32	46	19	*33.0*	*80.4*	134	58	67	9	*43.3*	*93.3*
Cricieth UD	All 3+	1345	357	878	107	*26.6*	*92.0*	562	151	372	37	*27.0*	*93.4*	783	206	506	70	*26.3*	*91.0*
	3–14	326	100	206	19	*30.8*	*94.2*	163	45	110	7	*27.8*	*95.7*	163	55	96	12	*33.7*	*92.6*
	15–24	281	51	211	18	*18.2*	*93.6*	109	24	78	7	*22.0*	*93.6*	172	27	133	11	*15.8*	*93.6*
	25–44	348	78	237	33	*22.4*	*90.5*	131	29	91	11	*22.1*	*91.6*	217	49	146	22	*22.6*	*89.9*
	45–64	287	85	176	26	*29.6*	*90.9*	118	40	70	8	*33.9*	*93.2*	169	45	106	18	*26.6*	*89.3*
	65–	103	43	48	11	*42.2*	*89.2*	41	13	23	4	*32.5*	*90.0*	62	30	25	7	*48.4*	*88.7*
Llandudno UD	All 3+	8766	331	4031	4379	*3.8*	*49.8*	3661	175	1816	1658	*4.8*	*54.4*	5105	156	2215	2721	*3.1*	*46.5*
	3–14	1753	65	832	850	*3.7*	*51.3*	841	36	388	414	*4.3*	*50.5*	912	29	444	436	*3.2*	*52.0*
	15–24	2089	56	1036	993	*2.7*	*52.3*	809	30	442	335	*3.7*	*58.4*	1280	26	594	658	*2.0*	*48.5*
	25–44	3087	98	1405	1573	*3.2*	*48.7*	1258	55	657	540	*4.4*	*56.6*	1829	43	748	1033	*2.4*	*43.3*
	45–64	1418	67	593	755	*4.7*	*46.5*	581	35	263	282	*6.0*	*51.3*	837	32	330	473	*3.8*	*43.2*
	65–	419	45	165	208	*10.7*	*50.1*	172	19	66	87	*11.0*	*49.4*	247	26	99	121	*10.5*	*50.6*
Llanfairfechan UD	All 3+	2587	850	1388	342	*32.9*	*86.7*	1231	474	636	114	*38.7*	*90.7*	1356	376	752	228	*27.7*	*83.2*
	3–14	654	256	340	57	*39.2*	*91.3*	316	126	166	23	*40.0*	*92.7*	338	130	174	34	*38.5*	*89.9*
	15–24	474	104	307	62	*22.0*	*86.9*	242	68	154	19	*28.2*	*92.1*	232	36	153	43	*15.5*	*81.5*
	25–44	846	255	461	127	*30.2*	*84.9*	397	152	194	48	*38.6*	*87.8*	449	103	267	79	*22.9*	*82.4*
	45–64	461	165	217	77	*35.9*	*83.2*	208	90	94	22	*43.7*	*89.3*	253	75	123	55	*29.6*	*78.3*
	65–	152	70	63	19	*46.1*	*87.5*	68	38	28	2	*55.9*	*97.1*	84	32	35	17	*38.1*	*79.8*
Penmaen-mawr UD	All 3+	3278	838	1852	583	*25.6*	*82.1*	1607	468	925	214	*29.1*	*86.7*	1671	370	927	369	*22.2*	*77.7*
	3–14	862	280	464	117	*32.5*	*86.3*	462	147	252	63	*31.8*	*86.4*	400	133	212	54	*33.3*	*86.3*
	15–24	694	97	486	108	*14.0*	*84.1*	334	60	239	35	*18.0*	*89.5*	360	37	247	73	*10.3*	*79.1*
	25–44	1002	246	554	201	*24.6*	*79.8*	481	144	275	62	*29.9*	*87.1*	521	102	279	139	*19.6*	*73.1*
	45–64	563	138	298	127	*24.5*	*77.4*	269	80	138	51	*29.7*	*81.0*	294	58	160	76	*19.7*	*74.1*
	65–	157	77	50	30	*49.0*	*80.9*	61	37	21	3	*60.7*	*95.1*	96	40	29	27	*41.7*	*71.9*

District[1]	Age last birth-day	Number[2] Total in age group	Welsh only	Both	English only	Percentage[3] Welsh only	Able to speak Welsh	Number[2] Total in age group	Welsh only	Both	English only	Percentage[3] Welsh only	Able to speak Welsh	Number[2] Total in age group	Welsh only	Both	English only	Percentage[3] Welsh only	Able to speak Welsh
		Persons						Males						Females					
Pwllheli MB	All 3+	3475	1256	1968	248	*36.2*	*92.9*	1582	584	901	97	*36.9*	*93.9*	1893	672	1067	151	*35.6*	*92.0*
	3–14	852	410	382	59	*48.2*	*93.1*	430	224	190	16	*52.1*	*96.3*	422	186	192	43	*44.2*	*89.8*
	15–24	750	173	535	41	*23.1*	*94.5*	360	89	251	20	*24.7*	*94.4*	390	84	284	21	*21.6*	*94.6*
	25–44	977	315	573	88	*32.3*	*91.0*	407	134	244	29	*32.9*	*92.9*	570	181	329	59	*31.8*	*89.6*
	45–64	669	233	390	46	*34.8*	*93.1*	299	100	171	28	*33.4*	*90.6*	370	133	219	18	*35.9*	*95.1*
	65–	227	125	88	14	*55.1*	*93.8*	86	37	45	4	*43.0*	*95.3*	141	88	43	10	*62.4*	*92.9*
Ynyscynhaearn UD	All 3+	4591	1599	2706	269	*34.9*	*93.9*	2160	729	1277	139	*33.8*	*93.0*	2431	870	1429	130	*35.8*	*94.6*
	3–14	1148	604	479	63	*52.7*	*94.5*	583	296	247	39	*50.9*	*93.3*	565	308	232	24	*54.6*	*95.7*
	15–24	958	187	724	38	*19.6*	*95.4*	451	91	327	24	*20.3*	*93.3*	507	96	397	14	*18.9*	*97.2*
	25–44	1289	299	858	126	*23.2*	*89.8*	589	137	391	56	*23.3*	*89.6*	700	162	467	70	*23.2*	*90.0*
	45–64	909	373	508	28	*41.0*	*96.9*	420	160	246	14	*38.1*	*96.7*	489	213	262	14	*43.6*	*97.1*
	65–	287	136	137	14	*47.4*	*95.1*	117	45	66	6	*38.5*	*94.9*	170	91	71	8	*53.5*	*95.3*
Conwy RD	All 3+	5841	2036	3084	712	*34.9*	*87.8*	2953	1109	1514	326	*37.6*	*88.9*	2888	927	1570	386	*32.2*	*86.6*
	3–14	1644	667	818	152	*40.7*	*90.7*	810	348	377	82	*43.1*	*89.8*	834	319	441	70	*38.4*	*91.6*
	15–24	1115	279	713	123	*25.0*	*89.0*	603	182	365	56	*30.2*	*90.7*	512	97	348	67	*18.9*	*86.9*
	25–44	1814	494	1038	280	*27.3*	*84.5*	909	273	523	112	*30.1*	*87.7*	905	221	515	168	*24.4*	*81.4*
	45–64	912	370	416	126	*40.6*	*86.2*	457	196	200	61	*42.9*	*86.7*	455	174	216	65	*38.2*	*85.7*
	65–	356	226	99	31	*63.5*	*91.3*	174	110	49	15	*63.2*	*91.4*	182	116	50	16	*63.7*	*91.2*
Geirionydd RD	All 3+	4708	2691	1814	201	*57.2*	*95.7*	2360	1395	881	84	*59.1*	*96.4*	2348	1296	933	117	*55.2*	*95.0*
	3–14	1189	759	390	40	*63.8*	*96.6*	592	376	197	19	*63.5*	*96.8*	597	383	193	21	*64.2*	*96.5*
	15–24	898	381	490	26	*42.5*	*97.1*	460	221	228	11	*48.0*	*97.6*	438	160	262	15	*36.6*	*96.6*
	25–44	1395	748	577	70	*53.6*	*95.0*	706	405	271	30	*57.4*	*95.8*	689	343	306	40	*49.8*	*94.2*
	45–64	897	552	293	52	*61.5*	*94.2*	451	279	151	21	*61.9*	*95.3*	446	273	142	31	*61.2*	*93.0*
	65–	329	251	64	13	*76.5*	*96.0*	151	114	34	3	*75.5*	*98.0*	178	137	30	10	*77.4*	*94.4*
Glaslyn RD	All 3+	3348	2496	752	94	*74.7*	*97.2*	1664	1250	373	39	*75.2*	*97.7*	1684	1246	379	55	*74.1*	*96.7*
	3–14	924	790	110	23	*85.6*	*97.5*	471	407	54	10	*86.4*	*97.9*	453	383	56	13	*84.7*	*97.1*
	15–24	664	463	185	16	*69.7*	*97.6*	348	254	86	8	*73.0*	*97.7*	316	209	99	8	*66.1*	*97.5*
	25–44	949	631	289	28	*66.5*	*96.9*	472	315	146	11	*66.7*	*97.7*	477	316	143	17	*66.2*	*96.2*
	45–64	581	427	129	22	*73.9*	*96.2*	279	199	70	8	*71.8*	*97.1*	302	228	59	14	*75.7*	*95.3*
	65–	230	185	39	5	*80.8*	*97.8*	94	75	17	2	*79.8*	*97.9*	136	110	22	3	*81.5*	*97.8*
Gwyrfai RD	All 3+	27771	20423	6870	446	*73.6*	*98.4*	14108	10645	3245	203	*75.5*	*98.6*	13663	9778	3625	243	*71.6*	*98.2*
	3–14	7111	5775	1242	82	*81.3*	*98.8*	3655	2986	622	41	*81.8*	*98.9*	3456	2789	620	41	*80.8*	*98.8*
	15–24	5500	3537	1890	61	*64.4*	*98.9*	2941	2035	875	25	*69.3*	*99.1*	2559	1502	1015	36	*58.8*	*98.6*
	25–44	8259	5681	2379	196	*68.8*	*97.6*	4239	3042	1112	83	*71.8*	*98.0*	4020	2639	1267	113	*65.7*	*97.2*
	45–64	5308	4110	1108	86	*77.5*	*98.4*	2592	2032	512	47	*78.4*	*98.2*	2716	2078	596	39	*76.6*	*98.6*
	65–	1593	1320	251	21	*82.9*	*98.7*	681	550	124	7	*80.8*	*99.0*	912	770	127	14	*84.5*	*98.5*

Llŷn RD	All 3+	15891	12290	3272	313	*77.4*	*98.0*	7785	5976	1618	182	*76.8*	*97.6*	8106	6314	1654	131	*78.0*	*98.4*
	3–14	3882	3324	521	32	*85.7*	*99.2*	2003	1734	257	10	*86.7*	*99.5*	1879	1590	264	22	*84.8*	*98.8*
	15–24	3026	2143	819	59	*70.9*	*97.9*	1560	1150	367	40	*73.7*	*97.2*	1466	993	452	19	*67.8*	*98.7*
	25–44	4380	3131	1121	125	*71.5*	*97.1*	2051	1443	525	80	*70.4*	*96.0*	2329	1688	596	45	*72.5*	*98.1*
	45–64	3151	2452	623	73	*77.9*	*97.7*	1494	1108	345	40	*74.2*	*97.3*	1657	1344	278	33	*81.2*	*98.0*
	65–	1452	1240	188	24	*85.4*	*98.3*	677	541	124	12	*79.9*	*98.2*	775	699	64	12	*90.2*	*98.5*
Ogwen RD	All 3+	6201	3355	2490	350	*54.1*	*94.3*	2998	1662	1176	156	*55.5*	*94.8*	3203	1693	1314	194	*52.9*	*93.9*
	3–14	1610	970	552	85	*60.4*	*94.7*	803	481	285	35	*60.0*	*95.6*	807	489	267	50	*60.7*	*93.8*
	15–24	1143	442	639	61	*38.7*	*94.6*	567	239	301	26	*42.2*	*95.2*	576	203	338	35	*35.2*	*93.9*
	25–44	1718	846	743	127	*49.3*	*92.5*	807	414	337	55	*51.4*	*93.2*	911	432	406	72	*47.4*	*92.0*
	45–64	1262	746	453	63	*59.1*	*95.0*	619	379	207	33	*61.2*	*94.7*	643	367	246	30	*57.1*	*95.3*
	65–	468	351	103	14	*75.0*	*97.0*	202	149	46	7	*73.8*	*96.5*	266	202	57	7	*75.9*	*97.4*
ANGLESEY																			
Beaumaris MB	All 3+	2210	205	1383	614	*9.3*	*72.1*	1054	112	643	297	*10.6*	*71.8*	1156	93	740	317	*8.1*	*72.4*
	3–14	517	55	321	141	*10.6*	*72.7*	251	29	157	65	*11.6*	*74.1*	266	26	164	76	*9.8*	*71.4*
	15–24	458	34	306	116	*7.5*	*74.6*	233	22	152	57	*9.5*	*75.3*	225	12	154	59	*5.3*	*73.8*
	25–44	687	44	416	225	*6.4*	*67.1*	327	20	189	118	*6.1*	*63.9*	360	24	227	107	*6.7*	*69.9*
	45–64	392	51	240	97	*13.1*	*75.0*	174	28	104	42	*16.1*	*75.9*	218	23	136	55	*10.7*	*74.3*
	65–	156	21	100	35	*13.5*	*77.6*	69	13	41	15	*18.8*	*78.3*	87	8	59	20	*9.2*	*77.0*
Holyhead UD	All 3+	9364	1455	6145	1675	*15.5*	*81.2*	4572	733	2896	862	*16.0*	*79.4*	4792	722	3249	813	*15.1*	*82.9*
	3–14	2496	510	1567	415	*20.4*	*83.3*	1257	274	787	193	*21.8*	*84.5*	1239	236	780	222	*19.1*	*82.1*
	15–24	1877	154	1389	303	*8.2*	*82.2*	900	97	634	139	*10.8*	*81.2*	977	57	755	164	*5.8*	*83.1*
	25–44	2896	351	1888	615	*12.1*	*77.4*	1451	184	892	336	*12.7*	*74.2*	1445	167	996	279	*11.6*	*80.5*
	45–64	1583	279	1010	282	*17.7*	*81.6*	756	131	449	167	*17.4*	*76.9*	827	148	561	115	*17.9*	*85.8*
	65–	512	161	291	60	*31.4*	*88.3*	208	47	134	27	*22.6*	*87.0*	304	114	157	33	*37.5*	*89.1*
Llangefni UD	All 3+	1658	770	830	56	*46.5*	*96.6*	753	360	367	25	*47.9*	*96.7*	905	410	463	31	*45.4*	*96.6*
	3–14	424	271	147	5	*64.1*	*98.8*	207	133	74	0	*64.3*	*100.0*	217	138	73	5	*63.9*	*97.7*
	15–24	317	103	203	11	*32.5*	*96.5*	128	49	75	4	*38.3*	*96.9*	189	54	128	7	*28.6*	*96.3*
	25–44	468	186	256	25	*39.8*	*94.6*	211	83	112	15	*39.5*	*92.9*	257	103	144	10	*40.1*	*96.1*
	45–64	313	127	173	13	*40.6*	*95.8*	144	59	80	5	*41.0*	*96.5*	169	68	93	8	*40.2*	*95.3*
	65–	136	83	51	2	*61.0*	*98.5*	63	36	26	1	*57.1*	*98.4*	73	47	25	1	*64.4*	*98.6*
Menai Bridge UD	All 3+	1614	314	1115	179	*19.5*	*88.8*	741	155	503	80	*21.0*	*89.2*	873	159	612	99	*18.3*	*88.5*
	3–14	355	103	208	43	*29.1*	*87.9*	181	54	100	26	*30.0*	*85.6*	174	49	108	17	*28.2*	*90.2*
	15–24	307	33	249	23	*10.8*	*92.5*	150	16	128	5	*10.7*	*96.6*	157	17	121	18	*10.9*	*88.5*
	25–44	511	84	371	55	*16.5*	*89.2*	233	42	168	23	*18.0*	*90.1*	278	42	203	32	*15.2*	*88.4*
	45–64	321	63	214	42	*19.7*	*86.6*	126	27	81	17	*21.6*	*86.4*	195	36	133	25	*18.5*	*86.7*
	65–	120	31	73	16	*25.8*	*86.7*	51	16	26	9	*31.4*	*82.4*	69	15	47	7	*21.7*	*89.9*
Aethwy RD	All 3+	8185	4279	3237	662	*52.3*	*91.9*	4067	2138	1518	406	*52.6*	*90.0*	4118	2141	1719	256	*52.0*	*93.8*
	3–14	2192	1268	694	230	*57.8*	*89.5*	1188	660	340	188	*55.6*	*84.2*	1004	608	354	42	*60.6*	*95.8*
	15–24	1606	682	761	162	*42.5*	*89.9*	827	378	347	101	*45.8*	*87.8*	779	304	414	61	*39.0*	*92.2*
	25–44	2212	1005	1038	165	*45.5*	*92.5*	1038	491	475	69	*47.4*	*93.3*	1174	514	563	96	*43.8*	*91.8*
	45–64	1474	834	554	84	*56.7*	*94.3*	694	395	261	37	*57.0*	*94.7*	780	439	293	47	*56.4*	*94.0*
	65–	701	490	190	21	*69.9*	*97.0*	320	214	95	11	*66.9*	*96.6*	381	276	95	10	*72.4*	*97.4*

District[1]	Age last birth-day	Number[2] Total in age group	Welsh only	Both	English only	Percentage[3] Welsh only	Percentage[3] Able to speak Welsh	Number[2] Total in age group	Welsh only	Both	English only	Percentage[3] Welsh only	Percentage[3] Able to speak Welsh	Number[2] Total in age group	Welsh only	Both	English only	Percentage[3] Welsh only	Percentage[3] Able to speak Welsh
		Persons						Males						Females					
Dwyran RD	All 3+	2870	2037	796	34	*71.0*	*98.8*	1346	973	354	18	*72.3*	*98.7*	1524	1064	442	16	*69.9*	*98.9*
	3–14	699	566	123	9	*81.1*	*98.7*	351	289	57	5	*82.3*	*98.6*	348	277	66	4	*79.8*	*98.8*
	15–24	504	324	180	0	*64.3*	*100.0*	236	166	70	0	*70.3*	*100.0*	268	158	110	0	*59.0*	*100.0*
	25–44	791	509	263	18	*64.4*	*97.7*	360	235	114	10	*65.5*	*97.2*	431	274	149	8	*63.6*	*98.1*
	45–64	605	435	165	5	*71.9*	*99.2*	275	195	77	3	*70.9*	*98.9*	330	240	88	2	*72.7*	*99.4*
	65–	271	203	65	2	*75.2*	*99.3*	124	88	36	0	*71.0*	*100.0*	147	115	29	2	*78.8*	*98.6*
Twrcelyn RD	All 3+	11788	7419	4014	323	*63.0*	*97.1*	5564	3636	1720	183	*65.5*	*96.5*	6224	3783	2294	140	*60.8*	*97.7*
	3–14	3042	2266	699	70	*74.7*	*97.7*	1564	1208	318	35	*77.4*	*97.8*	1478	1058	381	35	*71.8*	*97.6*
	15–24	2102	1196	863	34	*57.0*	*98.0*	990	641	323	17	*64.9*	*97.6*	1112	555	540	17	*49.9*	*98.5*
	25–44	3241	1733	1356	140	*53.6*	*95.5*	1491	822	575	85	*55.3*	*93.9*	1750	911	781	55	*52.1*	*96.9*
	45–64	2315	1455	796	61	*62.9*	*97.3*	1061	654	366	38	*61.8*	*96.3*	1254	801	430	23	*63.9*	*98.2*
	65–	1088	769	300	18	*70.7*	*98.3*	458	311	138	8	*68.1*	*98.2*	630	458	162	10	*72.7*	*98.4*
Valley RD	All 3+	9815	6312	3243	250	*64.4*	*97.5*	4787	3188	1495	98	*66.7*	*98.0*	5028	3124	1748	152	*62.2*	*97.0*
	3–14	2599	1980	538	80	*76.2*	*96.9*	1342	1052	253	36	*78.4*	*97.3*	1257	928	285	44	*73.8*	*96.5*
	15–24	1789	1003	743	42	*56.1*	*97.7*	880	556	314	9	*63.3*	*99.0*	909	447	429	33	*49.2*	*96.4*
	25–44	2698	1511	1109	73	*56.1*	*97.3*	1249	721	502	24	*57.8*	*98.1*	1449	790	607	49	*54.6*	*96.6*
	45–64	1870	1163	662	42	*62.3*	*97.8*	909	563	320	24	*62.1*	*97.4*	961	600	342	18	*62.5*	*98.1*
	65–	859	655	191	13	*76.3*	*98.5*	407	296	106	5	*72.7*	*98.8*	452	359	85	8	*79.4*	*98.2*

Source: *Census of Population for England and Wales*: 1901, *County Reports* (HMSO, 1902/3), Table 40.

1 Abbreviations as follows: UD Urban District; MB Municipal Borough; CB County Borough; RD Rural District.

2 The total numbers in age groups include small numbers who either gave no statement as to language spoken or who entered other languages. The totals for Wales are 2,757 and 3,893 respectively.

3 The denominator excludes those who gave no language statement but includes those who entered other languages.

Language 3.7 Census Returns. Ability to speak Welsh and English. Persons, males and females, by age. Numbers and percentage. Urban and Rural Districts. 1911

District[1]	Age last birth-day	Number[2] Total in age group	Welsh only	Both	English only	Percentage[3] *Welsh only*	*Able to speak Welsh*	Number[2] Total in age group	Welsh only	Both	English only	Percentage[3] *Welsh only*	*Able to speak Welsh*	Number[2] Total in age group	Welsh only	Both	English only	Percentage[3] *Welsh only*	*Able to speak Welsh*
		Persons						Males						Females					
MONMOUTHSHIRE																			
Aber-carn UD	All 3+	15072	47	2026	12648	*0.3*	*14.1*	8278	24	1072	7008	*0.3*	*13.5*	6794	23	954	5640	*0.3*	*14.8*
	3–4	878	0	31	779	*0.0*	*3.8*	457	0	17	407	*0.0*	*4.0*	421	0	14	372	*0.0*	*3.6*
	5–9	2087	1	93	1898	*0.1*	*4.7*	1062	1	45	961	*0.1*	*4.6*	1025	0	48	937	*0.0*	*4.9*
	10–14	1657	0	91	1518	*0.0*	*5.7*	863	0	45	789	*0.0*	*5.4*	794	0	46	729	*0.0*	*5.9*
	15–24	3240	4	257	2920	*0.1*	*8.2*	1756	4	121	1609	*0.2*	*7.2*	1484	0	136	1311	*0.0*	*9.4*
	25–44	4773	15	727	3973	*0.3*	*15.7*	2770	7	400	2336	*0.3*	*14.8*	2003	8	327	1637	*0.4*	*17.0*
	45–64	2008	15	631	1344	*0.8*	*32.4*	1156	8	354	788	*0.7*	*31.5*	852	7	277	556	*0.8*	*33.8*
	65–	429	12	196	216	*2.8*	*49.1*	214	4	90	118	*1.9*	*44.3*	215	8	106	98	*3.8*	*53.8*
Abergavenny MB	All 3+	8029	11	361	7415	*0.1*	*4.8*	3882	11	185	3585	*0.3*	*5.2*	4147	0	176	3830	*0.0*	*4.4*
	3–4	337	0	3	312	*0.0*	*1.0*	169	0	3	156	*0.0*	*1.9*	168	0	0	156	*0.0*	*0.0*
	5–9	813	0	12	733	*0.0*	*1.6*	406	0	8	365	*0.0*	*2.1*	407	0	4	368	*0.0*	*1.1*
	10–14	767	0	14	709	*0.0*	*1.9*	392	0	5	364	*0.0*	*1.4*	375	0	9	345	*0.0*	*2.5*
	15–24	1479	2	29	1397	*0.1*	*2.2*	664	2	16	622	*0.3*	*2.8*	815	0	13	775	*0.0*	*1.6*
	25–44	2519	5	129	2348	*0.2*	*5.4*	1217	5	68	1138	*0.4*	*6.0*	1302	0	61	1210	*0.0*	*4.8*
	45–64	1545	3	110	1417	*0.2*	*7.4*	761	3	54	701	*0.4*	*7.5*	784	0	56	716	*0.0*	*7.3*
	65–	569	1	64	499	*0.2*	*11.5*	273	1	31	239	*0.4*	*11.8*	296	0	33	260	*0.0*	*11.3*
Abersychan UD	All 3+	22540	8	905	21370	*0.0*	*4.1*	11949	6	493	11316	*0.1*	*4.2*	10591	2	412	10054	*0.0*	*4.0*
	3–4	1350	0	9	1269	*0.0*	*0.7*	683	0	4	643	*0.0*	*0.6*	667	0	5	626	*0.0*	*0.8*
	5–9	3204	0	22	3119	*0.0*	*0.7*	1623	0	9	1582	*0.0*	*0.6*	1581	0	13	1537	*0.0*	*0.8*
	10–14	2772	0	26	2721	*0.0*	*0.9*	1407	0	12	1376	*0.0*	*0.9*	1365	0	14	1345	*0.0*	*1.0*
	15–24	4739	1	84	4623	*0.0*	*1.8*	2603	0	50	2537	*0.0*	*1.9*	2136	1	34	2086	*0.0*	*1.7*
	25–44	6819	5	317	6447	*0.1*	*4.8*	3728	4	179	3517	*0.1*	*4.9*	3091	1	138	2930	*0.0*	*4.5*
	45–64	2951	2	299	2636	*0.1*	*10.2*	1566	2	165	1396	*0.1*	*10.7*	1385	0	134	1240	*0.0*	*9.8*
	65–	705	0	148	555	*0.0*	*21.1*	339	0	74	265	*0.0*	*21.8*	366	0	74	290	*0.0*	*20.3*
Abertillery UD	All 3+	32078	79	2164	28284	*0.3*	*7.3*	17698	40	1206	15693	*0.2*	*7.3*	14380	39	958	12591	*0.3*	*7.3*
	3–4	2028	1	29	1741	*0.1*	*1.7*	969	0	15	837	*0.0*	*1.8*	1059	1	14	904	*0.1*	*1.6*
	5–9	4680	8	58	4204	*0.2*	*1.5*	2397	1	23	2156	*0.0*	*1.1*	2283	7	35	2048	*0.3*	*2.0*
	10–14	3686	5	89	3370	*0.1*	*2.7*	1840	3	49	1669	*0.2*	*3.0*	1846	2	40	1701	*0.1*	*2.4*
	15–24	6900	11	266	6340	*0.2*	*4.2*	3990	8	138	3683	*0.2*	*3.8*	2910	3	128	2657	*0.1*	*4.7*
	25–44	10681	26	943	9426	*0.2*	*9.3*	6202	16	559	5518	*0.3*	*9.4*	4479	10	384	3908	*0.2*	*9.2*
	45–64	3495	21	627	2772	*0.6*	*18.9*	2008	9	353	1617	*0.5*	*18.3*	1487	12	274	1155	*0.8*	*19.8*
	65–	608	7	152	431	*1.2*	*26.9*	292	3	69	213	*1.1*	*25.3*	316	4	83	218	*1.3*	*28.4*

Bedwellte UD[3]	All 3+	20506	229	4141	14939	*1.2*	*22.6*	11315	120	2299	8294	*1.1*	*22.6*	9191	109	1842	6645	*1.3*	*22.7*
	3–4	1332	5	90	1009	*0.5*	*8.6*	657	2	39	499	*0.4*	*7.6*	675	3	51	510	*0.5*	*9.6*
	5–9	3022	7	318	2387	*0.3*	*12.0*	1517	1	156	1199	*0.1*	*11.6*	1505	6	162	1188	*0.4*	*12.4*
	10–14	2377	11	344	1834	*0.5*	*16.2*	1217	2	168	956	*0.2*	*15.1*	1160	9	176	878	*0.8*	*17.4*
	15–24	4160	37	658	3252	*0.9*	*17.6*	2408	20	362	1901	*0.9*	*16.7*	1752	17	296	1351	*1.0*	*18.8*
	25–44	6888	84	1644	4951	*1.3*	*25.9*	3997	48	958	2903	*1.2*	*25.7*	2891	36	686	2048	*1.3*	*26.0*
	45–64	2290	71	866	1313	*3.2*	*41.6*	1309	42	509	743	*3.2*	*42.5*	981	29	357	570	*3.0*	*40.4*
	65–	437	14	221	193	*3.3*	*54.8*	210	5	107	93	*2.4*	*54.4*	227	9	114	100	*4.0*	*55.2*
Blaenafon UD	All 3+	11087	11	616	10080	*0.1*	*5.9*	5952	3	310	5450	*0.1*	*5.4*	5135	8	306	4630	*0.2*	*6.3*
	3–4	591	0	1	535	*0.0*	*0.2*	284	0	1	247	*0.0*	*0.4*	307	0	0	288	*0.0*	*0.0*
	5–9	1432	0	7	1336	*0.0*	*0.5*	747	0	4	696	*0.0*	*0.6*	685	0	3	640	*0.0*	*0.5*
	10–14	1281	0	10	1221	*0.0*	*0.8*	647	0	6	617	*0.0*	*1.0*	634	0	4	604	*0.0*	*0.7*
	15–24	2208	2	48	2087	*0.1*	*2.3*	1247	0	23	1193	*0.0*	*1.9*	961	2	25	894	*0.2*	*2.9*
	25–44	3382	0	157	3148	*0.0*	*4.7*	1870	0	84	1754	*0.0*	*4.6*	1512	0	73	1394	*0.0*	*5.0*
	45–64	1694	3	244	1410	*0.2*	*14.9*	912	2	126	765	*0.2*	*14.3*	782	1	118	645	*0.1*	*15.6*
	65–	499	6	149	343	*1.2*	*31.1*	245	1	66	178	*0.4*	*27.3*	254	5	83	165	*2.0*	*34.8*
Caerleon UD	All 3+	1935	2	73	1828	*0.1*	*3.9*	897	1	32	855	*0.1*	*3.7*	1038	1	41	973	*0.1*	*4.1*
	3–4	82	0	0	79	*0.0*	*0.0*	42	0	0	40	*0.0*	*0.0*	40	0	0	39	*0.0*	*0.0*
	5–9	175	0	2	166	*0.0*	*1.2*	80	0	2	76	*0.0*	*2.6*	95	0	0	90	*0.0*	*0.0*
	10–14	174	0	2	167	*0.0*	*1.2*	85	0	1	84	*0.0*	*1.2*	89	0	1	83	*0.0*	*1.2*
	15–24	326	0	6	317	*0.0*	*1.9*	142	0	2	140	*0.0*	*1.4*	184	0	4	177	*0.0*	*2.2*
	25–44	594	1	29	557	*0.2*	*5.1*	282	0	11	268	*0.0*	*3.9*	312	1	18	289	*0.3*	*6.1*
	45–64	427	1	25	397	*0.2*	*6.1*	203	1	12	189	*0.5*	*6.4*	224	0	13	208	*0.0*	*5.9*
	65–	157	0	9	145	*0.0*	*5.8*	63	0	4	58	*0.0*	*6.5*	94	0	5	87	*0.0*	*5.4*
Chepstow UD	All 3+	2809	1	41	2660	*0.0*	*1.6*	1353	0	17	1279	*0.0*	*1.3*	1456	1	24	1381	*0.1*	*1.8*
	3–4	109	0	0	98	*0.0*	*0.0*	69	0	0	60	*0.0*	*0.0*	40	0	0	38	*0.0*	*0.0*
	5–9	236	0	0	217	*0.0*	*0.0*	111	0	0	100	*0.0*	*0.0*	125	0	0	117	*0.0*	*0.0*
	10–14	283	0	2	271	*0.0*	*0.7*	132	0	0	126	*0.0*	*0.0*	151	0	2	145	*0.0*	*1.4*
	15–24	536	0	10	513	*0.0*	*1.9*	237	0	6	224	*0.0*	*2.6*	299	0	4	289	*0.0*	*1.4*
	25–44	772	0	12	733	*0.0*	*1.6*	370	0	2	355	*0.0*	*0.6*	402	0	10	378	*0.0*	*2.6*
	45–64	620	1	14	586	*0.2*	*2.5*	302	0	8	287	*0.0*	*2.7*	318	1	6	299	*0.3*	*2.3*
	65–	253	0	3	242	*0.0*	*1.2*	132	0	1	127	*0.0*	*0.8*	121	0	2	115	*0.0*	*1.7*
Ebbw Vale UD	All 3+	27857	113	3435	23035	*0.4*	*13.3*	15037	55	1806	12487	*0.4*	*12.9*	12820	58	1629	10548	*0.5*	*13.8*
	3–4	1697	1	36	1461	*0.1*	*2.5*	838	1	14	725	*0.1*	*2.0*	859	0	22	736	*0.0*	*2.9*
	5–9	3869	4	95	3502	*0.1*	*2.7*	1869	1	37	1686	*0.1*	*2.2*	2000	3	58	1816	*0.2*	*3.2*
	10–14	3145	5	105	2857	*0.2*	*3.7*	1595	3	56	1454	*0.2*	*3.9*	1550	2	49	1403	*0.1*	*3.5*
	15–24	5501	16	390	4898	*0.3*	*7.6*	3013	10	224	2670	*0.3*	*8.0*	2488	6	166	2228	*0.2*	*7.2*
	25–44	9049	26	1278	7466	*0.3*	*14.9*	5115	14	655	4301	*0.3*	*13.4*	3934	12	623	3165	*0.3*	*16.7*
	45–64	3820	35	1196	2455	*0.9*	*33.3*	2214	15	660	1443	*0.7*	*31.8*	1606	20	536	1012	*1.3*	*35.4*
	65–	776	26	335	396	*3.4*	*47.7*	393	11	160	208	*2.9*	*45.1*	383	15	175	188	*4.0*	*50.3*

District[1]	Age last birth-day	Number[2] Total in age group	Welsh only	Both	English only	Percentage[3] Welsh only	Able to speak Welsh	Number[2] Total in age group	Welsh only	Both	English only	Percentage[3] Welsh only	Able to speak Welsh	Number[2] Total in age group	Welsh only	Both	English only	Percentage[3] Welsh only	Able to speak Welsh
		Persons						Males						Females					
Llanfrechfa Upper UD	All 3+	4093	8	203	3774	*0.2*	*5.3*	2128	4	112	1967	*0.2*	*5.6*	1965	4	91	1807	*0.2*	*5.0*
	3–4	235	0	4	214	*0.0*	*1.8*	114	0	1	106	*0.0*	*0.9*	121	0	3	108	*0.0*	*2.7*
	5–9	548	0	3	529	*0.0*	*0.6*	278	0	2	267	*0.0*	*0.7*	270	0	1	262	*0.0*	*0.4*
	10–14	465	0	8	441	*0.0*	*1.8*	229	0	3	220	*0.0*	*1.3*	236	0	5	221	*0.0*	*2.2*
	15–24	841	0	20	795	*0.0*	*2.5*	452	0	6	434	*0.0*	*1.4*	389	0	14	361	*0.0*	*3.7*
	25–44	1290	4	74	1188	*0.3*	*6.2*	692	1	50	633	*0.1*	*7.5*	598	3	24	555	*0.5*	*4.6*
	45–64	564	2	73	480	*0.4*	*13.5*	297	2	42	250	*0.7*	*15.0*	267	0	31	230	*0.0*	*11.9*
	65–	150	2	21	127	*1.3*	*15.3*	66	1	8	57	*1.5*	*13.6*	84	1	13	70	*1.2*	*16.7*
Llantarnam UD	All 3+	6475	10	250	5962	*0.2*	*4.2*	3422	7	132	3158	*0.2*	*4.2*	3053	3	118	2804	*0.1*	*4.1*
	3–4	384	0	1	335	*0.0*	*0.3*	198	0	0	171	*0.0*	*0.0*	186	0	1	164	*0.0*	*0.6*
	5–9	875	1	11	817	*0.1*	*1.4*	453	1	6	421	*0.2*	*1.6*	422	0	5	396	*0.0*	*1.2*
	10–14	741	1	8	690	*0.1*	*1.3*	367	0	5	342	*0.0*	*1.4*	374	1	3	348	*0.3*	*1.1*
	15–24	1309	0	27	1226	*0.0*	*2.1*	710	0	13	666	*0.0*	*1.9*	599	0	14	560	*0.0*	*2.4*
	25–44	1936	5	73	1824	*0.3*	*4.1*	1055	4	40	999	*0.4*	*4.2*	881	1	33	825	*0.1*	*4.0*
	45–64	958	2	92	846	*0.2*	*10.0*	508	2	52	446	*0.4*	*10.8*	450	0	40	400	*0.0*	*9.1*
	65–	272	1	38	224	*0.4*	*14.8*	131	0	16	113	*0.0*	*12.4*	141	1	22	111	*0.7*	*17.2*
Monmouth MB[3]	All 3+	4985	6	54	3124	*0.2*	*1.9*	2464	5	28	1614	*0.3*	*2.0*	2521	1	26	1510	*0.1*	*1.7*
	3–4	176	0	0	118	*0.0*	*0.0*	87	0	0	58	*0.0*	*0.0*	89	0	0	60	*0.0*	*0.0*
	5–9	458	0	3	298	*0.0*	*1.0*	232	0	3	152	*0.0*	*1.9*	226	0	0	146	*0.0*	*0.0*
	10–14	519	0	2	287	*0.0*	*0.7*	258	0	0	134	*0.0*	*0.0*	261	0	2	153	*0.0*	*1.3*
	15–24	1086	3	12	626	*0.5*	*2.3*	568	2	6	348	*0.6*	*2.2*	518	1	6	278	*0.3*	*2.4*
	25–44	1380	3	23	893	*0.3*	*2.8*	662	3	13	456	*0.6*	*3.3*	718	0	10	437	*0.0*	*2.2*
	45–64	917	0	9	578	*0.0*	*1.5*	454	0	3	312	*0.0*	*0.9*	463	0	6	266	*0.0*	*2.2*
	65–	449	0	5	324	*0.0*	*1.5*	203	0	3	154	*0.0*	*1.9*	246	0	2	170	*0.0*	*1.2*
Mynyddislwyn UD	All 3+	9014	60	2061	6766	*0.7*	*23.9*	4943	37	1134	3701	*0.8*	*24.0*	4071	23	927	3065	*0.6*	*23.7*
	3–4	598	5	58	490	*0.9*	*11.4*	310	2	29	256	*0.7*	*10.8*	288	3	29	234	*1.1*	*12.0*
	5–9	1312	7	155	1118	*0.5*	*12.7*	665	3	81	562	*0.5*	*13.0*	647	4	74	556	*0.6*	*12.3*
	10–14	924	4	129	775	*0.4*	*14.6*	469	4	59	395	*0.9*	*13.8*	455	0	70	380	*0.0*	*15.6*
	15–24	1747	2	315	1418	*0.1*	*18.3*	973	2	176	789	*0.2*	*18.4*	774	0	139	629	*0.0*	*18.1*
	25–44	3145	29	804	2295	*0.9*	*26.6*	1800	20	467	1305	*1.1*	*27.2*	1345	9	337	990	*0.7*	*25.9*
	45–64	1086	9	486	587	*0.8*	*45.7*	623	4	271	344	*0.6*	*44.4*	463	5	215	243	*1.1*	*47.5*
	65–	202	4	114	83	*2.0*	*58.7*	103	2	51	50	*1.9*	*51.5*	99	2	63	33	*2.0*	*66.3*

Nant-y-glo and Blaenau UD	All 3+	14055	79	1844	11796	0.6	14.0	7485	44	797	6363	0.6	11.7	6570	35	1047	5433	0.5	16.6
	3–4	878	1	6	744	0.1	0.9	463	1	2	402	0.2	0.7	415	0	4	342	0.0	1.2
	5–9	2091	5	25	1888	0.3	1.6	1053	2	14	954	0.2	1.6	1038	3	11	934	0.3	1.5
	10–14	1733	3	33	1595	0.2	2.2	896	2	11	834	0.2	1.5	837	1	22	761	0.1	2.9
	15–24	2688	12	104	2470	0.5	4.5	1426	6	55	1313	0.4	4.4	1262	6	49	1157	0.5	4.5
	25–44	4397	26	577	3693	0.6	14.0	2415	15	306	2066	0.6	13.4	1982	11	271	1627	0.6	14.8
	45–64	1886	21	627	1211	1.1	34.8	1067	12	342	704	1.1	33.4	819	9	285	507	1.1	36.7
	65–	382	11	472	195	1.6	71.0	165	6	67	90	3.6	44.2	217	5	405	105	1.0	79.6
Newport CB	All 3+	77686	26	2032	72891	0.0	2.7	39187	14	1072	36521	0.0	2.9	38499	12	960	36370	0.0	2.6
	3–4	3983	1	20	3654	0.0	0.6	2027	0	8	1857	0.0	0.4	1956	1	12	1797	0.1	0.7
	5–9	9130	2	42	8650	0.0	0.5	4514	0	22	4270	0.0	0.5	4616	2	20	4380	0.0	0.5
	10–14	8307	1	65	7914	0.0	0.8	4058	0	30	3867	0.0	0.8	4249	1	35	4047	0.0	0.9
	15–24	16133	7	256	15225	0.0	1.7	7900	3	119	7332	0.0	1.6	8233	4	137	7893	0.0	1.8
	25–44	25283	10	861	23682	0.0	3.5	13039	8	481	12106	0.1	3.8	12244	2	380	11576	0.0	3.2
	45–64	11876	5	553	11079	0.0	4.8	6224	3	299	5793	0.0	4.9	5652	2	254	5286	0.0	4.6
	65–	2974	0	235	2687	0.0	8.0	1425	0	113	1296	0.0	8.0	1549	0	122	1391	0.0	8.1
Pant-teg UD	All 3+	9364	8	374	8833	0.1	4.1	4933	3	197	4662	0.1	4.1	4431	5	177	4171	0.1	4.2
	3–4	483	0	1	467	0.0	0.2	261	0	0	258	0.0	0.0	222	0	1	209	0.0	0.5
	5–9	1177	0	8	1139	0.0	0.7	594	0	5	578	0.0	0.9	583	0	3	561	0.0	0.5
	10–14	1016	0	15	977	0.0	1.5	482	0	9	460	0.0	1.9	534	0	6	517	0.0	1.1
	15–24	1838	2	47	1757	0.1	2.7	1011	1	22	968	0.1	2.3	827	1	25	789	0.1	3.2
	25–44	2926	3	125	2765	0.1	4.4	1582	0	70	1496	0.0	4.5	1344	3	55	1269	0.2	4.4
	45–64	1475	3	120	1338	0.2	8.4	778	2	63	706	0.3	8.4	697	1	57	632	0.1	8.4
	65–	449	0	58	390	0.0	12.9	225	0	28	196	0.0	12.4	224	0	30	194	0.0	13.4
Pontypool UD	All 3+	6021	4	246	5716	0.1	4.2	3178	0	136	2999	0.0	4.3	2843	4	110	2717	0.1	4.0
	3–4	307	0	2	302	0.0	0.7	145	0	2	141	0.0	1.4	162	0	0	161	0.0	0.0
	5–9	673	0	6	663	0.0	0.9	349	0	4	343	0.0	1.2	324	0	2	320	0.0	0.6
	10–14	625	0	6	614	0.0	1.0	299	0	2	295	0.0	0.7	326	0	4	319	0.0	1.2
	15–24	1291	0	35	1253	0.0	2.7	653	0	17	634	0.0	2.6	638	0	18	619	0.0	2.8
	25–44	1927	3	90	1812	0.2	4.9	1076	0	54	1004	0.0	5.1	851	3	36	808	0.4	4.6
	45–64	950	1	77	856	0.1	8.4	529	0	43	471	0.0	8.4	421	1	34	385	0.2	8.3
	65–	248	0	30	216	0.0	12.2	127	0	14	111	0.0	11.2	121	0	16	105	0.0	13.2
Rhymni UD[3]	All 3+	10489	526	5340	4049	5.3	59.1	5610	275	2795	2292	5.1	57.2	4879	251	2545	1757	5.5	61.4
	3–4	655	31	211	304	5.7	44.3	320	20	104	149	7.3	45.4	335	11	107	155	4.0	43.2
	5–9	1427	46	609	606	3.6	51.9	690	22	289	301	3.6	50.8	737	24	320	305	3.7	52.9
	10–14	1183	47	571	469	4.3	56.9	607	27	289	242	4.8	56.6	576	20	282	227	3.8	57.1
	15–24	2193	66	1088	946	3.1	54.9	1231	31	567	587	2.6	50.4	962	35	521	359	3.8	60.8
	25–44	3294	144	1786	1283	4.5	60.0	1849	82	981	767	4.5	58.0	1445	62	805	516	4.5	62.6
	45–64	1421	117	909	371	8.4	73.4	778	63	492	215	8.2	72.1	643	54	417	156	8.6	75.1
	65–	316	75	166	70	24.1	77.5	135	30	73	31	22.4	76.9	181	45	93	39	25.4	78.0

District[1]	Age last birth-day	Persons: Number[2] Total in age group	Welsh only	Both	English only	Percentage[3] *Welsh only*	*Able to speak Welsh*	Males: Number[2] Total in age group	Welsh only	Both	English only	Percentage[3] *Welsh only*	*Able to speak Welsh*	Females: Number[2] Total in age group	Welsh only	Both	English only	Percentage[3] *Welsh only*	*Able to speak Welsh*
Risca UD	All 3+	12981	17	678	11848	*0.1*	*5.5*	6918	6	360	6326	*0.1*	*5.5*	6063	11	318	5522	*0.2*	*5.6*
	3–4	734	0	4	662	*0.0*	*0.6*	357	0	1	329	*0.0*	*0.3*	377	0	3	333	*0.0*	*0.9*
	5–9	1668	0	18	1572	*0.0*	*1.1*	859	0	10	809	*0.0*	*1.2*	809	0	8	763	*0.0*	*1.0*
	10–14	1502	0	19	1403	*0.0*	*1.3*	780	0	7	736	*0.0*	*0.9*	722	0	12	667	*0.0*	*1.8*
	15–24	2841	4	70	2697	*0.1*	*2.7*	1512	1	38	1433	*0.1*	*2.6*	1329	3	32	1264	*0.2*	*2.7*
	25–44	4110	3	224	3779	*0.1*	*5.7*	2262	1	133	2071	*0.0*	*6.1*	1848	2	91	1708	*0.1*	*5.2*
	45–64	1695	7	238	1419	*0.4*	*14.7*	953	3	128	800	*0.3*	*14.1*	742	4	110	619	*0.5*	*15.6*
	65–	431	3	105	316	*0.7*	*25.5*	195	1	43	148	*0.5*	*22.9*	236	2	62	168	*0.9*	*27.6*
Tredegar UD	All 3+	21572	198	4063	16363	*1.0*	*20.7*	11721	107	2114	9041	*0.9*	*19.7*	9851	91	1949	7322	*1.0*	*21.8*
	3–4	1257	6	66	1017	*0.6*	*6.6*	620	5	25	510	*0.9*	*5.6*	637	1	41	507	*0.2*	*7.7*
	5–9	2918	16	230	2435	*0.6*	*9.2*	1471	8	103	1231	*0.6*	*8.3*	1447	8	127	1204	*0.6*	*10.1*
	10–14	2315	6	238	1919	*0.3*	*11.3*	1162	3	123	961	*0.3*	*11.6*	1153	3	115	958	*0.3*	*11.0*
	15–24	4418	23	518	3739	*0.5*	*12.6*	2424	15	265	2071	*0.6*	*11.9*	1994	8	253	1668	*0.4*	*13.5*
	25–44	6800	60	1451	5112	*0.9*	*22.8*	3868	34	794	2975	*0.9*	*21.8*	2932	26	657	2137	*0.9*	*24.2*
	45–64	2956	56	1114	1732	*1.9*	*40.3*	1682	29	582	1047	*1.7*	*36.8*	1274	27	532	685	*2.2*	*44.9*
	65–	908	31	446	409	*3.5*	*53.7*	494	13	222	246	*2.7*	*48.8*	414	18	224	163	*4.4*	*59.6*
Usk UD	All 3+	1423	0	43	1359	*0.0*	*3.1*	742	0	24	711	*0.0*	*3.3*	681	0	19	648	*0.0*	*2.8*
	3–4	56	0	0	54	*0.0*	*0.0*	36	0	0	35	*0.0*	*0.0*	20	0	0	19	*0.0*	*0.0*
	5–9	139	0	0	134	*0.0*	*0.0*	76	0	0	72	*0.0*	*0.0*	63	0	0	62	*0.0*	*0.0*
	10–14	124	0	0	122	*0.0*	*0.0*	64	0	0	63	*0.0*	*0.0*	60	0	0	59	*0.0*	*0.0*
	15–24	250	0	7	241	*0.0*	*2.8*	120	0	2	118	*0.0*	*1.7*	130	0	5	123	*0.0*	*3.9*
	25–44	469	0	22	441	*0.0*	*4.8*	255	0	17	237	*0.0*	*6.7*	214	0	5	204	*0.0*	*2.4*
	45–64	271	0	11	257	*0.0*	*4.1*	138	0	2	136	*0.0*	*1.4*	133	0	9	121	*0.0*	*6.9*
	65–	114	0	3	110	*0.0*	*2.7*	53	0	3	50	*0.0*	*5.7*	61	0	0	60	*0.0*	*0.0*
Abergavenny RD	All 3+	8283	14	607	7363	*0.2*	*7.8*	4186	5	312	3731	*0.1*	*7.8*	4097	9	295	3632	*0.2*	*7.7*
	3–4	329	1	2	290	*0.3*	*1.0*	183	1	0	162	*0.6*	*0.6*	146	0	2	128	*0.0*	*1.5*
	5–9	836	2	15	760	*0.3*	*2.2*	426	0	7	384	*0.0*	*1.8*	410	2	8	376	*0.5*	*2.6*
	10–14	754	1	20	681	*0.1*	*3.0*	371	0	8	344	*0.0*	*2.3*	383	1	12	337	*0.3*	*3.7*
	15–24	1434	0	49	1326	*0.0*	*3.6*	686	0	20	635	*0.0*	*3.0*	748	0	29	691	*0.0*	*4.0*
	25–44	2406	2	174	2182	*0.1*	*7.5*	1190	0	90	1087	*0.0*	*7.6*	1216	2	84	1095	*0.2*	*7.3*
	45–64	1793	4	213	1542	*0.2*	*12.3*	971	3	121	832	*0.3*	*13.0*	822	1	92	710	*0.1*	*11.6*
	65–	731	4	134	582	*0.6*	*19.1*	359	1	66	287	*0.3*	*18.9*	372	3	68	295	*0.8*	*19.3*

Chepstow RD[3]	All 3+	7432	2	131	6884	*0.0*	*1.9*	3716	0	69	3457	*0.0*	*2.0*	3716	2	62	3427	*0.1*	*1.8*
	3–4	369	0	2	304	*0.0*	*0.7*	195	0	0	162	*0.0*	*0.0*	174	0	2	142	*0.0*	*1.4*
	5–9	897	0	2	802	*0.0*	*0.2*	466	0	1	416	*0.0*	*0.2*	431	0	1	386	*0.0*	*0.3*
	10–14	928	0	3	848	*0.0*	*0.4*	449	0	1	403	*0.0*	*0.2*	479	0	2	445	*0.0*	*0.4*
	15–24	1291	0	19	1211	*0.0*	*1.5*	640	0	5	601	*0.0*	*0.8*	651	0	14	610	*0.0*	*2.2*
	25–44	2082	1	64	1941	*0.0*	*3.2*	1027	0	37	970	*0.0*	*3.7*	1055	1	27	971	*0.1*	*2.8*
	45–64	1351	0	29	1293	*0.0*	*2.2*	693	0	16	673	*0.0*	*2.3*	658	0	13	620	*0.0*	*2.1*
	65–	514	1	12	485	*0.2*	*2.6*	246	0	9	232	*0.0*	*3.7*	268	1	3	253	*0.4*	*1.6*
Magor RD	All 3+	4551	3	100	4240	*0.1*	*2.4*	2247	2	38	2116	*0.1*	*1.9*	2304	1	62	2124	*0.0*	*2.9*
	3–4	229	0	1	209	*0.0*	*0.5*	107	0	1	99	*0.0*	*1.0*	122	0	0	110	*0.0*	*0.0*
	5–9	530	0	3	485	*0.0*	*0.6*	261	0	1	243	*0.0*	*0.4*	269	0	2	242	*0.0*	*0.8*
	10–14	505	0	2	469	*0.0*	*0.4*	247	0	0	230	*0.0*	*0.0*	258	0	2	239	*0.0*	*0.8*
	15–24	822	1	6	793	*0.1*	*0.9*	385	0	1	374	*0.0*	*0.3*	437	1	5	419	*0.2*	*1.4*
	25–44	1376	2	37	1287	*0.2*	*2.9*	694	2	18	649	*0.3*	*3.0*	682	0	19	638	*0.0*	*2.9*
	45–64	739	0	29	683	*0.0*	*4.1*	374	0	11	355	*0.0*	*3.0*	365	0	18	328	*0.0*	*5.2*
	65–	350	0	22	314	*0.0*	*6.5*	179	0	6	166	*0.0*	*3.5*	171	0	16	148	*0.0*	*9.7*
Monmouth RD	All 3+	6146	2	142	5716	*0.0*	*2.5*	3054	0	72	2863	*0.0*	*2.5*	3092	2	70	2853	*0.1*	*2.5*
	3–4	281	0	0	239	*0.0*	*0.0*	147	0	0	123	*0.0*	*0.0*	134	0	0	116	*0.0*	*0.0*
	5–9	623	0	3	552	*0.0*	*0.5*	316	0	3	281	*0.0*	*1.1*	307	0	0	271	*0.0*	*0.0*
	10–14	651	0	5	591	*0.0*	*0.8*	327	0	1	299	*0.0*	*0.3*	324	0	4	292	*0.0*	*1.4*
	15–24	1113	0	11	1064	*0.0*	*1.0*	552	0	4	536	*0.0*	*0.7*	561	0	7	528	*0.0*	*1.3*
	25–44	1729	1	42	1632	*0.1*	*2.6*	850	0	21	813	*0.0*	*2.5*	879	1	21	819	*0.1*	*2.6*
	45–64	1234	0	61	1151	*0.0*	*5.0*	615	0	33	575	*0.0*	*5.4*	619	0	28	576	*0.0*	*4.6*
	65–	515	1	20	487	*0.2*	*4.1*	247	0	10	236	*0.0*	*4.1*	268	1	10	251	*0.4*	*4.2*
Pontypool RD	All 3+	4754	3	224	4495	*0.1*	*4.8*	2413	0	111	2285	*0.0*	*4.6*	2341	3	113	2210	*0.1*	*5.0*
	3–4	241	0	0	231	*0.0*	*0.0*	115	0	0	109	*0.0*	*0.0*	126	0	0	122	*0.0*	*0.0*
	5–9	534	0	7	521	*0.0*	*1.3*	252	0	5	243	*0.0*	*2.0*	282	0	2	278	*0.0*	*0.7*
	10–14	539	0	9	526	*0.0*	*1.7*	272	0	3	268	*0.0*	*1.1*	267	0	6	258	*0.0*	*2.3*
	15–24	830	0	24	801	*0.0*	*2.9*	432	0	12	417	*0.0*	*2.8*	398	0	12	384	*0.0*	*3.0*
	25–44	1378	0	68	1307	*0.0*	*4.9*	701	0	30	670	*0.0*	*4.3*	677	0	38	637	*0.0*	*5.6*
	45–64	862	3	74	782	*0.3*	*9.0*	457	0	38	418	*0.0*	*8.3*	405	3	36	364	*0.7*	*9.7*
	65–	370	0	42	327	*0.0*	*11.4*	184	0	23	160	*0.0*	*12.6*	186	0	19	167	*0.0*	*10.2*
St Mellons RD	All 3+	13353	29	1897	11092	*0.2*	*14.8*	6897	13	909	5816	*0.2*	*13.7*	6456	16	988	5276	*0.3*	*16.0*
	3–4	646	1	33	549	*0.2*	*5.8*	338	0	16	289	*0.0*	*5.2*	308	1	17	260	*0.4*	*6.5*
	5–9	1593	1	90	1412	*0.1*	*6.1*	775	1	44	684	*0.1*	*6.2*	818	0	46	728	*0.0*	*5.9*
	10–14	1463	0	93	1327	*0.0*	*6.5*	725	0	42	660	*0.0*	*6.0*	738	0	51	667	*0.0*	*7.1*
	15–24	2564	2	172	2345	*0.1*	*6.9*	1338	1	76	1242	*0.1*	*5.8*	1226	1	96	1103	*0.1*	*8.1*
	25–44	4277	6	624	3579	*0.1*	*15.0*	2253	3	308	1916	*0.1*	*14.0*	2024	3	316	1663	*0.2*	*16.1*
	45–64	2155	8	583	1547	*0.4*	*27.6*	1157	3	293	852	*0.3*	*25.8*	998	5	290	695	*0.5*	*29.8*
	65–	655	11	302	333	*1.7*	*48.5*	311	5	130	173	*1.6*	*43.8*	344	6	172	160	*1.8*	*52.7*

District[1]	Age last birth-day	Number[2] Total in age group	Welsh only	Both	English only	Percentage[3] Welsh only	Percentage[3] Able to speak Welsh	Number[2] Total in age group	Welsh only	Both	English only	Percentage[3] Welsh only	Percentage[3] Able to speak Welsh	Number[2] Total in age group	Welsh only	Both	English only	Percentage[3] Welsh only	Percentage[3] Able to speak Welsh
		Persons						Males						Females					
GLAMORGAN																			
Aberafan MB	All 3+	9688	68	2992	6407	*0.7*	*32.2*	5073	28	1484	3452	*0.6*	*30.3*	4615	40	1508	2955	*0.9*	*34.4*
	3–4	546	2	75	423	*0.4*	*15.4*	250	0	33	198	*0.0*	*14.3*	296	2	42	225	*0.7*	*16.3*
	5–9	1221	5	234	943	*0.4*	*20.2*	608	3	111	480	*0.5*	*19.2*	613	2	123	463	*0.3*	*21.3*
	10–14	1050	3	245	777	*0.3*	*24.2*	511	1	102	393	*0.2*	*20.8*	539	2	143	384	*0.4*	*27.4*
	15–24	2066	10	543	1471	*0.5*	*27.2*	1036	4	247	760	*0.4*	*24.7*	1030	6	296	711	*0.6*	*29.8*
	25–44	3074	16	1050	1949	*0.5*	*35.1*	1745	8	568	1138	*0.5*	*33.3*	1329	8	482	811	*0.6*	*37.6*
	45–64	1382	18	650	705	*1.3*	*48.6*	759	7	331	416	*0.9*	*44.7*	623	11	319	289	*1.8*	*53.3*
	65–	349	14	195	139	*4.0*	*60.1*	164	5	92	67	*3.0*	*59.1*	185	9	103	72	*4.9*	*60.9*
Aberdare UD	All 3+	46844	3068	26894	15988	*6.7*	*65.2*	24425	1515	13830	8630	*6.3*	*64.0*	22419	1553	13064	7358	*7.1*	*66.5*
	3–4	2377	223	871	1027	*10.5*	*51.6*	1182	108	424	517	*10.3*	*50.7*	1195	115	447	510	*10.7*	*52.4*
	5–9	5807	297	2934	2370	*5.3*	*57.7*	2920	157	1458	1203	*5.6*	*57.3*	2887	140	1476	1167	*5.0*	*58.1*
	10–14	5196	194	2980	1909	*3.8*	*62.4*	2574	97	1483	943	*3.8*	*62.6*	2622	97	1497	966	*3.8*	*62.3*
	15–24	9213	373	5557	3158	*4.1*	*65.2*	4798	192	2829	1713	*4.1*	*63.8*	4415	181	2728	1445	*4.2*	*66.8*
	25–44	15633	742	9423	5343	*4.8*	*65.5*	8498	417	4982	3038	*4.9*	*63.9*	7135	325	4441	2305	*4.6*	*67.4*
	45–64	6938	835	4287	1761	*12.1*	*74.4*	3743	408	2286	1017	*11.0*	*72.6*	3195	427	2001	744	*13.5*	*76.5*
	65–	1680	404	842	420	*24.2*	*74.7*	710	136	368	199	*19.3*	*71.6*	970	268	474	221	*27.8*	*77.0*
Barry UD	All 3+	31411	101	3537	26014	*0.3*	*12.1*	16302	46	1738	13425	*0.3*	*11.5*	15109	55	1799	12589	*0.4*	*12.8*
	3–4	1599	7	62	1360	*0.5*	*4.8*	798	5	32	684	*0.7*	*5.1*	801	2	30	676	*0.3*	*4.5*
	5–9	4001	13	303	3422	*0.3*	*8.4*	2009	6	161	1732	*0.3*	*8.8*	1992	7	142	1690	*0.4*	*8.1*
	10–14	3834	7	320	3328	*0.2*	*8.9*	1914	2	163	1661	*0.1*	*9.0*	1920	5	157	1667	*0.3*	*8.9*
	15–24	6230	16	450	5319	*0.3*	*7.9*	3200	7	208	2654	*0.2*	*7.2*	3030	9	242	2665	*0.3*	*8.6*
	25–44	10047	29	1304	8195	*0.3*	*13.7*	5249	11	610	4251	*0.2*	*12.3*	4798	18	694	3944	*0.4*	*15.3*
	45–64	4755	17	881	3707	*0.4*	*19.4*	2666	10	453	2111	*0.4*	*17.9*	2089	7	428	1596	*0.3*	*21.4*
	65–	945	12	217	683	*1.3*	*25.1*	466	5	111	332	*1.1*	*25.9*	479	7	106	351	*1.5*	*24.3*
Bridgend UD	All 3+	7453	43	1694	5602	*0.6*	*23.7*	3691	19	837	2783	*0.5*	*23.5*	3762	24	857	2819	*0.6*	*23.8*
	3–4	362	1	15	312	*0.3*	*4.9*	177	0	7	150	*0.0*	*4.5*	185	1	8	162	*0.6*	*5.3*
	5–9	862	2	74	754	*0.2*	*9.2*	423	1	37	368	*0.2*	*9.4*	439	1	37	386	*0.2*	*9.0*
	10–14	777	3	102	657	*0.4*	*13.8*	379	3	47	321	*0.8*	*13.5*	398	0	55	336	*0.0*	*14.1*
	15–24	1452	6	253	1179	*0.4*	*18.0*	657	1	96	556	*0.2*	*14.9*	795	5	157	623	*0.6*	*20.6*
	25–44	2443	14	574	1842	*0.6*	*24.2*	1205	5	273	924	*0.4*	*23.1*	1238	9	301	918	*0.7*	*25.2*
	45–64	1167	7	479	678	*0.6*	*41.8*	639	3	267	369	*0.5*	*42.3*	528	4	212	309	*0.8*	*41.1*
	65–	390	10	197	180	*2.6*	*53.5*	211	6	110	95	*2.8*	*55.0*	179	4	87	85	*2.3*	*51.7*

Briton Ferry UD	All 3+	7885	118	2860	4561	*1.6*	*39.4*	4100	61	1340	2463	*1.6*	*36.1*	3785	57	1520	2098	*1.6*	*42.9*
	3–4	407	2	65	291	*0.6*	*18.7*	199	2	30	143	*1.1*	*18.3*	208	0	35	148	*0.0*	*19.1*
	5–9	1008	10	212	726	*1.1*	*23.4*	500	1	98	370	*0.2*	*21.1*	508	9	114	356	*1.9*	*25.7*
	10–14	854	9	121	573	*1.3*	*18.5*	452	4	12	301	*1.3*	*5.0*	402	5	109	272	*1.3*	*29.5*
	15–24	1598	19	502	1048	*1.2*	*33.0*	857	13	247	574	*1.5*	*30.9*	741	6	255	474	*0.8*	*35.5*
	25–44	2555	29	1056	1424	*1.2*	*43.1*	1365	18	530	797	*1.3*	*40.6*	1190	11	526	627	*0.9*	*46.1*
	45–64	1151	35	697	411	*3.1*	*64.0*	592	16	340	234	*2.7*	*60.3*	559	19	357	177	*3.4*	*68.0*
	65–	312	14	207	88	*4.5*	*71.3*	135	7	83	44	*5.2*	*67.2*	177	7	124	44	*4.0*	*74.4*
Caerphilly UD	All 3+	29893	742	9281	18867	*2.6*	*34.7*	16480	452	5094	10460	*2.8*	*34.6*	13413	290	4187	8407	*2.2*	*34.7*
	3–4	1797	44	290	1264	*2.8*	*20.9*	890	23	139	627	*2.9*	*20.5*	907	21	151	637	*2.6*	*21.2*
	5–9	4086	68	834	2932	*1.8*	*23.5*	2064	36	428	1480	*1.9*	*23.9*	2022	32	406	1452	*1.7*	*23.2*
	10–14	3297	46	762	2336	*1.5*	*25.7*	1657	27	373	1186	*1.7*	*25.2*	1640	19	389	1150	*1.2*	*26.2*
	15–24	6031	107	1702	4064	*1.8*	*30.8*	3476	73	944	2375	*2.2*	*30.0*	2555	34	758	1689	*1.4*	*31.9*
	25–44	10442	295	3660	6311	*2.9*	*38.5*	6062	193	2126	3670	*3.2*	*38.7*	4380	102	1534	2641	*2.4*	*38.2*
	45–64	3549	141	1688	1665	*4.0*	*52.3*	1991	82	924	965	*4.2*	*51.0*	1558	59	764	700	*3.9*	*54.0*
	65–	691	41	345	295	*6.0*	*56.5*	340	18	160	157	*5.4*	*53.0*	351	23	185	138	*6.6*	*59.9*
Cardiff City CB	All 3+	170016	262	11053	150547	*0.2*	*6.9*	83552	118	5192	74040	*0.1*	*6.6*	86464	144	5861	76507	*0.2*	*7.3*
	3–4	7875	12	106	6853	*0.2*	*1.7*	3884	5	42	3392	*0.1*	*1.4*	3991	7	64	3461	*0.2*	*2.0*
	5–9	19698	18	549	17681	*0.1*	*3.1*	9779	10	269	8787	*0.1*	*3.1*	9919	8	280	8894	*0.1*	*3.1*
	10–14	18493	17	686	16717	*0.1*	*4.0*	8967	7	263	8172	*0.1*	*3.2*	9526	10	423	8545	*0.1*	*4.8*
	15–24	34980	41	1533	31762	*0.1*	*4.7*	16729	21	667	15065	*0.1*	*4.3*	18251	20	866	16697	*0.1*	*5.0*
	25–44	54543	78	3877	48504	*0.1*	*7.5*	27008	34	1878	23985	*0.1*	*7.3*	27535	44	1999	24519	*0.2*	*7.7*
	45–64	27467	59	3183	23419	*0.2*	*12.1*	14040	23	1575	12077	*0.2*	*11.6*	13427	36	1608	11342	*0.3*	*12.6*
	65–	6960	37	1119	5611	*0.5*	*17.0*	3145	18	498	2562	*0.6*	*16.7*	3815	19	621	3049	*0.5*	*17.3*
Cowbridge MB	All 3+	1113	6	215	891	*0.5*	*19.9*	543	3	96	443	*0.6*	*18.3*	570	3	119	448	*0.5*	*21.4*
	3–4	37	0	1	35	*0.0*	*2.8*	14	0	0	13	*0.0*	*0.0*	23	0	1	22	*0.0*	*4.3*
	5–9	94	0	6	88	*0.0*	*6.4*	50	0	4	46	*0.0*	*8.0*	44	0	2	42	*0.0*	*4.5*
	10–14	124	1	11	112	*0.8*	*9.7*	64	1	3	60	*1.6*	*6.3*	60	0	8	52	*0.0*	*13.3*
	15–24	241	1	20	220	*0.4*	*8.7*	110	0	5	105	*0.0*	*4.5*	131	1	15	115	*0.8*	*12.2*
	25–44	305	0	63	242	*0.0*	*20.7*	142	0	31	111	*0.0*	*21.8*	163	0	32	131	*0.0*	*19.6*
	45–64	238	2	69	167	*0.8*	*29.8*	130	1	34	95	*0.8*	*26.9*	108	1	35	72	*0.9*	*33.3*
	65–	74	2	45	27	*2.7*	*63.5*	33	1	19	13	*3.0*	*60.6*	41	1	26	14	*2.4*	*65.9*
Gelli-gaer UD	All 3+	32288	866	12391	18654	*2.7*	*41.5*	17807	499	6660	10446	*2.8*	*40.6*	14481	367	5731	8208	*2.6*	*42.6*
	3–4	1999	65	463	1315	*3.5*	*28.6*	987	28	218	667	*3.1*	*26.9*	1012	37	245	648	*4.0*	*30.3*
	5–9	4533	81	1314	3041	*1.8*	*31.4*	2271	48	664	1512	*2.2*	*32.0*	2262	33	650	1529	*1.5*	*30.9*
	10–14	3468	38	1236	2171	*1.1*	*37.0*	1739	21	616	1089	*1.2*	*36.9*	1729	17	620	1082	*1.0*	*37.1*
	15–24	6784	101	2410	4246	*1.5*	*37.2*	3920	64	1295	2546	*1.6*	*34.8*	2864	37	1115	1700	*1.3*	*40.4*
	25–44	10965	259	4561	6098	*2.4*	*44.1*	6358	166	2538	3619	*2.6*	*42.7*	4607	93	2023	2479	*2.0*	*46.1*
	45–64	3827	234	2005	1568	*6.1*	*58.8*	2185	134	1133	904	*6.2*	*58.3*	1642	100	872	664	*6.1*	*59.4*
	65–	712	88	402	215	*12.5*	*69.5*	347	38	196	109	*11.1*	*68.2*	365	50	206	106	*13.8*	*70.7*

District[1]	Age last birth-day	Persons: Number[2] Total in age group	Welsh only	Both	English only	Percentage[3] Welsh only	Able to speak Welsh	Males: Number[2] Total in age group	Welsh only	Both	English only	Percentage[3] Welsh only	Able to speak Welsh	Females: Number[2] Total in age group	Welsh only	Both	English only	Percentage[3] Welsh only	Able to speak Welsh
Glyncorrwg UD	All 3+	7868	308	4170	3297	*4.0*	*57.6*	4250	161	2236	1808	*3.8*	*57.0*	3618	147	1934	1489	*4.1*	*58.3*
	3–4	537	32	198	266	*6.5*	*46.4*	275	17	98	140	*6.7*	*45.1*	262	15	100	126	*6.2*	*47.7*
	5–9	1176	41	520	594	*3.5*	*48.6*	570	20	243	298	*3.6*	*46.9*	606	21	277	296	*3.5*	*50.2*
	10–14	974	24	493	450	*2.5*	*53.5*	483	10	256	211	*2.1*	*55.8*	491	14	237	239	*2.9*	*51.2*
	15–24	1649	35	923	682	*2.1*	*58.4*	927	21	497	405	*2.3*	*56.1*	722	14	426	277	*2.0*	*61.4*
	25–44	2465	85	1408	962	*3.5*	*60.8*	1407	45	802	555	*3.2*	*60.4*	1058	40	606	407	*3.8*	*61.3*
	45–64	912	68	544	299	*7.5*	*67.2*	516	38	304	174	*7.4*	*66.3*	396	30	240	125	*7.6*	*68.4*
	65–	155	23	84	44	*15.2*	*70.9*	72	10	36	25	*14.1*	*64.8*	83	13	48	19	*16.3*	*76.3*
Maesteg UD	All 3+	22687	1196	12537	8411	*5.4*	*62.0*	12235	626	6717	4616	*5.2*	*61.4*	10452	570	5820	3795	*5.6*	*62.7*
	3–4	1428	93	546	636	*7.3*	*50.1*	714	45	289	304	*7.1*	*52.4*	714	48	257	332	*7.5*	*47.9*
	5–9	3263	142	1606	1397	*4.5*	*55.6*	1605	65	772	710	*4.2*	*54.1*	1658	77	834	687	*4.8*	*57.0*
	10–14	2579	94	1416	1005	*3.7*	*60.0*	1340	52	735	517	*4.0*	*60.4*	1239	42	681	488	*3.5*	*59.7*
	15–24	4491	156	2556	1695	*3.5*	*61.5*	2427	83	1321	974	*3.5*	*59.0*	2064	73	1235	721	*3.6*	*64.4*
	25–44	7517	333	4300	2795	*4.5*	*62.3*	4299	190	2454	1612	*4.5*	*62.0*	3218	143	1846	1183	*4.5*	*62.6*
	45–64	2826	290	1790	717	*10.4*	*74.4*	1560	157	985	406	*10.1*	*73.8*	1266	133	805	311	*10.6*	*75.1*
	65–	583	88	323	166	*15.3*	*71.2*	290	34	161	93	*11.8*	*67.7*	293	54	162	73	*18.7*	*74.7*
Margam UD	All 3+	13593	224	6252	6649	*1.7*	*48.7*	7188	111	3160	3571	*1.6*	*46.7*	6405	113	3092	3078	*1.8*	*51.0*
	3–4	725	31	183	444	*4.7*	*32.5*	358	19	81	223	*5.9*	*31.0*	367	12	102	221	*3.6*	*34.0*
	5–9	1721	25	642	1002	*1.5*	*39.9*	866	13	298	523	*1.6*	*37.2*	855	12	344	479	*1.4*	*42.6*
	10–14	1438	13	609	791	*0.9*	*43.9*	720	9	283	416	*1.3*	*41.1*	718	4	326	375	*0.6*	*46.7*
	15–24	2834	24	1310	1353	*0.9*	*47.9*	1551	12	673	732	*0.8*	*45.3*	1283	12	637	621	*0.9*	*51.1*
	25–44	4487	35	2089	2219	*0.8*	*48.2*	2470	15	1127	1216	*0.6*	*47.2*	2017	20	962	1003	*1.0*	*49.4*
	45–64	1906	52	1123	700	*2.8*	*62.4*	1014	25	578	392	*2.5*	*60.1*	892	27	545	308	*3.1*	*65.0*
	65–	482	44	296	140	*9.2*	*70.8*	209	18	120	69	*8.7*	*66.7*	273	26	176	71	*9.5*	*74.0*
Merthyr Tydfil CB	All 3+	74597	2643	34826	35882	*3.6*	*50.9*	39778	1405	18098	19608	*3.6*	*49.6*	34819	1238	16728	16274	*3.6*	*52.3*
	3–4	4089	159	1172	2418	*4.2*	*35.4*	2063	75	588	1223	*4.0*	*35.1*	2026	84	584	1195	*4.5*	*35.7*
	5–9	9554	191	3585	5518	*2.0*	*40.5*	4791	101	1827	2721	*2.2*	*41.3*	4763	90	1758	2797	*1.9*	*39.7*
	10–14	8126	136	3475	4401	*1.7*	*45.0*	4060	69	1700	2235	*1.7*	*44.1*	4066	67	1775	2166	*1.7*	*45.9*
	15–24	14991	332	6940	7570	*2.2*	*48.8*	7991	201	3584	4120	*2.5*	*47.7*	7000	131	3356	3450	*1.9*	*50.2*
	25–44	24437	717	12145	11306	*3.0*	*52.9*	13630	423	6488	6579	*3.1*	*50.9*	10807	294	5657	4727	*2.7*	*55.5*
	45–64	10734	734	6068	3845	*6.9*	*63.7*	5970	383	3229	2303	*6.4*	*60.8*	4764	351	2839	1542	*7.4*	*67.3*
	65–	2666	374	1441	824	*14.1*	*68.6*	1273	153	682	427	*12.1*	*66.0*	1393	221	759	397	*16.0*	*71.0*

Mountain Ash UD	All 3+	38475	1161	14130	21997	*3.1*	*41.0*	20780	635	7438	12119	*3.1*	*39.9*	17695	526	6692	9878	*3.1*	*42.2*
	3–4	2338	48	455	1576	*2.3*	*24.2*	1125	18	214	753	*1.8*	*23.6*	1213	30	241	823	*2.7*	*24.7*
	5–9	5451	71	1450	3640	*1.4*	*29.4*	2716	33	720	1813	*1.3*	*29.3*	2735	38	730	1827	*1.5*	*29.5*
	10–14	4445	67	1404	2789	*1.6*	*34.5*	2234	36	664	1447	*1.7*	*32.6*	2211	31	740	1342	*1.5*	*36.5*
	15–24	7778	126	2813	4661	*1.7*	*38.6*	4291	81	1467	2646	*1.9*	*36.8*	3487	45	1346	2015	*1.3*	*40.8*
	25–44	12590	379	5111	6890	*3.1*	*44.3*	7204	230	2812	4075	*3.2*	*42.7*	5386	149	2299	2815	*2.8*	*46.5*
	45–64	4956	358	2492	2055	*7.3*	*58.0*	2817	192	1392	1214	*6.8*	*56.5*	2139	166	1100	841	*7.9*	*60.1*
	65–	917	112	405	386	*12.4*	*57.2*	393	45	169	171	*11.7*	*55.4*	524	67	236	215	*12.9*	*58.5*
Neath MB	All 3+	16345	191	4742	11016	*1.2*	*30.9*	8320	96	2322	5700	*1.2*	*29.8*	8025	95	2420	5316	*1.2*	*32.1*
	3–4	879	10	73	715	*1.3*	*10.4*	418	3	41	343	*0.8*	*11.4*	461	7	32	372	*1.7*	*9.5*
	5–9	1979	12	261	1611	*0.6*	*14.5*	998	7	135	810	*0.7*	*14.9*	981	5	126	801	*0.5*	*14.1*
	10–14	1686	12	279	1351	*0.7*	*17.7*	847	9	132	685	*1.1*	*17.1*	839	3	147	666	*0.4*	*18.4*
	15–24	3374	29	769	2523	*0.9*	*24.0*	1693	13	364	1285	*0.8*	*22.7*	1681	16	405	1238	*1.0*	*25.4*
	25–44	5281	58	1769	3367	*1.1*	*35.2*	2775	33	897	1792	*1.2*	*34.1*	2506	25	872	1575	*1.0*	*36.3*
	45–64	2442	48	1217	1152	*2.0*	*52.3*	1274	24	582	653	*1.9*	*48.1*	1168	24	635	499	*2.1*	*56.9*
	65–	704	22	374	297	*3.2*	*57.1*	315	7	171	132	*2.3*	*57.4*	389	15	203	165	*3.9*	*56.9*
Ogmore and Garw UD	All 3+	24350	1016	10252	12346	*4.3*	*47.7*	13366	557	5555	6898	*4.3*	*47.0*	10984	459	4697	5448	*4.3*	*48.6*
	3–4	1531	55	361	935	*4.1*	*30.8*	775	31	172	473	*4.6*	*30.0*	756	24	189	462	*3.6*	*31.6*
	5–9	3577	94	1125	2161	*2.8*	*36.1*	1776	44	559	1080	*2.6*	*35.8*	1801	50	566	1081	*2.9*	*36.3*
	10–14	2785	59	1075	1542	*2.2*	*42.4*	1386	29	539	768	*2.2*	*42.5*	1399	30	536	774	*2.2*	*42.2*
	15–24	4778	138	2013	2525	*3.0*	*46.0*	2690	90	1079	1468	*3.4*	*44.3*	2088	48	934	1057	*2.4*	*48.2*
	25–44	8036	316	3723	3881	*4.0*	*51.0*	4651	188	2084	2331	*4.1*	*49.3*	3385	128	1639	1550	*3.9*	*53.3*
	45–64	3090	265	1678	1119	*8.6*	*63.4*	1812	139	982	679	*7.7*	*62.2*	1278	126	696	440	*10.0*	*65.1*
	65–	553	89	277	183	*16.2*	*66.7*	276	36	140	99	*13.1*	*64.0*	277	53	137	84	*19.3*	*69.3*
Oystermouth UD	All 3+	5739	2	405	5248	*0.0*	*7.2*	2539	0	131	2369	*0.0*	*5.2*	3200	2	274	2879	*0.1*	*8.7*
	3–4	259	0	4	244	*0.0*	*1.6*	129	0	1	124	*0.0*	*0.8*	130	0	3	120	*0.0*	*2.4*
	5–9	612	0	5	585	*0.0*	*0.8*	319	0	4	306	*0.0*	*1.3*	293	0	1	279	*0.0*	*0.4*
	10–14	545	0	5	537	*0.0*	*0.9*	253	0	4	248	*0.0*	*1.6*	292	0	1	289	*0.0*	*0.3*
	15–24	1039	1	63	965	*0.1*	*6.2*	437	0	11	420	*0.0*	*2.5*	602	1	52	545	*0.2*	*8.8*
	25–44	1902	0	156	1722	*0.0*	*8.3*	788	0	46	731	*0.0*	*5.9*	1114	0	110	991	*0.0*	*10.0*
	45–64	971	1	121	840	*0.1*	*12.7*	430	0	46	378	*0.0*	*10.8*	541	1	75	462	*0.2*	*14.1*
	65–	411	0	51	355	*0.0*	*12.6*	183	0	19	162	*0.0*	*10.5*	228	0	32	193	*0.0*	*14.2*
Penarth UD	All 3+	14597	8	808	13130	*0.1*	*5.8*	6793	3	338	6025	*0.0*	*5.2*	7804	5	470	7105	*0.1*	*6.3*
	3–4	618	1	10	565	*0.2*	*1.9*	305	1	7	277	*0.4*	*2.8*	313	0	3	288	*0.0*	*1.0*
	5–9	1534	0	35	1413	*0.0*	*2.4*	779	0	14	721	*0.0*	*1.9*	755	0	21	692	*0.0*	*2.9*
	10–14	1539	0	33	1434	*0.0*	*2.2*	784	0	22	718	*0.0*	*3.0*	755	0	11	716	*0.0*	*1.5*
	15–24	3135	1	113	2835	*0.0*	*3.8*	1323	0	32	1145	*0.0*	*2.5*	1812	1	81	1690	*0.1*	*4.6*
	25–44	4741	3	281	4258	*0.1*	*6.2*	2168	1	116	1915	*0.0*	*5.6*	2573	2	165	2343	*0.1*	*6.6*
	45–64	2379	0	227	2095	*0.0*	*9.7*	1169	0	101	1035	*0.0*	*8.8*	1210	0	126	1060	*0.0*	*10.6*
	65–	651	3	109	530	*0.5*	*17.4*	265	1	46	214	*0.4*	*18.0*	386	2	63	316	*0.5*	*17.0*

District[1]	Age last birth-day	Number[2] Total in age group	Welsh only	Both	English only	Percentage[3] Welsh only	Able to speak Welsh	Number[2] Total in age group	Welsh only	Both	English only	Percentage[3] Welsh only	Able to speak Welsh	Number[2] Total in age group	Welsh only	Both	English only	Percentage[3] Welsh only	Able to speak Welsh
		Persons						Males						Females					
Pontypridd UD	All 3+	39542	589	11265	26597	*1.5*	*30.8*	21126	313	5904	14391	*1.5*	*30.1*	18416	276	5361	12206	*1.5*	*31.6*
	3–4	2082	29	244	1569	*1.6*	*14.8*	1071	17	132	815	*1.8*	*15.5*	1011	12	112	754	*1.4*	*14.1*
	5–9	5135	50	882	3930	*1.0*	*19.2*	2563	28	414	1986	*1.2*	*18.2*	2572	22	468	1944	*0.9*	*20.1*
	10–14	4329	22	895	3265	*0.5*	*21.9*	2171	6	462	1632	*0.3*	*22.3*	2158	16	433	1633	*0.8*	*21.6*
	15–24	8059	62	1998	5854	*0.8*	*26.0*	4202	36	972	3114	*0.9*	*24.4*	3857	26	1026	2740	*0.7*	*27.7*
	25–44	13241	179	4151	8705	*1.4*	*33.2*	7440	106	2258	4991	*1.4*	*32.1*	5801	73	1893	3714	*1.3*	*34.6*
	45–64	5602	192	2533	2808	*3.5*	*49.2*	3145	102	1396	1614	*3.3*	*48.0*	2457	90	1137	1194	*3.7*	*50.6*
	65–	1094	55	562	466	*5.1*	*56.9*	534	18	270	239	*3.4*	*54.4*	560	37	292	227	*6.7*	*59.2*
Porthcawl UD	All 3+	3279	41	869	2281	*1.3*	*28.5*	1486	17	392	1039	*1.2*	*28.2*	1793	24	477	1242	*1.4*	*28.7*
	3–4	94	0	12	72	*0.0*	*14.3*	49	0	9	34	*0.0*	*20.9*	45	0	3	38	*0.0*	*7.3*
	5–9	302	3	37	244	*1.1*	*14.1*	163	1	20	134	*0.6*	*13.5*	139	2	17	110	*1.6*	*14.7*
	10–14	317	1	58	247	*0.3*	*19.3*	131	0	22	105	*0.0*	*17.3*	186	1	36	142	*0.6*	*20.7*
	15–24	709	8	120	565	*1.1*	*18.4*	288	2	38	239	*0.7*	*14.3*	421	6	82	326	*1.4*	*21.2*
	25–44	1036	7	276	727	*0.7*	*28.0*	496	5	138	343	*1.0*	*29.4*	540	2	138	384	*0.4*	*26.7*
	45–64	609	16	258	329	*2.7*	*45.4*	273	7	119	146	*2.6*	*46.3*	336	9	139	183	*2.7*	*44.7*
	65–	212	6	108	97	*2.8*	*54.0*	86	2	46	38	*2.3*	*55.8*	126	4	62	59	*3.2*	*52.8*
Rhondda UD	All 3+	139235	6100	70696	60056	*4.5*	*56.1*	76424	3187	38154	33858	*4.2*	*54.9*	62811	2913	32542	26198	*4.7*	*57.5*
	3–4	7952	351	2688	4145	*4.9*	*42.3*	3941	179	1299	2052	*5.1*	*41.9*	4011	172	1389	2093	*4.7*	*42.7*
	5–9	18673	465	8186	9464	*2.6*	*47.8*	9291	239	4005	4752	*2.7*	*47.2*	9382	226	4181	4712	*2.5*	*48.3*
	10–14	15554	313	7705	7242	*2.1*	*52.5*	7846	162	3788	3727	*2.1*	*51.4*	7708	151	3917	3515	*2.0*	*53.6*
	15–24	28683	635	14738	13017	*2.2*	*54.1*	16104	365	7925	7664	*2.3*	*51.9*	12579	270	6813	5353	*2.2*	*56.9*
	25–44	46702	1833	25136	19394	*4.0*	*58.1*	27178	1036	14327	11675	*3.8*	*56.8*	19524	797	10809	7719	*4.1*	*60.0*
	45–64	18245	1845	10438	5849	*10.2*	*67.7*	10444	963	5934	3493	*9.3*	*66.3*	7801	882	4504	2356	*11.4*	*69.6*
	65–	3426	658	1805	945	*19.3*	*72.2*	1620	243	876	495	*15.0*	*69.3*	1806	415	929	450	*23.1*	*74.9*
Swansea CB	All 3+	106776	2013	26860	73628	*2.0*	*28.0*	53907	940	12955	37677	*1.8*	*26.7*	52869	1073	13905	35951	*2.1*	*29.4*
	3–4	5204	125	636	3928	*2.7*	*16.2*	2617	66	317	1978	*2.8*	*16.2*	2587	59	319	1950	*2.5*	*16.2*
	5–9	12121	195	2030	9222	*1.7*	*19.4*	6100	98	988	4664	*1.7*	*18.9*	6021	97	1042	4558	*1.7*	*20.0*
	10–14	10804	122	2148	8057	*1.2*	*21.9*	5372	54	1034	4044	*1.0*	*21.2*	5432	68	1114	4013	*1.3*	*22.7*
	15–24	22218	273	5316	15745	*1.3*	*26.0*	11059	136	2507	7887	*1.3*	*24.7*	11159	137	2809	7858	*1.3*	*27.2*
	25–44	35230	471	9446	24144	*1.4*	*28.9*	18282	244	4709	12657	*1.4*	*27.8*	16948	227	4737	11487	*1.4*	*30.1*
	45–64	16696	537	5634	10090	*3.3*	*37.8*	8640	241	2735	5421	*2.9*	*35.3*	8056	296	2899	4669	*3.8*	*40.6*
	65–	4503	290	1650	2442	*6.6*	*44.1*	1837	101	665	1026	*5.6*	*42.6*	2666	189	985	1416	*7.3*	*45.2*

Cowbridge RD	All 3+	7396	41	2419	4799	*0.6*	*33.9*	3773	19	1214	2477	*0.5*	*33.2*	3623	22	1205	2322	*0.6*	*34.6*
	3–4	385	5	52	290	*1.4*	*16.4*	189	1	26	147	*0.6*	*15.5*	196	4	26	143	*2.3*	*17.3*
	5–9	940	1	184	724	*0.1*	*20.4*	472	0	88	373	*0.0*	*19.1*	468	1	96	351	*0.2*	*21.7*
	10–14	738	2	147	572	*0.3*	*20.7*	367	1	71	283	*0.3*	*20.3*	371	1	76	289	*0.3*	*21.0*
	15–24	1480	3	370	1088	*0.2*	*25.5*	727	2	164	550	*0.3*	*23.1*	753	1	206	538	*0.1*	*27.8*
	25–44	2222	13	736	1451	*0.6*	*34.0*	1176	9	380	777	*0.8*	*33.3*	1046	4	356	674	*0.4*	*34.8*
	45–64	1193	9	621	556	*0.8*	*53.1*	629	4	328	294	*0.6*	*53.0*	564	5	293	262	*0.9*	*53.2*
	65–	438	8	309	118	*1.8*	*72.9*	213	2	157	53	*0.9*	*75.0*	225	6	152	65	*2.7*	*70.9*
Gower RD	All 3+	8030	137	2873	4862	*1.7*	*38.2*	3996	64	1445	2425	*1.6*	*38.4*	4034	73	1428	2437	*1.9*	*38.1*
	3–4	418	28	140	228	*7.1*	*42.4*	220	17	68	123	*8.2*	*40.9*	198	11	72	105	*5.9*	*44.1*
	5–9	966	26	357	555	*2.8*	*40.8*	489	11	176	292	*2.3*	*39.0*	477	15	181	263	*3.3*	*42.7*
	10–14	881	15	327	521	*1.7*	*39.6*	438	7	171	253	*1.6*	*41.3*	443	8	156	268	*1.9*	*38.0*
	15–24	1558	16	572	930	*1.1*	*38.7*	800	9	278	497	*1.1*	*36.6*	758	7	294	433	*1.0*	*41.0*
	25–44	2377	24	929	1398	*1.0*	*40.5*	1161	10	478	664	*0.9*	*42.4*	1216	14	451	734	*1.2*	*38.8*
	45–64	1297	16	428	835	*1.3*	*34.7*	627	7	215	399	*1.1*	*35.7*	670	9	213	436	*1.4*	*33.7*
	65–	533	12	120	395	*2.3*	*25.0*	261	3	59	197	*1.2*	*23.9*	272	9	61	198	*3.4*	*26.1*
Llandaff and Dinas Powys RD	All 3+	30974	134	5086	24824	*0.4*	*17.4*	14900	66	2440	12009	*0.5*	*17.2*	16074	68	2646	12815	*0.4*	*17.5*
	3–4	1449	2	89	1196	*0.2*	*7.1*	711	2	44	594	*0.3*	*7.2*	738	0	45	602	*0.0*	*7.0*
	5–9	3605	4	295	3071	*0.1*	*8.9*	1788	2	146	1539	*0.1*	*8.8*	1817	2	149	1532	*0.1*	*9.0*
	10–14	3225	5	294	2776	*0.2*	*9.7*	1593	4	138	1372	*0.3*	*9.4*	1632	1	156	1404	*0.1*	*10.1*
	15–24	5879	7	672	5055	*0.1*	*11.8*	2599	2	276	2258	*0.1*	*11.0*	3280	5	396	2797	*0.2*	*12.5*
	25–44	10165	40	1673	8296	*0.4*	*17.1*	4827	18	812	3957	*0.4*	*17.3*	5338	22	861	4339	*0.4*	*16.9*
	45–64	4926	43	1426	3391	*0.9*	*30.2*	2487	23	717	1721	*0.9*	*30.1*	2439	20	709	1670	*0.8*	*30.4*
	65–	1725	33	637	1039	*1.9*	*39.2*	895	15	307	568	*1.7*	*36.2*	830	18	330	471	*2.2*	*42.5*
Llantrisant and Llantwit Fardre RD	All 3+	15984	273	6285	9058	*1.7*	*42.0*	8436	139	3251	4873	*1.7*	*41.0*	7548	134	3034	4185	*1.8*	*43.1*
	3–4	1003	14	194	662	*1.6*	*23.9*	481	5	88	320	*1.2*	*22.5*	522	9	106	342	*2.0*	*25.2*
	5–9	2239	15	626	1521	*0.7*	*29.6*	1119	7	313	761	*0.6*	*29.6*	1120	8	313	760	*0.7*	*29.7*
	10–14	1854	15	590	1208	*0.8*	*33.4*	912	4	286	605	*0.4*	*32.4*	942	11	304	603	*1.2*	*34.3*
	15–24	3076	28	1153	1855	*0.9*	*38.9*	1645	18	571	1036	*1.1*	*36.2*	1431	10	582	819	*0.7*	*42.0*
	25–44	5178	64	2240	2818	*1.2*	*44.9*	2878	42	1213	1604	*1.5*	*43.9*	2300	22	1027	1214	*1.0*	*46.3*
	45–64	2077	77	1161	821	*3.7*	*60.0*	1152	40	634	469	*3.5*	*58.8*	925	37	527	352	*4.0*	*61.6*
	65–	557	60	321	173	*10.8*	*68.8*	249	23	146	78	*9.3*	*68.4*	308	37	175	95	*12.1*	*69.1*
Neath RD	All 3+	38176	1614	23784	12136	*4.3*	*67.7*	20142	791	12366	6662	*4.0*	*66.4*	18034	823	11418	5474	*4.6*	*69.1*
	3–4	2259	279	906	821	*13.9*	*59.0*	1123	135	440	419	*13.6*	*57.8*	1136	144	466	402	*14.2*	*60.3*
	5–9	5112	216	2983	1781	*4.3*	*64.2*	2600	112	1509	905	*4.4*	*64.2*	2512	104	1474	876	*4.2*	*64.3*
	10–14	4347	79	2779	1414	*1.8*	*66.9*	2221	34	1412	739	*1.6*	*66.2*	2126	45	1367	675	*2.2*	*67.7*
	15–24	7773	123	4984	2607	*1.6*	*66.2*	4213	63	2644	1482	*1.5*	*64.6*	3560	60	2340	1125	*1.7*	*68.1*
	25–44	12173	329	7858	3905	*2.7*	*67.7*	6601	175	4162	2222	*2.7*	*66.1*	5572	154	3696	1683	*2.8*	*69.6*
	45–64	5226	371	3495	1325	*7.1*	*74.4*	2785	191	1822	758	*6.9*	*72.6*	2441	180	1673	567	*7.4*	*76.5*
	65–	1286	217	779	283	*17.0*	*77.9*	599	81	377	137	*13.6*	*77.0*	687	136	402	146	*19.9*	*78.7*

District[1]	Age last birth-day	Number[2] Total in age group	Welsh only	Both	English only	Percentage[3] Welsh only	Able to speak Welsh	Number[2] Total in age group	Welsh only	Both	English only	Percentage[3] Welsh only	Able to speak Welsh	Number[2] Total in age group	Welsh only	Both	English only	Percentage[3] Welsh only	Able to speak Welsh
		Persons						Males						Females					
Pen-y-bont RD[3]	All 3+	20649	393	9320	9738	*2.0*	*49.9*	10989	203	4816	5304	*2.0*	*48.6*	9660	190	4504	4434	*2.1*	*51.4*
	3–4	1094	32	300	618	*3.4*	*34.9*	580	22	150	336	*4.3*	*33.8*	514	10	150	282	*2.3*	*36.2*
	5–9	2448	35	836	1363	*1.6*	*39.0*	1240	19	410	692	*1.7*	*38.3*	1208	16	426	671	*1.4*	*39.6*
	10–14	2078	29	859	1040	*1.5*	*46.0*	1059	15	434	530	*1.5*	*45.8*	1019	14	425	510	*1.5*	*46.2*
	15–24	3904	41	1674	1988	*1.1*	*46.3*	2125	20	864	1117	*1.0*	*44.2*	1779	21	810	871	*1.2*	*48.8*
	25–44	6832	99	3176	3252	*1.5*	*50.1*	3774	58	1712	1835	*1.6*	*49.1*	3058	41	1464	1417	*1.4*	*51.5*
	45–64	3353	93	1908	1201	*2.9*	*62.5*	1745	43	965	654	*2.6*	*60.6*	1608	50	943	547	*3.2*	*64.5*
	65–	940	64	567	276	*7.1*	*69.6*	466	26	281	140	*5.8*	*68.7*	474	38	286	136	*8.3*	*70.4*
Pontardawe RD	All 3+	28861	4835	18350	4742	*17.3*	*83.0*	15140	2410	9395	2888	*16.4*	*80.3*	13721	2425	8955	1854	*18.3*	*86.0*
	3–4	1665	508	566	312	*36.7*	*77.5*	808	247	272	149	*37.0*	*77.7*	857	261	294	163	*36.4*	*77.3*
	5–9	3652	887	2029	482	*26.1*	*85.8*	1818	448	992	242	*26.6*	*85.6*	1834	439	1037	240	*25.6*	*86.0*
	10–14	3117	408	2310	271	*13.7*	*90.9*	1515	210	1122	123	*14.4*	*91.5*	1602	198	1188	148	*12.9*	*90.4*
	15–24	6012	590	4338	983	*10.0*	*83.3*	3173	329	2198	601	*10.5*	*80.7*	2839	261	2140	382	*9.4*	*86.2*
	25–44	9696	1126	6307	2147	*11.7*	*77.5*	5376	576	3340	1424	*10.8*	*73.2*	4320	550	2967	723	*13.0*	*82.9*
	45–64	3697	877	2305	467	*24.0*	*87.2*	2009	436	1238	310	*22.0*	*84.3*	1688	441	1067	157	*26.5*	*90.6*
	65–	1022	439	495	80	*43.3*	*92.1*	441	164	233	39	*37.6*	*91.1*	581	275	262	41	*47.6*	*92.9*
Swansea RD	All 3+	39973	3526	25018	10691	*9.0*	*72.7*	20802	1715	12797	5920	*8.4*	*71.0*	19171	1811	12221	4771	*9.6*	*74.6*
	3–4	2133	402	777	675	*21.7*	*63.6*	1078	207	406	324	*22.1*	*65.4*	1055	195	371	351	*21.3*	*61.7*
	5–9	5042	503	2964	1389	*10.4*	*71.4*	2488	253	1425	720	*10.6*	*70.0*	2554	250	1539	669	*10.2*	*72.8*
	10–14	4433	255	2973	1141	*5.8*	*73.9*	2236	120	1486	605	*5.4*	*72.6*	2197	135	1487	536	*6.3*	*75.2*
	15–24	8151	385	5593	2110	*4.8*	*73.9*	4343	203	2930	1180	*4.7*	*72.6*	3808	182	2663	930	*4.8*	*75.4*
	25–44	12834	772	8320	3647	*6.1*	*71.4*	6872	390	4337	2092	*5.7*	*69.3*	5962	382	3983	1555	*6.5*	*73.7*
	45–64	5786	789	3534	1426	*13.7*	*75.2*	3026	375	1788	839	*12.5*	*72.0*	2760	414	1746	587	*15.1*	*78.6*
	65–	1594	420	857	303	*26.6*	*80.8*	759	167	425	160	*22.2*	*78.7*	835	253	432	143	*30.6*	*82.7*
CARMARTHENSHIRE																			
Ammanford UD	All 3+	5574	498	3902	1091	*9.1*	*80.1*	2982	243	2025	666	*8.3*	*77.3*	2592	255	1877	425	*22.4*	*72.8*
	3–4	323	70	139	78	*24.4*	*72.8*	159	37	65	38	*26.4*	*72.9*	164	33	74	40	*11.5*	*82.2*
	5–9	711	76	499	124	*10.9*	*82.3*	339	34	240	59	*10.2*	*82.3*	372	42	259	65	*4.4*	*87.2*
	10–14	524	24	426	71	*4.6*	*86.4*	272	13	219	39	*4.8*	*85.6*	252	11	207	32	*4.3*	*86.6*
	15–24	1203	60	903	226	*5.0*	*81.0*	684	38	479	157	*5.6*	*76.7*	519	22	424	69	*7.3*	*81.2*
	25–44	1960	129	1362	458	*6.6*	*76.5*	1087	66	720	295	*6.1*	*72.7*	873	63	642	163	*15.3*	*84.7*
	45–64	691	94	474	118	*13.7*	*82.8*	376	46	256	70	*12.4*	*81.2*	315	48	218	48	*37.1*	*91.8*
	65–	162	45	99	16	*28.1*	*90.0*	65	9	46	8	*14.3*	*87.3*	97	36	53	8	*10.0*	*83.4*

Burry Port UD	All 3+	4258	410	3030	745	9.8	82.2	2111	199	1499	375	9.6	81.9	2147	211	1531	370	28.6	75.5
	3–4	213	54	78	46	30.3	74.2	105	26	32	22	32.5	72.5	108	28	46	24	12.0	78.5
	5–9	513	60	333	105	12.0	78.9	252	30	166	51	12.1	79.4	261	30	167	54	8.3	84.3
	10–14	497	36	371	82	7.4	83.2	250	16	187	44	6.5	82.2	247	20	184	38	4.9	82.6
	15–24	796	34	611	143	4.3	81.9	406	15	313	76	3.7	81.2	390	19	298	67	6.9	83.2
	25–44	1332	101	1004	221	7.6	83.3	679	56	508	112	8.3	83.4	653	45	496	109	10.8	82.9
	45–64	691	72	503	115	10.4	83.3	328	33	242	53	10.1	83.8	363	39	261	62	24.0	87.2
	65–	216	53	130	33	24.4	84.3	91	23	51	17	25.0	80.4	125	30	79	16	10.0	82.5
Carmarthen MB	All 3+	9731	686	6858	2118	7.1	78.1	4490	261	3113	1079	5.9	75.8	5241	425	3745	1039	11.8	60.2
	3–4	337	34	168	114	10.8	63.9	166	15	90	50	9.7	67.7	171	19	78	64	5.1	73.5
	5–9	830	43	566	207	5.3	74.6	393	21	271	93	5.5	75.8	437	22	295	114	2.1	77.5
	10–14	867	26	654	183	3.0	78.8	389	16	295	76	4.1	80.4	478	10	359	107	1.9	81.4
	15–24	1963	44	1456	453	2.3	76.8	919	24	629	260	2.6	71.5	1044	20	827	193	5.9	79.5
	25–44	3043	143	2183	703	4.7	76.8	1457	50	1021	379	3.4	73.8	1586	93	1162	324	14.6	83.1
	45–64	1943	246	1342	351	12.7	81.9	879	91	615	171	10.4	80.5	1064	155	727	180	23.0	87.6
	65–	748	150	489	107	20.1	85.7	287	44	192	50	15.4	82.5	461	106	297	57	8.2	80.0
Kidwelly MB	All 3+	2813	325	2095	320	11.9	88.3	1394	153	1038	166	11.3	87.8	1419	172	1057	154	34.0	79.2
	3–4	152	46	54	20	38.3	83.3	82	28	30	9	41.8	86.6	70	18	24	11	11.8	87.7
	5–9	366	51	259	44	14.4	87.6	165	28	111	20	17.6	87.4	201	23	148	24	4.3	91.3
	10–14	288	14	240	25	5.0	91.0	148	8	120	13	5.7	90.8	140	6	120	12	6.1	94.2
	15–24	619	30	528	55	4.9	91.0	322	12	270	38	3.8	88.1	297	18	258	17	9.3	83.7
	25–44	788	62	589	130	7.9	83.4	398	26	302	67	6.6	83.0	390	36	287	63	19.5	93.2
	45–64	456	82	338	32	18.1	92.9	218	36	164	16	16.7	92.6	238	46	174	16	30.5	86.6
	65–	144	40	87	14	28.4	90.1	61	15	41	3	25.4	94.9	83	25	46	11	12.4	88.9
Llandeilo UD	All 3+	1837	73	1446	287	4.0	84.1	831	30	636	147	3.7	81.9	1006	43	810	140	10.0	83.3
	3–4	64	6	43	10	10.2	83.1	32	3	21	5	10.3	82.8	32	3	22	5	1.3	81.8
	5–9	154	5	115	29	3.4	80.5	75	4	53	15	5.6	79.2	79	1	62	14	0.0	87.0
	10–14	151	2	122	22	1.4	84.9	81	2	62	13	2.6	83.1	70	0	60	9	0.4	88.3
	15–24	382	2	318	57	0.5	84.9	156	1	122	31	0.6	79.9	226	1	196	26	2.5	83.5
	25–44	594	12	471	103	2.0	82.4	269	4	210	50	1.5	81.1	325	8	261	53	7.9	88.9
	45–64	353	24	282	44	6.9	87.4	161	9	128	23	5.6	85.6	192	15	154	21	18.3	85.4
	65–	139	22	95	22	15.8	84.2	57	7	40	10	12.3	82.5	82	15	55	12	4.3	85.9
Llandovery MB	All 3+	1870	102	1295	457	5.5	75.4	966	40	633	283	4.2	70.4	904	62	662	174	18.4	78.9
	3–4	78	13	40	21	17.6	71.6	40	6	17	13	16.7	63.9	38	7	23	8	2.3	75.9
	5–9	194	8	135	46	4.2	75.7	105	6	71	25	5.9	75.5	89	2	64	21	0.0	85.0
	10–14	208	1	148	58	0.5	72.0	127	1	80	46	0.8	63.8	81	0	68	12	0.6	74.7
	15–24	387	5	255	127	1.3	67.2	221	4	132	85	1.8	61.5	166	1	123	42	2.6	79.9
	25–44	536	11	394	128	2.1	76.0	261	4	182	73	1.5	71.8	275	7	212	55	11.5	85.1
	45–64	324	27	236	60	8.4	81.4	150	7	108	34	4.7	77.2	174	20	128	26	31.6	87.3
	65–	143	37	87	17	26.2	87.9	62	12	43	7	19.4	88.7	81	25	44	10	6.9	80.6

District[1]	Age last birth-day	Persons: Number[2] Total in age group	Welsh only	Both	English only	Percentage[3] Welsh only	Able to speak Welsh	Males: Number[2] Total in age group	Welsh only	Both	English only	Percentage[3] Welsh only	Able to speak Welsh	Females: Number[2] Total in age group	Welsh only	Both	English only	Percentage[3] Welsh only	Able to speak Welsh
Llanelli UD	All 3+	29970	1653	21135	6667	*5.6*	*77.3*	15429	795	10638	3712	*5.2*	*75.4*	14541	858	10497	2955	*12.6*	*66.0*
	3–4	1405	153	694	411	*12.2*	*67.3*	712	74	358	197	*11.8*	*68.7*	693	79	336	214	*5.3*	*74.7*
	5–9	3372	168	2281	846	*5.1*	*74.3*	1700	82	1151	434	*4.9*	*74.0*	1672	86	1130	412	*3.4*	*77.9*
	10–14	2986	102	2237	643	*3.4*	*78.4*	1500	52	1140	318	*3.4*	*78.9*	1486	50	1097	325	*3.1*	*80.5*
	15–24	6410	207	4771	1339	*3.3*	*78.6*	3327	111	2412	746	*3.4*	*76.9*	3083	96	2359	593	*4.0*	*79.0*
	25–44	9736	383	6877	2339	*4.0*	*75.6*	5163	202	3485	1391	*4.0*	*72.5*	4573	181	3392	948	*9.3*	*84.6*
	45–64	4695	401	3383	863	*8.6*	*81.4*	2427	191	1688	518	*8.0*	*78.4*	2268	210	1695	345	*20.5*	*84.5*
	65–	1366	239	892	226	*17.6*	*83.3*	600	83	404	108	*13.9*	*81.7*	766	156	488	118	*6.0*	*79.3*
Newcastle Emlyn UD	All 3+	879	143	664	70	*16.3*	*91.9*	406	51	304	49	*12.6*	*87.7*	473	92	360	21	*41.2*	*88.2*
	3–4	31	12	14	4	*40.0*	*86.7*	14	5	6	2	*38.5*	*84.6*	17	7	8	2	*21.1*	*100.0*
	5–9	72	14	56	2	*19.4*	*97.2*	34	6	26	2	*17.6*	*94.1*	38	8	30	0	*0.0*	*100.0*
	10–14	56	1	55	0	*1.8*	*100.0*	34	1	33	0	*2.9*	*100.0*	22	0	22	0	*4.9*	*97.1*
	15–24	175	8	155	12	*4.6*	*93.1*	72	3	60	9	*4.2*	*87.5*	103	5	95	3	*9.9*	*92.2*
	25–44	278	25	213	39	*9.0*	*85.6*	137	11	97	28	*8.0*	*78.8*	141	14	116	11	*28.0*	*95.0*
	45–64	176	44	119	13	*25.0*	*92.6*	76	16	52	8	*21.1*	*89.5*	100	28	67	5	*57.7*	*100.0*
	65–	91	39	52	0	*42.9*	*100.0*	39	9	30	0	*23.1*	*100.0*	52	30	22	0	*19.5*	*95.6*
Carmarthen RD	All 3+	22670	6773	13449	2200	*30.2*	*90.2*	10783	2946	6563	1152	*27.6*	*89.2*	11887	3827	6886	1048	*65.6*	*87.4*
	3–4	978	582	194	100	*66.4*	*88.6*	489	296	99	45	*67.3*	*89.8*	489	286	95	55	*38.4*	*89.3*
	5–9	2361	900	1183	224	*39.0*	*90.3*	1115	432	561	94	*39.7*	*91.4*	1246	468	622	130	*18.9*	*91.2*
	10–14	2316	478	1619	197	*20.8*	*91.4*	1101	251	748	91	*23.0*	*91.7*	1215	227	871	106	*18.2*	*90.6*
	15–24	4746	788	3268	671	*16.7*	*85.8*	2405	364	1580	453	*15.2*	*81.1*	2341	424	1688	218	*26.5*	*91.1*
	25–44	6407	1539	4263	574	*24.1*	*91.0*	3026	646	2091	273	*21.5*	*90.9*	3381	893	2172	301	*43.0*	*93.0*
	45–64	4113	1591	2192	316	*38.8*	*92.3*	1929	655	1101	164	*34.1*	*91.5*	2184	936	1091	152	*57.8*	*91.6*
	65–	1749	895	730	118	*51.3*	*93.2*	718	302	383	32	*42.1*	*95.5*	1031	593	347	86	*32.5*	*91.1*
Llandeilo Fawr RD	All 3+	23373	5864	14468	2293	*25.9*	*89.9*	12082	2935	7477	1439	*24.8*	*87.8*	11291	2929	6991	854	*61.2*	*89.8*
	3–4	1237	647	309	122	*60.0*	*88.7*	614	318	155	67	*58.9*	*87.6*	623	329	154	55	*38.7*	*92.0*
	5–9	2833	1076	1450	204	*39.4*	*92.5*	1425	553	729	96	*40.1*	*93.0*	1408	523	721	108	*20.5*	*91.6*
	10–14	2541	547	1779	183	*21.8*	*92.7*	1238	283	865	75	*23.1*	*93.9*	1303	264	914	108	*14.1*	*92.4*
	15–24	4824	642	3510	632	*13.4*	*86.8*	2604	332	1788	464	*12.8*	*82.0*	2220	310	1722	168	*21.3*	*91.0*
	25–44	7290	1377	5010	837	*19.1*	*88.4*	3887	658	2654	533	*17.1*	*86.1*	3403	719	2356	304	*27.9*	*93.3*
	45–64	3451	939	1902	266	*30.2*	*91.4*	1803	567	1030	176	*32.0*	*90.1*	1648	372	872	90	*60.1*	*96.9*
	65–	1197	636	508	49	*53.3*	*95.9*	511	224	256	28	*44.1*	*94.5*	686	412	252	21	*27.2*	*92.1*

Llandovery RD	All 3+	7013	1715	4505	710	24.7	89.8	3465	734	2251	443	21.4	87.1	3548	981	2254	267	63.2	90.4
	3–4	250	137	67	18	61.7	91.9	122	65	36	7	60.2	93.5	128	72	31	11	33.0	93.3
	5–9	642	223	354	41	36.1	93.4	314	119	164	20	39.3	93.4	328	104	190	21	12.5	92.4
	10–14	674	80	541	46	12.0	93.1	342	39	278	21	11.5	93.8	332	41	263	25	11.5	87.8
	15–24	1503	146	1055	294	9.8	80.3	786	64	512	207	8.2	73.6	717	82	543	87	17.8	91.3
	25–44	1934	298	1429	197	15.5	89.8	961	126	718	113	13.2	88.2	973	172	711	84	41.2	95.7
	45–64	1375	486	795	90	35.4	93.4	649	188	401	59	29.0	90.9	726	298	394	31	62.0	97.7
	65–	635	345	264	24	54.5	96.2	291	133	142	16	45.7	94.5	344	212	122	8	28.0	92.4
Llanelli RD	All 3+	25218	5836	16682	2080	23.7	91.4	13019	2819	8603	1261	22.1	89.7	12199	3017	8079	819	56.8	90.3
	3–4	1420	681	427	113	55.8	90.7	699	322	215	52	54.7	91.2	721	359	212	61	30.4	93.5
	5–9	3270	971	1917	206	31.4	93.3	1678	516	970	109	32.4	93.2	1592	455	947	97	14.7	94.2
	10–14	2812	432	2181	149	15.6	94.6	1353	220	1038	65	16.6	95.1	1459	212	1143	84	11.8	94.2
	15–24	5254	615	4104	463	11.9	91.0	2828	332	2131	325	11.9	88.2	2426	283	1973	138	19.6	91.6
	25–44	7887	1433	5542	822	18.3	89.0	4202	717	2913	516	17.1	86.7	3685	716	2629	306	38.8	94.2
	45–64	3483	1161	2036	261	33.6	92.5	1781	504	1099	163	28.5	90.8	1702	657	937	98	55.1	94.2
	65–	1092	543	475	66	50.1	93.9	478	208	237	31	43.7	93.5	614	335	238	35	25.3	93.1
Llanybydder RD	All 3+	3421	1632	1624	119	48.4	96.5	1613	685	819	83	43.2	94.8	1808	947	805	36	77.8	92.1
	3–4	147	107	14	8	82.9	93.8	78	58	5	3	87.9	95.5	69	49	9	5	68.7	98.7
	5–9	330	214	96	5	67.9	98.4	175	111	51	3	67.3	98.2	155	103	45	2	34.9	98.8
	10–14	340	124	210	3	36.8	99.1	165	64	100	1	38.8	99.4	175	60	110	2	28.9	97.5
	15–24	594	154	390	47	26.1	92.0	308	72	195	40	23.5	87.0	286	82	195	7	39.3	97.1
	25–44	958	329	589	37	34.5	96.1	434	124	287	22	28.6	94.9	524	205	302	15	67.9	99.2
	45–64	686	412	257	14	60.3	98.0	302	152	137	11	50.7	96.3	384	260	120	3	87.9	99.1
	65–	366	292	68	5	80.0	98.6	151	104	44	3	68.9	98.0	215	188	24	2	53.0	98.0
Newcastle Emlyn RD	All 3+	6134	3307	2655	116	54.4	98.1	2836	1393	1336	81	49.6	97.1	3298	1914	1319	35	90.4	98.3
	3–4	248	210	18	2	91.3	99.1	124	106	9	0	92.2	100.0	124	104	9	2	75.9	99.7
	5–9	655	477	158	3	74.8	99.5	332	237	83	2	73.6	99.4	323	240	75	1	40.4	100.0
	10–14	669	291	369	3	43.9	99.5	338	159	174	3	47.3	99.1	331	132	195	0	38.9	98.1
	15–24	1206	410	739	55	34.1	95.4	570	163	363	43	28.6	92.4	636	247	376	12	51.8	98.5
	25–44	1703	802	860	34	47.3	98.0	752	311	418	20	41.5	97.3	951	491	442	14	71.8	99.2
	45–64	1171	751	399	16	64.4	98.6	524	290	223	11	55.3	97.9	647	461	176	5	83.6	99.7
	65–	482	366	112	3	76.1	99.4	196	127	66	2	65.1	99.0	286	239	46	1	58.6	98.9
Whitland RD	All 3+	4930	1388	2753	718	28.6	85.2	2314	598	1282	392	26.3	82.7	2616	790	1471	326	60.2	80.7
	3–4	182	87	38	32	55.4	79.6	87	34	20	15	49.3	78.3	95	53	18	17	45.3	84.2
	5–9	509	211	201	81	42.8	83.6	267	105	110	44	40.5	83.0	242	106	91	37	23.6	86.3
	10–14	459	104	291	62	22.8	86.4	226	49	145	30	21.9	86.6	233	55	146	32	16.0	84.9
	15–24	1021	175	640	200	17.2	80.3	481	89	269	119	18.7	75.1	540	86	371	81	22.9	86.7
	25–44	1403	292	881	219	21.0	84.3	626	115	388	116	18.6	81.3	777	177	493	103	40.2	92.6
	45–64	993	346	547	90	35.2	90.8	473	140	278	52	29.8	88.9	520	206	269	38	51.4	91.3
	65–	363	173	155	34	47.8	90.6	154	66	72	16	42.9	89.6	209	107	83	18	30.5	87.4

District[1]	Age last birth-day	Persons: Number[2] Total in age group	Welsh only	Both	English only	Percentage[3] *Welsh only*	*Able to speak Welsh*	Males: Number[2] Total in age group	Welsh only	Both	English only	Percentage[3] *Welsh only*	*Able to speak Welsh*	Females: Number[2] Total in age group	Welsh only	Both	English only	Percentage[3] *Welsh only*	*Able to speak Welsh*
PEMBROKESHIRE																			
Fishguard UD	All 3+	2656	218	1819	661	*8.1*	*75.5*	1273	151	838	347	*11.3*	*74.0*	1383	67	981	314	*16.4*	*68.9*
	3–4	127	25	59	35	*21.0*	*70.6*	63	15	27	16	*25.9*	*72.4*	64	10	32	19	*5.1*	*70.6*
	5–9	325	24	201	88	*7.7*	*71.9*	141	15	85	36	*11.0*	*73.5*	184	9	116	52	*2.6*	*70.9*
	10–14	263	8	184	67	*3.1*	*74.1*	146	5	104	33	*3.5*	*76.8*	117	3	80	34	*0.8*	*77.6*
	15–24	469	4	343	118	*0.9*	*74.6*	227	2	158	64	*0.9*	*71.4*	242	2	185	54	*3.4*	*76.5*
	25–44	920	112	625	258	*11.2*	*74.0*	445	96	283	149	*18.2*	*71.8*	475	16	342	109	*6.0*	*82.6*
	45–64	401	20	296	80	*5.1*	*79.8*	181	7	129	42	*3.9*	*76.4*	220	13	167	38	*17.3*	*90.1*
	65–	151	25	111	15	*16.6*	*90.1*	70	11	52	7	*15.7*	*90.0*	81	14	59	8	*4.9*	*76.9*
Haverfordwest MB	All 3+	5613	9	559	4934	*0.2*	*10.3*	2577	3	242	2289	*0.1*	*9.7*	3036	6	317	2645	*0.0*	*6.2*
	3–4	220	0	7	193	*0.0*	*3.5*	110	0	1	102	*0.0*	*1.0*	110	0	6	91	*0.0*	*0.8*
	5–9	537	0	9	498	*0.0*	*1.8*	255	0	7	237	*0.0*	*2.9*	282	0	2	261	*0.7*	*3.3*
	10–14	641	2	22	591	*0.3*	*3.9*	323	0	14	296	*0.0*	*4.5*	318	2	8	295	*0.0*	*7.0*
	15–24	1087	0	68	1009	*0.0*	*6.3*	494	0	27	461	*0.0*	*5.5*	593	0	41	548	*0.5*	*12.2*
	25–44	1594	6	198	1378	*0.4*	*12.9*	719	2	96	618	*0.3*	*13.7*	875	4	102	760	*0.0*	*17.3*
	45–64	1096	0	169	919	*0.0*	*15.5*	502	0	67	433	*0.0*	*13.4*	594	0	102	486	*0.0*	*21.5*
	65–	438	1	86	346	*0.2*	*20.1*	174	1	30	142	*0.6*	*17.9*	264	0	56	204	*0.2*	*10.9*
Milford Haven UD	All 3+	5877	3	218	5405	*0.1*	*3.9*	2880	2	99	2643	*0.1*	*3.6*	2997	1	119	2762	*0.0*	*1.3*
	3–4	316	0	4	281	*0.0*	*1.4*	146	0	2	130	*0.0*	*1.5*	170	0	2	151	*0.0*	*1.1*
	5–9	791	0	6	736	*0.0*	*0.8*	390	0	2	365	*0.0*	*0.5*	401	0	4	371	*0.0*	*0.0*
	10–14	664	0	6	612	*0.0*	*1.0*	321	0	6	291	*0.0*	*2.0*	343	0	0	321	*0.0*	*2.9*
	15–24	1245	0	24	1159	*0.0*	*2.0*	620	0	6	567	*0.0*	*1.0*	625	0	18	592	*0.0*	*5.3*
	25–44	1850	1	99	1702	*0.1*	*5.5*	914	1	51	843	*0.1*	*5.8*	936	0	48	859	*0.3*	*8.6*
	45–64	768	2	57	698	*0.3*	*7.8*	380	1	25	347	*0.3*	*7.0*	388	1	32	351	*0.0*	*11.4*
	65–	243	0	22	217	*0.0*	*9.2*	109	0	7	100	*0.0*	*6.5*	134	0	15	117	*0.0*	*4.2*
Narberth UD	All 3+	1052	4	320	718	*0.4*	*31.1*	476	2	149	318	*0.4*	*32.2*	576	2	171	400	*0.0*	*6.3*
	3–4	36	0	3	33	*0.0*	*8.3*	20	0	2	18	*0.0*	*10.0*	16	0	1	15	*0.0*	*2.6*
	5–9	92	0	5	85	*0.0*	*5.6*	52	0	4	47	*0.0*	*7.8*	40	0	1	38	*0.0*	*13.2*
	10–14	134	0	18	114	*0.0*	*13.6*	65	0	9	55	*0.0*	*14.1*	69	0	9	59	*0.0*	*29.1*
	15–24	181	0	52	125	*0.0*	*29.4*	77	0	22	52	*0.0*	*29.7*	104	0	30	73	*0.5*	*31.4*
	25–44	323	1	113	208	*0.3*	*35.4*	135	0	55	79	*0.0*	*41.0*	188	1	58	129	*1.0*	*43.8*
	45–64	185	1	81	103	*0.5*	*44.3*	80	0	36	44	*0.0*	*45.0*	105	1	45	59	*0.0*	*50.0*
	65–	101	2	48	50	*2.0*	*50.0*	47	2	21	23	*4.3*	*50.0*	54	0	27	27	*0.3*	*30.2*

Neyland UD	All 3+	2288	5	133	2100	*0.2*	*6.2*	1083	2	70	981	*0.2*	*6.8*	1205	3	63	1119	*0.0*	*0.0*
	3–4	102	0	0	97	*0.0*	*0.0*	50	0	0	48	*0.0*	*0.0*	52	0	0	49	*0.0*	*0.7*
	5–9	275	0	7	264	*0.0*	*2.6*	137	0	6	129	*0.0*	*4.4*	138	0	1	135	*0.0*	*2.3*
	10–14	291	0	5	275	*0.0*	*1.8*	154	0	2	146	*0.0*	*1.4*	137	0	3	129	*0.9*	*4.0*
	15–24	409	4	12	382	*1.0*	*4.0*	181	2	5	166	*1.2*	*4.0*	228	2	7	216	*0.3*	*6.9*
	25–44	665	1	51	603	*0.2*	*7.9*	299	0	27	266	*0.0*	*9.2*	366	1	24	337	*0.0*	*7.0*
	45–64	390	0	35	348	*0.0*	*9.1*	188	0	21	162	*0.0*	*11.5*	202	0	14	186	*0.0*	*17.3*
	65–	156	0	23	131	*0.0*	*14.9*	74	0	9	64	*0.0*	*12.3*	82	0	14	67	*0.3*	*5.6*
Pembroke MB	All 3+	14755	9	515	13887	*0.1*	*3.6*	7606	4	287	7125	*0.1*	*3.9*	7149	5	228	6762	*0.0*	*0.4*
	3–4	576	0	2	529	*0.0*	*0.4*	285	0	1	265	*0.0*	*0.4*	291	0	1	264	*0.0*	*0.0*
	5–9	1518	0	3	1464	*0.0*	*0.2*	792	0	3	763	*0.0*	*0.4*	726	0	0	701	*0.0*	*1.5*
	10–14	1466	0	15	1419	*0.0*	*1.0*	721	0	4	700	*0.0*	*0.6*	745	0	11	719	*0.0*	*1.7*
	15–24	3270	0	91	3122	*0.0*	*2.8*	1866	0	67	1768	*0.0*	*3.7*	1404	0	24	1354	*0.1*	*3.9*
	25–44	4321	7	184	4016	*0.2*	*4.5*	2209	4	105	2018	*0.2*	*5.1*	2112	3	79	1998	*0.1*	*5.3*
	45–64	2644	2	144	2469	*0.1*	*5.6*	1284	0	75	1200	*0.0*	*5.9*	1360	2	69	1269	*0.0*	*8.8*
	65–	960	0	76	868	*0.0*	*8.0*	449	0	32	411	*0.0*	*7.2*	511	0	44	457	*0.1*	*3.3*
Tenby MB	All 3+	4156	2	195	3812	*0.0*	*4.9*	1706	2	81	1563	*0.1*	*5.0*	2450	0	114	2249	*0.0*	*1.6*
	3–4	128	0	1	114	*0.0*	*0.9*	60	0	0	53	*0.0*	*0.0*	68	0	1	61	*0.0*	*0.6*
	5–9	376	0	3	347	*0.0*	*0.9*	185	0	2	171	*0.0*	*1.2*	191	0	1	176	*0.0*	*1.2*
	10–14	345	0	4	322	*0.0*	*1.2*	174	0	2	162	*0.0*	*1.2*	171	0	2	160	*0.0*	*3.5*
	15–24	767	0	28	718	*0.0*	*3.7*	300	0	12	277	*0.0*	*4.1*	467	0	16	441	*0.0*	*5.2*
	25–44	1319	1	68	1209	*0.1*	*5.4*	500	1	27	462	*0.2*	*5.7*	819	0	41	747	*0.0*	*7.8*
	45–64	857	1	61	775	*0.1*	*7.4*	363	1	23	332	*0.3*	*6.7*	494	0	38	443	*0.0*	*6.4*
	65–	364	0	30	327	*0.0*	*8.4*	124	0	15	106	*0.0*	*12.4*	240	0	15	221	*0.0*	*4.8*
Haverfordwest RD	All 3+	19929	1682	7885	9881	*8.6*	*49.2*	9822	774	3698	5143	*8.0*	*46.5*	10107	908	4187	4738	*23.5*	*42.2*
	3–4	968	212	141	503	*24.8*	*41.2*	512	120	68	277	*25.8*	*40.4*	456	92	73	226	*12.7*	*43.3*
	5–9	2193	279	633	1192	*13.3*	*43.3*	1087	145	312	595	*13.8*	*43.4*	1106	134	321	597	*4.5*	*47.5*
	10–14	2071	104	821	1068	*5.2*	*46.4*	1053	60	402	557	*5.9*	*45.3*	1018	44	419	511	*3.2*	*49.3*
	15–24	4026	138	1687	2132	*3.5*	*46.1*	2034	75	785	1138	*3.8*	*43.0*	1992	63	902	994	*5.7*	*51.6*
	25–44	5684	293	2437	2876	*5.2*	*48.7*	2766	128	1116	1486	*4.7*	*45.6*	2918	165	1321	1390	*12.2*	*58.3*
	45–64	3514	362	1545	1565	*10.4*	*54.9*	1720	147	729	829	*8.6*	*51.4*	1794	215	816	736	*24.0*	*65.1*
	65–	1473	294	621	545	*20.1*	*62.7*	650	99	286	261	*15.3*	*59.6*	823	195	335	284	*9.2*	*51.8*
Llanfyrnach RD	All 3+	2281	1254	979	41	*55.1*	*98.2*	1074	543	498	29	*50.7*	*97.3*	1207	711	481	12	*94.9*	*97.4*
	3–4	83	67	10	2	*84.8*	*97.5*	41	30	9	1	*75.0*	*97.5*	42	37	1	1	*67.3*	*100.0*
	5–9	247	168	74	3	*68.6*	*98.8*	137	94	38	3	*69.6*	*97.8*	110	74	36	0	*45.0*	*99.1*
	10–14	251	112	136	3	*44.6*	*98.8*	140	62	76	2	*44.3*	*98.6*	111	50	60	1	*32.8*	*99.5*
	15–24	400	149	238	13	*37.3*	*96.8*	196	82	102	12	*41.8*	*93.9*	204	67	136	1	*52.6*	*98.3*
	25–44	632	301	317	13	*47.7*	*97.9*	273	112	153	7	*41.2*	*97.4*	359	189	164	6	*74.7*	*98.9*
	45–64	483	317	159	7	*65.6*	*98.6*	210	113	93	4	*53.8*	*98.1*	273	204	66	3	*83.3*	*100.0*
	65–	185	140	45	0	*75.7*	*100.0*	77	50	27	0	*64.9*	*100.0*	108	90	18	0	*59.1*	*99.0*

District[1]	Age last birth-day	Number[2] Total in age group	Welsh only	Both	English only	Percentage[3] Welsh only	Percentage[3] Able to speak Welsh	Number[2] Total in age group	Welsh only	Both	English only	Percentage[3] Welsh only	Percentage[3] Able to speak Welsh	Number[2] Total in age group	Welsh only	Both	English only	Percentage[3] Welsh only	Percentage[3] Able to speak Welsh
		Persons						Males						Females					
Narberth RD	All 3+	10387	869	3373	5964	*8.5*	*41.6*	4897	372	1586	2854	*7.7*	*40.7*	5490	497	1787	3110	*22.9*	*34.4*
	3–4	442	88	47	256	*22.5*	*34.5*	223	44	25	130	*22.1*	*34.7*	219	44	22	126	*13.2*	*35.0*
	5–9	1119	148	218	707	*13.8*	*34.1*	569	78	103	363	*14.3*	*33.3*	550	70	115	344	*6.5*	*35.0*
	10–14	1061	62	328	649	*6.0*	*37.5*	516	27	176	301	*5.4*	*40.3*	545	35	152	348	*3.9*	*36.9*
	15–24	1946	66	624	1237	*3.4*	*35.8*	954	28	299	616	*3.0*	*34.7*	992	38	325	621	*5.8*	*46.0*
	25–44	2830	156	1091	1562	*5.6*	*44.4*	1331	70	494	761	*5.3*	*42.6*	1499	86	597	801	*11.5*	*47.2*
	45–64	2086	213	758	1100	*10.3*	*46.9*	930	81	350	495	*8.7*	*46.5*	1156	132	408	605	*17.5*	*49.5*
	65–	903	136	307	453	*15.2*	*49.4*	374	44	139	188	*11.9*	*49.3*	529	92	168	265	*9.2*	*42.3*
Pembroke RD	All 3+	7977	16	403	7375	*0.2*	*5.4*	3964	8	170	3690	*0.2*	*4.6*	4013	8	233	3685	*0.0*	*0.6*
	3–4	339	1	2	315	*0.3*	*0.9*	167	1	1	153	*0.6*	*1.3*	172	0	1	162	*0.0*	*1.6*
	5–9	859	1	8	817	*0.1*	*1.1*	465	1	2	448	*0.2*	*0.7*	394	0	6	369	*0.0*	*0.7*
	10–14	896	2	8	869	*0.2*	*1.1*	458	2	5	443	*0.4*	*1.6*	438	0	3	426	*0.2*	*3.3*
	15–24	1683	3	59	1591	*0.2*	*3.8*	862	1	34	807	*0.1*	*4.2*	821	2	25	784	*0.2*	*8.2*
	25–44	2105	4	135	1912	*0.2*	*6.8*	1006	2	49	925	*0.2*	*5.2*	1099	2	86	987	*0.4*	*9.5*
	45–64	1513	4	127	1359	*0.3*	*8.8*	741	1	58	672	*0.1*	*8.1*	772	3	69	687	*0.3*	*14.0*
	65–	582	1	64	512	*0.2*	*11.3*	265	0	21	242	*0.0*	*8.0*	317	1	43	270	*0.2*	*6.1*
St Dogmaels RD	All 3+	7492	2527	4480	346	*34.4*	*95.3*	3336	1076	2017	182	*32.8*	*94.4*	4156	1451	2463	164	*69.2*	*93.1*
	3–4	295	176	55	20	*70.1*	*92.0*	141	86	24	11	*71.1*	*90.9*	154	90	31	9	*42.0*	*96.2*
	5–9	723	317	356	24	*45.5*	*96.6*	366	172	169	11	*48.9*	*96.9*	357	145	187	13	*21.9*	*97.6*
	10–14	707	159	512	25	*22.8*	*96.4*	368	86	259	17	*23.8*	*95.3*	339	73	253	8	*19.6*	*93.3*
	15–24	1275	250	897	108	*19.9*	*91.3*	595	118	402	63	*20.2*	*89.0*	680	132	495	45	*26.3*	*96.1*
	25–44	2038	515	1408	93	*25.5*	*95.4*	855	208	595	47	*24.5*	*94.5*	1183	307	813	46	*41.3*	*96.7*
	45–64	1575	619	892	53	*39.6*	*96.6*	641	236	379	22	*37.0*	*96.5*	934	383	513	31	*63.7*	*97.6*
	65–	879	491	360	23	*56.2*	*97.4*	370	170	189	11	*45.9*	*97.0*	509	321	171	12	*35.6*	*96.0*
CARDIGANSHIRE																			
Aberaeron UD	All 3+	1289	225	964	87	*17.6*	*93.2*	522	95	370	50	*18.4*	*90.3*	767	130	594	37	*40.0*	*70.0*
	3–4	34	14	7	7	*50.0*	*75.0*	22	10	4	4	*55.6*	*77.8*	12	4	3	3	*24.0*	*96.0*
	5–9	102	29	70	3	*28.4*	*97.1*	52	17	34	1	*32.7*	*98.1*	50	12	36	2	*10.3*	*98.7*
	10–14	138	22	114	1	*16.1*	*99.3*	59	14	45	0	*23.7*	*100.0*	79	8	69	1	*5.3*	*97.0*
	15–24	218	14	188	15	*6.5*	*93.1*	85	7	66	11	*8.3*	*86.9*	133	7	122	4	*7.4*	*94.0*
	25–44	334	28	272	32	*8.4*	*90.4*	117	12	86	19	*10.3*	*83.8*	217	16	186	13	*21.7*	*93.9*
	45–64	306	56	227	21	*18.4*	*93.1*	125	17	97	10	*13.7*	*91.9*	181	39	130	11	*46.3*	*96.8*
	65–	157	62	86	8	*39.7*	*94.9*	62	18	38	5	*29.5*	*91.8*	95	44	48	3	*17.1*	*95.1*

Aberystwyth MB	All 3+	8042	370	5192	2285	*4.7*	*70.8*	3337	132	2229	894	*4.1*	*72.5*	4705	238	2963	1391	*12.9*	*66.2*
	3–4	285	32	131	88	*12.7*	*64.9*	127	14	57	41	*12.5*	*63.4*	158	18	74	47	*8.0*	*71.6*
	5–9	690	43	413	191	*6.6*	*70.3*	319	15	191	92	*5.0*	*68.7*	371	28	222	99	*3.9*	*71.7*
	10–14	657	23	445	167	*3.6*	*73.6*	314	10	220	74	*3.3*	*75.7*	343	13	225	93	*1.8*	*65.1*
	15–24	1797	28	1160	582	*1.6*	*67.1*	710	9	480	208	*1.3*	*70.2*	1087	19	680	374	*3.4*	*68.2*
	25–44	2520	80	1666	732	*3.2*	*70.4*	1019	30	710	265	*3.0*	*73.6*	1501	50	956	467	*6.9*	*74.4*
	45–64	1537	93	1038	386	*6.1*	*74.6*	636	32	439	159	*5.1*	*74.8*	901	61	599	227	*14.4*	*75.3*
	65–	556	71	339	139	*12.9*	*74.7*	212	22	132	55	*10.5*	*73.7*	344	49	207	84	*5.2*	*69.7*
Cardigan MB	All 3+	3391	410	2642	297	*12.2*	*91.1*	1466	156	1140	141	*10.9*	*90.2*	1925	254	1502	156	*38.6*	*84.1*
	3–4	111	35	46	16	*36.1*	*83.5*	63	18	26	9	*34.0*	*83.0*	48	17	20	7	*11.2*	*87.0*
	5–9	343	51	245	41	*15.1*	*87.8*	173	32	117	19	*19.0*	*88.7*	170	19	128	22	*5.6*	*93.3*
	10–14	344	21	299	21	*6.2*	*93.8*	163	11	141	9	*6.8*	*94.4*	181	10	158	12	*3.1*	*94.1*
	15–24	638	21	569	41	*3.3*	*93.5*	277	10	243	20	*3.7*	*92.7*	361	11	326	21	*9.1*	*89.9*
	25–44	966	77	769	116	*8.0*	*87.9*	383	24	299	57	*6.3*	*85.0*	583	53	470	59	*19.0*	*92.7*
	45–64	666	110	501	47	*16.7*	*92.9*	278	37	217	19	*13.6*	*93.0*	388	73	284	28	*36.6*	*96.4*
	65–	323	95	213	15	*29.4*	*95.4*	129	24	97	8	*18.6*	*93.8*	194	71	116	7	*13.3*	*91.8*
Lampeter MB	All 3+	1712	212	1300	189	*12.5*	*88.9*	760	73	575	105	*9.7*	*86.1*	952	139	725	84	*45.8*	*91.7*
	3–4	53	18	25	5	*37.5*	*89.6*	28	7	14	3	*29.2*	*87.5*	25	11	11	2	*16.9*	*84.7*
	5–9	128	16	89	19	*12.9*	*84.7*	67	6	49	10	*9.2*	*84.6*	61	10	40	9	*4.7*	*90.6*
	10–14	156	5	136	14	*3.2*	*91.0*	71	1	63	6	*1.4*	*91.4*	85	4	73	8	*2.7*	*94.0*
	15–24	339	13	296	30	*3.8*	*91.2*	157	8	130	19	*5.1*	*87.9*	182	5	166	11	*8.5*	*89.0*
	25–44	548	43	429	76	*7.8*	*86.1*	231	16	174	41	*6.9*	*82.3*	317	27	255	35	*20.3*	*93.8*
	45–64	333	60	238	34	*18.1*	*89.8*	140	21	97	22	*15.0*	*84.3*	193	39	141	12	*48.3*	*92.1*
	65–	155	57	87	11	*36.8*	*92.9*	66	14	48	4	*21.2*	*93.9*	89	43	39	7	*14.7*	*91.1*
New Quay UD	All 3+	1132	184	864	64	*16.5*	*94.2*	438	55	339	33	*12.9*	*92.3*	694	129	525	31	*44.4*	*72.2*
	3–4	37	18	6	8	*56.3*	*75.0*	17	10	1	3	*71.4*	*78.6*	20	8	5	5	*21.3*	*89.4*
	5–9	99	22	63	10	*23.2*	*89.5*	50	12	31	5	*25.0*	*89.6*	49	10	32	5	*9.1*	*92.7*
	10–14	106	7	93	5	*6.7*	*95.2*	51	2	47	1	*4.0*	*98.0*	55	5	46	4	*1.8*	*98.2*
	15–24	170	5	155	9	*3.0*	*94.7*	55	3	45	7	*5.5*	*87.3*	115	2	110	2	*8.1*	*93.0*
	25–44	288	21	240	21	*7.4*	*92.6*	100	6	82	8	*6.3*	*91.7*	188	15	158	13	*23.4*	*99.4*
	45–64	270	51	209	8	*19.0*	*97.0*	98	11	79	7	*11.3*	*92.8*	172	40	130	1	*52.1*	*98.9*
	65–	162	60	98	3	*37.3*	*98.1*	67	11	54	2	*16.4*	*97.0*	95	49	44	1	*18.8*	*95.5*
Aberaeron RD	All 3+	7338	3821	3221	185	*52.9*	*97.4*	3298	1598	1513	133	*49.3*	*95.9*	4040	2223	1708	52	*88.6*	*97.9*
	3–4	290	240	20	3	*91.3*	*98.9*	141	116	7	0	*94.3*	*100.0*	149	124	13	3	*71.0*	*99.7*
	5–9	699	492	174	5	*73.3*	*99.3*	375	272	85	4	*75.3*	*98.9*	324	220	89	1	*42.7*	*99.7*
	10–14	719	312	392	7	*43.9*	*99.0*	351	157	185	6	*45.1*	*98.3*	368	155	207	1	*31.0*	*98.8*
	15–24	1282	386	817	63	*30.5*	*95.0*	623	184	375	55	*30.0*	*91.0*	659	202	442	8	*40.7*	*97.7*
	25–44	1870	719	1068	65	*38.8*	*96.5*	748	268	436	39	*36.1*	*94.8*	1122	451	632	26	*70.3*	*99.1*
	45–64	1625	1005	577	34	*62.2*	*97.9*	718	372	317	26	*52.0*	*96.4*	907	633	260	8	*86.2*	*99.0*
	65–	853	667	173	8	*78.7*	*99.1*	342	229	108	3	*67.4*	*99.1*	511	438	65	5	*55.8*	*98.7*

District[1]	Age last birth-day	Number[2] Total in age group	Welsh only	Both	English only	Percentage[3] Welsh only	Able to speak Welsh	Number[2] Total in age group	Welsh only	Both	English only	Percentage[3] Welsh only	Able to speak Welsh	Number[2] Total in age group	Welsh only	Both	English only	Percentage[3] Welsh only	Able to speak Welsh
		Persons						Males						Females					
Aberystwyth RD	All 3+	12429	4232	7043	924	*34.7*	*92.4*	5699	1815	3308	481	*32.4*	*91.4*	6730	2417	3735	443	*75.4*	*93.4*
	3–4	464	293	80	23	*74.0*	*94.2*	245	155	47	11	*72.8*	*94.8*	219	138	33	12	*54.9*	*94.7*
	5–9	1229	658	465	59	*55.7*	*95.0*	602	328	226	27	*56.5*	*95.4*	627	330	239	32	*27.3*	*95.8*
	10–14	1283	353	857	42	*28.2*	*96.6*	620	177	416	15	*29.1*	*97.5*	663	176	441	27	*18.3*	*92.5*
	15–24	2162	407	1536	182	*19.1*	*91.4*	1042	205	717	99	*20.1*	*90.2*	1120	202	819	83	*23.4*	*91.1*
	25–44	3295	748	2211	316	*22.8*	*90.4*	1443	318	970	152	*22.1*	*89.4*	1852	430	1241	164	*42.5*	*93.6*
	45–64	2673	1017	1400	237	*38.3*	*91.1*	1233	411	671	146	*33.5*	*88.1*	1440	606	729	91	*66.7*	*95.8*
	65–	1323	756	494	65	*57.5*	*95.1*	514	221	261	31	*43.1*	*94.0*	809	535	233	34	*36.6*	*93.3*
Cardigan RD	All 3+	3117	892	1876	274	*29.2*	*90.6*	1379	331	830	168	*24.7*	*86.6*	1738	561	1046	106	*71.1*	*93.3*
	3–4	104	61	23	4	*69.3*	*95.5*	56	29	13	1	*67.4*	*97.7*	48	32	10	3	*37.1*	*95.7*
	5–9	282	107	145	7	*41.3*	*97.3*	131	55	63	1	*46.2*	*99.2*	151	52	82	6	*16.8*	*97.8*
	10–14	294	48	222	12	*17.0*	*95.7*	153	25	111	9	*17.2*	*93.8*	141	23	111	3	*16.1*	*90.9*
	15–24	610	81	406	117	*13.3*	*80.2*	311	33	183	90	*10.7*	*69.9*	299	48	223	27	*20.1*	*92.4*
	25–44	874	169	622	76	*19.4*	*90.9*	345	63	241	37	*18.4*	*88.6*	529	106	381	39	*48.8*	*95.9*
	45–64	628	264	319	38	*42.2*	*93.1*	259	85	146	23	*32.8*	*89.2*	369	179	173	15	*60.5*	*93.5*
	65–	325	162	139	20	*50.2*	*93.2*	124	41	73	7	*33.3*	*92.7*	201	121	66	13	*32.7*	*93.8*
Lampeter RD	All 3+	3398	1527	1692	109	*45.9*	*96.7*	1598	663	821	77	*42.5*	*95.1*	1800	864	871	32	*83.8*	*100.0*
	3–4	105	78	9	3	*86.7*	*96.7*	64	47	3	3	*88.7*	*94.3*	41	31	6	0	*58.7*	*99.3*
	5–9	320	194	110	2	*63.4*	*99.3*	165	106	49	1	*67.9*	*99.4*	155	88	61	1	*22.9*	*98.7*
	10–14	342	97	233	7	*28.8*	*97.9*	189	62	117	5	*33.7*	*97.3*	153	35	116	2	*19.4*	*98.3*
	15–24	606	117	443	26	*20.0*	*95.6*	299	60	211	21	*20.5*	*92.8*	307	57	232	5	*36.9*	*96.5*
	25–44	913	298	559	48	*32.9*	*94.7*	399	110	256	30	*27.8*	*92.4*	514	188	303	18	*67.4*	*98.5*
	45–64	734	441	263	22	*60.7*	*97.0*	329	172	139	16	*52.6*	*95.1*	405	269	124	6	*87.1*	*100.0*
	65–	378	302	75	1	*79.9*	*99.7*	153	106	46	1	*69.3*	*99.3*	225	196	29	0	*48.9*	*98.2*
Llandysul RD	All 3+	7617	3701	3515	281	*49.4*	*96.3*	3465	1493	1722	196	*43.8*	*94.3*	4152	2208	1793	85	*88.6*	*97.0*
	3–4	268	217	20	8	*88.6*	*96.7*	123	100	9	4	*88.5*	*96.5*	145	117	11	4	*74.8*	*99.7*
	5–9	687	493	164	5	*74.5*	*99.2*	355	253	84	4	*74.2*	*98.8*	332	240	80	1	*40.7*	*98.8*
	10–14	734	293	415	6	*41.0*	*99.2*	391	158	222	2	*41.4*	*99.5*	343	135	193	4	*30.0*	*97.4*
	15–24	1480	392	929	139	*26.8*	*90.5*	729	170	430	120	*23.6*	*83.3*	751	222	499	19	*42.0*	*97.1*
	25–44	2047	769	1191	73	*37.8*	*96.4*	862	275	544	39	*32.1*	*95.5*	1185	494	647	34	*66.6*	*97.9*
	45–64	1619	956	603	44	*59.6*	*97.3*	702	351	318	25	*50.6*	*96.4*	917	605	285	19	*82.8*	*99.2*
	65–	782	581	193	6	*74.5*	*99.2*	303	186	115	2	*61.4*	*99.3*	479	395	78	4	*54.0*	*97.9*

Tregaron RD	All 3+	7180	3772	3075	229	53.3	96.8	3391	1599	1563	180	47.8	94.6	3789	2173	1512	49	85.2	98.3
	3–4	243	187	22	5	87.4	97.7	113	89	7	3	89.9	97.0	130	98	15	2	69.0	96.7
	5–9	692	479	172	16	71.8	97.6	346	250	80	5	74.6	98.5	346	229	92	11	43.0	99.4
	10–14	732	310	398	9	43.2	98.7	377	159	200	7	43.4	98.1	355	151	198	2	34.0	98.9
	15–24	1337	415	841	70	31.3	94.7	698	199	429	63	28.8	90.9	639	216	412	7	45.2	98.1
	25–44	1817	755	982	68	41.8	96.2	817	308	458	49	37.8	94.0	1000	447	524	19	73.1	99.0
	45–64	1534	973	501	51	63.8	96.7	699	367	286	43	52.7	93.8	835	606	215	8	88.4	100.0
	65–	825	653	159	10	79.4	98.8	341	227	103	10	66.8	97.1	484	426	56	0	58.2	98.7
Ysgubor-y-coed CP (admin. by Machynlleth (Mont) RD)	All 3+	394	151	196	45	38.5	88.5	184	68	98	17	37.2	90.7	210	83	98	28	100.0	100.0
	3–4	14	10	3	0	76.9	100.0	7	3	3	0	50.0	100.0	7	7	0	0	59.1	95.5
	5–9	46	21	23	2	45.7	95.7	24	8	15	1	33.3	95.8	22	13	8	1	20.0	85.0
	10–14	39	13	21	5	33.3	87.2	19	9	8	2	47.4	89.5	20	4	13	3	28.6	96.4
	15–24	59	19	38	2	32.2	96.6	31	11	19	1	35.5	96.8	28	8	19	1	20.9	77.6
	25–44	121	30	69	22	24.8	81.8	54	16	31	7	29.6	87.0	67	14	38	15	53.7	82.9
	45–64	70	33	26	11	47.1	84.3	29	11	14	4	37.9	86.2	41	22	12	7	62.5	95.8
	65–	45	25	16	3	56.8	93.2	20	10	8	2	50.0	90.0	25	15	8	1	39.7	86.6
BRECONSHIRE																			
Brecon UD	All 3+	5587	18	954	4507	0.3	17.7	2729	6	455	2226	0.2	17.2	2858	12	499	2281	0.0	2.8
	3–4	241	0	4	215	0.0	1.8	117	0	1	109	0.0	0.9	124	0	3	106	0.4	2.8
	5–9	582	1	12	530	0.2	2.4	278	0	5	254	0.0	1.9	304	1	7	276	0.0	3.4
	10–14	613	0	27	573	0.0	4.5	317	0	17	293	0.0	5.5	296	0	10	280	0.0	10.3
	15–24	1126	0	125	983	0.0	11.3	565	0	68	491	0.0	12.2	561	0	57	492	0.3	18.5
	25–44	1703	5	306	1380	0.3	18.4	834	2	150	679	0.2	18.3	869	3	156	701	0.2	33.6
	45–64	919	4	302	609	0.4	33.4	439	3	143	293	0.7	33.3	480	1	159	316	3.1	50.9
	65–	403	8	178	217	2.0	46.2	179	1	71	107	0.6	40.2	224	7	107	110	0.4	18.3
Bryn-mawr UD	All 3+	6996	15	1129	5744	0.2	16.6	3604	10	605	2944	0.3	17.3	3392	5	524	2800	0.0	3.3
	3–4	369	1	12	324	0.3	3.9	165	1	6	148	0.6	4.5	204	0	6	176	0.0	3.0
	5–9	882	0	26	831	0.0	3.0	432	0	13	407	0.0	3.1	450	0	13	424	0.0	5.0
	10–14	751	0	35	708	0.0	4.7	371	0	16	350	0.0	4.4	380	0	19	358	0.0	6.3
	15–24	1432	0	100	1314	0.0	7.1	715	0	56	654	0.0	7.9	717	0	44	660	0.2	17.7
	25–44	2257	6	410	1825	0.3	18.5	1229	4	231	984	0.3	19.2	1028	2	179	841	0.6	39.6
	45–64	1069	7	418	637	0.7	40.0	590	4	233	350	0.7	40.3	479	3	185	287	0.0	59.1
	65–	236	1	128	105	0.4	55.1	102	1	50	51	1.0	50.0	134	0	78	54	0.2	15.9
Builth Wells UD	All 3+	1635	3	228	1393	0.2	14.2	733	2	103	627	0.3	14.3	902	1	125	766	0.0	8.8
	3–4	64	0	3	58	0.0	4.9	28	0	0	27	0.0	0.0	36	0	3	31	0.0	2.9
	5–9	149	0	8	139	0.0	5.4	77	0	6	71	0.0	7.8	72	0	2	68	0.0	7.3
	10–14	137	0	9	128	0.0	6.6	55	0	3	52	0.0	5.5	82	0	6	76	0.0	9.6
	15–24	286	0	25	258	0.0	8.8	116	0	9	107	0.0	7.8	170	0	16	151	0.0	12.5
	25–44	520	0	72	446	0.0	13.9	238	0	37	201	0.0	15.5	282	0	35	245	0.0	24.3
	45–64	337	1	75	260	0.3	22.6	159	1	32	126	0.6	20.8	178	0	43	134	1.2	25.6
	65–	142	2	36	104	1.4	26.8	60	1	16	43	1.7	28.3	82	1	20	61	0.1	14.1

District[1]	Age last birth-day	Number[2] Total in age group	Welsh only	Both	English only	Percentage[3] Welsh only	Able to speak Welsh	Number[2] Total in age group	Welsh only	Both	English only	Percentage[3] Welsh only	Able to speak Welsh	Number[2] Total in age group	Welsh only	Both	English only	Percentage[3] Welsh only	Able to speak Welsh
		Persons						Males						Females					
Hay UD	All 3+	1541	0	44	1488	*0.0*	*2.9*	715	0	24	685	*0.0*	*3.4*	826	0	20	803	*0.0*	*0.0*
	3–4	73	0	1	70	*0.0*	*1.4*	30	0	1	28	*0.0*	*3.4*	43	0	0	42	*0.0*	*1.2*
	5–9	153	0	1	151	*0.0*	*0.7*	70	0	0	69	*0.0*	*0.0*	83	0	1	82	*0.0*	*3.8*
	10–14	155	0	4	151	*0.0*	*2.6*	77	0	1	76	*0.0*	*1.3*	78	0	3	75	*0.0*	*0.7*
	15–24	266	0	4	259	*0.0*	*1.5*	124	0	3	118	*0.0*	*2.5*	142	0	1	141	*0.0*	*2.2*
	25–44	425	0	17	407	*0.0*	*4.0*	197	0	12	185	*0.0*	*6.1*	228	0	5	222	*0.0*	*3.8*
	45–64	305	0	11	293	*0.0*	*3.6*	148	0	5	143	*0.0*	*3.4*	157	0	6	150	*0.0*	*4.2*
	65–	164	0	6	157	*0.0*	*3.7*	69	0	2	66	*0.0*	*2.9*	95	0	4	91	*0.0*	*2.4*
Llanwrtyd UD	All 3+	722	119	442	150	*16.7*	*78.9*	331	47	193	82	*14.6*	*74.5*	391	72	249	68	*25.0*	*68.8*
	3–4	30	7	11	8	*26.9*	*69.2*	13	3	4	3	*30.0*	*70.0*	17	4	7	5	*10.0*	*73.3*
	5–9	69	9	37	18	*14.1*	*71.9*	38	6	18	10	*17.6*	*70.6*	31	3	19	8	*13.8*	*82.8*
	10–14	56	7	39	10	*12.5*	*82.1*	27	3	19	5	*11.1*	*81.5*	29	4	20	5	*11.4*	*75.0*
	15–24	152	16	97	39	*10.5*	*74.3*	64	6	41	17	*9.4*	*73.4*	88	10	56	22	*15.9*	*84.1*
	25–44	207	31	128	48	*15.0*	*76.8*	94	13	51	30	*13.8*	*68.1*	113	18	77	18	*24.7*	*92.2*
	45–64	143	32	92	17	*22.7*	*87.9*	66	13	40	11	*20.3*	*82.8*	77	19	52	6	*38.9*	*88.9*
	65–	65	17	38	10	*26.2*	*84.6*	29	3	20	6	*10.3*	*79.3*	36	14	18	4	*18.5*	*82.5*
Brecon RD	All 3+	8613	505	4248	3792	*5.9*	*55.6*	4349	236	2132	1958	*5.5*	*54.7*	4264	269	2116	1834	*12.7*	*34.5*
	3–4	356	36	69	217	*11.2*	*32.6*	169	15	33	109	*9.6*	*30.6*	187	21	36	108	*5.0*	*38.1*
	5–9	910	51	286	559	*5.7*	*37.6*	487	30	148	301	*6.3*	*37.2*	423	21	138	258	*3.5*	*39.5*
	10–14	849	25	305	511	*3.0*	*39.2*	410	10	149	249	*2.5*	*39.0*	439	15	156	262	*1.6*	*44.5*
	15–24	1642	33	682	925	*2.0*	*43.6*	834	20	338	479	*2.4*	*42.8*	808	13	344	446	*4.3*	*59.3*
	25–44	2529	97	1376	1049	*3.8*	*58.4*	1257	43	679	533	*3.4*	*57.5*	1272	54	697	516	*8.6*	*76.3*
	45–64	1588	134	1055	395	*8.5*	*75.1*	827	69	541	215	*8.4*	*73.9*	761	65	514	180	*21.3*	*82.9*
	65–	739	129	475	136	*17.4*	*81.6*	365	49	244	72	*13.4*	*80.3*	374	80	231	64	*6.4*	*56.5*
Builth RD	All 3+	3984	280	1647	2008	*7.1*	*49.0*	2041	133	854	1034	*6.6*	*48.8*	1943	147	793	974	*20.0*	*36.5*
	3–4	163	28	26	93	*19.0*	*36.7*	70	11	12	39	*17.7*	*37.1*	93	17	14	54	*6.7*	*37.2*
	5–9	414	28	121	252	*7.0*	*37.2*	224	16	66	139	*7.2*	*37.1*	190	12	55	113	*1.4*	*39.0*
	10–14	438	15	155	263	*3.5*	*39.3*	227	12	76	135	*5.4*	*39.5*	211	3	79	128	*3.0*	*44.9*
	15–24	779	22	302	446	*2.9*	*42.1*	413	11	151	247	*2.7*	*39.6*	366	11	151	199	*4.7*	*46.5*
	25–44	1112	49	476	584	*4.4*	*47.3*	553	23	243	286	*4.2*	*48.2*	559	26	233	298	*10.7*	*59.0*
	45–64	771	79	388	302	*10.3*	*60.7*	403	40	211	152	*9.9*	*62.3*	368	39	177	150	*25.2*	*79.4*
	65–	307	59	179	68	*19.3*	*77.8*	151	20	95	36	*13.2*	*76.2*	156	39	84	32	*7.7*	*49.1*

Crickhowell RD	All 3+	7217	24	1299	5818	*0.3*	*18.5*	3615	14	654	2912	*0.4*	*18.7*	3602	10	645	2906	*0.0*	*2.0*
	3–4	347	0	6	325	*0.0*	*1.8*	190	0	3	179	*0.0*	*1.6*	157	0	3	146	*0.0*	*2.6*
	5–9	932	0	33	871	*0.0*	*3.7*	466	0	21	427	*0.0*	*4.7*	466	0	12	444	*0.0*	*3.6*
	10–14	797	0	34	750	*0.0*	*4.3*	394	0	20	370	*0.0*	*5.1*	403	0	14	380	*0.2*	*7.4*
	15–24	1316	2	82	1226	*0.2*	*6.4*	648	1	34	611	*0.2*	*5.4*	668	1	48	615	*0.0*	*18.1*
	25–44	2036	2	370	1657	*0.1*	*18.3*	1010	2	185	820	*0.2*	*18.6*	1026	0	185	837	*0.3*	*40.9*
	45–64	1273	8	502	757	*0.6*	*40.3*	663	6	257	400	*0.9*	*39.7*	610	2	245	357	*2.6*	*53.3*
	65–	516	12	272	232	*2.3*	*55.0*	244	5	134	105	*2.0*	*57.0*	272	7	138	127	*0.3*	*18.4*
Hay RD	All 3+	3381	12	505	2808	*0.4*	*15.5*	1688	7	237	1414	*0.4*	*14.7*	1693	5	268	1394	*0.0*	*0.0*
	3–4	136	0	2	124	*0.0*	*1.6*	71	0	2	63	*0.0*	*3.1*	65	0	0	61	*0.0*	*0.0*
	5–9	325	0	2	311	*0.0*	*0.6*	176	0	2	167	*0.0*	*1.2*	149	0	0	144	*0.0*	*3.5*
	10–14	293	1	9	273	*0.4*	*3.5*	145	1	4	135	*0.7*	*3.6*	148	0	5	138	*0.0*	*8.6*
	15–24	651	2	52	588	*0.3*	*8.4*	321	2	24	291	*0.6*	*8.2*	330	0	28	297	*0.2*	*17.8*
	25–44	978	2	157	815	*0.2*	*16.3*	494	1	72	419	*0.2*	*14.8*	484	1	85	396	*0.3*	*25.1*
	45–64	688	2	173	503	*0.3*	*25.8*	341	1	88	247	*0.3*	*26.5*	347	1	85	256	*1.8*	*40.0*
	65–	310	5	110	194	*1.6*	*37.2*	140	2	45	92	*1.4*	*33.8*	170	3	65	102	*0.3*	*16.4*
Faenor and Penderyn RD	All 3+	5124	281	3179	1585	*5.6*	*68.6*	2678	131	1610	901	*5.0*	*65.9*	2446	150	1569	684	*11.4*	*68.6*
	3–4	260	26	112	89	*11.5*	*60.8*	134	14	52	56	*11.5*	*54.1*	126	12	60	33	*5.1*	*64.6*
	5–9	635	30	372	216	*4.9*	*65.0*	327	15	195	111	*4.7*	*65.4*	308	15	177	105	*4.6*	*65.6*
	10–14	561	24	358	171	*4.3*	*69.1*	298	12	200	82	*4.1*	*72.1*	263	12	158	89	*3.7*	*71.6*
	15–24	938	30	627	275	*3.2*	*70.5*	480	13	318	146	*2.7*	*69.4*	458	17	309	129	*3.8*	*70.5*
	25–44	1616	54	997	558	*3.4*	*65.3*	871	26	501	339	*3.0*	*60.9*	745	28	496	219	*9.0*	*80.8*
	45–64	857	68	568	214	*8.0*	*74.7*	453	32	279	137	*7.1*	*69.3*	404	36	289	77	*21.1*	*77.5*
	65–	257	49	145	62	*19.1*	*75.8*	115	19	65	30	*16.7*	*73.7*	142	30	80	32	*6.2*	*71.5*
Ystradgynlais RD	All 3+	9541	1701	5790	1814	*18.1*	*79.8*	5297	859	3143	1166	*16.4*	*76.6*	4244	842	2647	648	*33.2*	*76.8*
	3–4	550	185	190	114	*37.6*	*76.2*	263	102	81	59	*42.1*	*75.6*	287	83	109	55	*24.9*	*86.3*
	5–9	1226	301	718	164	*25.3*	*85.7*	621	154	355	85	*25.8*	*85.1*	605	147	363	79	*14.7*	*88.8*
	10–14	1086	164	783	120	*15.3*	*88.4*	558	88	399	64	*15.9*	*88.1*	528	76	384	56	*11.1*	*85.6*
	15–24	1954	197	1342	376	*10.2*	*79.4*	1100	103	712	260	*9.4*	*74.6*	854	94	630	116	*15.8*	*78.7*
	25–44	3246	424	1950	814	*13.1*	*73.6*	1943	219	1134	552	*11.4*	*70.1*	1303	205	816	262	*29.3*	*87.5*
	45–64	1214	310	694	194	*25.7*	*83.1*	698	160	396	131	*23.0*	*79.9*	516	150	298	63	*57.6*	*88.7*
	65–	265	120	113	32	*45.3*	*87.9*	114	33	66	15	*28.9*	*86.8*	151	87	47	17	*20.2*	*83.8*
Llanwrthwl CP (admin. by Rhayader (Rad) RD)	All 3+	387	5	80	301	*1.3*	*22.0*	210	4	46	160	*1.9*	*23.8*	177	1	34	141	*0.0*	*0.0*
	3–4	15	0	0	14	*0.0*	*0.0*	5	0	0	5	*0.0*	*0.0*	10	0	0	9	*0.0*	*4.8*
	5–9	44	0	2	42	*0.0*	*4.5*	23	0	1	22	*0.0*	*4.3*	21	0	1	20	*0.0*	*0.0*
	10–14	46	0	2	44	*0.0*	*4.3*	29	0	2	27	*0.0*	*6.9*	17	0	0	17	*0.0*	*13.5*
	15–24	78	0	8	70	*0.0*	*10.3*	41	0	3	38	*0.0*	*7.3*	37	0	5	32	*2.0*	*26.0*
	25–44	107	2	31	74	*1.9*	*30.8*	57	1	19	37	*1.8*	*35.1*	50	1	12	37	*0.0*	*31.3*
	45–64	74	2	24	48	*2.7*	*35.1*	42	2	14	26	*4.8*	*38.1*	32	0	10	22	*0.0*	*60.0*
	65–	23	1	13	9	*4.3*	*60.9*	13	1	7	5	*7.7*	*61.5*	10	0	6	4	*0.6*	*19.9*

District[1]	Age last birth-day	Persons: Number[2] Total in age group	Persons: Welsh only	Persons: Both	Persons: English only	Persons: Percentage[3] Welsh only	Persons: Percentage[3] Able to speak Welsh	Males: Number[2] Total in age group	Males: Welsh only	Males: Both	Males: English only	Males: Percentage[3] Welsh only	Males: Percentage[3] Able to speak Welsh	Females: Number[2] Total in age group	Females: Welsh only	Females: Both	Females: English only	Females: Percentage[3] Welsh only	Females: Percentage[3] Able to speak Welsh
Ystradfellte CP (admin. by Neath (Glam) RD)	All 3+	587	52	342	178	*9.1*	*68.8*	329	27	176	116	*8.4*	*63.4*	258	25	166	62	*22.2*	*77.8*
	3–4	32	5	11	9	*19.2*	*61.5*	22	3	6	7	*17.6*	*52.9*	10	2	5	2	*17.9*	*64.3*
	5–9	65	9	32	17	*15.5*	*70.7*	33	4	19	7	*13.3*	*76.7*	32	5	13	10	*0.0*	*83.3*
	10–14	47	2	35	9	*4.3*	*80.4*	23	2	15	5	*9.1*	*77.3*	24	0	20	4	*0.0*	*76.7*
	15–24	83	0	63	20	*0.0*	*75.9*	40	0	30	10	*0.0*	*75.0*	43	0	33	10	*10.1*	*76.4*
	25–44	206	16	127	63	*7.8*	*69.4*	117	7	68	42	*6.0*	*64.1*	89	9	59	21	*12.8*	*72.3*
	45–64	123	12	58	53	*9.8*	*56.9*	76	6	30	40	*7.9*	*47.4*	47	6	28	13	*23.1*	*84.6*
	65–	31	8	16	7	*25.8*	*77.4*	18	5	8	5	*27.8*	*72.2*	13	3	8	2	*9.9*	*75.5*
RADNORSHIRE																			
Knighton UD	All 3+	1774	0	43	1681	*0.0*	*2.5*	837	0	20	800	*0.0*	*2.4*	937	0	23	881	*0.0*	*0.0*
	3–4	70	0	0	60	*0.0*	*0.0*	28	0	0	27	*0.0*	*0.0*	42	0	0	33	*0.0*	*0.0*
	5–9	194	0	0	178	*0.0*	*0.0*	100	0	0	95	*0.0*	*0.0*	94	0	0	83	*0.0*	*1.1*
	10–14	196	0	1	185	*0.0*	*0.5*	104	0	0	98	*0.0*	*0.0*	92	0	1	87	*0.0*	*1.7*
	15–24	301	0	5	294	*0.0*	*1.7*	125	0	2	122	*0.0*	*1.6*	176	0	3	172	*0.0*	*5.0*
	25–44	495	0	20	469	*0.0*	*4.1*	232	0	7	224	*0.0*	*3.0*	263	0	13	245	*0.0*	*2.1*
	45–64	362	0	12	349	*0.0*	*3.3*	166	0	8	158	*0.0*	*4.8*	196	0	4	191	*0.0*	*2.8*
	65–	156	0	5	146	*0.0*	*3.3*	82	0	3	76	*0.0*	*3.8*	74	0	2	70	*0.0*	*2.5*
Llandrindod Wells UD	All 3+	2644	3	210	2423	*0.1*	*8.1*	1173	1	87	1080	*0.1*	*7.5*	1471	2	123	1343	*0.0*	*4.8*
	3–4	89	0	2	81	*0.0*	*2.4*	45	0	0	41	*0.0*	*0.0*	44	0	2	40	*0.0*	*0.0*
	5–9	221	0	0	220	*0.0*	*0.0*	116	0	0	115	*0.0*	*0.0*	105	0	0	105	*0.0*	*3.1*
	10–14	207	0	6	201	*0.0*	*2.9*	109	0	3	106	*0.0*	*2.8*	98	0	3	95	*0.0*	*7.8*
	15–24	609	0	47	562	*0.0*	*7.7*	238	0	18	220	*0.0*	*7.6*	371	0	29	342	*0.2*	*10.1*
	25–44	982	2	91	888	*0.2*	*9.5*	437	1	37	399	*0.2*	*8.7*	545	1	54	489	*0.0*	*11.3*
	45–64	416	0	47	369	*0.0*	*11.3*	176	0	20	156	*0.0*	*11.4*	240	0	27	213	*1.5*	*13.2*
	65–	120	1	17	102	*0.8*	*15.0*	52	0	9	43	*0.0*	*17.3*	68	1	8	59	*0.1*	*8.5*
Presteigne UD	All 3+	1082	0	14	1061	*0.0*	*1.3*	507	0	5	501	*0.0*	*1.0*	575	0	9	560	*0.0*	*0.0*
	3–4	41	0	0	40	*0.0*	*0.0*	21	0	0	20	*0.0*	*0.0*	20	0	0	20	*0.0*	*0.0*
	5–9	112	0	0	112	*0.0*	*0.0*	58	0	0	58	*0.0*	*0.0*	54	0	0	54	*0.0*	*0.0*
	10–14	103	0	0	103	*0.0*	*0.0*	52	0	0	52	*0.0*	*0.0*	51	0	0	51	*0.0*	*0.0*
	15–24	184	0	1	182	*0.0*	*0.5*	81	0	1	80	*0.0*	*1.2*	103	0	0	102	*0.0*	*1.8*
	25–44	288	0	3	281	*0.0*	*1.1*	120	0	0	120	*0.0*	*0.0*	168	0	3	161	*0.0*	*4.2*
	45–64	239	0	7	231	*0.0*	*2.9*	119	0	2	117	*0.0*	*1.7*	120	0	5	114	*0.0*	*1.7*
	65–	115	0	3	112	*0.0*	*2.6*	56	0	2	54	*0.0*	*3.6*	59	0	1	58	*0.0*	*1.6*

Colwyn RD	All 3+	1935	0	146	1742	0.0	7.7	990	0	74	890	0.0	7.7	945	0	72	852	0.0	0.0
	3–4	89	0	2	80	0.0	2.4	46	0	2	39	0.0	4.9	43	0	0	41	0.0	2.9
	5–9	211	0	5	191	0.0	2.6	99	0	2	90	0.0	2.2	112	0	3	101	0.0	4.3
	10–14	205	0	6	192	0.0	3.0	109	0	2	104	0.0	1.9	96	0	4	88	0.0	5.5
	15–24	380	0	21	353	0.0	5.6	195	0	11	181	0.0	5.7	185	0	10	172	0.0	10.4
	25–44	563	0	53	503	0.0	9.5	283	0	24	254	0.0	8.6	280	0	29	249	0.0	8.8
	45–64	362	0	36	324	0.0	10.0	191	0	21	169	0.0	11.1	171	0	15	155	0.0	19.3
	65–	125	0	23	99	0.0	18.9	67	0	12	53	0.0	18.5	58	0	11	46	0.0	7.8
Knighton RD	All 3+	4155	1	91	4034	0.0	2.2	2201	1	48	2135	0.0	2.2	1954	0	43	1899	0.0	0.0
	3–4	198	0	0	193	0.0	0.0	93	0	0	92	0.0	0.0	105	0	0	101	0.0	0.0
	5–9	499	0	5	487	0.0	1.0	277	0	5	269	0.0	1.8	222	0	0	218	0.0	2.1
	10–14	456	0	8	443	0.0	1.8	215	0	3	208	0.0	1.4	241	0	5	235	0.0	1.9
	15–24	808	0	12	793	0.0	1.5	441	0	5	433	0.0	1.1	367	0	7	360	0.0	2.8
	25–44	1128	0	28	1096	0.0	2.5	582	0	13	567	0.0	2.2	546	0	15	529	0.0	3.7
	45–64	733	0	30	699	0.0	4.1	406	0	18	385	0.0	4.5	327	0	12	314	0.0	2.7
	65–	333	1	8	323	0.3	2.7	187	1	4	181	0.5	2.7	146	0	4	142	0.0	2.2
New Radnor RD	All 3+	2604	0	36	2529	0.0	1.4	1369	0	23	1332	0.0	1.7	1235	0	13	1197	0.0	2.4
	3–4	96	0	2	76	0.0	2.6	40	0	1	36	0.0	2.7	56	0	1	40	0.0	0.9
	5–9	254	0	1	248	0.0	0.4	134	0	0	133	0.0	0.0	120	0	1	115	0.0	0.0
	10–14	293	0	0	286	0.0	0.0	165	0	0	162	0.0	0.0	128	0	0	124	0.0	0.5
	15–24	468	0	1	465	0.0	0.2	245	0	0	244	0.0	0.0	223	0	1	221	0.0	1.9
	25–44	742	0	20	720	0.0	2.7	380	0	13	366	0.0	3.4	362	0	7	354	0.0	0.9
	45–64	516	0	9	503	0.0	1.8	283	0	7	272	0.0	2.5	233	0	2	231	0.0	0.9
	65–	235	0	3	231	0.0	1.3	122	0	2	119	0.0	1.7	113	0	1	112	0.0	1.1
Painscastle RD	All 3+	2193	0	73	2090	0.0	3.4	1102	0	36	1047	0.0	3.3	1091	0	37	1043	0.0	5.9
	3–4	86	0	2	74	0.0	2.6	48	0	0	42	0.0	0.0	38	0	2	32	0.0	1.6
	5–9	233	0	2	224	0.0	0.9	103	0	0	98	0.0	0.0	130	0	2	126	0.0	0.9
	10–14	214	0	3	208	0.0	1.4	102	0	2	98	0.0	2.0	112	0	1	110	0.0	1.7
	15–24	442	0	6	431	0.0	1.4	209	0	2	204	0.0	1.0	233	0	4	227	0.0	3.5
	25–44	595	0	22	569	0.0	3.7	311	0	12	297	0.0	3.9	284	0	10	272	0.0	7.1
	45–64	438	0	28	409	0.0	6.4	228	0	13	214	0.0	5.7	210	0	15	195	0.0	3.6
	65–	185	0	10	175	0.0	5.4	101	0	7	94	0.0	6.9	84	0	3	81	0.0	3.4
Rhayader RD	All 3+	4892	7	515	4312	0.1	10.8	2472	1	276	2168	0.0	11.3	2420	6	239	2144	0.0	5.4
	3–4	199	0	9	173	0.0	4.9	97	0	4	86	0.0	4.4	102	0	5	87	0.4	2.0
	5–9	521	1	13	498	0.2	2.7	266	0	9	253	0.0	3.4	255	1	4	245	0.0	3.5
	10–14	524	0	17	504	0.0	3.3	269	0	8	259	0.0	3.0	255	0	9	245	0.2	5.5
	15–24	853	1	51	797	0.1	6.1	430	0	29	398	0.0	6.8	423	1	22	399	0.1	10.9
	25–44	1408	1	160	1236	0.1	11.5	696	0	84	606	0.0	12.1	712	1	76	630	0.2	15.1
	45–64	932	1	141	781	0.1	15.4	482	0	75	403	0.0	15.7	450	1	66	378	0.9	26.9
	65–	455	3	124	323	0.7	28.2	232	1	67	163	0.4	29.4	223	2	57	160	0.3	10.3

District[1]	Age last birth-day	Persons: Number[2] Total in age group	Welsh only	Both	English only	Percentage[3] Welsh only	Able to speak Welsh
MONTGOMERYSHIRE							
Llanfyllin MB	All 3+	1548	166	973	404	*10.8*	*73.8*
	3–4	79	17	29	30	*22.4*	*60.5*
	5–9	171	13	92	66	*7.6*	*61.4*
	10–14	166	7	116	43	*4.2*	*74.1*
	15–24	243	20	165	58	*8.2*	*76.1*
	25–44	429	23	289	116	*5.4*	*72.9*
	45–64	318	53	197	67	*16.7*	*78.9*
	65–	142	33	85	24	*23.2*	*83.1*
Llanidloes MB	All 3+	2437	28	1018	1347	*1.2*	*43.7*
	3–4	92	1	5	76	*1.2*	*7.3*
	5–9	284	0	41	234	*0.0*	*14.9*
	10–14	241	0	52	187	*0.0*	*21.8*
	15–24	447	1	131	309	*0.2*	*29.9*
	25–44	721	9	341	368	*1.3*	*48.7*
	45–64	433	5	284	131	*1.2*	*68.8*
	65–	219	12	164	42	*5.5*	*80.7*
Machynlleth UD	All 3+	1859	168	1423	255	*9.1*	*86.2*
	3–4	58	16	20	15	*31.4*	*70.6*
	5–9	175	22	134	16	*12.8*	*90.7*
	10–14	221	11	190	19	*5.0*	*91.4*
	15–24	331	8	266	56	*2.4*	*83.0*
	25–44	566	28	441	97	*4.9*	*82.9*
	45–64	376	41	297	38	*10.9*	*89.9*
	65–	132	42	75	14	*32.1*	*89.3*
Montgomery MB	All 3+	942	9	48	873	*1.0*	*6.1*
	3–4	32	1	0	28	*3.4*	*3.4*
	5–9	95	0	0	93	*0.0*	*0.0*
	10–14	85	0	3	81	*0.0*	*3.6*
	15–24	165	5	8	150	*3.1*	*8.0*
	25–44	253	1	14	237	*0.4*	*6.0*
	45–64	215	2	15	195	*0.9*	*8.0*
	65–	97	0	8	89	*0.0*	*8.2*

District[1]	Age last birth-day	Males: Number[2] Total in age group	Welsh only	Both	English only	Percentage[3] Welsh only	Able to speak Welsh
MONTGOMERYSHIRE							
Llanfyllin MB	All 3+	757	91	467	198	*12.0*	*73.8*
	3–4	44	11	21	12	*25.0*	*72.7*
	5–9	93	8	53	32	*8.6*	*65.6*
	10–14	82	2	55	25	*2.4*	*69.5*
	15–24	112	12	73	27	*10.7*	*75.9*
	25–44	198	12	134	51	*6.1*	*74.1*
	45–64	159	29	91	39	*18.2*	*75.5*
	65–	69	17	40	12	*24.6*	*82.6*
Llanidloes MB	All 3+	1115	8	437	640	*0.7*	*41.0*
	3–4	60	0	3	49	*0.0*	*5.8*
	5–9	131	0	13	113	*0.0*	*10.3*
	10–14	128	0	26	101	*0.0*	*20.5*
	15–24	196	0	54	140	*0.0*	*27.8*
	25–44	322	3	159	158	*0.9*	*50.6*
	45–64	184	2	107	63	*1.2*	*63.4*
	65–	94	3	75	16	*3.2*	*83.0*
Machynlleth UD	All 3+	849	69	667	107	*8.2*	*87.3*
	3–4	32	9	11	9	*31.0*	*69.0*
	5–9	91	10	72	8	*11.1*	*91.1*
	10–14	114	8	101	5	*7.0*	*95.6*
	15–24	132	1	112	18	*0.8*	*86.3*
	25–44	259	12	203	44	*4.6*	*83.0*
	45–64	171	17	136	18	*9.9*	*89.5*
	65–	50	12	32	5	*24.5*	*89.8*
Montgomery MB	All 3+	441	3	23	409	*0.7*	*6.0*
	3–4	16	1	0	14	*6.7*	*6.7*
	5–9	48	0	0	47	*0.0*	*0.0*
	10–14	37	0	1	35	*0.0*	*2.8*
	15–24	78	2	3	72	*2.6*	*6.5*
	25–44	119	0	7	112	*0.0*	*5.9*
	45–64	102	0	8	92	*0.0*	*8.0*
	65–	41	0	4	37	*0.0*	*9.8*

District[1]	Age last birth-day	Females: Number[2] Total in age group	Welsh only	Both	English only	Percentage[3] Welsh only	Able to speak Welsh
MONTGOMERYSHIRE							
Llanfyllin MB	All 3+	791	75	506	206	*9.5*	*73.8*
	3–4	35	6	8	18	*18.8*	*43.8*
	5–9	78	5	39	34	*6.4*	*56.4*
	10–14	84	5	61	18	*6.0*	*78.6*
	15–24	131	8	92	31	*6.1*	*76.3*
	25–44	231	11	155	65	*4.8*	*71.9*
	45–64	159	24	106	28	*15.2*	*82.3*
	65–	73	16	45	12	*21.9*	*83.6*
Llanidloes MB	All 3+	1322	20	581	707	*1.5*	*45.9*
	3–4	32	1	2	27	*3.3*	*10.0*
	5–9	153	0	28	121	*0.0*	*18.8*
	10–14	113	0	26	86	*0.0*	*23.2*
	15–24	251	1	77	169	*0.4*	*31.6*
	25–44	399	6	182	210	*1.5*	*47.2*
	45–64	249	3	177	68	*1.2*	*72.6*
	65–	125	9	89	26	*7.3*	*79.0*
Machynlleth UD	All 3+	1010	99	756	148	*9.9*	*85.2*
	3–4	26	7	9	6	*31.8*	*72.7*
	5–9	84	12	62	8	*14.6*	*90.2*
	10–14	107	3	89	14	*2.8*	*86.8*
	15–24	199	7	154	38	*3.5*	*80.9*
	25–44	307	16	238	53	*5.2*	*82.7*
	45–64	205	24	161	20	*11.7*	*90.2*
	65–	82	30	43	9	*36.6*	*89.0*
Montgomery MB	All 3+	501	6	25	464	*1.2*	*6.3*
	3–4	16	0	0	14	*0.0*	*0.0*
	5–9	47	0	0	46	*0.0*	*0.0*
	10–14	48	0	2	46	*0.0*	*4.2*
	15–24	87	3	5	78	*3.5*	*9.3*
	25–44	134	1	7	125	*0.8*	*6.0*
	45–64	113	2	7	103	*1.8*	*8.0*
	65–	56	0	4	52	*0.0*	*7.1*

Newtown and Llanllwchaearn UD	All 3+	5722	6	592	4984	*0.1*	*10.7*	2663	2	253	2350	*0.1*	*9.8*	3059	4	339	2634	*0.1*	*11.5*
	3–4	221	0	5	204	*0.0*	*2.4*	113	0	5	101	*0.0*	*4.7*	108	0	0	103	*0.0*	*0.0*
	5–9	619	0	25	566	*0.0*	*4.2*	320	0	13	295	*0.0*	*4.2*	299	0	12	271	*0.0*	*4.2*
	10–14	603	0	22	555	*0.0*	*3.8*	295	0	1	276	*0.0*	*0.3*	308	0	21	279	*0.0*	*7.0*
	15–24	1173	0	94	1058	*0.0*	*8.2*	544	0	36	499	*0.0*	*6.7*	629	0	58	559	*0.0*	*9.4*
	25–44	1642	2	191	1416	*0.1*	*12.0*	716	1	81	627	*0.1*	*11.5*	926	1	110	789	*0.1*	*12.3*
	45–64	1045	1	162	869	*0.1*	*15.8*	485	0	79	403	*0.0*	*16.4*	560	1	83	466	*0.2*	*15.3*
	65–	419	3	93	316	*0.7*	*23.3*	190	1	38	149	*0.5*	*20.7*	229	2	55	167	*0.9*	*25.4*
Welshpool MB	All 3+	5581	10	533	4961	*0.2*	*9.9*	2687	5	265	2385	*0.2*	*10.2*	2894	5	268	2576	*0.2*	*9.6*
	3–4	245	1	6	224	*0.4*	*3.0*	117	1	2	106	*0.9*	*2.8*	128	0	4	118	*0.0*	*3.3*
	5–9	576	1	15	533	*0.2*	*2.9*	285	1	8	265	*0.4*	*3.3*	291	0	7	268	*0.0*	*2.5*
	10–14	545	0	15	521	*0.0*	*2.8*	279	0	5	270	*0.0*	*1.8*	266	0	10	251	*0.0*	*3.8*
	15–24	994	2	69	912	*0.2*	*7.2*	462	0	30	425	*0.0*	*6.6*	532	2	39	487	*0.4*	*7.8*
	25–44	1635	1	187	1440	*0.1*	*11.5*	794	1	100	693	*0.1*	*12.7*	841	0	87	747	*0.0*	*10.4*
	45–64	1080	1	144	930	*0.1*	*13.5*	519	1	75	441	*0.2*	*14.7*	561	0	69	489	*0.0*	*12.4*
	65–	506	4	97	401	*0.8*	*20.1*	231	1	45	185	*0.4*	*19.9*	275	3	52	216	*1.1*	*20.2*
Forden RD	All 3+	5364	21	488	4800	*0.4*	*9.6*	2728	11	242	2441	*0.4*	*9.4*	2636	10	246	2359	*0.4*	*9.8*
	3–4	272	2	11	246	*0.8*	*5.0*	134	0	6	120	*0.0*	*4.8*	138	2	5	126	*1.5*	*5.3*
	5–9	586	5	24	544	*0.9*	*5.1*	298	4	9	276	*1.4*	*4.5*	288	1	15	268	*0.4*	*5.6*
	10–14	571	3	27	538	*0.5*	*5.3*	289	2	15	269	*0.7*	*5.9*	282	1	12	269	*0.4*	*4.6*
	15–24	961	2	64	890	*0.2*	*6.9*	502	1	31	467	*0.2*	*6.4*	459	1	33	423	*0.2*	*7.4*
	25–44	1414	6	146	1249	*0.4*	*10.8*	694	3	70	613	*0.4*	*10.6*	720	3	76	636	*0.4*	*11.0*
	45–64	1058	2	131	923	*0.2*	*12.6*	545	1	69	475	*0.2*	*12.8*	513	1	62	448	*0.2*	*12.3*
	65–	502	1	85	410	*0.2*	*17.3*	266	0	42	221	*0.0*	*16.0*	236	1	43	189	*0.4*	*18.9*
Llanfyllin RD	All 3+	11773	2173	5775	3715	*18.6*	*68.1*	5964	1161	2935	1812	*19.7*	*69.3*	5809	1012	2840	1903	*17.6*	*66.9*
	3–4	493	188	72	191	*41.7*	*57.6*	255	93	40	101	*39.7*	*56.8*	238	95	32	90	*43.8*	*58.5*
	5–9	1282	349	412	495	*27.8*	*60.6*	661	200	200	248	*30.9*	*61.7*	621	149	212	247	*24.5*	*59.4*
	10–14	1362	172	665	514	*12.7*	*62.0*	670	101	313	251	*15.2*	*62.3*	692	71	352	263	*10.3*	*61.7*
	15–24	2105	266	1086	740	*12.7*	*64.6*	1108	157	583	362	*14.2*	*67.2*	997	109	503	378	*11.0*	*61.8*
	25–44	3104	425	1734	935	*13.7*	*69.8*	1549	232	863	447	*15.0*	*71.0*	1555	193	871	488	*12.4*	*68.6*
	45–64	2346	452	1285	602	*19.3*	*74.3*	1191	229	668	291	*19.3*	*75.5*	1155	223	617	311	*19.4*	*73.0*
	65–	1081	321	521	238	*29.7*	*78.0*	530	149	268	112	*28.2*	*78.8*	551	172	253	126	*31.2*	*77.1*
Machynlleth RD	All 3+	3897	1917	1844	109	*49.5*	*97.2*	1895	950	878	49	*50.6*	*97.4*	2002	967	966	60	*48.5*	*97.0*
	3–4	167	135	14	6	*87.1*	*96.1*	86	67	8	2	*87.0*	*97.4*	81	68	6	4	*87.2*	*94.9*
	5–9	392	271	100	16	*70.0*	*95.9*	195	146	37	9	*76.0*	*95.3*	197	125	63	7	*64.1*	*96.4*
	10–14	403	168	229	4	*41.9*	*99.0*	195	90	103	1	*46.4*	*99.5*	208	78	126	3	*37.7*	*98.6*
	15–24	658	213	426	15	*32.6*	*97.7*	338	117	214	5	*34.8*	*98.5*	320	96	212	10	*30.2*	*96.9*
	25–44	1111	453	610	47	*40.8*	*95.8*	518	226	269	23	*43.6*	*95.6*	593	227	341	24	*38.3*	*95.9*
	45–64	812	415	380	15	*51.2*	*98.1*	409	194	206	7	*47.7*	*98.3*	403	221	174	8	*54.8*	*98.0*
	65–	354	262	85	6	*74.2*	*98.3*	154	110	41	2	*71.9*	*98.7*	200	152	44	4	*76.0*	*98.0*

District[1]	Age last birth-day	Number[2] Total in age group	Welsh only	Both	English only	Percentage[3] Welsh only	Percentage[3] Able to speak Welsh	Number[2] Total in age group	Welsh only	Both	English only	Percentage[3] Welsh only	Percentage[3] Able to speak Welsh	Number[2] Total in age group	Welsh only	Both	English only	Percentage[3] Welsh only	Percentage[3] Able to speak Welsh
		Persons						Males						Females					
Newtown and Llanidloes RD	All 3+	10885	869	4315	5555	*8.1*	*48.3*	5560	430	2180	2889	*7.8*	*47.5*	5325	439	2135	2666	*8.4*	*49.1*
	3–4	511	82	85	309	*17.2*	*35.1*	284	56	53	155	*21.2*	*41.3*	227	26	32	154	*12.3*	*27.4*
	5–9	1205	154	309	713	*13.1*	*39.4*	621	81	160	363	*13.4*	*39.9*	584	73	149	350	*12.8*	*38.8*
	10–14	1239	82	413	730	*6.7*	*40.4*	639	42	206	384	*6.6*	*39.2*	600	40	207	346	*6.7*	*41.7*
	15–24	2096	87	861	1139	*4.2*	*45.4*	1060	47	417	590	*4.5*	*44.0*	1036	40	444	549	*3.9*	*46.9*
	25–44	2921	183	1252	1468	*6.3*	*49.4*	1436	86	590	752	*6.0*	*47.3*	1485	97	662	716	*6.6*	*51.5*
	45–64	1987	151	953	847	*7.7*	*56.6*	1036	67	515	453	*6.5*	*56.2*	951	84	438	394	*9.2*	*57.0*
	65–	926	130	442	349	*14.1*	*62.1*	484	51	239	192	*10.6*	*60.2*	442	79	203	157	*18.0*	*64.2*
FLINTSHIRE																			
Buckley UD	All 3+	5825	24	496	5162	*0.4*	*9.2*	3101	13	258	2768	*0.4*	*8.9*	2724	11	238	2394	*0.4*	*9.4*
	3–4	297	1	10	261	*0.4*	*4.0*	128	0	7	111	*0.0*	*5.9*	169	1	3	150	*0.6*	*2.6*
	5–9	803	1	25	738	*0.1*	*3.4*	393	1	11	364	*0.3*	*3.2*	410	0	14	374	*0.0*	*3.6*
	10–14	716	1	26	670	*0.1*	*3.9*	388	1	19	357	*0.3*	*5.3*	328	0	7	313	*0.0*	*2.2*
	15–24	1022	1	52	957	*0.1*	*5.2*	643	1	25	611	*0.2*	*4.1*	379	0	27	346	*0.0*	*7.2*
	25–44	1737	9	171	1533	*0.5*	*10.5*	928	5	83	833	*0.5*	*9.6*	809	4	88	700	*0.5*	*11.6*
	45–64	904	8	148	732	*0.9*	*17.6*	457	4	75	369	*0.9*	*17.6*	447	4	73	363	*0.9*	*17.5*
	65–	346	3	64	271	*0.9*	*19.8*	164	1	38	123	*0.6*	*24.1*	182	2	26	148	*1.1*	*15.9*
Connah's Quay UD	All 3+	4216	29	478	3532	*0.7*	*12.5*	2150	14	262	1790	*0.7*	*13.3*	2066	15	216	1742	*0.8*	*11.7*
	3–4	239	1	7	199	*0.5*	*3.9*	111	1	5	88	*1.1*	*6.4*	128	0	2	111	*0.0*	*1.8*
	5–9	620	2	27	554	*0.3*	*5.0*	308	1	14	277	*0.3*	*5.1*	312	1	13	277	*0.3*	*4.8*
	10–14	519	2	26	469	*0.4*	*5.6*	263	0	14	243	*0.0*	*5.4*	256	2	12	226	*0.8*	*5.8*
	15–24	799	7	91	673	*0.9*	*12.7*	435	5	59	355	*1.2*	*15.3*	364	2	32	318	*0.6*	*9.7*
	25–44	1321	7	173	1095	*0.5*	*14.1*	685	3	90	567	*0.5*	*14.0*	636	4	83	528	*0.6*	*14.1*
	45–64	539	4	110	417	*0.8*	*21.5*	267	2	62	201	*0.8*	*24.2*	272	2	48	216	*0.8*	*18.8*
	65–	179	6	44	125	*3.4*	*28.6*	81	2	18	59	*2.5*	*25.3*	98	4	26	66	*4.2*	*31.3*
Flint MB	All 3+	5062	77	1705	3152	*1.6*	*36.1*	2583	44	864	1606	*1.7*	*36.0*	2479	33	841	1546	*1.4*	*36.1*
	3–4	261	5	30	203	*2.1*	*14.7*	125	2	15	100	*1.7*	*14.5*	136	3	15	103	*2.5*	*14.9*
	5–9	608	8	91	478	*1.4*	*17.2*	300	2	44	236	*0.7*	*16.3*	308	6	47	242	*2.0*	*18.0*
	10–14	560	2	98	440	*0.4*	*18.5*	284	2	58	213	*0.7*	*22.0*	276	0	40	227	*0.0*	*15.0*
	15–24	981	10	260	696	*1.0*	*27.9*	520	6	141	363	*1.2*	*28.8*	461	4	119	333	*0.9*	*26.9*
	25–44	1500	14	568	893	*0.9*	*39.4*	788	8	286	480	*1.0*	*37.8*	712	6	282	413	*0.9*	*41.1*
	45–64	842	22	461	348	*2.6*	*58.1*	442	14	244	177	*3.2*	*59.3*	400	8	217	171	*2.0*	*56.8*
	65–	310	16	197	94	*5.2*	*69.4*	124	10	76	37	*8.1*	*69.9*	186	6	121	57	*3.3*	*69.0*

Holywell UD	All 3+	2413	53	1387	920	2.2	61.0	1123	26	660	408	2.4	62.7	1290	27	727	512	2.1	59.5
	3–4	78	2	22	47	2.8	33.8	37	0	11	24	0.0	31.4	41	2	11	23	5.6	36.1
	5–9	225	4	80	132	1.9	38.9	109	3	40	62	2.9	41.0	116	1	40	70	0.9	36.9
	10–14	269	2	129	131	0.8	50.0	141	2	70	64	1.5	52.9	128	0	59	67	0.0	46.8
	15–24	471	5	272	181	1.1	60.5	218	3	121	84	1.4	59.6	253	2	151	97	0.8	61.2
	25–44	724	7	448	259	1.0	63.7	332	2	216	110	0.6	66.5	392	5	232	149	1.3	61.4
	45–64	460	18	316	121	4.0	73.4	212	9	152	47	4.3	77.4	248	9	164	74	3.6	70.0
	65–	186	15	120	49	8.1	73.0	74	7	50	17	9.5	77.0	112	8	70	32	7.2	70.3
Mold UD	All 3+	4495	83	2267	2020	1.9	53.8	2211	40	1148	963	1.9	55.2	2284	43	1119	1057	1.9	52.4
	3–4	241	4	75	128	1.9	38.2	131	3	43	64	2.7	41.8	110	1	32	64	1.0	34.0
	5–9	551	7	207	303	1.4	41.4	265	4	96	143	1.6	41.2	286	3	111	160	1.1	41.6
	10–14	497	6	196	283	1.2	41.6	249	4	99	141	1.6	42.2	248	2	97	142	0.8	41.1
	15–24	857	8	376	458	1.0	45.6	435	0	197	233	0.0	45.8	422	8	179	225	1.9	45.4
	25–44	1352	21	762	549	1.6	58.8	648	14	384	245	2.2	61.9	704	7	378	304	1.0	55.9
	45–64	720	19	465	230	2.7	67.8	361	7	246	107	1.9	70.3	359	12	219	123	3.4	65.3
	65–	277	18	186	69	6.6	74.7	122	8	83	30	6.6	75.2	155	10	103	39	6.6	74.3
Prestatyn UD	All 3+	1955	39	878	1003	2.0	47.8	815	18	421	366	2.2	54.5	1140	21	457	637	1.9	42.9
	3–4	61	3	24	29	5.4	48.2	33	1	13	18	3.1	43.8	28	2	11	11	8.3	54.2
	5–9	165	1	66	91	0.6	42.4	97	1	41	52	1.1	44.7	68	0	25	39	0.0	39.1
	10–14	190	0	75	111	0.0	40.3	99	0	42	56	0.0	42.9	91	0	33	55	0.0	37.5
	15–24	310	1	171	134	0.3	56.2	115	1	67	47	0.9	59.1	195	0	104	87	0.0	54.5
	25–44	612	7	300	299	1.2	50.7	245	4	150	88	1.7	63.6	367	3	150	211	0.8	42.0
	45–64	446	10	175	253	2.3	42.2	158	4	80	72	2.6	53.8	288	6	95	181	2.1	35.8
	65–	171	17	67	86	10.0	49.4	68	7	28	33	10.3	51.5	103	10	39	53	9.8	48.0
Rhyl UD	All 3+	8559	138	3331	4862	1.7	41.6	3510	67	1445	1914	2.0	44.1	5049	71	1886	2948	1.4	39.9
	3–4	289	6	59	189	2.4	25.6	134	3	23	88	2.6	22.8	155	3	36	101	2.1	27.9
	5–9	799	10	186	558	1.3	26.0	425	5	98	298	1.2	25.7	374	5	88	260	1.4	26.3
	10–14	836	2	227	570	0.3	28.7	420	2	109	289	0.5	27.8	416	0	118	281	0.0	29.6
	15-24	1705	27	681	958	1.6	42.5	620	15	263	332	2.5	45.6	1085	12	418	626	1.1	40.7
	25–44	2723	31	1140	1519	1.2	43.5	1051	16	494	536	1.5	48.8	1672	15	646	983	0.9	40.2
	45–64	1617	33	767	785	2.1	50.5	652	14	355	278	2.2	57.0	965	19	412	507	2.0	45.9
	65–	590	29	271	283	5.0	51.4	208	12	103	93	5.8	55.3	382	17	168	190	4.5	49.2
Hawarden RD	All 3+	19064	301	3403	14827	1.6	20.0	9992	154	1815	7757	1.6	20.2	9072	147	1588	7070	1.7	19.7
	3–4	968	29	77	771	3.3	12.1	469	17	38	366	4.0	13.1	499	12	39	405	2.6	11.2
	5–9	2314	42	306	1853	1.9	15.8	1174	24	160	932	2.2	16.5	1140	18	146	921	1.7	15.1
	10–14	2140	24	303	1730	1.2	15.9	1114	11	154	913	1.0	15.3	1026	13	149	817	1.3	16.5
	15–24	3658	29	559	2988	0.8	16.4	2055	15	312	1678	0.7	16.3	1603	14	247	1310	0.9	16.6
	25–44	5999	89	1190	4616	1.5	21.7	3152	50	655	2406	1.6	22.6	2847	39	535	2210	1.4	20.6
	45–64	3033	59	708	2213	2.0	25.7	1585	29	361	1166	1.9	25.0	1448	30	347	1047	2.1	26.5
	65–	952	29	260	656	3.1	30.6	443	8	135	296	1.8	32.6	509	21	125	360	4.2	28.9

District[1]	Age last birth-day	Persons: Number[2] Total in age group	Persons: Welsh only	Persons: Both	Persons: English only	Persons: Percentage[3] Welsh only	Persons: Percentage[3] Able to speak Welsh	Males: Number[2] Total in age group	Males: Welsh only	Males: Both	Males: English only	Males: Percentage[3] Welsh only	Males: Percentage[3] Able to speak Welsh	Females: Number[2] Total in age group	Females: Welsh only	Females: Both	Females: English only	Females: Percentage[3] Welsh only	Females: Percentage[3] Able to speak Welsh
Holywell RD	All 3+	23682	1711	15530	5912	*7.4*	*74.5*	11800	946	7965	2618	*8.2*	*77.3*	11882	765	7565	3294	*6.6*	*71.6*
	3–4	1057	204	400	329	*21.9*	*64.7*	506	98	193	151	*22.2*	*65.8*	551	106	207	178	*21.6*	*63.7*
	5–9	2680	220	1558	755	*8.7*	*70.2*	1313	110	791	340	*8.9*	*72.6*	1367	110	767	415	*8.5*	*67.9*
	10–14	2706	85	1745	791	*3.2*	*69.8*	1297	51	897	304	*4.1*	*75.7*	1409	34	848	487	*2.5*	*64.4*
	15–24	4153	127	2822	1151	*3.1*	*71.9*	2263	88	1583	560	*3.9*	*74.9*	1890	39	1239	591	*2.1*	*68.3*
	25–44	6860	308	4772	1712	*4.5*	*74.8*	3403	172	2458	741	*5.1*	*78.0*	3457	136	2314	971	*4.0*	*71.6*
	45–64	4366	404	3054	872	*9.3*	*79.8*	2162	238	1519	387	*11.1*	*81.9*	2204	166	1535	485	*7.6*	*77.8*
	65–	1860	363	1179	302	*19.7*	*83.6*	856	189	524	135	*22.3*	*84.1*	1004	174	655	167	*17.5*	*83.2*
Overton RD	All 3+	4878	4	127	4620	*0.1*	*2.8*	2350	2	45	2248	*0.1*	*2.0*	2528	2	82	2372	*0.1*	*3.4*
	3–4	213	0	0	189	*0.0*	*0.0*	98	0	0	88	*0.0*	*0.0*	115	0	0	101	*0.0*	*0.0*
	5–9	525	0	2	505	*0.0*	*0.4*	270	0	2	255	*0.0*	*0.8*	255	0	0	250	*0.0*	*0.0*
	10–14	532	0	6	503	*0.0*	*1.2*	261	0	2	252	*0.0*	*0.8*	271	0	4	251	*0.0*	*1.6*
	15–24	995	1	26	950	*0.1*	*2.8*	457	0	7	445	*0.0*	*1.5*	538	1	19	505	*0.2*	*3.8*
	25–44	1371	1	49	1296	*0.1*	*3.7*	643	1	16	613	*0.2*	*2.7*	728	0	33	683	*0.0*	*4.6*
	45–64	881	2	33	831	*0.2*	*4.0*	459	1	16	437	*0.2*	*3.7*	422	1	17	394	*0.2*	*4.4*
	65–	361	0	11	346	*0.0*	*3.1*	162	0	2	158	*0.0*	*1.3*	199	0	9	188	*0.0*	*4.6*
St Asaph (Flint) RD	All 3+	6421	487	3985	1876	*7.7*	*70.4*	3047	246	1911	851	*8.2*	*71.7*	3374	241	2074	1025	*7.2*	*69.3*
	3–4	255	58	86	93	*24.5*	*60.8*	119	25	34	50	*22.9*	*54.1*	136	33	52	43	*25.8*	*66.4*
	5–9	628	44	357	214	*7.2*	*65.2*	338	24	190	117	*7.3*	*64.7*	290	20	167	97	*7.0*	*65.8*
	10–14	635	25	380	222	*4.0*	*64.6*	339	11	191	134	*3.3*	*60.1*	296	14	189	88	*4.8*	*69.8*
	15–24	1091	38	735	312	*3.5*	*71.2*	518	18	363	134	*3.5*	*74.0*	573	20	372	178	*3.5*	*68.8*
	25–44	1901	87	1241	560	*4.6*	*70.3*	887	42	616	222	*4.8*	*74.8*	1014	45	625	338	*4.5*	*66.5*
	45–64	1314	123	827	353	*9.4*	*72.9*	596	72	370	146	*12.2*	*75.0*	718	51	457	207	*7.1*	*71.0*
	65–	597	112	359	122	*18.9*	*79.4*	250	54	147	48	*21.7*	*80.7*	347	58	212	74	*16.9*	*78.5*
DENBIGHSHIRE																			
Abergele and Pen-sarn UD	All 3+	2011	81	1474	418	*4.1*	*78.8*	892	42	673	161	*4.8*	*81.6*	1119	39	801	257	*3.6*	*76.6*
	3–4	87	16	44	18	*20.5*	*76.9*	51	10	25	10	*22.2*	*77.8*	36	6	19	8	*18.2*	*75.8*
	5–9	196	14	132	43	*7.4*	*77.2*	95	7	61	24	*7.6*	*73.9*	101	7	71	19	*7.2*	*80.4*
	10–14	186	2	147	32	*1.1*	*82.3*	93	1	75	15	*1.1*	*83.5*	93	1	72	17	*1.1*	*81.1*
	15–24	374	4	301	64	*1.1*	*82.7*	176	2	147	24	*1.2*	*86.1*	198	2	154	40	*1.0*	*79.6*
	25–44	555	5	425	120	*0.9*	*78.2*	231	3	185	41	*1.3*	*82.1*	324	2	240	79	*0.6*	*75.4*
	45–64	451	27	318	101	*6.1*	*77.4*	190	16	137	37	*8.4*	*80.5*	261	11	181	64	*4.3*	*75.0*
	65–	162	13	107	40	*8.1*	*75.0*	56	3	43	10	*5.4*	*82.1*	106	10	64	30	*9.6*	*71.2*

Colwyn Bay and Colwyn UD	All 3+	12108	419	4508	6849	*3.6*	*41.8*	4759	212	2026	2398	*4.6*	*48.2*	7349	207	2482	4451	*2.9*	*37.6*
	3–4	379	41	87	201	*12.5*	*38.9*	190	21	46	97	*12.8*	*40.9*	189	20	41	104	*12.1*	*37.0*
	5–9	1007	47	378	517	*5.0*	*45.1*	496	26	184	260	*5.5*	*44.7*	511	21	194	257	*4.4*	*45.6*
	10–14	958	21	418	480	*2.3*	*47.8*	466	12	222	219	*2.6*	*51.7*	492	9	196	261	*1.9*	*44.0*
	15–24	2335	46	1084	1153	*2.0*	*49.3*	877	23	437	391	*2.7*	*53.5*	1458	23	647	762	*1.6*	*46.7*
	25–44	4225	82	1604	2474	*2.0*	*40.5*	1579	42	714	806	*2.7*	*48.4*	2646	40	890	1668	*1.5*	*35.8*
	45–64	2410	114	733	1515	*4.8*	*35.8*	872	56	341	464	*6.5*	*46.1*	1538	58	392	1051	*3.9*	*29.9*
	65–	794	68	204	509	*8.7*	*34.8*	279	32	82	161	*11.6*	*41.5*	515	36	122	348	*7.1*	*31.2*
Denbigh MB	All 3+	6564	900	4566	994	*13.9*	*84.6*	3143	500	2194	413	*16.1*	*86.7*	3421	400	2372	581	*11.9*	*82.7*
	3–4	217	65	96	33	*33.5*	*83.0*	112	41	48	15	*39.4*	*85.6*	105	24	48	18	*26.7*	*80.0*
	5–9	605	87	417	78	*14.9*	*86.6*	305	46	211	39	*15.5*	*86.8*	300	41	206	39	*14.3*	*86.4*
	10–14	620	29	501	79	*4.8*	*87.0*	295	22	238	33	*7.5*	*88.7*	325	7	263	46	*2.2*	*85.4*
	15–24	1058	49	863	132	*4.7*	*87.4*	500	29	418	46	*5.9*	*90.7*	558	20	445	86	*3.6*	*84.4*
	25–44	2062	217	1463	364	*10.6*	*82.2*	1001	139	696	158	*14.0*	*84.1*	1061	78	767	206	*7.4*	*80.4*
	45–64	1443	298	902	230	*20.8*	*83.9*	703	161	450	90	*23.0*	*87.2*	740	137	452	140	*18.8*	*80.8*
	65–	559	155	324	78	*27.8*	*86.0*	227	62	133	32	*27.3*	*85.9*	332	93	191	46	*28.2*	*86.1*
Llangollen UD	All 3+	3081	164	1939	919	*5.4*	*69.6*	1370	74	918	354	*5.5*	*73.7*	1711	90	1021	565	*5.4*	*66.3*
	3–4	116	12	51	44	*11.2*	*58.9*	60	4	31	20	*7.3*	*63.6*	56	8	20	24	*15.4*	*53.8*
	5–9	288	14	161	99	*5.1*	*63.9*	144	10	80	48	*7.2*	*65.2*	144	4	81	51	*2.9*	*62.5*
	10–14	311	8	197	95	*2.7*	*68.3*	159	4	102	49	*2.6*	*68.4*	152	4	95	46	*2.8*	*68.3*
	15–24	533	12	344	170	*2.3*	*67.7*	207	2	142	58	*1.0*	*71.3*	326	10	202	112	*3.1*	*65.4*
	25–44	960	46	623	282	*4.8*	*70.3*	416	21	308	86	*5.1*	*79.3*	544	25	315	196	*4.7*	*63.4*
	45–64	618	36	408	168	*5.9*	*72.5*	281	20	187	72	*7.2*	*74.2*	337	16	221	96	*4.8*	*71.2*
	65–	255	36	155	61	*14.3*	*75.8*	103	13	68	21	*12.7*	*79.4*	152	23	87	40	*15.3*	*73.3*
Llanrwst UD	All 3+	2364	352	1751	208	*15.2*	*91.0*	1064	166	772	100	*16.0*	*90.4*	1300	186	979	108	*14.6*	*91.5*
	3–4	99	43	23	14	*53.8*	*82.5*	53	27	6	6	*69.2*	*84.6*	46	16	17	8	*39.0*	*80.5*
	5–9	232	51	149	17	*23.5*	*92.2*	111	25	75	5	*23.8*	*95.2*	121	26	74	12	*23.2*	*89.3*
	10–14	239	14	209	11	*6.0*	*95.3*	89	9	75	3	*10.3*	*96.6*	150	5	134	8	*3.4*	*94.6*
	15–24	417	14	383	15	*3.4*	*96.4*	173	6	155	10	*3.5*	*94.2*	244	8	228	5	*3.3*	*97.9*
	25–44	726	61	572	84	*8.5*	*88.3*	339	28	271	38	*8.3*	*88.7*	387	33	301	46	*8.7*	*87.9*
	45–64	460	85	324	51	*18.5*	*88.9*	220	41	147	32	*18.6*	*85.5*	240	44	177	19	*18.3*	*92.1*
	65–	191	84	91	16	*44.0*	*91.6*	79	30	43	6	*38.0*	*92.4*	112	54	48	10	*48.2*	*91.1*
Ruthin MB	All 3+	2678	181	1939	513	*6.9*	*80.4*	1276	85	931	235	*6.8*	*81.1*	1402	96	1008	278	*6.9*	*79.8*
	3–4	94	14	43	24	*17.3*	*70.4*	53	9	23	16	*18.8*	*66.7*	41	5	20	8	*15.2*	*75.8*
	5–9	261	14	186	51	*5.6*	*79.7*	138	7	94	29	*5.4*	*77.7*	123	7	92	22	*5.8*	*81.8*
	10–14	292	10	218	57	*3.5*	*80.0*	123	2	92	24	*1.7*	*79.7*	169	8	126	33	*4.8*	*80.2*
	15–24	473	9	357	102	*1.9*	*78.0*	230	4	178	43	*1.8*	*80.5*	243	5	179	59	*2.1*	*75.7*
	25–44	805	23	616	163	*2.9*	*79.7*	389	6	309	74	*1.5*	*81.0*	416	17	307	89	*4.1*	*78.5*
	45–64	518	53	379	82	*10.3*	*83.9*	246	27	179	40	*11.0*	*83.7*	272	26	200	42	*9.7*	*84.0*
	65–	235	58	140	34	*24.9*	*85.0*	97	30	56	9	*31.3*	*89.6*	138	28	84	25	*20.4*	*81.8*

District[1]	Age last birth-day	Persons: Number[2] Total in age group	Welsh only	Both	English only	Percentage[3] Welsh only	Able to speak Welsh	Males: Number[2] Total in age group	Welsh only	Both	English only	Percentage[3] Welsh only	Able to speak Welsh	Females: Number[2] Total in age group	Welsh only	Both	English only	Percentage[3] Welsh only	Able to speak Welsh
Wrexham MB	All 3+	17152	72	2688	14186	*0.4*	*16.3*	8586	34	1273	7172	*0.4*	*15.4*	8566	38	1415	7014	*0.4*	*17.2*
	3–4	799	7	45	700	*0.9*	*6.9*	410	6	24	354	*1.6*	*7.8*	389	1	21	346	*0.3*	*6.0*
	5–9	1969	6	113	1803	*0.3*	*6.2*	987	3	53	900	*0.3*	*5.9*	982	3	60	903	*0.3*	*6.5*
	10–14	1837	4	156	1649	*0.2*	*8.8*	912	0	75	823	*0.0*	*8.4*	925	4	81	826	*0.4*	*9.3*
	15–24	3292	10	486	2770	*0.3*	*15.2*	1690	4	191	1478	*0.2*	*11.6*	1602	6	295	1292	*0.4*	*18.9*
	25–44	5683	20	1027	4599	*0.4*	*18.5*	2841	12	519	2296	*0.4*	*18.8*	2842	8	508	2303	*0.3*	*18.3*
	45–64	2774	14	643	2099	*0.5*	*23.8*	1406	4	327	1070	*0.3*	*23.6*	1368	10	316	1029	*0.7*	*24.0*
	65–	798	11	218	566	*1.4*	*28.8*	340	5	84	251	*1.5*	*26.2*	458	6	134	315	*1.3*	*30.8*
Chirk RD	All 3+	4271	485	1420	2274	*11.6*	*45.6*	2238	271	737	1199	*12.3*	*45.7*	2033	214	683	1075	*10.8*	*45.5*
	3–4	201	23	23	129	*13.1*	*26.3*	103	22	10	64	*22.9*	*33.3*	98	1	13	65	*1.3*	*17.7*
	5–9	546	84	129	309	*16.1*	*40.8*	273	40	64	161	*15.1*	*39.2*	273	44	65	148	*17.1*	*42.4*
	10–14	489	36	159	282	*7.5*	*40.9*	253	16	80	150	*6.5*	*39.0*	236	20	79	132	*8.7*	*42.9*
	15–24	827	54	290	470	*6.6*	*42.3*	449	33	147	263	*7.4*	*40.6*	378	21	143	207	*5.7*	*44.2*
	25–44	1223	108	452	655	*8.9*	*46.1*	650	62	251	336	*9.6*	*48.2*	573	46	201	319	*8.1*	*43.6*
	45–64	745	116	288	337	*15.7*	*54.5*	388	65	140	182	*16.8*	*53.0*	357	51	148	155	*14.4*	*56.2*
	65–	240	64	79	92	*27.2*	*60.9*	122	33	45	43	*27.3*	*64.5*	118	31	34	49	*27.2*	*57.0*
Llangollen RD	All 3+	3389	499	2084	703	*15.2*	*78.6*	1739	264	1106	321	*15.6*	*81.0*	1650	235	978	382	*14.7*	*76.1*
	3–4	179	55	54	48	*35.0*	*69.4*	100	33	26	33	*35.9*	*64.1*	79	22	28	15	*33.8*	*76.9*
	5–9	420	60	249	81	*15.4*	*79.2*	205	27	118	44	*14.3*	*76.7*	215	33	131	37	*16.4*	*81.6*
	10–14	380	35	258	70	*9.6*	*80.7*	189	17	131	33	*9.4*	*81.8*	191	18	127	37	*9.9*	*79.7*
	15–24	572	49	387	124	*8.8*	*77.9*	329	27	241	53	*8.4*	*83.5*	243	22	146	71	*9.2*	*70.3*
	25–44	987	111	636	228	*11.4*	*76.6*	480	56	326	95	*11.7*	*80.1*	507	55	310	133	*11.0*	*73.3*
	45–64	628	115	394	112	*18.5*	*82.0*	336	69	214	49	*20.8*	*85.2*	292	46	180	63	*15.9*	*78.2*
	65–	223	74	106	40	*33.6*	*81.8*	100	35	50	14	*35.4*	*85.9*	123	39	56	26	*32.2*	*78.5*
Llanrwst RD	All 3+	4132	1950	1888	227	*48.0*	*94.4*	2124	1060	932	102	*50.6*	*95.1*	2008	890	956	125	*45.2*	*93.7*
	3–4	175	137	10	6	*89.5*	*96.1*	94	75	6	2	*90.4*	*97.6*	81	62	4	4	*88.6*	*94.3*
	5–9	397	253	114	14	*66.4*	*96.3*	221	140	66	6	*66.0*	*97.2*	176	113	48	8	*66.9*	*95.3*
	10–14	398	146	232	12	*37.4*	*96.9*	177	69	100	7	*39.2*	*96.0*	221	77	132	5	*36.0*	*97.7*
	15–24	727	254	431	35	*35.3*	*95.1*	372	141	216	11	*38.3*	*97.0*	355	113	215	24	*32.1*	*93.2*
	25–44	1280	475	694	104	*37.3*	*91.8*	660	274	338	45	*41.7*	*93.2*	620	201	356	59	*32.6*	*90.4*
	45–64	791	440	305	41	*56.0*	*94.8*	415	240	151	22	*58.1*	*94.7*	376	200	154	19	*53.6*	*94.9*
	65–	364	245	102	15	*67.7*	*95.9*	185	121	55	9	*65.4*	*95.1*	179	124	47	6	*70.1*	*96.6*

Llansilin RD	All 3+	3006	563	2159	262	18.9	91.2	1578	295	1160	112	18.8	92.9	1428	268	999	150	18.9	89.4
	3–4	127	59	41	16	50.9	86.2	65	31	19	9	52.5	84.7	62	28	22	7	49.1	87.7
	5–9	334	98	198	34	29.7	89.7	156	51	88	15	33.1	90.3	178	47	110	19	26.7	89.2
	10–14	322	44	256	21	13.7	93.5	171	24	140	6	14.1	96.5	151	20	116	15	13.2	90.1
	15–24	556	42	460	51	7.6	90.8	291	25	243	23	8.6	92.1	265	17	217	28	6.5	89.3
	25–44	841	119	630	90	14.2	89.3	449	60	351	37	13.4	91.7	392	59	279	53	15.1	86.4
	45–64	597	128	428	40	21.5	93.3	323	66	241	15	20.5	95.3	274	62	187	25	22.6	90.9
	65–	229	73	146	10	31.9	95.6	123	38	78	7	30.9	94.3	106	35	68	3	33.0	97.2
Ruthin RD	All 3+	8608	2212	5348	943	26.0	88.9	4316	1159	2705	404	27.2	90.5	4292	1053	2643	539	24.8	87.2
	3–4	289	167	49	35	66.5	86.1	151	86	21	22	66.7	82.9	138	81	28	13	66.4	89.3
	5–9	784	343	358	60	45.1	92.1	359	155	171	26	44.0	92.6	425	188	187	34	46.0	91.7
	10–14	846	166	627	46	19.8	94.5	443	96	327	17	21.8	96.1	403	70	300	29	17.5	92.7
	15–24	1617	219	1196	194	13.6	87.9	876	138	637	96	15.8	89.0	741	81	559	98	11.0	86.6
	25–44	2556	426	1749	365	16.8	85.6	1234	216	866	146	17.6	88.1	1322	210	883	219	16.0	83.2
	45–64	1763	560	1018	178	31.9	89.9	889	300	516	70	33.9	92.1	874	260	502	108	29.9	87.6
	65–	753	331	351	65	44.3	91.3	364	168	167	27	46.4	92.5	389	163	184	38	42.3	90.1
St Asaph (Denb) RD	All 3+	6325	2095	3445	675	33.7	89.1	3190	1146	1725	271	36.5	91.4	3135	949	1720	404	30.9	86.9
	3–4	264	142	56	26	63.4	88.4	117	68	24	6	69.4	93.9	147	74	32	20	58.7	84.1
	5–9	617	278	260	52	47.1	91.2	310	148	122	27	49.8	90.9	307	130	138	25	44.4	91.5
	10–14	656	161	413	76	24.8	88.3	346	80	217	47	23.3	86.3	310	81	196	29	26.5	90.5
	15–24	1198	306	760	120	25.8	89.9	615	183	385	45	29.9	92.7	583	123	375	75	21.5	86.9
	25–44	1950	537	1185	216	27.7	88.9	954	297	587	65	31.3	93.2	996	240	598	151	24.3	84.7
	45–64	1178	440	588	140	37.7	88.0	616	245	304	61	40.2	90.0	562	195	284	79	34.9	85.8
	65–	462	231	183	45	50.3	90.2	232	125	86	20	54.1	91.3	230	106	97	25	46.5	89.0
Uwchaled RD	All 3+	2115	1134	837	121	54.2	94.2	1123	607	424	77	54.8	93.1	992	527	413	44	53.6	95.5
	3–4	84	68	6	3	88.3	96.1	37	29	2	1	90.6	96.9	47	39	4	2	86.7	95.6
	5–9	207	134	56	12	66.3	94.1	100	64	27	7	65.3	92.9	107	70	29	5	67.3	95.2
	10–14	201	91	101	7	45.7	96.5	106	49	51	5	46.7	95.2	95	42	50	2	44.7	97.9
	15–24	428	181	215	28	42.7	93.4	234	110	106	15	47.6	93.5	194	71	109	13	36.8	93.3
	25–44	606	258	293	53	42.7	91.2	326	141	145	38	43.5	88.3	280	117	148	15	41.8	94.6
	45–64	402	252	130	17	63.2	95.7	216	133	71	10	62.1	95.3	186	119	59	7	64.3	96.2
	65–	187	150	36	1	80.2	99.5	104	81	22	1	77.9	99.0	83	69	14	0	83.1	100.0
Wrexham RD	All 3+	56210	2196	26192	27004	4.0	51.2	29472	1168	13950	13985	4.0	51.9	26738	1028	12242	13019	3.9	50.5
	3–4	3068	352	810	1683	12.4	40.8	1540	189	402	845	13.2	41.2	1528	163	408	838	11.6	40.5
	5–9	7493	427	2808	4048	5.9	44.4	3819	226	1399	2093	6.1	43.7	3674	201	1409	1955	5.6	45.1
	10–14	6848	137	3031	3563	2.0	47.0	3531	78	1558	1843	2.2	47.0	3317	59	1473	1720	1.8	47.1
	15–24	10291	145	4782	5274	1.4	48.3	5951	90	2803	3006	1.5	49.0	4340	55	1979	2268	1.3	47.3
	25–44	16883	376	8551	7846	2.2	53.2	8771	200	4589	3944	2.3	54.8	8112	176	3962	3902	2.2	51.5
	45–64	8840	473	4833	3478	5.4	60.4	4548	258	2564	1710	5.7	62.3	4292	215	2269	1768	5.1	58.4
	65–	2787	286	1377	1112	10.3	59.9	1312	127	635	544	9.7	58.3	1475	159	742	568	10.8	61.3

District[1]	Age last birth-day	Number[2] Total in age group	Welsh only	Both	English only	Percentage[3] Welsh only	Able to speak Welsh	Number[2] Total in age group	Welsh only	Both	English only	Percentage[3] Welsh only	Able to speak Welsh	Number[2] Total in age group	Welsh only	Both	English only	Percentage[3] Welsh only	Able to speak Welsh
		Persons						Males						Females					
Llaneilian CP & Llansanffraid CP (admin. by Conwy (Caern) RD)	All 3+	1593	324	986	203	*21.4*	*86.6*	804	184	497	87	*24.0*	*88.7*	789	140	489	116	*18.8*	*84.4*
	3–4	78	38	18	8	*59.4*	*87.5*	43	22	10	4	*61.1*	*88.9*	35	16	8	4	*57.1*	*85.7*
	5–9	176	46	101	12	*28.9*	*92.5*	91	29	47	7	*34.9*	*91.6*	85	17	54	5	*22.4*	*93.4*
	10–14	163	20	115	17	*13.2*	*88.8*	79	14	51	9	*18.9*	*87.8*	84	6	64	8	*7.7*	*89.7*
	15–24	276	27	205	31	*10.3*	*88.2*	147	15	113	11	*10.8*	*92.1*	129	12	92	20	*9.7*	*83.9*
	25–44	499	72	336	76	*14.9*	*84.3*	248	38	172	32	*15.7*	*86.8*	251	34	164	44	*14.0*	*81.8*
	45–64	266	70	148	39	*27.2*	*84.8*	133	40	77	14	*30.5*	*89.3*	133	30	71	25	*23.8*	*80.2*
	65–	135	51	63	20	*38.1*	*85.1*	63	26	27	10	*41.3*	*84.1*	72	25	36	10	*35.2*	*85.9*
MERIONETH																			
Bala UD	All 3+	1462	256	1047	150	*17.6*	*89.6*	692	110	499	79	*16.0*	*88.4*	770	146	548	71	*19.1*	*90.7*
	3–4	48	29	10	6	*64.4*	*86.7*	16	9	5	1	*60.0*	*93.3*	32	20	5	5	*66.7*	*83.3*
	5–9	108	46	54	6	*43.4*	*94.3*	57	24	28	3	*43.6*	*94.5*	51	22	26	3	*43.1*	*94.1*
	10–14	141	16	121	4	*11.3*	*97.2*	69	6	60	3	*8.7*	*95.7*	72	10	61	1	*13.9*	*98.6*
	15–24	264	15	222	25	*5.7*	*90.5*	120	5	103	12	*4.2*	*90.0*	144	10	119	13	*7.0*	*90.8*
	25–44	436	30	341	63	*6.9*	*85.3*	211	13	161	36	*6.2*	*82.5*	225	17	180	27	*7.6*	*87.9*
	45–64	309	60	211	38	*19.4*	*87.7*	142	25	97	20	*17.6*	*85.9*	167	35	114	18	*21.0*	*89.2*
	65–	156	60	88	8	*38.5*	*94.9*	77	28	45	4	*36.4*	*94.8*	79	32	43	4	*40.5*	*94.9*
Barmouth UD	All 3+	2023	196	1299	450	*10.1*	*76.9*	823	92	521	183	*11.6*	*77.0*	1200	104	778	267	*9.1*	*76.8*
	3–4	67	26	17	11	*48.1*	*79.6*	31	15	6	6	*55.6*	*77.8*	36	11	11	5	*40.7*	*81.5*
	5–9	144	24	82	23	*18.6*	*82.2*	72	14	40	10	*21.9*	*84.4*	72	10	42	13	*15.4*	*80.0*
	10–14	168	13	118	28	*8.2*	*82.4*	76	7	49	15	*9.9*	*78.9*	92	6	69	13	*6.8*	*85.2*
	15–24	384	18	278	73	*4.9*	*80.2*	152	11	102	33	*7.5*	*77.4*	232	7	176	40	*3.1*	*82.1*
	25–44	657	29	430	178	*4.6*	*72.1*	252	12	173	64	*4.8*	*74.3*	405	17	257	114	*4.4*	*70.6*
	45–64	432	43	279	105	*10.1*	*75.4*	168	18	108	41	*10.8*	*75.4*	264	25	171	64	*9.6*	*75.4*
	65–	171	43	95	32	*25.3*	*81.2*	72	15	43	14	*20.8*	*80.6*	99	28	52	18	*28.6*	*81.6*
Dolgellau UD	All 3+	2060	425	1418	165	*21.2*	*91.8*	922	191	638	64	*21.4*	*92.8*	1138	234	780	101	*21.0*	*90.9*
	3–4	77	39	21	3	*61.9*	*95.2*	38	22	9	0	*71.0*	*100.0*	39	17	12	3	*53.1*	*90.6*
	5–9	202	68	105	13	*36.6*	*93.0*	99	35	49	9	*37.6*	*90.3*	103	33	56	4	*35.5*	*95.7*
	10–14	209	25	163	11	*12.6*	*94.5*	95	11	72	4	*12.6*	*95.4*	114	14	91	7	*12.5*	*93.8*
	15–24	329	24	273	29	*7.4*	*91.1*	157	10	135	10	*6.5*	*93.5*	172	14	138	19	*8.2*	*88.9*
	25–44	613	86	462	59	*14.2*	*90.3*	265	38	206	18	*14.5*	*93.1*	348	48	256	41	*13.9*	*88.1*
	45–64	429	100	289	39	*23.4*	*90.9*	189	41	130	17	*21.8*	*91.0*	240	59	159	22	*24.6*	*90.8*
	65–	201	83	105	11	*41.7*	*94.5*	79	34	37	6	*44.2*	*92.2*	122	49	68	5	*40.2*	*95.9*

Ffestiniog UD	All 3+	9087	3995	4688	178	45.1	98.0	4512	2026	2304	82	45.9	98.1	4575	1969	2384	96	44.2	97.8
	3–4	375	293	27	9	89.1	97.3	187	148	10	3	91.9	98.1	188	145	17	6	86.3	96.4
	5–9	1049	735	237	19	74.2	98.1	528	372	117	8	74.8	98.4	521	363	120	11	73.5	97.8
	10–14	1081	423	615	12	40.3	98.9	533	226	290	5	43.4	99.0	548	197	325	7	37.2	98.7
	15–24	1411	293	1078	13	21.2	99.0	765	182	558	10	24.3	98.7	646	111	520	3	17.5	99.4
	25–44	2745	858	1776	74	31.7	97.3	1371	457	873	32	33.6	97.7	1374	401	903	42	29.8	96.9
	45–64	1835	998	772	42	55.0	97.6	893	486	380	21	54.7	97.5	942	512	392	21	55.4	97.7
	65–	591	395	183	9	67.3	98.5	235	155	76	3	66.2	98.7	356	240	107	6	68.0	98.3
Mallwyd UD	All 3+	726	294	364	63	40.8	91.3	352	140	177	33	40.0	90.6	374	154	187	30	41.5	91.9
	3–4	22	16	3	2	76.2	90.5	10	7	2	0	77.8	100.0	12	9	1	2	75.0	83.3
	5–9	60	28	26	5	47.5	91.5	30	16	12	2	53.3	93.3	30	12	14	3	41.4	89.7
	10–14	67	16	49	2	23.9	97.0	40	11	28	1	27.5	97.5	27	5	21	1	18.5	96.3
	15–24	93	19	64	10	20.4	89.2	48	12	29	7	25.0	85.4	45	7	35	3	15.6	93.3
	25–44	209	60	122	27	28.7	87.1	93	27	55	11	29.0	88.2	116	33	67	16	28.4	86.2
	45–64	182	90	73	17	50.0	90.6	90	39	38	12	43.8	86.5	92	51	35	5	56.0	94.5
	65–	93	65	27	0	70.7	100.0	41	28	13	0	68.3	100.0	52	37	14	0	72.5	100.0
Tywyn UD	All 3+	3755	514	2591	609	13.8	83.5	1654	252	1138	237	15.4	85.1	2101	262	1453	372	12.6	82.2
	3–4	105	35	36	17	39.8	80.7	46	17	14	5	47.2	86.1	59	18	22	12	34.6	76.9
	5–9	358	75	223	51	21.5	85.4	171	33	106	25	20.1	84.8	187	42	117	26	22.7	85.9
	10–14	396	39	301	51	10.0	87.0	203	24	149	28	11.9	86.1	193	15	152	23	7.9	87.9
	15–24	712	39	550	116	5.5	83.1	338	26	255	52	7.7	83.4	374	13	295	64	3.5	82.8
	25–44	1106	93	798	212	8.4	80.6	429	40	321	65	9.3	84.3	677	53	477	147	7.8	78.3
	45–64	749	133	510	106	17.8	85.8	323	71	215	37	22.0	88.5	426	62	295	69	14.6	83.8
	65–	329	100	173	56	30.4	83.0	144	41	78	25	28.5	82.6	185	59	95	31	31.9	83.2
Deudraeth RD	All 3+	7361	3480	3222	405	48.9	94.2	3589	1660	1558	260	47.7	92.5	3772	1820	1664	145	50.0	95.8
	3–4	318	230	28	10	85.8	96.3	165	121	13	6	86.4	95.7	153	109	15	4	85.2	96.9
	5–9	808	574	141	19	78.2	97.4	392	274	70	9	77.6	97.5	416	300	71	10	78.7	97.4
	10–14	789	357	385	8	47.6	98.9	386	179	186	5	48.4	98.6	403	178	199	3	46.8	99.2
	15–24	1251	349	783	74	28.7	93.2	645	189	387	52	30.0	91.6	606	160	396	22	27.3	94.9
	25–44	2148	745	1185	185	35.2	91.2	1042	364	539	125	35.4	87.8	1106	381	646	60	35.0	94.4
	45–64	1450	835	517	89	57.9	93.8	720	399	268	53	55.4	92.6	730	436	249	36	60.5	95.0
	65–	597	390	183	20	65.8	96.6	239	134	95	10	56.1	95.8	358	256	88	10	72.3	97.2
Dolgellau RD	All 3+	7595	3001	3757	671	40.4	91.0	3523	1509	1689	247	43.8	92.8	4072	1492	2068	424	37.4	89.4
	3–4	282	192	37	22	76.5	91.2	130	88	14	12	77.2	89.5	152	104	23	10	75.9	92.7
	5–9	750	427	243	46	59.6	93.6	374	216	116	22	61.0	93.8	376	211	127	24	58.3	93.4
	10–14	833	221	530	56	27.4	93.1	398	122	228	33	31.9	91.4	435	99	302	23	23.3	94.6
	15–24	1334	332	847	136	25.2	89.7	650	197	399	45	30.7	93.0	684	135	448	91	20.0	86.5
	25–44	2100	642	1216	215	31.0	89.6	925	324	531	64	35.2	92.9	1175	318	685	151	27.6	86.9
	45–64	1603	762	675	147	48.1	90.7	745	371	311	55	50.3	92.5	858	391	364	92	46.2	89.1
	65–	693	425	209	49	62.2	92.8	301	191	90	16	64.3	94.6	392	234	119	33	60.6	91.5

District[1]	Age last birth-day	Persons: Number[2] Total in age group	Welsh only	Both	English only	Percentage[3] Welsh only	Able to speak Welsh	Males: Number[2] Total in age group	Welsh only	Both	English only	Percentage[3] Welsh only	Able to speak Welsh	Females: Number[2] Total in age group	Welsh only	Both	English only	Percentage[3] Welsh only	Able to speak Welsh
Edeirnion RD	All 3+	4860	1508	2878	436	*31.3*	*91.0*	2432	796	1437	185	*32.9*	*92.3*	2428	712	1441	251	*29.6*	*89.6*
	3–4	158	92	38	18	*62.2*	*87.8*	75	50	17	6	*68.5*	*91.8*	83	42	21	12	*56.0*	*84.0*
	5–9	472	222	192	49	*47.9*	*89.4*	228	110	94	20	*49.1*	*91.1*	244	112	98	29	*46.9*	*87.9*
	10–14	503	131	340	30	*26.1*	*94.0*	265	77	173	14	*29.2*	*94.7*	238	54	167	16	*22.8*	*93.2*
	15–24	866	155	638	71	*17.9*	*91.8*	447	88	326	33	*19.7*	*92.6*	419	67	312	38	*16.1*	*90.9*
	25–44	1422	309	948	161	*21.8*	*88.6*	690	158	465	66	*22.9*	*90.4*	732	151	483	95	*20.7*	*87.0*
	45–64	1014	389	541	78	*38.6*	*92.3*	527	216	272	36	*41.2*	*93.1*	487	173	269	42	*35.7*	*91.3*
	65–	425	210	181	29	*50.0*	*93.1*	200	97	90	10	*49.2*	*94.9*	225	113	91	19	*50.7*	*91.5*
Penllyn RD	All 3+	3868	2074	1594	176	*53.9*	*95.4*	1947	1074	787	78	*55.4*	*96.0*	1921	1000	807	98	*52.5*	*94.8*
	3–4	135	108	9	5	*88.5*	*95.9*	60	50	5	1	*89.3*	*98.2*	75	58	4	4	*87.9*	*93.9*
	5–9	373	293	62	16	*79.0*	*95.7*	176	141	29	6	*80.1*	*96.6*	197	152	33	10	*77.9*	*94.9*
	10–14	352	198	145	6	*56.7*	*98.3*	173	107	63	2	*62.2*	*98.8*	179	91	82	4	*51.4*	*97.7*
	15–24	745	292	415	37	*39.2*	*94.9*	403	183	203	17	*45.4*	*95.8*	342	109	212	20	*31.9*	*93.9*
	25–44	1146	481	591	72	*42.0*	*93.7*	561	239	289	32	*42.7*	*94.3*	585	242	302	40	*41.4*	*93.2*
	45–64	740	421	286	30	*57.1*	*95.9*	393	225	150	16	*57.5*	*95.9*	347	196	136	14	*56.6*	*96.0*
	65–	377	281	86	10	*74.5*	*97.3*	181	129	48	4	*71.3*	*97.8*	196	152	38	6	*77.6*	*96.9*
Pennal CP	All 3+	412	114	261	37	*27.7*	*91.0*	181	55	113	13	*30.4*	*92.8*	231	59	148	24	*25.5*	*89.6*
(admin. by	3–4	8	4	3	1	*50.0*	*87.5*	4	3	1	0	*75.0*	*100.0*	4	1	2	1	*25.0*	*75.0*
Machynlleth	5–9	42	16	23	3	*38.1*	*92.9*	25	10	14	1	*40.0*	*96.0*	17	6	9	2	*35.3*	*88.2*
(Mont) RD)	10–14	30	4	24	2	*13.3*	*93.3*	14	1	12	1	*7.1*	*92.9*	16	3	12	1	*18.8*	*93.8*
	15–24	71	12	54	5	*16.9*	*93.0*	30	7	21	2	*23.3*	*93.3*	41	5	33	3	*12.2*	*92.7*
	25–44	131	25	94	12	*19.1*	*90.8*	50	11	36	3	*22.0*	*94.0*	81	14	58	9	*17.3*	*88.9*
	45–64	90	26	52	12	*28.9*	*86.7*	39	10	24	5	*25.6*	*87.2*	51	16	28	7	*31.4*	*86.3*
	65–	40	27	11	2	*67.5*	*95.0*	19	13	5	1	*68.4*	*94.7*	21	14	6	1	*66.7*	*95.2*
CAERNARFONSHIRE																			
Bangor City MB	All 3+	10658	597	7672	2238	*5.7*	*78.7*	4871	278	3562	959	*5.8*	*80.0*	5787	319	4110	1279	*5.6*	*77.6*
	3–4	393	87	182	91	*24.2*	*74.7*	201	47	97	38	*25.8*	*79.1*	192	40	85	53	*22.5*	*70.2*
	5–9	1071	101	751	195	*9.6*	*81.4*	520	51	359	101	*10.0*	*80.2*	551	50	392	94	*9.3*	*82.5*
	10–14	1053	20	797	216	*1.9*	*79.1*	522	9	405	99	*1.8*	*80.7*	531	11	392	117	*2.1*	*77.5*
	15–24	2127	25	1587	490	*1.2*	*76.7*	894	10	713	157	*1.1*	*82.1*	1233	15	874	333	*1.2*	*72.7*
	25–44	3389	117	2495	745	*3.5*	*77.8*	1521	55	1130	323	*3.6*	*78.6*	1868	62	1365	422	*3.4*	*77.2*
	45–64	1985	145	1430	395	*7.4*	*79.9*	964	63	691	202	*6.6*	*78.9*	1021	82	739	193	*8.1*	*81.0*
	65–	640	102	430	106	*16.0*	*83.3*	249	43	167	39	*17.3*	*84.3*	391	59	263	67	*15.1*	*82.6*

Bethesda UD	All 3+	4455	2467	1887	43	56.1	99.0	2143	1224	873	16	57.9	99.2	2312	1243	1014	27	54.4	98.8
	3–4	199	167	11	1	93.3	99.4	93	78	4	0	95.1	100.0	106	89	7	1	91.8	99.0
	5–9	442	343	85	2	79.8	99.5	224	170	47	2	77.6	99.1	218	173	38	0	82.0	100.0
	10–14	423	179	235	0	43.2	100.0	205	84	116	0	42.0	100.0	218	95	119	0	44.4	100.0
	15–24	675	249	413	5	37.3	99.3	367	156	201	3	43.3	99.2	308	93	212	2	30.3	99.3
	25–44	1283	581	673	24	45.5	98.1	613	289	315	8	47.2	98.7	670	292	358	16	43.8	97.6
	45–64	974	608	357	6	62.6	99.4	459	310	146	2	67.7	99.6	515	298	211	4	58.1	99.2
	65–	459	340	113	5	74.2	98.9	182	137	44	1	75.3	99.5	277	203	69	4	73.6	98.6
Betws-y-coed UD[3]	All 3+	886	123	606	111	14.6	86.8	399	60	274	42	16.0	88.8	487	63	332	69	13.6	85.1
	3–4	25	9	8	1	50.0	94.4	15	6	5	1	50.0	91.7	10	3	3	0	50.0	100.0
	5–9	85	15	57	5	19.5	93.5	48	9	30	3	21.4	92.9	37	6	27	2	17.1	94.3
	10–14	81	5	69	3	6.5	96.1	50	4	42	1	8.5	97.9	31	1	27	2	3.3	93.3
	15–24	164	12	125	20	7.6	87.3	61	7	48	5	11.7	91.7	103	5	77	15	5.2	84.5
	25–44	276	24	196	42	9.2	84.0	119	13	84	16	11.5	85.8	157	11	112	26	7.4	82.6
	45–64	183	31	115	32	17.4	82.0	81	12	53	13	15.4	83.3	102	19	62	19	19.0	81.0
	65–	72	27	36	8	38.0	88.7	25	9	12	3	37.5	87.5	47	18	24	5	38.3	89.4
Caernarfon MB	All 3+	8647	1469	6285	840	17.1	90.2	3995	687	2894	386	17.3	90.2	4652	782	3391	454	16.9	90.2
	3–4	321	179	92	32	59.1	89.4	164	95	48	15	60.1	90.5	157	84	44	17	57.9	88.3
	5–9	834	275	474	85	33.0	89.8	432	148	244	40	34.3	90.7	402	127	230	45	31.6	88.8
	10–14	842	96	688	58	11.4	93.1	404	49	329	26	12.1	93.6	438	47	359	32	10.7	92.7
	15–24	1579	133	1325	113	8.5	92.7	682	57	579	43	8.4	93.5	897	76	746	70	8.5	92.0
	25–44	2688	287	2071	312	10.7	88.3	1225	129	940	141	10.7	88.3	1463	158	1131	171	10.8	88.3
	45–64	1762	323	1252	181	18.4	89.7	822	143	585	91	17.5	88.9	940	180	667	90	19.2	90.4
	65–	621	176	383	59	28.5	90.5	266	66	169	30	24.9	88.7	355	110	214	29	31.2	91.8
Conwy MB	All 3+	4962	229	3185	1452	4.7	70.2	2315	113	1534	632	5.0	72.3	2647	116	1651	820	4.5	68.3
	3–4	193	39	82	57	21.9	68.0	90	21	36	29	24.4	66.3	103	18	46	28	19.6	69.6
	5–9	483	26	303	120	5.8	73.3	228	19	135	59	8.9	72.3	255	7	168	61	3.0	74.2
	10–14	491	7	376	95	1.5	80.1	239	1	181	50	0.4	78.4	252	6	195	45	2.4	81.7
	15–24	938	23	671	234	2.5	74.8	450	10	343	92	2.2	79.3	488	13	328	142	2.7	70.6
	25–44	1607	41	1001	552	2.6	65.4	731	19	481	230	2.6	68.5	876	22	520	322	2.5	62.7
	45–64	971	59	599	306	6.1	68.3	452	27	288	134	6.0	70.2	519	32	311	172	6.2	66.6
	65–	279	34	153	88	12.4	68.0	125	16	70	38	12.9	69.4	154	18	83	50	11.9	66.9
Cricieth UD	All 3+	1333	243	968	107	18.4	91.9	513	107	372	30	21.0	94.1	820	136	596	77	16.8	90.5
	3–4	51	32	11	3	69.6	93.5	22	15	6	0	71.4	100.0	29	17	5	3	68.0	88.0
	5–9	113	45	59	4	41.7	96.3	48	24	21	1	52.2	97.8	65	21	38	3	33.9	95.2
	10–14	110	14	94	1	12.8	99.1	59	11	46	1	19.0	98.3	51	3	48	0	5.9	100.0
	15–24	232	16	203	12	6.9	94.8	75	3	70	2	4.0	97.3	157	13	133	10	8.3	93.6
	25–44	395	37	315	42	9.4	89.3	149	12	126	11	8.1	92.6	246	25	189	31	10.2	87.3
	45–64	302	55	213	33	18.3	89.0	112	27	73	12	24.1	89.3	190	28	140	21	14.8	88.9
	65–	130	44	73	12	34.1	90.7	48	15	30	3	31.3	93.8	82	29	43	9	35.8	88.9

District[1]	Age last birth-day	Number[2] Total in age group	Welsh only	Both	English only	Percentage[3] Welsh only	Able to speak Welsh	Number[2] Total in age group	Welsh only	Both	English only	Percentage[3] Welsh only	Able to speak Welsh	Number[2] Total in age group	Welsh only	Both	English only	Percentage[3] Welsh only	Able to speak Welsh
		Persons						Males						Females					
Llandudno UD	All 3+	10008	129	4243	5410	*1.3*	*44.7*	4018	64	1842	2034	*1.6*	*48.3*	5990	65	2401	3376	*1.1*	*42.2*
	3–4	345	9	107	182	*3.0*	*38.9*	152	4	44	86	*3.0*	*35.8*	193	5	63	96	*3.0*	*41.5*
	5–9	830	7	287	494	*0.9*	*37.3*	417	3	148	247	*0.8*	*37.9*	413	4	139	247	*1.0*	*36.6*
	10–14	883	3	413	438	*0.4*	*48.7*	423	2	194	212	*0.5*	*48.0*	460	1	219	226	*0.2*	*49.3*
	15–24	2041	11	971	1017	*0.5*	*49.1*	741	7	373	346	*1.0*	*52.1*	1300	4	598	671	*0.3*	*47.3*
	25–44	3440	37	1417	1946	*1.1*	*42.7*	1303	18	632	649	*1.4*	*50.0*	2137	19	785	1297	*0.9*	*38.2*
	45–64	1892	39	825	1008	*2.1*	*46.1*	755	20	371	359	*2.7*	*52.1*	1137	19	454	649	*1.7*	*42.1*
	65–	577	23	223	325	*4.0*	*43.1*	227	10	80	135	*4.4*	*40.0*	350	13	143	190	*3.8*	*45.1*
Llanfairfechan UD	All 3+	2792	547	1712	454	*20.2*	*83.3*	1319	323	789	168	*25.2*	*86.9*	1473	224	923	286	*15.6*	*80.0*
	3–4	137	65	27	17	*59.6*	*84.4*	69	36	12	6	*66.7*	*88.9*	68	29	15	11	*52.7*	*80.0*
	5–9	305	90	156	35	*32.0*	*87.5*	161	56	72	19	*38.1*	*87.1*	144	34	84	16	*25.4*	*88.1*
	10–14	266	31	205	23	*12.0*	*91.1*	120	14	95	8	*12.0*	*93.2*	146	17	110	15	*12.0*	*89.4*
	15–24	425	32	334	53	*7.6*	*87.4*	208	22	162	21	*10.7*	*89.8*	217	10	172	32	*4.7*	*85.0*
	25–44	915	140	609	161	*15.4*	*82.3*	431	86	286	57	*20.0*	*86.7*	484	54	323	104	*11.2*	*78.4*
	45–64	532	120	287	120	*22.8*	*77.2*	227	69	119	39	*30.4*	*82.8*	305	51	168	81	*17.0*	*73.0*
	65–	212	69	94	45	*33.2*	*78.4*	103	40	43	18	*39.6*	*82.2*	109	29	51	27	*27.1*	*74.8*
Penmaen-mawr UD	All 3+	3826	482	2491	726	*13.0*	*80.3*	1861	279	1235	284	*15.5*	*84.1*	1965	203	1256	442	*10.7*	*76.7*
	3–4	157	58	54	26	*41.7*	*80.6*	80	34	24	14	*46.6*	*79.5*	77	24	30	12	*36.4*	*81.8*
	5–9	427	78	262	58	*19.5*	*85.2*	223	48	135	29	*22.5*	*85.9*	204	30	127	29	*16.1*	*84.4*
	10–14	392	28	294	45	*7.6*	*87.7*	204	15	146	27	*8.0*	*85.6*	188	13	148	18	*7.3*	*89.9*
	15–24	654	16	515	101	*2.5*	*84.0*	324	7	268	33	*2.3*	*89.3*	330	9	247	68	*2.8*	*79.0*
	25–44	1249	131	845	255	*10.6*	*79.3*	597	79	419	93	*13.4*	*84.3*	652	52	426	162	*8.1*	*74.7*
	45–64	713	117	418	167	*16.7*	*76.2*	332	65	199	62	*19.9*	*81.0*	381	52	219	105	*13.8*	*72.1*
	65–	234	54	103	74	*23.4*	*68.0*	101	31	44	26	*30.7*	*74.3*	133	23	59	48	*17.7*	*63.1*
Pwllheli MB	All 3+	3587	897	2332	255	*25.7*	*92.7*	1616	428	1039	110	*27.1*	*93.0*	1971	469	1293	145	*24.6*	*92.4*
	3–4	150	87	30	9	*69.0*	*92.9*	78	48	14	6	*70.6*	*91.2*	72	39	16	3	*67.2*	*94.8*
	5–9	378	179	149	22	*51.1*	*93.7*	193	97	73	7	*54.8*	*96.0*	185	82	76	15	*47.4*	*91.3*
	10–14	331	60	243	14	*18.9*	*95.6*	164	39	119	2	*24.4*	*98.8*	167	21	124	12	*13.4*	*92.4*
	15–24	648	80	520	41	*12.5*	*93.6*	293	40	228	22	*13.8*	*92.4*	355	40	292	19	*11.4*	*94.6*
	25–44	1140	185	837	98	*16.5*	*91.3*	481	83	356	37	*17.4*	*92.2*	659	102	481	61	*15.8*	*90.5*
	45–64	678	185	427	59	*27.6*	*91.2*	304	84	191	28	*27.7*	*90.8*	374	101	236	31	*27.4*	*91.6*
	65–	262	121	126	12	*46.7*	*95.4*	103	37	58	8	*35.9*	*92.2*	159	84	68	4	*53.8*	*97.4*

Ynyscynhaearn UD	All 3+	4193	1098	2772	201	*27.0*	*95.0*	1848	494	1222	81	*27.5*	*95.4*	2345	604	1550	120	*26.6*	*94.7*
	3–4	182	119	28	9	*76.3*	*94.2*	81	50	14	4	*73.5*	*94.1*	101	69	14	5	*78.4*	*94.3*
	5–9	472	271	164	8	*61.2*	*98.2*	240	147	73	3	*65.9*	*98.7*	232	124	91	5	*56.4*	*97.7*
	10–14	429	92	309	10	*22.4*	*97.6*	195	50	136	4	*26.3*	*97.9*	234	42	173	6	*19.0*	*97.3*
	15–24	656	63	549	28	*9.8*	*95.6*	283	35	227	14	*12.7*	*94.9*	373	28	322	14	*7.7*	*96.2*
	25–44	1317	192	1007	96	*14.8*	*92.5*	563	73	451	34	*13.1*	*93.7*	754	119	556	62	*16.1*	*91.6*
	45–64	775	208	524	36	*27.1*	*95.3*	329	75	238	14	*22.9*	*95.7*	446	133	286	22	*30.2*	*95.0*
	65–	362	153	191	14	*42.7*	*96.1*	157	64	83	8	*41.3*	*94.8*	205	89	108	6	*43.8*	*97.0*
Conwy RD	All 3+	6698	1197	4141	1185	*18.3*	*81.8*	3341	653	2068	518	*20.1*	*84.0*	3357	544	2073	667	*16.6*	*79.7*
	3–4	319	111	100	65	*40.2*	*76.4*	166	63	47	37	*42.9*	*74.8*	153	48	53	28	*37.2*	*78.3*
	5–9	782	166	476	95	*22.5*	*87.1*	376	77	233	43	*21.8*	*87.8*	406	89	243	52	*23.2*	*86.5*
	10–14	736	75	562	82	*10.4*	*88.6*	357	40	269	36	*11.6*	*89.6*	379	35	293	46	*9.4*	*87.7*
	15–24	1092	106	796	173	*9.8*	*83.8*	585	72	428	72	*12.5*	*87.1*	507	34	368	101	*6.8*	*79.9*
	25–44	2180	270	1415	462	*12.6*	*78.5*	1096	170	707	197	*15.8*	*81.7*	1084	100	708	265	*9.3*	*75.3*
	45–64	1207	297	645	248	*25.0*	*79.2*	593	148	324	110	*25.4*	*81.1*	614	149	321	138	*24.5*	*77.3*
	65–	382	172	147	60	*45.4*	*84.2*	168	83	60	23	*50.0*	*86.1*	214	89	87	37	*41.8*	*82.6*
Geirionydd RD[3]	All 3+	4251	2023	1712	230	*51.0*	*94.2*	2107	1036	814	114	*52.7*	*94.2*	2144	987	898	116	*49.3*	*94.2*
	3–4	176	132	8	6	*90.4*	*95.9*	93	70	3	4	*90.9*	*94.8*	83	62	5	2	*89.9*	*97.1*
	5–9	451	296	89	21	*72.9*	*94.8*	222	148	42	11	*73.6*	*94.5*	229	148	47	10	*72.2*	*95.1*
	10–14	479	196	228	8	*45.4*	*98.1*	239	93	114	6	*43.7*	*97.2*	240	103	114	2	*47.0*	*99.1*
	15–24	702	211	403	32	*32.7*	*95.0*	371	125	202	12	*36.9*	*96.5*	331	86	201	20	*28.0*	*93.5*
	25–44	1265	528	593	90	*43.6*	*92.6*	622	272	277	47	*45.6*	*92.1*	643	256	316	43	*41.6*	*93.0*
	45–64	867	455	306	57	*55.6*	*93.0*	433	242	145	26	*58.6*	*93.7*	434	213	161	31	*52.6*	*92.3*
	65–	311	205	85	16	*67.0*	*94.8*	127	86	31	8	*68.8*	*93.6*	184	119	54	8	*65.7*	*95.6*
Glaslyn RD	All 3+	3131	1950	1005	94	*63.9*	*96.9*	1525	971	480	42	*65.0*	*97.2*	1606	979	525	52	*62.9*	*96.6*
	3–4	146	119	6	1	*94.4*	*99.2*	66	57	3	0	*95.0*	*100.0*	80	62	3	1	*93.9*	*98.5*
	5–9	373	317	35	4	*89.0*	*98.9*	182	158	17	0	*90.3*	*100.0*	191	159	18	4	*87.8*	*97.8*
	10–14	334	210	108	5	*65.0*	*98.5*	168	113	51	1	*68.5*	*99.4*	166	97	57	4	*61.4*	*97.5*
	15–24	544	264	248	17	*49.8*	*96.6*	290	157	113	10	*56.1*	*96.4*	254	107	135	7	*42.8*	*96.8*
	25–44	916	487	389	28	*53.9*	*96.9*	453	243	194	12	*54.1*	*97.3*	463	244	195	16	*53.6*	*96.5*
	45–64	575	364	180	27	*63.7*	*95.3*	271	168	88	14	*62.2*	*94.8*	304	196	92	13	*65.1*	*95.7*
	65–	243	189	39	12	*78.8*	*95.0*	95	75	14	5	*79.8*	*94.7*	148	114	25	7	*78.1*	*95.2*
Gwyrfai RD	All 3+	26661	16092	9576	418	*61.7*	*98.4*	13277	8326	4481	177	*64.1*	*98.6*	13384	7766	5095	241	*59.3*	*98.2*
	3–4	1133	885	72	23	*90.3*	*97.7*	549	427	30	15	*90.5*	*96.8*	584	458	42	8	*90.2*	*98.4*
	5–9	2931	2293	457	26	*82.6*	*99.1*	1494	1188	204	13	*84.6*	*99.1*	1437	1105	253	13	*80.6*	*99.1*
	10–14	2852	1537	1215	17	*55.5*	*99.4*	1464	844	567	8	*59.5*	*99.4*	1388	693	648	9	*51.3*	*99.3*
	15–24	4173	1749	2310	66	*42.4*	*98.4*	2273	1062	1157	21	*47.4*	*99.1*	1900	687	1153	45	*36.4*	*97.6*
	25–44	8018	4290	3479	167	*54.1*	*97.9*	3919	2234	1586	63	*57.5*	*98.4*	4099	2056	1893	104	*50.7*	*97.4*
	45–64	5457	3709	1608	97	*68.5*	*98.2*	2683	1881	745	47	*70.4*	*98.2*	2774	1828	863	50	*66.7*	*98.1*
	65–	2097	1629	435	22	*78.1*	*98.9*	895	690	192	10	*77.4*	*98.9*	1202	939	243	12	*78.6*	*99.0*

District[1]	Age last birth-day	Persons: Number[2] Total in age group	Persons: Welsh only	Persons: Both	Persons: English only	Persons: Percentage[3] *Welsh only*	Persons: Percentage[3] *Able to speak Welsh*	Males: Number[2] Total in age group	Males: Welsh only	Males: Both	Males: English only	Males: Percentage[3] *Welsh only*	Males: Percentage[3] *Able to speak Welsh*	Females: Number[2] Total in age group	Females: Welsh only	Females: Both	Females: English only	Females: Percentage[3] *Welsh only*	Females: Percentage[3] *Able to speak Welsh*
Llŷn RD	All 3+	15947	10138	5111	353	*65.0*	*97.7*	7757	4999	2420	169	*65.9*	*97.8*	8190	5139	2691	184	*64.1*	*97.7*
	3–4	637	506	31	21	*90.7*	*96.2*	334	258	13	14	*90.5*	*95.1*	303	248	18	7	*90.8*	*97.4*
	5–9	1501	1174	242	19	*81.8*	*98.7*	752	580	121	12	*81.3*	*98.3*	749	594	121	7	*82.3*	*99.0*
	10–14	1516	881	580	17	*59.6*	*98.8*	796	489	278	11	*62.9*	*98.6*	720	392	302	6	*56.0*	*99.1*
	15–24	2718	1372	1241	52	*51.5*	*98.0*	1373	768	549	25	*57.2*	*98.1*	1345	604	692	27	*45.7*	*98.0*
	25–44	4624	2638	1784	138	*57.9*	*97.0*	2170	1282	802	66	*59.6*	*96.9*	2454	1356	982	72	*56.3*	*97.0*
	45–64	3354	2329	920	73	*70.1*	*97.8*	1600	1091	473	27	*68.6*	*98.3*	1754	1238	447	46	*71.5*	*97.3*
	65–	1597	1238	313	33	*78.1*	*97.9*	732	531	184	14	*72.7*	*97.9*	865	707	129	19	*82.7*	*97.8*
Ogwen RD	All 3+	6309	2416	3452	347	*38.9*	*94.4*	3129	1249	1680	151	*40.6*	*95.1*	3180	1167	1772	196	*37.2*	*93.7*
	3–4	275	192	39	16	*77.7*	*93.5*	144	107	16	8	*81.7*	*93.9*	131	85	23	8	*73.3*	*93.1*
	5–9	644	331	269	24	*53.0*	*96.2*	322	169	134	9	*54.2*	*97.1*	322	162	135	15	*51.9*	*95.2*
	10–14	655	183	439	21	*28.5*	*96.7*	320	95	206	9	*30.6*	*97.1*	335	88	233	12	*26.4*	*96.4*
	15–24	1066	230	761	70	*21.7*	*93.4*	592	141	409	39	*23.9*	*93.4*	474	89	352	31	*18.9*	*93.4*
	25–44	1830	565	1116	133	*31.1*	*92.6*	883	294	532	50	*33.6*	*94.3*	947	271	584	83	*28.9*	*91.1*
	45–64	1317	611	631	66	*46.7*	*95.0*	640	319	288	29	*50.2*	*95.4*	677	292	343	37	*43.5*	*94.5*
	65–	522	304	197	17	*58.7*	*96.7*	228	124	95	7	*54.9*	*96.9*	294	180	102	10	*61.6*	*96.6*
ANGLESEY																			
Amlwch UD	All 3+	2570	884	1557	77	*35.1*	*96.9*	1118	418	643	33	*38.2*	*97.0*	1452	466	914	44	*32.7*	*96.9*
	3–4	115	82	11	5	*83.7*	*94.9*	55	41	4	3	*85.4*	*93.8*	60	41	7	2	*82.0*	*96.0*
	5–9	288	175	95	5	*63.6*	*98.2*	148	96	42	3	*68.1*	*97.9*	140	79	53	2	*59.0*	*98.5*
	10–14	272	73	187	6	*27.4*	*97.7*	150	41	103	3	*27.9*	*98.0*	122	32	84	3	*26.9*	*97.5*
	15–24	403	79	310	10	*19.8*	*97.5*	165	38	122	3	*23.3*	*98.2*	238	41	188	7	*17.4*	*97.0*
	25–44	681	167	484	22	*24.8*	*96.7*	274	73	191	7	*26.9*	*97.4*	407	94	293	15	*23.4*	*96.3*
	45–64	538	179	337	20	*33.4*	*96.3*	211	78	122	10	*37.1*	*95.2*	327	101	215	10	*31.0*	*96.9*
	65–	273	129	133	9	*47.6*	*96.7*	115	51	59	4	*44.7*	*96.5*	158	78	74	5	*49.7*	*96.8*
Beaumaris MB	All 3+	2131	101	1261	742	*4.8*	*64.7*	1025	61	586	364	*6.0*	*63.9*	1106	40	675	378	*3.7*	*65.4*
	3–4	88	14	25	44	*16.9*	*47.0*	45	11	9	22	*26.2*	*47.6*	43	3	16	22	*7.3*	*46.3*
	5–9	200	14	94	84	*7.3*	*56.3*	118	11	52	50	*9.7*	*55.8*	82	3	42	34	*3.8*	*57.0*
	10–14	219	2	144	70	*0.9*	*67.6*	99	1	73	23	*1.0*	*76.3*	120	1	71	47	*0.8*	*60.5*
	15–24	400	12	251	132	*3.0*	*66.2*	192	7	115	67	*3.7*	*63.9*	208	5	136	65	*2.4*	*68.4*
	25–44	668	23	364	277	*3.5*	*58.3*	325	10	173	141	*3.1*	*56.5*	343	13	191	136	*3.8*	*60.0*
	45–64	420	28	288	102	*6.7*	*75.6*	199	17	134	48	*8.5*	*75.9*	221	11	154	54	*5.0*	*75.3*
	65–	136	8	95	33	*5.9*	*75.7*	47	4	30	13	*8.5*	*72.3*	89	4	65	20	*4.5*	*77.5*

Holyhead UD	All 3+	10019	876	7078	1709	*9.1*	*82.3*	4879	415	3419	830	*8.9*	*82.1*	5140	461	3659	879	*9.2*	*82.4*
	3–4	423	122	165	68	*34.4*	*80.8*	226	75	80	37	*39.1*	*80.7*	197	47	85	31	*28.8*	*81.0*
	5–9	1195	183	756	199	*16.1*	*82.5*	623	102	388	104	*17.2*	*82.5*	572	81	368	95	*14.9*	*82.5*
	10–14	1087	43	839	172	*4.1*	*83.7*	539	20	425	78	*3.8*	*85.1*	548	23	414	94	*4.3*	*82.3*
	15–24	1795	57	1390	292	*3.3*	*83.1*	890	36	699	114	*4.2*	*86.3*	905	21	691	178	*2.4*	*80.0*
	25–44	3131	164	2296	577	*5.4*	*81.0*	1508	72	1083	290	*5.0*	*79.9*	1623	92	1213	287	*5.8*	*82.0*
	45–64	1805	176	1259	326	*10.0*	*81.4*	868	73	599	166	*8.7*	*80.0*	937	103	660	160	*11.2*	*82.7*
	65–	583	131	373	75	*22.6*	*87.0*	225	37	145	41	*16.6*	*81.6*	358	94	228	34	*26.4*	*90.4*
Llangefni UD	All 3+	1658	572	990	67	*35.1*	*95.8*	740	264	439	26	*36.2*	*96.3*	918	308	551	41	*34.2*	*95.3*
	3–4	68	49	10	3	*79.0*	*95.2*	27	19	6	2	*70.4*	*92.6*	41	30	4	1	*85.7*	*97.1*
	5–9	159	101	50	1	*66.4*	*99.3*	77	52	22	0	*70.3*	*100.0*	82	49	28	1	*62.8*	*98.7*
	10–14	160	52	103	3	*32.7*	*97.5*	73	28	42	2	*38.4*	*95.9*	87	24	61	1	*27.9*	*98.8*
	15–24	294	60	216	13	*20.7*	*95.2*	120	28	88	2	*23.7*	*98.3*	174	32	128	11	*18.6*	*93.0*
	25–44	507	125	348	30	*24.9*	*94.0*	220	53	151	13	*24.4*	*94.0*	287	72	197	17	*25.2*	*94.1*
	45–64	318	112	191	14	*35.3*	*95.6*	150	50	93	7	*33.3*	*95.3*	168	62	98	7	*37.1*	*95.8*
	65–	152	73	72	3	*49.3*	*98.0*	73	34	37	0	*47.9*	*100.0*	79	39	35	3	*50.6*	*96.1*
Menai Bridge UD	All 3+	1557	171	1151	188	*11.3*	*87.5*	702	86	529	65	*12.6*	*90.4*	855	85	622	123	*10.2*	*85.2*
	3–4	76	34	18	12	*53.1*	*81.3*	47	22	12	6	*55.0*	*85.0*	29	12	6	6	*50.0*	*75.0*
	5–9	160	25	116	10	*16.6*	*93.4*	81	15	58	5	*19.2*	*93.6*	79	10	58	5	*13.7*	*93.2*
	10–14	124	6	103	11	*5.0*	*90.8*	58	1	49	5	*1.8*	*90.9*	66	5	54	6	*7.7*	*90.8*
	15–24	258	15	212	26	*5.9*	*89.7*	118	8	103	4	*7.0*	*96.5*	140	7	109	22	*5.1*	*84.1*
	25–44	475	28	376	60	*6.0*	*87.1*	215	12	182	17	*5.7*	*91.9*	260	16	194	43	*6.3*	*83.0*
	45–64	312	37	216	53	*12.1*	*82.7*	131	17	88	24	*13.2*	*81.4*	181	20	128	29	*11.3*	*83.6*
	65–	152	26	110	16	*17.1*	*89.5*	52	11	37	4	*21.2*	*92.3*	100	15	73	12	*15.0*	*88.0*
Aethwy RD	All 3+	8212	3241	4017	693	*40.8*	*91.3*	4168	1646	1956	440	*40.7*	*89.1*	4044	1595	2061	253	*40.8*	*93.5*
	3–4	323	208	44	13	*78.5*	*95.1*	163	110	18	4	*83.3*	*97.0*	160	98	26	9	*73.7*	*93.2*
	5–9	855	487	253	47	*61.9*	*94.0*	441	255	133	25	*61.7*	*93.9*	414	232	120	22	*62.0*	*94.1*
	10–14	1007	299	486	186[4]	*30.8*	*80.8*	588	151	240	173[4]	*26.8*	*69.3*	419	148	246	13	*36.4*	*96.8*
	15–24	1411	379	865	130[4]	*27.6*	*90.5*	757	202	441	95[4]	*27.4*	*87.1*	654	177	424	35	*27.8*	*94.5*
	25–44	2287	728	1332	191	*32.3*	*91.5*	1101	368	634	86	*33.8*	*92.1*	1186	360	698	105	*31.0*	*91.0*
	45–64	1624	723	781	99	*45.1*	*93.8*	792	373	367	44	*47.6*	*94.4*	832	350	414	55	*42.7*	*93.3*
	65–	705	417	256	27	*59.6*	*96.1*	326	187	123	13	*57.9*	*96.0*	379	230	133	14	*61.0*	*96.3*
Dwyran RD	All 3+	2819	1687	1026	37	*61.3*	*98.7*	1296	798	449	19	*63.0*	*98.5*	1523	889	577	18	*59.9*	*98.8*
	3–4	127	105	6	2	*92.9*	*98.2*	68	54	5	2	*88.5*	*96.7*	59	51	1	0	*98.1*	*100.0*
	5–9	304	243	45	3	*83.5*	*99.0*	149	119	21	1	*84.4*	*99.3*	155	124	24	2	*82.7*	*98.7*
	10–14	299	163	123	3	*56.4*	*99.0*	142	83	54	2	*59.7*	*98.6*	157	80	69	1	*53.3*	*99.3*
	15–24	436	183	233	9	*43.1*	*97.9*	198	94	96	4	*48.5*	*97.9*	238	89	137	5	*38.5*	*97.8*
	25–44	781	410	346	15	*53.2*	*98.1*	342	189	141	8	*55.9*	*97.6*	439	221	205	7	*51.0*	*98.4*
	45–64	571	355	203	3	*63.3*	*99.5*	258	155	98	1	*61.0*	*99.6*	313	200	105	2	*65.1*	*99.3*
	65–	301	228	70	2	*76.0*	*99.3*	139	104	34	1	*74.8*	*99.3*	162	124	36	1	*77.0*	*99.4*

District[1]	Age last birth-day	Number[2] Total in age group	Welsh only	Both	English only	Percentage[3] Welsh only	Able to speak Welsh	Number[2] Total in age group	Welsh only	Both	English only	Percentage[3] Welsh only	Able to speak Welsh	Number[2] Total in age group	Welsh only	Both	English only	Percentage[3] Welsh only	Able to speak Welsh
		Persons						Males						Females					
Twrcelyn RD	All 3+	8813	4618	3778	177	*53.9*	*97.9*	4133	2279	1664	74	*56.7*	*98.2*	4680	2339	2114	103	*51.3*	*97.7*
	3–4	355	262	25	13	*87.3*	*95.7*	174	124	13	8	*85.5*	*94.5*	181	138	12	5	*89.0*	*96.8*
	5–9	874	604	190	15	*74.7*	*98.1*	428	294	88	6	*75.8*	*98.5*	446	310	102	9	*73.6*	*97.9*
	10–14	875	394	442	7	*46.7*	*99.2*	450	213	219	2	*49.1*	*99.5*	425	181	223	5	*44.3*	*98.8*
	15–24	1541	586	898	28	*38.8*	*98.1*	727	334	362	12	*47.2*	*98.3*	814	252	536	16	*31.3*	*98.0*
	25–44	2361	1112	1155	66	*47.7*	*97.2*	1073	549	490	26	*51.5*	*97.6*	1288	563	665	40	*44.4*	*96.8*
	45–64	1919	1073	785	41	*56.5*	*97.8*	900	518	360	18	*57.8*	*98.0*	1019	555	425	23	*55.3*	*97.7*
	65–	888	587	283	7	*66.9*	*99.2*	381	247	132	2	*64.8*	*99.5*	507	340	151	5	*68.5*	*99.0*
Valley RD	All 3+	10316	5284	4374	403	*52.5*	*96.0*	5087	2735	2057	167	*55.1*	*96.6*	5229	2549	2317	236	*50.0*	*95.4*
	3–4	445	341	34	13	*87.9*	*96.6*	225	162	18	9	*85.7*	*95.2*	220	179	16	4	*89.9*	*98.0*
	5–9	1104	771	247	33	*73.4*	*96.9*	591	418	129	17	*74.1*	*97.0*	513	353	118	16	*72.5*	*96.7*
	10–14	1055	475	524	30	*46.2*	*97.1*	546	267	253	14	*50.0*	*97.4*	509	208	271	16	*42.0*	*96.8*
	15–24	1832	699	1009	84	*39.0*	*95.3*	937	401	475	38	*43.8*	*95.7*	895	298	534	46	*33.9*	*94.8*
	25–44	2834	1208	1445	138	*43.3*	*95.1*	1312	595	649	50	*46.0*	*96.1*	1522	613	796	88	*40.9*	*94.1*
	45–64	2119	1167	843	77	*55.9*	*96.3*	1036	594	406	26	*57.9*	*97.5*	1083	573	437	51	*54.0*	*95.2*
	65–	927	623	272	28	*67.5*	*97.0*	440	298	127	13	*68.0*	*97.0*	487	325	145	15	*67.0*	*96.9*

Source: *Census of Population for England and Wales*: 1911, *Vol. XII, Language Spoken in Wales and Monmouthshire* (HMSO, 1913), Table 1; reprinted in *County Reports*, Table 33.

1 Abbreviations as follows: UD Urban District; MB Municipal Borough; CB County Borough; RD Rural District.

2 The totals for population aged 3 years and over include small numbers of those who either gave no statement as to language spoken or who entered other languages. The totals for Wales are as follows: no language statement: 58,517; other languages: 3,762.

3 The denominator excludes those who gave no language statement but includes those who entered other languages. In general the percentage giving no language statement was less than 3 per cent. In the following districts, however, in 1911 the percentage was greater than 5 per cent: Bedwellte UD (1,188, 5.8%), Monmouth MB (1,781, 35.7%), Rhymni (569, 5.4%), Chepstow RD (414, 5.6%), Pen-y-bont RD (1,185, 5.7%), Betws-y-coed UD (465, 5.2%), Geirionydd RD (285, 6.7%).

4 A note in the census remarks that the figures include a considerable number of English boys enumerated on board the Industrial School Ship 'Clio'.

Language 4.1 Local Surveys. Social surveys of the ironworks towns of Pontypool and Blaenafon, 1840; Merthyr Tydfil, 1841

	Pontypool[1] 1840[4]		Blaenafon[2] 1840[4]		Merthyr Tydfil[3] 1841[5]	
Population	17196		5115		32968	
Number of houses	2908		811		6145	
Sleeping rooms	5496		1602		10835	
Children under 3 yrs of age	1884		499		3203	
Children from 3 to 12 yrs	3547		982		6857	
Married people	5952		1670		..	
Lodgers	3537		1464		6140	
Welsh people	8821	*(51%)*	3134	*(61%)*	27802	*(84%)*
English people	7554	*(44%)*	1895	*(38%)*	4181	*(13%)*
Irish people	821	*(5%)*	86	*(1%)*	985	*(3%)*
Persons who cannot speak English	106		21		–	
as percentage of population from 3 yrs	*0.7%*		*0.5%*			
Persons who can speak English intelligibly	–		–		10917	
as percentage of population from 3 yrs					*36.7%*	
Children who go to school[6]	1022		306		1272	
Persons who say they do not go to any place of worship	2161		490		11759	
Houses having Bibles[7]	*80%*		701 (*86%*)		–	
Drunkards[8]	1962		400		2587	

Source: G. S. Kenrick, 'Statistics of the Population in the Parish of Trevethin (Pontypool) and at the Neighbouring Works of Blaenavon in Monmouthshire, chiefly employed in the Iron Trade, and inhabiting part of the District recently disturbed', *Journal of the Statistical Society of London*, III (1840–1), 366–75; idem, 'Statistics of Merthyr Tydvil', *Journal of the Royal Statistical Society of London*, IX (1846), 14–21.

1 The whole parish of Trevethin which includes the township of Pontypool.
2 Includes part of the adjoining parish to Trevethin containing workers in the Blaenafon Ironworks.
3 Excluding Coedcymer, hamlet of Faenor, Taff, and Cynon, and Forest-hill.
4 Kenrick fails to give the exact date of his Monmouthshire surveys. They were published in January 1841, and include Savings Bank returns for the year ending 30 November 1839, which suggest the surveys were undertaken sometime during early 1840.
5 Survey taken during Spring 1841.
6 For Pontypool and Blaenafon this number is of children 'who say they go to school'; for Merthyr Tydfil it is the number of children 'go to day-schools by report of their parents'.
7 Kenrick gave only the percentage and not the number of houses for Pontypool. For Merthyr Tydfil the equivalent information obtained was of the number of 'persons among the labouring classes who have other books besides religious books' (445).
8 For Blaenafon and Merthyr Tydfil, this is the number of 'persons who say they are drunkards' and 'workmen occasionally intoxicated' respectively. For Pontypool there is no qualification.

Language 4.2 Local Surveys. Montgomery survey. Language knowledge, by sex and age, in three parishes: Llanfair Caereinion, Castle Caereinion, and Manafon, 1846

a) Llanfair Caereinion[1]

Age in years	Number Welsh only	Welsh and English	English only	Total[2]	*Percentage in age group* *Welsh only*	*Welsh and English*	*English only*	*Total*
Males								
0–4	109	20	16	145	*75.2*	*13.8*	*11.0*	*100.0*
5–9	102	65	6	173	*59.0*	*37.6*	*3.5*	*100.0*
10–14	86	77	5	168	*51.2*	*45.8*	*3.0*	*100.0*
15–19	62	83	0	145	*42.8*	*57.2*	*0.0*	*100.0*
20–29	26	129	2	157	*16.6*	*82.2*	*1.3*	*100.0*
30–39	28	112	7[3]	147	*19.0*	*76.2*	*4.8*	*100.0*
40–49	29	89	1	119	*24.4*	*74.8*	*0.8*	*100.0*
50–59	16	89	2	107	*15.0*	*83.2*	*1.9*	*100.0*
60–69	15	66	2	83	*18.1*	*79.5*	*2.4*	*100.0*
70–	14	43	1	58	*24.1*	*74.1*	*1.7*	*100.0*
n.g.	8	7	4	19				
Total	**495**	**780**	**46**	**1321**	***37.5***	***59.0***	***3.5***	***100.0***
Females								
0–4	112	24	9	145	*77.2*	*16.6*	*6.2*	*100.0*
5–9	106	57	8	171	*62.0*	*33.3*	*4.7*	*100.0*
10–14	86	78	2	166	*51.8*	*47.0*	*1.2*	*100.0*
15–19	56	73	3[3]	132	*42.4*	*55.3*	*2.3*	*100.0*
20–29	56	109	6[3]	171	*59.1*	*63.7*	*3.5*	*100.0*
30–39	56	101	5	162	*34.6*	*62.3*	*3.1*	*100.0*
40–49	54	90	2	146	*37.0*	*61.6*	*1.4*	*100.0*
50–59	37	65	1	103	*35.9*	*63.1*	*1.0*	*100.0*
60–69	28	54	1	83	*33.7*	*65.1*	*1.2*	*100.0*
70–	25	39	0	64	*39.0*	*60.9*	*0.0*	*100.0*
n.g	3	7	6	16				
Total	**619**	**697**	**43**	**1359**	***45.5***	***51.3***	***3.2***	***100.0***

b) Castle Caereinion[4]

Age in years	Number Welsh only	Welsh and English	English only	Total[5]	*Percentage in age group[6]* *Welsh only*	*Welsh and English*	*English only*	*Total*
Males								
0–4	14	5	23	42	*33*	*12*	*55*	*100.0*
5–9	7	19	16	42	*17*	*45*	*38*	*100.0*
10–14	0	22	18	40	*0*	*55*	*45*	*100.0*
15–19	0	20	19	39	*0*	*51*	*49*	*100.0*
20–29	3	49	17	69	*4*	*71*	*25*	*100.0*
30–39	0	22	6	28	*0*	*79*	*21*	*100.0*
40–49	0	26	10	36	*0*	*72*	*28*	*100.0*
50–59	0	23	0	23	*0*	*100*	*0*	*100.0*
60–69	1	19	2	22	*5*	*86*	*9*	*100.0*
70–	1	6	1	8	*13*	*75*	*13*	*100.0*
n.g.	0	2	3	5				
Total	**26**	**213**	**115**	**354**	***7.3***	***60.2***	***32.5***	***100.0***
Females								
0–4	7	9	15	31	*23*	*29*	*48*	*100.0*
5–9	4	15	13	32	*13*	*47*	*41*	*100.0*
10–14	2	17	14	33	*6*	*52*	*42*	*100.0*
15–19	1	21	7	29	*3*	*72*	*24*	*100.0*
20–29	3	35	13	51	*6*	*69*	*25*	*100.0*
30–39	2	24	7	33	*6*	*73*	*21*	*100.0*
40–49	3	19	4	26	*12*	*73*	*15*	*100.0*
50–59	0	12	7	19	*0*	*63*	*37*	*100.0*
60–69	2	12	4	18	*11*	*67*	*22*	*100.0*
70–	2	9	0	11	*18*	*82*	*0*	*100.0*
n.g	0	5	1	6				
Total	**26**	**178**	**85**	**289**	***9.0***	***61.6***	***29.4***	***100.0***

c) Manafon[7]

Age in years	Number Welsh only	Welsh and English	English only	Total[8]	Percentage in age group[6] Welsh only	Welsh and English	English only	Total
Males								
0–4	25	7	24	56	*45*	*13*	*43*	*100.0*
5–9	15	11	14	40	*38*	*28*	*35*	*100.0*
10–14	13	32	12	57	*23*	*56*	*21*	*100.0*
15–19	10	23	8	41	*24*	*56*	*20*	*100.0*
20–29	5	39	7	51	*10*	*76*	*14*	*100.0*
30–39	7	36	8	51	*14*	*71*	*16*	*100.0*
40–49	4	24	2	30	*13*	*80*	*7*	*100.0*
50–59	4	21	0	25	*16*	*84*	*0*	*100.0*
60–69	3	14	3	20	*15*	*70*	*15*	*100.0*
70–	6	15	0	21	*29*	*71*	*0*	*100.0*
n.g.	0	9	0	9				
Total	**92**	**231**	**78**	**401**	***22.9***	***57.6***	***19.5***	***100.0***
Females								
0–4	26	3	20	49	*53*	*6*	*41*	*100.0*
5–9	18	22	25	65	*28*	*34*	*38*	*100.0*
10–14	14	24	13	51	*27*	*47*	*25*	*100.0*
15–19	11	19	7	37	*30*	*51*	*19*	*100.0*
20–29	11	35	7	53	*21*	*66*	*13*	*100.0*
30–39	8	33	4	45	*18*	*73*	*9*	*100.0*
40–49	7	19	7	33	*21*	*58*	*21*	*100.0*
50–59	4	18	3	25	*16*	*72*	*12*	*100.0*
60–69	3	15	1	19	*16*	*79*	*5*	*100.0*
70–	12	11	1	24	*50*	*46*	*4*	*100.0*
n.g	0	5	0	5				
Total	**114**	**204**	**88**	**406**	***28.1***	***50.2***	***21.7***	***100.0***

Source: NLW MS 23220E, A survey of the state of education in and around the parishes of Castle Caereinion, Llanfair Caereinion and Manafon, county Montgomery, carried out, December 1846, by representatives of local nonconformist denominations under the supervision of the Reverend Robert David Thomas ('Iorthryn Gwynedd', 1817–88), minister of Penarth Congregational chapel, Llanfair Caereinion.

1 Figures in this table exclude seven whose sex could not be ascertained from the information given.
2 Excludes 26 males and 23 females whose language ability was not given; nearly all were in the age group 0–4.
3 Includes one of a family with additional language knowledge of Hindustani, having lived for some time in India.
4 Figures in this table exclude five whose sex could not be ascertained from the information given.
5 Excludes four males and five females whose language ability was not given; nearly all were in the age group 0–4 years.
6 As the totals in each age group are relatively small, the percentages are given only to the nearest whole number.
7 Figures in this table exclude one whose sex could not be ascertained from the information given.
8 Excludes seven males and eight females whose language ability was not given; nearly all were in the age group 0–4 years.

Language 4.3 Local Surveys. Montgomery survey. Language of heads of households, males and females, in three parishes: Llanfair Caereinion, Castle Caereinion, and Manafon, 1846

Parish	Number Welsh only	Welsh and English	English only	Total	Percentage Welsh only	Welsh and English	English only	Total
Llanfair Caereinion								
Males	98	373	13[1]	484	*20.2*	*77.1*	*2.7*	*100.0*
Females	23	40	0	63	*36.5*	*63.5*	–	*100.0*
Total	121	413	13	547	*22.1*	*75.5*	*2.4*	*100.0*
Castle Caereinion								
Males	2	94	20	116	*1.7*	*81.0*	*17.2*	*100.0*
Females	0	5	3	8	–	*62.5*	*37.5*	*100.0*
Total	2	99	23	124	*1.6*	*79.8*	*18.5*	*100.0*
Manafon								
Males	14	100	14	128	*10.9*	*78.1*	*10.9*	*100.0*
Females	4	16	3	23	*17.4*	*69.6*	*13.0*	*100.0*
Total	18	116	17	151	*11.9*	*76.8*	*11.3*	*100.0*

Source: As Table 4.2.
1 Includes one also able to speak Hindustani.

Language 4.4 Local Surveys. Montgomery survey. Language knowledge, by nationality, males and females, in three parishes: Llanfair Caereinion, Castle Caereinion, and Manafon, 1846

Nationality	Welsh only	Welsh and English	English only	Total	*Per-centage*	Welsh only	Welsh and English	English only	Total	*Per-centage*
	Males					Females				
Llanfair Caereinion[1]										
Welsh	495	764	20	1279	*97.1*	619	684	19	1322	*97.3*
English	–	15	25[2]	40	*3.0*	–	12[3]	24[4]	36	*2.7*
Total	495	779	45	1319	*100.0*	619	696	43	1358	*100.0*
Castle Caereinion[5]										
Welsh	25	206	64	295	*84.0*	25	177	50	252	*87.2*
English	1	7	48	56	*16.0*	1	1	35	37	*12.8*
Total	26	213	112	351	*100.0*	26	178	85	289	*100.0*
Manafon[6]										
Welsh	92	231	65	388	*96.8*	114	204	74	392	*96.6*
English	–	–	13	13	*3.2*	–	–	14	14	*3.4*
Total	92	231	88	401	*100.0*	114	204	88	406	*100.0*

Source: As Table 4.2.

1 These figures exclude two males and one female whose nationality is not given.
2 Includes three Scots.
3 Includes one Irish.
4 Includes one Scot.
5 These figures exclude four males and five females whose nationality or language ability is not given.
6 These figures exclude seven males and eight females whose nationality or language ability is not given.

Language 4.5 Local Surveys. Montgomery survey. Language knowledge, by occupation, males and females, in three parishes: Llanfair Caereinion, Castle Caereinion, and Manafon, 1846

a) Llanfair Caereinion

Males[1] Occupation	Knowledge of language: Welsh only	Welsh & English	English only	Total
Gentleman	–	1	1	2
Minister	–	7	–	7
Schoolmaster	–	3	–	3
Parish/govt. official[3]	1	4	1	6
Surgeon	–	3	–	3
Auctioneer	–	1	–	1
Farmer	32	147	1	180
Farmers' relatives	20	71	–	91
Farm servants	46	49	1	96
Rural craftsmen etc.[4]	13	103	3	119
Manufacturer[5]	–	1	–	1
Woollen worker[6]	6	10	–	16
Innkeeper	–	2	–	2
Shopkeeper/dealer	–	23	–	23
Tollgate-keeper	1	4	–	5
Carrier	–	6	–	6
Labourer	47	89	2	138
Servant	8	29	1	38
Pauper[7]	2	2	–	4
Other	–	11	–	11
Not given	20	52	6	78
Total	**196**	**618**	**17**	**831**
Percentage	*23.6*	*73.4*	*2.0*	*100.0*

Females[2] Occupation	Knowledge of language: Welsh only	Welsh & English	English only	Total
Day school-keeper	–	1	–	1
Farmer	3	4	–	7
Farm servant	49	21	–	70
Shopkeeper	1	4	–	5
Chandler	–	1	–	1
Coal dealer	–	1	–	1
Dressmaker	–	2	–	2
Innkeeper	–	1	–	1
Turnpike-gate keeper	–	1	–	1
Weaver	1	–	–	1
Servant	14	37	1	52
Prostitute[8]	–	1	–	1
Pauper[7]	3	3	–	6
Other[9]	–	2	–	2
Total	**71**	**80**	**1**	**152**
Percentage	*46.7*	*52.6*	*0.7*	*100.0*

b) Castle Caereinion

Males[1] Occupation	Knowledge of language Welsh only	Welsh & English	English only	Total
Gentleman	–	–	2	2
Minister	–	1	–	1
Schoolmaster	–	1	–	1
Farmer	1	42	9	52
Farmers' relatives	–	18	11	29
Farm servants	3	34	9	46
Rural craftsmen	–	19	8	27
Labourer	1	34	4	39
Servant	–	10	6	16
Other	–	1	–	1
Not given	–	7	9	16
Total	**5**	**167**	**58**	**230**
Percentage	*2.2*	*72.6*	*25.2*	*100.0*

Females[2] Occupation	Knowledge of language Welsh only	Welsh & English	English only	Total
Farmer	–	1	–	1
Farm servant	3	19	5	27
Shopkeeper	–	1	–	1
Servant	1	7	2	10
Total	**4**	**28**	**7**	**39**

c) Manafon

Males[1] Occupation	Knowledge of language Welsh only	Welsh & English	English only	Total
Gentleman	–	–	1	1
Minister	–	1	–	1
Schoolmaster	–	1	–	1
Farmer	8	54	6	68
Farmers' relatives	6	20	3	29
Farm servants	12	26	6	44
Rural craftsmen	2	17	4	23
Manufacturer[10]	–	7	–	7
Woollen worker[11]	2	7	3	12
Innkeeper	–	1	2	3
Servant	1	6	1	8
Labourer	2	16	2	20
Pauper[7]	–	2	–	2
Not given	6	10	1	17
Total	**39**	**173**	**29**	**241**
Percentage	*16.2*	*71.8*	*12.0*	*100.0*

Females[2] Occupation	Knowledge of language Welsh only	Welsh & English	English only	Total
Farmer	–	2	2	4
Farm servant	10	13	5	28
Dressmaker	–	2	–	2
Spinner	1	–	–	1
Shopkeeper	–	1	–	1
Servant	1	1	1	3
Pauper[7]	1	–	–	1
Total	**13**	**19**	**8**	**40**

Source: As Table 4.2.

[1] Males aged 15 years and over. Unless otherwise indicated, sons and other male relatives are classified according to the occupation of the household head. Thus a 'carpenter's son' is classified as a rural craftsman.
[2] Females aged 15 years and over, included only where an occupation is defined *not* in relation to the male head of household (i.e. excludes carpenter's wife etc.).
[3] Includes parish clerk, relieving officer, assistant overseer, excise officer.
[4] Includes carpenter, cooper, mason, miller, sadler, sawyer, shoemaker, smith, tailor, tanner, wheelwright.
[5] Unspecified but probably woollen goods.
[6] Includes carder, dyer, spinner, weaver.
[7] Receiving 'outdoor' Poor Law relief.
[8] This description of a 39 year-old woman living alone with four children was inserted in the comments column, with an exclamation mark.
[9] Illegible entry.
[10] Probably all woollen manufacturers.
[11] Includes carder, fuller, spinner, weaver.

Map A: Language zones in the mid-nineteenth century

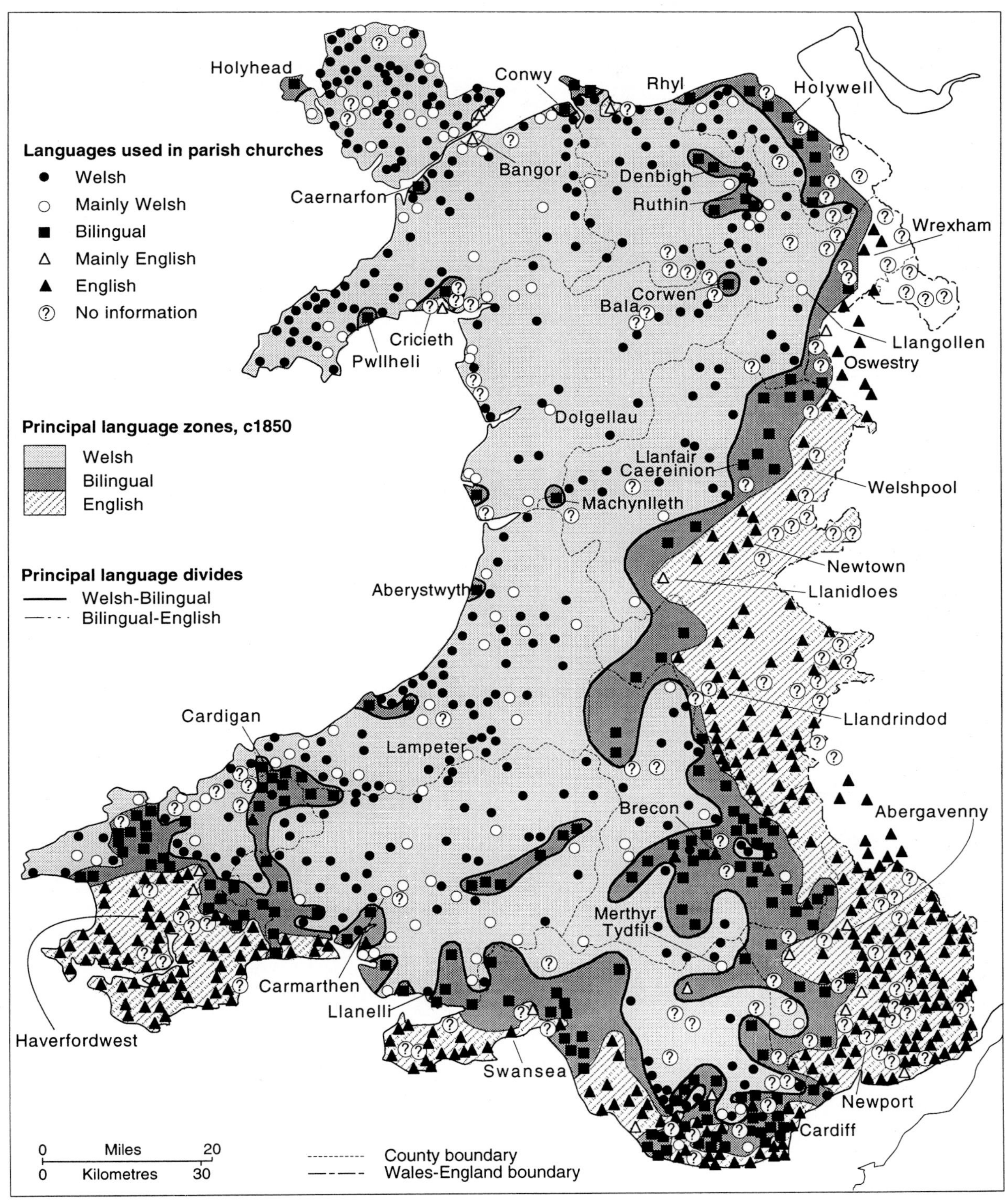

Sources: NLW MSS: SA/RD/52 (*c.* 1844); SD/QA/18, 77, 140, 206 (1848); LL/QA/35–7 (1848); B/QA/27 (*c.* 1850).

Map B: Language changes 1749–*c.*1900

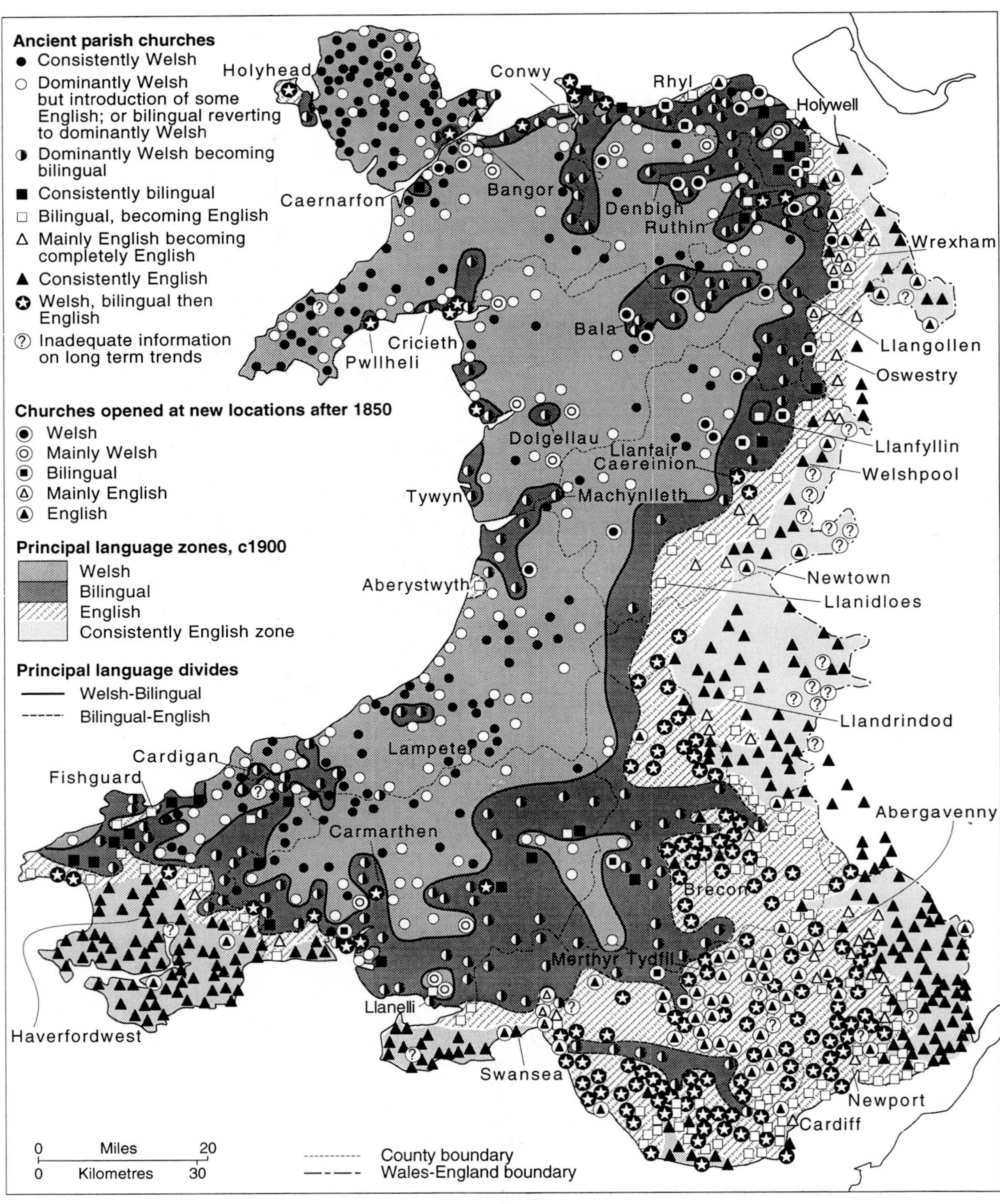

Sources: (1) NLW MSS: B/QA/2 (1749), 19–20 (1811), 27 (*c.* 1850), 33 (1900); SA/RD/26 (1749), 52 (*c.* 1844), SA/QA/15 (1809), 28 (1902); SD/QA/1, 61, 120, 180 (1755), 5–6, 65, 124–5, 187 (1807), 18, 77, 140, 206 (1848), 54, 114, 175, 248 (1900); LL/QA/4–5 (1771), 22 (1809), 35–7 (1848); (2) 'Report by Sir John Williams', *Report, Royal Commission on the Church of England and Other Religious Bodies in Wales and Monmouthshire* (London, 1910), pp. 301–95; (3) See also W. T. R. Pryce, 'Welsh and English in Wales, 1750–1971: A Spatial Analysis based on the Linguistic Affiliation of Parochial Communities', *Bulletin of the Board of Celtic Studies* XXVIII, pt. 1 (1978), 1–36.

Map C: Percentage of the population aged 2 and over able to speak Welsh, 1891 Census

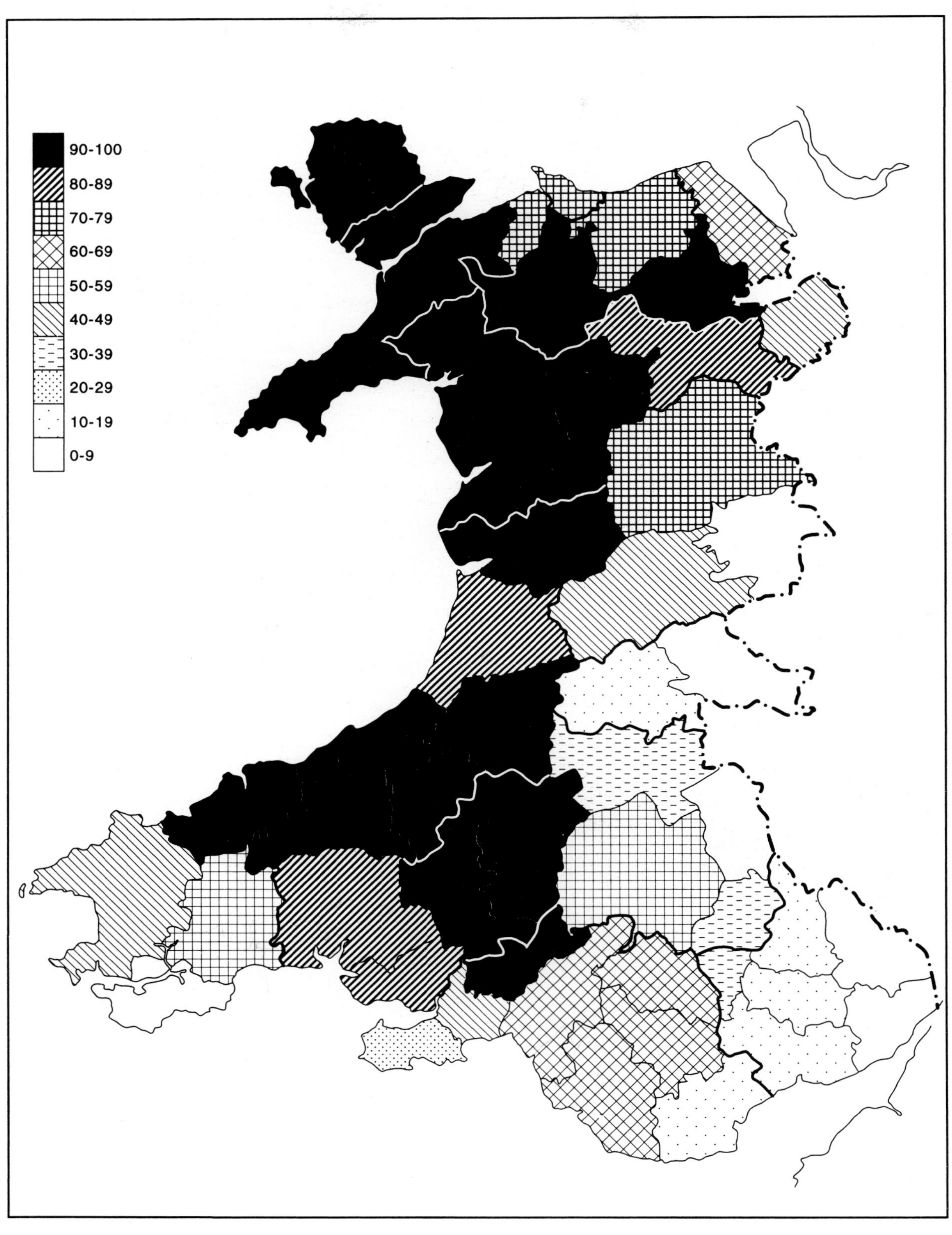

Source: 1891 Census by Registration Districts.

Map D: Percentage of the population aged 3 and over able to speak Welsh, 1901 Census

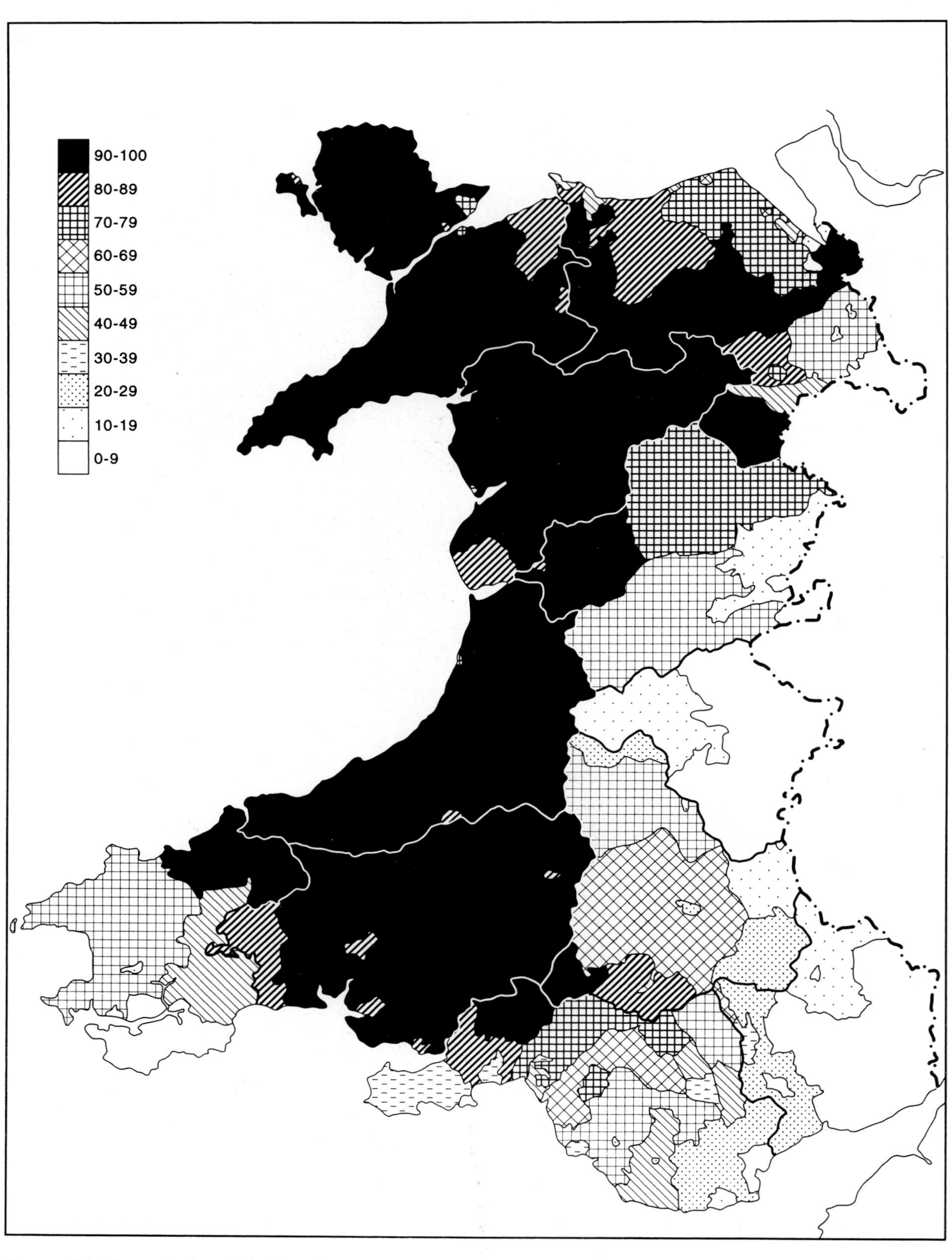

Source: 1901 Census by Local Administration Areas.

Map E: Percentage of the population aged 3 and over able to speak Welsh, 1911 Census

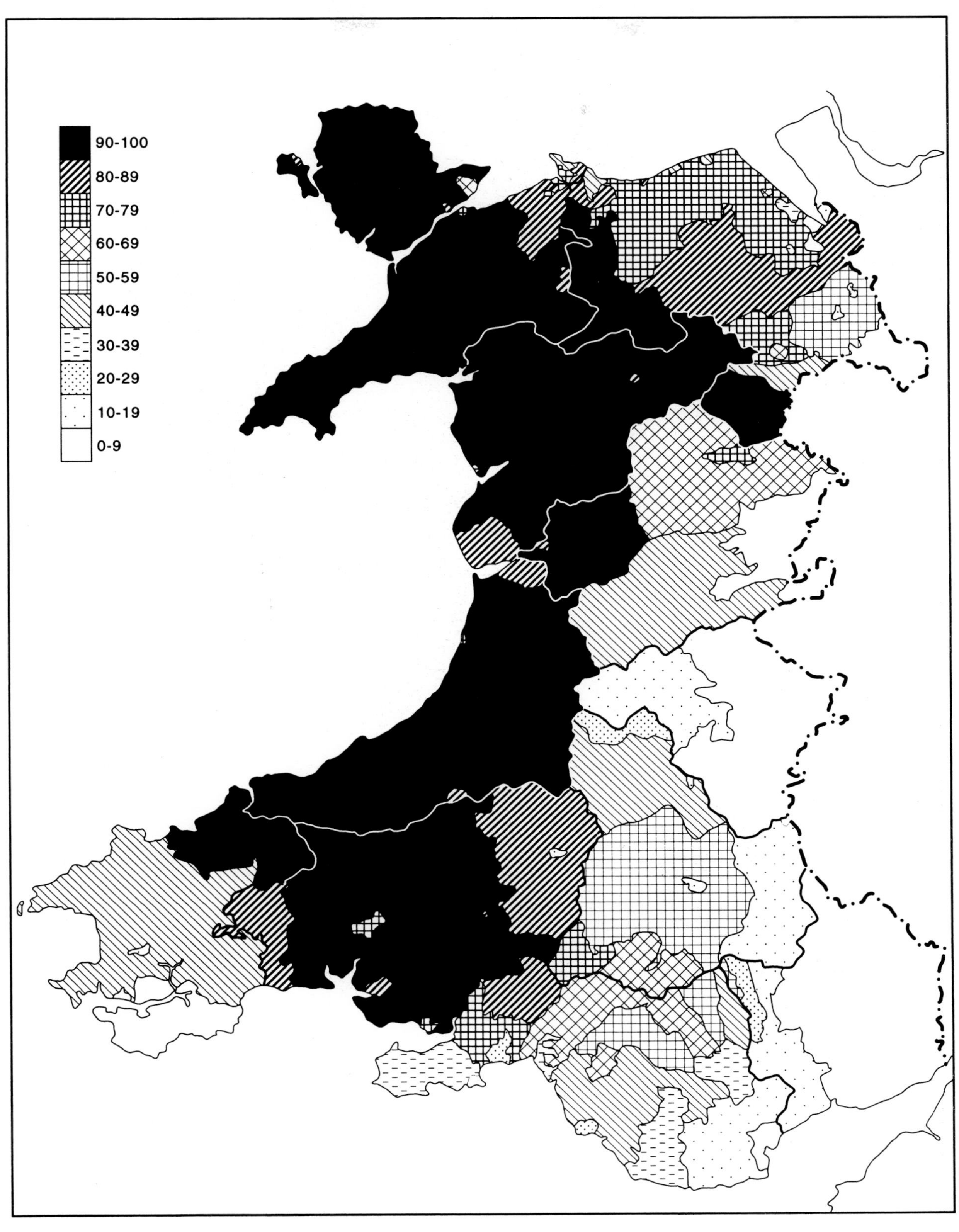

Source: 1911 Census by Local Administration Areas.

III

Education

Addysg

Rhagymadrodd

O'r holl feysydd cyhoeddus allweddol y mae a wnelont â'r iaith Gymraeg, addysg oedd yr un a ddioddefodd fwyaf yn sgil dylanwadau Seisnig yn ystod y bedwaredd ganrif ar bymtheg. Amlygwyd rhagfarn ddofn a hyd yn oed elyniaeth at y Gymraeg nid yn unig gan gomisiynwyr y llywodraeth ac Arolygwyr Ysgolion Ei Mawrhydi ond hefyd gan y dosbarth canol 'blaengar' Cymreig. Gan fynnu bod y Saesneg yn hanfodol well, fe'u gyrrid gan argyhoeddiad fod y Gymraeg yn rhwystr cymdeithasol difrifol i bobl Cymru.

Am ran helaethaf y bedwaredd ganrif ar bymtheg, y mae'n anodd darganfod unrhyw dystiolaeth, ystadegol nac fel arall, sy'n awgrymu i'r Gymraeg gael ei defnyddio naill ai yn gyfrwng hyfforddiant neu yn bwnc a deilyngai ei astudio yn ysgolion dyddiol cyffredin Cymru.[1] Gellir priodoli'r ffaith fod cymaint yn parhau i siarad Cymraeg yn eu bywyd bob dydd nid yn unig i amherthnasedd llawer o'u haddysg ysgol ddyddiol brin, ond yn fwy neilltuol i sefydliad yr ysgol Sul Ymneilltuol Cymraeg yr oedd ei gweithgareddau'n cwmpasu'r gymuned gyfan. Gan ddilyn meysydd llafur penodol, a hynny mewn dosbarthiadau bychain, dysgai oedolion yn ogystal â phlant ddarllen Cymraeg, adrodd holwyddoregau, a thrafod cynnwys y Beibl a thestunau crefyddol yn bur fanwl. Cynhelid arholiadau blynyddol a chyflwynid tystysgrifau. Trefnid eisteddfodau a chyhoeddid papurau newydd, cyfnodolion a thestunau crefyddol Cymraeg gan y gwahanol enwadau. Mewn un flwyddyn, sef 1907, honnwyd bod 100,000 o gopïau o bum llyfr yn *Cyfres Newydd y Plant*, cyfres a baratowyd ar gyfer dosbarthiadau ysgol Sul yr Annibynwyr, wedi eu gwerthu am ddwy geiniog yr un.[2] Fel hyn y câi crefydd, addysg a diwylliant eu clymu ynghyd mewn ffordd gwbl Gymreig. Fel yr adroddodd y Pwyllgor Adrannol ar y Gymraeg yng Nghyfundrefn Addysg Cymru ym 1927: 'Y mae'n bwysig iawn inni gofio am y dylanwad dirfawr a gafodd yr Ysgol Sul a'r sefydliadau a oedd ynglŷn â hi, ar addysg Cymru ... Oni wneir hynny, ni bydd modd deall paham yr ymddangosai'r bobl mor ddifraw wrth weled esgeuluso eu hiaith yn yr ysgolion bob dydd ... Yn wir, nid gormod dywedud iddi [h.y. yr ysgol Sul] wneuthur mwy nag un sefydliad arall i ddiogelu'r iaith fel cyfrwng mynegiant i'r llenor.'[3] Y mae pob cyfiawnhad, felly, dros y ffaith mai deunydd yn ymwneud ag ysgolion Sul yw crynswth yr adran hon.[4]

Introduction

Of all the key public domains concerning the Welsh language, education was the most adversely affected by Anglicizing influences during the course of the nineteenth century. Deep-seated prejudice and even hostility towards the use of Welsh was exhibited not only by government commissioners and Her Majesty's Inspectors of Schools but also by the 'progressive' Welsh middle class. Driven by their conviction of the innate superiority of the English language, they believed that Welsh was a grave social handicap to the people of Wales.

For the greater part of the nineteenth century, it is difficult to find any evidence, statistical or otherwise, to suggest that Welsh was used either as a medium of instruction or as a subject worthy of study in the ordinary day schools of Wales.[1] That so many continued to speak Welsh in everyday life may be attributed not only to the irrelevance of much of their limited day school education, but more particularly to the institution of the Welsh Nonconformist Sunday school whose activities formed an alternative system of education involving the whole community. In small classes, following set syllabuses, adults as well as children learnt to read Welsh, recite catechisms, and discuss the content of the Bible and religious tracts in considerable detail. Annual examinations were held and certificates presented. The cultural competitions of the eisteddfodau and the publishing of Welsh language newspapers, periodicals and religious writings were organized on a denominational basis. In one year, 1907, it was claimed that 100,000 copies of five books in a series prepared for Congregational Sunday school classes, *Cyfres Newydd y Plant*, had been sold at 2d. each.[2] Religion, education and culture were thus closely bound together in a uniquely Welsh way. As the Departmental Committee on Welsh in the Educational System of Wales reported in 1927: 'It is of the utmost importance to bear in mind the dominating influence of the Sunday school and its ancillary organisations in the educational life of Wales ... otherwise it will be impossible to understand the seeming apathy of the people towards the neglect of the language in the day schools ... The Sunday School has done more to preserve Welsh as a cultured and flexible organ of expression than any institution in the land.'[3] Material concerning Sunday schools, therefore,

Serch hynny, â llythrennedd cyffredinol y mae a wnelo'r ddau dabl cyntaf, 1.1 ac 1.2. Ceir ynddynt ffigurau swyddogol y Cofrestrydd Cyffredinol am y ganran o ddynion a merched a lofnodai gofrestrau priodas â marc yn hytrach na llofnod. Fe'u cynhwyswyd fel arwydd bras o'r gyfradd o welliant a gafwyd mewn llythrennedd oddi ar ddechreuadau isel yng nghanol y ganrif. Yng Nghymru gyfan ym 1845 llofnododd 46.3 y cant o'r dynion a 69.5 y cant o'r merched y gofrestr briodas â marc; erbyn 1910 yr oedd y cyfrannau cymharol wedi disgyn i 1.6 y cant i'r naill ac 1.7 y cant i'r llall. Er bod rhaid bod yn wyliadwrus wrth wneud tybiaethau cyffredinol ar sail niferoedd bychain, y mae'r gwahaniaethau ystadegol sy'n dod i'r amlwg rhwng dynion a merched a rhwng dosbarthau cofrestru yng Nghymru yn codi cwestiynau diddorol. Y mae gwahaniaeth nodedig, er enghraifft, rhwng y ganran o ddynion a merched a allai lofnodi'r gofrestr briodas mewn siroedd gwledig yng ngorllewin Cymru. Ym 1845 32.7 y cant yn unig o ddynion sir Aberteifi a lofnododd y gofrestr briodas â marc, o gymharu ag 80.5 y cant o ferched. Er mai sir Faesyfed sy'n cofnodi, yn gyson, y ganran leiaf o bobl a lofnodai â marc, yn sicr nid oes cydberthynas syml yn bodoli ym mhob sir neu ddosbarth rhwng lefelau llythrennedd fel y'u hamlygir yn y ffigurau hyn a chryfder ieithyddol y Gymraeg neu'r Saesneg. Er gwaethaf problemau dehongli, y mae'r gyfres yn cynnig fframwaith y gellir cysylltu cyfresi ac arolygon diweddarach wrtho.

Y mae'r ail grŵp o dablau yn ymwneud â chasgliadau'r Comisiwn Adrannol, a benodwyd ym 1846, i ymchwilio i Gyflwr Addysg yng Nghymru. Enynnodd adroddiadau'r Comisiynwyr, a gyhoeddwyd y flwyddyn ganlynol, ddadl ffyrnig a enillodd ei lle ym mytholeg hanes Cymru fel 'Brad y Llyfrau Gleision'.[5] Nid oedd hanfod casgliadau'r adroddiadau – sef bod safon addysg gyffredinol yng Nghymru yn isel – yn syndod yn y byd, ond ysgogodd sylwadau digymell y Comisiynwyr ynglŷn â moesau, crefydd, cyflwr cymdeithasol ac iaith pobl Cymru wrth-ensyniadau dig ynglŷn ag anwybodaeth, rhagfarn a chymhellion swyddogion Seisnig y llywodraeth.[6]

Er i destun yr adroddiadau a'r atodiadau o dystiolaeth ysgrifenedig a llafar gael eu harchwilio'n drwyadl gan haneswyr, yn rhyfedd iawn prin fu'r sylw a roddwyd i'r cyfoeth o ddeunydd a gynhwysir yn y 505 tudalen o ystadegau plwyfol. Trwy gyfrwng ymweliadau, llythyrau, a chylchlythyrau, casglodd y tri Chomisiynydd wybodaeth fanwl o 1,687 o ysgolion dyddiol a 2,713 o ysgolion Sul ledled Cymru. Cyflwynwyd yr wybodaeth ynglŷn ag ysgolion dyddiol mewn tablau ar gyfer pob ysgol dan 91 o benawdau yn ymestyn dros bedwar tudalen ac, yn achos ysgolion Sul, dan 52 o benawdau; cynhwyswyd crynodebau yn yr adroddiadau eu hunain. Cynhwyswyd manylion am ddyddiad sefydlu, cyflwr adeiladau, y corff rheoli, yr athrawon, y disgyblion, y pynciau a ddysgid, cyfrwng

justifiably forms the bulk of this section.[4]

However, Tables 1.1 and 1.2 are concerned with general literacy. They present the official returns of the Registrar General of the number and percentage of men and women signing marriage registers with a mark rather than a signature. They have been included as a crude indicator of the rate of improvement in literacy from low beginnings in mid-century. In 1845, in Wales as a whole 46.3 per cent of men and 69.5 per cent of women signed the marriage register with a mark; by 1910 the comparative proportions had fallen to 1.6 per cent and 1.7 per cent respectively. Although care must be taken in making general assumptions based on small numbers, the statistical differences which emerge between men and women and between registration districts within Wales raise interesting questions. There is a marked disparity, for instance, between the percentage of men and women who were able to sign the marriage register in counties located in rural west Wales. In 1845 only 32.7 per cent of Cardiganshire men signed the marriage register with a mark, compared to 80.5 per cent of women. Although Radnorshire consistently records the lowest percentage signing with a mark, there is certainly no straightforward correlation in every county or district between levels of literacy as indicated by these figures and the linguistic strength of either Welsh or English. Despite problems of interpretation, the series does provide a framework to which later series and snapshot surveys can be attached.

The second group of tables relate to the findings of the Departmental Commission, appointed in 1846, to inquire into the State of Education in Wales. The Commissioners' reports, published in the following year, ignited a fierce debate which entered the mythology of Welsh history as 'Brad y Llyfrau Gleision' (The Treachery of the Blue Books).[5] The essential findings of the reports – that the standard of general education in Wales was poor – came as no surprise, but the Commissioners' gratuitous comments regarding the morals, religion, social condition and the language of the Welsh people prompted angry countercharges concerning the ignorance, prejudice and motives of English government officials.[6]

Although the text of the reports and the appendices of written and verbal evidence have been thoroughly examined by historians, the wealth of material contained in the 505 pages of parochial statistics has been strangely neglected. By means of visits, letters, and circulars, the three Commissioners gathered detailed information from 1,687 day schools and 2,713 Sunday schools throughout Wales. The information for day schools was tabulated for each school under 91 headings extending over four pages; for Sunday schools under 52 headings; summaries were included in the reports themselves. Details were supplied about the date of establishment, the condition of school premises,

yr hyfforddiant, ariannu'r ysgol, a chyrhaeddiad y disgyblion.

Yr oedd casglu gwybodaeth feintiol ac ansoddol ar addysgu a dysgu'r iaith Saesneg yn ganolog i'r ymchwiliad. Rhoddai ffurflenni'r ysgolion dyddiol gyfle i gofnodi medr mewn addysg grefyddol, darllen, ysgrifennu, rhifyddeg ac amrediad o bynciau eraill yn amrywio o hanes Lloegr i forwriaeth, y cyfan yn Saesneg. Ond yr unig wybodaeth sydd ar gael ar gyfer y Gymraeg yw cyfrwng yr hyfforddiant mewn ysgolion dyddiol ac ysgolion Sul ac, yn achos ysgolion Sul, y nifer o ddisgyblion a allai 'ddarllen yn yr ysgrythurau'. Aildrefnwyd yr wybodaeth hon yn Nhablau 2.1 i 2.8. Yr oedd ffurflenni'r ysgolion dyddiol yn cynnwys y penawdau ychwanegol 'Grammar of English', 'Grammar of Welsh', 'Grammar of both languages' dan 'Language of instruction', ond gan fod cyn lleied o ysgolion wedi ymateb ni chynhwyswyd yr atebion.

Y mae amheuon, wrth gwrs, ynglŷn â pha mor ddibynadwy a chyflawn oedd yr wybodaeth hon. Yr unig ran o sir Fynwy a arolygwyd oedd y deunaw plwyf diwydiannol a ffiniai â siroedd Morgannwg a Brycheiniog. Ceir bylchau yn y tablau lle na roddwyd yr wybodaeth y gofynnwyd amdani neu lle nad oedd yr wybodaeth honno ar gael. Weithiau y mae'n rhaid inni fodloni ar sylwadau fel 'ychydig', 'llawer', a 'newid trwy'r amser', a hynny pan ofynnid am atebion rhifol manwl. Yr oedd problemau, rhaid cyfaddef, yn enwedig ynglŷn â chasglu gwybodaeth o ysgolion Sul, gan nad oeddynt yn cwrdd ond unwaith yr wythnos. Cwynai Jelinger C. Symons, y Comisiynydd yr oedd ei ardal yn cynnwys siroedd Aberteifi, Brycheiniog, Maesyfed a rhan o Fynwy, am hynodrwydd y wlad, lleoliad gwasgaredig y capeli, yr anhawster i gael hyd i berson cymwys i gasglu gwybodaeth, y ffaith fod y bobl yn byw mewn mannau anghysbell, a'r diffyg llyfrau a chofnodion ynglŷn â nifer disgyblion yr ysgolion Sul, os nad yr ysgolion dyddiol yn ogystal. Dwysaodd ei broblemau oherwydd y tywydd anarferol o arw yn ystod gaeaf 1846–7. Ar waethaf tywydd Cymru, ymddengys i'r Comisiynwyr wneud eu gorau i gasglu'r wybodaeth ofynnol. Er enghraifft, argraffwyd ffurflenni mewn cyfnodolion Cymraeg a Saesneg fel y gallai arolygwyr ysgolion Sul baratoi'r wybodaeth angenrheidiol erbyn ymweliad y comisiynydd neu ei gynorthwyydd. O ganlyniad i'r ymdrechion hyn, y mae cwmpas yr wybodaeth a gasglwyd yn drawiadol ac yn cymharu'n ffafriol â'r cyfrifo trwyadl ar ysgolion a disgyblion yng Nghyfrifiad Addysg 1851.

Atebodd bron y cyfan o'r ysgolion y cwestiwn am iaith yr hyfforddiant. Yn Nhablau 2.1 a 2.2 rhoddir cyfansymiau'r atebion yn achos yr ysgolion dyddiol ar gyfer pob sir a dosbarth cofrestru yn ôl y math o ysgol a'r nifer o ddisgyblion. Dengys y ffigurau fod ysgolion dyddiol yn brin a bod y defnydd o'r iaith Gymraeg yn brinnach fyth. Traean yn unig o boblogaeth Cymru rhwng 5 a 14 oed oedd 'ar y llyfrau' (78,265). Os

the controlling body, the teachers, the pupils, the subjects taught, the language of instruction, school funding, and pupils' attainment.

The assembling of quantitative and qualitative information on English language teaching and learning was central to the enquiry. Day school schedules gave the opportunity to record proficiency in religious instruction, reading, writing, arithmetic and a variety of other subjects from English history to navigation, all in the English language. But the only information available for the Welsh language is the language of instruction for day and Sunday schools, and the number of scholars 'able to read in the scriptures' for Sunday schools. This information has been reworked in Tables 2.1 to 2.8. Day school schedules contained the additional headings 'Grammar of English', 'Grammar of Welsh', 'Grammar of both languages' under 'Language of instruction', but so few schools responded that the replies have not been included.

Of course there are questions about the reliability and completeness of this information. The only parts of Monmouthshire inspected were the eighteen industrial parishes adjoining Glamorgan and Breconshire. There are gaps in the tabulation where the information required was either not given or not available. Sometimes we have to be satisfied with comments like 'a few', 'many', and 'always fluctuating', where convenient, precise numerical replies were required. Admittedly there were problems, particularly relating to the collection of information from Sunday schools, which assembled only once a week. Jelinger C. Symons, the Commissioner whose district included the counties of Brecon, Cardigan, Radnor and part of Monmouth, complained of 'the peculiarities of the country, the scattered position of the chapels, the difficulty of finding the proper persons to give information, their remote residences, and the frequent absence of any books or record of the number of scholars in Sunday-schools, and not infrequently even in day schools'. Unusually inclement weather during the winter of 1846–7 compounded his problems. Notwithstanding the Welsh weather, the Commissioners seem to have done their best to collect the required information. For example, schedules were printed in both Welsh and English periodicals so that the superintendents of Sunday schools might have the necessary information prepared before the visit of the Commissioner or his assistant. As a result of these efforts, the coverage of the returns is impressive and stands comparison with the thorough counting of schools and scholars in the 1851 Census of Education.

Nearly all schools responded to the question about the language of instruction. In Tables 2.1 and 2.2 the replies from day schools are aggregated for each county and registration district by type of school and number of scholars. The figures indicate the paucity of day schools and the almost total absence of the Welsh

cymerir y 'nifer sy'n mynychu fel rheol' fel mesuriad mwy priodol, y mae'r gyfran yn disgyn i chwarter. Er bod y rhestr o ddosbarthau lle'r awgryma'r ffigurau amgylchedd cwbl Saesneg – Penfro, Llanfair-ym-Muallt, Y Gelli, Llanandras, Trefyclo, Y Drenewydd, Trefaldwyn – i'w gweld yn fyr o bosibl, ac er bod y mannau hynny mewn ardaloedd hir-Seisnigedig, eto tair ysgol ddyddiol yn unig yng Nghymru gyfan a oedd yn dysgu trwy gyfrwng 'Cymraeg yn unig'. Ysgolion Eglwys Ymddiriedolwyr Madam Bridget Bevan yn sir Aberteifi oedd dwy ohonynt: ym mhlwyf Llandyfriog, addysgid chwech ar hugain o ddisgyblion gan gyn-ffermwr 63 mlwydd oed, ac ym mhlwyf Llanfihangel Ystrad addysgid ugain o ddisgyblion gan gyn-labrwr 47 mlwydd oed.[7] Ysgol breifat ac ynddi ddau ar bymtheg o ddisgyblion (merched yn bennaf) yn cael ei rhedeg gan gyn-felinydd 68 mlwydd oed (menyw) yng Nghapel Pisgah ym mhlwyf Llandwrog, Caernarfon, oedd y drydedd ysgol 'Gymraeg yn unig'. Ceir peth tystiolaeth arall o ddefnyddio'r Gymraeg pan oedd angen. Yn sir Gaerfyrddin, er enghraifft, ac eithrio'r ysgolion mewn plwyfi o amgylch Llanelli a thref Caerfyrddin, cyfaddefai llawer o ysgolion dyddiol fod y Gymraeg yn cael ei defnyddio i egluro llyfrau Saesneg. Serch hynny, amlygir yn glir bresenoldeb dra-arglwyddiaethol y Saesneg mewn ysgolion ledled Cymru yng nghanol y bedwaredd ganrif ar bymtheg.

Y mae'r atodiadau i'r adroddiadau yn frith o dystiolaeth leol am safon wael y dysgu yn achos Saesneg a chyraeddiadau isel yn yr iaith honno. Cafodd cyflwr adeiladau'r ysgolion dyddiol ac ansawdd y dysgu eu condemnio yn unfryd gan y Comisiynwyr. Mewn gwrthgyferbyniad, derbyniodd yr ysgolion Sul Cymraeg glod unfrydol. Gyda thros chwarter miliwn o ddisgyblion – bron hanner cyfanswm y boblogaeth – yr oeddynt yn sicr yn boblogaidd. Yn nhref Aberystwyth, er enghraifft, yr oedd 666 o ddisgyblion yn bresennol yn ysgol Sul y Tabernacl, capel y Methodistiaid Calfinaidd yn Stryd y Felin, pan ymwelwyd â'r ysgol (honnid bod 812 o ddisgyblion 'ar y llyfrau'); yr oedd 116 wedi eu cofrestru yn ysgol Sul arall y Methodistiaid Calfinaidd yn Stryd y Crwynwr; 392 wedi eu cofrestru mewn dwy ysgol Sul gan y Methodistiaid Wesleaidd, a 175 gan yr Annibynwyr a 295 gan y Bedyddwyr yn eu hysgolion Sul hwythau yn Stryd y Frenhines. Yr oedd cyfanswm o 396 wedi eu cofrestru yn y tair ysgol Sul a oedd gan Eglwys Loegr yn y dref, er mai 182 yn unig a oedd yn bresennol pan ymwelwyd â hwy. Yr oedd cyfanswm y nifer o ddisgyblion ysgol Sul cofrestredig (2,186) yn 44.5 y cant o gyfanswm poblogaeth y dref (4,916).

Y mae Tablau 2.3 a 2.4 yn datgelu'r nifer o ysgolion Sul a disgyblion ym mhob sir a dosbarth cofrestru yn ôl y math o ysgol a chyfrwng yr hyfforddiant. Dengys y ffigurau yn y tablau hyn i ba raddau yr oedd y prif enwadau Ymneilltuol – Methodistiaid Calfinaidd, Annibynwyr, Bedyddwyr, a Methodistiaid Wesleaidd –

language. The total number of 'children on the books' (78,265) represents only a third of the population of Wales aged 5–14 years. If the 'number who usually attend' is taken as a more appropriate measurement, the proportion falls to one quarter. Although the list of districts where the returns suggest an exclusively English school environment – Pembroke, Builth, Hay, Presteigne, Knighton, Newtown, Montgomery – may seem short and were located in long-standing Anglicized areas, yet only three day schools in the whole of Wales were marked under 'Welsh only' for the language of instruction. Two were Madam Bridget Bevan's Trustees' Church schools in Cardiganshire: in the parish of Llandyfriog twenty-six pupils were taught by a 63 year old ex-farmer, and in the parish of Llanfihangel Ystrad twenty pupils were taught by a 47 year old ex-labourer.[7] The third 'Welsh only' school was a private school with seventeen pupils (mainly girls) run by a 68 year old ex-miller (female) in Pisgah Chapel in the parish of Llandwrog, Caernarfon. There is some other evidence that Welsh was used when necessary. In Carmarthenshire, for example, apart from those in parishes around Llanelli and the town of Carmarthen, many day schools admitted that 'Welsh [was] spoken in explanation of English books'. Nevertheless, the dominating presence of the English language in schools throughout Wales in the mid-nineteenth century is clearly demonstrated by these figures.

The appendices to the reports are densely scattered with local evidence about the poor standard of English language teaching and attainment. Both the condition of day school premises and the quality of teaching were unanimously condemned by the Commissioners. In contrast, Welsh Sunday schools received unanimous praise. With over a quarter of a million scholars – equivalent to almost half the total population – they were certainly popular. In the town of Aberystwyth, for example, 666 pupils were present at the Tabernacl Calvinistic Methodist Sunday school in Mill Street when the school was visited (812 scholars were claimed to be 'on the books'); 116 were registered at the other Calvinistic Methodist Sunday school in Skinner Street; 392 were registered at two Wesleyan Methodist Sunday schools, and 175 and 295 respectively at the Independent and Baptist Sunday schools in Queen Street. Sunday pupils registered at three Church of England Sunday schools in the town totalled 396, although only 182 were actually present when the schools were visited. The total number (2,186) of registered Sunday school pupils represented 44.5 per cent of the town's total population of 4,916.

Tables 2.3 and 2.4 reveal the number of Sunday schools and scholars for each county and registration district according to the type of school and the language of instruction. The figures in these tables show the extent to which the major Nonconformist denominations – Calvinistic Methodists, Independents,

yn gryfach na'r Eglwys sefydledig ym mhob rhan o Gymru. Dangosant hefyd i ba raddau y câi'r Gymraeg ei defnyddio yn gyfrwng hyfforddiant mewn ysgolion Sul. Pymtheg y cant yn unig o ddisgyblion ysgol Sul, yn bennaf yn siroedd Penfro, Maesyfed a Mynwy, a gâi eu dysgu trwy gyfrwng y Saesneg yn unig. Yn wir, a barnu oddi wrth faint yr ysgolion, yr ysgolion Sul Cymraeg oedd fwyaf poblogaidd. Gellir gweld cryfder y Methodistiaid Calfinaidd – enwad Cymraeg i raddau helaeth iawn – ledled y Gymru Gymraeg. Fel enwad, dim ond yn siroedd Morgannwg a Chaerfyrddin, lle'r oedd yr Annibynwyr gryfaf, yr ildiai ei le o ychydig yn safle cyntaf y cynghrair.

Rhydd Tablau 2.5 a 2.6 ddadansoddiad o ddisgyblion Sul yn ôl oedran a rhyw ym mhob sir a dosbarth cofrestru. Dengys y ffigurau fod yr un faint o ferched a bechgyn yn mynychu ysgol Sul, bod bron cymaint o oedolion ag o blant, a bod rhagor o ddynion nag o fenywod. Rhoddai presenoldeb cynifer o oedolion gymeriad unigryw i'r ysgol Sul Gymraeg, oherwydd byddai ei haelodau yn parhau'n ddisgyblion ar hyd eu hoes. O ran cyfraneddau grŵp oedran, Meirionnydd oedd yn flaenaf gyda 50.6 y cant o'r boblogaeth dan 15 oed a 35.2 y cant o'r boblogaeth dros 15 oed 'ar lyfrau' ysgolion Sul, rhai Cymraeg eu cyfrwng bron i gyd. Nid oedd siroedd gwledig Aberteifi, Caernarfon a Môn ymhell ar ei hôl. O gofio'r trosiant (nas mesurwyd) o ddisgyblion cofrestredig, y mae'n amlwg fod addysg grefyddol yng nghanol y bedwaredd ganrif ar bymtheg yn cyrraedd y rhan fwyaf o bobl ar ryw adeg yn ystod eu hoes ac mai trwy gyfrwng y Gymraeg y câi ei chyflwyno.[8]

Ymhlith yr holl ystadegau a gyflwynwyd yn adroddiad 1847, yr unig fesur o allu i ddarllen Cymraeg yw'r niferoedd a allai 'ddarllen yn yr ysgrythurau' mewn ysgolion Sul. Cyflwynir y rhain yn ôl sir a dosbarth cofrestru yn Nhablau 2.7 a 2.8. Ar ben y rhestr o ran gallu i ddarllen Cymraeg y mae'r nifer mawr o Fethodistiaid Calfinaidd Cymraeg, y cofnodwyd bod 75 y cant o ddisgyblion eu hysgolion Sul yn gallu darllen yr Ysgrythurau. Nid ymddengys fod disgyblion a fynychai ysgolion lle y câi'r ddwy iaith eu defnyddio mor hyfedr â disgyblion mewn ysgolion un-iaith. Y mae'r dadansoddiad yn ôl sir yn rhoi Aberteifi ar frig y rhestr gydag 86 y cant a Morgannwg ar y gwaelod gyda 54 y cant. Er mai natur grefyddol a oedd i'r addysg at ei gilydd, arweiniodd y gallu cyffredinol i ddarllen Cymraeg a enillwyd trwy ymdrechion athrawon ysgol Sul at alw am ragor o gyhoeddiadau Cymraeg cyffredinol i blant ac oedolion. Ym marn Jelinger C. Symons, yr oedd tri chwarter yr atebion cywir a dderbyniodd mewn arholiadau ysgolion dyddiol yn ganlyniad yr addysg a gafwyd mewn ysgol Sul. Canodd ef a'i gyd-gomisiynwyr glodydd ysgolion Sul yr Ymneilltuwyr, gan honni bod y werin Gymraeg yn gallu darllen ac ysgrifennu eu hiaith eu hunain yn well na'r dosbarth cymdeithasol cyfatebol yn Lloegr.

Baptists, and Wesleyan Methodists – prevailed over the established Church throughout Wales. They also show the extent to which the Welsh language was used in Sunday school teaching. Only fifteen per cent of Sunday school pupils, mainly concentrated in the counties of Pembroke, Radnor and Monmouth, were being taught solely through the medium of English. Indeed, judging by school size, the Welsh Sunday schools were the most popular. The strength of Calvinistic Methodism – very much a Welsh denomination – can be identified throughout Welsh-speaking Wales. As a denomination, it was narrowly ousted from its premier position only in Glamorgan and Carmarthen, where the Independents were strongest.

Tables 2.5 and 2.6 give a breakdown of Sunday scholars by age and sex for counties and registration districts. The overall figures show that girls and boys attended in equal numbers, that almost as many adults as children attended, and that more adult males than females attended. The attendance of such a large proportion of adults gave the Welsh Sunday school a unique character, for its members continued to attend into old age. In terms of age group proportions, Merioneth led the field with the equivalent of 50.6 per cent of the population under 15 years and 35.2 per cent of the population over 15 years returned as 'on the books' of Sunday schools, nearly all of which were Welsh language schools. The other rural counties of Cardigan, Caernarfon and Anglesey were not far behind. Bearing in mind the (unmeasured) turnover of registered pupils, it is apparent that in the mid-nineteenth century religious teaching reached most people in Wales at some stage in their lives and that it was mainly conducted through the Welsh language.[8]

Among all the statistics presented in the 1847 report, the only measure of Welsh reading ability is the number 'able to read in the scriptures' in Sunday schools. These are presented by county and by registration district in Tables 2.7 and 2.8. At the head of the Welsh reading proficiency league is the large number of Welsh language Calvinistic Methodists, 75 per cent of whose Sunday school scholars were returned as being able to read the Scriptures. Pupils attending schools where both languages were used do not appear to have been as proficient as pupils in single language schools. The breakdown by county shows Cardigan at the top with 86 per cent and Glamorgan at the bottom with 54 per cent. Although the teaching was predominantly of a religious nature, general reading ability in Welsh achieved through the efforts of Sunday school teachers was sufficient to create a demand for more general Welsh language publications for both children and adults. Jelinger C. Symons judged that 'three-fourths of all correct answers made to me in day-school examinations have been the result of Sunday school teaching'. He and his fellow Commissioners warmly praised the Welsh Nonconformist Sunday schools and

Er nad yw'n cynnwys unrhyw wybodaeth am iaith, cynhwyswyd Tabl 2.9 gan ei fod yn cynnig cymhariaeth werthfawr rhwng adroddiad 1847 a Chyfrifiad Addysg 1851, y cyflogodd awdurdodau'r cyfrifiad wasanaeth 30,610 o rifwyr ledled Cymru a Lloegr i'w gynnal. Ceir anghysonderau mawr mewn rhai ardaloedd ond, o gofio pa mor fyrhoedlog oedd llawer o ysgolion dyddiol preifat a faint o drafod a fu ar gyflwr addysg yng Nghymru dros y pum mlynedd flaenorol, y mae'r gymhariaeth yn cadarnhau dilysrwydd deunydd 1847 yn hytrach na bwrw amheuaeth arno.

Yn Nhabl 3.1 cyflwynir yr holl dystiolaeth ystadegol ynglŷn â'r iaith Gymraeg a ymddangosodd yn adroddiad John Jenkins, Comisiynydd Cynorthwyol ar Gomisiwn Cross a benodwyd ym 1858 i ymchwilio i gyflwr addysg boblogaidd yng Nghymru a Lloegr. Dewiswyd ysgolion mewn dwy ardal enghreifftiol i'w hastudio'n fanwl, y naill, sef rhan o sir Feirionnydd, yn cynrychioli'r Gymru wledig, a'r llall, sef Castell-nedd, y Gymru ddiwydiannol. Er bod Jenkins yn cyfaddef mai ofer oedd pob ymdrech i gynnal yr iaith Gymraeg ac yn disgrifio sut yr oedd y Gymraeg yn ildio ei lle i'r Saesneg, argymhellodd, serch hynny, wneud mwy o ddefnydd o'r Gymraeg wrth ddysgu Saesneg. Y mae canlyniadau ei arolwg cymedrol ei faint yn ddiddorol. Y mae'r gyfran o blant dan ddeg oed a allai siarad Cymraeg (87.3 y cant yn ysgolion Meirionnydd a 78.3 y cant yn ysgolion Castell-nedd) yn awgrymu mai Cymraeg oedd prif iaith yr aelwyd yn y ddwy ardal. Ac eto, ymhlith plant dros ddeg oed, honnir bod gan 42.9 y cant o blant Meirionnydd a 62.7 y cant o blant Castell-nedd afael dda ar y Saesneg a bod y gyfran o siaradwyr Cymraeg uniaith wedi disgyn yn drawiadol. Yr unig wahaniaeth nodedig rhwng ysgolion 'tref' a 'gwlad' ym Meirionnydd oedd bod y plant hŷn yn ysgolion y 'trefi' yn fwy rhugl yn Saesneg. Pa faint bynnag oedd y cyfiawnhad dros feirniadu'r dulliau dysgu, y mae'r ffigurau hyn o leiaf yn awgrymu bod disgyblion ysgolion dyddiol Cymru yn y bedwaredd ganrif ar bymtheg yn dod i siarad Saesneg.

Arweiniodd y galw cynyddol am ddatgysylltiad yng Nghymru yn y 1890au at benodi Comisiwn Brenhinol ym 1906 'to inquire into ... the provision made, and the work done, by the Churches of all Denominations in Wales and Monmouthshire for the spiritual welfare of the people, and the extent to which the people avail themselves of such provision'. Yr oedd yr adroddiad, a gyhoeddwyd ym 1910, yn cynnwys 500 o dudalennau o atodiadau ystadegol wedi eu rhannu'n ddwy – Eglwys Loegr (yn ôl esgobaeth, deoniaeth, a phlwyf) ac enwadau Ymneilltuol (fel rheol fesul plwyf ym mhob sir).[9] Nid yw'r wybodaeth ar ysgolion Sul, a gynhwysir yn Nhablau 4.1 i 4.4, mor gyflawn ag yn yr atodiadau i adroddiad Comisiwn 1846 i Ymchwilio i Gyflwr Addysg yng Nghymru. Ni chaiff iaith yr hyfforddiant ei nodi'n bendant bob tro; ni rannwyd y disgyblion yn wrywod/benywod; ac ni cheir unrhyw arwydd o'r

claimed that 'the Welsh peasantry are better able to read and write in their own language than the same classes in England'.

Although it contains no information about language, Table 2.9 has been included since it offers a valuable comparison between the 1847 report and the 1851 Census of Education, for which the census authorities employed the services of 30,610 enumerators throughout England and Wales. There are major discrepancies in a few districts but, taking into account the ephemeral nature of many small private day schools and the five year period during which the topic of education in Wales had been the focus of much discussion and activity, the comparison serves more to confirm the validity of the 1847 material than to query it.

Table 3.1 presents all the statistical evidence relating to the Welsh language which appeared in the report of John Jenkins, Assistant Commissioner on the Cross Commission appointed in 1858 to inquire into the state of popular education in England and Wales. Schools in two sample areas representing rural and industrial Wales, namely part of Merioneth and Neath, were chosen for close scrutiny. Although Jenkins readily confessed the 'futility of all efforts to maintain the Welsh language' and described the ways in which Welsh was yielding to English, he nevertheless advocated increased use of Welsh in the teaching of English. The results of his modest survey are interesting. The proportion of children under ten years of age who were able to speak Welsh (87.3 per cent in the Merioneth schools and 78.3 per cent in the Neath schools) suggest that Welsh was the dominant language in homes in both areas. Yet, of the children over ten years of age, it was claimed that 42.9 per cent in Merioneth and 62.7 per cent in Neath had good knowledge of English and the proportion of monoglot Welsh speakers had fallen dramatically. The only marked difference between 'town' and 'country' schools in Merioneth was a greater proficiency in English among the older children in the 'town' schools. However justified the criticism of teaching methods might have been, these figures at least suggest that in the mid-nineteenth century English was actually being acquired by pupils in the day schools of Wales.

The increasing clamour for disestablishment in Wales in the 1890s led to the appointment of a Royal Commission in 1906 'to inquire into ... the provision made, and the work done, by the Churches of all Denominations in Wales and Monmouthshire for the spiritual welfare of the people, and the extent to which the people avail themselves of such provision'. The report, published in 1910, contained 500 pages of statistical appendices divided into two parts – Church of England (by diocese, deanery, and parish) and Nonconformist denominations (usually on a parish by parish basis for each county).[9] The information on Sunday schools, included in Tables 4.1 to 4.4, is not as

hyfedredd a enillwyd. Serch hynny, y mae'r ffigurau'n bwrw cryn oleuni ar yr hyn a gyflawnwyd yn y maes hwn dros y trigain mlynedd flaenorol.

Y mae Tabl 4.1 yn cyfuno ffigurau a gyflwynwyd i'r Comisiynwyr ar ran eglwysi'r Annibynwyr a'r Methodistiaid Calfinaidd Cymraeg yng Nghymru. Er nad yw'r tabl yn rhoi gwybodaeth am iaith, y mae'n dangos parhad dylanwad ysgolion Sul y ddau enwad Ymneilltuol cryfaf yng Nghymru gydol ail hanner y bedwaredd ganrif ar bymtheg. Y mae Tabl 4.2, fodd bynnag, yn gwahaniaethu rhwng Cymraeg (77 y cant), Saesneg (22 y cant) a'r Ddwy (1 y cant) yn achos ysgolion Sul yr Annibynwyr yn ôl siroedd ym 1906, ac yn dystiolaeth bellach fod goruchafiaeth y Gymraeg mewn ysgolion Sul Ymneilltuol yn parhau ym mhob sir yng Nghymru, ac eithrio siroedd Mynwy, Brycheiniog, a Maesyfed.

Dengys Tablau 4.3 a 4.4 y nifer o ysgolion Sul, athrawon a disgyblion yn ôl enwad, am bob sir a dosbarth. Lle y mae'r wybodaeth ar gael, rhannwyd nifer y disgyblion yn rhai dan bymtheg a thros bymtheng mlwydd oed. O ran cyfansymiau'r niferoedd a fynychai ysgolion Sul, ymddengys mai'r un oedd trefn poblogrwydd yr enwadau ym 1906 ag ym 1846: Methodistiaid Calfinaidd, Annibynwyr, Eglwys Loegr, Bedyddwyr, a Methodistiaid Wesleaidd. Ond er yr ymddengys fod gan yr Annibynwyr (21.1 y cant), y Bedyddwyr (18.5 y cant) a Methodistiaid eraill (11.7 y cant) tua'r un gyfran o fynychwyr ysgol Sul ym 1906 ag a oedd ganddynt ym 1846, yr oedd cyfran gyfatebol yr Eglwys sefydledig wedi codi o 14.0 y cant i 20.4 y cant. Yn Aberystwyth, serch hynny, yr oedd y Methodistiaid Calfinaidd wedi mynd o nerth i nerth. Cofnododd yr ysgolion Sul a oedd yn gysylltiedig â'r Tabernacl gyfanswm o 898 o athrawon a disgyblion; cofnodwyd 729 yn Seilo ac yn ysgol capel Stryd y Crwynwr a 258 yn Salem. Ond fel llawer o enwadau Cymraeg traddodiadol eraill, yr oedd y Methodistiaid Calfinaidd wedi sefydlu capel Saesneg, yn Stryd y Baddon, a oedd â chyfanswm cymharol fychan o athrawon a disgyblion ysgol Sul. Serch hynny, os cynhwysir ffigurau o'r holl gapeli Cymraeg Ymneilltuol, y mae'r cyfanswm rhyfeddol o 2,927 o athrawon a disgyblion yn 35.5 y cant o gyfanswm poblogaeth Aberystwyth. Gwaetha'r modd, nid yw bob amser yn bosibl penderfynu beth oedd iaith pob ysgol Sul a restrir yn y canlyniadau, ond y mae crynswth y dystiolaeth ystadegol a gyflwynwyd i Gomisiwn 1906 yn datgelu'n bendant fod yr ysgol Sul yn parhau'n gyfrwng grymus i addysg Gymraeg ar ddechrau'r ugeinfed ganrif.

Yn Nhablau 5.1 i 5.4 dangosir canlyniadau'r ymgyrch i gyflwyno'r Gymraeg yn bwnc astudiaeth yn y gyfundrefn addysg ffurfiol. Creodd diddordeb cynyddol mewn hyrwyddo'r Gymraeg a phryder cynyddol am oblygiadau cymdeithasol prosesau Seisnig alw am fwy o ddefnydd o'r Gymraeg mewn ysgolion yn chwarter olaf y bedwaredd ganrif ar bymtheg. Yn

complete as in the appendices to the report of the 1846 Commission of Inquiry into the State of Education in Wales. The language of instruction is not always explicitly stated; there is no male/female division in the number of scholars given; any indication of proficiency attained is missing. Nevertheless, the figures throw considerable light on what had been achieved in this field over the previous sixty years.

Table 4.1 combines figures submitted to the Commissioners on behalf of the Independent and Welsh Calvinistic Methodist churches of Wales. Although the table gives no language information, it indicates the sustained influence of the Sunday schools of the two largest Nonconformist denominations in Wales throughout the second half of the nineteenth century. Table 4.2, however, distinguishes between Welsh (77 per cent), English (22 per cent), and Both (1 per cent) for Independent Sunday schools by counties in 1906, and provides evidence of the continued dominance of the Welsh language in Nonconformist Sunday schools in every county of Wales except Monmouth, Brecon, and Radnor.

Tables 4.3 and 4.4 show the number of Sunday schools, teachers and scholars by denomination, for each county and district. Where the information is available, the number of scholars has been subdivided into those under fifteen years of age and those over fifteen years of age. In terms of total numbers attending Sunday schools, the order of denominational primacy appears to have been the same in 1906 as it was in 1846: Calvinistic Methodists, Independents, Church of England, Baptists, and Wesleyan Methodists. However, although the Independents (21.1 per cent), Baptists (18.5 per cent) and other Methodists (11.7 per cent) appear to have retained approximately the same proportion of Sunday school attenders in 1906 as they had in 1846, the Calvinistic Methodist share of the total had fallen from 40.8 per cent to 25.5 per cent, and the equivalent share of the established Church had increased from 14.0 per cent to 20.4 per cent. At Aberystwyth, however, the Calvinistic Methodists had gone from strength to strength. Sunday schools associated with Tabernacl entered a total of 898 teachers and scholars; Seilo and the Skinner Street chapel school entered 729 and Salem 258. But, like many other traditionally Welsh denominations, the Calvinistic Methodists had established an English language chapel, in Bath Street, which had a relatively small total of 188 Sunday school teachers and scholars. Nevertheless, if returns from all the Nonconformist Welsh chapels are included, the remarkable total of 2,927 teachers and scholars constitutes 35.5 per cent of the total population of Aberystwyth. Unfortunately, it is not always possible to determine the language of every Sunday school listed in the returns, but the weight of the statistical evidence presented to the 1906 Commission reveals conclusively that the Sunday

Nhabl 5.1 atgynhyrchir canlyniadau arolwg o brif-athrawon a drefnwyd gan Gymdeithas y Cymmrodorion ym 1884. Dangosant fod 54.0 y cant o blaid cyflwyno'r Gymraeg fel pwnc, a 40.9 y cant yn erbyn. Anogodd canlyniadau'r arolwg sefydlu Cymdeithas yr Iaith Gymraeg ym 1885. Cyflwynodd nifer o'i haelodau, yn enwedig Dan Isaac Davies,[10] Beriah Gwynfe Evans, Isambard Owen, a'r Archddiacon John Griffiths dystiolaeth drawiadol gerbron y Comisiwn Brenhinol ar Addysg Elfennol ym 1887. Yr oedd ymchwiliadau eang y Comisiwn yn cynnwys materion megis 'Ysgolion arbennig a'u hanawsterau – ysgolion Cymraeg' a 'Hyfforddiant secwlar – a) i ba raddau yr atebir yr anhawster dwyieithog yng Nghymru? b) yr iaith Gymraeg'. Nid arweiniodd ymchwiliadau'r Comisiwn at unrhyw ddeunydd ystadegol ar ddefnyddio'r iaith Gymraeg mewn ysgolion ond yn ei adroddiad terfynol argymhellodd fel a ganlyn: 'in Wales permission should be given to take up the Welsh language as a specific subject; to adopt an optional scheme to take the place of English as a class subject, founded on the principle of substituting a graduated system of translation from Welsh to English for the present requirements in English grammar; to teach Welsh along with English as a class subject; and to include Welsh among the languages in which candidates for Queen's scholarships and for certificates of merit may be examined'.[11] Yn sgil hyn cafwyd Deddf Addysg Ganolraddol Cymru 1889 a greodd gyfundrefn newydd o ysgolion uwchradd sirol. Saith mlynedd yn ddiweddarach, ffurfiwyd y Bwrdd Canol fel corff i arolygu ac arholi, ac er mai prin fu ei sêl, o leiaf bu gan y corff hwnnw gydymdeimlad at le'r Gymraeg yn ysgolion uwchradd Cymru.

Yn Nhablau 5.2 i 5.5 dangosir cynnydd araf y Gymraeg fel pwnc cydnabyddedig mewn ysgolion elfennol, ysgolion uwchradd sirol, ac ym Mhrifysgol Cymru, yn y ddau ddegawd olaf cyn y Rhyfel Byd Cyntaf. Er gwaethaf ymdrechion gwiw unigolion ymroddedig ac awdurdod addysg canolog a oedd â chydymdeimlad, y prif rwystrau a barhaodd i'r ugeinfed ganrif oedd agwedd wrthwynebus rhieni a phrinder difrifol o athrawon cymwys. I'r rhan fwyaf o bobl, felly, yr ysgol Sul Ymneilltuol oedd yr unig gyfrwng o hyd a gynigiai addysg Gymraeg.

1 Am fanylion pellach ynglŷn â lle'r Gymraeg mewn addysg, gw. W. R. Jones, *Addysg Ddwyieithog yng Nghymru* (Caernarfon, 1963), tt. 50–69; idem, 'National Revival and Education', pennod II yn *Bilingualism in Welsh Education* (Cardiff, 1966), tt. 44–85; Gareth Elwyn Jones, 'Education in Wales: the need for a historical perspective', *Education for Development*, 10, rhifyn 1 (1986), 2–12; W. Gareth Evans, 'The "bilingual difficulty": H.M.I. and the Welsh language in the Victorian age', *Cylchgrawn Hanes Cymru*, 16, rhifyn 4 (1993), 494–513.

2 Yr oedd y gyfres hon o lyfrau gan Abel J. Jones, wedi eu darlunio ar gyfer plant dan ddeuddeg oed, yn cynnwys gwersi darllen Cymraeg, stori Iesu Grist, storïau o'r Hen Destament, a moeswersi.

3 Pwyllgor Adrannol ar y Gymraeg yng Nghyfundrefn Addysg

school was still a powerful agent of Welsh language education at the beginning of the twentieth century.

The results of the campaign to introduce Welsh as a subject of study in the formal education system are shown in Tables 5.1 to 5.4. Growing interest in the promotion of the Welsh language and mounting concern about the social implications of Anglicizing processes created a demand for greater use of Welsh in schools in the final quarter of the nineteenth century. The results of a survey of head teachers organized by the Cymmrodorion Society in 1884 are reproduced in Table 5.1. They show that 54.0 per cent were in favour of introducing Welsh as a subject, but that 40.9 per cent were opposed. Encouraged by the results of the Cymmrodorion survey, the Society for the Utilisation of the Welsh Language in Education was founded in 1885. Several of its members, notably Dan Isaac Davies,[10] Beriah Gwynfe Evans, Isambard Owen, and the Archdeacon John Griffiths gave impressive evidence before the Royal Commission on the Working of the Elementary Education Acts in 1887. The Commission's wide-ranging inquiry included matters such as 'Special schools and their difficulties – Welsh schools' and 'Secular instruction – a) how far is the bilingual difficulty met in Wales? b) the Welsh language'. The Commission's investigations yielded no statistical material on Welsh language use in schools but in its final report it recommended that 'in Wales permission should be given to take up the Welsh language as a specific subject; to adopt an optional scheme to take the place of English as a class subject, founded on the principle of substituting a graduated system of translation from Welsh to English for the present requirements in English Grammar; to teach Welsh along with English as a class subject; and to include Welsh among the languages in which candidates for Queen's scholarships and for certificates of merit maybe examined'.[11] The resultant Welsh Intermediate Education Act of 1889 created a new system of county secondary schools. Seven years later, the Central Welsh Board for Intermediate Education was formed as a body for inspection and examination which, although it proved lacking in zeal, was at least sympathetic to the place of Welsh in the secondary schools of Wales.

Tables 5.2 to 5.5 show the slow progress of Welsh as a recognized subject of study in elementary schools, county secondary schools, and in the University of Wales, in the last two decades before the First World War. Despite the dedicated efforts of committed individuals and a sympathetic central education authority, the main obstacles which were carried into the twentieth century were the hostile attitude of parents and the serious lack of qualified teachers. For most people, therefore, the Nonconformist Sunday school continued to provide the only means of access to Welsh language education.

Cymru, *Y Gymraeg mewn Addysg a Bywyd* (Llundain, 1927), tt. 42, 143.

4 Ceir ystadegau blynyddol manwl am y nifer o ysgolion dyddiol, disgyblion, athrawon a myfyrwyr prifysgol yn John Williams, *Digest of Welsh Historical Statistics* (2 gyf., Cardiff, 1985), II, tt. 195–248.

5 Tasg y Comisiwn a sefydlwyd ym mis Hydref 1846 oedd: 'to direct an inquiry to be made into the state of education in the principality of Wales, especially into the means afforded to the labouring classes of acquiring a knowledge of the English language'.

6 Am ragor o fanylion am yr Adroddiadau a'u canlyniadau, gw. David Salmon, 'The Story of a Welsh Education Commission (1846–7)', *Y Cymmrodor*, XXIV (1913), 189–237; Frank Price Jones, 'The Blue Books of 1847' yn Jac L. Williams a Gwilym Rees Hughes (goln.), *The History of Education in Wales, 1* (Swansea, 1978), tt. 127–44; Prys Morgan, 'From Long Knives to Blue Books' yn R. R. Davies et al. (goln.), *Welsh Society and Nationhood* (Cardiff, 1984), tt. 199–215; idem (gol.), *Brad y Llyfrau Gleision: Ysgrifau ar Hanes Cymru* (Llandysul, 1991).

7 Y mae peth dryswch ynglŷn ag ysgol Llandyfrïog gan fod marc yn y golofn 'cyfrwng hyfforddiant' dan 'Cymraeg a Saesneg' yn ogystal â than 'Cymraeg yn unig'.

8 Gw. David Evans, *The Sunday Schools of Wales* (London, 1884) am hanes y mudiad ysgolion Sul yng Nghymru, a ysgrifennwyd fel teyrnged adeg y canmlwyddiant.

9 Esgeuluswyd yr ystadegau hyn gan haneswyr yn ogystal. Ond, ar gyfer sir Forgannwg, gw. R. Tudur Jones, 'Glamorgan Christianity in 1905–6: A Statistical Survey' yn Prys Morgan (gol.), *Glamorgan County History, Vol. VI, Glamorgan Society 1780–1980* (Cardiff, 1988), tt. 245–63.

10 Y mae W. R. Jones yn talu teyrnged i Dan Isaac Davies, Arolygwr ei Mawrhydi: 'No other person in the second half of the nineteenth century contributed as much as Dan Isaac Davies towards popularising the concept of a bilingual education in Wales.' *Bilingualism in Welsh Education*, t. 61. Am gyfraniad Dan Isaac Davies i addysg Gymraeg, gw. J. Elwyn Hughes, *Arloeswr Dwyieithedd: Dan Isaac Davies 1839–1887* (Caerdydd, 1984).

11 *Final Report of the Commissioners appointed to inquire into the Elementary Education Acts, England and Wales*, par. 108, PP 1888 (c5485) XXXV.

1 For further details of the place of Welsh in education, see 'National Revival and Education', chapter II in W. R. Jones, *Bilingualism in Welsh Education* (Cardiff, 1966), pp. 44–85; Gareth Elwyn Jones, 'Education in Wales: the need for a historical perspective', *Education for Development*, 10, no. 1 (1986), 2–12; W. Gareth Evans, 'The "bilingual difficulty": H.M.I. and the Welsh language in the Victorian age', *Welsh History Review*, 16, no. 4 (1993), 494–513.

2 The series, by Abel J. Jones, included Welsh reading lessons, the story of Jesus Christ, Old Testament stories, and moral lessons, in illustrated books for children under the age of twelve.

3 Departmental Committee on Welsh in the Educational System of Wales, *Welsh in Education and Life* (London, 1927), pp. 42, 151.

4 Detailed statistical information on an annual basis concerning the number of day schools, pupils, teachers, and university students, may be found in John Williams, *Digest of Welsh Historical Statistics* (2 vols., Cardiff, 1985), II, pp. 195–248.

5 The Commission, established in October 1846, was instructed 'to direct an inquiry to be made into the state of education in the principality of Wales, especially into the means afforded to the labouring classes of acquiring a knowledge of the English language'.

6 For more detail about the Reports and the aftermath, see David Salmon, 'The Story of a Welsh Education Commission (1846–7)', *Y Cymmrodor*, XXIV (1913), 189–237; Frank Price Jones, 'The Blue Books of 1847' in Jac L. Williams and Gwilym Rees Hughes (eds.), *The History of Education in Wales 1* (Swansea, 1978), pp. 127–44; Prys Morgan, 'From Long Knives to Blue Books' in R. R. Davies et al. (eds.), *Welsh Society and Nationhood* (Cardiff, 1984), pp. 199–215; idem (ed.), *Brad y Llyfrau Gleision: Ysgrifau ar Hanes Cymru* (Llandysul, 1991).

7 There is some confusion about the Llandyfrïog school since the 'language of instruction' heading was also marked under 'Welsh and English' as well as 'Welsh only'.

8 See David Evans, *The Sunday Schools of Wales* (London, 1884) for a history of the Sunday school movement in Wales written as a centenary tribute.

9 These statistics have also been neglected by historians. But, for Glamorgan, see R. Tudur Jones, 'Glamorgan Christianity in 1905–6: A Statistical Survey' in Prys Morgan (ed.), *Glamorgan County History, Vol. VI, Glamorgan Society 1780–1980* (Cardiff, 1988), pp. 245–63.

10 W. R. Jones pays warm tribute to Dan Isaac Davies, an HM Inspector of Schools: 'No other person in the second half of the nineteenth century contributed as much as Dan Isaac Davies towards popularising the concept of a bilingual education in Wales.' *Bilingualism in Welsh Education*, p. 61. For a full account of Dan Isaac Davies's contribution to Welsh education, see J. Elwyn Hughes, *Arloeswr Dwyieithedd: Dan Isaac Davies 1839–1887* (Caerdydd, 1984).

11 *Final Report of the Commissioners appointed to inquire into the Elementary Education Acts, England and Wales*, para. 108, PP 1888 (c5485) XXXV.

Education 1.1 Literacy. Number and percentage of men and women signing the marriage register with a mark. Wales and Registration Counties. Various years. 1845–1910

	Year	Total marriages	Marriages signed with marks Number Men	Women	*Percentage Men*	*Women*
WALES	1845	8304	3846	5770	*46.3*	*69.5*
	1850	9323	4188	6231	*44.9*	*66.8*
	1855	9721	4242	6151	*43.6*	*63.3*
	1860	10009	3789	5573	*37.9*	*55.7*
	1865	11279	4001	5701	*35.5*	*50.5*
	1870	10953	3375	4884	*30.8*	*44.6*
	1875	11856	2888	4110	*24.4*	*34.7*
	1880	10952	2434	3322	*22.2*	*30.3*
	1884[1]	12226	2407	2981	*19.7*	*24.4*
	1885	11751	2011	2694	*17.1*	*22.9*
	1890	14457	1651	2125	*11.4*	*14.7*
	1895	14203	907	1106	*6.4*	*7.8*
	1900	16214	688	859	*4.2*	*5.3*
	1905	16331	359	496	*2.2*	*3.0*
	1910	17062	267	288	*1.6*	*1.7*
Registration Counties						
MONMOUTH	1845	1429	758	964	*53.0*	*67.5*
	1855	1668	804	1004	*48.2*	*60.2*
	1860	1658	721	848	*43.5*	*51.1*
	1865	1871	760	890	*40.6*	*47.6*
	1870	1839	674	816	*36.7*	*44.4*
	1875	1829	495	574	*27.1*	*31.4*
	1880	1676	480	531	*28.6*	*31.7*
	1884	2030	500	484	*24.6*	*23.8*
	1905	2681	64	91	*2.4*	*3.4*
	1910	2906	56	54	*1.9*	*1.9*
GLAMORGAN	1845	1785	955	1320	*53.5*	*73.9*
	1855	2723	1383	1896	*50.8*	*69.6*
	1860	2860	1173	1778	*41.0*	*62.2*
	1865	3552	1437	2072	*40.5*	*58.3*
	1870	3524	1230	1777	*34.9*	*50.4*
	1875	4111	1085	1521	*26.4*	*37.0*
	1880	4088	938	1339	*22.9*	*32.8*
	1884	5057	1058	1332	*20.9*	*26.3*
	1905	7707	170	237	*2.2*	*3.1*
	1910	8448	121	125	*1.4*	*1.5*
CARMARTHEN	1845	681	279	501	*41.0*	*73.6*
	1855	739	280	504	*37.9*	*68.2*
	1860	710	233	437	*32.8*	*61.5*
	1865	740	246	405	*33.2*	*54.7*
	1870	833	224	405	*26.9*	*48.6*
	1875	857	180	328	*21.0*	*38.3*
	1880	767	142	297	*18.5*	*38.7*
	1884	754	89	206	*11.8*	*27.3*
	1905	969	22	42	*2.3*	*4.3*
	1910	1084	11	17	*1.0*	*1.6*
PEMBROKE	1845	589	190	334	*32.3*	*56.7*
	1855	570	170	294	*29.8*	*51.6*
	1860	658	178	283	*27.1*	*43.0*
	1865	654	147	232	*22.5*	*35.5*
	1870	632	101	212	*16.0*	*33.5*
	1875	646	87	202	*13.5*	*31.3*
	1880	563	79	145	*14.0*	*25.8*
	1884	552	60	86	*10.9*	*15.6*
	1905	630	6	10	*1.0*	*1.6*
	1910	589	12	14	*2.0*	*2.4*

County	Year	Total marriages	Marriages signed with marks Number Men	Women	*Percentage Men*	*Women*
CARDIGAN	1845	636	208	512	*32.7*	*80.5*
	1855	646	181	434	*28.0*	*67.2*
	1860	647	168	396	*26.0*	*61.2*
	1865	667	145	342	*21.7*	*51.3*
	1870	626	111	296	*17.7*	*47.3*
	1875	616	83	232	*13.5*	*37.7*
	1880	543	74	147	*13.6*	*27.1*
	1884	499	55	147	*11.0*	*29.5*
	1905	517	10	13	*1.9*	*2.5*
	1910	442	3	9	*0.7*	*2.0*
BRECON	1845	454	222	303	*48.9*	*66.7*
	1855	454	191	262	*42.1*	*57.7*
	1860	432	156	226	*36.1*	*52.3*
	1865	468	182	250	*38.9*	*53.4*
	1870	430	152	186	*35.3*	*43.3*
	1875	421	124	140	*29.5*	*33.3*
	1880	370	91	91	*24.6*	*24.6*
	1884	371	107	94	*28.8*	*25.3*
	1905	461	9	18	*2.0*	*3.9*
	1910	386	11	11	*2.8*	*2.8*
RADNOR	1845	197	69	85	*35.0*	*43.1*
	1855	179	73	85	*40.8*	*47.5*
	1860	226	63	85	*27.9*	*37.6*
	1865	225	68	72	*30.2*	*32.0*
	1870	190	56	48	*29.5*	*25.3*
	1875	146	35	36	*24.0*	*24.7*
	1880	130	29	30	*22.3*	*23.1*
	1884	134	27	13	*20.1*	*9.7*
	1905	113	3	1	*2.7*	*0.9*
	1910	105	1	0	*1.0*	*0.0*
MONTGOMERY	1845	487	203	298	*41.7*	*61.2*
	1855	494	190	258	*38.5*	*52.2*
	1860	516	174	251	*33.7*	*48.6*
	1865	540	154	216	*28.5*	*40.0*
	1870	505	138	189	*27.3*	*37.4*
	1875	486	118	149	*24.3*	*30.7*
	1880	404	76	99	*18.8*	*24.5*
	1884	444	75	81	*16.9*	*18.2*
	1905	457	16	12	*3.5*	*2.6*
	1910	329	8	6	*2.4*	*1.8*
FLINT	1845	598	317	419	*53.0*	*70.1*
	1855	267	125	161	*46.8*	*60.3*
	1860	248	110	141	*44.4*	*56.9*
	1865	285	120	140	*42.1*	*49.1*
	1870	214	84	81	*39.3*	*37.9*
	1875	297	88	102	*29.6*	*34.3*
	1880	241	80	76	*33.2*	*31.5*
	1884	235	65	59	*27.7*	*25.1*
	1905	363	6	3	*1.7*	*0.8*
	1910	474	9	10	*1.9*	*2.1*
DENBIGH	1845	317	161	219	*50.8*	*69.1*
	1855	690	348	436	*50.4*	*63.2*
	1860	721	339	415	*47.0*	*57.6*
	1865	771	292	372	*37.9*	*48.2*
	1870	726	247	298	*34.0*	*41.0*
	1875	824	241	280	*29.2*	*34.0*
	1880	738	184	185	*24.9*	*25.1*
	1884	773	170	195	*22.0*	*25.2*
	1905	877	18	25	*2.1*	*2.9*
	1910	917	16	19	*1.7*	*2.1*

County	Year	Total marriages	Marriages signed with marks: Number: Men	Women	*Percentage* *Men*	*Women*
MERIONETH	1845	343	126	228	*36.7*	*66.5*
	1855	349	121	205	*34.7*	*58.7*
	1860	326	105	160	*32.2*	*49.1*
	1865	490	145	244	*29.6*	*49.8*
	1870	444	102	156	*23.0*	*35.1*
	1875	453	93	143	*20.5*	*31.6*
	1880	407	64	97	*15.7*	*23.8*
	1884	337	50	66	*14.8*	*19.6*
	1905	388	5	6	*1.3*	*1.5*
	1910	327	3	4	*0.9*	*1.2*
CAERNARFON	1845	569	245	414	*43.1*	*72.8*
	1855	689	264	437	*38.3*	*63.4*
	1860	764	275	416	*36.0*	*54.5*
	1865	783	211	339	*26.9*	*43.3*
	1870	789	186	320	*23.6*	*40.6*
	1875	934	195	303	*20.9*	*32.4*
	1880	808	138	207	*17.1*	*25.6*
	1884	847	113	174	*13.3*	*20.5*
	1905	945	20	33	*2.1*	*3.5*
	1910	844	11	12	*1.3*	*1.4*
ANGLESEY	1845	219	113	173	*51.6*	*79.0*
	1855	253	112	175	*44.3*	*69.2*
	1860	243	94	137	*38.7*	*56.4*
	1865	233	94	127	*40.3*	*54.5*
	1870	201	70	100	*34.8*	*49.8*
	1875	236	64	100	*27.1*	*42.4*
	1880	217	59	78	*27.2*	*35.9*
	1884	193	38	44	*19.7*	*22.8*
	1905	223	10	5	*4.5*	*2.2*
	1910	211	5	7	*2.4*	*3.3*

Source: Registrar General, *Annual Reports* (for years ending 31 December).

[1] The Annual Reports from 1885 to 1904 did not give separate Welsh county figures for this period but instead divided Wales into Monmouthshire, North Wales and South Wales. The figures for 1884 for Wales have been inserted to enable comparison with the county figures.

Education 1.2 Literacy. Number and percentage of men and women signing the marriage register with a mark. Registration Districts. Various years. 1845–84

County	Registration District	Year	Total marriages	Marriages signed with marks: Number Men	Women	Percentage *Men*	*Women*
MONMOUTHSHIRE	Chepstow, Monmouth	1845	322	135	158	*41.9*	*49.1*
	Chepstow	1855	94	40	41	*42.6*	*43.6*
		1860	98	36	30	*36.7*	*30.6*
		1865	89	28	22	*31.5*	*24.7*
		1870	91	22	18	*24.2*	*19.8*
		1875	96	18	11	*18.8*	*11.5*
		1880	80	14	10	*17.5*	*12.5*
		1884	137	23	25	*16.8*	*18.2*
	Monmouth	1855	163	47	62	*28.8*	*38.0*
		1860	207	80	55	*38.6*	*26.6*
		1865	221	74	64	*33.5*	*29.0*
		1870	197	55	49	*27.9*	*24.9*
		1875	241	61	42	*25.3*	*17.4*
		1880	165	33	26	*20.0*	*15.8*
		1884	188	49	24	*26.1*	*12.8*
	Abergavenny, Pontypool	1845	800	487	623	*60.9*	*77.9*
	Abergavenny	1855	560	331	413	*59.1*	*73.8*
		1860	589	320	399	*54.3*	*67.7*
		1865	156	54	62	*34.6*	*39.7*
		1870	180	70	87	*38.9*	*48.3*
		1875	128	36	35	*28.1*	*27.3*
		1880	128	35	44	*27.3*	*34.4*
		1884	154	35	33	*22.7*	*21.4*
	Bedwellte[1]	1870	460	245	303	*53.3*	*65.9*
		1875	405	157	218	*38.8*	*53.8*
		1880	420	154	209	*36.7*	*49.8*
		1884	467	166	182	*35.5*	*39.0*
		1865	479	257	329	*53.7*	*68.7*
	Pontypool	1855	348	196	228	*56.3*	*65.5*
		1860	304	145	181	*47.7*	*59.5*
		1865	382	197	217	*51.6*	*56.8*
		1870	337	158	189	*46.9*	*56.1*
		1875	258	83	116	*32.2*	*45.0*
		1880	308	121	125	*39.3*	*40.6*
		1884	325	100	94	*30.8*	*28.9*
	Newport	1845	307	136	183	*44.3*	*59.6*
		1855	503	190	260	*37.8*	*51.7*
		1860	460	140	183	*30.4*	*39.8*
		1865	544	150	196	*27.6*	*36.0*
		1870	574	124	170	*21.6*	*29.6*
		1875	701	140	152	*20.0*	*21.7*
		1880	575	123	117	*21.4*	*20.3*
		1884	759	127	126	*16.7*	*16.6*
GLAMORGAN	Cardiff, Bridgend, Neath	1845	741	380	517	*51.3*	*69.8*
	Cardiff	1855	665	302	377	*45.4*	*56.7*
		1860	656	220	328	*33.5*	*50.0*
		1865	644	185	244	*28.7*	*37.9*
		1870	657	144	206	*21.9*	*31.4*
		1875	887	159	225	*17.9*	*25.4*
		1880	892	132	181	*14.8*	*20.3*
		1884	1310	173	205	*13.2*	*15.6*
	Merthyr Tydfil	1845	695	431	585	*62.0*	*84.2*
	Pontypridd[2]	1865	315	151	200	*47.9*	*63.5*
		1870	430	186	248	*43.3*	*57.7*
		1875	557	172	246	*30.9*	*44.2*
		1880	700	216	286	*30.9*	*40.9*
		1884	1019	293	331	*28.8*	*32.5*

County	Registration District	Year	Total marriages	Marriages signed with marks: Number Men	Women	*Percentage Men*	*Women*
	Merthyr Tydfil	1855	1036	609	842	*58.8*	*81.3*
		1860	952	483	716	*50.7*	*75.2*
		1865	1129	596	841	*52.8*	*74.5*
		1870	1058	462	710	*43.7*	*67.1*
		1875	769	251	354	*32.6*	*46.0*
		1880	851	240	350	*28.2*	*41.1*
		1884	908	237	315	*26.1*	*34.7*
	Bridgend	1855	195	99	116	*50.8*	*59.5*
		1860	224	100	124	*44.6*	*55.4*
		1865	230	96	118	*41.7*	*51.3*
		1870	231	75	88	*32.5*	*38.1*
		1875	310	80	98	*25.8*	*31.6*
		1880	243	56	71	*23.0*	*29.2*
		1884	329	91	80	*27.7*	*24.3*
	Neath	1855	408	222	320	*54.4*	*78.4*
		1860	434	194	289	*44.7*	*66.6*
		1865	570	222	345	*38.9*	*60.5*
		1870	489	154	254	*31.5*	*51.9*
		1875	542	151	228	*27.9*	*42.1*
		1880	400	96	138	*24.0*	*34.5*
		1884	391	76	113	*19.4*	*28.9*
	Pontardawe[3]	1875	66	26	29	*39.4*	*43.9*
		1880	128	28	48	*21.9*	*37.5*
		1884	148	21	40	*14.2*	*27.0*
	Swansea	1845	349	144	218	*41.3*	*62.5*
		1855	419	151	241	*36.0*	*57.5*
		1860	538	165	296	*30.7*	*55.0*
		1865	609	175	300	*28.7*	*49.3*
		1870	602	194	245	*32.2*	*40.7*
		1875	924	235	319	*25.4*	*34.5*
		1880	823	165	247	*20.0*	*30.0*
		1884	896	162	240	*18.1*	*26.8*
	Gower[4]	1860	56	11	25	*19.6*	*44.6*
		1865	55	12	24	*21.8*	*43.6*
		1870	57	15	26	*26.3*	*45.6*
		1875	56	11	22	*19.6*	*39.3*
		1880	51	5	18	*9.8*	*35.3*
		1884	56	5	8	*8.9*	*14.3*
CARMARTHENSHIRE	Llanelli, Llandovery, Llandeilo Fawr	1845	368	159	288	*43.2*	*78.3*
	Llanelli	1855	215	85	153	*39.5*	*71.2*
		1860	210	73	134	*34.8*	*63.8*
		1865	219	67	119	*30.6*	*54.3*
		1870	247	76	132	*30.8*	*53.4*
		1875	336	67	122	*19.9*	*36.3*
		1880	306	62	131	*20.3*	*42.8*
		1884	306	43	83	*14.1*	*27.1*
	Llandovery	1855	101	37	71	*36.6*	*70.3*
		1860	111	38	71	*34.2*	*64.0*
		1865	102	37	58	*36.3*	*56.9*
		1870	123	31	54	*25.2*	*43.9*
		1875	112	19	45	*17.0*	*40.2*
		1880	95	18	36	*18.9*	*37.9*
		1884	77	8	22	*10.4*	*28.6*
	Llandeilo Fawr	1855	142	59	101	*41.5*	*71.1*
		1860	103	31	65	*30.1*	*63.1*
		1865	136	44	77	*32.4*	*56.6*
		1870	164	44	85	*26.8*	*51.8*
		1875	129	33	44	*25.6*	*34.1*
		1880	121	24	40	*19.8*	*33.1*
		1884	116	11	31	*9.5*	*26.7*

County	Registration District	Year	Total marriages	Marriages signed with marks Number Men	Women	*Percentage Men*	*Women*
	Carmarthen	1845	313	120	213	*38.3*	*68.1*
		1855	281	99	179	*35.2*	*63.7*
		1860	286	91	167	*31.8*	*58.4*
		1865	283	98	151	*34.6*	*53.4*
		1870	299	73	134	*24.4*	*44.8*
		1875	280	61	117	*21.8*	*41.8*
		1880	245	38	90	*15.5*	*36.7*
		1884	255	27	70	*10.6*	*27.5*
PEMBROKESHIRE	Narberth, Pembroke	1845	319	102	175	*32.0*	*54.9*
	Narberth	1855	110	40	71	*36.4*	*64.5*
		1860	130	39	74	*30.0*	*56.9*
		1865	121	31	54	*25.6*	*44.6*
		1870	148	26	56	*17.6*	*37.8*
		1875	151	19	51	*12.6*	*33.8*
		1880	132	17	40	*12.9*	*30.3*
		1884	112	17	19	*15.2*	*17.0*
	Pembroke	1855	172	42	67	*24.4*	*39.0*
		1860	268	68	113	*25.4*	*42.2*
		1865	290	53	90	*18.3*	*31.0*
		1870	234	26	65	*11.1*	*27.8*
		1875	276	35	70	*12.7*	*25.4*
		1880	208	24	43	*11.5*	*20.7*
		1884	242	17	31	*7.0*	*12.8*
	Haverfordwest	1845	270	88	159	*32.6*	*58.9*
		1855	288	88	156	*30.6*	*54.2*
		1860	260	71	96	*27.3*	*36.9*
		1865	243	63	88	*25.9*	*36.2*
		1870	250	49	91	*19.6*	*36.4*
		1875	219	33	81	*15.1*	*37.0*
		1880	223	38	62	*17.0*	*27.8*
		1884	198	26	36	*13.1*	*18.2*
CARDIGANSHIRE	Cardigan, Aberaeron	1845	232	69	180	*29.7*	*77.6*
	Cardigan	1855	118	32	69	*27.1*	*58.5*
		1860	105	19	48	*18.1*	*45.7*
		1865	121	20	52	*16.5*	*43.0*
		1870	105	13	38	*12.4*	*36.2*
		1875	106	13	41	*12.3*	*38.7*
		1880	107	17	33	*15.9*	*30.8*
		1884	117	14	36	*12.0*	*30.8*
	Tregaron, Lampeter, Newcastle Emlyn	1845	269	92	219	*34.2*	*81.4*
	Newcastle Emlyn	1855	122	40	93	*32.8*	*76.2*
		1860	143	31	97	*21.7*	*67.8*
		1865	120	33	63	*27.5*	*52.5*
		1870	112	23	58	*20.5*	*51.8*
		1875	111	18	43	*16.2*	*38.7*
		1880	90	10	20	*11.1*	*22.2*
		1884	92	8	32	*8.7*	*34.8*
	Lampeter	1855	75	27	56	*36.0*	*74.7*
		1860	59	21	43	*35.6*	*72.9*
		1865	67	16	42	*23.9*	*62.7*
		1870	77	17	41	*22.1*	*53.2*
		1875	58	7	24	*12.1*	*41.4*
		1880	70	13	20	*18.6*	*28.6*
		1884	50	10	22	*20.0*	*44.0*
	Aberaeron	1855	96	17	55	*17.7*	*57.3*
		1860	102	14	54	*13.7*	*52.9*
		1865	82	9	36	*11.0*	*43.9*
		1870	88	10	37	*11.4*	*42.0*
		1875	80	8	23	*10.0*	*28.8*
		1880	76	5	17	*6.6*	*22.4*
		1884	71	7	15	*9.9*	*21.1*

County	Registration District	Year	Total marriages	Marriages signed with marks: Number Men	Women	*Percentage Men*	*Women*
	Aberystwyth	1845	135	47	113	*34.8*	*83.7*
		1855	176	47	119	*26.7*	*67.6*
		1860	178	62	113	*34.8*	*63.5*
		1865	227	53	124	*23.3*	*54.6*
		1870	189	33	85	*17.5*	*45.0*
		1875	192	24	61	*12.5*	*31.8*
		1880	152	19	38	*12.5*	*25.0*
		1884	127	10	30	*7.9*	*23.6*
	Tregaron	1855	59	18	42	*30.5*	*71.2*
		1860	60	21	41	*35.0*	*68.3*
		1865	50	14	25	*28.0*	*50.0*
		1870	55	15	37	*27.3*	*67.3*
		1875	69	13	40	*18.8*	*58.0*
		1880	48	10	19	*20.8*	*39.6*
		1884	42	6	12	*14.3*	*28.6*
BRECONSHIRE	Builth, Brecon, Crickhowell, Hay	1845	454	222	303	*48.9*	*66.7*
	Builth	1855	54	19	31	*35.2*	*57.4*
		1860	48	12	20	*25.0*	*41.7*
		1865	88	28	39	*31.8*	*44.3*
		1870	48	9	16	*18.8*	*33.3*
		1875	58	8	9	*13.8*	*15.5*
		1880	59	5	7	*8.5*	*11.9*
		1884	37	6	4	*16.2*	*10.8*
	Brecon	1855	147	49	81	*33.3*	*55.1*
		1860	142	42	78	*29.6*	*54.9*
		1865	139	40	67	*28.8*	*48.2*
		1870	144	30	53	*20.8*	*36.8*
		1875	133	28	43	*21.1*	*32.3*
		1880	102	19	16	*18.6*	*15.7*
		1884	88	13	17	*14.8*	*19.3*
	Crickhowell	1855	187	105	132	*56.1*	*70.6*
		1860	148	73	99	*49.3*	*66.9*
		1865	178	93	124	*52.2*	*69.7*
		1870	176	99	106	*56.3*	*60.2*
		1875	162	77	81	*47.5*	*50.0*
		1880	135	57	61	*42.2*	*45.2*
		1884	177	75	69	*42.4*	*39.0*
	Hay	1855	66	18	18	*27.3*	*27.3*
		1860	94	29	29	*30.9*	*30.9*
		1865	63	21	20	*33.3*	*31.7*
		1870	62	14	11	*22.6*	*17.7*
		1875	68	11	7	*16.2*	*10.3*
		1880	74	10	7	*13.5*	*9.5*
		1884	69	13	4	*18.8*	*5.8*
RADNORSHIRE	Presteigne, Knighton, Rhayader	1845	197	69	85	*35.0*	*43.1*
	Kington[5]	1870	55	14	11	*25.5*	*20.0*
	Presteigne[6]	1855	92	40	42	*43.5*	*45.7*
		1860	102	25	40	*24.5*	*39.2*
		1865	106	41	35	*38.7*	*33.0*
		1870	27	6	6	*22.2*	*22.2*
		1875	22	6	6	*27.3*	*27.3*
	Knighton	1855	48	16	21	*33.3*	*43.8*
		1860	78	26	32	*33.3*	*41.0*
		1865	66	15	21	*22.7*	*31.8*
		1870	70	23	22	*32.9*	*31.4*
		1875	72	20	17	*27.8*	*23.6*
		1880	77	20	16	*26.0*	*20.8*
		1884	97	20	10	*20.6*	*10.3*

County	Registration District	Year	Total marriages	Marriages signed with marks: Number Men	Women	*Percentage Men*	*Women*
	Rhayader	1355	39	17	22	*43.6*	*56.4*
		1860	46	12	13	*26.1*	*28.3*
		1865	53	12	16	*22.6*	*30.2*
		1870	38	13	9	*34.2*	*23.7*
		1875	52	9	13	*17.3*	*25.0*
		1880	53	9	14	*17.0*	*26.4*
		1884	37	7	3	*18.9*	*8.1*
MONTGOMERYSHIRE	Machynlleth, Llanfyllin	1845	182	78	126	*42.9*	*69.2*
	Machynlleth	1855	76	35	43	*46.1*	*56.6*
		1860	73	23	39	*31.5*	*53.4*
		1865	110	24	46	*21.8*	*41.8*
		1870	90	27	38	*30.0*	*42.2*
		1875	79	14	24	*17.7*	*30.4*
		1880	66	10	16	*15.2*	*24.2*
		1884	66	12	11	*18.2*	*16.7*
	Llanfyllin	1855	140	52	74	*37.1*	*52.9*
		1860	135	52	59	*38.5*	*43.7*
		1865	130	36	50	*27.7*	*38.5*
		1870	121	38	45	*31.4*	*37.2*
		1875	101	34	32	*33.7*	*31.7*
		1880	106	22	26	*20.8*	*24.5*
		1884	116	21	23	*18.1*	*19.8*
	Newtown, Montgomery	1845	305	125	172	*41.0*	*56.4*
	Newtown	1855	148	49	83	*33.1*	*56.1*
		1860	188	56	107	*29.8*	*56.9*
		1865	171	57	82	*33.3*	*48.0*
		1870	192	47	77	*24.5*	*40.1*
		1875	207	46	74	*22.2*	*35.7*
		1880	135	27	38	*20.0*	*28.1*
		1884	159	23	32	*14.5*	*20.1*
	Montgomery/Forden[7]	1855	130	54	58	*41.5*	*44.6*
		1860	120	43	46	*35.8*	*38.3*
		1865	129	37	38	*28.7*	*29.5*
		1870	102	26	29	*25.5*	*28.4*
		1875	99	24	19	*24.2*	*19.2*
		1880	97	17	19	*17.5*	*19.6*
		1884	103	19	15	*18.4*	*14.6*
FLINTSHIRE	Holywell	1845	257	143	175	*55.6*	*68.1*
		1855	267	125	161	*46.8*	*60.3*
		1860	248	110	141	*44.4*	*56.9*
		1865	285	120	140	*42.1*	*49.1*
		1870	214	84	81	*39.3*	*37.9*
		1875	297	88	102	*29.6*	*34.3*
		1880	241	80	76	*33.2*	*31.5*
		1884	235	65	59	*27.7*	*25.1*
DENBIGHSHIRE	Wrexham	1845[8]	341	174	244	*51.0*	*71.6*
		1855	352	199	227	*56.5*	*64.5*
		1860	373	184	223	*49.3*	*59.8*
		1865	399	186	215	*46.6*	*53.9*
		1870	362	134	168	*37.0*	*46.4*
		1875	440	151	170	*34.3*	*38.6*
		1880	367	105	117	*28.6*	*31.9*
		1884	455	112	132	*24.6*	*29.0*

County	Registration District	Year	Total marriages	Marriages signed with marks: Number Men	Women	*Percentage Men*	*Women*
	Ruthin, Llanrwst, St Asaph	1845	317	161	219	*50.8*	*69.1*
	Ruthin	1855	103	53	71	*51.5*	*68.9*
		1860	84	41	45	*48.8*	*53.6*
		1865	89	30	44	*33.7*	*49.4*
		1870	85	24	32	*28.2*	*37.6*
		1875	76	19	21	*25.0*	*27.6*
		1880	86	22	26	*25.6*	*30.2*
		1884	60	12	17	*20.0*	*28.3*
	St Asaph	1855	147	56	83	*38.1*	*56.5*
		1860	186	86	99	*46.2*	*53.2*
		1865	201	53	70	*26.4*	*34.8*
		1870	217	74	78	*34.1*	*35.9*
		1875	224	56	60	*25.0*	*26.8*
		1880	194	42	26	*21.6*	*13.4*
		1884	190	33	32	*17.4*	*16.8*
	Llanrwst	1855	88	40	55	*45.5*	*62.5*
		1860	78	28	48	*35.9*	*61.5*
		1865	82	23	43	*28.0*	*52.4*
		1870	62	15	20	*24.2*	*32.3*
		1875	84	15	29	*17.9*	*34.5*
		1880	91	15	16	*16.5*	*17.6*
		1884	68	13	14	*19.1*	*20.6*
MERIONETH	Merioneth	1845	343	126	228	*36.7*	*66.5*
	Corwen	1855	106	47	72	*44.3*	*67.9*
		1860	94	36	38	*38.3*	*40.4*
		1865	140	49	79	*35.0*	*56.4*
		1870	123	36	45	*29.3*	*36.6*
		1875	117	38	37	*32.5*	*31.6*
		1880	87	14	14	*16.1*	*16.1*
		1884	91	19	15	*20.9*	*16.5*
	Bala	1855	44	9	23	*20.5*	*52.3*
		1860	45	11	23	*24.4*	*51.1*
		1865	40	10	21	*25.0*	*52.5*
		1870	52	8	14	*15.4*	*26.9*
		1875	39	5	11	*12.8*	*28.2*
		1880	35	2	6	*5.7*	*17.1*
		1884	35	3	5	*8.6*	*14.3*
	Dolgellau	1855	87	23	39	*26.4*	*44.8*
		1860	75	24	33	*32.0*	*44.0*
		1865	120	28	41	*23.3*	*34.2*
		1870	103	20	32	*19.4*	*31.1*
		1875	110	15	36	*13.6*	*32.7*
		1880	87	11	14	*12.6*	*16.1*
		1884	70	7	17	*10.0*	*24.3*
	Ffestiniog	1855	112	42	71	*37.5*	*63.4*
		1860	112	34	66	*30.4*	*58.9*
		1865	190	58	103	*30.5*	*54.2*
		1870	166	38	65	*22.9*	*39.2*
		1875	187	35	59	*18.7*	*31.6*
		1880	198	37	63	*18.7*	*31.8*
		1884	141	21	29	*14.9*	*20.6*
CAERNARFONSHIRE	Pwllheli, Caernarfon	1845	313	131	235	*41.9*	*75.1*
	Pwllheli	1855	113	49	74	*43.4*	*65.5*
		1860	134	43	82	*32.1*	*61.2*
		1865	138	44	73	*31.9*	*52.9*
		1870	133	23	63	*17.3*	*47.4*
		1875	149	37	50	*24.8*	*33.6*
		1880	134	38	50	*28.4*	*37.3*
		1884	138	17	34	*12.3*	*24.6*

County	Registration District	Year	Total marriages	Marriages signed with marks: Number Men	Number Women	*Percentage Men*	*Percentage Women*
	Caernarfon	1855	214	81	146	*37.9*	*68.2*
		1860	252	103	149	*40.9*	*59.1*
		1865	274	65	129	*23.7*	*47.1*
		1870	287	81	132	*28.2*	*46.0*
		1875	332	73	128	*22.0*	*38.6*
		1880	305	48	82	*15.7*	*26.9*
		1884	296	42	68	*14.2*	*23.0*
	Bangor, Conwy	1845	256	114	179	*44.5*	*69.9*
	Bangor	1855	261	92	160	*35.2*	*61.3*
		1860	286	101	151	*35.3*	*52.8*
		1865	282	82	112	*29.1*	*39.7*
		1870	279	64	102	*22.9*	*36.6*
		1875	328	69	102	*21.0*	*31.1*
		1880	254	36	51	*14.2*	*20.1*
		1884	279	39	53	*14.0*	*19.0*
	Conwy	1855	101	42	57	*41.6*	*56.4*
		1860	92	28	34	*30.4*	*37.0*
		1865	89	20	25	*22.5*	*28.1*
		1870	90	18	23	*20.0*	*25.6*
		1875	125	16	23	*12.8*	*18.4*
		1880	115	16	24	*13.9*	*20.9*
		1884	134	15	19	*11.2*	*14.2*
ANGLESEY	Anglesey	1845	219	113	173	*51.6*	*79.0*
		1855	253	112	175	*44.3*	*69.2*
		1860	243	94	137	*38.7*	*56.4*
		1865	233	94	127	*40.3*	*54.5*
		1870	201	70	100	*34.8*	*49.8*
		1875	236	64	100	*27.1*	*42.4*
		1880	217	59	78	*27.2*	*35.9*
		1884	193	38	44	*19.7*	*22.8*

Source: Registrar General, *Annual Reports* (for years ending 31 December).

For full details of boundary changes affecting Registration Districts from 1851, see Population Table 1.2.

[1] Bedwellte District was created from part of Abergavenny District on 1 July 1861.
[2] Pontypridd District was created from parts of Cardiff and Merthyr Tydfil Districts on 18 July 1863.
[3] Pontardawe District was created from parts of Neath and Swansea Districts on 1 July 1875.
[4] Gower District was created from part of Swansea District on 19 July 1858.
[5] Kington District was created from part of Presteigne District on 1 April 1870 and transferred to Hereford Registration County.
[6] Presteigne District was abolished on 1 July 1877; most parts were transferred to Knighton District.
[7] Montgomery District was renamed Forden on 1 July 1870.
[8] Wrexham District was included in Flint in 1845.

Education 2.1 Reports of the Commissioners of Inquiry into the state of education in Wales, 1847. Day schools. Number of schools and scholars, by type of school and language of instruction. Wales and Registration Counties. 1847

	Type of school	Number of schools[1] Language of instruction[3] Welsh	Both	English	Total	Number of scholars[2] Language of instruction[3] Welsh	Both	English	Total	*Percentage*
Wales[4]	Church of England	2	128	486	616	46	6506	30066	36618	*47.6*
	Nonconformist[5]	0	25	24	49	0	946	1391	2337	*3.0*
	Roman Catholic	0	0	5	5	0	0	208	208	*0.3*
	British[6]	0	12	61	73	0	953	7383	8336	*10.8*
	Private[7]	1	100	669	770	17	3208	17353	20578	*26.7*
	Union[8]	0	6	21	27	0	182	885	1067	*1.4*
	Company[9]	0	7	30	37	0	523	3346	3869	*5.0*
	Other[10]	0	40	40	80	0	1566	2396	3962	*5.1*
	Total	**3**	**318**	**1336**	**1657**	**63**	**13884**	**63028**	**76975**	***100.0***
	Percentage					*0.1*	*18.0*	*81.9*	*100.0*	
Registration Counties										
Monmouth[4]	Church of England	0	2	26	28	0	140	2571	2711	*40.8*
	Nonconformist[5]	0	0	1	1	0	0	84	84	*1.3*
	Roman Catholic	0	0	1	1	0	0	97	97	*1.5*
	British[6]	0	0	6	6	0	0	682	682	*10.3*
	Private[7]	0	5	81	86	0	254	2117	2371	*35.6*
	Company[9]	0	0	5	5	0	0	707	707	*10.6*
	Total	**0**	**7**	**120**	**127**	**0**	**394**	**6258**	**6652**	***100.0***
	Percentage					*0.0*	*5.9*	*94.1*	*100.0*	
Glamorgan	Church of England	0	24	69	93	0	1128	3642	4770	*30.1*
	Nonconformist[5]	0	13	7	20	0	530	424	954	*6.0*
	Roman Catholic	0	0	1	1	0	0	40	40	*0.3*
	British[6]	0	1	9	10	0	130	1308	1438	*9.1*
	Private[7]	0	19	162	181	0	670	4336	5006	*31.6*
	Union[8]	0	2	2	4	0	81	76	157	*1.0*
	Company[9]	0	7	22	29	0	523	2509	3032	*19.1*
	Other[10]	0	0	7	7	0	0	449	449	*2.8*
	Total	**0**	**66**	**279**	**345**	**0**	**3062**	**12784**	**15846**	***100.0***
	Percentage					*0.0*	*19.3*	*80.7*	*100.0*	
Carmarthen	Church of England	0	46	10	56	0	2218	621	2839	*43.9*
	Nonconformist[5]	0	21	4	25	0	637	195	832	*12.9*
	British[6]	0	1	2	3	0	101	325	426	*6.6*
	Private[7]	0	26	45	71	0	743	1351	2094	*32.4*
	Union[8]	0	2	2	4	0	74	52	126	*1.9*
	Company[9]	0	0	1	1	0	0	40	40	*0.6*
	Other[10]	0	3	0	3	0	114	0	114	*1.8*
	Total	**0**	**99**	**64**	**163**	**0**	**3887**	**2584**	**6471**	***100.0***
	Percentage					*0.0*	*60.1*	*39.9*	*100.0*	
Pembroke	Church of England	0	10	49	59	0	437	3123	3560	*50*
	Nonconformist[5]	0	12	6	18	0	559	173	732	*10.3*
	British[6]	0	2	1	3	0	175	158	333	*4.7*
	Private[7]	0	9	88	97	0	207	1946	2153	*30.2*
	Union[8]	0	0	5	5	0	0	253	253	*3.6*
	Other[10]	0	2	1	3	0	50	40	90	*1.3*
	Total	**0**	**35**	**150**	**185**	**0**	**1428**	**5693**	**7121**	***100.0***
	Percentage					*0*	*20.1*	*79.9*	*100.0*	
Cardigan	Church of England	2	20	28	50	46	1086	1307	2439	*44.0*
	Nonconformist[5]	0	8	5	13	0	390	307	697	*12.5*
	British[6]	0	2	2	4	0	70	136	206	*3.7*
	Private[7]	0	27	42	69	0	933	1181	2114	*38.2*
	Union[8]	0	2	0	2	0	27	0	27	*0.5*
	Company[9]	0	0	1	1	0	0	60	60	*1.1*
	Total	**2**	**59**	**78**	**139**	**46**	**2506**	**2991**	**5543**	***100.0***
	Percentage					*0.8*	*45.2*	*54.0*	*100.0*	

Registration County	Type of school	Number of schools[1] Language of instruction[3] Welsh	Both	English	Total	Number of scholars[2] Language of instruction[3] Welsh	Both	English	Total	*Percentage*
Brecon	Church of England	0	2	41	43	0	86	2011	2097	*53.1*
	Nonconformist[5]	0	0	1	1	0	0	63	63	*1.6*
	Roman Catholic	0	0	1	1	0	0	16	16	*0.4*
	British[6]	0	1	2	3	0	96	176	272	*6.9*
	Private[7]	0	2	48	50	0	51	1453	1504	*38.0*
	Total	**0**	**5**	**93**	**98**	**0**	**233**	**3719**	**3952**	***100.0***
	Percentage						*5.9*	*94.1*	*100.0*	
Radnor	Church of England	0	0	20	20	0	0	685	685	*67.9*
	Private[7]	0	0	12	12	0	0	283	283	*28.1*
	Union[8]	0	0	1	1	0	0	41	41	*4.1*
	Total	**0**	**0**	**33**	**33**	**0**	**0**	**1009**	**1009**	***100.0***
	Percentage							*100.0*	*100.0*	
Montgomery	Church of England	0	3	52	55	0	126	2634	2760	*52.4*
	Nonconformist[5]	0	0	2	2	0	0	248	248	*4.7*
	British[6]	0	0	6	6	0	0	461	461	*8.8*
	Private[7]	0	1	62	63	0	25	1326	1351	*25.7*
	Union[8]	0	0	5	5	0	0	192	192	*3.6*
	Other[10]	0	1	4	5	0	60	195	255	*4.8*
	Total	**0**	**5**	**131**	**136**	**0**	**211**	**5056**	**5267**	***100.0***
	Percentage						*4.0*	*96.0*	*100.0*	
Flint	Church of England	0	2	29	31	0	163	2232	2395	*52.9*
	Nonconformist[5]	0	0	3	3	0	0	151	151	*3.4*
	Roman Catholic	0	0	2	2	0	0	55	55	*1.2*
	British[6]	0	0	6	6	0	0	806	806	*17.8*
	Private[7]	0	0	36	36	0	0	821	821	*18.2*
	Union[8]	0	0	1	1	0	0	63	63	*1.4*
	Company[9]	0	0	1	1	0	0	30	30	*0.7*
	Other[10]	0	0	3	3	0	0	205	205	*4.5*
	Total	**0**	**2**	**81**	**83**	**0**	**163**	**4363**	**4526**	***100.0***
	Percentage						*3.6*	*96.4*	*100.0*	
Denbigh	Church of England	0	3	68	71	0	234	4312	4546	*57.4*
	Nonconformist[5]	0	1	3	4	0	36	183	219	*2.8*
	British[6]	0	0	10	10	0	0	1413	1413	*17.8*
	Private[7]	0	4	40	44	0	96	848	944	*12.0*
	Union[8]	0	0	4	4	0	0	172	172	*2.2*
	Other[10]	0	1	9	10	0	36	587	623	*7.9*
	Total	**0**	**9**	**134**	**143**	**0**	**402**	**7515**	**7917**	***100.0***
	Percentage						*5.1*	*94.9*	*100.0*	
Merioneth	Church of England	0	5	33	38	0	238	1713	1951	*52.2*
	Nonconformist[5]	0	0	2	2	0	0	82	82	*2.2*
	British[6]	0	2	11	13	0	112	1123	1235	*33.0*
	Private[7]	0	3	13	16	0	96	304	400	*10.7*
	Other[10]	0	2	1	3	0	50	21	71	*1.9*
	Total	**0**	**12**	**60**	**72**	**0**	**496**	**3243**	**3739**	***100.0***
	Percentage						*13.3*	*86.7*	*100.0*	
Caernarfon	Church of England	0	6	50	56	0	321	4240	4561	*71.0*
	British[6]	0	1	3	4	0	81	534	615	*9.6*
	Private[7]	1	1	27	29	17	30	941	988	*15.3*
	Union[8]	0	0	1	1	0	0	36	36	*0.6*
	Other[10]	0	0	2	2	0	0	225	225	*3.5*
	Total	**1**	**8**	**83**	**92**	**17**	**432**	**5976**	**6425**	***100.0***
	Percentage					*0.3*	*6.7*	*93.0*	*100.0*	
Anglesey	Church of England	0	5	11	16	0	329	975	1304	*52.0*
	Nonconformist[5]	0	0	2	2	0	0	65	65	*2.6*
	British[6]	0	2	3	5	0	188	261	449	*17.9*
	Private[7]	0	3	13	16	0	103	446	549	*21.9*
	Other[10]	0	1	1	2	0	50	90	140	*5.6*
	Total	**0**	**11**	**30**	**41**	**0**	**670**	**1837**	**2507**	***100.0***
	Percentage						*26.7*	*73.3*	*100.0*	

Parts of Wales in English Registration Counties

Registration County	Type of school	Number of schools[1] Language of instruction[3] Welsh	Both	English	Total	Number of scholars[2] Language of instruction[3] Welsh	Both	English	Total	*Percentage*
Shropshire[11]	Church of England	0	0	10	10	0	0	575	575	*60.5*
	Private[7]	0	0	9	9	0	0	235	235	*24.7*
	Other[10]	0	0	2	2	0	0	141	141	*14.8*
	Total	0	0	21	21	0	0	951	951	*100.0*
Cheshire[12]	Church of England	0	0	8	8	0	0	625	625	*93.8*
	Private[7]	0	0	1	1	0	0	16	16	*2.4*
	Other[10]	0	0	1	1	0	0	25	25	*3.8*
	Total	**0**	**0**	**10**	**10**	**0**	**0**	**666**	**666**	***100.0***

Source: *Reports of the Commissioners of Inquiry into the State of Education in Wales*; Part I, Carmarthen, Glamorgan and Pembroke [PP 1847 (870) XXVII]; Part II, Brecknock, Cardigan, Radnor and Monmouth [PP 1847 (871) XXVIII]; Part III, North Wales [PP 1847 (872) XXVII]; Parochial tables.

1 Excludes seven day schools listed without information concerning number of scholars on the books and/or language of instruction.
2 These are numbers of 'Children on the Books', giving an average of 47 per school. Where given, the equivalent for 'Average Attendance last Year' is 41.
3 At source marks are placed under the following headings: 'Welsh only', 'Welsh spoken in explanation of English books', 'English books only'.
4 For Monmouthshire, only those 18 industrial parishes adjoining Glamorgan and Brecon were included in the returns, viz. Aberystruth, Basaleg, Bedwellte, Caerleon, Llanelen, Llanfihangel Llantarnam, Llanfihangel Pont-y-moel, Llanfoist, Llanfrechfa, Llanhilleth, Llanofer, Llanwenarth, Machen, Mynyddislwyn, Newport, Pant-teg, Risca, Trevethin with Pontypool. In 1841 these parishes contained 60% of the total population of Monmouthshire.
5 'British and Foreign' schools were non-denominational.
6 Includes chapel schools established by Independents, Methodists and Baptists. The comparatively large number of Nonconformist day schools in Carmarthen were mainly Baptist.
7 'Private adventure' and 'Dame' schools.
8 Workhouse schools governed by the Poor Law authorities.
9 Schools funded by company owners' philanthropy and workers' subscriptions; for example, the Dowlais Iron Company's separate schools for boys and girls at Merthyr Tydfil.
10 A residual group, including 'no sect', and unspecified schools.
11 Includes returns from: Hanmer, Overton, and Malpas, and Penley in the Ancient County of Flint; Hyssington and Crugion in the Ancient County of Montgomery; Chirk and Llansilin in the Ancient County of Montgomery.
12 Includes returns from Hawarden in the Ancient County of Flint.

Education 2.2 Reports of the Commissioners of Inquiry into the state of education in Wales, 1847. Day schools. Number of schools and scholars, by type of school and language of instruction. Registration Districts. 1847

Registration District	Type of school	Number of schools[1] Language of instruction[3] Welsh	Both	English	Total	Number of scholars[2] Language of instruction[3] Welsh	Both	English	Total
MONMOUTHSHIRE									
Abergavenny[4]	Church of England	0	1	8	9	0	47	904	951
	British[5]	0	0	2	2	0	0	198	198
	Private[6]	0	4	24	28	0	159	680	839
	Company[7]	0	0	3	3	0	0	459	459
	Total	**0**	**5**	**37**	**42**	**0**	**206**	**2241**	**2447**
Pontypool[4]	Church of England	0	1	5	6	0	93	616	709
	British[5]	0	0	1	1	0	0	180	180
	Private[6]	0	0	17	17	0	0	438	438
	Company[7]	0	0	2	2	0	0	248	248
	Nonconformist[8]	0	0	1	1	0	0	84	84
	Total	**0**	**1**	**26**	**27**	**0**	**93**	**1566**	**1659**
Newport[4]	Church of England	0	0	13	13	0	0	1051	1051
	British[5]	0	0	3	3	0	0	304	304
	Roman Catholic	0	0	1	1	0	0	97	97
	Private[6]	0	1	40	41	0	95	999	1094
	Total	**0**	**1**	**57**	**58**	**0**	**95**	**2451**	**2546**
GLAMORGAN									
Cardiff	Church of England	0	6	28	34	0	320	1340	1660
	British[5]	0	0	3	3	0	0	592	592
	Roman Catholic	0	0	1	1	0	0	40	40
	Private[6]	0	1	44	45	0	33	1262	1295
	Company[7]	0	1	2	3	0	40	105	145
	Nonconformist[8]	0	3	3	6	0	98	206	304
	Union[9]	0	0	1	1	0	0	54	54
	Total	**0**	**11**	**82**	**93**	**0**	**491**	**3599**	**4090**
Merthyr Tydfil	Church of England	0	2	7	9	0	83	593	676
	Private[6]	0	11	33	44	0	472	1041	1513
	Company[7]	0	2	4	6	0	90	645	735
	Nonconformist[8]	0	6	0	6	0	286	0	286
	Union[9]	0	1	0	1	0	65	0	65
	Other[10]	0	0	2	2	0	0	60	60
	Total	**0**	**22**	**46**	**68**	**0**	**996**	**2339**	**3335**
Bridgend	Church of England	0	9	14	23	0	349	626	975
	Private[6]	0	3	13	16	0	80	298	378
	Nonconformist[8]	0	0	1	1	0	0	92	92
	Total	**0**	**12**	**28**	**40**	**0**	**429**	**1016**	**1445**
Neath	Church of England	0	3	6	9	0	184	324	508
	British[5]	0	0	3	3	0	0	220	220
	Private[6]	0	4	21	25	0	85	594	679
	Company[7]	0	4	15	19	0	393	1640	2033
	Nonconformist[8]	0	3	0	3	0	138	0	138
	Other[10]	0	0	2	2	0	0	214	214
	Total	**0**	**14**	**47**	**61**	**0**	**800**	**2992**	**3792**
Swansea	Church of England	0	4	14	18	0	192	759	951
	British[5]	0	1	3	4	0	130	496	626
	Private[6]	0	0	51	51	0	0	1141	1141
	Company[7]	0	0	1	1	0	0	119	119
	Nonconformist[8]	0	1	3	4	0	8	126	134
	Union[9]	0	1	1	2	0	16	22	38
	Other[10]	0	0	3	3	0	0	175	175
	Total	**0**	**7**	**76**	**83**	**0**	**346**	**2838**	**3184**

Registration District	Type of school	Number of schools[1] Language of instruction[3] Welsh	Both	English	Total	Number of scholars[2] Language of instruction[3] Welsh	Both	English	Total
CARMARTHENSHIRE									
Llanelli	Church of England	0	2	5	7	0	172	241	413
	British[5]	0	0	1	1	0	0	180	180
	Private[6]	0	1	19	20	0	9	663	672
	Company[7]	0	0	1	1	0	0	40	40
	Nonconformist[8]	0	1	4	5	0	25	195	220
	Union[9]	0	0	1	1	0	0	19	19
	Other[10]	0	1	0	1	0	36	0	36
	Total	**0**	**5**	**31**	**36**	**0**	**242**	**1338**	**1580**
Llandovery	Church of England	0	6	1	7	0	250	74	324
	British[5]	0	1	0	1	0	101	0	101
	Private[6]	0	7	1	8	0	256	21	277
	Nonconformist[8]	0	4	0	4	0	126	0	126
	Union[9]	0	1	0	1	0	16	0	16
	Other[10]	0	1	0	1	0	59	0	59
	Total	**0**	**20**	**2**	**22**	**0**	**808**	**95**	**903**
Llandeilo Fawr	Church of England	0	17	0	17	0	714	0	714
	Private[6]	0	7	5	12	0	218	119	337
	Nonconformist[8]	0	4	0	4	0	151	0	151
	Union[9]	0	0	1	1	0	0	33	33
	Total	**0**	**28**	**6**	**34**	**0**	**1083**	**152**	**1235**
Carmarthen	Church of England	0	21	4	25	0	1082	306	1388
	British[5]	0	0	1	1	0	0	145	145
	Private[6]	0	11	20	31	0	260	548	808
	Nonconformist[8]	0	12	0	12	0	335	0	335
	Union[9]	0	1	0	1	0	58	0	58
	Other[10]	0	1	0	1	0	19	0	19
	Total	**0**	**46**	**25**	**71**	**0**	**1754**	**999**	**2753**
PEMBROKESHIRE									
Narberth	Church of England	0	6	14	20	0	260	797	1057
	Private[6]	0	4	12	16	0	126	255	381
	Nonconformist[8]	0	2	3	5	0	71	77	148
	Union[9]	0	0	1	1	0	0	17	17
	Total	**0**	**12**	**30**	**42**	**0**	**457**	**1146**	**1603**
Pembroke	Church of England	0	0	15	15	0	0	1281	1281
	Private[6]	0	0	40	40	0	0	879	879
	Union[9]	0	0	1	1	0	0	62	62
	Total	**0**	**0**	**56**	**56**	**0**	**0**	**2222**	**2222**
Haverfordwest	Church of England	0	4	20	24	0	177	1045	1222
	British[5]	0	2	1	3	0	175	158	333
	Private[6]	0	5	36	41	0	81	812	893
	Nonconformist[8]	0	10	3	13	0	488	96	584
	Union[9]	0	0	3	3	0	0	174	174
	Other[10]	0	2	1	3	0	50	40	90
	Total	**0**	**23**	**64**	**87**	**0**	**971**	**2325**	**3296**
CARDIGANSHIRE									
Cardigan	Church of England	0	6	7	13	0	400	294	694
	British[5]	0	1	0	1	0	40	0	40
	Private[6]	0	5	11	16	0	144	250	394
	Nonconformist[8]	0	4	1	5	0	210	25	235
	Union[9]	0	1	0	1	0	15	0	15
	Total	**0**	**17**	**19**	**36**	**0**	**809**	**569**	**1378**
Newcastle Emlyn	Church of England	1	7	0	8	26	323	0	349
	British[5]	0	1	0	1	0	30	0	30
	Private[6]	0	7	6	13	0	246	206	452
	Nonconformist[8]	0	3	1	4	0	112	35	147
	Union[9]	0	1	0	1	0	12	0	12
	Total	**1**	**19**	**7**	**27**	**26**	**723**	**241**	**990**
Lampeter	Church of England	0	2	2	4	0	109	70	179
	Private[6]	0	3	4	7	0	60	125	185
	Nonconformist[8]	0	1	0	1	0	68	0	68
	Total	**0**	**6**	**6**	**12**	**0**	**237**	**195**	**432**

Registration District	Type of school	Number of schools[1] Language of instruction[3] Welsh	Both	English	Total	Number of scholars[2] Language of instruction[3] Welsh	Both	English	Total
Aberaeron	Church of England	1	1	3	5	20	67	161	248
	British[5]	0	0	1	1	0	0	67	67
	Private[6]	0	6	6	12	0	236	164	400
	Total	**1**	**7**	**10**	**18**	**20**	**303**	**392**	**715**
Aberystwyth	Church of England	0	4	14	18	0	187	673	860
	British[5]	0	0	1	1	0	0	69	69
	Private[6]	0	5	13	18	0	194	371	565
	Nonconformist[8]	0	0	2	2	0	0	212	212
	Total	**0**	**9**	**30**	**39**	**0**	**381**	**1325**	**1706**
Tregaron	Church of England	0	0	2	2	0	0	109	109
	Private[6]	0	1	2	3	0	53	65	118
	Company[7]	0	0	1	1	0	0	60	60
	Nonconformist[8]	0	0	1	1	0	0	35	35
	Total	**0**	**1**	**6**	**7**	**0**	**53**	**269**	**322**
BRECONSHIRE									
Builth	Church of England	0	0	5	5	0	0	188	188
	Private[6]	0	0	3	3	0	0	73	73
	Total	**0**	**0**	**8**	**8**	**0**	**0**	**261**	**261**
Brecon	Church of England	0	1	18	19	0	45	847	892
	British[5]	0	1	0	1	0	96	0	96
	Roman Catholic	0	0	1	1	0	0	16	16
	Private[6]	0	1	16	17	0	25	420	445
	Total	**0**	**3**	**35**	**38**	**0**	**166**	**1283**	**1449**
Crickhowell	Church of England	0	1	9	10	0	41	426	467
	British[5]	0	0	1	1	0	0	74	74
	Private[6]	0	1	22	23	0	26	807	833
	Total	**0**	**2**	**32**	**34**	**0**	**67**	**1307**	**1374**
Hay	Church of England	0	0	9	9	0	0	550	550
	British[5]	0	0	1	1	0	0	102	102
	Private[6]	0	0	7	7	0	0	153	153
	Nonconformist[8]	0	0	1	1	0	0	63	63
	Total	**0**	**0**	**18**	**18**	**0**	**0**	**868**	**868**
RADNORSHIRE									
Presteigne	Church of England	0	0	10	10	0	0	348	348
	Private[6]	0	0	7	7	0	0	159	159
	Total	**0**	**0**	**17**	**17**	**0**	**0**	**507**	**507**
Knighton	Church of England	0	0	6	6	0	0	227	227
	Private[6]	0	0	3	3	0	0	49	49
	Union[9]	0	0	1	1	0	0	41	41
	Total	**0**	**0**	**10**	**10**	**0**	**0**	**317**	**317**
Rhayader	Church of England	0	0	4	4	0	0	110	110
	Private[6]	0	0	2	2	0	0	75	75
	Total	**0**	**0**	**6**	**6**	**0**	**0**	**185**	**185**
MONTGOMERYSHIRE									
Machynlleth	Church of England	0	1	6	7	0	43	361	404
	British[5]	0	0	2	2	0	0	197	197
	Private[6]	0	1	6	7	0	25	143	168
	Nonconformist[8]	0	0	1	1	0	0	48	48
	Other[10]	0	0	1	1	0	0	57	57
	Total	**0**	**2**	**16**	**18**	**0**	**68**	**806**	**874**
Newtown	Church of England	0	0	17	17	0	0	868	868
	Private[6]	0	0	21	21	0	0	472	472
	Nonconformist[8]	0	0	1	1	0	0	200	200
	Union[9]	0	0	2	2	0	0	85	85
	Total	**0**	**0**	**41**	**41**	**0**	**0**	**1625**	**1625**
Montgomery	Church of England	0	0	16	16	0	0	785	785
	British[5]	0	0	2	2	0	0	89	89
	Private[6]	0	0	20	20	0	0	337	337
	Union[9]	0	0	1	1	0	0	28	28
	Total	**0**	**0**	**39**	**39**	**0**	**0**	**1239**	**1239**

Registration District	Type of school	Number of schools[1] Language of instruction[3] Welsh	Both	English	Total	Number of scholars[2] Language of instruction[3] Welsh	Both	English	Total
Llanfyllin	Church of England	0	2	13	15	0	83	620	703
	British[5]	0	0	2	2	0	0	175	175
	Private[6]	0	0	15	15	0	0	374	374
	Union[9]	0	0	2	2	0	0	79	79
	Other[10]	0	1	3	4	0	60	138	198
	Total	**0**	**3**	**35**	**38**	**0**	**143**	**1386**	**1529**
FLINTSHIRE									
Holywell	Church of England	0	2	29	31	0	163	2232	2395
	British[5]	0	0	6	6	0	0	806	806
	Roman Catholic	0	0	2	2	0	0	55	55
	Private[6]	0	0	36	36	0	0	821	821
	Company[7]	0	0	1	1	0	0	30	30
	Nonconformist[8]	0	0	3	3	0	0	151	151
	Union[9]	0	0	1	1	0	0	63	63
	Other[10]	0	0	3	3	0	0	205	205
	Total	**0**	**2**	**81**	**83**	**0**	**163**	**4363**	**4526**
DENBIGHSHIRE									
Wrexham	Church of England	0	1	25	26	0	90	1626	1716
	British[5]	0	0	4	4	0	0	702	702
	Private[6]	0	2	19	21	0	41	385	426
	Nonconformist[8]	0	0	1	1	0	0	85	85
	Union[9]	0	0	1	1	0	0	76	76
	Other[10]	0	0	3	3	0	0	195	195
	Total	**0**	**3**	**53**	**56**	**0**	**131**	**3069**	**3200**
Ruthin	Church of England	0	0	14	14	0	0	935	935
	British[5]	0	0	2	2	0	0	239	239
	Private[6]	0	1	3	4	0	44	62	106
	Nonconformist[8]	0	1	0	1	0	36	0	36
	Union[9]	0	0	1	1	0	0	47	47
	Other[10]	0	1	0	1	0	36	0	36
	Total	**0**	**3**	**20**	**23**	**0**	**116**	**1283**	**1399**
St Asaph	Church of England	0	1	22	23	0	60	1342	1402
	British[5]	0	0	2	2	0	0	282	282
	Private[6]	0	0	17	17	0	0	372	372
	Nonconformist[8]	0	0	1	1	0	0	48	48
	Union[9]	0	0	2	2	0	0	49	49
	Other[10]	0	0	3	3	0	0	223	223
	Total	**0**	**1**	**47**	**48**	**0**	**60**	**2316**	**2376**
Llanrwst	Church of England	0	1	7	8	0	84	409	493
	British[5]	0	0	2	2	0	0	190	190
	Private[6]	0	1	1	2	0	11	29	40
	Nonconformist[8]	0	0	1	1	0	0	50	50
	Other[10]	0	0	3	3	0	0	169	169
	Total	**0**	**2**	**14**	**16**	**0**	**95**	**847**	**942**
MERIONETH									
Corwen	Church of England	0	1	10	11	0	34	528	562
	British[5]	0	0	2	2	0	0	346	346
	Private[6]	0	0	3	3	0	0	42	42
	Nonconformist[8]	0	0	1	1	0	0	42	42
	Other[10]	0	0	1	1	0	0	21	21
	Total	**0**	**1**	**17**	**18**	**0**	**34**	**979**	**1013**
Bala	Church of England	0	0	4	4	0	0	141	141
	British[5]	0	2	2	4	0	112	135	247
	Private[6]	0	1	1	2	0	24	40	64
	Nonconformist[8]	0	0	1	1	0	0	40	40
	Total	**0**	**3**	**8**	**11**	**0**	**136**	**356**	**492**
Dolgellau	Church of England	0	3	10	13	0	144	533	677
	British[5]	0	0	4	4	0	0	451	451
	Private[6]	0	2	5	7	0	72	69	141
	Other[10]	0	1	0	1	0	20	0	20
	Total	**0**	**6**	**19**	**25**	**0**	**236**	**1053**	**1289**

Registration District	Type of school	Number of schools[1] Language of instruction[3] Welsh	Both	English	Total	Number of scholars[2] Language of instruction[3] Welsh	Both	English	Total
Ffestiniog	Church of England	0	1	9	10	0	60	511	571
	British[5]	0	0	3	3	0	0	191	191
	Private[6]	0	0	4	4	0	0	153	153
	Other[10]	0	1	0	1	0	30	0	30
	Total	**0**	**2**	**16**	**18**	**0**	**90**	**855**	**945**
CAERNARFONSHIRE									
Pwllheli	Church of England	0	2	16	18	0	137	983	1120
	British[5]	0	1	0	1	0	81	0	81
	Private[6]	0	0	5	5	0	0	198	198
	Total	**0**	**3**	**21**	**24**	**0**	**218**	**1181**	**1399**
Caernarfon	Church of England	0	2	9	11	0	99	1019	1118
	British[5]	0	0	2	2	0	0	424	424
	Private[6]	1	0	5	6	17	0	154	171
	Total	**1**	**2**	**16**	**19**	**17**	**99**	**1597**	**1713**
Bangor	Church of England	0	1	14	15	0	20	1493	1513
	Private[6]	0	1	14	15	0	30	479	509
	Union[9]	0	0	1	1	0	0	36	36
	Other[10]	0	0	2	2	0	0	225	225
	Total	**0**	**2**	**31**	**33**	**0**	**50**	**2233**	**2283**
Conwy	Church of England	0	1	11	12	0	65	745	810
	British[5]	0	0	1	1	0	0	110	110
	Private[6]	0	0	3	3	0	0	110	110
	Total	**0**	**1**	**15**	**16**	**0**	**65**	**965**	**1030**
ANGLESEY									
Anglesey	Church of England	0	5	11	16	0	329	975	1304
	British[5]	0	2	3	5	0	188	261	449
	Private[6]	0	3	13	16	0	103	446	549
	Nonconformist[8]	0	0	2	2	0	0	65	65
	Other[10]	0	1	1	2	0	50	90	140
	Total	**0**	**11**	**30**	**41**	**0**	**670**	**1837**	**2507**

Source: *Reports of the Commissioners of Inquiry into the State of Education in Wales*; Part I, Carmarthen, Glamorgan and Pembroke [PP 1847 (870) XXVII]; Part II, Brecknock, Cardigan, Radnor and Monmouth [PP 1847 (871) XXVIII]; Part III, North Wales [PP 1847 (872) XXVII]; Parochial tables.

1 Excludes seven day schools listed without figures for number of scholars on the books and/or language of instruction.

2 These are numbers of 'Children on the Books', giving an average of 47 per school. Where given, the equivalent for 'Average Attendance last Year' is 41.

3 At source marks are placed under the following headings: 'Welsh only', 'Welsh spoken in explanation of English books', 'English books only'.

4 Monmouthshire includes only the following parishes: Abergavenny – Bedwellte, Llanover, Llanwenarth, Aberystruth, Llanfoist, Llanelen; Pontypool – Trevethin, Llanfrechfa, Llanhilleth, Llanfihangel Pont-y-moel; Newport – Caerleon, Risca, Newport, Llanfihangel Llantarnam, Basaleg, Mynyddislwyn, Machen.

5 'British and Foreign' schools were non-denominational.

6 'Private adventure' and 'Dame' schools.

7 Schools funded by company owners' philanthropy and workers' subscriptions; for example, the Dowlais Iron Company's separate schools for boys and girls at Merthyr Tydfil.

8 Includes chapel schools established by Independents, Methodists and Baptists. The comparatively large number of Nonconformist day schools in Carmarthen were mainly Baptist.

9 Workhouse schools run by the Poor Law authorities.

10 A residual group, including 'no sect', and unspecified schools.

Education 2.3 Reports of the Commissioners of Inquiry into the state of education in Wales, 1847. Sunday schools. Number of schools and scholars, by denomination and language of instruction. Wales and Registration Counties. 1847

	Denomination	Number of schools[1] Language of instruction Welsh	Both	English	Total	Number of scholars[2] Language of instruction Welsh	Both	English	Total
Wales[3]	Church of England	83	128	254	465	6271	11970	17133	35374
	Independent	358	220	47	625	31142	23159	4358	58659
	Baptist	131	155	47	333	9496	14487	4072	28055
	Calvinistic Methodist	710	124	52	886	86618	12569	3901	103088
	Wesleyan Methodist	106	114	76	296	7113	11087	7869	26069
	Other	1	3	15	19	82	315	1289	1686
	Total	**1389**	**744**	**491**	**2624**	**140722**	**73587**	**38622**	**252931**
	as % total scholars	*52.9*	*28.4*	*18.7*	*100.0*	*55.6*	*29.1*	*15.3*	*100.0*
Registration Counties									
Monmouth[3]	Church of England	1	5	23	29	36	821	2334	3191
	Independent	5	23	7	35	622	2434	779	3835
	Baptist	2	29	9	40	215	3336	845	4396
	Calvinistic Methodist	7	7	0	14	1203	997	0	2200
	Wesleyan Methodist	1	7	19	27	160	716	2809	3685
	Other	0	1	1	2	0	40	37	77
	Total	**16**	**72**	**59**	**147**	**2236**	**8344**	**6804**	**17384**
	as % total scholars					*12.9*	*48.0*	*39.1*	*100.0*
Glamorgan	Church of England	5	14	74	93	407	795	4737	5939
	Independent	58	41	5	104	5416	4673	387	10476
	Baptist	10	45	5	60	595	4249	773	5617
	Calvinistic Methodist	72	22	7	101	7418	1593	596	9607
	Wesleyan Methodist	0	9	14	23	0	520	1337	1857
	Other	0	1	7	8	0	198	882	1080
	Total	**145**	**132**	**112**	**389**	**13836**	**12028**	**8712**	**34576**
	as % total scholars					*40.0*	*34.8*	*25.2*	*100.0*
Carmarthen	Church of England	6	25	12	43	335	2225	948	3508
	Independent	32	53	1	86	3022	6284	151	9457
	Baptist	20	25	0	45	1489	1766	0	3255
	Calvinistic Methodist	51	23	1	75	5169	1726	60	6955
	Wesleyan Methodist	2	7	3	12	51	504	351	906
	Other	0	0	1	1	0	0	40	40
	Total	**111**	**133**	**18**	**262**	**10066**	**12505**	**1550**	**24121**
	as % total scholars					*41.7*	*51.8*	*6.4*	*100.0*
Pembroke	Church of England	2	5	42	49	94	226	2678	2998
	Independent	14	19	17	50	1249	1820	1724	4793
	Baptist	11	11	18	40	850	812	1318	2980
	Calvinistic Methodist	12	11	11	34	741	730	850	2321
	Wesleyan Methodist	1	2	12	15	53	47	1244	1344
	Other	0	0	2	2	0	0	65	65
	Total	**40**	**48**	**102**	**190**	**2987**	**3635**	**7879**	**14501**
	as % total scholars					*20.6*	*25.1*	*54.3*	*100.0*
Cardigan	Church of England	42	15	7	64	3294	1043	291	4628
	Independent	67	9	1	77	7399	1091	99	8589
	Baptist	31	10	0	41	2622	1503	0	4125
	Calvinistic Methodist	74	9	1	84	13282	1331	331	14944
	Wesleyan Methodist	8	8	2	18	718	880	81	1679
	Other	1	0	0	1	82	0	0	82
	Total	**223**	**51**	**11**	**285**	**27397**	**5848**	**802**	**34047**
	as % total scholars					*80.5*	*17.2*	*2.4*	*100.0*
Brecon	Church of England	3	3	35	41	168	111	1980	2259
	Independent	12	27	3	42	988	2304	80	3372
	Baptist	5	17	4	26	190	1459	238	1887
	Calvinistic Methodist	26	8	2	36	2290	986	99	3375
	Wesleyan Methodist	2	5	7	14	93	188	598	879
	Other	0	0	1	1	0	0	17	17
	Total	**48**	**60**	**52**	**160**	**3729**	**5048**	**3012**	**11789**
	as % total scholars					*31.6*	*42.8*	*25.5*	*100.0*

Registration County	Denomination	Number of schools[1] Language of instruction Welsh	Both	English	Total	Number of scholars[2] Language of instruction Welsh	Both	English	Total
Radnor	Church of England	0	0	19	19	0	0	991	991
	Independent	0	4	2	6	0	248	65	313
	Baptist	0	1	8	9	0	35	267	302
	Calvinistic Methodist	0	2	5	7	0	105	194	299
	Wesleyan Methodist	0	0	4	4	0	0	183	183
	Other	0	0	1	1	0	0	26	26
	Total	**0**	**7**	**39**	**46**	**0**	**388**	**1726**	**2114**
	as % total scholars					*0.0*	*18.4*	*81.6*	*100.0*
Montgomery	Church of England	5	9	14	28	363	674	1037	2074
	Independent	31	12	6	49	1921	1031	536	3488
	Baptist	3	5	1	9	117	357	502	976
	Calvinistic Methodist	76	21	14	111	6092	2283	1149	9524
	Wesleyan Methodist	22	22	6	50	1364	2181	536	4081
	Other	0	0	1	1	0	0	50	50
	Total	**137**	**69**	**42**	**248**	**9857**	**6526**	**3810**	**20193**
	as % total scholars					*48.8*	*32.3*	*18.9*	*100.0*
Flint	Church of England	1	11	1	13	27	2269	173	2469
	Independent	5	14	1	20	516	1269	155	1940
	Baptist	0	1	0	1	0	141	0	141
	Calvinistic Methodist	23	7	2	32	2845	799	114	3758
	Wesleyan Methodist	5	19	3	27	446	2207	307	2960
	Total	**34**	**52**	**7**	**93**	**3834**	**6685**	**749**	**11268**
	as % total scholars					*34.0*	*59.3*	*6.6*	*100.0*
Denbigh	Church of England	3	21	8	32	304	2392	690	3386
	Independent	31	10	3	44	1960	921	272	3153
	Baptist	7	5	2	14	400	342	129	871
	Calvinistic Methodist	77	7	8	92	10287	1327	467	12081
	Wesleyan Methodist	15	15	3	33	1266	1596	224	3086
	Other	0	1	1	2	0	77	172	249
	Total	**133**	**59**	**25**	**217**	**14217**	**6655**	**1954**	**22826**
	as % total scholars					*62.3*	*29.2*	*8.6*	*100.0*
Merioneth	Church of England	7	6	6	19	404	286	266	956
	Independent	46	4	0	50	3184	394	0	3578
	Baptist	12	1	0	13	765	160	0	925
	Calvinistic Methodist	122	2	0	124	13334	90	0	13424
	Wesleyan Methodist	27	7	0	34	1557	493	0	2050
	Total	**214**	**20**	**6**	**240**	**19244**	**1423**	**266**	**20933**
	as % total scholars					*91.9*	*6.8*	*1.3*	*100.0*
Caernarfon	Church of England	6	10	3	19	702	884	128	1714
	Independent	40	3	1	44	3312	595	110	4017
	Baptist	14	3	0	17	973	194	0	1167
	Calvinistic Methodist	119	2	0	121	17764	211	0	17975
	Wesleyan Methodist	16	11	1	28	855	1466	50	2371
	Total	**195**	**29**	**5**	**229**	**23606**	**3350**	**288**	**27244**
	as % total scholars					*86.6*	*12.3*	*1.1*	*100.0*
Anglesey	Church of England	2	3	2	7	137	144	258	539
	Independent	16	1	0	17	1493	95	0	1588
	Baptist	16	0	0	16	1280	0	0	1280
	Calvinistic Methodist	51	2	0	53	6193	348	0	6541
	Wesleyan Methodist	7	1	1	9	550	201	89	840
	Total	**92**	**7**	**3**	**102**	**9653**	**788**	**347**	**10788**
	as % total scholars					*89.5*	*7.3*	*3.2*	*100.0*
Parts of Wales in English Registration Counties									
Shropshire[4]	Church of England	0	1	4	5	0	100	336	436
	Independent	1	0	0	1	60	0	0	60
	Baptist	0	2	0	2	0	133	0	133
	Calvinistic Methodist	0	1	0	1	0	43	0	43
	Wesleyan Methodist	0	1	1	2	0	88	60	148
	Total	**1**	**5**	**5**	**11**	**60**	**364**	**396**	**820**
	as % total scholars					*7.3*	*44.4*	*48.3*	*100.0*

Registration County	Denomination	Number of schools[1] Language of instruction Welsh	Both	English	Total	Number of scholars[2] Language of instruction Welsh	Both	English	Total
Cheshire[5]	Church of England	0	0	4	4	0	0	286	286
	Calvinistic Methodist	0	0	1	1	0	0	41	41
	Total	**0**	**0**	**5**	**5**	**0**	**0**	**327**	**327**
	as % total scholars							*100.0*	*100.0*

Source: *Reports of the Commissioners of Inquiry into the State of Education in Wales*; Part I, Carmarthen, Glamorgan and Pembroke [PP 1847 (870) XXVII]; Part II, Brecknock, Cardigan, Radnor and Monmouth [PP 1847 (871) XXVIII]; Part III, North Wales [PP 1847 (872) XXVII]; Parochial tables.

1 Excludes 86 Sunday schools listed in the returns without figures for the 'number on books'.
2 This is the 'number on books', giving an average of 96 per Sunday school; the equivalent average for 'those who usually attend' is 86.
3 For Monmouth, only the 18 industrial parishes adjoining Glamorgan and Brecon were included in the returns, viz. Aberystruth, Basaleg, Bedwellte, Caerleon, Llanelen, Llanfihangel Llantarnam, Llanfihangel Pont-y-moel, Llanfoist, Llanfrechfa, Llanhilleth, Llanover, Llanwenarth, Machen, Mynyddislwyn, Newport, Pant-teg, Risca, Trevethin with Pontypool. In 1841 these parishes contained 60% of the total population of Monmouthshire. The total for Wales includes parts of Flint and Denbigh in English Registration Counties.
4 Includes returns from: Hanmer and Penley in the Ancient County of Flint; Chirk and Llansilin in the Ancient County of Denbigh.
5 Includes returns from Hawarden in the Ancient County of Flint.

Education 2.4 Reports of the Commissioners of Inquiry into the state of education in Wales, 1847. Sunday schools. Number of schools and scholars, by denomination and language of instruction. Registration Districts. 1847

Registration District	Denomination	Number of schools[1] Language of instruction Welsh	Both	English	Total	Number of scholars[2] Language of instruction Welsh	Both	English	Total
MONMOUTHSHIRE[3]									
Abergavenny[3]	Church of England	0	5	7	12	0	821	852	1673
	Independent	3	9	2	14	409	1318	107	1834
	Baptist	2	10	3	15	215	1048	149	1412
	Calvinistic Methodist	5	4	0	9	1029	833	0	1862
	Wesleyan Methodist	1	3	9	13	160	492	1160	1812
	Total	**11**	**31**	**21**	**63**	**1813**	**4512**	**2268**	**8593**
	% of total scholars					*21.1*	*52.5*	*26.4*	*100.0*
Pontypool[3]	Church of England	0	0	7	7	0	0	825	825
	Independent	1	3	2	6	123	209	160	492
	Baptist	0	11	4	15	0	1465	369	1834
	Calvinistic Methodist	1	1	0	2	121	90	0	211
	Wesleyan Methodist	0	2	6	8	0	90	1137	1227
	Other	0	0	1	1	0	0	37	37
	Total	**2**	**17**	**20**	**39**	**244**	**1854**	**2528**	**4626**
	% of total scholars					*5.3*	*40.1*	*54.6*	*100.0*
Newport[3]	Church of England	1	0	9	10	36	0	657	693
	Independent	1	11	3	15	90	907	512	1509
	Baptist	0	8	2	10	0	823	327	1150
	Calvinistic Methodist	1	2	0	3	53	74	0	127
	Wesleyan Methodist	0	2	4	6	0	134	512	646
	Other	0	1	0	1	0	40	0	40
	Total	**3**	**24**	**18**	**45**	**179**	**1978**	**2008**	**4165**
	% of total scholars					*4.3*	*47.5*	*48.2*	*100.0*
GLAMORGAN									
Cardiff	Church of England	0	3	24	27	0	121	1360	1481
	Independent	7	6	1	14	317	555	74	946
	Baptist	2	8	2	12	99	633	280	1012
	Calvinistic Methodist	15	7	0	22	1218	510	0	1728
	Wesleyan Methodist	0	2	2	4	0	126	299	425
	Other	0	0	2	2	0	0	201	201
	Total	**24**	**26**	**31**	**81**	**1634**	**1945**	**2214**	**5793**
	% of total scholars					*28.2*	*33.6*	*38.2*	*100.0*
Merthyr Tydfil	Church of England	3	2	7	12	295	96	834	1225
	Independent	11	9	1	21	1710	1622	93	3425
	Baptist	4	17	1	22	218	2222	170	2610
	Calvinistic Methodist	13	2	0	15	2283	251	0	2534
	Wesleyan Methodist	0	2	5	7	0	182	377	559
	Other	0	1	0	1	0	198	0	198
	Total	**31**	**33**	**14**	**78**	**4506**	**4571**	**1474**	**10551**
	% of total scholars					*42.7*	*43.3*	*14.0*	*100.0*
Bridgend	Church of England	0	4	19	23	0	162	889	1051
	Independent	14	4	0	18	1074	277	0	1351
	Baptist	0	9	0	9	0	538	0	538
	Calvinistic Methodist	15	4	0	19	1023	126	0	1149
	Wesleyan Methodist	0	1	3	4	0	51	365	416
	Other	0	0	1	1	0	0	45	45
	Total	**29**	**22**	**23**	**74**	**2097**	**1154**	**1299**	**4550**
	% of total scholars					*46.1*	*25.4*	*28.5*	*100.0*
Neath	Church of England	2	2	9	13	112	203	763	1078
	Independent	21	8	0	29	1767	1113	0	2880
	Baptist	3	5	1	9	229	346	180	755
	Calvinistic Methodist	24	7	0	31	2391	513	0	2904
	Wesleyan Methodist	0	2	1	3	0	63	110	173
	Other	0	0	3	3	0	0	616	616
	Total	**50**	**24**	**14**	**88**	**4499**	**2238**	**1669**	**8406**
	% of total scholars					*53.5*	*26.6*	*19.9*	*100.0*

Registration District	Denomination	Number of schools[1] Language of instruction Welsh	Both	English	Total	Number of scholars[2] Language of instruction Welsh	Both	English	Total
Swansea	Church of England	0	3	15	18	0	213	891	1104
	Independent	5	14	3	22	548	1106	220	1874
	Baptist	1	6	1	8	49	510	143	702
	Calvinistic Methodist	5	2	7	14	503	193	596	1292
	Wesleyan Methodist	0	2	3	5	0	98	186	284
	Other	0	0	1	1	0	0	20	20
	Total	**11**	**27**	**30**	**68**	**1100**	**2120**	**2056**	**5276**
	% of total scholars					*20.8*	*40. 2*	*39.0*	*100.0*
CARMARTHENSHIRE									
Llanelli	Church of England	0	6	2	8	0	289	260	549
	Independent	5	8	1	14	673	1233	151	2057
	Baptist	6	4	0	10	769	429	0	1198
	Calvinistic Methodist	8	1	0	9	1231	82	0	1313
	Wesleyan Methodist	0	1	1	2	0	36	173	209
	Total	**19**	**20**	**4**	**43**	**2673**	**2069**	**584**	**5326**
	% of total scholars					*50.2*	*38.8*	*11.0*	*100.0*
Llandovery	Church of England	2	4	2	8	135	271	79	485
	Independent	6	15	0	21	316	1786	0	2102
	Baptist	5	4	0	9	236	213	0	449
	Calvinistic Methodist	11	8	0	19	766	654	0	1420
	Wesleyan Methodist	0	1	0	1	0	83	0	83
	Total	**24**	**32**	**2**	**58**	**1453**	**3007**	**79**	**4539**
	% of total scholars					*32.0*	*66.2*	*1.7*	*100.0*
Llandeilo Fawr	Church of England	0	7	3	10	0	624	139	763
	Independent	5	5	0	10	582	602	0	1184
	Baptist	5	5	0	10	263	202	0	465
	Calvinistic Methodist	11	6	0	17	1041	361	0	1402
	Wesleyan Methodist	1	3	1	5	30	185	28	243
	Total	**22**	**26**	**4**	**52**	**1916**	**1974**	**167**	**4057**
	% of total scholars					*47.2*	*48.7*	*4.1*	*100.0*
Carmarthen	Church of England	4	8	5	17	200	1041	470	1711
	Independent	16	25	0	41	1451	2663	0	4114
	Baptist	4	12	0	16	221	922	0	1143
	Calvinistic Methodist	21	8	1	30	2131	629	60	2820
	Wesleyan Methodist	1	2	1	4	21	200	150	371
	Other	0	0	1	1	0	0	40	40
	Total	**46**	**55**	**8**	**109**	**4024**	**5455**	**720**	**10199**
	% of total scholars					*39.5*	*53.5*	*7.1*	*100.0*
PEMBROKESHIRE									
Narberth	Church of England	1	2	13	16	24	71	819	914
	Independent	11	8	2	21	1074	821	180	2075
	Baptist	3	5	2	10	252	406	100	758
	Calvinistic Methodist	0	2	3	5	0	115	189	304
	Wesleyan Methodist	0	0	2	2	0	0	224	224
	Other	0	0	1	1	0	0	21	21
	Total	**15**	**17**	**23**	**55**	**1350**	**1413**	**1533**	**4296**
	% of total scholars					*31.4*	*32.9*	*35.7*	*100.0*
Pembroke	Church of England	0	0	15	15	0	0	1060	1060
	Independent	0	0	4	4	0	0	560	560
	Baptist	0	0	8	8	0	0	535	535
	Calvinistic Methodist	0	0	7	7	0	0	623	623
	Wesleyan Methodist	0	0	4	4	0	0	400	400
	Total	**0**	**0**	**38**	**38**	**0**	**0**	**3178**	**3178**
	% of total scholars							*100.0*	*100.0*
Haverfordwest	Church of England	1	3	14	18	70	155	799	1024
	Independent	3	11	11	25	175	999	984	2158
	Baptist	8	6	8	22	598	406	683	1687
	Calvinistic Methodist	12	9	1	22	741	615	38	1394
	Wesleyan Methodist	1	2	6	9	53	47	620	720
	Other	0	0	1	1	0	0	44	44
	Total	**25**	**31**	**41**	**97**	**1637**	**2222**	**3168**	**7027**
	% of total scholars					*23.3*	*31.6*	*45.1*	*100.0*

Registration District	Denomination	Number of schools[1] Language of instruction Welsh	Both	English	Total	Number of scholars[2] Language of instruction Welsh	Both	English	Total
CARDIGANSHIRE									
Cardigan	Church of England	3	3	4	10	314	238	265	817
	Independent	16	1	1	18	1525	118	99	1742
	Baptist	15	4	0	19	1331	808	0	2139
	Calvinistic Methodist	14	0	1	15	1411	0	331	1742
	Wesleyan Methodist	0	1	0	1	0	97	0	97
	Other	1	0	0	1	82	0	0	82
	Total	**49**	**9**	**6**	**64**	**4663**	**1261**	**695**	**6619**
	% of total scholars					*70.4*	*19.1*	*10.5*	*100.0*
Newcastle Emlyn	Church of England	7	3	0	10	498	144	0	642
	Independent	21	1	0	22	2466	150	0	2616
	Baptist	8	0	0	8	574	0	0	574
	Calvinistic Methodist	11	1	0	12	1675	29	0	1704
	Wesleyan Methodist	2	0	0	2	105	0	0	105
	Total	**49**	**5**	**0**	**54**	**5318**	**323**	**0**	**5641**
	% of total scholars					*94.3*	*5.7*	*0.0*	*100.0*
Lampeter	Church of England	0	3	0	3	0	306	0	306
	Independent	10	5	0	15	791	396	0	1187
	Baptist	0	3	0	3	0	151	0	151
	Calvinistic Methodist	1	2	0	3	31	104	0	135
	Wesleyan Methodist	0	1	0	1	0	51	0	51
	Total	**11**	**14**	**0**	**25**	**822**	**1008**	**0**	**1830**
	% of total scholars					*44.9*	*55.1*	*0.0*	*100.0*
Aberaeron	Church of England	5	6	0	11	423	355	0	778
	Independent	10	2	0	12	1387	427	0	1814
	Baptist	1	0	0	1	50	0	0	50
	Calvinistic Methodist	10	0	0	10	1793	0	0	1793
	Wesleyan Methodist	1	1	0	2	63	12	0	75
	Total	**27**	**9**	**0**	**36**	**3716**	**794**	**0**	**4510**
	% of total scholars					*82.4*	*17.6*	*0.0*	*100.0*
Aberystwyth	Church of England	18	0	3	21	1463	0	26	1489
	Independent	8	0	0	8	1067	0	0	1067
	Baptist	5	3	0	8	496	544	0	1040
	Calvinistic Methodist	24	3	0	27	5882	566	0	6448
	Wesleyan Methodist	3	4	2	9	445	632	81	1158
	Total	**58**	**10**	**5**	**73**	**9353**	**1742**	**107**	**11202**
	% of total scholars					*83.5*	*15.6*	*1.0*	*100.0*
Tregaron	Church of England	9	0	0	9	596	0	0	596
	Independent	2	0	0	2	163	0	0	163
	Baptist	2	0	0	2	171	0	0	171
	Calvinistic Methodist	14	3	0	17	2490	632	0	3122
	Wesleyan Methodist	2	1	0	3	105	88	0	193
	Total	**29**	**4**	**0**	**33**	**3525**	**720**	**0**	**4245**
	% of total scholars					*83.0*	*17.0*	*0.0*	*100.0*
BRECONSHIRE									
Builth	Church of England	0	0	6	6	0	0	239	239
	Independent	1	10	1	12	47	628	31	706
	Baptist	2	2	2	6	91	80	65	236
	Calvinistic Methodist	1	1	1	3	126	140	75	341
	Total	**4**	**13**	**10**	**27**	**264**	**848**	**410**	**1522**
	% of total scholars					*17.3*	*55.7*	*26.9*	*100.0*
Brecon	Church of England	3	2	11	16	168	81	720	969
	Independent	7	7	1	15	424	490	30	944
	Baptist	2	7	1	10	59	371	66	496
	Calvinistic Methodist	16	2	0	18	1104	182	0	1286
	Wesleyan Methodist	0	3	1	4	0	108	75	183
	Other	0	0	1	1	0	0	17	17
	Total	**28**	**21**	**15**	**64**	**1755**	**1232**	**908**	**3895**
	% of total scholars					*45.1*	*31.6*	*23.3*	*100.0*

Registration District	Denomination	Number of schools[1] Language of instruction Welsh	Both	English	Total	Number of scholars[2] Language of instruction Welsh	Both	English	Total
Crickhowell	Church of England	0	1	8	9	0	30	476	506
	Independent	4	9	0	13	517	1097	0	1614
	Baptist	1	8	0	9	40	1008	0	1048
	Calvinistic Methodist	7	3	0	10	858	583	0	1441
	Wesleyan Methodist	1	2	5	8	44	80	483	607
	Total	**13**	**23**	**13**	**49**	**1459**	**2798**	**959**	**5216**
	% of total scholars					*28.0*	*53.6*	*18.4*	*100.0*
Hay	Church of England	0	0	10	10	0	0	545	545
	Independent	0	1	1	2	0	89	19	108
	Baptist	0	0	1	1	0	0	107	107
	Calvinistic Methodist	2	2	1	5	202	81	24	307
	Wesleyan Methodist	1	0	1	2	49	0	40	89
	Total	**3**	**3**	**14**	**20**	**251**	**170**	**735**	**1156**
	% of total scholars					*21.7*	*14.7*	*63.6*	*100.0*
RADNORSHIRE									
Presteigne	Church of England	0	0	10	10	0	0	496	496
	Independent	0	0	1	1	0	0	50	50
	Baptist	0	0	2	2	0	0	68	68
	Calvinistic Methodist	0	0	2	2	0	0	65	65
	Wesleyan Methodist	0	0	3	3	0	0	109	109
	Other	0	0	1	1	0	0	26	26
	Total	**0**	**0**	**19**	**19**	**0**	**0**	**814**	**814**
	% of total scholars					*0*	*0*	*100*	*100*
Knighton	Church of England	0	0	5	5	0	0	323	323
	Calvinistic Methodist	0	0	2	2	0	0	59	59
	Total	**0**	**0**	**7**	**7**	**0**	**0**	**382**	**382**
	% of total scholars					*0*	*0*	*100*	*100*
Rhayader	Church of England	0	0	4	4	0	0	172	172
	Independent	0	4	1	5	0	248	15	263
	Baptist	0	1	6	7	0	35	199	234
	Calvinistic Methodist	0	2	1	3	0	105	70	175
	Wesleyan Methodist	0	0	1	1	0	0	74	74
	Total	**0**	**7**	**13**	**20**	**0**	**388**	**530**	**918**
	% of total scholars					*0.0*	*42.3*	*57.7*	*100.0*
MONTGOMERYSHIRE									
Machynlleth	Church of England	3	3	0	6	268	250	0	518
	Independent	13	0	0	13	961	0	0	961
	Baptist	3	0	0	3	117	0	0	117
	Calvinistic Methodist	21	0	0	21	2315	0	0	2315
	Wesleyan Methodist	11	2	0	13	763	242	0	1005
	Total	**51**	**5**	**0**	**56**	**4424**	**492**	**0**	**4916**
	% of total scholars					*90.0*	*10.0*	*0.0*	*100.0*
Newtown	Church of England	1	3	3	7	30	277	191	498
	Independent	0	4	4	8	0	425	386	811
	Baptist	0	4	1	5	0	302	502	804
	Calvinistic Methodist	30	11	7	48	2133	1677	591	4401
	Wesleyan Methodist	3	8	2	13	207	857	324	1388
	Total	**34**	**30**	**17**	**81**	**2370**	**3538**	**1994**	**7902**
	% of total scholars					*30.0*	*44.8*	*25.2*	*100.0*
Montgomery	Church of England	0	0	7	7	0	0	616	616
	Independent	1	2	2	5	33	142	150	325
	Calvinistic Methodist	0	6	6	12	0	313	478	791
	Wesleyan Methodist	0	0	4	4	0	0	212	212
	Other	0	0	1	1	0	0	50	50
	Total	**1**	**8**	**20**	**29**	**33**	**455**	**1506**	**1994**
	% of total scholars					*1.7*	*22.8*	*75.5*	*100.0*
Llanfyllin	Church of England	1	3	4	8	65	147	230	442
	Independent	17	6	0	23	927	464	0	1391
	Baptist	0	1	0	1	0	55	0	55
	Calvinistic Methodist	25	4	1	30	1644	293	80	2017
	Wesleyan Methodist	8	12	0	20	394	1082	0	1476
	Total	**51**	**26**	**5**	**82**	**3030**	**2041**	**310**	**5381**
	% of total scholars					*56.3*	*37.9*	*5.8*	*100.0*

Registration District	Denomination	Number of schools[1] Language of instruction Welsh	Both	English	Total	Number of scholars[2] Language of instruction Welsh	Both	English	Total
FLINTSHIRE									
Holywell	Church of England	1	11	1	13	27	2269	173	2469
	Independent	5	14	1	20	516	1269	155	1940
	Baptist	0	1	0	1	0	141	0	141
	Calvinistic Methodist	23	7	2	32	2845	799	114	3758
	Wesleyan Methodist	5	19	3	27	446	2207	307	2960
	Total	**34**	**52**	**7**	**93**	**3834**	**6685**	**749**	**11268**
	% of total scholars					*34.0*	*59.3*	*6.6*	*100.0*
DENBIGHSHIRE									
Wrexham	Church of England	0	4	6	10	0	1005	547	1552
	Independent	6	2	3	11	598	147	272	1017
	Baptist	0	0	2	2	0	0	129	129
	Calvinistic Methodist	15	3	8	26	1950	207	467	2624
	Wesleyan Methodist	6	1	3	10	498	99	224	821
	Other	0	1	1	2	0	77	172	249
	Total	**27**	**11**	**23**	**61**	**3046**	**1535**	**1811**	**6392**
	% of total scholars					*47.7*	*24.0*	*28.3*	*100.0*
Ruthin	Church of England	1	7	2	10	28	403	143	574
	Independent	8	1	0	9	431	129	0	560
	Baptist	3	1	0	4	212	139	0	351
	Calvinistic Methodist	21	2	0	23	3133	200	0	3333
	Wesleyan Methodist	4	5	0	9	278	424	0	702
	Total	**37**	**16**	**2**	**55**	**4082**	**1295**	**143**	**5520**
	% of total scholars					*73.9*	*23.5*	*2.6*	*100.0*
St Asaph	Church of England	1	7	0	8	224	670	0	894
	Independent	6	7	0	13	230	645	0	875
	Baptist	1	4	0	5	43	203	0	246
	Calvinistic Methodist	14	2	0	16	2059	920	0	2979
	Wesleyan Methodist	3	7	0	10	340	865	0	1205
	Total	**25**	**27**	**0**	**52**	**2896**	**3303**	**0**	**6199**
	% of total scholars					*46.7*	*53.3*	*0.0*	*100.0*
Llanrwst	Church of England	1	3	0	4	52	314	0	366
	Independent	11	0	0	11	701	0	0	701
	Baptist	3	0	0	3	145	0	0	145
	Calvinistic Methodist	27	0	0	27	3145	0	0	3145
	Wesleyan Methodist	2	2	0	4	150	208	0	358
	Total	**44**	**5**	**0**	**49**	**4193**	**522**	**0**	**4715**
	% of total scholars					*88.9*	*11.1*	*0.0*	*100.0*
MERIONETH									
Corwen	Church of England	1	4	1	6	62	169	57	288
	Independent	8	2	0	10	559	209	0	768
	Baptist	6	1	0	7	542	160	0	702
	Calvinistic Methodist	36	1	0	37	3918	60	0	3978
	Wesleyan Methodist	11	6	0	17	522	441	0	963
	Total	**62**	**14**	**1**	**77**	**5603**	**1039**	**57**	**6699**
	% of total scholars					*83.6*	*15.5*	*0.9*	*100.0*
Bala	Church of England	1	1	1	3	39	23	25	87
	Independent	12	0	0	12	825	0	0	825
	Baptist	2	0	0	2	40	0	0	40
	Calvinistic Methodist	24	0	0	24	2716	0	0	2716
	Wesleyan Methodist	1	0	0	1	26	0	0	26
	Total	**40**	**1**	**1**	**42**	**3646**	**23**	**25**	**3694**
	% of total scholars					*98.7*	*0.6*	*0.7*	*100.0*
Dolgellau	Church of England	5	0	0	5	303	0	0	303
	Independent	15	2	0	17	953	185	0	1138
	Baptist	3	0	0	3	171	0	0	171
	Calvinistic Methodist	33	1	0	34	3016	30	0	3046
	Wesleyan Methodist	7	0	0	7	645	0	0	645
	Total	**63**	**3**	**0**	**66**	**5088**	**215**	**0**	**5303**
	% of total scholars					*95.9*	*4.1*	*0.0*	*100.0*

Registration District	Denomination	Number of schools[1] Language of instruction Welsh	Both	English	Total	Number of scholars[2] Language of instruction Welsh	Both	English	Total
Ffestiniog	Church of England	0	1	4	5	0	94	184	278
	Independent	11	0	0	11	847	0	0	847
	Baptist	1	0	0	1	12	0	0	12
	Calvinistic Methodist	29	0	0	29	3684	0	0	3684
	Wesleyan Methodist	8	1	0	9	364	52	0	416
	Total	**49**	**2**	**4**	**55**	**4907**	**146**	**184**	**5237**
	% of total scholars					*93.7*	*2.8*	*3.5*	*100.0*
CAERNARFONSHIRE									
Pwllheli	Church of England	2	5	0	7	121	288	0	409
	Independent	13	0	0	13	995	0	0	995
	Baptist	7	0	0	7	567	0	0	567
	Calvinistic Methodist	36	1	0	37	4762	56	0	4818
	Wesleyan Methodist	4	3	0	7	172	201	0	373
	Total	**62**	**9**	**0**	**71**	**6617**	**545**	**0**	**7162**
	% of total scholars					*92.4*	*7.6*	*0.0*	*100.0*
Caernarfon	Church of England	2	0	1	3	394	0	20	414
	Independent	16	0	0	16	1323	0	0	1323
	Baptist	4	0	0	4	240	0	0	240
	Calvinistic Methodist	39	0	0	39	6900	0	0	6900
	Wesleyan Methodist	6	1	0	7	285	158	0	443
	Total	**67**	**1**	**1**	**69**	**9142**	**158**	**20**	**9320**
	% of total scholars					*98.1*	*1.7*	*0.2*	*100.0*
Bangor	Church of England	2	4	1	7	187	541	60	788
	Independent	6	2	1	9	586	540	110	1236
	Baptist	1	1	0	2	50	40	0	90
	Calvinistic Methodist	31	0	0	31	4564	0	0	4564
	Wesleyan Methodist	4	5	1	10	297	774	50	1121
	Total	**44**	**12**	**3**	**59**	**5684**	**1895**	**220**	**7799**
	% of total scholars					*72.9*	*24.3*	*2.8*	*100.0*
Conwy	Church of England	0	1	1	2	0	55	48	103
	Independent	5	1	0	6	408	55	0	463
	Baptist	2	2	0	4	116	154	0	270
	Calvinistic Methodist	13	1	0	14	1538	155	0	1693
	Wesleyan Methodist	2	2	0	4	101	333	0	434
	Total	**22**	**7**	**1**	**30**	**2163**	**752**	**48**	**2963**
	% of total scholars					*73.0*	*25.4*	*1.6*	*100.0*
ANGLESEY									
Anglesey	Church of England	2	3	2	7	137	144	258	539
	Independent	16	1	0	17	1493	95	0	1588
	Baptist	16	0	0	16	1280	0	0	1280
	Calvinistic Methodist	51	2	0	53	6193	348	0	6541
	Wesleyan Methodist	7	1	1	9	550	201	89	840
	Total	**92**	**7**	**3**	**102**	**9653**	**788**	**347**	**10788**
	% of total scholars					*89.5*	*7.3*	*3.2*	*100.0*
Parts of Wales included in the returns situated in English Registration Districts									
SHROPSHIRE									
Oswestry[4]	Church of England	0	1	2	3	0	100	166	266
	Independent	1	0	0	1	60	0	0	60
	Baptist	0	2	0	2	0	133	0	133
	Calvinistic Methodist	0	1	0	1	0	43	0	43
	Wesleyan Methodist	0	1	0	1	0	88	0	88
	Total	**1**	**5**	**2**	**8**	**60**	**364**	**166**	**590**
	% of total scholars					*10.2*	*61.7*	*28.1*	*100.0*
Ellesmere[5]	Church of England	0	0	2	2	0	0	170	170
	Wesleyan Methodist	0	0	1	1	0	0	60	60
	Total	**0**	**0**	**3**	**3**	**0**	**0**	**230**	**230**
	% of total scholars					*0.0*	*0.0*	*100.0*	*100.0*

Registration District	Denomination	Number of schools[1] Language of instruction Welsh	Both	English	Total	Number of scholars[2] Language of instruction Welsh	Both	English	Total
CHESHIRE									
Hawarden[6]	Church of England	0	0	4	4	0	0	286	286
	Calvinistic Methodist	0	0	1	1	0	0	41	41
	Total	**0**	**0**	**5**	**5**	**0**	**0**	**327**	**327**
	% of total scholars					*0.0*	*0.0*	*100.0*	*100.0*

Source: *Reports of the Commissioners of Inquiry into the State of Education in Wales*; Part I, Carmarthen, Glamorgan and Pembroke [PP 1847 (870) XXVII]; Part II, Brecknock, Cardigan, Radnor and Monmouth [PP 1847 (871) XXVIII]; Part III, North Wales [PP 1847 (872) XXVII]; Parochial tables.

1 Excludes 86 Sunday schools listed in the returns without figures for the 'number on books'.
2 This is the 'number on books', giving an average of 96 per Sunday school; the equivalent average for 'those who usually attend' is 86.
3 Monmouthshire includes only the following parishes: Abergavenny – Bedwellte, Llanover, Llanwenarth, Aberystruth, Llanfoist, Llanelen; Pontypool – Trevethin, Llanfrechfa, Llanhilleth, Llanfihangel Pont-y-moel; Newport – Caerleon, Risca, Newport, Llanfihangel Llantarnam, Basaleg, Mynyddislwyn, Machen.
4 Includes returns from: Chirk and Llansilin in the Ancient County of Denbigh.
5 Includes returns from: Hanmer and Penley in the Ancient County of Flint.
6 Returns from the parish of Hawarden in the Ancient County of Flint.

Education 2.5 Reports of the Commissioners of Inquiry into the state of education in Wales, 1847. Sunday schools. Number of schools, age and sex of scholars, by language of instruction. Wales and Registration Counties. 1847

	Language	Sunday[1] schools	Scholars 'on books' Under 15 years Males	Females	Total	Over 15 years Males	Females	Total	All ages Total
Wales[2]	Welsh	1389	32231	30691	62922	42731	35069	77800	140722
	Both	744	21459	19861	41320	18521	13746	32267	73587
	English	489	16392	16456	32848	3037	2870	5907	38755
	Total	**2622**	**70082**	**67008**	**137090**	**64289**	**51685**	**115974**	**253064**
Registration Counties									
Monmouth[2]	Welsh	16	683	560	1243	581	412	993	2236
	Both	72	2646	2294	4940	1966	1438	3404	8344
	English	59	3002	2825	5827	550	427	977	6804
	Total	**147**	**6331**	**5679**	**12010**	**3097**	**2277**	**5374**	**17384**
Glamorgan	Welsh	145	4261	3380	7641	3975	2220	6195	13836
	Both	132	4083	3521	7604	2784	1640	4424	12028
	English	112	3804	3815	7619	543	550	1093	8712
	Total	**389**	**12148**	**10716**	**22864**	**7302**	**4410**	**11712**	**34576**
Carmarthen	Welsh	111	2385	2253	4638	3062	2366	5428	10066
	Both	133	3422	3295	6717	3347	2441	5788	12505
	English	18	584	736	1320	123	107	230	1550
	Total	**262**	**6391**	**6284**	**12675**	**6532**	**4914**	**11446**	**24121**
Pembroke	Welsh	40	691	691	1382	782	823	1605	2987
	Both	48	1029	899	1928	908	799	1707	3635
	English	102	3448	3381	6829	496	554	1050	7879
	Total	**190**	**5168**	**4971**	**10139**	**2186**	**2176**	**4362**	**14501**
Cardigan	Welsh	223	4913	5334	10247	8292	8858	17150	27397
	Both	51	1256	1273	2529	1630	1689	3319	5848
	English	10	391	280	671	146	152	298	969
	Total	**284**	**6560**	**6887**	**13447**	**10068**	**10699**	**20767**	**34214**
Brecon	Welsh	48	853	761	1614	1310	805	2115	3729
	Both	60	1367	1146	2513	1583	952	2535	5048
	English	52	1211	1459	2670	186	156	342	3012
	Total	**160**	**3431**	**3366**	**6797**	**3079**	**1913**	**4992**	**11789**
Radnor	Both	7	106	117	223	84	81	165	388
	English	39	776	779	1555	109	62	171	1726
	Total	**46**	**882**	**896**	**1778**	**193**	**143**	**336**	**2114**
Montgomery	Welsh	137	2066	2082	4148	2925	2784	5709	9857
	Both	69	1721	1603	3324	1607	1595	3202	6526
	English	42	1216	1400	2616	616	578	1194	3810
	Total	**248**	**5003**	**5085**	**10088**	**5148**	**4957**	**10105**	**20193**
Flint	Welsh	34	1051	799	1850	1270	714	1984	3834
	Both	52	2045	2038	4083	1600	1002	2602	6685
	English	7	319	288	607	97	45	142	749
	Total	**93**	**3415**	**3125**	**6540**	**2967**	**1761**	**4728**	**11268**
Denbigh	Welsh	133	3304	3074	6378	4264	3575	7839	14217
	Both	59	2068	2080	4148	1397	1110	2507	6655
	English	25	869	778	1647	124	183	307	1954
	Total	**217**	**6241**	**5932**	**12173**	**5785**	**4868**	**10653**	**22826**
Merioneth	Welsh	214	4055	4175	8230	5916	5098	11014	19244
	Both	20	459	436	895	298	230	528	1423
	English	6	160	94	254	8	4	12	266
	Total	**240**	**4674**	**4705**	**9379**	**6222**	**5332**	**11554**	**20933**
Caernarfon	Welsh	195	5636	5471	11107	7365	5134	12499	23606
	Both	29	947	857	1804	1016	530	1546	3350
	English	5	134	141	275	6	7	13	288
	Total	**229**	**6717**	**6469**	**13186**	**8387**	**5671**	**14058**	**27244**

Registration County	Language	Sunday[1] schools	Scholars 'on books' Under 15 years Males	Females	Total	Over 15 years Males	Females	Total	All ages Total
Anglesey	Welsh	92	2318	2091	4409	2979	2265	5244	9653
	Both	7	181	188	369	226	193	419	788
	English	3	140	165	305	17	25	42	347
	Total	**102**	**2639**	**2444**	**5083**	**3222**	**2483**	**5705**	**10788**
Parts of Wales in English Registration Counties									
Shropshire[3]	Welsh	1	15	20	35	10	15	25	60
	Both	5	129	114	243	75	46	121	364
	English	5	168	223	391	1	4	5	396
	Total	**11**	**312**	**357**	**669**	**86**	**65**	**151**	**820**
Cheshire[4]	English	4	170	92	262	15	16	31	293
	Total	**4**	**170**	**92**	**262**	**15**	**16**	**31**	**293**

Source: *Reports of the Commissioners of Inquiry into the State of Education in Wales*; Part I, Carmarthen, Glamorgan and Pembroke [PP 1847 (870) XXVII]; Part II, Brecknock, Cardigan, Radnor and Monmouth [PP 1847 (871) XXVIII]; Part III, North Wales [PP 1847 (872) XXVII]; Parochial tables.

1 Excludes 88 Sunday schools listed in the returns without figures for the 'number on books'.

2 For Monmouth, only the 18 industrial parishes adjoining Glamorgan and Brecon were included in the returns, viz. Aberystruth, Basaleg, Bedwellte, Caerleon, Llanelen, Llanfihangel Llantarnam, Llanfihangel Pont-y-moel, Llanfoist, Llanfrechfa, Llanhilleth, Llanover, Llanwenarth, Machen, Mynyddislwyn, Newport, Pant-teg, Risca, Trevethin with Pontypool. In 1841 these parishes contained 60% of the total population of Monmouthshire. The total for Wales includes parts of Flint and Denbigh in English Registration Counties.

3 Includes returns from: Hanmer and Penley in the Ancient County of Flint; Chirk and Llansilin in the Ancient County of Denbigh.

4 Includes returns from Hawarden in the Ancient County of Flint.

Education 2.6 Reports of the Commissioners of Inquiry into the state of education in Wales, 1847. Sunday schools. Number of schools, age and sex of scholars, by language of instruction. Registration Districts. 1847

Registration District	Language	Sunday[1] schools	Scholars 'on books' Under 15 years Males	Females	Total	Over 15 years Males	Females	Total	All ages Total
MONMOUTHSHIRE[2]									
Abergavenny[2]	Welsh	11	556	443	999	475	339	814	1813
	Both	31	1276	1130	2406	1284	822	2106	4512
	English	21	925	886	1811	259	198	457	2268
	Total	**63**	**2757**	**2459**	**5216**	**2018**	**1359**	**3377**	**8593**
Pontypool[2]	Welsh	2	79	74	153	54	37	91	244
	Both	17	586	534	1120	357	377	734	1854
	English	20	1167	1026	2193	191	144	335	2528
	Total	**39**	**1832**	**1634**	**3466**	**602**	**558**	**1160**	**4626**
Newport[2]	Welsh	3	48	43	91	52	36	88	179
	Both	24	784	630	1414	325	239	564	1978
	English	18	910	913	1823	100	85	185	2008
	Total	**45**	**1742**	**1586**	**3328**	**477**	**360**	**837**	**4165**
GLAMORGAN									
Cardiff	Welsh	24	461	382	843	501	290	791	1634
	Both	26	627	727	1354	371	220	591	1945
	English	31	961	1025	1986	115	113	228	2214
	Total	**81**	**2049**	**2134**	**4183**	**987**	**623**	**1610**	**5793**
Merthyr Tydfil	Welsh	31	1380	1120	2500	1328	678	2006	4506
	Both	33	1441	1154	2595	1215	761	1976	4571
	English	14	635	633	1268	119	87	206	1474
	Total	**78**	**3456**	**2907**	**6363**	**2662**	**1526**	**4188**	**10551**
Bridgend	Welsh	29	675	507	1182	571	344	915	2097
	Both	22	424	365	789	234	131	365	1154
	English	23	555	647	1202	50	47	97	1299
	Total	**74**	**1654**	**1519**	**3173**	**855**	**522**	**1377**	**4550**
Neath	Welsh	50	1390	1049	2439	1330	730	2060	4499
	Both	24	762	632	1394	547	297	844	2238
	English	14	836	622	1458	116	95	211	1669
	Total	**88**	**2988**	**2303**	**5291**	**1993**	**1122**	**3115**	**8406**
Swansea	Welsh	11	355	322	677	245	178	423	1100
	Both	27	829	643	1472	417	231	648	2120
	English	30	817	888	1705	143	208	351	2056
	Total	**68**	**2001**	**1853**	**3854**	**805**	**617**	**1422**	**5276**
CARMARTHENSHIRE									
Llanelli	Welsh	19	714	673	1387	736	550	1286	2673
	Both	20	722	630	1352	472	245	717	2069
	English	4	210	278	488	42	54	96	584
	Total	**43**	**1646**	**1581**	**3227**	**1250**	**849**	**2099**	**5326**
Llandovery	Welsh	24	337	283	620	504	329	833	1453
	Both	32	769	755	1524	855	628	1483	3007
	English	2	32	31	63	11	5	16	79
	Total	**58**	**1138**	**1069**	**2207**	**1370**	**962**	**2332**	**4539**
Llandeilo Fawr	Welsh	22	427	398	825	628	463	1091	1916
	Both	26	550	570	1120	518	336	854	1974
	English	4	81	66	147	11	9	20	167
	Total	**52**	**1058**	**1034**	**2092**	**1157**	**808**	**1965**	**4057**
Carmarthen	Welsh	46	907	899	1806	1194	1024	2218	4024
	Both	55	1381	1340	2721	1502	1232	2734	5455
	English	8	261	361	622	59	39	98	720
	Total	**109**	**2549**	**2600**	**5149**	**2755**	**2295**	**5050**	**10199**
PEMBROKESHIRE									
Narberth	Welsh	15	310	311	621	384	345	729	1350
	Both	17	421	345	766	370	277	647	1413
	English	23	627	619	1246	133	154	287	1533
	Total	**55**	**1358**	**1275**	**2633**	**887**	**776**	**1663**	**4296**

Registration District	Language	Sunday[1] schools	Scholars 'on books' Under 15 years Males	Females	Total	Over 15 years Males	Females	Total	All ages Total
Pembroke	English	38	1428	1480	2908	105	165	270	3178
	Total	**38**	**1428**	**1480**	**2908**	**105**	**165**	**270**	**3178**
Haverford-west	Welsh	25	381	380	761	398	478	876	1637
	Both	31	608	554	1162	538	522	1060	2222
	English	41	1393	1282	2675	258	235	493	3168
	Total	**97**	**2382**	**2216**	**4598**	**1194**	**1235**	**2429**	**7027**
CARDIGANSHIRE									
Cardigan	Welsh	49	834	961	1795	1296	1572	2868	4663
	Both	9	274	332	606	257	398	655	1261
	English	6	254	160	414	138	143	281	695
	Total	**64**	**1362**	**1453**	**2815**	**1691**	**2113**	**3804**	**6619**
Newcastle Emlyn	Welsh	49	955	1083	2038	1561	1719	3280	5318
	Both	5	82	66	148	104	71	175	323
	Total	**54**	**1037**	**1149**	**2186**	**1665**	**1790**	**3455**	**5641**
Lampeter	Welsh	11	158	142	300	278	244	522	822
	Both	14	256	258	514	273	221	494	1008
	Total	**25**	**414**	**400**	**814**	**551**	**465**	**1016**	**1830**
Aberaeron	Welsh	27	553	561	1114	1258	1344	2602	3716
	Both	9	181	150	331	232	231	463	794
	Total	**36**	**734**	**711**	**1445**	**1490**	**1575**	**3065**	**4510**
Aberystwyth	Welsh	58	1831	1918	3749	2749	2855	5604	9353
	Both	10	331	344	675	534	533	1067	1742
	English	4	137	120	257	8	9	17	274
	Total	**72**	**2299**	**2382**	**4681**	**3291**	**3397**	**6688**	**11369**
Tregaron	Welsh	29	582	669	1251	1150	1124	2274	3525
	Both	4	132	123	255	230	235	465	720
	Total	**33**	**714**	**792**	**1506**	**1380**	**1359**	**2739**	**4245**
BRECONSHIRE									
Builth	Welsh	4	58	56	114	81	69	150	264
	Both	13	195	181	376	290	182	472	848
	English	10	178	184	362	19	29	48	410
	Total	**27**	**431**	**421**	**852**	**390**	**280**	**670**	**1522**
Brecon	Welsh	28	379	337	716	595	444	1039	1755
	Both	21	288	310	598	350	284	634	1232
	English	15	311	492	803	47	58	105	908
	Total	**64**	**978**	**1139**	**2117**	**992**	**786**	**1778**	**3895**
Crickhowell	Welsh	13	334	323	657	556	246	802	1459
	Both	23	838	616	1454	891	453	1344	2798
	English	13	411	436	847	80	32	112	959
	Total	**49**	**1583**	**1375**	**2958**	**1527**	**731**	**2258**	**5216**
Hay	Welsh	3	82	45	127	78	46	124	251
	Both	3	46	39	85	52	33	85	170
	English	14	311	347	658	40	37	77	735
	Total	**20**	**439**	**431**	**870**	**170**	**116**	**286**	**1156**
RADNORSHIRE									
Presteigne	English	19	383	372	755	41	18	59	814
	Total	**19**	**383**	**372**	**755**	**41**	**18**	**59**	**814**
Knighton	English	7	192	177	369	10	3	13	382
	Total	**7**	**192**	**177**	**369**	**10**	**3**	**13**	**382**
Rhayader	Both	7	106	117	223	84	81	165	388
	English	13	201	230	431	58	41	99	530
	Total	**20**	**307**	**347**	**654**	**142**	**122**	**264**	**918**
MONTGOMERYSHIRE									
Machynlleth	Welsh	51	818	833	1651	1400	1373	2773	4424
	Both	5	127	131	258	131	103	234	492
	Total	**56**	**945**	**964**	**1909**	**1531**	**1476**	**3007**	**4916**

Registration District	Language	Sunday[1] schools	Scholars 'on books' Under 15 years Males	Females	Total	Over 15 years Males	Females	Total	All ages Total
Newtown	Welsh	34	528	528	1056	668	646	1314	2370
	Both	30	956	849	1805	827	906	1733	3538
	English	17	546	571	1117	453	424	877	1994
	Total	**81**	**2030**	**1948**	**3978**	**1948**	**1976**	**3924**	**7902**
Montgomery	Welsh	1	2	3	5	18	10	28	33
	Both	8	131	107	238	104	113	217	455
	English	20	531	685	1216	152	138	290	1506
	Total	**29**	**664**	**795**	**1459**	**274**	**261**	**535**	**1994**
Llanfyllin	Welsh	51	718	718	1436	839	755	1594	3030
	Both	26	507	516	1023	545	473	1018	2041
	English	5	139	144	283	11	16	27	310
	Total	**82**	**1364**	**1378**	**2742**	**1395**	**1244**	**2639**	**5381**
FLINTSHIRE									
Holywell	Welsh	34	1051	799	1850	1270	714	1984	3834
	Both	52	2045	2038	4083	1600	1002	2602	6685
	English	7	319	288	607	97	45	142	749
	Total	**93**	**3415**	**3125**	**6540**	**2967**	**1761**	**4728**	**11268**
DENBIGHSHIRE									
Wrexham	Welsh	27	753	733	1486	881	679	1560	3046
	Both	11	607	590	1197	228	110	338	1535
	English	23	823	722	1545	108	158	266	1811
	Total	**61**	**2183**	**2045**	**4228**	**1217**	**947**	**2164**	**6392**
Ruthin	Welsh	37	900	788	1688	1284	1110	2394	4082
	Both	16	441	377	818	271	206	477	1295
	English	2	46	56	102	16	25	41	143
	Total	**55**	**1387**	**1221**	**2608**	**1571**	**1341**	**2912**	**5520**
St Asaph	Welsh	25	629	546	1175	986	735	1721	2896
	Both	27	836	905	1741	835	727	1562	3303
	Total	**52**	**1465**	**1451**	**2916**	**1821**	**1462**	**3283**	**6199**
Llanrwst	Welsh	44	1022	1007	2029	1113	1051	2164	4193
	Both	5	184	208	392	63	67	130	522
	Total	**49**	**1206**	**1215**	**2421**	**1176**	**1118**	**2294**	**4715**
MERIONETH									
Corwen	Welsh	62	1180	1194	2374	1714	1515	3229	5603
	Both	14	314	340	654	213	172	385	1039
	English	1	57	0	57	0	0	0	57
	Total	**77**	**1551**	**1534**	**3085**	**1927**	**1687**	**3614**	**6699**
Bala	Welsh	40	682	745	1427	1135	1084	2219	3646
	Both	1	14	7	21	0	2	2	23
	English	1	0	25	25	0	0	0	25
	Total	**42**	**696**	**777**	**1473**	**1135**	**1086**	**2221**	**3694**
Dolgellau	Welsh	63	1036	1108	2144	1616	1328	2944	5088
	Both	3	50	62	112	67	36	103	215
	Total	**66**	**1086**	**1170**	**2256**	**1683**	**1364**	**3047**	**5303**
Ffestiniog	Welsh	49	1157	1128	2285	1451	1171	2622	4907
	Both	2	81	27	108	18	20	38	146
	English	4	103	69	172	8	4	12	184
	Total	**55**	**1341**	**1224**	**2565**	**1477**	**1195**	**2672**	**5237**
CAERNARFONSHIRE									
Pwllheli	Welsh	62	1421	1448	2869	2120	1628	3748	6617
	Both	9	154	165	319	142	84	226	545
	Total	**71**	**1575**	**1613**	**3188**	**2262**	**1712**	**3974**	**7162**
Caernarfon	Welsh	67	2337	2258	4595	2630	1917	4547	9142
	Both	1	22	39	61	82	15	97	158
	English	1	10	10	20	0	0	0	20
	Total	**69**	**2369**	**2307**	**4676**	**2712**	**1932**	**4644**	**9320**
Bangor	Welsh	44	1336	1266	2602	1930	1152	3082	5684
	Both	12	536	502	1038	564	293	857	1895
	English	3	112	98	210	6	4	10	220
	Total	**59**	**1984**	**1866**	**3850**	**2500**	**1449**	**3949**	**7799**

Registration District	Language	Sunday[1] schools	Scholars 'on books' Under 15 years Males	Females	Total	Over 15 years Males	Females	Total	All ages Total
Conwy	Welsh	22	542	499	1041	685	437	1122	2163
	Both	7	235	151	386	228	138	366	752
	English	1	12	33	45	0	3	3	48
	Total	**30**	**789**	**683**	**1472**	**913**	**578**	**1491**	**2963**
ANGLESEY									
Anglesey	Welsh	92	2318	2091	4409	2979	2265	5244	9653
	Both	7	181	188	369	226	193	419	788
	English	3	140	165	305	17	25	42	347
	Total	**102**	**2639**	**2444**	**5083**	**3222**	**2483**	**5705**	**10788**
Parts of Wales in English Registration Counties									
SHROPSHIRE									
Oswestry[3]	Welsh	1	15	20	35	10	15	25	60
	Both	5	129	114	243	75	46	121	364
	English	2	45	117	162	0	4	4	166
	Total	**8**	**189**	**251**	**440**	**85**	**65**	**150**	**590**
Ellesmere[4]	English	3	123	106	229	1	0	1	230
	Total	**3**	**123**	**106**	**229**	**1**	**0**	**1**	**230**
CHESHIRE									
Hawarden[5]	English	4	170	141	311	15	16	31	342
	Total	**4**	**170**	**141**	**311**	**15**	**16**	**31**	**342**

Source: *Reports of the Commissioners of Inquiry into the State of Education in Wales*; Part I, Carmarthen, Glamorgan and Pembroke [PP 1847 (870) XXVII]; Part II, Brecknock, Cardigan, Radnor and Monmouth [PP 1847 (871) XXVIII]; Part III, North Wales [PP 1847 (872) XXVII]; Parochial tables.

1 Excludes 88 Sunday schools listed in the returns without figures for the 'number on books' or age of scholars.
2 Monmouthshire includes only the following parishes: Abergavenny – Bedwellte, Llanover, Llanwenarth, Aberystruth, Llanfoist, Llanelen; Pontypool – Trevethin, Llanfrechfa, Llanhilleth, Llanfihangel Pont-y-moel; Newport – Caerleon, Risca, Newport, Llanfihangel Llantarnam, Basaleg, Mynyddislwyn, Machen.
3 Includes returns from: Chirk and Llansilin in the Ancient County of Denbigh.
4 Includes returns from: Hanmer and Penley in the Ancient County of Flint.
5 Returns from the parish of Hawarden in the Ancient County of Flint.

Education 2.7 Reports of the Commissioners of Inquiry into the state of education in Wales, 1847. Sunday schools. Number of scholars 'able to read in the scriptures', by denomination and language of instruction. Wales and Registration Counties. 1847

	Denomination	Sunday schools[1]	Scholars 'able to read in the scriptures' Number Language of instruction Welsh	Both	English	Total	*as percentage of total scholars[2] Language of instruction Welsh*	*Both*	*English*	*Total*
Wales[3]	Church of England	453	3979	6091	8630	18700	*63.5*	*52.5*	*54.2*	*55.3*
	Independent	617	19848	12797	2572	35217	*64.7*	*56.0*	*59.0*	*60.8*
	Baptist	326	5784	7317	2319	15420	*61.0*	*53.4*	*58.1*	*56.7*
	Calvinistic Methodist	879	58806	7784	2345	68935	*68.5*	*62.9*	*60.8*	*67.5*
	Wesleyan Methodist[4]	291	4000	6441	4029	14470	*59.5*	*59.8*	*51.6*	*57.2*
	Other	19	30	187	562	779	*36.6*	*59.4*	*43.6*	*46.2*
	Total	**2584**	**92447**	**40617**	**20457**	**153521**	***66.5***	***56.7***	***55.0***	***61.9***
Registration Counties										
Monmouth[3]	Church of England	29	18	399	1200	1617	*50.0*	*48.6*	*51.4*	*50.7*
	Independent	35	330	1218	422	1970	*53.1*	*50.0*	*54.2*	*51.4*
	Baptist	40	120	1599	435	2154	*55.8*	*47.9*	*51.5*	*49.0*
	Calvinistic Methodist	14	719	596	0	1315	*59.8*	*59.8*	–	*59.8*
	Wesleyan Methodist	27	120	327	1353	1800	*75.0*	*45.7*	*48.2*	*48.8*
	Other	2	0	25	20	45	–	*62.5*	*54.1*	*58.4*
	Total	**147**	**1307**	**4164**	**3430**	**8901**	***58.5***	***49.9***	***50.4***	***51.2***
Glamorgan	Church of England	89	150	266	2059	2475	*36.9*	*39.8*	*46.4*	*44.9*
	Independent	103	2860	2290	247	5397	*53.7*	*49.0*	*63.8*	*52.0*
	Baptist	58	335	1840	402	2577	*56.3*	*49.1*	*52.0*	*50.4*
	Calvinistic Methodist	101	3623	806	330	4759	*48.8*	*50.6*	*55.4*	*49.5*
	Wesleyan Methodist	23	0	298	643	941	–	*57.3*	*48.1*	*50.7*
	Other	8	0	122	317	439	–	*61.6*	*35.9*	*40.6*
	Total	**382**	**6968**	**5622**	**3998**	**16588**	***50.7***	***49.3***	***47.5***	***49.4***
Carmarthen	Church of England	43	188	1150	376	1714	*56.1*	*51.7*	*39.7*	*48.9*
	Independent	86	1963	3388	99	5450	*65.0*	*53.9*	*65.6*	*57.6*
	Baptist	45	670	969	0	1639	*45.0*	*54.9*	–	*50.4*
	Calvinistic Methodist	74	3117	1007	45	4169	*61.2*	*58.3*	*75.0*	*60.6*
	Wesleyan Methodist	12	25	263	203	491	*49.0*	*52.2*	*57.8*	*54.2*
	Other	1	0	0	20	20	–	–	*50.0*	*50.0*
	Total	**261**	**5963**	**6777**	**743**	**13483**	***59.7***	***54.2***	***47.9***	***56.1***
Pembroke	Church of England	48	47	122	1497	1666	*50.0*	*54.0*	*57.9*	*57.3*
	Independent	50	843	1273	1150	3266	*67.5*	*69.9*	*66.7*	*68.1*
	Baptist	40	505	470	856	1831	*59.4*	*57.9*	*64.9*	*61.4*
	Calvinistic Methodist	34	484	457	454	1395	*65.3*	*62.6*	*53.4*	*60.1*
	Wesleyan Methodist	15	35	27	749	811	*66.0*	*57.4*	*60.2*	*60.3*
	Other	2	0	0	47	47	–	–	*72.3*	*72.3*
	Total	**189**	**1914**	**2349**	**4753**	**9016**	***64.1***	***64.6***	***61.0***	***62.6***
Cardigan	Church of England	63	2294	542	191	3027	*69.6*	*52.0*	*41.7*	*63.1*
	Independent	74	5211	526	60	5797	*71.8*	*65.9*	*60.6*	*71.1*
	Baptist	38	1794	981	0	2775	*68.9*	*67.6*	–	*68.4*
	Calvinistic Methodist	83	9602	983	300	10885	*73.7*	*73.9*	*90.6*	*74.1*
	Wesleyan Methodist	18	469	553	56	1078	*65.3*	*62.8*	*69.1*	*64.2*
	Other	1	30	0	0	30	*36.6*	–	–	*36.6*
	Total	**277**	**19400**	**3585**	**607**	**23592**	***71.9***	***65.1***	***62.6***	***70.5***
Brecon	Church of England	41	100	79	1163	1342	*59.5*	*71.2*	*58.7*	*59.4*
	Independent	42	534	1470	52	2056	*54.0*	*63.8*	*65.0*	*61.0*
	Baptist	26	143	713	108	964	*75.3*	*48.9*	*45.4*	*51.1*
	Calvinistic Methodist	36	1490	636	66	2192	*65.1*	*64.5*	*66.7*	*64.9*
	Wesleyan Methodist	14	42	120	254	416	*45.2*	*63.8*	*42.5*	*47.3*
	Other	1	0	0	8	8	–	–	*47.1*	*47.1*
	Total	**160**	**2309**	**3018**	**1651**	**6978**	***61.9***	***59.8***	***54.8***	***59.2***

Registration District	Denomination	Sunday schools[1]	Scholars 'able to read in the scriptures' Number Language of instruction Welsh	Both	English	Total	*as percentage of total scholars[2] Language of instruction Welsh*	*Both*	*English*	*Total*
Radnor	Church of England	18	0	0	505	505	–	–	*58.0*	*58.0*
	Independent	6	0	140	40	180	–	*56.5*	*61.5*	*57.5*
	Baptist	9	0	20	130	150	–	*57.1*	*48.7*	*49.7*
	Calvinistic Methodist	7	0	65	127	192	–	*61.9*	*65.5*	*64.2*
	Wesleyan Methodist	4	0	0	85	85	–	–	*46.4*	*46.4*
	Other	1	0	0	20	20	–	–	*76.9*	*76.9*
	Total	**45**	**0**	**225**	**907**	**1132**	**–**	***58.0***	***56.5***	***56.8***
Montgomery	Church of England	28	243	356	587	1186	*66.9*	*52.8*	*56.6*	*57.2*
	Independent	48	1378	627	231	2236	*73.0*	*60.8*	*43.1*	*64.7*
	Baptist	8	80	152	370	602	*68.4*	*58.7*	*73.7*	*68.6*
	Calvinistic Methodist	110	4468	1529	710	6707	*73.3*	*68.4*	*61.8*	*70.8*
	Wesleyan Methodist	50	796	1275	373	2444	*58.4*	*58.5*	*69.6*	*59.9*
	Other	1	0	0	30	30	–	–	*60.0*	*60.0*
	Total	**245**	**6965**	**3939**	**2301**	**13205**	***70.9***	***61.7***	***60.4***	***66.0***
Flint	Church of England	13	19	1303	75	1397	*70.4*	*57.4*	*43.4*	*56.6*
	Independent	20	288	652	66	1006	*55.8*	*51.4*	*42.6*	*51.9*
	Baptist	1	0	110	0	110	–	*78.0*	–	*78.0*
	Calvinistic Methodist	32	1995	494	30	2519	*70.1*	*61.8*	*26.3*	*67.0*
	Wesleyan Methodist	27	187	1259	165	1611	*41.9*	*57.0*	*53.7*	*54.4*
	Total	**93**	**2489**	**3818**	**336**	**6643**	***64.9***	***57.1***	***44.9***	***59.0***
Denbigh	Church of England	28	192	1222	227	1641	*63.2*	*54.1*	*51.7*	*54.7*
	Independent	44	1385	567	165	2117	*70.7*	*61.6*	*60.7*	*67.1*
	Baptist	13	237	188	18	443	*59.3*	*55.0*	*36.0*	*55.9*
	Calvinistic Methodist	91	6928	757	250	7935	*67.3*	*61.4*	*53.5*	*66.2*
	Wesleyan Methodist	31	698	991	68	1757	*56.4*	*64.9*	*30.4*	*58.8*
	Other	2	0	40	100	140	–	*51.9*	*58.1*	*56.2*
	Total	**209**	**9440**	**3765**	**828**	**14033**	***66.5***	***59.2***	***51.0***	***63.3***
Merioneth	Church of England	19	257	120	136	513	*63.6*	*42.0*	*51.1*	*53.7*
	Independent	50	2232	223	0	2455	*70.1*	*56.6*	–	*68.6*
	Baptist	13	472	80	0	552	*61.7*	*50.0*	–	*59.7*
	Calvinistic Methodist	124	9690	42	0	9732	*72.7*	*46.7*	–	*72.5*
	Wesleyan Methodist	34	1025	299	0	1324	*65.8*	*60.6*	–	*64.6*
	Total	**240**	**13676**	**764**	**136**	**14576**	***71.1***	***53.7***	***51.1***	***69.6***
Caernarfon	Church of England	19	416	416	70	902	*59.3*	*47.1*	*54.7*	*52.6*
	Independent	41	1966	353	40	2359	*62.4*	*59.3*	*36.4*	*61.2*
	Baptist	17	534	128	0	662	*54.9*	*66.0*	–	*56.7*
	Calvinistic Methodist	119	12428	146	0	12574	*71.0*	*69.2*	–	*71.0*
	Wesleyan Methodist [4]	26	452	910	30	1392	*60.9*	*69.6*	*60.0*	*66.3*
	Total	**222**	**15796**	**1953**	**140**	**17889**	***68.5***	***61.2***	***48.6***	***67.4***
Anglesey	Church of England	7	55	61	150	266	*40.1*	*42.4*	*58.1*	*49.4*
	Independent	17	818	70	0	888	*54.8*	*73.7*	–	*55.9*
	Baptist	16	894	0	0	894	*69.8*	–	–	*69.8*
	Calvinistic Methodist	52	4262	248	0	4510	*70.2*	*71.3*	–	*70.2*
	Wesleyan Methodist	7	151	69	35	255	*50.8*	*34.3*	*39.3*	*43.4*
	Total	**99**	**6180**	**448**	**185**	**6813**	***66.6***	***56.9***	***53.3***	***65.4***
Parts of Wales in English Registration Counties										
Shropshire[5]	Church of England	5	0	55	197	252	–	*55.0*	*58.6*	*57.8*
	Independent	1	40	0	0	40	*66.7*	–	–	*66.7*
	Baptist	2	0	67	0	67	–	*50.4*	–	*50.4*
	Calvinistic Methodist	1	0	18	0	18	–	*41.9*	–	*41.9*
	Wesleyan Methodist	2	0	50	15	65	–	*56.8*	*25.0*	*43.9*
	Total	**11**	**40**	**190**	**212**	**442**	***66.7***	***52.2***	***53.5***	***53.9***
Cheshire[6]	Church of England	3	0	0	197	197	–	–	*65.4*	*65.4*
	Calvinistic Methodist	1	0	0	33	33	–	–	*80.5*	*80.5*
	Total	**4**	**0**	**0**	**230**	**230**	**–**	**–**	***67.3***	***67.3***

Source: *Reports of the Commissioners of Inquiry into the State of Education in Wales*; Part I, Carmarthen, Glamorgan and Pembroke [PP 1847 (870) XXVII]; Part II, Brecknock, Cardigan, Radnor and Monmouth [PP 1847 (871) XXVIII]; Part III, North Wales [PP 1847 (872) XXVII]; Parochial tables.

1 Excludes126 Sunday schools listed in the returns without figures for numbers 'on books' or 'able to read in the scriptures'.
2 This percentage is read as the number of scholars 'able to read in the scriptures' as a percentage of the number of scholars 'on books' in each language group, for each denomination.
3 For Monmouth, only the 18 industrial parishes adjoining Glamorgan and Brecon were included in the returns, viz. Aberystruth, Basaleg, Bedwellte, Caerleon, Llanelen, Llanfihangel Llantarnam, Llanfihangel Pont-y-moel, Llanfoist, Llanfrechfa, Llanhilleth, Llanover, Llanwenarth, Machen, Mynyddislwyn, Newport, Pant-teg, Risca, Trevethin with Pontypool. In 1841 these parishes contained 60% of the total population of Monmouthshire. The total for Wales includes parts of Flint and Denbigh in English Registration Counties.
4 The returns for the Wesleyan Methodist chapel in Caernarfon, in which instruction is given in both languages have been excluded from this table because the number given as 'able to read in the scriptures' (172) is greater than the total 'number on books' (158).
5 Includes returns from: Hanmer and Penley in the Ancient County of Flint; Chirk and Llansilin in the Ancient County of Denbigh.
6 Includes returns from Hawarden in the Ancient County of Flint.

Education 2.8 Reports of the Commissioners of Inquiry into the state of education in Wales, 1847. Sunday schools. Number of scholars 'able to read in the scriptures', by denomination and language of instruction. Registration Districts. 1847

			Scholars 'able to read in the scriptures'							
			Number				*as percentage of total scholars*[2]			
			Language of instruction				*Language of instruction*			
Registration District	Denomination	Sunday schools[1]	Welsh	Both	English	Total	*Welsh*	*Both*	*English*	*Total*
MONMOUTHSHIRE[3]										
Abergavenny[3]	Church of England	12	0	399	341	740	–	*48.6*	*40.0*	*44.2*
	Independent	14	199	688	43	930	*48.7*	*52.2*	*40.2*	*50.7*
	Baptist	15	120	465	71	656	*55.8*	*44.4*	*47.7*	*46.5*
	Calvinistic Methodist	9	599	516	0	1115	*58.2*	*61.9*	–	*59.9*
	Wesleyan Methodist	13	120	224	509	853	*75.0*	*45.5*	*43.9*	*47.1*
	Total	**63**	**1038**	**2292**	**964**	**4294**	***57.3***	***50.8***	***42.5***	***50.0***
Pontypool[3]	Church of England	7	0	0	399	399	–	–	*48.4*	*48.4*
	Independent	6	77	100	70	247	*62.6*	*47.8*	*43.8*	*50.2*
	Baptist	15	0	810	210	1020	–	*55.3*	*56.9*	*55.6*
	Calvinistic Methodist	2	90	50	0	140	*74.4*	*55.6*	–	*66.4*
	Wesleyan Methodist	8	0	55	543	598	–	*61.1*	*47.8*	*48.7*
	Other	1	0	0	20	20	–	–	*54.1*	*54.1*
	Total	**39**	**167**	**1015**	**1242**	**2424**	***68.4***	***54.7***	***49.1***	***52.4***
Newport[3]	Church of England	10	18	0	460	478	*50.0*	–	*70.0*	*69.0*
	Independent	15	54	430	309	793	*60.0*	*47.4*	*60.4*	*52.6*
	Baptist	10	0	324	154	478		*39.4*	*47.1*	*41.6*
	Calvinistic Methodist	3	30	30	0	60	*56.6*	*40.5*	–	*47.2*
	Wesleyan Methodist	6	0	48	301	349	–	*35.8*	*58.8*	*54.0*
	Other	1	0	25	0	25	–	*62.5*	–	*62.5*
	Total	**45**	**102**	**857**	**1224**	**2183**	***57.0***	***43.3***	***61.0***	***52.4***
GLAMORGAN										
Cardiff	Church of England	27	0	54	716	770	–	*44.6*	*52.6*	*52.0*
	Independent	14	165	250	40	455	*52.1*	*45.0*	*54.1*	*48.1*
	Baptist	12	47	320	173	540	*47.5*	*50.6*	*61.8*	*53.4*
	Calvinistic Methodist	22	645	244	0	889	*53.0*	*47.8*	–	*51.4*
	Wesleyan Methodist	4	0	89	156	245	–	*70.6*	*52.2*	*57.6*
	Other	2	0	0	47	47	–	–	*23.4*	*23.4*
	Total	**81**	**857**	**957**	**1132**	**2946**	***52.4***	***49.2***	***51.1***	***50.9***
Merthyr Tydfil	Church of England	12	101	25	278	404	*34.2*	*26.0*	*33.3*	*33.0*
	Independent	21	1008	799	36	1843	*58.9*	*49.3*	*38.7*	*53.8*
	Baptist	20	121	732	59	912	*55.5*	*42.6*	*34.7*	*43.3*
	Calvinistic Methodist	15	1149	97	0	1246	*50.3*	*38.6*	–	*49.2*
	Wesleyan Methodist	7	0	85	135	220	–	*46.7*	*35.8*	*39.4*
	Other	1	0	122	0	122	–	*61.6*	–	*61.6*
	Total	**76**	**2379**	**1860**	**508**	**4747**	***52.8***	***45.7***	***34.5***	***47.2***
Bridgend	Church of England	22	0	70	321	391	–	*43.2*	*39.1*	*39.8*
	Independent	17	458	118	0	576	*46.8*	*42.6*	–	*45.9*
	Baptist	9	0	312	0	312	–	*58.0*	–	*58.0*
	Calvinistic Methodist	19	504	92	0	596	*49.3*	*73.0*	–	*51.9*
	Wesleyan Methodist	4	0	30	157	187	–	*58.8*	*43.0*	*45.0*
	Other	1	0	0	20	20	–	–	*44.4*	*44.4*
	Total	**72**	**962**	**622**	**498**	**2082**	***48.1***	***53.9***	***40.5***	***47.5***
Neath	Church of England	10	49	30	241	320	*43.8*	*39.5*	*45.2*	*44.4*
	Independent	29	939	503	0	1442	*53.1*	*45.2*	–	*50.1*
	Baptist	9	146	172	90	408	*63.8*	*49.7*	*50.0*	*54.0*
	Calvinistic Methodist	31	1124	278	0	1402	*47.0*	*54.2*	–	*48.3*
	Wesleyan Methodist	3	0	35	80	115	–	*55.6*	*72.7*	*66.5*
	Other	3	0	0	230	230	–	–	*37.3*	*37.3*
	Total	**85**	**2258**	**1018**	**641**	**3917**	***50.2***	***48.2***	***44.5***	***48.7***
Swansea	Church of England	18	0	87	503	590	–	*40.8*	*56.5*	*53.4*
	Independent	22	290	620	171	1081	*52.9*	*56.1*	*77.7*	*57.7*
	Baptist	8	21	304	80	405	*42.9*	*59.6*	*55.9*	*57.7*
	Calvinistic Methodist	14	201	95	330	626	*40.0*	*49.2*	*55.4*	*48.5*
	Wesleyan Methodist	5	0	59	115	174	–	*60.2*	*61.8*	*61.3*
	Other	1	0	0	20	20	–	–	*100*	*100*
	Total	**68**	**512**	**1165**	**1219**	**2896**	***46.5***	***55.0***	***59.3***	***54.9***

Registration District	Denomination	Sunday schools[1]	Scholars 'able to read in the scriptures' Number Language of instruction Welsh	Both	English	Total	*as percentage of total scholars*[2] *Language of instruction* *Welsh*	*Both*	*English*	*Total*
CARMARTHENSHIRE										
Llanelli	Church of England	8	0	125	93	218	–	*43.3*	*35.8*	*39.7*
	Independent	14	375	588	99	1062	*55.7*	*47.7*	*65.6*	*51.6*
	Baptist	10	285	257	0	542	*37.1*	*59.9*	–	*45.2*
	Calvinistic Methodist	9	746	35	0	781	*60.6*	*42.7*	–	*59.5*
	Wesleyan Methodist	2	0	10	84	94	–	*27.8*	*48.6*	*45.0*
	Total	**43**	**1406**	**1015**	**276**	**2697**	***52.6***	***49.1***	***47.3***	***50.6***
Llandovery	Church of England	8	80	129	43	252	*59.3*	*47.6*	*54.4*	*52.0*
	Independent	21	206	894	0	1100	*65.2*	*50.1*	–	*52.3*
	Baptist	9	172	125	0	297	*72.9*	*58.7*	–	*66.1*
	Calvinistic Methodist	18	444	464	0	908	*64.3*	*70.9*	–	*67.5*
	Wesleyan Methodist	1	0	40	0	40	–	*48.2*	–	*48.2*
	Total	**57**	**902**	**1652**	**43**	**2597**	***65.5***	***54.9***	***54.4***	***58.2***
Llandeilo Fawr	Church of England	10	0	261	43	304	–	*41.8*	*30.9*	*39.8*
	Independent	10	447	365	0	812	*76.8*	*60.6*	–	*68.6*
	Baptist	10	120	88	0	208	*45.6*	*43.6*	–	*44.7*
	Calvinistic Methodist	17	703	175	0	878	*67.5*	*48.5*	–	*62.6*
	Wesleyan Methodist	5	15	119	19	153	*50.0*	*64.3*	*67.9*	*63.0*
	Total	**52**	**1285**	**1008**	**62**	**2355**	***67.1***	***51.1***	***37.1***	***58.0***
Carmarthen	Church of England	17	108	635	197	940	*54.0*	*61.0*	*41.9*	*54.9*
	Independent	41	935	1541	0	2476	*64.4*	*57.9*	–	*60.2*
	Baptist	16	93	499	0	592	*42.1*	*54.1*	–	*51.8*
	Calvinistic Methodist	30	1224	333	45	1602	*57.4*	*52.9*	*75.0*	*56.8*
	Wesleyan Methodist	4	10	94	100	204	*47.6*	*47.0*	*66.7*	*55.0*
	Other	1	0	0	20	20	–	–	*50.0*	*50.0*
	Total	**109**	**2370**	**3102**	**362**	**5834**	***58.9***	***56.9***	***50.3***	***57.2***
PEMBROKESHIRE										
Narberth	Church of England	16	12	35	431	478	*50.0*	*49.3*	*52.6*	*52.3*
	Independent	21	691	566	120	1377	*64.3*	*68.9*	*66.7*	*66.4*
	Baptist	10	123	236	53	412	*48.8*	*58.1*	*53.0*	*54.4*
	Calvinistic Methodist	5	0	40	112	152	–	*34.8*	*59.3*	*50.0*
	Wesleyan Methodist	2	0	0	140	140	–	–	*62.5*	*62.5*
	Other	1	0	0	17	17	–	–	*81.0*	*81.0*
	Total	**55**	**826**	**877**	**873**	**2576**	***61.2***	***62.1***	***56.9***	***60.0***
Pembroke	Church of England	14	0	0	597	597	–	–	*61.7*	*61.7*
	Independent	4	0	0	392	392	–	–	*70.0*	*70.0*
	Baptist	8	0	0	333	333	–	–	*62.2*	*62.2*
	Calvinistic Methodist	7	0	0	317	317	–	–	*50.9*	*50.9*
	Wesleyan Methodist	4	0	0	212	212	–	–	*53.0*	*53.0*
	Total	**37**	**0**	**0**	**1851**	**1851**	**–**	**–**	***60.0***	***60.0***
Haverfordwest	Church of England	18	35	87	469	591	*50.0*	*56.1*	*58.7*	*57.7*
	Independent	25	152	707	638	1497	*86.9*	*70.8*	*64.8*	*69.4*
	Baptist	22	382	234	470	1086	*63.9*	*57.6*	*68.8*	*64.4*
	Calvinistic Methodist	22	484	417	25	926	*65.3*	*67.8*	*65.8*	*66.4*
	Wesleyan Methodist	9	35	27	397	459	*66.0*	*57.4*	*64.0*	*63.8*
	Other	1	0	0	30	30	–	–	*68.2*	*68.2*
	Total	**97**	**1088**	**1472**	**2029**	**4589**	***66.5***	***66.2***	***64.0***	***65.3***
CARDIGANSHIRE										
Cardigan	Church of England	10	209	137	141	487	*66.6*	*57.6*	*53.2*	*59.6*
	Independent	17	985	63	60	1108	*70.0*	*53.4*	*60.6*	*68.2*
	Baptist	18	859	606	0	1465	*65.5*	*75.0*	–	*69.1*
	Calvinistic Methodist	15	1031	0	300	1331	*73.1*	–	*90.6*	*76.4*
	Wesleyan Methodist	1	0	38	0	38	–	*39.2*	–	*39.2*
	Other	1	30	0	0	30	*36.6*	–	–	*36.6*
	Total	**62**	**3114**	**844**	**501**	**4459**	***68.8***	***66.9***	***72.1***	***68.8***
Newcastle Emlyn	Church of England	10	345	77	0	422	*69.3*	*53.5*	–	*65.7*
	Independent	22	1878	140	0	2018	*76.2*	*93.3*	–	*77.1*
	Baptist	8	368	0	0	368	*64.1*	–	–	*64.1*
	Calvinistic Methodist	12	1177	10	0	1187	*70.3*	*34.5*	–	*69.7*
	Wesleyan Methodist	2	60	0	0	60	*57.1*	–	–	*57.1*
	Total	**54**	**3828**	**227**	**0**	**4055**	***72.0***	***70.3***	**–**	***71.9***

Registration District	Denomination	Sunday schools[1]	Scholars 'able to read in the scriptures' Number Language of instruction Welsh	Both	English	Total	*as percentage of total scholars*[2] *Language of instruction* *Welsh*	*Both*	*English*	*Total*
Lampeter	Church of England	3	0	139	0	139	–	*45.4*	–	*45.4*
	Independent	14	408	228	0	636	*52.9*	*57.6*	–	*54.5*
	Baptist	1	0	60	0	60	–	*60.0*	–	*60.0*
	Calvinistic Methodist	3	20	32	0	52	*64.5*	*30.8*	–	*38.5*
	Wesleyan Methodist	1	0	40	0	40	–	*78.4*	–	*78.4*
	Total	**22**	**428**	**499**	**0**	**927**	***53.4***	***52.1***	**–**	***52.7***
Aberaeron	Church of England	11	338	189	0	527	*79.9*	*53.2*	–	*67.7*
	Independent	11	979	95	0	1074	*70.6*	*70.9*	–	*70.6*
	Baptist	1	30	0	0	30	*60.0*	–	–	*60.0*
	Calvinistic Methodist	9	1197	0	0	1197	*77.7*	–	–	*77.7*
	Wesleyan Methodist	2	55	9	0	64	*87.3*	*75.0*	–	*85.3*
	Total	**34**	**2599**	**293**	**0**	**2892**	***75.0***	***58.5***	**–**	***72.9***
Aberystwyth	Church of England	20	937	0	50	987	*64.0*	–	*25.9*	*59.6*
	Independent	8	866	0	0	866	*81.2*	–	–	*81.2*
	Baptist	8	400	315	0	715	*80.6*	*57.9*	–	*68.8*
	Calvinistic Methodist	27	4338	442	0	4780	*73.8*	*78.1*	–	*74.1*
	Wesleyan Methodist	9	269	408	56	733	*60.4*	*64.6*	*69.1*	*63.3*
	Total	**72**	**6810**	**1165**	**106**	**8081**	***72.8***	***66.9***	***38.7***	***71.1***
Tregaron	Church of England	9	465	0	0	465	*78.0*	–	–	*78.0*
	Independent	2	95	0	0	95	*58.3*	–	–	*58.3*
	Baptist	2	137	0	0	137	*80.1*	–	–	*80.1*
	Calvinistic Methodist	17	1839	499	0	2338	*73.9*	*79.0*	–	*74.9*
	Wesleyan Methodist	3	85	58	0	143	*81.0*	*65.9*	–	*74.1*
	Total	**33**	**2621**	**557**	**0**	**3178**	***74.4***	***77.4***	**–**	***74.9***
BRECONSHIRE										
Builth	Church of England	6	0	0	126	126	–	–	*52.7*	*52.7*
	Independent	12	13	435	12	460	*27.7*	*69.3*	*38.7*	*65.2*
	Baptist	6	58	42	30	130	*63.7*	*52.5*	*46.2*	*55.1*
	Calvinistic Methodist	3	100	130	50	280	*79.4*	*92.9*	*66.7*	*82.1*
	Wesleyan Methodist	0	0	0	0	0	–	–	–	–
	Total	**27**	**171**	**607**	**218**	**996**	***64.8***	***71.6***	***53.2***	***65.4***
Brecon	Church of England	16	100	59	502	661	*59.5*	*72.8*	*69.7*	*68.2*
	Independent	15	211	340	25	576	*49.8*	*69.4*	*83.3*	*61.0*
	Baptist	10	52	224	33	309	*88.1*	*60.4*	*50.0*	*62.3*
	Calvinistic Methodist	18	750	121	0	871	*67.9*	*66.5*	–	*67.7*
	Wesleyan Methodist	4	0	80	46	126	–	*74.1*	*61.3*	*68.9*
	Other	1	0	0	8	8	–	–	*47.1*	*47.1*
	Total	**64**	**1113**	**824**	**614**	**2551**	***63.4***	***66.9***	***67.6***	***65.5***
Crickhowell	Church of England	9	0	20	256	276	–	*66.7*	*53.8*	*54.5*
	Independent	13	310	647	0	957	*60.0*	*59.0*	–	*59.3*
	Baptist	9	33	447	0	480	*82.5*	*44.3*	–	*45.8*
	Calvinistic Methodist	10	519	331	0	850	*60.5*	*56.8*	–	*59.0*
	Wesleyan Methodist	8	22	40	183	245	*50.0*	*50.0*	*37.9*	*40.4*
	Total	**49**	**884**	**1485**	**439**	**2808**	***60.6***	***53.1***	***45.8***	***53.8***
Hay	Church of England	10	0	0	279	279	–	–	*51.2*	*51.2*
	Independent	2	0	48	15	63	–	*53.9*	*78.9*	*58.3*
	Baptist	1	0	0	45	45	–	–	*42.1*	*42.1*
	Calvinistic Methodist	5	121	54	16	191	*59.9*	*66.7*	*66.7*	*62.2*
	Wesleyan Methodist	2	20	0	25	45	*40.8*	–	*62.5*	*50.6*
	Total	**20**	**141**	**102**	**380**	**623**	***56.2***	***60.0***	***51.7***	***53.9***
RADNORSHIRE										
Presteigne	Church of England	10	0	0	300	300	–	–	*60.5*	*60.5*
	Independent	1	0	0	30	30	–	–	*60.0*	*60.0*
	Baptist	2	0	0	36	36	–	–	*52.9*	*52.9*
	Calvinistic Methodist	2	0	0	51	51	–	–	*78.5*	*78.5*
	Wesleyan Methodist	3	0	0	48	48	–	–	*44.0*	*44.0*
	Other	1	0	0	20	20	–	–	*76.9*	*76.9*
	Total	**19**	**0**	**0**	**485**	**485**	**–**	**–**	***59.6***	***59.6***
Knighton	Church of England	4	0	0	90	90	–	–	*44.3*	*44.3*
	Calvinistic Methodist	2	0	0	36	36	–	–	*61.0*	*61.0*
	Total	**6**	**0**	**0**	**126**	**126**	**–**	**–**	***48.1***	***48.1***

Registration District	Denomination	Sunday schools[1]	Scholars 'able to read in the scriptures' Number Language of instruction Welsh	Both	English	Total	*as percentage of total scholars[2] Language of instruction* *Welsh*	*Both*	*English*	*Total*
Rhayader	Church of England	4	0	0	115	115	–	–	*66.9*	*66.9*
	Independent	5	0	140	10	150	–	*56.5*	*66.7*	*57.0*
	Baptist	7	0	20	94	114	–	*57.1*	*47.2*	*48.7*
	Calvinistic Methodist	3	0	65	40	105	–	*61.9*	*57.1*	*60.0*
	Wesleyan Methodist	1	0	0	37	37	–	–	*50.0*	*50.0*
	Total	**20**	**0**	**225**	**296**	**521**	**–**	***58.0***	***55.8***	***56.8***
MONTGOMERYSHIRE										
Machynlleth	Church of England	6	170	131	0	301	*63.4*	*52.4*	–	*58.1*
	Independent	13	763	0	0	763	*79.4*	–	–	*79.4*
	Baptist	3	80	0	0	80	*68.4*	–	–	*68.4*
	Calvinistic Methodist	21	1788	0	0	1788	*77.2*	–	–	*77.2*
	Wesleyan Methodist	13	474	141	0	615	*62.1*	*58.3*	–	*61.2*
	Total	**56**	**3275**	**272**	**0**	**3547**	***74.0***	***55.3***	**–**	***72.2***
Newtown	Church of England	7	8	120	160	288	*26.7*	*43.3*	*83.8*	*57.8*
	Independent	8	0	257	145	402	–	*60.5*	*37.6*	*49.6*
	Baptist	4	0	120	370	490	–	*58.8*	*73.7*	*69.4*
	Calvinistic Methodist	48	1570	1136	385	3091	*73.6*	*67.7*	*65.1*	*70.2*
	Wesleyan Methodist	13	117	535	220	872	*56.5*	*62.4*	*67.9*	*62.8*
	Total	**80**	**1695**	**2168**	**1280**	**5143**	***71.5***	***63.0***	***64.2***	***65.9***
Montgomery	Church of England	7	0	0	299	299	–	–	*48.5*	*48.5*
	Independent	5	33	80	86	199	*100.0*	*56.3*	*57.3*	*61.2*
	Baptist	0	0	0	0	0	–	–	–	–
	Calvinistic Methodist	11	0	200	285	485	–	*75.2*	*59.6*	*65.2*
	Wesleyan Methodist	4	0	0	153	153	–	–	*72.2*	*72.2*
	Other	1	0	0	30	30	–	–	*60.0*	*60.0*
	Total	**28**	**33**	**280**	**853**	**1166**	***100.0***	***68.6***	***56.6***	***59.9***
Llanfyllin	Church of England	8	65	105	128	298	*100.0*	*71.4*	*55.7*	*67.4*
	Independent	22	582	290	0	872	*65.2*	*62.5*	–	*64.3*
	Baptist	1	0	32	0	32	–	*58.2*	–	*58.2*
	Calvinistic Methodist	30	1110	193	40	1343	*67.5*	*65.9*	*50.0*	*66.6*
	Wesleyan Methodist	20	205	599	0	804	*52.0*	*55.4*	–	*54.5*
	Total	**81**	**1962**	**1219**	**168**	**3349**	***65.5***	***59.7***	***54.2***	***62.6***
FLINTSHIRE										
Holywell	Church of England	13	19	1303	75	1397	*70.4*	*57.4*	*43.4*	*56.6*
	Independent	20	288	652	66	1006	*55.8*	*51.4*	*42.6*	*51.9*
	Baptist	1	0	110	0	110	–	*78.0*	–	*78.0*
	Calvinistic Methodist	32	1995	494	30	2519	*70.1*	*61.8*	*26.3*	*67.0*
	Wesleyan Methodist	27	187	1259	165	1611	*41.9*	*57.0*	*53.7*	*54.4*
	Total	**93**	**2489**	**3818**	**336**	**6643**	***64.9***	***57.1***	***44.9***	***59.0***
DENBIGHSHIRE										
Wrexham	Church of England	6	0	575	124	699	–	*66.0*	*41.9*	*59.9*
	Independent	11	423	63	165	651	*70.7*	*42.9*	*60.7*	*64.0*
	Baptist	1	0	0	18	18	–	–	*36.0*	*36.0*
	Calvinistic Methodist	26	1216	98	250	1564	*62.4*	*47.3*	*53.5*	*59.6*
	Wesleyan Methodist	10	286	55	68	409	*57.4*	*55.6*	*30.4*	*49.8*
	Other	2	0	40	100	140	–	*51.9*	*58.1*	*56.2*
	Total	**56**	**1925**	**831**	**725**	**3481**	***63.2***	***59.3***	***49.0***	***58.7***
Ruthin	Church of England	10	18	196	103	317	*64.3*	*48.6*	*72.0*	*55.2*
	Independent	9	285	93	0	378	*66.1*	*72.1*	–	*67.5*
	Baptist	4	147	80	0	227	*69.3*	*57.6*	–	*64.7*
	Calvinistic Methodist	23	2133	159	0	2292	*68.1*	*79.5*	–	*68.8*
	Wesleyan Methodist	9	168	244	0	412	*60.4*	*57.5*	–	*58.7*
	Total	**55**	**2751**	**772**	**103**	**3626**	***67.4***	***59.6***	***72.0***	***65.7***
St Asaph	Church of England	8	150	327	0	477	*67.0*	*48.8*	–	*53.4*
	Independent	13	141	411	0	552	*61.3*	*63.7*	–	*63.1*
	Baptist	5	20	108	0	128	*46.5*	*53.2*	–	*52.0*
	Calvinistic Methodist	15	1366	500	0	1866	*66.3*	*60.6*	–	*64.7*
	Wesleyan Methodist	8	149	567	0	716	*47.8*	*71.2*	–	*64.6*
	Total	**49**	**1826**	**1913**	**0**	**3739**	***63.7***	***60.9***	**–**	***62.2***

Registration District	Denomination	Sunday schools[1]	Scholars 'able to read in the scriptures' Number Language of instruction Welsh	Both	English	Total	*as percentage of total scholars[2]* *Language of instruction* *Welsh*	*Both*	*English*	*Total*
Llanrwst	Church of England	4	24	124	0	148	*46.2*	*39.5*	–	*40.4*
	Independent	11	536	0	0	536	*76.5*	–	–	*76.5*
	Baptist	3	70	0	0	70	*48.3*	–	–	*48.3*
	Calvinistic Methodist	27	2213	0	0	2213	*70.4*	–	–	*70.4*
	Wesleyan Methodist	4	95	125	0	220	*63.3*	*60.1*	–	*61.5*
	Total	**49**	**2938**	**249**	**0**	**3187**	***70.1***	***47.7***	**–**	***67.6***
MERIONETH										
Corwen	Church of England	6	30	72	28	130	*48.4*	*42.6*	*49.1*	*45.1*
	Independent	10	374	102	0	476	*66.9*	*48.8*	–	*62.0*
	Baptist	7	326	80	0	406	*60.1*	*50.0*	–	*57.8*
	Calvinistic Methodist	37	2773	19	0	2792	*70.8*	*31.7*	–	*70.2*
	Wesleyan Methodist	17	289	274	0	563	*55.4*	*62.1*	–	*58.5*
	Total	**77**	**3792**	**547**	**28**	**4367**	***67.7***	***52.6***	***49.1***	***65.2***
Bala	Church of England	3	20	13	4	37	*51.3*	*56.5*	*16.0*	*42.5*
	Independent	12	598	0	0	598	*72.5*	–	–	*72.5*
	Baptist	2	29	0	0	29	*72.5*	–	–	*72.5*
	Calvinistic Methodist	24	2048	0	0	2048	*75.4*	–	–	*75.4*
	Wesleyan Methodist	1	14	0	0	14	*53.8*	–	–	*53.8*
	Total	**42**	**2709**	**13**	**4**	**2726**	***74.3***	***56.5***	***16.0***	***73.8***
Dolgellau	Church of England	5	207	0	0	207	*68.3*	–	–	*68.3*
	Independent	17	679	121	0	800	*71.2*	*65.4*	–	*70.3*
	Baptist	3	111	0	0	111	*64.9*	–	–	*64.9*
	Calvinistic Methodist	34	2292	23	0	2315	*76.0*	*76.7*	–	*76.0*
	Wesleyan Methodist	7	502	0	0	502	*77.8*	–	–	*77.8*
	Total	**66**	**3791**	**144**	**0**	**3935**	***74.5***	***67.0***	**–**	***74.2***
Ffestiniog	Church of England	5	0	35	104	139	–	*37.2*	*56.5*	*50.0*
	Independent	11	581	0	0	581	*68.6*	–	–	*68.6*
	Baptist	1	6	0	0	6	*50.0*	–	–	*50.0*
	Calvinistic Methodist	29	2577	0	0	2577	*70.0*	–	–	*70.0*
	Wesleyan Methodist	9	220	25	0	245	*60.4*	*48.1*	–	*58.9*
	Total	**55**	**3384**	**60**	**104**	**3548**	***69.0***	***41.1***	***56.5***	***67.7***
CAERNARFONSHIRE										
Pwllheli	Church of England	7	84	201	0	285	*69.4*	*69.8*	–	*69.7*
	Independent	12	606	0	0	606	*63.6*	–	–	*63.6*
	Baptist	7	303	0	0	303	*53.4*	–	–	*53.4*
	Calvinistic Methodist	36	3523	40	0	3563	*76.0*	*71.4*	–	*76.0*
	Wesleyan Methodist	7	99	119	0	218	*57.6*	*59.2*	–	*58.4*
	Total	**69**	**4615**	**360**	**0**	**4975**	***71.6***	***66.1***	**–**	***71.1***
Caernarfon	Church of England	3	186	0	14	200	*47.2*	–	*70.0*	*48.3*
	Independent	15	837	0	0	837	*65.8*	–	–	*65.8*
	Baptist	4	129	0	0	129	*53.8*	–	–	*53.8*
	Calvinistic Methodist	39	4896	0	0	4896	*71.0*	–	–	*71.0*
	Wesleyan Methodist[4]	6	163	–[4]	0	163	*57.2*	–[4]	–	*57.2*
	Total	**67**	**6211**	**0[4]**	**14**	**6225**	***68.3***	–[4]	***70.0***	***68.3***
Bangor	Church of England	7	146	195	30	371	*78.1*	*36.0*	*50.0*	*47.1*
	Independent	9	309	320	40	669	*52.7*	*59.3*	*36.4*	*54.1*
	Baptist	2	25	20	0	45	*50.0*	*50.0*	–	*50.0*
	Calvinistic Methodist	30	3029	0	0	3029	*68.5*	–	–	*68.5*
	Wesleyan Methodist	9	145	566	30	741	*78.8*	*73.1*	*60.0*	*73.5*
	Total	**57**	**3654**	**1101**	**100**	**4855**	***67.3***	***58.1***	***45.5***	***64.3***
Conwy	Church of England	2	0	20	26	46	–	*36.4*	*54.2*	*44.7*
	Independent	5	214	33	0	247	*63.1*	*60.0*	–	*62.7*
	Baptist	4	77	108	0	185	*66.4*	*70.1*	–	*68.5*
	Calvinistic Methodist	14	980	106	0	1086	*63.7*	*68.4*	–	*64.1*
	Wesleyan Methodist	4	45	225	0	270	*44.6*	*67.6*	–	*62.2*
	Total	**29**	**1316**	**492**	**26**	**1834**	***62.8***	***65.4***	***54.2***	***63.4***

Registration District	Denomination	Sunday schools[1]	Scholars 'able to read in the scriptures' Number Language of instruction Welsh	Both	English	Total	*as percentage of total scholars*[2] *Language of instruction* *Welsh*	*Both*	*English*	*Total*
ANGLESEY										
Anglesey	Church of England	7	55	61	150	266	*40.1*	*42.4*	*58.1*	*49.4*
	Independent	17	818	70	0	888	*54.8*	*73.7*	–	*55.9*
	Baptist	16	894	0	0	894	*69.8*	–	–	*69.8*
	Calvinistic Methodist	52	4262	248	0	4510	*70.2*	*71.3*	–	*70.2*
	Wesleyan Methodist	7	151	69	35	255	*50.8*	*34.3*	*39.3*	*43.4*
	Total	**99**	**6180**	**448**	**185**	**6813**	***66.6***	***56.9***	***53.3***	***65.4***
Parts of Wales in English Registration Counties										
SHROPSHIRE										
Oswestry[5]	Church of England	3	0	55	117	172	–	*55.0*	*70.5*	*64.7*
	Independents	1	40	0	0	40	*66.7*	–	–	*66.7*
	Baptists	2	0	67	0	67	–	*50.4*	–	*50.4*
	Calvinistic Methodist	1	0	18	0	18	–	*41.9*	–	*41.9*
	Wesleyan Methodist	1	0	50	0	50	–	*56.8*	–	*56.8*
	Total	**8**	**40**	**190**	**117**	**347**	***66.7***	***52.2***	***70.5***	***58.8***
Ellesmere[6]	Church of England	2	0	0	80	80	–	–	*47.1*	*47.1*
	Calvinistic Methodist	1	0	0	15	15	–	–	*25.0*	*25.0*
	Total	**3**	**0**	**0**	**95**	**95**	**–**	**–**	***41.3***	***41.3***
CHESHIRE										
Hawarden[7]	Church of England	3	0	0	197	197	–	–	*65.4*	*65.4*
	Calvinistic Methodist	1	0	0	33	33	–	–	*80.5*	*80.5*
	Total	**4**	**0**	**0**	**230**	**230**	**–**	**–**	***67.3***	***67.3***

Source: *Reports of the Commissioners of Inquiry into the State of Education in Wales*; Part I, Carmarthen, Glamorgan and Pembroke [PP 1847 (870) XXVII]; Part II, Brecknock, Cardigan, Radnor and Monmouth [PP 1847 (871) XXVIII]; Part III, North Wales [PP 1847 (872) XXVII]; Parochial tables.

1 Excludes126 Sunday schools listed in the returns without figures for numbers 'on books' or 'able to read in the scriptures'.
2 This percentage is read as the number of pupils 'able to read in the scriptures' as a percentage of the number of scholars 'on books' in each language group, for each denomination.
3 Monmouthshire includes only the following parishes: Abergavenny – Bedwellte, Llanover, Llanwenarth, Aberystruth, Llanfoist, Llanelen; Pontypool – Trevethin, Llanfrechfa, Llanhilleth, Llanfihangel Pont-y-moel; Newport – Caerleon, Risca, Newport, Llanfihangel Llantarnam, Basaleg, Mynyddislwyn, Machen.
4 The returns for the Wesleyan Methodist chapel in Caernarfon, in which instruction is given in both languages have been excluded from this table because the number given as 'able to read in the scriptures' (172) is greater than the total 'number on books' (158).
5 Includes returns from: Chirk and Llansilin in the Ancient County of Denbigh.
6 Includes returns from: Hanmer and Penley in the Ancient County of Flint.
7 Returns from the parish of Hawarden in the Ancient County of Flint.

Education 2.9 Reports of the Commissioners of Inquiry into the state of education in Wales, 1847. Day and Sunday schools. Number of schools and scholars. Registration Districts, Wales excluding Monmouthshire. 1847, 1851

Registration District[1]	Day schools[2] 1846 schools	scholars	1851 schools	scholars	Sunday schools 1846 schools	scholars	1851 schools	scholars
Wales	1530 (1528)[3]	70033	1684	88092	2546 (2485)[3]	235502	2764	269272
GLAMORGAN								
Cardiff	92	4055	73	4167	82	5793	75	5795
Merthyr Tydfil	68	3335	73	4422	78	10551	97	15716
Bridgend	39	1423	45	2298	83 (74)	4550	70	4940
Neath	61	3792	65	4445	89 (88)	8405	108	11135
Swansea	84	3180	92	4925	73 (70)	5352	81	7977
CARMARTHENSHIRE								
Llanelli	36	1580	36	2142	44 (43)	5326	43	5784
Llandovery	23	903	21	1255	58	4539	53	5102
Llandeilo Fawr	36	1235	31	1612	53 (52)	4057	56	4477
Carmarthen	73	2753	83	3664	100 (109)	10199	113	11973
PEMBROKESHIRE								
Narberth	40	1491	40	1956	55	4296	58	4902
Pembroke	55	2325	63	2746	38	3158	37	3351
Haverfordwest	86	3246	81	3377	99 (98)	7064	84	6593
CARDIGANSHIRE								
Cardigan	37 (36)	1378	28	1611	64	6520	49	6257
Newcastle Emlyn	27	990	36	1869	55	5632	60	6423
Lampeter	12	432	17	713	25	1830	29	1798
Aberaeron	18	715	27	1467	36	4510	44	5121
Aberystwyth	39	1706	47	2141	73	11400	67	9835
Tregaron	6	262	10	452	33	4245	38	4281
BRECONSHIRE								
Builth	8	261	17	474	27	1522	30	1736
Brecknock	38	1449	41	1739	64	3895	62	3545
Crickhowell	34	1374	23	1326	49	5216	61	6038
Hay[1]	18	868	23	863	20	1155	29	1643
RADNORSHIRE								
Presteigne[1]	16	479	44	1306	19	814	26	1205
Knighton[1]	10	317	28	680	7	381	5	312
Rhayader	6	185	11	444	20	884	20	1002
MONTGOMERYSHIRE								
Machynlleth	18	874	15	1022	63 (56)	4894	77	6026
Newtown	41 (40)	1617	31	1451	83	7983	90	7697
Montgomery[1]	39	1239	53	2162	32 (31)	2053	52	3413
Llanfyllin	38	1529	28	1559	88 (87)	5667	93	5865
FLINTSHIRE								
Holywell	83	4526	67	4573	95 (93)	11296	122	14900
DENBIGHSHIRE								
Wrexham[1]	56	3200	88	4447	64 (62)	6477	95	9451
Ruthin	23	1399	30	1491	57 (55)	5520	59	6005
St Asaph	48	2376	50	2535	53 (52)	6199	76	8208
Llanrwst	16	942	19	1036	51	4699	57	5696
MERIONETH								
Corwen	19	1137	19	1103	80 (77)	6699	44	3370
Bala	11	492	11	458	42	3694	39	3079
Dolgellau	24	1165	21	1094	67 (66)	5315	73	5405
Ffestiniog	18	945	16	1055	60 (58)	5464	70	6422
CAERNARFONSHIRE								
Pwllheli	23	1325	35	1518	76 (73)	7245	89	8508
Caernarfon	19	1713	41	2823	73 (70)	9380	89	11973
Bangor	33	2283	44	3490	65 (60)	7865	76	10143
Conwy	16	1030	14	1292	33 (30)	2963	53	4508
ANGLESEY								
Anglesey	41	2507	47	2889	110 (102)	10795	115	11662

Sources: 1846: as Table 1; 1851: *Census of Population for England and Wales: Education. England and Wales. Report and Tables* (HMSO, 1854), pp. 202–12.

[1] Registration districts in Monmouthshire have been excluded because the returns for 1846 are incomplete (see Table 2.1 note 4). Parts of other registration districts in the Welsh division – Hay, Presteigne, Knighton, Montgomery, and Wrexham – lie in England and were also excluded from the 1846 returns. This means that the figures for 1846 and 1851 for these districts are not comparable.

[2] The figures for 1846 are mainly for schools 'for the working classes' and are therefore not as inclusive as those for 1851.

[3] Figures in brackets are the numbers of schools corresponding to the numbers of scholars given in the next column.

Education 3.1 Reports of the Assistant Commissioners appointed to inquire into the state of popular education in England, 1861. Day schools. Knowledge of Welsh and English in schools in Merioneth and Neath. 1861

	Children under 10 years of age				Children over 10 years of age			
	Total[1]	Welsh	English knowledge		Total[1]	Welsh	English knowledge	
Schools	pupils	only	Imperfect	Good	pupils	only	Imperfect	Good
Merioneth								
Beddgelert (British)	71	0	62	9	30	14	0	16
Glyndyfrdwy	56	22	30	4	12	0	2	10
Betws	40	25	15	0	14	2	11	1
Llwynygell	50	2	38	10	44	7	12	25
Dolgellau (National)	120	64	50	6	40	10	10	20
Llangollen Girls (British)[2]	84	22	36	26	35	11	24	0
Llangollen Boys (British)[2]	93	30	43	20	39	1	18	20
Llangollen (National)[2]	92	59	23	10	75	18	36	21
Bala Free School[2]	5	0	2	3	34	0	14	20
Ffestiniog Slate Quarries (British)	90	54	30	6[3]	77	11	26	40
Bala (British)[2]	106	42	49	15	66	0	21	45
Dolgellau (British)[2]	102	36	59	7	91	0	70	21
Total	**909**	**356**	**437**	**116**	**557**	**74**	**244**	**239**
Percentage	*100.0*	*39.2*	*48.1*	*12.8*	*100.0*	*13.3*	*43.8*	*42.9*
Neath, Glamorgan								
Ynysgedwyn Ironworks	46	11	20	15	29	4	16	9
Margam Copperworks	98	8	58	32	52	3	15	34
Margam Tinworks	25	0	9	16	39	0	8	31
Ystradgynlais (National)	54	37	17	0	27	0	14	13
Aber-craf	69	33	16	20	24	5	5	14
Ystalyfera (Boys)	82	14	40	28	41	0	9	32
Total	**374**	**103**	**160**	**111**	**212**	**12**	**67**	**133**
Percentage	*100.0*	*27.5*	*42.8*	*29.7*	*100.0*	*5.7*	*31.6*	*62.7*

Source: 'Report of Assistant Commissioner John Jenkins, Esq., on the State of Popular Education in the Welsh Specimen Districts in the Poor Law Unions of Corwen, Dolgelly, Bala, Ffestiniog, Neath, and Merthyr Tydfil in North and South Wales' in *Reports of the Assistant Commissioners appointed to inquire into the state of popular education in England. Vol. II* (HMSO, 1861), Appendix D, p. 631 [PP 1861 (2792-ii) XX!, pt. 2].

1 This column is simply the sum of the three following columns. It therefore differs in some cases from figures given in the corresponding column at source where either the column has been left blank or the value given does not equal the sum. In the latter case it may be that the source figure represents the 'number on the books' or 'those usually present' rather than the total of pupils whose linguistic knowledge has been judged.

2 Described as 'schools in towns' in an otherwise rural area.

3 Given as 'few' at source but can be calculated from the other figures given.

Education 4.1 Report of the Royal Commission on the Church of England and Other Religious Bodies in Wales and Monmouthshire, 1910. Independent and Calvinistic Methodist Sunday schools. Number of scholars. Wales. 1846–1905

Year	Sunday scholars Calvinistic Methodist Wales Number	*as % pop.*	Independent Wales excl. Mon. Number	Mon.	Wales incl. Mon.	*as % pop.*
1846	103088[1]	*9+*	–	–	58659[1]	*5+*
1855	123570					
1860	137732	*10.7*				
1861			78404	8042	86446	*6.7*
1865	143607					
1870	162525					
1875	174148					
1880	185635	*11.8*				
1882			105825	10193	116018	*7.4*
1885	186740					
1890	192806	*10.9*				
1895	194793		133598	–		
1896			139939	–		
1897			135736	12702	148438	
1898			135628	12737	148365	
1899			137196	14131	151327	
1900	202759	*10.1*	132150	13894	146044	
1901			136488	14054	150542	*7.3*
1902			135246	14326	149572	
1903			137190	14413	151603	
1904			147298	15187	162487	
1905	222880	*10.1*	150135	15783	165918	*7.5*

Source: 1846, Table 2.3; 1855–1905, Royal Commission on the Church of England and Other Religious Bodies in Wales, *Report, Vol. I* (HMSO, 1910), Appendix H, Table M, p. 112 [PP 1910 (Cd 5432-i) XIV]; ibid., *Report, Vol. VII, Appendices to Minutes of Evidence (Nonconformists)* (HMSO, 1911), Appendix II, Table II, p. 6 [PP 1910 (Cd 5438) XIX].

[1] The figures for 1846 do not include parts of Monmouth which accounted for about 40% of the population of the county.

Education 4.2 Report of the Royal Commission on the Church of England and Other Religious Bodies in Wales and Monmouthshire, 1910. Independent Sunday schools. Number of scholars by language and age. Wales and Counties. 1906

Language	Age of scholars under 14	over 14	All ages
Welsh			
Monmouth	2116	2242	4358
Glamorgan	26738	30666	57404
Carmarthen	7531	9876	17407
Pembroke	1388	2525	3913
Cardigan	3306	5486	8792
Montgomery	1241	2319	3560
Flint	766	1304	2070
Denbigh	2162	3138	5300
Merioneth	3718	3000	6718
Caernarfon	5345	6589	11934
Anglesey	1199	1835	3034
Total	**55510**	**68980**	**124490**
as % total scholars	*71.3*	*82.3*	*77.0*
Welsh and English			
Brecon	739	895	1634
as % total scholars	*0.9*	*1.1*	*1.0*

Language	Age of scholars under 14	over 14	All ages
English			
Monmouth	7012	3549	10561
Glamorgan East	7000	3683	10683
Carmarthen and Glamorgan West	3791	2492	6283
Pembroke	1458	1748	3206
Brecon and Radnor	421	265	686
Montgomery	660	377	1037
Flint	233	967	1200
Denbigh	830	660	1490
Merioneth	50	30	80
Caernarfon	185	145	330
Total	**21640**	**13916**	**35556**
as % total scholars	*27.8*	*16.6*	*22.0*

Source: Royal Commission on the Church of England and Other Religious Bodies in Wales, *Report, Vol. I* (HMSO, 1910), Appendix H, Table N, p. 113 [PP 1910 (Cd 5432-i) XIV].

Education 4.3 Report of the Royal Commission on the Church of England and Other Religious Bodies in Wales and Monmouthshire, 1910. Sunday schools. Number of schools and age of scholars, by denomination. Wales and Administrative Counties. 1906

	Denomination	Number Sunday schools[1]	Teachers	Age of scholars[2] under 15	over 15	age not given	Total in Sunday school[3]	*as % total pop.*[4]
Wales	Church of England	1755	11095	93597	48694	20751	172337	
	Baptists	941	12159	65042	54071	16001	155683	
	Calvinistic Methodists	1418	21900	52119	58173	58942	215490	
	Independents	1154	15800	64063	60485	29252	178008	
	Wesleyan Methodists	603	6882	29997	23015	10249	78425	
	Primitive Methodists	128	1973	10078	4983	264	19822	
	Others[4]	227	1891	9525	4468	7036	23690	
	Total	**6146**	**71700**	**324421**	**253889**	**142495**	**843455**	***41.9***
Administrative Counties								
Monmouth	Church of England	239	1604	17286	6193	–	25083	
	Baptists	126	1948	16059	11760	310	30077	
	Calvinistic Methodists[5]	57	809	4680	3494	436	9419	
	Independents	86	1213	8565	5686	160	15624	
	Wesleyan Methodists	71	1115	7535	3925	0	12575	
	Primitive Methodists	41	783	4815	2237	0	7835	
	Others[4]	30	311	1609	773	450	3143	
	Total	**650**	**7783**	**60549**	**34068**	**1356**	**103756**	***34.8***
Glamorgan	Church of England	343	4576	46614	19832	–	71022	
	Baptists	291	5772	30505	24705	9486	70468	
	Calvinistic Methodists	254	5737	22955	22638	7579	58909	
	Independents	310	6451	31120	29950	8804	76325	
	Wesleyan Methodists	130	2265	13442	8328	1447	25482	
	Primitive Methodists	16	761	3144	1693	264	5862	
	Others[4]	121	1050	5314	2069	5515	13948	
	Total	**1465**	**26612**	**153094**	**109215**	**33095**	**322016**	***32.4***
Carmarthen	Church of England	157	1034	6970	6248	–	14252	
	Baptists	110	1301	6816	7481	171	15769	
	Calvinistic Methodists	103	1204	3679	5247	1482	11612	
	Independents	172	2194	9694	11764	55	23707	
	Wesleyan Methodists	21	141	693	653	0	1487	
	Others[4]	9	24	160	85	0	269	
	Total	**572**	**5898**	**28012**	**31478**	**1708**	**67096**	***49.6***
Pembroke	Church of England	168	702	5468	2052	–	8222	
	Baptists	80	899	4324	3897	270	9390	
	Calvinistic Methodists	48	395	1816	1604	130	3945	
	Independents	76	757	3809	3327	110	8003	
	Wesleyan Methodists	21	240	1356	601	27	2224	
	Primitive Methodists	4	17	71	39	0	127	
	Others[4]	3	10	84	32	0	126	
	Total	**400**	**3020**	**16928**	**11552**	**537**	**32037**	***36.4***
Cardigan	Church of England	106	685	3008	3592	–	7285	
	Baptists	27	240	–	–	1972	2212	
	Calvinistic Methodists	146	1992	–	–	13329	15321	
	Independents	66	908	–	–	7677	8585	
	Wesleyan Methodists	21	225	–	–	1624	1849	
	Others[4]	15	95	–	–	1071	1166	
	Total	**381**	**4145**	**3008**	**3592**	**25673**	**36418**	***59.6***
Brecon	Church of England	103	438	3386	1314	–	5138	
	Baptists	42	300	1758	1428	140	3626	
	Calvinistic Methodists	52	479	1913	1706	332	4430	
	Independents	57	539	2841	2580	92	6052	
	Wesleyan Methodists	16	119	673	391	0	1183	
	Primitive Methodists	3	56	307	190	0	553	
	Others[4]	2	12	97	75	0	184	
	Total	**275**	**1943**	**10975**	**7684**	**564**	**21166**	***39.0***

Administrative County	Denomination	Number Sunday schools[1]	Teachers	Age of scholars[2] under 15	over 15	age not given	Total in Sunday school[3]	*as % total pop.*[4]
Radnor	Church of England	58	162	1435	1453	–	1865	
	Baptists	30	181	1360	687	–	2228	
	Calvinistic Methodists	10	60	405	217	–	682	
	Independents	9	51	269	160	–	480	
	Wesleyan Methodists	7	31	151	53	–	235	
	Primitive Methodists	9	51	268	55	–	374	
	Others[4]	5	21	125	54	–	200	
	Total	**128**	**557**	**4013**	**2679**	**–**	**6064**	***26.0***
Montgomery	Church of England	78	110	582	548	2740	3980	
	Baptists	24	201	1010	859	–	2070	
	Calvinistic Methodists	89	977	3004	4625	–	8606	
	Independents	57	432	1868	2347	–	4647	
	Wesleyan Methodists	56	469	1637	1928	–	4034	
	Primitive Methodists	14	79	390	169	–	638	
	Others[4]	2	2	18	0	–	20	
	Total	**320**	**2270**	**8509**	**10476**	**2740**	**23995**	***43.7***
Flint	Church of England	86	–	–	–	7172	7172	
	Baptists	24	133	606	517	–	1256	
	Calvinistic Methodists	66	1012	3242	3375	–	7629	
	Independents	43	386	1730	1601	–	3717	
	Wesleyan Methodists	61	695	2751	2506	–	5952	
	Primitive Methodists	22	226	1083	600	–	1909	
	Others[4]	31	366	2118	1380	–	3864	
	Total	**333**	**2818**	**11530**	**9979**	**7172**	**31499**	***38.7***
Denbigh	Church of England	120	–	–	–	9265	9265	
	Baptists	71	–	–	–	8410	8410	
	Calvinistic Methodists	173	–	–	–	24356	24356	
	Independents	67	–	–	–	8408	8408	
	Wesleyan Methodists	82	–	–	–	8282	8282	
	Primitive Methodists	19	–	–	–	2524	2524	
	Others[4]	9	–	–	–	770	770	
	Total	**541**	**–**	**–**	**–**	**62015**	**62015**	***47.1***
Merioneth	Church of England	71	270	1100	1072	1227	3669	
	Baptists	30	312	971	1389	130	2802	
	Calvinistic Methodists	132	2198	5351	8534	0	16083	
	Independents	77	859	2732	1758	86	5435	
	Wesleyan Methodists	35	390	997	4037	0	5424	
	Total	**345**	**4029**	**11151**	**16790**	**1443**	**33413**	***68.4***
Caernarfon	Church of England	133	1063	5261	4210	347	10881	
	Baptists	44	480	–	–	3522	4002	
	Calvinistic Methodists	188	5227	–	–	35654	40881	
	Independents	97	1597	–	–	12268	13865	
	Wesleyan Methodists	58	961	–	–	7151	8112	
	Total	**520**	**9328**	**5261**	**4210**	**58942**	**77741**	***61.9***
Anglesey[6]	Church of England	93	451	2469	1583	–	4503	
	Baptists	42	392	1633	1348	–	3373	
	Calvinistic Methodists	100	1810	5074	6733	–	13617	
	Independents	37	413	1435	1312	–	3160	
	Wesleyan Methodists	24	231	762	593	–	1586	
	Total	**296**	**3297**	**11373**	**11569**	**–**	**26239**	***51.8***

Source: Royal Commission on the Church of England and Other Religious Bodies in Wales and Monmouthshire, *Report, Vol. V, Appendices to Minutes of Evidence. Church of England,* Statistical Returns for the Dioceses of Bangor, Llandaff, St Asaph, and St David's, pp. 1–244 [PP 1910 (Cd. 5436) XVIII]; ibid.,*Vol. VI, Appendices to Minutes of Evidence. Nonconformist County Statistics*, pp. 437–42, with amendments given in the county statistics for Cardiganshire and Glamorgan, pp. 66–7, 234, 294–5 [PP 1910 (Cd. 5437) XVIII].

1 For the Church of England this is the total number of Churches and Missions, not all of which would have necessarily held Sunday schools. For the remainder, this refers to the number of chapels and separate school rooms for which information is given in the returns regarding Sunday school attenders.

[2] Church of England returns from the Diocese of St Asaph, affecting the counties of Denbigh and Merioneth, give only the total number of teachers and scholars. Nonconformist returns for Cardigan and Caernarfon give separate figures for teachers and scholars, but do not distinguish the ages of scholars.

[3] These figures are simply the total number of those attending Sunday schools as a percentage of the total population in 1901. There are two major reasons why they should be used only as very crude comparisons. First, the returns are mainly for 1905. Therefore, for counties such as Monmouth and Glamorgan, which experienced substantial population growth during this period, the percentages may overestimate the influence of Sunday schools in relation to other counties. Second, comments in the Nonconformist statistics suggest that some teachers were counted twice in the figures for scholars. In particular, for Anglesey no figure was given for the total number attending Sunday school because it was claimed that 'In the majority of cases, examination of the original schedules has shown that the teachers are included for scholars over 15'. Here, in order to provide such a total without deliberate overcounting, the number of Nonconformist teachers (total 2,846) has been subtracted from the number given for scholars over 15. This means that the percentage for Anglesey is low in strict comparison with other counties. Without this subtraction, the total for those attending Sunday schools in Anglesey would be 29,085, and the total (including an unknown element of double counting) as a percentage of the total population would be 57.5%. One sixth is generally given as the school-age proportion of the population.

[4] This is a residual group including Bible Christians, Christadelphians, Church of Christ, Plymouth Brethren, Presbyterians, Salvation Army, Seventh Day Adventists, Society of Friends.

[5] For Monmouth, the figures for Calvinistic Methodists include a small number of Presbyterians.

[6] See note 3 regarding the calculation of the total number of Nonconformist Sunday school pupils in Anglesey.

Education 4.4 Report of the Royal Commission on the Church of England and Other Religious Bodies in Wales and Monmouthshire, 1910. Sunday schools. Number of schools and age of scholars, by denomination. Various districts. 1906

District[1]	Denomination	Number Sunday schools[2]	Teachers	Age of scholars under 15	over 15	age not given	Total in Sunday school
MONMOUTHSHIRE							
Monmouth	Church of England	56	220	2082	249	0	2551
	Baptist	8	54	283	116	50	503
	Calvinistic Methodists	1	2	18	0	0	20
	Independents	4	31	211	29	0	271
	Wesleyan Methodists	9	50	451	61	0	562
	Primitive Methodists	3	14	76	1	0	91
	Others	9	54	271	26	0	351
	Total	**90**	**425**	**3392**	**482**	**50**	**4349**
Abergavenny	Church of England	25	133	1351	183	0	1667
	Baptist	16	176	1616	990	0	2782
	Calvinistic Methodists	6	64	299	239	0	602
	Independents	5	80	611	382	0	1073
	Wesleyan Methodists	4	83	475	253	0	811
	Primitive Methodists	1	19	118	80	0	217
	Others	1	7	40	12	0	59
	Total	**58**	**562**	**4510**	**2139**	**0**	**7211**
Abertillery	Church of England	14	185	2172	1187	0	3544
	Baptist	11	243	2273	1792	0	4308
	Calvinistic Methodists	8	111	555	770	0	1436
	Independents	8	122	1058	694	0	1874
	Wesleyan Methodists	6	93	651	382	0	1126
	Primitive Methodists	9	210	1237	770	0	2217
	Others	4	48	360	119	0	527
	Total	**60**	**1012**	**8306**	**5714**	**0**	**15032**
Tredegar	Church of England	14	276	2427	1529	0	4232
	Baptist	21	345	2899	1670	0	4914
	Calvinistic Methodists	15	256	1494	981	0	2731
	Independents	23	387	2576	1705	0	4668
	Wesleyan Methodists	13	220	1283	788	0	2291
	Primitive Methodists	8	185	1329	221	0	1735
	Others	1	12	12	126	0	150
	Total	**95**	**1681**	**12020**	**7020**	**0**	**20721**
Pontypool	Church of England	35	251	2720	857	0	3828
	Baptist	20	285	2191	1854	0	4330
	Calvinistic Methodists	4	74	515	250	0	839
	Independents	17	251	1470	1144	160	3025
	Wesleyan Methodists	14	243	1754	1117	0	3114
	Primitive Methodists	8	169	1069	697	0	1935
	Others	7	75	450	301	97	923
	Total	**105**	**1348**	**10169**	**6220**	**257**	**17994**
Newport	Church of England	9	201	2548	1092	0	3841
	Baptist	10	284	2616	1521	260	4681
	Calvinistic Methodists	8	161	1088	776	436	2461
	Independents	6	117	987	494	0	1598
	Wesleyan Methodists	6	182	1353	440	0	1975
	Primitive Methodists	3	44	189	83	0	316
	Others	5	96	328	155	353	932
	Total	**47**	**1085**	**9109**	**4561**	**1049**	**15804**
Risca	Church of England	51	338	3986	1096	0	5420
	Baptist	40	561	4181	3817	0	8559
	Calvinistic Methodists	15	141	711	478	0	1330
	Independents	23	225	1652	1238	0	3115
	Wesleyan Methodists	19	244	1568	884	0	2696
	Primitive Methodists	9	142	797	385	0	1324
	Others	3	19	148	34	0	201
	Total	**160**	**1670**	**13043**	**7932**	**0**	**22645**

District[1]	Denomination	Number Sunday schools[2]	Teachers	Age of scholars under 15	over 15	age not given	Total in Sunday school
GLAMORGAN							
Cardiff CB	Church of England	25	726	9735	2763	0	13224
	Welsh						
	Baptist	4	89	294	426	0	809
	Calvinistic Methodists	5	103	297	590	0	990
	Independents	5	77	394	444	0	915
	Wesleyan Methodists	1	3	4	16	0	23
	Total	**15**	**272**	**989**	**1476**	**0**	**2737**
	English						
	Baptist	15	411	3211	2162	406	6190
	Calvinistic Methodists	13	330	2888	1276	384	4878
	Independents	11	219	1348	587	682	2836
	Wesleyan Methodists	15	529	4215	2063	0	6807
	Primitive Methodists	5	76	287	245	0	608
	Others	31	503	2694	648	2955	6800
	Total	**90**	**2068**	**14643**	**6981**	**4427**	**28119**
	Grand Total	**130**	**3066**	**25367**	**11220**	**4427**	**44080**
Cowbridge, Barry, Penarth	Church of England	60	381	3629	876	0	4886
	Baptist	20	273	1587	809	481	3150
	Calvinistic Methodists	15	201	1307	1017	31	2556
	Independents	22	216	1099	696	0	2011
	Wesleyan Methodists	14	217	1800	581	0	2598
	Primitive Methodists	2	28	70	30	0	128
	Others	10	106	880	356	0	1342
	Total	**143**	**1422**	**10372**	**4363**	**512**	**16671**
Caerphilly	Church of England	34	374	3945	1598	0	5917
	Baptist	21	262	1608	1310	60	3240
	Calvinistic Methodists	23	259	1208	1204	54	2725
	Independents	26	354	2157	1618	0	4129
	Wesleyan Methodists	12	162	966	454	0	1582
	Others	11	120	576	505	0	1201
	Total	**127**	**1531**	**10460**	**6689**	**114**	**18794**
Pontypridd	Church of England	5	123	1103	334	0	1560
	Welsh						
	Baptist	5	92	505	443	0	1040
	Calvinistic Methodists	7	187	912	670	0	1769
	Independents	4	92	458	491	0	1041
	Wesleyan Methodists	3	35	180	108	0	323
	Others	1	15	116	45	0	176
	Total	**20**	**421**	**2171**	**1757**	**0**	**4349**
	English						
	Baptist	7	137	1123	807	0	2067
	Calvinistic Methodists	5	78	651	423	0	1152
	Independents	3	52	562	395	0	1009
	Wesleyan Methodists	6	89	616	370	0	1075
	Others	6	61	414	149	0	624
	Total	**27**	**417**	**3366**	**2144**	**0**	**5927**
	Grand Total	**52**	**946**	**6640**	**4235**	**0**	**11821**
Merthyr Tydfil	Church of England*	16	380	3948	1698	0	6024
	Baptist	34	764	4117	3177	200	8258
	Calvinistic Methodists	21	407	1788	1904	80	4179
	Independents	27	643	3469	3445	0	7557
	Wesleyan Methodists	11	110	543	453	0	1106
	Others	12	119	769	364	0	1252
	Total	**121**	**2423**	**14632**	**11041**	**280**	**28376**
	* Language of Sunday services in the 3 churches in St David's diocese: 3 Welsh, 3 English						
Aberdare	Church of England	25	380	4337	1583	0	6300
	Baptist	30	633	2880	2124	1192	6829
	Calvinistic Methodists	25	642	2259	2597	337	5835
	Independents	35	789	3997	3919	135	8840
	Wesleyan Methodists	8	115	448	546	0	1109
	Others	13	246	897	356	0	1499
	Total	**136**	**2805**	**14818**	**11125**	**1664**	**30412**

District[1]	Denomination	Number Sunday schools[2]	Teachers	Age of scholars under 15	over 15	age not given	Total in Sunday school
Rhondda UD	Church of England	20	410	4219	2011	0	6640
	Welsh						
	Baptist	31	783	4173	3779	0	8735
	Calvinistic Methodists	25	1014	3323	4559	0	8896
	Independents	29	946	4605	5053	0	10604
	Wesleyan Methodists	11	195	530	891	0	1616
	Total	**96**	**2938**	**12631**	**14282**	**0**	**29851**
	English						
	Baptist	15	256	1801	1499	0	3556
	Calvinistic Methodists	9	161	1095	1153	0	2409
	Independents	8	114	897	552	0	1563
	Wesleyan Methodists	14	264	1726	1171	0	3161
	Primitive Methodists	9	163	960	485	0	1608
	Total	**55**	**958**	**6479**	**4860**	**0**	**12297**
	Grand Total	**171**	**4306**	**23329**	**21153**	**0**	**48788**
Neath	Church of England	31	444	4108	1963	0	6515
	Baptist	24	494	2979	2671	370	6514
	Calvinistic Methodists	33	777	3426	3520	276	7999
	Independents	32	707	3773	4051	150	8681
	Wesleyan Methodists	9	145	901	728	0	1774
	Others	8	105	676	493	0	1274
	Total	**137**	**2672**	**15863**	**13426**	**796**	**32757**
Swansea Urban	Church of England	22	617	5295	2815	0	8727
	Welsh						
	Baptist	8	228	0	0	2588	2816
	Calvinistic Methodists	12	322	0	0	2965	3287
	Independents	11	405	0	0	4385	4790
	Wesleyan Methodists	1	4	0	0	35	39
	Total	**32**	**959**	**0**	**0**	**9973**	**10932**
	English						
	Baptist	14	293	0	0	3966	4259
	Calvinistic Methodists	9	166	0	0	1640	1806
	Independents	13	266	0	0	3079	3345
	Wesleyan Methodists	6	113	0	0	1412	1525
	Others	19	203	0	0	2726	2929
	Total	**61**	**1041**	**0**	**0**	**12823**	**13864**
	Grand total	**115**	**2617**	**0**	**0**	**22796**	**33523**
Swansea Rural	Church of England	44	444	3555	2555	0	6554
	Baptist	29	487	2785	2528	0	5800
	Calvinistic Methodists	23	427	1846	1997	0	4270
	Independents	50	1004	4999	5610	277	11890
	Wesleyan Methodists	14	137	683	437	0	1257
	Others	3	29	187	100	0	316
	Total	**163**	**2528**	**14055**	**13227**	**277**	**30087**
Bridgend	Church of England	37	369	3316	1892	0	5577
	Baptist	34	560	3460	2920	98	7038
	Calvinistic Methodists	29	441	2214	2145	0	4800
	Independents	34	557	3038	2723	65	6383
	Wesleyan Methodists	7	83	451	293	0	827
	Others	7	68	280	155	98	601
	Total	**148**	**2078**	**12759**	**10128**	**261**	**25226**
CARMARTHENSHIRE							
Llanelli	Church of England*	22	358	2772	2100	0	5230
	Baptist	29	683	3608	4314	0	8605
	Calvinistic Methodists	17	336	1316	1674	53	3379
	Independents	26	683	3399	3374	0	7456
	Wesleyan Methodists	7	74	414	370	0	858
	Others	1	20	150	50	0	220
	Total	**102**	**2154**	**11659**	**11882**	**53**	**25748**

Excludes Loughor parish (included in Swansea Rural)

* Language of Sunday Services: 28 Welsh, 15 Bilingual, 28 English

District[1]	Denomination	Number Sunday schools[2]	Teachers	Age of scholars under 15	over 15	age not given	Total in Sunday school
Llandovery	Church of England*	16	86	368	402	0	856
	Baptist	11	71	320	271	62	719
	Calvinistic Methodists	19	221	251	300	1337	2109
	Independents	18	220	846	1188	92	2346
	Total	**64**	**598**	**1785**	**2161**	**1491**	**6035**
	* Language of Sunday Services: 12 Welsh, 14 Bilingual, 7 English						
Llandeilo Fawr	Church of England*	22	182	1326	1135	0	2643
	Baptist	15	165	970	804	109	1883
	Calvinistic Methodists	18	255	757	1088	302	2147
	Independents	20	378	1972	1782	30	3784
	Wesleyan Methodists	6	44	156	180	0	336
	Total	**81**	**1024**	**5181**	**4989**	**441**	**10793**
	* Language of Sunday Services: 24 Welsh, 12 Bilingual, 10 English						
Carmarthen	Church of England*	44	280	1752	1691	0	3723
	Baptist	29	240	1189	1379	0	2568
	Calvinistic Methodists	29	333	1084	1739	70	2893
	Independents	39	543	2132	3196	25	5353
	Wesleyan Methodists	3	22	123	92	0	215
	Total	**144**	**1418**	**6280**	**8097**	**95**	**14752**
	* Language of Sunday Services: 38 Welsh, 28 Bilingual, 25 English						
PEMBROKESHIRE							
Narberth	Church of England*	43	126	821	386	0	1333
	Baptist	17	181	877	972	60	2090
	Calvinistic Methodists	10	55	268	264	0	587
	Independents	25	283	1133	1871	0	3287
	Wesleyan Methodists	4	27	86	101	0	214
	Primitive Methodists	2	3	16	14	0	33
	Total	**101**	**675**	**3201**	**3608**	**60**	**7544**
	* Language of Sunday Services: 6 Welsh, 21 Bilingual, 47 English						
Pembroke	Church of England*	34	286	2487	606	0	3379
	Baptist	11	183	1062	666	0	1911
	Calvinistic Methodists	10	133	660	457	130	1380
	Independents	12	144	1070	480	0	1694
	Wesleyan Methodists	11	132	764	295	27	1218
	Primitive Methodists	1	4	15	15	0	34
	Others	3	10	84	32	0	126
	Total	**82**	**892**	**6142**	**2551**	**157**	**9742**
	* Language of Sunday Services: 76 English						
Haverfordwest	Church of England*	67	212	1918	688	0	2818
	Baptist	38	361	1885	1552	60	3858
	Calvinistic Methodists	23	140	657	636	0	1433
	Independents	33	261	1505	1005	0	2771
	Wesleyan Methodists	7	82	506	216	0	804
	Primitive Methodists	1	10	40	10	0	60
	Total	**169**	**1066**	**6511**	**4107**	**60**	**11744**
	* Language of Sunday Services: 14 Welsh, 23 Bilingual, 78 English						
CARDIGANSHIRE							
Cardigan	Church of England*	31	133	587	690	0	1410
	Baptists	20	257	704	774	755	2490
	Calvinistic Methodists	15	204	234	262	1042	1742
	Independents	15	203	323	560	806	1892
	Total	**81**	**797**	**1848**	**2286**	**2603**	**7534**
	* Language of Sunday Services: 24 Welsh, 20 Bilingual, 8 English						
Newcastle Emlyn	Church of England*	31	157	806	1066	0	2029
	Baptist	12	132	480	571	193	1376
	Calvinistic Methodists	17	237	250	409	809	1705
	Independents	34	525	850	1189	2214	4778
	Wesleyan Methodists	2	11	0	0	110	121
	Unitarian	3	25	0	0	275	300
	Total	**99**	**1087**	**2386**	**3235**	**3601**	**10309**
	* Language of Sunday Services: 33 Welsh, 19 Bilingual						

District[1]	Denomination	Number Sunday schools[2]	Teachers	Age of scholars under 15	over 15	age not given	Total in Sunday school
Lampeter	Church of England*	17	118	594	666	0	1378
	Baptist	6	47	70	100	235	452
	Calvinistic Methodists	4	47	30	43	244	364
	Independents	16	166	273	446	758	1643
	Wesleyan Methodists	2	8	0	0	51	59
	Others	7	45	10	35	473	570
	Total	**52**	**431**	**977**	**1290**	**1761**	**4459**
	* Language of Sunday Services: 25 Welsh, 4 Bilingual, 3 English						
Aberaeron	Church of England*	21	159	563	884	0	1606
	Baptist	3	15	0	0	95	110
	Calvinistic Methodists	13	216	0	0	1843	2059
	Independents	17	309	0	0	2681	2990
	Wesleyan Methodists	3	16	0	0	100	116
	Unitarian	4	26	0	0	293	319
	Total	**61**	**741**	**563**	**884**	**5012**	**7200**
	* Language of Sunday Services: 32 Welsh, 3 Bilingual, 3 English						
Aberystwyth	Church of England*	27	243	1100	1133	0	2476
	Baptist	9	89	0	0	661	750
	Calvinistic Methodists	60	886	0	0	5838	6724
	Independents	18	142	0	0	1167	1306
	Wesleyan Methodists	11	156	0	0	1154	1310
	Others	1	3	0	0	30	33
	Total	**126**	**1519**	**1100**	**1133**	**8850**	**12599**
	* Language of Sunday Services: 35 Welsh, 12 Bilingual, 18 English						
Tregaron	Church of England*	13	88	382	467	0	937
	Baptist	4	22	0	0	243	265
	Calvinistic Methodists	45	553	0	0	3269	3822
	Independents	2	11	0	0	73	84
	Wesleyan Methodists	2	21	0	0	130	151
	Total	**66**	**695**	**382**	**467**	**3715**	**5259**
	* Language of Sunday Services: 19 Welsh, 4 Bilingual, 0 English						
BRECONSHIRE							
Builth	Church of England*	26	71	587	168	0	826
	Baptist	8	40	265	172	0	477
	Calvinistic Methodists	6	58	327	216	30	631
	Independents	10	90	304	406	0	800
	Wesleyan Methodists	2	15	72	55	0	142
	Primitive Methodists	2	5	33	6	0	44
	Others	2	13	75	48	0	136
	Total	**56**	**292**	**1663**	**1071**	**30**	**3056**
	* Language of Sunday Services: 10 Welsh, 2 Bilingual, 39 English						
Brecon	Church of England*	44	184	1364	649	0	2197
	Baptist	10	47	233	121	140	541
	Calvinistic Methodists	19	126	484	473	22	1105
	Independents	16	94	486	452	0	1032
	Wesleyan Methodists	2	24	115	52	0	191
	Total	**91**	**475**	**2682**	**1747**	**162**	**5066**
	* Language of Sunday Services: 10 Welsh, 19 Bilingual, 61 English						
Crickhowell	Church of England*	15	97	818	198	0	1113
	Baptist	11	121	861	807	0	1789
	Calvinistic Methodists	9	100	486	430	0	1016
	Independents	12	120	851	631	0	1602
	Wesleyan Methodists	5	44	265	168	0	477
	Primitive Methodists	1	27	183	104	0	314
	Others	1	1	22	0	0	23
	Total	**54**	**510**	**3486**	**2338**	**0**	**6334**
	* Language of Sunday Services: 1 Welsh, 0 Bilingual, 31 English						

District[1]	Denomination	Number Sunday schools[2]	Teachers	Age of scholars under 15	over 15	age not given	Total in Sunday school
Hay	Church of England*	18	71	669	79	0	819
	Baptist	6	34	172	96	0	302
	Calvinistic Methodists	7	33	198	136	0	367
	Independents	7	41	231	191	0	463
	Wesleyan Methodists	2	11	68	10	0	89
	Primitive Methodists	2	7	41	7	0	55
	Total	**42**	**197**	**1379**	**519**	**0**	**2095**
	* Language of Sunday Services: 0 Welsh, 0 Bilingual, 32 English						
RADNORSHIRE							
Presteigne	Church of England*	9	12	112	8	0	132
	Baptist	7	37	267	79	0	383
	Calvinistic Methodists	3	8	54	22	0	84
	Independents	1	7	51	7	0	65
	Wesleyan Methodists	1	2	5	0	0	7
	Primitive Methodists	1	6	30	10	0	46
	Others	1	2	12	0	0	14
	Total	**23**	**74**	**531**	**126**	**0**	**731**
	* Language of Sunday Services: 0 Welsh, 0 Bilingual, 16 English						
Knighton	Church of England*	10	23	177	41	0	241
	Baptist	11	71	593	241	0	905
	Calvinistic Methodists	2	7	75	6	0	88
	Wesleyan Methodists	3	13	83	17	0	113
	Primitive Methodists	5	38	175	36	0	249
	Total	**31**	**152**	**1103**	**341**	**0**	**1596**
	* Language of Sunday Services: 0 Welsh, 0 Bilingual, 19 English						
Rhayader	Church of England*	13	63	508	143	0	714
	Baptist	6	38	255	209	0	502
	Calvinistic Methodists	4	33	186	119	0	338
	Independents	3	20	90	79	0	189
	Wesleyan Methodists	1	5	10	20	0	35
	Others	2	6	38	6	0	50
	Total	**29**	**165**	**1087**	**576**	**0**	**1828**
	* Language of Sunday Services: 0 Welsh, 0 Bilingual, 28 English						
MONTGOMERYSHIRE							
Machynlleth	Church of England*	14	83	393	448	0	924
	Baptist	6	31	104	166	0	301
	Calvinistic Methodists	29	360	859	1480	101	2800
	Independents	18	197	585	1063	28	1873
	Wesleyan Methodists	14	127	279	569	79	1054
	Total	**81**	**798**	**2220**	**3726**	**208**	**6952**
	* Language of Sunday Services: 23 Welsh, 2 Bilingual, 11 English						
Newtown	Church of England*	22	–	–	–	–	1368
	Baptist	14	144	753	598	0	1495
	Calvinistic Methodists	33	474	1381	2349	0	4204
	Independents	11	84	542	466	0	1092
	Wesleyan Methodists	16	158	582	655	0	1395
	Primitive Methodists	1	13	30	43	0	86
	Others	2	2	18	0	0	20
	Total	**99**	**875**	**3306**	**4111**	**0**	**9660**
	* Language of Sunday Services: 3 Welsh, 3 Bilingual, 45 English						
Montgomery	Church of England*	9	–	–	–	–	935
	Baptist	3	16	116	54	0	186
	Calvinistic Methodists	10	88	414	308	0	810
	Independents	8	40	216	203	0	459
	Wesleyan Methodists	10	67	310	199	0	576
	Primitive Methodists	7	43	222	68	0	333
	Total	**47**	**254**	**1278**	**832**	**0**	**3299**
	* Language of Sunday Services: 0 Welsh, 0 Bilingual, 31 English						

District[1]	Denomination	Number Sunday schools[2]	Teachers	Age of scholars under 15	over 15	age not given	Total in Sunday school
Llanfyllin	Church of England*	26	–	–	–	–	1154
	Baptist	6	23	80	98	0	233
	Calvinistic Methodists	34	230	698	1198	0	2590
	Independents	29	170	684	913	0	1841
	Wesleyan Methodists	23	177	558	761	0	1613
	Primitive Methodists	3	8	74	16	0	98
	Others	1	2	8	12	0	22
	Total	**122**	**610**	**2102**	**2998**	**0**	**7551**
	* Language of Sunday Services: 36 Welsh, 0 Bilingual, 28 English						
FLINTSHIRE							
Holywell	Church of England*	30	–	–	–	–	4055
	Baptist	14	75	335	297	0	707
	Calvinistic Methodists	41	635	2003	2001	0	4642
	Independents	31	278	1148	1154	0	2580
	Wesleyan Methodists	34	429	1694	1542	0	3665
	Primitive Methodists	2	20	140	93	0	253
	Others	10	138	922	649	0	1709
	Total	**162**	**1575**	**6242**	**5739**	**0**	**17611**
	* Language of Sunday Services: 36 Welsh, 1 Bilingual, 58 English						
DENBIGHSHIRE							
Wrexham	Church of England*	33	–	–	–	–	6874
	Baptist	32	0	0	0	0	5185
	Calvinistic Methodists	49	0	0	0	0	8852
	Independents	29	0	0	0	0	5045
	Wesleyan Methodists	35	0	0	0	0	5031
	Primitive Methodists	16	0	0	0	0	2066
	Others	5	0	0	0	0	335
	Total	**199**	**0**	**0**	**0**	**0**	**33388**
	* Language of Sunday Services: 11 Welsh, 0 Bilingual, 109 English						
Ruthin	Church of England*	21	–	–	–	–	772
	Baptist	4	0	0	0	0	228
	Calvinistic Methodists	36	0	0	0	0	4041
	Independents	9	0	0	0	0	533
	Wesleyan Methodists	11	0	0	0	0	501
	Total	**81**	**0**	**0**	**0**	**0**	**6075**
	* Language of Sunday Services: 30 Welsh, 0 Bilingual, 20 English						
St Asaph	Church of England*	29	–	–	–	–	2499
	Baptist	10	0	0	0	0	724
	Calvinistic Methodists	29	0	0	0	0	3763
	Independents	9	0	0	0	0	961
	Wesleyan Methodists	8	0	0	0	0	811
	Others	3	0	0	0	0	165
	Total	**88**	**0**	**0**	**0**	**0**	**8923**
	* Language of Sunday Services: 39 Welsh, 0 Bilingual, 36 English						
Llanrwst	Church of England*	17	50			425	895
	Baptist	5	0	0	0	263	263
	Calvinistic Methodists	28	308	0	0	1595	4549
	Independents	11	51	0	0	381	993
	Wesleyan Methodists	9	66	0	0	356	826
	Total	**70**	**475**	**228**	**192**	**3020**	**7526**
	The figures of 425 and 263 for C.of E. and Baptist Sunday scholars 'age not given' include some teachers						
	* Language of Sunday Services: 29 Welsh, 0 Bilingual, 10 English						
MERIONETH							
Corwen	Church of England*	19	–	–	–	–	1144
	Baptist	18	58	141	279	130	2085
	Calvinistic Methodists	37	201	576	914	0	4724
	Independents	15	59	162	272	86	1318
	Wesleyan Methodists	14	40	132	190	0	956
	Primitive Methodists	1	0	0	0	0	116
	Total	**104**	**358**	**1011**	**1655**	**216**	**10343**
	* Language of Sunday Services: 30 Welsh, 0 Bilingual, 23 English						

District[1]	Denomination	Number Sunday schools[2]	Teachers	Age of scholars under 15	over 15	age not given	Total in Sunday school
Bala	Church of England*	9	–	–	–	–	334
	Baptist	1	7	19	32	0	58
	Calvinistic Methodists	21	322	722	1575	0	2619
	Independents	10	97	292	456	0	845
	Total	**41**	**426**	**1033**	**2063**	**0**	**3856**
	* Language of Sunday Services: 13 Welsh, 1 Bilingual, 6 English						
Dolgellau	Church of England*	22	123	497	546	0	1166
	Baptist	6	45	144	244	0	433
	Calvinistic Methodists	42	482	1299	1989	0	3770
	Independents	34	293	885	1423	0	2601
	Wesleyan Methodists	14	137	340	620	0	1097
	Total	**118**	**1080**	**3165**	**4822**	**0**	**9067**
	* Language of Sunday Services: 35 Welsh, 0 Bilingual, 19 English						
Ffestiniog	Church of England*	21	181	739	593	0	1513
	Baptist	22	233	657	804	249	1943
	Calvinistic Methodists	67	1499	2348	3336	2715	9898
	Independents	27	481	1234	1588	820	4123
	Wesleyan Methodists	14	196	425	680	182	1483
	Total	**150**	**2590**	**5403**	**6461**	**3966**	**18960**
	* Language of Sunday Services: 43 Welsh, 0 Bilingual, 17 English						
CAERNARFONSHIRE							
Pwllheli	Church of England*	40	190	766	649	0	1605
	Baptist	11	96	0	0	564	660
	Calvinistic Methodists	57	1140	0	0	6449	7589
	Independents	27	302	0	0	1838	2140
	Wesleyan Methodists	10	124	0	0	837	961
	Total	**145**	**1852**	**766**	**649**	**9688**	**12955**
	* Language of Sunday Services: 61 Welsh, 0 Bilingual, 15 English						
Caernarfon	Church of England*	31	375	1714	1639	0	3728
	Baptist	15	159	15	10	879	1063
	Calvinistic Methodists	60	2273	415	620	12387	15695
	Independents	26	637	76	59	4121	4893
	Wesleyan Methodists	14	239	0	0	1358	1597
	Total	**146**	**3683**	**2220**	**2328**	**18745**	**26976**
	* Language of Sunday Services: 57 Welsh, 0 Bilingual, 15 English						
Bangor	Church of England*	33	409	2186	1652	0	4247
	Baptist	13	149	173	149	528	999
	Calvinistic Methodists	46	1206	1080	1400	4787	8473
	Independents	25	388	184	183	2159	2914
	Wesleyan Methodists	19	301	127	86	1859	2373
	Total	**136**	**2453**	**3750**	**3470**	**9333**	**19006**
	* Language of Sunday Services: 61 Welsh, 1 Bilingual, 35 English						
Conwy	Church of England*	25	140	866	488	1090	2584
	Baptist	12	98	0	0	822	1305
	Calvinistic Methodists	29	366	0	0	2494	4183
	Independents	17	178	0	0	1358	1979
	Wesleyan Methodists	21	253	0	0	1598	2442
	Total	**104**	**1035**	**866**	**488**	**7362**	**12493**
	The figure of 1090 for C.of E. Sunday scholars 'age not given' includes some teachers * Language of Sunday Services: 31 Welsh, 0 Bilingual, 44 English						
ANGLESEY							
Anglesey	Church of England*	64	294	1723	996	0	3013
	Baptist	34	332	1448	1209	0	2989
	Calvinistic Methodists	74	1269	3576	4693	0	9538
	Independents	30	329	1175	1070	0	2574
	Wesleyan Methodists	19	177	635	507	0	1319
	Total	**221**	**2401**	**8557**	**8475**	**0**	**19433**
	* Language of Sunday Services: 102 Welsh, 0 Bilingual, 17 English						

Source: Royal Commission on the Church of England and Other Religious Bodies in Wales and Monmouthshire, *Report, Vol. V, Appendices to Minutes of Evidence. Church of England,* Statistical Returns for the Dioceses of Bangor, Llandaff, St Asaph, and St

David's, pp. 1–244 [PP 1910 (Cd. 5436) XVIII]; ibid., *Vol. VI, Appendices to Minutes of Evidence. Nonconformist County Statistics*, pp. 1–433 [PP 1910 (Cd. 5437) XVIII].

[1] For most counties, the Nonconformist statistics have been grouped according to Registration District boundaries in 1851 to enable comparison with Education tables 2.4, 2.6 and 2.8. However, for Monmouth and Glamorgan, districts are based on the divisions given in the Nonconformist statistics as listed below, with the addition of the Breconshire parishes of Penderyn, Vaynor, Ystradgynlais and Ystradfellte. The Diocesan statistics, originally grouped according to Diocese, Archdeaconry and Rural Deanery, have been reclassified on the same basis. Returns from the diocese of Llandaff contain no details of the language of services.

MONMOUTHSHIRE

Monmouth: Chapel Hill and Penteri, Chepstow, Caldicot, Caer-went, Kilgwrrwg, Llandogo, Llanishen, Llanvihangel Torymynydd, Llantilio Crossenny, Trelleck, Wonastow, Wolvesnewton, Llandenny, Llanvapley, Raglan, Skenfrith, Pen-rhos, Pen-allt.

Abergavenny: Abergavenny, Llanwenarth, Llanddewi Rhydderch, Blaenafon, Llanover, Llanvetherine, Cwm-iou Lower, Llanvihangel Crucorney, Llansanffraid.

Abertillery: Abertillery, Llanhilleth, Aberystruth.

Tredegar: Tredegar, Rhymni, Ebbw Vale.

Pontypool: Usk, Llanfrechfa Upper, Pontypool, Caerleon, Gwehelog, Goytre, Llantrisant, Llan-gwm Ucha, Llangybi, Llanfrechfa Lower, Llansoy, Llanbadog, Abersychan, Llanfihangel Llantarnam, Griffithstown.

Newport: Newport County Borough and parish.

Risca: Bedwas Lower, Pontllan-fraith, Ynys-ddu and Pen-maen, Marshfield, Upper Machen, Upper Bedwas, Fleur-de-lys, Magor, Peterstone, Rumney, Risca and Pontymister, St Mellons, Malpas, Redwick, Aber-carn and Cwm-carn, Llanvaches, Blackwood and Pengam, Goldcliff, Henllys, Langstone and Llan-bedr, Nash, Michaelston-y-Vedw, Rogerstone, St Bride's Wentlloog, Undy, Bishton, Graig, Llanmartin and Llandevaud, Newbridge, Crymlyn, Crosskeys, Christchurch.

GLAMORGAN

Cardiff: Cardiff County Borough (Canton, Roath, St John, St Mary).

Cowbridge, Barry, Penarth: Barry UD, Penarth UD (Cogan, Llandough, Penarth), Cowbridge UD, Cowbridge RD (St Athan, Colwinston, Llanblethian, Llan-gan, Llanhari, Llanharan, Llantwit Major, Lisworney, Pen-llin, St Mary Hill), Llandaff and Dinas Powys (Caerau, Llancarfan, Pendoylan, St Andrews, St Nicholas, Wenvoe, Pen-marc).

Caerphilly: Llantrisant, Llantwit Fardre, Caerphilly UD (Eglwysilan, Llanfabon), Llandaff and Dinas Powys UD (Whitchurch, Pentyrch, St Fagans, Llandaff, Llanishen, Lisvane, Llanedern, Radur, St Brides-super-Ely, Rudry).

Pontypridd: Pontypridd Urban District (includes parts of the parishes of Llanwynno, Llanfabon, Eglwysilan, Llantwit Fardre, and Llantrisant).

Merthyr Tydfil: Merthyr Tydfil, Gelli-gaer and Vaynor (Brec).

Aberdare: UD Aberdare, UD Llanwynno (Mountain Ash, Abercynon, Penrhiw-ceibr, Ynys-boeth, Ynys-y-bŵl), Rhigos, Penderyn (Brec).

Rhondda: Rhondda Urban District.

Neath: UD Neath, RD Neath (Michaelston Higher, Llantwit Lower, Cwm-gwrach, Baglan Higher, Blaenhonddan, Neath Higher, Coed-ffranc, Dulais Higher, Michaelston Lower, Dyffryn Clydach, Resolfen), Glyncorrwg, Briton Ferry, Aberafan, Margam, Ystradgynlais (Brec) and Ystradfellte (Brec).

Swansea Urban: Swansea County Borough.

Swansea Rural: Swansea RD (Clas Rural, Cockett, Gowerton, Llandeilo Tal-y-bont, Llansamlet, Loughor, Llangyfelach) and Pontardawe RD (Llanguicke, Cilybebyll, Rhyndwyglydach Mawr, Ynysymwn), Oystermouth, and the Gower.

Bridgend: Bridgend UD (Newcastle Lower, Oldcastle), Maes-teg UD (Cwm-du, Llangynwyd Higher), Ogmore and Garw UD (Betws, Llandyfodwg, Llangeinor), Pen-y-bont RD (Coychurch Higher and Lower, Ewenni, Llangynwyd Lower and Middle, Newcastle Higher, St Brides Minor, Tythegston Higher, Wick, Ynysawdre), Porthcawl UD (Newton Nottage).

[2] For the Church of England this is the total number of Churches and Missions not all of which would have necessarily held Sunday schools. For the remainder, it is the number of chapels and separate school rooms for which information is given in the returns regarding Sunday school attenders.

Education 5.1 Welsh as an academic subject. The attitude of head teachers to the teaching of Welsh as a subject. 1884

Replies to the question: 'Do you consider that advantage would result from the introduction of the Welsh language as a "specific subject" into the course of elementary education in Wales?'

County	Yes	No	Neutral	Total
Monmouthshire	27	23	3	53
Glamorgan	77	48	7	132
Carmarthenshire	34	25	3	62
Pembrokeshire	18	21	6	45
Cardiganshire	33	18	–	51
Breconshire	10	10	1	21
Radnorshire	4	4	1	9
Montgomeryshire	19	17	–	36
Flintshire	8	13	1	22
Denbighshire	19	18	3	40
Merioneth	29	12	2	43
Caernarfonshire	38	30	2	70
Anglesey	20	10	3	33
Oswestry district	1	5	–	6
Anonymous	2	3	–	5
Total	**339**	**257**	**32**	**628**

REASON FOR

Would assist in acquiring English.
In Welsh-speaking districts intelligent farmers wish their children to write Welsh letters.
Parents' desire for children to write Welsh letters.
English boys try to learn it when teachers explain in Welsh, and race jealousy diminishes.
Would be a pecuniary, an educational, and a moral advantage.
Young people *now* unable to compose Welsh letters.
Successful teachers use Welsh freely.
Would aid in securing inspectors who could properly understand the difficulties of Welsh children.
Children could then be taught to translate properly.
Stimulative to the mind.
English children insist on speaking Welsh every chance they get.
Means of menial discipline – *systematic* knowledge of great value.
Should be COMPULSORY ON ALL SCHOOLS.
English taught more thoroughly thus.
Would require little extra work.
Children would be greatly delighted.
Would foster a love of study.
Open the field for more extensive reading.
Would induce parents to bring up their children in their mother-tongue.
Easier to teach French when Welsh is learnt.
Would enlarge both vocabularies.
Especially [wanted] where Welsh is likely to be forgotten.

RESULT OF PRESENT SYSTEM

Present mode has lamentably failed except to a few.
Parrot-like knowledge of English in most elementary schools.
Many 'Sunday' school scholars does [*sic*] not distinguish between *i'w* and *yw*.
Best teachers groan under drudgery of the Code.[2]
Present methods dreary and unnatural.
Welsh as a written language going into disuse.
Present slipshod way of teaching, or rather not teaching English.
Children ashamed of their mother-tongue.
Weary work.

REASON AGAINST

Would hinder English conversation.
Children would have to unlearn colloquial Welsh.
Parents would object.
Would isolate Wales from complete assimilation with England.
Want of utility.
'Sunday' schools and literary meetings provide for it.
Some successful teachers do not understand it. Inspectors rank Englishmen.[1]
Present Code gives sufficient latitude.
Language too inflectional.
English predominant in certain districts.
Most teachers ignorant of Welsh and would require special training.
Because a special Code for Wales is wanted worst.

PREDICTED RESULTS OF PROPOSED SYSTEM

Would create a thorough love for higher education and science.
The study of it would give full command of a beautiful and expressive language.
Would be an introduction to a classical education.
Would keep alive the Welsh national spirit.
Welsh literature would gain immensely.
Would relieve over pressure.
Would sharpen the intellects of the children for the reception of moral impressions during preaching.
[Under a Welsh Code] in twenty or thirty years a revolution would have taken place in the mental condition of the people.

Source: Honourable Society of Cymmrodorion, Report of the Committee appointed by the Council to inquire into the Advisability of the Introduction of the Welsh Language into the Course of Elementary Education in Wales (1884), as tabulated in John E. Southall, *Wales and her Language* (Newport, 1892), pp. 133–5, and Appendix D, p. 386.

Notes: [quoted from Southall]

1 It would not be fair to speak of the Inspectors of 1891 as *rank Englishmen*. There are now notable exceptions to the old rule, but the Department is not yet sufficiently alive to the advantage of having Welsh-speaking Inspectors and assistants, even in bilingual districts.

2 This was written under the old Code, but doubtless is still true to a large extent in Wales.

Education 5.2 Welsh as an academic subject. Subjects inspected in elementary schools. Wales and Counties. 1898–9

Administrative Counties	Number of Schools	Scholars[2]	Number of Departments in which scholars examined[1] Total	Class subjects Welsh	English	Geography	Science	History	Occupations[3]	Domestic Economy[4]	Needlework[4]
Wales	1679	372408	1852	15	1482	1447	1611	280	3	25	489
Monmouth	182	44778	194	1	135	149	171	50	0	2	73
Glamorgan	313	115877	376	5	328	304	311	25	1	7	110
Cardiff CB	35	30661	57	0	30	50	56	16	0	3	14
Swansea CB	28	20171	39	0	36	38	11	3	0	0	1
Glam. incl CBs	376	166709	472	5	394	392	378	44	1	10	125
Carmarthen	167	27723	176	6	165	153	167	11	0	0	52
Pembroke	127	17061	135	0	123	118	130	10	0	0	32
Cardigan	107	11117	109	1	106	96	103	5	0	0	24
Brecon	87	11085	91	0	73	56	92	19	0	1	45
Radnor	51	3815	52	0	30	38	51	12	0	0	20
Montgomery	94	9799	97	2	60	79	78	23	0	4	4
Flint	97	15934	104	0	58	69	101	40	0	3	30
Denbigh	123	24103	136	0	83	96	115	40	1	3	32
Merioneth	76	9609	80	0	73	60	55	5	0	1	13
Caernarfon	128	22037	139	0	123	98	119	16	1	1	32
Anglesey	64	8638	67	0	59	43	51	5	0	0	7

Source: *Report of the Board of Education, 1899–1900, Vol. III* – Appendix to the Report (Elementary Education), Table 9 (HMSO, 1900).

1 Departments were separate groups within a school (e.g. Boys, Girls, Mixed, Infants). Some schools included Infants with the Girls Department.

2 This is the number of scholars on the registers on the last day of the school year. The average number of scholars in attendance throughout the school year 1898–9 for the whole of Wales was 288,709.

3 These are 'Suitable Occupations'.

4 Domestic Economy and Needlework were subjects for girls only.

Education 5.3 Welsh as an academic subject. Day scholars presented for examination in Welsh in elementary schools. Wales. 1886–99

Year	Number of day scholars presented for examination in Welsh (1886–98) or qualifying for a grant (1899)
1886	0
1887	192
1888	369
1889	419
1890	459
1891	576
1892	393
1893	402
1894	534
1895	548
1896	678
1897	745
1898	783
1899	3004

Source: *Report of the Board of Education 1899–1900, Vol. III* – Appendix to Report (Elementary Education), Table 52.

Education 5.4 Welsh as an academic subject. Written examinations of the Central Welsh Board in Welsh in County Secondary Schools. Wales. 1897–1914

Year	Schools	Pupils	Schools offering Welsh	Number of pupils presented[1] Examination grades: Stage 4		Stage 3		Stage 2		Stage 1	
1897	80	6427	31								
1898[2]	88	6912	35	87 (10)		80 (8)		145 (15)		257 (23)	
1899	93	7390	38	5 (3)		84 (24)		126 (29)		159 (22)	
1900	94	7445	38	11 (6)		61 (26)		176 (30)		178 (21)	
1901	95	7668	41	29 (15)		104 (26)		224 (33)		219 (26)	
1902	95	8322	42	17 (9)		143 (31)		219 (32)		214 (24)	
				Honours		Senior		Junior			
1903	95	8789	40	14 (7)		154 (34)		242 (35)			
1904	95	9284	39	12 (6)		145 (33)		306 (37)			
1905	95	10413	45	13 (6)		212 (38)		324 (41)			
1906	95	11577	49	22 (10)		290 (41)		389 (45)			
1907	95	12499	49	Higher 32) (21)[3] Lower 23)		279 (44)		453 (46)			
				Higher Honours		Lower Honours		Senior		Junior	
				Entries	Passes	Entries	Passes	Entries	Passes	Entries	Passes
1908	96	12962	60	14	14	39	38	368	312	630	499
1909	96	13760	64	14	9	37	24	408	355	721	494
1910	96	13729	69	3	3	42	40	460	411	716	567
1911	96	13335	69	4	4	29	26	528	408	686	543
1912	96	13217	71	5	5	25	25	573	467	672	507
1913	96	13528	74	5	5	26	23	565	459	733	576
1914	100	14192	90	5	5	42	40	602	478	836	697

Source: Central Welsh Board, *Annual Reports*, 1898–1914.

[1] Figures in brackets are the number of schools presenting pupils for each grade.
[2] In 1898, a 5th grade paper was taken by 14 pupils from 3 schools.
[3] Total number of schools presenting pupils at the Higher and Lower grades.

Education 5.5 Welsh as an academic subject. University of Wales Degree examinations. Number of successful candidates in Welsh in the constituent colleges. 1896–1914

College	Year	Number of students in classes[1]	Degree Examinations passed: Intermediate Men	Intermediate Women	Ordinary Men	Ordinary Women	Special Men	Special Women	Honours[2] Men	Honours[2] Women
Aberystwyth	1896	–	1	0	–	–	–	–	–	–
	1897	54	5	1	1	0	–	–	–	–
	1898	–	7	2	6	1	1	0	–	–
	1899	–	7	2	3	1	0	0	0	0
	1900	–	7	2	2	1	3	1	1	0
	1901	–	4	5	1	0	1	1	0	1
	1902	–	7	5	3	2	1	0	2	0
	1903	50	12	1	4	1	1	0	2	1
	1904	44	22	7	6	1	1	0	0	1
	1905	47	6	6	9	5	2	0	0	0
	1906	51	11	5	4	3	5	0	5	4
	1907	59	6	7	6	8	0	1	5	0
	1908	67	15	9	10	1	4	2	1	4
	1909	66	13	5	10	8	4	0	4	1
	1910	66	12	8	10	7	3	3	3	3
	1911	69	9	4	13	3	3	1	4	2
	1912	49	11	4	6	4	8	1	2	1
	1913	41	6	5	7	3	4	5	3	1
	1914[2]	32	3	5	3	4	4	0	3	4
Bangor	1896	–	3	0	–	–	–	–	–	–
	1897	87	11	1	3	0	–	–	–	–
	1898	88	18	2	9	0	1	0	–	–
	1899	87	10	1	9	2	5	0	1	0
	1900	89	15	1	7	1	4	2	4	0
	1901	81	12	0	8	1	2	0	3	0
	1902	74	18	7	8	0	6	0	0	0
	1903	81	14	4	11	3	2	0	2	0
	1904	72	11	0	7	5	6	0	0	1
	1905	68	16	7	2	2	3	0	1	0
	1906	80	13	8	10	2	1	0	2	1
	1907	91	17	11	18	3	3	2	2	1
	1908	111	26	9	11	9	8	0	6	0
	1909	109	25	15	17	8	2	6	5	0
	1910	98	35	7	17	11	6	3	2	0
	1911	93	25	9	19	4	5	5	6	1
	1912	77	14	12	20	8	5	2	6	0
	1913	74	14	5	15	12	11	1	4	2
	1914[2]	67	13	8	13	2	8	0	5	0
Cardiff	1896	–	7	0	–	–	–	–	–	–
	1897	–	2	0	3	0	–	–	–	–
	1898	63	6	0	1	0	3	0	–	–
	1899	65	9	1	4	0	0	0	1	0
	1900	71	5	0	6	0	3	0	0	0
	1901	66	8	1	4	0	0	0	3	0
	1902	53	12	1	4	1	0	0	2	0
	1903	55	11	4	5	0	3	0	1	0
	1904	43	17	2	5	0	1	0	4	0
	1905	38	8	1	5	1	3	0	3	0
	1906	45	10	2	9	1	0	0	3	0
	1907	37	8	0	9	0	2	0	2	0
	1908	53	17	7	8	0	1	1	3	0
	1909	45	14	2	7	2	4	0	3	0
	1910	47	21	0	6	0	1	0	4	1
	1911	41	17	1	9	0	3	0	2	0
	1912	49	13	3	8	1	7	1	3	0
	1913	37	6	6	9	0	2	0	2	1
	1914[2]	36	6	0	5	3	4	0	4	0

Source: *The Calendar of the University of Wales for 1897–8,* then annually to 1914–15.

1 These figures include students taking non-degree course Welsh classes. At Cardiff, for example, the figures for 1900 include 41 students studying for Matriculation qualifications. The proportion of such students decreased considerably.

2 In 1914, the figures include the following taking Honours examinations under new regulations: Aberystwyth – 2 men, 2 women, Bangor – 1 man, Cardiff – 1 man.

IV

Religion

Crefydd

Rhagymadrodd

Yng nghanol y bedwaredd ganrif ar bymtheg, honnodd y Parchedig Thomas Rees mai'r Cymry oedd y genedl fwyaf crefyddol ar y ddaear.[1] Dan ddylanwad y naill ddiwygiad lleol a chenedlaethol ar ôl y llall, ymledai sêl crefyddol fel tân gwyllt o bryd i'w gilydd trwy wlad a thref. Sefydlwyd mannau cyfarfod mewn ffermydd a thai; codwyd capeli ac ysgoldai hyd yn oed yn y rhannau mwyaf diarffordd o'r wlad. Golygai hyblygrwydd trefniadaeth yr Ymneilltuwyr y gallent ymateb nid yn unig i'r ffrwydrad mewn poblogaeth yn yr ardaloedd gwledig yn hanner cyntaf y bedwaredd ganrif ar bymtheg ond hefyd i her diwydiannaeth. Yr oedd crefydd fel y'i harferid gan yr enwadau Ymneilltuol, sef y Methodistiaid Calfinaidd, yr Annibynwyr (yr eglwysi Cynulleidfaol), y Methodistiaid Wesleaidd a'r Bedyddwyr, yn mynnu mwy o ymroddiad gan ddilynwyr na'r weithred unigol o addoliad wythnosol, a honno'n aml yn un oddefol, a ddisgwylid gan gymunwyr yr Eglwys sefydledig. Yr oedd ymlyniad o ddifrif wrth Ymneilltuaeth yn effeithio ar bob agwedd ar fywyd. Yn ogystal â'r moddion gras ar fore a nos Sul, byddai'r ysgolion Sul yn dysgu mynychwyr i ddarllen Cymraeg ac yn annog trafodaeth ar faterion Beiblaidd a moesol. Rhoddai'r Gobeithlu a'r mudiad dirwest arweiniad moesol pellach. Cynhelid gweithgareddau diwylliannol megis eisteddfodau capel a gwyliau corawl. Cafwyd cynnydd mewn cyhoeddiadau Cymraeg – yn gyfnodolion, papurau newydd, esboniadau crefyddol, storïau moesol, a chyfresi darllen ar gyfer disgyblion ysgol Sul – ac yr oedd iddynt farchnad barod ymhlith cynulleidfaoedd yr enwadau Ymneilltuol. Yr oedd gan ddiaconiaid a blaenoriaid, fel swyddogion etholedig y capeli, fwy o rym o lawer ym materion lleol eu cymuned na'u cymheiriaid yn yr Eglwys sefydledig. Prin y gellir gorbwysleisio cyfraniad crefydd at gynnal yr iaith Gymraeg y tu allan i'r cartref a'r fferm yn wyneb y dylanwadau Seisnig a oedd yn araf ymledu. Yn wir, cryfder crefydd yng Nghymru oedd yr union beth a ddallodd lawer rhag gweld peryglon dwyieithrwydd yn ail hanner y bedwaredd ganrif ar bymtheg.

Ceir cyfoeth o dystiolaeth ystadegol, yn enwedig o ganol y ganrif, i gefnogi'r farn fod yr ymlyniad wrth grefydd yn gryf yng Nghymru. Cyhoeddai'r enwadau Ymneilltuol lawlyfrau neu flwyddlyfrau rheolaidd yn cynnwys ffigurau manwl yn cofnodi aelodaeth a

Introduction

In the mid-nineteenth century it was claimed by the Reverend Thomas Rees that 'the Welsh were the most religious nation on earth'.[1] Fuelled by successive local and national revivals, a blaze of Nonconformist religious fervour swept from time to time through town and country. Meeting places were established in farms and houses; chapels and schoolrooms were built even in the remotest corners of Wales. The flexibility of Nonconformist organization enabled it to respond both to the population explosion in rural areas in the first half of the nineteenth century and also to the challenges of industrialization. Religion as practised by the Nonconformist denominations of Calvinistic Methodists, Independents (Congregationalists), Wesleyan Methodists and Baptists demanded greater involvement from followers than the single and often passive act of Sunday worship which was expected of communicants of the established Church. Serious commitment to Nonconformity affected every aspect of life. Besides the morning and evening services of worship on Sundays, Sunday schools taught the reading of Welsh and encouraged discussion of biblical and moral issues. Moral guidance was further supplied by the Bands of Hope and the temperance movement. Cultural activities included chapel eisteddfodau and choral festivals. The growth of Welsh language publications – periodicals, newspapers, religious commentaries, moral stories, and reading series for Sunday scholars – found a ready market in the congregations of the Nonconformist denominations. Chapel deacons and elders, as elected chapel officials, wielded far more power in local community affairs than their equivalents in the established Church. The role of religion in protecting the Welsh language beyond the base of home and farm against creeping Anglicization can hardly be overestimated. Indeed, it was precisely the strength of the religious domain in Wales which blinded many to the dangers of bilingualism in the second half of the nineteenth century.

There is an abundance of statistical evidence, particularly from mid-century, to support the assertion of high levels of religious observance in Wales. Nonconformist denominations published regular handbooks or yearbooks with detailed figures of membership and finances.[2] They have been expertly assembled in a large section on Religion in Volume II of John Williams's

chyllid.[2] Fe'u casglwyd ynghyd yn fedrus mewn adran sylweddol ar Grefydd yn yr ail gyfrol o *Digest of Welsh Historical Statistics* gan John Williams. Yn y gyfrol hon, fodd bynnag, er mwyn gallu cymharu cyfansoddiad crefyddol gwahanol ardaloedd yn fanwl a chysylltu'r patrymau enwadol â defnydd o iaith a newid iaith, y mae'r rhan fwyaf o'r ystadegau wedi eu codi o ddwy ymgais uchelgeisiol ar ran y llywodraeth ganolog i ddarganfod cryfderau cymharol y gwahanol enwadau a chrefyddolder y boblogaeth yn gyffredinol. Y ffynhonnell gyntaf yw Cyfrifiad Crefydd 1851, a wnaed ar yr un diwrnod â'r cyfrifiad cyffredinol o'r boblogaeth ac a gwmpasai Gymru, Lloegr a'r Alban. Dyma'r unig ymgais swyddogol erioed i fesur cyflwr crefydd ym Mhrydain. Cyhoeddwyd y canlyniadau llawysgrif ar gyfer Cymru, gyda rhagarweiniad esboniadol manwl, yn *The Religious Census of 1851. A Calendar of the Returns relating to Wales*, a olygwyd gan Ieuan Gwynedd Jones a David Williams.[3] Yr ail ffynhonnell yw'r dystiolaeth a gasglwyd gan y Comisiwn Brenhinol ar Eglwys Loegr a Chyrff Crefyddol eraill yng Nghymru a sir Fynwy a sefydlwyd ym 1906 ond na chyflwynodd ei adroddiad tan 1910. Y mae problemau dehongli difrifol ynglŷn â'r ddwy set o ffigurau. Fel y dywed E. T. Davies yn ei astudiaeth ragorol, *Religion in the Industrial Revolution in South Wales*: 'the figures that are available for ecclesiastical purposes are all unsatisfactory to some degree or other. But they are the only figures to hand, and the best use must be made of them.'[4]

Cymerwyd y ffigurau yn Nhablau 1.1 ac 1.2, dan y penawdau nifer o addoldai, eisteddleoedd (h.y. lle a oedd ar gael), a phresenoldeb yn y gwasanaethau ar fore, prynhawn a nos Sul, 30 Mawrth 1851, yn syth o'r Cyfrifiad Crefydd. Cyhoeddwyd yr wybodaeth yn ôl dosbarth cofrestru. Addaswyd y ffigurau i ganiatáu ar gyfer ffigurau a aeth ar goll a'u cydgrynhoi i roi'r un wybodaeth fesul sir.[5] Rhydd Tabl 1.3 fanylion am eglwysi'r Methodistiaid Calfinaidd Cymraeg mewn ardaloedd cofrestru yn Lloegr. Er mwyn cael yr wybodaeth hon, anfonwyd ffurflenni cyfrifiad at offeiriaid Eglwys Loegr a gweinidogion enwadau eraill yn gofyn am fanylion dan naw pennawd, gan gynnwys adran olaf ar gyfer unrhyw sylwadau yr hoffai'r gweinidog neu'r swyddog eu cofnodi.[6]

Y ffigurau presenoldeb yw'r rhai y mae mwyaf o amheuaeth yn eu cylch, o ran eu cywirdeb ac o ran eu harwyddocâd. Pan wnaed y cyfrifiad, a phan gyhoeddwyd yr adroddiad wedi hynny, honnai eglwyswyr fod maint cynulleidfaoedd Ymneilltuol wedi cael eu chwyddo'n fwriadol.[7] Ond ni ddarganfu Ieuan Gwynedd Jones unrhyw dystiolaeth uniongyrchol i ategu'r cyhuddiad hwn a phwysleisia y byddai'r clerigwyr wedi cael mwy o amser i gynnull eu praidd gan fod y ffurflenni ar gyfer addoldai'r Eglwys sefydledig wedi cael eu danfon cyn rhai'r Ymneilltuwyr. Ond yn y canlyniadau llawysgrif, ceir llawer rheswm paham yr oedd maint cynulleidfaoedd yn ansefydlog, ffaith sy'n

Digest of Welsh Historical Statistics. In the present volume, however, in order to enable comparison of the religious composition between different districts in detail and to relate the denominational patterns to language use and change, most statistics have been derived from two ambitious attempts by central government to discover the relative strengths of the different denominations and the overall religiosity of the population. The first is the Religious Census of 1851, which was taken on the same day as the general census of population and covered England, Wales and Scotland. It remains the only official attempt to quantify the state of religion in Britain. The manuscript returns for Wales have been published, with a detailed explanatory introduction, in *The Religious Census of 1851. A Calendar of the Returns relating to Wales,* edited by Ieuan Gwynedd Jones and David Williams.[3] The second source is the evidence collected by the Royal Commission on the Church of England and other Religious Bodies in Wales and Monmouthshire which was set up in 1906 but did not report until 1910. Both sets of figures pose severe problems of interpretation. As E. T. Davies comments in his excellent study on *Religion in the Industrial Revolution in South Wales*: 'the figures that are available for ecclesiastical purposes are all unsatisfactory to some degree or other. But they are the only figures to hand, and the best use must be made of them.'[4]

Figures in Tables 1.1 and 1.2, under the headings of number of places of worship, sittings (i.e. accommodation available), and attendants at morning, afternoon and evening services on Sunday, 30 March 1851, are taken directly from the Religious Census. The information was published according to registration district. The figures have been adjusted to include an allowance for missing returns and aggregated to give the same information on a county basis.[5] Table 1.3 gives details of the Welsh Calvinistic Methodist Churches in English registration divisions. To obtain this information, census schedules were sent to clergy of the Church of England and to ministers of other denominations, requesting details under nine headings, including a final section for any remarks the minister or official might wish to record.[6]

The attendance figures are most open to question, both in terms of accuracy and significance. At the time the census was taken, and subsequently, when the report was published, members of the established Church claimed that the size of Nonconformist congregations had been deliberately inflated.[7] However, Ieuan Gwynedd Jones has uncovered no direct evidence to substantiate this accusation and he makes the point that because the schedules for places of worship of the established Church were delivered before those of the Nonconformists, clergymen had more time to assemble their flocks. There are, however, many reasons given in the manuscript returns which indicate the fluctuating size of congregations and which

bwrw amheuaeth ar ddilysrwydd ffigurau presenoldeb un Sul arbennig. Effaith y tymhorau a'r tywydd yw'r rheswm a grybwyllir amlaf dros bresenoldeb isel. Ddydd Sul, 30 Mawrth, yr oedd y tywydd yn arbennig o wael, a chofnodwyd disgrifiadau megis 'gwlyb a stormus', 'gwlyb iawn a garw', 'gwlyb ac oer', yn enwedig yng nghanol a gogledd-ddwyrain Cymru. Yn sir Fynwy, yr oedd Sul y Cyfrifiad yn cyd-daro â Chanol y Grawys neu Sul y Fam, pan fyddai gweision a morynion yn draddodiadol yn ymweld â'u teuluoedd. Yr oedd salwch ymhlith gweinidogion neu gynulleidfaoedd yn rheswm arall a roddwyd am bresenoldeb isel.[8] Ar y llaw arall, prin yw'r honiadau fod cynulleidfaoedd yn fwy na'r arfer.[9] Awgryma hyn fod y ffigurau presenoldeb a gofnodwyd ar y dydd hwnnw yn debygol o fod yn is yn hytrach nag yn uwch na'r cofnod presenoldeb cyfartalog. Ar ôl astudio'r canlyniadau llawysgrif yn fanwl, daeth Ieuan Gwynedd Jones i'r casgliad fod y ffurflenni, at ei gilydd, wedi cael eu llenwi'n onest a bod y ffynhonnell hon yn gwbl ddibynadwy o safbwynt y nifer a'r mathau o addoldai, ychydig yn llai dibynadwy o safbwynt nifer yr adeiladau ac yn llai dibynadwy fyth o safbwynt faint yn union o bobl a fynychodd wasanaeth crefyddol ar 30 Mawrth 1851.[10]

Hyd yn oed os gellir amddiffyn cywirdeb y ffigurau presenoldeb, erys problemau dehongli. Trwy gyfrif y rhai a fynychodd fan o addoliad dair gwaith yr un dydd, methodd y cyfrifiad ag ateb un o'i brif ddibenion, sef canfod faint o unigolion a fynychodd fan o addoliad ar un Sul penodol.[11] Dyfeisiodd Horace Mann, trefnydd y cyfrifiad, fformwla i drosi 'presenoldebau' yn 'unigolion', ond petaem yn cymhwyso'r fformwla hon yn yr un modd at fynychwyr gwasanaethau'r Eglwys wladol a'r enwadau Ymneilltuol fel ei gilydd, byddai'n chwyddo nifer yr unigolion a fynychodd wasanaethau Ymneilltuol.

Serch hynny, y mae'n ddiogel defnyddio'r ffigurau i gymharu cryfder yr enwadau mewn gwahanol ardaloedd ac i fesur 'crefyddolder' yn nhermau cyfanswm presenoldebau yn hytrach na mynychwyr unigol. Y mae'r ffigur yng ngholofn olaf Tablau 1.1 ac 1.2 yn ymgais i roi mynegrif presenoldeb er mwyn gallu cymharu 'crefyddolder' gwahanol ardaloedd. Gan mai cyfanswm y presenoldebau yn y gwasanaethau yn y bore, y prynhawn a'r nos yw'r mynegrif, y mae'n amlwg y gallai'r un person gael ei gyfrif ddwywaith neu hyd yn oed dair gwaith pe bai wedi mynychu mwy nag un gwasanaeth. Felly y mae modd i'r rhif hwn fod yn fwy na chant. Defnyddiwyd yr un mynegrif gan Ieuan Gwynedd Jones ac eraill i ddehongli'r Cyfrifiad Crefydd.[12]

Pa ffordd bynnag y mynegir y ffigurau, y mae'r tablau cyfrifiad anaddasedig yn profi y tu hwnt i amheuaeth mai Cymru oedd y rhan fwyaf crefyddol o Brydain yng nghanol y bedwaredd ganrif ar bymtheg.[13] O ran cyfle i addoli yr oedd hi'n well ar y Cymry nag

therefore question the validity of one Sunday's attendance figures. The effect of season and weather is the most constantly cited reason for poor attendance. The weather on Sunday, 30 March, was particularly poor, with descriptions such as 'wet and stormy', 'very wet and boisterous', 'wet and cold' recorded, especially in central and north-east Wales. In Monmouthshire, Census Sunday coincided with Mid-Lent or Mothering Sunday, when servants traditionally visited their families. Illness among ministers or congregations was yet another reason given for poor attendance.[8] On the other hand, claims that congregations were larger than usual are rare.[9] This suggests that the attendance returns for that day probably understate rather than overstate the average attendance record. A close examination of the manuscript returns led Ieuan Gwynedd Jones to conclude that, for the most part, the returns were completed with honest intent and that 'this source enables us to count with complete accuracy the numbers and types of places of worship ..., to count with rather less accuracy the accommodation provided by them, and with least accuracy the actual number of people who attended religious services on 30 March 1851'.[10]

Even if the accuracy of the attendance figures can be defended, problems of interpretation remain. By counting the number of those who attended on three occasions on the same day, the census failed in one of its primary purposes, which was to establish the number of individuals who attended church on a given Sunday.[11] Horace Mann, the organizer of the census, devised a formula to convert 'attendances' into 'individuals', but if we were to apply this equally to attenders of services of the established Church and Nonconformist denominations alike it would inflate the number of individuals attending Nonconformist services.

Nevertheless, these statistics can be safely used to compare the strength of the different denominations between districts and also to quantify 'religiosity' in terms of total attendances rather than individual attenders. The figure in the last column of Tables 1.1 and 1.2 is an attempt to provide an attendance index to enable comparison of 'religiosity' between different areas. As the index is simply the sum of the attendance at morning, afternoon and evening services given as a percentage of the total population, it is clear that one person may be counted twice or even three times if they attend more than one service. Therefore, it is possible for this figure to exceed one hundred. The same index has been used by Ieuan Gwynedd Jones and others in their interpretation of the Religious Census.[12]

Whichever way the figures are expressed, the unadjusted summary census tables prove beyond doubt that Wales was the most religious part of Britain in the mid-nineteenth century.[13] In terms of opportunity for

ar y Saeson a'r Albanwyr. Yr oedd lle (i eistedd) ar gael mewn eglwysi neu gapeli ar gyfer o leiaf 75.6 y cant o boblogaeth Cymru, o'i gymharu â 51.2 y cant yn Lloegr a 49.2 y cant yn yr Alban. O ran presenoldeb, os rhoddir presenoldeb yng ngwasanaeth y bore yn unig fel canran o gyfanswm y boblogaeth, y mae'r canlyniad yn 31.7 y cant yng Nghymru, 24.2 y cant yn Lloegr, a 25.6 y cant yn yr Alban. Os cymerir cyfanswm presenoldeb yng ngwasanaethau'r bore, y prynhawn a'r hwyr yn fesur o ymlyniad crefyddol, yna y mae arfer yr Ymneilltuwyr o fynychu mwy nag un gwasanaeth yn lledu'r bwlch ymhellach: 82.6 y cant ar gyfer Cymru, 56.4 y cant yn Lloegr a 48.3 y cant yn yr Alban.[14]

Er nad yw tablau cyhoeddedig y cyfrifiad yn cynnwys unrhyw wybodaeth am iaith y gwasanaethau, cyhoeddwyd ym 1850 ganlyniadau cyfrifiad seneddol o'r nifer o wasanaethau Cymraeg a Saesneg, gan wahaniaethu rhwng y gwasanaethau a oedd yn gyfan gwbl Saesneg a'r rhai a oedd yn gyfan gwbl Gymraeg, am dri mis olaf 1848, ym mhedair esgobaeth Cymru, sef Bangor, Llanelwy, Tyddewi a Llandaf.[15] Ychwanegwyd yr atebion yn y ffurflenni fel atodiad i dablau'r cyfrifiad fel arwydd o'r dewis iaith ym mhob ardal. Y mae'n debygol iawn fod y ffigurau hyn yn gorddatgan Seisnigrwydd plwyfi cymysg eu hiaith.

Y mae'r ffigurau addasedig yn Nhabl 1.1 yn dadlennu'r patrwm enwadol yng Nghymru ac yn siroedd cofrestru Cymru. Yng Nghymru gyfan, y mae 20 y cant o'r mynychwyr yn Eglwyswyr, 25.6 y cant yn Fethodistiaid Calfinaidd Cymraeg, 21.8 y cant yn Annibynwyr (Cynulleidfaol) a 17.4 y cant yn Fedyddwyr. Yn Eglwys Loegr, yr oedd oddeutu 50 y cant o'r gwasanaethau yn Gymraeg, 42 y cant yn Saesneg, ac 8 y cant yn gymysg neu'n Gymraeg a Saesneg bob yn ail. Dengys ffigurau'r siroedd amrywiaeth o sefyllfaoedd ieithyddol sy'n cyfateb i ymlyniad crefyddol penodol. Er enghraifft, Maesyfed, y sir fwyaf Seisnigedig, oedd â'r mynegrif presenoldeb isaf (50.4), gyda 43.4 y cant o'r mynychwyr yn mynychu Eglwys Loegr, a dim ond 7.0 y cant yn addoli yn eglwysi'r Methodistiaid Calfinaidd. Ymddengys fod cysylltiad agos rhwng cryfder yr enwadau Ymneilltuol, yn enwedig y Methodistiaid Calfinaidd, a chryfder yr iaith Gymraeg. Yn un o'r siroedd Cymreiciaf, sef sir Gaernarfon, yr oedd y mynegrif presenoldeb yn 100.1, gyda 13.4 y cant yn unig yn Eglwyswyr o gymharu â 49.6 y cant a oedd yn Fethodistiaid Calfinaidd. Nid yw'r gydberthynas rhwng iaith ac enwad Ymneilltuol arbennig mor glir ym mhob sir. Yn sir Aberteifi (mynegrif presenoldeb 104.8), y sir fwyaf crefyddol ohonynt oll, yr oedd nifer y Methodistiaid Calfinaidd a fynychai le o addoliad yn is (37.1 y cant) nag yn sir Gaernarfon, ond yr oedd cefnogaeth gryfach yn sir Aberteifi ymhlith enwadau Ymneilltuol eraill, yn enwedig y Bedyddwyr (16.4 y cant) a'r Annibynwyr (21.7 y cant), a oedd hefyd yn Gymraeg eu hiaith yn bennaf.

religious worship, the Welsh were far better endowed than either the English or the Scots. Accommodation (sittings) was available in churches or chapels for at least 75.6 per cent of the population of Wales, whereas the English and Scots had accommodation for only 51.2 per cent and 49.2 per cent respectively. In terms of attendance, if attendance at morning service only is given as a percentage of the total population, the result is 31.7 per cent for Wales, 24.2 per cent for England, and 25.6 per cent for Scotland. If the total attendance for morning, afternoon, and evening services is taken as a measure of religious attachment, then the Nonconformist practice of attending more than one service widens the gap still further: 82.6 per cent for Wales, 56.4 per cent for England, and 48.3 per cent for Scotland.[14]

Although the published census tables contain no information about the language of services, a parliamentary return of the number of services in English and Welsh, 'distinguishing the English entire Services from the Welsh entire Services' for the last three months of 1848, for the four Welsh dioceses of St Asaph, Bangor, St David's, and Llandaff, was published in 1850.[15] The answers in the returns have been appended to the census tables as an indicator of language preference in each district. It is most likely that these returns overstate the Englishness of a mixed language parish.

The adjusted figures in Table 1.1 reveal the denominational pattern in Wales and the Welsh registration counties. In Wales as a whole, attendants of the Church of England account for 20 per cent of the total, compared with 25.6 per cent Welsh Calvinistic Methodists, 21.8 per cent Independents (Congregationalists) and 17.4 per cent Baptists. In the Church of England, approximately 50 per cent of services were in Welsh, 42 per cent in English, and 8 per cent mixed or alternately Welsh and English. The county figures show a variety of linguistic situations which correlate with specific religious allegiance. For example, Radnor, the most Anglicized county, had the lowest (50.4) attendance index, with 43.4 per cent of attendants belonging to the Church of England and only 7.0 per cent worshipping in Calvinistic Methodist churches. The strength of Nonconformist denominations, in particular the Calvinistic Methodists, appears to have been closely linked to the strength of the Welsh language. In one of the most Welsh counties, Caernarfonshire, the attendance index was 100.1, with only 13.4 per cent of attendants belonging to the Church of England as opposed to 49.6 per cent who belonged to the Calvinistic Methodists. The correlation between a particular Nonconformist denomination and language is not so clear in every county. In Cardiganshire (attendance index 104.8), the most religious county of all, Calvinistic Methodists had fewer attendants (37.1 per cent) than Caernarfonshire, but there was stronger

Y mae Tabl 1.2 yn datgelu'r un wybodaeth ar sail dosbarthau cofrestru. Daw patrwm mwy cymhleth i'r amlwg yma nag ar lefel sirol ac amlygir mwy o amrywiaeth yn lleol. At ei gilydd yr oedd Eglwys Loegr gryfaf a'r mynegrif presenoldeb isaf yn yr ardaloedd mwyaf Seisnigedig (megis Cas-gwent, Llanandras a Threfyclo, er enghraifft). Yn Nosbarth Cofrestru Trefynwy, fodd bynnag, lle'r oedd Eglwys Loegr hefyd yn gryf, rhoddodd cryfder y Methodistiaid Wesleaidd a'r Bedyddwyr hwb i'r mynegrif presenoldeb. Ar ben arall y raddfa, yr oedd y lefelau presenoldeb ar eu huchaf (yn fwy na 100 y cant yn Aberteifi, Castellnewydd Emlyn, Aberaeron, Aberystwyth, Crucywel, Machynlleth, Dolgellau, Caernarfon, Bangor a Chonwy) ymhlith y tri enwad Cymraeg cryfaf, sef y Methodistiaid Calfinaidd, y Bedyddwyr a'r Annibynwyr. Y mae ffigurau Merthyr Tudful yn enghraifft loyw o lwyddiant yr ymateb Ymneilltuol i'r newid mewn poblogaeth yng Nghymru. Yn y ddau ddegawd rhwng 1831 a 1851 yr oedd poblogaeth Merthyr Tudful wedi mwy na dyblu, gan gyrraedd 76,804. Gadawyd Eglwys Loegr, a'i threfniadaeth drwsgl, ar ôl gydag 11.2 y cant yn unig o eisteddleoedd a 6.5 y cant o fynychwyr, tra gallai'r enwadau Ymneilltuol, yn enwedig y Bedyddwyr a'r Annibynwyr, a oedd wedi llenwi'r bwlch yn llwyddiannus, ymffrostio mewn mynegrif presenoldeb o 82.9 y cant. Yr oedd y ganran o drigolion Merthyr – rhai digon stwrllyd, yn ôl pob sôn – a oedd yn mynychu gwasanaeth crefyddol ar y Sul ddwywaith cymaint â chanran Trefyclo dawel.

Y mae Tabl 1.3 yn tystio i bresenoldeb y Methodistiaid Calfinaidd Cymraeg yn Lloegr. Yr oedd eglwysi Cymraeg Lloegr yn fannau cyfarfod ar gyfer Cymry Cymraeg oddi cartref, lle y gallent gyfnewid newyddion yn eu hiaith eu hunain, a pharhau ag arferion crefyddol tebyg. Y Cymry yn swydd Gaerhirfryn a swydd Gaer a gynrychiolir gliriaf; mynychai cyfanswm o dros 2,000 o bobl wasanaeth yr hwyr yn y pedwar capel Cymraeg yn Lerpwl yn unig. Codwyd capel Princes Road i ddal dros 1,200 o bobl, y gynulleidfa unigol fwyaf yn enwad y Methodistiaid.[16]

Y mae'r ail grŵp o dablau yn ymwneud â'r Comisiwn Brenhinol ar Eglwys Loegr a Chyrff Crefyddol eraill yng Nghymru a sir Fynwy, a sefydlwyd ym 1906 i ddarparu tystiolaeth ar gyfer y drafodaeth ar ddatgysylltiad yng Nghymru. Bu'n Gomisiwn anffodus ar sawl ystyr. Arweiniodd anghytuno ac anfodlonrwydd ymhlith yr aelodau penodedig, yn enwedig ynglŷn â'r dystiolaeth ystadegol, at ymddiswyddo a phenodiadau newydd yn ystod yr ymchwiliad. Y Comisiynydd John Greaves oedd yr unig un a lofnododd adroddiad y cadeirydd heb ychwanegu nodyn neu femorandwm amodol. Gwrthododd Syr John Williams lofnodi a lluniodd adroddiad ar wahân gydag atodiad ystadegol sylweddol o'i eiddo ef ei hun. Yn eu memorandwm hynod feirniadol, rhoddodd dau aelod arall, yr Archddiacon Owen Evans a'r Arglwydd Hugh Cecil,

support amongst other Nonconformist denominations, notably the Baptists (16.4 per cent) and Independents (21.7 per cent), which were also predominantly Welsh-speaking.

Table 1.2 reveals the same information on the basis of registration districts. A more complex pattern emerges here than at county level. In general the Church of England was strongest and the attendance index lowest in the most Anglicized districts (for example, Chepstow, Knighton, Presteigne). In Monmouth Registration District, however, where the Church of England was also strong, the attendance index was boosted by the strength of Wesleyan Methodists and Baptists. At the other end of the scale, attendance levels were highest (greater than 100 per cent in Cardigan, Newcastle Emlyn, Aberaeron, Aberystwyth, Crickhowell, Machynlleth, Dolgellau, Caernarfon, Bangor and Conwy) among the three major Welsh language denominations of Calvinistic Methodists, Baptists, and Independents. The figures for Merthyr Tydfil provide a spectacular example of the success of Nonconformist response to population change in Wales. In the two decades between 1831 and 1851 the population of Merthyr Tydfil District more than doubled in reaching 76,804. The Church of England, with its cumbersome administration, was left behind with only 11.2 per cent of sittings and 6.5 per cent of attendants, whereas Nonconformist denominations, particularly the Baptists and Independents, who had successfully filled the void, could boast an attendance index of 82.9 per cent. Reputedly rowdy Merthyr had twice as many attenders of religious services on Sundays as a proportion of the population than did sleepy Knighton.

Table 1.3 reveals the presence of Welsh Calvinistic Methodists in England. Welsh chapels in England provided focal points where Welsh-speaking exiles could meet, exchange news from home in their own language, and continue to observe familiar religious practices. The Lancashire and Cheshire Welsh overspill is most clearly represented; over 2,000 people attended the evening service in the four Liverpool chapels alone. The Princes Road chapel was built to accommodate over 1,200 people, the largest single congregation in the Calvinistic Methodist denomination.[16]

The second group of tables relates to the Royal Commission on the Church of England and other Religious Bodies in Wales and Monmouthshire, which was established in 1906 in order to provide evidence for the debate on disestablishment in Wales. The Commission was ill-fated in several respects. Disagreement and disaffection among the appointed members, particularly concerning the statistical evidence, led to resignations and replacements during the course of the inquiry. Only Commissioner John Greaves signed the chairman's report without adding a qualifying note or memorandum. Sir John Williams refused to sign and

ddadansoddiad mwy trwyadl o'r hanner nag y ceisiwyd ei gynnwys yn y prif adroddiad.[17] Ychydig o sylw a roddwyd i'w holl ymdrechion, serch hynny. Erbyn i'r Comisiwn gyflwyno ei adroddiad ym 1910, nid oedd datgysylltu yn bwnc mor llosg ag yr oedd yn y 1890au.

Byddai'n hawdd beirniadu gwerth tystiolaeth ystadegol y Comisiwn. Ni pharatowyd rhestr o gwestiynau fel y gwnaed cyn cyfrifiad 1851. Ac nid oedd y pwyllgorau sirol wedi derbyn cyfarwyddiadau clir ar gasglu tystiolaeth ystadegol. Dibynnwyd ar ffigurau gan awdurdodau'r esgobaethau yn achos yr Eglwys sefydledig ac ar ffigurau gan gapeli unigol, ynghyd ag ystadegau o flwyddlyfrau enwadol yn achos yr eglwysi Ymneilltuol. Y canlyniad oedd anghysondeb nid yn unig rhwng enwadau ond hefyd rhwng capeli unigol. Yr oedd anghysonderau o'r fath yn ymwneud â'r dyddiadau y cyfeiriai'r ystadegau atynt, y diffiniad o dermau megis 'aelodau' a 'gwrandawyr', ac a gâi plant eu cynnwys ai peidio. Yr oedd hyd yn oed fesuriad safonol yr 'eisteddle' yn amrywio, o ddeunaw modfedd i Ymneilltuwyr i un fodfedd ar hugain yn achos yr Eglwys wladol.[18]

Y ffigurau mwyaf amheus yw'r niferoedd a roddir ar gyfer 'gwrandawyr', sef y grŵp pwysig iawn o bobl a fynychai eglwysi Ymneilltuol, rhai yn fwy cyson na'i gilydd, ond heb yr un ymroddiad â'r aelodau llawn. Y mae'r grŵp hwn yn un anodd ei fesur, a dim ond y Methodistiaid Calfinaidd a fyddai'n cynnwys eu niferoedd yn gyson ym mlwyddiadur eu henwad. Ystyrid bod niferoedd y gwrandawyr yn rhy annibynadwy i'w cynnwys yn y tablau crynhoi yn yr adroddiad. Datganodd yr Archddiacon Owen Evans fod y golofn o wrandawyr yn y tablau crynhoi sirol yn 'gymysgedd anobeithiol o ffigurau ... o ddim gwerth i'w cyfrif hyd yn oed ar gyfer yr amcangyfrifon brasaf oll'.[19] Serch hynny, y mae'r wybodaeth hon wedi ei chynnwys yn Nhablau 2.1 a 2.2, ac felly hefyd amcangyfrifon yr Archddiacon Evans yn Nhabl 2.3, gan eu bod yn grŵp pwysig na ddylid eu hanwybyddu. Er y dylid eu trin yn hynod ochelgar, y mae'r ystadegau hyn yn dystiolaeth ategol werthfawr o gryfder ymlyniad pobl wrth Ymneilltuaeth.

Er gwaethaf problemau dehongli, y mae Tablau 2.1 a 2.2 yn cyfuno ffigurau yn ymwneud â niferoedd addoldai, eisteddleoedd, cymunwyr (neu aelodau), gwrandawyr a chyfanswm aelodau ysgol Sul, ar sail y ddau brif atodiad ystadegol i'r Adroddiad, ar gyfer Eglwys Loegr a'r enwadau Ymneilltuol. Fe'u cynhwyswyd mewn tablau hyd y bo modd er mwyn caniatáu mesur y newid enwadol mewn bywyd crefyddol yn yr hanner canrif wedi Cyfrifiad Crefydd 1851. Nid yw'r ffigurau sirol yn hollol gymaradwy; y mae'r ffigurau yn Nhabl 2.1 yn ymwneud â siroedd gweinyddol, tra bod a wnelo'r ffigurau yn Nhabl 1.1 â siroedd cofrestru. Ond, ac eithrio siroedd Morgannwg a Mynwy, dosbarthwyd y ffigurau ar gyfer capeli a phlwyfi unigol mewn grwpiau yn Nhabl 2.2 ar yr un sail â'r

produced a separate report with a substantial statistical appendix of his own. In their highly critical memorandum, two other members, Archdeacon Owen Evans and Lord Hugh Cecil, gave a much more rigorous analysis of the Nonconformist statistical evidence than was attempted in the main report.[17] In the event, little notice was taken of all their efforts. By the time the Commission presented its report in 1910, disestablishment was no longer the burning issue it had been in the 1890s.

It would be easy to criticize the value of the Commission's statistical evidence. No schedule of questions had been prepared as had been done prior to the 1851 census. Neither had clear instructions been given to county committees on the collection of statistical evidence. Reliance was placed on returns from diocesan authorities for the established Church and on individual chapel returns, together with statistics from denominational yearbooks for the Nonconformist churches. The result was inconsistency not only between denominations but also between individual chapels. Such inconsistencies concerned the dates to which statistics related, the definition of terms such as 'members', 'adherents', and the inclusion of children. Even the standard measurement of a 'sitting' varied, from eighteen inches for Nonconformists to twenty-one inches for the established Church.[18]

The most suspect figures are the numbers given for adherents or 'hearers' (*y gwrandawyr*), the very important group of people who attended Nonconformist churches with varying degrees of regularity but without the commitment of full members. This group is difficult to quantify, and only the Calvinistic Methodists regularly included their numbers in their denomination yearbook. Their numbers were considered too untrustworthy to be included in the summary tables in the report. Archdeacon Owen Evans declared that the column of adherents in the county summary tables was 'a hopeless medley of figures ... useless to add up even for the roughest estimates'.[19] Nevertheless, this data has been included in Tables 2.1 and 2.2, as have Archdeacon Evans's estimates in Table 2.3, because they were an important group that should not be ignored. Although they need to be treated with utmost caution, these statistics provide valuable supplementary evidence of the strength of the attachment of people to the Nonconformist religion.

In spite of problems of interpretation, Tables 2.1 and 2.2 combine figures for the number of places of worship, sittings (i.e. accommodation), communicants (or members), adherents and totals in Sunday schools, derived from the two main statistical appendices to the Report, for the Church of England and Nonconformist denominations. They have been tabulated as far as possible to enable quantification of the denominational change in the religious domain in the half century following the 1851 Religious Census. The county

dosbarthau cofrestru ym 1851 (Tabl 1.2).

Y mae'n bwysig nodi i'r enwadau Ymneilltuol, o ran cyfle i addoli (h.y. niferoedd eisteddleoedd), fynd o nerth i nerth, tra methodd yr Eglwys sefydledig o ychydig â chydgerdded â'r cynnydd mewn poblogaeth ar ôl 1851. Y mae'r ffigurau ar gyfer Cymru yn Nhablau 1.1 a 2.1 yn dangos bod nifer yr eisteddleoedd yn yr Eglwys sefydledig wedi disgyn peth, o'r hyn a oedd yn cyfateb i 24 y cant i 23 y cant o gyfanswm y boblogaeth ym 1901, tra cododd nifer yr eisteddleoedd yn yr holl enwadau eraill o 55 y cant i 80 y cant o'r boblogaeth. Ym 1906, yr oedd, mewn gwirionedd, fwy o eisteddleoedd mewn addoldai yng Nghymru nag ydoedd o bobl i'w llenwi.

Cwestiwn anos i'w ateb yw faint o seddi a gâi eu llenwi a pha gysylltiad sydd rhwng patrymau o ymlyniad crefyddol ac iaith. Honnai'r Eglwys sefydledig fod 10 y cant o'r boblogaeth yn cymuno ynddi. Yr oedd pedwar enwad 'mawr' Cymru, sef y Methodistiaid Calfinaidd, yr Annibynwyr, y Bedyddwyr a'r Methodistiaid Wesleaidd, yn honni bod 27 y cant yn cymuno ynddynt neu'n aelodau ohonynt ond, os cynhwysir gwrandawyr, y mae'r ffigur hwn yn codi i 59 y cant. Sut bynnag y dehonglir y ffigurau, y mae'n eglur fod yr enwadau Ymneilltuol wedi llwyddo'n llawer gwell na'r Eglwys sefydledig i ymateb i her newid mewn poblogaeth a diwydiannu.

O ran iaith, dim ond ffigurau'r Eglwys sefydledig – ar gyfer esgobaethau Bangor, Llanelwy a Thyddewi – a oedd yn cynnwys yn gyson fanylion am iaith y gwasanaethau. Cynhwyswyd yr wybodaeth hon mewn atodiadau i Dablau 2.1 a 2.2 yn yr un modd ag y cyplyswyd gwybodaeth gyffelyb am ganol y bedwaredd ganrif ar bymtheg â Thablau 1.1 a 1.2. Ynghyd â ffigurau yn yr Adran Iaith, y mae'r tablau hyn yn darparu tystiolaeth sy'n caniatáu i ni edrych ar y berthynas rhwng yr Eglwys ac iaith y gymuned. Yn achos yr enwadau Ymneilltuol, y mae'r ffigurau yn Nhabl 2.2 am ddosbarthau Caerdydd, Pontypridd, y Rhondda, ac Abertawe ym Morgannwg yn gwahaniaethu rhwng capeli Cymraeg a Saesneg, ond, ar gyfer Cymru a siroedd Cymru gyda'i gilydd, rhaid inni ddibynnu ar amcangyfrifon yr Archddiacon Owen Evans (Tabl 2.3) a'r dystiolaeth ystadegol a gyflwynwyd ar wahân i'r Comisiwn gan gyrff Ymneilltuol unigol (Tablau 2.4 i 2.7).

Dengys Tabl 2.3 gyfrifiadau'r Archddiacon Evans ynglŷn â gwrandawyr Cymraeg a Saesneg eu hiaith yn y prif enwadau Ymneilltuol ar sail ffigurau a ddarparwyd gan y Methodistiaid Calfinaidd. Y Methodistiaid Calfinaidd oedd yr unig enwad i gynnwys ffigurau 'holl-gynhwysol' am wrandawyr (h.y. yn cynnwys aelodau) yn eu *Blwyddiadur* ac i wahaniaethu rhwng aelodau o oedolion a phlant. I amcangyfrif niferoedd yr oedolion a oedd yn wrandawyr, defnyddiodd yr Archddiacon gymarebau plant i oedolion a oedd yn aelodau o gapeli Methodistiaid Calfinaidd Cymraeg a Saesneg.

figures are not exactly comparable; those in Table 2.1 relate to administrative counties, while those in Table 1.1 relate to registration counties. But in Table 2.2, with the exception of Glamorgan and Monmouthshire, the returns for individual chapels and parishes have been grouped on the same basis as registration districts in 1851 (Table 1.2).

It is important to note that, in terms of opportunity for worship (i.e. number of sittings), Nonconformist denominations went from strength to strength, whereas the established Church marginally failed to keep up with the increase in population after 1851. The figures for Wales in Tables 1.1 and 2.1, reveal that sittings in the established Church fell slightly from the equivalent of 24 per cent to 23 per cent of the total population in 1901, whereas sittings in all other denominations rose from 55 per cent to 80 per cent of the population. In 1906 there was, in fact, more accommodation available in places of worship in Wales than the total population of Wales.

The question of how many seats were filled and how the pattern of religious observance relates to language is more difficult to answer. The established Church claimed 10 per cent of the population as communicants. The 'big four' Welsh denominations of Calvinistic Methodists, Independents, Baptists, and Wesleyan Methodists claimed 27 per cent as communicants or members but, if adherents are included, this figure rises to 59 per cent. Whichever way the figures are interpreted, it is clear that the Nonconformist denominations were more successful than the established Church in responding to the challenges of population change and industrialization.

Regarding language, only the returns for the established Church – for the dioceses of Bangor, St Asaph and St David's – consistently included details about the language of services. This information has been appended to Tables 2.1 and 2.2 in the same way as similar information for the mid-nineteenth century has been attached to Tables 1.1 and 1.2. Together with figures in the Language Section, these tables provide evidence which enables us to examine the relationship between the Church and the language of the community. For the Nonconformist denominations, figures in Table 2.2 for the Glamorgan districts of Cardiff, Pontypridd, Rhondda, and Swansea distinguish between Welsh and English chapels, but, for Wales and Welsh counties as a whole, we must rely on Archdeacon Owen Evans's estimates (Table 2.3) and the statistical evidence presented separately to the Commission by individual Nonconformist bodies (Tables 2.4 to 2.7).

Table 2.3 shows the calculations made by Archdeacon Evans about Welsh and English adherents in the main Nonconformist denominations based on figures supplied by the Calvinistic Methodists. The Calvinistic Methodists were the only denomination to

Yna cymhwyswyd y cymarebau hyn i'r ffigurau am aelodau o oedolion yn y prif enwadau Ymneilltuol eraill er mwyn cael amcangyfrifon o'r nifer o wrandawyr 'holl-gynhwysol' a'r gwrandawyr o oedolion. Cyfaddefodd Evans na ellid dibynnu ar yr amcangyfrifon. Serch hynny, y mae'n werth nodi, fel y gwnaeth yntau, fod cyfanswm y gwrandawyr Ymneilltuol 'holl-gynhwysol' a geir trwy'r cyfrifiadau hyn (1,032,254) yn cyfateb i 52 y cant o gyfanswm amcangyfrifiedig poblogaeth Cymru ym 1901. Er bod y gyfran hon yn llai na'r hyn a amlygir yn y prif atodiadau ystadegol, y mae'n cynrychioli dwywaith cymaint o gymunwyr ag a oedd gan yr Eglwys sefydledig. Dylid tynnu sylw at ddau fater arall. Yn gyntaf, yn ôl y cyfrifiadau hyn, dyma oedd canran y gwrandawyr yn y capeli Cymraeg: Methodistiaid Calfinaidd 78.1 y cant, Annibynwyr 76 y cant, Bedyddwyr 47.9 y cant, a'r Methodistiaid Wesleaidd 42.6 y cant. Yr oedd hyn ar adeg pan oedd 50 y cant o boblogaeth Cymru wedi datgan yng nghyfrifiad 1901 eu bod yn gallu siarad Cymraeg. Awgryma hyn fod y Methodistiaid Calfinaidd a'r Annibynwyr yn enwedig yn ymladd brwydr enbyd yn erbyn newid ieithyddol. Yn ail, y mae'r gyfran uwch o blant ymhlith aelodaeth capeli'r Methodistiaid Calfinaidd Saesneg (39 y cant o gymharu â 29 y cant mewn capeli Cymraeg) yn awgrymu bod hyd yn oed y Methodistiaid Calfinaidd, er gwaethaf y frwydr hon, wedi eu gorfodi i ymateb i'r newid trwy agor capeli Saesneg newydd er mwyn denu dilynwyr iau.

Rhydd Tabl 2.4 ffigurau ynglŷn â sefydlu capeli Annibynnol Cymraeg a Saesneg, a hynny yn ôl sir mewn tri chyfnod gwahanol hyd at 1907. Y maent hefyd yn dangos sut yr ymatebodd yr Annibynwyr i newid ieithyddol er mwyn 'achub eneidiau' a hefyd gryfhau eu cryfder enwadol. Cyn 1800, dim ond 12 y cant o'r capeli a sefydlwyd a oedd yn rhai Saesneg, ond yn y cyfnod rhwng 1850 a 1907, capeli Saesneg oedd 25 y cant o'r capeli newydd a sefydlwyd. Ar y llaw arall, y mae'n arwyddocaol fod cynifer â 187 o gapeli Annibynnol Cymraeg newydd wedi cael eu sefydlu ym Morgannwg rhwng 1850 a 1907. Rhydd Tabl 2.5, sydd hefyd yn ymwneud â chapeli Annibynnol, ddadansoddiad Cymraeg/Saesneg o wahanol ddosbarthiadau o fynychwyr (ond nid gwrandawyr) fesul sir ac ar gyfer capeli Cymraeg yn Lloegr. Y mae'r ddau dabl yn dystiolaeth bellach o gryfder y Gymraeg yn y byd crefyddol Ymneilltuol.

Y mae Tabl 2.6 yn ymwneud â'r Methodistiaid Wesleaidd, y mwyaf Seisnig o'r prif enwadau Ymneilltuol yng Nghymru. Morgannwg oedd eu cadarnle Saesneg, ond yr oedd ganddynt gefnogaeth arwyddocaol hefyd yn siroedd gogledd Cymru a thros 7,000 o aelodau a gwrandawyr mewn capeli Cymraeg yn Lloegr.

Rhydd Tabl 2.7 wahanol ffigurau ar gyfer y Methodistiaid Calfinaidd fesul sir, ynghyd â manylion am

publish regularly figures for 'all inclusive' adherents (i.e. including members) in their Yearbook and to distinguish between adult and child members. Archdeacon Evans used the ratios of children to adult members for Welsh and English Calvinistic Methodist chapels to calculate estimates for adult adherents. These ratios were then applied to the figures for adult members of the other main Nonconformist denominations to obtain estimates of the number of 'all inclusive' adherents and adult adherents. Evans admitted that the estimates were 'too precarious to be relied upon'. Nevertheless, it is worth noting, as he did, that the total of 'all inclusive' Nonconformist adherents reached by these calculations (1,032,254) is equivalent to 52 per cent of the estimated total population of Wales in 1901. Although this represents a smaller proportion than that derived from figures in the main statistical appendices, it constitutes twice the number of communicants claimed by the established Church. Two further points should be highlighted. First, according to these calculations, the percentage of adherents in Welsh chapels was: Calvinistic Methodists 78.1 per cent, Independents 76 per cent, Baptists 47.9 per cent, and Wesleyan Methodists 42.6 per cent. This was at a time when 50 per cent of the population of Wales had been entered in the 1901 Census as 'able to speak Welsh'. This suggests that the Calvinistic Methodist and Independent chapels in particular were fighting a fierce rearguard action against language change. Second, the higher proportion of children within the membership of English Calvinistic Methodist chapels (39 per cent compared to 29 per cent in Welsh chapels) suggests that, despite this rearguard action, even the Calvinistic Methodists had been forced to respond to change by opening new English chapels in order to attract younger followers.

Table 2.4 reveals figures for the establishment of Welsh and English Independent chapels by county in three different periods up to 1907. They also quantify the manner by which Independents responded to language change in order to 'save souls' and also to increase their denominational strength. Before 1800, only 12 per cent of chapels established were English, but in the period from 1850 to 1907, 25 per cent of new chapels established were English. On the other hand, it is significant that as many as 187 new Welsh Independent chapels were established in Glamorgan between 1850 and 1907. Table 2.5, which also relates to Independent chapels, gives a Welsh/English breakdown of various categories of attenders (but not adherents) on a county basis and for Welsh churches in England. Both tables provide further indications of the strength of the Welsh language in the Nonconformist religious domain.

Table 2.6 relates to Wesleyan Methodists, the most English of the major Nonconformist denominations in Wales. Their English stronghold was in Glamorgan,

gapeli yn Lloegr a thramor. Er bod y ffigurau sirol a atgynhyrchir yn nwy ran gyntaf y tabl hwn yn dod yn wreiddiol o'r un ffynhonnell, sef *Blwyddiadur* 1907, ymddangosant hefyd mewn dau dabl ar wahân yn *Denominational Statistics* y Comisiwn lle y ceir rhai mân anghysonderau. Honnir mai wedi eu haddasu 'cyn belled ag yr oedd modd' ar gyfer Cymru yr oedd y ffigurau yn y rhan gyntaf, tra bod ffigurau'r ail ran wedi eu tablu 'yn ôl ardaloedd Sirol' gyda digon o hyder i ychwanegu colofn olaf yn rhoi ffigurau'r gwrandawyr fel canran o boblogaeth yr hen ardaloedd sirol ym 1901. Dadlennir cryfder y Methodistiaid Calfinaidd, yr unig enwad Cymraeg gwreiddiol, yn y ffigurau hyn. Yr oedd cyfanswm nifer y gwrandawyr, gan gynnwys aelodau, yn cyfateb i 16 y cant o boblogaeth Cymru gyfan, a chymaint â 40 y cant o boblogaeth siroedd Môn a Chaernarfon.

Ychydig o ystadegau sydd yn Nhabl 2.8. Yn hytrach atgynhyrchir ynddo atebion i holiadur ynglŷn â gwasanaethau Sul dwyieithog a anfonwyd i bob plwyf yn esgobaeth Tyddewi fel rhan o ymchwiliadau'r Comisiwn Brenhinol. Ni chyhoeddwyd yr wybodaeth hon yn llawn o'r blaen. Ar y pryd yr oedd esgobaeth Tyddewi – a gynhwysai siroedd Aberteifi, Caerfyrddin, Maesyfed, Penfro, a Gorllewin Morgannwg – yn cynnwys llawer o gymunedau a oedd dan bwysau i newid iaith. Oherwydd hynny, y mae sylwadau clerigwyr lleol hyd yn oed yn fwy diddorol ac yn gymorth i roi cig ar esgyrn y tablau ystadegol. Dengys yr atebion, a restrir yn ôl dosbarthau cofrestru ar yr un sail â'r ffigurau yn Nhabl 2.2, yr amrywiol resymau – annisgwyl, weithiau – dros gychwyn cynnal gwasanaethau Saesneg mewn eglwysi plwyf yn ne a gorllewin Cymru; yn eu plith yr oedd presenoldeb teuluoedd bonheddig a'u gweision, ymwelwyr yn ystod yr haf, dylanwad staff a gweithwyr rheilffordd, a phlant o ysgolion diwydiannol Saesneg a weithiai ar ffermydd. Ymddengys nad oedd gweinidogion Ymneilltuol yn gyndyn i recriwtio'r newydd-ddyfodiaid. Cwynodd ficer Meidrim, er enghraifft, fod y capeli Ymneilltuol cyfagos yn defnyddio ychydig o Saesneg 'er mwyn "dal" ein hieuenctid Diwygiadol'. Y mae digon o dystiolaeth fod y glerigaeth yn fwy na pharod i gynnal gwasanaethau Saesneg mewn eglwysi plwyf hyd yn oed lle'r oedd nifer y rhai na ddeallent y Gymraeg yn fychan iawn. A lle y ceid gwahaniaeth rhwng iaith gwasanaethau'r Eglwys a gwasanaethau Ymneilltuol, byddai'r enwadau Ymneilltuol, yn ddieithriad, yn darparu rhagor o wasanaethau Cymraeg na'r Eglwys sefydledig.

Efallai mai Syr John Williams a grynhodd gliriaf y dystiolaeth ynglŷn ag iaith: maentumiai fod y nifer o wasanaethau Saesneg a geid yn yr Eglwys sefydledig yn dibynnu ar y nifer mewn ardal a fedrai siarad Saesneg, tra bod y nifer o wasanaethau Cymraeg yn dibynnu ar y nifer a allai siarad Cymraeg *yn unig*. Mewn capeli Ymneilltuol, ar y llaw arall, dibynnai'r nifer o wasanaethau

but they also retained a significant Welsh presence in the counties of north Wales and over 7,000 members and adherents in Welsh chapels in England.

Table 2.7 gives various figures for Calvinistic Methodists on a county basis, together with details of chapels in England and abroad. Although the county figures reproduced in the first two parts of this table were originally compiled from the same source – the *Blwyddiadur* for 1907 – they also appear in two separate tables in the Commission's *Denominational Statistics* in which they show some minor discrepancies. Those in the first part claim only to have been adapted 'as far as possible' for Wales, whereas those in the second part were tabulated 'according to County areas' with sufficient confidence that a final column was inserted giving figures for adherents as a percentage of the population of ancient county areas in 1901. The strength of the Calvinistic Methodists, the only originally Welsh denomination, is quantified in these figures. The total number of adherents, including members, was equivalent to 16 per cent of the population of Wales as a whole, and as great as 40 per cent of the population of Anglesey and Caernarfonshire.

Table 2.8 contains few statistics. Instead it simply reproduces the answers to a questionnaire concerning bilingual Sunday services which was sent to every parish in the diocese of St David's as part of the enquiries of the Royal Commission. This data has never been published in full. The diocese of St David's comprised, for the most part, the counties of Cardigan, Carmarthen, Pembroke, Radnor, and West Glamorgan, and therefore contained many communities under pressure to change language at this time. This renders the observations of local clergymen all the more interesting and helps to add meat to the bones of the statistical tables. The answers, listed according to registration districts on the same basis as the figures in Table 2.2, illustrate the various, and sometimes unexpected, reasons for the introduction of English language services in parish churches in south and west Wales; among them were the presence of gentry families and their servants, the arrival of summer visitors, the influence of railway staff and workers, and of children from English industrial schools working on farms. It would appear that Nonconformist ministers were not averse to recruiting the newcomers. The vicar of Meidrim, for example, complained that the nearby Nonconformist chapels were introducing a little English 'so as to "catch" our Reformatory youths'. Overwhelmingly, the evidence indicates a greater willingness on the part of the clergy to introduce English services in parish churches even when the number of those who did not understand Welsh was very small indeed. And where there was a difference in the language of Church services and Nonconformist services, without exception the Nonconformist denominations provided more Welsh language services than did the established Church.

Cymraeg ar y nifer a allai siarad Cymraeg a'r nifer o wasanaethau Saesneg ar y nifer a allai siarad Saesneg *yn unig*. Pan fynnai twf cynulleidfaoedd neu ostyngiad mewn niferoedd fod yn rhaid wrth wasanaethau Saesneg, byddai'r enwadau Ymneilltuol yn ymateb trwy sefydlu capeli Saesneg ar wahân yn hytrach na chynnal gwasanaethau dwyieithog neu Saesneg.[20]

Er gwaethaf yr anawsterau ynglŷn â dehongli llawer o'r tablau yn yr adran hon, y mae'r casgliadau cyffredinol yn glir. Yr oedd cyfraniad crefydd i gynnal maes iaith egnïol a byw i'r Gymraeg y tu allan i'r aelwyd a'i gwarchod rhag pwysau moderniaeth yn hanfodol i oroesiad yr iaith i'r ugeinfed ganrif.

1 Thomas Rees, yn ysgrifennu 7 Mai 1850 i'r *Christian Witness* ynglŷn â Diwygiad 1849. Dyfynnwyd yn E. T. Davies, *Religion in the Industrial Revolution in South Wales* (Cardiff, 1965), t. 37.

2 Cyhoeddwyd y prif flwyddlyfrau enwadol fel a ganlyn: *Church of England Yearbook*, 1882, ac wedyn *The Official Handbook of the Church of England*, 1883– ; *Congregational Yearbook*, 1846– ; *Baptist Handbook*, 1851– ; *Eglwys Methodistiaid Calfinaidd Cymru, Y Blwyddiadur*, 1898– ; *Minutes of the Methodist Conference* 1812 (o 1744–1812), ac wedyn yn flynyddol (o 1855 dan y teitl *Minutes of the Wesleyan Methodist Conference*). Ceir adran faith ar Grefydd yn John Williams, *Digest of Welsh Historical Statistics*, cyf. II; cafwyd llawer o'r wybodaeth ym mlwyddlyfrau'r gwahanol enwadau ac fe'i cyflwynwyd yn ôl sir. Y mae dehongli'r ffigurau a geir yn y blwyddlyfrau yn llawn peryglon: cafwyd ambell enghraifft o ailadrodd yr un rhifau aelodaeth o'r naill flwyddyn i'r llall.

3 Gw. Ieuan Gwynedd Jones a David Williams (goln.), *The Religious Census of 1851. A Calendar of the Returns relating to Wales. Volume I South Wales* (Cardiff, 1976); Ieuan Gwynedd Jones (gol.), *The Religious Census of 1851. A Calendar of the Returns relating to Wales. Volume II North Wales* (Cardiff, 1981).

4 Davies, *Religion in the Industrial Revolution*, t. 185.

5 Yn achos Cymru, yn wahanol i Loegr, ni cheir tablau ar gyfer siroedd unigol, ond yn hytrach dablau ar gyfer gogledd a de Cymru yn unig.

6 Y penawdau oedd: I. Enw'r man o addoliad; II. Safle'r man o addoliad; III. Enwad crefyddol; IV. Pryd y'i codwyd; V. A oedd yn adeilad ar wahân; VI. A oedd yn cael ei ddefnyddio yn unig fel man o addoliad (neu ysgol Sul); VII. Faint o le a oedd ar gael ar gyfer addoliad cyhoeddus; VIII. Amcangyfrif o faint o bobl a fynychodd wasanaeth ar fore, prynhawn a nos Sul 30 Mawrth 1851, gan wahaniaethu rhwng y Gynulleidfa Gyffredinol a'r disgyblion ysgol Sul, ac os oedd y rhifau hyn yn anghynrychioliadol, i roi hefyd gyfartaledd y mynychwyr; IX. Sylwadau.

7 Yng ngeiriau Ebenezer Williams, curad eglwys plwyf Bryneglwys, sir Ddinbych: 'Forcible appeals have lately been made by dissenters in their small publications for a full attendance on Sunday last in order to show numerical strength.' *Calendar of Returns*, II, t. 240.

8 E.e. lleihawyd cynulleidfaoedd oherwydd gwres a'r clefyd coch yn Nhŷ-du, sir Fynwy; rhyw salwch difrifol yn Nhyddewi, sir Benfro; y frech wen ac anhwylderau eraill yn Llanbadarn Fawr, sir Aberteifi, a'r frech goch ac annwyd yn Llanrhaeadr-yng-Nghinmeirch, sir Ddinbych. *Calendar of Returns*, I, tt. 109, 439, 536; II, t. 179.

9 Nododd Richard Owen, gweinidog Hermon, eglwys y Bedyddwyr, Abergwaun, fod y cynulleidfaoedd yn fwy niferus yn ystod y gaeaf pan oedd y morwyr gartref. Cynyddodd y gynulleidfa o 20 i 30 yn eglwys y plwyf

Perhaps Sir John Williams most clearly summed up the evidence of language: he maintained that within the established Church the number of English services was dependent on the number in a district who could speak English, while the number of Welsh services was dependent on the number who could speak *Welsh only*. In Nonconformist chapels, on the other hand, the number of Welsh services depended on the number who could speak Welsh and the number of English services upon the number of persons who could speak *English only*. It was also true that when swelling congregations or falling numbers demanded the inclusion of English language services, Nonconformist denominations responded by establishing separate English language chapels rather than by introducing bilingual or English services.[20]

In spite of the difficulties attached to the interpretation of many of the tables in this section, the overall conclusions are clear. The role of religion in maintaining a vibrant Welsh language domain outside the hearth and protecting it against the pressures of modernity was crucial to the survival of the language into the twentieth century.

1 Thomas Rees, writing 7 May 1850 to the *Christian Witness* about the 1849 Revival. Quoted in E. T. Davies, *Religion in the Industrial Revolution in South Wales* (Cardiff, 1965), p. 37.

2 The main denominational yearbooks were published as follows: *Church of England Yearbook*, 1882, thereafter *The Official Handbook of the Church of England*, 1883– ; *Congregational Yearbook*, 1846– ; *Baptist Handbook*, 1851– ; *Eglwys Methodistiaid Calfinaidd Cymru, Y Blwyddiadur*, 1898– ; *Minutes of the Methodist Conference* 1812 (for 1744–1812), thereafter annually (from 1855 entitled *Minutes of the Wesleyan Methodist Conference*). John Williams, *Digest of Welsh Historical Statistics*, volume II, contains a large section on Religion, much of which has been extracted from the yearbooks of the various denominations and is assembled on a county basis. Interpretation of yearbook figures is fraught with dangers; the figures of membership, for example, were occasionally repeated year after year.

3 See Ieuan Gwynedd Jones and David Williams (eds.), *The Religious Census of 1851. A Calendar of the Returns relating to Wales. Volume I South Wales* (Cardiff, 1976); Ieuan Gwynedd Jones (ed.), *The Religious Census of 1851. A Calendar of the Returns relating to Wales. Volume II North Wales* (Cardiff, 1981).

4 Davies, *Religion in the Industrial Revolution*, p. 185.

5 Unlike England, the Census tables for Wales contain separate tables for north Wales and south Wales only, instead of for individual counties.

6 The headings were: I. Name of place of worship; II. Situation of place of worship; III. Religious denomination; IV. When built; V. Whether a separate building; VI. Whether used exclusively as a place of worship (or Sunday School); VII. Space available for public worship; VIII. Estimated number of persons attending Divine Service, in the Morning, Afternoon, and Evening of Sunday 30 March 1851, distinguishing the General Congregation from Sunday Scholars, and if these numbers were unrepresentative, to also give the average number of attendants; IX. Remarks.

7 Ebenezer Williams, curate of Bryneglwys parish church, Denbighshire, complained that 'forcible appeals have lately been made by dissenters in their small publications for a full attendance on Sunday last in order to show numerical

Llanarmon-yn-Iâl, sir Ddinbych, brynhawn Sul 30 Mawrth, gan fod bedydd yn cael ei gynnal yno. *Calendar of Returns*, I, t. 446; II, t. 165.

[10] Ieuan Gwynedd Jones, 'Denominationalism in Caernarvonshire in the mid-nineteenth century as shown in the Religious Census of 1851', *Trafodion Cymdeithas Hanes Sir Gaernarfon*, 31 (1970), 78–114; adargraffwyd yn Ieuan Gwynedd Jones, *Explorations and Explanations: Essays in the Social History of Victorian Wales* (Llandysul, 1981), tt. 17–52.

[11] W. S. Pickering, 'The 1851 Religious Census – a useless experiment?' *British Journal of Sociology*, XVII (1967), 382–407.

[12] Defnyddiwyd gan K. S. Inglis, *Churches and the Working Classes in Victorian England* (London, 1963), gan R. M. Goodridge yn 'The religious condition of the West country in 1851', *Social Compass*, XIV, rhifyn 4 (1967), 285–96, a chan Ieuan Gwynedd Jones yn 'Denominationalism in Caernarvonshire in the mid-nineteenth century as shown in the Religious Census of 1851' and 'Denominationalism in Swansea and District: A Study of the Ecclesiastical Census of 1851', *Morgannwg*, XII (1968), 67–96, a adargraffwyd yn Jones, *Explorations and Explanations*, tt. 17–52, 53–80. Ceir astudiaethau lleol eraill ar Gyfrifiad Crefydd 1851 yng Nghymru gan David Williams, 'The Census of Religious Worship of 1851 in Cardiganshire', *Ceredigion*, IV, rhifyn 2 (1961), 113–28; Ieuan Gwynedd Jones, 'The Religious Condition of the Counties of Brecon and Radnor as Revealed in the Census of Religious Worship of 1851' yn Owain W. Jones a David Walker (goln.), *Links with the Past. Swansea and Brecon Historical Essays* (Llandybïe, 1974), tt. 185–214.

[13] Yr oedd hyn yn wir, fwy na thebyg, ers canol y 1830au. Gw. Ieuan Gwynedd Jones, 'Language and Community in Nineteenth-century Wales' yn idem, *Mid-Victorian Wales. The Observers and the Observed* (Cardiff, 1992), t. 61.

[14] Cafwyd y ffigurau hyn yn nhablau cryno'r Cyfrifiad. Tynnwyd y rhifau ar gyfer Adran Cofrestru Cymru allan o'r cyfanswm am Gymru a Lloegr er mwyn cael y rhifau ar gyfer Lloegr. *Census of Great Britain, 1851. Religious Worship. England and Wales. Report and Tables* (London, 1853), PP 1852–3 LXXXIX. *Census of Great Britain, 1851. Religious Worship and Education. Scotland. Report and Tables* (London, 1854), PP 1854 (1690) LIX.

[15] *Churches and Chapels (Wales). Returns of the number of services performed in each Church or Chapel in the Dioceses of St Asaph, Bangor, St Davids, and Llandaff, for the three months ending 31st day of December 1848* (London, 1850). PP 1850 (4) XLII.

[16] R. Merfyn Jones a D. Ben Rees, *Cymry Lerpwl a'u Crefydd: Dwy Ganrif o Fethodistiaeth Galfinaidd Gymreig* (Lerpwl, 1984), t. 25.

[17] Ar y llaw arall, gwnaeth J. H. Davies, aelod arall o'r Comisiwn, sylw mwy cadarnhaol: 'a very large portion of the time of the Commission was spent in criticism of the Nonconformist figures, and as a result the totals of communicants were not reduced by more than 500'.

[18] Comisiwn Brenhinol ar Eglwys Loegr a Chyrff Crefyddol eraill yng Nghymru a sir Fynwy. *Adroddiad*, t. 54. PP 1910 (cd 5432) XIV.

[19] Adroddiad Comisiwn yr Eglwys. Memorandwm gan yr Archddiacon Owen Evans ac Arglwydd Hugh Cecil, t. 149.

[20] Adroddiad Comisiwn yr Eglwys gan Syr John Williams, tt. 297–8. Gw. hefyd R. Tudur Jones, 'Yr Eglwysi a'r Iaith yn Oes Victoria', *Llên Cymru*, 19 (1996), 146–67.

strength'. *Calendar of Returns*, II, p. 240.

[8] For example, congregations were reduced by 'fever and scarletina' at Rogerstone, Monmouthshire; an undefined 'great sickness' at St David's, Pembrokeshire; 'small pox and other complaints' in Llanbadarn Fawr, Cardiganshire, and 'measles and colds' at Llanrhaeadr-yng-Nghinmeirch, Denbighshire. *Calendar of Returns*, I, pp. 109, 439, 536; II, p. 179.

[9] Richard Owen, minister of Hermon Baptist chapel in Fishguard, remarked: 'During the winter when Sailors are at home Congregations are more numerous.' A christening at Llanarmon-yn-Iâl parish church, Denbighshire, increased the size of the congregation from 20 to 30 for the afternoon service on 30 March. *Calendar of Returns*, I, p. 446; II, p. 165.

[10] Ieuan Gwynedd Jones, 'Denominationalism in Caernarvonshire in the mid-nineteenth century as shown in the Religious Census of 1851', *Caernarfonshire Historical Society Transactions*, 31 (1970), 78–114; reprinted in Ieuan Gwynedd Jones, *Explorations and Explanations: Essays in the Social History of Victorian Wales* (Llandysul, 1981), pp. 17–52.

[11] W. S. Pickering, 'The 1851 Religious Census – a useless experiment?', *British Journal of Sociology*, XVII (1967), 382–407.

[12] Used by K. S. Inglis, *Churches and the Working Classes in Victorian England* (London, 1963), by R. M. Goodridge in 'The religious condition of the West country in 1851', *Social Compass*, XIV, no. 4 (1967), 285–96, and by Ieuan Gwynedd Jones, in 'Denominationalism in Caernarvonshire in the mid-nineteenth century as shown in the Religious Census of 1851' and 'Denominationalism in Swansea and District: A Study of the Ecclesiastical Census of 1851', *Morgannwg*, XII (1968), 67–96, reprinted in Jones, *Explorations and Explanations*, pp. 17–52, 53–80. Local Welsh studies based on the 1851 Religious Census also include David Williams, 'The Census of Religious Worship of 1851 in Cardiganshire', *Ceredigion*, IV, no. 2 (1961), 113–28; Ieuan Gwynedd Jones, 'The Religious Condition of the Counties of Brecon and Radnor as Revealed in the Census of Religious Worship of 1851' in Owain W. Jones and David Walker (eds.), *Links with the Past. Swansea and Brecon Historical Essays* (Llandybïe, 1974), pp. 185–214.

[13] This had probably been the case since the mid-1830s. See Ieuan Gwynedd Jones, 'Language and Community in Nineteenth-century Wales' in idem, *Mid-Victorian Wales. The Observers and the Observed* (Cardiff, 1992), p. 61.

[14] These figures are taken from the Census summary tables. Figures for the Welsh Registration Division have been subtracted from the figures for England and Wales as a whole to obtain totals for England. *Census of Great Britain, 1851. Religious Worship. England and Wales. Report and Tables* (London, 1853), PP 1852–3 LXXXIX. *Census of Great Britain, 1851. Religious Worship and Education. Scotland. Report and Tables* (London, 1854), PP 1854 (1690) LIX.

[15] *Churches and Chapels (Wales). Returns of the number of services performed in each Church or Chapel in the Dioceses of St Asaph, Bangor, St Davids, and Llandaff, for the three months ending 31st day of December 1848* (London, 1850). PP 1850 (4) XLII.

[16] R. Merfyn Jones and D. Ben Rees, *The Liverpool Welsh and their Religion. Two Centuries of Welsh Calvinistic Methodism* (Liverpool, 1984), p. 26.

[17] On the other hand, another member of the Commission, J. H. Davies, more positively commented that 'a very large portion of the time of the Commission was spent in criticism of the Nonconformist figures, and as a result the totals of communicants were not reduced by more than 500'.

[18] Royal Commission on the Church of England and Other Religious Bodies in Wales and Monmouthshire. *Report*, p. 54. PP 1910 (cd 5432) XIV.

[19] *Church Commission Report.* Memorandum by Archdeacon Owen Evans and Lord Hugh Cecil, p. 149.

[20] *Church Commission Report* by Sir John Williams, pp. 297–8.

See also R. Tudur Jones, 'Yr Eglwysi a'r Iaith yn Oes Victoria', *Llên Cymru,* 19 (1996), 146–67.

Religion 1.1 Religious Census, 1851. Number of places of worship, sittings and total attendants, by denomination. Wales and Registration Counties

	Denomination	Places of worship	Sittings[2]	Attendance[2]	*Attendance as % total[3]*	*Attendance Index[4]*
Wales	Church of England	1180	289746	199265	*20.0*	
Pop. 1,188,914	Independents	700	178782	218052	*21.8*	
	Baptists	533	135003	173446	*17.4*	
	Wesleyan Methodists					
	Methodist Original Connexion	499	96297	103970	*10.4*	
	Methodist New Connexion	10	1420	1471	*0.1*	
	Primitive Methodists	118	13440	14083	*1.4*	
	Bible Christians	14	1228	1221	*0.1*	
	Wesleyan Association	10	1186	1562	*0.2*	
	Wesleyan Reformers	8	1743	1628	*0.2*	
	Total Wesleyan Methodists	**659**	**115314**	**123935**	***12.4***	
	Calvinistic Methodists					
	Welsh Calvinistic Methodists	807	196442	255830	*25.6*	
	Lady Huntingdon's Connexion	1	650	1050	*0.1*	
	Total Calvinistic Methodists	**808**	**197092**	**256880**	***25.7***	
	Society of Friends	8	790	145	*0.0*	
	Unitarians	27	5730	3812	*0.4*	
	Moravians	1	200	280	–	
	Brethren	1	200	263	–	
	Undefined Protestant	33	6115	7169	*0.7*	
	Roman Catholics	22	5713	8423	*0.8*	
	Latter Day Saints	32	4655	6807	*0.7*	
	Jews	2	112	218	–	
	Total	**4006**	**939452**	**998695**	***100.0***	***84.0***

1848 Church of England[5]	Places of worship: 1016 Language of services: 744 Welsh, 623 English, 67 mixed, 49 'alternate'

Registration Counties[1]

	Denomination	Places of worship	Sittings	Attendance	*Attendance as % total*	*Attendance Index*
Monmouth	Church of England	182	40506	34162	*26.5*	
Pop. 177,130	Independents	52	14619	18231	*14.2*	
	Baptists	89	28952	33836	*26.3*	
	Wesleyan Methodists				*0.0*	
	Wesleyan Methodists	71	17157	19580	*15.2*	
	Primitive Methodists	32	4650	6088	*4.7*	
	Bible Christians	13	1088	1101	*0.9*	
	Wesleyan Reformers	5	1118	1099	*0.9*	
	Total Wesleyan Methodists	**121**	**24013**	**27868**	***21.6***	
	Calvinistic Methodists	25	7239	8457	*6.6*	
	Moravians	1	200	280	*0.2*	
	Roman Catholic	10	2890	3857	*3.0*	
	Latter Day Saints	6	835	1559	*1.2*	
	Undefined	4	780	544	*0.4*	
	Total	**490**	**120034**	**128794**	***100.0***	***72.7***

1848 Church of England[5]	Places of worship: 139 Language of services: 12 Welsh, 185 English, 1 mixed, 2 'alternate'

Registration County[1]	Denomination	Places of worship	Sittings[2]	Attendance[2]	*Attendance as % total*[3]	*Attendance Index*[4]
Glamorgan	Church of England	159	35764	25341	*13.6*	
Pop. 240,095	Independents	114	40549	57529	*31.0*	
	Baptists	100	31433	44425	*23.9*	
	Wesleyan Methodists					
	Wesleyan Methodists	65	12865	11934	*6.4*	
	Primitive Methodists	9	1382	1650	*0.9*	
	Bible Christians	1	140	120	*0.1*	
	Wesleyan Reformers	2	155	155	*0.1*	
	Total Wesleyan Methodists	**77**	**14542**	**13859**	***7.5***	
	Calvinistic Methodists	85	28574	34451	*18.5*	
	Lady Huntingdon's Connexion	1	650	1050	*0.6*	
	Society of Friends	3	594	99	*0.1*	
	Unitarians	7	1549	1036	*0.6*	
	Roman Catholic	3	1454	2700	*1.5*	
	Latter Day Saints	12	2685	3783	*2.0*	
	Undefined	6	1241	1318	*0.7*	
	Jews	2	112	218	*0.1*	
	Total	**569**	**159147**	**185809**	***100.0***	***77.4***
	1848 Church of England[5]	Places of worship: 150 Language of services: 75 Welsh, 101 English, 6 mixed, 25 'alternate'				
Carmarthen	Church of England	79	23563	19933	*22.5*	
Pop. 94,672	Independents	72	22610	29504	*33.3*	
	Baptists	50	12412	17410	*19.6*	
	Wesleyan Methodists	19	3757	3136	*3.5*	
	Calvinistic Methodists	61	15033	17522	*19.8*	
	Unitarians	3	416	400	*0.5*	
	Roman Catholic	1	120	145	*0.2*	
	Latter Day Saints	3	360	652	*0.7*	
	Total	**288**	**78271**	**88702**	***100.0***	***93.7***
	1848 Church of England[5]	Places of worship: 66 Language of services: 56 Welsh, 20 English, 15 mixed, 1 'alternate'				
Pembroke	Church of England	136	25987	18303	*27.1*	
Pop. 84,472	Independents	59	14973	16393	*24.3*	
	Baptists	50	14060	17021	*25.2*	
	Wesleyan Methodists					
	Wesleyan Methodists	29	6909	7194	*10.7*	
	Primitive Methodists	6	725	800	*1.2*	
	Total Wesleyan Methodists	**35**	**7634**	**7994**	***11.8***	
	Calvinistic Methodists	27	5841	6808	*10.1*	
	Society of Friends	1	60	5	*0.0*	
	Unitarians	1	80	76	*0.1*	
	Roman Catholic	2	214	210	*0.3*	
	Latter Day Saints	1	50	110	*0.2*	
	Brethren	1	200	263	*0.4*	
	Undefined	4	339	346	*0.5*	
	Total	**317**	**69438**	**67529**	***100.0***	***79.9***
	1848 Church of England[5]	Places of worship: 132 Language of services: 29 Welsh, 101 English, 26 mixed, 2 'alternate'				
Cardigan	Church of England	110	24344	18845	*18.4*	
Pop. 97,614	Independents	71	21890	22177	*21.7*	
	Baptists	48	12573	16785	*16.4*	
	Wesleyan Methodists					
	Wesleyan Methodists	20	4006	4223	*4.1*	
	Primitive Methodists	1	212	211	*0.2*	
	Wesleyan Association	1	258	222	*0.2*	
	Total Wesleyan Methodists	**22**	**4476**	**4656**	***4.5***	
	Calvinistic Methodists	82	23795	37950	*37.1*	
	Unitarians	14	2975	1825	*1.8*	
	Latter Day Saints	2	90	106	*0.1*	
	Total	**349**	**90143**	**102344**	***100.0***	***104.8***
	1848 Church of England[5]	Places of worship: 96 Language of services: 95 Welsh, 11 English, 10 mixed				

Registration County[1]	Denomination	Places of worship	Sittings[2]	Attendance[2]	*Attendance as % total*[3]	*Attendance Index*[4]
Brecon	Church of England	99	18192	12041	*23.8*	
Pop. 59,178	Independents	46	10993	15167	*30.0*	
	Baptists	36	9015	9618	*19.0*	
	Wesleyan Methodists					
	Wesleyan Methodists	23	3840	4187	*8.3*	
	Primitive Methodists	11	1559	1503	*3.0*	
	Total Wesleyan Methodists	**34**	**5399**	**5690**	***11.2***	
	Calvinistic Methodists	39	7152	7320	*14.5*	
	Society of Friends	1	40	3	*0.0*	
	Roman Catholic	1	150	242	*0.5*	
	Latter Day Saints	1	18	18	*0.0*	
	Undefined	2	304	524	*1.0*	
	Total	**259**	**51263**	**50623**	***100.0***	***85.5***

1848 Church of England[5] Places of worship: 89
Language of services: 38 Welsh, 56 English, 2 mixed, 13 'alternate'

Registration County[1]	Denomination	Places of worship	Sittings[2]	Attendance[2]	*Attendance as % total*[3]	*Attendance Index*[4]
Radnor	Church of England	59	13238	6874	*43.4*	
Pop. 31,425	Independents	11	2102	1969	*12.4*	
	Baptists	17	3436	2799	*17.7*	
	Wesleyan Methodists					
	Wesleyan Methodists	16	1897	1417	*8.9*	
	Primitive Methodists	23	1823	1647	*10.4*	
	Total Wesleyan Methodists	**39**	**3720**	**3064**	***19.3***	
	Calvinistic Methodists	11	1451	1107	*7.0*	
	Society of Friends	2	36	30	*0.2*	
	Total	**139**	**23983**	**15843**	***100.0***	***50.4***

1848 Church of England[5] Places of worship: 28
Language of services: 0 Welsh, 25 English, 4 mixed

Registration County[1]	Denomination	Places of worship	Sittings[2]	Attendance[2]	*Attendance as % total*[3]	*Attendance Index*[4]
Montgomery	Church of England	66	22382	14257	*23.9*	
Pop. 77,142	Independents	58	10369	9890	*16.6*	
	Baptists	26	4227	4609	*7.7*	
	Wesleyan Methodists					
	Wesleyan Methodists	78	11906	13213	*22.2*	
	Primitive Methodists	23	1782	1112	*1.9*	
	Wesleyan Association	1	57	105	*0.2*	
	Total Wesleyan Methodists	**102**	**13745**	**14430**	***24.2***	
	Calvinistic Methodists	89	13145	15551	*26.1*	
	Latter Day Saints	1	35	65	*0.1*	
	Undefined	4	529	845	*1.4*	
	Total	**346**	**64432**	**59647**	***100.0***	***77.3***

1848 Church of England[5] Places of worship: 55
Language of services: 56 Welsh, 48 English, 2 'alternate'

Registration County[1]	Denomination	Places of worship	Sittings[2]	Attendance[2]	*Attendance as % total*[3]	*Attendance Index*[4]
Flint	Church of England	22	10660	9235	*24.2*	
Pop. 41,047	Independents	21	4933	5032	*13.2*	
	Baptists	11	1614	2577	*6.7*	
	Wesleyan Methodists					
	Wesleyan Methodists	31	6899	8450	*22.1*	
	Methodists New Connexion	4	531	577	*1.5*	
	Primitive Methodists	2	281	326	*0.9*	
	Wesleyan Reformers	1	470	374	*1.0*	
	Total Wesleyan Methodists	**38**	**8181**	**9727**	***25.5***	
	Calvinistic Methodists	32	6675	10008	*26.2*	
	Roman Catholic	2	340	624	*1.6*	
	Latter Day Saints	1	16	28	*0.1*	
	Undefined	2	324	979	*2.6*	
	Total	**129**	**32743**	**38210**	***100.0***	***93.1***

1848 Church of England[5] Places of worship: 20
Language of services: 25 Welsh, 16 English, 1 mixed, 1 'alternate'

Registration County[1]	Denomination	Places of worship	Sittings[2]	Attendance[2]	*Attendance as % total*[3]	*Attendance Index*[4]
Denbigh	Church of England	76	28608	18013	*22.3*	
Pop. 96,915	Independents	49	9072	9361	*11.6*	
	Baptists	31	6253	9562	*11.9*	
	Wesleyan Methodists					
	Wesleyan Methodists	49	9411	10808	*13.4*	
	Methodist New Connexion	6	889	894	*1.1*	
	Primitive Methodists	11	1026	746	*0.9*	
	Wesleyan Association	7	811	1105	*1.4*	
	Total Wesleyan Methodists	**73**	**12137**	**13553**	***16.8***	
	Calvinistic Methodists	98	20998	28170	*34.9*	
	Society of Friends	1	60	8	*0.0*	
	Unitarians	2	710	475	*0.6*	
	Roman Catholic	2	345	472	*0.6*	
	Latter Day Saints	3	428	242	*0.3*	
	Undefined	6	1107	809	*1.0*	
	Total	**341**	**79718**	**80665**	***100.0***	***83.2***

1848 Church of England[5]	Places of worship: 65 Language of services: 93 Welsh, 39 English, 2 mixed, 2 'alternate'

Registration County	Denomination	Places of worship	Sittings	Attendance	Attendance as % total	Attendance Index
Merioneth	Church of England	50	12208	4858	*9.9*	
Pop. 51,307	Independents	56	8944	9646	*19.7*	
	Baptists	26	3192	5572	*11.4*	
	Wesleyan Methodists					
	Wesleyan Methodists	39	5937	5481	*11.2*	
	Wesleyan Association	1	60	130	*0.3*	
	Total Wesleyan Methodists	**40**	**5997**	**5611**	***11.4***	
	Calvinistic Methodists	93	19351	22893	*46.7*	
	Undefined	2	428	467	*1.0*	
	Total	**267**	**50120**	**49047**	***100.0***	***95.6***

1848 Church of England[5]	Places of worship: 48 Language of services: 77 Welsh, 6 English, 1 'alternate'

Registration County	Denomination	Places of worship	Sittings	Attendance	Attendance as % total	Attendance Index
Caernarfon	Church of England	89	25183	12726	*13.4*	
Pop. 94,674	Independents	66	13122	17506	*18.5*	
	Baptists	34	4836	5512	*5.8*	
	Wesleyan Methodists	45	9207	10848	*11.4*	
	Calvinistic Methodists	113	33731	47007	*49.6*	
	Roman Catholic	1	200	173	*0.2*	
	Latter Day Saints	2	138	244	*0.3*	
	Undefined	2	734	727	*0.8*	
	Total	**352**	**87151**	**94743**	***100.0***	***100.1***

1848 Church of England[5]	Places of worship: 78 Language of services: 124 Welsh, 10 English

Registration County	Denomination	Places of worship	Sittings	Attendance	Attendance as % total	Attendance Index
Anglesey	Church of England	53	9111	4677	*12.7*	
Pop. 43,243	Independents	25	4606	5647	*15.4*	
	Baptists	15	3000	3720	*10.1*	
	Wesleyan Methodists	14	2506	3499	*9.5*	
	Calvinistic Methodists	52	13457	18586	*50.6*	
	Undefined	1	329	610	*1.7*	
	Total	**160**	**33009**	**36739**	***100.0***	***85.0***

1848 Church of England[5]	Places of worship: 50 Language of services: 64 Welsh, 5 English

Source: Census of Great Britain, 1851. *Religious Worship in England and Wales. Report and Tables* (London, 1853). *Churches and Chapels (Wales). Returns of the numbers of Services performed in each Church and Chapel in the Dioceses of St Asaph, Bangor, St David's and Llandaff, for Three Months ending the 31st of December 1848* (PP 1850 (4) XLII) as given in Ieuan Gwynedd Jones and David Williams (eds.), *The Religious Census of 1851. A Calendar of the Returns relating to Wales, Volume I, South Wales* (Cardiff, 1976); Ieuan Gwynedd Jones (ed.), *The Religious Census of 1851. A Calendar of the Returns relating to Wales, Volume II, North Wales* (Cardiff, 1981).

1. Registration counties as constituted in 1851. See Appendix I and maps for details of constituent parishes.
2. Estimates for missing returns have been included as follows: if sittings not given, the figure for maximum attendance has been used if possible; if sittings are given, but not attendance, then a figure in the same proportion as others in the same denomination is used; if neither sittings nor attendance is given, the average of others in the same denomination in the district is used.
3. This column is given as a guide to enable comparison of the strengths of the various denominations in different areas.
4. This figure, an Index of Attendance, has been calculated by expressing the sum of attendances at all three Sunday services as a percentage of the total population to give a measure of religiosity. As explained in the introduction, this figure can be greater than 100 if sufficient people attend more than one service.
5. These figures are the number of regular weekly services during October–December 1848 for which the language used is clearly defined. Additional information is given as follows:

MONMOUTHSHIRE
Abergavenny — Welsh monthly at Llantilio Pertholey, Welsh in summer at Llanover.
Newport — Welsh 'occasionally' at St Bride's Wentlloog.

GLAMORGAN
Cardiff — Welsh 'occasionally' at Cadoxton-juxta-Barry.
Bridgend — 'Occasional' Welsh at Pen-llin, Welsh fortnightly at Wick, 1 Welsh and 3 English monthly at Tythegston.
Swansea — Extra English in summer at Oystermouth.

CARMARTHENSHIRE
Llanelli — Extra Welsh in summer at Llanedi.
Carmarthen — Welsh fortnightly at Tre-lech a'r Betws, English monthly at Llanarthne, Llandyfaelog, Abergwili. Welsh once a year at Laugharne with Llansadyrnin.

PEMBROKESHIRE
Haverfordwest — Welsh fortnightly at Hayscastle and Letterston.

CARDIGANSHIRE
Cardigan — Welsh fortnightly at Nevern (Pemb), Llantood (Pemb), Monington (Pemb).
Aberaeron — Extra Welsh fortnightly at Llanfihangel Ystrad.
Aberystwyth — English fortnightly at Llanafan, English monthly at Llanilar.
Tregaron — Extra Welsh fortnightly at Caron-is-clawdd (Tregaron).

BRECONSHIRE
Builth — English monthly at Gwenddwr.
Brecon — Extra Welsh fortnightly at Llanfilo, extra 'alternate' in summer at Llanddeti, Llansanffraid, Llangasty-Tal-y-Llyn.
Crickhowell — Welsh monthly at Llanfihangel Cwm-du, extra 'alternate' in summer at Llangynidr, Llanbedr.

MONTGOMERYSHIRE
Llanfyllin — Welsh fortnightly at Llangedwyn (Denb).

FLINTSHIRE
Holywell — English fortnightly at Caerwys, Ysgeifiog. English sermon fortnightly at Nannerch.

DENBIGHSHIRE
Ruthin — English monthly at Llanrhaeadr-yng-Nghinmeirch.
St Asaph — English fortnightly at Diserth (Flint), English monthly at Betws-yn-Rhos.
Llanrwst — English monthly at Eglwys-bach.

MERIONETH
Corwen — English monthly at Betws Gwerful Goch.
Bala — English monthly at Llanfor.

CAERNARFONSHIRE
Pwllheli — Extra Welsh monthly at Nefyn.
Caernarfon — Extra summer Welsh at Llandwrog.
Bangor — Extra summer Welsh at Llansadyrnin (Angl), summer English at Llan-faes (Angl), Llandygái.

ANGLESEY
Anglesey — Welsh monthly at Rhosbeirio, Welsh in summer at Rhodogeidio.

Religion 1.2 Religious Census, 1851. Number of places of worship, sittings and total attendants, by denomination. Registration Districts

Registration District[1]	Denomination	Places of worship	Sittings[2]	Attendance[2]	*Attendance as % total[3]*	*Attendance Index[4]*
MONMOUTHSHIRE						
Chepstow	Church of England	37	7324	5866	*59.9*	
Pop. 19,057	Independents	4	650	269	*2.7*	
	Baptists	7	891	1010	*10.3*	
	Moravians	1	200	280	*2.9*	
	Wesleyan Methodists	11	1557	1106	*11.3*	
	Primitive Methodists	1	100	300	*3.1*	
	Bible Christians	6	429	657	*6.7*	
	Total Wesleyan Methodists	**18**	**2086**	**2063**	***21.1***	
	Calvinistic Methodists	1	100	69	*0.7*	
	Roman Catholic	2	260	230	*2.4*	
	Total	**70**	**11511**	**9787**	***100.0***	***51.4***

1848 Church of England[5] Places of worship: 26
Language of services: 0 Welsh, 35 English (excl. Lydney)

Registration District[1]	Denomination	Places of worship	Sittings[2]	Attendance[2]	*Attendance as % total[3]*	*Attendance Index[4]*
Monmouth	Church of England	47	11421	9895	*54.9*	
Pop. 27,379	Independents	3	977	861	*4.8*	
	Baptists	16	2517	3134	*17.4*	
	Wesleyan Methodists	14	2146	1640	*9.1*	
	Primitive Methodists	14	1216	1745	*9.7*	
	Bible Christians	4	245	190	*1.1*	
	Wesleyan Reformers	2	402	250	*1.4*	
	Total Wesleyan Methodists	**34**	**4009**	**3825**	***21.2***	
	Roman Catholic	3	420	323	*1.8*	
	Total	**103**	**19344**	**18038**	***100.0***	***65.9***

1848 Church of England[5] Places of worship: 26
Language of services: 0 Welsh, 38 English (excl. Coleford)

Registration District[1]	Denomination	Places of worship	Sittings[2]	Attendance[2]	*Attendance as % total[3]*	*Attendance Index[4]*
Abergavenny	Church of England	34	9182	8922	*18.4*	
Pop. 59,229	Independents	13	5904	8309	*17.1*	
	Baptists	30	12811	14502	*29.9*	
	Wesleyan Methodists	16	5886	6952	*14.3*	
	Primitive Methodists	11	2194	2374	*4.9*	
	Total Wesleyan Methodists	**27**	**8080**	**9326**	***19.2***	
	Calvinistic Methodists	13	5111	6086	*12.5*	
	Undefined	1	200	358	*0.7*	
	Roman Catholic	2	510	484	*1.0*	
	Latter Day Saints	4	135	539	*1.1*	
	Total	**124**	**41933**	**48526**	***100.0***	***81.9***

1848 Church of England[5] Places of worship: 32
Language of services: 7 Welsh, 45 English

Registration District[1]	Denomination	Places of worship	Sittings[2]	Attendance[2]	*Attendance as % total[3]*	*Attendance Index[4]*
Pontypool	Church of England	28	6347	5772	*23.7*	
Pop. 27,993	Independents	12	2299	2989	*12.3*	
	Baptists	16	5921	6722	*27.6*	
	Wesleyan Methodists	15	4304	5943	*24.4*	
	Primitive Methodists	4	840	1331	*5.5*	
	Bible Christians	1	100	61	*0.3*	
	Total Wesleyan Methodists	**20**	**5244**	**7335**	***30.1***	
	Calvinistic Methodists	3	635	770	*3.2*	
	Undefined	1	120	128	*0.5*	
	Roman Catholic	2	400	620	*2.5*	
	Total	**82**	**20966**	**24336**	***100.0***	***86.9***

1848 Church of England[5] Places of worship: 22
Language of services: 2 Welsh, 27 English, 1 mixed

Registration District[1]	Denomination	Places of worship	Sittings[2]	Attendance[2]	*Attendance as % total[3]*	*Attendance Index[4]*
Newport	Church of England	36	6232	3707	*13.2*	
Pop. 43,472	Independents	20	4789	5803	*20.6*	
	Baptists	20	6812	8468	*30.1*	
	Wesleyan Methodists	15	3264	3939	*14.0*	
	Primitive Methodists	2	300	338	*1.2*	
	Bible Christians	2	314	193	*0.7*	
	Wesleyan Reformers	3	716	849	*3.0*	
	Total Wesleyan Methodists	**22**	**4594**	**5319**	***18.9***	
	Calvinistic Methodists	8	1393	1532	*5.5*	
	Undefined	2	460	58	*0.2*	
	Roman Catholic	1	1300	2200	*7.8*	
	Latter Day Saints	2	700	1020	*3.6*	
	Total	**111**	**26280**	**28107**	***100.0***	***64.7***

1848 Church of England[5]	Places of worship: 33 Language of services: 3 Welsh, 40 English, 2 'alternate'

GLAMORGAN

Registration District[1]	Denomination	Places of worship	Sittings[2]	Attendance[2]	*Attendance as % total[3]*	*Attendance Index[4]*
Cardiff	Church of England	50	9293	5575	*17.0*	
Pop. 46,491	Independents	19	5147	5087	*15.6*	
	Baptists	24	6308	7998	*24.5*	
	Society of Friends	1	200	8	*0.0*	
	Wesleyan Methodists	18	3058	3796	*11.6*	
	Calvinistic Methodists	25	6172	8146	*24.9*	
	Undefined	1	60	140	*0.4*	
	Roman Catholic	1	942	1450	*4.4*	
	Latter Day Saints	1	250	500	*1.5*	
	Total	**140**	**31430**	**32700**	***100.0***	***70.3***

1848 Church of England[5]	Places of worship: 44 Language of services: 21 Welsh, 28 English, 13 'alternate'

Registration District[1]	Denomination	Places of worship	Sittings[2]	Attendance[2]	*Attendance as % total[3]*	*Attendance Index[4]*
Merthyr Tydfil	Church of England	17	4894	4162	*6.5*	
Pop. 76,804	Independents	26	10306	18955	*29.8*	
	Baptists	30	13128	23006	*36.1*	
	Unitarians	2	461	467	*0.7*	
	Wesleyan Methodists	16	4225	3379	*5.3*	
	Primitive Methodists	4	702	720	*1.1*	
	Wesleyan Reformers	2	155	155	*0.2*	
	Total Wesleyan Methodists	**22**	**5082**	**4254**	**6.7**	
	Calvinistic Methodists	15	6936	8548	*13.4*	
	Undefined	1	305	688	*1.1*	
	Roman Catholic	1	300	750	*1.2*	
	Latter Day Saints	7	2139	2798	*4.4*	
	Jews	1	40	78	*0.1*	
	Total	**122**	**43591**	**63706**	***100.0***	***82.9***

1848 Church of England[5]	Places of worship: 14 Language of services: 15 Welsh, 10 English, 1 'alternate'

Registration District[1]	Denomination	Places of worship	Sittings[2]	Attendance[2]	*Attendance as % total[3]*	*Attendance Index[4]*
Bridgend	Church of England	40	5510	3661	*18.8*	
Pop. 23,422	Independents	17	5041	5524	*28.4*	
	Baptists	14	3036	3792	*19.5*	
	Unitarians	1	40	9	*0.0*	
	Wesleyan Methodists	11	1860	1506	*7.7*	
	Calvinistic Methodists	15	4619	4975	*25.6*	
	Total	**98**	**20106**	**19467**	***100.0***	***83.1***

1848 Church of England[5]	Places of worship: 46 Language of services: 19 Welsh, 28 English, 1 mixed, 9 'alternate'

Registration District[1]	Denomination	Places of worship	Sittings[2]	Attendance[2]	*Attendance as % total[3]*	*Attendance Index[4]*
Neath	Church of England	25	6255	4839	*13.6*	
Pop. 46,471	Independents	27	10291	15831	*44.5*	
	Baptists	17	4325	4767	*13.4*	
	Society of Friends	1	154	56	*0.2*	
	Unitarians	2	148	218	*0.6*	
	Wesleyan Methodists	6	1255	904	*2.5*	
	Primitive Methodists	1	60	140	*0.4*	
	Bible Christians	1	140	120	*0.3*	
	Total Wesleyan Methodists	**8**	**1455**	**1164**	**3.3**	
	Calvinistic Methodists	17	5892	8538	*24.0*	
	Latter Day Saints	3	96	165	*0.5*	
	Total	**100**	**28616**	**35578**	***100.0***	***76.6***

1848 Church of England[5]	Places of worship: 22
	Language of services: 14 Welsh, 12 English, 4 mixed, 2 'alternate'

Registration District	Denomination	Places of worship	Sittings	Attendance	*Attendance as % total*	*Attendance Index*
Swansea	Church of England	27	9812	7104	*20.7*	
Pop. 46,907	Independents	25	9764	12132	*35.3*	
	Baptists	15	4636	4862	*14.2*	
	Society of Friends	1	240	35	*0.1*	
	Unitarians	2	900	342	*1.0*	
	Wesleyan Methodists	14	2467	2349	*6.8*	
	Primitive Methodists	4	620	790	*2.3*	
	Total Wesleyan Methodists	**18**	**3087**	**3139**	***9.1***	
	Calvinistic Methodists	13	4955	4244	*12.4*	
	Lady Huntingdon's Connexion	1	650	1050	*3.1*	
	Undefined	4	876	490	*1.4*	
	Roman Catholic	1	212	500	*1.5*	
	Latter Day Saints	1	200	320	*0.9*	
	Jews	1	72	140[6]	*0.4*	
	Total	**109**	**35404**	**34358**	***100.0***	***73.2***

1848 Church of England[5]	Places of worship: 24
	Language of services: 6 Welsh, 23 English, 1 mixed

CARMARTHENSHIRE

Registration District	Denomination	Places of worship	Sittings	Attendance	*Attendance as % total*	*Attendance Index*
Llanelli	Church of England	11	4020	5125	*22.2*	
Pop. 23,507	Independents	13	4719	6328	*27.5*	
	Baptists	14	4187	7015	*30.4*	
	Wesleyan Methodists	5	1005	887	*3.8*	
	Calvinistic Methodists	7	2134	3259	*14.1*	
	Latter Day Saints	1	160	436	*1.9*	
	Total	**51**	**16225**	**23050**	***100.0***	***98.1***

1848 Church of England[5]	Places of worship: 9
	Language of services: 10 Welsh, 9 English

Registration District	Denomination	Places of worship	Sittings	Attendance	*Attendance as % total*	*Attendance Index*
Llandovery	Church of England	15	4069	2992	*21.6*	
Pop. 15,055	Independents	15	4686	5708	*41.1*	
	Baptists	8	1595	1409	*10.2*	
	Wesleyan Methodists	2	275	236	*1.7*	
	Calvinistic Methodists	12	3604	3528	*25.4*	
	Total	**52**	**14229**	**13873**	***100.0***	***92.1***

1848 Church of England[5]	Places of worship: 13
	Language of services: 12 Welsh, 2 English, 2 mixed

Registration District[1]	Denomination	Places of worship	Sittings[2]	Attendance[2]	*Attendance as % total[3]*	*Attendance Index[4]*
Llandeilo Fawr	Church of England	18	5780	4013	*23.8*	
Pop. 17,968	Independents	12[7]	3991	5339	*31.7*	
	Baptists	11	1904	2997	*17.8*	
	Unitarians	1	100	50	*0.3*	
	Wesleyan Methodists	6	988	930	*5.5*	
	Calvinistic Methodists	13	2963	3475	*20.6*	
	Latter Day Saints	1	100	56	*0.3*	
	Total	**62[7]**	**15826**	**16860**	***100.0***	***93.8***

1848 Church of England[5]	Places of worship: 14 Language of services: 12 Welsh, 2 English, 3 mixed, 1 'alternate'

Registration District[1]	Denomination	Places of worship	Sittings[2]	Attendance[2]	*Attendance as % total[3]*	*Attendance Index[4]*
Carmarthen	Church of England	35	9694	7803	*22.3*	
Pop. 38,142	Independents	32	9214	12129	*34.7*	
	Baptists	17	4726	5989	*17.2*	
	Unitarians	2	316	350	*1.0*	
	Wesleyan Methodists	6	1489	1083	*3.1*	
	Calvinistic Methodists	29	6332	7260	*20.8*	
	Roman Catholic	1	120	145	*0.4*	
	Latter Day Saints	1	100	160	*0.5*	
	Total	**123**	**31991**	**34919**	***100.0***	***91.5***

1848 Church of England[5]	Places of worship: 30 Language of services: 21 Welsh, 7 English, 10 mixed

PEMBROKESHIRE

Registration District[1]	Denomination	Places of worship	Sittings[2]	Attendance[2]	*Attendance as % total[3]*	*Attendance Index[4]*
Narberth	Church of England	41	7204	4738	*27.2*	
Pop. 22,130	Independents	23	6385	6145	*35.3*	
	Baptists	13	3700	4289	*24.6*	
	Unitarians	1	80	76	*0.4*	
	Wesleyan Methodists	4	541	732	*4.2*	
	Primitive Methodists	2	320	350	*2.0*	
	Total Wesleyan Methodists	**6**	**861**	**1082**	***6.2***	
	Calvinistic Methodists	6	967	1074	*6.2*	
	Total	**90**	**19197**	**17404**	***100.0***	***78.6***

1848 Church of England[5]	Places of worship: 41 Language of services: 13 Welsh, 22 English, 9 mixed

Registration District[1]	Denomination	Places of worship	Sittings[2]	Attendance[2]	*Attendance as % total[3]*	*Attendance Index[4]*
Pembroke	Church of England	28	8077	7162	*38.3*	
Pop. 22,960	Independents	10	2212	2642	*14.1*	
	Baptists	11	3106	3484	*18.7*	
	Wesleyan Methodists	8	2451	2973	*15.9*	
	Primitive Methodists	3	305	360	*1.9*	
	Total Wesleyan Methodists	**11**	**2756**	**3333**	***17.8***	
	Calvinistic Methodists	7	1353	1750	*9.4*	
	Undefined	3	250	168	*0.9*	
	Roman Catholic	1	130	140	*0.7*	
	Total	**71**	**17884**	**18679**	***100.0***	***81.4***

1848 Church of England[5]	Places of worship: 27 Language of services: 0 Welsh, 36 English, 2 mixed

Registration District[1]	Denomination	Places of worship	Sittings[2]	Attendance[2]	*Attendance as % total*[3]	*Attendance Index*[4]
Haverfordwest Pop. 39,382	Church of England	67	10706	6403	*20.4*	
	Independents	26	6376	7606	*24.2*	
	Baptists	26	7254	9248	*29.4*	
	Society of Friends	1	60	5	*0.0*	
	Wesleyan Methodists	17	3917	3489	*11.1*	
	Primitive Methodists	1	100	90	*0.3*	
	Total Wesleyan Methodists	**18**	**4017**	**3579**	***11.4***	
	Calvinistic Methodists	14	3521	3984	*12.7*	
	Brethren	1	200	263	*0.8*	
	Undefined	1	89	178	*0.6*	
	Roman Catholic	1	84	70	*0.2*	
	Latter Day Saints	1	50	110	*0.3*	
	Total	**156**	**32357**	**31446**	***100.0***	***79.8***

1848 Church of England[5] Places of worship: 64
Language of services: 16 Welsh, 43 English, 15 mixed, 2 'alternate'

CARDIGANSHIRE

Registration District[1]	Denomination	Places of worship	Sittings[2]	Attendance[2]	*Attendance as % total*[3]	*Attendance Index*[4]
Cardigan Pop. 20,186	Church of England	27	4723	4305	*19.2*	
	Independents	17	5251	4973	*22.2*	
	Baptists	20	6659	8377	*37.4*	
	Wesleyan Methodists	1	196	116	*0.5*	
	Calvinistic Methodists	13	3456	4640	*20.7*	
	Total	**78**	**20285**	**22411**	***100.0***	***111.0***

1848 Church of England[5] Places of worship: 28
Language of services: 21 Welsh, 7 English, 3 mixed

Registration District[1]	Denomination	Places of worship	Sittings[2]	Attendance[2]	*Attendance as % total*[3]	*Attendance Index*[4]
Newcastle Emlyn Pop. 20,173	Church of England	22	4142	3227	*15.6*	
	Independents	23	7378	7551	*36.5*	
	Baptists	10	2089	3522	*17.0*	
	Unitarians	5	1002	710	*3.4*	
	Wesleyan Methodists	3	561	515	*2.5*	
	Calvinistic Methodists	13	3170	5093	*24.6*	
	Latter Day Saints	1	60	76	*0.4*	
	Total	**77**	**18402**	**20694**	***100.0***	***102.6***

1848 Church of England[5] Places of worship: 18
Language of services: 18 Welsh, 1 English, 6 mixed

Registration District[1]	Denomination	Places of worship	Sittings[2]	Attendance[2]	*Attendance as % total*[3]	*Attendance Index*[4]
Lampeter Pop. 9,874	Church of England	15	2085	1445	*20.0*	
	Independents	13	3697	3179	*44.0*	
	Baptists	5	1010	926	*12.8*	
	Unitarians	5	1175	600	*8.3*	
	Wesleyan Methodists	2	305	238	*3.3*	
	Calvinistic Methodists	3	730	799	*11.1*	
	Latter Day Saints	1	30	30	*0.4*	
	Total	**44**	**9032**	**7217**	***100.0***	***73.1***

1848 Church of England[5] Places of worship: 13
Language of services: 14 Welsh, 0 English

Registration District[1]	Denomination	Places of worship	Sittings[2]	Attendance[2]	*Attendance as % total*[3]	*Attendance Index*[4]
Aberaeron Pop. 13,224	Church of England	16	3737	2734	*19.9*	
	Independents	11	3568	3970	*28.9*	
	Baptists	2	360	647	*4.7*	
	Unitarians	4	798	515	*3.8*	
	Wesleyan Methodists	3	365	258	*1.9*	
	Calvinistic Methodists	11	3260	5594	*40.8*	
	Total	**47**	**12088**	**13718**	***100.0***	***103.7***

1848 Church of England[5] Places of worship: 15
Language of services: 14 Welsh, 1 English, 1 mixed

Registration District[1]	Denomination	Places of worship	Sittings[2]	Attendance[2]	*Attendance as % total[3]*	*Attendance Index[4]*
Aberystwyth	Church of England	20	7638	5363	*18.2*	
Pop. 23,753	Independents	7	1996	2504	*8.5*	
	Baptists	9	2095	2363	*8.0*	
	Wesleyan Methodists	10	2519	3011	*10.2*	
	Primitive Methodists	1	212	211	*0.7*	
	Wesleyan Association	1	258	222	*0.8*	
	Total Wesleyan Methodists	**12**	**2989**	**3444**	***11.7***	
	Calvinistic Methodists	27	8605	15831	*53.7*	
	Total	**75**	**23323**	**29505**	***100.0***	***124.2***
	1848 Church of England[5]	Places of worship: 14 Language of services: 20 Welsh, 2 English				
Tregaron	Church of England	10	2019	1771	*20.1*	
Pop. 10,404	Baptists	2	360	950	*10.8*	
	Wesleyan Methodists	1	60	85	*1.0*	
	Calvinistic Methodists	15	4574	5993	*68.1*	
	Total	**28**	**7013**	**8799**	***100.0***	***84.6***
	1848 Church of England[5]	Places of worship: 8 Language of services: 8 Welsh, 0 English				
BRECONSHIRE						
Builth	Church of England	26	3109	1303	*25.7*	
Pop. 8,345	Independents	12	1584	1862	*36.7*	
	Baptists	5	830	739	*14.6*	
	Primitive Methodists	1	20	20	*0.4*	
	Calvinistic Methodists	5	1282	1150	*22.7*	
	Total	**49**	**6825**	**5074**	***100.0***	***60.8***
	1848 Church of England[5]	Places of worship: 26 Language of services: 10 Welsh, 16 English, 1 mixed				
Brecon	Church of England	41	6504	6081	*36.7*	
Pop. 18,174	Independents	14	3330	3898	*23.5*	
	Baptists	12	2411	2358	*14.2*	
	Wesleyan Methodists	5	815	852	*5.1*	
	Calvinistic Methodists	18	2780	3139	*18.9*	
	Roman Catholic	1	150	242	*1.5*	
	Total	**91**	**15990**	**16570**	***100.0***	***91.2***
	1848 Church of England[5]	Places of worship: 38 Language of services: 26 Welsh, 12 English, 9 'alternate'				
Crickhowell	Church of England	11	4339	2145	*9.8*	
Pop. 21,697	Independents	16	4981	8448	*38.6*	
	Baptists	12	4417	4835	*22.1*	
	Wesleyan Methodists	13	2291	2835	*13.0*	
	Primitive Methodists	5	1077	1112	*5.1*	
	Total Wesleyan Methodists	**18**	**3368**	**3947**	***18.1***	
	Calvinistic Methodists	7	1949	2016	*9.2*	
	Undefined	1	254	474	*2.2*	
	Total	**65**	**19308**	**21865**	***100.0***	***100.8***
	1848 Church of England[5]	Places of worship: 8 Language of services: 2 Welsh, 7 English, 3 'alternate'				

Registration District[1]	Denomination	Places of worship	Sittings[2]	Attendance[2]	*Attendance as % total[3]*	*Attendance Index[4]*
Hay	Church of England	21	4240	2512	*35.3*	
Pop. 10,962	Independents	4	1098	959	*13.5*	
	Baptists	7	1357	1686	*23.7*	
	Society of Friends	1	40	3	*0.0*	
	Wesleyan Methodists	5	734	500	*7.0*	
	Primitive Methodists	5	462	371	*5.2*	
	Total Wesleyan Methodists	**10**	**1196**	**871**	***12.2***	
	Calvinistic Methodists	9	1141	1015	*14.3*	
	Undefined	1	50	50	*0.7*	
	Latter Day Saints	1	18	18	*0.3*	
	Total	**54**	**9140**	**7114**	***100.0***	***64.9***

1848 Church of England[5] Places of worship: 17
Language of services: 0 Welsh, 21 English, 1 mixed, 1 'alternate'

RADNORSHIRE

Registration District	Denomination	Places of worship	Sittings	Attendance	*Attendance as % total*	*Attendance Index*
Presteigne	Church of England	33	6908	3746	*50.5*	
Pop. 15,149	Independents	4	642	388	*5.2*	
	Baptists	5	1357	1058	*14.3*	
	Society of Friends	2	36	30	*0.4*	
	Wesleyan Methodists	8	1199	707	*9.5*	
	Primitive Methodists	14	1262	917	*12.4*	
	Total Wesleyan Methodists	**22**	**2461**	**1624**	***21.9***	
	Calvinistic Methodists	7	848	578	*7.8*	
	Total	**73**	**12252**	**7424**	***100.0***	***49.0***

1848 Church of England[5] Places of worship: 9
Language of services: 0 Welsh, 9 English

Registration District	Denomination	Places of worship	Sittings	Attendance	*Attendance as % total*	*Attendance Index*
Knighton	Church of England	15	3724	1955	*55.8*	
Pop. 9,480	Independents	2	70	37	*1.1*	
	Baptists	4	480	316	*9.0*	
	Wesleyan Methodists	3	369	465	*13.3*	
	Primitive Methodists	9	561	730	*20.8*	
	Total Wesleyan Methodists	**12**	**930**	**1195**	***34.1***	
	Total	**33**	**5204**	**3503**	***100.0***	***37.0***

1848 Church of England[5] Places of worship: 9
Language of services: 0 Welsh, 9 English

Registration District	Denomination	Places of worship	Sittings	Attendance	*Attendance as % total*	*Attendance Index*
Rhayader	Church of England	11	2606	1173	*23.9*	
Pop. 6,796	Independents	5	1390	1544	*31.4*	
	Baptists	8	1599	1425	*29.0*	
	Wesleyan Methodists	5	329	245	*5.0*	
	Calvinistic Methodists	4	603	529	*10.8*	
	Total	**33**	**6527**	**4916**	***100.0***	***72.3***

1848 Church of England[5] Places of worship: 10
Language of services: 0 Welsh, 7 English, 4 mixed

MONTGOMERYSHIRE

Registration District	Denomination	Places of worship	Sittings	Attendance	*Attendance as % total*	*Attendance Index*
Machynlleth	Church of England	10	4479	1937	*14.1*	
Pop. 12,116	Independents	16	3032	3353	*24.4*	
	Baptists	2	160	302	*2.2*	
	Wesleyan Methodists	13	2154	2803	*20.4*	
	Wesleyan Association	1	57	105	*0.8*	
	Total Wesleyan Methodists	**14**	**2211**	**2908**	***21.2***	
	Calvinistic Methodists	20	3625	4540	*33.1*	
	Undefined	3	429	626	*4.6*	
	Latter Day Saints	1	35	65	*0.5*	
	Total	**66**	**13971**	**13731**	***100.0***	***113.3***

1848 Church of England[5] Places of worship: 10
Language of services: 15 Welsh, 4 English

Registration District[1]	Denomination	Places of worship	Sittings[2]	Attendance[2]	*Attendance as % total[3]*	*Attendance Index[4]*
Newtown	Church of England	16	3772	2828	*18.7*	
Pop. 25,107	Independents	7	1693	1392	*9.2*	
	Baptists	15	3080	3260	*21.6*	
	Wesleyan Methodists	15	2756	2899	*19.2*	
	Primitive Methodists	1	600	80	*0.5*	
	Total Wesleyan Methodists	**16**	**3356**	**2979**	***19.7***	
	Calvinistic Methodists	23	4090	4667	*30.9*	
	Total	**77**	**15991**	**15126**	***100.0***	***60.2***
	1848 Church of England[5]	Places of worship: 18 Language of services: 15 Welsh, 16 English				
Montgomery	Church of England	20	8309	6511	*51.9*	
Pop. 20,381	Independents	10	1529	1288	*10.3*	
	Baptists	4	432	394	*3.1*	
	Wesleyan Methodists	14	1501	1527	*12.2*	
	Primitive Methodists	21	1112	962	*7.7*	
	Total Wesleyan Methodists	**35**	**2613**	**2489**	***19.8***	
	Calvinistic Methodists	17	1827	1874	*14.9*	
	Total	**86**	**14710**	**12556**	***100.0***	***61.6***
	1848 Church of England[5]	Places of worship: 7 Language of services: 1 Welsh, 13 English				
Llanfyllin	Church of England	20	5822	2981	*16.3*	
Pop. 19,538	Independents	25	4115	3857	*21.2*	
	Baptists	5	555	653	*3.6*	
	Wesleyan Methodists	36	5495	5984	*32.8*	
	Primitive Methodists	1	70	70	*0.4*	
	Total Wesleyan Methodists	**37**	**5565**	**6054**	***33.2***	
	Calvinistic Methodists	29	3603	4470	*24.5*	
	Undefined	1	100	219	*1.2*	
	Total	**117**	**19760**	**18234**	***100.0***	***93.3***
	1848 Church of England[5]	Places of worship: 20 Language of services: 25 Welsh, 15 English, 2 'alternate'				
FLINTSHIRE						
Holywell	Church of England	22	10660	9235	*24.2*	
Pop. 41,047	Independents	21	4933	5032	*13.2*	
	Baptists	11	1614	2577	*6.7*	
	Wesleyan Methodists	31	6899	8450	*22.1*	
	Methodist New Connexion	4	531	577	*1.5*	
	Primitive Methodists	2	281	326	*0.9*	
	Wesleyan Reformers	1	470	374	*1.0*	
	Total Wesleyan Methodists	**38**	**8181**	**9727**	***25.5***	
	Calvinistic Methodists	32	6675	10008	*26.2*	
	Undefined	2	324	979	*2.6*	
	Roman Catholic	2	340	624	*1.6*	
	Latter Day Saints	1	16	28	*0.1*	
	Total	**129**	**32743**	**38210**	***100.0***	***93.1***
	1848 Church of England[5]	Places of worship: 20 Language of services: 25 Welsh, 16 English, 1 mixed, 1 'alternate'				

Registration District[1]	Denomination	Places of worship	Sittings[2]	Attendance[2]	*Attendance as % total*[3]	*Attendance Index*[4]
DENBIGHSHIRE						
Wrexham	Church of England	21	12255	8376	*26.6*	
Pop. 42,295	Independents	19	3049	3348	*10.6*	
	Baptists	13	3392	6326	*20.1*	
	Unitarians	2	710	475	*1.5*	
	Wesleyan Methodists	19	3171	3930	*12.5*	
	Methodist New Connexion	6	889	894	*2.8*	
	Primitive Methodists	11	1026	746	*2.4*	
	Wesleyan Association	7	811	1105	*3.5*	
	Total Wesleyan Methodists	**43**	**5897**	**6675**	***21.2***	
	Calvinistic Methodists	25	4939	5695	*18.1*	
	Undefined	4	257	164	*0.5*	
	Roman Catholic	1	305	360	*1.1*	
	Latter Day Saints	1	68	111	*0.4*	
	Total	**129**	**30872**	**31530**	***100.0***	***74.5***
	1848 Church of England[5]	Places of worship: 14 Language of services: 6 Welsh, 21 English, 1 'alternate'				
Ruthin	Church of England	21	5148	3503	*23.6*	
Pop. 16,853	Independents	9	1583	1677	*11.3*	
	Baptists	4	795	1005	*6.8*	
	Society of Friends	1	60	8	*0.1*	
	Wesleyan Methodists	9	1652	1746	*11.7*	
	Calvinistic Methodists	25	5205	6422	*43.2*	
	Undefined	1	800	510[5]	*3.4*	
	Total	**70**	**15243**	**14871**	***100.0***	***88.2***
	1848 Church of England[5]	Places of worship: 19 Language of services: 40 Welsh, 4 English				
St Asaph	Church of England	19	7704	4648	*21.2*	
Pop. 25,288	Independents	13	2807	2398	*10.9*	
	Baptists	10	1466	1810	*8.3*	
	Wesleyan Methodists	15	3535	3658	*16.7*	
	Calvinistic Methodists	25	5841	9043	*41.2*	
	Undefined	1	50	135	*0.6*	
	Roman Catholic	1	40	112	*0.5*	
	Latter Day Saints	2	360	131	*0.6*	
	Total	**86**	**21803**	**21935**	***100.0***	***86.7***
	1848 Church of England[5]	Places of worship: 18 Language of services: 26 Welsh, 10 English, 2 mixed, 1 'alternate'				
Llanrwst	Church of England	15	3501	1486	*12.1*	
Pop. 12,479	Independents	8	1633	1938	*15.7*	
	Baptists	4	600	421	*3.4*	
	Wesleyan Methodists	6	1053	1474	*12.0*	
	Calvinistic Methodists	23	5013	7010	*56.9*	
	Total	**56**	**11800**	**12329**	***100.0***	***98.8***
	1848 Church of England[5]	Places of worship: 14 Language of services: 21 Welsh, 4 English				
MERIONETH						
Corwen	Church of England	12	2977	1553	*11.0*	
Pop. 15,418	Independents	9	1570	1646	*11.6*	
	Baptists	10	1190	3226	*22.8*	
	Wesleyan Methodists	17	2638	2184	*15.4*	
	Calvinistic Methodists	27	5188	5544	*39.2*	
	Total	**75**	**13563**	**14153**	***100.0***	***91.8***
	1848 Church of England[5]	Places of worship: 14 Language of services: 25 Welsh, 3 English, 1 'alternate'				

Registration District[1]	Denomination	Places of worship	Sittings[2]	Attendance[2]	*Attendance as % total[3]*	*Attendance Index[4]*
Bala	Church of England	7	1686	491	*7.8*	
Pop. 6,736	Independents	10	1419	1624	*25.8*	
	Baptists	1	132	57	*0.9*	
	Wesleyan Methodists	1	178	80	*1.3*	
	Calvinistic Methodists	18	2968	4037	*64.2*	
	Total	**37**	**6383**	**6289**	***100.0***	***93.4***
	1848 Church of England[5]	Places of worship: 6 Language of services: 11 Welsh, 2 English				
Dolgellau	Church of England	13	3175	1259	*9.6*	
Pop. 12,971	Independents	23	3394	3413	*26.0*	
	Baptists	3	543	612	*4.7*	
	Wesleyan Methodists	12	1819	2261	*17.2*	
	Wesleyan Association	1	60	130	*1.0*	
	Total Wesleyan Methodists	**13**	**1879**	**2391**	***18.2***	
	Calvinistic Methodists	26	4599	5205	*39.6*	
	Undefined	1	257	257	*2.0*	
	Total	**79**	**13847**	**13137**	***100.0***	***101.3***
	1848 Church of England[5]	Places of worship: 13 Language of services: 20 Welsh, 1 English				
Ffestiniog	Church of England	18	4370	1555	*10.1*	
Pop. 16,182	Independents	14	2561	2963	*19.2*	
	Baptists	12	1327	1677	*10.8*	
	Wesleyan Methodists	9	1302	956	*6.2*	
	Calvinistic Methodists	22	6596	8107	*52.4*	
	Undefined	1	171	210	*1.4*	
	Total	**76**	**16327**	**15468**	***100.0***	***95.6***
	1848 Church of England[5]	Places of worship: 15 Language of services: 21 Welsh, 0 English				

CAERNARFONSHIRE

Registration District[1]	Denomination	Places of worship	Sittings[2]	Attendance[2]	*Attendance as % total[3]*	*Attendance Index[4]*
Pwllheli	Church of England	30	7735	1865	*8.7*	
Pop. 21,788	Independents	20	3191	3405	*15.9*	
	Baptists	12	1603	1773	*8.3*	
	Wesleyan Methodists	9	1205	1941	*9.0*	
	Calvinistic Methodists	35	9132	12216	*56.9*	
	Undefined	1	444	267	*1.2*	
	Total	**107**	**23310**	**21467**	***100.0***	***98.5***
	1848 Church of England[5]	Places of worship: 29 Language of services: 42 Welsh, 2 English				
Caernarfon	Church of England	21	5797	2616	*9.4*	
Pop. 30,446	Independents	23	4453	5898	*21.3*	
	Baptists	8	1250	1158	*4.2*	
	Wesleyan Methodists	9	2159	1932	*7.0*	
	Calvinistic Methodists	36	11868	15996	*57.7*	
	Latter Day Saints	1	58	108	*0.4*	
	Total	**98**	**25585**	**27708**	***100.0***	***109.6***
	1848 Church of England[5]	Places of worship: 16 Language of services: 24 Welsh, 3 English				

Registration District[1]	Denomination	Places of worship	Sittings[2]	Attendance[2]	*Attendance as % total[3]*	*Attendance Index[4]*
Bangor	Church of England	24	7243	5954	*17.8*	
Pop. 30,810	Independents	16	4018	6331	*19.0*	
	Baptists	8	945	1527	*4.6*	
	Wesleyan Methodists	15	3907	4337	*13.0*	
	Calvinistic Methodists	24	9593	14923	*44.7*	
	Roman Catholic	1	200	173	*0.5*	
	Latter Day Saints	1	80	136	*0.4*	
	Total	**89**	**25986**	**33381**	***100.0***	***108.3***
	1848 Church of England[5]	Places of worship: 20	Language of services: 34 Welsh, 2 English			
Conwy	Church of England	14	4408	2291	*18.8*	
Pop. 11,630	Independents	7	1460	1872	*15.4*	
	Baptists	6	1038	1054	*8.6*	
	Wesleyan Methodists	12	1936	2638	*21.6*	
	Calvinistic Methodists	18	3138	3872	*31.8*	
	Undefined	1	290	460	*3.8*	
	Total	**58**	**12270**	**12187**	***100.0***	***104.8***
	1848 Church of England[5]	Places of worship: 13	Language of services: 24 Welsh, 3 English			
ANGLESEY						
Anglesey	Church of England	53	9111	4677	*12.7*	
Pop. 43,243	Independents	25	4606	5647	*15.4*	
	Baptists	15	3000	3720	*10.1*	
	Wesleyan Methodists	14	2506	3499	*9.5*	
	Calvinistic Methodists	52	13457	18586	*50.6*	
	Undefined	1	329	610	*1.7*	
	Total	**160**	**33009**	**36739**	***100.0***	***85.0***
	1848 Church of England[5]	Places of worship: 50	Language of services: 64 Welsh, 5 English			

Source: Census of Great Britain, 1851. *Religious Worship in England and Wales. Report and Tables* (London, 1853). *Churches and Chapels (Wales). Returns of the numbers of Services performed in each Church and Chapel in the Dioceses of St Asaph, Bangor, St David's and Llandaff, for Three Months ending the 31st of December 1848* (PP 1850 (4) XLII) as given in Ieuan Gwynedd Jones and David Williams (eds.), *The Religious Census of 1851. A Calendar of the Returns relating to Wales, Volume I, South Wales* (Cardiff, 1976); Ieuan Gwynedd Jones (ed.), *The Religious Census of 1851. A Calendar of the Returns relating to Wales, Volume II, North Wales* (Cardiff, 1981).

1 Registration counties as constituted in 1851. See Appendix I and maps for details of constituent parishes.

2 Estimates for missing returns have been included as follows: if sittings are not given, the figure for maximum attendance has been used if possible; if sittings are given, but not attendance, a figure in the same proportion as others in the same denomination is used; if neither sittings nor attendance is given, the average of others in the same denomination in the district is used.

3 This column is given as a guide to enable comparison of the strengths of the various denominations in different areas.

4 This figure, an Index of Attendance, has been calculated by expressing the sum of attendances at all three Sunday services as a percentage of the total population to give a measure of religiosity. As explained in the introduction, this figure can be greater than 100 if sufficient people attend more than one service.

5 These figures are the number of regular weekly services during October–December 1848 for which the language used is clearly defined. Additional information is given in Table 1.1, note 5.

6 This figure is a rough estimate only, based only on the number of sittings given and attendants at the Jewish synagogue at Merthyr Tydfil.

7 There is a discrepancy in the printed census tables. The sum of places of worship for the District of Llandeilo Fawr is 72, whereas the sum given is 62. Comparing the returns from individual chapels given in the *Calendar*, it seems likely that the number of Independent chapels should have been 12, as given here, not 22 as given in the Census tables.

Religion 1.3 Religious Census, 1851. Number of places of worship, sittings and total attendants. Calvinistic Methodists. England

Registration area Division	County	District	Chapels	Total Sittings	Attendance Morning	Afternoon	Evening	Total
Total England		*Welsh Calvinistic Methodists*	30	9223	4001	1821	5145	10967
		Calvinistic Methodists	19	5216	2762	417	2769	5948
		Total	**49**	**14439**	**6763**	**2238**	**7914**	**16915**
London		*Welsh Calvinistic Methodists*						
		Westminster	1	200	120	120	0	240
		Strand	1	500	280	0	130	410
		St Olave, Southwark	1	100	0	100	60	160
		Calvinistic Methodists						
		Marylebone	1	206	45	0	80	125
		East London	1	820	400	0	600	1000
		Shoreditch	1	822	533	0	429	962
South Midland		Daventry	1	14	9	10	0	19
		Peterborough	2	80	55	13	12	80
South Western	Wilts	Westbury	1	140	0	66	64	130
West Midland		*Welsh Calvinistic Methodists*						
	Salop	Shrewsbury	1	250	200	0	190	390
	Salop	Oswestry	2	390	149	150	146	445
		Wolverhampton	1	180	0	150	150	300
		Birmingham	1	32	130	0	0	130
		Calvinistic Methodists						
	Gloucs	Bristol	1	1150	702	0	725	1427
		Thornbury	1	n.g.	85	78	120	283
	Salop	Atcham	1	125	0	100	60	160
		Oswestry	7	1059	803	0	406	1209
North Western		*Welsh Calvinistic Methodists*						
	Ches	Runcorn	2	506	305	0	420	725
		Northwich	1	200	60	125	0	185
		Great Broughton	8	1362	487	326	647	1460
		Wirrall	2	512	0	266	251	517
	Lancs	Liverpool	4	2807	1717	242	2126	4085
		West Derby	2	1584	523	146	919	1588
		Ormskirk	2	500	0	146	50	196
		Wigan	1	100	30	50	56	136
		Calvinistic Methodists						
	Lancs	Salford	1	500	130	0	127	257
		Manchester	1	300	0	150	146	296

Source: Census of Great Britain, 1851. *Religious Worship in England and Wales. Report and Tables* (London, 1853).

Religion 2.1 Report of the Royal Commission on the Church of England and Other Religious Bodies in Wales and Monmouthshire, 1910. Number of places of worship, sittings, communicants, adherents, and total in Sunday schools, by denomination. Wales and Administrative Counties. 1905

	Denomination	Places of worship[1]	Sittings	Communicants/ members[2]	Adherents[3]	Total in Sunday Schools	*Communicants as % total*[4]	*Total communicants as % pop.*[5]
Wales	Church of England*	1835	452683	190546	–	172337	*25.6*	
Pop. 1,998,118	Independents	1196	444468	174897	159623	176942	*23.5*	
	Baptists	985	387717	142151	160569	154377	*19.1*	
	Wesleyan Methodists	708	198636	47405	92781	83264	*6.4*	
	Primitive Methodists	161	38063	8308	22834	19922	*1.1*	
	Calvinistic Methodists	1509	477867	170365	231925	210710	*22.9*	
	English Presbyterians	24	8174	2398	4010	3502	*0.3*	
	Society of Friends	6	1010	271	285	373	*0.0*	
	Unitarians	27	7444	1898	1686	1925	*0.3*	
	Roman Catholics	4	250	12	20	9	*0.0*	
	Jews	2	300	31	10	23	*0.0*	
	Other	137	28287	4894	10444	9769	*0.7*	
	Total	**6594**	**2044899**	**743176**	**684187**	**833153**	***100.0***	***37.2***
	* Language of Sunday services:[6] 975 Welsh, 1239 English, 220 bilingual							
Administrative Counties								
Monmouth	Church of England*	239	56621	22913	–	25083	*31.5*	
Pop. 299,156	Independents	87	35550	12097	21590	15624	*16.6*	
	Baptists	132	63770	21653	41447	30077	*29.8*	
	Wesleyan Methodists	100	31163	6690	16238	14583	*9.2*	
	Primitive Methodists	43	12354	3022	8295	7835	*4.2*	
	Calvinistic Methodists	56	24850	6158	16867	9419	*8.5*	
	Unitarians	1	110	0	100	0	*0.0*	
	Jews	1	150	0	0	0	*0.0*	
	Other	34	3900	217	1791	1135	*0.3*	
	Total	**693**	**228468**	**72750**	**106328**	**103756**	***100.0***	***24.3***
	* Language of Sunday services: Not given							
Glamorgan	Church of England*	423	125618	61196	–	71022	*23.1*	
Pop. 855,309	Independents	325	176061	73287	58733	76325	*27.6*	
	Baptists	306	161990	63845	61214	70468	*24.1*	
	Wesleyan Methodists	168	61360	13926	26918	29440	*5.3*	
	Primitive Methodists	44	12789	2600	7097	5962	*1.0*	
	Calvinistic Methodists	284	137588	44201	54212	58886	*16.7*	
	English Presbyterians	6	3830	1271	835	1282	*0.5*	
	Society of Friends	2	550	130	120	238	*0.0*	
	Unitarians	11	3464	478	871	631	*0.2*	
	Roman Catholics	2	200	0	0	0	*0.0*	
	Other	69	20700	4282	7396	7763	*1.6*	
	Total	**1640**	**704150**	**265216**	**217396**	**322017**	***100.0***	***31.0***
	* Language of Sunday services: (West Glamorgan only) 21 Welsh, 142 English, 15 bilingual							
Carmarthen	Church of England*	157	38343	18968	–	14252	*24.3*	
Pop. 141,068	Independents	173	61762	28813	8849	21603	*37.0*	
	Baptists	110	42331	17760	10256	14468	*22.8*	
	Wesleyan Methodists	21	5130	1006	862	1346	*1.3*	
	Calvinistic Methodists	102	34163	11286	7169	10318	*14.5*	
	Other	9	620	100	320	245	*0.1*	
	Total	**572**	**182349**	**77933**	**27456**	**62232**	***100.0***	***55.2***
	* Language of Sunday services: 131 Welsh, 72 English, 83 bilingual							

Administrative County	Denomination	Places of worship[1]	Sittings	Communicants/ members[2]	Adherents[3]	Total in Sunday Schools	*Communicants as % total*[4]	*Total communicants as % pop.*[5]
Pembroke	Church of England*	168	32080	11568	–	8222	*30.6*	
Pop. 88,101	Independents	78	24046	8792	6705	7943	*23.3*	
	Baptists	87	30503	12348	8078	9450	*32.7*	
	Wesleyan Methodists	26	6741	1321	2194	2224	*3.5*	
	Primitive Methodists	4	850	112	134	127	*0.3*	
	Calvinistic Methodists	50	12404	3559	2908	3945	*9.4*	
	Roman Catholics	1	0	0	0	0	*0.0*	
	Other	11	860	59	80	126	*0.2*	
	Total	**425**	**107484**	**37759**	**20099**	**32037**	***100.0***	***42.9***
	* Language of Sunday services: 34 Welsh, 197 English, 51 bilingual							
Cardigan	Church of England*	106	20731	8928	–	7285	*24.0*	
Pop. 58,386	Independents	66	23894	9402	3089	8582	*25.3*	
	Baptists	27	8462	2536	1113	2212	*6.8*	
	Wesleyan Methodists	22	6768	1625	697	1882	*4.4*	
	Calvinistic Methodists	145	37229	13338	7072	15321	*35.9*	
	Unitarians	14	3620	1325	635	1133	*3.6*	
	Total	**380**	**100704**	**37154**	**12606**	**36415**	***100.0***	***63.6***
	* Language of Sunday services: 125 Welsh, 30 English, 36 bilingual							
Brecon	Church of England*	103	19925	6937	–	5138	*31.1*	
Pop. 50,637	Independents	59	17418	6533	4780	6052	*29.2*	
	Baptists	42	12608	3695	3704	3626	*16.5*	
	Wesleyan Methodists	16	3692	715	934	1183	*3.2*	
	Primitive Methodists	3	980	261	670	553	*1.2*	
	Calvinistic Methodists	52	15553	4069	3956	4430	*18.2*	
	Unitarians	1	250	95	80	161	*0.4*	
	Jews	1	150	31	10	23	*0.1*	
	Other	1	200	0	60	0	*0.0*	
	Total	**278**	**70776**	**22336**	**14194**	**21166**	***100.0***	***44.1***
	* Language of Sunday services: 21 Welsh, 133 English, 27 bilingual							
Radnor	Church of England*	58	10422	3347	–	1865	*40.8*	
Pop. 20,259	Independents	13	2800	545	588	480	*6.6*	
	Baptists	36	8200	2964	3331	2228	*36.1*	
	Wesleyan Methodists	15	2428	299	506	235	*3.6*	
	Primitive Methodists	12	1709	295	425	374	*3.6*	
	Calvinistic Methodists	16	4026	617	767	682	*7.5*	
	Society of Friends	4	460	141	165	135	*1.7*	
	Other	2	240	0	110	65	*0.0*	
	Total	**156**	**30285**	**8208**	**5892**	**6064**	***100.0***	***40.5***
	* Language of Sunday services: 0 Welsh, 101 English, 0 bilingual							
Montgomery	Church of England*	78	19319	7098	–	3980	*30.9*	
Pop. 50,917	Independents	64	12290	3946	2673	4647	*17.2*	
	Baptists	25	5725	1988	1585	2070	*8.7*	
	Wesleyan Methodists	61	11199	3175	2364	4034	*13.8*	
	Primitive Methodists	14	1800	362	478	638	*1.6*	
	Calvinistic Methodists	96	17019	6339	5241	8606	*27.6*	
	Roman Catholics	1	50	12	20	9	*0.1*	
	Other	3	430	32	71	11	*0.1*	
	Total	**342**	**67832**	**22952**	**12432**	**23995**	***100.0***	***45.1***
	* Language of Sunday services: 53 Welsh, 108 English, 5 bilingual							
Flint	Church of England*	86	25730	11009	–	7172	*44.0*	
Pop. 81,902	Independents	44	10500	2707	5701	3717	*10.8*	
	Baptists	24	5340	759	1943	1256	*3.0*	
	Wesleyan Methodists	72	17491	3520	11357	7512	*14.1*	
	Primitive Methodists	22	3966	765	2769	1909	*3.1*	
	Calvinistic Methodists	65	15601	5054	9871	7629	*20.2*	
	English Presbyterians	18	4344	1127	3175	2220	*4.5*	
	Other	2	410	84	140	84	*0.3*	
	Total	**333**	**83382**	**25025**	**34956**	**31499**	***100.0***	***30.6***
	* Language of Sunday services: 53 Welsh, 132 English, 1 bilingual							

Administrative County	Denomination	Places of worship[1]	Sittings	Communicants/ members[2]	Adherents[3]	Total in Sunday Schools	*Communicants as % total*[4]	*Total communicants as % pop.*[5]
Denbigh	Church of England*	120	32608	15317	–	9265	*30.2*	
Pop. 122,991	Independents	71	19549	6316	11244	8408	*12.5*	
	Baptists	77	18986	5867	12551	8410	*11.6*	
	Wesleyan Methodists	88	19935	5360	12709	8712	*10.6*	
	Primitive Methodists	19	3615	891	2966	2524	*1.8*	
	Calvinistic Methodists	182	44108	16785	32572	24356	*33.1*	
	Other	6	927	120	476	340	*0.2*	
	Total	**563**	**139728**	**50656**	**72518**	**62015**	***100.0***	***41.2***
	* Language of Sunday services: 104 Welsh, 147 English, 0 bilingual							
Merioneth	Church of England*	71	16453	5000	–	3669	*16.8*	
Pop. 54,894	Independents	77	17792	6663	10514	7714	*22.4*	
	Baptists	31	6655	2075	3450	2802	*7.0*	
	Wesleyan Methodists	36	9052	2695	4576	3145	*9.1*	
	Calvinistic Methodists	134	34204	13300	20474	16083	*44.7*	
	Total	**349**	**84156**	**29733**	**39014**	**33413**	***100.0***	***54.2***
	* Language of Sunday services: 102 Welsh, 55 English, 1 bilingual							
Caernarfon	Church of England*	133	37642	13458	–	10881	*20.0*	
Pop. 123,892	Independents	101	33492	12117	20192	12274	*18.0*	
	Baptists	45	12659	3564	6992	3522	*5.3*	
	Wesleyan Methodists	58	18047	5590	10804	7151	*8.3*	
	Calvinistic Methodists	216	71357	32667	50210	35654	*48.5*	
	Total	**553**	**173197**	**67396**	**88198**	**69482**	***100.0***	***54.4***
	* Language of Sunday services: 195 Welsh, 89 English, 0 bilingual							
Anglesey	Church of England*	93	17191	4807	–	4503	*18.4*	
Pop. 50,606	Independents	38	9314	3679	4965	3573	*14.1*	
	Baptists	43	10488	3097	4905	3788	*11.9*	
	Wesleyan Methodists	25	5630	1483	2622	1817	*5.7*	
	Calvinistic Methodists	111	29765	12992	20606	15381	*49.9*	
	Total	**310**	**72388**	**26058**	**33098**	**29062**	***100.0***	***51.5***
	* Language of Sunday services: 136 Welsh, 33 English, 1 bilingual							

Source: Royal Commission on the Church of England and Other Religious Bodies in Wales and Monmouthshire, *Report, Vol. V, Appendices to Minutes of Evidence. Church of England,* Statistical Returns for the Dioceses of Bangor, Llandaff, St Asaph, and St David's, pp. 1–244 [PP 1910 (Cd. 5436) XVIII]; ibid.,*Vol. VI, Appendices to Minutes of Evidence. Nonconformist County Statistics*, pp. 1–433 [PP 1910 (Cd. 5437) XVIII].

1 For the established Church this represents the total of churches and missions. For the remainder, it is the total of chapels and separate preaching stations or schoolrooms.
2 Communicants in the Church of England were understood to be the equivalent of members in Nonconformist denominations.
3 The statistics given in this column represent adherents rather than members. The accuracy of this data is discussed in the introduction.
4 This column represents the relative strengths of the different denominations in each district.
5 This proportion, the total number of communicants/members as a percentage of the population in 1901 given in the first column, can be used in a similar way, as an indicator of 'religiosity', but should not be confused with the Index of Attendance given in Tables 1.1 and 1.2.
6 Excludes parishes in Monmouthshire and east Glamorgan in the diocese of Llandaff.

Religion 2.2 Report of the Royal Commission on the Church of England and Other Religious Bodies in Wales and Monmouthshire, 1910. Number of places of worship, sittings, communicants, adherents, and total in Sunday schools, by denomination. Registration Districts. 1905

District[1]	Denomination	Places of worship[2]	Sittings	Commun-icants/ members[3]	Adher-ents[4]	Total in Sunday Schools	*Commun-icants as % total* [5]
MONMOUTHSHIRE							
Newport	Church of England	12	5911	2818		3841	*28.0*
	Independents	6	3800	1400	2490	1598	*13.9*
	Baptists	13	7870	2969	5359	4681	*29.5*
	Wesleyan Methodists	12	5740	1343	3340	2696	*13.3*
	Primitive Methodists	3	980	148	340	316	*1.5*
	Calvinistic Methodists	8	6500	1330	5725	2461	*13.2*
	Unitarians	1	110	0	100	0	*0.0*
	Jews	1	150	0	0	0	*0.0*
	Other	11	600	67	180	211	*0.7*
	Total	**67**	**31661**	**10075**	**17534**	**15804**	***100.0***
Monmouth	Church of England	61	10707	3080		2551	*74.6*
	Independents	5	1410	234	520	271	*5.7*
	Baptists	12	2010	316	842	503	*7.6*
	Wesleyan Methodists	24	3217	438	1231	913	*10.6*
	Primitive Methodists	4	454	63	147	91	*1.5*
	Calvinistic Methodists	1	0	0	0	20	*0.0*
	Total	**107**	**17798**	**4131**	**2740**	**4349**	***100.0***
Abergavenny	Church of England	29	5498	2032		1667	*32.9*
	Independents	4	2100	718	1528	1073	*11.6*
	Baptists	15	6320	2031	4010	2782	*32.9*
	Wesleyan Methodists	5	1768	658	1150	870	*10.7*
	Primitive Methodists	1	900	163	450	217	*2.6*
	Calvinistic Methodists	6	1430	571	1258	602	*9.2*
	Other	5	0	0	0	0	*0.0*
	Total	**65**	**18016**	**6173**	**8396**	**7211**	***100.0***
Tredegar	Church of England	18	7400	3265		4232	*20.9*
	Independents	25	12680	4357	6318	5048	*27.9*
	Baptists	23	12650	4165	7020	4994	*26.7*
	Wesleyan Methodists	15	5710	1202	2457	2413	*7.7*
	Primitive Methodists	9	2703	694	2050	1954	*4.4*
	Calvinistic Methodists	16	7540	1940	4297	2841	*12.4*
	Other	1	300	0	274	150	*0.0*
	Total	**107**	**48983**	**15623**	**22416**	**21632**	***100.0***
Abertillery	Church of England	19	6061	2786		3544	*29.3*
	Independents	8	2860	1321	2454	1874	*13.9*
	Baptists	11	7750	3218	6077	4308	*33.8*
	Wesleyan Methodists	8	2855	568	1600	1290	*6.0*
	Primitive Methodists	9	2900	740	2600	2217	*7.8*
	Calvinistic Methodists	8	3850	887	2170	1436	*9.3*
	Other	4	950	0	555	363	*0.0*
	Total	**67**	**27226**	**9520**	**15456**	**15032**	***100.0***
Pontypool	Church of England	41	8981	3919		3828	*33.3*
	Independents	17	6070	2110	3741	3025	*17.9*
	Baptists	21	10095	3021	6483	4330	*25.7*
	Wesleyan Methodists	17	5979	1343	3404	3804	*11.4*
	Primitive Methodists	8	2407	759	1581	1935	*6.5*
	Calvinistic Methodists	4	2000	485	1232	839	*4.1*
	Other	9	1510	120	567	233	*1.0*
	Total	**117**	**37042**	**11757**	**17008**	**17994**	***100.0***

District[1]	Denomination	Places of worship[2]	Sittings	Communicants/ members[3]	Adherents[4]	Total in Sunday Schools	*Communicants as % total* [5]
Risca	Church of England	59	12063	5013		5420	*31.0*
	Independents	24	7930	2355	4769	3115	*14.6*
	Baptists	38	17215	5963	11756	8559	*36.9*
	Wesleyan Methodists	21	6344	1203	3160	2719	*7.4*
	Primitive Methodists	10	2360	563	1427	1324	*3.5*
	Calvinistic Methodists	14	3980	1037	2285	1330	*6.4*
	Other	4	540	30	215	178	*0.2*
	Total	**170**	**50432**	**16164**	**23612**	**22645**	***100.0***
GLAMORGAN							
Cardiff	Church of England	38	16874	9354		13224	*33.8*
	English						
	Independents	12	8545	1614	4576	2836	*5.8*
	Baptists	17	10820	4167	4350	6190	*15.1*
	Wesleyan Methodists	15	10351	2485	5855	6807	*9.0*
	Calvinistic Methodists	14	10030	2457	6688	4878	*8.9*
	Total	**58**	**39746**	**10723**	**21469**	**20711**	***38.8***
	Welsh						
	Independents	5	2750	1187	522	915	*4.3*
	Baptists	5	2810	1226	530	809	*4.4*
	Wesleyan Methodists	1	325	53	10	23	*0.2*
	Calvinistic Methodists	5	2630	1027	643	990	*3.7*
	Total	**16**	**8515**	**3493**	**1705**	**2737**	***12.6***
	Methodist Free Church	3	1066	262	400	522	*0.9*
	Bible Christians	4	1981	584	725	987	*2.1*
	Primitive Methodists	5	1825	355	650	608	*1.3*
	Presbyterian	3	1850	789	335	730	*2.9*
	Society of Friends	1	300	80	20	41	*0.3*
	Unitarians	1	200	0	231	117	*0.0*
	Plymouth Brethren	5	3200	1080	1100	3119	*3.9*
	Salvation Army	10	3270	613	869	803	*2.2*
	Other	14	3000	302	1295	481	*1.1*
	Total	**158**	**81827**	**27635**	**28799**	**44080**	***100.0***
Cowbridge	Church of England	68	11938	4909		4886	*39.4*
	Independents	16	6286	2012	1899	2556	*16.1*
	Baptists	20	7785	2288	2384	3150	*18.4*
	Wesleyan Methodists	19	7156	1464	3130	3324	*11.7*
	Primitive Methodists	2	328	54	120	128	*0.4*
	Calvinistic Methodists	22	6833	1475	2261	2011	*11.8*
	Roman Catholics	1	200	0	0	0	*0.0*
	Other	11	1480	261	434	616	*2.1*
	Total	**159**	**42006**	**12463**	**10228**	**16671**	***100.0***
Caerphilly	Church of England	41	10669	5239		5917	*35.3*
	Independents	27	11954	3514	2161	4129	*23.7*
	Baptists	21	9230	2812	2670	3240	*19.0*
	Wesleyan Methodists	15	3425	724	1390	1871	*4.9*
	Primitive Methodists	5	840	308	475	603	*2.1*
	Calvinistic Methodists	26	9936	2131	2304	3129	*14.4*
	Presbyterians	1	330	62	250	139	*0.4*
	Other	2	350	49	80	170	*0.3*
	Total	**138**	**46734**	**14839**	**9330**	**19198**	***100.0***
Pontypridd	Church of England	6	2250	1123	–	1560	*13.7*
	Welsh						
	Independents	5	2220	1104	1095	1217	*13.4*
	Baptists	5	3050	1092	1040	1040	*13.3*
	Wesleyan Methodists	3	1110	180	172	323	*2.2*
	Calvinistic Methodists	7	3300	1427	1149	1769	*17.4*
	Total	**20**	**9680**	**3803**	**3456**	**4349**	***46.3***

District[1]	Denomination	Places of worship[2]	Sittings	Communicants/ members[3]	Adherents[4]	Total in Sunday Schools	*Communicants as % total*[5]
Pontypridd cont.	*English*						
	Independents	3	1320	449	630	1009	*5.5*
	Baptists	8	2935	1468	1575	2116	*17.9*
	Wesleyan Methodists	6	1835	416	810	1075	*5.1*
	Primitive Methodists	2	300	89	180	222	*1.1*
	Calvinistic Methodists	7	2150	823	1110	1455	*10.0*
	Unitarians	1	70	45	35	50	*0.5*
	Other	2	350	0	0	0	*0.0*
	Total	**29**	**8960**	**3290**	**4340**	**5927**	***40.0***
	Grand Total	**55**	**20890**	**8216**	**7796**	**11836**	***100.0***
Merthyr Tydfil	Church of England*	40	12075	5728		6024	*20.8*
	Independents	31	18340	7907	5067	7983	*28.7*
	Baptists	41	22411	8533	6520	8693	*30.9*
	Wesleyan Methodists	14	4100	786	1107	1348	*2.8*
	Primitive Methodists	5	1570	243	440	543	*0.9*
	Calvinistic Methodists	26	12720	3833	3819	4788	*13.9*
	Unitarians	3	680	150	125	250	*0.5*
	Other	4	1760	411	420	502	*1.5*
	Total	**164**	**73656**	**27591**	**17498**	**30131**	***100.0***
	* Language of Sunday services in the 3 churches in St David's diocese: 3 Welsh, 3 English						
Aberdare	Church of England*	34	10109	4906		6300	*17.8*
	Independents	35	18968	8612	5757	8840	*31.2*
	Baptists	30	16585	7422	5492	6829	*26.9*
	Wesleyan Methodists	11	4480	1002	445	1109	*3.6*
	Primitive Methodists	9	2510	535	1052	1306	*1.9*
	Calvinistic Methodists	24	12994	4879	4777	5719	*17.7*
	Presbyterians	1	400	83	50	116	*0.3*
	Unitarians	3	1050	142	220	174	*0.5*
	Other	1	90	30	0	19	*0.1*
	Total	**148**	**67186**	**27611**	**17793**	**30412**	***100.0***
	* Language of Sunday services at Penderyn Church in St David's diocese: 1 Welsh, 1 English						
Rhondda	Church of England*	38	12016	5039	–	6640	*12.7*
	Welsh						
	Independents	29	21092	10505	13425	10604	*26.4*
	Baptists	31	21565	9245	11110	8735	*23.3*
	Wesleyan Methodists	11	4309	1231	1260	1616	*3.1*
	Calvinistic Methodists	25	15168	6873	11490	8896	*17.3*
	Total	**96**	**62134**	**27854**	**37285**	**29851**	***70.1***
	English						
	Independents	8	2830	1066	2486	1563	*2.7*
	Baptists	15	7890	2658	5900	3556	*6.7*
	Wesleyan Methodists	14	4986	1142	5550	3161	*2.9*
	Primitive Methodists	9	2895	530	3080	1608	*1.3*
	Calvinistic Methodists	8	4120	1444	3725	2248	*3.6*
	Total	**54**	**22721**	**6840**	**20741**	**12136**	***17.2***
	Grand Total	**188**	**96871**	**39733**	**58026**	**48627**	***100.0***
Neath	Church of England*	48	15770	7123		6844	*23.1*
	Independents	46	23422	9538	6095	10150	*31.0*
	Baptists	29	13615	5506	5012	6950	*17.9*
	Wesleyan Methodists	13	4196	1240	1635	2381	*4.0*
	Primitive Methodists	2	745	173	390	356	*0.6*
	Calvinistic Methodists	40	23325	7114	6134	8992	*23.1*
	Other	2	350	110	200	311	*0.4*
	Total	**180**	**81423**	**30804**	**19466**	**35984**	***100.0***
	* Language of Sunday services at the 10 churches in St David's diocese: 7 Welsh, 6 English, 4 Bilingual						

District[1]	Denomination	Places of worship[2]	Sittings	Commun-icants/ members[3]	Adher-ents[4]	Total in Sunday Schools	*Commun-icants as % total*[5]
Swansea UD	Church of England*	31	13556	6916		8727	*25.1*
	Welsh						
	Independents		11620	5554	2950	4790	*20.1*
	Baptists	8	7344	3251	2276	2816	*11.8*
	Wesleyan Methodists	1	350	54	6	39	*0.2*
	Calvinistic Methodists	15	8262	2787	1714	3287	*10.1*
	Total	**43**	**27576**	**11646**	**6946**	**10932**	***42.2***
	English						
	Independents	14	8380	2733	2725	3345	*9.9*
	Baptists	15	7880	2592	3340	4259	*9.4*
	Wesleyan Methodists	10	4550	1060	2146	2197	*3.8*
	Primitive Methodists	3	876	209	460	305	*0.8*
	Calvinistic Methodists	12	5130	929	1564	1806	*3.4*
	Presbyterians	1	1250	337	200	297	*1.2*
	Society of Friends	1	250	50	100	197	*0.2*
	Unitarians	1	314	0	150	49	*0.0*
	Other	13	5860	1115	2680	1409	*4.0*
	Total	**70**	**34490**	**9025**	**13365**	**13864**	***32.7***
	Language not given						
	Baptists	1	150	0	0	0	*0.0*
	Total	**145**	**75772**	**27587**	**20311**	**33523**	***100.0***
	* Language of Sunday services: 4 Welsh, 69 English, 3 Bilingual						
Swansea Rural	Church of England*	51	13737	7270		6554	*22.8*
	Independents	52	27593	13543	7680	11900	*42.4*
	Baptists	32	13423	5948	3903	5800	*18.6*
	Wesleyan Methodists	16	3620	865	1167	1257	*2.7*
	Calvinistic Methodists	26	11348	3922	3162	4530	*12.3*
	Unitarians	1	950	172	80	111	*0.5*
	Roman Catholics	1	0	0	0	0	*0.0*
	Other	3	540	231	218	205	*0.7*
	Total	**182**	**71211**	**31951**	**16210**	**30357**	***100.0***
	* Language of Sunday services in 49 churches in St David's diocese: 17 Welsh, 73 English, 12 Bilingual						
Bridgend	Church of England*	43	10259	4896		5577	*22.5*
	Independents	34	15605	5822	3178	6383	*26.7*
	Baptists	35	16417	6306	5511	7038	*29.0*
	Wesleyan Methodists	15	4240	539	1220	1642	*2.5*
	Primitive Methodists	2	900	104	250	283	*0.5*
	Calvinistic Methodists	35	13622	3960	4476	5411	*18.2*
	Unitarians	2	450	64	110	41	*0.3*
	Other	2	450	80	100	128	*0.4*
	Total	**168**	**61943**	**21771**	**14845**	**26503**	***100.0***
CARMARTHENSHIRE							
Llanelli	Church of England*	33	11514	6816		5733	*24.5*
	Independents	31	16510	8234	3902	6773	*29.6*
	Baptists	37	18983	8902	6000	7922	*32.0*
	Wesleyan Methodists	9	2480	491	521	784	*1.8*
	Calvinistic Methodists	20	8934	3233	2595	3043	*11.6*
	Other	2	300	100	250	200	*0.4*
	Total	**132**	**58721**	**27776**	**13268**	**24455**	***100.0***
	* Language of Sunday services: 28 Welsh, 28 English, 15 Bilingual						
Llandovery	Church of England*	21	4448	1339		856	*17.5*
	Independents	24	7041	3097	521	2140	*40.5*
	Baptists	11	3220	1013	436	659	*13.2*
	Calvinistic Methodists	20	6410	2207	1825	1925	*28.8*
	Total	**76**	**21119**	**7656**	**2782**	**5580**	***100.0***
	* Language of Sunday services: 12 Welsh, 7 English, 14 Bilingual						

District[1]	Denomination	Places of worship[2]	Sittings	Commun-icants/ members[3]	Adher-ents[4]	Total in Sunday Schools	*Commun-icants as % total* [5]
Llandeilo Fawr	Church of England*	25	5947	3324		2643	*25.4*
	Independents	34	10778	4861	1220	3784	*37.2*
	Baptists	19	5365	2187	1051	1883	*16.7*
	Wesleyan Methodists	6	1324	303	122	336	*2.3*
	Calvinistic Methodists	25	7173	2409	1103	2147	*18.4*
	Other	2	200	0	0	0	*0.0*
	Total	**111**	**30787**	**13084**	**3496**	**10793**	***100.0***
	* Language of Sunday services: 24 Welsh, 10 English, 12 Bilingual						
Carmarthen	Church of England*	50	12033	5536		3723	*28.1*
	Independents	52	17004	7583	1988	5443	*38.5*
	Baptists	31	9939	3589	1967	2568	*18.2*
	Wesleyan Methodists	5	1286	204	199	215	*1.0*
	Calvinistic Methodists	30	9872	2804	1617	2803	*14.2*
	Other	2	0	0	0	0	*0.0*
	Total	**170**	**50134**	**19716**	**5771**	**14752**	***100.0***
	* Language of Sunday services: 38 Welsh, 25 English, 28 Bilingual						
PEMBROKESHIRE							
Narberth	Church of England*	48	7890	2297		1333	*25.4*
	Independents	26	7780	3608	1426	3159	*39.9*
	Baptists	18	5809	2439	1455	2032	*27.0*
	Wesleyan Methodists	6	688	150	148	213	*1.7*
	Primitive Methodists	2	250	28	48	33	*0.3*
	Calvinistic Methodists	10	1789	527	607	576	*5.8*
	Total	**110**	**24206**	**9049**	**3684**	**7346**	***100.0***
	* Language of Sunday services: 6 Welsh, 47 English, 21 Bilingual						
Pembroke	Church of England*	37	10014	4160		3379	*43.6*
	Independents	12	4786	1339	1552	1694	*14.0*
	Baptists	12	5120	2158	1921	1911	*22.6*
	Wesleyan Methodists	12	3537	725	988	1218	*7.6*
	Primitive Methodists	1	400	40	50	34	*0.4*
	Calvinistic Methodists	11	2738	1083	951	1380	*11.3*
	Other	6	710	44	80	126	*0.5*
	Total	91	27305	9549	5542	9742	*100.0*
	* Language of Sunday services: 76 English						
Haverfordwest	Church of England*	72	11970	4014		2818	*28.2*
	Independents	33	9057	3291	3307	2771	*23.1*
	Baptists	41	12054	5052	3457	3858	*35.5*
	Wesleyan Methodists	9	2556	454	1078	804	*3.2*
	Primitive Methodists	1	200	44	36	60	*0.3*
	Calvinistic Methodists	24	5381	1357	1066	1433	*9.5*
	Roman Catholics	1	0	0	0	0	*0.0*
	Other	5	150	15	0	0	*0.1*
	Total	**186**	**41368**	**14227**	**8944**	**11744**	***100.0***
	* Language of Sunday services: 14 Welsh, 78 English, 23 Bilingual						
CARDIGANSHIRE							
Cardigan	Church of England*	32	5697	2257		1410	*21.8*
	Independents	17	6527	2409	1005	1892	*23.3*
	Baptists	21	9914	3870	1782	2490	*37.5*
	Calvinistic Methodists	15	5790	1797	817	1742	*17.4*
	Total	**85**	**27928**	**10333**	**3604**	**7534**	***100.0***
	* Language of Sunday services: 24 Welsh, 8 English, 20 Bilingual						

District[1]	Denomination	Places of worship[2]	Sittings	Commun-icants/ members[3]	Adher-ents[4]	Total in Sunday Schools	*Commun-icants as % total* [5]
Newcastle Emlyn	Church of England*	32	5543	2547		2029	*20.1*
	Independents	35	13330	5927	1473	4612	*46.8*
	Baptists	13	4800	1782	572	1303	*14.1*
	Wesleyan Methodists	2	540	117	27	121	*0.9*
	Calvinistic Methodists	17	4850	1894	801	1817	*14.9*
	Unitarians	3	1100	409	172	300	*3.2*
	Other	2	0	0	0	0	*0.0*
	Total	**104**	**30163**	**12676**	**3045**	**10182**	***100.0***
	* Language of Sunday services: 33 Welsh, 19 Bilingual						
Lampeter	Church of England*	19	2718	1724		1378	*30.2*
	Independents	16	4770	2280	521	1553	*39.9*
	Baptists	6	1862	641	315	435	*11.2*
	Wesleyan Methodists	2	550	72	14	59	*1.3*
	Calvinistic Methodists	4	900	439	161	350	*7.7*
	Unitarians	6	1400	557	225	514	*9.7*
	Other	1	120	0	70	45	*0.0*
	Total	**54**	**12320**	**5713**	**1306**	**4334**	***100.0***
	* Language of Sunday services: 25 Welsh, 3 English, 4 Bilingual						
Aberaeron	Church of England*	23	4392	1723		1606	*24.5*
	Independents	17	6931	2922	1052	2990	*41.6*
	Baptists	3	660	116	37	110	*1.6*
	Wesleyan Methodists	3	470	89	28	116	*1.3*
	Calvinistic Methodists	13	4940	1822	873	2059	*25.9*
	Unitarians	4	1070	359	218	319	*5.1*
	Total	**63**	**18463**	**7031**	**2208**	**7200**	***100.0***
	* Language of Sunday services: 32 Welsh, 3 English, 3 Bilingual						
Aberystwyth	Church of England*	33	8088	3234		2476	*26.4*
	Independents	18	4960	1537	652	1306	*12.5*
	Baptists	9	2960	773	355	750	*6.3*
	Wesleyan Methodists	12	3978	1134	594	1343	*9.2*
	Calvinistic Methodists	62	15434	5585	3235	6724	*45.5*
	Unitarians	1	50	0	20	0	*0.0*
	Total	**135**	**35470**	**12263**	**4856**	**12599**	***100.0***
	* Language of Sunday services: 35 Welsh, 18 English, 12 Bilingual						
Tregaron	Church of England*	13	2480	1007		937	*21.5*
	Independents	2	400	52	4	84	*1.1*
	Baptists	4	860	247	129	265	*5.3*
	Wesleyan Methodists	2	970	150	28	151	*3.2*
	Calvinistic Methodists	45	9705	3235	1817	3822	*69.0*
	Total	**66**	**14415**	**4691**	**1978**	**5259**	***100.0***
	* Language of Sunday services: 19 Welsh, 4 Bilingual						
BRECONSHIRE							
Builth	Church of England*	26	3285	1341		826	*33.6*
	Independents	14	3482	1001	730	800	*25.1*
	Baptists	9	2642	768	650	477	*19.3*
	Wesleyan Methodists	2	800	120	225	142	*3.0*
	Primitive Methodists	2	172	56	60	44	*1.4*
	Calvinistic Methodists	8	3295	639	801	631	*16.0*
	Society of Friends	1	200	64	50	71	*1.6*
	Other	1	100	0	30	65	*0.0*
	Total	**63**	**13976**	**3989**	**2546**	**3056**	***100.0***
	* Language of Sunday services: 10 Welsh, 39 English, 2 Bilingual						
Brecon	Church of England*	48	9581	3169		2197	*49.2*
	Independents	17	3490	1324	698	1032	*20.6*
	Baptists	11	2736	715	833	541	*11.1*
	Wesleyan Methodists	4	740	125	156	191	*1.9*
	Calvinistic Methodists	20	4633	1107	916	1105	*17.2*
	Total	**100**	**21180**	**6440**	**2603**	**5066**	***100.0***
	* Language of Sunday services: 10 Welsh, 61 English, 19 Bilingual						

District[1]	Denomination	Places of worship[2]	Sittings	Commun-icants/ members[3]	Adher-ents[4]	Total in Sunday Schools	*Commun-icants as % total* [5]
Crickhowell	Church of England*	19	3350	1389		1113	*25.1*
	Independents	12	3900	1457	1357	1602	*26.3*
	Baptists	11	4890	1424	1647	1789	*25.7*
	Wesleyan Methodists	5	1282	249	439	477	*4.5*
	Primitive Methodists	1	480	133	300	314	*2.4*
	Calvinistic Methodists	9	2917	852	1034	1016	*15.4*
	Jews	1	150	31	10	23	*0.6*
	Total	**58**	**16969**	**5535**	**4787**	**6334**	***100.0***
	* Language of Sunday services: 1 Welsh, 31 English						
Hay	Church of England*	18	3694	1261		819	*46.8*
	Independents	10	1950	554	490	463	*20.6*
	Baptists	8	1830	438	543	302	*16.3*
	Wesleyan Methodists	2	450	57	91	89	*2.1*
	Primitive Methodists	3	400	28	120	55	*1.0*
	Calvinistic Methodists	7	1178	354	211	367	*13.2*
	Other (SA)	1	200	0	60	0	*0.0*
	Total	**49**	**9702**	**2692**	**1515**	**2095**	***100.0***
	* Language of Sunday services: 32 English						
RADNORSHIRE							
Presteigne	Church of England*	9	993	303		132	*26.0*
	Independents	2	170	42	158	65	*3.6*
	Baptists	10	1460	608	916	383	*52.2*
	Wesleyan Methodists	4	510	58	141	7	*5.0*
	Primitive Methodists	1	260	60	90	46	*5.2*
	Calvinistic Methodists	4	390	63	155	84	*5.4*
	Society of Friends	1	60	30	45	14	*2.6*
	Other	1	140	0	80	0	*0.0*
	Total	**32**	**3983**	**1164**	**1585**	**731**	***100.0***
	* Language of Sunday services: 16 English						
Knighton	Church of England*	11	1817	409		241	*22.4*
	Baptists	11	2360	1047	1023	905	*57.4*
	Wesleyan Methodists	4	618	103	75	113	*5.6*
	Primitive Methodists	7	1027	171	225	249	*9.4*
	Calvinistic Methodists	3	400	95	55	88	*5.2*
	Total	**36**	**6222**	**1825**	**1378**	**1596**	***100.0***
	* Language of Sunday services: 19 English						
Rhayader	Church of England*	16	4246	1369		714	*50.3*
	Independents	3	770	261	192	189	*9.6*
	Baptists	7	1930	675	824	502	*24.8*
	Wesleyan Methodists	3	550	69	81	35	*2.5*
	Calvinistic Methodists	6	1496	303	282	338	*11.1*
	Society of Friends	2	200	47	70	50	*1.7*
	Total	**37**	**9192**	**2724**	**1449**	**1828**	***100.0***
	* Language of Sunday services: 28 English						
MONTGOMERYSHIRE							
Machynlleth	Church of England*	16	3759	1169		924	*18.4*
	Independents	25	5102	1545	1189	1873	*24.3*
	Baptists	6	1350	383	278	301	*6.0*
	Wesleyan Methodists	17	3290	912	782	1054	*14.3*
	Calvinistic Methodists	31	6008	2354	2357	2800	*37.0*
	Total	**95**	**19509**	**6363**	**4606**	**6952**	***100.0***
	* Language of Sunday services: 23 Welsh, 11 English, 2 Bilingual						

District[1]	Denomination	Places of worship[2]	Sittings	Communicants/ members[3]	Adherents[4]	Total in Sunday Schools	*Communicants as % total*[5]
Newtown	Church of England*	25	6235	2394		1368	*26.6*
	Independents	11	2504	895	767	1092	*9.9*
	Baptists	15	4015	1542	1148	1495	*17.1*
	Wesleyan Methodists	17	3980	1099	653	1395	*12.2*
	Primitive Methodists	1	350	66	50	86	*0.7*
	Calvinistic Methodists	37	7810	2957	2411	4204	*32.9*
	Roman Catholics	1	50	12	20	9	*0.1*
	Other	3	430	32	71	11	*0.4*
	Total	**110**	**25374**	**8997**	**5120**	**9660**	***100.0***
	* Language of Sunday services: 3 Welsh, 45 English, 3 Bilingual						
Montgomery	Church of England*	15	4916	2042		935	*53.7*
	Independents	8	1500	399	408	459	*10.5*
	Baptists	3	540	133	175	186	*3.5*
	Wesleyan Methodists	11	1715	381	438	576	*10.0*
	Primitive Methodists	7	860	194	260	333	*5.1*
	Calvinistic Methodists	10	1702	653	821	810	*17.2*
	Total	**54**	**11233**	**3802**	**2102**	**3299**	***100.0***
	* Language of Sunday services: 31 English						
Llanfyllin	Church of England*	30	6184	2166		1154	*30.1*
	Independents	29	4939	1646	1075	1841	*22.9*
	Baptists	6	820	164	174	233	*2.3*
	Wesleyan Methodists	25	4074	1336	1411	1635	*18.6*
	Primitive Methodists	3	320	30	88	98	*0.4*
	Calvinistic Methodists	35	4892	1860	1823	2590	*25.8*
	Total	**128**	**21229**	**7202**	**4571**	**7551**	***100.0***
	* Language of Sunday services: 36 Welsh, 28 English						
FLINTSHIRE							
Holywell	Church of England*	48	14322	5285		4055	*40.6*
	Independents	31	7185	1745	3548	2580	*13.4*
	Baptists	14	3294	427	1104	707	*3.3*
	Wesleyan Methodists	36	9789	1927	6044	4294	*14.8*
	Primitive Methodists	2	530	87	330	253	*0.7*
	Calvinistic Methodists	41	9616	2988	5782	4642	*22.9*
	English Presbyterians	7	2114	531	1470	1034	*4.1*
	Other	1	300	34	40	46	*0.3*
	Total	**180**	**47150**	**13024**	**18318**	**17611**	***100.0***
	* Language of Sunday services: 36 Welsh, 58 English, 1 Bilingual						
DENBIGHSHIRE							
Wrexham	Church of England*	59	16926	9883		6874	*37.8*
	Independents	36	10755	3721	6694	5399	*14.2*
	Baptists	37	10541	3208	7504	5240	*12.3*
	Wesleyan Methodists	47	10936	2944	7789	5823	*11.3*
	Primitive Methodists	18	3215	778	2465	2149	*3.0*
	Calvinistic Methodists	55	15684	5316	12657	9441	*20.3*
	English Presbyterians	4	860	172	535	324	*0.7*
	Other	3	587	120	370	175	*0.5*
	Total	**259**	**69504**	**26142**	**38014**	**35425**	***100.0***
	* Language of Sunday services: 11 Welsh, 109 English						
Ruthin	Church of England*	23	5013	1360		772	*25.7*
	Independents	9	1845	463	1001	533	*8.7*
	Baptists	4	900	189	390	228	*3.6*
	Wesleyan Methodists	11	1900	399	906	501	*7.5*
	Calvinistic Methodists	39	7588	2883	5205	4041	*54.5*
	Total	**86**	**17246**	**5294**	**7502**	**6075**	***100.0***
	* Language of Sunday services: 30 Welsh, 20 English						

District[1]	Denomination	Places of worship[2]	Sittings	Communicants/ members[3]	Adherents[4]	Total in Sunday Schools	*Communicants as % total*[5]
St Asaph	Church of England*	30	10806	5294		2499	*39.1*
	Independents	18	4544	1230	2438	1453	*9.1*
	Baptists	18	3646	900	1632	1098	*6.6*
	Wesleyan Methodists	23	5648	1504	3747	2141	*11.1*
	Calvinistic Methodists	47	11865	4447	8369	6010	*32.8*
	English Presbyterians	2	470	170	330	186	*1.3*
	Other	3	340	0	106	165	*0.0*
	Total	**141**	**37319**	**13545**	**16622**	**13552**	***100.0***
	* Language of Sunday services: 39 Welsh, 36 English						
Llanrwst	Church of England*	20	3989	1122		895	*16.1*
	Independents	12	2795	1044	1644	993	*15.0*
	Baptists	5	830	256	487	263	*3.7*
	Wesleyan Methodists	9	2030	787	1289	826	*11.3*
	Calvinistic Methodists	38	8857	3748	5837	4549	*53.9*
	Total	**84**	**18501**	**6957**	**9257**	**7526**	***100.0***
	* Language of Sunday services: 29 Welsh, 10 English						
MERIONETH							
Corwen	Church of England*	25	4772	1849		1144	*21.0*
	Independents	15	2990	1037	1633	1318	*11.8*
	Baptists	19	4159	1488	2870	2085	*16.9*
	Wesleyan Methodists	15	2942	828	1475	956	*9.4*
	Primitive Methodists	1	130	60	186	116	*0.7*
	Calvinistic Methodists	38	8130	3529	5943	4724	*40.1*
	Total	**113**	**23123**	**8791**	**12107**	**10343**	***100.0***
	* Language of Sunday services: 30 Welsh, 23 English						
Bala	Church of England*	9	1780	515		334	*15.2*
	Independents	10	2200	768	1274	845	*22.7*
	Baptists	2	220	65	96	58	*1.9*
	Calvinistic Methodists	21	4331	2041	3095	2619	*60.2*
	Total	**42**	**8531**	**3389**	**4465**	**3856**	***100.0***
	* Language of Sunday services: 13 Welsh, 6 English, 1 Bilingual						
Dolgellau	Church of England*	25	6348	1609		1166	*18.6*
	Independents	34	6422	2454	3668	2601	*28.4*
	Baptists	6	1120	326	494	433	*3.8*
	Wesleyan Methodists	14	3577	970	1596	1097	*11.2*
	Calvinistic Methodists	44	9495	3293	5035	3770	*38.1*
	Total	**123**	**26962**	**8652**	**10793**	**9067**	***100.0***
	* Language of Sunday services: 35 Welsh, 19 English						
Ffestiniog	Church of England*	27	5613	1696		1513	*10.3*
	Independents	27	9616	3460	5866	4123	*21.0*
	Baptists	21	5199	1582	2666	1943	*9.6*
	Wesleyan Methodists	15	3970	1295	2261	1483	*7.9*
	Calvinistic Methodists	68	21278	8438	13116	9898	*51.2*
	Total	**158**	**45676**	**16471**	**23909**	**18960**	***100.0***
	* Language of Sunday services: 43 Welsh, 17 English						
CAERNARFONSHIRE							
Pwllheli	Church of England*	41	9951	1845		1605	*13.4*
	Independents	28	6969	2408	3804	2140	*17.5*
	Baptists	12	2406	726	1281	660	*5.3*
	Wesleyan Methodists	10	2840	813	1402	961	*5.9*
	Calvinistic Methodists	61	18654	7978	12473	7589	*57.9*
	Total	**152**	**40820**	**13770**	**18960**	**12955**	***100.0***
	* Language of Sunday services: 61 Welsh, 15 English						

District[1]	Denomination	Places of worship[2]	Sittings	Commun-icants/ members[3]	Adher-ents[4]	Total in Sunday Schools	*Commun-icants as % total* [5]
Caernarfon	Church of England*	35	9509	3223		3728	*13.4*
	Independents	28	10553	4524	7578	4915	*18.8*
	Baptists	15	3802	1130	1924	1068	*4.7*
	Wesleyan Methodists	15	3654	1182	2172	1597	*4.9*
	Calvinistic Methodists	69	27481	13978	20862	15820	*58.2*
	Total	**162**	**54999**	**24037**	**32536**	**27128**	***100.0***
	* Language of Sunday services: 57 Welsh, 15 English						
Bangor	Church of England*	39	12462	5561		4247	*29.5*
	Independents	25	9463	2927	4643	2976	*15.5*
	Baptists	13	4245	1003	1677	1054	*5.3*
	Wesleyan Methodists	19	6808	1898	3569	2427	*10.1*
	Calvinistic Methodists	53	16881	7458	11908	8866	*39.6*
	Total	**149**	**49859**	**18847**	**21797**	**19570**	***100.0***
	* Language of Sunday services: 61 Welsh, 35 English, 1 Bilingual						
Conwy	Church of England*	32	11277	5477		2584	*38.8*
	Independents	17	5520	1916	3368	1979	*13.6*
	Baptists	12	4163	1162	2857	1305	*8.2*
	Wesleyan Methodists	21	6671	1796	4197	2442	*12.7*
	Calvinistic Methodists	33	9847	3775	6177	4183	*26.7*
	Total	**115**	**37478**	**14126**	**16599**	**12493**	***100.0***
	* Language of Sunday services: 31 Welsh, 44 English						
ANGLESEY							
Anglesey	Church of England*	69	12014	3101		3013	*16.2*
	Independents	31	7455	2984	4066	2903	*15.6*
	Baptists	35	8623	2713	4356	3321	*14.1*
	Wesleyan Methodists	19	4280	1182	2118	1496	*6.2*
	Calvinistic Methodists	81	21259	9202	14523	10807	*48.0*
	Total	**235**	**53631**	**19182**	**25063**	**21540**	***100.0***
	* Language of Sunday services: 102 Welsh, 17 English						

Source: Royal Commission on the Church of England and Other Religious Bodies in Wales and Monmouthshire, *Report, Vol. V, Appendices to Minutes of Evidence. Church of England,* Statistical Returns for the Dioceses of Bangor, Llandaff, St Asaph, and St David's, pp. 1–244 [PP 1910 (Cd. 5436) XVIII]; ibid.,*Vol. VI, Appendices to Minutes of Evidence. Nonconformist County Statistics*, pp. 1–433 [PP 1910 (Cd. 5437) XVIII].

[1] For most counties, the Nonconformist statistics have been grouped according to Registration District boundaries in 1851 to enable comparison with Religion Table 1.2. However, for Monmouthshire and Glamorgan, districts are based on the divisions given in the Nonconformist statistics as listed below, with the addition of the Breconshire parishes of Penderyn, Vaynor, Ystradgynlais and Ystradfellte. The diocesan statistics, originally grouped according to diocese, archdeaconry and rural deanery, have been reclassified on the same basis. Returns from the diocese of Llandaff contain no details of the language of services.

MONMOUTHSHIRE

Monmouth: Chapel Hill and Penteri, Chepstow, Caldicot, Caer-went, Kilgwrrwg, Llandogo, Llanishen, Llanvihangel Torymynydd, Llantilio Crossenny, Trelleck, Wonastow, Wolvesnewton, Llandenny, Llanvapley, Raglan, Skenfrith, Pen-rhos, Pen-allt.

Abergavenny: Abergavenny, Llanwenarth, Llanddewi Rhydderch, Blaenafon, Llanover, Llanvetherine, Cwm-iou Lower, Llanvihangel Crucorney, Llansanffraid.

Abertillery: Abertillery, Llanhilleth, Aberystruth.

Tredegar: Tredegar, Rhymni, Ebbw Vale.

Pontypool: Usk, Llanfrechfa Upper, Pontypool, Caerleon, Gwehelog, Goytre, Llantrisant, Llan-gwm Ucha, Llangybi, Llanfrechfa Lower, Llansoy, Llanbadog, Abersychan, Llanfihangel Llantarnam, Griffithstown.

Newport: Newport County Borough and parish.

Risca: Bedwas Lower, Pontllan-fraith, Ynys-ddu and Pen-maen, Marshfield, Upper Machen, Upper Bedwas, Fleur-de-lys, Magor, Peterstone, Rumney, Risca and Pontymister, St Mellons, Malpas, Redwick, Aber-carn and Cwm-carn, Llanvaches, Blackwood and Pengam, Goldcliff, Henllys, Langstone and Llan-bedr, Nash, Michaelston-y-Vedw, Rogerstone, St Bride's Wentlloog, Undy, Bishton, Graig, Llanmartin and Llandevaud, Newbridge, Crymlyn, Crosskeys, Christchurch.

GLAMORGAN

Cardiff: Cardiff County Borough (Canton, Roath, St John, St Mary).

Cowbridge, Barry, Penarth: Barry UD, Penarth UD (Cogan, Llandough, Penarth), Cowbridge UD, Cowbridge RD (St Athan, Colwinston, Llanblethian, Llan-gan, Llanhari, Llanharan, Llantwit Major, Lisworney, Pen-llin, St Mary Hill), Llandaff and Dinas Powys (Caerau, Llancarfan, Pendoylan, St Andrews, St Nicholas, Wenvoe, Pen-marc).

Caerphilly: Llantrisant, Llantwit Fardre, Caerphilly UD (Eglwysilan, Llanfabon), Llandaff and Dinas Powys UD (Whitchurch, Pentyrch, St Fagans, Llandaff, Llanishen, Lisvane, Llanedern, Radur, St Brides-super-Ely, Rudry).

Pontypridd: Pontypridd Urban District (includes parts of the parishes of Llanwynno, Llanfabon, Eglwysilan, Llantwit Fardre, and Llantrisant).

Merthyr Tydfil: Merthyr Tydfil, Gelli-gaer and Vaynor (Brec).

Aberdare: UD Aberdare, UD Llanwynno (Mountain Ash, Abercynon, Penrhiw-ceibr, Ynys-boeth, Ynys-y-bŵl), Rhigos, Penderyn (Brec).

Rhondda: Rhondda Urban District.

Neath: UD Neath, RD Neath (Michaelston Higher, Llantwit Lower, Cwm-gwrach, Baglan Higher, Blaenhonddan, Neath Higher, Coed-ffranc, Dulais Higher, Michaelston Lower, Dyffryn Clydach, Resolfen), Glyncorrwg, Briton Ferry, Aberafan, Margam, Ystradgynlais (Brec) and Ystradfellte (Brec).

Swansea Urban: Swansea County Borough.

Swansea Rural: Swansea RD (Clas Rural, Cockett, Gowerton, Llandeilo Tal-y-bont, Llansamlet, Loughor, Llangyfelach) and Pontardawe RD (Llanguicke, Cilybebyll, Rhyndwyglydach Mawr, Ynysymwn), Oystermouth, and the Gower.

Bridgend: Bridgend UD (Newcastle Lower, Oldcastle), Maes-teg UD (Cwm-du, Llangynwyd Higher), Ogmore and Garw UD (Betws, Llandyfodwg, Llangeinor), Pen-y-bont RD (Coychurch Higher and Lower, Ewenni, Llangynwyd Lower and Middle, Newcastle Higher, St Brides Minor, Tythegston Higher, Wick, Ynysawdre), Porthcawl UD (Newton Nottage).

[2] For the established Church this represents the total of churches and missions. For the remainder, it represents the total of chapels and separate preaching stations or schoolrooms.

[3] Communicants in the Church of England were understood to be the equivalent of members of Nonconformist denominations.

[4] The statistics given in this column represent adherents rather than members. The accuracy of this data is discussed in the introduction.

[5] This column reflects the relative strengths of the different denominations in each district.

Religion 2.3 Report of the Royal Commission on the Church of England and Other Religious Bodies in Wales and Monmouthshire, 1910. Archdeacon Owen Evans's estimates. Number of members and adherents. Welsh and English chapels. Calvinistic Methodists, Independents, Baptists, Wesleyan Methodists. Wales. 1905

Calvinistic Methodists	Members[1] Adult	Children	Total	*% children*	All adherents[2]	Adherents less members Adult[3]	Children[3]	Total
Total Wales	**170617**	**74207**	**244824**	***30.3***	**313292**	**47715**	**20753**	**68468**
English Chapels	24613	15511	40124	*38.7*	68552	17438	10990	28428
Welsh Chapels	146004	58696	204700	*28.7*	244740	28559	11481	40040
Welsh as % total	*85.6*	*79.1*	*83.6*		*78.1*	–	–	
Glam and Mon	50308	25624	75932	*33.7*	111303	23435	11936	35371
Rest of Wales	120309	48583	168892	*28.8*	201989	23577	9520	33097

Denomination	Adult members[4] Welsh	English	Total	*% Welsh*
Calvinistic Methodists	146004	24613	170617	*85.6*
Independents	147155	27992	175147	*84.0*
Baptists	86949	56886	143835	*60.5*
Wesleyan Methodists	22524	18287	40811	*55.2*
Total	**402632**	**127778**	**530410**	***75.9***

Denomination	All adherents (including members, adults and children) Welsh[5]	English[5]	Total	*% Welsh*	Adult adherents Welsh[6]	English[6]
Calvinistic Methodists	244740	68552	313292	*78.1*	28559	17438
Independents	247220	78097	325317	*76.0*	28783	19829
Baptists	146074	158711	304785	*47.9*	17007	40298
Wesleyan Methodists	37840	51020	88860	*42.6*	4405	12954
Total	**675874**	**356380**	**1032254**	***65.5***	**78754**	**90519**

Source: Royal Commission on the Church of England and Other Religious Bodies in Wales and Monmouthshire, *Report, Vol. I,* Memorandum by Archdeacon Owen Evans and Lord Hugh Cecil, M.P., Tables III, IV and V, pp. 138–9 [PP 1910 (Cd. 5432) XIV].

Calvinistic Methodists were the only denomination to publish figures for 'all inclusive' adherents (i.e. including members) in its Yearbook as well as distinguishing between adult and child members. Archdeacon Evans used the ratios of children to adult members for Welsh and English Calvinistic Methodist chapels to calculate estimates for adult adherents. These ratios were then applied to the figures for adult members of the other main Nonconformist denominations to obtain estimates for the number of 'all inclusive' adherents and adult adherents. He admitted that the estimates were 'too precarious to be relied upon'. Nevertheless, it is worth noting, as he did, that the total of 'all inclusive' Nonconformist adherents reached by these calculations (1,032,254) is equivalent to 48% of the estimated total population of Wales in 1905.

1 Includes ministers, deacons, probationers as well as ordinary full members.
2 Includes members and all others who attended.
3 Calculated from the total by using the ratio of children to adults in the previous columns.
4 These statistics derived from the denominational Yearbooks.
5 The statistics for Independents, Baptists and Wesleyan Methodists are calculated by applying ratios taken from the Calvinistic Methodist figures of 168 and 279 adherents per 100 members, for Welsh and English chapels respectively, to the figures for adult members given above.
6 The statistics for Independents, Baptists and Wesleyan Methodists are calculated by applying ratios taken from the Calvinistic Methodist figures of 19.56 and 70.84 adult adherents per 100 members, for Welsh and English chapels respectively. Since this final calculation involves three sets of assumptions, the results are necessarily the most 'precarious' of all.

Religion 2.4 Report of the Royal Commission on the Church of England and Other Religious Bodies in Wales and Monmouthshire, 1910. Independents. Dates of establishment of Welsh and English chapels. Wales and Counties

County	Date of chapel formation Welsh Before 1800	1800–50	1850–1907	English Before 1800	1800–50	1850–1907
Wales (excl. Mon.)	**123**	**423**	**385**	**17**	**63**	**126**
Glamorgan	26	83	187	1	10	83
Carmarthenshire	24	49	56	1	1	3
Pembrokeshire	12	20	11	4	23	9
Cardiganshire	16	38	20	0	1	1
Breconshire	11	18	7	–	–	–
Radnorshire and Breconshire	–	–	–	3	10	3
Montgomeryshire	7	42	8	4	9	2
Denbighshire	1	29	17	2	5	7
Flintshire	2	23	5	1	3	8
Merioneth	8	37	25	0	0	3
Caernarfonshire	8	58	43	1	1	7
Anglesey	8	26	6	–	–	–
	Welsh and English					
Monmouthshire	11	42	47			

Source: Royal Commission on the Church of England and Other Religious Bodies in Wales and Monmouthshire, *Report, Vol. VII, Appendices to Minutes of Evidence. Nonconformists.* Denominational Statistics. Appendix XXXIX, A Sketch of the Progress of Congregationalism, 1800–1906, p. 154 [PP 1910 (Cd. 5438) XIX].

Religion 2.5 Report of the Royal Commission on the Church of England and Other Religious Bodies in Wales and Monmouthshire, 1910. Independents. Welsh and English Associations. Number of churches and mission rooms, sittings, communicants, deacons, Sunday school teachers and pupils, members of temperance societies. Wales and Counties. Welsh churches in England. 1906

County	Language[1]	Chapels and Mission Rooms[2]	Sittings[2]	Deacons	Communicants[3] Number	Communicants[3] *Welsh as % Total*	Sunday Schools Teachers	Sunday Schools On Registers Under 14 years	Sunday Schools On Registers Over 14 years	Members of Temperance Societies[9]
Wales[4]	Welsh	1029	367840	5322	144488		13244	56249	69875	38522
	English	266	91972	1439	26884		2975	21691	13923	11236
	Total	**1295**	**459812**	**6761**	**171372**	***84.3***	**16219**	**77940**	**83798**	**49758**
Monmouth	Welsh	38	16360	254	5136		449	2116	2242	1082
	English	59	22874	364	7299		821	7012	3549	3457
	Total	**97**	**39234**	**618**	**12435**	***41.3***	**1270**	**9128**	**5791**	**4539**
Glamorgan	Welsh	311	149871	2094	63581		5436	26738	30666	20128
	English[5]	63	25014	359	6733		876	7000	3683	2379
	Total[5]	**374**	**174885**	**2453**	**70314**	***90.4***	**6312**	**33738**	**34349**	**22507**
Carmarthen	Welsh	149	51612	812	23436		1617	7531	9876	5343
	English[6]	38	15648	258	5289		495	3791	2492	2633
	Total[6]	**187**	**67260**	**1070**	**28725**	***81.6***	**2112**	**11322**	**12368**	**7976**
Pembroke	Welsh	41	14117	239	5636		426	1388	2525	1554
	English	38	11797	180	3493		309	1458	1748	1340
	Total	**79**	**25914**	**419**	**9129**	***61.7***	**735**	**2846**	**4273**	**2894**
Cardigan	Welsh	78	28788	444	11465	*100.0*	1030	3306	5486	3143
Brecon	Welsh	34	7553	125	2749		192	739	895	178
Brecon and Radnor	English	18	4184	76	1048		88	472	272	276
Brecon and Radnor	**Total**	**52**	**11737**	**201**	**3797**	***72.4***	**280**	**1211**	**1167**	**454**
Montgomery	Welsh	57	12471	196	3770		393	1241	2319	686
	English	15	2860	58	816		96	660	377	188
	Total	**72**	**15331**	**254**	**4586**	***82.2***	**489**	**1901**	**2696**	**874**
Flint	Welsh	32	7070	109	1756		252	766	1304	696
	English	14	3345	48	852		108	233	967	300
	Total	**46**	**10415**	**157**	**2608**	***67.3***	**360**	**999**	**2271**	**996**
Denbigh	Welsh	45	13120	164	4179		573	2162	3138	1025
	English	13	3420	52	832		136	830	660	515
	Total	**58**	**16540**	**216**	**5011**	***83.4***	**709**	**2992**	**3798**	**1540**
Merioneth	Welsh	74	18086	236	6409		819	3718[7]	3000[7]	1930
	English	3	720	9	92		13	50[7]	30[7]	18
	Total	**77**	**18806**	**245**	**6501**	***98.6***	**832**	**3768**[7]	**3030**[7]	**1948**
Caernarfon	Welsh	129	38554[8]	495	12654		1671	5345	6589	1918[8]
	English	5	2110	35	430		33	185	145	130[8]
	Total	**134**	**40664**[8]	**530**	**13084**	***96.7***	**1704**	**5530**	**6734**	**2048**[8]
Anglesey	Welsh	41	10238	154	3717	*100.0*	386	1199	1835	839
WELSH CHURCHES IN ENGLAND										
Liverpool, Manchester		27	11050	135	3734		283	665	2097	715
London		7	2320	42	1527		62	147	594	196

Source: Royal Commission on the Church of England and Other Religious Bodies in Wales and Monmouthshire, *Report, Vol. VII, Appendices to Minutes of Evidence. Nonconformists.* Denominational Statistics. Appendix IV, Statistics of the Congregational Churches of Wales and Monmouthshire and Welsh Churches in England for 1906, pp. 16–17 [PP 1910 (Cd. 5438) XIX].

1 The Independent (or Congregational) Churches were grouped into County (or part County) Associations according to language; for example, the Monmouthshire (Welsh) and Monmouthshire (English) Associations were separate bodies.

2 The total number of Chapels and Mission Rooms in Wales is 1,078 and 219 respectively; the corresponding number of sittings is 420,868 and 38,944 respectively.

3 These are the Communicants at 31 December 1906.

4 See following notes.

5 West Glam (English) is included with Carm (English).

6 Carmarthenshire (English) includes West Glam (English).

7 Estimated age groupings.

8 Includes an estimated figure of 1,700 given as the sittings of 17 Mission Rooms in South Caernarfonshire (Welsh).

9 The statistics for Adult and Juvenile members of Temperance societies in Caernarfonshire are incomplete. A footnote for North Caernarfonshire (Welsh), which gives a figure of only 50 adult members, states that 'many Churches are affiliated with District Total Abstinence Societies'. This suggests that these figures underestimate the extent to which the Independent Churches were involved in the Temperance movement.

Religion 2.6 Report of the Royal Commission on the Church of England and Other Religious Bodies in Wales and Monmouthshire, 1910. Wesleyan Methodists. Number of churches, sittings, ministers, members, adherents, Sunday school teachers and pupils. Wales and Counties. Welsh churches in England. 1905

	Language[1]	Chapels[2]	Sittings[3]	Ministers and Lay Preachers	Members Number	*Welsh as % Total*	Adherents[4]	Sunday Schools Teachers	Scholars under 15 yr	over 15 yr
Wales	Welsh	339	91039	451	24682		38050	4090	12632	16661
	English	280	81294	–	19508		–	9194	56705	30380
	Total	**619**	**172333**	**–**	**44190**	***55.9***	**–**	**13284**	**69337**	**47041**
Counties										
Monmouth	Welsh	5	2500	8	447		265	69	245	316
	English	70	21577	–	5555		–	1199	7234	3732
	Total	**75**	**24077**	**–**	**6002**	***7.4***	**–**	**1268**	**7479**	**4048**
Glamorgan	Welsh	40	14384	64	3507		1274	497	1640	2122
	English	118	38877	–	9821		–	2059	13984	6674
	Total	**158**	**53261**	**–**	**13328**	***26.3***	**–**	**2556**	**15624**	**8796**
Carmarthen	Welsh	9	2634	10	541		205	67	278	297
	English	11	2521	–	489		–	5179	31526	17889
	Total	**20**	**5155**	**–**	**1030**	***52.5***	**–**	**5246**	**31804**	**18186**
Pembroke	Welsh	1	250	2	37		7	6	20	12
	English	27	6569	–	1377		–	258	1478	548
	Total	**28**	**6819**	**–**	**1414**	***2.6***	**–**	**264**	**1498**	**560**
Cardigan	Welsh	20	6068	29	1505	*100.0*	999	207	538	988
Brecon	Welsh	6	1150	3	154		67	31	70	105
Brecon and Radnor	English	11	1846	–	352		–	58	262	140
Brecon and Radnor	**Total**	**17**	**2996**	**–**	**506**	***30.4***	**–**	**89**	**332**	**245**
Montgomery	Welsh	42	7974	39	2419		2721	350	1104	1433
	English	9	1325	15	302		620	56	253	145
	Total	**51**	**9299**	**54**	**2721**	***88.9***	**3341**	**406**	**1357**	**1578**
Flint	Welsh	47	12436	68	2541		7017	587	2026	2267
	English	10	2170	29	402		1610	111	700	288
	Total	**57**	**14606**	**97**	**2943**	***86.3***	**8627**	**698**	**2726**	**2555**
Denbigh	Welsh	60	13458	90	4143		8998	769	2528	3258
	English	16	4150	40	832		2670	194	999	674
	Total	**76**	**17608**	**130**	**4975**	***83.3***	**11668**	**963**	**3527**	**3932**
Merioneth	Welsh	34	8677	42	2633	*100.0*	4207	391	1036	1750
Caernarfon	Welsh	53	16418	81	5365		9838	901	2479	3365
	English	6	1779	10	285		1063	69	205	224
	Total	**59**	**18197**	**91**	**5650**	***95.0***	**10901**	**970**	**2684**	**3589**
Anglesey	Welsh	22	5090	15	1390		2452	215	668	748
	English	2	480	3	93		170	11	64	66
	Total	**24**	**5570**	**18**	**1483**	***93.7***	**2622**	**226**	**732**	**814**
WELSH CHURCHES IN ENGLAND										
1st North Wales District										
Liverpool	Welsh	4[6]	2193[6]	9	647		950	76	208	382
Manchester	Welsh	5[6]	1216[6]	4	381		558	50	105	251
Others[5]	Welsh	28[6]	5512[6]	51	1434		2546	223	611	933
1st London District										
London	Welsh				334		448			

Source: Royal Commission on the Church of England and Other Religious Bodies in Wales and Monmouthshire, *Report, Vol. VII, Appendices to Minutes of Evidence. Nonconformists.* Denominational Statistics. Appendices V–XII, pp. 29–75 [PP 1910 (Cd. 5438) XIX].

1 For most counties, chapels are listed under a Welsh or English heading. However, the language of chapels in Anglesey, Caernarfonshire and the parts of Denbighshire and Merioneth, listed in Appendix VI, has been assumed Welsh unless otherwise indicated.

2 Includes Chapels and Mission rooms.

3 Excludes Schoolrooms and Classrooms.

4 Excluding members.

5 Includes Chapels and Mission Rooms at Birkenhead, Bootle, Egremont, Garston, Widnes, Rock Ferry, Eccles, Leeds, Stubshaw Cross, Earlestown, Golborne, Spring View, Leigh, St Helens, Hanley, Butt Lane, Stockton-on-Tees, Coundon, Crook, Spennymoor, South Hetton, Chester (2), Oswestry, Cefnblodwel, Llynclys, Birmingham.

6 Includes Mission Rooms.

Religion 2.7 Report of the Royal Commission on the Church of England and Other Religious Bodies in Wales and Monmouthshire, 1910. Calvinistic Methodists. Number of chapels, sittings, ministers, elders, communicants, adherents, children, Sunday school teachers and pupils. Wales and Counties. Number of churches, sittings, communicants, adherents and Sunday school teachers and scholars outside Wales. 1905

Monthly Meetings[1]	Chapels and Preaching Stations[2]	Sittings	Ordained Ministers and Preachers	Elders	Communicants[3] Number Welsh	English	*Welsh as % Total*	Adherents[4] Welsh	English
Wales	1481	447897	1130	5459	145973	24738	*85.5*	28475	65432
					3435*			10385*	
Monmouth	63	25670	61	221	2765	4328	*39.0*	5840	13375
Glamorgan	289	136469	275	1219	33522	10609	*76.0*	62866	31539
Carmarthen	93	33000	85	500	10749	354	*96.8*	17391	1105
Pembroke	48	11840	35	174	1922	1733	*52.6*	2877	3646
Cardigan	131	33815	89	403	12848	166	*98.7*	10721	300
Brecon, Radnor, Hereford	56	11395	32	147	1934	1595		6419*	
					3435*				
Montgomery	108	17304	48	343	5338	1725	*75.6*	4978	3565
								3966*	
Flint	93	23285	70	321	8336	307	*96.4*	15891	1056
Denbigh	144	31833	84	495	13082	697	*94.9*	22426	1440
Lancashire, Cheshire†	36	7900	32	78	0	2176	*0.0*	0	7272
Merioneth	139	30585	97	431	14143	298	*97.9*	21754	609
Caernarfon	179	58901	147	763	28583	509	*98.3*	43794	995
Anglesey	102	25900	75	364	12751	241	*98.1*	19937	530

† including Flint and Denbigh

* No language given

Monthly Meetings[1]	Children Number Welsh	English	*Welsh as % Total*	Sunday Schools Teachers	Total
Wales	59194	14983	*79.8*	25115	205535
	1357*				
Monmouth	390	2941	*11.7*	1037	10848
Glamorgan	14425	8214	*63.7*	5977	56662
Carmarthen	4663	134	*97.2*	1163	11045
Pembroke	573	591	*49.2*	355	3371
Cardigan	4689	45	*99.0*	1943	14137
Brecon, Rad, Her	1357		–	384	3591
Montgomery	2813	774	*78.4*	1193	9008
Flint	4145	244	*94.4*	1700	13287
Denbigh	6169	200	*96.9*	2263	16751
Lancs and Cheshire†	0	1347	*0.0*	445	4700
Merioneth	6202	165	*97.4*	2289	17219
Caernarfon	10714	228	*97.9*	4662	31565
Anglesey	4411	100	*97.8*	1704	13351

† including Flint and Denbigh

Ancient Counties[1]	Chapels and Preaching Stations	Adher-ents	*Adher-ents as % pop.*
Wales	1486	313292	*15.6*
Monmouth	58	17384	*5.9*
Glamorgan	287	93919	*10.9*
Carmarthen	94	18661	*13.8*
Pembroke	47	6758	*7.6*
Cardigan	131	20021	*33.2*
Brecon	52	7055	*11.8*
Radnor	13	1367	*5.9*
Montgomery	93	11345	*20.7*
Flint	91	13412	*16.4*
Denbigh	183	32114	*24.7*
Merioneth	131	20428	*41.6*
Caernarfon	204	50361	*39.7*
Anglesey	102	20467	*40.4*

* No language given

	Churches	Sittings	Commun-icants	Adher-ents	Total in Sun-day Schools
England					
London (*Welsh*)[5]	16	4550	4398	6045	2810
Liverpool (*Welsh*)[6]	55	14962	8094	12748	7891
Liverpool and Cheshire (*English*)	18	6290	2492	5665	3046
Cheshire (*Welsh*)	4	1180	475	700	442
Manchester (*Welsh*)[7]	18	4150	1765	2866	1413
Shropshire[8]	16	3134	1247	2506	1387
Hereford, Gloucester (*English*)	5	980	129	790	267
Somerset (*Welsh*)[9]	1	500	31	70	11
Dublin (*Welsh*)	1	168	48	75	38
USA, Canada, Australia[10]	167	–	12576	25650	–

Source: Royal Commission on the Church of England and Other Religious Bodies in Wales and Monmouthshire, *Report, Vol. VII, Appendices to Minutes of Evidence. Nonconformists.* Denominational Statistics. Appendix II, Statistics of the Welsh Calvinistic Methodist Church for 1905, Tables I and IV, pp. 5, 7. Appendix XXXII, Welshmen outside of Wales – Calvinistic Methodists, p. 131 [PP 1910 (Cd. 5438) XIX].

[1] Combinations of associations of Calvinistic Methodist Churches (Monthly Meetings) approximate to county areas, with some notable exceptions. Montgomeryshire Lower, for example, contained 10 Chapels (9 Welsh, 1 English) in England. Conversely, the Lancashire and Cheshire group contained 36 Churches and preaching stations in Flintshire and Denbighshire. Although the figures reproduced in both parts of this table were originally compiled from the same source – the Yearbook for 1907 – they appear in two separate tables in *Denominational Statistics Appendix II* and show some discrepancies. Those in the first part claim only to have been adapted 'as far as possible' for Wales, whereas those in the second part were tabulated 'according to County areas' with sufficient confidence to include a final column giving statistics for adherents as a percentage of the population of Ancient County areas in 1901.

[2] The language of Chapels and Preaching Stations is given for some counties as follows: Monmouthshire – 25 Welsh, 38 English; Glamorgan – 211 Welsh, 78 English; Carmarthenshire – 87 Welsh, 6 English; Pembrokeshire – 28 Welsh, 20 English; Cardiganshire – 129 Welsh, 2 English.

[3] Adult members.

[4] All inclusive, i.e. members and any other attenders, adult and children.

[5] At Jewin Newydd, Charing Cross Road, Wilton Square, Falmouth Road, Mile End Road, Shirland Road, Holloway, Hammersmith, Stratford, Clapham Junction, Walham Green, Willesden Green, Lewisham, Tottenham, Walthamstow, Wood Green.

[6] Includes chapels at Runcorn, Widnes, Wigan, St Helens, Dalton in Furness, Millom, Workington, Spennymoor, Sunderland, Middlesborough, Stockton on Tees, Skelmersdale, Preston, Whitehaven.

[7] Includes chapels at Bolton, Bury, Stockport, Rochdale, Tyldesley, Ashton, Oldham, Warrington, Leigh, Farnworth, Earlstown, Altrincham, Sheffield, Blackburn.

[8] 9 Welsh, 7 English. Includes 2 chapels in Birmingham, 1 chapel in Wolverhampton, 1 chapel in Old Hill (Staffs), all Welsh.

[9] In Bristol.

[10] Appendix XXXII, p.131, states that collections were made for Welsh Calvinistic Methodist churches abroad as follows:

	Churches	Communicants	Adherents
Australia	3	196	270
USA	157	12000	25000
Canada (Llewelyn Settlement)	1	60	–
Patagonia	6	320	–
Cape Town (Undenominational)	1	–	–

Religion 2.8 Report of the Royal Commission on the Church of England and Other Religious Bodies in Wales and Monmouthshire, 1910. Questionnaire on bilingual Sunday services. Returns from the parishes in the Diocese of St David's. 1908

Answers to questions:[1]	A: For what class or classes of people are the English portions of your bilingual services provided? B: If you happen to know, please state whether any portions of the services (or sermons) in the Nonconformist chapels in your parish are in English.

GLAMORGAN

Neath District

Ystradfellte (Brec)
A: A goodly number of Radnorshire labourers have settled in this parish and they have mixed with the old nations thro' marriage and their descendants are English for all intents and purpose, there are also two families of Scotchmen here, Employed as Shepherds by Mr N(orth?) – besides at this time we have a few English in connection with the Neath District Waterworks Reservoir which is in this parish.
B: The Services of the Nonconformists to the utmost of my knowledge are in Welsh, but I think they have introduced a little English in Special Services, in their Prayers but this is a new thing for the district. I don't think my predecessor ever had any English in the Services or English Sermons with the exception of Harvest festival.

Ystradgynlais (Brec)
A: Working class. Colliers without exception.
B: –

Llanguicke
A: 1. Colliers. 2. Railway men. 3. A few English servant maids and many people who enjoy both languages indifferently.
B: No English at the principal Nonconformist Chapel but the Baptist cause recently begun provide a little English.

Llansamlet
A: All of the working classes.
B: There are two English Chapels. Some of the Welsh Chapels hold occasional English Services on Sundays.

Swansea District

Llangyfelach
A: The English services are held for the benefit of English residents in these districts.
B: There are no Nonconformist chapels in the parish in which there is a mixed service, but there are several English Chapels in Morriston but none in the outlying districts.

Waunarlwydd (Swansea Higher)
A: Chiefly the working class.
B: So far as I know all the services in the chapel are in Welsh.

Cwmbwrla
A: All services are in English.
B: –

Swansea (St Peter's)
A: For all classes, chiefly members of the working class.
B: In one of the chapels here the services are all English and in the others Welsh.

CARMARTHENSHIRE

Llanelli District

Dafen and Llwynhendy
A: Working classes chiefly Railway men (English), Miners and Tin-platers (Welsh).
B: None in English. All Welsh (except perhaps the Text).

Llanelli
A: Monoglot English of the working Class Welsh people versed in the English Language of the same Class.
B: Yes, in Three Chapels in the Parish. The Services and Sermons are entirely English.

Felinfoel
A: For all classes.
B: No.

Pembrey
A: Llandyry – Manager of Colliery and his wife and a few people of the working class.
Pwll – Families of Stradey Castle and Kilymaenllwyd and majority of the Church people of the district of the working class.
B: Burry Port – two Baptist Chapels, one Congregational Chapel, Entirely English. There are no bilingual services in Chapels to my knowledge.

Llandovery District

Llangadog (Gwynfe)
A: For different classes – working people – English boys as servants and some people in better circumstances than the above.
B: I do not think there is much English in the Chapels (Nonconformist).

Llanwrda
A: As a rule the same people attend our English and Welsh Services, quite the same people take part in the services, singing, responding, etc., the people in this district are practically bilinguists. The English services are a great help to boys and girls from English Industrial Schools who are here in strong numbers, also a few monoglot English people connected with the station and a few connected with the Llwyn-y-brain Estate.
B: There is no English provided at any of the Chapels, an occasional hymn sung in English when there may be some important English visitor. I should like to point out that no provision is made for the boys and girls from English Industrial Schools.

Llansadwrn	A: As a rule the same people attend our English and Welsh service quite the same people take part in the services, singing, responding etc., the people in this district are practically bilinguists. These English services are a great help to boys and girls from industrial Schools in England who are found here in rather large numbers, and also a few monoglot English people who are connected with Abermarlais Park. B: There is no English given at any of the Chapels in the parish with the occasional hymn in English. I would like to point out the fact that no provision is made for boys and girls from the English Industrial Schools, although in some cases pressure is brought to bear upon them by their employers to attend Dissenting Chapels rather than the service Church where they have a tendency to go.
Myddfai	A: For servants and the working class. B: To the best of my knowledge, there is no English in any of the Chapels.
Llanfair-ar-y-bryn (Ystrad-ffin)	A: Farm hands, who come to service in the Parish from industrial Schools, etc. in England. B: To the best of my knowledge, the English language is never heard in the Chapels in this parish.
Tirabad (Brec) (Llanddulas)	A: An artisan and his wife, and the Schoolmistress. [Only three English people in the parish.] B: No English whatever.
Llanwrtyd (Brec)	A: Residents and Visitors. English rapidly increasing. B: Calvinistic Methodist – entirely Welsh. Congregationalists and Baptists have an English sermon during the Season, followed by a Welsh Sermon, as a rule their Sermons are by different preachers.
Cil-y-cwm	A: For all classes. B: As far as I can gather all services and Sermons in the Nonconformist chapels in parish are Welsh. At Tynewydd (Meth.) an occasional chapter is read in English.
Cynwyl Gaeo	A: Families residen[t] in Country Seats and their servants and a number of English boys and girls in service in farms. B: I am not aware that there is any English given in any Nonconformist place of worship in the parish, though I know that a few English boys are taken to Chapel.

Llandeilo Fawr District

Llansawel	A: Families residen[t] in country seats and their servants – a number of English boys in service in farms. B: I am not aware that there is any English given in any chapel in the Parish, though I know that a few English boys are taken to Chapel.
Talley	A: For Edwinsford family of Talley House, also their servants and very many English boys from the different schools, our English Services are attended better than the Welsh as the Welsh people attend both services. B: There is no English in either of the two chapels and no provision whatever for the 30 Industrial school boys in the parish though the farmers often insist on taking their servants with them to Chapels.
Llanfynydd	A: They are provided for the family of Pantglas, their domestics, and some industrial boys, drawn from English Schools. B: I believe there is no English given in the Nonconformist chapels in my Parish.
Llanegwad	A: For all those of the congregation who do not understand Welsh. B: To the best of my knowledge and belief there is no English given in any of the chapels in the Parish.
Brynaman (Llandeilo Fawr)	A: 1. Colliers and colliery officials 2. Railway servants 3. Young people in business houses. B: In the Nonconformist Chapels the service and sermon are Welsh.
Taliaris (Llandeilo Fawr)	A: For the Squire (Mr Herbert Peel) and his family. A Gamekeeper and his family. A farm Bailiff and his family. Domestic Servants. English Industrial School boys at farms. A solicitor and sometimes his family. B: There are only 2 chapels in our parish, both Independent (or Congregationalist). I know that there is no portion of the service nor sermon in these two chapels conducted in English.
Cwmaman (Llandeilo Fawr)	A: Mainly Colliers, Tin Plate workers – and officials – with a few farmers. B: Of all the Nonconformist Chapels in this large and populous parish, there is only one small English gathering, the service being held in a vestry room underneath Bethel chapel only on Sunday evenings – the services often conducted by females and sometimes by an itinerant student – this service is only thinly attended.
Llandybïe	A: 1. Gentry 2. Colliers, Quarrymen, Railwaymen and a few domestic servants. B: There is an English Service once a month on Sunday afternoon at Llandebie in the Congregational Chapel. At Ammanford the Wesleyans and the Baptists have English Services every Sunday both morning and evening.

Carmarthen District

Llanddarog	A: For the Gentry and some Industrial School boys. B: There is no English in the Nonconformist Chapels.
Llanarthne (Gors-las)	A: For the gentry and some of the Industrial School boys. B: No English in Nonconformist chapels. (Gorslas) A: The Working Class. B: I hear that they give a portion of the Service in English, and occasionally English addresses.

Llangynnwr	A: Mostly for the better class of people, but some of the railway people from Pensarn attend the Church ... and few of the lads – servants in the farms from the Industrial Schools also appreciate the English Services. B: I do not think that any English is given in any of the two chapels in the Parish. It is possible that some English is given in Pen-sarn chapel but I am not aware of it.
Llangyndeyrn (Pontyberem)	A: For all classes. B: No.
Llansteffan	A: For all; except a small sprinkling of old Welsh people. The young people all appear to prefer English as they can read it with greater ease, and they understand an English Sermon better. I regret it personally, as I like a Welsh Service best; I have done my best to teach young boys in the Choir to read Welsh but they do not seem to take to it well. B: As far as I know there is no English as a rule, but when there are visitors in the summer they have to 'give a little English'. The Chapels are however beginning to feel the difficulty, since some of their young people have come over to Church because there is more English in Church. And there are several adults also in Church regularly because there is no English in Chapel. Yesterday I was asked to Church a Nonconformist woman who has come here to live from England. She could not go to Chapel as they were Welsh. I did so.
Llan-y-bri	A: For farmers and farm servants. B: No, none whatever.
Llanddowror	A: Gentry, Teachers, Farmers and Labourers. B: There is only one Chapel in this parish. The services in this as well as the Sermons are entirely in Welsh. Some Nonconformists who only know English have to my knowledge joined the church for this reason.
Llangynin	*There is no English given unless it is noticed that some English people are at the Services.* A: – B: In most Dissenting meeting-houses in the locality there is a demand for English and it is given by the preachers.
St Clears	A: The monoglot English especially (not the 'upper ten', but rather the 'lower five'). I may mention that I believe the majority of our Church Welsh people really prefer both service and sermon in English as they understand them better. Most of our Welsh speaking people cannot follow a real Welsh Sermon unless it is studded pretty thickly with English words and phrases! B: At the Wesleyan Chapel it is practically all English now. They often give portions of sermons in English at the 2 Independent Chapels here. I know there are some monoglot English people attending one, at least, of the Chapels; and there are Welsh people attending who practically do not understand and cannot at all follow the Welsh Sermons.
Llanfihangel Abercywyn	A: There are 3 families in the parish who prefer English although they understand Welsh. There are few others who prefer English. The bulk of the congregation is thorough Welsh; and we try and bear this in mind, though there are a few who clamour for more English – but they are only a few. B: Salem (Baptist) entirely Welsh. Trinity (Calvinistic Methodist) little English sometimes – but very little. Bankyfelin (Calvinistic Methodist) same as Trinity.
Llandeilo Abercywyn	A: – B: There is not a single Nonconformist Chapel in this small parish.
Llangynog	A: For all classes attending our Church who do not understand Welsh. B: In the two Chapels in my Parish Welsh only is the invariable language in which Services are conducted.
Llan-gain	*When some English families visit ... in summer, a little more of the service is read in English.* A: Chiefly for servants that have come to the parish from Industrial Schools, and other institutions from England. B: There is only one chapel in the parish and English is never given there.
Carmarthen (St Peter's)	A: Welsh services, English occasionally if English people present. B: –
Llanllawddog	A: For the squire of the Parish and family, residing at Glangwili Mansion, and his employees. There are also employed on the farms in the Parish many English boys from the Industrial Schools and they invariably attend Church. B: I am not aware and I do not believe that any portions of the services (or sermons) in the Nonconformist Chapels in this Parish are in English.
Aber-nant	*For boys from Industrial Schools and others.* A: – B: There is no English in any Chapel in the parish.
Cynwyl Elfed with Cwmduad	A: Working class – young men from England from Industrial Establishments some of whom settle here in the first instance from Industrial Schools. B: There is no English in any Chapel in either of these parishes.
Meidrim	A: In the morning, 2 or 3 English gentry attend, and their children, and by their own 'request'; the one 'mixed' Service. In the Evening, their servants attend, and some reformatory boys, and girls – farm-servants. B: Not, so far, within my parish. In the near district, Nonconformist chapels are introducing English, a little, into services, and sermons, so as to 'catch' our Reformatory youths!
Llanwinio	A: There are several English boys from Industrial Schools in this parish and English is chiefly provided for these.

B: Services and sermons are entirely Welsh in all the Nonconformist chapels in this parish.

PEMBROKESHIRE

Narberth District

Llanboidy (Carms) A: The gentry of the parish are English and there is a good number of male and female servants in the district and a few families of the working class. The farmers nearly all understand English. The gentry are never present at Evening service but the service is the same as the morning one.
B: I understand that a short English sermon is given every Sunday Evening at the chapel in the village.

Henllan Amgoed (Carms) A: Some farmers, and a few well-to-do people, with boys from Industrial Schools are English.
B: Sometimes, I believe, a few words are said by the Independent Minister in English before the Welsh sermon.

Llanglydwen (Carms) A: Dolwilym and Glyntaf families and their dependents – Porters Railway Station – and few English farm servants.
B: At Hebron the only Nonconformist Chapel in parish, services are I believe, entirely in Welsh.

Mynachlog-ddu A: Two families (Farmers) and a few boys from the Industrial Schools which are in service in the neighbourhood.
B: No English at all, I am told, in the Baptist chapel which is the only chapel in the parish.

Llangolman A: The English portion of the service is provided for five English members who cannot speak Welsh; and for two children belonging to one of the families.
B: Llandilo Congregational Chapel, about a mile from Llangolman Church has a part of the service in English (very likely a part of the sermon) for the benefit of an English farmer and his family who have not been in the neighbourhood long; and for a few industrial school girls.

Maenclochog A: A fair number of our congregation do not speak Welsh.
B: I am not aware that any portion of the services, at either of the two Congregational Chapels in Maenclochog, are in English.

New Moat A: For farmers and farm servants.
B: We have no Chapel in the parish.

Llys-y-frân A: Farmers and farm labourers.
B: General Rule Welsh. Sometimes English.

Llan-y-cefn A: There are some English people from the English part who prefer English and English boys from England. There is no 'parish Esquire'.
B: There is none in this parish.

Llandysilio (Carms and Pembs) A: Farmers and working people without one single exception.
B: 1. At the Independent Chapel there is some little English occasionally. 2. At Blaenconin (Baptist) Sermon is supposed to be given once a month, but this depends on the Minister present being able to do so. 3. No English at Rhydwilym Baptist. It is the most Welsh part of the Parish. 4. At the new chapel (Methodist) at Clynderwen the Services are bilingual but more Welsh than English.

Egrmwnt (Carms) A: All that attend are farmers and working people without one single exception.
B: No Chapels in the Parish.

Llan-gan (Carms and Pembs) A: For farmers and artizans; and at Whitland many Railway Men.
B: I am given to understand that at Whitland the New Ministers lately appointed were selected, principally, to give parts of their Services and Sermons in English.

Cyffig (Carms) A: For all alike as the English language predominates considerably: All would understand English, but a few prefer Welsh as they are Welsh by descent.
B: I have made enquiries and find that there is a portion of the Services and Sermon delivered in English every Sunday in both the Nonconformist Chapels of Kiffig.

Llanddewi Velfrey A: The Trewern and Henllan Families attend Church with some of their Servants. All the other Church people of the parish are farm labourers and artizans with their families. There are no Church Farmers in the parish.
B: Yes. English sermons are often delivered in the two Chapels of the parish and always when there are Special Services. The parish is on the border line between the English and Welsh part of Pembrokeshire and the inhabitants judging from what I know of the parish understand English better than Welsh. They do not understand and cannot follow the Services in Welsh.

Castelldwyran (Cilymaenllwyd) (Carms) A: Farmers and working people without one single exception.
B: No Chapel in this Parish.

Pembroke District – no returns

Haverfordwest District

St Lawrence A: For all classes, except those that are thoroughly English.
B: Some English is given in the nearest chapels (one in my parish and one in Hayscastle) I do not know how much.

Hayscastle A: The majority of our Churchpeople are English or prefer English – our young people are becoming more and more English every year.

B: Yes: an English Sermon is given at the Baptist, Independent and Methodist Chapels whenever they find even one English person present. Their Hymn Books contain English Hymns.

St Edrens
A: All classes.
B: There is some English, I am informed, given in the Nonconformist Chapel.

Llandeloy with Llanrheithan
A: For those who find it difficult to respond or read in Welsh. For the monoglot English people.
B: I understand that the Services (and sermons) are entirely in Welsh.

Brawdy
A: For the main body of Churchpeople (squire, farmers, workmen, servants).
B: No English I believe as a rule in Independent Chapel. Most Baptists go to Chapel in adjoining parish which is English.

Whitchurch (Solva)
A: For the majority of Churchpeople – farmers, shopkeepers, servants (farm and domestic).
B: Not as a rule – but if monoglot English are present I am told English is occasionally given.

Llanhowel
A: For farmers and farm labourers.
B: I understand the Nonconformist Chapels in the district generally have some English at their services.

Llanrhian
A: The principal farmer's wife and her nephews, the schoolmaster and a few farm servants. In the summer months, English visitors at Trevine.
B: The text is sometimes given in English in the Chapels in this parish.

Mathri
A: Four farmers with large families. Two tailors with numerous families. One Carpenter's wife and four children. The family of a blacksmith also our Butcher's family though Welsh speaking prefer English.
B: It is not the rule to preach English in the Chapels as no English people belong to them in the parish. When some of my flock rarely stray they get English.

Granston with St Nicholas
A: Gentry, English Farmers and Labourers.
B: In the Baptist chapel in Llangloffan and in a branch of it in the village of St Nicholas no English is employed in the Services. In the Independent Chapel in the parish of St Nicholas English is used in the service sometimes if any English are present. English Hymn, prayer in English by the Minister and sermon in English so I have been informed by one of the congregation.

Llanstinan
A: [?] family, Sunday school children, wife of a Gentleman farmer, a few farmers who understand English as well as Welsh.
B: –

Jordanston
A: Agricultural labourers, navvies, and their families and Farmers. (no resident gentry).
B: There is only a branch chapel in the Parish, right on the border of Manorowen Parish, only Sunday Evening Welsh services and Sunday School in the afternoon. Nothing in the morning.

Llanfair Nant-y-gof
A: Schoolteachers, Gardeners, artizans, and some English people in the District.
B: Have no knowledge – most likely Welsh.

Letterston
A: For all classes – from the chief inhabitant to the labourer. Since the Advent of the Railway through the parish, a good many English have come in. Even the Welsh prefer English Services.
B: Have no knowledge – must be bilingual.

Ambleston
A: For all classes.
B: In the two chapels (Calvinistic Methodist) the services and sermons are usually in Welsh – but if the itinerant ministers prefer English then all the services and sermons are in English.

East Walton
A: Farmers, Mechanics, and farm Labourers.
B: I do not know. I think as a general rule it is Welsh. Maids and servants come from the upper parts of the County and are Welsh, and nonconformists and the chapel provides for them.

CARDIGANSHIRE

Cardigan District

Dinas (Pembs)
A: The English portion of my Congregation is made up of monoglot middle class English people (about 15 in number) – Coastguards and families make up about 10 of the number. From Easter to October the English portion increases considerably owing to sea-side visitors from England – this accounts for the separate English service during that period.
B: I make occasional enquiries and do not think anything more than the text is given in English. I attended the Quarterly Meetings of the Babtist [*sic*] two weeks ago, heard 8 Sermons all Welsh. The only English spoken was by a Missionary from Congo and he spoke in English, not for the sake of his hearers, but because he felt his Welsh would be weak. The only place where English is regularly given is at Church.

Newport (Pembs)
A: All classes – rich and Poor.
B: In the Summer English Sermons are preached occasionally – and in the Baptist Chapel in the morning, the substance of the Welsh sermon is given in English.

Nevern (Pembs)
A: Squire of Parish and family and Dependents. English speaking resident farmers and families, English speaking boys and girls in service on farms.
B: Gethesmane [*sic*] Calvinistic Methodist – short English sermon generally. Velindre Congregationalist – short English occasionally. Penuel Baptist – short English occasionally.

Cilgwyn (Pembs)
A: For English boy servants in the service of farmers in the district.
B: –

Meline (Pembs)
A: For those who are monoglot English, old residents, and new comers, and Industrial Homes Boys and Girls.

	B: I believe portions of the services (or sermons) in Cana, Congregational Chapel, Velindre, are occasionally in English.
Whitchurch with Llanfair Nant-gwyn (Pembs)	A: Mostly for English working men in neighbourhood. For English boys and girls from industrial Schools. B: Not a word of English used in any Nonconformist Chapel in the neighbourhood.
Llantood (Pembs)	A: English gentry and their domestics. B: There is one (Glanrhyd) in Llantood Parish. Services, I believe, are entirely Welsh there.
Monington (Pembs)	A: English gentry and their domestics. B: No Nonconformist chapel in Monington Parish.
Bridell (Pembs)	A: All classes that are generally found in agricultural parishes – gentry, some of their servants, and some boys and girls from the Homes engaged at farms in the parish or district. B: There is no portion of the services, or sermons, ever in English in the only Nonconformist Chapel in my parish – this I ascertained from the Chief Deacon yesterday. His reply to my question was 'Dim Seisneg un amser'.
Cilgerran (Pembs)	A: For all Classes, gentry and ordinary parishioners who may be English. Nearly all that attend the Church understand English, though most of them are Welsh. B: I have been told that if a person known to be English (without a knowledge of Welsh) should be present, the minister gives the text, and makes a few remarks, in English. The occasion seldom arises.
St Dogmaels (Pembs)	A: Chiefly coastguardsmen. B: I believe their services are exclusively Welsh,[2] unless they may be giving some little English in Summer-time when there are English visitors in the village.
Llangoedmor	A: For the gentry residing in the parish and also for English servants. B: The services and sermons in the Nonconformist Chapels in the parish are entirely Welsh.
Aber-porth	A: For the gentry and their dependents. English visitors and some English residents in the place. B: The chapels about here make no provision for English. They might in the summer give a little English. The English people of the place and the English visitors are nearly entirely dependent on the provisions made by the Church.
Blaen-porth	A: 1. For two gentlemen's families. 2. For some half a dozen 'Industrial School' boys in service at different farms. B: No English whatever is used in the Nonconformist Chapels.
Llanfihangel Penbedw (Pembs)	A: With two or three exceptions the English portion of the congregation is composed of the industrial classes – Farm boys from Industrial schools. Servants in gentlemen's houses, Labourers, etc. B: Seldom there is any English in the Chapels. Only sometimes at Special meetings a few words in English are spoken.

Newcastle Emlyn District

Capel Colman (Pembs)	A: With two or three exceptions they are of the working class. B: As a rule I believe no English is to be heard in the Chapel – now and again when some special services are held, a short address is given in English.
Penrhydd (Pembs)	A: Boy and girl from School at service on a farm close by. Last year we had four boys from School here. We have no English people in the place … B: Only one Chapel in the Parish. There is no English at all there.
Cenarth (Carms) (Newcastle Emlyn)	A: The upper and middle classes. B: An occasional English sermon preceding the Welsh.
Llangeler (Carms)	A: Rich and poor, masters and servants. B: As a rule none from what I hear. There are no English people belonging to them. I believe that an English Sermon is preached at the quarterly meetings of the denomination.
Brongwyn	A: I For the best class in the Parish. II For Industrial School boys. B: There is no English whatever in the Nonconformist chapels in this parish. Not even the text is given out in English.
Troed-yr-aur	A: For two English Families together with Industrial School Children in the employ of farmers. B: If any of our school children happen to stray into Chapels the minister will read a chapter of the Bible in English.
Betws Ifan	A: I For the best class in the parish. II For Industrial School boys. B: There is no English whatever in the Nonconformist chapels in this parish. Not even the text is given out in English.
Penbryn	A: Mainly for Visitors to the Seaside, but there are a few servants and others that prefer English, though they understand little Welsh. B: There are no English Services or Sermons in any of the Nonconformist Chapels in this parish except in a small Branch in Traethsaith where they have an occasional service and sermon during the summer months. Last summer they had only one service in English and the preacher could not preach in English, so they procured an interpreter. The Chapel is Methodist.
Llangrannog	A: Mixed Visitors, but chiefly of the better class from all parts of the Country as well as for the family who happens to occupy Llynsford[?] their visitors and some of the servants.

	B: Not to my knowledge. A considerable percentage of the English Nonconformist visitors attend church on Sunday mornings because it is partly English.
Llangynllo	A: Monoglot English people residents in the Parish and their Servants. B: Not to my knowledge.
Bangor Teifi and Henllan	A: Two families of the upper class in each church and a few others. B: No English.
Llandysul	A: More especially the Middle Class – but there is a certain number of monoglot English people belonging to the upper and lower classes. B: No regular English Services or Sermons at any of the Nonconformist Chapels. I am informed that a little English is occasionally given at one or two Chapels.
Llanfihangel-ar-arth (Carms)	A: Upper and middle classes resident in the Parish, as well as for visitors during the summer and autumn. B: I cannot say. I believe an occasional sermon is given at the Congregational Chapel, Pencader.
Pencader (Carms)	A: Middle and working classes. B: I cannot say. I believe an occasional English Sermon is given at Congregational Chapel, Pencader.

Lampeter District

Llanybydder (Carms)	A: The artisan class, and for English visitors. B: I do not think that either Services or Sermons in English are ever held in the Nonconformist Chapels in the parish.
Llan-y-crwys (Carms)	A: Boys and girls from Church Homes and a few English who are married and settled down here. B: All Welsh.
Lampeter	A: For the servants and the families of workmen at Falcondale. B: No English is given in any chapel here, so far as I can ascertain.
Llanwenog	A: The English service is provided for a few gentlefolk and their dependents. B: No English Services are ever held in the Nonconformist Chapels.

Aberaeron District

Llannarth with Llanina	[Llanina more English in the service than Llannarth] A: The Landowners and household dependents; and the English boys from Industrial Schools in service in the neighbourhood. B: The Rev. J. M. Prytherch, Minister of the Congregational Chapels of Wern and Pencae, gives a portion of the sermon only in English occasionally when English visitors happen to attend either of his chapels.
Llanfihangel Ystrad	A: The families of Llanlear, and Brynog, and their dependents. B: No English.
Cilcennin with LlanbadarnTref-eglwys	A: For English boys from Industrial schools that are in service in the parish. B: All Welsh.

Aberystwyth District

Llanrhystud	A: Rich and poor. B: I am not aware of any English services being held anywhere.
Llanddeiniol	A: At present there are only two persons attending our church who are unable to follow the service in Welsh – the Vicar's wife and a man in service in the parish. It has always been a custom here to have a portion of the service in English. The parishioners approve of it. B: No portion of the services is ever carried on in English in the Nonconformist Chapel in this parish.
Llanilar	A: Servants and working people. A mixture of all classes attend the 11.30 a.m. service in English. B: Only one sermon delivered in the memory of the oldest inhabitants. I can give fuller information with regard to this particular sermon if required.
Llanychaearn	*One Welsh, one English service each Sunday morning, bilingual afternoon Sunday school and bilingual evening service.* A: – B: I am not able to say.
Llanfihangel-Genau'r-glyn[3]	A: It is only at the Mission Church in Talybont we have a bilingual service on Sunday mornings – a few of the collects are had in English, one lesson and sometimes the Psalms. Then is a short English sermon, with another short one in Welsh, and this arrangement is made to suit the convenience of one English family. We have English and Welsh services regularly every Sunday at the parish Church and also at Borth. B: No bilingual services are held in the Chapels as far as I know except in Borth for five or six Sundays during the summer and this arrangement is made to meet some of the Nonconformist visitors.
Llangynfelyn	A: There are a few English people in the Parish who frequent the Bilingual service on Sunday Evenings in addition to the English service at 11.15 on Sunday morning. One is a Medical man, another (with a family) is a gardener, two or three are servants and there are a few English women married to Welshmen. B: Occasionally parts of the sermon are given in English at one of the Nonconformist chapels in the parish. Still this must be regarded as the exception and not the rule.
Llangorwen	A: For a few people of all classes living in the Parish.

(Llanbadarn Fawr)	B: None.
Cwmrheidol (Llanbadarn Fawr)	A: They are provided for working men, really tramps, who have settled down in the Parish, since my advent here, and I have prevailed on them to attend Church, and now they are useful members of society. I have also some boys who come from Birmingham. B: None whatever.
Capel Bangor (Llanbadarn Fawr)	A: (a) For the better class, viz the squire of the parish, his family, and several others. (b) The working class, of whom we have a good few. B: –
Llanfihangel-y-Creuddyn	A: For domestic Servants, gardeners, and Farm labourers. B: To the best of my knowledge, no portions of the Services or Sermons are ever given in English, in Nonconformist Chapels, in my Parish.

Tregaron District

Llangeitho	A: There are always some English servants, in the neighbourhood, they have been here for years, and few of them are regular communicants. B: There is no Dissenting Chapel in the parish, there is no English in the neighbouring chapels.
Strata Florida (Caron-is-clawdd)	A: Visitors etc. B: None.
Tregaron (Caron-is-clawdd)	A: Very varied. At present we have three families residing in the immediate neighbourhood, viz. Sunnyhill, Brynygôg, Plas Waunfawr. Masters at Intermediate School. Excise officer, a Painter, Plumber and families, Servant men and boys and girls etc. All grades are represented. B: There is no English in the Chapel, except an occasional sermon preached by a Visitor.

BRECONSHIRE

Builth District

Llanfihangel Abergwesyn	A: English residents – few labourers – schoolmistress – farmer (Visitors in summer). B: –
Llanafan Fawr (with Llanfihangel Brynpabuan)	*The Church people young and old understand and speak English. There are very few who understand sermon Welsh. The young with few exceptions monoglot English. I preach a Welsh sermon occasionally – but when I do so I know that I speak almost in an unknown tongue.* A: All my people are Farmers, farm servants, and tradesmen. B: Independent Chapels – Troedrhywdar, Capel Groes, Partly English, Partly Welsh. Baptist – Pisgah, entirely English.

Brecon District

Merthyr Cynog	A: All my people are farmers and labourers. A good many families are English who come from Radnorshire and other English districts. Several of the farm labourers come from East Breconshire and Herefordshire. Two families of farmers are Scotch. The young people habitually speak English. B: In the two Methodist chapels, part of the sermon is nearly always in English and a hymn or two. The prayers in prayer meetings nearly always Welsh, I believe. In the two Independent Chapels, the sermons are nearly always mixed, and in the evening often entirely English as far as I can make out. The prayers in prayer meetings are in both tongues and also hymns.
Garthbrengi	A: For Welsh people who have no knowledge of the vernacular. B: No chapel in Parish.
Llanfihangel Fechan (Chapelry)	*Services all English – Except at Harvest Festival services.* A: – B: There is a Methodist Chapel where the services and sermons are bilingual.
Llanfihangel Nant Brân	A: Farm servants. B: I do not know.
Llandeilo'r-fân	A: Farm servants and people of a higher class who have come to live in the parish. B: I do not know.
Llywel	A: I may say that most of the people who attend the services understand English as well as Welsh – and I think this is the case in most of the Brecon parishes. The congregations are made up of all classes. B: I believe a special English sermon is given at Cwmwysg Independent Chapel once if not twice a month. I believe that there is a good deal of English given in the other Chapels especially when English servants are employed in the neighbourhood and attend the chapels.
Traean-glas	A: Servant Boys and Girls from English Schools; Mr and Mrs Jeffrey, Camden House who attend regularly with their 4 children and Governess. Three other English families attend occasionally. B: There used to be an English Service once a month at Cwmwysg Congregational Chapel but I am given to understand that this is discontinued – the English family that attended has left the district.
Trallong	*Bilingual service on Sunday morning – all the members of my Congregation understand English fairly well.* A: –

	B: There is only one Chapel in the Parish, and the Services as a rule, are all in Welsh. A small portion of the Service and Sermon is given occasionally in English – but the younger members of the Congregation, I am told, are anxious for more English.
Defynnog	A: A few of the upper Class, the remainder would be of the labouring class. B: The services and sermons in the Wesleyan Chapel are in English.
Llanilltyd	A: We have only one class; viz the working people, labourers etc. in this Parish. English is given because our Evening Service is largely attended by farm servants, (men and women) who are unable to understand Welsh. Over half the evening congregation is made up of such. English is the only language understood by the children and the young people of this Parish. English is generally the language of the home even when the parents prefer Welsh. B: The only Nonconformists in this Parish are Congregationalists. Their Services and Sermons are Bilingual almost without an exception. I am told that there is almost, if not quite, as much English as Welsh employed in their Services, and more English still will have to be given in the immediate future.
Crai	A: Some well to do English people, and also servant men and women especially in the evening. B: As a rule no English in Chapel.
Llanfigan	*All the Congregation know English. By far the greater part are young people who do not know Welsh sufficiently well to understand a Welsh sermon.* A: Working farmers and their families and servants – the latter chiefly English. B: Benaiah Chapel – Independent – 30 years ago when I came here, was all Welsh. It is now, I am given to understand nearly all English. The Aber chapel Welsh [?of the] Welsh formerly. Now service in both languages. The rising generation of Dissenters do not know Welsh.

MONTGOMERYSHIRE

Machynlleth District

Eglwys-fach (Llanfihangel Genau'r-glyn)	A: As a rule for the working class. B: To the best of my knowledge the Services and sermons in the Nonconformist Chapels in this Parish are at the present time entirely in Welsh.

Source: National Library of Wales, St David's Diocesan Papers. Papers relating to the Royal Commission on the Church of England in Wales and Monmouthshire, 1906–10. Returns on bilingual Sunday services in the Diocese of St David's, 1908.

These are the full written replies, given by Church officials to the last two questions on a printed two-page questionnaire sent to each parish in the Diocese of St David's. In some cases, comments about language use, contained in answers to other questions have been appended in italics. A question mark in brackets indicates illegibility in the returns. The returns have been grouped according to Registration Districts, as constituted in 1851, to enable comparison with Religion tables 1.2 and 2.2.

[1] Answers A and B correspond to questions 3 and 4 on the questionnaire. Other questions were as follows:

1. Please state what portion of each bilingual service is in Welsh and in English respectively –
(a) On Sunday morning
  (1) As a general rule
  (2) On certain Sundays in the month
  (3) At different times of the year
(b) On Sunday afternoon
  (1) As a general rule
  (2) On certain Sundays in the month
  (3) At different times of the year
(c) On Sunday evening
  (1) As a general rule
  (2) On certain Sundays in the month
  (3) At different times of the year
2. Please state what your arrangements are in regard to the language of sermons at bilingual services.

[2] 'English', not 'Welsh', was the word actually written. However, from the sense of the sentence and from other comment given, this was clearly an error and has been corrected here.

[3] The questionnaire was not properly completed. This information was written in a signed statement in the space for answers to question 1.

V

Culture

Diwylliant

Rhagymadrodd

Drwy gydol y bedwaredd ganrif ar bymtheg, diogelwyd yr iaith Gymraeg gan amryfal weithgareddau diwylliannol yn perthyn i draddodiad hir o farddoniaeth, drama, canu baledi ac arferion gwerin. Yr oedd yr eisteddfodau, y cyfarfodydd llenyddol a'r traddodiad cerddorol i gyd yn gysylltiedig ag etifeddiaeth ddiwylliannol gyfoethog Cymru. At hynny, gellir priodoli twf a llwyddiant y gweisg argraffu Cymraeg yn y bedwaredd ganrif ar bymtheg i lwyddiant yr ysgolion Sul Ymneilltuol i ddysgu plant ac oedolion fel ei gilydd i ddarllen yn eu mamiaith. Er mor ddibris oedd y Comisiynwyr Addysg ym 1847 o'r gyfundrefn addysg ffurfiol (Saesneg) a'r arferion cymdeithasol a ganfuwyd ganddynt yng Nghymru, gorfodwyd hwythau hyd yn oed i gydnabod bod y dosbarthiadau gweithiol yng Nghymru yn fwy llythrennog yn eu hiaith eu hunain na'u cymheiriaid yn Lloegr. Daeth gweisg argraffu Cymraeg fel Gwasg Gee a Hughes a'i Fab yn enwau cyfarwydd ac yr oedd eu cyfraniad i'r proses o ailgynnau hunaniaeth a balchder cenedlaethol ymhlith y werin addysgedig yn ail hanner y bedwaredd ganrif ar bymtheg yn allweddol. Ac eto ni ellir yn rhwydd fesur cyfraniad diwylliant i hynt a helynt y Gymraeg mewn ystadegau. Y mae bron y cyfan o'r dystiolaeth sydd ar gael yn ansoddol yn hytrach na meintiol. Serch hynny, gobeithir y bydd y deunydd a geir yma, nad yw'r cyfan ohono yn ystadegol ei natur, yn taflu peth goleuni ar rai o'r sefydliadau diwylliannol a fu'n gymorth i feithrin y Gymraeg mewn cyfnod tyngedfennol yn ei hanes.

Y mae a wnelo'r grŵp cyntaf o dablau â'r enwocaf, yn ôl pob tebyg, o sefydliadau diwylliannol Cymru, sef yr eisteddfod. Tua diwedd y ddeunawfed ganrif a rhan gyntaf y bedwaredd ganrif ar bymtheg daeth y gwyliau cystadleuol hyn – a ailsefydlwyd ar batrwm hen draddodiad barddol – yn rhan hanfodol o weithgaredd y nifer cynyddol o gymdeithasau a sefydlwyd i hyrwyddo llenyddiaeth a cherddoriaeth Cymru. Cynhaliai'r Gwyneddigion, y Cymmrodorion, a'r Cymreigyddion yn Llundain eisteddfodau yn gyson, fel y gwnâi'r Gordofigion yn Lerpwl a chymdeithasau rhanbarthol cyffelyb yng Nghymru, gan ennyn dadlau brwd weithiau ynglŷn â rhagoriaethau gwahanol feirdd a cherddorion. Datblygwyd y cystadlu ar raddfa fwy yn yr Eisteddfod Genedlaethol, a gynhaliwyd yn flynyddol bron yn ddi-fwlch o 1861 ymlaen. Meddai'r *Carnarvon*

Introduction

Throughout the nineteenth century the well-being of the Welsh language was sustained by a range of cultural activities which followed a long oral tradition of poetry, drama, ballad-singing and folk customs. Eisteddfodau, literary meetings and music-making all had direct links to a rich Welsh cultural heritage. In addition, the growth and success of Welsh printing presses in the nineteenth century can be attributed to the success of Welsh Nonconformist Sunday schools in teaching children and adults alike to read in their native tongue. Even the notorious Education Commissioners in 1847, while dismissive of the formal (English) education system and the social customs they discovered in Wales, were forced to acknowledge that the labouring classes in Wales were more literate in their own tongue than their English counterparts. Welsh printing presses such as Gwasg Gee and Hughes a'i Fab became household names in Wales and played a vital role in reawakening a sense of national identity and a pride in an educated *gwerin* in the second half of the nineteenth century. Yet the contribution of culture to the fortunes of the Welsh language cannot easily be represented in quantitative terms. Almost all available evidence is qualitative rather than quantitative. Nevertheless, it is hoped that the material displayed here, not all of which is statistical in nature, will provide an insight into some of the cultural institutions which helped to nourish the Welsh language during a critical period.

The first group of tables deal with perhaps the most famous of Welsh cultural institutions, the eisteddfod. These competitive festivals of poetry, prose and music were re-established in the pattern of an ancient bardic tradition towards the end of the eighteenth century and during the early nineteenth century as an essential part of the growing number of societies established to promote Welsh literature and music. The *Gwyneddigion,* the *Cymmrodorion*, and the *Cymreigyddion* in London, the *Gordofigion* in Liverpool, and similar provincial societies within Wales, all held regular eisteddfodau which sometimes generated heated arguments over the respective merits of competing poets and musicians. The competitions were developed on a grander scale in official National Eisteddfodau, held annually, with a few intervals, from 1861 onwards. It was claimed in the *Carnarvon and Denbigh Herald* in 1866: 'What the

and Denbigh Herald ym 1866: 'What the "Derby Day" is to the Londoner, or the "Leger" to the Yorkshireman, the Eisteddfod is to the Welshman.'[1] Dengys Tabl 1.1, sy'n rhestru lleoliadau a dyddiadau'r Eisteddfod Genedlaethol, oruchafiaeth gogledd Cymru yn y 1870au; wedi hynny, fe'i cynhaliwyd yng ngogledd a de Cymru bob yn ail, er iddi ymweld â Lloegr hefyd nifer o weithiau. Er nad oes ffigurau mynychu swyddogol ar gael, nid oes amheuaeth ynglŷn â phoblogrwydd yr Eisteddfod. Yng nghyfarfod cyntaf Eisteddfod Genedlaethol Lerpwl ym 1890, dywedir bod cynulleidfa enfawr yn bresennol ar gyfer y brif gystadleuaeth gorawl, gyda phob sedd a phob modfedd o le sefyll yn llawn.[2]

Rhydd Tabl 1.2 ffigurau ar gyfer nifer yr eisteddfodau a gynhaliwyd yng Nghymru rhwng 1802 a 1900, fel y nodir gan David Morgan Richards yn *Rhestr Eisteddfodau hyd y flwyddyn 1901*.[3] Er bod yr ystadegau yn dangos cynnydd amlwg, nid ydynt wrth reswm yn adlewyrchu'r holl weithgarwch eisteddfodol mewn capeli, ysgolion, cymdeithasau cyfeillgar, a phentrefi ledled Cymru. Y mae Tabl 1.3, a seiliwyd ar yr un ffynhonnell, yn rhestru eisteddfodau a gynhaliwyd y tu allan i Gymru ac yn dangos i ba raddau y glynodd y Cymry oddi cartref wrth eu hunaniaeth ddiwylliannol Gymreig. Yn yr eisteddfod ddeuddydd a gynhaliwyd yn Hyde Park, Pennsylvania, ym 1875, er enghraifft, yr oedd pabell yr eisteddfod dan ei sang, gyda 6,000 yn mynychu pob un o'r chwe sesiwn.[4] Yr oedd eisteddfod y Cymry, fe ymddengys, mor boblogaidd dramor ag ydoedd gartref.

Dengys Tablau 1.4 i 1.6, sy'n rhestru testunau a nifer y cystadleuwyr yn Eisteddfodau Cenedlaethol Aberystwyth (1865), Caerdydd (1883) a Lerpwl (1900), fod natur yr Eisteddfod yn newid ac nad oedd pob un o'i hyrwyddwyr yn awyddus i ddiogelu'r famiaith. Yn sgil 'Brad y Llyfrau Gleision' ym 1847, dadleuai iwtilitariaid yn frwd fod y gallu i siarad Saesneg yn hanfodol os oedd y Cymry i gael gwared ar eu diffygion deallusol a moesol. Trwy gyflwyno cystadlaethau Saesneg ar bynciau cymdeithasol yn nhestunau 1862, mynnodd Hugh Owen hyrwyddo'r iaith Saesneg o fewn prif sefydliad diwylliannol Cymru. Yr oedd ffrwyth ei bolisi eisoes yn amlwg yn y dewis o destunau yn yr Eisteddfod Genedlaethol a gynhaliwyd yn Aberystwyth ym 1865 (Tabl 1.4), ond gwelir effaith y Seisnigo orau yng nghystadlaethau Eisteddfod Caerdydd ym 1883 (Tabl 1.5). Un gân Gymraeg yn unig a gynhwyswyd yn y cystadlaethau lleisiol; Saesneg oedd iaith un ar ddeg o'r ddwy gystadleuaeth ar hugain yn yr adran ryddiaith; yr oedd hyd yn oed gystadleuaeth y bryddest, sef cerdd y goron, yn agored i gerddi Saesneg yn ogystal â rhai Cymraeg. Erbyn 1900, fodd bynnag, pan gynhaliwyd yr Eisteddfod yn Lerpwl, yr oedd y llanw yn amlwg wedi troi, fel y dengys Tabl 1.6. Yr oedd yr adran farddoniaeth yn gwbl Gymraeg ac, er bod dewis mewn rhai dosbarthiadau, gellid cynnig yn Gymraeg ar

"Derby Day" is to the Londoner, or the "Leger" to the Yorkshireman, the Eisteddfod is to the Welshman.'[1] Table 1.1, which simply lists the location and dates of the National Eisteddfod, reveals the dominance of north Wales in the 1870s, and the fact that the venue thereafter alternated between north and south Wales, though it also moved to England on several occasions. Although no official attendance figures are available, there is no doubt of the popularity of the Eisteddfod. At the first meeting of the National Eisteddfod held at Liverpool in 1890, a 'huge attendance' was claimed for the chief choral competition, 'every seat and every inch of standing room being occupied'.[2]

Table 1.2 gives figures for the number of eisteddfodau held in Wales between 1802 and 1900, as noted by David Morgan Richards in *Rhestr Eisteddfodau hyd y flwyddyn 1901*.[3] Although the statistics clearly indicate a rising trend, they necessarily fail to reflect the widespread popular involvement of chapel groups, schools, friendly societies, and villages in local eisteddfodau throughout Wales. Derived from the same source, Table 1.3 lists eisteddfodau held outside Wales. It suggests the extent to which Welsh exiles clung to their distinctive Welsh cultural identity. For instance, at the two-day eisteddfod held at Hyde Park, Pennsylvania, in 1875, the eisteddfod tent was full to its 6,000 capacity during all six sessions.[4] The Welsh eisteddfod, it would appear, was as popular abroad as it was at home.

Tables 1.4 to 1.6 list the subjects and the number of competitors for three National Eisteddfodau, held at Aberystwyth, Cardiff, and Liverpool in the years 1865, 1883, and 1900 respectively. They are included to illustrate the changing character of the National Eisteddfod. It is clear that not all promoters of the National Eisteddfod were anxious to preserve the mother tongue. In the wake of the 'Treachery of the Blue Books' in 1847, middle-class utilitarians argued strongly that the acquisition of English was a necessity if the Welsh were to rid themselves of their intellectual and moral deficiencies. By introducing a 'Social Science Section' into the Eisteddfod programme from 1862 onwards, Hugh Owen resolved to promote the English language in the premier cultural institution in Wales. The fruits of his policy were already apparent in the choice of subjects at the National Eisteddfod held at Aberystwyth in 1865 (Table 1.4), but the degree of Anglicization is best reflected in competitions at the Cardiff Eisteddfod in 1883 (Table 1.5). Only one Welsh song was included in the vocal competitions; eleven of the twenty-two categories of prose competition were English only; even the competition for the principal *pryddest,* the crown poem, was open to English as well as Welsh entries. However, by 1900, when the Eisteddfod was held in Liverpool (Table 1.6), this trend had clearly been reversed. The poetry

yr holl destunau rhyddiaith, a gosodwyd caneuon Cymraeg a Saesneg ar gyfer y pedair prif gystadleuaeth gorawl. Serch hynny, y mae enwau'r corau a oedd yn cystadlu yn dangos i ba raddau yr oedd diddordeb yn yr Eisteddfod Genedlaethol yn ymestyn y tu draw i Glawdd Offa. Denwyd y Blackpool Glee and Madrigal Society, y Birmingham Welsh Musical Society, y Liverpool Juveniles, a'r Millgirls Industrial Choir o Fanceinion, ymhlith nifer o gorau eraill o Loegr, i gystadlu yn erbyn corau Cymru yn y prif gystadlaethau corawl.

Y mae'r tabl olaf yng ngrŵp yr Eisteddfod (Tabl 1.7) yn rhestru'r testunau a'r awduron arobryn yng nghystadlaethau drama yr Eisteddfod Genedlaethol rhwng 1884 a 1913, ac yn ein hatgoffa unwaith eto o'r modd y llwyddodd Ymneilltuaeth Gymreig i ddylanwadu ar bron pob agwedd ar fywyd yng Nghymru. Amlygir yr effaith sobreiddiol a gafodd cyfres o ddiwygiadau crefyddol ar y traddodiad drama cyfoethog a phoblogaidd a fodolai yng Nghymru yn y ddeunawfed ganrif, ac a gâi ei fynegi trwy gyfrwng anterliwtiau hwyliog, a masweddus weithiau, defodau cymunedol fel y ceffyl pren, ac arferion dathlu tymhorol theatrig fel y Fari Lwyd.[5] Ni osodwyd drama yn destun cystadleuaeth yn yr Eisteddfod Genedlaethol tan 1884, ac yn achlysurol yn unig ar ôl hynny. Bu'n rhaid aros tan 1906 cyn cael perfformiad o ddrama yn yr Eisteddfod, a hyd yn oed wedi hynny yn araf y diflannai agweddau piwritanaidd. Yr oedd y rhan fwyaf o'r testunau yn rhai difrifol, ac arwyr a digwyddiadau hanesyddol yn amlwg yn eu plith. Amhosibl barnu ar sail y rhestr hon pa mor boblogaidd oedd y dramâu hyn, ond y mae'r ffaith nad oedd cystadlu o gwbl ambell flwyddyn yn awgrymu bod sylwadau difrïol yr Ymneilltuwyr yn dal i ffrwyno'r dramodwyr.

Y wasg Gymraeg yw testun yr ail grŵp o dablau. Gan fod y pulpud a'r wasg fel rheol yn cael eu portreadu fel gwarcheidwaid yr iaith Gymraeg yn y bedwaredd ganrif ar bymtheg, y mae'n bwysig cyflwyno peth tystiolaeth ynglŷn â natur y wasg Gymraeg mewn cyfnod a oedd yn cynnwys yr hyn a elwir yn 'oes aur' rhwng 1860 a 1890. Er mai materion crefyddol a llenyddol a gâi'r lle blaenaf, câi pynciau gwleidyddol a chymdeithasol eu trafod hefyd ar dudalennau'r cyfnodolion Cymraeg. Y mae llawer o'r deunydd a gyflwynir yma ar ffurf rhestrau. Rhydd Tablau 2.1 a 2.2, sy'n rhestru cyfnodolion Cymraeg a gyhoeddwyd yn y cyfnodau 1735–1850 a 1851–1900, wybodaeth am eu cynnwys a hyd eu parhad. Câi cylchgronau crefyddol ac enwadol, ar gyfer oedolion a phlant, eu darllen yn eang a byddai trafod ar eu cynnwys mewn dosbarthiadau ysgol Sul ledled Cymru.[6] Yn Nhabl 2.3 ceir rhestr o bapurau newydd Cymraeg a dyddiadau eu cyhoeddi. Byrhoedlog fu parhad llawer o bapurau newydd a chyfnodolion, ond llwyddodd eraill i oroesi'n rhyfeddol. Yn ôl D. Lleufer Thomas, mewn atodiad i Adroddiad y Comisiwn Tir Cymreig,

section was entirely Welsh and, although choice was available in some categories, all prose competitions could be entered in Welsh. Both Welsh and English songs were included in the four main choir competitions. However, the names of competing choirs indicate how far interest in the National Eisteddfod extended beyond Wales. The Blackpool Glee and Madrigal Society, the Birmingham Welsh Musical Society, the Liverpool Juveniles, and the Millgirls Industrial Choir from Manchester were among a number of English choirs which competed against local Welsh choirs in the main choral competitions.

The final table in the Eisteddfod group, Table 1.7, lists subjects and prizewinners in the National Eisteddfod drama competition from 1884 to 1913. It serves as a further reminder of the capacity of Welsh Nonconformity to influence almost every aspect of life in Wales. Following a rich tradition of drama in popular culture in the eighteenth century, expressed in entertaining and sometimes bawdy *anterliwtiau* (interludes), in rituals of community sanction such as the *ceffyl pren* (wooden horse), and in theatrical seasonal customs of celebration such as the *Mari Lwyd* (Grey Mare), the sobering effect of a succession of religious revivals is reflected in this list.[5] Drama was not included as a subject for competition in the National Eisteddfod until 1884, and thereafter only as an irregular event. It was not until 1906 that a play was actually performed at the Eisteddfod, but even afterwards puritanical attitudes were slow to soften. Most of the titles were devoted to serious subjects, notably Welsh heroes and historic events. It is impossible from this list to judge the popularity of such plays but the fact that there were no entries in some years suggests that the vituperative comments of Welsh Nonconformists continued to discourage dramatists.

The second group of tables is concerned with the Welsh language press. Since the pulpit and the press are generally portrayed as the guardians of the Welsh language in the nineteenth century, it is important to present some evidence of the character of the Welsh language press during a period which included a so-called 'golden age' between 1860 and 1890. Although religious and literary matters predominated, political and social questions were also discussed in the pages of the Welsh periodical press. Much of the material presented here is in the form of lists. Tables 2.1 and 2.2, which list Welsh periodicals published in the periods 1735–1850, and 1851–1900 respectively, give information about their content and lifespan. Religious and denominational magazines, for adults and children, were widely read and their contents were discussed in Sunday school classes throughout Wales.[6] Table 2.3 lists Welsh language newspapers and includes dates of publication. The lifespan of many newspapers and periodicals was clearly very short, while others proved remarkably durable. According to D. Lleufer Thomas,

yr oedd tri ar ddeg o'r pum deg tri o bapurau newydd a chyfnodolion Cymraeg wythnosol neu fisol a gyhoeddwyd yng Nghymru neu Lerpwl ym 1895 wedi ymddangos gyntaf cyn 1850.[7]

Y mae ffigurau cylchrediad gwahanol bapurau newydd a chyfnodolion ynghyd â maint yr argraffiadau (Tabl 2.4) yn datgelu poblogrwydd cymharol gwahanol deitlau. Ym 1850 yr oedd llawer o'r cyfnodolion mwyaf poblogaidd yn gysylltiedig ag enwadau arbennig: cylchredai *Y Geiniogwerth* (12,900 o ddarllenwyr) ymhlith y Methodistiaid Calfinaidd; *Y Cronicl* (7,320 o ddarllenwyr) a'r *Golygydd* (3,000 o ddarllenwyr) ymhlith yr Annibynwyr; *Athraw i Blentyn* (3,000 o ddarllenwyr) ymhlith disgyblion ysgol Sul y Bedyddwyr; *Yr Haul* (1,000 o ddarllenwyr) ymhlith aelodau'r Eglwys sefydledig. Ond câi diddordebau ehangach eu cynrychioli hefyd: cylchgrawn i ferched oedd *Y Gymraes*; cynhwysai'r *Traethodydd* ddeunydd llenyddol; bwriedid *Ifor Hael* ar gyfer aelodau cymdeithas gyfeillgar yr Iforiaid. Yr oedd pob un o'r rhain yn honni cylchrediad o dros 1,000 yng nghanol y ganrif (Tabl 2.4 (a)). Wedi 'oes aur' cyhoeddi yn Gymraeg, cafodd ymdreiddiad cynyddol teitlau Saesneg i'r farchnad o ddarllenwyr ei gelu gan gynnydd yn y boblogaeth Gymraeg ei hiaith ym Maes Glo De Cymru a chan y ffaith fod y Gymraeg yn dal ei thir fel iaith y capel. Yr oedd ffigurau cylchrediad *Trysorfa y Plant*, cylchgrawn y Methodistiaid Calfinaidd i blant, a gyhoeddwyd o 1862 ymlaen, yn rhyfeddol. Gwerthwyd dros 40,000 o gopïau y mis ym 1893, ynghyd â 5,000 o gopïau o'r *Drysorfa*, y cylchgrawn cyfatebol ar gyfer oedolion (Tabl 2.4 (b) ac (c)).

Er nad oes ffigurau cylchredeg papurau newydd i'w cael dros gyfnod o amser, y mae Philip Henry Jones wedi llunio cyfrifiadau gofalus ar sail llyfrau cyfrifon ystafell argraffu Thomas Gee, yr argraffwyr a'r cyhoeddwyr o Ddinbych, sy'n olrhain llwyddiant y papur Cymraeg dylanwadol, *Baner Cymru*, sef *Baner ac Amserau Cymru* yn ddiweddarach (Tabl 2.4 (d)). Gyda chymorth rhwydwaith trawiadol o ddosbarthwyr lleol at eu gwasanaeth, yr oedd papurau wythnosol fel *Y Faner* yn llywio barn y cyhoedd Cymraeg ei iaith trwy gyfrwng sylwebaeth fyw ac, ar brydiau, ohebiaeth frwd ar faterion gwleidyddol a chymdeithasol y dydd. Y mae Tablau 2.4(d)–(f) hefyd yn dangos sut y brwydrodd tri chyhoeddiad Cymraeg gwahanol iawn i'w gilydd i gynnal cylchrediad iach yn yr ugeinfed ganrif. Cyrhaeddodd *Y Faner* ei benllanw yn y 1870au; ni lwyddodd *Cymru'r Plant* i adennill y cylchrediad cyson o rhwng naw a deng mil a fwynhâi yn y blynyddoedd cyn y rhyfel; a methodd *Y Llenor*, a gyhoeddwyd gyntaf ym 1895, â chynnal nifer yr argraffiad cychwynnol, sef 3,000.

Y mae Tabl 2.5 yn canolbwyntio ar nifer y llyfrau a'r pamffledi Cymraeg a gyhoeddwyd, yn ôl cofnodion yr argraffwyr Hughes a'i Fab, Wrecsam, a Thomas Gee, Dinbych. Gwerthai *Almanac y Miloedd*, *Egwyddorig o'r*

in an appendix to the Report of the Welsh Land Commission, thirteen of the fifty-three weekly or monthly Welsh language newspapers and periodicals published in Wales or Liverpool in 1895 were first published prior to 1850.[7]

Circulation figures and print runs of various newspapers and periodicals are presented in Table 2.4 and reveal the relative popularity of various titles. In 1850 many of the most popular periodicals were associated with particular denominations: *Y Geiniogwerth* (12,900 readers) circulated among Calvinistic Methodists; *Y Cronicl* (7,320 readers) and *Y Golygydd* (3,000 readers) among Independents; *Athraw i Blentyn* (3,000 readers) among Baptist Sunday school pupils; *Yr Haul* (1,000 readers) among members of the established Church. However, wider interests were also represented: *Y Gymraes* was a women's magazine; *Y Traethodydd* contained literary material; *Ifor Hael* was intended for members of the Ivorites friendly society. Each of these claimed a circulation of over 1,000 at mid-century (Table 2.4 (a)). Following the 'golden age' of Welsh publishing, increasing penetration of the readers' market by English titles was hidden by an increase in the Welsh-speaking population in the South Wales Coalfield and by the continuing survival of Welsh as the language of the chapel. Circulation figures for *Trysorfa y Plant*, the Calvinistic Methodist magazine for children, published from 1862, were astonishing. Over 40,000 copies were sold per month in 1893, as well as 5,000 copies of *Y Drysorfa*, the adult equivalent (Table 2.4 (b) and (c)).

Although it is impossible to obtain accurate circulation figures over time for newspapers, Philip Henry Jones has made careful calculations based on the print-room ledgers of Thomas Gee, printers and publishers of Denbigh, which chart the success of the influential Welsh language newspaper, *Baner Cymru*, later *Baner ac Amserau Cymru* (Table 2.4 (d)). Served by an impressive network of local distributors, weekly newspapers such as '*Y Faner*' actively shaped Welsh-speaking public opinion by including lively comment and sometimes heated correspondence on the political and social matters of the day. Tables 2.4(d)–(f) also illustrate how three very different Welsh language publications struggled to maintain a healthy circulation in the twentieth century. *Y Faner* reached a peak in the 1870s, *Cymru'r Plant* never recovered its consistent pre-war circulation of between nine and ten thousand, and *Y Llenor,* first published in 1895, failed to sustain an initial print run of 3,000.

Table 2.5 focuses on the publication of Welsh language books and pamphlets by reproducing figures compiled from the records of the printers Hughes a'i Fab, Wrexham, and Thomas Gee, Denbigh. A small penny almanac (*Almanac y Miloedd*), a Welsh grammar (*Egwyddorig o'r Iaith Gymraeg*), and a Sunday school catechism (*Rhodd Mam*) sold in their tens of thousands.

Iaith Gymraeg, a *Rhodd Mam* yn eu degau o filoedd, ac yr oedd gweithiau crefyddol yn hynod o boblogaidd.[8] I'r gwrthwyneb, ac eithrio chwedlau hanesyddol neu foesegol, y mae'r diffyg ffuglen yn y Gymraeg yn amlwg. Ym marn Ymneilltuwyr, yr oedd darllen nofel, fel gwylio drama, yn rhy debyg i adloniant pur i'w gymeradwyo, er nad oes amheuaeth na fyddai teuluoedd a ymhyfrydai mewn llenyddiaeth yn gwbl gyfarwydd, erbyn diwedd y ganrif, ag enwau cymeriadau fel Wil Bryan, Tomos Bartley, Enoc Huws a Gwen Tomos.

Tynnwyd sylw eisoes trwy gyfrwng y rhestr o gystadlaethau mewn Eisteddfodau Cenedlaethol a gyflwynwyd yn Nhablau 1.4 i 1.6 at un agwedd ffyniannus ar ddiwylliant Cymru a ddaeth i amlygrwydd yn ystod ail hanner y bedwaredd ganrif ar bymtheg, sef datblygiad traddodiad corawl cryf. Yr oedd gwreiddiau'r traddodiad yn yr hen ganu penillion, ond fe'i lliwiwyd bellach â sêl canu emynau yr Ymneilltuwyr, a ddaeth i fri mawr yn y cymanfaoedd canu.[9] Rhoddodd cyflwyno nodiant y tonic sol-ffa hwb i'r datblygiad hwn trwy alluogi oedolion a phlant i ganu ar yr olwg gyntaf; yr oedd hwn yn ddull rhwydd ei ddysgu a chafodd ei ddefnyddio'n helaeth mewn ysgolion a chymdeithasau capeli ledled Cymru o'r 1860au ymlaen. Yn Nhabl 2.6 ceir ymgais i ddangos pa mor boblogaidd oedd canu corawl. Rhwng 1861 a 1891 sefydlwyd saith cyfnodolyn Cymraeg yn un swydd at ddibenion cerddorol, a'r cyfan yn cynnwys caneuon Cymraeg. Dros gyfnod o ddeng mlynedd ar hugain, argraffodd Hughes a'i Fab 106,350 o gopïau o Ran 1 *Swn y Juwbili, neu Ganiadau y Diwygiad*, llyfr o emynau a chaneuon ysbrydol Ira D. Sankey wedi eu cyfieithu i'r Gymraeg gan y Parchedig John Roberts ('Ieuan Gwyllt'). Y mae'r nifer yn cyfateb i un tŷ mewn tri yng Nghymru ym 1891.

Daw'r pwyslais yn ôl at lenyddiaeth Gymraeg yn Nhabl 2.7, lle y rhestrir, fesul pwnc, y nifer o lyfrau Cymraeg a Saesneg a fenthyciwyd o Sefydliad Llenyddol a Gwyddonol Glynebwy yn y flwyddyn 1870–1, a nifer y llyfrau a geid yn adran fenthyg Ystafell Ddarllen a Llyfrgell Llanrwst *c.*1895. Y mae'r ffigurau'n dangos y prinder cymharol o deitlau Cymraeg yn ogystal â'r gwahaniaeth yn nhestunau'r llyfrau a fenthyciwyd. Yng Nglynebwy, er enghraifft, yr oedd 43 y cant o'r llyfrau Cymraeg a fenthyciwyd yn llyfrau ar grefydd a barddoniaeth o gymharu ag wyth y cant o fenthyciadau Saesneg; tri y cant o'r benthyciadau Cymraeg oedd yn storïau a nofelau, ond yr oedd 57 y cant o'r benthyciadau Saesneg yn y dosbarth hwn. Yr oedd y nifer o lyfrau Cymraeg a fenthyciwyd yn cyfateb o ran cyfrannedd i'r nifer o lyfrau Cymraeg mewn stoc – tua un mewn deg – ond y mae'r anghydbwysedd yn y math o ddeunydd yn drawiadol. Dangosir yn eglur y pwyslais ar farddoniaeth a chrefydd wrth ddarllen Cymraeg.[10]

Cyfeiria'r tabl olaf (Tabl 3.1) at aelodaeth o Urdd

Religious works in particular were extremely popular.[8] Conversely, apart from historical or moralizing tales, Welsh language fiction was conspicuous by its absence. Reading novels, like watching drama, was considered by Nonconformists too akin to mere entertainment to be encouraged, though it is inconceivable that, by the end of the century, families with a taste for literature would not have been thoroughly familiar with the names of Wil Bryan, Tomos Bartley, Enoc Huws and Gwen Tomos, characters in the novels of Daniel Owen.

One flourishing aspect of Welsh culture, which has already been highlighted by the list of competitions in National Eisteddfodau presented in Tables 1.4 to 1.6, and which increased in popularity during the latter half of the nineteenth century, was the development of a strong choral tradition, whose roots in ancient *penillion* singing were now flavoured with the zeal of Nonconformist hymn-singing, exemplified by *cymanfaoedd canu* (singing festivals).[9] The introduction of the tonic sol-fa notation of music encouraged this development by enabling adults and children to become proficient in sight-singing; the system was easily learnt and was widely used in schools and chapel societies throughout Wales from the 1860s onwards. Table 2.6 attempts to show the extent of popular involvement. Between 1861 and 1891 seven Welsh language periodicals, all containing Welsh songs, were established specifically for musical interests. Over a thirty-year period, Hughes a'i Fab of Wrexham printed 106,350 copies of Part 1 of *Swn y Juwbili, neu Ganiadau y Diwygiad*, a book of hymns and uplifting songs by Ira D. Sankey translated into Welsh by the Reverend John Roberts ('Ieuan Gwyllt'). This number is equivalent to one in three houses in Wales in 1891.

Table 2.7 returns the focus to Welsh literature. It gives the number of Welsh and English books loaned by Ebbw Vale Literary and Scientific Institute in the year 1870–1, and the number of books in the circulating library section of Llanrwst Reading Room and Library *c.*1895, according to subject. The figures illustrate both the relative paucity of Welsh titles and also the differences in subject matter. At Ebbw Vale, for example, books on religion and poetry comprised 43 per cent of the Welsh book loans compared with eight per cent of English book loans; stories and novels comprised three per cent of Welsh loans and 57 per cent of English loans. The number of Welsh books loaned was in the same proportion as the number of Welsh books stocked – approximately one in ten – but the imbalance in the type of material read is very marked indeed. An emphasis on poetry and religion in Welsh language reading is clearly shown.[10]

The final table (Table 3.1) refers to the membership of the Philanthropic Order of True Ivorites, a friendly society established in Wrexham in 1836, whose first object, apart from the provision of benefit in times of

Ddyngarol y Gwir Iforiaid, cymdeithas gyfeillgar a sefydlwyd yn Wrecsam ym 1836. Prif amcan y gymdeithas, heblaw darparu er budd ei haelodau ar adegau o salwch ac angen, oedd 'cadw'r iaith Gymraeg yn ei phurdeb'. Un o'i rheolau cynnar oedd y dylai holl lyfrau a chyfrifon y gymdeithas gael eu cadw yn Gymraeg, ac un arall oedd ei bod yn ofynnol i bob swyddog, ac eithrio'r trysorydd, allu siarad Cymraeg yn rhugl.[11] Yn sgil dadl ymhlith ei harweinwyr, symudwyd y pencadlys i Gaerfyrddin ym 1838 ac ymhen dwy flynedd yr oedd un gyfrinfa ar bymtheg a thrigain wedi eu sefydlu yng Nghaerfyrddin a'r cylch.[12] Ychydig o gyfrinfeydd a fyddai'n cofrestru â Chofrestrydd y Cymdeithasau Cyfeillgar yn y blynyddoedd cynnar, ac felly y mae'n debygol fod yr aelodaeth yn uwch o lawer nag yr awgryma'r ffigurau swyddogol.[13] Yr oedd y gweithgareddau diwylliannol yn cynnwys cynnal eisteddfodau, a gwnaed sawl ymgais i gyhoeddi cylchgronau rheolaidd ar gyfer yr aelodau, yn eu plith *Y Gwir Iforydd*, *Yr Iforydd*, *Ifor Hael*, a'r *Gwladgarwr* (gweler Tablau 2.1 a 2.2).[14] Yn y 1860au a'r 1870au, yr oedd dylanwad yr Iforiaid yn ymestyn i'r cymunedau glofaol a oedd yn blodeuo ym Morgannwg, ac y mae gwybodaeth fwy dibynadwy ar gael am nifer y cyfrinfeydd a'r aelodau yn y cyfnod hwn. Y mae Tabl 3.1a yn cynnwys ffigurau sy'n seiliedig ar ystadegau swyddogol cymdeithasau cyfeillgar, sy'n dangos aelodaeth o dros 10,000 yn gyson o'r 1870au i'r ugeinfed ganrif, a'r aelodaeth honno wedi ei chyfyngu bron yn llwyr i dde Cymru. Ond ceir tystiolaeth o edwino yn y tabl hwn ac yn Nhabl 3.1b, sy'n rhoi ffigurau am drosiant yr aelodau mewn cant namyn tri o gyfrinfeydd ym 1886. Yn y flwyddyn honno, yr oedd nifer yr aelodau a gollwyd, boed trwy farwolaeth neu achosion eraill, 45 y cant yn fwy na nifer yr aelodau newydd. Yn Nhabl 3.1c rhoddir dyddiadau sefydlu cyfrinfeydd y Gwir Iforiaid (er na chynhwysir cyfrinfeydd y daeth eu gweithgareddau i ben cyn 1910) a chadarnheir tystiolaeth o'r lleihad yn yr aelodaeth. Yn fwyaf nodedig, y mae'r tabl yn datgelu bod dechrau'r lleihad cymharol mewn aelodaeth yn cyd-daro â'r cynnydd arwyddocaol ym mhoblogaeth de Cymru yn negawdau olaf y bedwaredd ganrif ar bymtheg. Fel y cymdeithasau cyfeillgar eraill, ni allai'r Iforiaid gystadlu yn erbyn mathau eraill o weithgareddau hamdden a chwmnïau yswiriant a oedd hefyd yn cynnig darpariaeth i rai mewn angen mewn adeg o gyni. Er bod lle cryf i amau yr honiad pleidiol fod yr achos Iforaidd mewn gwell sefyllfa i ddiogelu'r Gymraeg na'r ysgol Sul,[15] rhaid cyfaddef bod y gymdeithas yn ffynhonnell seciwlar bwysig o gefnogaeth i weithgareddau diwylliannol Cymraeg, a'i bod yn haeddu mwy o sylw gan haneswyr diwylliannol.

Ar lawer ystyr, ni all y deunydd ystadegol a geir yn yr adran hon gyfleu cyfraniad cyfoethog a lliwgar pobl fel Dic Dywyll, Talhaiarn, Llew Llwyfo, Ceiriog, Daniel Owen a Beriah Gwynfe Evans i fywyd diwylliannol y

illness and need, was 'to preserve the Welsh language in its purity'. Early regulations ruled that 'all books and accounts belonging to this Society be kept in the Welsh language' and 'no Member shall be an Officer in this Union, unless he is able to speak the Welsh language properly, except the Treasurer'.[11] Following an argument among its leaders, the headquarters were moved to Carmarthen in 1838 and within two years seventy-six lodges had been established in Carmarthen and the surrounding area.[12] Few lodges enrolled with the Registrar of Friendly Societies in the early years, so it is likely that membership was much larger than official returns suggest.[13] Cultural activities included the holding of eisteddfodau, and several attempts were made to publish regular magazines for members, among them *Y Gwir Iforydd*, *Yr Iforydd*, *Ifor Hael*, and *Y Gwladgarwr* (see Tables 2.1 and 2.2).[14] In the 1860s and 1870s, the influence of the Ivorites extended into the growing coalfield communities of Glamorgan, and it is from this period that we have more reliable information concerning the number of lodges and members. Table 3.1a contains figures compiled from official friendly society returns, showing that a membership of over 10,000 was maintained from the 1870s into the twentieth century, almost exclusively restricted to south Wales. However, evidence of declining interest is revealed both in this table and in Table 3.1b, which gives figures for the turnover of members in ninety-seven lodges in 1886. Members leaving in that year, whether through death or 'other causes', exceeded new members by 45 per cent. Table 3.1c reveals the dates when lodges of True Ivorites were established (although it excludes lodges ceasing activities before 1910) and confirms evidence of the decline in membership. Most notably, it reveals that the beginning of the relative decline in membership coincided with the appreciable increase in the population in south Wales in the last decades of the nineteenth century. In common with other friendly societies, the Ivorites were unable to compete against new forms of leisure activities and insurance companies which also offered provision for those in need in times of hardship. Although a partisan claim that the Ivorite cause was better equipped to preserve Welsh than the Sunday school does not bear scrutiny,[15] nevertheless the society did represent an important secular source of support for Welsh cultural activities and deserves more attention from cultural historians.

In many ways, the statistical material included in this section cannot convey the rich and colourful contribution of the likes of Dic Dywyll, Talhaiarn, Llew Llwyfo, Ceiriog, Daniel Owen and Beriah Gwynfe Evans to the cultural life of Welsh-speaking Wales. Nor can it reflect cultural influences in the English language which promoted new and exciting alternatives to chapel-based activities. By 1901 nearly half the population of Wales spoke English only, and Welsh

Gymru Gymraeg. Ac ni all ychwaith adlewyrchu dylanwadau diwylliannol yn Saesneg a hyrwyddodd ddewisiadau a oedd yn newydd a chyffrous o'u cymharu â gweithgareddau a oedd yn gysylltiedig â'r capeli. Erbyn 1901 Saesneg oedd unig iaith bron hanner poblogaeth Cymru, ac yr oedd Ymneilltuaeth Gymraeg yn colli ei hapêl wrth i glybiau gweithwyr, undebau llafur, clybiau rygbi, pêl-droed a phaffio, theatrau a theatrau cerdd ddenu niferoedd cynyddol o bobl a allai siarad Saesneg naill ai fel iaith gyntaf neu ail iaith. Yr oedd y cynnydd carlamus yn nifer y siaradwyr uniaith Saesneg a'r siaradwyr dwyieithog yn cynnig llawer her newydd i'r rhai hynny a oedd yn dal i goleddu heniaith eu gwlad.

[1] Hywel Teifi Edwards, '*Gŵyl Gwalia': Yr Eisteddfod Genedlaethol yn Oes Aur Victoria 1858–1868* (Llandysul, 1980), t. 387.

[2] *Liverpool Daily Post*, 19 Medi 1900.

[3] David Morgan Richards, *Rhestr Eisteddfodau hyd y flwyddyn 1901, gyda nodiadau ar amryw o honynt* (Llandysul, 1914).

[4] William D. Jones, *Wales in America: Scranton and the Welsh 1860–1920* (Cardiff, 1993), t. 102. Gw. hefyd Hywel Teifi Edwards, *Eisteddfod Ffair y Byd* (Llandysul, 1989).

[5] Fel y dywed H. Idris Bell yn ei bennod atodol ar yr ugeinfed ganrif yn ei gyfieithiad o waith Thomas Parry, *A History of Welsh Literature* (Oxford, 1955), t. 485: 'the atmosphere of nineteenth-century Puritanism ... was apt to regard the theatre as the gateway to Hell and actors as social outcasts'.

[6] Honnodd William Rees, cyhoeddwr *Yr Haul*, wrth roi tystiolaeth gerbron y Comisiynwyr Addysg ym 1846: 'The Welsh peasantry are better able to read and write in their own language than the same classes in England. Among them are found many contributors to Welsh periodicals.' *Reports of the Commissioners of Inquiry into the State of Education in Wales*. Part I. Carmarthen, Glamorgan, and Pembroke, t. 235 [PP 1847 (870) XXVII].

[7] *Report of the Royal Commission on Land in Wales and Monmouthshire*, Atodiad C Tabl III (a), 'Periodicals and Newspapers published in the Welsh language' [PP 1896 XXXIII]. Y mae'r atodiad defnyddiol hwn hefyd yn cynnwys rhestr o newyddiaduron Saesneg a gyhoeddwyd yng Nghymru ym 1895, yn ogystal â chylchgronau Saesneg a chanddynt gysylltiad â Chymru.

[8] Cyhoeddwyd o leiaf un argraffiad newydd neu adargraffiad o'r Beibl Cymraeg bob blwyddyn yn ystod y bedwaredd ganrif ar bymtheg, weithiau ar ffurf cyfres o rannau a werthid am chwe cheiniog neu swllt yr un fel y gallai cynifer o bobl â phosibl eu prynu. Am wybodaeth fanwl ynglŷn ag argraffu'r Beibl yn Gymraeg, gw. John Ballinger, *The Bible in Wales* (London, 1906).

[9] Amcangyfrifwyd bod 134,000 o gantorion wedi cymryd rhan mewn 280 o gymanfaoedd canu ym 1895. Gw. Trefor M. Owen, *The Customs and Traditions of Wales* (Cardiff, 1991), t. 111.

[10] Ceir ffigurau eraill ar gyfer llyfrau Cymraeg/Saesneg yn Philip H. Jones, 'Welsh Public Libraries to 1914', a C. M. Baggs, 'The Miners' Institute Libraries of South Wales 1875–1939' yn Philip H. Jones ac Eiluned Rees (goln.), *A Nation and its Books* (Aberystwyth, i'w gyhoeddi).

[11] *Laws and Regulations to be Observed by the Members of the True Ivorites Society* (Carmarthen, 1839). Galwyd y gymdeithas ar ôl Ifor ap Llywelyn ('Ifor Hael'), prif noddwr Dafydd ap Gwilym.

[12] David Williams, *The Rebecca Riots* (Cardiff, 1955), t. 156.

[13] Yn ôl *A Return relating to Friendly Societies enrolled in the Several*

Nonconformity was losing its appeal as working men's clubs, trade unions, rugby, soccer and boxing clubs, theatres and music halls attracted growing numbers who were able to speak English either as a first or a second language. The swiftly increasing number of monoglot English and of bilingual speakers posed new challenges for those who still cherished their native tongue.

[1] Hywel Teifi Edwards, *'Gŵyl Gwalia': Yr Eisteddfod Genedlaethol yn Oes Aur Victoria 1858–1868* (Llandysul, 1980), p. 387.

[2] *Liverpool Daily Post*, 19 September 1900.

[3] David Morgan Richards, *Rhestr Eisteddfodau hyd y flwyddyn 1901, gyda nodiadau ar amryw o honynt* (Llandysul, 1914).

[4] William D. Jones, *Wales in America; Scranton and the Welsh 1860–1920* (Cardiff, 1993), p. 102. See also Hywel Teifi Edwards, *Eisteddfod Ffair y Byd* (Llandysul, 1989).

[5] As H. Idris Bell states in the Appendix to his translation of Thomas Parry, *A History of Welsh Literature* (Oxford, 1955), p. 485: 'the atmosphere of nineteenth-century Puritanism ... was apt to regard the theatre as the gateway to Hell and actors as social outcasts'.

[6] William Rees, the publisher of *Yr Haul*, giving written evidence before the Education Commissioners in 1846, claimed that 'The Welsh peasantry are better able to read and write in their own language than the same classes in England. Among them are found many contributors to Welsh periodicals.' *Reports of the Commissioners of Inquiry into the State of Education in Wales*. Part I, Carmarthen, Glamorgan, and Pembroke, p. 235 [PP 1847 (870) XXVII].

[7] *Report of the Royal Commission on Land in Wales and Monmouthshire*, Appendix C table III (a), 'Periodicals and Newspapers published in the Welsh language' [PP 1896 XXXIII]. This useful appendix also contains a list of English newspapers published in Wales, and English periodicals issued in connection with Wales, in 1895.

[8] At least one new edition or reprint of the Welsh Bible was published every year during the nineteenth century, sometimes in the form of a series of parts selling at 6d. or 1s. each to enable purchase by as many as possible. Detailed information about the printing of the Bible in Welsh can be found in John Ballinger, *The Bible in Wales* (London, 1906).

[9] It was estimated that 134,000 singers took part in 280 singing festivals held in 1895. See Trefor M. Owen, *The Customs and Traditions of Wales* (Cardiff, 1991), p. 111.

[10] Other figures for Welsh/English books can be found in Philip H. Jones, 'Welsh Public Libraries to 1914', and C. M. Baggs, 'The Miners' Institute Libraries of South Wales 1875–1939' in Philip H. Jones and Eiluned Rees (eds.), *A Nation and its Books* (Aberystwyth, forthcoming).

[11] *Laws and Regulations to be Observed by the Members of the True Ivorites Society* (Carmarthen, 1839). The society was named after Ifor ap Llywelyn ('Ifor Hael'), the chief patron of the celebrated poet Dafydd ap Gwilym.

[12] David Williams, *The Rebecca Riots* (Cardiff, 1955), p. 156.

[13] In *A Return relating to Friendly Societies enrolled in the Several Counties of England and Wales* [PP 1842 (73) XXVI], only two True Ivorites Friendly Societies, at Mold and at an unspecified location in Merioneth, can be positively identified.

[14] Richards, in *Rhestr Eisteddfodau*, lists notable Ivorite eisteddfodau as follows: 1839, Wrexham; 1845, Castleton (Mon.); 1846, Caernarfon; 1853, Dowlais; 1854, Treforest; 1856, Cardiff; 1861, Cardiff; 1863, Brecon; 1867, Llanelli.

[15] 'Yr ydych yn crybwyll fod gennych well sefydliad na'r Ysgol Sabothol at gadw yr hen iaith, sef Iforiaeth.' T. Morgan Bassett, 'Iforiaeth', *Seren Gomer*, XXXII (1940), 195.

Counties of England and Wales [PP 1842 (73) XXVI], dwy gymdeithas gyfeillgar yn unig y gellir eu lleoli, y naill yn Yr Wyddgrug a'r llall mewn man anhysbys yn sir Feirionnydd.

[14] Yn *Rhestr Eisteddfodau*, rhestra Richards eisteddfodau nodedig yr Iforiaid fel a ganlyn: 1839, Wrecsam; 1845, Cas-bach (sir Fynwy); 1846, Caernarfon; 1853, Dowlais; 1854, Trefforest; 1856, Caerdydd; 1861, Caerdydd; 1863, Aberhonddu; 1867, Llanelli.

[15] 'Yr ydych yn crybwyll fod gennych well sefydliad na'r Ysgol Sabothol at gadw yr hen iaith, sef Iforiaeth.' T. Morgan Bassett, 'Iforiaeth', *Seren Gomer*, XXXII (1940), 195.

Culture 1.1 Eisteddfodau. Location and date of the National Eisteddfod. 1861–1914

Year[1]	Date	Place
1861	20–22 Aug.	Aberdare
1862	26–29 Aug.	Caernarfon
1863	1–4 Sept.	Swansea
1864	23–26 Aug.	Llandudno
1865	12–15 Sept.	Aberystwyth
1866	4–7 Sept.	Chester
1867	2–6 Sept.	Carmarthen
1868	4–7 Aug.	Ruthin
1869	1–4 Sept.	Holywell
1870	7–12 Aug.	Rhyl
1871		*none held*
1872	28–30 Aug.	Portmadog
1873	19–22 Aug.	Mold
1874	18–21 Aug.	Bangor
1875	24–27 Aug.	Pwllheli
1876	22–25 Aug.	Wrexham
1877	21–24 Aug.	Caernarfon
1878[2]	17–20 Sept.	Birkenhead
1879	5–7 Aug.	Conwy[3]
1880	24–27 Aug.	Caernarfon
1881	30 Aug.– 2 Sept.	Merthyr Tydfil
1882	22–25 Aug.	Denbigh
1883	6–9 Aug.	Cardiff
1884	15–20 Sept.	Liverpool
1885	25–28 Aug.	Aberdare
1886	14–17 Sept.	Caernarfon
1887	9–12 Aug.	London

Year	Date	Place
1888	4–7 Sept.	Wrexham
1889	27–29 Aug.	Brecon
1890	2–5 Sept.	Bangor
1891	18–21 Aug.	Swansea
1892	6–9 Sept.	Rhyl
1893	1–4 Aug.	Pontypridd
1894	10–13 July	Caernarfon
1895	30 July– 2 Aug.	Llanelli
1896	30 June–4 July	Llandudno
1897	2–6 Aug.	Newport
1898	19–23 July	Blaenau Ffestiniog
1899	18–21 July	Cardiff
1900	18–22 Sept.	Liverpool
1901	6–9 Aug.	Merthyr Tydfil
1902	9–13 Sept.	Bangor
1903	3–7 Aug.	Llanelli
1904	6–10 Sept.	Rhyl
1905	7–11 Aug.	Mountain Ash
1906	21–24 Aug.	Caernarfon
1907	20–24 Aug.	Swansea
1908	1–4 Sept.	Llangollen
1909	15–18 June	London
1910	13–16 Sept.	Colwyn Bay
1911	7–11 Aug.	Carmarthen
1912	2–7 Sept.	Wrexham
1913	4–8 Aug.	Abergavenny
1914		*none held* [4]

Sources: Official Eisteddfod programmes; John May, *Reference Wales* (Cardiff, 1994), p. 73.

1 The eisteddfodau held between 1869 and 1880 were not held under the auspices of a national organization but were *ad hoc* arrangements.
2 John May does not give any information for this year.
3 The location of the National Eisteddfod for this year is wrongly given as Birkenhead in John May.
4 The National Eisteddfod scheduled for Bangor in September 1914 was postponed until the following year.

Culture 1.2 Eisteddfodau. Number of places holding eisteddfodau in Wales. 1802–1900

Year	Number of places[1]	Year	Number of places[1]	Year	Number of places[1]	Year	Number of places[1]	Year	Number of places[1]
1802	1	1822	4	1842	5	1862	21	1882	26
1803	1	1823	7	1843	8	1863	25	1883	31
1804	1	1824	9	1844	7	1864	30	1884	29
1805	–	1825	9	1845	8	1865	26	1885	24
1806	–	1826	8	1846	15	1866	24	1886	37
1807	–	1827	4	1847	7	1867	30	1887	32
1808	1	1828	6	1848	13	1868	36	1888	34
1809	1	1829	6	1849	16	1869	44	1889	42
1810	1	1830	4	1850	17	1870	40	1890	37
1811	1	1831	7	1851	21	1871	18	1891	54
1812	–	1832	3	1852	14	1872	25	1892	46
1813	3	1833	3	1853	23	1873	31	1893	50
1814	1	1834	11	1854	17	1874	26	1894	56
1815	1	1835	10	1855	19	1875	24	1895	46
1816	2	1836	7	1856	28	1876	23	1896	41
1817	2	1837	11	1857	39	1877	24	1897	35
1818	1	1838	14	1858	31	1878	35	1898	68
1819	3	1839	9	1859	39	1879	28	1899	141
1820	4	1840	6	1860	26	1880	30	1900	198
1821	3	1841	8	1861	15	1881	28		

Source: David Morgan Richards, *Rhestr Eisteddfodau hyd y flwyddyn 1901* (Llandysul, 1914).

These figures have been compiled directly from the lists of locations and dates of eisteddfodau given at source. They only suggest trends and fail to reflect popular involvement in activities connected with school, chapel, and village eisteddfodau.

[1] This is the number of locations listed rather than the number of eisteddfodau. It was not unusual for several eisteddfodau to be held in one year in one location. For example, according to Richards, there were four eisteddfodau in Merthyr Tydfil in 1824, and six in Cardiff in 1900.

Culture 1.3 Eisteddfodau. Location and date of eisteddfodau in England and overseas. 1803–1900

Year	Location
1803	London (Gwyneddigion)[1]
1804	London (Gwyneddigion)
1813	London (Gwyneddigion)
1815	London (Cymmrodorion)
1820	London (Cymmrodorion)[1]
1821	London (Cymmrodorion)
1822	London (Cymmrodorion), 22 May
1823	London (Cymreigyddion);[1] London, 22 May
1824	–
1825	Birmingham; Liverpool; London (Gwyneddigion); London (Cymmrodorion)
1826	(Cymmrodorion)[2]
1827	(Cymmrodorion)[2]
1828	–
1829	London (Eisteddfod and Cambrian Concert)
1830	London (Cymreigyddion) (2); London (Gwyneddigion)
1831	London (Eisteddfod and Cambrian Concert)
1832	–
1833	London, 29 May
1834	London, 23 Oct.
1835	–
1836	Liverpool; London, 31 May
1837	–
1838	Liverpool (2) (Gwyneddigion), 1 March
1839	Liverpool (2), 1 March, June
1840	Liverpool, 17–20 June; London (Cymreigyddion), 23 Dec.
1841	Liverpool; London
1842	Liverpool
1843	London (Cymreigyddion Caerludd)
1844	–
1845	Liverpool (Gordofigion)[1]
1846	–
1847	–
1848	–
1849	–
1850	–
1851	Liverpool
1852	Liverpool, March; London; Manchester, 1 March
1853	Ironbridge; Liverpool, 22 March; Manchester, St David's Day
1854	Liverpool, 22 March
1855	London, 25 July; Manchester
1856	London; Manchester; Racine (Wis., USA), 1 March *(1st Eisteddfod in USA)*
1857	Racine (USA), 1–2 July; Utica (Pa., USA), New Year[3]
1858	Racine (USA), 7 Jan.; Rome (Wis., USA)
1859	Manchester; Utica (USA), New Year; Ebenezburg (USA)
1860	–
1861	–
1862	–
1863	Hyde Park (Scranton, Pa., USA)[4]
1864	Johnstown (Pa., USA), Christmas
1865	Birkenhead, Christmas; London, Jan.
1866	Chester (National Eisteddfod), 4–7 Sept.; Melbourne (Australia), Christmas
1867	Liverpool; Oswestry; Paris (Musical Competition), July 8; St Brieux (Brittany);[5] Utica (USA), 1 Jan.
1868	Liverpool (Gordofigion)
1869	Liverpool (Gordofigion); Utica (USA), St David's Day
1870	Liverpool; London 18 May; Utica (USA), 1 Jan.; Youngstown (Ohio, USA), 4 July
1871	Birkenhead; Liverpool; Miles (Ohio, USA); Utica, St David's Day
1872	Liverpool, London, 4 July;[6] Miles (USA), Jan.; Utica (USA), St David's Day
1873	Birkenhead; Cincinnati (USA); Liverpool; Utica (USA), St David's Day; Wyoming (USA),[7] 1 Jan.
1874	Liverpool, Middlesborough; Utica (USA), St David's Day
1875	Hyde Park (USA); Liverpool; Milwaukee (USA), 25 Dec.; Pennsylvania, (USA); Scranton (Pa., USA)
1876	Birkenhead; Liverpool (Gordofigion)
1877	Liverpool (Christmas)
1878	Birkenhead (National Eisteddfod); Birmingham; Liverpool, Christmas; London, 10 April; Wilkes-Barre (Pa., USA) (St David's Day)
1879	Liverpool; London; Oswestry
1880	Hyde Park (USA), Schuylkill (Pa., USA); London; Youngstown (Ohio, USA)
1881	Liverpool, 25 Jan.; Oswestry
1882	Ballarat (Victoria, Australia), 1 March; Liverpool, Christmas; Philadelphia (USA)
1883	Colorado (USA); Emporia (Kan., USA); Liverpool, 10 Nov.; Stratford (Essex); Utica (USA)
1884	Birkenhead, St David's Day; New York (USA), Feb.; Liverpool (National Eisteddfod), 15–20 Sept.; Mineapolis (USA); Stratford (Essex); Venedocia (Ohio, USA), 12 June
1885	Birkenhead; London; Stratford (Essex)
1886	Stratford (Essex)
1887	Birkenhead; New York; Hyde Park (USA); Liverpool; London (National Eisteddfod), 9–12 Aug.; Oakland (USA), 22 Feb.; Stratford (Essex); Utica (USA); Youngstown (USA)
1888	Ballarat (Australia); Denver (Col., USA); New York (USA), New Year; Liverpool; Scranton (USA); Stratford (Essex); Washington (USA)

Year	Location
1889	London; Powell (Ipswich County; Dakota, USA), 20 June; Stratford (Essex); Toronto (Canada), Christmas; Utica (USA), New Year
1890	Chester, Christmas; Liverpool; Stratford (Essex); Utica (USA)
1891	Chester, Christmas; Liverpool (2), St David's Day, 26 Dec.; Racine (USA); Stratford (Essex); Utica (USA)
1892	Chester, Christmas; Birkenhead, 10 May; Liverpool, Christmas; London; Stratford (Essex)
1893	Bootle (2), 14 April, May; Chicago (USA), *World Fair*; Liverpool (3); Middle Granville (USA); St Helens; Stratford (Essex)
1894	Bootle; Liverpool; Scranton (USA); Stratford (Essex)
1895	Liverpool (2), 26 Dec.; Oswestry; Stratford (Essex)
1896	Stratford (Essex)
1897	Birkenhead; Liverpool, 14 Oct.; Scranton (USA), 11 May; Stratford (Essex); Workington (Lancs.), 1–2 June
1898	Cleveland, Ohio, USA; Hunstanton; Johannesburg, Good Friday; Liverpool, Christmas; London, 23 Nov.; Luzerne (Pa., USA); Manchester, Nov.; Oban (Scotland), 1 Sept.; Oswestry; Stratford (Essex); Utah (USA)
1899	Birkenhead, Easter Monday; Birmingham, Christmas; Hunstanton; Chester, 26 Dec.; Ipswich (Queensland, Australia); Hay Johannesburg, Good Friday; Liverpool, May; London (5), Jan., Feb.,16, 23 Nov.; Manchester, 9 Dec.; Middlesborough, 1 Jan.; Nantichoke (Pa., USA); Calon; Plains (USA); Stockton-on-Tees (*Cymric Eisteddfod*); Stratford (Essex); Utica (USA), 17 March; Workington (Lancs), 1–2 Jan.
1900	Atlanta City (USA), July; Birkenhead, 16 April; Birmingham (3), 16 April, 2 May, 25 Dec.; Chester (2), 28 Nov., 26 Dec.; Cincinnati (USA), 1 Jan.; Cleveland and Durham, 1 Jan.; Columba (USA), 31 Dec.; Edward's Dale (USA), 14 March; Liverpool (National Eisteddfod) 18–22 Sept.; Liverpool, 26 Dec.; London (4), 26 Jan., 21–22 Feb., 29 Sept., 29 Nov.; Mount Morgan (Queensland, Australia), 13 April; Oswestry, 1 March; Ottumwa (USA), Christmas; Scranton (USA), 3 Sept.; Stratford (Essex), 26 March; Utica (USA), (4), 1 Jan., 16 Aug., Nov., Christmas; West Kirby (Cheshire), 4 June

Source: David Morgan Richards, *Rhestr Eisteddfodau hyd y flwyddyn 1901* (Llandysul, 1914).

Figures in brackets indicate when more than one eisteddfod was held.

[1] Societies promoting Welsh culture for Welsh exiles in England, such as the Gwyneddigion, Cymmrodorion, and Cymreigyddion in London, and the Gordofigion in Liverpool, were also established during the first quarter of the nineteenth century in many parts of Wales.

[2] Location not given at source; presumably the London society.

[3] According to Richards, this was the first Eisteddfod in Utica.

[4] Detailed information on eisteddfodau in north-east Pennsylvania can be found in 'Welsh cultural life in Scranton', in William D. Jones, *Wales in America; Scranton and the Welsh 1860–1920* (Cardiff, 1993), pp. 87–145.

[5] The first Pan-Celtic Eisteddfod.

[6] Held at the Crystal Palace.

[7] Almost certainly Wyoming County, Pennsylvania.

Culture 1.4 Eisteddfodau. Subjects for competition and number of competitors. The National Eisteddfod, Aberystwyth. 1865

	Subject[1]	Number of Competitors[2]
	POETRY[3]	
1	St. Paul: Chair Poem – *Awdl*[4] ... recommended that this poem should not exceed 1,000 lines.	
2	David: The Principal *Pryddest*[5] (in Welsh) ... recommended that this Poem should not exceed 2,000 lines.	10
3	Home: A *Cywydd*, not to exceed 1,000 lines.[6]	3
4	English Ode: On any subject. The Ode not to exceed 1,000 lines, and competitors to be natives of Wales.	
5	Aberystwyth Castle: Historical and Descriptive Ode. (In Welsh)	5
6	The Wedding Ring: Song. (In Welsh)	
7	Aberystwyth as a Watering Place: Six *Hir a Thoddaid*.[7]	
8	Lewis Morris' Grave at Llanbadarn Fawr: Six verses – *Penillion*.[8] (In Welsh)	
9	Monach Bridge (*Pontarfynach*): One *Englyn*.[9]	
10	The Aberystwyth Railway: Six *Englynion*.	
11	Translation: For the best translation into English, in any metre the poet may select, of *'Gwrthddrych Henaidd'*, in the Pryddest of the Rev. Wm. Jones ('Myvyr Môn') on the Resurrection, appended to the Treatise on 'Swyddogaeth Barn a Darvelydd', beginning at page 127 and ending at the last line of page 130. (Published by Isaac Clarke, Ruthin).	
12	Awdl, To the memory of the late John Vaughan, Esq., Penmaen Dyfi, Merionethshire.	2[10]
	PROSE	
1	The Origin of the English Nation: More especially with reference to the question, – 'How far are they descended from the Ancient Britons?' (In English, Welsh, French, or German)	
2	The Industrial Classes of Wales: Giving a full account of the nature of their various callings, their present condition, and future prospects. (In Welsh)	8
3	Eben Vardd: A Biographical and Critical Essay on his Life and Genius. (In Welsh)	
4	The Geology of South Wales: The Cambrian and Silurian Rocks of South Wales. (In English) ... must be written in a popular style.	
5	Llanbadarn Fawr: The Ecclesiastical and Secular History of Llanbadarn Fawr. (In English)	
6	The Eminent Men of Cardiganshire. (In Welsh) ... not to include any of the living celebrities of Cardiganshire.	
7	The Antiquities and Legends of Cardiganshire. (In Welsh)	1
8	On the Selection, Breeding, and Management of the Live Stock best suited for Wales. (In Welsh)	3
9	The Truth against the World, And the advantages of exercising and conforming with this wise proverb. (In Welsh)	9
	MUSIC Compositions	
1	Cantata: 'The Prodigal Son', Libretto published in 'Yr Eisteddfod', No. 3, (Hughes and Son, Publishers, Wrexham).	3[10]
2	Congregational Tune: ... on the metre 8, 8, 6 ('Yn Eden, cofiaf hyny byth, &c.').	148
3	Glees: ... three Glees or Part Songs to any Welsh words.	27
4	Duett: Suitable for Two Females (Sopranos).	
	Choral Singing	
1	The Swansea Prize Motett, From 'Y Gyfres Gerddol', published by Messrs Hughes & Son, Wrexham. By a Choir of not less than 30, and not more than 100 persons.	
2	'The Harp of Wales' (Brinley Richards): By a Choir of Mixed voices, not less than 16 in number, Welsh or English words.	
3	Choral Singing: Mixed voices, no less than 10 in number, – 'Sweet Day So Cool', 'Boat Song' – Brinley Richards. (Welsh or English words)	
4	Choral Singing: Male voices, 'God Bless the Prince of Wales' (Anthem Tywysog Cymru).	
5	Part Song: 'Up Quit thy Bower' (Brinley Richards) By a Choir of Mixed voices of not less than 14 in number.	
6	Solo: ... 'The people that walked in darkness' from Handel's 'Messiah'.	

	Subject[1]	Number of Competitors[2]
	Instrumental	
7	Brass Band: For the best Brass Band Performance of the March from 'Faust'.	
8	Playing on the Triple Harp:	
9	Playing on the Triple Harp: The successful Competitor on Prize No. 8, will not be allowed to compete for this prize.	
10	Pianoforte Playing: To the best Female Performer on the Pianoforte. (Age not to exceed 18 years.) Subject, – 'The Rising of the Lark' (No. 3, 'The Recollections of Wales').	1
11	Pianoforte Playing: To the best Male Performer on the Pianoforte (Under 15 years of age.) Subject, – 'Home, Sweet Home', arranged by James Bellak.	1
12	Vocal Scholarship: To the most promising Female Vocalist, towards her Musical Education under the direction of the Eisteddfod Council. Candidates to be between 16 and 21 years of age, to be natives of Wales, and conversant with the Welsh language. Winners of former Scholarships not allowed to compete.	6
	ART	
1	For the best specimen in Wood Carving, of some useful piece of Furniture.	
2	For the best Six specimens of small Carvings, suitable for a Drawing-room Table.	
3	For the best specimen of Stone Carving.	
4	For the best specimen of Slate Carving.	

Source: *The National Eisteddfod, for the year 1865: to be held at Aberystwyth, in the Autumn of the same Year* (Aberystwyth, 1865), a pamphlet for prospective competitors, listing subjects and prizes.

[1] In addition to the main competition performances and adjudication on the subjects listed below, the eisteddfod events included 'An Exhibition of the Art, Industry, and Produce of Wales', 'Concerts of National Music', and 'Papers on questions of Social Economy, &c. to be read at the Social Science Meetings ... to be followed by free discussion and conversation'. Papers delivered to the Social Science meetings included: 'The Welsh Language', 'Middle Class Education', 'Popular Education in Wales and the Union of its promoters', and 'A Bundle of Statistics or the Welsh People and Wales'.

[2] As reported in the *Aberystwyth Observer*, 16, 23 September 1865.

[3] A further competition was announced at the Eisteddfod, a prize for the best stanza on Prince Napoleon 'to be delivered next day'.

[4] A long poem in strict metre form.

[5] A long poem in free metre.

[6] A strict metre poem, composed of rhyming couplets.

[7] A strict metre poem, usually six lines of ten syllables.

[8] A folk song sung to harp accompaniment.

[9] A monorhymed stanza of four lines in strict metre.

[10] No prize awarded.

Culture 1.5 Eisteddfodau. Subjects for competition and number of competitors. The National Eisteddfod, Cardiff. 1883

Category	Subject	Competitors
	POETRY	
Awdl [1] (Welsh)	'*Y Llong*' [The Ship], not exceeding 1,000 lines	3
Pryddest [2] (Welsh or English)	'*Llandaf*' [Llandaff], not exceeding 1,000 lines	13
Awdl (Welsh)	On the late Sir Hugh Owen, not exceeding 1,000 lines	6
Pryddest (Welsh or English)	In memory of the late Marquess of Bute, not to exceed 250 lines	10
Galargerdd [3] (Welsh or English)	On the late Right Rev. Dr. Ollivant, Bishop of Llandaff, not to exceed 150 lines	19
Cywydd [4] (Welsh)	'Uchelgais' [Ambition]	4
Bugeilgerdd [5] (Welsh)	The author to choose his subject	15
Hymns (Welsh)	Eight hymns, for the use of Sunday Schools	21
Translation (Welsh)	Twelve Latin Hymns in the same metre as the original. Selected from H.10 to H.100 in Helmore's selection	3
Poem (Welsh or English)	'The New Tower of Cardiff Castle', not to exceed 100 lines	ng[6]
Englynion [7] (Welsh)	Three englynion on the late Bard 'Ioan Madoc'	36
Englyn unodl union (Welsh)	On the late 'Mr Isaac Harding, of Caerphilly'	43
Tuchangerdd [8] (Welsh)	'Ymhonwr' [The Egotist]	14
Song (Welsh)	'Y Weddw' [The Widow] (for females only)	4
Verses (Welsh)	'Gosteg o Englynion i'r Glo' [Verses on Coal]	12
Epitaph (Welsh)	On the late Bard Islwyn ('Beddargraph Islwyn')	45
Englyn (Welsh)	'Anadl' [Breath]	102
	PROSE	
Essay (Welsh or English)	History of Welsh Literature, from the year 1300 to the year 1650	7
Essay (Welsh or English)	On the Life and Labours of the late Sir Hugh Owen	3
Serial Story (English)	On Welsh Social Life, or Welsh Historical Events, consisting of not less than 13 or more than 16 weekly parts. The weekly parts to be not less than two nor more than three ordinary newspaper columns (i.e., not less than 4000 words nor more than 6000 words)	11
Short Story (Welsh)	On Welsh Social Life or Welsh Historical Events. Complete in not less than 4000 or more than 6000 words	8
Essay (Welsh or English)	'The Periodical Literature of Wales during the present century', with particulars of the character of the publications, their editors and publishers, in chronological order	5
Essay (English)	'History of the Principal Eisteddfodau of the present century', with a description of the chief prizes, in poetry and prose, and the successful competitors. The facts to appear in chronological order	2
Paper (English)	'Cymro-Celtic Names of Places still preserved in parts of Britain, now inhabitated by English or Saxons'	7
Essay (Welsh)	'Y modd i sicrhau adloniant iachus a theilwng mewn lleoedd poblogaidd y tu allan i gylch bwrdeisdrefi' [The best method of promoting healthy and rational recreation in populous districts outside the range of municipal boroughs]	8
Libretto (English)	For a pantomime, subject 'Sindbad the Sailor'	11
Essay (English)	'Cn the Coal Resources of South Wales and Monmouthshire'	1
Essay (Welsh)	'Arweddion diweddaraf Gwyddoneg yn eu perthynas a Datguddiad' [The bearings of recent discoveries of Science on Revelation, treated from a Christian point of view]	6
Essay (Welsh or English)	'Hanes a Nodweddion y Diarhebion Cymreig' [History and Characteristics of the Welsh Proverbs]	3
Essay (English)	'History of the Rise and Progress and present prospects of the Coal Trade, particularly Steam Coal, in South Wales and Monmouthshire'	3
Register (English)	Of existing Manuscripts relating to the History of the County of Glamorgan	1
Essay (Welsh and English)	'The Old Squire of Llanharran'	3
Essay (Welsh and English)	History of Cwm-yr-Ystrad (Rhondda Valley)	ng[6]

Category	Subject	Competitors
Essay (Welsh)	'Cynildeb Teuluol' [Thrift], by females only	5
Essay (English)	History of the Ancient Industries of Pontypool	3
Shorthand Transcription (English)	Take down in shorthand, and transcribe without the use of abbreviations, most correctly and expeditiously, a column of a speech by the late Earl of Beaconsfield	6
Descriptive Account (English)	Of the first day's proceedings of the National Eisteddfod, not to exceed in length one column of the *Western Mail*	14
Examination (Welsh)	Welsh Grammar	8
Examination (English)	Welsh History subsequent to the Norman Conquest	5
Translation	(at sight) English into Welsh, and Welsh into English	14
	MUSIC Vocal	
Choir, 150–200 voices	'Wretched Lovers' (*Acis and Galatea*, Handel) 'Lord of the Golden Day' (omitting the Contralto Solo and Chorus) (*Martyr of Antioch*, Sullivan) 'Cyfoded Duw' (Jenkins)	6[9]
Choir, 60–100 voices	Sight Singing, of an accompanied chorus, for mixed voices	4[10]
Choir, 50–60 voices	Anthem, *In That Day* (Elvey), Recitative and next three movements	7[11]
Church or Congregational Choir	Anthem (choice open to competitors). Conductor and performers to be *bonâ fidé* members of a Church or Congregational Choir	5[12]
Madrigal and Part-song, not less than 20 voices	'Come again, sweet love' (Dowland) 'Winter Days' (Caldicott)	9[13]
Male Voice Part-song, 16 voices	Unaccompanied. Choice open to competitors	14
Female Voice Part-song or Chorus	Accompanied. Choice open to competitors	1[14]
Quartette – soprano, alto, tenor, bass	'Quando Corpus' (Rossini)	7
Trio – soprano, tenor, bass	'The hour of vengeance' (Beethoven)	9
Duet – soprano and bass, or soprano and tenor, or tenor and bass	Choice open to competitors	20
Duet – female voices	'The Homestead' (Rubinstein)	5
Soprano Solo	'Beauteous Cradle' (Schumann)	32
Contralto Solo	'O Lord, Thou hast searched me out' (Bennett)	27
Tenor Solo	'The enemy said' (Handel)	46
Bass Solo	'Is not His word like a fire' (Mendelssohn)	41
	Instrumental	
Brass Band	March, 'Tannhauser' (Wagner) Grand Selection, 'Rigoletto' (Verdi)	5[15]
Full Orchestra	Overture 'Masaniello'	3[16]
String Quartette	No. 1 (Beethoven)	ng[6]
Solo Violin – Males	(with pianoforte accompaniment) Choice open to performers	ng[6]
Solo Violin – Ladies	(with pianoforte accompaniment) Choice open to performers	ng[6]
Solo Violincello	(with pianoforte accompaniment) Choice open to performers	1
Any Other Instrument Solo	(with pianoforte accompaniment) Choice open to performers	9
Solo Harp	'Autumn' (John Thomas)	9
Solo Harp	Choice open	14
Solo Pianoforte	'Novelette', no.1 in F (Schumann) 'Rondo Capriccioso' (Mendelssohn)	31
Duet, Piano and Harmonium	'Dinorah' (Engel)	2
Solo Harmonium	'Cujus Animam' (Rossini)	ng[6]
Organ Solo	Sixth Organ Sonata (Mendelssohn). Extempore playing upon a given initial subject; the time not to exceed five minutes	8

Category	Subject	Competitors
	Compositions	
Anthem	Four vocal parts, with solo or verse pianoforte or organ accompaniment	29
Part Song – four voices		28
Song – any voice		44
Duet – piano and harmonium		2
Hymn Tune		183
Double Chant		86
	ART AND SCIENCE	
Oil Painting	Open	
Oil Painting	Confined to natives of the Principality, whether resident or non-resident, and residents in Wales for two years before January, 1883, and at the time of the Eisteddfod	
Water Colour Painting	Open	
Water Colour Painting	Confined to natives of the Principality	
Sculpture		
Medallion	Cast in plaster, of an Ideal Bust or Figure, personifying the town of Cardiff, not less than 2ft. in diameter	
Portrait Bust	A Welsh Worthy	
Design	A coloured Almanack, suitable for reproduction by Chromolithography	
Artistic Bookbinding		
Wood Carving		
Stone Carving		
Artistic Metal Work	For Ecclesiastical or Domestic decoration	
Drawing	Crayon, Chalk, Charcoal, or Pencil Drawing	
Oil Monochrome		
Water-colour Monochrome		
Drawing	Pen-and-Ink, Sepia or Ink	
Etching, Mezzotint, Engraving, or Lithograph		
Lithography	For commercial purposes	
Architectural Design	A villa	
Applied Design		
Original Painting	On porcelain or earthenware	
Art Needlework	In crewels	
Decorative Painting	On Terra-Cotta, in Oil or Water-colour	
Painting	Upon Satin or Silk	
Mechanical Drawing	For Colliery Winding Engine	
Photograph	Artistic figure-subject	
Photograph	Any other subject	
Model	A skeleton of Plesiosaurus, suitable for educational purposes. Length of model not to be less than four feet, each bone to be separately modelled, and removable, except those of the cranium and phalanges	
Collection of Botanical Specimens	Accurately named, and collected by the exhibitor in any one county of Wales, including Monmouthshire	
Collection of Specimens	Illustrative of the Geology and Palaeontology of any one of the counties of Wales, including Monmouthshire, accurately named and collected by the exhibitor	

Source: *The National Eisteddfod of Wales (Eisteddfod Genedlaethol Cymru). Cardiff Meeting 1883 ... Complete and Official List of Prizes* (Cardiff, 1883). *Programme of the National Eisteddfod held at Cardiff, 6–9 Aug. 1883* (Cardiff, 1883).

[1] A long poem in strict metre form.
[2] A long poem in free metre.

[3] Elegy.
[4] A strict metre poem composed of rhyming couplets.
[5] Pastoral song.
[6] Included in the original list of competitions but not in the final programme.
[7] Monorhymed stanzas of four lines in strict metre.
[8] Satirical poem.
[9] Llanelly United Choir, Pembroke Dock Choral Union, Penrhyn Quarries Choral Union, Rhondda Choral Union, Dowlais Harmonic Society, Rhondda Philharmonic Society.
[10] Dowlais Glee Society, Cambrian Minstrels (Neath), Rhondda Choir (Ton Ystrad), Morlais Choral Society (Dowlais).
[11] Abergavenny Choir, Morlais Choral Society (Dowlais), Tabernacle Harmonic Society, Merthyr, Aberdulais Choir (Neath), The Pontypool and Abersychan United Choir, Tredegar Harmonic Society, Ton United Choir (Ystrad Rhondda).
[12] Wern Congregational Choir (Ystalyfera), English Wesleyan Choir (Tredegar), Horeb Choir (Skewen, Neath), Libanus Choir (Dowlais), Bethal Choir (Cwmparc, Rhondda).
[13] Llandaff Choral Society, Morlais Choral Society (Dowlais), Welsh Vocalists (Hirwaun), Ynysydarren Madrigal Society, Tredegar Glee Party, Newtown Musical Union, Taff Minstrels (Troedyrhiw), The Pontypool and Abersychan United Choir, Rhondda Minstrels (Porth).
[14] Ynysydarren Vocalists.
[15] Merthyr Town Band, D. Burns' Band (Cardiff), Cardiff Brass Band, 1st Glamorgan Artillery Volunteer Band, Irwell Bank Band (Manchester).
[16] Cardiff String Band, Merthyr Amateur Orchestral Band, Libanus String Band (Treherbert).

Culture 1.6 Eisteddfodau. Subjects for competition and number of competitors. The National Eisteddfod, Liverpool. 1900

Category	Subject	Competitors
	POETRY (Welsh)	
Awdl y Gadair [1]	*Y Bugail* [The Shepherd]	20
Pryddest y Goron [2]	*Williams Pant-y-Celyn*	11
Drama	*Yr Archesgob Williams, Conwy; ac adeg y Rhyfel Cartrefol yn Nghymru* [The Archbishop Williams, Conwy and the time of the Civil War in Wales]	2
Myfyrdraith [3]	*Ioan Fedyddiwr yn ngharchar* [John the Baptist in prison]	14
Cywydd [4]	*Y Gweledydd* [The Seer]	8
Rhiangerdd [5]	*Ardudfyl, mam Dafydd ap Gwilym* [Ardudfyl, mother of Dafydd ap Gwilym]	4
Cadwen o Englynion [6]	*Y Chwarelwr* [The Quarryman]	16
Englyn [7]	*Y Geirseinydd* [The Gramophone]	89
Cân Ddesgrifiadol [8]	*Glanfa Lerpwl* [Liverpool Landing Stage]	5
Duchangerdd [9]	*Y Grwgnachwr* [The Grumbler]	19
Telynegion [10]	*i) Modrwy y Cyfeillgarwch; ii) Modrwy y Dyweddiad; iii) Modrwy y Briodas; iv) Modrwy y Weddwdod* [i) Friendship Ring, ii) Engagement Ring, iii) Wedding Ring, iv) Ring of Widowhood]	7
	PROSE	
Essay (Welsh)	*Bywyd a Gwaith T. E. Ellis* [The life and work of T. E. Ellis]	0
Essay (Welsh or English)	*Cymru yn y Bedwaredd Ganrif ar Bymtheg: ei chynydd mewn dysg a moes.* Wales in the Nineteenth Century: its progress in Education and Morals	6
Essay (Welsh or English)	*Rhagarweiniad i'r Mabinogion, yn cynwys efrydiaeth gymharol ohonynt.* An Introduction to, and Comparative Study of, the Mabinogion	0
Novel (Welsh)	*Yn desgrifio Bywyd Cymreig yn ystod haner olaf y 18fed ganrif (1750–1800)* [A description of Welsh life during the second half of the 18th century (1750–1800)]	6
Handbook (Welsh)	*ar Feddyleg* [on Psychology]	3
Essay (Welsh or English)	*Prif rinweddau dinesydd da, pa rai ydynt, a'r moddion goreu tuag at eu meithrin.* The cardinal virtues of a good citizen, what they are, and by what means can their formation be best promoted	18
Essay (Welsh or English)	*Diwydianau Cymreig: eu hanes a'r moddion goreu i'w dadblygu.* Welsh Industries: their history and the best means for their development	
Essay (Welsh or English)	*Casgliad cyflawn o Lên Gwerin Cymru wedi eu cynull o Lyfrau Argraphedig Cymraeg (gan eithrio y Mabinogion) hyd ymddangosiad y Brython.* Complete collection of Welsh Folklore in Welsh printed books (excluding the *Mabinogion*) before the appearance of the *Brython*	3
Critical Essay (Welsh)	*Bywyd a Gwaith Robert Owen o'r Drefnewydd* [Life and Work of Robert Owen, Newtown]	6
Essay (Welsh)	*Lle a Dylanwad y chwedl yn nglyn â chrefyddau* [The Place and Influence of the Myth in relation to Religions]	3
Critical Essay (Welsh)	Y Monwyson – (a) Lewis Morris; (b) Richard Morris; (c) William Morris; (d) Goronwy Owen	2
Essay (Welsh or English)	*Dylanwad Sefydliadau Gwerinol ar Foesau a Moesgarwch.* The Influence of Democratic Institutions upon Morals and Manners	7
	Translations	
Into modern Welsh [11]		3
From Welsh into English	*Cywydd y March* by Tudur Aled	2
From English into Welsh	Faith and the Future by Mazzini	12
	Recitations	
English	Speech of King Henry (Shakespeare's *King Henry V*, act iv, scene iii)	50
Welsh	Glan Alaw, *Cwymp Pompeii* [The Fall of Pompeii]	

Category	Subject	Competitors
	MUSIC Vocal	
Choir, 150–180 voices	(a) Dyna'r gwyntoedd yn ymosod (Storm Tiberias, Stephens) (b) Why my soul (Last Chorus, 42nd Psalm, Mendelssohn) (c) (unaccompanied) The vale of rest (Mendelssohn)	5[12]
Choir, 60–75 voices	(a) There is joy in the presence (Prodigal Son, First Chorus, Sullivan) (b) (unaccompanied) Cwsg, fy anwylyd [Sleep my beloved] (J. H. Roberts)	10[13]
Male Choir, 50–60 voices	(a) Croesi'r anial [Crossing the Plain] (T. Maldwyn Price) (b) (unaccompanied) Cyrus in Babylon (Boulanger)	16[14]
Female Choir, 35–40 voices	(a) Sweet the balmy days (*Story of Sayid*, A. C. Mackenzie) (b) Iesu, Cyfaill f'enaid cu [Jesu, Lover of my soul] (D. Protheroe)	8[15]
Children's choir, 40–50 voices	(a) Don't forget the old folks (W. H. Jude) (b) Selene (John Henry)	11[16]
Mixed Quartette	Part song 'Moonlight and Music' (Pinsuti)	36
Male Quartette	(a) unaccompanied 'Meek twilight' (Martin) (b) unaccompanied 'Good night, beloved' (J. L. Hatton)	21
Trio – soprano, contralto, bass	'Queen of the Night' (Smart)	27
Duet – soprano, tenor	'A Night in Venice' Key G Flat (Lucantoni)	38
Duet – tenor, bass	'Hidden Gold' (*Dinorah*, Meyerbeer)	27
Soprano Solo	'With verdure clad' (*Creation*, Haydn)	75
Mezzo-Soprano Solo	'When this scene of trouble closes' (Calvary, Spohr)	63
Contralto Solo	'The voice that bids me come' Key E Flat (Hartwell Jones)	76
Tenor Solo	'Jerusalem' (J. H. Roberts)	88
Baritone Solo	'Wreck of the Hesperus' (J. L. Hatton)	94
Bass Solo	'O Isis and Osiris' (*Zauberflöte*, Mozart)	70
Treble Boy Solo	'Y Deryn Pur' [The Pure Bird] (Brinley Richards, *Songs of Wales*)	9
Penillion Singing[17] – North Wales style		19
Penillion Singing – North Wales style	(open to those who have not won at a National Eisteddfod)	15
Penillion Singing – South Wales style		11
	Instrumental	
Orchestral Band, 35–40 performers	Overture, 'Athalie' (Mendelssohn)	2[18]
String Quartette	Minuette and Trio and Finale (Op. 54 in E, Haydn)	0
Pianoforte (Seniors)	'Valse Caprice' (Rubenstein)	40
Pianoforte (Juniors – under 16 years)	'Pas Triste pas gai' (Sterndale Bennett)	54
Violin Solo (Seniors)	'Romance and Bolero' (Dancla)	15
Pedal Harp Solo	'Fantasia in C minor' (L. Spohr)	3
Triple Harp Solo	'Pêr Alaw' (Parry's *Welsh Harper*)	3
Cornet Solo	'Jenny Jones' (H. Round)	6
Organ Solo	(a) 'Funeral March' and 'Hymn of Seraphs' (Guilmant) (b) 'Short Fugue G minor' (Bach)	10
	Compositions	
Orchestral Suite	Suitable for small orchestra	0
Sacred Cantata	With accompaniment for Pianoforte and Stringed Instruments. Welsh and English words to be chosen by the Composer.	0
Anthem	To contain, among other movements, a Solo and Quartette, and to conclude with Fughetta. Separate Organ accompaniment. Welsh and English words, to be chosen by the composer. Not to occupy more than fifteen minutes in performance	8

Category	Subject	Competitors
Organ Sonata	In four movements. Not to occupy more than twenty minutes in performance	1
Choral Ballad for Male voices	With Welsh and English words, founded upon a Welsh historical incident. Not to occupy more than ten minutes in performance	4
Arrangement for Female voices	Of the Welsh melodies 'Ar hyd y nos' and 'Hela'r Ysgyfarnog'	9
Contralto Solo	With obligato for Wind or String. English and Welsh words	9
Tenor Song	With obligato for Wind or String. English and Welsh words	4
	ART AND SCIENCE Painting, etching, drawing	
Oil Painting	Of a Welsh Legendary or Historical Subject, Canvas 36in. x 28in.	4
Oil Painting	Of a Welsh landscape, Canvas 36in. x 28in.	9
Water Colour Painting	Of a Welsh Landscape, size not to exceed 30in. x 22in.	6
Water Colour Painting	Of an Interior of Welsh Cottage or Building, with figures, size not to exceed 30in. x 22in.	3
Drawing	In Sepia or Black and White, size 30in. x 22in.	11
Unpublished Etching	12in x 8in.	1
Series of Twelve Illustrations	In Black and White, to *Bardd Cwsc*, by Elis Wyn	2
Series of Six Illustrations	In Black and White, depicting incidents in the Welsh novel *Rhys Lewis*[19]	1
Set of Three Small Drawings	In any medium of a river or estuary	4
Set of Three Small Drawings	In any medium of mountain scenery	4
	Sculpture and Modelling	
Piece of Sculpture in Marble	Of a mythological or historical subject relating to Wales	0
Modelling of a Figure Subject	In Terra-cotta	0
Modelling of a Figure Subject Bas-relief Panel	In Terra-cotta	0
Specimen Carving in Stone		3
Specimen Carving in Slate		1
	Architecture[20]	
Architectural Design	Of a Village Club-house with newsroom, reading-room, billiard-room, and hall to accommodate 250 people, with caretaker's residence. Cost not to exceed £1,500	6
Architectural Design	Of a mountain church or chapel to seat 200 people. Cost not to exceed £1,000	5
Architectural Design	Of a row of four agricultural labourers' village cottages and small shop adjoining. Cost of each house not to exceed £100, and shop £150	
	Wood Carving	
Oak Dado	4 ft high x 3 ft 6in. wide, with carved panels	0
Carved Chimney-piece and Overmantel	In any hard wood	1
	Metal Work	
Ornamental Copper Door Handle	With Plate	1
Ecclesiastical or Domestic Entrance-door Furniture	In wrought iron	0
Artistic Hinges and Furniture	(Suitable for a cabinet)	0
Bracket for Electric Light	In wrought iron or copper	0
Wrought Iron Garden Gate	(suitable for a suburban villa)	0
Panel in Lead Light	For vestibule door, size 3 ft x 2 ft 6in.	0
	Pottery, Bookbinding, Design, Graining	
Specimen of Art Pottery		0
Specimen of Bookbinding	In Calf or Morocco, hand-tooled and lettered. No Blocking. Size not to exceed Royal 8vo.	1
Design of an Oak Bardic Chair		8

Category	Subject	Competitors
Design for Wall Paper		1
Design for Hall Fire Place		3
Design for Interior Decoration	Of a Place of worship in distemper or oils, showing dado, wall, frieze, and ceiling	1
Set of Five Panels	Showing specimen of graining in various woods	0
	Photography	
Set of Four Prints	From original negatives of Welsh mountain scenery	3
Enlargement	Any subject except portraits. To be not less than four times the size of the original, and to be accompanied by a direct print from the original negative	5
Set of not less than 25 Lantern Slides	Accompanied by a descriptive Lecturette to occupy not more than half-an-hour in delivery. Subject: 'A Holiday Tour in Wales'	1
Set of Four Prints	From original negatives. 'Fruit' or 'Flower' studies	1
Set of Four Prints	From original negatives of Marine Views	2
Set of Four Lantern Slides		2
Set of Four Prints	From original negatives, illustrating the following characters from Daniel Owen's novels: Mari Lewis, Tomos Bartley, Will Bryan (from *Rhys Lewis),* and Gwen Tomos (from *Gwen Tomos)*	0
	Domestic Arts	
Portiere or Screen	Embroidered in silk	3
Dining Table Centre	With six d'oyleys embroidered (natural flowers)	7
Linen Bedspread	Embroidered with threads in fancy stitches	5
Sideboard Cloth	Embroidered on Linen	13
Cushion	Embroidered in Crewel Wools	
Lady's Dressing Gown	Embroidered	0
Gentlemen's Hand Knitted Stockings	With fancy tops	23
Specimen of Welsh-made Tweed or Cloth	(7 yards) made entirely from Welsh wool	41
Specimen of Welsh Flannel	(6 yards)	22
	Botany, Geology, Mineralogy	
Collection of Ferns	From Wales (Classified and Mounted)	1
Collection of Geological Specimens	From Wales (Classified)	0
Collection of Mineral Specimens	From Wales	0

Source: *Official Programme of the National Eisteddfod held at Liverpool, 18–22 September 1900* (Liverpool, 1900).

[1] The 'Chair' Awdl. See Table 1.4 note 4.
[2] The 'Crown' Pryddest. See Table 1.4 note 5.
[3] Monologue.
[4] See Table 1.4 note 6.
[5] Maiden-song/eulogy of a woman. The modern form of spelling is *Rhieingerdd*.
[6] A chain or series of *englynion*.
[7] See Table 1.4 note 9.
[8] Descriptive song.
[9] Satirical poem. The modern form is *Dychangerdd.*
[10] Lyrics.
[11] On the model of Skene, *Four Ancient Books of Wales*.
[12] Carmarthen Choral Society, Caernarfon Choral Society, Pontypridd United Choir, Potteries and District Choral Society, Shrewsbury Choral Society.
[13] Blackpool Glee and Madrigal Society, Cardiff Blue Ribbon Choir, Cefn Mawr Choral Society, Graig Choral Society (Machynlleth), Holywell United Choir, Orpheus Choral Society (Ffestiniog), Pendref Choir (Bangor), Pontypridd Choral Society, St Helens Prize Choir, Talke and District Prize Choir.
[14] Abercarn Male Voice Party, Bangor Male Voice Society, The Birmingham Welsh Musical Society, Dowlais Male Voice Choir, The Ebbw Vale Male Voice Party, Gwalia Male Voice Society, The Manchester Orpheus Prize Glee Society, Moelwyn Male Voice Party, Nantlle Vale Male Voice Choir, Nelson Arion Prize Glee Union, Oldham Male Voice Society, Port Talbot Glee

Society, Porth and Cymer Male Voice Choir, Rhymney Male Voice Choir, Swansea Cymmrodorion Society, Workington United Male Voice Choir.

[15] Blackpool Glee and Madrigal Society, Cardiff United Ladies Choir, Holyhead Harmonic Ladies Choir, Millgirls Institute Choir (Manchester), Nantlle Vale Ladies Choir, Pontypridd Ladies Choir, Rhymney Ladies Vocal Society, Treherbert Ladies Choir.

[16] Birkenhead Orpheus Children's Choir, Blaenau Ffestiniog Juvenile Choir, Brymbo and Broughton United Juvenile Choir, Bwlchgwyn Board School Juvenile Choir, Ffynongroew Juvenile Choir, Gitana Children's Choir, Gobaith y Rhos (Mountain Ash), Mersey Juvenile Choir (Widnes), Mountain Ash United Juvenile Choir, The Liverpool Juveniles, Treorchy Juvenile Society.

[17] Singing a counter-melody to a tune played on the harp.

[18] Birkenhead Orpheus Orchestral Society, Cambrian Orchestral Society.

[19] The *List of Subjects* added that an English translation of *Rhys Lewis* was available published by Hughes & Son, Wrexham.

[20] Cost exclusive of land and architect's commission. All designs to be drawn to one-eighth scale and to include plans of each floor, sections and elevations of each front and a sketch perspective view. The drainage, sanitary arrangements and water supply to be clearly shown. Also size and height of rooms to be figured. To be accompanied with a short descriptive specification of the various materials used in the construction of the buildings. All the drawing to be in black and white line. Walls coloured black only on plans and sections. Architectural treatment as well as planning will be taken into consideration.

Culture 1.7 Eisteddfodau. Drama competitions at the National Eisteddfod. 1884–1913

Year	Place	Title	Winning author
1884[1]	Liverpool	*Gruffydd ab Cynan*	Elis o'r Nant and the Revd E. A. Jones, Buxton
		Cyfieithiad o 'King Lear' [Translation of 'King Lear']	Revd O. N. Jones, Pwllheli
1885	Aberdare	No competition	
1886	Caernarfon	*Buddug* [Boudicea]	E. Hevin Jones
1887	London	No competition	
1888	Wrexham	*Y Mwnwr Cymreig* [The Welsh Miner]	Elis o'r Nant and T. J. Powell
1889	Brecon	*Rhamant hanesyddol fer* [Short historical romance]	Pedr Hir
1890	Bangor	*Rhys Goch Eryri*	One entry. No prize awarded
1891	Swansea	*Traeth y Lafan* [Lafan Beach] (dramatic cantata)	Robert Bryan
1892	Rhyl	No competition	
1893	Cardiff	No competition	
1894	Caernarfon	*Owain Tudur*	Revd E. Gurnos Jones
1895	Llanelli	No competition	
1896	Llandudno	Any title	Six entries. No prize awarded.
1897	Newport	*Cyflafan y Fenni* [The Abergavenny Massacre]	Elphin and R. H. Roberts, Llanrwst
1898	Ffestiniog	No competition	
1899	Cardiff	*Ifor Bach*	Elphin
1900	Liverpool	*Yr Archesgob Williams* [Archbishop Williams]	Elphin
1901	Merthyr Tydfil	No competition	
1902	Bangor	Bywyd Cymreig yn y 18fed neu'r 19eg ganrif [Welsh life in the 18th or 19th century]	J. Ifano Jones
1903	Llanelli	No competition	
1904	Rhyl	The Banner of the Red Dragon	Miss Eilian Hughes
		Rhys ab Tewdwr Mawr	J. Ifano Jones
1905	Mountain Ash	Bywyd Cymdeithasol yn y 18fed ganrif [Social life in the 18th century]	No prize awarded
1906	Caernarfon	*Owain Lawgoch*	No prize awarded
1907	Swansea	Tair dramawd fer [Three short plays]	T. O. Jones ('Gwynfor') and R. H. Williams, Caernarfon
1908	Llangollen	Dramawd yn ymwneud â hanes Cymru [A play involving Welsh history]	No prize awarded
1909	London	Bywyd Cymreig yn yr oes hon [Welsh life in these times]	T. O. Jones ('Gwynfor')
1910	Colwyn Bay	No competition	
1911	Carmarthen	*Bob Morgan*	Mrs Bassett
		'68	T. O. Jones ('Gwynfor')
		Asgre Lân [Pure heart]	Revd R. G. Berry
1912	Wrexham	*Owain Gwynedd*	Pedr Hir and the Revd R. G. Berry
1913	Abergavenny	No competition	

Source: T. J. Williams, *Hanes y Ddrama Gymreig* (Bangor, 1915), pp. 37–8.

[1] Although drama was excluded from National Eisteddfod competitions before 1884, it had been included in earlier eisteddfodau.

Culture 2.1 The Welsh Press. Welsh Periodicals published between 1735 and 1850

Date of publication	Title	Description	Place of printing[1]
1735[2]	*Tlysau yr hen oesoedd* [Gems of past ages]	Quarterly. Intended to provide entertaining literature and to awaken the interest of the Welsh people in their language	Holyhead
1770	*Trysorfa gwybodaeth* [Treasury of knowledge]	Religious, literary and antiquarian	Carmarthen
1793–94	*Cylch-grawn Cynmraeg* (changed to *Y Cylchgrawn*, Nov. 1793) or *Welsh Magazine*	Quarterly. Largely religious, also articles on slavery and the French Revolution	Trefeca, Machynlleth, Carmarthen
1795–96	*The Miscellaneous repository neu, y drysorfa gymmysgedig*	Quarterly. General, radical and political	Carmarthen
1796	*Y Geirgrawn* [The Magazine]	Monthly. General, radical and political	Chester
1799–1827	*Trysorfa ysprydol* 1799–1801 (*Trysorfa* 1809–13; *Y Drysorfa* 1819–27) [Spiritual treasury]	Quarterly. Religious, serving the Calvinistic Methodist denomination	Chester, Bala
1800	*Greal, neu eurgrawn* [The Miscellany, or magazine]	Chiefly antiquarian and literary with foreign and home news	Caernarfon
1805–7	*Y Greal* [or Welsh magazine]	Quarterly. Literary and antiquarian	London
1806	*Trysorfa efangylaidd* [Evangelical treasury]	Quarterly. Religious, serving the Baptists of south Wales	Carmarthen
1807–8	*Trysorfa gwybodaeth* [Treasury of Knowledge]	Quarterly. Religious, literary and antiquarian	Carmarthen
1809–1983	*Yr Eurgrawn Wesleyaidd* [The Wesleyan Magazine] (*Y Drysorfa Wesleyaidd*, 1822; *Yr Eurgrawn*, 1822; *Yr Eurgrawn Wesleyaidd*, 1823; *Yr Eurgrawn,* 1933)	Monthly until 1961; quarterly 1962–83. Mainly religious – for Wesleyan Methodists	Dolgellau, London, Llanfair Caereinion, Llanidloes, Bangor, Denbigh, Llandysul, Caernarfon, Dolgellau
1812–20?*	*Trysorfa'r ysgol Sabbothol* [The Sunday school treasury]	Religious and educational, serving the Sunday schools	Aberystwyth
1814–15	*Cylchgrawn Cymru* [The Magazine of Wales]	Twice a year. General and literary, undenominational	Chester, Dolgellau, Bala
1816	*Cronicl cenhadol* [Missionary chronicle]	Every two months. Activities of missionary societies – mainly north Wales	Holywell
1817	*Greal y Bedyddwyr* [The Baptists' Miscellany]	Monthly. Chiefly religious – circulating among the Baptists of south Wales	Swansea
1818–23	*Cronicl cenadol*	Monthly. Undenominational digest of *The Missionary chronicle* in Welsh	Carmarthen
1818–30	*Goleuad Gwynedd, neu'n hytrach goleuad Cymru* (*Goleuad Cymru,* 1820) [The Illuminator of Gwynedd, or rather the illuminator of Wales]	Monthly. Religious and general – for the Calvinistic Methodists, mainly in north Wales	Chester
1818–1983	*Seren Gomer* [The Star of Gomer]	(Previously a newspaper, 1814) General, religious and literary. Undenominational up to 1859, but serving the Baptist denomination thereafter	Swansea, Carmarthen, Aberdare, Blaenau, Tonypandy, Barmouth, Denbigh, Blaenau Ffestiniog, Llandysul
1821–1968	*Y Dysgedydd crefyddol* [The Religious instructor] (*Y Dysgedydd*, 1840; *Yr Annibynwr*, 1865; *Y Diwygiwr*, 1912; joined *Y Drysorfa*, 1968, to form *Porfeydd*)	Monthly. Religious and general – for the Congregationalists	Dolgellau, Cardiff, Bala, Llanelli, Swansea
1822	*Cyfaill y Cymro* [The Welshman's friend]	Monthly. Literary, antiquarian and historical	Bala
1822	*Y Cymro* [The Welshman]	Monthly. General and undenominational	Liverpool
1822–37	*Y Gwyliedydd* [The Sentinel]	Monthly. Literary, antiquarian and historical	Bala
1822?	*Lloffion* [Gleanings]	Monthly. Mainly religious and educational	Denbigh
1823	*Addysgydd* [The Educator]	Monthly. For Sunday school pupils	Carmarthen
1823	*Hanesydd* [The Historian]	Monthly. Mainly religious, intended for the Sunday schools of Cardiganshire	Aberystwyth

Date of publication	Title	Description	Place of printing[1]
1825–7	*Y Drych* [The Mirror]	Monthly. For children and young Sunday school pupils	Carmarthen
1825?	*Y Drysorfa* [The Treasury]		?Aberystwyth
1825–6	*Eurgrawn Mon* [The Anglesey magazine]	Monthly (quarterly 1826). Mainly articles of a general nature, geography, astronomy, home and foreign news	Holyhead
1825–42	*Trysor i blentyn* [A child's treasure]	Monthly. Wesleyan Methodist publication for Sunday school children; undenominational 1841–2	Llanfair Caereinion, Llanidloes
1826?	*Yr Addysgydd* [The Educator]		Aberystwyth
1826–7	*Cydymaith yr ieuengctid* [The Young people's companion]	Monthly. Chiefly religious	Llanrwst
1826	*Yr Oes* [The Age] (followed by *Lleuad yr oes* 1827–30, *Yr Efangylydd* 1831–6)	Monthly. General and undenominational	Swansea
1826–9	*Pethau newydd a hen* [Things new and old]	Monthly. Religious, intended for Sunday school children of Montgomeryshire	Dolgellau, Chester
1826–7	*Trysor i'r ieuangc* (*Trysor i'r ieuengctid,* June 1826) [Treasure for young people]	Monthly. Chiefly religious, intended for Sunday school children of Caernarfonshire	Caernarfon
1827–30	*Yr Athraw, crefyddol, hanesyddol, eglwysig a gwladol* [The Teacher, religious, historical, ecclesiastical and civil]	Monthly. For Sunday school teachers and pupils	Merthyr Tydfil, Pontypool
1827–1918	*Athraw i blentyn* (*Y Tyst Apostolaidd* 1851–, *Yr Athraw* 1853–)	Monthly. Baptist Sunday school pupils	Llanrwst, Llangollen
1827	*Cyfrinach y Bedyddwyr* [The Baptists' association]	Monthly. Religious and literary – for the Baptists of Glamorgan and Monmouthshire	Merthyr Tydfil, Maesycwmwr
1827–37	*Greal y Bedyddwyr* [The Baptists' miscellany]	Monthly. Religious and literary – circulating among the Baptists of south Wales	Cardigan, Cardiff
1827–31	*Yr Hanesydd Cenadawl* [The Missionary historian]	Quarterly. Undenominational digest of *The Missionary chronicle* in Welsh with news of foreign missions	London
1827–30	*Lleuad yr oes* [The Moon of the age] (Preceded by *Yr Oes* 1826. Succeeded by *Yr Efangylydd* 1831)	Monthly. General and undenominational	Swansea, Aberystwyth, Llandovery
1827	*Y Meddyg teuluaidd/The Family physician*	Monthly. Bilingual medical magazine	Merthyr Tydfil
1828	*Y Brud a sylwydd: or the chronicle and observer*	Monthly. General knowledge, emphasis on science	Carmarthen, Liverpool
1828	*Trysorfa Ieuenctyd* [Young people's treasury]	Monthly. Mainly religious, intended for children	Aberystwyth
1829	*The Duoglott medical adviser* [or *Y Cynghorydd meddygol dwyieithog*]	Monthly. Bilingual	Carmarthen
1830–2	*Y Cymro* (*Y Cymmro*, 1831–) [The Welshman]	Monthly. General, variety of subjects from science to home and foreign news	London
1830	*Y Wawr-ddydd* [The Dawn of day]	Monthly. Religious periodical for children	Caernarfon
1831–42	*Darlun Cenadawl* [Missionary portrait]	Quarterly. Foreign missions and the activities of the London Missionary Society	London
1831–1968	*Y Drysorfa* (joined with *Y Dysgedydd* to form *Porfeydd,* 1968) [The Treasury]	Monthly. Mainly religious and general – for Calvinistic Methodists	Chester, Holywell, Caernarfon
1831–5	*Yr Efangylydd* [The Evangelist] (Preceded by *Lleuad yr oes,* 1827; *Yr Oes,* 1826)	Monthly. Religious in early years, later becoming more secular – circulation mainly among the Congregationalists of south Wales	Llandovery
1831	*Y Sylwedydd* [The Observer]	Monthly. Literary and general, home and foreign news, undenominational	Llannerch-y-medd, Caernarfon
1832	*Brud cenadawl* [Missionary chronicle]	Monthly. Foreign missions and the activities of the Baptist Missionary Society	Cardigan

Date of publication	Title	Description	Place of printing[1]
1832–6	*Y Rhosyn* [The Rose]	Monthly. Religious, intended for Sunday school children in the Swansea area	Swansea
1832–3	*Tywysog Cymru* [The Prince of Wales]	Monthly. Literary and general, circulating mainly in north Wales	Caernarfon
1833–41	*Y Gwladgarwr* [The Patriot]	Monthly. Undenominational with wide interests; including articles on religion, astronomy, farming, music and geography	Chester, Liverpool
1833	*Trysorfa rhyfeddodau, a hynodrwydd yr oesoedd* [A Treasury of wonders and peculiarities of the ages]	Monthly. Historical notes and news of a sensational nature	Dolgellau
1833–4	*Trysorfa yr ieuenctid* [Treasury for young people]	Monthly. Intended for Sunday school teachers and children	Caernarfon
1834–5	*Cylchgrawn y Gymdeithas er taenu gwybodaeth fuddiol* [The Magazine of the Society for the diffusion of useful knowledge]	Monthly. Undenominational, with articles on popular subjects, literature, science, geography and natural history	Llandovery, Carmarthen
1834	*Y Cynniweirydd* [The Wayfarer] (followed by newspapers: *Y Newyddiadur hanesyddol,* 1835; *Cronicl yr oes,* 1836)	Monthly. Mainly religious and general – for Sunday school teachers and pupils	Mold
1835–7	*Cyfaill Plentyn* [The Child's friend]	Monthly. Mainly religious – for Sunday school pupils	Merthyr Tydfil, Bryn-mawr
1835–6	*Y Cymedrolwr* [The Moderationist]	Monthly. Temperance – advocating moderation rather than total abstinence	Denbigh
1835–1911	*Y Diwygiwr* [The Reformer] (incorporated in *Y Dysgedydd* 1912)	Monthly. Radical, anti-Tory and anti-Church – for the Congregationalists of south Wales	Llanelli, Merthyr Tydfil
1835–1983	*Yr Haul* [The Sun] (joined with *Y Gangell* to form *Yr Haul a'r gangell* 1953. Contains *The Carmarthen chronicle and haul advertiser* 1860–84)	Religious and general, serving the Established Church	Llandovery, Carmarthen, Lampeter, London, Dolgellau, Aberystwyth, Denbigh, Caerphilly
1835–8	*Y Pregethwr* [The Preacher]	Published sermons by Calvinistic Methodist ministers	Liverpool
1835–6	*Y Seren ogleddol* [The Northern Star] (Succeeded by *Y Papyr newydd Cymraeg* – newspaper 1836)	Monthly. A nonconformist anti-Church and anti-Tory periodical circulating in north Wales	Caernarfon
1835–6	*Y Wenynen* [The Bee]	Monthly. Chiefly literary, containing prose and verse of the editor's own composition	Wrexham, Mold
1836–44	*Yr Athraw* [The Teacher]	Monthly. Religious, temperance, general magazine	Llanidloes
1836?	*The Crickhowell temperance advocate*/*Y Cymmedrolydd*	Monthly. Bilingual. For Crickhowell Temperance Society	Crickhowell
1836–9	*Y Dirwestydd* [The Abstainer]	Monthly. Undenominational temperance	Liverpool
1836, 1846– (with gaps)	*Ymdeithydd yr ysgolion Sabbathol* [The Sunday school companion]	Bimonthly. Mainly for children and young people	Llanrwst
1837–8	*Y Cerbyd dirwestol* [The Temperance chariot]	Monthly. Temperance – mainly north Wales	Mold
1837?	*Seren ddirwest* [The Temperance star]	?Monthly	?Crickhowell
1837	*Y Seren ddirwestol* [The Temperance star]	Monthly. Temperance periodical circulating mainly in north Wales	Chester
1837–1966	*Tywysydd yr ieuainc* [Guide for young people]	Monthly. Intended for Sunday school children of the Congregational denomination	Llanelli, Cardiff, Swansea, Bala, Caernarfon
1837	*Ymwelwr* [Visitor]	Monthly. Religious, serving the various temperance societies	Swansea
1838–9	*Yr Adolygydd* [The Reviewer]	Monthly. Anti-teetotal periodical	Caernarfon

Date of publication	Title	Description	Place of printing[1]
1838–1933	*Cyfaill o'r hen wlad yn America* [The friend from the old country in America] (*Y Cyfaill* 1844, *Y Cyfaill o'r hen wlad* 1848, *Y Cyfaill* 1881, The Friend 1884–1933)	Monthly (fortnightly 1865 only). Undenominational 1838–41. Religious, educational and general for Welsh Calvinistic Methodists in America. Bilingual 1921–33	New York, Scranton, New York
1838–9	*Y Dirwestwr deheuol* [The Southern abstainer] (followed by *Y Dirwestydd deheuol* ,1840–)	Monthly. Temperance – circulation in south Wales	Llanelli
1838–?1842	*Y Drysorfa Hynafiaethol* [or The Antiquarian magazine]	Welsh history, early Welsh poetry and antiquities	Llanrwst
1838–9	*Trysorfa grefyddol Gwent a Morganwg* [The Religious treasury of Gwent and Glamorgan] (Changed to *Trysorfa grefyddol Gymreig,* 1839)	A religious publication circulating among the Congregationalists of south-east Wales]	Cowbridge
1838	*Ystorfa weinidogaethol* [The Ministerial repository] (changed title to *Ystorfa y Bedyddwyr*)	Monthly. General, religious and literary, serving the Baptist denomination	Cardiff
1839	*Brud cenadol* [Missionary chronicle]	Quarterly. Activities of the Baptist Missionary Society	Cardigan
1839	*Yr Hanesydd* [The Historian]	A general periodical circulating among the Unitarians of south-west Wales	Aberystwyth
1839	*Tarian rhyddid a dymchwelydd gormes* [The Shield of freedom and overthrower of oppression]	Monthly. Radical and anti-Church with a large circulation among the Congregationalists	Llanrwst
1840–62, 1901	*Y Cenhadwr Americanaidd* [The American messenger]	Monthly. General, literary, religious – for Welsh Congregationalists in America	New York
1840–2	*Y Cenhadydd Cymreig* [The Welsh missionary] (*Y Cenhadydd,* 1841)	Monthly. Religious and general – for young Baptists	Merthyr Tydfil, Cardiff
1840–5	*Y Dirwestwr* [The Abstainer] (*Y Dirwestwr a'r hanesydd Rechabaidd* 1843)	Monthly. Temperance – the Temperance Association of Gwynedd	Dolgellau
1840–1	*Y Dirwestydd deheuol* [The Southern abstainer]	Monthly. Temperance – circulation in south Wales	Llanelli
1840	*Y Gwron odyddol* [The Oddfellows' hero]	Monthly. General and literary, serving the Oddfellows' friendly society	Cowbridge
1840?	*Yr Udgorn dirwestol* [The Temperance Trumpet]	?Monthly	?St Asaph
1841	*Cennad hedd* [The Messenger of peace]	Bimonthly. Activities of missionary societies in north Wales	Mold
1841–2	*Y Gwir Iforydd* [The True Ivorite]	Quarterly. Mainly general and literary, published by the Wrexham Union of the True Ivorites friendly society	Carmarthen
1841–2	*Yr Iforydd* [The Ivorite] (Succeeded by *Ifor Hael* 1850. Changed to *Y Gwladgarwr* 1851)	Monthly. General and literary, serving the Ivorites friendly society	Carmarthen
1841–2	*Y Pregethwr* [The Preacher]	Bimonthly. Published sermons by Calvinistic Methodist ministers	Mold
1841–2	*Y Rechabydd* [The Rechabite]	Monthly. Devoted to the spread of teetotalism and the progress of the Rechabite Order in Wales	Liverpool
1842–3	*Y Beread* [The Berean]	Fortnightly. Religious and general – for Welsh Baptists in America	New York
1842	*Blaguryn y diwygiad* [The Bud of the revival]	Monthly. Welsh Wesleyan Methodist – reform movement	Aberystwyth
1842–68	*Y Gwir Fedyddiwr* [The True Baptist] (*Y Bedyddiwr,* 1844)	Monthly. Mainly religious and literary serving the Baptists and their Sunday schools	Cardiff, Newport, Gelligroes, Aberdare, Blaenau
1842	*Yr Odydd Cymreig* [The Welsh Oddfellow]	Quarterly. General and literary serving the Oddfellows' friendly society	Cardiff
1843–1910	*Cronicl y cymdeithasau crefyddol* [The Chronicle of the religious societies] (*Y Cronicl* 1876)	Monthly. General, literary and radical – mainly Congregationalists	Dolgellau, Blaenau Ffestiniog, Bala, Bangor, Conwy

Date of publication	Title	Description	Place of printing[1]
1843–4	*Y Cwmwl* [The Cloud]	Monthly. Undenominational, general	Aberystwyth
1843	*Y Dyngarwr* [The Philanthropist]	Monthly. Welsh-American periodical, advocated freedom for slaves and other philanthropic causes	New York
1843	*Y Gwladgarwr* [The Patriot]	Monthly. Undenominational, religious, literary and general	Llanidloes
1843–4	*Y Gwyliedydd* [The Sentinel]	The organ of the Welsh Baptists in America	?Carbondale, Pa.
1843?	*Y Morgrugyn* [The Ant]		
1843–51	*Trysorfa Gynnulleidfaol Gwent a Morganwg* [Congregational treasury of Gwent and Glamorgan] (Changed to *Y Drysorfa Gynnulleidfaol* Aug. 1843)	Monthly. Religious and general, circulating among the Congregationalists of south-east Wales	Swansea, Carmarthen
1843	*Twr Gwalia* [The Tower of Walliae]	Monthly. Mainly articles of a general nature, home and foreign news	Bangor
1844–6	*Cyfaill rhinwedd* [The Friend of virtue]	Monthly. Temperance and religious periodical for children and young people	Llangollen
1844	*Yr Esboniwr* [The Expositor]	Monthly. Undenominational, mainly Biblical commentary for use in Sunday schools	Chester
1844–69	*Seren orllewinol* [The western star] (Changed to *Y Seren orllewinol* 1845)	Monthly. Religious, educational and general, serving the Welsh Baptists of America	Utica, New York, Pottsville
1845–6	*Yr Amaethydd* [The Farmer]	Monthly. Agricultural matters	Caernarfon
1845–6	*Y Beirniadur Cymreig* [The Welsh critic]	Monthly. Undenominational, religious, literary, general	St Asaph
1845	*Y Gwyliedydd* [The Sentinel]	A satirical periodical which derided Nonconformist itinerant preachers	Bryn-mawr
1845	*Y Traethodydd* [The Essayist]	Literary, with emphasis on theology, philosophy, education and reviews	Denbigh, Holywell, Caernarfon
1846–50	*Y Golygydd* [The Editor]	Monthly. Undenominational but generally associated with the Congregationalists; mainly religious and literary	Rhyd-y-bont, Merthyr Tydfil
1846	*Yr Hanesydd* [The Historian]	Monthly. A general periodical for children and young people	Llangollen
1846–8	*Prophwyd y jubili* [The Prophet of the jubilee] (Succeeded by *Udgorn Seion* 1849)	Monthly. Periodical of the Church of Jesus Christ of Latter Day Saints	Rhyd-y-bont, Carmarthen
1846–7	*Y Seren Foreu* [The Morning star]	Monthly. Religious periodical for children	Rhyd-y-bont
1846–51	*Y Tyst apostolaidd* [The Apostolic witness]	Religious and general, serving the Baptist denomination	Llangollen
1847–64	*Yr Eglwysydd* [The Churchman] (joined with *Cenadwr eglwysig* to form *Yr Eglwysydd a'r cenadwr eglwysig* 1855)	Monthly. Mainly religious – serving the interests of the Established Church	Holywell, Denbigh
1847–51	*Y Geiniogwerth* [The Pennyworth] (followed by *Y Methodist* 1852, *Y Methodist* 1854)	Monthly. Religious and general – for Calvinistic Methodists	Denbigh
1847–	*Yr Ymofynydd* [The Inquirer]	Monthly. Religious and general, serving the Unitarian denomination	Carmarthen, Bridgend, Cardiff, Aberdare, Merthyr Tydfil, Llandysul
1848–1965	*Y Winllan* [The Vineyard]	Monthly. Intended for Sunday school children of the Wesleyan Methodist denomination	Llanidloes, Bangor, Holywell, Bala, Swansea
1849?	*Yr Areithfa Gymreig* [The Welsh pulpit]		
1849–62	*Udgorn Seion* [The Trumpet of Zion] (following *Prophwyd y jubili* 1846)	Periodical of the Church of Jesus Christ of Latter Day Saints	Carmarthen, Merthyr Tydfil, Swansea, Liverpool
1850–3	*Yr Adolygydd* [The Reviewer] (Succeeded by *Y Beirniad* from 1859)	Quarterly. Literary	Cardiff, Llanelli

Date of publication	Title	Description	Place of printing[1]
1850	*Yr Athraw dirwestol* [The Temperance Teacher] (Succeeded by *Udgorn dirwest* 1850)	Monthly. Temperance	Caernarfon
1850–2	*Y Detholydd* [The Digest]	Monthly. General, including extracts from the Welsh periodical press – for the Welsh in America	New York
1850–1	*Y Gymraes* [The Welsh woman] (joined with *Tywysydd yr ieuainc* to form *Y Tywysydd a'r Gymraes* 1852)	Monthly. Women's magazine mainly devoted to literature	Cardiff
1850–1	*Ifor Hael* [Ivor the bountiful] (Preceded by *Yr Iforydd,* 1841. Succeeded by *Y Gwladgarwr,* 1851)	Monthly. General and literary, serving the Ivorites friendly society	Carmarthen
1850	*Udgorn dirwest* [The Temperance trumpet] (followed by *Yr Athraw dirwestol* 1850)	Monthly. Temperance periodical published by the Bethesda Temperance Association, Caernarfonshire	Bangor
1850–1	*Y Wawr* [The Dawn]	Monthly. Chiefly literary, but also included articles on scientific subjects	Cardiff
1850–1	*Y Wawrddydd* [The Dawn of day]	Monthly. Religious periodical for Sunday school children	Carmarthen

Source: Huw Walters, *Llyfryddiaeth Cylchgronau Cymreig 1735–1850: A Bibliography of Welsh Periodicals 1735–1850* (Aberystwyth, 1993).

[1] The place of printing has been given rather than the place of publication for two reasons. First, there is more information given concerning the place of printing, and, second, where information is given both as to the place of publication and the place of printing, it is generally (but not always) the same.

[2] 100 facsimile copies, 1902.